D1258127

HOLT SCIENCE & TECHNOLOGY

Physical
Science

HOLT, RINEHART AND WINSTON

A Harcourt Education Company

Orlando • Austin • New York • San Diego • Toronto • London

Acknowledgments

Contributing Authors

Christie Borgford, Ph.D.
Assistant Professor of Chemistry
Department of Chemistry
The University of Alabama
Birmingham, Alabama

Andrew Champagne
Former Physics Teacher
Ashland, Massachusetts

Mapi Cuevas, Ph.D.
Professor of Chemistry
Department of Natural Sciences
Santa Fe Community College
Gainesville, Florida

Leila Dumas
Former Physics Teacher
Austin, Texas

William G. Lamb, Ph.D.
Winningstad Chair in the Physical Sciences
Oregon Episcopal School
Portland, Oregon

Sally Ann Vonderbrink, Ph.D.
Chemistry Teacher (retired)
Cincinnati, Ohio

Inclusion Specialist

Ellen McPeek Glisan
Special Needs Consultant
San Antonio, Texas

Safety Reviewer

Jack Gerlovich, Ph.D.
Associate Professor
School of Education
Drake University
Des Moines, Iowa

Academic Reviewers

Howard L. Brooks, Ph.D.
Professor of Physics & Astronomy
Department of Physics & Astronomy
DePauw University
Greencastle, Indiana

Scott Darveau, Ph.D.
Associate Professor of Chemistry
Chemistry Department
University of Nebraska at Kearney
Kearney, Nebraska

Cassandra Eagle
Professor
Chemistry Department
Appalachian State University
Boone, North Carolina

Simonetta Frittelli, Ph.D.
Associate Professor
Department of Physics
Duquesne University
Pittsburgh, Pennsylvania

David S. Hall, Ph.D.
Assistant Professor of Physics
Department of Physics
Amherst College
Amherst, Massachusetts

William H. Ingham, Ph.D.
Professor of Physics
James Madison University
Harrisonburg, Virginia

Mark N. Kobrak, Ph.D.
Assistant Professor of Chemistry
Chemistry Department
Brooklyn College of the City University of New York
Brooklyn, New York

Daniela Kohen
Assistant Professor of Chemistry
Chemistry Department
Carleton College
North Field, Minnesota

David Lamp, Ph.D.
Associate Professor of Physics
Physics Department
Texas Tech University
Lubbock, Texas

Mark Mattson, Ph.D.
Assistant Professor
Physics Department
James Madison University
Harrisonburg, Virginia

Richard F. Niedziela, Ph.D.
Assistant Professor of Chemistry
Department of Chemistry
DePaul University
Chicago, Illinois

Enrique Peacock-López
Professor of Chemistry
Department of Chemistry
Williams College
Wiliamstown, Massachusetts

Kate Queeney, Ph.D.
Assistant Professor of Chemistry
Chemistry Department
Smith College
Northampton, Massachusetts

Fred Seaman, Ph.D.
Retired Research Associate
College of Pharmacy
The University of Texas at Austin
Austin, Texas

H. Michael Sommermann, Ph.D.
Professor of Physics
Physics Department
Westmont College
Santa Barbara, California

Richard S. Treptow, Ph.D.
Professor of Chemistry
Department of Chemistry and Physics
Chicago State University
Chicago, Illinois

Dale Wheeler
Assistant Professor of Chemistry
A. R. Smith Department of Chemistry
Appalachian State University
Boone, North Carolina

Acknowledgments
continued on page 816

Contents in Brief

UNIT 1 **Introduction to Matter** **2**
Chapter 1   The World of Physical Science 4
Chapter 2   The Properties of Matter 36
Chapter 3   States of Matter 64
Chapter 4   Elements, Compounds, and Mixtures 88

UNIT 2 **Motion and Forces** **114**
Chapter 5   Matter in Motion 116
Chapter 6   Forces and Motion 148
Chapter 7   Forces in Fluids 178

UNIT 3 **Work, Machines, and Energy** **206**
Chapter 8   Work and Machines 208
Chapter 9   Energy and Energy Resources 238
Chapter 10   Heat and Heat Technology 272

UNIT 4 **The Atom** **308**
Chapter 11   Introduction to Atoms 310
Chapter 12   The Periodic Table 334

UNIT 5 **Interactions of Matter** **360**
Chapter 13   Chemical Bonding 362
Chapter 14   Chemical Reactions 386
Chapter 15   Chemical Compounds 416
Chapter 16   Atomic Energy 446

UNIT 6 **Electricity** **470**
Chapter 17   Introduction to Electricity 472
Chapter 18   Electromagnetism 508
Chapter 19   Electronic Technology 538

UNIT 7 **Waves, Sound, and Light** **570**
Chapter 20   The Energy of Waves 572
Chapter 21   The Nature of Sound 598
Chapter 22   The Nature of Light 630
Chapter 23   Light and Our World 666

Contents

Safety First! xxvi

UNIT 1 ·· **Introduction to Matter**
TIMELINE **2**

CHAPTER 1 The World of Physical Science **4**

SECTION 1 Exploring Physical Science 6

SECTION 2 Scientific Methods 12

SECTION 3 Scientific Models 20

SECTION 4 Tools, Measurement, and Safety 24

Chapter Lab Skills Practice Measuring Liquid Volume 28

Chapter Review 30

Standardized Test Preparation 32

Science in Action 34
  Science Fiction "Inspiration"
  Weird Science A Palace of Ice
  Careers Julie Williams–Byrd: Electronics Engineer

LabBook   **Skills Practice** Exploring the Unseen 696

  Model Making Off to the Races 697

  Skills Practice Coin Operated 698

CHAPTER 2 The Properties of Matter **36**

SECTION 1 What Is Matter? 38

SECTION 2 Physical Properties 44

SECTION 3 Chemical Properties 50

Chapter Lab Skills Practice White Before Your Eyes 56

Chapter Review 58

Standardized Test Preparation 60

Science in Action 62
  Scientific Debate Paper or Plastic?
  Science, Technology, and Society Building a Better Body
  Careers Mimi So: Gemologist and Jewelry Designer

LabBook   **Skills Practice** Volumania! 700

  Skills Practice Determining Density 702

  Skills Practice Layering Liquids 703

CHAPTER ③ States of Matter 64

SECTION 1 Three States of Matter 66

SECTION 2 Behavior of Gases 70

SECTION 3 Changes of State 74

Chapter Lab Skills Practice A Hot and Cool Lab 80

Chapter Review 82

Standardized Test Preparation 84

Science in Action 86

Science, Technology, and Society Deep-sea Diving with Helium
Scientific Discoveries The Fourth State of Matter
People in Science Andy Goldsworthy: Nature Artist

LabBook **Skills Practice** Full of Hot Air! 704

Skills Practice Can Crusher 705

CHAPTER ④ Elements, Compounds, and Mixtures 88

SECTION 1 Elements 90

SECTION 2 Compounds 94

SECTION 3 Mixtures 98

Chapter Lab Skills Practice Flame Tests 106

Chapter Review 108

Standardized Test Preparation 110

Science in Action 112

Science, Technology, and Society Dry Cleaning: How Stains Are Dissolved
Science Fiction "The Strange Case of Dr. Jekyll and Mr. Hyde"
Careers Aundra Nix: Metallurgist

LabBook **Skills Practice** A Sugar Cube Race! 706

Skills Practice Making Butter 707

Model Making Unpolluting Water 708

Contents   **v**

UNIT 2 · Motion and Forces

TIMELINE **114**

CHAPTER 5 Matter in Motion **116**

SECTION 1 Measuring Motion 118

SECTION 2 What Is a Force? 124

SECTION 3 Friction: A Force That Opposes Motion 128

SECTION 4 Gravity: A Force of Attraction 134

Chapter Lab Skills Practice Detecting Acceleration 140

Chapter Review 142

Standardized Test Preparation 144

Science in Action 146

Science, Technology, and Society GPS Watch System
Weird Science The Segway™ Human Transporter
People in Science Victor Petrenko: Snowboard and Ski Brakes

LabBook   **Skills Practice** Built for Speed 710

             Skills Practice Relating Mass and Weight 711

             Skills Practice Science Friction 712

CHAPTER 6 Forces and Motion **148**

SECTION 1 Gravity and Motion 150

SECTION 2 Newton's Laws of Motion 158

SECTION 3 Momentum 166

Chapter Lab Skills Practice Inertia-Rama! 170

Chapter Review 172

Standardized Test Preparation 174

Science in Action 176

Scientific Discoveries The Millennium Bridge
Science, Technology, and Society Power Suit for Lifting Patients
Careers Steve Okamoto: Roller Coaster Designer

LabBook   **Skills Practice** A Marshmallow Catapult 714

             Model Making Blast Off! 715

             Skills Practice Quite a Reaction 716

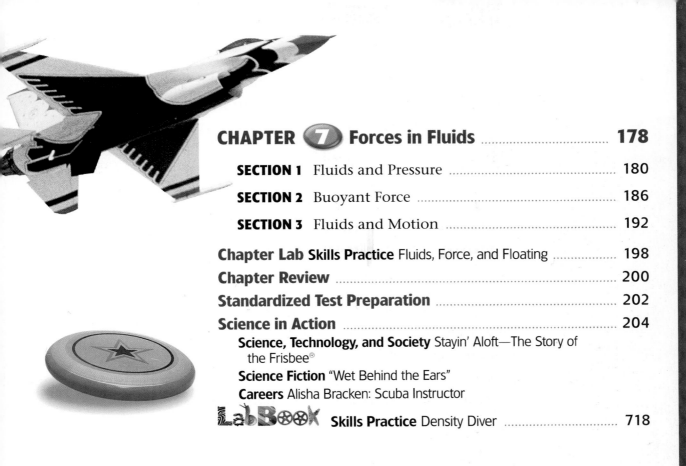

CHAPTER 7 Forces in Fluids 178

SECTION 1 Fluids and Pressure 180

SECTION 2 Buoyant Force 186

SECTION 3 Fluids and Motion 192

Chapter Lab Skills Practice Fluids, Force, and Floating 198

Chapter Review 200

Standardized Test Preparation 202

Science in Action 204

    Science, Technology, and Society Stayin' Aloft—The Story of
the Frisbee®

    Science Fiction "Wet Behind the Ears"

    Careers Alisha Bracken: Scuba Instructor

 **Skills Practice** Density Diver 718

UNIT 3 ···Work, Machines, and Energy
   TIMELINE 206

CHAPTER 8 Work and Machines 208

SECTION 1 Work and Power 210

SECTION 2 What Is a Machine? 216

SECTION 3 Types of Machines 222

Chapter Lab Skills Practice A Powerful Workout 230

Chapter Review 232

Standardized Test Preparation 234

Science in Action 236

    Science, Technology, and Society Kinetic Sculpture

    Weird Science Nanomachines

    People in Science Mike Hensler: The Surf Chair

 **Skills Practice** Inclined to Move 719

    Skills Practice Wheeling and Dealing 720

    Inquiry Building Machines 722

CHAPTER ⑨ Energy and Energy Resources ... 238

SECTION 1 What Is Energy? 240

SECTION 2 Energy Conversions 248

SECTION 3 Conservation of Energy 254

SECTION 4 Energy Resources 258

Chapter Lab Skills Practice Finding Energy 264

Chapter Review 266

Standardized Test Preparation 268

Science in Action 270

    Science, Technology, and Society Underwater Jet Engines
    Scientific Discoveries $E = mc^2$
    Careers Cheryl Mele: Power-Plant Manager

LabBook Skills Practice Energy of a Pendulum 723

CHAPTER ⑩ Heat and Heat Technology 272

SECTION 1 Temperature 274

SECTION 2 What Is Heat? 280

SECTION 3 Matter and Heat 288

SECTION 4 Heat Technology 292

Chapter Lab Skills Practice Feel the Heat 300

Chapter Review 302

Standardized Test Preparation 304

Science in Action 306

    Scientific Discoveries The Deep Freeze
    Science, Technology, and Society DiAPLEX®: The Intelligent Fabric
    Careers Michael Reynolds: Earthship Architect

LabBook Inquiry Save the Cube! 724

    Model Making Counting Calories 725

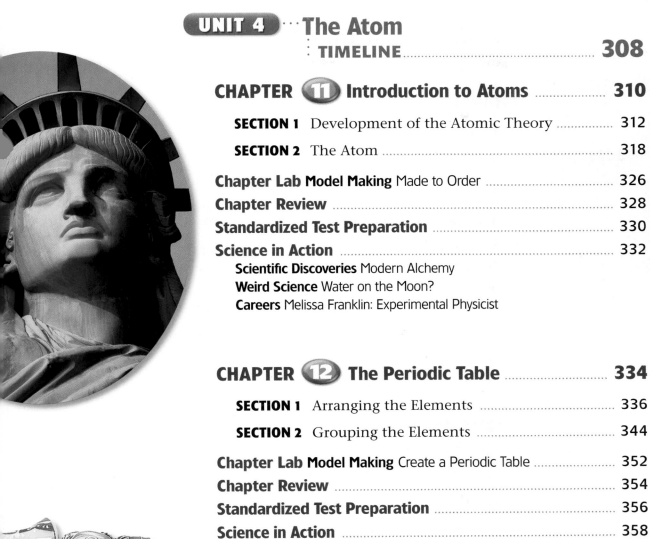

UNIT 4 ⋯ The Atom

TIMELINE **308**

CHAPTER 11 Introduction to Atoms **310**

SECTION 1 Development of the Atomic Theory 312

SECTION 2 The Atom 318

Chapter Lab Model Making Made to Order 326

Chapter Review 328

Standardized Test Preparation 330

Science in Action 332
 Scientific Discoveries Modern Alchemy
 Weird Science Water on the Moon?
 Careers Melissa Franklin: Experimental Physicist

CHAPTER 12 The Periodic Table **334**

SECTION 1 Arranging the Elements 336

SECTION 2 Grouping the Elements 344

Chapter Lab Model Making Create a Periodic Table 352

Chapter Review 354

Standardized Test Preparation 356

Science in Action 358
 Weird Science Buckyballs
 Science, Technology, and Society The Science of Fireworks
 People in Science Glenn T. Seaborg: Making Elements

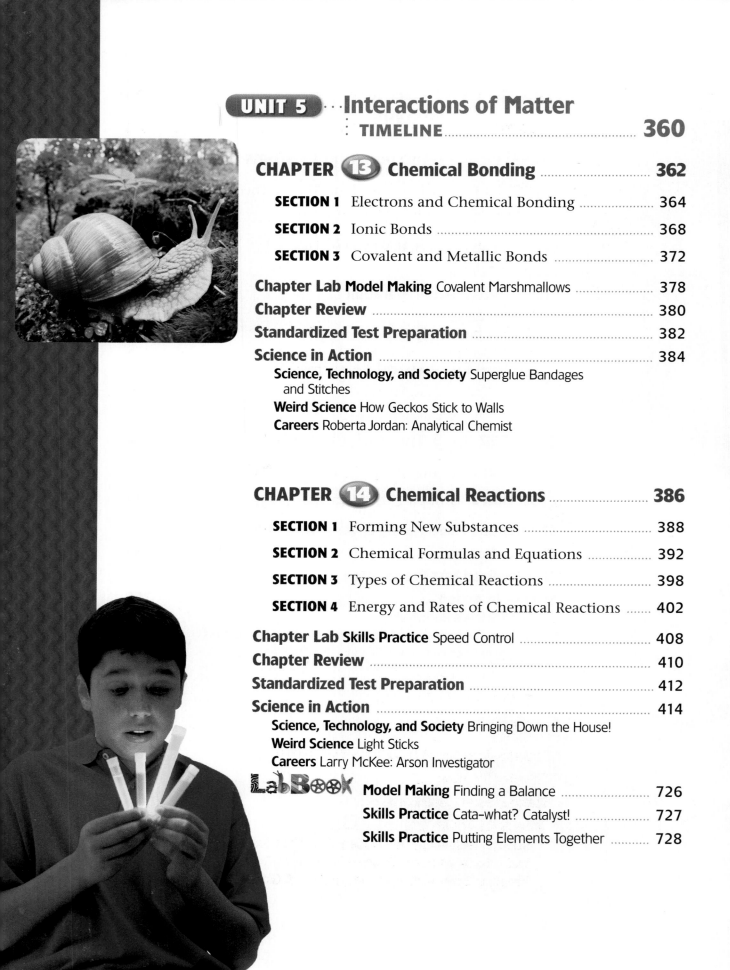

UNIT 5 ···Interactions of Matter
TIMELINE 360

CHAPTER 13 Chemical Bonding 362

SECTION 1 Electrons and Chemical Bonding 364

SECTION 2 Ionic Bonds 368

SECTION 3 Covalent and Metallic Bonds 372

Chapter Lab Model Making Covalent Marshmallows 378

Chapter Review 380

Standardized Test Preparation 382

Science in Action 384

    Science, Technology, and Society Superglue Bandages
    and Stitches

    Weird Science How Geckos Stick to Walls

    Careers Roberta Jordan: Analytical Chemist

CHAPTER 14 Chemical Reactions 386

SECTION 1 Forming New Substances 388

SECTION 2 Chemical Formulas and Equations 392

SECTION 3 Types of Chemical Reactions 398

SECTION 4 Energy and Rates of Chemical Reactions 402

Chapter Lab Skills Practice Speed Control 408

Chapter Review 410

Standardized Test Preparation 412

Science in Action 414

    Science, Technology, and Society Bringing Down the House!

    Weird Science Light Sticks

    Careers Larry McKee: Arson Investigator

LabBook

    Model Making Finding a Balance 726

    Skills Practice Cata-what? Catalyst! 727

    Skills Practice Putting Elements Together 728

CHAPTER ⑮ Chemical Compounds 416

SECTION 1 Ionic and Covalent Compounds 418

SECTION 2 Acids and Bases 422

SECTION 3 Solutions of Acids and Bases 428

SECTION 4 Organic Compounds 432

Chapter Lab Skills Practice Cabbage Patch Indicators 438

Chapter Review 440

Standardized Test Preparation 442

Science in Action 444

   Science, Technology, and Society Molecular Photocopying
   Weird Science Silly Putty®
   Careers Jeannie Eberhardt: Forensic Scientist

LabBook Skills Practice Making Salt 730

CHAPTER ⑯ Atomic Energy 446

SECTION 1 Radioactivity 448

SECTION 2 Energy from the Nucleus 456

Chapter Lab Model Making Domino Chain Reactions 462

Chapter Review 464

Standardized Test Preparation 466

Science in Action 468

   Science, Technology, and Society Irradiated Food
   Weird Science Nuclear-Powered Bacteria
   People in Science Marie and Pierre Curie: A Great Team

UNIT 6 ··· Electricity
TIMELINE **470**

CHAPTER 17 Introduction to Electricity **472**

SECTION 1 Electric Charge and Static Electricity 474

SECTION 2 Electric Current and Electrical Energy 482

SECTION 3 Electrical Calculations 490

SECTION 4 Electric Circuits 494

Chapter Lab Skills Practice Circuitry 101 500

Chapter Review 502

Standardized Test Preparation 504

Science in Action 506
  Weird Science Electric Eels
  Scientific Discoveries Sprites and Elves
  Careers Pete Perez: Electrician

LabBook   **Skills Practice** Stop the Static Electricity! 732

                Model Making Potato Power 733

CHAPTER 18 Electromagnetism **508**

SECTION 1 Magnets and Magnetism 510

SECTION 2 Magnetism from Electricity 518

SECTION 3 Electricity from Magnetism 524

Chapter Lab Model Making Build a DC Motor 530

Chapter Review 532

Standardized Test Preparation 534

Science in Action 536
  Weird Science Geomagnetic Storms
  Science, Technology, and Society Magnets in Medicine
  People in Science James Clerk Maxwell: Magnetic Math

LabBook   **Skills Practice** Magnetic Mystery 734

                Skills Practice Electricity from Magnetism 735

CHAPTER ⟨19⟩ Electronic Technology 538

SECTION 1 Electronic Devices 540

SECTION 2 Communication Technology 546

SECTION 3 Computers 554

Chapter Lab Skills Practice Sending Signals 562

Chapter Review 564

Standardized Test Preparation 566

Science in Action 568

    Science, Technology, and Society Wearable Computers
    Science Fiction "There Will Come Soft Rains"
    Careers Agnes Riley: Computer Technician

LabBook **Model Making** Tune In! 736

UNIT 7 ···· Waves, Sound, and Light
    TIMELINE 570

CHAPTER ⟨20⟩ The Energy of Waves 572

SECTION 1 The Nature of Waves 574

SECTION 2 Properties of Waves 580

SECTION 3 Wave Interactions 584

Chapter Lab Skills Practice Wave Energy and Speed 590

Chapter Review 592

Standardized Test Preparation 594

Science in Action 596

    Science, Technology, and Society The Ultimate Telescope
    Scientific Discoveries The Wave Nature of Light
    Careers Estela Zavala: Ultrasonographer

LabBook **Skills Practice** Wave Speed, Frequency,
    and Wavelength 740

CHAPTER 21 The Nature of Sound **598**

SECTION 1 What Is Sound? 600

SECTION 2 Properties of Sound 606

SECTION 3 Interactions of Sound Waves 612

SECTION 4 Sound Quality 618

Chapter Lab Skills Practice Easy Listening 622

Chapter Review 624

Standardized Test Preparation 626

Science in Action 628
  Scientific Discoveries Jurassic Bark
  Science Fiction "Ear"
  Careers Adam Dudley: Sound Engineer

LabBook **Inquiry** The Speed of Sound 742

  Skills Practice Tuneful Tube 743

  Skills Practice The Energy of Sound 744

CHAPTER 22 The Nature of Light **630**

SECTION 1 What Is Light? 632

SECTION 2 The Electromagnetic Spectrum 636

SECTION 3 Interactions of Light Waves 644

SECTION 4 Light and Color 652

Chapter Lab Skills Practice Mixing Colors 658

Chapter Review 660

Standardized Test Preparation 662

Science in Action 664
  Weird Science Fireflies Light the Way
  Science, Technology, and Society It's a Heat Wave
  People in Science Albert Einstein: A Light Pioneer

LabBook **Skills Practice** What Color of Light Is
    Best for Green Plants? 746

  Skills Practice Which Color Is Hottest? 747

CHAPTER ㉓ Light and Our World 666

SECTION 1 Mirrors and Lenses 668

SECTION 2 Light and Sight 674

SECTION 3 Light and Technology 678

Chapter Lab Skills Practice Images from Convex Lenses 686

Chapter Review 688

Standardized Test Preparation 690

Science in Action 692

    Science, Technology, and Society Bionic Eyes

    Scientific Debate Do Cellular Telephones Cause Cancer?

    People in Science Sandra Faber: Astronomer

LabBook Skills Practice Mirror Images 748

LabBook 694

Appendix 750

    Reading Check Answers 751

    Study Skills 757

    SI Measurement 763

    Temperature Scales 764

    Measuring Skills 765

    Scientific Methods 766

    Periodic Table of the Elements 768

    Making Charts and Graphs 770

    Math Refresher 773

    Physical Science Laws and Principles 777

Glossary 781

Spanish Glossary 789

Index 798

Chapter Labs and LabBook

Safety First! xxvi

CHAPTER ① The World of Physical Science

Chapter Lab
Skills Practice Measuring Liquid
Volume 28
LabBook
Skills Practice Exploring the Unseen 696
Model Making Off to the Races 697
Skills Practice Coin Operated 698

CHAPTER ② The Properties of Matter

Chapter Lab
Skills Practice White Before Your Eyes 56
LabBook
Skills Practice Volumania! 700
Skills Practice Determining Density 702
Skills Practice Layering Liquids 703

CHAPTER ③ States of Matter

Chapter Lab
Skills Practice A Hot and Cool Lab 80
LabBook
Skills Practice Full of Hot Air! 704
Skills Practice Can Crusher 705

CHAPTER ④ Elements, Compounds, and Mixtures

Chapter Lab
Skills Practice Flame Tests 106
LabBook
Skills Practice A Sugar Cube Race! 706
Skills Practice Making Butter 707
Model Making Unpolluting Water 708

CHAPTER ⑤ Matter in Motion

Chapter Lab
Skills Practice Detecting Acceleration ... 140
LabBook
Skills Practice Built for Speed 710
Skills Practice Relating Mass
and Weight 711
Skills Practice Science Friction 712

CHAPTER ⑥ Forces and Motion

Chapter Lab
Skills Practice Inertia-Rama! 170
LabBook
Skills Practice A Marshmallow
Catapult 714
Model Making Blast Off! 715
Skills Practice Quite a Reaction 716

CHAPTER ⑦ Forces in Fluids

Chapter Lab
Skills Practice Fluids, Force,
and Floating 198
LabBook
Skills Practice Density Diver 718

CHAPTER ⑧ Work and Machines

Chapter Lab
Skills Practice A Powerful Workout 230
LabBook
Skills Practice Inclined to Move 719
Skills Practice Wheeling and Dealing 720
Inquiry Building Machines 722

CHAPTER ⑨ Energy and Energy Resources

Chapter Lab
Skills Practice Finding Energy 264
LabBook
Skills Practice Energy of a Pendulum 723

CHAPTER ⑩ Heat and Heat Technology

Chapter Lab
Skills Practice Feel the Heat 300
LabBook
Inquiry Save the Cube! 724
Model Making Counting Calories 725

CHAPTER ⑪ Introduction to Atoms

Chapter Lab
Model Making Made to Order 326

CHAPTER ⑫ The Periodic Table

Chapter Lab
Model Making Create a Periodic Table ... 352

CHAPTER 13 Chemical Bonding

Chapter Lab
Model Making Covalent
Marshmallows 378

CHAPTER 14 Chemical Reactions

Chapter Lab
Skills Practice Speed Control 408
LabBook
Model Making Finding a Balance 726
Skills Practice Cata-what? Catalyst! 727
Skills Practice Putting Elements
Together 728

CHAPTER 15 Chemical Compounds

Chapter Lab
Skills Practice Cabbage Patch
Indicators 438
LabBook
Skills Practice Making Salt 730

CHAPTER 16 Atomic Energy

Chapter Lab
Model Making Domino Chain
Reactions 462

CHAPTER 17 Introduction to Electricity

Chapter Lab
Skills Practice Circuitry 101 500
LabBook
Skills Practice Stop the Static
Electricity! 732
Model Making Potato Power 733

CHAPTER 18 Electromagnetism

Chapter Lab
Model Making Build a DC Motor 530
LabBook
Skills Practice Magnetic Mystery 734
Skills Practice Electricity from
Magnetism 735

CHAPTER 19 Electronic Technology

Chapter Lab
Skills Practice Sending Signals 562
LabBook
Model Making Tune In! 736

CHAPTER 20 The Energy of Waves

Chapter Lab
Skills Practice Wave Energy
and Speed 590
LabBook
Skills Practice Wave Speed, Frequency,
and Wavelength 740

CHAPTER 21 The Nature of Sound

Chapter Lab
Skills Practice Easy Listening 622
LabBook
Inquiry The Speed of Sound 742
Skills Practice Tuneful Tube 743
Skills Practice The Energy of Sound 744

CHAPTER 22 The Nature of Light

Chapter Lab
Skills Practice Mixing Colors 658
LabBook
Skills Practice What Color of Light Is
Best for Green Plants? 746
Skills Practice Which Color Is Hottest? ... 747

CHAPTER 23 Light and Our World

Chapter Lab
Skills Practice Images from Convex
Lenses 686
LabBook
Skills Practice Mirror Images 748

The more labs, the better!
Take a minute to browse the variety of exciting **labs** in this textbook. Labs appear within the chapters and in a special LabBook in the back of the textbook. All labs are designed to help you experience science firsthand. But please don't forget to be safe. Read the Safety First! section before starting any of the labs.

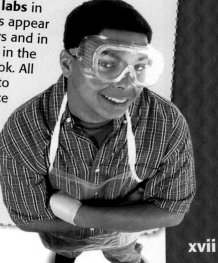

Start your engines with an activity!

Get motivated to learn by doing the two activities at the beginning of each chapter. The **Pre-Reading Activity** helps you organize information as you read the chapter. The **Start-up Activity** helps you gain scientific understanding of the topic through hands-on experience.

PRE-READING ACTIVITY

FOLDNOTES

Booklet 36
Three-Panel Flip Chart 64
Key-Term Fold 88
Four-Corner Fold 116
Booklet 178
Booklet 208
Layered Book 238
Two-Panel Flip Chart 272
Three-Panel Flip Chart 334
Three-Panel Flip Chart 362
Four-Corner Fold 386
Layered Book 416
Layered Book 472

Booklet 538
Three-Panel Flip Chart 572
Booklet 630
Tri-fold 666

Graphic Organizer

Spider Map 4
Spider Map 148
Chain-of-Events Chart 310
Spider Map 446
Comparison Table 508
Concept Map 598

START-UP ACTIVITY

Figure It Out 5
Sack Secrets 37
Vanishing Act 65
Mystery Mixture 89
The Domino Derby 117
Falling Water 149
Taking Flight 179
C'mon, Lever a Little! 209
Energy Swings! 239
Some Like It Hot 273
Where Is It? 311
Placement Pattern 335

From Glue to Goop 363
A Model Formula 387
Sticking Together 417
Watch Your Headsium! 447
Stick Together 473
Magnetic Attraction 509
Talking Long Distance 539
Energetic Waves 573
A Homemade Guitar 599
Colors of Light 631
Mirror, Mirror 667

READING STRATEGY

Brainstorming

Chapter 1 24
Chapter 5 128
Chapter 7 180
Chapter 9 248
Chapter 10 288
Chapter 17 494
Chapter 22 632

Discussion

Chapter 1 20
Chapter 5 118
Chapter 7 186
Chapter 9 240
Chapter 13 364
Chapter 14 392
Chapter 15 428
Chapter 19 546
Chapter 20 574
Chapter 22 652

Mnemonics

Chapter 2 44
Chapter 3 74
Chapter 8 222
Chapter 12 336
Chapter 14 398
Chapter 20 580
Chapter 22 636

Paired Summarizing

Chapter 3 66
Chapter 5 134
Chapter 6 158
Chapter 9 254
Chapter 10 280
Chapter 12 344
Chapter 13 368
Chapter 14 402
Chapter 15 432
Chapter 17 490
Chapter 18 524
Chapter 21 612

Prediction Guide

Chapter 1 6
Chapter 2 38
Chapter 4 94
Chapter 6 166
Chapter 8 216
Chapter 10 274
Chapter 18 510
Chapter 19 554
Chapter 21 600
Chapter 23 678

**Reading Organizer—
Concept Map**

Chapter 4 90
Chapter 11 318
Chapter 19 540
Chapter 20 584
Chapter 22 644
Chapter 23 668

**Reading Organizer—
Flowchart**

Chapter 1 12
Chapter 23 674

**Reading Organizer—
Outline**

Chapter 2 50
Chapter 4 98
Chapter 6 150
Chapter 7 192
Chapter 10 292
Chapter 11 312
Chapter 13 372
Chapter 14 388
Chapter 15 418
Chapter 16 448
Chapter 17 474
Chapter 21 606

**Reading Organizer—
Table**

Chapter 3 70
Chapter 5 124
Chapter 8 210
Chapter 9 258
Chapter 15 422
Chapter 16 456
Chapter 17 482
Chapter 18 518
Chapter 21 618

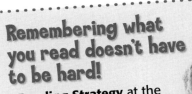

Remembering what you read doesn't have to be hard!

A **Reading Strategy** at the beginning of every section provides tips to help you remember and/or organize the information covered in the section.

Quick Lab

That's Swingin'! 17
Space Case 39
Changing Change 52
Physical or Chemical Change 54
Boiling Water Is Cool 78
Separating Elements 91
Compound Confusion 95
The Friction 500 129
Reducing Friction 132
Penny Projectile Motion 156
First Law Skateboard 159
First Law Magic 160
Blown Away 184
Ship Shape 190
Get to Work! 213
Hear That Energy! 245
Hot or Cold? 275
Heat Exchange 282
Conduction Connection 340
Bending with Bonds 376
Reaction Ready 391
Conservation of Mass 397
Identifying Reactions 400
Endo Alert 403
Which Is Quicker? 405
Blue to Red—Acid! 426
pHast Relief 429
Food Facts 435
Gone Fission 459
Detecting Charge 477
A Series of Circuits 496
A Parallel Lab 497
Model of Earth's Magnetic Field 515
Electromagnets 520
The Speed of a Simple
    Computer 555
Springy Waves 581
Good Vibrations 601
Sounding Board 609
Scattering Milk 647
Refraction Rainbow 649
Rose Colored Glasses? 656
Blackout! 683

School to Home

Weather Forecasting 21
Twenty Questions 47
Suspensions 104
What's Your Speed? 119
Comparing Friction 130
Newton Ball 163
Floating Fun 187
Useful Friction 220
Everyday Machines 228
Energy Conversions 256
Home Heating and Cooling 294
Atomic Diagrams 322
Patterns of Symbols 342
Studying Salt 369
Acids and Bases at Home 426
Saving Energy 493
TV Screen 551
What If Light Diffracted? 586
Decibel Levels 610
Making a Rainbow 640
Television Colors 655
Car Mirrors 671

Science brings you closer together!

Bring science into your home by doing **School-to-Home Activities** with a parent or another adult in your household.

INTERNET ACTIVITY

CHAPTER 1 The World of Physical Science HP5WPSW

CHAPTER 2 The Properties of Matter HP5MATW

CHAPTER 3 States of Matter HP5STAW

CHAPTER 4 Elements, Compounds, and Mixtures HP5MIXW

CHAPTER 5 Matter in Motion HP5MOTW

CHAPTER 6 Forces and Motion HP5FORW

CHAPTER 7 Forces in Fluids HP5FLUW

CHAPTER 8 Work and Machines .. HP5WRKW

CHAPTER 9 Energy and Energy Resources HP5ENGW

CHAPTER 10 Heat and Heat Technology HP5HOTW

CHAPTER 11 Introduction to Atoms HP5ATSW

Get caught in the Web!

Go to **go.hrw.com** for **Internet Activities** related to each chapter. To find the Internet Activity for a particular chapter, just type in the keyword listed below.

CHAPTER 12 The Periodic Table HP5PRTW

CHAPTER 13 Chemical Bonding HP5BNDW

CHAPTER 14 Chemical Reactions HP5REAW

CHAPTER 15 Chemical Compounds HP5CMPW

CHAPTER 16 Atomic Energy HP5RADW

CHAPTER 17 Introduction to Electricity HP5ELEW

CHAPTER 18 Electromagnetism HP5EMGW

CHAPTER 19 Electronic Technology HP5ELTW

CHAPTER 20 The Energy of Waves HP5WAVW

CHAPTER 21 The Nature of Sound HP5SNDW

CHAPTER 22 The Nature of Light HP5LGTW

CHAPTER 23 Light and Our World HP5LOWW

MATH PRACTICE

Units of Measurement 25

Calculating Acceleration 122

Finding the Advantage 219

Converting Temperatures 277

Percentages 341

Calculating Charge 370

Counting Atoms 393

How Old Is It? 453

Transformers and Voltage 528

Computer Memory 557

The Speed of Sound 607

Microscope Magnification 679

MATH FOCUS

Volume of a Rectangular Solid 40

Converting Mass to Weight 42

Calculating Concentration 102

Calculating Average Speed 120

Calculating the Velocity of Falling Objects 151

Second-Law Problems 162

Momentum Calculations 167

Pressure, Force, and Area 181

Finding Density 188

More Power to You 214

Mechanical Advantage of an Inclined Plane 226

Kinetic Energy 241

Gravitational Potential Energy 242

Calculating Heat 286

Atomic Mass 323

Using Ohm's Law 491

Power and Energy 492

Wave Calculations 582

How Fast Is Light? 634

Science and math go hand in hand.

The **Math Focus** and **Math Practice** items show you many ways that math applies directly to science and vice versa.

Connection to...

Astronomy
Black Holes 136
Hydrogen 320
Elements of the Stars 460
Light Speed 576
Gamma Ray Spectrometer 642
Moonlight? 646

Biology
Adaptations 15
Seeds and Gravity 135
Work in the Human Body 211
Energy from Plants 250
Water Treatment 349
Proteins 375
Enzymes and Inhibitors 406
Acids Can Curl Your Hair 424
Blood and pH 430
Help for a Heart 485
Nervous Impulses 495
Animal Compasses 512
Vocal Sounds 602
Color Deficiency and Genes 676

Environmental Science
Thermal Pollution 9
Acid Rain 54
Car Sizes and Pollution 161
Recycling Aluminum 347
Radon in the Home 452
Painting Cars 476

Geology
Erosion 48
Floating Rocks 189
Seismograms 547

Language Arts
Communicating Without Words 18
Alloys 101
Gravity Story 138
Momentum and Language 168
Horsepower 215
Hidden Help 337
Diatomic Molecules 396
Covalent Compounds 420
Storage Site 459
The Colors of the Rainbow 585

Oceanography
Energy from the Ocean 295

Physics
Is Glass a Liquid? 67
Electrolysis 96

Social Studies
The Right Stuff 51
Invention of the Wheel 131
The First Flight 194
Living Near Coastlines 285
History of a Noble Gas 366
The Strike-Anywhere Match 404
DNA Fingerprinting and
   Crime-Scene Investigation 436
Benjamin Franklin 480
History of the Compass 516
ENIAC 556
The Particle Model of Light 633
Navigation 684

One subject leads to another.

You may not realize it at first, but different subjects are related to each other in many ways. Each **Connection** explores a topic from the viewpoint of another discipline. In this way, all of the subjects you learn about in school merge to improve your understanding of the world around you.

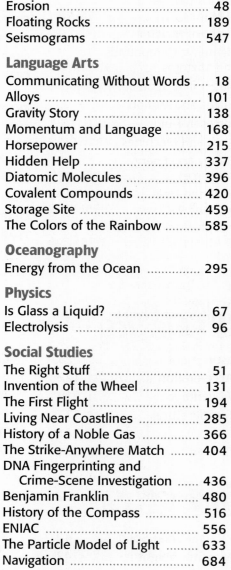

Science in Action

Science Fiction

"Inspiration" 34
"The Strange Case of Dr. Jekyll
   and Mr. Hyde" 112
"Wet Behind the Ears" 204
"There Will Come Soft Rains" 568
"Ear" 628

Science, Technology, and Society

Building a Better Body 62
Deep-sea Diving with Helium 86
Dry Cleaning: How Stains Are
   Dissolved 112
GPS Watch System 146
Power Suit for Lifting Patients 176
Stayin' Aloft—The Story of
   the Frisbee® 204
Kinetic Sculpture 236
Underwater Jet Engines 270
DiAPLEX®: The Intelligent Fabric 306
The Science of Fireworks 358
Superglue Bandages and Stitches 384
Bringing Down the House! 414
Molecular Photocopying 444
Irradiated Food 468
Magnets in Medicine 536
Wearable Computers 568
The Ultimate Telescope 596
It's a Heat Wave 664
Bionic Eyes 692

Scientific Debate

Paper or Plastic? 62
Do Cellular Telephones Cause
   Cancer? 692

Scientific Discoveries

The Fourth State of Matter 86
The Millennium Bridge 176
$E = mc^2$ 270
The Deep Freeze 306
Modern Alchemy 332
Sprites and Elves 506
The Wave Nature of Light 596
Jurassic Bark 628

Science moves beyond the classroom!

Read **Science in Action** articles to learn more about science in the real world. These articles will give you an idea of how interesting, strange, helpful, and action packed science is. At the end of each chapter, you will find three short articles. And if your thirst is still not quenched, go to **go.hrw.com** for in-depth coverage.

Weird Science

A Palace of Ice 34
The Segway™ Human Transporter 146
Nanomachines 236
Water on the Moon? 332
Buckyballs 358
How Geckos Stick to Walls 384
Light Sticks 414
Silly Putty® 444
Nuclear-Powered Bacteria 468
Electric Eels 506
Geomagnetic Storms 536
Fireflies Light the Way 664

Careers

Julie Williams-Byrd Electronics Engineer 35
Mimi So Gemologist and Jewelry Designer 63
Aundra Nix Metallurgist 113
Steve Okamoto Roller Coaster Designer 177
Alisha Bracken Scuba Instructor 205
Cheryl Mele Power-Plant Manager 271
Michael Reynolds Earthship Architect 307
Melissa Franklin Experimental Physicist 333
Roberta Jordan Analytical Chemist 385
Larry McKee Arson Investigator 415
Jeannie Eberhardt Forensic Scientist 445
Pete Perez Electrician 507
Agnes Riley Computer Technician 569
Estela Zavala Ultrasonographer 597
Adam Dudley Sound Engineer 629

People in Science

Andy Goldsworthy Nature Artist 87
Victor Petrenko Snowboard and Ski Brakes 147
Mike Hensler The Surf Chair 237
Glenn T. Seaborg Making Elements 359
Marie and Pierre Curie A Great Team 469
James Clerk Maxwell Magnetic Math 537
Albert Einstein A Light Pioneer 665
Sandra Faber Astronomer 693

How to Use Your Textbook

Your Roadmap for Success with Holt Science and Technology

Reading Warm-Up

A Reading Warm-Up at the beginning of every section provides you with the section's objectives and key terms. The objectives tell you what you'll need to know after you finish reading the section.

Key terms are listed for each section. Learn the definitions of these terms because you will most likely be tested on them. Each key term is highlighted in the text and is defined at point of use and in the margin. You can also use the glossary to locate definitions quickly.

STUDY TIP Reread the objectives and the definitions to the key terms when studying for a test to be sure you know the material.

Get Organized

A Reading Strategy at the beginning of every section provides tips to help you organize and remember the information covered in the section. Keep a science notebook so that you are ready to take notes when your teacher reviews the material in class. Keep your assignments in this notebook so that you can review them when studying for the chapter test.

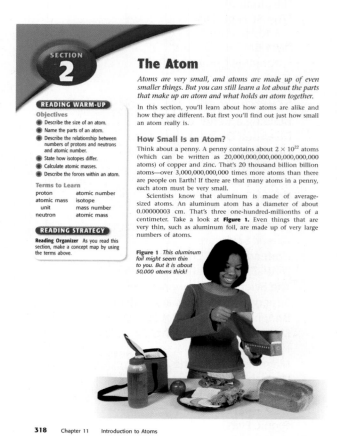

SECTION 2

The Atom

Atoms are very small, and atoms are made up of even smaller things. But you can still learn a lot about the parts that make up an atom and what holds an atom together.

In this section, you'll learn about how atoms are alike and how they are different. But first you'll find out just how small an atom really is.

How Small Is an Atom?

Think about a penny. A penny contains about 2×10^{22} atoms (which can be written as 20,000,000,000,000,000,000,000 atoms) of copper and zinc. That's 20 thousand billion billion atoms—over 3,000,000,000,000 times more atoms than there are people on Earth! If there are that many atoms in a penny, each atom must be very small.

Scientists know that aluminum is made of average-sized atoms. An aluminum atom has a diameter of about 0.00000003 cm. That's three one-hundred-millionths of a centimeter. Take a look at **Figure 1**. Even things that are very thin, such as aluminum foil, are made up of very large numbers of atoms.

Figure 1 This aluminum foil might seem thin to you. But it is about 50,000 atoms thick!

READING WARM-UP

Objectives
- Describe the size of an atom.
- Name the parts of an atom.
- Describe the relationship between numbers of protons and neutrons and atomic number.
- State how isotopes differ.
- Calculate atomic masses.
- Describe the forces within an atom.

Terms to Learn

proton   atomic number
atomic mass   isotope
unit   mass number
neutron   atomic mass

READING STRATEGY

Reading Organizer As you read this section, make a concept map by using the terms above.

318   Chapter 11   Introduction to Atoms

Be Resourceful—Use the Web

SCiLINKS

Internet Connect boxes in your textbook take you to resources that you can use for science projects, reports, and research papers. Go to scilinks.org, and type in the SciLinks code to get information on a topic.

go.hrw.com

Visit **go.hrw.com** Find worksheets, **Current Science** magazine articles online, and other materials that go with your textbook at **go.hrw.com**. Click on the textbook icon and the table of contents to see all of the resources for each chapter.

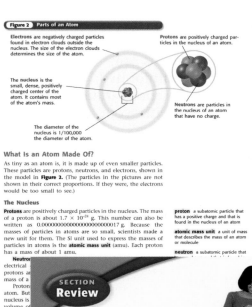

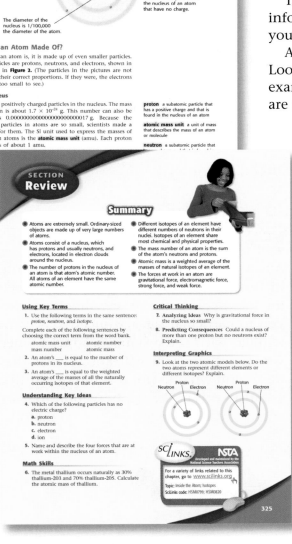

Use the Illustrations and Photos

Art shows complex ideas and processes. Learn to analyze the art so that you better understand the material you read in the text.

Tables and graphs display important information in an organized way to help you see relationships.

A picture is worth a thousand words. Look at the photographs to see relevant examples of science concepts that you are reading about.

Answer the Section Reviews

Section Reviews test your knowledge of the main points of the section. Critical Thinking items challenge you to think about the material in greater depth and to find connections that you infer from the text.

STUDY TIP When you can't answer a question, reread the section. The answer is usually there.

Do Your Homework

Your teacher may assign worksheets to help you understand and remember the material in the chapter.

STUDY TIP Don't try to answer the questions without reading the text and reviewing your class notes. A little preparation up front will make your homework assignments a lot easier. Answering the items in the Chapter Review will help prepare you for the chapter test.

Visit Holt Online Learning

If your teacher gives you a special password to log onto the Holt Online Learning site, you'll find your complete textbook on the Web. In addition, you'll find some great learning tools and practice quizzes. You'll be able to see how well you know the material from your textbook.

Visit CNN Student News

You'll find up-to-date events in science at **cnnstudentnews.com**.

SAFETY FIRST!

Exploring, inventing, and investigating are essential to the study of science. However, these activities can also be dangerous. To make sure that your experiments and explorations are safe, you must be aware of a variety of safety guidelines. You have probably heard of the saying, "It is better to be safe than sorry." This is particularly true in a science classroom where experiments and explorations are being performed. Being uninformed and careless can result in serious injuries. Don't take chances with your own safety or with anyone else's.

The following pages describe important guidelines for staying safe in the science classroom. Your teacher may also have safety guidelines and tips that are specific to your classroom and laboratory. Take the time to be safe.

Safety Rules!

Start Out Right

Always get your teacher's permission before attempting any laboratory exploration. Read the procedures carefully, and pay particular attention to safety information and caution statements. If you are unsure about what a safety symbol means, look it up or ask your teacher. You cannot be too careful when it comes to safety. If an accident does occur, inform your teacher immediately regardless of how minor you think the accident is.

If you are instructed to note the odor of a substance, wave the fumes toward your nose with your hand. Never put your nose close to the source.

Safety Symbols

All of the experiments and investigations in this book and their related worksheets include important safety symbols to alert you to particular safety concerns. Become familiar with these symbols so that when you see them, you will know what they mean and what to do. It is important that you read this entire safety section to learn about specific dangers in the laboratory.

Eye protection

Clothing protection

Hand safety

Heating safety

Electric safety

Chemical safety

Animal safety

Sharp object

Plant safety

xxvi

Eye Safety

Wear safety goggles when working around chemicals, acids, bases, or any type of flame or heating device. Wear safety goggles any time there is even the slightest chance that harm could come to your eyes. If any substance gets into your eyes, notify your teacher immediately and flush your eyes with running water for at least 15 minutes. Treat any unknown chemical as if it were a dangerous chemical. Never look directly into the sun. Doing so could cause permanent blindness.

Avoid wearing contact lenses in a laboratory situation. Even if you are wearing safety goggles, chemicals can get between the contact lenses and your eyes. If your doctor requires that you wear contact lenses instead of glasses, wear eye-cup safety goggles in the lab.

Safety Equipment

Know the locations of the nearest fire alarms and any other safety equipment, such as fire blankets and eyewash fountains, as identified by your teacher, and know the procedures for using the equipment.

Neatness

Keep your work area free of all unnecessary books and papers. Tie back long hair, and secure loose sleeves or other loose articles of clothing, such as ties and bows. Remove dangling jewelry. Don't wear open-toed shoes or sandals in the laboratory. Never eat, drink, or apply cosmetics in a laboratory setting. Food, drink, and cosmetics can easily become contaminated with dangerous materials.

Certain hair products (such as aerosol hair spray) are flammable and should not be worn while working near an open flame. Avoid wearing hair spray or hair gel on lab days.

Sharp/Pointed Objects

Use knives and other sharp instruments with extreme care. Never cut objects while holding them in your hands. Place objects on a suitable work surface for cutting.

Be extra careful when using any glassware. When adding a heavy object to a graduated cylinder, tilt the cylinder so that the object slides slowly to the bottom.

Heat

Wear safety goggles when using a heating device or a flame. Whenever possible, use an electric hot plate as a heat source instead of using an open flame. When heating materials in a test tube, always angle the test tube away from yourself and others. To avoid burns, wear heat-resistant gloves whenever instructed to do so.

Electricity

Be careful with electrical cords. When using a microscope with a lamp, do not place the cord where it could trip someone. Do not let cords hang over a table edge in a way that could cause equipment to fall if the cord is accidentally pulled. Do not use equipment with damaged cords. Be sure that your hands are dry and that the electrical equipment is in the "off" position before plugging it in. Turn off and unplug electrical equipment when you are finished.

Chemicals

Wear safety goggles when handling any potentially dangerous chemicals, acids, or bases. If a chemical is unknown, handle it as you would a dangerous chemical. Wear an apron and protective gloves when you work with acids or bases or whenever you are told to do so. If a spill gets on your skin or clothing, rinse it off immediately with water for at least 5 minutes while calling to your teacher.

Never mix chemicals unless your teacher tells you to do so. Never taste, touch, or smell chemicals unless you are specifically directed to do so. Before working with a flammable liquid or gas, check for the presence of any source of flame, spark, or heat.

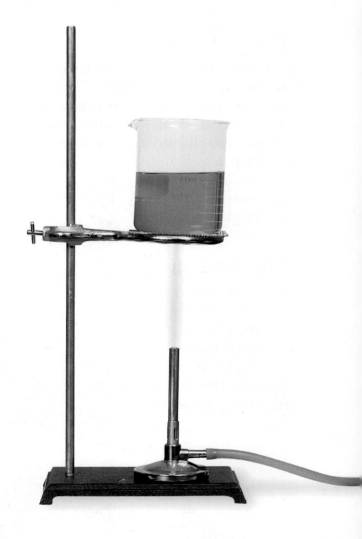

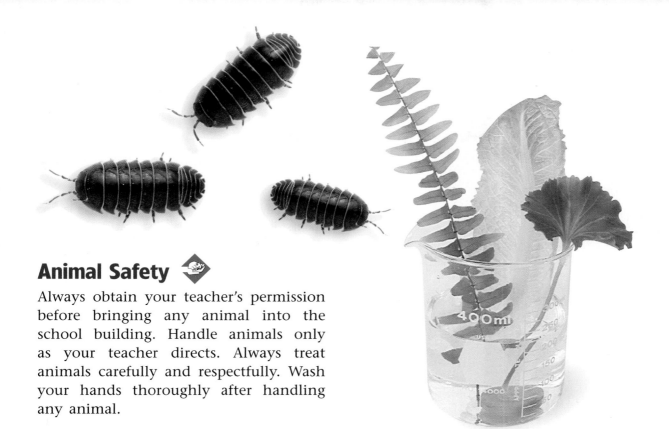

Animal Safety

Always obtain your teacher's permission before bringing any animal into the school building. Handle animals only as your teacher directs. Always treat animals carefully and respectfully. Wash your hands thoroughly after handling any animal.

Plant Safety

Do not eat any part of a plant or plant seed used in the laboratory. Wash your hands thoroughly after handling any part of a plant. When in nature, do not pick any wild plants unless your teacher instructs you to do so.

Glassware

Examine all glassware before use. Be sure that glassware is clean and free of chips and cracks. Report damaged glassware to your teacher. Glass containers used for heating should be made of heat-resistant glass.

TIMELINE

Introduction to Matter

In this unit, you will explore a basic question that people have been pondering for centuries: What is the nature of matter? You will learn how to define the word *matter* and the ways to describe matter and the changes it goes through. You will also learn about the different states of matter and how to classify different arrangements of matter as elements, compounds, or mixtures. This timeline shows some of the events and discoveries that have occurred throughout history as scientists have sought to understand the nature of matter.

1661

Robert Boyle, a chemist in England, determines that elements are substances that cannot be broken down into anything simpler by chemical processes.

1712

Thomas Newcomen invents the first practical steam engine.

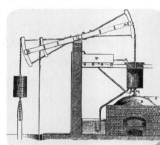

1937

The *Hindenburg* explodes while docking in Lakehurst, New Jersey. To make it lighter than air, the airship was filled with flammable hydrogen gas.

1971

The first commercially available "pocket" calculator is introduced. It has a mass of nearly 1 kg and a price of about $400, hardly the kind of pocket calculator that exists today.

1766

English chemist Henry Cavendish discovers and describes the properties of a highly flammable substance now known as hydrogen gas.

1800

Current from an electric battery is used to separate water into the elements hydrogen and oxygen for the first time.

1920

American women win the right to vote with the ratification of the 19th Amendment to the Constitution.

1950

Silly Putty® is sold in a toy store for the first time. The soft, gooey substance quickly becomes popular because of its strange properties, including the ability to "pick up" the print from a newspaper page.

1957

The space age begins when the Soviet Union launches *Sputnik I*, the first artificial satellite to circle the Earth.

1989

An oil tanker strikes a reef in Prince William Sound, Alaska, and spills nearly 11 million gallons of oil. The floating oil injures or kills thousands of marine mammals and seabirds and damages the Alaskan coastline.

2000

The World's Fair, an international exhibition featuring exhibits and participants from around the world, is held in Hanover, Germany. The theme is "Humankind, Nature, and Technology."

2003

Sally Ride, the first American woman in space, is inducted into the Astronaut Hall of Fame.

1

The World of Physical Science

SECTION ① Exploring Physical
Science   6

SECTION ② Scientific Methods. 12

SECTION ③ Scientific Models 20

SECTION ④ Tools, Measurement,
and Safety 24

Chapter Lab 28
Chapter Review 30
Standardized Test Preparation 32
Science in Action 34

About the PHOTO

Flippers work great to help penguins move through the water. But could flippers help ships, too? Two scientists have been trying to find out. By using scientific methods, they are asking questions such as, "Would flippers use less energy than propellers do?" As a result of these investigations, ships may have flippers like those of penguins someday!

PRE-READING ACTIVITY

Graphic Organizer

Spider Map Before you read the chapter, create the graphic organizer entitled "Spider Map" described in the **Study Skills** section of the Appendix. Label the circle "Scientific Models." Create a leg for each type of scientific model. As you read the chapter, fill in the map with details about each type of scientific model.

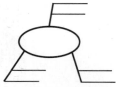

START-UP ACTIVITY

Figure It Out

In this activity, you will make observations and use them to solve a puzzle, just as scientists do.

Procedure

1. Get the **five shapes** shown here from your teacher.

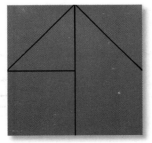

2. Observe the drawing at right. Predict how the five shapes could be arranged to make the fish.

3. Test your idea. You may have to try several times. (Hint: Shapes can be turned over.)

Analysis

1. Did you solve the puzzle just by making observations? What observations helped the most?

2. How did testing your ideas help?

Exploring Physical Science

You're eating breakfast. You look down and notice that your reflection in your spoon is upside down! You wonder, Why is my reflection upside down even though I'm holding the spoon right side up?

Congratulations! You just completed the first steps toward becoming a scientist. How did you do it? You observed the world around you. Then, you asked questions about your observations. That's what most of science is all about.

That's Science!

Science is a process of gathering knowledge about the natural world. Asking a question is often the first step in the process of gathering knowledge. The world around you is full of amazing things that can lead you to ask questions. The student in **Figure 1** didn't have to look very far to realize that she had some questions to ask.

✓ **Reading Check** What is often the first step in gathering knowledge? (*See the Appendix for answers to Reading Checks.*)

Everyday Science

Everyday actions such as timing the microwave popcorn and using the brakes on your bicycle use your knowledge of science. You learned how to do these things by making observations and asking questions. Making observations and asking questions is what science is all about. And because science is all around, you might not be surprised to learn that there are many branches of science. Physical science is the science you will learn about in this book. But physical science is just one of the many different branches of science.

Why can I see a reflection in a spoon?

What causes high and low tides?

Why do I feel pain when I stub my toe?

Figure 1 *Part of science is asking questions about the world around you.*

Figure 2 *The cheetah, the fastest land mammal, uses a lot of energy when running full speed. But a successful hunt will supply the energy the cheetah needs to live.*

What Is Physical Science?

Physical science is the study of matter and energy. *Matter* is the "stuff" that everything is made of. Even stuff so small that you can't see it is matter. Your shoes, your pencil, and even the air you breathe are made of matter. And all of this matter has energy. *Energy* is the ability to do work. But energy is easier to describe than to explain. For example, energy is partly responsible for rainbows in the sky. But energy isn't the rainbow itself. All moving objects have energy of motion, such as the cheetah shown in **Figure 2.**

Food also has energy. When you eat food, the energy in the food is transferred to you. You can use that energy to carry out your daily activities. But energy isn't always associated with motion or food. All matter, including matter that isn't moving, has energy. So, because the baseball in **Figure 3** is matter, it has energy even though it is not yet moving.

science the knowledge obtained by observing natural events and conditions in order to discover facts and formulate laws or principles that can be verified or tested

physical science the scientific study of nonliving matter

A Study of Matter and Energy

As you explore physical science, you'll learn more about matter and energy. And you will see how matter and energy relate to each other. For example, both paper and gold are matter. But why will paper burn, and gold will not? And why is throwing a bowling ball harder than throwing a baseball? How can water turn into steam and back into water? All of the answers to these questions have to do with matter and energy. It is hard to talk about matter without talking about energy. However, sometimes it is useful to focus on one or the other. Physical science is also often divided into two categories: chemistry and physics.

Figure 3 *The baseball has energy even before the boy throws it, because it is matter, and all matter has energy.*

Branches of Physical Science

Physical science is usually divided into chemistry and physics. But both chemistry and physics can be further broken down into many more specialized areas of study. For example, chemistry includes organic chemistry, which is the study of substances made of carbon. And geophysics, one of the branches of physics, includes the study of the vibrations deep inside the Earth that are caused by earthquakes.

Chemistry—A Matter of Reactions!

Chemistry is the study of all forms of matter, including how matter interacts with other matter. Chemistry looks at the structure and properties of matter. For example, some substances behave one way under high temperature and high pressure. But other substances will behave very differently under the same conditions. The scientist in **Figure 4** is studying the properties of different kinds of materials. He is trying to find materials that have unusual properties, such as the ability to withstand very high heat.

Chemistry is also the study of how substances change. A chemical reaction takes place when one substance reacts with another substance to make a new substance. Chemical reactions are taking place around you all of the time. When your body digests food, a chemical reaction is taking place. Chemical reactions are needed when you take a photo of your best friend, when your parent starts the car engine, and when you turn on a flashlight.

Reading Check What are three things that chemistry studies?

Figure 4 *A materials scientist uses his knowledge of chemistry to study the properties of different kinds of substances.*

Figure 5 *When you study physics, you'll learn how energy causes the motion that makes a roller-coaster ride so exciting.*

Physics—A Matter of Energy

Like chemistry, physics deals with matter. But physics looks mostly at energy and the way that energy affects matter. Studying different forms of energy is what studying physics is all about. Energy can make matter do some interesting things. For example, have you ever wondered what keeps a roller coaster, such as the one shown in **Figure 5,** on its tracks? The study of physics will help answer this question.

Motion, force, gravity, electricity, light, and heat are parts of physics. They are also things that you experience in your daily life. For example, if you have ever ridden a bike, you are aware that force causes motion. If you have ever used a compass, you have dealt with the concept of magnetism. Do you know why you see a rainbow after a rainstorm? Or, do you know why shifting gears on your bicycle makes it easier to pedal? You will learn the answers to these questions, as well as many others, as you study physical science.

INTERNET ACTIVITY

For another activity related to this chapter, go to **go.hrw.com** and type in the keyword **HP5WPSW.**

CONNECTION TO Environmental Science

Thermal Pollution Factories are often built along the banks of rivers. The factories use the river water to cool the engines of their machinery. Then, the hot water is poured back into the river. Energy, in the form of heat, is transferred from this water to the river water. The increase in temperature results in the death of many living things. Research how thermal pollution causes fish to die. Also, find out what many factories are doing to prevent thermal pollution. Make a brochure that explains what thermal pollution is and what is being done to prevent it.

ACTIVITY

Figure 6 *These meteorologists are risking their lives to gather data about tornadoes.*

Physical Science: All Around You

Believe it or not, matter and energy are not just concepts in physical science. What you learn about matter and energy is important for other science classes, too.

Meteorology

The study of Earth's atmosphere, especially in relation to weather and climate, is called *meteorology* (MEET ee uhr AHL uh jee). A *meteorologist* (MEET ee uhr AHL uh jist) is a person who studies the atmosphere. One of the most common careers meteorologists have is weather forecasting. But other meteorologists specialize in and even chase tornadoes! These meteorologists predict where a tornado is likely to form. Then, they drive very close to the site to gather data, as shown in **Figure 6.** By gathering data this way, scientists hope to understand tornadoes better. Meteorologists must have knowledge of physical science. They must understand high and low pressure, motion, and force before they can predict how tornadoes will behave.

Geology

The study of the origin, history, and structure of Earth is called *geology*. Some geologists are geochemists (JEE oh KEM ists). A *geochemist* is a person who specializes in the chemistry of rocks, minerals, and soil. Geochemists, such as the one in **Figure 7,** try to find out what the environment was like when these materials formed and what has happened to the materials since they formed. To understand how rocks and soil have changed over millions of years, a geochemist must have a knowledge of heat, force, and chemistry.

✓ Reading Check What does a geochemist study?

Figure 7 *This geochemist takes rock samples from the field. Then, she studies them in her laboratory.*

Biology

Students are often surprised that life science and physical science are related. But chemistry and physics explain many things that happen in biology. For example, a chemical reaction explains how animals, such as the cow in **Figure 8,** get energy from food. Sugar, $C_6H_{12}O_6$, which is produced by the plant, reacts with oxygen. As a result, carbon dioxide, water, and energy are produced. This reaction can be shown by the following chemical equation:

$$C_6H_{12}O_6 + 6O_2 \rightarrow 6CO_2 + 6H_2O + energy$$

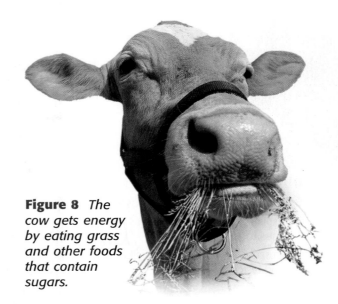

Figure 8 *The cow gets energy by eating grass and other foods that contain sugars.*

SECTION Review

Summary

- Science is a process of gathering knowledge about the natural world.
- Physical science is the study of matter and energy.
- Physical science is divided into the study of physics and chemistry.
- Chemistry studies the structure and properties of matter and how matter changes.
- Physics looks at energy and the way that energy affects matter.
- A knowledge of physical science is important for many areas of science, such as geology and biology.

Using Key Terms

1. In your own words, write a definition for each of the following terms: *science* and *physical science*.

Understanding Key Ideas

2. Which of the following statements is true?
   a. Energy is the ability to do work.
   b. Air is made of matter.
   c. All matter has energy.
   d. All of the above

3. What are three areas of science that rely on physical science?

4. What is the difference between chemistry and physics?

Math Skills

5. You want to know which month had the highest percentage of rainy days for your city last year. Your investigation gave the following results: March had 5 days of rain, April had 8 days of rain, and May had 3 days of rain. For each month, what percentage of the month had rainy days? Which month had the highest percentage of rainy days?

Critical Thinking

6. **Applying Concepts** How do you think science is used by a pharmacist? by a firefighter?

7. **Analyzing Ideas** You are building a go-cart and want to know how to make it go as fast as possible. Which branch, or branches, of science would you study? Explain your answer.

8. **Identifying Relationships** Describe three things that you do every day that use your experience with physical science.

9. **Making Inferences** Botany is the study of plants. What role do you think physical science plays in botany?

Scientific Methods

Imagine that you are trying to improve ships. Would you study the history of shipbuilding? Would you investigate different types of fuel? Would you observe animals that move easily through water, such as dolphins and penguins?

Two scientists from the Massachusetts Institute of Technology (MIT) thought that studying penguins was a great way to improve ships! James Czarnowski (zahr NOW SKEE) and Michael Triantafyllou (tree AHN ti FEE loo) used scientific methods to develop *Proteus* (PROH tee uhs), the penguin boat. In the next few pages, you will learn how these scientists used scientific methods to answer their questions.

What Are Scientific Methods?

Scientific methods are the ways in which scientists answer questions and solve problems. As scientists look for answers, they often use the same steps. But there is more than one way to use the steps. Look at **Figure 1.** This figure is an outline of the six steps on which scientific methods are based. Scientists may use all of the steps or just some of the steps during an investigation. They may even repeat some of the steps or do the steps in a different order. How they choose to use the steps depends on what works best to answer their question.

scientific methods a series of steps followed to solve problems

Figure 1 Steps of Scientific Methods

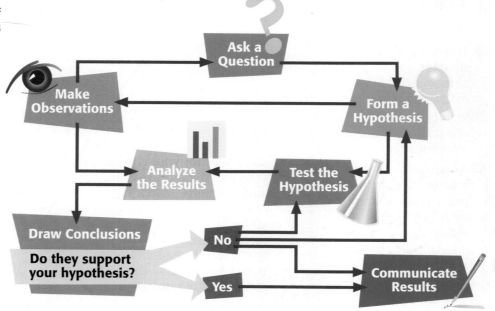

Asking a Question

Asking a question helps focus the purpose of an investigation. Scientists often ask a question after making many observations. **Observation** is any use of the senses to gather information. Noting that the sky is blue or that a cotton ball feels soft is an observation. Measurements are observations that are made with tools, such as the ones shown in **Figure 2.** Keep in mind that observations can be made (and should be accurately recorded) at any point during an investigation.

✓ **Reading Check** What is the purpose of asking questions? (*See the Appendix for answers to Reading Checks.*)

A Real-World Question

Czarnowski and Triantafyllou, shown in **Figure 3,** are engineers, scientists who put scientific knowledge to practical use. Czarnowski was a graduate student at the Massachusetts Institute of Technology. He and Triantafyllou, his professor, worked together to observe boat propulsion (proh PUHL shuhn) systems. Then, they investigated how to make these systems work better. A propulsion system is what makes a boat move. Most boats have propellers to move them through the water.

Czarnowski and Triantafyllou studied the efficiency (e FISH uhn see) of boat propulsion systems. *Efficiency* compares energy output (the energy used to move the boat forward) with energy input (the energy supplied by the boat's engine). From their observations, Czarnowski and Triantafyllou learned that boat propellers are not very efficient.

Figure 2 *Stopwatches and rulers are among the many tools used to make observations.*

observation the process of obtaining information by using the senses

Figure 3 *James Czarnowski* (left) *and Michael Triantafyllou* (right) *made observations about how boats work in order to develop* Proteus.

Figure 4 **Observations About the Efficiency of Boat Propellers**

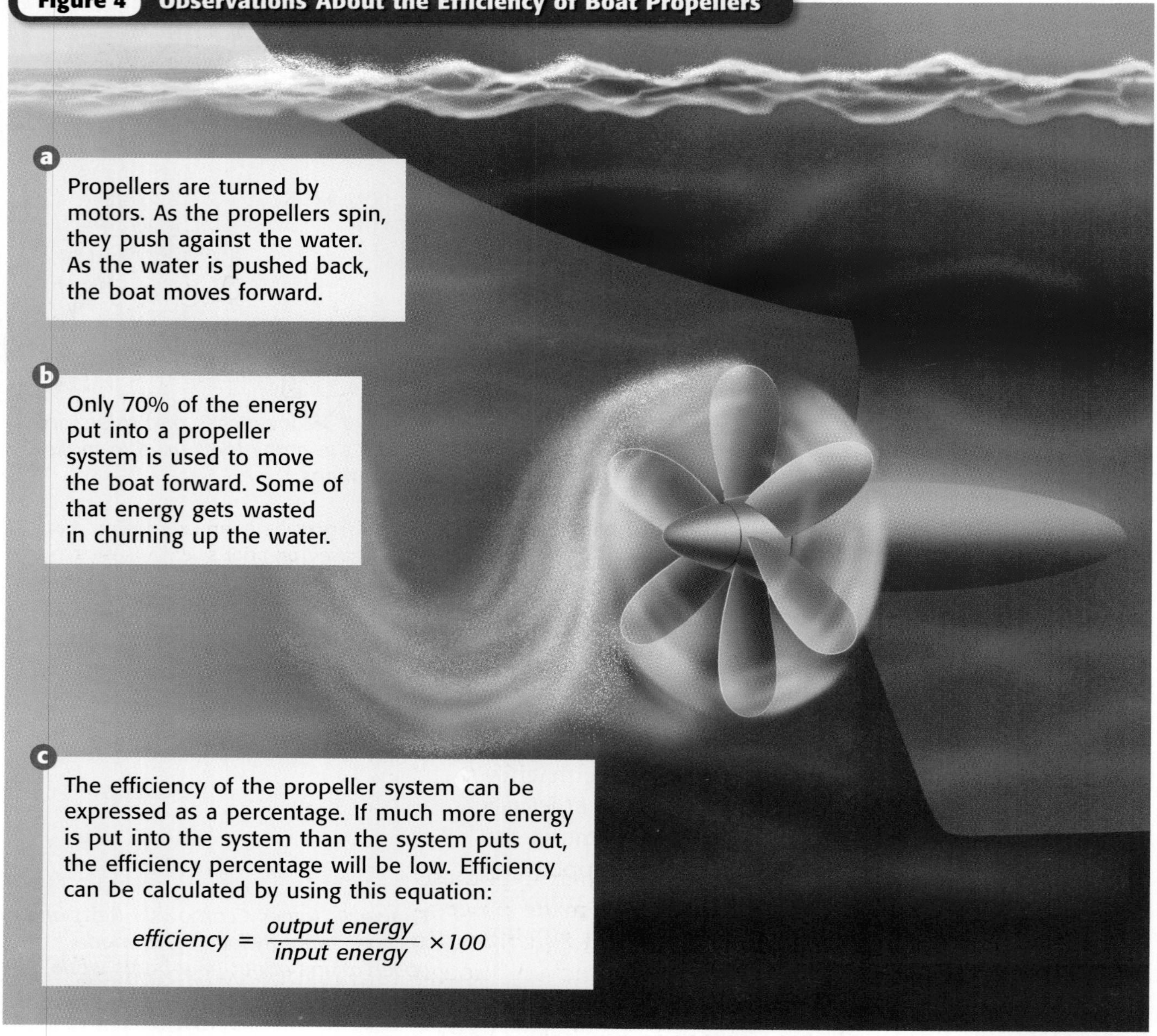

a Propellers are turned by motors. As the propellers spin, they push against the water. As the water is pushed back, the boat moves forward.

b Only 70% of the energy put into a propeller system is used to move the boat forward. Some of that energy gets wasted in churning up the water.

c The efficiency of the propeller system can be expressed as a percentage. If much more energy is put into the system than the system puts out, the efficiency percentage will be low. Efficiency can be calculated by using this equation:

$$efficiency = \frac{output\ energy}{input\ energy} \times 100$$

The Importance of Boat Efficiency

Most boats that have propellers, shown in **Figure 4,** are only about 70% efficient. But is boat efficiency important, and if so, why? Yes, boat efficiency is important because it saves many resources. Making only a small fraction of U.S. boats and ships just 10% more efficient would save millions of liters of fuel per year. Saving fuel means saving money. It also means using less of Earth's supply of fossil fuels. Based on their observations and all of this information, Czarnowski and Triantafyllou were ready to ask a question: How can boat propulsion systems be made more efficient?

Reading Check Why is boat efficiency important?

Figure 5 *Penguins use their flippers to "fly" underwater. As they pull their flippers toward their body, they push against the water, which propels them forward.*

Forming a Hypothesis

Once you've asked your question and made observations, you are ready to form a hypothesis (hie PAHTH uh sis). A **hypothesis** is a possible explanation or answer to a question. You can use what you already know and what you have observed to form a hypothesis.

A good hypothesis is testable. In other words, information can be gathered or an experiment can be designed to test the hypothesis. A hypothesis that is not testable isn't necessarily wrong. But there is no way to show whether the hypothesis is right or wrong.

hypothesis an explanation that is based on prior scientific research or observations and that can be tested

A Possible Answer from Nature

Czarnowski and Triantafyllou wanted to base their hypothesis on an example from nature. Czarnowski had made observations of penguins swimming at the New England Aquarium. He observed how quickly and easily the penguins moved through the water. **Figure 5** shows how penguins propel themselves. Czarnowski also observed that penguins, like boats, have a rigid body. These observations led to a hypothesis: A propulsion system that imitates the way that a penguin swims will be more efficient than a propulsion system that uses propellers.

Making Predictions

Before scientists test a hypothesis, they often predict what they think will happen when they test the hypothesis. Scientists usually state predictions in an if-then statement. The engineers at MIT might have made the following prediction: *If* two flippers are attached to a boat, *then* the boat will be more efficient than a boat powered by propellers.

CONNECTION TO Biology

Adaptations Penguins, though flightless, are better adapted to water and extreme cold than any other birds are. Research these amazing birds to learn how they are adapted to their environment. Also, investigate the speed at which penguins can swim. Present this information in a poster.

Quick Lab

That's Swingin'!

1. Make a pendulum. Tie a **piece of string** to a **ring stand.** Hang a **small weight** from the string.

2. Form a testable hypothesis about one factor (such as the mass of the small weight) that may affect the rate at which the pendulum swings.

3. Predict the results as you change this factor (the variable).

4. Test your hypothesis. Record the number of swings made in 10 s for each trial.

5. Was your hypothesis supported? Analyze your results.

Testing the Hypothesis

After you form a hypothesis, you must test it. You must find out if it is a reasonable answer to your question. Testing helps you find out if your hypothesis is pointing you in the right direction or is way off the mark. If your hypothesis is way off the mark, you may have to change it.

Controlled Experiments

One way to test a hypothesis is to do a controlled experiment. A *controlled experiment* compares the results from a control group with the results from experimental groups. The groups are the same except for one factor. This factor is called a *variable*. The results of the experiment will show the effect of the variable.

Sometimes, a controlled experiment is not possible. Stars, for example, are too far away to be used in an experiment. In such cases, you can make more observations or do research. Another investigation may require you to make or build a device to test. You can then test your device to see if it does what you expected it to do and if the results support your hypothesis. Czarnowski and Triantafyllou did such a controlled experiment. They built *Proteus,* the penguin boat, shown in **Figure 6.**

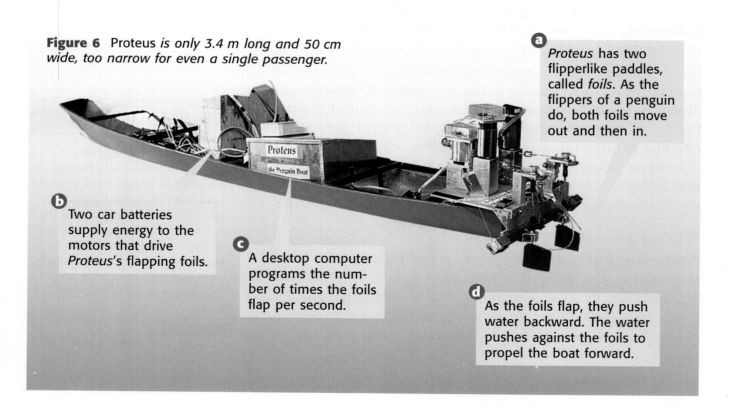

Figure 6 Proteus *is only 3.4 m long and 50 cm wide, too narrow for even a single passenger.*

a *Proteus* has two flipperlike paddles, called *foils*. As the flippers of a penguin do, both foils move out and then in.

b Two car batteries supply energy to the motors that drive *Proteus*'s flapping foils.

c A desktop computer programs the number of times the foils flap per second.

d As the foils flap, they push water backward. The water pushes against the foils to propel the boat forward.

Figure 7 Graphs of the Test Results

This line graph shows that *Proteus* was most efficient when its foils were flapping about 1.7 times per second.

This bar graph shows that *Proteus* is 17% more efficient than a propeller-driven boat.

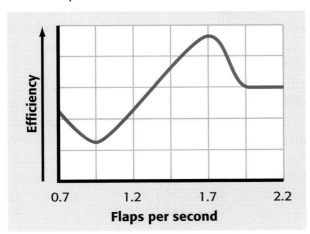

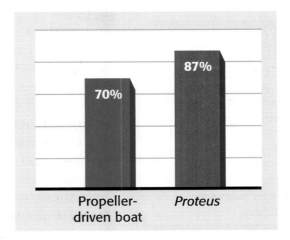

Testing *Proteus*

Czarnowski and Triantafyllou took *Proteus* out into the open water of the Charles River in Boston when they were ready to collect data. **Data** are any pieces of information acquired through experimentation. For each test, data such as the flapping rate, the energy used by the motors, and the speed achieved by the boat were carefully recorded. But the only factor the scientists changed was the flapping rate. The input energy was determined by how much energy was used. The output energy was determined from the speed *Proteus* reached.

data any pieces of information acquired through observation or experimentation

Analyzing the Results

After you collect and record your data, you must analyze them. You must find out if the results of your test support the hypothesis. Sometimes, doing calculations can help you learn more about your results. Organizing data into tables and graphs makes relationships between information easier to see.

✓ Reading Check Why are graphs and charts useful for analyzing results?

Analyzing *Proteus*

Czarnowski and Triantafyllou used the data for input energy and output energy to calculate *Proteus*'s efficiency for different flapping rates. These data are graphed in **Figure 7.** The scientists compared *Proteus*'s highest level of efficiency with the average efficiency of a propeller-driven boat. As you can see, the data support the scientists' hypothesis that penguin propulsion is more efficient than propeller propulsion.

Drawing Conclusions

At the end of an investigation, you must draw a conclusion. You could conclude that your results support your hypothesis. Or you could conclude that your results do *not* support your hypothesis. Or you might even conclude that you need more information. Your conclusion can help guide you in deciding what to do next. You could ask new questions, gather more information, or change the procedure.

The *Proteus* Conclusion

After Czarnowski and Triantafyllou analyzed the results of their test, they ran many more trials. Again, they found that the penguin propulsion system was more efficient than a propeller propulsion system. So, they concluded that their hypothesis was supported, which led to more questions, as **Figure 8** shows.

Communicating Results

One of the most important steps in any investigation is to communicate your results. You can write a scientific paper, make a presentation, or create a Web site. Telling others what you learned keeps science going. Other scientists can then conduct their own tests.

> **✓ Reading Check** What are some ways to communicate the results of an investigation?

Communicating About *Proteus*

Czarnowski and Triantafyllou published their results in academic papers, science magazines, and newspapers. They also displayed the results of their project on the Internet. These reports allow other scientists to conduct additional research about *Proteus*.

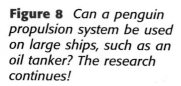

CONNECTION TO Language Arts

WRITING SKILL **Communicating Without Words**
Research methods of nonverbal communication. In the past, how did people communicate with each other without talking? Write a one-page essay describing what you have learned about nonverbal communication.

Figure 8 *Can a penguin propulsion system be used on large ships, such as an oil tanker? The research continues!*

Summary

- Scientific methods are the ways in which scientists answer questions and solve problems.

- Asking a question usually results from making an observation. Questioning is often the first step of using scientific methods.

- A hypothesis is a possible explanation or answer to a question. A good hypothesis is testable.

- After testing a hypothesis, you should analyze your results. Analyzing is usually done by using calculations, tables, and graphs.

- After analyzing your results, you should draw conclusions about whether your hypothesis is supported.

- Communicating your results allows others to check or continue your work. You can communicate through reports, posters, and the Internet.

Using Key Terms

The statements below are false. For each statement, replace the underlined term to make a true statement.

1. <u>Observations</u> are the ways in which scientists answer questions and solve problems.

2. <u>Hypotheses</u> are pieces of information that are gathered through experimentation.

3. <u>Data</u> are possible explanations or answers to a question.

Understanding Key Ideas

4. A controlled experiment
   a. is not always possible.
   b. contains a test group.
   c. has only one variable.
   d. All of the above

5. Name the steps that can be used in scientific methods.

Critical Thinking

6. **Analyzing Methods** Explain how the accuracy of your observations might affect how you develop a hypothesis.

7. **Applying Concepts** You want to test different shapes of kites to see which shape results in the strongest lift, or upward force, in the air. List some factors that need to be the same for each trial so that the only variable is the shape of the kite.

Interpreting Graphics

Use the graph below to answer the questions that follow.

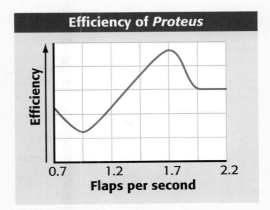

Efficiency of *Proteus*

Efficiency (vertical axis)

Flaps per second (horizontal axis): 0.7, 1.2, 1.7, 2.2

8. At what number of flaps per second is *Proteus* most efficient? least efficient?

9. At approximately what point does the efficiency appear neither to increase nor to decrease?

SCI LINKS®

NSTA
Developed and maintained by the
National Science Teachers Association

For a variety of links related to this chapter, go to www.scilinks.org

Topic: Scientific Methods
SciLinks code: HSM1359

19

Scientific Models

How much like a penguin is Proteus? Proteus *doesn't have feathers and isn't a living thing. But its "flippers" create the same kind of motion that a penguin's flippers do.*

The MIT engineers built *Proteus* to mimic the way a penguin swims so that they could gain a greater understanding about boat propulsion. In other words, they made a model.

Models in Science

A **model** is a representation of an object or system. A model uses something familiar to help you understand something that is not familiar. For example, models of human body systems can help you understand how the body works. Models can also be used to explain the past and the present. They can even be used to predict future events. There are three common kinds of scientific models. They are physical, mathematical, and conceptual (kuhn SEP choo uhl) models. However, models have limitations because they are never exactly like the real thing.

Physical Models

Model airplanes, dolls, and drawings are examples of physical models. A model of a molecule can show you the shape of the molecule, which you cannot see. But this model wouldn't let you see how the molecule interacts with other molecules. Other kinds of physical models can help you understand certain concepts. For example, look at the model space shuttle and the real space shuttle in **Figure 1.** Launching a model like the one on the left can help you understand how a real space shuttle blasts off into space.

Figure 1 *Using a model of a space shuttle can help you understand how a real space shuttle works.*

Mathematical Models

Every day, people try to predict the weather. One way to predict the weather is to use mathematical models. A mathematical model is made up of mathematical equations and data. Some mathematical models are simple. These models allow you to calculate things such as forces and acceleration. But other mathematical models are so complex that only computers can handle them. Some of these very complex models have many variables. Sometimes, certain variables that no one thought of exist in a model. A change in any variable could cause the model to fail.

✓ Reading Check Name a possible limitation of a mathematical model. (*See the Appendix for answers to Reading Checks.*)

Conceptual Models

The third kind of model is a conceptual model. Some conceptual models are systems of ideas. Others are based on making comparisons with familiar things to help illustrate or explain an idea. The big bang theory is a conceptual model that describes how the planets and galaxies formed. This model is described in **Figure 2.** Although the big bang theory is widely accepted by astronomers, some data do not fit the model. For example, scientists have calculated the ages of some old, nearby stars. If the calculations are right, some of these stars are older than the universe itself. So, conceptual models may not take certain data into account. Or the models may rely on certain ideas but not on others.

model a pattern, plan, representation, or description designed to show the structure or workings of an object, system, or concept

Weather Forecasting

Watch the weather forecast on TV. You will see several models that a weather reporter uses to inform you about the weather in your area. In your **science journal,** describe two of these models and explain how each model is used to represent the weather. Describe some of the advantages and disadvantages of each model.

Figure 2 *The big bang theory says that 12 billion to 15 billion years ago, an event called the* big bang *sent matter in all directions. This matter eventually formed the galaxies and planets.*

Figure 3 *The compressed coils on the spring toy can be used to model the way air particles are crowded together in a sound wave.*

theory an explanation that ties together many hypotheses and observations

law a summary of many experimental results and observations; a law tells how things work

Models: The Right Size

Models are often used to represent things that are very small or very large. Some particles of matter are too small to see. The Earth and the solar system are too large to see completely. So, a model can help you picture the thing in your mind. Sometimes, models are used to learn about things you cannot see, such as sound waves. Look at **Figure 3.** A coiled spring toy is often used as a model of sound waves because the spring toy behaves similar to the way sound waves do.

Using Models to Build Scientific Knowledge

Models not only can represent scientific ideas and objects but also can be tools that are useful to help you learn new information.

Scientific Theories

Models are often used to help illustrate and explain scientific theories. In science, a **theory** is an explanation for many hypotheses and observations. Usually, these hypotheses have been supported by repeated tests. A theory not only explains an observation you've made but also can predict what might happen in the future.

Scientists use models to help guide their search for new information. This information can help support a theory or can show that the theory is wrong. Keep in mind that models can be changed or replaced. These changes happen when scientists make new observations. Because of these new observations, scientists may have to change their theories. **Figure 4** compares an old model with a current model.

Reading Check What two things can a theory explain?

Figure 4 *These models show how scientists' idea of the atom has changed over time as new information was gathered.*

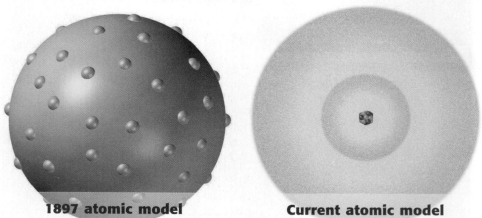

1897 atomic model   **Current atomic model**

Scientific Laws

What happens when a model correctly predicts the results of many different experiments? A scientific law can be constructed. In science, a **law** is a summary of many experimental results and observations. A law tells you how things work. Laws are not the same as theories. Laws tell you only what happens, not why it happens. Look at **Figure 5.** A chemical change took place when the flask was turned over. A light blue solid and a dark blue solution formed. Notice that the mass did not change, which demonstrates the *law of conservation of mass*. This law says that during a chemical change, the total mass of the materials formed is the same as the total mass of the starting materials. However, the law doesn't explain why. It tells you only what will happen during every chemical change.

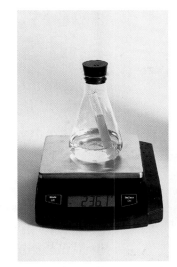

Figure 5 *The total mass before the chemical change is always the same as the total mass after the change.*

SECTION
Review

Summary

- A model uses familiar things to describe unfamiliar things.
- Physical, mathematical, and conceptual models are commonly used in science.
- A scientific theory is an explanation for many hypotheses and observations.
- A scientific law summarizes experimental results and observations. It describes what happens but not why.

Using Key Terms

1. In your own words, write a definition for the term *model*.

Understanding Key Ideas

2. Which kind of model would you use to represent a human heart?
   a. a mathematical model
   b. a physical model
   c. a conceptual model
   d. a natural model

3. Explain the difference between a theory and a law.

Critical Thinking

4. **Analyzing Methods** Both a globe and a flat world map can model features of Earth. Give an example of when you would use each of these models.

5. **Applying Concepts** Identify two limitations of physical models.

Math Skills

6. For a science fair, you want to make a model of the moon orbiting Earth by using two different balls. The diameter of the ball that will represent Earth will be about 62 cm. You want your model to be to scale. If the moon is about 4 times smaller than Earth, what should the diameter of the ball that represents the moon be?

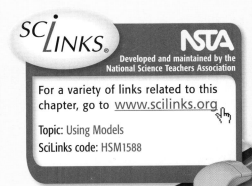

Tools, Measurement, and Safety

READING WARM-UP

Objectives

- Identify tools used to collect and analyze data.
- Explain the importance of the International System of Units.
- Identify the appropriate units to use for particular measurements.
- Identify safety symbols.

Terms to Learn

mass   density
volume   temperature

READING STRATEGY

Brainstorming The key idea of this section is scientific tools and measurements. Brainstorm what tools scientists use in their work and what the tools are used for.

Would you use a spoon to dig a hole to plant a tree? You wouldn't if you had a shovel!

To dig a hole, you need the correct tools. A *tool* is anything that helps you do a task. Scientists use many different tools to help them in their experiments.

Tools in Science

One way to collect data is to take measurements. To get the best measurements, you need the proper tools. Stopwatches, metersticks, and balances are some of the tools you can use to make measurements. Thermometers can be used to observe changes in temperature. Some of the uses for these tools are shown in **Figure 1.**

After you collect data, you need to analyze them. Calculators are handy tools to help you do calculations quickly. Or you might show your data in a graph or a figure. A computer that has the correct software can help you display your data. Of course, you can use a pencil and graph paper to graph your data.

✓ **Reading Check** Name two ways that scientists use tools. (*See the Appendix for answers to Reading Checks.*)

Making Measurements

Many years ago, different countries used different systems of measurement. In England, the standard for an inch used to be three grains of barley placed end to end. Other units were originally based on parts of the body, such as the foot.

| **Figure 1** | **Measurement Tools** |

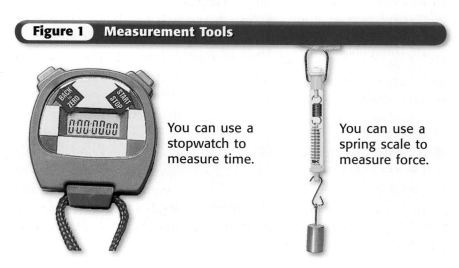

You can use a stopwatch to measure time.

You can use a spring scale to measure force.

Table 1 Common SI Units

Length	**meter (m)**	
	kilometer (km)	1 km = 1,000 m
	decimeter (dm)	1 dm = 0.1 m
	centimeter (cm)	1 cm = 0.01 m
	millimeter (mm)	1 mm = 0.001 m
	micrometer (μm)	1 μm = 0.000 001 m
	nanometer (nm)	1 nm = 0.000 000 001 m
Volume	**cubic meter (m³)**	
	cubic centimeter (cm³)	1 cm³ = 0.000 001 m³
	liter (L)	1 L = 1 dm³ = 0.001 m³
	milliliter (mL)	1 mL = 0.001 L = 1 cm³
Mass	**kilogram (kg)**	
	gram (g)	1 g = 0.001 kg
	milligram (mg)	1 mg = 0.000 001 kg
Temperature	**Kelvin (K)**	0°C = 273 K
	Celsius (°C)	100°C = 373 K

The International System of Units

In the late 1700s, the French Academy of Sciences set out to make a simple and reliable measurement system. Over the next 200 years, the metric system was formed. This system is now the International System of Units (SI). Because all SI units are expressed in multiples of 10, changing from one unit to another is easy. Prefixes are used to express SI units that are larger or smaller than basic units such as meter and gram. For example, *kilo-* means 1,000 times, and *milli-* indicates 1/1,000 times. The prefix used depends on the size of the object being measured. **Table 1** shows common SI units.

Length

To describe the length of an Olympic-sized swimming pool, a scientist would use meters (m). A *meter* is the basic SI unit of length. Other SI units of length are larger or smaller than the meter by multiples of 10. For example, if you divide 1 m into 1,000 parts, each part equals 1 millimeter (mm). So, 1 mm is one-thousandth of a meter.

Mass

Mass is the amount of matter in an object. The *kilogram* (kg) is the basic SI unit for mass. The kilogram is used to describe the mass of large objects. One kilogram equals 1,000 g. So, the gram is used to describe the mass of small objects. Masses of very large objects are expressed in metric tons. A metric ton equals 1,000 kg.

Units of Measure

Pick an object to use as a unit of measure. You can pick a pencil, your hand, or anything else. Find out how many units wide your desk is, and compare your measurement with those of your classmates. What were some of the units used? Now, choose two of the units that were used in your class, and make a conversion factor. For example, 1.5 pencils equal 1 board eraser.

mass a measure of the amount of matter in an object

Volume

Imagine that you need to move some lenses to a laser laboratory. How many lenses will fit into a crate? The answer depends on the volume of the crate and the volume of each lens. **Volume** is the amount of space that something occupies.

Liquid volume is expressed in *liters* (L). Liters are based on the meter. A cubic meter (1 m³) is equal to 1,000 L. So, 1,000 L will fit perfectly into a box that is 1 m on each side. A milliliter (mL) will fit perfectly into a box that is 1 cm on each side. So, 1 mL = 1 cm³. Graduated cylinders are used to measure the volume of liquids.

Volumes of solid objects are usually expressed in cubic meters (m³). Volumes of smaller objects can be expressed in cubic centimeters (cm³) or cubic millimeters (mm³). To find the volume of a crate—or any other rectangular shape—multiply the length by the width by the height.

Density

If you measure the mass and the volume of an object, you have the information you need to find the density of the object. **Density** is the amount of matter in a given volume. You cannot measure density directly. But after you measure the mass and the volume, you can calculate density by dividing the mass by the volume, as shown in the following equation:

$$D = \frac{m}{V}$$

Density is called a *derived quantity* because it is found by combining two basic quantities, mass and volume.

volume a measure of the size of an object or region in three-dimensional space

density the ratio of the mass of a substance to the volume of the substance

temperature a measure of how hot (or cold) something is; specifically, a measure of the average kinetic energy of the particles in an object

Figure 2 *Some common temperature measurements shown in degrees Fahrenheit and degrees Celsius*

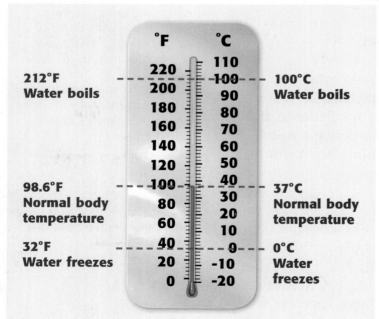

Temperature

The **temperature** of a substance is a measurement of how hot (or cold) the substance is. Degrees Fahrenheit (°F) and degrees Celsius (°C) are used to describe temperature. However, the *kelvin* (K), the SI unit for temperature, is also used. Notice that the degree sign (°) is not used with the Kelvin scale. The thermometer in **Figure 2** shows how the Celsius and Fahrenheit scales compare.

Reading Check What is the SI unit for temperature?

Safety Rules

Science is exciting and fun, but it can also be dangerous. Always follow your teacher's instructions. Don't take shortcuts, even when you think there is no danger. Read lab procedures carefully. Pay special attention to safety information and caution statements. **Figure 3** shows the safety symbols used in this book. Learn these symbols and their meanings by reading the safety information at the start of the book. If you are still not sure about what a safety symbol means, ask your teacher.

Figure 3 **Safety Symbols**

 Eye protection   Clothing protection   Hand safety   Chemical safety   Animal safety

 Heating safety    Electric safety   Sharp object    Plant safety

SECTION Review

Summary

- Tools are used to make observations, take measurements, and analyze data.
- The International System of Units (SI) is the standard system of measurement.
- Length, volume, mass, and temperature are types of measurement.
- Density is the amount of matter in a given volume.
- Safety symbols are for your protection.

Using Key Terms

1. Use each of the following terms in a separate sentence: *volume, density,* and *mass.*

Understanding Key Ideas

2. Which SI unit would you use to express the height of your desk?
   a. kilogram   c. meter
   b. gram   d. liter

3. Explain the relationship between mass and density.

4. What is normal body temperature in degrees Fahrenheit and degrees Celsius?

Math Skills

5. A certain bacterial cell has a diameter of 0.50 μm. The tip of a pin is about 1,100 μm in diameter. How many of these bacterial cells would fit on the tip of the pin?

Critical Thinking

6. **Analyzing Ideas** What safety icons would you expect to see for a lab activity that asks you to pour acid into a beaker? Explain your answer.

7. **Applying Concepts** To find the area of a rectangle, multiply the length by the width. Why is area called a *derived quantity*?

SCILINKS®   NSTA
Developed and maintained by the National Science Teachers Association

For a variety of links related to this chapter, go to www.scilinks.org

Topic: SI Units
SciLinks code: HSM1390

Skills Practice Lab

Measuring Liquid Volume

In this lab, you will use a graduated cylinder to measure and transfer precise amounts of liquids. Remember that, to accurately measure liquids in a graduated cylinder, you should first place the graduated cylinder flat on the lab table. Then, at eye level, read the volume of the liquid at the bottom of the meniscus, which is the curved surface of the liquid.

OBJECTIVES

Measure accurately different volumes of liquids with a graduated cylinder.

Transfer exact amounts of liquids from a graduated cylinder to a test tube.

MATERIALS

- beakers, filled with colored liquid (3)
- funnel, small
- graduated cylinder, 10 mL
- marker
- tape, masking
- test-tube rack
- test tubes, large (6)

SAFETY

Procedure

1. Using the masking tape and marker, label the test tubes A, B, C, D, E, and F. Place them in the test-tube rack.

2. Make a data table as shown on the next page.

3. Using the graduated cylinder and the funnel, pour 14 mL of the red liquid into test tube A. (To do this, first measure out 10 mL of the liquid in the graduated cylinder, and pour it into the test tube. Then, measure an additional 4 mL of liquid in the graduated cylinder, and add this liquid to the test tube.)

4. Rinse the graduated cylinder and funnel with water each time you measure a different liquid.

5. Measure 13 mL of the yellow liquid, and pour it into test tube C.

6. Measure 13 mL of the blue liquid, and pour it into test tube E. Record the initial color and the volume of the liquid in each test tube.

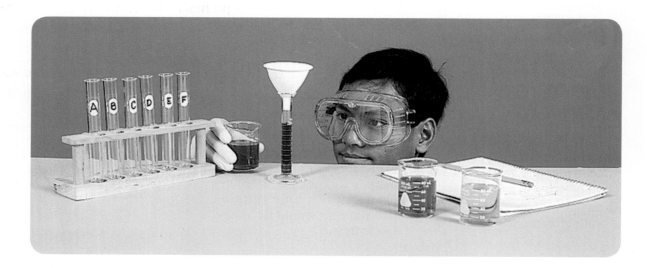

Data Table				
Test tube	Initial color	Initial volume	Final color	Final volume
A				
B				
C				
D				
E				
F				

DO NOT WRITE IN BOOK

7 Transfer 4 mL of liquid from test tube C into test tube D. Transfer 7 mL of liquid from test tube E into test tube D.

8 Measure 4 mL of blue liquid from the beaker, and pour it into test tube F. Measure 7 mL of red liquid from the beaker, and pour it into test tube F.

9 Transfer 8 mL of liquid from test tube A into test tube B. Transfer 3 mL of liquid from test tube C into test tube B.

Analyze the Results

1 **Analyzing Data** Record your final color observations in your data table.

2 **Examining Data** What is the final volume of all of the liquids? Use the graduated cylinder to measure the volume of liquid in each test tube. Record the volumes in your data table.

3 **Organizing Data** Record your final color observations and final volumes in a table of class data prepared by your teacher.

Draw Conclusions

4 **Interpreting Information** Did all of your classmates report the same colors? Form a hypothesis that could explain why the colors were the same or different after the liquids were combined.

5 **Evaluating Methods** Why should you not fill the graduated cylinder to the top?

Chapter Review

USING KEY TERMS

1 In your own words, write a definition for each of the following terms: *meter*, *temperature*, and *density*.

For each pair of terms, explain how the meanings of the terms differ.

2 *science* and *scientific methods*

3 *observation* and *hypothesis*

4 *theory* and *law*

5 *model* and *theory*

6 *volume* and *mass*

UNDERSTANDING KEY IDEAS

Multiple Choice

7 Physical science is

  a. the study of matter and energy.

  b. the study of physics and chemistry.

  c. important in most sciences.

  d. All of the above

8 The statement "Sheila has a stain on her shirt" is an example of a(n)

  a. law.

  b. hypothesis.

  c. observation.

  d. prediction.

9 A hypothesis

  a. may or may not be testable.

  b. is supported by evidence.

  c. is a possible answer to a question.

  d. All of the above

10 A variable

  a. is found in an uncontrolled experiment.

  b. is the factor that changes in an experiment.

  c. cannot change.

  d. is rarely included in experiments.

11 Organizing data into a graph is an example of

  a. collecting data.

  b. forming a hypothesis.

  c. asking a question.

  d. analyzing data.

12 How many milliliters are in 3.5 kL?

  a. 0.0035   **c.** 35,000

  b. 3,500   **d.** 3,500,000

13 A map of Seattle is an example of a

  a. physical model.

  b. mathematical model.

  c. conceptual model.

  d. All of the above

14 Ten meters is equal to

  a. 100 cm.   **c.** 100,000 mm.

  b. 1,000 cm.   **d.** 1,000 μm.

Short Answer

15 Describe three kinds of models used in science. Give an example and explain one limitation of each model.

16 Name two SI units that can be used to describe the volume of an object and two SI units that can be used to describe the mass of an object.

17 What are the steps used in scientific methods?

18 If a hypothesis is not testable, is the hypothesis wrong? Explain.

Math Skills

19 The cereal box on the right has a mass of 340 g. Its dimensions are 27 cm × 19 cm × 6 cm. What is the volume of the box? What is its density?

CRITICAL THINKING

20 Concept Mapping Use the following terms to create a concept map: *science, scientific methods, hypothesis, problems, questions, experiments,* and *observations*.

21 Applying Concepts A tailor is someone who makes or alters items of clothing. Why might a standard system of measurement be helpful to a tailor?

22 Analyzing Ideas Imagine that you are conducting an experiment. You are testing the effects of the height of a ramp on the speed at which a toy car goes down the ramp. What is the variable in this experiment? What factors must be controlled?

23 Evaluating Assumptions Suppose a classmate says, "I don't need to study science because I'm not going to be a scientist, and scientists are the only people who use science." How would you respond? In your answer, give several examples of careers that use physical science.

24 Making Inferences You build a model boat that you predict will float. However, your tests show that the boat sinks. What conclusion would you draw? Suggest some logical next steps.

INTERPRETING GRAPHICS

Use the picture below to answer the questions that follow.

25 How similar is this model to a real object?

26 What are some of the limitations of this model?

27 How might this model be useful?

Standardized Test Preparation

Read each of the passages below. Then, answer the questions that follow each passage.

Passage 1 The white light we see every day is actually composed of all of the colors of the visible spectrum. A laser emits a very small portion of this spectrum, so there can be blue lasers, red lasers, and so on. High-voltage sources called laser "pumps" cause laser materials to <u>emit</u> certain wavelengths of light depending on the material used. A laser material, such as a helium-neon (HeNe) gas mixture, emits radiation (light) as a result of electrons in high energy levels moving to lower energy levels. This process gives lasers their name: **l**ight **a**mplification of the **s**timulated **e**mission of **r**adiation.

1. Why are there blue lasers and red lasers?
   A White light is composed of all of the colors of the visible spectrum.
   B A laser emits a small portion of the visible spectrum.
   C A laser material emits radiation.
   D High-voltage sources are called laser "pumps."

2. In this passage, what is the meaning of the word *emit*?
   F to brighten
   G to compose
   H to change
   I to give off

3. Why does a laser produce radiation?
   A Only a small amount of light is used.
   B A laser is a high-voltage pump.
   C Light is made up of all of the colors in the visible spectrum.
   D Electrons in atoms change energy levels.

Passage 2 Researchers have created a new <u>class</u> of molecules. These molecules are called texaphyrins because of their large size and the five-pointed starlike shape at their center. Texaphyrins are similar to molecules that already exist in most living things. But texaphyrins are different because of their shape and their large size. The shape and large size of the molecules let scientists attach other elements to the molecules. Depending on what element is attached, texaphyrins can be used to locate tumors in the body or to help in treatments for some kinds of cancer.

1. Which of the following statements is true about texaphyrins, according to the passage?
   A They were just recently discovered.
   B They have the same shape that most natural molecules do.
   C They are used to treat certain cancers.
   D They are extremely small molecules.

2. In this passage, what is the meaning of the word *class*?
   F room
   G standing
   H rank
   I group

3. What is the main advantage of texaphyrin in treating tumors?
   A the small size of texaphyrin
   B the star shape of texaphyrin
   C the ability to attach to other substances
   D the man-made nature of the molecule

The graph below shows the changes in temperature during a chemical reaction. Use the graph below to answer the questions that follow.

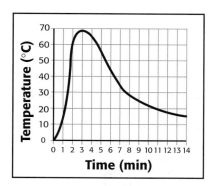

1. What was the highest temperature reached during the reaction?
   A 20°C
   B 40°C
   C 50°C
   D 70°C

2. During what period of time was the temperature increasing?
   F between 3 min and 14 min
   G between 0 min and 3 min
   H between 1 min and 13 min
   I between 0 min and 4 min

3. How many minutes did it take the temperature to increase from 10°C to 60°C?
   A less than 1 min
   B 1 min
   C 2 min
   D 3 min

4. About how many minutes passed from the time the highest temperature was reached until the time the temperature decreased to 20°C?
   F 7 min
   G 8 min
   H 11 min
   I 12 min

Read each question below, and choose the best answer.

1. What is the volume of a room that is 3.125 m high, 4.25 m wide, and 5.75 m long?
   A 13.1 m
   B 13.1 m³
   C 76.4 m
   D 76.4 m³

2. Yukiko has a storage box that measures 12 cm wide, 16.5 cm long, and 10 cm high. It has a mass of 850 g. What is the density of the box?
   F 1,980 cm³
   G 38.5 cm³
   H 2.3 g/cm³
   I .43 g/cm³

3. Remy traveled to Osaka, Japan, where the unit of currency is the yen. He spent 4,900 yen on train tickets. If the exchange rate was 113 yen to 1 U.S. dollar, approximately how much did the train tickets cost in U.S. dollars?
   A $25
   B $43
   C $49
   D $80

4. Lucia is measuring how fast bacteria grow in a Petri dish by measuring the area that the bacteria cover. On day 1, the bacteria cover 0.25 cm². On day 2, they cover 0.50 cm². On day 3, they cover 1.00 cm². What is the best prediction for the area covered on day 4?
   F 1.25 cm²
   G 1.50 cm²
   H 1.75 cm²
   I 2.00 cm²

Standardized Test Preparation

Science in Action

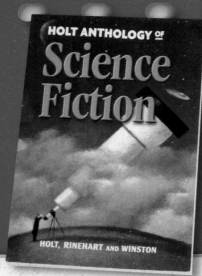

Science Fiction

"Inspiration" by Ben Bova

What if you were able to leap back and forth through time? Novelist H. G. Wells imagined such a possibility in his 1895 novelette *The Time Machine*. Most physicists said that time travel was against all the laws of physics. But what if Albert Einstein, then 16 and not a very good student, had met Wells and had an inspiration? Ben Bova's story "Inspiration" describes such a possibility. Young Einstein meets Wells and the great physicist of the time, Lord Kelvin. But was the meeting just a lucky coincidence or something else entirely? Escape to the *Holt Anthology of Science Fiction,* and read "Inspiration."

Weird Science

A Palace of Ice

An ice palace is just a fancy kind of igloo, but it takes a lot of ice and snow to make an ice palace. One ice palace was made from 27,215.5 metric tons of snow and 9,071.85 metric tons of ice! Making an ice palace takes time, patience, and temperatures below freezing. Sometimes, blocks of ice are cut with chain saws from a frozen river or lake and then transported in huge trucks. On location, the huge ice cubes are stacked on each other. Slush is used as mortar between the "bricks." The slush freezes and cements the blocks of ice together. Then, sculptors with chain saws, picks, and axes fashion elegant details in the ice.

Math ACTiViTY

One block of ice used to make the ice palace in the story above has a mass of 181.44 kg. How many blocks of ice were needed to make the ice palace if 9071.85 metric tons of ice was used?

Social Studies

Research the life of Albert Einstein from high school through college. Make a poster that describes some of his experiences during this time. Include information about how he matured as a student.

Julie Williams-Byrd

Electronics Engineer Julie Williams-Byrd uses her knowledge of physics to develop better lasers. She started working with lasers when she was a graduate student at Hampton University in Virginia. Today, Williams-Byrd works as an electronics engineer in the Laser Systems Branch (LSB) of NASA. She designs and builds lasers that are used to study wind and ozone in the atmosphere. Williams-Byrd uses scientific models to predict the nature of different aspects of laser design. For example, laser models are used to predict output energy, wavelength, and efficiency of the laser system.

Her most challenging project has been building a laser transmitter that will be used to measure winds in the atmosphere. This system, called *Lidar,* is very much like radar except that it uses light waves instead of sound waves to bounce off objects. Although Williams-Byrd works with high-tech lasers, she points out that lasers are a part of daily life for many people. For example, lasers are used in scanners at many retail stores. Ophthalmologists use lasers to correct vision problems. Some metal workers use them to cut metal. And lasers are even used to create spectacular light shows!

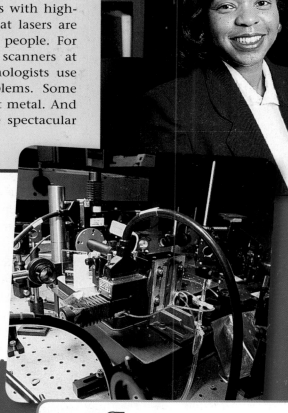

Language Arts ACTIVITY

WRITING SKILL Research lasers and how they can be used in everyday life. Then, write a one-page essay on how lasers have made life easier for people.

To learn more about these Science in Action topics, visit **go.hrw.com** and type in the keyword **HP5WPSF.**

Current Science

Check out Current Science® articles related to this chapter by visiting **go.hrw.com.** Just type in the keyword **HP5CS01.**

2

The Properties of Matter

SECTION 1 What Is Matter? 38

SECTION 2 Physical Properties 44

SECTION 3 Chemical Properties. . . . 50

Chapter Lab 56
Chapter Review 58
Standardized Test Preparation 60
Science in Action. 62

About the PHOTO

This giant ice dragon began as a 1,700 kg block of ice! Making the blocks of ice takes six weeks. Then, the ice blocks are stored at –30°C until the sculpting begins. The artist has to work at –10°C to keep the ice from melting. An ice sculptor has to be familiar with the many properties of water, including its melting point.

PRE-READING ACTIVITY

FOLDNOTES **Booklet** Before you read the chapter, create the FoldNote entitled "Booklet" described in the **Study Skills** section of the Appendix. Label each page of the booklet with a main idea from the chapter. As you read the chapter, write what you learn about each main idea on the appropriate page of the booklet.

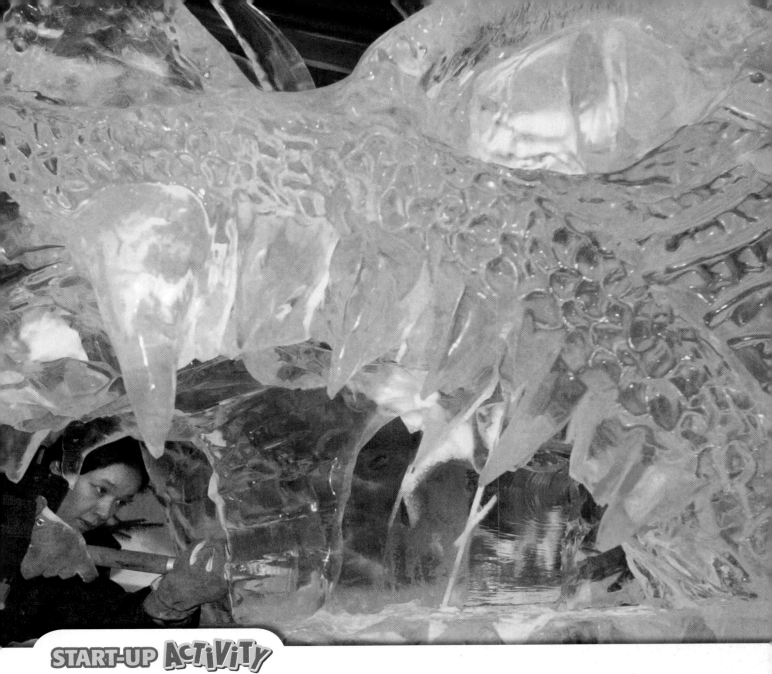

START-UP ACTIVITY

Sack Secrets

In this activity, you will test your skills in determining an object's identity based on the object's properties.

Procedure

1. You and two or three of your classmates will receive a **sealed paper sack** containing a **mystery object.** Do not open the sack!

2. For five minutes, make as many observations about the object as you can without opening the sack. You may touch, smell, shake, or listen to the object through the sack. Record your observations.

Analysis

1. At the end of five minutes, discuss your findings with your partners.

2. List the object's properties that you can identify. Make another list of properties that you cannot identify. Make a conclusion about the object's identity.

3. Share your observations, your list of properties, and your conclusion with the class. Then, open the sack.

4. Did you properly identify the object? If so, how? If not, why not? Record your answers.

What Is Matter?

What do you have in common with a toaster, a steaming bowl of soup, or a bright neon sign?

You are probably thinking that this is a trick question. It is hard to imagine that a person has anything in common with a kitchen appliance, hot soup, or a glowing neon sign.

Matter

From a scientific point of view, you have at least one characteristic in common with these things. You, the toaster, the bowl, the soup, the steam, the glass tubing of a neon sign, and the glowing gas are made of matter. But exactly what is matter? **Matter** is anything that has mass and takes up space. It's that simple! Everything in the universe that you can see is made up of some type of matter.

Matter and Volume

All matter takes up space. The amount of space taken up, or occupied, by an object is known as the object's **volume.** Your fingernails, the Statue of Liberty, the continent of Africa, and a cloud have volume. And because these things have volume, they cannot share the same space at the same time. Even the tiniest speck of dust takes up space. Another speck of dust cannot fit into that space without somehow bumping the first speck out of the way. **Figure 1** shows an example of how one object cannot share with another object the same space at the same time. Try the Quick Lab on the next page to see for yourself that matter takes up space.

matter anything that has mass and takes up space

volume a measure of the size of a body or region in three-dimensional space

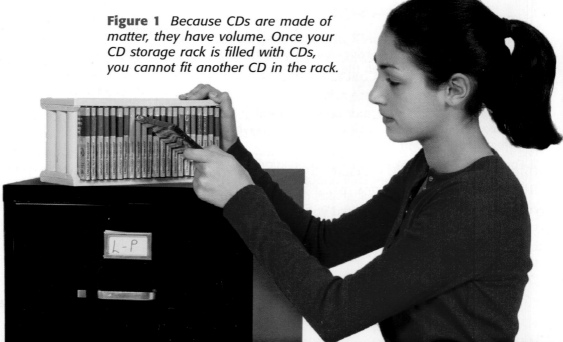

Figure 1 *Because CDs are made of matter, they have volume. Once your CD storage rack is filled with CDs, you cannot fit another CD in the rack.*

L–P

Quick Lab

Space Case

1. Crumple a **piece of paper.** Fit it tightly in the bottom of a **clear plastic cup** so that it won't fall out.

2. Turn the cup upside down. Lower the cup straight down into a **bucket** half-filled with **water.** Be sure that the cup is completely underwater.

3. Lift the cup straight out of the water. Turn the cup upright, and observe the paper. Record your observations.

4. Use the point of a **pencil** to punch a small hole in the bottom of the cup. Repeat steps 2 and 3.

5. How do the results show that air has volume? Explain your answer.

Liquid Volume

Lake Erie, the smallest of the Great Lakes, has a volume of approximately 483 trillion (that's 483,000,000,000,000) liters of water. Can you imagine that much water? Think of a 2-liter bottle of soda. The water in Lake Erie could fill more than 241 trillion 2-liter soda bottles. That's a lot of water! On a smaller scale, a can of soda has a volume of only 355 milliliters, which is about one-third of a liter. You can check the volume of the soda by using a large measuring cup from your kitchen.

Liters (L) and milliliters (mL) are the units used most often to express the volume of liquids. The volume of any amount of liquid, from one raindrop to a can of soda to an entire ocean, can be expressed in these units.

✓ Reading Check What are two units used to measure volume? (*See the Appendix for answers to Reading Checks.*)

Measuring the Volume of Liquids

In your science class, you'll probably use a graduated cylinder instead of a measuring cup to measure the volume of liquids. Graduated cylinders are used to measure the liquid volume when accuracy is important. The surface of a liquid in any container, including a measuring cup or a large beaker, is curved. The curve at the surface of a liquid is called a **meniscus** (muh NIS kuhs). To measure the volume of most liquids, such as water, you must look at the bottom of the meniscus, as shown in **Figure 2.** Note that you may not be able to see a meniscus in a large beaker. The meniscus looks flat because the liquid is in a wide container.

Volume = 15 mL

Figure 2 *To measure volume correctly, read the scale of the lowest part of the meniscus (as shown) at eye level.*

meniscus the curve at a liquid's surface by which one measures the volume of the liquid

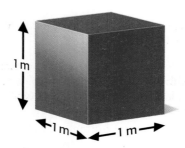

Figure 3 *A cubic meter (1 m³) is a cube that has a length, width, and height of 1 m.*

Volume of a Regularly Shaped Solid Object

The volume of any solid object is expressed in cubic units. The word *cubic* means "having three dimensions." In science, cubic meters (m^3) and cubic centimeters (cm^3) are the units most often used to express the volume of solid things. The 3 in these unit symbols shows that three quantities, or dimensions, were multiplied to get the final result. You can see the three dimensions of a cubic meter in **Figure 3.** There are formulas to find the volume of regularly shaped objects. For example, to find the volume of a cube or a rectangular object, multiply the length, width, and height of the object, as shown in the following equation:

$$volume = length \times width \times height$$

Volume of an Irregularly Shaped Solid Object

How do you find the volume of a solid that does not have a regular shape? For example, to find the volume of a 12-sided object, you cannot use the equation given above. But you can measure the volume of a solid object by measuring the volume of water that the object displaces. In **Figure 4,** when a 12-sided object is added to the water in a graduated cylinder, the water level rises. The volume of water displaced by the object is equal to its volume. Because 1 mL is equal to 1 cm^3, you can express the volume of the water displaced by the object in cubic centimeters. Although volumes of liquids can be expressed in cubic units, volumes of solids should not be expressed in liters or milliliters.

Figure 4 *The 12-sided object displaced 15 mL of water. Because 1 mL = 1 cm³, the volume of the object is 15 cm³.*

✓ Reading Check Explain how you would measure the volume of an apple.

MATH FOCUS

Volume of a Rectangular Solid What is the volume of a box that has a length of 5 cm, a width of 1 cm, and a height of 2 cm?

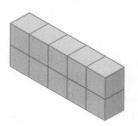

Step 1: Write the equation for volume.

$volume = length \times width \times height$

Step 2: Replace the variables with the measurements given to you, and solve.

$volume = 5$ cm $\times 1$ cm $\times 2$ cm $= 10$ cm^3

Now It's Your Turn

1. A book has a length of 25 cm, a width of 18 cm, and a height of 4 cm. What is its volume?
2. What is the volume of a suitcase that has a length of 95 cm, a width of 50 cm, and a height of 20 cm?
3. A CD case is 14.2 cm long, 12.4 cm wide, and 1 cm deep. What is its volume?

Matter and Mass

Another characteristic of all matter is mass. **Mass** is the amount of matter in an object. For example, you and a peanut are made of matter. But you are made of more matter than a peanut is, so you have more mass. The mass of an object is the same no matter where in the universe the object is located. The only way to change the mass of an object is to change the amount of matter that makes up the object.

mass a measure of the amount of matter in an object

weight a measure of the gravitational force exerted on an object; its value can change with the location of the object in the universe

The Difference Between Mass and Weight

The terms *mass* and *weight* are often used as though they mean the same thing, but they don't. **Weight** is a measure of the gravitational (GRAV i TAY shuh nuhl) force exerted on an object. Gravitational force keeps objects on Earth from floating into space. The gravitational force between an object and the Earth depends partly on the object's mass. The more mass an object has, the greater the gravitational force on the object and the greater the object's weight. But an object's weight can change depending on its location in the universe. An object would weigh less on the moon than it does on Earth because the moon has less gravitational force than Earth does. **Figure 5** explains the differences between mass and weight.

Figure 5 Differences Between Mass and Weight

Mass

- Mass is a measure of the amount of matter in an object.
- Mass is always constant for an object no matter where the object is located in the universe.
- Mass is measured by using a balance (shown below).
- Mass is expressed in kilograms (kg), grams (g), and milligrams (mg).

Weight

- Weight is a measure of the gravitational force on an object.
- Weight varies depending on where the object is in relation to the Earth (or any large body in the universe).
- Weight is measured by using a spring scale (shown at right).
- Weight is expressed in newtons (N).

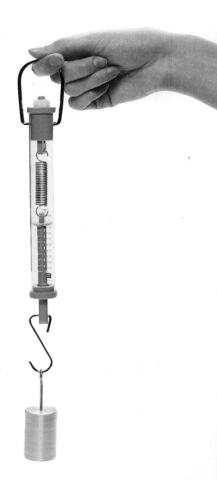

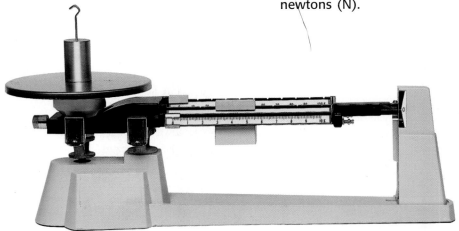

Figure 6 *The brick and the sponge take up the same amount of space. But the brick has more matter in it, so its mass—and thus its weight—is greater.*

Measuring Mass and Weight

The brick and the sponge in **Figure 6** have the same volume. But because the brick has more mass, a greater gravitational force is exerted on the brick than on the sponge. As a result, the brick weighs more than the sponge.

The SI unit of mass is the kilogram (kg), but mass is often expressed in grams (g) and milligrams (mg), too. These units can be used to express the mass of any object in the universe.

Weight is a measure of gravitational force and is expressed in the SI unit of force, the *newton* (N). One newton is about equal to the weight of an object that has a mass of 100 g on Earth. So, if you know the mass of an object, you can calculate the object's weight on Earth. Weight is a good estimate of the mass of an object because, on Earth, gravity doesn't change.

 **Reading Check** What units are often used to measure mass?

Inertia

Imagine kicking a soccer ball that has the mass of a bowling ball. It would be not only painful but also very difficult to get the ball moving in the first place! The reason is inertia (in UHR shuh). **Inertia** is the tendency of an object to resist a change in motion. So, an object at rest will remain at rest until something causes the object to move. Also, a moving object will keep moving at the same speed and in the same direction unless something acts on the object to change its speed or direction.

inertia the tendency of an object to resist being moved or, if the object is moving, to resist a change in speed or direction until an outside force acts on the object

MATH FOCUS

Converting Mass to Weight A student has a mass of 45,000 g. How much does this student weigh in newtons?

Step 1: Write the information given to you.

45,000 g

Step 2: Write the conversion factor to change grams into newtons.

1 N = 100 g

Step 3: Write the equation so that grams will cancel.

$$45,000 \text{ g} \times \frac{1 \text{ N}}{100 \text{ g}} = 450 \text{ N}$$

Now It's Your Turn

1. What is the weight of a car that has a mass of 1,362,000 g?

2. Your pair of boots has a mass of 850 g. If each boot has exactly the same mass, what is the weight of each boot?

Mass: The Measure of Inertia

Mass is a measure of inertia. An object that has a large mass is harder to get moving and harder to stop than an object that has less mass. The reason is that the object with the large mass has greater inertia. For example, imagine that you are going to push a grocery cart that has only one potato in it. Pushing the cart is easy because the mass and inertia are small. But suppose the grocery cart is stacked with potatoes, as in **Figure 7.** Now the total mass—and the inertia—of the cart full of potatoes is much greater. It will be harder to get the cart moving. And once the cart is moving, stopping the cart will be harder.

Figure 7 *Because of inertia, moving a cart full of potatoes is more difficult than moving a cart that is empty.*

SECTION Review

Summary

- Two properties of matter are volume and mass.
- Volume is the amount of space taken up by an object.
- The SI unit of volume is the liter (L).
- Mass is the amount of matter in an object.
- The SI unit of mass is the kilogram (kg).
- Weight is a measure of the gravitational force on an object, usually in relation to the Earth.
- Inertia is the tendency of an object to resist being moved or, if the object is moving, to resist a change in speed or direction. The more massive an object is, the greater its inertia.

Using Key Terms

1. Use the following terms in the same sentence: *volume* and *meniscus*.

2. In your own words, write a definition for each of the following terms: *mass, weight,* and *inertia.*

Understanding Key Ideas

3. Which of the following is matter?
   - **a.** dust
   - **b.** the moon
   - **c.** strand of hair
   - **d.** All of the above

4. A graduated cylinder is used to measure
   - **a.** volume.
   - **b.** weight.
   - **c.** mass.
   - **d.** inertia.

5. The volume of a solid is measured in
   - **a.** liters.
   - **b.** grams.
   - **c.** cubic centimeters.
   - **d.** All of the above

6. Mass is measured in
   - **a.** liters.
   - **b.** centimeters.
   - **c.** newtons.
   - **d.** kilograms.

7. Explain the relationship between mass and inertia.

Math Skills

8. A nugget of gold is placed in a graduated cylinder that contains 80 mL of water. The water level rises to 225 mL after the nugget is added to the cylinder. What is the volume of the gold nugget?

9. One newton equals about 100 g on Earth. How many newtons would a football weigh if it had a mass of 400 g?

Critical Thinking

10. **Identifying Relationships** Do objects with large masses always have large weights? Explain.

11. **Applying Concepts** Would an elephant weigh more or less on the moon than it would weigh on Earth? Explain your answer.

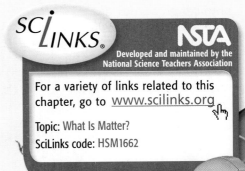

SCI**LINKS**®

NSTA
Developed and maintained by the
National Science Teachers Association

For a variety of links related to this chapter, go to www.scilinks.org

Topic: What Is Matter?
SciLinks code: HSM1662

Physical Properties

Have you ever played the game 20 Questions? The goal of this game is to figure out what object another person is thinking of by asking 20 yes/no questions or less.

If you can't figure out the object's identity after asking 20 questions, you may not be asking the right kinds of questions. What kinds of questions should you ask? You may want to ask questions about the physical properties of the object. Knowing the properties of an object can help you find out what it is.

Physical Properties

The questions in **Figure 1** help someone gather information about color, odor, mass, and volume. Each piece of information is a physical property of matter. A **physical property** of matter can be observed or measured without changing the matter's identity. For example, you don't have to change an apple's identity to see its color or to measure its volume.

Other physical properties, such as magnetism, the ability to conduct electric current, strength, and flexibility, can help someone identify how to use a substance. For example, think of a scooter with an electric motor. The magnetism produced by the motor is used to convert energy stored in a battery into energy that will turn the wheels.

✓ **Reading Check** List four physical properties. (*See the Appendix for answers to Reading Checks.*)

READING WARM-UP

Objectives

● Identify six examples of physical properties of matter.

● Describe how density is used to identify substances.

● List six examples of physical changes.

● Explain what happens to matter during a physical change.

Terms to Learn

physical property
density
physical change

READING STRATEGY

Mnemonics As you read this section, create a mnemonic device to help you remember examples of physical properties.

Figure 1 *Asking questions about the physical properties of an object can help you identify it.*

Could I hold it in my hand? **Yes.**
Does it have an odor? **Yes.**
Is it safe to eat? **Yes.**
Is it orange? **No.**
Is it yellow? **No.**
Is it red? **Yes.**
Is it an apple? **Yes!**

Figure 2 Examples of Physical Properties

Thermal conductivity (KAHN duhk TIV uh tee) is the rate at which a substance transfers heat. Plastic foam is a poor conductor.

State is the physical form in which a substance exists, such as a solid, liquid, or gas. Ice is water in the solid state.

Density is the mass per unit volume of a substance. Lead is very dense, so it makes a good sinker for a fishing line.

Solubility (SAHL yoo BIL uh tee) is the ability of a substance to dissolve in another substance. Flavored drink mix dissolves in water.

Ductility (duhk TIL uh tee) is the ability of a substance to be pulled into a wire. Copper is often used to make wiring because it is ductile.

Malleability (MAL ee uh BIL uh tee) is the ability of a substance to be rolled or pounded into thin sheets. Aluminum can be rolled into sheets to make foil.

Identifying Matter

You use physical properties every day. For example, physical properties help you determine if your socks are clean (odor), if your books will fit into your backpack (volume), or if your shirt matches your pants (color). **Figure 2** gives more examples of physical properties.

Density

Density is a physical property that describes the relationship between mass and volume. **Density** is the amount of matter in a given space, or volume. A golf ball and a table-tennis ball, such as those in **Figure 3**, have similar volumes. But a golf ball has more mass than a table-tennis ball does. So, the golf ball has a greater density.

physical property a characteristic of a substance that does not involve a chemical change, such as density, color, or hardness

density the ratio of the mass of a substance to the volume of the substance

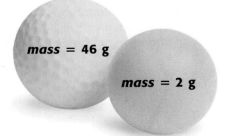

mass = 46 g

mass = 2 g

Figure 3 *A golf ball is denser than a table-tennis ball because the golf ball contains more matter in a similar volume.*

Liquid Layers

What do you think causes the liquid in **Figure 4** to look the way it does? Is it trick photography? No, it is differences in density! There are six liquids in the graduated cylinder. Each liquid has a different density. If the liquids are carefully poured into the cylinder, they can form six layers because of the differences in density. The densest layer is on the bottom. The least dense layer is on top. The order of the layers shows the order of increasing density. Yellow is the least dense, followed by the colorless layer, red, blue, green, and brown (the densest).

Density of Solids

Which would you rather carry around all day: a kilogram of lead or a kilogram of feathers? At first, you might say feathers. But both the feathers and the lead have the same mass, just as the cotton balls and the tomatoes have the same mass, as shown in **Figure 5.** So, the lead would be less awkward to carry around than the feathers would. The feathers are much less dense than the lead. So, it takes a lot of feathers to equal the same mass of lead.

Figure 4 *This graduated cylinder contains six liquids. From top to bottom, they are corn oil, water, shampoo, dish detergent, antifreeze, and maple syrup.*

Knowing the density of a substance can also tell you if the substance will float or sink in water. If the density of an object is less than the density of water, the object will float. Likewise, a solid object whose density is greater than the density of water will sink when the object is placed in water.

✓ Reading Check What will happen to an object placed in water if the object's density is less than water's density?

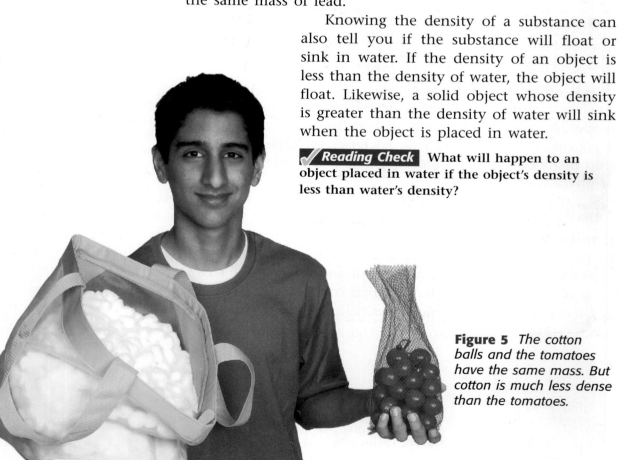

Figure 5 *The cotton balls and the tomatoes have the same mass. But cotton is much less dense than the tomatoes.*

Solving for Density

To find an object's density (D), first measure its mass (m) and volume (V). Then, use the equation below.

$$D = \frac{m}{V}$$

Units for density consist of a mass unit divided by a volume unit. Some units for density are g/cm^3, g/mL, kg/m^3, and kg/L. Remember that the volume of a solid is often given in cubic centimeters or cubic meters. So, the density of a solid should be given in units of g/cm^3 or kg/m^3.

Using Density to Identify Substances

Density is a useful physical property for identifying substances. Each substance has a density that differs from the densities of other substances. And the density of a substance is always the same at a given temperature and pressure. Look at **Table 1** to compare the densities of several common substances.

Table 1 Densities of Common Substances*			
Substance	**Density* (g/cm³)**	**Substance**	**Density* (g/cm³)**
Helium (gas)	0.00001663	Zinc (solid)	7.13
Oxygen (gas)	0.001331	Silver (solid)	10.50
Water (liquid)	1.00	Lead (solid)	11.35
Pyrite (solid)	5.02	Mercury (liquid)	13.55

*at 20°C and 1.0 atm

Calculating Density What is the density of an object whose mass is 25 g and whose volume is 10 cm³?

Step 1: Write the equation for density.

$$D = \frac{m}{V}$$

Step 2: Replace m and V with the measurements given in the problem, and solve.

$$D = \frac{25 \text{ g}}{10 \text{ cm}^3} = 2.5 \text{ g/cm}^3$$

The equation for density can also be rearranged to find mass and volume, as shown.

$m = D \times V$ (Rearrange by multiplying by V.)

$V = \frac{m}{D}$ (Rearrange by dividing by D.)

Now It's Your Turn

1. Find the density of a substance that has a mass of 45 kg and a volume of 43 m³. (Hint: Make sure your answer's units are units of density.)
2. Suppose you have a lead ball whose mass is 454 g. What is the ball's volume? (Hint: Use **Table 1** above.)
3. What is the mass of a 15 mL sample of mercury?

Figure 6 **Examples of Physical Changes**

Changing from a solid to a liquid is a physical change. All changes of state are physical changes.

This aluminum can has gone through the physical change of being crushed. The properties of the can are the same.

Physical Changes Do Not Form New Substances

physical change a change of matter from one form to another without a change in chemical properties

A **physical change** is a change that affects one or more physical properties of a substance. Imagine that a piece of silver is pounded and molded into a heart-shaped pendant. This change is a physical one because only the shape of the silver has changed. The piece of silver is still silver. Its properties are the same. **Figure 6** shows more examples of physical changes.

✓ *Reading Check* What is a physical change?

Examples of Physical Changes

Freezing water to make ice cubes and sanding a piece of wood are examples of physical changes. These changes do not change the identities of the substances. Ice is still water. And sawdust is still wood. Another interesting physical change takes place when certain substances dissolve in other substances. For example, when you dissolve sugar in water, the sugar seems to disappear. But if you heat the mixture, the water evaporates. Then, you will see that the sugar is still there. The sugar went through a physical change when it dissolved.

CONNECTION TO Geology

WRITING SKILL **Erosion** Erosion of soil is a physical change. Soil erodes when wind and water move soil from one place to another. Research the history of the Grand Canyon. Write a one-page report about how erosion formed the Grand Canyon.

Matter and Physical Changes

Physical changes do not change the identity of the matter involved. A stick of butter can be melted and poured over a bowl of popcorn, as shown in **Figure 7.** Although the shape of the butter has changed, the butter is still butter, so a physical change has occurred. In the same way, if you make a figure from a lump of clay, you change the clay's shape and cause a physical change. But the identity of the clay does not change. The properties of the figure are the same as those of the lump of clay.

Figure 7 *Melting butter for popcorn involves a physical change.*

SECTION Review

Summary

- Physical properties of matter can be observed without changing the identity of the matter.
- Examples of physical properties are conductivity, state, malleability, ductility, solubility, and density.
- Density is the amount of matter in a given space.
- Density is used to identify substances because the density of a substance is always the same at a given pressure and temperature.
- When a substance undergoes a physical change, its identity stays the same.
- Examples of physical changes are freezing, cutting, bending, dissolving, and melting.

Using Key Terms

1. Use each of the following terms in a separate sentence: *physical property* and *physical change*.

Understanding Key Ideas

2. The units of density for a rectangular piece of wood are
   a. grams per milliliter.
   b. cubic centimeters.
   c. kilograms per liter.
   d. grams per cubic centimeter.

3. Explain why a golf ball is heavier than a table-tennis ball even though the balls are the same size.

4. Describe what happens to a substance when it goes through a physical change.

5. Identify six examples of physical properties.

6. List six physical changes that matter can go through.

Math Skills

7. What is the density of an object that has a mass of 350 g and a volume of 95 cm^3? Would this object float in water? Explain.

8. The density of an object is 5 g/cm^3, and the volume of the object is 10 cm^3. What is the mass of the object?

Critical Thinking

9. **Applying Concepts** How can you determine that a coin is not pure silver if you know the mass and volume of the coin?

10. **Identifying Relationships** What physical property do the following substances have in common: water, oil, mercury, and alcohol?

11. **Analyzing Processes** Explain how you would find the density of an unknown liquid if you have all of the laboratory equipment that you need.

SC*LINKS*®

NSTA
Developed and maintained by the
National Science Teachers Association

For a variety of links related to this chapter, go to www.scilinks.org

Topic: Describing Matter; Physical Changes
SciLinks code: HSM0391; HSM1142

Chemical Properties

How would you describe a piece of wood before and after it is burned? Has it changed color? Does it have the same texture? The original piece of wood changed, and physical properties alone can't describe what happened to it.

READING WARM-UP

Objectives

● Describe two examples of chemical properties.

● Explain what happens during a chemical change.

● Distinguish between physical and chemical changes.

Terms to Learn

chemical property
chemical change

READING STRATEGY

Reading Organizer As you read this section, create an outline of the section. Use the headings from the section in your outline.

chemical property a property of matter that describes a substance's ability to participate in chemical reactions

Chemical Properties

Physical properties are not the only properties that describe matter. **Chemical properties** describe matter based on its ability to change into new matter that has different properties. For example, when wood is burned, ash and smoke are created. These new substances have very different properties than the original piece of wood had. Wood has the chemical property of flammability. *Flammability* is the ability of a substance to burn. Ash and smoke cannot burn, so they have the chemical property of nonflammability.

Another chemical property is reactivity. *Reactivity* is the ability of two or more substances to combine and form one or more new substances. The photo of the old car in **Figure 1** illustrates reactivity and nonreactivity.

✓ **Reading Check** What does the term *reactivity* mean? (*See the Appendix for answers to Reading Checks.*)

Figure 1 **Reactivity with Oxygen**

The iron used in this old car has the chemical property of **reactivity with oxygen**. When iron is exposed to oxygen, it rusts.

The bumper on this car still looks new because it is coated with chromium. Chromium has the chemical property of **nonreactivity with oxygen**.

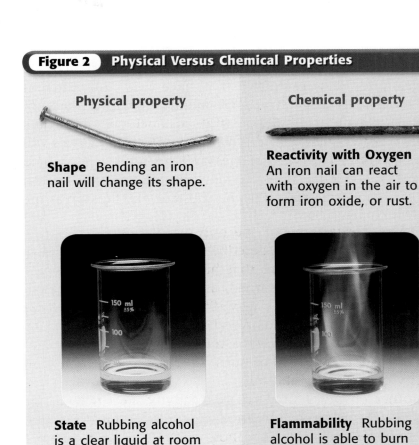

Figure 2 Physical Versus Chemical Properties

Physical property

Shape Bending an iron nail will change its shape.

State Rubbing alcohol is a clear liquid at room temperature.

Chemical property

Reactivity with Oxygen An iron nail can react with oxygen in the air to form iron oxide, or rust.

Flammability Rubbing alcohol is able to burn easily.

Comparing Physical and Chemical Properties

How do you tell a physical property from a chemical property? You can observe physical properties without changing the identity of the substance. For example, you can find the density and hardness of wood without changing anything about the wood.

Chemical properties, however, aren't as easy to observe. For example, you can see that wood is flammable only while it is burning. And you can observe that gold is nonflammable only when it won't burn. But a substance always has chemical properties. A piece of wood is flammable even when it's not burning. **Figure 2** shows examples of physical and chemical properties.

Characteristic Properties

The properties that are most useful in identifying a substance are *characteristic properties*. These properties are always the same no matter what size the sample is. Characteristic properties can be physical properties, such as density and solubility, as well as chemical properties, such as flammability and reactivity. Scientists rely on characteristic properties to identify and classify substances.

CONNECTION TO Social Studies

WRITING SKILL **The Right Stuff** When choosing materials to use in manufacturing, you must make sure their properties are suitable for their uses. For example, false teeth can be made from acrylic plastic, porcelain, or gold. According to legend, George Washington wore false teeth made of wood. Do research and find what Washington's false teeth were really made of. In your **science journal,** write a paragraph about what you have learned. Include information about the advantages of the materials used in modern false teeth.

Chemical Changes and New Substances

A **chemical change** happens when one or more substances are changed into new substances that have new and different properties. Chemical changes and chemical properties are not the same. Chemical properties of a substance describe which chemical changes will occur and which chemical changes will not occur. But chemical changes are the process by which substances actually change into new substances. You can learn about the chemical properties of a substance by looking at the chemical changes that take place.

You see chemical changes more often than you may think. For example, a chemical reaction happens every time a battery is used. Chemicals failing to react results in a dead battery. Chemical changes also take place within your body when the food you eat is digested. **Figure 3** describes other examples of chemical changes.

Reading Check How does a chemical change differ from a chemical property?

Figure 3 Examples of Chemical Changes

Soured milk smells bad because bacteria have formed new substances in the milk.

Effervescent tablets bubble when the citric acid and baking soda in them react in water.

The **hot gas** formed when hydrogen and oxygen join to make water helps blast the space shuttle into orbit.

The **Statue of Liberty** is made of orange-brown copper but it looks green from the metal's interaction with moist air. New copper compounds formed and these chemical changes made the statue turn green over time.

Figure 4 *Each of the original ingredients has different physical and chemical properties than the final product, the cake, does!*

What Happens During a Chemical Change?

A fun way to see what happens during chemical changes is to bake a cake. You combine eggs, flour, sugar, and other ingredients, as shown in **Figure 4.** When you bake the batter, you end up with something completely different. The heat of the oven and the interaction of the ingredients cause a chemical change. The result is a cake that has properties that differ from the properties of the ingredients.

Signs of Chemical Changes

Look back at **Figure 3.** In each picture, at least one sign indicates a chemical change. Other signs that indicate a chemical change include a change in color or odor, production of heat, fizzing and foaming, and sound or light being given off.

In the cake example, you would smell the cake as it baked. You would also see the batter rise and begin to brown. When you cut the finished cake, you would see the air pockets made by gas bubbles that formed in the batter. These signs show that chemical changes have happened.

Matter and Chemical Changes

Chemical changes change the identity of the matter involved. So, most of the chemical changes that occur in your daily life, such as a cake baking, would be hard to reverse. Imagine trying to unbake a cake. However, some chemical changes can be reversed by more chemical changes. For example, the water formed in the space shuttle's rockets could be split into hydrogen and oxygen by using an electric current.

chemical change a change that occurs when one or more substances change into entirely new substances with different properties

For another activity related to this chapter, go to **go.hrw.com** and type in keyword **HP5MATW.**

Figure 5 Physical and Chemical Changes

Change in Texture Grinding baking soda into a fine, powdery substance is a physical change.

Reactivity with Vinegar Gas bubbles are produced when vinegar is poured into baking soda.

Physical Versus Chemical Changes

The most important question to ask when trying to decide if a physical or chemical change has happened is, Did the composition change? The *composition* of an object is the type of matter that makes up the object and the way that the matter is arranged in the object. **Figure 5** shows both a physical and a chemical change.

A Change in Composition

Physical changes do not change the composition of a substance. For example, water is made of two hydrogen atoms and one oxygen atom. Whether water is a solid, liquid, or gas, its composition is the same. But chemical changes do alter the composition of a substance. For example, through a process called *electrolysis*, water is broken down into hydrogen and oxygen gases. The composition of water has changed, so you know that a chemical change has taken place.

CONNECTION TO Environmental Science

Acid Rain When fossil fuels are burned, a chemical change takes place. Sulfur from fossil fuels and oxygen from the air combine to produce sulfur dioxide, a gas. When sulfur dioxide enters the atmosphere, it undergoes another chemical change by interacting with water and oxygen. Research this chemical reaction. Make a poster describing the reaction and showing how the final product affects the environment.

ACTIVITY

Physical or Chemical Change?

1. Watch as your teacher places a burning **wooden stick** into a **test tube.** Record your observations.
2. Place a mixture of **powdered sulfur** and **iron filings** on a **sheet of paper.** Place a **bar magnet** underneath the paper, and try to separate the iron from the sulfur.
3. Drop an **effervescent tablet** into a **beaker of water.** Record your observations.
4. Identify whether each change is a physical change or a chemical change. Explain your answers.

Reversing Changes

Can physical and chemical changes be reversed? Many physical changes are easily reversed. They do not change the composition of a substance. For example, if an ice cube melts, you could freeze the liquid water to make another ice cube. But composition does change in a chemical change. So, most chemical changes are not easily reversed. Look at **Figure 6.** The chemical changes that happen when a firework explodes would be almost impossible to reverse, even if you collected all of the materials made in the chemical changes.

Figure 6 *This display of fireworks represents many chemical changes happening at the same time.*

SECTION Review

Summary

- Chemical properties describe a substance based on its ability to change into a new substance that has different properties.

- Chemical properties can be observed only when a chemical change might happen.

- Examples of chemical properties are flammability and reactivity.

- New substances form as a result of a chemical change.

- Unlike a chemical change, a physical change does not alter the identity of a substance.

Using Key Terms

1. In your own words, write a definition for each of the following terms: *chemical property* and *chemical change*.

Understanding Key Ideas

2. Rusting is an example of a
   a. physical property.
   b. physical change.
   c. chemical property.
   d. chemical change.

3. Which of the following is a characteristic property?
   a. density
   b. chemical reactivity
   c. solubility in water
   d. All of the above

4. Write two examples of chemical properties and explain what they are.

5. The Statue of Liberty was originally a copper color. After being exposed to the air, she turned a greenish color. What kind of change happened? Explain your answer.

6. Explain how to tell the difference between a physical and a chemical property.

Math Skills

7. The temperature of an acid solution is 25°C. A strip of magnesium is added, and the temperature rises 2°C each minute for the first 3 min. After another 5 min, the temperature has risen two more degrees. What is the final temperature?

Critical Thinking

8. **Making Comparisons** Describe the difference between physical and chemical changes in terms of what happens to the matter involved in each kind of change.

9. **Applying Concepts** Identify two physical properties and two chemical properties of a bag of microwave popcorn before popping and after.

SCiLINKS.

NSTA
Developed and maintained by the National Science Teachers Association

For a variety of links related to this chapter, go to www.scilinks.org

Topic: Chemical Changes
SciLinks code: HSM0266

Skills Practice Lab

OBJECTIVES

Describe the physical properties of four substances.

Identify physical and chemical changes.

Classify four substances by their chemical properties.

MATERIALS

- baking powder
- baking soda
- carton, egg, plastic-foam
- cornstarch
- eyedroppers (3)
- iodine solution
- spatulas (4)
- stirring rod
- sugar
- vinegar
- water

SAFETY

White Before Your Eyes

You have learned how to describe matter based on its physical and chemical properties. You have also learned some signs that can help you determine whether a change in matter is a physical change or a chemical change. In this lab, you'll use what you have learned to describe four substances based on their properties and the changes that they undergo.

Procedure

1 Copy Table 1 and Table 2 shown on the next page. Be sure to leave plenty of room in each box to write down your observations.

2 Using a spatula, place a small amount of baking powder into three cups of your egg carton. Use just enough baking powder to cover the bottom of each cup. Record your observations about the baking powder's appearance, such as color and texture, in the "Unmixed" column of Table 1.

3 Use an eyedropper to add 60 drops of water to the baking powder in the first cup. Stir with the stirring rod. Record your observations in Table 1 in the column labeled "Mixed with water." Clean your stirring rod.

4 Use a clean dropper to add 20 drops of vinegar to the second cup of baking powder. Stir. Record your observations in Table 1 in the column labeled "Mixed with vinegar." Clean your stirring rod.

5 Use a clean dropper to add five drops of iodine solution to the third cup of baking powder. Stir. Record your observations in Table 1 in the column labeled "Mixed with iodine solution." Clean your stirring rod. **Caution:** Be careful when using iodine. Iodine will stain your skin and clothes.

6 Repeat steps 2–5 for each of the other substances (baking soda, cornstarch, and sugar). Use a clean spatula for each substance.

Analyze the Results

1 **Examining Data** What physical properties do all four substances share?

2 **Analyzing Data** In Table 2, write the type of change—physical or chemical—that you observed for each substance. State the property that the change demonstrates.

Draw Conclusions

3 **Evaluating Results** Classify the four substances by the chemical property of reactivity. For example, which substances are reactive with vinegar (acid)?

Table 1 Observations				
Substance	**Unmixed**	**Mixed with water**	**Mixed with vinegar**	**Mixed with iodine solution**
Baking powder				
Baking soda				
Cornstarch				
Sugar				

Table 2 Changes and Properties						
	Mixed with water		**Mixed with vinegar**		**Mixed with iodine solution**	
Substance	**Change**	**Property**	**Change**	**Property**	**Change**	**Property**
Baking powder						
Baking soda						
Cornstarch						
Sugar						

Chapter Review

USING KEY TERMS

1 Use each of the following terms in a separate sentence: *physical property*, *chemical property*, *physical change*, and *chemical change*.

For each pair of terms, explain how the meanings of the terms differ.

2 *mass* and *weight*

3 *inertia* and *mass*

4 *volume* and *density*

UNDERSTANDING KEY IDEAS

Multiple Choice

5 Which of the following properties is NOT a chemical property?

a. reactivity with oxygen

b. malleability

c. flammability

d. reactivity with acid

6 The volume of a liquid can be expressed in all of the following units EXCEPT

a. grams.

b. liters.

c. milliliters.

d. cubic centimeters.

7 The SI unit for the mass of a substance is the

a. gram.

b. liter.

c. milliliter.

d. kilogram.

8 The best way to measure the volume of an irregularly shaped solid is to

a. use a ruler to measure the length of each side of the object.

b. weigh the solid on a balance.

c. use the water displacement method.

d. use a spring scale.

9 Which of the following statements about weight is true?

a. Weight is a measure of the gravitational force on an object.

b. Weight varies depending on where the object is located in relation to the Earth.

c. Weight is measured by using a spring scale.

d. All of the above

10 Which of the following statements does NOT describe a physical property of a piece of chalk?

a. Chalk is a solid.

b. Chalk can be broken into pieces.

c. Chalk is white.

d. Chalk will bubble in vinegar.

11 Which of the following statements about density is true?

a. Density is expressed in grams.

b. Density is mass per unit volume.

c. Density is expressed in milliliters.

d. Density is a chemical property.

Short Answer

12 In one or two sentences, explain how the process of measuring the volume of a liquid differs from the process of measuring the volume of a solid.

13 What is the formula for calculating density?

14 List three characteristic properties of matter.

Math Skills

15 What is the volume of a book that has a width of 10 cm, a length that is 2 times the width, and a height that is half the width? Remember to express your answer in cubic units.

16 A jar contains 30 mL of glycerin (whose mass is 37.8 g) and 60 mL of corn syrup (whose mass is 82.8 g). Which liquid is on top? Show your work, and explain your answer.

CRITICAL THINKING

17 **Concept Mapping** Use the following terms to create a concept map: *matter, mass, inertia, volume, milliliters, cubic centimeters, weight,* and *gravity.*

18 **Applying Concepts** Develop a set of questions that would be useful when identifying an unknown substance. The substance may be a liquid, a gas, or a solid.

19 **Analyzing Processes** You are making breakfast for your friend Filbert. When you take the scrambled eggs to the table, he asks, "Would you please poach these eggs instead?" What scientific reason do you give Filbert for not changing his eggs?

20 **Identifying Relationships** You look out your bedroom window and see your new neighbor moving in. Your neighbor bends over to pick up a small cardboard box, but he cannot lift it. What can you conclude about the item(s) in the box? Use the terms *mass* and *inertia* to explain how you came to your conclusion.

21 **Analyzing Ideas** You may sometimes hear on the radio or on TV that astronauts are weightless in space. Explain why this statement is not true.

INTERPRETING GRAPHICS

Use the photograph below to answer the questions that follow.

22 List three physical properties of this aluminum can.

23 When this can was crushed, did it undergo a physical change or a chemical change?

24 How does the density of the metal in the crushed can compare with the density of the metal before the can was crushed?

25 Can you tell what the chemical properties of the can are by looking at the picture? Explain your answer.

Standardized Test Preparation

Read each of the passages below. Then, answer the questions that follow each passage.

Passage 1 Astronomers were studying the motions of galaxies in space when they noticed something odd. They thought that the large gravitational force, which causes the galaxies to rotate rapidly, was due to a large amount of mass in the galaxies. Then, they discovered that the mass of the galaxies was not great enough to explain this large gravitational force. So, what was causing the additional gravitational force? One theory is that the universe contains matter that we cannot see with our eyes or our telescopes. Astronomers call this invisible matter <u>dark matter</u>.

1. According to this passage, what did astronomers originally think caused the rotation of the galaxies?
   A a lack of inertia
   B a large gravitational force
   C a small amount of mass in the galaxies
   D a small gravitational force

2. Why do you think astronomers use the term *dark matter*?
   F Dark matter refers to dark objects.
   G Dark matter refers to matter that we can't see.
   H You need a telescope to see dark matter.
   I All large objects are dark.

3. Which statement is the best summary of the passage?
   A The enormous amount of mass in the galaxies explains why the galaxies rotate.
   B Dark matter may be responsible for the gravitational force that causes the rotation of galaxies.
   C Invisible matter is called dark matter.
   D Galaxies rotate as they move through the universe.

Passage 2 Blimps and dirigibles are types of airships. An airship consists of an engine, a large balloon that contains gas, and a gondola that carries passengers and crew. Airships float in air because the gases that the airships contain are less dense than air. In the early 1900s, airships were commonly used for travel, including transatlantic flights. Airships were less frequently used after the 1937 explosion and crash of the *Hindenburg* in New Jersey. The *Hindenburg* was filled with <u>flammable</u> hydrogen gas instead of helium gas, which is nonflammable.

1. In this passage, what does *flammable* mean?
   A able to burn
   B able to float
   C able to sink
   D not able to burn

2. Which of the following statements is true according to the passage?
   F Hydrogen gas is nonflammable.
   G Airships float because they contain gases that are less dense than air.
   H Helium gas was used in the *Hindenburg*.
   I The gondola contains gas.

3. Which of the following statements about airships is true?
   A Airships are still a major mode of transportation.
   B Airships now contain nonflammable, hydrogen gas.
   C Airships consist of an engine, a gondola, and a large balloon.
   D Airships traveled only in the United States.

The table below shows the properties of different substances. Use the table below to answer the questions that follow.

Properties of Some Substances*

Substance	State	Density (g/cm³)
Helium	Gas	0.0001663
Pyrite	Solid	5.02
Mercury	Liquid	13.55
Gold	Solid	19.32

* at room temperature and pressure

1. What could you use to tell pyrite (fool's gold) and gold apart?

A volume

B density

C mass

D state

2. What do you think would happen if you placed a nugget of pyrite into a beaker of mercury?

F The pyrite would sink.

G The pyrite would dissolve.

H The mercury and the pyrite would react.

I The pyrite would float.

3. If a nugget of pyrite and a nugget of gold each have a mass of 50 g, what can you conclude about the volume of each nugget?

A The volume of pyrite is greater than the volume of gold.

B The volume of pyrite is less than the volume of gold.

C The volumes of the substances are equal.

D There is not enough information to determine the answer.

4. Which substance has the **lowest** density?

F helium

G pyrite

H mercury

I gold

Read each question below, and choose the best answer.

1. Imagine that you have discovered a new element, and you want to find its density. It has a mass of 78.8 g and a volume of 8 cm³. To find the density of the element, you must divide the element's mass by its volume. What is the density of the element?

A 0.102 g/cm³

B 0.98 g/cm³

C 9.85 g/cm³

D 630.4 g/cm³

2. Many soft drinks come in bottles that contain about 590 mL. If the density of a soft drink is 1.05 g/mL, what is the mass of the drink?

F 0.0018 g

G 498.2 g

H 561.9 g

I 619.5 g

3. If you have 150 g of pure gold and the density of gold is 19.32 g/cm³, what is the volume of your gold nugget?

A 2,898 cm³

B 7.76 cm³

C 0.98 cm³

D 0.13 cm³

4. Three objects have a mass of 16 g each. But their volumes differ. Object A, a liquid, has a volume of 1.2 mL. Object B, a solid, has a volume of 3.2 cm³. Object C, another solid, has a volume of 1.9 cm³. Which object is the least dense?

F object A

G object B

H object C

I There is not enough information to determine the answer.

Science in Action

Scientific Debate

Paper or Plastic?

What do you choose at the grocery store: paper or plastic bags? Plastic bags are waterproof and take up less space. You can use them to line waste cans and to pack lunches. Some places will recycle plastic bags. But making 1 ton of plastic bags uses 11 barrels of oil, which can't be replaced, and produces polluting chemicals. On the other hand, making 1 ton of paper bags destroys 13 to 17 trees, which take years to replace. Paper bags, too, can be reused for lining waste cans and wrapping packages. Recycling paper pollutes less than recycling plastic does. What is the answer? Maybe we should reuse both!

Language Arts ACTiViTY

WRITING SKILL There are advantages and disadvantages of each kind of bag. Write a one-page essay defending your position on this subject. Support your opinion with facts.

Science, Technology, and Society

Building a Better Body

Have you ever broken a bone? If so, you probably wore a cast while the bone healed. But what happens if the bone is too damaged to heal? Sometimes, a false bone made from titanium can replace the damaged bone. Titanium appears to be a great bone-replacement material. It is a lightweight but strong metal. It can attach to existing bone and resists chemical changes. But, friction can wear away titanium bones. Research has found that implanting a form of nitrogen on the titanium makes the metal last longer.

Social Studies ACTiViTY

Do some research on the history of bone-replacement therapy. Make a poster that shows a timeline of events leading up to current technology.

Mimi So

Gemologist and Jewelry Designer A typical day for gemologist and jewelry designer Mimi So involves deciding what materials to work with. When she chooses a gemstone for a piece of jewelry, she must consider the size, hardness, color, grade, and cut of the stone. When choosing a metal to use as a setting for a stone, she must look at the hardness, melting point, color, and malleability of the metal. She needs to choose a metal that not only looks good with a particular stone but also has physical properties that will work with that stone. For example, Mimi So says emeralds are soft and fragile. A platinum setting would be too hard and could damage the emerald. So, emeralds are usually set in a softer metal, such as 18-karat gold.

The chemical properties of stones must also be considered. Heating can burn or discolor some gemstones. Mimi So says, "If you are using pearls in a design that requires heating the metal, the pearl is not a stone, so you cannot heat the pearl, because it would destroy the pearl."

Math ACTIVITY

Pure gold is 24-karat (24K). Gold that contains 18 parts gold and 6 parts other metals is 18-karat gold. The percentage of gold in 18K gold is found by dividing the amount of gold by the total amount of the material and then multiplying by 100%. For example, (18 parts gold)/(24 parts total) equals 0.75 × 100% = 75% gold. Find the percentage of gold in 10K and 14K gold.

To learn more about these Science in Action topics, visit go.hrw.com and type in the keyword **HP5MATF**.

Current Science

Check out Current Science® articles related to this chapter by visiting go.hrw.com. Just type in the keyword **HP5CS02**.

3

States of Matter

SECTION ① Three States of Matter 66

SECTION ② Behavior of Gases 70

SECTION ③ Changes of State 74

Chapter Lab 80

Chapter Review 82

Standardized Test Preparation 84

Science in Action 86

About the PHOTO

This beautiful glass creation by artist Dale Chihuly is entitled "Mille Fiori" (A Thousand Flowers). The pieces that form the sculpture were not always solid and unchanging. Each individual piece started as a blob of melted glass on the end of a hollow pipe. The artist worked with his assistants to quickly form each shape before the molten glass cooled and became a solid again.

PRE-READING ACTIVITY

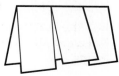

FOLDNOTES Three-Panel Flip Chart
Before you read the chapter, create the FoldNote entitled "Three-Panel Flip Chart" described in the **Study Skills** section of the Appendix. Label the flaps of the three-panel flip chart with "Solid," "Liquid," and "Gas." As you read the chapter, write information you learn about each category under the appropriate flap.

START-UP ACTIVITY

Vanishing Act

In this activity, you will use isopropyl alcohol (rubbing alcohol) to investigate a change of state.

Procedure

1. Pour **rubbing alcohol** into a **small plastic cup** until the alcohol just covers the bottom of the cup.
2. Moisten the tip of a **cotton swab** by dipping it into the alcohol in the cup.
3. Rub the cotton swab on the palm of your hand. Make sure there are no cuts or abrasions on your hands.
4. Record your observations.
5. Wash your hands thoroughly.

Analysis

1. Explain what happened to the alcohol after you rubbed the swab on your hand.
2. Did you feel a sensation of hot or cold? If so, how do you explain what you observed?
3. Record your answers.

Three States of Matter

You've just walked home on one of the coldest days of the year. A fire is blazing in the fireplace. And there is a pot of water on the stove to make hot chocolate.

The water begins to bubble. Steam rises from the pot. You make your hot chocolate, but it is too hot to drink. You don't want to wait for it to cool down. So, you add an ice cube. You watch the ice melt in the hot liquid until the drink is at just the right temperature. Then, you enjoy your hot drink while warming yourself by the fire.

The scene described above has examples of the three most familiar states of matter: solid, liquid, and gas. The **states of matter** are the physical forms in which a substance can exist. For example, water commonly exists in three states of matter: solid (ice), liquid (water), and gas (steam).

Particles of Matter

Matter is made up of tiny particles called *atoms* and *molecules* (MAHL i kyoolz). These particles are too small to see without a very powerful microscope. Atoms and molecules are always in motion and are always bumping into one another. The particles interact with each other, and the way they interact with each other helps determine the state of the matter. **Figure 1** describes three states of matter—solid, liquid, and gas—in terms of the speed and attraction of the particles.

READING WARM-UP

Objectives

● Describe the properties shared by particles of all matter.

● Describe three states of matter.

● Explain the differences between the states of matter.

Terms to Learn

states of matter
solid
liquid
surface tension
viscosity
gas

READING STRATEGY

Paired Summarizing Read this section silently. In pairs, take turns summarizing the material. Stop to discuss ideas that seem confusing.

Figure 1 **Models of a Solid, a Liquid, and a Gas**

Particles of a solid do not move fast enough to overcome the strong attraction between them. So, they are close together and vibrate in place.

Particles of a liquid move fast enough to overcome some of the attraction between them. The particles are close together but can slide past one another.

Particles of a gas move fast enough to overcome almost all of the attraction between them. The particles are far apart and move independently of one another.

Solids

Imagine dropping a marble into a bottle. Would anything happen to the shape or size of the marble? Would the shape or size of the marble change if you put it in a larger bottle?

Solids Have Definite Shape and Volume

Even in a bottle, a marble keeps its original shape and volume. The marble's shape and volume stay the same no matter what size bottle you drop it into because the marble is a solid. A **solid** is the state of matter that has a definite shape and volume.

The particles of a substance in a solid state are very close together. The attraction between them is stronger than the attraction between the particles of the same substance in the liquid or gaseous state. The particles in a solid move, but they do not move fast enough to overcome the attraction between them. Each particle vibrates in place. Therefore, each particle is locked in place by the particles around it.

There Are Two Kinds of Solids

There are two kinds of solids—*crystalline* (KRIS tuhl in) and *amorphous* (uh MAWR fuhs). Crystalline solids have a very orderly, three-dimensional arrangement of particles. The particles of crystalline solids are in a repeating pattern of rows. Iron, diamond, and ice are examples of crystalline solids.

Amorphous solids are made of particles that do not have a special arrangement. So, each particle is in one place, but the particles are not arranged in a pattern. Examples of amorphous solids are glass, rubber, and wax. **Figure 2** shows a photo of quartz (a crystalline solid) and glass (an amorphous solid).

✓ Reading Check How are the particles in a crystalline solid arranged? (*See the Appendix for answers to Reading Checks.*)

states of matter the physical forms of matter, which include solid, liquid, and gas

solid the state of matter in which the volume and shape of a substance are fixed

CONNECTION TO Physics

Is Glass a Liquid? At one time, there was a theory that glass was a liquid. This theory came about because of the observation that ancient windowpanes were often thicker at the bottom than at the top. People thought that the glass had flowed to the bottom of the pane, so glass must be a liquid. Research this theory. Present your research to your class in an oral presentation.

ACTIVITY

Figure 2 **Crystalline and Amorphous Solids**

The particles of crystalline solids, such as this quartz crystal, have an orderly three-dimensional pattern.

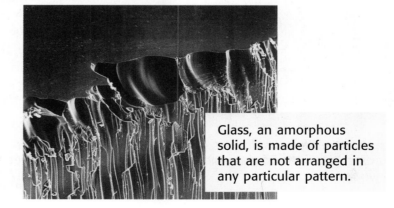

Glass, an amorphous solid, is made of particles that are not arranged in any particular pattern.

Figure 3 *Although their shapes are different, the beaker and the graduated cylinder each contain 350 mL of juice.*

liquid the state of matter that has a definite volume but not a definite shape

surface tension the force that acts on the surface of a liquid and that tends to minimize the area of the surface

viscosity the resistance of a gas or liquid to flow

gas a form of matter that does not have a definite volume or shape

Figure 4 *Water forms spherical drops as a result of surface tension.*

Liquids

What do you think would change about orange juice if you poured the juice from a can into a glass? Would the volume of juice be different? Would the taste of the juice change?

Liquids Change Shape but Not Volume

The only thing that would change when the juice is poured into the glass is the shape of the juice. The shape changes because juice is a liquid. **Liquid** is the state of matter that has a definite volume but takes the shape of its container. The particles in liquids move fast enough to overcome some of the attractions between them. The particles slide past each other until the liquid takes the shape of its container.

Although liquids change shape, they do not easily change volume. A can of juice contains a certain volume of liquid. That volume stays the same if you pour the juice into a large container or a small one. **Figure 3** shows the same volume of liquid in two different containers.

Liquids Have Unique Characteristics

A special property of liquids is surface tension. **Surface tension** is a force that acts on the particles at the surface of a liquid. Surface tension causes some liquids to form spherical drops, like the beads of water shown in **Figure 4.** Different liquids have different surface tensions. For example, gasoline has a very low surface tension and forms flat drops.

Another important property of liquids is viscosity. **Viscosity** is a liquid's resistance to flow. Usually, the stronger the attractions between the molecules of a liquid, the more viscous the liquid is. For example, honey flows more slowly than water. So, honey has a higher viscosity than water.

✓ **Reading Check** What is viscosity?

Gases

Would you believe that one small tank of helium can fill almost 700 balloons? How is this possible? After all, the volume of a tank is equal to the volume of only about five filled balloons. The answer has to do with helium's state of matter.

Gases Change in Both Shape and Volume

Helium is a gas. **Gas** is the state of matter that has no definite shape or volume. The particles of a gas move quickly. So, they can break away completely from one another. The particles of a gas have less attraction between them than do particles of the same substance in the solid or liquid state.

The amount of empty space between gas particles can change. Look at **Figure 5.** The particles of helium in the balloons are farther apart than the particles of helium in the tank. The particles spread out as helium fills the balloon. So, the amount of empty space among the gas particles increases.

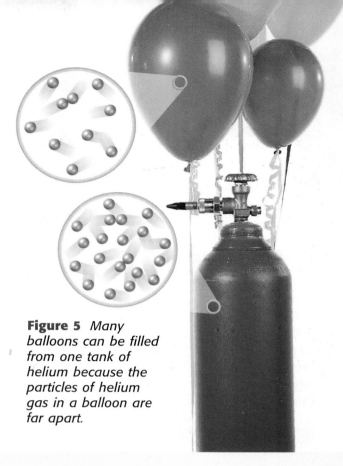

Figure 5 *Many balloons can be filled from one tank of helium because the particles of helium gas in a balloon are far apart.*

Using Key Terms

1. Use each of the following terms in a separate sentence: *viscosity* and *surface tension*.

Understanding Key Ideas

2. One property that all particles of matter have in common is they
   a. never move in solids.
   b. only move in gases.
   c. move constantly.
   d. None of the above

3. Describe solids, liquids, and gases in terms of shape and volume.

Critical Thinking

4. **Applying Concepts** Classify each substance according to its state of matter: apple juice, bread, a textbook, and steam.

5. **Identifying Relationships** The volume of a gas can change, but the volume of a solid cannot. Explain why this is true.

Interpreting Graphics

Use the image below to answer the questions that follow.

6. Identify the state of matter shown in the jar.

7. Discuss how the particles in the jar are attracted to each other.

For a variety of links related to this chapter, go to www.scilinks.org

Topic: Solids, Liquids, and Gases
SciLinks code: HSM1420

Behavior of Gases

Suppose you are watching a parade that you have been looking forward to for weeks. You may be fascinated by the giant balloons floating high overhead.

You may wonder how the balloons were arranged for the parade. How much helium was needed to fill all of the balloons? What role does the weather play in getting the balloons to float?

Describing Gas Behavior

Helium is a gas. Gases behave differently from solids or liquids. Unlike the particles that make up solids and liquids, gas particles have a large amount of empty space between them. The space that gas particles occupy is the gas's volume, which can change because of temperature and pressure.

Temperature

How much helium is needed to fill a parade balloon, like the one in **Figure 1?** The answer depends on the outdoor temperature. **Temperature** is a measure of how fast the particles in an object are moving. The faster the particles are moving, the more energy they have. So, on a hot day, the particles of gas are moving faster and hitting the inside walls of the balloon harder. Thus, the gas is expanding and pushing on the walls of the balloon with greater force. If the gas expands too much, the balloon will explode. But, what will happen if the weather is cool on the day of the parade? The particles of gas in the balloon will have less energy. And, the particles of gas will not push as hard on the walls of the balloon. So, more gas must be used to fill the balloons.

temperature a measure of how hot (or cold) something is; specifically, a measure of the movement of particles.

Figure 1 *To properly inflate a helium balloon, you must consider the temperature outside of the balloon.*

Volume

Volume is the amount of space that an object takes up. But because the particles of a gas spread out, the volume of any gas depends on the container that the gas is in. For example, have you seen inflated balloons that were twisted into different shapes? Shaping the balloons was possible because particles of gas can be compressed, or squeezed together, tightly into a smaller volume. But, if you tried to shape a balloon filled with water, the balloon would probably explode. It would explode because particles of liquids can't be compressed as much as particles of gases.

Pressure

The amount of force exerted on a given area of surface is called **pressure.** You can think of pressure as the number of times the particles of a gas hit the inside of their container.

The balls in **Figure 2** are the same size, which means they can hold the same volume of air, which is a gas. Notice, however, that there are more particles of gas in the basketball than in the beach ball. So, more particles hit the inside surface of the basketball than hit the inside surface of the beach ball. When more particles hit the inside surface of the basketball, the force on the inside surface of the ball increases. This increased force leads to greater pressure, which makes the basketball feel harder than the beach ball.

✓ **Reading Check** Why is the pressure greater in a basketball than in a beach ball? (*See the Appendix for answers to Reading Checks.*)

volume a measure of the size of a body or region in three-dimensional space

pressure the amount of force exerted per unit area of a surface

For another activity related to this chapter, go to **go.hrw.com** and type in the keyword **HP5STAW**.

Figure 2 **Gas and Pressure**

High pressure

The basketball has a higher pressure because there are more particles of gas in it, and they are closer together. The particles collide with the inside of the ball at a faster rate.

Low pressure

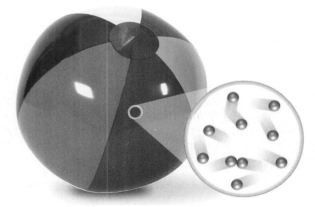

The beach ball has a lower pressure because there are fewer particles of gas, and they are farther apart. The particles in the beach ball collide with the inside of the ball at a slower rate.

Gas Behavior Laws

Scientists found that the temperature, pressure, and volume of a gas are linked. Changing one of the factors changes the other two factors. The relationships between temperature, pressure, and volume are described by gas laws.

Boyle's Law

Imagine that a diver 10 m below the surface of a lake blows a bubble of air. When the bubble reaches the surface, the bubble's volume has doubled. The difference in pressure between the surface and 10 m below the surface caused this change.

The relationship between the volume and pressure of a gas was first described by Robert Boyle, a 17th-century Irish chemist. The relationship is now known as Boyle's law. **Boyle's law** states that for a fixed amount of gas at a constant temperature, the volume of the gas is inversely related to the pressure. So, as the pressure of a gas increases, the volume decreases by the same amount, as shown in **Figure 3.**

Charles's Law

If you blow air into a balloon and leave it in the hot sun, the balloon might pop. **Charles's law** states that for a fixed amount of gas at a constant pressure, the volume of the gas changes in the same way that the temperature of the gas changes. So, if the temperature increases, the volume of gas also increases by the same amount. Charles's law is shown by the model in **Figure 4.**

✓ Reading Check State Charles's law in your own words.

Boyle's law the law that states that the volume of a gas is inversely proportional to the pressure of a gas when temperature is constant

Charles's law the law that states that the volume of a gas is directly proportional to the temperature of a gas when pressure is constant

---

Figure 3 Boyle's Law

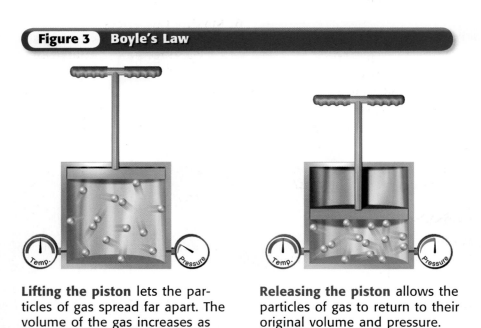

Lifting the piston lets the particles of gas spread far apart. The volume of the gas increases as the pressure decreases.

Releasing the piston allows the particles of gas to return to their original volume and pressure.

Pushing the piston forces the gas particles close together. The volume of the gas decreases as the pressure increases.

Figure 4   **Charles's Law**

Decreasing the temperature of the gas causes the particles to move more slowly. The gas particles hit the piston less often and with less force. So, the volume of the gas decreases.

Increasing the temperature of the gas causes the particles to move more quickly. The gas particles hit the piston more often and with greater force. So, the volume of the gas increases.

SECTION
Review

Summary

- Temperature measures how fast the particles in an object are moving.
- Gas pressure increases as the number of collisions of gas particles increases.
- Boyle's law states that the volume of a gas increases as the pressure decreases, if the temperature doesn't change.
- Charles's law states that the volume of a gas increases as the temperature increases, if the pressure doesn't change.

Using Key Terms

1. Use each of the following terms in the same sentence: *temperature, pressure, volume,* and *Charles's law.*

Understanding Key Ideas

2. Boyle's law describes the relationship between
   a. volume and pressure.
   b. temperature and pressure.
   c. temperature and volume.
   d. All of the above

3. What are the effects of a warm temperature on gas particles?

Math Skills

4. You have 3 L of gas at a certain temperature and pressure. What would the volume of the gas be if the temperature doubled and the pressure stayed the same?

Critical Thinking

5. **Applying Concepts** What happens to the volume of a balloon that is taken outside on a cold winter day? Explain.

6. **Making Inferences** When scientists record a gas's volume, they also record its temperature and pressure. Why?

7. **Analyzing Ideas** What happens to the pressure of a gas if the volume of gas is tripled at a constant temperature?

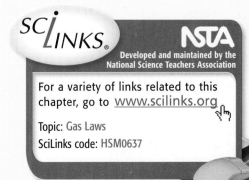

Developed and maintained by the National Science Teachers Association

For a variety of links related to this chapter, go to www.scilinks.org

Topic: Gas Laws
SciLinks code: HSM0637

Changes of State

It can be tricky to eat a frozen juice bar outside on a hot day. In just minutes, the juice bar will start to melt. Soon the solid juice bar becomes a liquid mess.

As the juice bar melts, it goes through a change of state. In this section, you will learn about the four changes of state shown in **Figure 1** as well as a fifth change of state called *sublimation* (SUHB luh MAY shuhn).

Energy and Changes of State

A **change of state** is the change of a substance from one physical form to another. All changes of state are physical changes. In a physical change, the identity of a substance does not change. In **Figure 1,** the ice, liquid water, and steam are all the same substance—water.

The particles of a substance move differently depending on the state of the substance. The particles also have different amounts of energy when the substance is in different states. For example, particles in liquid water have more energy than particles in ice. But particles of steam have more energy than particles in liquid water. So, to change a substance from one state to another, you must add or remove energy.

✓ **Reading Check** What is a change of state? (*See the Appendix for answers to Reading Checks.*)

change of state the change of a substance from one physical state to another

Figure 1 **Changes of State**

The terms in the arrows are changes of state. Water commonly goes through the changes of state shown here.

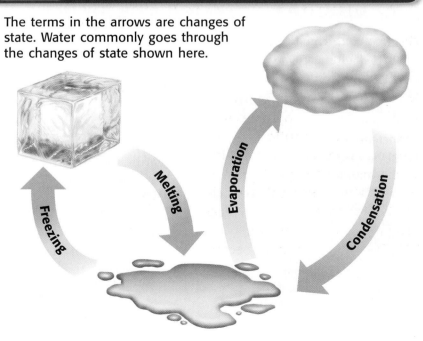

Melting: Solid to Liquid

One change of state that happens when you add energy to a substance is melting. **Melting** is the change of state from a solid to a liquid. This change of state is what happens when ice melts. Adding energy to a solid increases the temperature of the solid. As the temperature increases, the particles of the solid move faster. When a certain temperature is reached, the solid will melt. The temperature at which a substance changes from a solid to a liquid is the *melting point* of the substance. Melting point is a physical property. Different substances have different melting points. For example, gallium melts at about 30°C. Because your normal body temperature is about 37°C, gallium will melt in your hand! This is shown in **Figure 2.** Table salt, however, has a melting point of 801°C, so it will not melt in your hand.

Adding Energy

For a solid to melt, particles must overcome some of their attractions to each other. When a solid is at its melting point, any energy added to it is used to overcome the attractions that hold the particles in place. Melting is an *endothermic* (EN doh THUHR mik) change because energy is gained by the substance as it changes state.

Freezing: Liquid to Solid

The change of state from a liquid to a solid is called *freezing*. The temperature at which a liquid changes into a solid is the liquid's *freezing point*. Freezing is the reverse process of melting. Thus, freezing and melting occur at the same temperature, as shown in **Figure 3.**

Removing Energy

For a liquid to freeze, the attractions between the particles must overcome the motion of the particles. Imagine that a liquid is at its freezing point. Removing energy will cause the particles to begin locking into place. Freezing is an *exothermic* (EK so THUHR mik) change because energy is removed from the substance as it changes state.

Figure 2 *Even though gallium is a metal, it would not be very useful as jewelry!*

melting the change of state in which a solid becomes a liquid by adding energy

Figure 3 *Liquid water freezes at the same temperature at which ice melts—0°C.*

If energy is added at 0°C, the ice will melt.

If energy is removed at 0°C, the liquid water will freeze.

Evaporation: Liquid to Gas

One way to experience evaporation is to iron a shirt using a steam iron. You will notice steam coming up from the iron as the wrinkles disappear. This steam forms when the liquid water in the iron becomes hot and changes to gas.

Boiling and Evaporation

evaporation the change of a substance from a liquid to a gas

boiling the conversion of a liquid to a vapor when the vapor pressure of the liquid equals the atmospheric pressure

Evaporation (ee VAP uh RAY shuhn) is the change of a substance from a liquid to a gas. Evaporation can occur at the surface of a liquid that is below its boiling point. For example, when you sweat, your body is cooled through evaporation. Your sweat is mostly water. Water absorbs energy from your skin as the water evaporates. You feel cooler because your body transfers energy to the water. Evaporation also explains why water in a glass on a table disappears after several days.

Figure 4 explains the difference between boiling and evaporation. **Boiling** is the change of a liquid to a vapor, or gas, throughout the liquid. Boiling occurs when the pressure inside the bubbles, which is called *vapor pressure*, equals the outside pressure on the bubbles, or atmospheric pressure. The temperature at which a liquid boils is called its *boiling point*. No matter how much of a substance is present, neither the boiling point nor the melting point of a substance change. For example, 5 mL and 5 L of water both boil at 100°C.

✓ Reading Check What is evaporation?

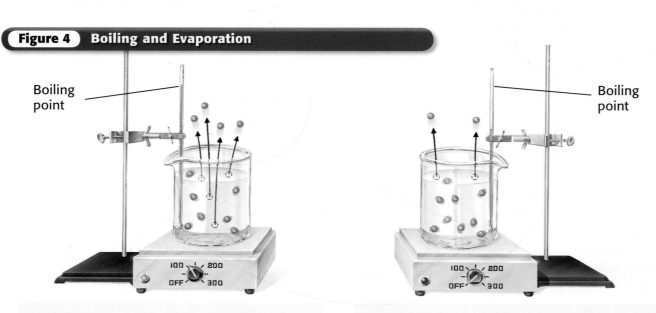

Figure 4 Boiling and Evaporation

Boiling point

Boiling point

Boiling occurs in a liquid at its boiling point. As energy is added to the liquid, particles throughout the liquid move faster. When they move fast enough to break away from other particles, they evaporate and become a gas.

Evaporation can also occur in a liquid below its boiling point. Some particles at the surface of the liquid move fast enough to break away from the particles around them and become a gas.

Effects of Pressure on Boiling Point

Earlier, you learned that water boils at 100°C. In fact, water boils at 100°C only at sea level, because of atmospheric pressure. Atmospheric pressure is caused by the weight of the gases that make up the atmosphere.

Atmospheric pressure varies depending on where you are in relation to sea level. Atmospheric pressure is lower at higher elevations. The higher you go above sea level, the fewer air particles there are above you. So, the atmospheric pressure is lower. Imagine boiling water at the top of a mountain. The boiling point would be lower than 100°C. For example, Denver, Colorado, is 1.6 km above sea level. In Denver, water boils at about 95°C.

Condensation: Gas to Liquid

Look at the dragonfly in **Figure 5.** Notice the beads of water that have formed on the wings. They form because of condensation of gaseous water in the air. **Condensation** is the change of state from a gas to a liquid. Condensation and evaporation are the reverse of each other. The *condensation point* of a substance is the temperature at which the gas becomes a liquid. And the condensation point is the same temperature as the boiling point at a given pressure.

For a gas to become a liquid, large numbers of particles must clump together. Particles clump together when the attraction between them overcomes their motion. For this to happen, energy must be removed from the gas to slow the movement of the particles. Because energy is removed, condensation is an exothermic change.

condensation the change of state from a gas to a liquid

Figure 5 *Beads of water form when water vapor in the air contacts a cool surface, such as the wings of this dragonfly.*

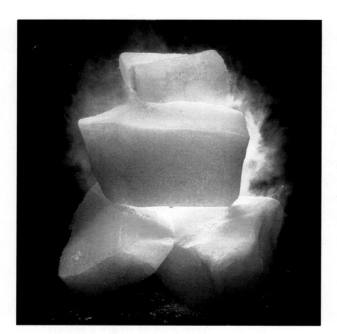

Figure 6 *Dry ice changes directly from a solid to a gas. This change of state is called* sublimation.

sublimation the process in which a solid changes directly into a gas

Sublimation: Solid to Gas

The solid in **Figure 6** is dry ice. Dry ice is carbon dioxide in a solid state. It is called *dry ice* because instead of melting into a liquid, it goes through sublimation. **Sublimation** is the change of state in which a solid changes directly into a gas. Dry ice is much colder than ice made from water.

For a solid to change directly into a gas, the particles of the substance must move from being very tightly packed to being spread far apart. So, the attractions between the particles must be completely overcome. The substance must gain energy for the particles to overcome their attractions. Thus, sublimation is an endothermic change because energy is gained by the substance as it changes state.

Change of Temperature Vs. Change of State

When most substances lose or gain energy, one of two things happens to the substance: its temperature changes or its state changes. The temperature of a substance is related to the speed of the substance's particles. So, when the temperature of a substance changes, the speed of the particles also changes. But the temperature of a substance does not change until the change of state is complete. For example, the temperature of boiling water stays at 100°C until it has all evaporated. In **Figure 7,** you can see what happens to ice as energy is added to the ice.

Reading Check What happens to the temperature of a substance as it changes state?

Boiling Water Is Cool

1. Remove the cap from a **syringe.**
2. Place the tip of the syringe in the **warm water** that is provided by your teacher. Pull the plunger out until you have 10 mL of water in the syringe.
3. Tighten the cap on the syringe.
4. Hold the syringe, and slowly pull the plunger out.
5. Observe any changes you see in the water. Record your observations.
6. Why are you not burned by the water in the syringe?

Figure 7 **Changing the State of Water**

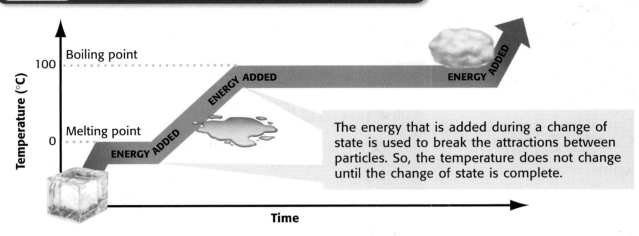

The energy that is added during a change of state is used to break the attractions between particles. So, the temperature does not change until the change of state is complete.

SECTION
Review

Summary

- A change of state is the conversion of a substance from one physical form to another.

- Energy is added during endothermic changes. Energy is removed during exothermic changes.

- The freezing point and the melting point of a substance are the same temperature.

- Both boiling and evaporation result in a liquid changing to a gas.

- Condensation is the change of a gas to a liquid. It is the reverse of evaporation.

- Sublimation changes a solid directly to a gas.

- The temperature of a substance does not change during a change of state.

Using Key Terms

For each pair of terms, explain how the meanings of the terms differ.

1. *melting* and *freezing*

2. *condensation* and *evaporation*

Understanding Key Ideas

3. The change from a solid directly to a gas is called
   a. evaporation.
   b. boiling.
   c. melting.
   d. sublimation.

4. Describe how the motion and arrangement of particles in a substance change as the substance freezes.

5. Explain what happens to the temperature of an ice cube as it melts.

6. How are evaporation and boiling different? How are they similar?

Math Skills

7. The volume of a substance in the gaseous state is about 1,000 times the volume of the same substance in the liquid state. How much space would 18 mL of water take up if it evaporated?

Critical Thinking

8. **Evaluating Data** The temperature of water in a beaker is 25°C. After adding a piece of magnesium to the water, the temperature increases to 28°C. Is this an exothermic or endothermic reaction? Explain your answer.

9. **Applying Concepts** Solid crystals of iodine were placed in a flask. The top of the flask was covered with aluminum foil. The flask was gently heated. Soon, the flask was filled with a reddish gas. What change of state took place? Explain your answer.

10. **Predicting Consequences** Would using dry ice in your holiday punch cause it to become watery after several hours? Why or why not?

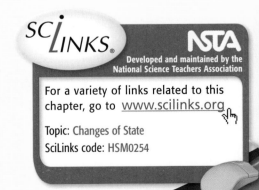

Skills Practice Lab

A Hot and Cool Lab

When you add energy to a substance through heating, does the substance's temperature always go up? When you remove energy from a substance through cooling, does the substance's temperature always go down? In this lab you'll investigate these important questions with a very common substance—water.

Procedure

1. Fill the beaker about one-third to one-half full with water.

2. Put on heat-resistant gloves. Turn on the hot plate, and put the beaker on it. Put the thermometer in the beaker. **Caution:** Be careful not to touch the hot plate.

3. Make a copy of Table 1. Record the temperature of the water every 30 seconds. Continue doing this until about one-fourth of the water boils away. Note the first temperature reading at which the water is steadily boiling.

Table 1								
Time (s)	30	60	90	120	150	180	210	etc.
Temperature (°C)	DO NOT WRITE IN BOOK							

4. Turn off the hot plate.

5. While the beaker is cooling, make a graph of temperature (y-axis) versus time (x-axis). Draw an arrow pointing to the first temperature at which the water was steadily boiling.

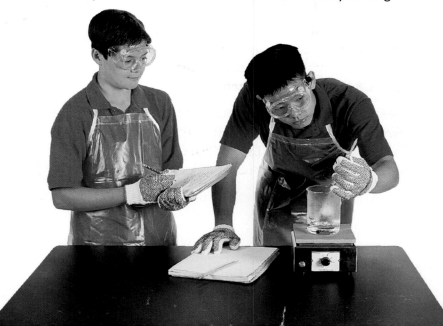

6 After you finish the graph, use heat-resistant gloves to pick up the beaker. Pour the warm water out, and rinse the warm beaker with cool water.
Caution: Even after cooling, the beaker is still too warm to handle without gloves.

7 Put approximately 20 mL of water in the graduated cylinder.

8 Put the graduated cylinder in the coffee can, and fill in around the graduated cylinder with crushed ice. Pour rock salt on the ice around the graduated cylinder. Place the thermometer and the wire-loop stirring device in the graduated cylinder.

9 As the ice melts and mixes with the rock salt, the level of ice will decrease. Add ice and rock salt to the can as needed.

10 Make another copy of Table I. Record the temperature of the water in the graduated cylinder every 30 seconds. Stir the water with the stirring device.
Caution: Do not stir with the thermometer.

11 Once the water begins to freeze, stop stirring. Do not try to pull the thermometer out of the solid ice in the cylinder.

12 Note the temperature when you first notice ice crystals forming in the water. Continue taking readings until the water in the graduated cylinder is completely frozen.

13 Make a graph of temperature (*y*-axis) versus time (*x*-axis). Draw an arrow to the temperature reading at which the first ice crystals form in the water in the graduated cylinder.

Analyze the Results

1 **Describing Events** What happens to the temperature of boiling water when you continue to add energy through heating?

2 **Describing Events** What happens to the temperature of freezing water when you continue to remove energy through cooling?

3 **Analyzing Data** What does the slope of each graph represent?

4 **Analyzing Results** How does the slope of the graph that shows water boiling compare with the slope of the graph before the water starts to boil? Why is the slope different for the two periods?

5 **Analyzing Results** How does the slope of the graph showing water freezing compare with the slope of the graph before the water starts to freeze? Why is the slope different for the two periods?

Draw Conclusions

6 **Evaluating Data** The particles that make up solids, liquids, and gases are in constant motion. Adding or removing energy causes changes in the movement of these particles. Using this idea, explain why the temperature graphs of the two experiments look the way they do.

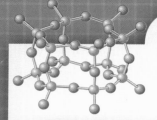

Chapter Review

USING KEY TERMS

For each pair of terms, explain how the meanings of the terms differ.

1 *solid* and *liquid*

2 *Boyle's law* and *Charles's law*

3 *evaporation* and *boiling*

4 *condensation* and *sublimation*

UNDERSTANDING KEY IDEAS

Multiple Choice

5 Which of the following statements best describes the particles of a liquid?

a. The particles are far apart and moving fast.

b. The particles are close together but moving past each other.

c. The particles are far apart and moving slowly.

d. The particles are closely packed and vibrating in place.

6 Which of the following statements describes what happens as the temperature of a gas in a balloon increases?

a. The speed of the particles decreases.

b. The volume of the gas increases, and the speed of the particles increases.

c. The volume of the gas decreases.

d. The pressure of the gas decreases.

7 Boiling points and freezing points are examples of

a. chemical properties.

b. physical properties.

c. energy.

d. matter.

8 Dew collecting on a spider web in the early morning is an example of

a. condensation.

c. sublimation.

b. evaporation.

d. melting.

9 During which change of state do atoms or molecules become more ordered?

a. boiling

c. melting

b. condensation

d. sublimation

10 Which of the following changes of state is exothermic?

a. evaporation

c. freezing

b. melting

d. All of the above

11 What happens to the volume of a gas inside a cylinder if the temperature does not change but the pressure is reduced?

a. The volume of the gas increases.

b. The volume of the gas stays the same.

c. The volume of the gas decreases.

d. There is not enough information to determine the answer.

12 The atoms and molecules in matter

a. are attracted to one another.

b. are constantly moving.

c. move faster at higher temperatures.

d. All of the above

Short Answer

13 Explain why liquid water takes the shape of its container but an ice cube does not.

14 Rank solids, liquids, and gases in order of particle speed from the highest speed to the lowest speed.

Math Skills

15 Kate placed 100 mL of water in five different pans, placed the pans on a windowsill for a week, and measured how much water evaporated from each pan. Draw a graph of her data, which is shown below. Place surface area on the x-axis and volume evaporated on the y-axis. Is the graph linear or non-linear? What does this information tell you?

Pan number	1	2	3	4	5
Surface area (cm²)	44	82	20	30	65
Volume evaporated (mL)	42	79	19	29	62

CRITICAL THINKING

16 Concept Mapping Use the following terms to create a concept map: *states of matter, solid, liquid, gas, changes of state, freezing, vaporization, condensation,* and *melting.*

17 Analyzing Ideas In the photo below, water is being split to form two new substances, hydrogen and oxygen. Is this a change of state? Explain your answer.

18 Applying Concepts After taking a shower, you notice that small droplets of water cover the mirror. Explain how this happens. Be sure to describe where the water comes from and the changes it goes through.

19 Analyzing Methods To protect their crops during freezing temperatures, orange growers spray water onto the trees and allow it to freeze. In terms of energy lost and energy gained, explain why this practice protects the oranges from damage.

20 Making Inferences At sea level, water boils at 100°C, while methane boils at –161°C. Which of these substances has a stronger force of attraction between its particles? Explain your reasoning.

INTERPRETING GRAPHICS

Use the graph below to answer the questions that follow.

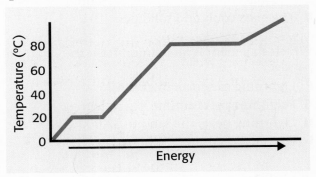

21 What is the boiling point of the substance? What is the melting point?

22 Which state is present at 30°C?

23 How will the substance change if energy is added to the liquid at 20°C?

Standardized Test Preparation

Read each of the passages below. Then, answer the questions that follow each passage.

Passage 1 Did you know that lightning can turn sand into glass? If lightning strikes sand, the sand can reach temperatures of up to 33,000°C. That temperature is as hot as the surface of the sun! This <u>intense</u> heat melts the sand into a liquid. The liquid quickly cools and hardens into glass. This glass is a rare and beautiful type of natural glass called *fulgurite*.

The same basic process is used to make light bulbs, windows, and bottles. But instead of lightning, glassmakers use hot ovens to melt solid silica (the main ingredient of sand) and other ingredients into liquid glass. Then, before the glass cools and solidifies, the glassmaker forms the glass into the desired shape.

1. In the glassmaking process, what happens after the glassmaker forms the material into the desired shape?
   A Solid silica melts in a hot oven.
   B Solid silica is struck by lightning.
   C The glass melts and becomes a liquid.
   D The glass cools and solidifies.

2. Which statement is an opinion from the passage?
   F Lightning can form fulgurites.
   G Fulgurites are beautiful.
   H Lightning heats the sand to 33,000°C.
   I Glassmakers use very hot ovens.

3. In the passage, what does *intense* mean?
   A a small amount
   B gaseous
   C a great amount
   D causing something to melt

Passage 2 For thousands of years, people used wind, water, gravity, dogs, horses, and cattle to do work. But until about 300 years ago, people had little success finding other things to help them do work. Then in 1690, Denis Papin, a French mathematician and physicist, noticed that steam <u>expanding</u> in a cylinder pushed a piston up. As the steam then cooled and contracted, the piston fell. Watching the motion of the piston, Papin had an idea. He connected a water-pump handle to the piston. As the pump handle rose and fell with the piston, water was pumped.

Throughout the next hundred years, other scientists and inventors improved upon Papin's design. In 1764, James Watt turned the steam pump into a true steam engine that could drive a locomotive. Watt's engine helped start the Industrial Revolution.

1. In the passage, what does *expanding* mean?
   A enlarging
   B enhancing
   C enforcing
   D disappearing

2. According to the passage, how was steam used?
   F as a source of power for thousands of years
   G by Denis Papin only in France
   H to pump water in the late 1600s
   I in the steam engine first

3. Which of the following statements is a fact from the passage?
   A Steam expands and causes a piston to fall.
   B When steam cools, it expands.
   C The invention of the water pump started the Industrial Revolution.
   D People began using steam as a source of power 300 years ago.

Use the chart below to answer the questions that follow.

Freezing Points of 50:50 Mixtures of Antifreeze and Water	
Brand	**Freezing Point (°C)**
Ice-B-Gone	−5
Freeze Free	−7
Liqui-Freeze	−9
Auntie Freeze	−11

1. Phillip wants to purchase antifreeze for his car. Antifreeze is added to the water in a car's radiator to lower the water's freezing point. The temperature in his area never falls below −10°C. Given the information in the chart above, which of the following brands of antifreeze would be the best for Phillip's car?

   A Ice-B-Gone
   B Freeze-Free
   C Liqui-Freeze
   D Auntie Freeze

2. Phillip wants to make a bar graph that compares the brands of antifreeze. If he puts the brand name of each antifreeze on the x-axis, what variable belongs on the y-axis?

   F Freezing point of water
   G Freezing point of water with antifreeze in it
   H Freezing point of the antifreeze only
   I Freezing point of the radiator

3. Phillip's cousin lives in an area where it rarely freezes. The record low temperature for winter is −2°C. Which brand should Phillip's cousin purchase?

   A Ice-B-Gone
   B Freeze-Free
   C Liqui-Freeze
   D Auntie Freeze

Read each question below, and choose the best answer.

1. Gerard and three of his friends each want to buy a kite. The kites regularly cost $7.95, but they are on sale for $4.50. How much will their total savings be if they all purchase their kites on sale?

   A $13.80
   B $18.00
   C $10.35
   D $23.85

2. Francis bought a 2 L bottle of juice. How many milliliters of juice does this bottle hold?

   F 0.002 mL
   G 0.2 mL
   H 200 mL
   I 2,000 mL

3. Which of the following lists contains ratios that are all equivalent to 3/4?

   A 3/4, 6/8, 15/22
   B 6/10, 15/20, 20/25
   C 3/4, 15/20, 20/25
   D 3/4, 6/8, 15/20

4. The Liu family went to the state fair in their home state. They purchased five tickets, which cost $6.50 each. Tickets for the rides cost $1.25 each, and all five family members rode six rides. Two daughters bought souvenirs that cost $5.25 each. Snacks cost a total of $12.00. What is the total amount of money the family spent on their outing?

   F $61.25
   G $140.50
   H $62.50
   I $92.50

Standardized Test Preparation

Science in Action

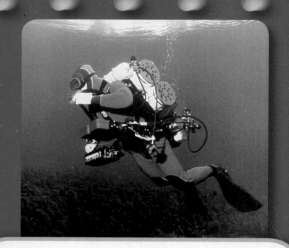

Science, Technology, and Society

Deep-sea Diving with Helium

Divers who breathe air while deep in the ocean run the risk of suffering from nitrogen narcosis. Nitrogen narcosis produces an alcohol-like effect, which can cause a diver to become disoriented and to use poor judgment. This toxic effect can lead to dangerous behavior. To avoid nitrogen narcosis, divers who work at depths of more than 60 m breathe heliox. *Heliox* is a mixture of helium and oxygen, instead of air. The main disadvantage of heliox is that helium conducts heat about six times faster than nitrogen does, so a diver using heliox will feel cold sooner than a diver who is breathing air.

Math ACTIVITY

There are 2.54 centimeters in one inch. How many feet deep could a diver go before he or she started experiencing nitrogen narcosis?

Scientific Discoveries

The Fourth State of Matter

If you heat water, it will eventually turn into a gas. But what would happen if you kept on heating the gas? Scientists only had to look to the sun for the answer. The sun, like other stars, is made of the fourth state of matter—plasma. Plasma is a superheated gas. Once a gas's temperature rises above 10,000°C to 20,000°C, its particles start to break apart and it becomes plasma. Unlike gas, plasma can create, and be affected by, electrical and magnetic fields. More than 99% of the known universe is made of plasma! Even Earth has some naturally occurring plasma. Plasma can be found in auroras, flames, and lightning.

Social Studies ACTIVITY

Research plasma. Find out how plasma is used in today's technology, such as plasma TVs. How will this new technology affect you and society in general? Describe your findings in a poster.

Andy Goldsworthy

Nature Artist Most of the art that Andy Goldsworthy creates will melt, decay, evaporate, or just blow away. He uses leaves, water, sticks, rocks, ice, and snow to create art. Goldsworthy observes how nature works and how it changes over time, and uses what he learns to create his art. For example, on cold, sunny mornings, Goldsworthy makes frost shadows. He stands with his back to the sun, which creates a shadow on the ground. The rising sun warms the ground and melts the frost around his shadow. When he steps away, he can see the shape of his body in the frost that is left on the ground.

In his art, Goldsworthy sometimes shows water in the process of changing states. For example, he made huge snowballs filled with branches, pebbles, and flowers. He then stored these snowballs in a freezer until summer, when they were displayed in a museum. As they melted, the snowballs slowly revealed their contents. Goldsworthy says his art reflects nature, because nature is constantly changing. Fortunately, he takes pictures of his art so we can enjoy it even after it disappears!

Language Arts ACTiViTY

WRITING SKILL Research Andy Goldsworthy's art. Write a one-page review of one of his creations. Be sure to include what you like or don't like about the art.

To learn more about these Science in Action topics, visit go.hrw.com and type in the keyword **HP5STAF.**

Current Science

Check out Current Science® articles related to this chapter by visiting go.hrw.com. Just type in the keyword **HP5CS03.**

Elements, Compounds, and Mixtures

SECTION 1 Elements 90

SECTION 2 Compounds 94

SECTION 3 Mixtures 98

Chapter Lab 106
Chapter Review 108
Standardized Test Preparation 110
Science in Action 112

About the PHOTO

Within these liquid-filled glass lamps, colored globs slowly rise and fall. But what are these liquids, and what keeps them from mixing together? The liquid inside these lamps is a mixture. This mixture is composed of four compounds, which include mineral oil, wax, water, and alcohol. The water and alcohol mix, but they remain separated from the globs of wax and oil.

PRE-READING ACTIVITY

FOLDNOTES **Key-Term Fold** Before you read the chapter, create the FoldNote entitled "Key-Term Fold" described in the **Study Skills** section of the Appendix. Write a key term from the chapter on each tab of the key-term fold. Under each tab, write the definition of the key term.

START-UP ACTIVITY

Mystery Mixture

In this activity, you will separate the different dyes found in an ink mixture.

Procedure

1. Place a **pencil** on top of a **clear plastic cup.** Tear a strip of paper (3 cm × 15 cm) from a **coffee filter.** Wrap one end of the strip around a pencil so that the other end will touch the bottom of the plastic cup. Use **tape** to attach the paper to the pencil.

2. Take the paper out of the cup. Using a **water-soluble black marker,** make a small dot in the center of the strip about 2 cm from the bottom.

3. Pour **water** in the cup to a depth of 1 cm. Lower the paper into the cup. Keep the dot above water.

4. Remove the paper when the water is 1 cm from the top. Record your observations.

Analysis

1. What happened as the paper soaked up the water?

2. Which colors make up the marker's black ink?

3. Compare your results with those of your classmates. Record your observations.

4. Is the process used to make the ink separate a physical or a chemical change? Explain.

Elements

Imagine that you work for the Break-It-Down Company. Your job is to break down materials into simpler substances.

You haven't had any trouble breaking down materials so far. But one rainy Monday morning, you get a material that seems very hard to break down. First, you try physical changes, such as crushing and melting. But these do not change the material into something simpler. Next, you try some chemical changes, such as passing an electric current through the material. These do not change it either. What's going on?

Elements, the Simplest Substances

You couldn't break down the material described above because it is an element. An **element** is a pure substance that cannot be separated into simpler substances by physical or chemical means. In this section, you'll learn about elements and the properties that help you classify them.

Only One Type of Particle

Elements are pure substances. A **pure substance** is a substance in which there is only one type of particle. So, each element contains only one type of particle. These particles, called *atoms*, are much too small for us to see. For example, every atom in a 5 g nugget of the element gold is like every other atom of gold. The particles of a pure substance are alike no matter where they are found, as shown in **Figure 1.**

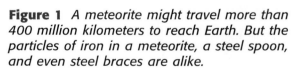 **Reading Check** Explain why an element is a pure substance. (*See the Appendix for answers to Reading Checks.*)

Figure 1 *A meteorite might travel more than 400 million kilometers to reach Earth. But the particles of iron in a meteorite, a steel spoon, and even steel braces are alike.*

Properties of Elements

Each element can be identified by its unique set of properties. For example, each element has its own *characteristic properties*. These properties do not depend on the amount of the element present. Characteristic properties include some physical properties, such as boiling point, melting point, and density. Chemical properties, such as reactivity with acid, are also characteristic properties.

An element may share a property with another element, but other properties can help you tell the elements apart. For example, the elements helium and krypton are both unreactive gases. However, the densities (mass per unit volume) of these elements are different. Helium is less dense than air. A helium-filled balloon will float up if it is released. Krypton is denser than air. A krypton-filled balloon will sink to the ground if it is released.

Identifying Elements by Their Properties

Look at the elements shown in **Figure 2.** These three elements have some similar properties. But each element can be identified by its unique set of properties.

Notice that the physical properties shown in **Figure 2** include melting point and density. Other physical properties, such as color, hardness, and texture, could be added to the list. Chemical properties might also be useful. For example, some elements, such as hydrogen and carbon, are flammable. Other elements, such as sodium, react with oxygen at room temperature. Still other elements, including zinc, are reactive with acid.

Quick Lab

Separating Elements

1. Examine a sample of nails provided by your teacher.

2. Your sample has **aluminum nails** and **iron nails.** Try to separate the two kinds of nails. Group similar nails into piles.

3. Pass a **bar magnet** over each pile of nails. Record your results.

4. Were you successful in completely separating the two types of nails? Explain.

5. Based on your observations, explain how the properties of aluminum and iron could be used to separate cans in a recycling plant.

element a substance that cannot be separated or broken down into simpler substances by chemical means

pure substance a sample of matter, either a single element or a single compound, that has definite chemical and physical properties

---

Figure 2 The Unique Properties of Elements

Cobalt	Iron	Nickel

Cobalt
- Melting point: 1,495°C
- Density: 8.9 g/cm³
- Conducts electric current and heat energy
- Unreactive with oxygen in the air

Iron
- Melting point: 1,535°C
- Density: 7.9 g/cm³
- Conducts electric current and heat energy
- Combines slowly with oxygen in the air to form rust

Nickel
- Melting point: 1,455°C
- Density: 8.9 g/cm³
- Conducts electric current and heat energy
- Unreactive with oxygen in the air

Figure 3 *Even though these dogs are different breeds, they have enough in common to be classified as terriers.*

Classifying Elements by Their Properties

Think about how many different breeds of dogs there are. Now, think about how you tell one breed from another. Most often, you can tell just by their appearance, or the physical properties, of the dogs. **Figure 3** shows several breeds of terriers. Many terriers are fairly small in size and have short hair. Not all terriers are alike, but they share enough properties to be classified in the same group.

Categories of Elements

Elements are also grouped into categories by the properties they share. There are three major categories of elements: metals, nonmetals, and metalloids. The elements iron, nickel, and cobalt are all metals. Not all metals are exactly alike, but they do have some properties in common. **Metals** are shiny, and they conduct heat energy and electric current. **Nonmetals** make up the second category of elements. They do not conduct heat or electric current, and solid nonmetals are dull in appearance. **Metalloids,** which have properties of both metals and nonmetals, make up the last category.

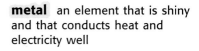 **Reading Check** What are three characteristics of metals?

Categories Are Similar

Imagine being in a music store. The CDs are categorized by type of music. If you like rock-and-roll, you would go to the rock-and-roll section. You might not know every CD, but you know that a CD has the characteristics of rock-and-roll for it to be in this section.

By knowing the category to which an unfamiliar element belongs, you can predict some of its properties. **Figure 4** shows examples of each category and describes the properties that identify elements in each category.

metal an element that is shiny and that conducts heat and electricity well

nonmetal an element that conducts heat and electricity poorly

metalloid an element that has properties of both metals and nonmetals

Figure 4 **The Three Major Categories of Elements**

Metals

Lead

Tin

Copper

Metals are elements that are shiny and are good conductors of heat and electric current. They are *malleable.* (They can be hammered into thin sheets.) They are also *ductile.* (They can be drawn into thin wires.)

Nonmetals

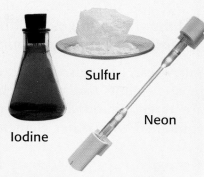

Sulfur

Neon

Iodine

Nonmetals are elements that are dull (not shiny) and that are poor conductors of heat and electric current. Solids tend to be brittle and unmalleable. Few familiar objects are made of only nonmetals.

Metalloids

Boron

Silicon

Antimony

Metalloids are also called semiconductors. They have properties of both metals and nonmetals. Some metalloids are shiny. Some are dull. Metalloids are somewhat malleable and ductile. Some metalloids conduct heat and electric current as well.

SECTION Review

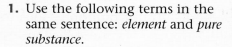

Summary

- A substance in which all of the particles are alike is a pure substance.
- An element is a pure substance that cannot be broken down into anything simpler by physical or chemical means.
- Each element has a unique set of physical and chemical properties.
- Elements are classified as metals, nonmetals, or metalloids, based on their properties.

Using Key Terms

1. Use the following terms in the same sentence: *element* and *pure substance*.

Understanding Key Ideas

2. A metalloid
   a. may conduct electric current.
   b. can be ductile.
   c. is also called a semiconductor.
   d. All of the above

3. What is a pure substance?

Math Skills

4. There are eight elements that make up 98.5% of the Earth's crust: 46.6% oxygen, 8.1% aluminum, 5.0% iron, 3.6% calcium, 2.8% sodium, 2.6% potassium, and 2.1% magnesium. The rest is silicon. What percentage of the Earth's crust is silicon?

Critical Thinking

5. **Applying Concepts** From which category of elements would you choose to make a container that wouldn't shatter if dropped? Explain your answer.

6. **Making Comparisons** Compare the properties of metals, nonmetals, and metalloids.

7. **Evaluating Assumptions** Your friend tells you that a shiny element has to be a metal. Do you agree? Explain.

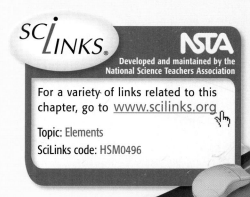

Developed and maintained by the National Science Teachers Association

For a variety of links related to this chapter, go to www.scilinks.org

Topic: Elements
SciLinks code: HSM0496

Compounds

What do salt, sugar, baking soda, and water have in common? You might use all of these to bake bread. Is there anything else similar about them?

Salt, sugar, baking soda, and water are all compounds. Because most elements take part in chemical changes fairly easily, they are rarely found alone in nature. Instead, they are found combined with other elements as compounds.

Compounds: Made of Elements

A **compound** is a pure substance composed of two or more elements that are chemically combined. Elements combine by reacting, or undergoing a chemical change, with one another. A particle of a compound is a molecule. Molecules of compounds are formed when atoms of two or more elements join together.

In **Figure 1,** you see magnesium reacting with oxygen. A compound called *magnesium oxide* is forming. The compound is a new pure substance. It is different from the elements that make it up. Most of the substances that you see every day are compounds. **Table 1** lists some familiar examples.

The Ratio of Elements in a Compound

Elements do not randomly join to form compounds. Elements join in a specific ratio according to their masses to form a compound. For example, the ratio of the mass of hydrogen to the mass of oxygen in water is 1 to 8. This mass ratio can be written as 1:8. This ratio is always the same. Every sample of water has a 1:8 mass ratio of hydrogen to oxygen. What happens if a sample of a compound has a different mass ratio of hydrogen to oxygen? The compound cannot be water.

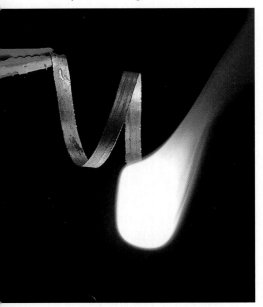

Figure 1 *As magnesium burns, it reacts with oxygen and forms the compound magnesium oxide.*

Table 1 Familiar Compounds	
Compound	**Elements combined**
Table salt	sodium and chlorine
Water	hydrogen and oxygen
Vinegar	hydrogen, carbon, and oxygen
Carbon dioxide	carbon and oxygen
Baking soda	sodium, hydrogen, carbon, and oxygen

Compound Confusion

1. Measure **4 g of compound A**, and place it in a **clear plastic cup**.

2. Measure **4 g of compound B**, and place it in a **second clear plastic cup**.

3. Observe the color and texture of each compound. Record your observations.

4. Add **5 mL of vinegar** to each cup. Record your observations.

5. Baking soda reacts with vinegar. Powdered sugar does not react with vinegar. Which compound is baking soda, and which compound is powdered sugar? Explain your answer.

Properties of Compounds

As an element does, each compound has its own physical properties. Physical properties include melting point, density, and color. Compounds can also be identified by their different chemical properties. Some compounds react with acid. For example, calcium carbonate, found in chalk, reacts with acid. Other compounds, such as hydrogen peroxide, react when exposed to light.

compound a substance made up of atoms of two or more different elements joined by chemical bonds

✓ **Reading Check** What are three physical properties used to identify compounds? (*See the Appendix for answers to Reading Checks.*)

Properties: Compounds Versus Elements

A compound has properties that differ from those of the elements that form it. Look at **Figure 2.** Sodium chloride, or table salt, is made of two very dangerous elements—sodium and chlorine. Sodium reacts violently with water. Chlorine is a poisonous gas. But when combined, these elements form a harmless compound with unique properties. Sodium chloride is safe to eat. It also dissolves (without exploding!) in water.

Figure 2 Forming Sodium Chloride

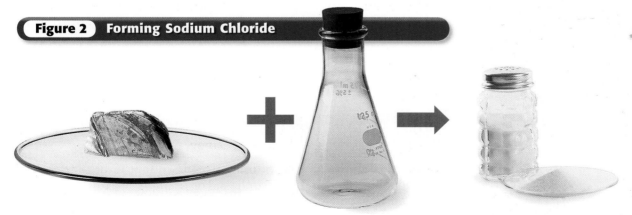

Sodium is a soft, silvery white metal that reacts violently with water.

Chlorine is a poisonous, greenish yellow gas.

Sodium chloride, or table salt, is a white solid. It dissolves easily in water and is safe to eat.

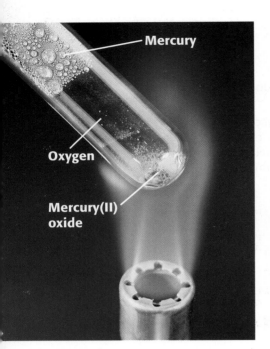

Figure 3 *Heating mercury(II) oxide causes a chemical change that separates it into the elements mercury and oxygen.*

Labels on figure: Mercury, Oxygen, Mercury(II) oxide

Breaking Down Compounds

Some compounds can be broken down into their elements by chemical changes. Other compounds break down to form simpler compounds instead of elements. These simpler compounds can then be broken down into elements through more chemical changes. For example, carbonic acid is a compound that helps give carbonated beverages their "fizz." When you open a carbonated beverage, carbonic acid breaks down into carbon dioxide and water. Carbon dioxide and water can then be broken down into the elements carbon, oxygen, and hydrogen through chemical changes.

✓ **Reading Check** Compounds can be broken down into what two types of substances?

Methods of Breaking Down Compounds

The only way to break down a compound is through a chemical change. Sometimes, energy is needed for a chemical change to happen. Two ways to add energy to break down a compound are to apply heat and to apply an electric current. For example, heating the compound mercury(II) oxide breaks it down into the elements mercury and oxygen, as shown in **Figure 3.**

Compounds in Your World

You are surrounded by compounds. Compounds make up the food you eat, the school supplies you use, and the clothes you wear—even you!

Compounds in Industry

The compounds found in nature are not usually the raw materials needed by industry. Often, these compounds must be broken down to provide elements or other compounds that can be used as raw material. For example, aluminum is used in cans and airplanes. But aluminum is not found alone in nature. Aluminum is produced by breaking down the compound aluminum oxide. Ammonia is another important compound used in industry. It is used to make fertilizers. Ammonia is made by combining the elements nitrogen and hydrogen.

INTERNET ACTIVITY

For another activity related to this chapter, go to **go.hrw.com** and type in the keyword **HP5MIXW.**

CONNECTION TO Physics

Electrolysis The process of using electric current to break down compounds is known as *electrolysis*. For example, electrolysis can be used to separate water into hydrogen and oxygen. Research ways that electrolysis is used in industry. Make a poster of what you learn, and present a report to your class.

ACTiViTY

Compounds in Nature

Proteins are compounds found in all living things. The element nitrogen is one of the elements needed to make proteins. **Figure 4** shows how some plants get the nitrogen they need. Other plants use nitrogen compounds that are in the soil. Animals get the nitrogen they need by eating plants or by eating animals that have eaten plants. The proteins in the food are broken down as an animal digests the food. The simpler compounds that form are used by the animal's cells to make new proteins.

Another compound that plays an important role in life is carbon dioxide. You exhale carbon dioxide that was made in your body. Plants take in carbon dioxide, which is used in photosynthesis. Plants use photosynthesis to make compounds called carbohydrates. These carbohydrates can then be broken down for energy through other chemical changes by plants or animals.

Figure 4 *The bumps on the roots of this pea plant are home to bacteria that form compounds from nitrogen in the air. The pea plant makes proteins from these compounds.*

SECTION Review

Summary

- A compound is a pure substance composed of two or more elements.
- The elements that form a compound always combine in a specific ratio according to their masses.
- Each compound has a unique set of physical and chemical properties that differ from those of the elements that make up the compound.
- Compounds can be broken down into simpler substances only by chemical changes.

Using Key Terms

1. In your own words, write a definition for the term *compound*.

Understanding Key Ideas

2. The elements in a compound
   a. join in a specific ratio according to their masses.
   b. combine by reacting with one another.
   c. can be separated by chemical changes.
   d. All of the above

3. What type of change is needed to break down a compound?

Math Skills

4. Table sugar is a compound made of carbon, hydrogen, and oxygen. If sugar contains 41.86% carbon and 6.98% hydrogen, what percentage of sugar is oxygen?

Critical Thinking

5. **Applying Concepts** Iron is a solid, gray metal. Oxygen is a colorless gas. When they chemically combine, rust is made. Rust has a reddish brown color. Why is rust different from the iron and oxygen that it is made of?

6. **Analyzing Ideas** A jar contains samples of the elements carbon and oxygen. Does the jar contain a compound? Explain your answer.

SCI LINKS.

NSTA
Developed and maintained by the
National Science Teachers Association

For a variety of links related to this chapter, go to www.scilinks.org

Topic: Compounds
SciLinks code: HSM0332

mixture a combination of two
or more substances that are not
chemically combined

Mixtures

*Imagine that you roll out some dough, add tomato sauce,
and sprinkle some cheese on top. Then, you add green
peppers, mushrooms, olives, and pepperoni! What have
you just made?*

A pizza, of course! But that's not all. You have also created a
mixture—and a delicious one at that! In this section, you will
learn about mixtures and their properties.

Properties of Mixtures

All mixtures—even pizza—share certain properties. A **mixture** is
a combination of two or more substances that are not chemically combined. When two or more materials are put together,
they form a mixture if they do not react to form a compound.
For example, cheese and tomato sauce do not react when they
are used to make a pizza. So, a pizza is a mixture.

No Chemical Changes in a Mixture

No chemical change happens when a mixture is made. So,
each substance in a mixture has the same chemical makeup
it had before the mixture formed. That is, each substance in a
mixture keeps its identity. In some mixtures, such as the pizza
in **Figure 1,** you can see each of the components. In other mixtures, such as salt water, you cannot see all the components.

✓ **Reading Check** Why do substances in a mixture keep their
identities? (*See the Appendix for answers to Reading Checks.*)

Separating Mixtures Through Physical Methods

You don't like mushrooms on your pizza? Just pick them off.
This change is a physical change of the mixture. The identities
of the substances do not change. But not all mixtures are as
easy to separate as a pizza. You cannot just pick salt out of
a saltwater mixture. One way to separate the salt from the
water is to heat the mixture until the water evaporates. The
salt is left behind. Other ways to separate mixtures are shown
in **Figure 2.**

Figure 1 *You can see each topping
on this mixture, which is better
known as a pizza.*

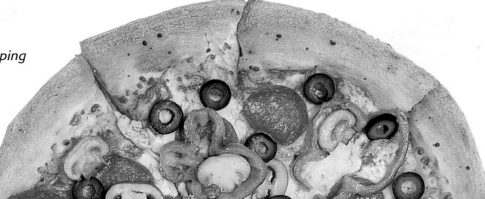

Figure 2 **Common Ways to Separate Mixtures**

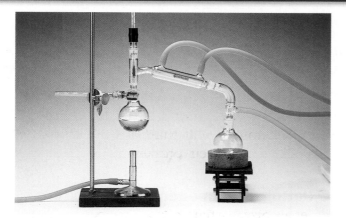

Distillation (DIS tuh LAY shuhn) is a process that separates a mixture based on the boiling points of the components. Here, pure water (at right) is being distilled from a salt-water mixture (at left). Distillation is also used to separate crude oil into components, such as gasoline and kerosene.

A **magnet** can be used to separate a mixture of the elements iron and aluminum. Iron is attracted to the magnet, but aluminum is not.

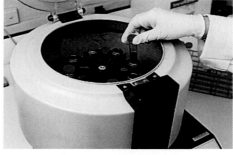

The different parts of blood are separated using a machine called a **centrifuge** (SEN truh FYOOJ). In the test tube at left, a layer of plasma rests above a layer of red blood cells. A centrifuge separates mixtures by the densities of the components.

Separating a mixture of sodium chloride (table salt) and sulfur takes more than one step.

❶ In the first step, water is added, and the mixture is stirred. Salt dissolves in water. Sulfur does not.

❷ In the second step, the mixture is poured through a filter. The filter traps the solid sulfur.

❸ In the third step, the water is evaporated. The sodium chloride is left behind.

Table 1 Mixtures and Compounds

Mixtures	Compounds
Made of elements, compounds, or both	Made of elements
No change in original properties of components	Change in original properties of components
Separated by physical means	Separated by chemical means
Formed using any ratio of components	Formed using a set ratio of components

The Ratio of Components in a Mixture

A compound is made of elements in a specific mass ratio. However, the components of a mixture do not need to be mixed in a definite ratio. For example, granite is a mixture made of three minerals: feldspar, mica, and quartz. Feldspar is pink in color. Mica is black. Quartz is colorless. Look at the egg-shaped paperweights in **Figure 3.** The pink one is made from granite that has more feldspar than mica or quartz. That is why it is pink. The black one is made from granite that has more mica than the other minerals. The gray one is made from granite that has more quartz than the other minerals. Even though the proportions of the minerals change, this combination of minerals is always a mixture called *granite*. **Table 1** above summarizes the differences between mixtures and compounds.

Figure 3 *These paperweights are made of granite. They are different colors because the granite used in each has different ratios of minerals.*

Solutions

A **solution** is a mixture that appears to be a single substance. A solution is composed of particles of two or more substances that are distributed evenly among each other. Solutions have the same appearance and properties throughout the mixture.

The process in which particles of substances separate and spread evenly throughout a mixture is known as *dissolving*. In solutions, the **solute** is the substance that is dissolved. The **solvent** is the substance in which the solute is dissolved. A solute must be *soluble,* or able to dissolve, in the solvent. A substance that is *insoluble,* or unable to dissolve, forms a mixture that is not a solution.

Salt water is a solution. Salt is soluble in water, meaning that salt dissolves in water. Therefore, salt is the solute, and water is the solvent. When two liquids or two gases form a solution, the substance with the greater amount is the solvent.

solution a homogeneous mixture of two or more substances uniformly dispersed throughout a single phase

solute in a solution, the substance that dissolves in the solvent

solvent in a solution, the substance in which the solute dissolves

Table 2 Examples of Different States in Solutions	
States	**Examples**
Gas in gas	dry air (oxygen in nitrogen)
Gas in liquid	soft drinks (carbon dioxide in water)
Liquid in liquid	antifreeze (alcohol in water)
Solid in liquid	salt water (salt in water)
Solid in solid	brass (zinc in copper)

Examples of Solutions

You may think that all solutions are liquids. And in fact, tap water, soft drinks, gasoline, and many cleaning supplies are liquid solutions. However, solutions may also be gases, such as air. Solutions may even be solids, such as steel. *Alloys* are solid solutions of metals or nonmetals dissolved in metals. Brass is an alloy of the metal zinc dissolved in copper. Steel is an alloy made of the nonmetal carbon and other elements dissolved in iron. **Table 2** lists more examples of solutions.

✓ Reading Check What is an alloy?

Particles in Solutions

The particles in solutions are so small that they never settle out. They also cannot be removed by filtering. In fact, the particles are so small that they don't even scatter light. Both of the jars in **Figure 4** contain mixtures. The mixture in the jar on the left is a solution of table salt in water. The jar on the right holds a mixture—but not a solution—of gelatin in water.

CONNECTION TO Language Arts

WRITING SKILL **Alloys** Research an alloy. Find out what the alloy is made of and the amount of each substance in the alloy. Also, identify different ways that the alloy is used. Then, write a song or poem about the alloy to recite in class.

Figure 4 *Both of these jars contain mixtures. The mixture in the jar on the left, however, is a solution. The particles in solutions are so small that they don't scatter light. Therefore, you can't see the path of light through the solution.*

Figure 5 *The dilute solution (left) contains less solute than the concentrated solution (right).*

Concentration of Solutions

A measure of the amount of solute dissolved in a solvent is **concentration.** Concentration can be expressed in grams of solute per milliliter of solvent (g/mL).

concentration the amount of a particular substance in a given quantity of a mixture, solution, or ore

solubility the ability of one substance to dissolve in another at a given temperature and pressure

Concentrated or Dilute?

Solutions can be described as being concentrated or dilute. In **Figure 5,** both solutions have the same amount of solvent. However, the solution on the left contains less solute than the solution on the right. The solution on the left is dilute. The solution on the right is concentrated. Keep in mind that the terms *dilute* and *concentrated* do not tell you the amount of solute that is dissolved.

Solubility

If you add too much sugar to a glass of lemonade, not all of the sugar can dissolve. Some of it sinks to the bottom. To find the maximum amount of sugar that can dissolve, you would need to know the solubility of sugar. The **solubility** of a solute is the ability of the solute to dissolve in a solvent at a certain temperature. **Figure 6** shows how the solubility of several different solid substances changes with temperature.

Calculating Concentration What is the concentration of a solution that has 35 g of salt dissolved in 175 mL of water?

Step 1: One equation for finding concentration is the following:

$$\text{concentration} = \frac{grams\ of\ solute}{milliliters\ of\ solvent}$$

Step 2: Replace grams of solute and milliliters of solvent with the values given, and solve.

$$\frac{35\ \text{g salt}}{175\ \text{mL water}} = 0.2\ \text{g/mL}$$

Now It's Your Turn
1. What is the concentration of solution A if it has 55 g of sugar dissolved in 500 mL of water?
2. What is the concentration of solution B if it has 36 g of sugar dissolved in 144 mL of water?
3. Which solution is more concentrated?

Figure 6 Solubility of Different Solids In Water

The solubility of most solids increases as the temperature gets higher. So, more solute can dissolve at higher temperatures. However, some solids, such as cerium sulfate, are less soluble at higher temperatures.

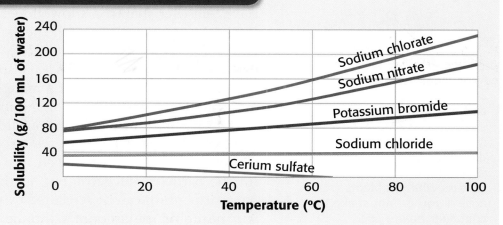

Dissolving Gases in Liquids

Most solids are more soluble in liquids at higher temperatures. But gases become less soluble in liquids as the temperature is raised. A soft drink goes flat faster when warm. The gas that is dissolved in the soft drink cannot stay dissolved when the temperature increases. So, the gas escapes, and the soft drink becomes "flat."

✓**Reading Check** How does the solubility of gases change with temperature?

Dissolving Solids Faster in Liquids

Several things affect how fast a solid will dissolve. Look at **Figure 7** to see three ways to make a solute dissolve faster. You can see why you will enjoy a glass of lemonade sooner if you stir granulated sugar into the lemonade before adding ice!

Figure 7 How to Dissolve Solids Faster

Mixing by stirring or shaking causes the solute particles to separate from one another and spread out more quickly among the solvent particles.

Heating causes particles to move more quickly. The solvent particles can separate the solute particles and spread them out more quickly.

Crushing the solute increases the amount of contact it has with the solvent. The particles of the crushed solute mix with the solvent more quickly.

suspension a mixture in which particles of a material are more or less evenly dispersed throughout a liquid or gas

colloid a mixture consisting of tiny particles that are intermediate in size between those in solutions and those in suspensions and that are suspended in a liquid, solid, or gas

Suspensions

Have you ever shaken a snow globe? If so, you have seen the solid snow particles mix with the water, as shown in **Figure 8.** When you stop shaking the globe, the snow settles to the bottom. This mixture is called a suspension. A **suspension** is a mixture in which particles of a material are dispersed throughout a liquid or gas but are large enough that they settle out.

The particles in a suspension are large enough to scatter or block light. The particles are also too large to stay mixed without being stirred or shaken. If a suspension is allowed to sit, the particles will settle out, as they do in a snow globe.

A suspension can be separated by passing it through a filter. So, the liquid or gas passes through the filter, but the solid particles are large enough to be trapped by the filter.

✓ Reading Check How can the particles of a suspension be separated?

Colloids

Some mixtures have properties between those of solutions and suspensions. These mixtures are known as colloids (KAHL OYDZ). A **colloid** is a mixture in which the particles are dispersed throughout but are not heavy enough to settle out. The particles in a colloid are relatively small and are fairly well mixed. You might be surprised at the number of colloids you see each day. Milk, mayonnaise, and stick deodorant—even the gelatin and whipped cream in **Figure 8**—are colloids.

The particles in a colloid are much smaller than the particles in a suspension. However, the particles are large enough to scatter light. A colloid cannot be separated by filtration. The particles are small enough to pass through a filter.

Figure 8 **Properties of Suspensions and Colloids**

Suspension This snow globe contains solid particles that will mix with the clear liquid when you shake it up. But the particles will soon fall to the bottom when the globe is at rest.

Colloid This dessert includes two tasty examples of colloids—fruity gelatin and whipped cream.

SECTION
Review

Summary

- A mixture is a combination of two or more substances, each of which keeps its own characteristics.
- Mixtures can be separated by physical means, such as filtration and evaporation.
- A solution is a mixture that appears to be a single substance but is composed of a solute dissolved in a solvent.
- Concentration is a measure of the amount of solute dissolved in a solvent.
- The solubility of a solute is the ability of the solute to dissolve in a solvent at a certain temperature.
- Suspensions are mixtures that contain particles large enough to settle out or be filtered and to block or scatter light.
- Colloids are mixtures that contain particles that are too small to settle out or be filtered but are large enough to scatter light.

Using Key Terms

The statements below are false. For each statement, replace the underlined term to make a true statement.

1. The <u>solvent</u> is the substance that is dissolved.

2. A <u>suspension</u> is composed of substances that are spread evenly among each other.

3. A measure of the amount of solute dissolved in a solvent is <u>solubility</u>.

4. A <u>colloid</u> contains particles that will settle out of the mixture if left sitting.

Understanding Key Ideas

5. A mixture
   a. has substances in it that are chemically combined.
   b. can always be separated using filtration.
   c. contains substances that are not mixed in a definite ratio.
   d. All of the above

6. List three ways to dissolve a solid faster.

Critical Thinking

7. **Making Comparisons** How do solutions, suspensions, and colloids differ?

8. **Applying Concepts** Suggest a procedure to separate iron filings from sawdust. Explain why this procedure works.

9. **Analyzing Ideas** Identify the solute and solvent in a solution made of 15 mL of oxygen and 5 mL of helium.

Interpreting Graphics

Use the graph below to answer the questions that follow.

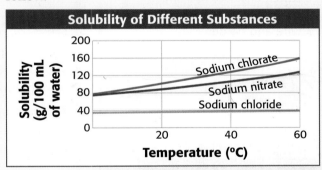

10. At what temperature is 120 g of sodium nitrate soluble in 100 mL of water?

11. At 60°C, how much more sodium chlorate than sodium chloride will dissolve in 100 mL of water?

SC**LINKS**.

NSTA
Developed and maintained by the
National Science Teachers Association

For a variety of links related to this chapter, go to www.scilinks.org

Topic: Mixtures
SciLinks code: HSM0974

Skills Practice Lab

OBJECTIVES

Observe flame colors emitted by various compounds.

Determine the composition of an unknown compound.

MATERIALS

- Bunsen burner
- chloride test solutions (4)
- hydrochloric acid, dilute, in a small beaker
- spark igniter
- tape, masking
- test tubes, small (4)
- test-tube rack
- water, distilled, in a small beaker
- wire and holder

SAFETY

Flame Tests

Fireworks produce fantastic combinations of color when they are ignited. The different colors are the results of burning different compounds. Imagine that you are the head chemist for a fireworks company. The label has fallen off one box, and you must identify the unknown compound inside so that the fireworks may be used in the correct fireworks display. To identify the compound, you will use your knowledge that every compound has a unique set of properties.

Ask a Question

1. How can you identify an unknown compound by heating it in a flame?

Form a Hypothesis

2. Write a hypothesis that is a possible answer to the question above. Explain your reasoning.

Test the Hypothesis

3. Arrange the test tubes in the test-tube rack. Use masking tape to label each tube with one of the following names: calcium chloride, potassium chloride, sodium chloride, and unknown.

4. Copy the table below. Then, ask your teacher for your portions of the solutions. **Caution:** Be very careful in handling all chemicals. Tell your teacher immediately if you spill a chemical.

Test Results	
Compound	**Color of flame**
Calcium chloride	
Potassium chloride	*DO NOT WRITE IN BOOK*
Sodium chloride	
Unknown	

5 Light the burner. Clean the wire by dipping it into the dilute hydrochloric acid and then into distilled water. Holding the wooden handle, heat the wire in the blue flame of the burner until the wire is glowing and it no longer colors the flame. **Caution:** Use extreme care around an open flame.

6 Dip the clean wire into the first test solution. Hold the wire at the tip of the inner cone of the burner flame. Record in the table the color given to the flame.

7 Clean the wire by repeating step 5. Then, repeat steps 5 and 6 for the other solutions.

8 Follow your teacher's instructions for cleanup and disposal.

Analyze the Results

1 **Identifying Patterns** Is the flame color a test for the metal or for the chloride in each compound? Explain your answer.

2 **Analyzing Data** What is the identity of your unknown solution? How do you know?

Draw Conclusions

3 **Evaluating Methods** Why is it necessary to carefully clean the wire before testing each solution?

4 **Making Predictions** Would you expect the compound sodium fluoride to produce the same color as sodium chloride in a flame test? Why or why not?

5 **Interpreting Information** Each of the compounds you tested is made from chlorine, which is a poisonous gas at room temperature. Why is it safe to use these compounds without a gas mask?

Chapter Review

USING KEY TERMS

Complete each of the following sentences by choosing the correct term from the word bank.

compound   element
suspension   solubility
solution   metal
nonmetal   solute

1 A(n) ___ has a definite ratio of components.

2 The ability of one substance to dissolve in another substance is the ___ of the solute.

3 A(n) ___ can be separated by filtration.

4 A(n) ___ is a pure substance that cannot be broken down into simpler substances by chemical means.

5 A(n) ___ is an element that is brittle and dull.

6 The ___ is the substance that dissolves to form a solution.

UNDERSTANDING KEY IDEAS

Multiple Choice

7 Which of the following increases the solubility of a gas in a liquid?

   a. increasing the temperature of the liquid

   b. increasing the amount of gas in the liquid

   c. decreasing the temperature of the liquid

   d. decreasing the amount of liquid

8 Which of the following best describes chicken noodle soup?

   a. element   **c.** compound
   b. mixture   **d.** solution

9 Which of the following statements describes elements?

   a. All of the particles in the same element are different.

   b. Elements can be broken down into simpler substances.

   c. Elements have unique sets of properties.

   d. Elements cannot be joined together in chemical reactions.

10 A solution that contains a large amount of solute is best described as

   a. insoluble.   **c.** dilute.
   b. concentrated.   **d.** weak.

11 Which of the following substances can be separated into simpler substances only by chemical means?

   a. sodium   **c.** water
   b. salt water   **d.** gold

12 Which of the following would not increase the rate at which a solid dissolves?

   a. decreasing the temperature

   b. crushing the solid

   c. stirring

   d. increasing the temperature

13 In which classification of matter are components chemically combined?

a. a solution   c. a compound

b. a colloid   d. a suspension

14 An element that conducts thermal energy well and is easily shaped is a

a. metal.

b. metalloid.

c. nonmetal.

d. None of the above

Short Answer

15 What is the difference between an element and a compound?

16 When nail polish is dissolved in acetone, which substance is the solute, and which is the solvent?

Math Skills

17 What is the concentration of a solution prepared by mixing 50 g of salt with 200 mL of water?

18 How many grams of sugar must be dissolved in 150 mL of water to make a solution that has a concentration of 0.6 g/mL?

CRITICAL THINKING

19 **Concept Mapping** Use the following terms to create a concept map: *matter, element, compound, mixture, solution, suspension,* and *colloid.*

20 **Forming Hypotheses** To keep the "fizz" in carbonated beverages after they have been opened, should you store them in a refrigerator or in a cabinet? Explain.

21 **Making Inferences**
A light green powder is heated in a test tube. A gas is given off, and the solid becomes black. In which classification of matter does the green powder belong? Explain your reasoning.

22 **Predicting Consequences** Why is it desirable to know the exact concentration of solutions rather than whether they are concentrated or dilute?

23 **Applying Concepts** Describe a procedure to separate a mixture of salt, finely ground pepper, and pebbles.

INTERPRETING GRAPHICS

Dr. Sol Vent did an experiment to find the solubility of a compound. The data below were collected using 100 mL of water. Use the table below to answer the questions that follow.

Temperature (°C)	10	25	40	60	95
Dissolved solute (g)	150	70	34	25	15

24 Use a computer or graph paper to construct a graph of Dr. Vent's results. Examine the graph. To increase the solubility, would you increase or decrease the temperature? Explain.

25 If 200 mL of water were used instead of 100 mL, how many grams of the compound would dissolve at 40°C?

26 Based on the solubility of this compound, is this compound a solid, liquid, or gas? Explain your answer.

READING

Read each of the passages below. Then, answer the questions that follow each passage.

Passage 1 In 1912, the *Titanic* was the largest ship ever to set sail. This majestic ship was considered to be unsinkable. Yet, on April 15, 1912, the *Titanic* hit a large iceberg. The resulting damage caused the *Titanic* to sink, killing 1,500 of its passengers and crew.

How could an iceberg destroy the 2.5 cm thick steel plates that made up the *Titanic's* hull? Analysis of a recovered piece of steel showed that the steel contained large amounts of sulfur. Sulfur is a normal component of steel. However, the recovered piece has much more sulfur than today's steel does. The excess sulfur may have made the steel <u>brittle</u>, much like glass. Scientists suspect that this brittle steel may have cracked on impact with the iceberg, allowing water to enter the hull.

1. In this passage, what does the word *brittle* mean?

A likely to break or crack

B very strong

C clear and easily seen through

D lightweight

2. What is the main idea of the second paragraph of this passage?

F The *Titanic's* hull was 2.5 cm thick.

G The steel in the *Titanic's* hull may have been brittle.

H The large amount of sulfur in the *Titanic's* hull may be responsible for the hull's cracking.

I Scientists were able to recover a piece of steel from the *Titanic's* hull.

3. What was the *Titanic* thought to be in 1912?

A the fastest ship afloat

B the smallest ship to set sail

C a ship not capable of being sunk

D the most luxurious ship to set sail

Passage 2 Perfume making is an ancient art. It was practiced by the ancient Egyptians, who rubbed their bodies with a substance made by soaking fragrant woods and resins in water and oil. Ancient Israelites also practiced the art of perfume making. This art was also known to the early Chinese, Arabs, Greeks, and Romans.

Over time, perfume making has developed into a fine art. A good perfume may contain more than 100 ingredients. The most familiar ingredients come from fragrant plants, such as sandalwood or roses. These plants get their pleasant odor from essential oils, which are stored in tiny, baglike parts called *sacs*. The parts of plants that are used for perfumes include the flowers, roots, and leaves. Other perfume ingredients come from animals and from human-made chemicals.

1. How did ancient Egyptians make perfume?

A by using 100 different ingredients

B by soaking woods and resins in water and oil

C by using plants or flowers

D by making tiny, baglike parts called sacs

2. What is the main idea of the second paragraph?

F Perfume making hasn't changed since ancient Egypt.

G The ancient art of perfume making has been replaced by simple science.

H Perfume making is a complex procedure involving many ingredients.

I Natural ingredients are no longer used in perfume.

3. How are good perfumes made?

A from plant oils only

B by combining one or two ingredients

C according to early Chinese formulas

D by blending as many as 100 ingredients

The graph below was constructed from data collected during a laboratory investigation. Use the graph below to answer the questions that follow.

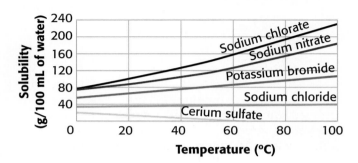

1. Which of the following values is the amount of sodium nitrate that can dissolve in 100 mL of water at 40°C?

A 0 g

B 40 g

C 80 g

D 100 g

2. How many grams of sodium chloride can dissolve in 100 mL of water at 60°C?

F 40 g

G 80 g

H 125 g

I 160 g

3. At what temperature will 80 g of potassium bromide completely dissolve in 100 mL of water?

A approximately 20°C

B approximately 42°C

C approximately 88°C

D approximately 100°C

4. At 20°C, which solid is the most soluble?

F sodium chloride

G sodium chlorate

H potassium bromide

I sodium nitrate

Read each question below, and choose the best answer.

Use the rectangle below to answer questions 1 and 2.

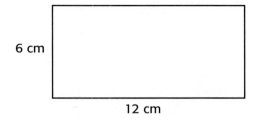

1. What is the perimeter of the rectangle shown above?

A 12 cm

B 18 cm

C 36 cm

D 72 cm

2. If the length of all the sides of the rectangle shown above were doubled, what would be the area of the larger rectangle?

F 36 cm²

G 72 cm²

H 144 cm²

I 288 cm²

3. One way to calculate the concentration of a solution is to divide the grams of solute by the milliliters of solvent. What is the concentration of a solution that is made by dissolving 65 g of sugar (the solute) in 500 mL of water (the solvent)?

A 0.13 g·mL

B 0.13 g/mL

C 7.7 g·mL

D 7.7 g/mL

4. If $16/n = 1/2$, what is the value of n?

F 2

G 8

H 16

I 32

Standardized Test Preparation

Science in Action

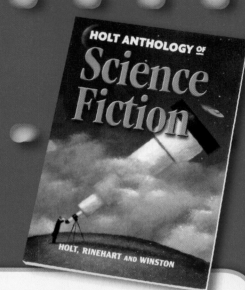

Science, Technology, and Society

Dry Cleaning: How Stains Are Dissolved

Sometimes, just water and detergent won't remove stains. For example, have you gotten ink on your favorite sweater? Or have you spilled something greasy on your shirt? In that case, your clothes will probably have to be dry-cleaned. In spite of its name, dry cleaning does involve liquids. First, the kind of stain on your clothing must be determined. If the stain will dissolve in water, a stain remover for that particular stain is applied. Then, the stain is removed with a steam gun. But some stains, such as grease or oil, won't dissolve in water. This kind of stain is treated with a liquid solvent. The clothing is then cleaned in a dry-cleaning machine.

Language Arts ACTiViTY

WRITING SKILL Imagine that you are a stained article of clothing. Write a five-paragraph short story describing how you became stained and how the stain was removed by the dry-cleaning process. You may have to research the dry-cleaning process before writing your story.

Science Fiction

"The Strange Case of Dr. Jekyll and Mr. Hyde" by Robert Louis Stevenson

Although Dr. Henry Jekyll was wild as a young man, he has become a respected doctor and scientist. Dr. Jekyll wants to understand the nature of human identity. His theory is that if he can separate his personality into "good" and "evil" parts, he can get rid of his evil side. Then, he can lead a happy, useful life.

Into Dr. Jekyll's life comes the mysterious Mr. Hyde, a man of action and anger. He sparks fear in the hearts of people he meets. Who is he? And what does he have to do with the deaths of two people? To find out more, read Stevenson's "The Strange Case of Dr. Jekyll and Mr. Hyde" in the *Holt Anthology of Science Fiction*.

Social Studies ACTiViTY

"The Strange Case of Dr. Jekyll and Mr. Hyde" was published in 1886. The story takes place in London, England. What was London like in the 1870s and 1880s? Use the library or the Internet to find information about London and its people at that time. Make a chart that compares London in the 1870s with your hometown today.

Aundra Nix

Metallurgist Aundra Nix is a chief metallurgist for a copper mine in Sahuarita, Arizona, where she supervises laboratories and other engineers. "To be able to look at rock in the ground and follow it through a process of drilling, blasting, hauling, crushing, grinding, and finally mineral separation—where you can hold a mineral that is one-third copper in your hand—is exciting."

Although she is a supervisor, Nix enjoys the flexible nature of her job. "My work environment includes office and computer work, plant work, and outdoor work. In this field you can 'get your hands into it,' which I always prefer," says Nix. "I did not want a career where it may be years before you see the results of your work." Aundra Nix enjoyed math and science, "so engineering seemed to be a natural area to study," she says. Nix's advice to students planning their own career is to learn all they can in science and technology, because that is the future.

Math ACTIVITY

A large copper-mining company employed about 2,300 people at three locations in New Mexico. Because of an increase in demand for copper, 570 of these workers were hired over a period of a year. Of the 570 new workers, 115 were hired within a three-week period. What percentage of the total work force do the newly hired employees represent? Of the new workers who were hired, what percentage was hired during the three-week hiring period?

UNIT 2

TIMELINE

Motion and Forces

It's hard to imagine a world where nothing ever moves. Without motion or forces to cause motion, life would be very dull! The relationship between force and motion is the subject of this unit. You will learn how to describe the motion of objects, how forces affect motion, and how fluids exert force. This timeline shows some events and discoveries that have occurred as scientists have worked to understand the motion of objects here on Earth and in space.

Around 250 BCE

Archimedes, a Greek mathematician, develops the principle that bears his name. The principle relates the buoyant force on an object in a fluid to the amount of fluid displaced by the object.

1764

In London, Wolfgang Amadeus Mozart composes his first symphony—at the age of 8.

1846

After determining that the orbit of Uranus is different from what is predicted from the law of universal gravitation, scientists discover Neptune whose gravitational force is causing Uranus's unusual orbit.

1947

While flying a Bell X-1 rocket-powered airplane, American pilot Chuck Yeager becomes the first human to travel faster than the speed of sound.

PHILOSOPHIÆ

NATURALIS

PRINCIPIA

MATHEMATICA

Autore *JS. NEWTON*, Trin. Coll. Cantab. Soc. Matheseos
Profeſſore Lucaſiano, & Societatis Regalis Sodali.

Around 240 BCE

Chinese astronomers are the first to record a sighting of Halley's Comet.

1519

Portuguese explorer Ferdinand Magellan begins the first voyage around the world.

1687

Sir Isaac Newton, a British mathematician and scientist, publishes *Principia*, a book describing his laws of motion and the law of universal gravitation.

1905

While employed as a patent clerk, German physicist Albert Einstein publishes his special theory of relativity. The theory states that the speed of light is constant no matter what the reference frame is.

1921

Bessie Coleman becomes the first African American woman licensed to fly an airplane.

1971

American astronaut Alan Shepard takes a break from gathering lunar data to play golf on the moon during the *Apollo 14* mission.

1990

The *Magellan* spacecraft begins orbiting Venus for a four-year mission to map the planet. By using the sun's gravitational forces, it propels itself to Venus without burning much fuel.

2003

NASA launches *Spirit* and *Opportunity*, two Mars Exploration Rovers, to study Mars.

5

Matter in Motion

SECTION ① **Measuring Motion** 118

SECTION ② **What Is a Force?** 124

SECTION ③ **Friction: A Force That Opposes Motion** 128

SECTION ④ **Gravity: A Force of Attraction** 134

Chapter Lab 140
Chapter Review 142
Standardized Test Preparation 144
Science in Action 146

About the

Speed skaters are fast. In fact, some skaters can skate at a rate of 12 m/s! That's equal to a speed of 27 mi/h. To reach such a speed, skaters must exert large forces. They must also use friction to turn corners on the slippery surface of the ice.

PRE-READING ACTIVITY

FOLDNOTES **Four-Corner Fold**
Before you read the chapter, create the FoldNote entitled "Four-Corner Fold" described in the **Study Skills** section of the Appendix. Label the flaps of the four-corner fold with "Motion," "Forces," "Friction," and "Gravity." Write what you know about each topic under the appropriate flap. As you read the chapter, add other information that you learn.

START-UP ACTIVITY

The Domino Derby

Speed is the distance traveled by an object in a certain amount of time. In this activity, you will observe one factor that affects the speed of falling dominoes.

Procedure

1. Set up **25 dominoes** in a straight line. Try to keep equal spacing between the dominoes.

2. Use a **meterstick** to measure the total length of your row of dominoes, and record the length.

3. Use a **stopwatch** to time how long it takes for the dominoes to fall. Record this measurement.

4. Predict what would happen to that amount of time if you changed the distance between the dominoes. Write your predictions.

5. Repeat steps 2 and 3 several times using distances between the dominoes that are smaller and larger than the distance used in your first setup. Use the same number of dominoes in each trial.

Analysis

1. Calculate the average speed for each trial by dividing the total distance (the length of the domino row) by the time the dominoes take to fall.

2. How did the spacing between dominoes affect the average speed? Is this result what you expected? If not, explain.

Measuring Motion

Look around you—you are likely to see something in motion. Your teacher may be walking across the room, or perhaps your friend is writing with a pencil.

Even if you don't see anything moving, motion is still occurring all around you. Air particles are moving, the Earth is circling the sun, and blood is traveling through your blood vessels!

Observing Motion by Using a Reference Point

You might think that the motion of an object is easy to detect—you just watch the object. But you are actually watching the object in relation to another object that appears to stay in place. The object that appears to stay in place is a *reference point*. When an object changes position over time relative to a reference point, the object is in **motion.** You can describe the direction of the object's motion with a reference direction, such as north, south, east, west, up, or down.

✓ **Reading Check** What is a reference point? (*See the Appendix for answers to Reading Checks.*)

Common Reference Points

The Earth's surface is a common reference point for determining motion, as shown in **Figure 1.** Nonmoving objects, such as trees and buildings, are also useful reference points.

A moving object can also be used as a reference point. For example, if you were on the hot-air balloon shown in **Figure 1,** you could watch a bird fly by and see that the bird was changing position in relation to your moving balloon.

Figure 1 *During the interval between the times that these pictures were taken, the hot-air balloon changed position relative to a reference point–the mountain.*

Speed Depends on Distance and Time

Speed is the distance traveled by an object divided by the time taken to travel that distance. Look again at **Figure 1.** Suppose the time interval between the pictures was 10 s and that the balloon traveled 50 m in that time. The speed of the balloon is (50 m)/(10 s), or 5 m/s.

The SI unit for speed is meters per second (m/s). Kilometers per hour (km/h), feet per second (ft/s), and miles per hour (mi/h) are other units commonly used to express speed.

Determining Average Speed

Most of the time, objects do not travel at a constant speed. For example, you probably do not walk at a constant speed from one class to the next. So, it is very useful to calculate *average speed* using the following equation:

$$average\ speed = \frac{total\ distance}{total\ time}$$

Recognizing Speed on a Graph

Suppose a person drives from one city to another. The blue line in the graph in **Figure 2** shows the total distance traveled during a 4 h period. Notice that the distance traveled during each hour is different. The distance varies because the speed is not constant. The driver may change speed because of weather, traffic, or varying speed limits. The average speed for the entire trip can be calculated as follows:

$$average\ speed = \frac{360\ km}{4\ h} = 90\ km/h$$

The red line on the graph shows how far the driver must travel each hour to reach the same city if he or she moved at a constant speed. The slope of this line is the average speed.

motion an object's change in position relative to a reference point

speed the distance traveled divided by the time interval during which the motion occurred

What's Your Speed?

Measure a distance of 5 m or a distance of 25 ft inside or outside. Ask an adult at home to use a stopwatch or a watch with a second hand to time you as you travel the distance you measured. Then, find your average speed. Find the average speed of other members of your family in the same way.

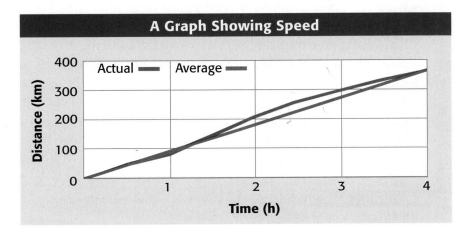

A Graph Showing Speed

Figure 2 *Speed can be shown on a graph of distance versus time.*

Calculating Average Speed An athlete swims a distance from one end of a 50 m pool to the other end in a time of 25 s. What is the athlete's average speed?

Step 1: Write the equation for average speed.

$$average\ speed = \frac{total\ distance}{total\ time}$$

Step 2: Replace the total distance and total time with the values given, and solve.

$$average\ speed = \frac{50\ m}{25\ s} = 2\ m/s$$

Now It's Your Turn

1. Kira jogs to a store 72 m away in a time of 36 s. What is Kira's average speed?
2. If you travel 7.5 km and walk for 1.5 h, what is your average speed?
3. An airplane traveling from San Francisco to Chicago travels 1,260 km in 3.5 h. What is the airplane's average speed?

Velocity: Direction Matters

Imagine that two birds leave the same tree at the same time. They both fly at 10 km/h for 5 min, 12 km/h for 8 min, and 5 km/h for 10 min. Why don't they end up at the same place?

Have you figured out the answer? The birds went in different directions. Their speeds were the same, but they had different velocities. **Velocity** (vuh LAHS uh tee) is the speed of an object in a particular direction.

Be careful not to confuse the terms *speed* and *velocity*. They do not have the same meaning. Velocity must include a reference direction. If you say that an airplane's velocity is 600 km/h, you would not be correct. But you could say the plane's velocity is 600 km/h south. **Figure 3** shows an example of the difference between speed and velocity.

Changing Velocity

You can think of velocity as the rate of change of an object's position. An object's velocity is constant only if its speed and direction don't change. Therefore, constant velocity is always motion along a straight line. An object's velocity changes if either its speed or direction changes. For example, as a bus traveling at 15 m/s south speeds up to 20 m/s south, its velocity changes. If the bus continues to travel at the same speed but changes direction to travel east, its velocity changes again. And if the bus slows down at the same time that it swerves north to avoid a cat, the velocity of the bus changes, too.

✓ **Reading Check** What are the two ways that velocity can change?

Figure 3 *The speeds of these cars may be similar, but the velocities of the cars differ because the cars are going in different directions.*

Figure 4 Finding Resultant Velocity

Person's resultant velocity
15 m/s east + 1 m/s east = 16 m/s east

When you combine two velocities that are **in the same direction,** add them together to find the resultant velocity.

Person's resultant velocity
15 m/s east − 1 m/s west = 14 m/s east

When you combine two velocities that are **in opposite directions,** subtract the smaller velocity from the larger velocity to find the resultant velocity. The resultant velocity is in the direction of the larger velocity.

Combining Velocities

Imagine that you are riding in a bus that is traveling east at 15 m/s. You and the other passengers are also traveling at a velocity of 15 m/s east. But suppose you stand up and walk down the bus's aisle while the bus is moving. Are you still moving at the same velocity as the bus? No! **Figure 4** shows how you can combine velocities to find the *resultant velocity.*

Acceleration

Although the word *accelerate* is commonly used to mean "speed up," the word means something else in science. **Acceleration** (ak SEL uhr AY shuhn) is the rate at which velocity changes. Velocity changes if speed changes, if direction changes, or if both change. So, an object accelerates if its speed, its direction, or both change.

An increase in velocity is commonly called *positive acceleration*. A decrease in velocity is commonly called *negative acceleration,* or *deceleration.* Keep in mind that acceleration is not only how much velocity changes but also how fast velocity changes. The faster the velocity changes, the greater the acceleration is.

velocity the speed of an object in a particular direction

acceleration the rate at which velocity changes over time; an object accelerates if its speed, direction, or both change

1 m/s   2 m/s   3 m/s   4 m/s   5 m/s

South

Figure 5 *This cyclist is accelerating at 1 m/s² south.*

Calculating Acceleration

Use the equation for average acceleration to do the following problem.

A plane passes over point A at a velocity of 240 m/s north. Forty seconds later, it passes over point B at a velocity of 260 m/s north. What is the plane's average acceleration?

Calculating Average Acceleration

You can find average acceleration by using the equation:

$$average\ acceleration = \frac{final\ velocity - starting\ velocity}{time\ it\ takes\ to\ change\ velocity}$$

Velocity is expressed in meters per second (m/s), and time is expressed in seconds (s). So acceleration is expressed in meters per second per second, or (m/s)/s, which equals m/s². For example, look at **Figure 5.** Every second, the cyclist's southward velocity increases by 1 m/s. His average acceleration can be calculated as follows:

$$average\ acceleration = \frac{5\ m/s - 1\ m/s}{4\ s} = 1\ m/s^2\ south$$

Reading Check What are the units of acceleration?

Recognizing Acceleration on a Graph

Suppose that you are riding a roller coaster. The roller-coaster car moves up a hill until it stops at the top. Then, you are off! The graph in **Figure 6** shows your acceleration for the next 10 s. During the first 8 s, you move down the hill. You can tell from the graph that your acceleration is positive for the first 8 s because your velocity increases as time passes. During the last 2 s, your car starts climbing the next hill. Your acceleration is negative because your velocity decreases as time passes.

Figure 6 *Acceleration can be shown on a graph of velocity versus time.*

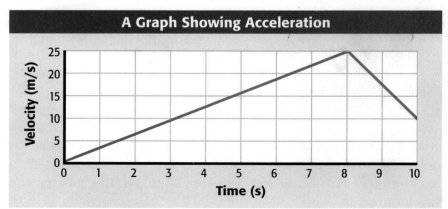

A Graph Showing Acceleration

Circular Motion: Continuous Acceleration

You may be surprised to know that even when you are completely still, you are experiencing acceleration. You may not seem to be changing speed or direction, but you are! You are traveling in a circle as the Earth rotates. An object traveling in a circular motion is always changing its direction. Therefore, its velocity is always changing, so it is accelerating. The acceleration that occurs in circular motion is known as *centripetal acceleration* (sen TRIP uht uhl ak SEL uhr AY shuhn). Centripetal acceleration occurs on a Ferris wheel at an amusement park or as the moon orbits Earth. Another example of centripetal acceleration is shown in **Figure 7.**

Figure 7 *The blades of these windmills are constantly changing direction. Thus, centripetal acceleration is occurring.*

SECTION Review

Summary

- An object is in motion if it changes position over time in relation to a reference point.
- Speed is the distance traveled by an object divided by the time the object takes to travel that distance.
- Velocity is speed in a given direction.
- Acceleration is the rate at which velocity changes.
- An object can accelerate by changing speed, direction, or both.
- Speed can be represented on a graph of distance versus time.
- Acceleration can be represented by graphing velocity versus time.

Using Key Terms

1. In your own words, write definitions for each of the following terms: *motion* and *acceleration*.

2. Use each of the following terms in a separate sentence: *speed* and *velocity*.

Understanding Key Ideas

3. Which of the following is NOT an example of acceleration?
   a. a person jogging at 3 m/s along a winding path
   b. a car stopping at a stop sign
   c. a cheetah running 27 m/s east
   d. a plane taking off

4. Which of the following would be a good reference point to describe the motion of a dog?
   a. the ground
   b. another dog running
   c. a tree
   d. All of the above

5. Explain the difference between speed and velocity.

6. What two things must you know to determine speed?

7. How are velocity and acceleration related?

Math Skills

8. Find the average speed of a person who swims 105 m in 70 s.

9. What is the average acceleration of a subway train that speeds up from 9.6 m/s to 12 m/s in 0.8 s on a straight section of track?

Critical Thinking

10. **Applying Concepts** Why is it more helpful to know a tornado's velocity rather than its speed?

11. **Evaluating Data** A wolf is chasing a rabbit. Graph the wolf's motion using the following data: 15 m/s at 0 s, 10 m/s at 1 s, 5 m/s at 2 s, 2.5 m/s at 3 s, 1 m/s at 4 s, and 0 m/s at 5 s. What does the graph tell you?

SCiLINKS®

NSTA
Developed and maintained by the
National Science Teachers Association

For a variety of links related to this chapter, go to www.scilinks.org

Topic: Measuring Motion
SciLinks code: HSM0927

What Is a Force?

You have probably heard the word force *in everyday conversation. People say things such as "That storm had a lot of force" or "Our football team is a force to be reckoned with." But what, exactly, is a force?*

In science, a **force** is simply a push or a pull. All forces have both size and direction. A force can change the acceleration of an object. This acceleration can be a change in the speed or direction of the object. In fact, any time you see a change in an object's motion, you can be sure that the change in motion was created by a force. Scientists express force using a unit called the **newton** (N).

Forces Acting on Objects

All forces act on objects. For any push to occur, something has to receive the push. You can't push nothing! The same is true for any pull. When doing schoolwork, you use your fingers to pull open books or to push the buttons on a computer keyboard. In these examples, your fingers are exerting forces on the books and the keys. So, the forces act on the books and keys. Another example of a force acting on an object is shown in **Figure 1.**

However, just because a force acts on an object doesn't mean that motion will occur. For example, you are probably sitting on a chair. But the force you are exerting on the chair does not cause the chair to move. The chair doesn't move because the floor is also exerting a force on the chair.

Figure 1 *The bulldozer is exerting a force on the pile of soil. But the pile of soil also exerts a force by just sitting on the ground!*

Unseen Sources and Receivers of Forces

It is not always easy to tell what is exerting a force or what is receiving a force, as shown in **Figure 2.** You cannot see what exerts the force that pulls magnets to refrigerators. And you cannot see that the air around you is held near Earth's surface by a force called *gravity.*

Determining Net Force

Usually, more than one force is acting on an object. The **net force** is the combination all of the forces acting on an object. So, how do you determine the net force? The answer depends on the directions of the forces.

Forces in the Same Direction

Suppose the music teacher asks you and a friend to move a piano. You pull on one end and your friend pushes on the other end, as shown in **Figure 3.** The forces you and your friend exert on the piano act in the same direction. The two forces are added to determine the net force because the forces act in the same direction. In this case, the net force is 45 N. This net force is large enough to move the piano—if it is on wheels, that is!

Reading Check How do you determine the net force on an object if all forces act in the same direction? (*See the Appendix for answers to Reading Checks.*)

Figure 2 *Something that you cannot see exerts a force that makes this cat's fur stand up.*

force a push or a pull exerted on an object in order to change the motion of the object; force has size and direction

newton the SI unit for force (symbol, N)

net force the combination of all of the forces acting on an object

25 N

Net force
25 N + 20 N = 45 N
to the right

20 N

Figure 3 *When forces act in the same direction, you add the forces to determine the net force. The net force will be in the same direction as the individual forces.*

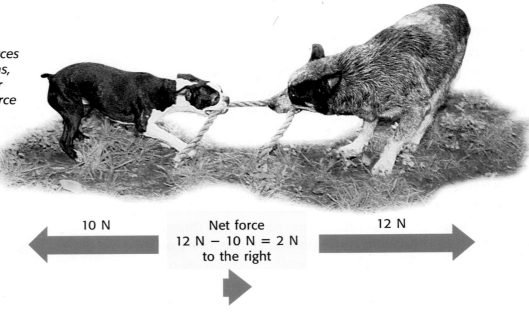

Figure 4 *When two forces act in opposite directions, you subtract the smaller force from the larger force to determine the net force. The net force will be in the same direction as the larger force.*

10 N

Net force
12 N − 10 N = 2 N
to the right

12 N

Forces in Different Directions

Look at the two dogs playing tug of war in **Figure 4.** Each dog is exerting a force on the rope. But the forces are in opposite directions. Which dog will win the tug of war?

Because the forces are in opposite directions, the net force on the rope is found by subtracting the smaller force from the larger one. In this case, the net force is 2 N in the direction of the dog on the right. Give that dog a dog biscuit!

✓ Reading Check What is the net force on an object when you combine a force of 7 N north with a force of 5 N south?

Balanced and Unbalanced Forces

If you know the net force on an object, you can determine the effect of the net force on the object's motion. Why? The net force tells you whether the forces on the object are balanced or unbalanced.

Balanced Forces

When the forces on an object produce a net force of 0 N, the forces are *balanced*. Balanced forces will not cause a change in the motion of a moving object. And balanced forces do not cause a nonmoving object to start moving.

Many objects around you have only balanced forces acting on them. For example, a light hanging from the ceiling does not move because the force of gravity pulling down on the light is balanced by the force of the cord pulling upward. A bird's nest in a tree and a hat resting on your head are also examples of objects that have only balanced forces acting on them. **Figure 5** shows another example of balanced forces.

Figure 5 *Because all the forces on this house of cards are balanced, none of the cards move.*

Unbalanced Forces

When the net force on an object is not 0 N, the forces on the object are *unbalanced*. Unbalanced forces produce a change in motion, such as a change in speed or a change in direction. Unbalanced forces are necessary to cause a nonmoving object to start moving.

Unbalanced forces are also necessary to change the motion of moving objects. For example, consider the soccer game shown in **Figure 6.** The soccer ball is already moving when it is passed from one player to another. When the ball reaches another player, that player exerts an unbalanced force—a kick—on the ball. After the kick, the ball moves in a new direction and has a new speed.

An object can continue to move when the unbalanced forces are removed. For example, when it is kicked, a soccer ball receives an unbalanced force. The ball continues to roll on the ground long after the force of the kick has ended.

Figure 6 *The soccer ball moves because the players exert an unbalanced force on the ball each time they kick it.*

SECTION Review

Summary

- A force is a push or a pull. Forces have size and direction and are expressed in newtons.
- Force is always exerted by one object on another object.
- Net force is determined by combining forces. Forces in the same direction are added. Forces in opposite directions are subtracted.
- Balanced forces produce no change in motion. Unbalanced forces produce a change in motion.

Using Key Terms

1. In your own words, write a definition for each of the following terms: *force* and *net force*.

Understanding Key Ideas

2. Which of the following may happen when an object receives unbalanced forces?
   a. The object changes direction.
   b. The object changes speed.
   c. The object starts to move.
   d. All of the above

3. Explain the difference between balanced and unbalanced forces.

4. Give an example of an unbalanced force causing a change in motion.

5. Give an example of an object that has balanced forces acting on it.

6. Explain the meaning of the phrase "Forces act on objects."

Math Skills

7. A boy pulls a wagon with a force of 6 N east as another boy pushes it with a force of 4 N east. What is the net force?

Critical Thinking

8. **Making Inferences** When finding net force, why must you know the directions of the forces acting on an object?

9. **Applying Concepts** List three forces that you exert when riding a bicycle.

SCiLINKS.®

NSTA
Developed and maintained by the
National Science Teachers Association

For a variety of links related to this chapter, go to www.scilinks.org

Topic: Forces
SciLinks code: HSM0604

Friction: A Force That Opposes Motion

While playing ball, your friend throws the ball out of your reach. Rather than running for the ball, you walk after it. You know that the ball will stop. But do you know why?

You know that the ball is slowing down. An unbalanced force is needed to change the speed of a moving object. So, what force is stopping the ball? The force is called friction. **Friction** is a force that opposes motion between two surfaces that are in contact. Friction can cause a moving object, such as a ball, to slow down and eventually stop.

The Source of Friction

Friction occurs because the surface of any object is rough. Even surfaces that feel smooth are covered with microscopic hills and valleys. When two surfaces are in contact, the hills and valleys of one surface stick to the hills and valleys of the other surface, as shown in **Figure 1.** This contact causes friction.

The amount of friction between two surfaces depends on many factors. Two factors include the force pushing the surfaces together and the roughness of the surfaces.

The Effect of Force on Friction

The amount of friction depends on the force pushing the surfaces together. If this force increases, the hills and valleys of the surfaces can come into closer contact. The close contact increases the friction between the surfaces. Objects that weigh less exert less downward force than objects that weigh more do, as shown in **Figure 2.** But changing how much of the surfaces come in contact does not change the amount of friction.

friction a force that opposes motion between two surfaces that are in contact

Figure 1 *When the hills and valleys of one surface stick to the hills and valleys of another surface, friction is created.*

Figure 2 Force and Friction

ⓐ There is more friction between the book with more weight and the table than there is between the book with less weight and the table. A harder push is needed to move the heavier book.

ⓑ Turning a book on its edge does not change the amount of friction between the table and the book.

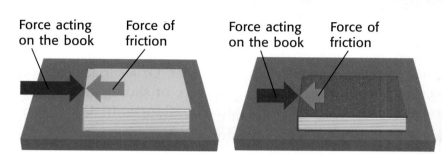

Force acting on the book · Force of friction

Force acting on the book · Force of friction

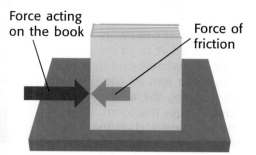

Force acting on the book · Force of friction

The Effect of Rougher Surfaces on Friction

Rough surfaces have more microscopic hills and valleys than smooth surfaces do. So, the rougher the surface is, the greater the friction is. For example, a ball rolling on the ground slows down because of the friction between the ball and the ground. A large amount of friction is produced because the ground has a rough surface. But imagine that you were playing ice hockey. If the puck passed out of your reach, it would slide across the ice for a long while before stopping. The reason the puck would continue to slide is that the ice is a smooth surface that has very little friction.

✓ Reading Check Why is friction greater between surfaces that are rough? (*See the Appendix for answers to Reading Checks.*)

The Friction 500

1. Make a short ramp out of **a piece of cardboard** and **one or two books** on a table.

2. Put a **toy car** at the top of the ramp, and let go of the car. If necessary, adjust the ramp height so that your car does not roll off the table.

3. Put the car at the top of the ramp again, and let go of the car. Record the distance the car travels after leaving the ramp.

4. Repeat step 3 two more times, and calculate the average for your results.

5. Change the surface of the table by covering the table with **sandpaper.** Repeat steps 3 and 4.

6. Change the surface of the table one more time by covering the table with **cloth.** Repeat steps 3 and 4 again.

7. Which surface had the most friction? Why? What do you predict would happen if the car were heavier?

Types of Friction

There are two types of friction. The friction you observe when sliding books across a tabletop is called *kinetic friction*. The other type of friction is *static friction*. You observe static friction when you push on a piece of furniture and it does not move.

Kinetic Friction

The word *kinetic* means "moving." So, kinetic friction is friction between moving surfaces. The amount of kinetic friction between two surfaces depends in part on how the surfaces move. Surfaces can slide past each other. Or a surface can roll over another surface. Usually, the force of sliding kinetic friction is greater than the force of rolling kinetic friction. Thus, it is usually easier to move objects on wheels than to slide the objects along the floor, as shown in **Figure 3.**

Kinetic friction is very useful in everyday life. You use sliding kinetic friction when you apply the brakes on a bicycle and when you write with a pencil or a piece of chalk. You also use sliding kinetic friction when you scratch a part of your body that is itchy!

Rolling kinetic friction is an important part of almost all means of transportation. Anything that has wheels—bicycles, in-line skates, cars, trains, and planes—uses rolling kinetic friction.

Comparing Friction

Ask an adult at home to sit on the floor. Try to push the adult across the room. Next, ask the adult to sit on a chair that has wheels and to keep his or her feet off the floor. Try pushing the adult and the chair across the room. If you do not have a chair that has wheels, try pushing the adult on different kinds of flooring. Explain why there was a difference between the two trials in your **science journal.**

Figure 3 Comparing Kinetic Friction

a Moving a heavy piece of furniture in your room can be hard work because **the force of sliding kinetic friction is large.**

b Moving a heavy piece of furniture is easier if you put it on wheels. **The force of rolling kinetic friction is smaller** and easier to overcome.

Figure 4 Static Friction

Block		
Table		

a There is no friction between the block and the table when no force is applied to the block.

Force applied — Static friction

b If a small force (purple arrow) is exerted on the block, the block does not move. The force of static friction (green arrow) balances the force applied.

Force applied — Kinetic friction

c When the force exerted on the block is greater than the force of static friction, the block starts moving. When the block starts moving, all static friction is gone, and only kinetic friction (green arrow) opposes the force applied.

Static Friction

When a force is applied to an object but does not cause the object to move, *static friction* occurs. The word *static* means "not moving." The object does not move because the force of static friction balances the force applied. Static friction can be overcome by applying a large enough force. Static friction disappears as soon as an object starts moving, and then kinetic friction immediately occurs. Look at **Figure 4** to understand under what conditions static friction affects an object.

✓ **Reading Check** What does the word *static* mean?

Friction: Harmful and Helpful

Think about how friction affects a car. Without friction, the tires could not push against the ground to move the car forward, and the brakes could not stop the car. Without friction, a car is useless. However, friction can also cause problems in a car. Friction between moving engine parts increases their temperature and causes the parts to wear down. A liquid coolant is added to the engine to keep the engine from overheating. And engine parts need to be changed as they wear out.

Friction is both harmful and helpful to you and the world around you. Friction can cause holes in your socks and in the knees of your jeans. Friction by wind and water can cause erosion of the topsoil that nourishes plants. On the other hand, friction between your pencil and your paper is necessary to allow the pencil to leave a mark. Without friction, you would just slip and fall when you tried to walk. Because friction can be both harmful and helpful, it is sometimes necessary to decrease or increase friction.

For another activity related to this chapter, go to **go.hrw.com** and type in the keyword **HP5MOTW**.

CONNECTION TO Social Studies

WRITING SKILL **Invention of the Wheel** Archeologists have found evidence that the first vehicles with wheels were used in ancient Mesopotamia sometime between 3500 and 3000 BCE. Before wheels were invented, people used planks or sleds to carry loads. In your **science journal,** write a paragraph about how your life would be different if wheels did not exist.

Some Ways to Reduce Friction

One way to reduce friction is to use lubricants (LOO bri kuhnts). *Lubricants* are substances that are applied to surfaces to reduce the friction between the surfaces. Some examples of common lubricants are motor oil, wax, and grease. Lubricants are usually liquids, but they can be solids or gases. An example of a gas lubricant is the air that comes out of the tiny holes of an air-hockey table. **Figure 5** shows one use of a lubricant.

Friction can also be reduced by switching from sliding kinetic friction to rolling kinetic friction. Ball bearings placed between the wheels and axles of in-line skates and bicycles make it easier for the wheels to turn by reducing friction.

Another way to reduce friction is to make surfaces that rub against each other smoother. For example, rough wood on a park bench is painful to slide across because there is a large amount of friction between your leg and the bench. Rubbing the bench with sandpaper makes the bench smoother and more comfortable to sit on. The reason the bench is more comfortable is that the friction between your leg and the bench is reduced.

Reading Check List three common lubricants.

Figure 5 *When you work on a bicycle, watch out for the chain! You might get dirty from the grease or oil that keeps the chain moving freely. Without this lubricant, friction between the sections of the chain would quickly wear the chain out.*

Some Ways to Increase Friction

One way to increase friction is to make surfaces rougher. For example, sand scattered on icy roads keeps cars from skidding. Baseball players sometimes wear textured batting gloves to increase the friction between their hands and the bat so that the bat does not fly out of their hands.

Another way to increase friction is to increase the force pushing the surfaces together. For example, if you are sanding a piece of wood, you can sand the wood faster by pressing harder on the sandpaper. Pressing harder increases the force pushing the sandpaper and wood together. So, the friction between the sandpaper and wood increases. **Figure 6** shows another example of friction increased by pushing on an object.

Figure 6 *No one likes cleaning dirty pans. To get this chore done quickly, press down with the scrubber to increase friction.*

SECTION Review

Summary

- Friction is a force that opposes motion.
- Friction is caused by hills and valleys on the surfaces of two objects touching each other.
- The amount of friction depends on factors such as the roughness of the surfaces and the force pushing the surfaces together.
- Two kinds of friction are kinetic friction and static friction.
- Friction can be helpful or harmful.

Using Key Terms

1. In your own words, write a definition for the term *friction*.

Understanding Key Ideas

2. Why is it easy to slip when there is water on the floor?
   a. The water is a lubricant and reduces the friction between your feet and the floor.
   b. The friction between your feet and the floor changes from kinetic to static friction.
   c. The water increases the friction between your feet and the floor.
   d. The friction between your feet and the floor changes from sliding kinetic friction to rolling kinetic friction.

3. Explain why friction occurs.

4. How does the roughness of surfaces that are touching affect the friction between the surfaces?

5. Describe how the amount of force pushing two surfaces together affects friction.

6. Name two ways in which friction can be increased.

7. List the two types of friction, and give an example of each.

Interpreting Graphics

8. Why do you think the sponge shown below has a layer of plastic bristles attached to it?

Critical Thinking

9. **Applying Concepts** Name two ways that friction is harmful and two ways that friction is helpful to you when riding a bicycle.

10. **Making Inferences** Describe a situation in which static friction is useful.

Developed and maintained by the
National Science Teachers Association

For a variety of links related to this chapter, go to www.scilinks.org

Topic: Force and Friction
SciLinks code: HSM0601

133

Gravity: A Force of Attraction

Have you ever seen a video of astronauts on the moon? They bounce around like beach balls even though they wear big, bulky spacesuits. Why is leaping on the moon easier than leaping on Earth?

The answer is gravity. **Gravity** is a force of attraction between objects that is due to their masses. The force of gravity can change the motion of an object by changing its speed, direction, or both. In this section, you will learn about gravity and its effects on objects, such as the astronaut in **Figure 1.**

The Effects of Gravity on Matter

All matter has mass. Gravity is a result of mass. Therefore, all matter is affected by gravity. That is, all objects experience an attraction toward all other objects. This gravitational force pulls objects toward each other. Right now, because of gravity, you are being pulled toward this book, your pencil, and every other object around you.

These objects are also being pulled toward you and toward each other because of gravity. So why don't you see the effects of this attraction? In other words, why don't you notice objects moving toward each other? The reason is that the mass of most objects is too small to cause a force large enough to move objects toward each other. However, you are familiar with one object that is massive enough to cause a noticeable attraction—the Earth.

gravity a force of attraction between objects that is due to their masses

Figure 1 *Because the moon has less gravity than the Earth does, walking on the moon's surface was a very bouncy experience for the Apollo astronauts.*

The Size of Earth's Gravitational Force

Compared with all objects around you, Earth has a huge mass. Therefore, Earth's gravitational force is very large. You must apply forces to overcome Earth's gravitational force any time you lift objects or even parts of your body.

Earth's gravitational force pulls everything toward the center of Earth. Because of this force, the books, tables, and chairs in the room stay in place, and dropped objects fall to Earth rather than moving together or toward you.

Reading Check **Why must you exert a force to pick up an object?** (*See the Appendix for answers to Reading Checks.*)

Newton and the Study of Gravity

For thousands of years, people asked two very puzzling questions: Why do objects fall toward Earth, and what keeps the planets moving in the sky? The two questions were treated separately until 1665 when a British scientist named Sir Isaac Newton realized that they were two parts of the same question.

The Core of an Idea

The legend is that Newton made the connection between the two questions when he watched a falling apple, as shown in **Figure 2.** He knew that unbalanced forces are needed to change the motion of objects. He concluded that an unbalanced force on the apple made the apple fall. And he reasoned that an unbalanced force on the moon kept the moon moving circularly around Earth. He proposed that these two forces are actually the same force—a force of attraction called *gravity*.

The Birth of a Law

Newton summarized his ideas about gravity in a law now known as the *law of universal gravitation*. This law describes the relationships between gravitational force, mass, and distance. The law is called *universal* because it applies to all objects in the universe.

CONNECTION TO Biology

Seeds and Gravity Seeds respond to gravity. The ability to respond to gravity causes seeds to send roots down and the green shoot up. But scientists do not understand how seeds can sense gravity. Plan an experiment to study how seedlings respond to gravity. After getting your teacher's approval, do your experiment and report your observations in a poster.

ACTIVITY

Figure 2 *Sir Isaac Newton realized that the same unbalanced force affected the motions of the apple and the moon.*

The Law of Universal Gravitation

The law of universal gravitation is the following: All objects in the universe attract each other through gravitational force. The size of the force depends on the masses of the objects and the distance between the objects. Understanding the law is easier if you consider it in two parts.

Part 1: Gravitational Force Increases as Mass Increases

Imagine an elephant and a cat. Because an elephant has a larger mass than a cat does, the amount of gravity between an elephant and Earth is greater than the amount of gravity between a cat and Earth. So, a cat is much easier to pick up than an elephant! There is also gravity between the cat and the elephant, but that force is very small because the cat's mass and the elephant's mass are so much smaller than Earth's mass. **Figure 3** shows the relationship between mass and gravitational force.

This part of the law of universal gravitation also explains why the astronauts on the moon bounce when they walk. The moon has less mass than Earth does. Therefore, the moon's gravitational force is less than Earth's. The astronauts bounced around on the moon because they were not being pulled down with as much force as they would have been on Earth.

✓ **Reading Check** How does mass affect gravitational force?

CONNECTION TO Astronomy

WRITING SKILL **Black Holes** Black holes are 4 times to 1 billion times as massive as our sun. So, the gravitational effects around a black hole are very large. The gravitational force of a black hole is so large that objects that enter a black hole can never get out. Even light cannot escape from a black hole. Because black holes do not emit light, they cannot be seen. Research how astronomers can detect black holes without seeing them. Write a one-page paper that details the results of your research.

Figure 3 **How Mass Affects Gravitational Force**

The gravitational force between objects increases as the masses of the objects increase. The arrows indicate the gravitational force between two objects. The length of the arrows indicates the strength of the force.

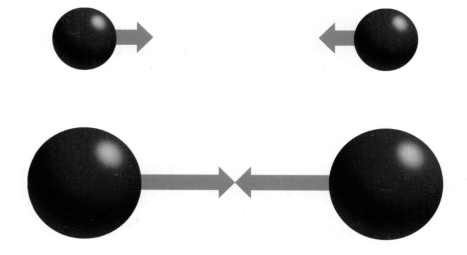

ⓐ Gravitational force is small between objects that have small masses.

ⓑ Gravitational force is large when the mass of one or both objects is large.

Part 2: Gravitational Force Decreases as Distance Increases

The gravitational force between you and Earth is large. Whenever you jump up, you are pulled back down by Earth's gravitational force. On the other hand, the sun is more than 300,000 times more massive than Earth. So why doesn't the sun's gravitational force affect you more than Earth's does? The reason is that the sun is so far away.

You are about 150 million kilometers (93 million miles) away from the sun. At this distance, the gravitational force between you and the sun is very small. If there were some way you could stand on the sun, you would find it impossible to move. The gravitational force acting on you would be so great that you could not move any part of your body!

Although the sun's gravitational force on your body is very small, the force is very large on Earth and the other planets, as shown in **Figure 4.** The gravity between the sun and the planets is large because the objects have large masses. If the sun's gravitational force did not have such an effect on the planets, the planets would not stay in orbit around the sun. **Figure 5** will help you understand the relationship between gravitational force and distance.

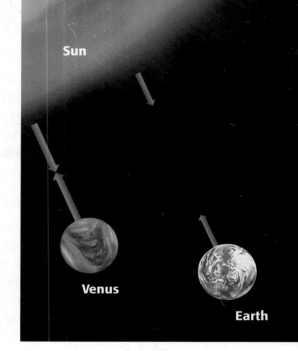

Figure 4 *Venus and Earth have approximately the same mass. But because Venus is closer to the sun, the gravitational force between Venus and the sun is greater than the gravitational force between Earth and the sun.*

Figure 5 **How Distance Affects Gravitational Force**

The gravitational force between objects decreases as the distance between the objects increases. The length of the arrows indicates the strength of the gravitational force between two objects.

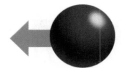 **a** Gravitational force is strong when the distance between two objects is small.

 **b** If the distance between two objects increases, the gravitational force pulling them together decreases rapidly.

Weight as a Measure of Gravitational Force

Gravity is a force of attraction between objects. **Weight** is a measure of the gravitational force on an object. When you see or hear the word *weight*, it usually refers to Earth's gravitational force on an object. But weight can also be a measure of the gravitational force exerted on objects by the moon or other planets.

The Differences Between Weight and Mass

Weight is related to mass, but they are not the same. Weight changes when gravitational force changes. **Mass** is the amount of matter in an object. An object's mass does not change. Imagine that an object is moved to a place that has a greater gravitational force—such as the planet Jupiter. The object's weight will increase, but its mass will remain the same. **Figure 6** shows the weight and mass of an astronaut on Earth and on the moon. The moon's gravitational force is about one-sixth of Earth's gravitational force.

Gravitational force is about the same everywhere on Earth. So, the weight of any object is about the same everywhere. Because mass and weight are constant on Earth, the terms *weight* and *mass* are often used to mean the same thing. This can be confusing. Be sure you understand the difference!

Reading Check How is gravitational force related to the weight of an object?

weight a measure of the gravitational force exerted on an object; its value can change with the location of the object in the universe

mass a measure of the amount of matter in an object

Figure 6 *The astronaut's weight on the moon is about one-sixth of his weight on Earth, but his mass remains constant.*

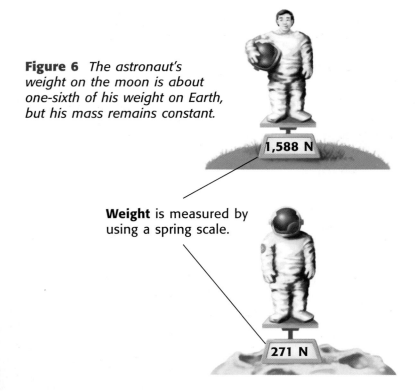

Weight is measured by using a spring scale.

1,588 N

271 N

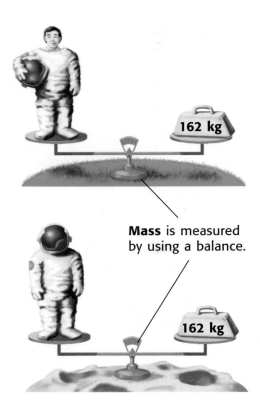

162 kg

Mass is measured by using a balance.

162 kg

Units of Weight and Mass

You have learned that the SI unit of force is a newton (N). Gravity is a force, and weight is a measure of gravity. So, weight is also measured in newtons. The SI unit of mass is the kilogram (kg). Mass is often measured in grams (g) and milligrams (mg) as well. On Earth, a 100 g object, such as the apple shown in **Figure 7,** weighs about 1 N.

When you use a bathroom scale, you are measuring the gravitational force between your body and Earth. So, you are measuring your weight, which should be given in newtons. However, many bathroom scales have units of pounds and kilograms instead of newtons. Thus, people sometimes mistakenly think that the kilogram (like the pound) is a unit of weight.

Figure 7 *A small apple weighs approximately 1 N.*

SECTION Review

Summary

- Gravity is a force of attraction between objects that is due to their masses.
- The law of universal gravitation states that all objects in the universe attract each other through gravitational force.
- Gravitational force increases as mass increases.
- Gravitational force decreases as distance increases.
- Weight and mass are not the same. Mass is the amount of matter in an object. Weight is a measure of the gravitational force on an object.

Using Key Terms

1. In your own words, write a definition for the term *gravity*.

2. Use each of the following terms in a separate sentence: *mass* and *weight*.

Understanding Key Ideas

3. If Earth's mass doubled without changing its size, your weight would

    a. increase because gravitational force increases.

    b. decrease because gravitational force increases.

    c. increase because gravitational force decreases.

    d. not change because you are still on Earth.

4. What is the law of universal gravitation?

5. How does the mass of an object relate to the gravitational force that the object exerts on other objects?

6. How does the distance between objects affect the gravitational force between them?

7. Why are mass and weight often confused?

Math Skills

8. The gravitational force on Jupiter is approximately 2.3 times the gravitational force on Earth. If an object has a mass of 70 kg and a weight of 686 N on Earth, what would the object's mass and weight on Jupiter be?

Critical Thinking

9. **Applying Concepts** Your friend thinks that there is no gravity in space. How could you explain to your friend that there must be gravity in space?

10. **Making Comparisons** Explain why it is your weight and not your mass that would change if you landed on Mars.

Skills Practice Lab

Detecting Acceleration

Have you ever noticed that you can "feel" acceleration? In a car or in an elevator, you may notice changes in speed or direction—even with your eyes closed! You are able to sense these changes because of tiny hair cells in your ears. These cells detect the movement of fluid in your inner ear. The fluid accelerates when you do, and the hair cells send a message about the acceleration to your brain. This message allows you to sense the acceleration. In this activity, you will build a device that detects acceleration. This device is called an *accelerometer* (ak SEL uhr AHM uht uhr).

OBJECTIVES

Build an accelerometer.

Explain how an accelerometer works.

MATERIALS

- container, 1 L, with watertight lid
- cork or plastic-foam ball, small
- modeling clay
- pushpin
- scissors
- string
- water

SAFETY

Procedure

1. Cut a piece of string that reaches three-quarters of the way into the container.

2. Use a pushpin to attach one end of the string to the cork or plastic-foam ball.

3. Use modeling clay to attach the other end of the string to the center of the inside of the container lid. The cork or ball should hang no farther than three-quarters of the way into the container.

4. Fill the container with water.

5. Put the lid tightly on the container. The string and cork or ball should be inside the container.

6. Turn the container upside down. The cork should float about three-quarters of the way up inside the container, as shown at right. You are now ready to detect acceleration by using your accelerometer and completing the following steps.

7. Put the accelerometer on a tabletop. The container lid should touch the tabletop. Notice that the cork floats straight up in the water.

8. Now, gently push the accelerometer across the table at a constant speed. Notice that the cork quickly moves in the direction you are pushing and then swings backward. If you did not see this motion, repeat this step until you are sure you can see the first movement of the cork.

9 After you are familiar with how to use your accelerometer, try the following changes in motion. For each change, record your observations of the cork's first motion.

a. As you move the accelerometer across the table, gradually increase its speed.

b. As you move the accelerometer across the table, gradually decrease its speed.

c. While moving the accelerometer across the table, change the direction in which you are pushing.

d. Make any other changes in motion you can think of. You should make only one change to the motion for each trial.

Analyze the Results

1 **Analyzing Results** When you move the bottle at a constant speed, why does the cork quickly swing backward after it moves in the direction of acceleration?

2 **Explaining Events** The cork moves forward (in the direction you were moving the bottle) when you speed up but moves backward when you slow down. Explain why the cork moves this way. (Hint: Think about the direction of acceleration.)

Draw Conclusions

3 **Making Predictions** Imagine you are standing on a corner and watching a car that is waiting at a stoplight. A passenger inside the car is holding some helium balloons. Based on what you observed with your accelerometer, what do you think will happen to the balloons when the car begins moving?

Applying Your Data

If you move the bottle in a circle at a constant speed, what do you predict the cork will do? Try it, and check your answer.

Chapter Review

USING KEY TERMS

Complete each of the following sentences by choosing the correct term from the word bank.

mass	gravity
friction	weight
speed	velocity
net force	newton

1 ___ opposes motion between surfaces that are touching.

2 The ___ is the unit of force.

3 ___ is determined by combining forces.

4 Acceleration is the rate at which ___ changes.

5 ___ is a measure of the gravitational force on an object.

UNDERSTANDING KEY IDEAS

Multiple Choice

6 If a student rides her bicycle on a straight road and does not speed up or slow down, she is traveling with a

  a. constant acceleration.

  b. constant velocity.

  c. positive acceleration.

  d. negative acceleration.

7 A force

  a. is expressed in newtons.

  b. can cause an object to speed up, slow down, or change direction.

  c. is a push or a pull.

  d. All of the above

8 If you are in a spacecraft that has been launched into space, your weight would

  a. increase because gravitational force is increasing.

  b. increase because gravitational force is decreasing.

  c. decrease because gravitational force is decreasing.

  d. decrease because gravitational force is increasing.

9 The gravitational force between 1 kg of lead and Earth is ___ the gravitational force between 1 kg of marshmallows and Earth.

  a. greater than   **c.** the same as

  b. less than   **d.** None of the above

10 Which of the following is a measurement of velocity?

  a. 16 m east   **c.** 55 m/h south

  b. 25 m/s^2 **d.** 60 km/h

Short Answer

11 Describe the relationship between motion and a reference point.

12 How is it possible to be accelerating and traveling at a constant speed?

13 Explain the difference between mass and weight.

Math Skills

14 A kangaroo hops 60 m to the east in 5 s. Use this information to answer the following questions.

   a. What is the kangaroo's average speed?

   b. What is the kangaroo's average velocity?

   c. The kangaroo stops at a lake for a drink of water and then starts hopping again to the south. Each second, the kangaroo's velocity increases 2.5 m/s. What is the kangaroo's acceleration after 5 s?

CRITICAL THINKING

15 **Concept Mapping** Use the following terms to create a concept map: *speed, velocity, acceleration, force, direction,* and *motion.*

16 **Applying Concepts** Your family is moving, and you are asked to help move some boxes. One box is so heavy that you must push it across the room rather than lift it. What are some ways you could reduce friction to make moving the box easier?

17 **Analyzing Ideas** Considering the scientific meaning of the word *acceleration,* how could using the term *accelerator* when talking about a car's gas pedal lead to confusion?

18 **Identifying Relationships** Explain why it is important for airplane pilots to know wind velocity and not just wind speed during a flight.

INTERPRETING GRAPHICS

Use the figures below to answer the questions that follow.

19 Is the graph below showing positive acceleration or negative acceleration? How can you tell?

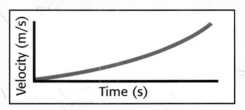

20 You know how to combine two forces that act in one or two directions. The same method can be used to combine several forces acting in several directions. Look at the diagrams, and calculate the net force in each diagram. Predict the direction each object will move.

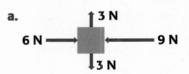

a.

6 N → ☐ ← 9 N
    ↑ 3 N   ↓ 3 N

b.

5 N → ☐ ← 5 N
   ↑ 5 N

c.

8 N → ☐
   ↑ 4 N   ↓ 4 N

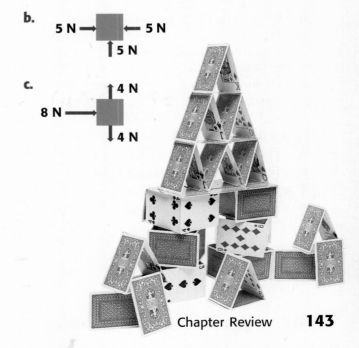

READING

Read each of the passages below. Then, answer the questions that follow each passage.

Passage 1 If you look closely at the surface of a golf ball, you'll see dozens of tiny dimples. When air flows past these dimples, the air is stirred up and stays near the surface of the ball. By keeping air moving near the surface of the ball, the dimples help the golf ball move faster and farther through the air. Jeff DiTullio, a teacher at MIT in Cambridge, Massachusetts, decided to apply this principle to a baseball bat. When DiTullio tested his dimpled bat in a <u>wind tunnel</u>, he found that the bat could be swung 3% to 5% faster than a bat without dimples. That increase may not seem like much, but the dimpled bat could add about 5 m of distance to a fly ball!

1. Who is Jeff DiTullio?
   A the inventor of the dimpled golf ball
   B a teacher at Cambridge University
   C the inventor of the dimpled bat
   D a professional baseball player

2. Which of the following ideas is NOT stated in the passage?
   F Dimples make DiTullio's bat move faster.
   G MIT is in Cambridge, Massachusetts.
   H Air that is stirred up near the surface of DiTullio's bat makes it easier to swing the bat faster.
   I DiTullio will make a lot of money from his invention.

3. In the passage, what does *wind tunnel* mean?
   A a place to practice batting
   B a place to test the speed of objects in the air
   C a baseball stadium
   D a passageway that is shielded from the wind

Passage 2 The Golden Gate Bridge in San Francisco, California, is one of the most famous <u>landmarks</u> in the world. Approximately 9 million people from around the world visit the bridge each year.

The Golden Gate Bridge is a suspension bridge. A suspension bridge is one in which the roadway is hung, or suspended, from huge cables that extend from one end of the bridge to the other. The main cables on the Golden Gate Bridge are 2.33 km long. Many forces act on the main cables. For example, smaller cables pull down on the main cables to connect the roadway to the main cables. And two towers that are 227 m tall push up on the main cables. The forces on the main cable must be balanced, or the bridge will collapse.

1. In this passage, what does *landmarks* mean?
   A large areas of land
   B well-known places
   C street signs
   D places where people meet

2. Which of the following statements is a fact from the passage?
   F The roadway of the Golden Gate Bridge is suspended from huge cables.
   G The towers of the Golden Gate Bridge are 2.33 km tall.
   H The main cables connect the roadway to the towers.
   I The forces on the cables are not balanced.

3. According to the passage, why do people from around the world visit the Golden Gate Bridge?
   A It is the longest bridge in the world.
   B It is a suspension bridge.
   C It is the only bridge that is painted orange.
   D It is a famous landmark.

The graph below shows the data collected by a student as she watched a squirrel running on the ground. Use the graph below to answer the questions that follow.

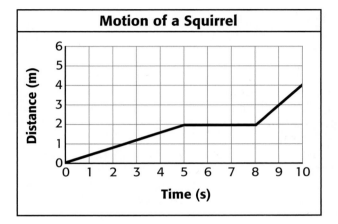

Motion of a Squirrel

1. Which of the following best describes the motion of the squirrel between 5 s and 8 s?
   A The squirrel's speed increased.
   B The squirrel's speed decreased.
   C The squirrel's speed did not change.
   D The squirrel moved backward.

2. Which of the following statements about the motion of the squirrel is true?
   F The squirrel moved with the greatest speed between 0 s and 5 s.
   G The squirrel moved with the greatest speed between 8 s and 10 s.
   H The squirrel moved with a constant speed between 0 s and 8 s.
   I The squirrel moved with a constant speed between 5 s and 10 s.

3. What is the average speed of the squirrel between 8 s and 10 s?
   A 0.4 m/s
   B 1 m/s
   C 2 m/s
   D 4 m/s

Read each question below, and choose the best answer.

1. The distance between Cedar Rapids, Iowa, and Sioux Falls, South Dakota, is about 660 km. How long will it take a car traveling with an average speed of 95 km/h to drive from Cedar Rapids to Sioux Falls?
   A less than 1 h
   B about 3 h
   C about 7 h
   D about 10 h

2. Martha counted the number of people in each group that walked into her school's cafeteria. In the first 10 groups, she counted the following numbers of people: 6, 4, 9, 6, 4, 10, 9, 5, 9, and 8. What is the mode of this set of data?
   F 6
   G 7
   H 9
   I 10

3. Which of the following terms describes the angle marked in the triangle below.

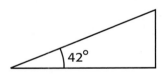

   A acute
   B obtuse
   C right
   D None of the above

4. Donnell collected money for a charity fundraiser. After one hour, he counted the money and found that he had raised $10.00 in bills and $3.74 in coins. Which of the following represents the number of coins he collected?
   F 4 pennies, 9 nickels, 18 dimes, and 6 quarters
   G 9 pennies, 7 nickels, 18 dimes, and 6 quarters
   H 6 pennies, 7 nickels, 15 dimes, and 8 quarters
   I 9 pennies, 8 nickels, 12 dimes, and 3 quarters

Standardized Test Preparation

Science in Action

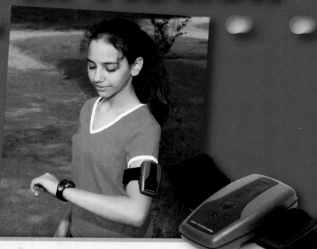

Science, Technology, and Society

GPS Watch System

Some athletes are concerned about knowing their speed during training. To calculate speed, they need to know distance and time. Finding time by using a watch is easy to do. But determining distance is more difficult. However, a GPS watch system is now available to help with this problem. *GPS* stands for *global positioning system*. A GPS unit, which is worn on an athlete's upper arm, monitors the athlete's position by using signals from satellites. As the athlete moves, the GPS unit calculates the distance traveled. The GPS unit sends a signal to the watch, which keeps the athlete's time, and the watch displays the athlete's speed.

Weird Science

The Segway™ Human Transporter

In November 2002, a new people-moving machine was introduced, and people have been fascinated by the odd-looking device ever since. The device is called the *Segway Human Transporter*. The Segway is a two-wheeled device that is powered by a rechargeable battery. To move forward, the rider simply leans forward. Sensors detect this motion and send signals to the on-board computer. The computer, in turn, tells the motor to start going. To slow down, the rider leans backward, and to stop, the rider stands straight up. The Segway has a top speed of 20 km/h (about 12.5 mi/h) and can travel up to 28 km (about 17.4 mi) on a single battery charge.

Math

Suppose an athlete wishes to finish a 5 K race in under 25 min. The distance of a 5 K is 5 km. (Remember that 1 km = 1,000 m.) If the athlete runs the race at a constant speed of 3.4 m/s, will she meet her goal?

Language Arts ACTiViTY

WRITING SKILL The inventor of the Segway thinks that the machine will make a good alternative to walking and bicycle riding. Write a one-page essay explaining whether you think using a Segway is better or worse than riding a bicycle.

Victor Petrenko

Snowboard and Ski Brakes Have you ever wished for emergency brakes on your snowboard or skis? Thanks to Victor Petrenko and the Ice Research Lab of Dartmouth College, snowboards and skis that have braking systems may soon be available.

Not many people know more about the properties of ice and ice-related technologies than Victor Petrenko does. He has spent most of his career researching the electrical and mechanical properties of ice. Through his research, Petrenko learned that ice can hold an electric charge. He used this property to design a braking system for snowboards. The system is a form of electric friction control.

The power source for the brakes is a battery. The battery is connected to a network of wires embedded on the bottom surface of a snowboard. When the battery is activated, the bottom of the snowboard gains a negative charge. This negative charge creates a positive charge on the surface of the snow. Because opposite charges attract, the snowboard and the snow are pulled together. The force that pulls the surfaces together increases friction, and the snowboard slows down.

Social Studies ACTIVITY

Research the history of skiing. Make a poster that includes a timeline of significant dates in the history of skiing. Illustrate your poster with photos or drawings.

To learn more about these Science in Action topics, visit **go.hrw.com** and type in the keyword **HP5MOTF.**

Current Science

Check out Current Science® articles related to this chapter by visiting go.hrw.com. Just type in the keyword **HP5CS05.**

6

Forces and Motion

SECTION ① Gravity and Motion . . . 150

SECTION ② Newton's Laws
of Motion 158

SECTION ③ Momentum 166

Chapter Lab 170
Chapter Review 172
Standardized Test Preparation 174
Science in Action 176

About the PHOTO

To train for space flight, astronauts fly in a modified KC-135 cargo airplane. The airplane first flies upward at a steep angle. Then, it flies downward at a 45° angle, which causes the feeling of reduced gravity inside. Under these conditions, the astronauts in the plane can float and can practice carrying out tasks that they will need to perform when they are in orbit. Because the floating makes people queasy, this KC-135 is nicknamed the "Vomit Comet."

PRE-READING ACTIVITY

Graphic Organizer

Spider Map Before you read the chapter, create the graphic organizer entitled "Spider Map" described in the **Study Skills** section of the Appendix. Label the circle "Motion." Create a leg for each law of motion, a leg for gravity, and a leg for momentum. As you read the chapter, fill in the map with details about how motion is related to the laws of motion, gravity, and momentum.

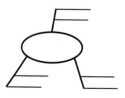

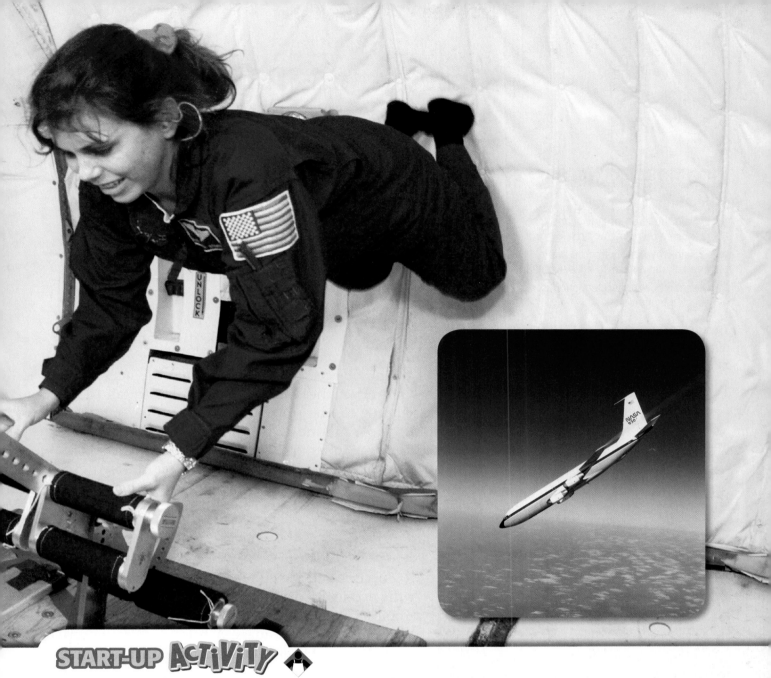

START-UP ACTIVITY

Falling Water

Gravity is one of the most important forces in your life. In this activity, you will observe the effect of gravity on a falling object.

Procedure

1. Place a **wide plastic tub** on the floor. Punch a small hole in the side of a **paper cup,** near the bottom.

2. Hold your finger over the hole, and fill the cup with **water.** Keep your finger over the hole, and hold the cup waist-high above the tub.

3. Uncover the hole. Record your observations as Trial 1.

4. Predict what will happen to the water if you drop the cup at the same time you uncover the hole.

5. Cover the hole, and refill the cup with water.

6. Uncover the hole, and drop the cup at the same time. Record your observations as Trial 2.

7. Clean up any spilled water with **paper towels.**

Analysis

1. What differences did you observe in the behavior of the water during the two trials?

2. In Trial 2, how fast did the cup fall compared with how fast the water fell?

3. How did the results of Trial 2 compare with your prediction?

Gravity and Motion

Suppose you dropped a baseball and a marble at the same time from the top of a tall building. Which do you think would land on the ground first?

Objectives

● Explain the effect of gravity and air resistance on falling objects.

● Explain why objects in orbit are in free fall and appear to be weightless.

● Describe how projectile motion is affected by gravity.

Terms to Learn

terminal velocity
free fall
projectile motion

Reading Organizer As you read this section, create an outline of the section. Use the headings from the section in your outline.

In ancient Greece around 400 BCE, a philosopher named Aristotle (AR is TAWT uhl) thought that the rate at which an object falls depended on the object's mass. If you asked Aristotle whether the baseball or the marble would land first, he would have said the baseball. But Aristotle never tried dropping objects with different masses to test his idea about falling objects.

Gravity and Falling Objects

In the late 1500s, a young Italian scientist named Galileo Galilei (GAL uh LAY oh GAL uh LAY) questioned Aristotle's idea about falling objects. Galileo argued that the mass of an object does not affect the time the object takes to fall to the ground. According to one story, Galileo proved his argument by dropping two cannonballs of different masses from the top of the Leaning Tower of Pisa in Italy. The people watching from the ground below were amazed to see the two cannonballs land at the same time. Whether or not this story is true, Galileo's work changed people's understanding of gravity and falling objects.

Gravity and Acceleration

Objects fall to the ground at the same rate because the acceleration due to gravity is the same for all objects. Why is this true? Acceleration depends on both force and mass. A heavier object experiences a greater gravitational force than a lighter object does. But a heavier object is also harder to accelerate because it has more mass. The extra mass of the heavy object exactly balances the additional gravitational force. **Figure 1** shows objects that have different masses falling with the same acceleration.

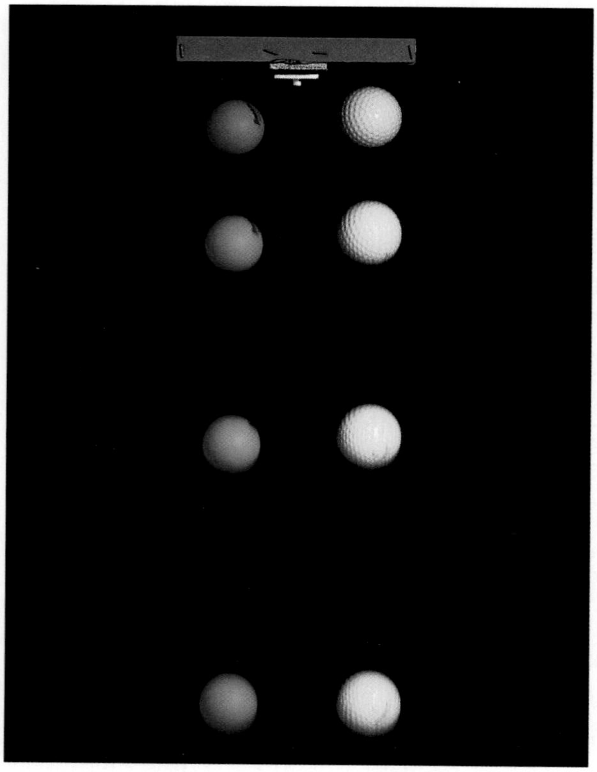

Figure 1 *This stop-action photo shows that a table-tennis ball and a golf ball fall at the same rate even though they have different masses.*

Acceleration Due to Gravity

Acceleration is the rate at which velocity changes over time. So, the acceleration of an object is the object's change in velocity divided by the amount of time during which the change occurs. All objects accelerate toward Earth at a rate of 9.8 meters per second per second. This rate is written as 9.8 m/s/s, or 9.8 m/s^2. So, for every second that an object falls, the object's downward velocity increases by 9.8 m/s, as shown in **Figure 2.**

✓ Reading Check What is the acceleration due to gravity? (*See the Appendix for answers to Reading Checks.*)

Velocity of Falling Objects

You can calculate the change in velocity (Δv) of a falling object by using the following equation:

$$\Delta v = g \times t$$

In this equation, g is the acceleration due to gravity on Earth (9.8 m/s^2), and t is the time the object takes to fall (in seconds). The change in velocity is the difference between the final velocity and the starting velocity. If the object starts at rest, this equation yields the velocity of the object after a certain time period.

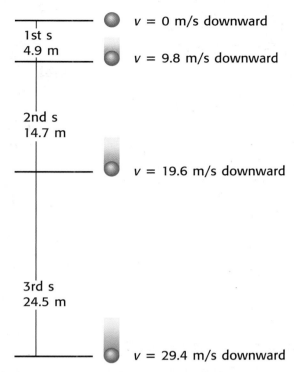

$v = 0$ m/s downward

1st s
4.9 m

$v = 9.8$ m/s downward

2nd s
14.7 m

$v = 19.6$ m/s downward

3rd s
24.5 m

$v = 29.4$ m/s downward

Figure 2 *A falling object accelerates at a constant rate. The object falls faster and farther each second than it did the second before.*

MATH FOCUS

Calculating the Velocity of Falling Objects A stone at rest is dropped from a cliff, and the stone hits the ground after a time of 3 s. What is the stone's velocity when it hits the ground?

Step 1: Write the equation for change in velocity.

$$\Delta v = g \times t$$

Step 2: Replace g with its value and t with the time given in the problem, and solve.

$$\Delta v = 9.8 \, \frac{m/s}{s} \times 3 \, s$$
$$= 29.4 \text{ m/s}$$

To rearrange the equation to find time, divide by the acceleration due to gravity:

$$t = \frac{\Delta v}{g}$$

Now It's Your Turn

1. A penny at rest is dropped from the top of a tall stairwell. What is the penny's velocity after it has fallen for 2 s?
2. The same penny hits the ground in 4.5 s. What is the penny's velocity as it hits the ground?
3. A marble at rest is dropped from a tall building. The marble hits the ground with a velocity of 98 m/s. How long was the marble in the air?
4. An acorn at rest falls from an oak tree. The acorn hits the ground with a velocity of 14.7 m/s. How long did it take the acorn to land?

Figure 3 **Effect of Air Resistance on a Falling Object**

a The **force of gravity** is pulling down on the apple. If gravity were the only force acting on the apple, the apple would accelerate at a rate of 9.8 m/s².

b The **force of air resistance** is pushing up on the apple. This force is subtracted from the force of gravity to yield the net force.

c The **net force** on the apple is equal to the force of air resistance subtracted from the force of gravity. Because the net force is not 0 N, the apple accelerates downward. But the apple does not accelerate as fast as it would without air resistance.

Air Resistance and Falling Objects

Try dropping two sheets of paper—one crumpled in a tight ball and the other kept flat. What happened? Does this simple experiment seem to contradict what you just learned about falling objects? The flat paper falls more slowly than the crumpled paper because of *air resistance*. Air resistance is the force that opposes the motion of objects through air.

The amount of air resistance acting on an object depends on the size, shape, and speed of the object. Air resistance affects the flat sheet of paper more than the crumpled one. The larger surface area of the flat sheet causes the flat sheet to fall slower than the crumpled one. **Figure 3** shows the effect of air resistance on the downward acceleration of a falling object.

✓ **Reading Check** Will air resistance have more effect on the acceleration of a falling leaf or the acceleration of a falling acorn?

Acceleration Stops at the Terminal Velocity

As the speed of a falling object increases, air resistance increases. The upward force of air resistance continues to increase until it is equal to the downward force of gravity. At this point, the net force is 0 N and the object stops accelerating. The object then falls at a constant velocity called the **terminal velocity.**

Terminal velocity can be a good thing. Every year, cars, buildings, and vegetation are severely damaged in hailstorms. The terminal velocity of hailstones is between 5 and 40 m/s, depending on their size. If there were no air resistance, hailstones would hit the Earth at velocities near 350 m/s! **Figure 4** shows another situation in which terminal velocity is helpful.

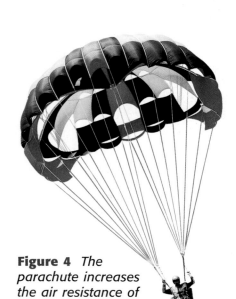

Figure 4 *The parachute increases the air resistance of this sky diver and slows him to a safe terminal velocity.*

terminal velocity the constant velocity of a falling object when the force of air resistance is equal in magnitude and opposite in direction to the force of gravity

Free Fall Occurs When There Is No Air Resistance

Sky divers are often described as being in free fall before they open their parachutes. However, that is an incorrect description, because air resistance is always acting on the sky diver.

An object is in **free fall** only if gravity is pulling it down and no other forces are acting on it. Because air resistance is a force, free fall can occur only where there is no air. Two places that have no air are in space and in a vacuum. A vacuum is a place in which there is no matter. **Figure 5** shows objects falling in a vacuum. Because there is no air resistance in a vacuum, the two objects are in free fall.

Orbiting Objects Are in Free Fall

Look at the astronaut in **Figure 6.** Why is the astronaut floating inside the space shuttle? You may be tempted to say that she is weightless in space. However, it is impossible for any object to be weightless anywhere in the universe.

Weight is a measure of gravitational force. The size of the force depends on the masses of objects and the distances between them. Suppose you traveled in space far away from all the stars and planets. The gravitational force acting on you would be very small because the distance between you and other objects would be very large. But you and all the other objects in the universe would still have mass. Therefore, gravity would attract you to other objects—even if just slightly—so you would still have weight.

Astronauts float in orbiting spacecrafts because of free fall. To better understand why astronauts float, you need to know what *orbiting* means.

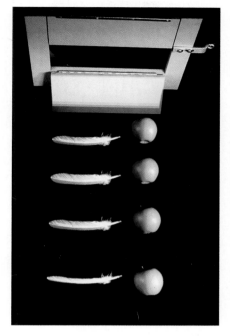

Figure 5 *Air resistance usually causes a feather to fall more slowly than an apple falls. But in a vacuum, a feather and an apple fall with the same acceleration because both are in free fall.*

free fall the motion of a body when only the force of gravity is acting on the body

Figure 6 *Astronauts appear to be weightless while they are floating inside the space shuttle— but they are not weightless!*

Figure 7 **How an Orbit Is Formed**

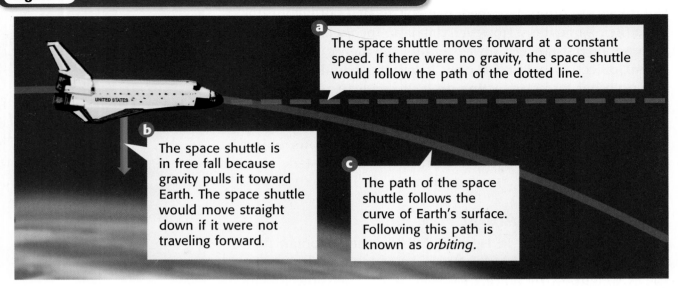

a The space shuttle moves forward at a constant speed. If there were no gravity, the space shuttle would follow the path of the dotted line.

b The space shuttle is in free fall because gravity pulls it toward Earth. The space shuttle would move straight down if it were not traveling forward.

c The path of the space shuttle follows the curve of Earth's surface. Following this path is known as *orbiting*.

Two Motions Combine to Cause Orbiting

An object is orbiting when it is traveling around another object in space. When a spacecraft orbits Earth, it is moving forward. But the spacecraft is also in free fall toward Earth. **Figure 7** shows how these two motions combine to cause orbiting.

As you can see in **Figure 7,** the space shuttle is always falling while it is in orbit. So why don't astronauts hit their heads on the ceiling of the falling shuttle? Because they are also in free fall—they are always falling, too. Because astronauts are in free fall, they float.

Orbiting and Centripetal Force

Besides spacecrafts and satellites, many other objects in the universe are in orbit. The moon orbits the Earth. Earth and the other planets orbit the sun. In addition, many stars orbit large masses in the center of galaxies. Many of these objects are traveling in a circular or nearly circular path. Any object in circular motion is constantly changing direction. Because an unbalanced force is necessary to change the motion of any object, there must be an unbalanced force working on any object in circular motion.

The unbalanced force that causes objects to move in a circular path is called a *centripetal force* (sen TRIP uht uhl FOHRS). Gravity provides the centripetal force that keeps objects in orbit. The word *centripetal* means "toward the center." As you can see in **Figure 8,** the centripetal force on the moon points toward the center of the moon's circular orbit.

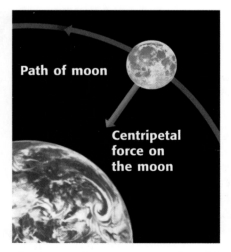

Path of moon

Centripetal force on the moon

Figure 8 *The moon stays in orbit around Earth because Earth's gravitational force provides a centripetal force on the moon.*

✓ **Reading Check** What does the word *centripetal* mean?

Projectile Motion and Gravity

The motion of a hopping grasshopper is an example of projectile motion (proh JEK tuhl MOH shuhn). **Projectile motion** is the curved path an object follows when it is thrown or propelled near the surface of the Earth. Projectile motion has two components—horizontal motion and vertical motion. The two components are independent, so they have no effect on each other. When the two motions are combined, they form a curved path, as shown in **Figure 9.** Some examples of projectile motion include the following:

- a frog leaping
- water sprayed by a sprinkler
- a swimmer diving into water
- balls being juggled
- an arrow shot by an archer

Horizontal Motion

When you throw a ball, your hand exerts a force on the ball that makes the ball move forward. This force gives the ball its horizontal motion, which is motion parallel to the ground.

After you release the ball, no horizontal forces are acting on the ball (if you ignore air resistance). Even gravity does not affect the horizontal component of projectile motion. So, there are no forces to change the ball's horizontal motion. Thus, the horizontal velocity of the ball is constant after the ball leaves your hand, as shown in **Figure 9.**

projectile motion the curved path that an object follows when thrown, launched, or otherwise projected near the surface of Earth

---

Figure 9 Projectile Motion

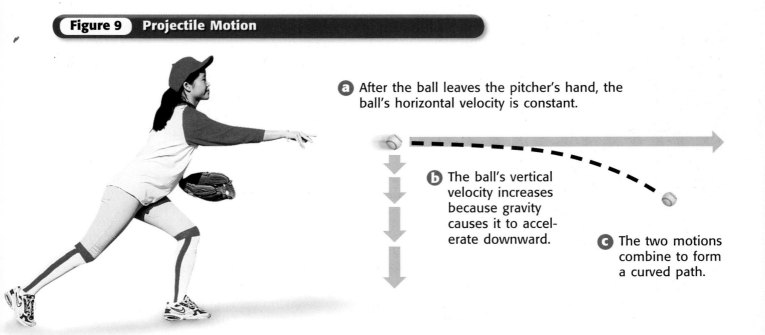

a After the ball leaves the pitcher's hand, the ball's horizontal velocity is constant.

b The ball's vertical velocity increases because gravity causes it to accelerate downward.

c The two motions combine to form a curved path.

INTERNET ACTIVITY

For another activity related to this chapter, go to **go.hrw.com** and type in the keyword **HP5FORW**.

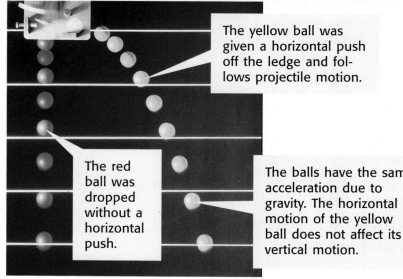

Figure 10 Projectile Motion and Acceleration Due to Gravity

The yellow ball was given a horizontal push off the ledge and follows projectile motion.

The red ball was dropped without a horizontal push.

The balls have the same acceleration due to gravity. The horizontal motion of the yellow ball does not affect its vertical motion.

Vertical Motion

Gravity pulls everything on Earth downward toward the center of Earth. A ball in your hand is prevented from falling by your hand. After you throw the ball, gravity pulls it downward and gives the ball vertical motion. Vertical motion is motion that is perpendicular to the ground. Gravity pulls objects in projectile motion down at an acceleration of 9.8 m/s² (if air resistance is ignored). This rate is the same for all falling objects. **Figure 10** shows that the downward acceleration of a thrown object and a falling object are the same.

Because objects in projectile motion accelerate downward, you always have to aim above a target if you want to hit it with a thrown or propelled object. That's why when you aim an arrow directly at a bull's-eye, your arrow strikes the bottom of the target rather than the middle of the target.

✓ **Reading Check** What gives an object in projectile motion its vertical motion?

Quick Lab

Penny Projectile Motion

1. Position a **flat ruler** and **two pennies** on a **desk or table** as shown below.

2. Hold the ruler by the end that is on the desk. Move the ruler quickly in the direction shown so that the ruler knocks the penny off the table and so that the other penny also drops. Repeat this step several times.

3. Which penny travels with projectile motion? In what order do the pennies hit the ground? Record and explain your answers.

SECTION Review

Summary

- Gravity causes all objects to accelerate toward Earth at a rate of 9.8 m/s^2.
- Air resistance slows the acceleration of falling objects. An object falls at its terminal velocity when the upward force of air resistance equals the downward force of gravity.
- An object is in free fall if gravity is the only force acting on it.
- Objects in orbit appear to be weightless because they are in free fall.

- A centripetal force is needed to keep objects in circular motion. Gravity acts as a centripetal force to keep objects in orbit.
- Projectile motion is the curved path an object follows when thrown or propelled near the surface of Earth.
- Projectile motion has two components—horizontal motion and vertical motion. Gravity affects only the vertical motion of projectile motion.

Using Key Terms

1. Use each of the following terms in a separate sentence: *terminal velocity* and *free fall*.

Understanding Key Ideas

2. Which of the following is in projectile motion?
   a. a feather falling in a vacuum
   b. a cat leaping on a toy
   c. a car driving up a hill
   d. a book laying on a desk

3. How does air resistance affect the acceleration of falling objects?

4. How does gravity affect the two components of projectile motion?

5. How is the acceleration of falling objects affected by gravity?

6. Why is the acceleration due to gravity the same for all objects?

Math Skills

7. A rock at rest falls off a tall cliff and hits the valley below after 3.5 s. What is the rock's velocity as it hits the ground?

Critical Thinking

8. **Applying Concepts** Think about a sport that uses a ball. Identify four examples from that sport in which an object is in projectile motion.

9. **Making Inferences** The moon has no atmosphere. Predict what would happen if an astronaut on the moon dropped a hammer and a feather at the same time from the same height.

Interpreting Graphics

10. Whenever Jon delivers a newspaper to the Zapanta house, the newspaper lands in the bushes, as shown below. What should Jon do to make sure the newspaper lands on the porch?

For a variety of links related to this chapter, go to www.scilinks.org
Topic: Gravity and Orbiting Objects; Projectile Motion
SciLinks code: HSM0692; HSM1223

Developed and maintained by the National Science Teachers Association

Newton's Laws of Motion

Imagine that you are playing baseball. The pitch comes in, and—crack—you hit the ball hard! But instead of flying off the bat, the ball just drops to the ground. Is that normal?

You would probably say no. You know that force and motion are related. When you exert a force on a baseball by hitting it with a bat, the baseball should move. In 1686, Sir Isaac Newton explained this relationship between force and the motion of an object with his three laws of motion.

Newton's First Law of Motion

> *An object at rest remains at rest, and an object in motion remains in motion at constant speed and in a straight line unless acted on by an unbalanced force.*

Newton's first law of motion describes the motion of an object that has a net force of 0 N acting on it. This law may seem complicated when you first read it. But, it is easy to understand when you consider its two parts separately.

Part 1: Objects at Rest

An object that is not moving is said to be at rest. A chair on the floor and a golf ball balanced on a tee are examples of objects at rest. Newton's first law says that objects at rest will stay at rest unless they are acted on by an unbalanced force. For example, objects will not start moving until a push or a pull is exerted on them. So, a chair won't slide across the room unless you push the chair. And, a golf ball won't move off the tee unless the ball is struck by a golf club, as shown in **Figure 1.**

Figure 1 *A golf ball will remain at rest on a tee until it is acted on by the unbalanced force of a moving club.*

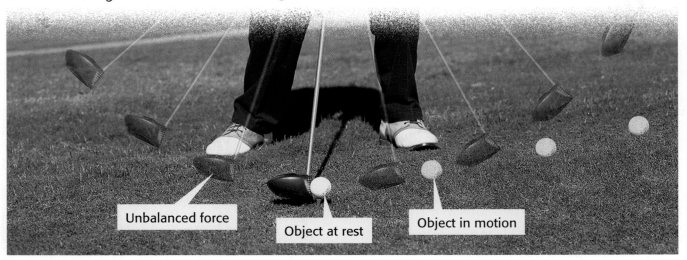

Unbalanced force

Object at rest

Object in motion

Part 2: Objects in Motion

The second part of Newton's first law is about objects moving with a certain velocity. Such objects will continue to move forever with the same velocity unless an unbalanced force acts on them.

Think about driving a bumper car at an amusement park. Your ride is pleasant as long as you are driving in an open space. But the name of the game is bumper cars! Sooner or later you are likely to run into another car, as shown in **Figure 2.** Your bumper car stops when it hits another car. But, you continue to move forward until the force from your seat belt stops you.

Friction and Newton's First Law

An object in motion will stay in motion forever unless it is acted on by an unbalanced force. So, you should be able to give your desk a push and send it sliding across the floor. If you push your desk, the desk quickly stops. Why?

There must be an unbalanced force that acts on the desk to stop its motion. That unbalanced force is friction. The friction between the desk and the floor works against the motion of the desk. Because of friction, observing the effects of Newton's first law is often difficult. For example, friction will cause a rolling ball to slow down and stop. Friction will also make a car slow down if the driver lets up on the gas pedal. Because of friction, the motion of objects changes.

Reading Check When you ride a bus, why do you fall forward when the bus stops moving? (*See the Appendix for answers to Reading Checks.*)

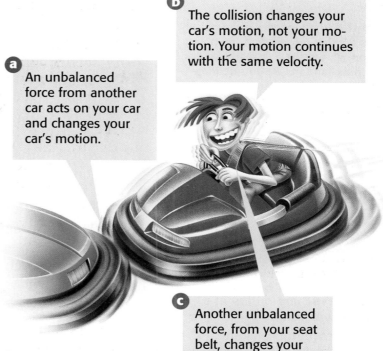

b The collision changes your car's motion, not your motion. Your motion continues with the same velocity.

a An unbalanced force from another car acts on your car and changes your car's motion.

c Another unbalanced force, from your seat belt, changes your motion.

Figure 2 *Bumper cars let you have fun with Newton's first law.*

First Law Skateboard

1. Place an **empty soda can** on top of a **skateboard.**

2. Ask a friend to catch the skateboard after you push it. Now, give the skateboard a quick, firm push. What happened to the soda can?

3. Put the can on the skateboard again. Push the skateboard gently so that the skateboard moves quickly but so that the can does not fall.

4. Ask your friend to stop the skateboard after he or she allows it to travel a short distance. What happened to the can?

5. Explain how Newton's first law applies to what happened.

inertia the tendency of an object to resist being moved or, if the object is moving, to resist a change in speed or direction until an outside force acts on the object

First-Law Magic

1. On a **table or desk**, place a **large, empty plastic cup** on top of a **paper towel.**

2. Without touching the cup or tipping it over, remove the paper towel from under the cup. How did you accomplish this? Repeat this step.

3. Fill the cup half full with **water,** and place the cup on the paper towel.

4. Once again, remove the paper towel from under the cup. Was it easier or harder to do this time?

5. Explain your observations in terms of mass, inertia, and Newton's first law of motion.

Inertia and Newton's First Law

Newton's first law of motion is sometimes called the *law of inertia.* **Inertia** (in UHR shuh) is the tendency of all objects to resist any change in motion. Because of inertia, an object at rest will remain at rest until a force makes it move. Likewise, inertia is the reason a moving object stays in motion with the same velocity unless a force changes its speed or direction. For example, because of inertia, you slide toward the side of a car when the driver turns a corner. Inertia is also why it is impossible for a plane, car, or bicycle to stop immediately.

Mass and Inertia

Mass is a measure of inertia. An object that has a small mass has less inertia than an object that has a large mass. So, changing the motion of an object that has a small mass is easier than changing the motion of an object that has a large mass. For example, a softball has less mass and therefore less inertia than a bowling ball. Because the softball has a small amount of inertia, it is easy to pitch a softball and to change its motion by hitting it with a bat. Imagine how difficult it would be to play softball with a bowling ball! **Figure 3** further shows the relationship between mass and inertia.

Figure 3 *Inertia makes it harder to accelerate a car than to accelerate a bicycle. Inertia also makes it easier to stop a moving bicycle than a car moving at the same speed.*

Newton's Second Law of Motion

The acceleration of an object depends on the mass of the object and the amount of force applied.

Newton's second law describes the motion of an object when an unbalanced force acts on the object. As with Newton's first law, you should consider the second law in two parts.

Part 1: Acceleration Depends on Mass

Suppose you are pushing an empty cart. You have to exert only a small force on the cart to accelerate it. But, the same amount of force will not accelerate the full cart as much as the empty cart. Look at the first two photos in **Figure 4.** They show that the acceleration of an object decreases as its mass increases and that its acceleration increases as its mass decreases.

Part 2: Acceleration Depends on Force

Suppose you give the cart a hard push, as shown in the third photo in **Figure 4.** The cart will start moving faster than if you gave it only a soft push. So, an object's acceleration increases as the force on the object increases. On the other hand, an object's acceleration decreases as the force on the object decreases.

The acceleration of an object is always in the same direction as the force applied. The cart in **Figure 4** moved forward because the push was in the forward direction.

Reading Check What is the relationship between the force on an object and the object's acceleration?

Figure 4 **Mass, Force, and Acceleration**

Acceleration   **Acceleration**   **Acceleration**

If the force applied to the carts is the same, the acceleration of the empty cart is greater than the acceleration of the loaded cart.

Acceleration will increase when a larger force is exerted.

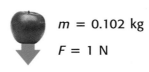 **Figure 5** Newton's Second Law and Acceleration Due to Gravity

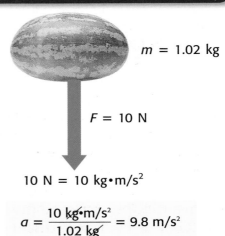

$m = 0.102$ kg

$F = 1$ N

$m = 1.02$ kg

$F = 10$ N

1 N $= 1$ kg•m/s²

$$a = \frac{1 \text{ kg•m/s}^2}{0.102 \text{ kg}} = 9.8 \text{ m/s}^2$$

10 N $= 10$ kg•m/s²

$$a = \frac{10 \text{ kg•m/s}^2}{1.02 \text{ kg}} = 9.8 \text{ m/s}^2$$

The apple has less mass than the watermelon does. So, less force is needed to give the apple the same acceleration that the watermelon has.

Expressing Newton's Second Law Mathematically

The relationship of acceleration (*a*) to mass (*m*) and force (*F*) can be expressed mathematically with the following equation:

$$a = \frac{F}{m}, \text{ or } F = m \times a$$

Notice that the equation can be rearranged to find the force applied. Both forms of the equation can be used to solve problems.

Newton's second law explains why objects fall to Earth with the same acceleration. In **Figure 5,** you can see how the large force of gravity on the watermelon is offset by its large mass. Thus, you find that the accelerations of the watermelon and the apple are the same when you solve for acceleration.

MATH FOCUS

Second-Law Problems What is the acceleration of a 3 kg mass if a force of 14.4 N is used to move the mass? (Note: 1 N is equal to 1 kg•m/s²)

Step 1: Write the equation for acceleration.

$$a = \frac{F}{m}$$

Step 2: Replace *F* and *m* with the values given in the problem, and solve.

$$a = \frac{14.4 \text{ kg•m/s}^2}{3 \text{ kg}} = 4.8 \text{ m/s}^2$$

Now It's Your Turn

1. What is the acceleration of a 7 kg mass if a force of 68.6 N is used to move it toward Earth?
2. What force is necessary to accelerate a 1,250 kg car at a rate of 40 m/s²?
3. Zookeepers carry a stretcher that holds a sleeping lion. The total mass of the lion and the stretcher is 175 kg. The lion's forward acceleration is 2 m/s². What is the force necessary to produce this acceleration?

Newton's Third Law of Motion

> *Whenever one object exerts a force on a second object, the second object exerts an equal and opposite force on the first.*

Newton's third law can be simply stated as follows: All forces act in pairs. If a force is exerted, another force occurs that is equal in size and opposite in direction. The law itself addresses only forces. But the way that force pairs interact affects the motion of objects.

How do forces act in pairs? Study **Figure 6** to learn how one force pair helps propel a swimmer through water. Action and reaction force pairs are present even when there is no motion. For example, you exert a force on a chair when you sit on it. Your weight pushing down on the chair is the action force. The reaction force is the force exerted by the chair that pushes up on your body. The force is equal to your weight.

✓ Reading Check How are the forces in each force pair related?

Force Pairs Do Not Act on the Same Object

A force is always exerted by one object on another object. This rule is true for all forces, including action and reaction forces. However, action and reaction forces in a pair do not act on the same object. If they did, the net force would always be 0 N and nothing would ever move! To understand how action and reaction forces act on objects, look at **Figure 6** again. The action force was exerted on the water by the swimmer's hands. But the reaction force was exerted on the swimmer's hands by the water. The forces did not act on the same object.

Newton Ball
Play catch with an adult. As you play, discuss how Newton's laws of motion are involved in the game. After you finish your game, make a list in your **science journal** of what you discussed.

ACTiViTY

Figure 6 *The action force and reaction force are a pair. The two forces are equal in size but opposite in direction.*

The action force is the swimmer's hands pushing on the water.

The reaction force is the water pushing on the hands. The reaction force moves the swimmer forward.

Figure 7 Examples of Action and Reaction Force Pairs

The space shuttle's thrusters push the exhaust gases downward as the gases push the shuttle upward with an equal force.

The rabbit's legs exert a force on Earth. Earth exerts an equal force on the rabbit's legs and causes the rabbit to accelerate upward.

The bat exerts a force on the ball and sends the ball flying. The ball exerts an equal force on the bat, but the bat does not move backward because the batter is exerting another force on the bat.

All Forces Act in Pairs—Action and Reaction

Newton's third law says that all forces act in pairs. When a force is exerted, there is always a reaction force. A force never acts by itself. **Figure 7** shows some examples of action and reaction force pairs. In each example, the action force is shown in yellow and the reaction force is shown in red.

The Effect of a Reaction Can Be Difficult to See

Another example of a force pair is shown in **Figure 8.** Gravity is a force of attraction between objects that is due to their masses. If you drop a ball, gravity pulls the ball toward Earth. This force is the action force exerted by Earth on the ball. But gravity also pulls Earth toward the ball. The force is the reaction force exerted by the ball on Earth.

It's easy to see the effect of the action force—the ball falls to Earth. Why don't you notice the effect of the reaction force—Earth being pulled upward? To find the answer to this question, think about Newton's second law. It states that the acceleration of an object depends on the force applied to it and on the mass of the object. The force on Earth is equal to the force on the ball. But the mass of Earth is much larger than the mass of the ball. Thus, the acceleration of Earth is much smaller than the acceleration of the ball. The acceleration of the Earth is so small that you can't see or feel the acceleration. So, it is difficult to observe the effect of Newton's third law on falling objects.

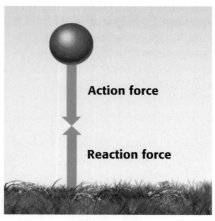

Figure 8 *The force of gravity between Earth and a falling object is a force pair.*

Action force

Reaction force

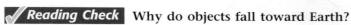

Reading Check Why do objects fall toward Earth?

Summary

- Newton's first law of motion states that the motion of an object will not change if no unbalanced forces act on it.
- Objects at rest will not move unless acted upon by an unbalanced force.
- Objects in motion will continue to move at a constant speed and in a straight line unless acted upon by an unbalanced force.
- Inertia is the tendency of matter to resist a change in motion. Mass is a measure of inertia.

- Newton's second law of motion states that the acceleration of an object depends on its mass and on the force exerted on it.
- Newton's second law is represented by the following equation: $F = m \times a$.
- Newton's third law of motion states that whenever one object exerts a force on a second object, the second object exerts an equal and opposite force on the first object.

Using Key Terms

1. In your own words, write a definition for the term *inertia*.

Understanding Key Ideas

2. Which of the following will increase the acceleration of an object that is pushed by a force?
   a. decreasing the mass of the object
   b. increasing the mass of the object
   c. increasing the force pushing the object
   d. Both (a) and (c)

3. Give three examples of force pairs that occur when you do your homework.

4. What does Newton's first law of motion say about objects at rest and objects in motion?

5. Use Newton's second law to describe the relationship between force, mass, and acceleration.

Math Skills

6. What force is necessary to accelerate a 70 kg object at a rate of 4.2 m/s^2?

Critical Thinking

7. **Applying Concepts** When a truck pulls a trailer, the trailer and truck accelerate forward even though the action and reaction forces are the same size but are in opposite directions. Why don't these forces balance each other?

8. **Making Inferences** Use Newton's first law of motion to explain why airbags in cars are important during head-on collisions.

Interpreting Graphics

9. Imagine you accidentally bumped your hand against a table, as shown in the photo below. Your hand hurts after it happens. Use Newton's third law of motion to explain what caused your hand to hurt.

Momentum

Imagine a compact car and a large truck traveling with the same velocity. The drivers of both vehicles put on the brakes at the same time. Which vehicle will stop first?

You would probably say that the compact car will stop first. You know that smaller objects are easier to stop than larger objects. But why? The answer is momentum (moh MEN tuhm).

Momentum, Mass, and Velocity

The **momentum** of an object depends on the object's mass and velocity. The more momentum an object has, the harder it is to stop the object or change its direction. In the example above, the truck has more mass and more momentum than the car has. So, a larger force is needed to stop the truck. Similarly, a fast-moving car has a greater velocity and thus more momentum than a slow-moving car of the same mass. So, a fast-moving car is harder to stop than a slow-moving car. **Figure 1** shows another example of an object that has momentum.

Calculating Momentum

Momentum (*p*) can be calculated with the equation below:

$$p = m \times v$$

In this equation, *m* is the mass of an object in kilograms and *v* is the object's velocity in meters per second. The units of momentum are kilograms multiplied by meters per second, or kg•m/s. Like velocity, momentum has a direction. Its direction is always the same as the direction of the object's velocity.

READING WARM-UP

Objectives
● Calculate the momentum of moving objects.
● Explain the law of conservation of momentum.

Terms to Learn
momentum

READING STRATEGY

Prediction Guide Before reading this section, write the title of each heading in this section. Next, under each heading, write what you think you will learn.

momentum a quantity defined as the product of the mass and velocity of an object

Figure 1 *The teen on the right has less mass than the teen on the left. But, the teen on the right can have a large momentum by moving quickly when she kicks.*

Momentum Calculations What is the momentum of an ostrich with a mass of 120 kg that runs with a velocity of 16 m/s north?

Step 1: Write the equation for momentum.

$$p = m \times v$$

Step 2: Replace m and v with the values given in the problem, and solve.

$$p = 120 \text{ kg} \times 16 \text{ m/s north}$$
$$p = 19{,}200 \text{ kg} \bullet \text{m/s north}$$

Now It's Your Turn

1. What is the momentum of a 6 kg bowling ball that is moving at 10 m/s down the alley toward the pins?
2. An 85 kg man is jogging with a velocity of 2.6 m/s to the north. Nearby, a 65 kg person is skateboarding and is traveling with a velocity of 3 m/s north. Which person has greater momentum? Show your calculations.

The Law of Conservation of Momentum

When a moving object hits another object, some or all of the momentum of the first object is transferred to the object that is hit. If only some of the momentum is transferred, the rest of the momentum stays with the first object.

Imagine that a cue ball hits a billiard ball so that the billiard ball starts moving and the cue ball stops, as shown in **Figure 2.** The white cue ball had a certain amount of momentum before the collision. During the collision, all of the cue ball's momentum was transferred to the red billiard ball. After the collision, the billiard ball moved away with the same amount of momentum the cue ball had. This example shows the *law of conservation of momentum.* The law of conservation of momentum states that any time objects collide, the total amount of momentum stays the same. The law of conservation of momentum is true for any collision if no other forces act on the colliding objects. This law applies whether the objects stick together or bounce off each other after they collide.

✓ Reading Check What can happen to momentum when two objects collide? (*See the Appendix for answers to Reading Checks.*)

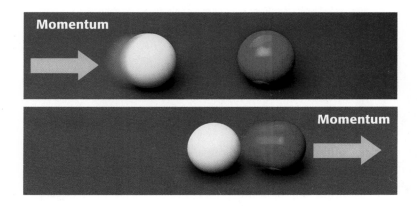

Figure 2 *The momentum before a collision is equal to the momentum after the collision.*

Objects Sticking Together

Sometimes, objects stick together after a collision. The football players shown in **Figure 3** are an example of such a collision. A dog leaping and catching a ball and a teen jumping on a skateboard are also examples. After two objects stick together, they move as one object. The mass of the combined objects is equal to the masses of the two objects added together. In a head-on collision, the combined objects move in the direction of the object that had the greater momentum before the collision. But together, the objects have a velocity that differs from the velocity of either object before the collision. The objects have a different velocity because momentum is conserved and depends on mass and velocity. So, when mass changes, the velocity must change, too.

Objects Bouncing Off Each Other

In some collisions, the objects bounce off each other. The bowling ball and bowling pins shown in **Figure 3** are examples of objects that bounce off each other after they collide. Billiard balls and bumper cars are other examples. During these types of collisions, momentum is usually transferred from one object to another object. The transfer of momentum causes the objects to move in different directions at different speeds. However, the total momentum of all the objects will remain the same before and after the collision.

Reading Check What are two ways that objects may interact after a collision?

CONNECTION TO Language Arts

WRITING SKILL **Momentum and Language**
The word *momentum* is often used in everyday language. For example, a sports announcer may say that the momentum of a game has changed. Or you may read that an idea is gaining momentum. In your **science journal,** write a paragraph that explains how the everyday use of the word *momentum* differs from momentum in science.

Figure 3 Examples of Conservation of Momentum

When football players tackle another player, they stick together. The velocity of each player changes after the collision because of conservation of momentum.

Although the bowling ball and bowling pins bounce off each other and move in different directions after a collision, momentum is neither gained nor lost.

Conservation of Momentum and Newton's Third Law

Conservation of momentum can be explained by Newton's third law of motion. In the example of the billiard ball, the cue ball hit the billiard ball with a certain amount of force. This force was the action force. The reaction force was the equal but opposite force exerted by the billiard ball on the cue ball. The action force made the billiard ball start moving, and the reaction force made the cue ball stop moving, as shown in **Figure 4.** Because the action and reaction forces are equal and opposite, momentum is neither gained nor lost.

Action force   Reaction force

Figure 4 *The action force makes the billiard ball begin moving, and the reaction force stops the cue ball's motion.*

SECTION Review

Summary

● Momentum is a property of moving objects.

● Momentum is calculated by multiplying the mass of an object by the object's velocity.

● When two or more objects collide, momentum may be transferred, but the total amount of momentum does not change. This is the law of conservation of momentum.

Using Key Terms

1. Use the following term in a sentence: *momentum.*

Understanding Key Ideas

2. Which of the following has the smallest amount of momentum?
   a. a loaded truck driven at highway speeds
   b. a track athlete running a race
   c. a baby crawling on the floor
   d. a jet airplane being towed toward an airport

3. Explain the law of conservation of momentum.

4. How is Newton's third law of motion related to the law of conservation of momentum?

Math Skills

5. Calculate the momentum of a 2.5 kg puppy that is running with a velocity of 4.8 m/s south.

Critical Thinking

6. **Applying Concepts** A car and a train are traveling with the same velocity. Do the two objects have the same momentum? Explain your answer.

7. **Analyzing Ideas** When you catch a softball, your hand and glove move in the same direction that the ball is moving. Analyze the motion of your hand and glove in terms of momentum.

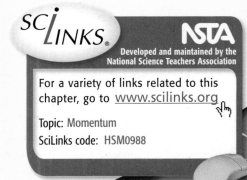

SCILINKS®

NSTA
Developed and maintained by the
National Science Teachers Association

For a variety of links related to this chapter, go to www.scilinks.org

Topic: Momentum
SciLinks code: HSM0988

Skills Practice Lab

OBJECTIVES

Observe several effects of inertia.

Describe the motion of objects in terms of inertia.

MATERIALS

Station 1
• egg, hard-boiled
• egg, raw

Station 2
• card, index
• coin
• cup

Station 3
• mass, hanging, 1 kg
• meterstick
• scissors
• thread, spool

SAFETY

Inertia-Rama!

Inertia is a property of all matter, from small particles of dust to enormous planets and stars. In this lab, you will investigate the inertia of various shapes and kinds of matter. Keep in mind that each investigation requires you to either overcome or use the object's inertia.

Station 1: Magic Eggs

Procedure

1. There are two eggs at this station—one is hard-boiled (solid all the way through) and the other is raw (liquid inside). The masses of the two eggs are about the same. The eggs are not marked. You should not be able to tell them apart by their appearance. Without breaking them open, how can you tell which egg is raw and which egg is hard-boiled?

2. Before you do anything to either egg, make some predictions. Will there be any difference in the way the two eggs spin? Which egg will be the easier to stop?

3. First, spin one egg. Then, place your finger on it gently to make it stop spinning. Record your observations.

4. Repeat step 3 with the second egg.

5. Compare your predictions with your observations. (Repeat steps 3 and 4 if necessary.)

6. Which egg is hard-boiled and which one is raw? Explain.

Analyze the Results

1. **Explaining Events** Explain why the eggs behave differently when you spin them even though they should have the same inertia. (Hint: Think about what happens to the liquid inside the raw egg.)

Draw Conclusions

2. **Drawing Conclusions** Explain why the eggs react differently when you try to stop them.

Station 2: Coin in a Cup

Procedure

1. At this station, you will find a coin, an index card, and a cup. Place the card over the cup. Then, place the coin on the card over the center of the cup, as shown below.

2. Write down a method for getting the coin into the cup without touching the coin and without lifting the card.

3. Try your method. If it doesn't work, try again until you find a method that does work.

Analyze the Results

1. **Describing Events** Use Newton's first law of motion to explain why the coin falls into the cup if you remove the card quickly.

Draw Conclusions

2. **Defending Conclusions** Explain why pulling on the card slowly will not work even though the coin has inertia. (Hint: Friction is a force.)

Station 3: The Magic Thread

Procedure

1. At this station, you will find a spool of thread and a mass hanging from a strong string. Cut a piece of thread about 40 cm long. Tie the thread around the bottom of the mass, as shown at right.

2. Pull gently on the end of the thread. Observe what happens, and record your observations.

3. Stop the mass from moving. Now hold the end of the thread so that there is a lot of slack between your fingers and the mass.

4. Give the thread a quick, hard pull. You should observe a very different event. Record your observations. Throw away the thread.

Analyze the Results

1. **Analyzing Results** Use Newton's first law of motion to explain why the result of a gentle pull is different from the result of a hard pull.

Draw Conclusions

2. **Applying Conclusions** Both moving and nonmoving objects have inertia. Explain why throwing a bowling ball and catching a thrown bowling ball are hard.

3. **Drawing Conclusions** Why is it harder to run with a backpack full of books than to run with an empty backpack?

Chapter Review

USING KEY TERMS

Complete each of the following sentences by choosing the correct term from the word bank.

free fall   projectile motion
inertia   terminal velocity
momentum

1 An object in motion has ___, so it tends to stay in motion.

2 An object is falling at its ___ if it falls at a constant velocity.

3 ___ is the path that a thrown object follows.

4 ___ is a property of moving objects that depends on mass and velocity.

5 ___ occurs only when air resistance does not affect the motion of a falling object.

UNDERSTANDING KEY IDEAS

Multiple Choice

6 When a soccer ball is kicked, the action and reaction forces do not cancel each other out because

  a. the forces are not equal in size.

  b. the forces act on different objects.

  c. the forces act at different times.

  d. All of the above

7 An object is in projectile motion if it

  a. is thrown with a horizontal push.

  b. is accelerated downward by gravity.

  c. does not accelerate horizontally.

  d. All of the above

8 Newton's first law of motion applies to

  a. moving objects.

  b. objects that are not moving.

  c. objects that are accelerating.

  d. Both (a) and (b)

9 To accelerate two objects at the same rate, the force used to push the object that has more mass should be

  a. smaller than the force used to push the object that has less mass.

  b. larger than the force used to push the object that has less mass.

  c. the same as the force used to push the object that has less mass.

  d. equal to the object's weight.

10 A golf ball and a bowling ball are moving at the same velocity. Which of the two has more momentum?

  a. The golf ball has more momentum because it has less mass.

  b. The bowling ball has more momentum because it has more mass.

  c. They have the same momentum because they have the same velocity.

  d. There is not enough information to determine the answer.

Short Answer

11 Give an example of an object that is in free fall.

12 Describe how gravity and air resistance are related to an object's terminal velocity.

13 Why can friction make observing Newton's first law of motion difficult?

Math Skills

14 A 12 kg rock falls from rest off a cliff and hits the ground in 1.5 s.

a. Without considering air resistance, what is the rock's velocity just before it hits the ground?

b. What is the rock's momentum just before it hits the ground?

CRITICAL THINKING

15 Concept Mapping Use the following terms to create a concept map: *gravity, free fall, terminal velocity, projectile motion,* and *air resistance.*

16 Identifying Relationships During a space shuttle launch, about 830,000 kg of fuel is burned in 8 min. The fuel provides the shuttle with a constant thrust, or forward force. How does Newton's second law of motion explain why the shuttle's acceleration increases as the fuel is burned?

17 Analyzing Processes When using a hammer to drive a nail into wood, you have to swing the hammer through the air with a certain velocity. Because the hammer has both mass and velocity, it has momentum. Describe what happens to the hammer's momentum after the hammer hits the nail.

18 Applying Concepts Suppose you are standing on a skateboard or on in-line skates and you toss a backpack full of heavy books toward your friend. What do you think will happen to you? Explain your answer in terms of Newton's third law of motion.

INTERPRETING GRAPHICS

19 The picture below shows a common desk toy. If you pull one ball up and release it, it hits the balls at the bottom and comes to a stop. In the same instant, the ball on the other side swings up and repeats the cycle. How does conservation of momentum explain how this toy works?

Standardized Test Preparation

Read each of the passages below. Then, answer the questions that follow each passage.

Passage 1   How do astronauts prepare for trips in the space shuttle? One method is to use simulations on Earth that mimic the conditions in space. For example, underwater training lets astronauts experience reduced gravity. They can also ride on NASA's modified KC-135 airplane. NASA's KC-135 simulates how it feels to be in a space shuttle. How does this airplane work? It flies upward at a steep angle and then flies downward at a 45° angle. When the airplane flies downward, the effect of reduced gravity is produced. As the plane falls, the astronauts inside the plane can float like astronauts in the space shuttle do!

1. What is the purpose of this passage?

   A to explain how astronauts prepare for missions in space

   B to convince people to become astronauts

   C to show that space is similar to Earth

   D to describe what it feels like to float in space

2. What can you conclude about NASA's KC-135 from the passage?

   F NASA's KC-135 is just like other airplanes.

   G All astronauts train in NASA's KC-135.

   H NASA's KC-135 simulates the space shuttle by reducing the effects of gravity.

   I Being in NASA's KC-135 is not very much like being in the space shuttle.

3. Based on the passage, which of the following statements is a fact?

   A Astronauts always have to train underwater.

   B Flying in airplanes is similar to riding in the space shuttle.

   C People in NASA's KC-135 float at all times.

   D Astronauts use simulations to learn what reduced gravity is like.

Passage 2   There once was a game that could be played by as few as 5 or as many as 1,000 players. The game could be played on a small field for a few hours or on a huge tract of land for several days. The game was not just for fun—in fact, it was often used as a <u>substitute</u> for war. One of the few rules was that the players couldn't touch the ball with their hands—they had to use a special stick with webbing on one end. Would you believe that this game is the same as the game of lacrosse that is played today?

   Lacrosse is a game that was originally played by Native Americans. They called the game *baggataway*, which means "little brother of war." Although lacrosse has changed and is now played all over the world, it still requires special, webbed sticks.

1. What is the purpose of this passage?

   A to explain the importance of rules in lacrosse

   B to explain why sticks are used in lacrosse

   C to describe the history of lacrosse

   D to describe the rules of lacrosse

2. Based on the passage, what does the word *substitute* mean?

   F something that occurs before war

   G something that is needed to play lacrosse

   H something that is of Native American origin

   I something that takes the place of something else

Read each question below, and choose the best answer.

1. Which of the following images shows an object with no momentum that is about to be set in motion by an unbalanced force?

A

B

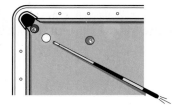

C

D

2. During a laboratory experiment, liquid was collected in a graduated cylinder. What is the volume of the liquid?

F 30 mL
G 35 mL
H 40 mL
I 45 mL

Read each question below, and choose the best answer.

1. The table below shows the accelerations produced by different forces for a 5 kg mass. Assuming that the pattern continues, use this data to predict what acceleration would be produced by a 100 N force.

Force	Acceleration
25 N	5 m/s^2
50 N	10 m/s^2
75 N	15 m/s^2

A 10 m/s^2
B 20 m/s^2
C 30 m/s^2
D 100 m/s^2

2. The average radius of the moon is 1.74×10^6 m. What is another way to express the radius of the moon?

F 0.00000174 m
G 0.000174 m
H 174,000 m
I 1,740,000 m

3. The half price bookstore is selling 4 paperback books for a total of $5.75. What would the price of 20 paperback books be?

A $23.00
B $24.75
C $28.75
D $51.75

4. A 75 kg speed skater is moving with a velocity of 16 m/s east. What is the speed skater's momentum? (Momentum is calculated with the equation: *momentum = mass × velocity*.)

F 91 kg•m/s
G 91 kg•m/s east
H 1,200 kg•m/s east
I 1,200 kg•m/s^2 east

Standardized Test Preparation

Science in Action

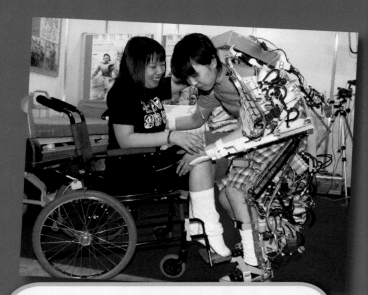

Scientific Discoveries

The Millennium Bridge

You may have heard the children's song, "London Bridge is falling down . . .". London Bridge never fell. But some people who walked on the Millennium Bridge thought that it might fall instead! The Millennium Bridge is a pedestrian bridge in London, England. The bridge opened on June 10, 2000, and more than 80,000 people crossed it that day. Immediately, people noticed something wrong—the bridge was swaying! The bridge was closed after two days so that engineers could determine what was wrong. After much research, the engineers learned that the force of the footsteps of the people crossing the bridge caused the bridge to sway.

Language Arts ACTiViTY

WRITING SKILL Imagine that you were in London on June 10, 2000 and walked across the Millennium Bridge. Write a one-page story about what you think it was like on the bridge that day.

Science, Technology, and Society

Power Suit for Lifting Patients

Imagine visiting a hospital and seeing someone who looked half human and half robot. No, it isn't a scene from a science fiction movie—it is a new invention that may some day help nurses lift patients easily. The invention, called a power suit, is a metal framework that a nurse would wear on his or her back. The suit calculates how much force a nurse needs to lift a patient, and then the robotic joints on the suit help the nurse exert the right amount of force. The suit will also help nurses avoid injuring their backs.

Math ACTiViTY

The pound (symbol £) is the currency in England. The inventor of the suit thinks that it will be sold for £1200. How much will the suit cost in dollars if $1 is equal to £0.60?

Steve Okamoto

Roller Coaster Designer Roller coasters have fascinated Steve Okamoto ever since his first ride on one. "I remember going to Disneyland as a kid. My mother was always upset with me because I kept looking over the sides of the rides, trying to figure out how they worked," he says. To satisfy his curiosity, Okamoto became a mechanical engineer. Today he uses his scientific knowledge to design and build machines, systems, and buildings. But his specialty is roller coasters.

Roller coasters really do coast along the track. A motor pulls the cars up a high hill to start the ride. After that, the cars are powered by only gravity. Designing a successful roller coaster is not a simple task. Okamoto has to calculate the cars' speed and acceleration on each part of the track. He must also consider the safety of the ride and the strength of the structure that supports the track.

Social Studies ACTiViTY

Research the history of roller coasters to learn how roller coaster design has changed over time. Make a poster to summarize your research.

To learn more about these Science in Action topics, visit **go.hrw.com** and type in the keyword **HP5FORF.**

Current Science

Check out Current Science® articles related to this chapter by visiting go.hrw.com. Just type in the keyword **HP5CS06.**

Forces
in Fluids

SECTION **1** Fluids and Pressure . . . 180

SECTION **2** Buoyant Force 186

SECTION **3** Fluids and Motion 192

Chapter Lab 198
Chapter Review 200
Standardized Test Preparation 202
Science in Action 204

About the PHOTO

As you race downhill on your bicycle, the air around you pushes on your body and slows you down. "What a drag!" you say. Well, actually, it is a drag. When designing bicycle gear and clothing, manufacturers consider more than just looks and comfort. They also try to decrease drag, a fluid force that opposes motion. This photo shows cyclists riding their bikes in a wind tunnel in a study of how a fluid—air—affects their ride.

PRE-READING ACTIVITY

FOLDNOTES **Booklet** Before you read the chapter, create the FoldNote entitled "Booklet" described in the **Study Skills** section of the Appendix. Label each page of the booklet with a main idea from the chapter. As you read the chapter, write what you learn about each main idea on the appropriate page of the booklet.

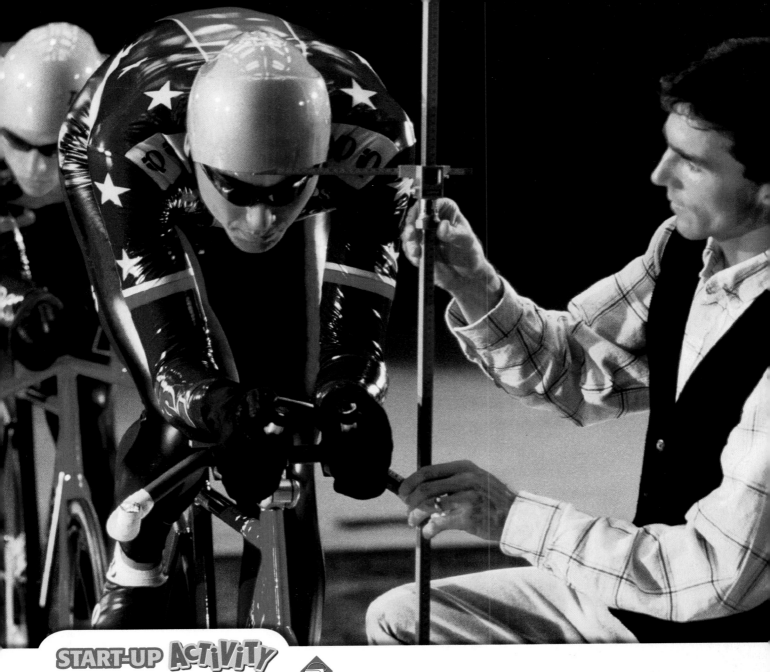

Taking Flight

In this activity, you will build a model airplane to learn how wing size affects flight.

Procedure

1. Fold a **sheet of paper** in half lengthwise. Then, open it. Fold the top corners toward the center crease. Keep the corners folded down, and fold the entire sheet in half along the center crease.

2. With the plane on its side, fold the top front edge down so that it meets the bottom edge. Fold the top edge down again so that it meets the bottom edge. Turn the plane over, and repeat.

3. Raise the wings so that they are perpendicular to the body.

4. Point the plane slightly upward, and gently throw it. Repeat several times. Describe what you see.

5. Make the wings smaller by folding them one more time. Gently throw the plane. Repeat several times. Describe what you see.

6. Using the smaller wings, try to achieve the same flight path you saw when the wings were bigger.

Analysis

1. What happened to the plane's flight when you reduced the size of its wings? What did you have to do to achieve the same flight path as when the wings were bigger?

2. What gave your plane its forward motion?

Fluids and Pressure

What does a dolphin have in common with a sea gull? What does a dog have in common with a fly? What do you have in common with all these living things?

One answer to these questions is that you and all these other living things spend a lifetime moving through fluids. A **fluid** is any material that can flow and that takes the shape of its container. Fluids include liquids and gases. Fluids can flow because the particles in fluids move easily past each other.

Fluids Exert Pressure

You probably have heard the terms *air pressure* and *water pressure*. Air and water are fluids. All fluids exert pressure. So, what is pressure? Think about this example. When you pump up a bicycle tire, you push air into the tire. And like all matter, air is made of tiny particles that are constantly moving.

Look at **Figure 1.** Inside the tire, the air particles collide with each other and with the walls of the tire. Together, these collisions create a force on the tire. The amount of force exerted on a given area is **pressure.**

Calculating Pressure

Pressure can be calculated by using the following equation:

$$pressure = \frac{force}{area}$$

The SI unit for pressure is the **pascal.** One pascal (1 Pa) is the force of one newton exerted over an area of one square meter (1 N/m²).

READING WARM-UP

Objectives
- Describe how fluids exert pressure.
- Analyze how atmospheric pressure varies with depth.
- Explain how depth and density affect water pressure.
- Give examples of fluids flowing from high to low pressure.

Terms to Learn
fluid
pressure
pascal
atmospheric pressure

READING STRATEGY

Brainstorming The key idea of this section is pressure. Brainstorm words and phrases related to pressure.

fluid a nonsolid state of matter in which the atoms or molecules are free to move past each other, as in a gas or liquid

pressure the amount of force exerted per unit area of a surface

pascal the SI unit of pressure (symbol, Pa)

atmospheric pressure the pressure caused by the weight of the atmosphere

Figure 1 *The force of the air particles hitting the inner surface of the tire creates pressure, which keeps the tire inflated.*

Pressure, Force, and Area What is the pressure exerted by a book that has an area of 0.2 m² and a weight of 10 N?

Step 1: Write the equation for pressure.

$$pressure = \frac{force}{area}$$

Step 2: Replace *force* and *area* with the values given, and solve. (Hint: Weight is a measure of gravitational force.)

$$pressure = \frac{10 \text{ N}}{0.2 \text{ m}^2} = 50 \text{ N/m}^2 = 50 \text{ Pa}$$

The equation for pressure can be rearranged to find force or area, as shown below.

$force = pressure \times area$ *(Rearrange by multiplying by area.)*

$area = \dfrac{force}{pressure}$ *(Rearrange by multiplying by area and then dividing by pressure.)*

Now It's Your Turn

1. Find the pressure exerted by a 3,000 N crate that has an area of 2 m².
2. Find the weight of a rock that has an area of 10 m² and that exerts a pressure of 250 Pa.

Pressure and Bubbles

When you blow a soap bubble, you blow in only one direction. So, why does the bubble get rounder instead of longer as you blow? The shape of the bubble partly depends on an important property of fluids: Fluids exert pressure evenly in all directions. The air you blow into the bubble exerts pressure evenly in all directions. So, the bubble expands in all directions to create a sphere.

Atmospheric Pressure

The *atmosphere* is the layer of nitrogen, oxygen, and other gases that surrounds Earth. Earth's atmosphere is held in place by gravity, which pulls the gases toward Earth. The pressure caused by the weight of the atmosphere is called **atmospheric pressure.**

Atmospheric pressure is exerted on everything on Earth, including you. At sea level, the atmosphere exerts a pressure of about 101,300 N on every square meter, or 101,300 Pa. So, there is a weight of about 10 N (about 2 lbs) on every square centimeter of your body. Why don't you feel this crushing pressure? Like the air inside a balloon, the fluids inside your body exert pressure. **Figure 2** can help you understand why you don't feel the pressure.

✓Reading Check Name two gases in the atmosphere. *(See the Appendix for answers to Reading Checks.)*

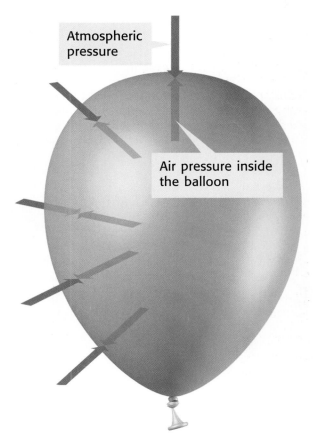

Atmospheric pressure

Air pressure inside the balloon

Figure 2 *The air inside a balloon exerts pressure that keeps the balloon inflated against atmospheric pressure. Similarly, fluid inside your body exerts pressure that works against atmospheric pressure.*

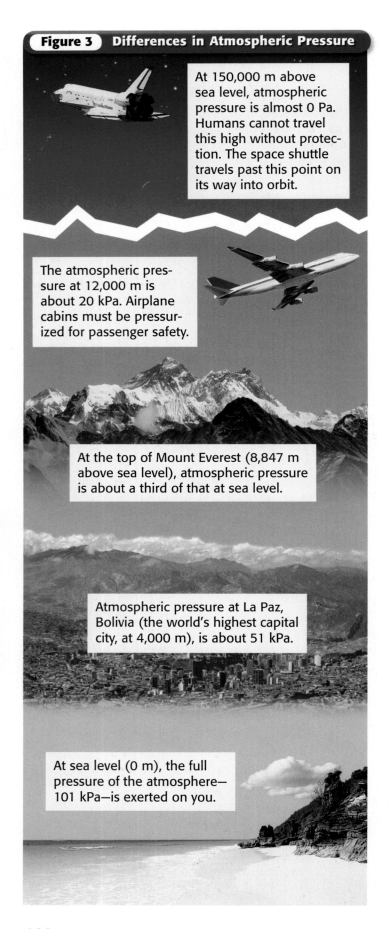

Figure 3 Differences in Atmospheric Pressure

At 150,000 m above sea level, atmospheric pressure is almost 0 Pa. Humans cannot travel this high without protection. The space shuttle travels past this point on its way into orbit.

The atmospheric pressure at 12,000 m is about 20 kPa. Airplane cabins must be pressurized for passenger safety.

At the top of Mount Everest (8,847 m above sea level), atmospheric pressure is about a third of that at sea level.

Atmospheric pressure at La Paz, Bolivia (the world's highest capital city, at 4,000 m), is about 51 kPa.

At sea level (0 m), the full pressure of the atmosphere—101 kPa—is exerted on you.

Variation of Atmospheric Pressure

The atmosphere stretches about 150 km above Earth's surface. However, about 80% of the atmosphere's gases are found within 10 km of Earth's surface. At the top of the atmosphere, pressure is almost nonexistent. The pressure is close to 0 Pa because the gas particles are far apart and rarely collide. Mount Everest in south-central Asia is the highest point on Earth. At the top of Mount Everest, atmospheric pressure is about 33,000 Pa, or 33 kilopascals (33 kPa). (Remember that the prefix *kilo-* means 1,000. So, 1 kPa is equal to 1,000 Pa.) At sea level, atmospheric pressure is about 101 kPa.

Atmospheric Pressure and Depth

Take a look at **Figure 3.** Notice how atmospheric pressure changes as you travel through the atmosphere. The further down through the atmosphere you go, the greater the pressure is. In other words, the pressure increases as the atmosphere gets "deeper." An important point to remember about fluids is that pressure varies depending on depth. At lower levels of the atmosphere, there is more fluid above that is being pulled by Earth's gravitational force. So, there is more pressure at lower levels of the atmosphere.

✓ **Reading Check** Describe how pressure changes with depth.

Pressure Changes and Your Body

So, what happens to your body when atmospheric pressure changes? If you travel to higher or lower points in the atmosphere, the fluids in your body have to adjust to maintain equal pressure. You may have experienced this adjustment if your ears have "popped" when you were in a plane taking off or in a car traveling down a steep mountain road. The "pop" happens because of pressure changes in pockets of air behind your eardrums.

Water Pressure

Water is a fluid. So, it exerts pressure like the atmosphere does. Water pressure also increases as depth increases, as shown in **Figure 4.** The deeper a diver goes in the water, the greater the pressure is. The pressure increases because more water above the diver is being pulled by Earth's gravitational force. In addition, the atmosphere presses down on the water, so the total pressure on the diver includes water pressure and atmospheric pressure.

Water Pressure and Depth

Like atmospheric pressure, water pressure depends on depth. Water pressure does not depend on the total amount of fluid present. A swimmer would feel the same pressure swimming at 3 m below the surface of a small pond and at 3 m below the surface of an ocean. Even though there is more water in the ocean than in the pond, the pressure on the swimmer in the pond would be the same as the pressure on the swimmer in the ocean.

Density Making a Difference

Water is about 1,000 times more dense than air. *Density* is the amount of matter in a given volume, or mass per unit volume. Because water is more dense than air, a certain volume of water has more mass—and weighs more—than the same volume of air. So, water exerts more pressure than air.

For example, if you climb a 10 m tree, the decrease in atmospheric pressure is too small to notice. But if you dive 10 m underwater, the pressure on you increases to 201 kPa, which is almost twice the atmospheric pressure at the surface!

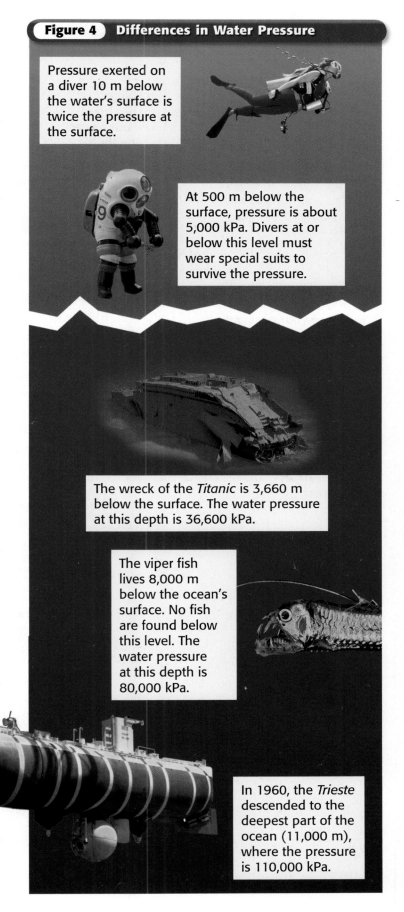

Figure 4 Differences in Water Pressure

Pressure exerted on a diver 10 m below the water's surface is twice the pressure at the surface.

At 500 m below the surface, pressure is about 5,000 kPa. Divers at or below this level must wear special suits to survive the pressure.

The wreck of the *Titanic* is 3,660 m below the surface. The water pressure at this depth is 36,600 kPa.

The viper fish lives 8,000 m below the ocean's surface. No fish are found below this level. The water pressure at this depth is 80,000 kPa.

In 1960, the *Trieste* descended to the deepest part of the ocean (11,000 m), where the pressure is 110,000 kPa.

Blown Away

1. Lay an **empty plastic soda bottle** on its side.
2. Wad a **small piece of paper** (about 4 × 4 cm) into a ball.
3. Place the paper ball just inside the bottle's opening.
4. Blow straight into the opening.
5. Record your observations.
6. Explain your results in terms of high and low fluid pressures.

Pressure Differences and Fluid Flow

When you drink through a straw, you remove some of the air in the straw. Because there is less air inside the straw, the pressure in the straw is reduced. But the atmospheric pressure on the surface of the liquid remains the same. Thus, there is a difference between the pressure inside the straw and the pressure outside the straw. The outside pressure forces the liquid up the straw and into your mouth. So, just by drinking through a straw, you can observe an important property of fluids: Fluids flow from areas of high pressure to areas of low pressure.

Reading Check When drinking through a straw, how do you decrease the pressure inside the straw?

Pressure Differences and Breathing

Take a deep breath—fluid is flowing from high to low pressure! When you inhale, a muscle increases the space in your chest and gives your lungs room to expand. This expansion decreases the pressure in your lungs. The pressure in your lungs becomes lower than the air pressure outside your lungs. Air then flows into your lungs—from high to low pressure. This air carries oxygen that you need to live. **Figure 5** shows how exhaling also causes fluids to flow from high to low pressure. You can see a similar flow of fluid when you open a carbonated beverage or squeeze toothpaste onto your toothbrush.

Figure 5 Exhaling, Pressure, and Fluid Flow

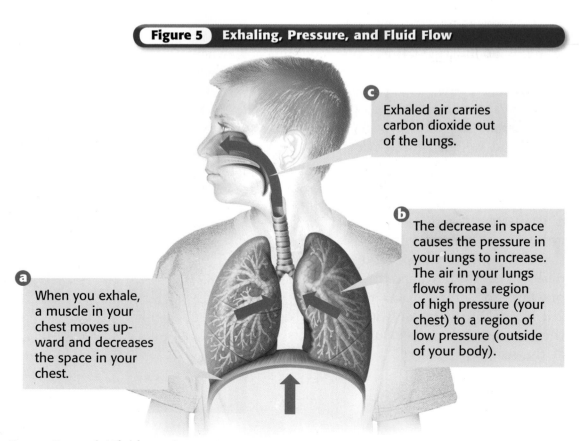

c Exhaled air carries carbon dioxide out of the lungs.

b The decrease in space causes the pressure in your lungs to increase. The air in your lungs flows from a region of high pressure (your chest) to a region of low pressure (outside of your body).

a When you exhale, a muscle in your chest moves upward and decreases the space in your chest.

Pressure Differences and Tornadoes

Look at the tornado in **Figure 6.** Some of the damaging winds caused by tornadoes are the result of pressure differences. The air pressure inside a tornado is very low. Because the air pressure outside of the tornado is higher than the pressure inside, air rushes into the tornado. The rushing air causes the tornado to be like a giant vacuum cleaner—objects are pushed into the tornado. The winds created are usually very strong and affect the area around the tornado. So, objects, such as trees and buildings, can be severely damaged by wind even if they are not in the direct path of a tornado.

Figure 6 *Tornadoes are like giant vacuum cleaners because of pressure differences.*

SECTION Review

Summary

- A fluid is any material that flows and takes the shape of its container.
- Pressure is force exerted on a given area.
- Moving particles of matter create pressure by colliding with one another and with the walls of their container.
- The pressure caused by the weight of the atmosphere is called *atmospheric pressure*.
- Fluid pressure increases as depth increases.
- As depth increases, water pressure increases faster than atmospheric pressure does because water is denser than air.
- Fluids flow from areas of high pressure to areas of low pressure.

Using Key Terms

1. In your own words, write a definition for each of the following terms: *fluid* and *atmospheric pressure*.

2. Use the following terms in the same sentence: *pressure* and *pascal*.

Understanding Key Ideas

3. Which of the following statements about fluids is true?
   a. Fluids rarely take the shape of their container.
   b. Fluids include liquids and gases.
   c. Fluids flow from low pressure to high pressure.
   d. Fluids exert the most pressure in the downward direction.

4. How do fluids exert pressure on a container?

5. Why are you not crushed by atmospheric pressure?

6. Explain why atmospheric pressure changes as depth changes.

7. Give three examples of fluids flowing from high pressure to low pressure in everyday life.

Math Skills

8. The water in a glass has a weight of 2.4 N. The bottom of the glass has an area of 0.012 m^2. What is the pressure exerted by the water on the bottom of the glass?

Critical Thinking

9. **Identifying Relationships** Mercury is a liquid that has a density of 13.5 g/mL. Water has a density of 1.0 g/mL. Equal volumes of mercury and water are in identical containers. Explain why the pressures exerted on the bottoms of the containers are different.

10. **Making Inferences** Why do airplanes need to be pressurized for passenger safety when flying high in the atmosphere?

Buoyant Force

Why does an ice cube float on water? Why doesn't it sink to the bottom of your glass?

Imagine that you use a straw to push an ice cube under water. Then, you release the cube. A force pushes the ice back to the water's surface. The force, called **buoyant force** (BOY uhnt FAWRS), is the upward force that fluids exert on all matter.

Buoyant Force and Fluid Pressure

Look at **Figure 1.** Water exerts fluid pressure on all sides of an object. The pressure exerted horizontally on one side of the object is equal to the pressure exerted on the opposite side. These equal pressures cancel one another. So, the only fluid pressures affecting the net force on the object are at the top and at the bottom. Pressure increases as depth increases. So, the pressure at the bottom of the object is greater than the pressure at the top. The water exerts a net upward force on the object. This upward force is buoyant force.

Determining Buoyant Force

Archimedes (AHR kuh MEE deez), a Greek mathematician who lived in the third century BCE, discovered how to determine buoyant force. **Archimedes' principle** states that the buoyant force on an object in a fluid is an upward force equal to the weight of the fluid that the object takes the place of, or displaces. Suppose the object in **Figure 1** displaces 250 mL of water. The weight of that volume of displaced water is about 2.5 N. So, the buoyant force on the object is 2.5 N. Notice that only the weight of the displaced fluid determines the buoyant force on an object. The weight of the object does not affect buoyant force.

buoyant force the upward force that keeps an object immersed in or floating on a liquid

Archimedes' principle the principle that states that the buoyant force on an object in a fluid is an upward force equal to the weight of the volume of fluid that the object displaces

Figure 1 *There is more pressure at the bottom of an object because pressure increases with depth. This results in an upward buoyant force on the object.*

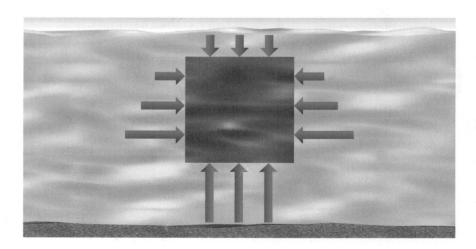

Weight Versus Buoyant Force

An object in a fluid will sink if its weight is greater than the buoyant force (the weight of the fluid it displaces). An object floats only when the buoyant force on the object is equal to the object's weight.

Sinking

The rock in **Figure 2** weighs 75 N. It displaces 5 L of water. Archimedes' principle says that the buoyant force is equal to the weight of the displaced water—about 50 N. The rock's weight is greater than the buoyant force. So, the rock sinks.

Floating

The fish in **Figure 2** weighs 12 N. It displaces a volume of water that weighs 12 N. Because the fish's weight is equal to the buoyant force, the fish floats in the water. In fact, the fish is suspended in the water as it floats. Now, look at the duck. The duck does not sink. So, the buoyant force on the duck must be equal to the duck's weight. But the duck isn't all the way underwater! Only the duck's feet, legs, and stomach have to be underwater to displace 9 N of water, which is equal to the duck's weight. So, the duck floats on the surface of the water.

Buoying Up

If the duck dove underwater, it would displace more than 9 N of water. So, the buoyant force on the duck would be greater than the duck's weight. When the buoyant force on an object is greater than the object's weight, the object is *buoyed up* (pushed up) in water. An object is buoyed up until the part of the object underwater displaces an amount of water that equals the object's entire weight. Thus, an ice cube pops to the surface when it is pushed to the bottom of a glass of water.

✓ Reading Check What causes an object to buoy up? (*See the Appendix for answers to Reading Checks.*)

Figure 2 *Will an object sink or float? That depends on whether the buoyant force is less than or equal to the object's weight.*

Weight = 12 N
Buoyant force = 12 N
Fish floats and is suspended in the water.

Weight = 9 N
Buoyant force = 9 N
Duck floats on the surface.

Weight = 75 N
Buoyant force = 50 N
Rock sinks.

Floating, Sinking, and Density

Think again about the rock in the lake. The rock displaces 5 L of water. But volumes of solids are measured in cubic centimeters (cm³). Because 1 mL is equal to 1 cm³, the volume of the rock is 5,000 cm³. But 5,000 cm³ of rock weighs more than an equal volume of water. So, the rock sinks.

Because mass is proportional to weight, you can say that the rock has more mass per volume than water has. Mass per unit volume is density. The rock sinks because it is more dense than water is. The duck floats because it is less dense than water is. The density of the fish is equal to the density of the water.

More Dense Than Air

Why does an ice cube float on water but not in air? An ice cube floats on water because it is less dense than water. But most substances are *more* dense than air. So, there are few substances that float in air. The ice cube is more dense than air, so the ice cube doesn't float in air.

Less Dense Than Air

One substance that is less dense than air is helium, a gas. In fact, helium has one-seventh the density of air under normal conditions. A given volume of helium displaces an equal volume of air that is much heavier than itself. So, helium floats in air. Because helium floats in air, it is used in parade balloons, such as the one shown in **Figure 3.**

✓ **Reading Check** Name a substance that is less dense than air.

Figure 3 *Helium in a balloon floats in air for the same reason an ice cube floats on water—helium is less dense than the surrounding fluid.*

MATH FOCUS

Finding Density Find the density of a rock that has a mass of 10 g and a volume of 2 cm³.

Step 1: Write the equation for density. Density is calculated by using this equation:

$$density = \frac{mass}{volume}$$

Step 2: Replace *mass* and *volume* with the values in the problem, and solve.

$$density = \frac{10 \text{ g}}{2 \text{ cm}^3} = 5 \text{ g/cm}^3$$

Now It's Your Turn

1. What is the density of a 20 cm³ object that has a mass of 25 g?
2. A 546 g fish displaces 420 mL of water. What is the density of the fish? (Note: 1 mL = 1 cm³)
3. A beaker holds 50 mL of a slimy green liquid. The mass of the liquid is 163 g. What is the density of the liquid?

Changing Overall Density

Steel is almost 8 times denser than water. And yet huge steel ships cruise the oceans with ease. But hold on! You just learned that substances that are more dense than water will sink in water. So, how does a steel ship float?

Changing Shape

The secret of how a ship floats is in the shape of the ship. What if a ship were just a big block of steel, as shown in **Figure 4**? If you put that block into water, the block would sink because it is more dense than water. So, ships are built with a hollow shape. The amount of steel in the ship is the same as in the block. But the hollow shape increases the volume of the ship. Remember that density is mass per unit volume. So, an increase in the ship's volume leads to a decrease in its density. Thus, ships made of steel float because their *overall density* is less than the density of water.

Most ships are built to displace more water than is necessary for the ship to float. Ships are made this way so that they won't sink when people and cargo are loaded on the ship.

CONNECTION TO Geology

Floating Rocks The rock that makes up Earth's continents is about 15% less dense than the molten (melted) mantle rock below it. Because of this difference in density, the continents are floating on the mantle. Research the structure of Earth, and make a poster that shows Earth's interior layers.

ACTIVITY

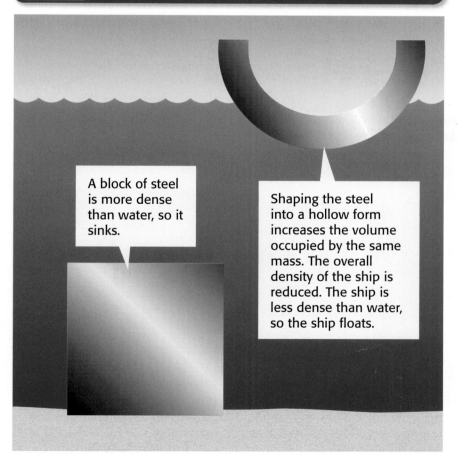

Figure 4 **Shape and Overall Density**

A block of steel is more dense than water, so it sinks.

Shaping the steel into a hollow form increases the volume occupied by the same mass. The overall density of the ship is reduced. The ship is less dense than water, so the ship floats.

INTERNET ACTIVITY

For another activity related to this chapter, go to **go.hrw.com** and type in the keyword **HP5FLUW**.

Ship Shape

1. Roll a **piece of clay** into a ball the size of a golf ball, and drop it into a **container of water.** Record your observations.

2. With your hands, flatten the ball of clay until it is a bit thinner than your little finger, and press it into the shape of a bowl or canoe.

3. Place the clay boat gently in the water. How does the change of shape affect the buoyant force on the clay? How is that change related to the overall density of the clay boat? Record your answers.

Changing Mass

A submarine is a special kind of ship that can travel both on the surface of the water and underwater. Submarines have *ballast tanks* that can be opened to allow sea water to flow in. As water is added, the submarine's mass increases, but its volume stays the same. The submarine's overall density increases so that it can dive under the surface. Crew members control the amount of water taken in. In this way, they control how dense the submarine is and how deep it dives. Compressed air is used to blow the water out of the tanks so that the submarine can rise. Study **Figure 5** to learn how ballast tanks work.

✓ Reading Check How do crew members control the density of a submarine?

Figure 5 Controlling Density Using Ballast Tanks

When a submarine is floating on the ocean's surface, its ballast tanks are filled mostly with air.

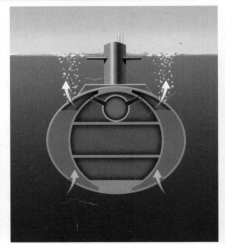

Vent holes on the ballast tanks are opened to allow the submarine to dive. Air escapes as the tanks fill with water.

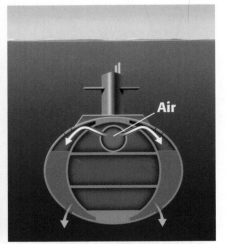

Vent holes are closed, and compressed air is pumped into the ballast tanks to force the water out, so the submarine rises.

Changing Volume

Like a submarine, some fish adjust their overall density to stay at a certain depth in the water. Most bony fishes have an organ called a *swim bladder,* shown in **Figure 6.** This swim bladder is filled with gases produced in a fish's blood. The inflated swim bladder increases the fish's volume and thereby decreases the fish's overall density, which keeps the fish from sinking in the water. The fish's nervous system controls the amount of gas in the bladder. Some fish, such as sharks, do not have a swim bladder. These fish must swim constantly to keep from sinking.

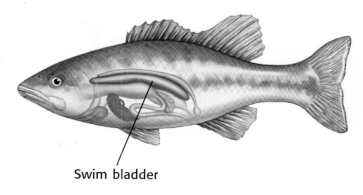

Swim bladder

Figure 6 *Most bony fishes have an organ called a* swim bladder *that allows them to adjust their overall density.*

SECTION Review

Summary

- All fluids exert an upward force called *buoyant force.*
- Buoyant force is caused by differences in fluid pressure.
- Archimedes' principle states that the buoyant force on an object is equal to the weight of the fluid displaced by the object.
- Any object that is more dense than the surrounding fluid will sink. An object that is less dense than the surrounding fluid will float.
- The overall density of an object can be changed by changing the object's shape, mass, or volume.

Using Key Terms

1. Use the following terms in the same sentence: *buoyant force* and *Archimedes' principle.*

Understanding Key Ideas

2. Which of the following changes increases the overall density of the object?

   a. A block of iron is formed into a hollow shape.

   b. A submarine fills its ballast tanks with water.

   c. A submarine fills its ballast tanks with air.

   d. A fish increases the amount of gas in its swim bladder.

3. Explain how differences in fluid pressure create buoyant force on an object.

4. How does an object's density determine whether the object will sink or float in water?

5. Name three methods that can be used to change the overall density of an object.

Math Skills

6. What is the density of an object that has a mass of 184 g and a volume of 50 cm^3?

Critical Thinking

7. **Applying Concepts** An object weighs 20 N. It displaces a volume of water that weighs 15 N.

   a. What is the buoyant force on the object?

   b. Will this object float or sink? Explain your answer.

8. **Predicting Consequences** Iron has a density of 7.9 g/cm^3. Mercury is a liquid that has a density of 13.5 g/cm^3. Will iron float or sink in mercury? Explain your answer.

9. **Evaluating Hypotheses** Imagine that your brother tells you that all heavy objects sink in water. Explain why you agree or disagree with his statement.

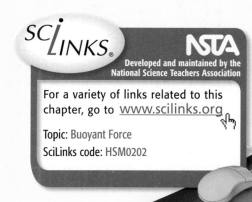

SCILINKS.

NSTA

Developed and maintained by the National Science Teachers Association

For a variety of links related to this chapter, go to www.scilinks.org

Topic: Buoyant Force
SciLinks code: HSM0202

Fluids and Motion

Hold two sheets of paper so that the edges are hanging in front of your face about 4 cm apart. The flat faces of the paper should be parallel to each other. Now, blow as hard as you can between the two sheets of paper.

What's going on? You can't separate the sheets by blowing between them. In fact, the sheets move closer together the harder you blow. You may be surprised that the explanation for this unusual occurrence also includes how wings help birds and planes fly and how pitchers throw curve balls.

Fluid Speed and Pressure

The strange reaction of the paper is caused by a property of moving fluids. This property was first described in the 18th century by Daniel Bernoulli (ber NOO lee), a Swiss mathematician. **Bernoulli's principle** states that as the speed of a moving fluid increases, the fluid's pressure decreases. In the case of the paper, air speed between the two sheets increased when you blew air between them. Because air speed increased, the pressure between the sheets decreased. Thus, the higher pressure on the outside of the sheets pushed them together.

Science in a Sink

Bernoulli's principle is at work in **Figure 1.** A table-tennis ball is attached to a string and swung into a stream of water. Instead of being pushed out of the water, the ball is held in the water. Why? The water is moving faster than the air around it, so the water has a lower pressure than the surrounding air. The higher air pressure pushes the ball into the area of lower pressure—the water stream. Try this at home to see for yourself!

Bernoulli's principle the principle that states that the pressure in a fluid decreases as the fluid's velocity increases

Figure 1 *This ball is pushed by the higher pressure of the air into an area of reduced pressure—the water stream.*

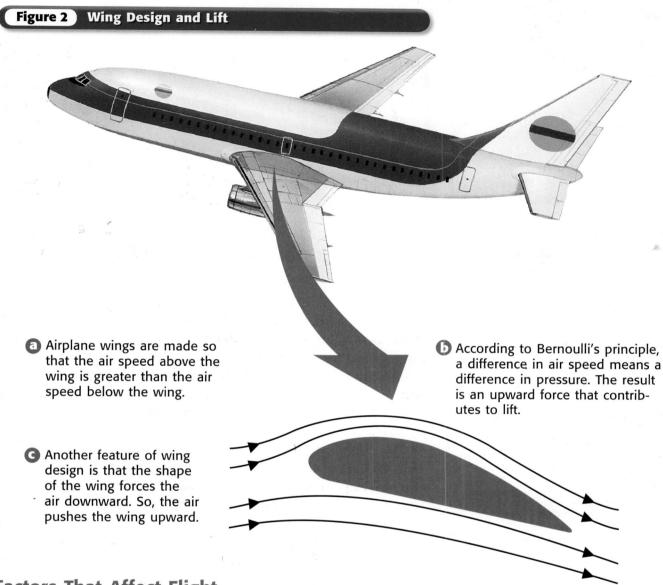

Figure 2 Wing Design and Lift

a Airplane wings are made so that the air speed above the wing is greater than the air speed below the wing.

b According to Bernoulli's principle, a difference in air speed means a difference in pressure. The result is an upward force that contributes to lift.

c Another feature of wing design is that the shape of the wing forces the air downward. So, the air pushes the wing upward.

Factors That Affect Flight

A common commercial airplane in the skies today is the Boeing 737 jet. Even without passengers, the plane weighs 350,000 N. How can something so big and heavy get off the ground and fly? Wing shape plays a role in helping these big planes—as well as smaller planes and birds—achieve flight, as shown in **Figure 2.**

According to Bernoulli's principle, the fast-moving air above the wing exerts less pressure than the slow-moving air below the wing. The greater pressure below the wing exerts an upward force. This upward force, known as **lift,** pushes the wings (and the rest of the airplane or bird) upward against the downward pull of gravity.

lift an upward force on an object that moves in a fluid

✓ **Reading Check** **What is lift?** (*See the Appendix for answers to Reading Checks.*)

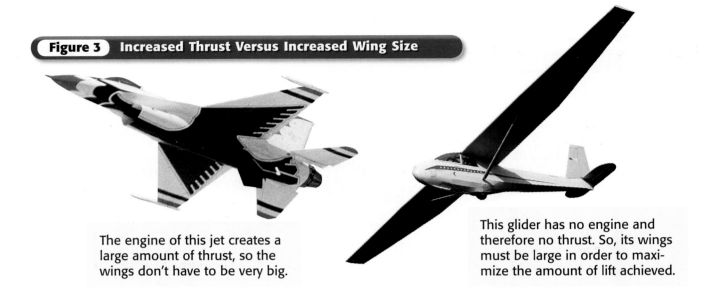

Figure 3 Increased Thrust Versus Increased Wing Size

The engine of this jet creates a large amount of thrust, so the wings don't have to be very big.

This glider has no engine and therefore no thrust. So, its wings must be large in order to maximize the amount of lift achieved.

Thrust and Lift

The amount of lift created by a plane's wing is determined partly by the speed at which air travels around the wing. The speed of a plane is determined mostly by its thrust. **Thrust** is the forward force produced by the plane's engine. In general, a plane with a large amount of thrust moves faster than a plane that has less thrust does. This faster speed means air travels around the wing at a higher speed, which increases lift.

thrust the pushing or pulling force exerted by the engine of an aircraft or rocket

Wing Size, Speed, and Lift

The amount of lift also depends partly on the size of a plane's wings. Look at the jet plane in **Figure 3.** This plane can fly with a relatively small wing size because its engine gives a large amount of thrust. This thrust pushes the plane through the sky at great speeds. So, the jet creates a large amount of lift with small wings by moving quickly through the air. Smaller wings keep a plane's weight low, which also helps it move faster.

Compared with the jet, the glider in **Figure 3** has a large wing area. A glider is an engineless plane. It rides rising air currents to stay in flight. Without engines, gliders produce no thrust and move more slowly than many other kinds of planes. Thus, a glider must have large wings to create the lift it needs to stay in the air.

Bernoulli and Birds

Birds don't have engines, so birds must flap their wings to push themselves through the air. A small bird must flap its wings at a fast pace to stay in the air. But a hawk flaps its wings only occasionally because it has larger wings than the small bird has. A hawk uses its large wings to fly with very little effort. Fully extended, a hawk's wings allow the hawk to glide on wind currents and still have enough lift to stay in the air.

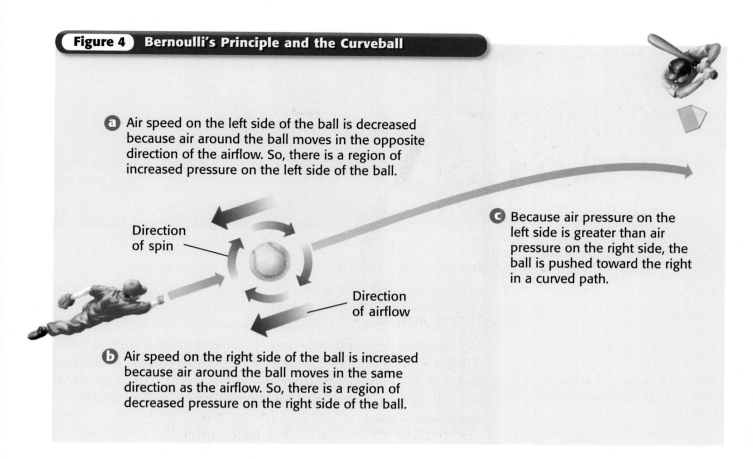

Figure 4 Bernoulli's Principle and the Curveball

a Air speed on the left side of the ball is decreased because air around the ball moves in the opposite direction of the airflow. So, there is a region of increased pressure on the left side of the ball.

Direction of spin

Direction of airflow

c Because air pressure on the left side is greater than air pressure on the right side, the ball is pushed toward the right in a curved path.

b Air speed on the right side of the ball is increased because air around the ball moves in the same direction as the airflow. So, there is a region of decreased pressure on the right side of the ball.

Bernoulli and Baseball

You don't have to look up at a bird or a plane flying through the sky to see Bernoulli's principle in your world. Any time fluids are moving, Bernoulli's principle is at work. **Figure 4** shows how a baseball pitcher can take advantage of Bernoulli's principle to throw a confusing curveball that is difficult for a batter to hit.

Drag and Motion in Fluids

Have you ever walked into a strong wind and noticed that the wind seemed to slow you down? It may have felt like the wind was pushing you backward. Fluids exert a force that opposes the motion of objects moving through the fluids. The force that opposes or restricts motion in a fluid is called **drag.**

In a strong wind, air "drags" on your body and makes it difficult for you to move forward. Drag also works against the forward motion of a plane or bird in flight. Drag is usually caused by an irregular flow of air. An irregular or unpredictable flow of fluids is known as *turbulence.*

drag a force parallel to the velocity of the flow; it opposes the direction of an aircraft and, in combination with thrust, determines the speed of the aircraft

✓ Reading Check What is turbulence?

Figure 5 *The pilot of this airplane can adjust these flaps to help increase lift when the airplane lands or takes off.*

Turbulence and Lift

Lift is often reduced when turbulence causes drag. Drag can be a serious problem for airplanes moving at high speeds. So, airplanes are equipped with ways to reduce turbulence as much as possible when in flight. For example, flaps like those shown in **Figure 5** can be used to change the shape or area of a wing. This change can reduce drag and increase lift. Similarly, birds can adjust their wing feathers in response to turbulence.

✔ **Reading Check** How do airplanes reduce turbulence?

Pascal's Principle

Imagine that the water-pumping station in your town increases the water pressure by 20 Pa. Will the water pressure be increased more at a store two blocks away or at a home 2 km away?

Believe it or not, the increase in water pressure will be the same at both locations. This equal change in water pressure is explained by Pascal's principle. **Pascal's principle** states that a change in pressure at any point in an enclosed fluid will be transmitted equally to all parts of that fluid. This principle was discovered by the 17th-century French scientist Blaise Pascal.

Pascal's principle the principle that states that a fluid in equilibrium contained in a vessel exerts a pressure of equal intensity in all directions

Pascal's Principle and Motion

Hydraulic (hie DRAW lik) devices use Pascal's principle to move or lift objects. Liquids are used in hydraulic devices because liquids cannot be easily compressed, or squeezed, into a smaller space. Cranes, forklifts, and bulldozers have hydraulic devices that help them lift heavy objects.

Hydraulic devices can multiply forces. Car brakes are a good example. In **Figure 6,** a driver's foot exerts pressure on a cylinder of liquid. This pressure is transmitted to all parts of the liquid-filled brake system. The liquid moves the brake pads. The pads press against the wheels, and friction stops the car. The force is multiplied because the pistons that push the brake pads are larger than the piston that is pushed by the brake pedal.

Figure 6 *Because of Pascal's principle, the touch of a foot can stop tons of moving metal.*

1 When the driver pushes the brake pedal, a small piston exerts pressure on the fluid inside the brake system.

2 The change in pressure is transmitted to the large pistons that push on the brake pads.

SECTION Review

Summary

- Bernoulli's principle states that fluid pressure decreases as the speed of the fluid increases.
- Wing shape allows airplanes to take advantage of Bernoulli's principle to achieve flight.
- Lift on an airplane is determined by wing size and thrust.
- Drag opposes motion through fluids.
- Pascal's principle states that a change in pressure in an enclosed fluid is transmitted equally to all parts of the fluid.

Using Key Terms

For each pair of terms, explain how the meanings of the terms differ.

1. *Bernoulli's principle* and *Pascal's principle*

2. *thrust* and *drag*

Understanding Key Ideas

3. The shape of an airplane's wing helps it gain
   a. drag.
   b. lift.
   c. thrust.
   d. turbulence.

4. What is the relationship between pressure and fluid speed?

5. What is Pascal's principle?

6. What force opposes motion through a fluid? How does this force affect lift?

7. How do thrust and lift help an airplane achieve flight?

Critical Thinking

8. **Applying Concepts** Air moving around a speeding race car can create lift. Upside-down wings, or spoilers, are mounted on the rear of race cars. Use Bernoulli's principle to explain how spoilers reduce the danger of accidents.

9. **Making Inferences** When you squeeze a balloon, where is the pressure inside the balloon increased the most? Explain.

Interpreting Graphics

10. Look at the image below. When the space through which a fluid flows becomes narrow, fluid speed increases. Using this information, explain how the two boats could collide.

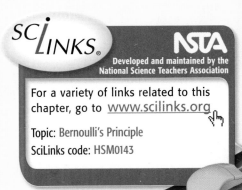

Developed and maintained by the National Science Teachers Association

For a variety of links related to this chapter, go to www.scilinks.org

Topic: Bernoulli's Principle
SciLinks code: HSM0143

Skills Practice Lab

Fluids, Force, and Floating

Why do some objects sink in fluids but others float? In this lab, you'll get a sinking feeling as you determine that an object floats when its weight equals the buoyant force exerted by the surrounding fluid.

OBJECTIVES

Calculate the buoyant force on an object.

Compare the buoyant force on an object with its weight.

MATERIALS

- balance
- mass set
- pan, rectangular baking
- paper towels
- ruler, metric
- tub, plastic, large rectangular
- water

SAFETY

Procedure

1. Copy the table shown below.

Measurement	Trial 1	Trial 2
Length (l), cm		
Width (w), cm		
Initial height (h_1), cm		
Initial volume (V_1), cm^3 $V_1 = l \times w \times h_1$		
New height (h_2), cm		
New total volume (V_2), cm^3 $V_2 = l \times w \times h_2$		
Displaced volume (ΔV), cm^3 $\Delta V = V_2 - V_1$		
Mass of displaced water, g $m = \Delta V \times 1$ g/cm^3		
Weight of displaced water, N (buoyant force)		
Weight of pan and masses, N		

DO NOT WRITE IN BOOK

2. Fill the tub half full with water. Measure (in centimeters) the length, width, and initial height of the water. Record your measurements in the table.

3. Using the equation given in the table, determine the initial volume of water in the tub. Record your results in the table.

4. Place the pan in the water, and place masses in the pan, as shown on the next page. Keep adding masses until the pan sinks to about three-quarters of its height. Record the new height of the water in the table. Then, use this value to determine and record the new total volume of water plus the volume of water displaced by the pan.

⑤ Determine the volume of the water that was displaced by the pan and masses, and record this value in the table. The displaced volume is equal to the new total volume minus the initial volume.

⑥ Determine the mass of the displaced water by multiplying the displaced volume by its density (1 g/cm^3). Record the mass in the table.

⑦ Divide the mass by 100. The value you get is the weight of the displaced water in newtons (N). This is equal to the buoyant force. Record the weight of the displaced water in the table.

⑧ Remove the pan and masses, and determine their total mass (in grams) using the balance. Convert the mass to weight (N), as you did in step 7. Record the weight of the masses and pan in the table.

⑨ Place the empty pan back in the tub. Perform a second trial by repeating steps 4–8. This time, add masses until the pan is just about to sink.

Analyze the Results

① **Identifying Patterns** Compare the buoyant force (the weight of the displaced water) with the weight of the pan and masses for both trials.

② **Examining Data** How did the buoyant force differ between the two trials? Explain.

Draw Conclusions

③ **Drawing Conclusions** Based on your observations, what would happen if you were to add even more mass to the pan than you did in the second trial? Explain your answer in terms of the buoyant force.

④ **Making Predictions** What would happen if you put the masses in the water without the pan? What difference does the pan's shape make?

Chapter Review

USING KEY TERMS

In each of the following sentences, replace the incorrect term with the correct term from the word bank.

thrust   pressure
drag   lift
buoyant force fluid
Pascal's principle
Bernoulli's principle

1 Lift increases with the depth of a fluid.

2 A plane's engines produce drag to push the plane forward.

3 A pascal can be a liquid or a gas.

4 A hydraulic device uses Archimedes' principle to lift or move objects.

5 Atmospheric pressure is the upward force exerted on objects by fluids.

UNDERSTANDING KEY IDEAS

Multiple Choice

6 The design of a wing
   a. causes the air above the wing to travel faster than the air below the wing.
   b. helps create lift.
   c. creates a low-pressure zone above the wing.
   d. All of the above

7 Fluid pressure is always directed
   a. up.   **c.** sideways.
   b. down. **d.** in all directions.

8 An object surrounded by a fluid will displace a volume of fluid that is
   a. equal to its own volume.
   b. less than its own volume.
   c. greater than its own volume.
   d. denser than itself.

9 If an object weighing 50 N displaces a volume of water that weighs 10 N, what is the buoyant force on the object?
   a. 60 N   **c.** 40 N
   b. 50 N   **d.** 10 N

10 A helium-filled balloon will float in air because
   a. there is more air than helium.
   b. helium is less dense than air.
   c. helium is as dense as air.
   d. helium is more dense than air.

11 Materials that can flow to fit their containers include
   a. gases.
   b. liquids.
   c. both gases and liquids.
   d. gases, liquids, and solids.

Short Answer

12 Where is water pressure greater, at a depth of 1 m in a large lake or at a depth of 2 m in a small pond? Explain your answer.

13 Why are bubbles round?

14 Why are tornadoes like giant vacuum cleaners?

Math Skills

15 Calculate the area of a 1,500 N object that exerts a pressure of 500 Pa (500 N/m^2). Then, calculate the pressure exerted by the same object over twice that area.

CRITICAL THINKING

16 **Concept Mapping** Use the following terms to create a concept map: *fluid, pressure, depth, density,* and *buoyant force.*

17 **Forming Hypotheses** Gases can be easily compressed into smaller spaces. Why would this property of gases make gases less useful than liquids in hydraulic brakes?

18 **Making Comparisons** Will a ship loaded with beach balls float higher or lower in the water than an empty ship? Explain your reasoning.

19 **Applying Concepts** Inside all vacuum cleaners is a high-speed fan. Explain how this fan causes the vacuum cleaner to pick up dirt.

20 **Evaluating Hypotheses** A 600 N girl on stilts says to two 600 N boys sitting on the ground, "I am exerting over twice as much pressure as the two of you are exerting together!" Could this statement be true? Explain your reasoning.

INTERPRETING GRAPHICS

Use the diagram of an iceberg below to answer the questions that follow.

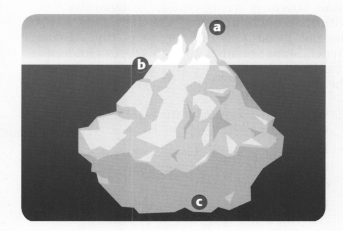

21 At what point (a, b, or c) is water pressure greatest on the iceberg?

22 How much of the iceberg has a weight equal to the buoyant force?

  a. all of it

  b. the section from a to b

  c. the section from b to c

  d. None of the above

23 How does the density of ice compare with the density of water?

24 Why do you think icebergs are dangerous to passing ships?

Standardized Test Preparation

Read each of the passages below. Then, answer the questions that follow each passage.

Passage 1 The Mariana Trench is about 11 km deep—that's deep enough to swallow Mount Everest, the tallest mountain in the world. Fewer than a dozen undersea vessels have ever ventured this deep into the ocean. Why? Water exerts tremendous pressure at this depth. A <u>revolutionary</u> new undersea vessel, *Deep Flight,* has a hull made of an extremely strong ceramic material that can withstand such pressure. Although *Deep Flight* has not made it to the bottom of the Mariana Trench, some scientists think this type of undersea vessel will one day be used routinely to explore the ocean floor.

1. What is the meaning of the word *revolutionary* in this passage?

  A strange

  B overthrowing the government

  C radically different

  D disgusting

2. Based on the name of the undersea vessel described in this passage, what does the vessel look like?

  F a robot

  G a house

  H a car

  I an airplane

3. Based on the passage, which of the following statements is a fact?

  A Scientists hope to fly *Deep Flight* to the top of Mount Everest.

  B *Deep Flight* can withstand very high pressures.

  C Scientists cannot explore the ocean without using *Deep Flight.*

  D *Deep Flight* has gone to the bottom of the Mariana Trench a dozen times.

Passage 2 Buoyancy is an object's ability to float. An object will float if the water it displaces has a mass greater than the object's mass. It will sink if the water it displaces has a mass less than its own mass. But if an object displaces its own mass in water, it will neither float nor sink. Instead, it will remain <u>suspended</u> in the water because of what is called *neutral buoyancy.*

A goldfish has neutral buoyancy. A goldfish has a sac in its body called a *swim bladder.* Gases from blood vessels can diffuse into and out of the swim bladder. When the goldfish needs to rise in the water, for example, gases diffuse into the swim bladder and cause it to inflate. The swim bladder helps the goldfish maintain neutral buoyancy.

1. What is the purpose of this passage?

  A to explain how a goldfish maintains neutral buoyancy

  B to explain how to change the buoyancy of an object

  C to convince people to buy goldfish

  D to describe objects that float and sink

2. What is the meaning of the word *suspended* in this passage?

  F not allowed to attend school

  G stopped for a period of time

  H weighed down

  I supported from sinking

3. What is buoyancy?

  A a sac in a goldfish's body

  B the ability to float

  C the mass of an object

  D an inflated balloon

The graph below shows the water pressure measured by a scientist at different depths in the ocean. Use the graph below to answer the questions that follow.

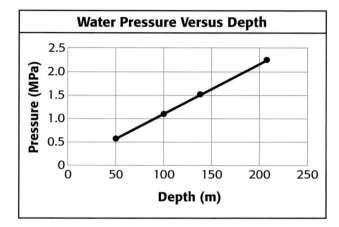

Water Pressure Versus Depth

1. What is the pressure on the object when it is 100 m underwater?

   A 1.0 MPa
   B 1.1 MPa
   C 1.5 MPa
   D 2.0 MPa

2. Based on the data in the graph, which of the following is the best estimate of the pressure at 250 m below the surface of the ocean?

   F 1.7 MPa
   G 2.2 MPa
   H 2.6 MPa
   I 5.0 MPa

3. Which of the following statements best describes the relationship between the water pressure on an object and the depth of the object in the ocean?

   A Water pressure increases as the depth increases.
   B Water pressure decreases as the depth increases.
   C Water pressure does not change as the depth increases.
   D Water pressure has no predictable relationship to the depth.

Read each question below, and choose the best answer.

1. Anna-Marie has a coil of wire. She uses a balance to find that the wire has a mass of 17.8 g. She uses water displacement to find that the volume of the wire is 2.0 cm^3. Density is equal to mass divided by volume. What is the density of the wire?

   A 0.11 g/cm^3
   B 8.9 g/cm^3
   C 19.8 g/cm^3
   D 35.6 g/cm^3

2. Hussain rode his bike 30 km this weekend. What is this distance expressed in meters?

   F 0.3 m
   G 300 m
   H 30,000 m
   I 300,000 m

3. Olivia purchased 21 tubes of oil paint at $3.95 per tube, which includes tax. What was the total cost of the 21 tubes of paint?

   A $65.15
   B $82.95
   C $89.10
   D $93.50

4. Javi filled a container halfway full with water. The container measures 2 m wide, 3 m long, and 1 m high. How many cubic meters of water are in the container?

   F 2 m^3
   G 3 m^3
   H 5 m^3
   I 6 m^3

5. Pressure is equal to force divided by area. Jenny pushes a door with a force of 12 N. The area of her hand is 96 cm^2. What is the pressure exerted by Jenny's hand on the door?

   A 0.125 N/cm
   B 0.125 N/cm^2
   C 8 N/cm
   D 8 N/cm^2

Standardized Test Preparation

Science in Action

Science, Technology, and Society

Stayin' Aloft—The Story of the Frisbee®
In the late 1800s, a few fun-loving college students invented a game that involved tossing an empty tin pie plate. The pie plate was stamped with the name of a bakery: Frisbie's Pies. So, the game of Frisbie was created. Unfortunately, the metal pie plates tended to develop sharp edges that caused injuries. In 1947, plastic disks were made to replace the metal pie plates. These plastic disks were called Frisbees. How do Frisbees stay in the air? When you throw a Frisbee, you give it thrust. And as it moves through the air, lift is created because of Bernoulli's principle. But you don't have to think about the science behind Frisbees to have fun with them!

Math Activity

A Frisbee landed 10 m away from where it is thrown. The Frisbee was in the air for 2.5 s. What was the average speed of the Frisbee?

Science Fiction

"Wet Behind the Ears" by Jack C. Haldeman II
Willie Joe Thomas cheated to get a swimming scholarship. Now, he is faced with a major swim meet, and his coach told him that he has to swim or be kicked off the team. Willie Joe could lose his scholarship.

One day, Willie Joe's roommate, Frank, announces that he has developed a new "sliding compound." And Frank also said something about using the compound to make ships go faster. So, Willie Joe thought, if it works for ships, it might work for swimming.

See what happens when Willie Joe tries to save his scholarship by using Frank's compound at the swim meet. Read "Wet Behind the Ears," by Jack C. Haldeman II in the *Holt Anthology of Science Fiction*.

Language Arts Activity

Analyze the story structure of "Wet Behind the Ears." In your analysis, identify the introduction, the rising action, the climax, and the denouement. Summarize your analysis in a chart.

Alisha Bracken

Scuba Instructor Alisha Bracken first started scuba diving in her freshman year of college. Her first dives were in a saltwater hot spring near Salt Lake City, Utah. "It was awesome," Bracken says. "There were nurse sharks, angelfish, puffer fish and brine shrimp!" Bracken enjoyed her experience so much that she wanted to share it with other people. The best way to do that was to become an instructor and teach other people to dive.

Bracken says one of the biggest challenges of being a scuba instructor is teaching people to adapt and function in a foreign environment. She believes that learning to dive properly is important not only for the safety of the diver but also for the protection of the underwater environment. She relies on science principles to help teach people how to control their movements and protect the natural environment. "Buoyancy is the foundation of teaching people to dive comfortably," she explains. "Without it, we cannot float on the surface or stay off the bottom. Underwater life can be damaged if students do not learn and apply the concepts of buoyancy."

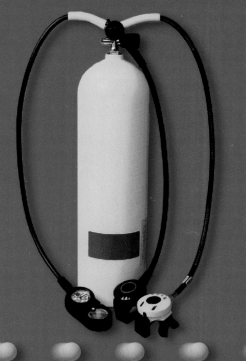

Social Studies ACTIVITY

Scuba divers and other underwater explorers sometimes investigate shipwrecks on the bottom of the ocean. Research the exploration of a specific shipwreck. Make a poster showing what artifacts were retrieved from the shipwreck and what was learned from the exploration.

To learn more about these Science in Action topics, visit **go.hrw.com** and type in the keyword **HP5FLUF**.

Current Science

Check out Current Science® articles related to this chapter by visiting **go.hrw.com**. Just type in the keyword **HP5CS07**.

UNIT 3

TIMELINE

Work, Machines, and Energy

Can you imagine living in a world with no machines? In this unit, you will explore the scientific meaning of *work* and learn how machines make work easier. You will find out how energy allows you to do work and how different forms of energy can be converted into other forms of energy. You will also learn about heat and how heating and cooling systems work. This timeline shows some of the inventions and discoveries made throughout history as people have advanced their understanding of work, machines, and energy.

Around 3000 BCE

The sail is used in Egypt. Sails use the wind rather than human power to move boats through the water.

1818

German inventor Baron Karl von Drais de Sauerbrun exhibits the first two-wheeled, rider-propelled machine. Made of wood, this early machine paves the way for the invention of the bicycle.

1948

Maria Telkes, a Hungarian-born physicist, designs the heating system for the first solar-heated house.

1972

The first American self-service gas station opens.

Around 200 BCE

Under the Han dynasty, the Chinese become one of the first civilizations to use coal as fuel.

1656

Dutch scientist Christiaan Huygens invents the pendulum clock.

1776

The American colonies declare their independence from Great Britain.

1893

The "Clasp Locker," an early zipper, is patented.

1908

The automobile age begins with the mass production of the Ford Model T.

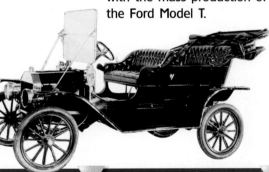

1926

American scientist Robert Goddard launches the first rocket powered by liquid fuel. The rocket reaches a height of 12.5 m and a speed of 97 km/h.

1988

A wind-powered generator begins generating electrical energy in Scotland's Orkney Islands.

2000

The 2000 Olympic Summer Games are held in Sydney, Australia.

2001

A two-wheeled, battery-powered "people mover" is introduced. Gyroscopes and tilt sensors allow riders to guide the scooter-like transporter by leaning.

8

Work and Machines

SECTION **1** Work and Power 210

SECTION **2** What Is a Machine? . . . 216

SECTION **3** Types of Machines 222

Chapter Lab 230
Chapter Review 232
Standardized Test Preparation 234
Science in Action 236

About the PHOTO

"One, two, stroke!" shouts the coach as the team races to the finish line. This paddling team is competing in Hong Kong's annual Dragon Boat Races. The Dragon Boat Festival is a 2,000-year-old Chinese tradition that commemorates Qu Yuan, a national hero. The paddlers that you see here are using the paddles to move the boat forward. Even though they are celebrating by racing their dragon boat, in scientific terms, this team is doing work.

PRE-READING ACTIVITY

FOLDNOTES **Booklet** Before you read the chapter, create the FoldNote entitled "Booklet" described in the **Study Skills** section of the Appendix. Label each page of the booklet with a main idea from the chapter. As you read the chapter, write what you learn about each main idea on the appropriate page of the booklet.

START-UP ACTIVITY

C'mon, Lever a Little!

In this activity, you will use a simple machine, a lever, to make your task a little easier.

Procedure

1. Stack **two books,** one on top of the other, on a **table.**

2. Slide your index finger underneath the edge of the bottom book. Using only the force of your finger, try to lift one side of the books 2 or 3 cm off the table. Is it hard to do so? Write your observations.

3. Slide the end of a **wooden ruler** underneath the edge of the bottom book. Then, slip a **large pencil eraser** or similar object under the ruler.

4. Again, using only your index finger, push down on the edge of the ruler and try to lift the books. Record your observations. **Caution:** Push down slowly to keep the ruler and eraser from flipping.

Analysis

1. Which was easier: lifting the books with your finger or lifting the books with the ruler? Explain your answer.

2. In what way did the direction of the force that your finger applied on the books differ from the direction of the force that your finger applied on the ruler?

Work and Power

Your science teacher has just given you tonight's homework assignment. You have to read an entire chapter by tomorrow! That sounds like a lot of work!

Actually, in the scientific sense, you won't be doing much work at all! How can that be? In science, **work** is done when a force causes an object to move in the direction of the force. In the example above, you may have to put a lot of mental effort into doing your homework, but you won't be using force to move anything. So, in the scientific sense, you will not be doing work—except the work to turn the pages of your book!

What Is Work?

The student in **Figure 1** is having a lot of fun, isn't she? But she is doing work, even though she is having fun. She is doing work because she is applying a force to the bowling ball and making the ball move through a distance. However, she is doing work on the ball only as long as she is touching it. The ball will keep moving away from her after she releases it. But she will no longer be doing work on the ball because she will no longer be applying a force to it.

Transfer of Energy

One way you can tell that the bowler in **Figure 1** has done work on the bowling ball is that the ball now has *kinetic energy.* This means that the ball is now moving. The bowler has transferred energy to the ball.

Differences Between Force and Work

Applying a force doesn't always result in work being done. Suppose that you help push a stalled car. You push and push, but the car doesn't budge. The pushing may have made you tired. But you haven't done any work on the car, because the car hasn't moved.

You do work on the car as soon as the car moves. Whenever you apply a force to an object and the object moves in the direction of the force, you have done work on the object.

✓ **Reading Check** Is work done every time a force is applied to an object? Explain. (*See the Appendix for answers to Reading Checks.*)

READING WARM-UP

Objectives

● Determine when work is being done on an object.

● Calculate the amount of work done on an object.

● Explain the difference between work and power.

Terms to Learn

work   power
joule   watt

READING STRATEGY

Reading Organizer As you read this section, make a table comparing work and power.

Figure 1
You might be surprised to find out that bowling is work!

Force and Motion in the Same Direction

Suppose you are in the airport and late for a flight. You have to run through the airport carrying a heavy suitcase. Because you are making the suitcase move, you are doing work on it, right? Wrong! For work to be done on an object, the object must move in the *same direction* as the force. You are applying a force to hold the suitcase up, but the suitcase is moving forward. So, no work is done on the suitcase. But work *is* done on the suitcase when you lift it off the ground.

Work is done on an object if two things happen: (1) the object moves as a force is applied and (2) the direction of the object's motion is the same as the direction of the force. The pictures and arrows in **Figure 2** will help you understand when work is being done on an object.

work the transfer of energy to an object by using a force that causes the object to move in the direction of the force

Figure 2 Work or Not Work?

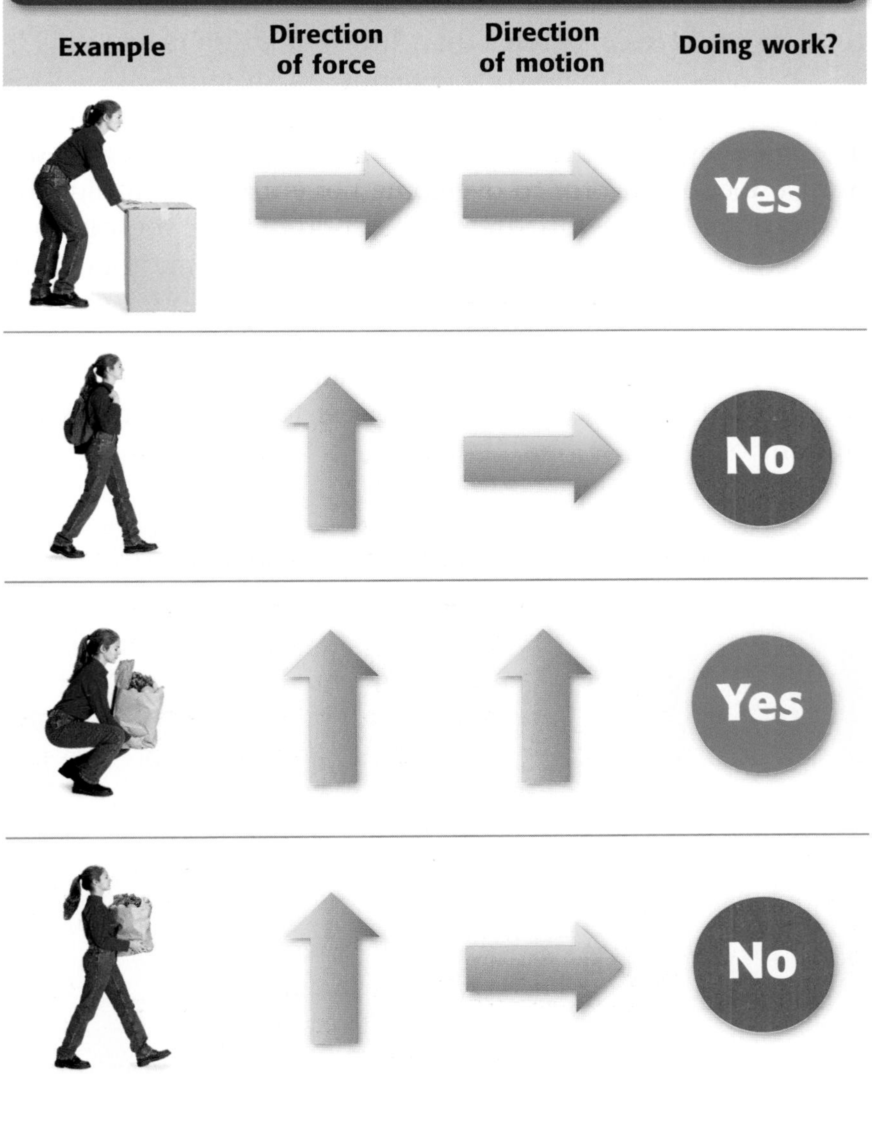

Example	Direction of force	Direction of motion	Doing work?
	→	→	Yes
	↑	→	No
	↑	↑	Yes
	↑	→	No

CONNECTION TO Biology

WRITING SKILL **Work in the Human Body**

You may not be doing any work on a suitcase if you are just holding it in your hands, but your body will still get tired from the effort because you are doing work on the muscles inside your body. Your muscles can contract thousands of times in just a few seconds while you try to keep the suitcase from falling. What other situations can you think of that might involve work being done somewhere inside your body? Describe these situations in your **science journal.**

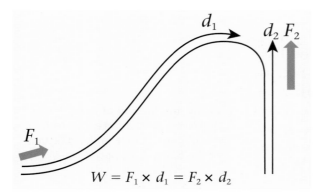

$$W = F_1 \times d_1 = F_2 \times d_2$$

Figure 3 *For each path, the same work is done to move the car to the top of the hill, although distance and force along the two paths differ.*

How Much Work?

Would you do more work on a car by pushing it up a long road to reach the top of a hill or by using a cable to raise the car up the side of a cliff to the top of the same hill? You would certainly need a different amount of force. Common use of the word *work* may make it seem that there would be a difference in the amount of work done in the two cases as well.

Same Work, Different Forces

You may be surprised to learn that the same amount of work is being done to push the car up a road as to raise it up the cliff. Look at **Figure 3.** A certain amount of energy is needed to move the car from the bottom to the top of the hill. Because the car ends up at the same place either way, the work done on the car is the same. However, pushing the car along the road up a hill seems easier than lifting it straight up. Why?

The reason is that work depends on distance as well as force. Consider a mountain climber who reaches the top of a mountain by climbing straight up a cliff, as in **Figure 4.** She must use enough force to overcome her entire weight. But the distance she travels up the cliff is shorter than the distance traveled by hikers who reach the top of the same mountain by walking up a slope. Either way, the same amount of work is done. But the hikers going up a slope don't need to use as much force as if they were going straight up the side of the cliff. This shows how you can use less force to do the same amount of work.

Figure 4 *Climbers going to the top of a mountain do the same amount of work whether they hike up a slope or go straight up a cliff.*

Calculating Work

The amount of work (W) done in moving an object, such as the barbell in **Figure 5,** can be calculated by multiplying the force (F) applied to the object by the distance (d) through which the force is applied, as shown in the following equation:

$$W = F \times d$$

Force is expressed in newtons, and the meter is the basic SI unit for length or distance. Therefore, the unit used to express work is the newton-meter (N $\times$ m), which is more simply called the **joule.** Because work is the transfer of energy to an object, the joule (J) is also the unit used to measure energy.

joule the unit used to express energy; equivalent to the amount of work done by a force of 1 N acting through a distance of 1 m in the direction of the force (symbol, J)

✓ **Reading Check** How is work calculated?

Figure 5 Force Times Distance

80 N

160 N

80 N

W = 80 N × 1 m = 80 J
The force needed to lift an object is equal to the gravitational force on the object—in other words, the object's weight.

W = 160 N × 1 m = 160 J
If you increase the weight, an increased force is needed to lift the object. This increases the amount of work done.

W = 80 N × 2 m = 160 J
Increasing the distance also increases the amount of work done.

Get to Work!

1. Use a **loop of string** to attach a **spring scale** to a **weight.**

2. Slowly pull the weight across a **table** by dragging the spring scale. Record the amount of force that you exerted on the weight.

3. Use a **metric ruler** to measure the distance that you pulled the weight.

4. Now, use the spring scale to slowly pull the weight up a **ramp.** Pull the weight the same distance that you pulled it across the table.

5. Calculate the work you did on the weight for both trials.

6. How were the amounts of work and force affected by the way you pulled the weight? What other ways of pulling the weight could you test?

Power: How Fast Work Is Done

power the rate at which work is done or energy is transformed

watt the unit used to express power; equivalent to joules per second (symbol, W)

Like the term *work*, the term *power* is used a lot in everyday language but has a very specific meaning in science. **Power** is the rate at which energy is transferred.

Calculating Power

To calculate power (*P*), you divide the amount of work done (*W*) by the time (*t*) it takes to do that work, as shown in the following equation:

$$P = \frac{W}{t}$$

The unit used to express power is joules per second (J/s), also called the **watt.** One watt (W) is equal to 1 J/s. So if you do 50 J of work in 5 s, your power is 10 J/s, or 10 W.

Power measures how fast work happens, or how quickly energy is transferred. When more work is done in a given amount of time, the power output is greater. Power output is also greater when the time it takes to do a certain amount of work is decreased, as shown in **Figure 6.**

Reading Check How is power calculated?

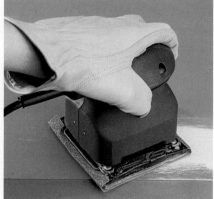

Figure 6 *No matter how fast you can sand by hand, an electric sander can do the same amount of work faster. Therefore, the electric sander has more power.*

MATH FOCUS

More Power to You A stage manager at a play raises the curtain by doing 5,976 J of work on the curtain in 12 s. What is the power output of the stage manager?

Step 1: Write the equation for power.

$$P = \frac{W}{t}$$

Step 2: Replace *W* and *t* with work and time.

$$P = \frac{5,976\,\text{J}}{12\,\text{s}} = 498\ \text{W}$$

Now It's Your Turn

1. If it takes you 10 s to do 150 J of work on a box to move it up a ramp, what is your power output?

2. A light bulb is on for 12 s, and during that time it uses 1,200 J of electrical energy. What is the wattage (power) of the light bulb?

Increasing Power

It may take you longer to sand a wooden shelf by hand than by using an electric sander, but the amount of energy needed is the same either way. Only the power output is lower when you sand the shelf by hand (although your hand may get more tired). You could also dry your hair with a fan, but it would take a long time! A hair dryer is more powerful. It can give off energy more quickly than a fan does, so your hair dries faster.

Car engines are usually rated with a certain power output. The more powerful the engine is, the more quickly the engine can move a car. And for a given speed, a more powerful engine can move a heavier car than a less powerful engine can.

CONNECTION TO Language Arts

WRITING SKILL **Horsepower** The unit of power most commonly used to rate car engines is the *horsepower* (hp). Look up the word *horsepower* in a dictionary. How many watts is equal to 1 hp? Do you think all horses output exactly 1 hp? Why or why not? Write your answers in your **science journal.**

SECTION Review

Summary

- In scientific terms, *work* is done when a force causes an object to move in the direction of the force.
- Work is calculated as force times distance. The unit of work is the newton-meter, or joule.
- *Power* is a measure of how fast work is done.
- Power is calculated as work divided by time. The unit of power is the joule per second, or watt.

Using Key Terms

For each pair of terms, explain how the meanings of the terms differ.

1. *work* and *joule*

2. *power* and *watt*

Understanding Key Ideas

3. How is work calculated?
   a. force times distance
   b. force divided by distance
   c. power times distance
   d. power divided by distance

4. What is the difference between work and power?

Math Skills

5. Using a force of 10 N, you push a shopping cart 10 m. How much work did you do?

6. If you did 100 J of work in 5 s, what was your power output?

Critical Thinking

7. **Analyzing Processes** Work is done on a ball when a pitcher throws it. Is the pitcher still doing work on the ball as it flies through the air? Explain.

8. **Applying Concepts** You lift a chair that weighs 50 N to a height of 0.5 m and carry it 10 m across the room. How much work do you do on the chair?

Interpreting Graphics

9. What idea about work and force does the following diagram describe? Explain your answer.

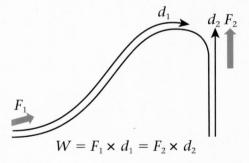

$$W = F_1 \times d_1 = F_2 \times d_2$$

Developed and maintained by the National Science Teachers Association

For a variety of links related to this chapter, go to www.scilinks.org

Topic: Work and Power
SciLinks code: HSM1675

What Is a Machine?

You are in the car with your mom on the way to a party when suddenly—KABLOOM hisssss—a tire blows out. "Now I'm going to be late!" you think as your mom pulls over to the side of the road.

You watch as she opens the trunk and gets out a jack and a tire iron. Using the tire iron, she pries the hubcap off and begins to unscrew the lug nuts from the wheel. She then puts the jack under the car and turns the jack's handle several times until the flat tire no longer touches the ground. After exchanging the flat tire with the spare, she lowers the jack and puts the lug nuts and hubcap back on the wheel.

"Wow!" you think, "That wasn't as hard as I thought it would be." As your mom drops you off at the party, you think how lucky it was that she had the right equipment to change the tire.

Machines: Making Work Easier

Now, imagine changing a tire without the jack and the tire iron. Would it have been easy? No, you would have needed several people just to hold up the car! Sometimes, you need the help of machines to do work. A **machine** is a device that makes work easier by changing the size or direction of a force.

When you think of machines, you might think of things such as cars, big construction equipment, or even computers. But not all machines are complicated. In fact, you use many simple machines in your everyday life. **Figure 1** shows some examples of machines.

READING WARM-UP

Objectives

- Explain how a machine makes work easier.
- Describe and give examples of the force-distance trade-off that occurs when a machine is used.
- Calculate mechanical advantage.
- Explain why machines are not 100% efficient.

Terms to Learn

machine
work input
work output
mechanical advantage
mechanical efficiency

READING STRATEGY

Prediction Guide Before reading this section, write the title of each heading in this section. Next, under each heading, write what you think you will learn.

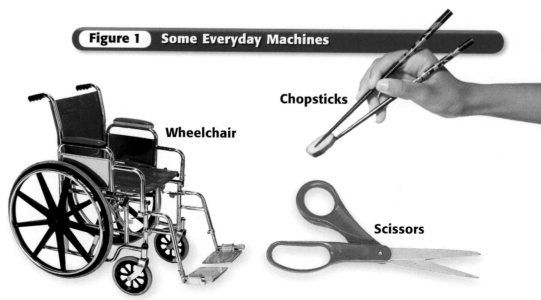

Figure 1 Some Everyday Machines

Wheelchair

Chopsticks

Scissors

Work In, Work Out

Suppose that you need to get the lid off a can of paint. What do you do? One way to pry the lid off is to use a common machine known as a *lever*. **Figure 2** shows a screwdriver being used as a lever. You place the tip of the screwdriver under the edge of the lid and then push down on the screwdriver's handle. The tip of the screwdriver lifts the lid as you push down. In other words, you do work on the screwdriver, and the screwdriver does work on the lid.

Work is done when a force is applied through a distance. Look again at **Figure 2.** The work that you do on a machine is called **work input.** You apply a force, called the *input force,* to the machine through a distance. The work done by the machine on an object is called **work output.** The machine applies a force, called the *output force,* through a distance.

How Machines Help

You might think that machines help you because they increase the amount of work done. But that's not true. If you multiplied the forces by the distances through which the forces are applied in **Figure 2** (remember that $W = F \times d$), you would find that the screwdriver does not do more work on the lid than you do on the screwdriver. Work output can never be greater than work input. Machines allow force to be applied over a greater distance, which means that less force will be needed for the same amount of work.

✓ Reading Check How do machines make work easier? (*See the Appendix for answers to Reading Checks.*)

machine a device that helps do work by either overcoming a force or changing the direction of the applied force

work input the work done on a machine; the product of the input force and the distance through which the force is exerted

work output the work done by a machine; the product of the output force and the distance through which the force is exerted

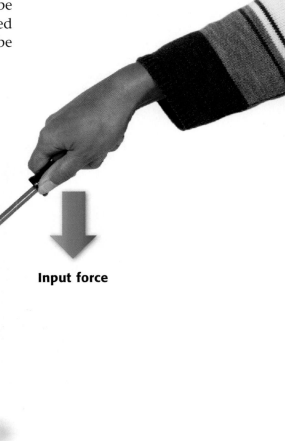

Output force

Input force

Figure 2 *When you use a machine, you do work on the machine, and the machine does work on something else.*

Same Work, Different Force

Machines make work easier by changing the size or direction (or both) of the input force. When a screwdriver is used as a lever to open a paint can, both the size and direction of the input force change. Remember that using a machine does not change the amount of work you will do. As **Figure 3** shows, the same amount of work is done with or without the ramp. The ramp decreases the size of the input force needed to lift the box but increases the distance over which the force is exerted. So, the machine allows a smaller force to be applied over a longer distance.

The Force-Distance Trade-Off

When a machine changes the size of the force, the distance through which the force is exerted must also change. Force or distance can increase, but both cannot increase. When one increases, the other must decrease.

Figure 4 shows how machines change force and distance. Whenever a machine changes the size of a force, the machine also changes the distance through which the force is applied. **Figure 4** also shows that some machines change only the direction of the force, not the size of the force or the distance through which the force is exerted.

✓ Reading Check What are the two things that a machine can change about how work is done?

Figure 3 Input Force and Distance

Lifting this box straight up requires an input force equal to the weight of the box.

$$W = 450 \text{ N} \times 1 \text{ m} = 450 \text{ J}$$

Using a ramp to lift the box requires an input force less than the weight of the box, but the input force must be exerted over a greater distance than if you didn't use a ramp.

$$W = 150 \text{ N} \times 3 \text{ m} = 450 \text{ J}$$

Figure 4 Machines Change the Size and/or Direction of a Force

Input force

Output force

A nutcracker *increases* the force but applies it over a *shorter* distance.

A hammer *decreases* the force, but applies it over a *greater* distance.

Output force

Input force

A simple pulley changes the *direction* of the input force, but the size of the output force is the same as the input force.

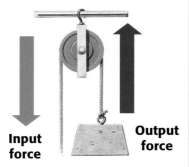
Input force

Output force

When a screwdriver is used as a lever, it *increases* the force and *decreases* the distance over which the force is applied.

Output force

Input force

Mechanical Advantage

Some machines make work easier than others do because they can increase force more than other machines can. A machine's **mechanical advantage** is the number of times the machine multiplies force. In other words, the mechanical advantage compares the input force with the output force.

mechanical advantage a number that tells how many times a machine multiplies force

Calculating Mechanical Advantage

You can find mechanical advantage by using the following equation:

$$\text{mechanical advantage (MA)} = \frac{output\ force}{input\ force}$$

For example, imagine that you had to push a 500 N weight up a ramp and only needed to push with 50 N of force the entire time. The mechanical advantage of the ramp would be calculated as follows:

$$MA = \frac{500\ \text{N}}{50\ \text{N}} = 10$$

A machine that has a mechanical advantage that is greater than 1 can help move or lift heavy objects because the output force is greater than the input force. A machine that has a mechanical advantage that is less than 1 will reduce the output force but can increase the distance an object moves. **Figure 4** shows an example of such a machine—a hammer.

Finding the Advantage

A grocer uses a handcart to lift a heavy stack of canned food. Suppose that he applies an input force of 40 N to the handcart. The cart applies an output force of 320 N to the stack of canned food. What is the mechanical advantage of the handcart?

Mechanical Efficiency

The work output of a machine can never be greater than the work input. In fact, the work output of a machine is always less than the work input. Why? Some of the work done by the machine is used to overcome the friction created by the use of the machine. But keep in mind that no work is lost. The work output plus the work done to overcome friction is equal to the work input.

The less work a machine has to do to overcome friction, the more efficient the machine is. **Mechanical efficiency** (muh KAN i kuhl e FISH uhn see) is a comparison of a machine's work output with the work input.

Calculating Efficiency

A machine's mechanical efficiency is calculated using the following equation:

$$mechanical\ efficiency = \frac{work\ output}{work\ input} \times 100$$

The 100 in this equation means that mechanical efficiency is expressed as a percentage. Mechanical efficiency tells you what percentage of the work input gets converted into work output.

Figure 5 shows a machine that is used to drill holes in metal. Some of the work input is used to overcome the friction between the metal and the drill. This energy cannot be used to do work on the steel block. Instead, it heats up the steel and the machine itself.

Reading Check How is mechanical efficiency calculated?

Useful Friction

Friction is always present when two objects touch or rub together, and friction usually slows down moving parts in a machine and heats them up. In some cases, parts in a machine are designed to increase friction. While at home, observe three situations in which friction is useful. Describe them in your **science journal.**

Figure 5 In this machine, some of the work input is converted into sound and heat energy.

Perfect Efficiency?

An *ideal machine* would be a machine that had 100% mechanical efficiency. An ideal machine's useful work output would equal the work done on the machine. Ideal machines are impossible to build, because every machine has moving parts. Moving parts always use some of the work input to overcome friction. But new technologies help increase efficiency so that more energy is available to do useful work. The train in **Figure 6** is floating on magnets, so there is almost no friction between the train and the tracks. Other machines use lubricants, such as oil or grease, to lower the friction between their moving parts, which makes the machines more efficient.

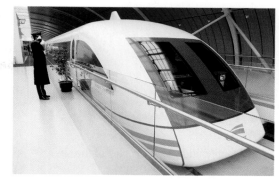

Figure 6 *There is very little friction between this magnetic levitation train and its tracks, so it is highly efficient.*

SECTION Review

Summary

- A machine makes work easier by changing the size or direction (or both) of a force.
- A machine can increase force or distance, but not both.
- Mechanical advantage tells how many times a machine multiplies force.
- Mechanical efficiency is a comparison of a machine's work output with work input.
- Machines are not 100% efficient because some of the work done is used to overcome friction.

Using Key Terms

For each pair of terms, explain how the meanings of the terms differ.

1. *work input* and *work output*

2. *mechanical advantage* and *mechanical efficiency*

Understanding Key Ideas

3. Which of the following is the correct way to calculate mechanical advantage?

   a. input force ÷ output force
   b. output force ÷ input force
   c. work input ÷ work output
   d. work output ÷ work input

4. Explain how using a ramp makes work easier.

5. Give a specific example of a machine, and describe how its mechanical efficiency might be calculated.

6. Why can't a machine be 100% efficient?

Math Skills

7. Suppose that you exert 60 N on a machine and the machine exerts 300 N on another object. What is the machine's mechanical advantage?

8. What is the mechanical efficiency of a machine whose work input is 100 J and work output is 30 J?

Critical Thinking

9. **Making Inferences** For a machine with a mechanical advantage of 3, how does the distance through which the output force is exerted differ from the distance through which the input force is exerted?

10. **Analyzing Processes** Describe the effect that friction has on a machine's mechanical efficiency. How do lubricants increase a machine's mechanical efficiency?

SECTION 3

Types of Machines

Imagine that it's a hot summer day. You have a whole ice-cold watermelon in front of you. It would taste cool and delicious—if only you had a machine that could cut it!

The machine you need is a knife. But how is a knife a machine? A knife is actually a very sharp wedge, which is one of the six simple machines. The six simple machines are the lever, the inclined plane, the wedge, the screw, the pulley, and the wheel and axle. All machines are made from one or more of these simple machines.

Levers

Have you ever used the claw end of a hammer to remove a nail from a piece of wood? If so, you were using the hammer as a lever. A **lever** is a simple machine that has a bar that pivots at a fixed point, called a *fulcrum*. Levers are used to apply a force to a load. There are three classes of levers, which are based on the locations of the fulcrum, the load, and the input force.

First-Class Levers

With a first-class lever, the fulcrum is between the input force and the load, as shown in **Figure 1.** First-class levers always change the direction of the input force. And depending on the location of the fulcrum, first-class levers can be used to increase force or to increase distance.

Figure 1 Examples of First-Class Levers

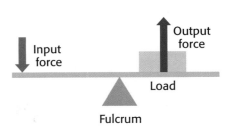

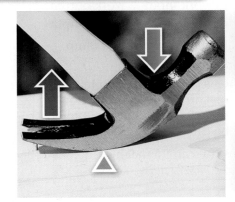

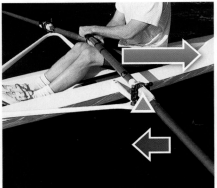

When the fulcrum is closer to the load than to the input force, the lever has a **mechanical advantage of greater than 1.** The output force is increased because it is exerted over a shorter distance.

When the fulcrum is exactly in the middle, the lever has a **mechanical advantage of 1.** The output force is not increased because the input force's distance is not increased.

When the fulcrum is closer to the input force than to the load, the lever has a **mechanical advantage of less than 1.** Although the output force is less than the input force, distance increases.

Figure 2 Examples of Second-Class Levers

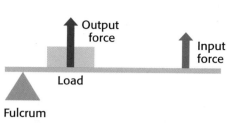

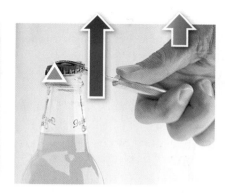

In a **second-class lever,** the output force, or load, is between the input force and the fulcrum.

Using a second-class lever results in a **mechanical advantage of greater than 1.** The closer the load is to the fulcrum, the more the force is increased and the greater the mechanical advantage is.

Second-Class Levers

The load of a second-class lever is between the fulcrum and the input force, as shown in **Figure 2.** Second-class levers do not change the direction of the input force. But they allow you to apply less force than the force exerted by the load. Because the output force is greater than the input force, you must exert the input force over a greater distance.

lever a simple machine that consists of a bar that pivots at a fixed point called a *fulcrum*

Third-Class Levers

The input force in a third-class lever is between the fulcrum and the load, as shown in **Figure 3.** Third-class levers do not change the direction of the input force. In addition, they do not increase the input force. Therefore, the output force is always less than the input force.

✓ **Reading Check** How do the three types of levers differ from one another? (*See the Appendix for answers to Reading Checks.*)

Figure 3 Examples of Third-Class Levers

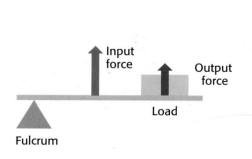

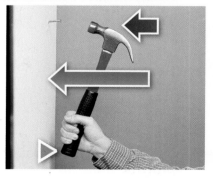

In a **third-class lever,** the input force is between the fulcrum and the load.

Using a third-class lever results in a **mechanical advantage of less than 1** because force is decreased. But third-class levers increase the distance through which the output force is exerted.

Pulleys

When you open window blinds by pulling on a cord, you're using a pulley. A **pulley** is a simple machine that has a grooved wheel that holds a rope or a cable. A load is attached to one end of the rope, and an input force is applied to the other end. Types of pulleys are shown in **Figure 4.**

Fixed Pulleys

A fixed pulley is attached to something that does not move. By using a fixed pulley, you can pull down on the rope to lift the load up. The pulley changes the direction of the force. Elevators make use of fixed pulleys.

Movable Pulleys

Unlike fixed pulleys, movable pulleys are attached to the object being moved. A movable pulley does not change a force's direction. Movable pulleys do increase force, but they also increase the distance over which the input force must be exerted.

Block and Tackles

When a fixed pulley and a movable pulley are used together, the pulley system is called a *block and tackle*. The mechanical advantage of a block and tackle depends on the number of rope segments.

pulley a simple machine that consists of a wheel over which a rope, chain, or wire passes

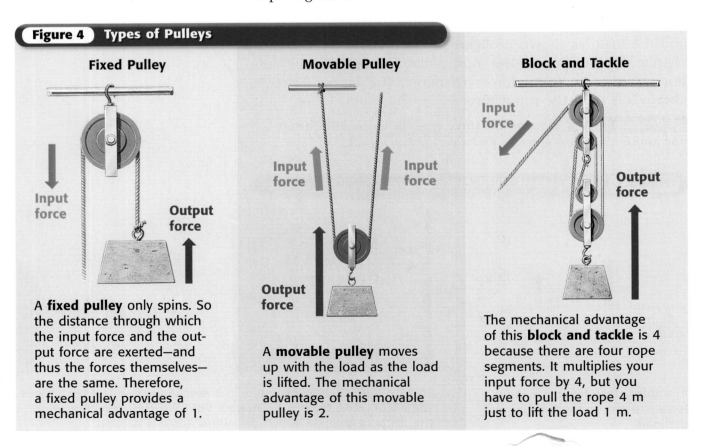

Figure 4 Types of Pulleys

Fixed Pulley

Input force

Output force

A **fixed pulley** only spins. So the distance through which the input force and the output force are exerted—and thus the forces themselves—are the same. Therefore, a fixed pulley provides a mechanical advantage of 1.

Movable Pulley

Input force

Input force

Output force

A **movable pulley** moves up with the load as the load is lifted. The mechanical advantage of this movable pulley is 2.

Block and Tackle

Input force

Output force

The mechanical advantage of this **block and tackle** is 4 because there are four rope segments. It multiplies your input force by 4, but you have to pull the rope 4 m just to lift the load 1 m.

Figure 5 **How a Wheel and Axle Works**

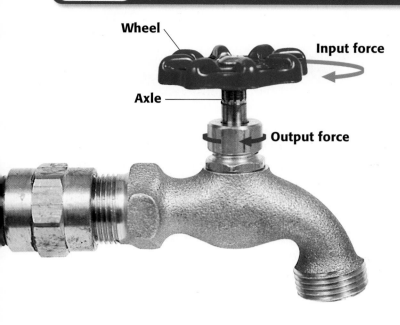

Wheel

Input force

Axle

Output force

ⓐ When a small input force is applied to the wheel, the wheel rotates through a circular distance.

ⓑ As the wheel turns, so does the axle. But because the axle is smaller than the wheel, it rotates through a smaller distance, which makes the output force larger than the input force

Wheel and Axle

Did you know that a faucet is a machine? The faucet shown in **Figure 5** is an example of a **wheel and axle,** a simple machine consisting of two circular objects of different sizes. Doorknobs, wrenches, and steering wheels all use a wheel and axle. **Figure 5** shows how a wheel and axle works.

wheel and axle a simple machine consisting of two circular objects of different sizes; the wheel is the larger of the two circular objects

Mechanical Advantage of a Wheel and Axle

The mechanical advantage of a wheel and axle can be found by dividing the *radius* (the distance from the center to the edge) of the wheel by the radius of the axle, as shown in **Figure 6.** Turning the wheel results in a mechanical advantage of greater than 1 because the radius of the wheel is larger than the radius of the axle.

✓ **Reading Check** How is the mechanical advantage of a wheel and axle calculated?

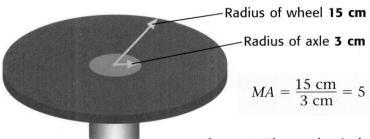

Radius of wheel **15 cm**

Radius of axle **3 cm**

$$MA = \frac{15 \text{ cm}}{3 \text{ cm}} = 5$$

Figure 6 *The mechanical advantage of a wheel and axle is the radius of the wheel divided by the radius of the axle.*

Figure 7 *The work you do on the piano to roll it up the ramp is the same as the work you would do to lift it straight up. An inclined plane simply allows you to apply a smaller force over a greater distance.*

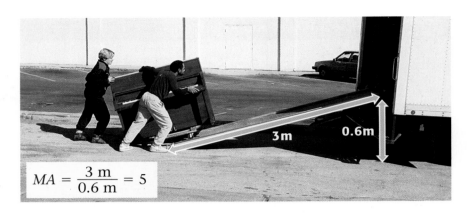

$$MA = \frac{3\ m}{0.6\ m} = 5$$

Inclined Planes

Do you remember the story about how the Egyptians built the Great Pyramid? One of the machines they used was the **inclined plane.** An *inclined plane* is a simple machine that is a straight, slanted surface. A ramp is an inclined plane.

Using an inclined plane to load a piano into a truck, as **Figure 7** shows, is easier than lifting the piano into the truck. Rolling the piano along an inclined plane requires a smaller input force than is needed to lift the piano into the truck. The same work is done on the piano, just over a longer distance.

 **Reading Check** What is an inclined plane?

inclined plane a simple machine that is a straight, slanted surface, which facilitates the raising of loads; a ramp

Mechanical Advantage of Inclined Planes

The greater the ratio of an inclined plane's length to its height is, the greater the mechanical advantage is. The mechanical advantage (*MA*) of an inclined plane can be calculated by dividing the *length* of the inclined plane by the *height* to which the load is lifted. The inclined plane in **Figure 7** has a mechanical advantage of 3 m/0.6 m = 5.

MATH FOCUS

Mechanical Advantage of an Inclined Plane A heavy box is pushed up a ramp that has an incline of 4.8 m long and 1.2 m high. What is the mechanical advantage of the ramp?

Step 1: Write the equation for the mechanical advantage of an inclined plane.

$$MA = \frac{l}{h}$$

Step 2: Replace *l* and *h* with length and height.

$$MA = \frac{4.8\ m}{1.2\ m} = 4$$

Now It's Your Turn

1. A wheelchair ramp is 9 m long and 1.5 m high. What is the mechanical advantage of the ramp?
2. As a pyramid is built, a stone block is dragged up a ramp that is 120 m long and 20 m high. What is the mechanical advantage of the ramp?
3. If an inclined plane were 2 m long and 8 m high, what would be its mechanical advantage?

$$MA = \frac{8\ \text{cm}}{2\ \text{cm}} = 4$$

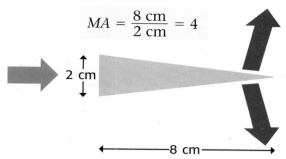

Figure 8 *A knife is a common example of a wedge, a simple machine consisting of two inclined planes back to back.*

Wedges

Imagine trying to cut a melon in half with a spoon. It wouldn't be easy, would it? A knife is much more useful for cutting because it is a **wedge.** A *wedge* is a pair of inclined planes that move. A wedge applies an output force that is greater than your input force, but you apply the input force over a greater distance. For example, a knife is a common wedge that can easily cut into a melon and push apart its two halves, as shown in **Figure 8.** Other useful wedges include doorstops, plows, ax heads, and chisels.

Mechanical Advantage of Wedges

The longer and thinner the wedge is, the greater its mechanical advantage is. That's why axes and knives cut better when you sharpen them—you are making the wedge thinner. Therefore, less input force is required. The mechanical advantage of a wedge can be found by dividing the length of the wedge by its greatest thickness, as shown in **Figure 8.**

Screws

A **screw** is an inclined plane that is wrapped in a spiral around a cylinder, as you can see in **Figure 9.** When a screw is turned, a small force is applied over the long distance along the inclined plane of the screw. Meanwhile, the screw applies a large force through the short distance it is pushed. Screws are used most commonly as fasteners.

Mechanical Advantage of Screws

If you could unwind the inclined plane of a screw, you would see that the plane is very long and has a gentle slope. Recall that the longer an inclined plane is compared with its height, the greater its mechanical advantage. Similarly, the longer the spiral on a screw is and the closer together the threads are, the greater the screw's mechanical advantage is. A jar lid is a screw that has a large mechanical advantage.

wedge a simple machine that is made up of two inclined planes and that moves; often used for cutting

screw a simple machine that consists of an inclined plane wrapped around a cylinder

Figure 9 *If you could unwind a screw, you would see that it is actually a very long inclined plane.*

Compound Machines

You are surrounded by machines. You even have machines in your body! But most of the machines in your world are **compound machines,** machines that are made of two or more simple machines. You have already seen one example of a compound machine: a block and tackle. A block and tackle consists of two or more pulleys.

Figure 10 shows a common example of a compound machine. A can opener may seem simple, but it is actually three machines combined. It consists of a second-class lever, a wheel and axle, and a wedge. When you squeeze the handle, you are making use of a second-class lever. The blade of the can opener acts as a wedge as it cuts into the can's top. The knob that you turn to open the can is a wheel and axle.

Mechanical Efficiency of Compound Machines

The mechanical efficiency of most compound machines is low. The efficiency is low because compound machines have more moving parts than simple machines do, thus there is more friction to overcome. Compound machines, such as automobiles and airplanes, can involve many simple machines. It is very important to reduce friction as much as possible, because too much friction can damage the simple machines that make up the compound machine. Friction can be lowered by using lubrication and other techniques.

✓ **Reading Check** What special disadvantage do compound machines have?

compound machine a machine made of more than one simple machine

Wheel and axle

Wedge

Second class lever

Figure 10 *A can opener is a compound machine. The handle is a second-class lever, the knob is a wheel and axle, and a wedge is used to open the can.*

Summary

- In a first-class lever, the fulcrum is between the force and the load. In a second-class lever, the load is between the force and the fulcrum. In a third-class lever, the force is between the fulcrum and the load.

- The mechanical advantage of an inclined plane is length divided by height. Wedges and screws are types of inclined planes.

- A wedge is a type of inclined plane. Its mechanical advantage is its length divided by its greatest thickness.

- The mechanical advantage of a wheel and axle is the radius of the wheel divided by the radius of the axle.

- Types of pulleys include fixed pulleys, movable pulleys, and block and tackles.

- Compound machines consist of two or more simple machines.

- Compound machines have low mechanical efficiencies because they have more moving parts and therefore more friction to overcome.

Using Key Terms

1. In your own words, write a definition for the term *lever*.

2. Use the following terms in the same sentence: *inclined plane*, *wedge*, and *screw*.

Understanding Key Ideas

3. Which class of lever always has a mechanical advantage of greater than 1?
   a. first-class
   b. second-class
   c. third-class
   d. None of the above

4. Give an example of each of the following simple machines: first-class lever, second-class lever, third-class lever, inclined plane, wedge, and screw.

Math Skills

5. A ramp is 0.5 m high and has a slope that is 4 m long. What is its mechanical advantage?

6. The radius of the wheel of a wheel and axle is 4 times the radius of the axle. What is the mechanical advantage of the wheel and axle?

Critical Thinking

7. **Applying Concepts** A third-class lever has a mechanical advantage of less than 1. Explain why it is useful for some tasks.

8. **Making Inferences** Which compound machine would you expect to have the lowest mechanical efficiency: a can opener or a pair of scissors? Explain your answer.

Interpreting Graphics

9. Indicate two simple machines being used in the picture below.

For a variety of links related to this chapter, go to www.scilinks.org

Topic: Simple Machines; Compound Machines

SciLinks code: HSM1395; HSM0331

Skills Practice Lab

A Powerful Workout

Does the amount of work that you do depend on how fast you do it? No! But the amount of time in which you do work does affect your power—the rate of work done. In this lab, you'll calculate your work and power for climbing a flight of stairs at different speeds. Then you'll compare your power with that of an ordinary household object—a 100 W light bulb.

OBJECTIVES

Calculate the work and power used to climb a flight of stairs.

Compare your work and power with that of a 100 W light bulb.

MATERIALS

- flight of stairs
- ruler, metric
- stopwatch

Ask a Question

1 How does your power in climbing a flight of stairs compare with the power of a 100 W light bulb?

Form a Hypothesis

2 Write a hypothesis that answers the question in step 1. Explain your reasoning.

Data Collection Table

Height of step (cm)	Number of steps	Height of stairs (m)	Time for slow walk (s)	Time for quick walk (s)
		DO NOT WRITE IN BOOK		

Test the Hypothesis

3 Copy the Data Collection Table onto a separate sheet of paper.

4 Use a metric ruler to measure the height of one stair step. Record the measurement in your Data Collection Table. Be sure to include units for all measurements.

5 Count the number of stairs, including the top step, and record this number in your Data Collection Table.

6 Calculate the height of the climb by multiplying the number of steps by the height of one step. Record your answer in meters. (You will need to convert your answer from centimeters to meters.)

7 Use a stopwatch to measure how many seconds it takes you to walk slowly up a flight of stairs. Record your measurement in your Data Collection Table.

8 Now measure how many seconds it takes you to walk quickly up a flight of stairs. Be careful not to overexert yourself. This is not a race to see who can get the fastest time!

Analyze the Results

1 **Constructing Tables** Copy the Calculations Table below onto a separate sheet of paper.

Calculations Table			
Weight (N)	Work (J)	Power for slow walk (W)	Power for quick walk (W)
DO NOT WRITE IN BOOK			

2 **Examining Data** Determine your weight in newtons, and record it in your Calculations Table. Your weight in newtons is your weight in pounds (lb) multiplied by 4.45 N/lb.

3 **Examining Data** Calculate and record your work done in climbing the stairs by using the following equation:

$$work = force \times distance$$

(Hint: If you are having trouble determining the force exerted, remember that force is measured in newtons.)

4 **Examining Data** Calculate and record your power output by using the following equation:

$$power = \frac{work}{time}$$

The unit for power is the watt (1 watt = 1 joule/second).

Draw Conclusions

5 **Evaluating Methods** In step 3 of "Analyze the Results," you were asked to calculate your work done in climbing the stairs. Why weren't you asked to calculate your work for each trial (slow walk and quick walk)?

6 **Drawing Conclusions** Look at your hypothesis. Was your hypothesis correct? Now that you have measured your power, write a statement that describes how your power compares with that of a 100 W light bulb.

7 **Applying Conclusions** The work done to move one electron in a light bulb is very small. Write down two reasons why the power used is large. (Hint: How many electrons are in the filament of a light bulb? How did you use more power in trial 2?)

Communicating Your Data

Your teacher will provide a class data table on the board. Add your average power to the table. Then calculate the average power from the class data. How many students would it take to create power equal to the power of a 100 W bulb?

Chapter Review

USING KEY TERMS

For each pair of terms, explain how the meanings of the terms differ.

1 *work* and *power*

2 *lever* and *inclined plane*

3 *wheel and axle* and *pulley*

UNDERSTANDING KEY IDEAS

Multiple Choice

4 Work is being done when

  a. you apply a force to an object.

  b. an object is moving after you applied a force to it.

  c. you exert a force that moves an object in the direction of the force.

  d. you do something that is difficult.

5 What is the unit for work?

  a. joule

  b. joule per second

  c. newton

  d. watt

6 Which of the following is a simple machine?

  a. a bicycle

  b. a jar lid

  c. a pair of scissors

  d. a can opener

7 A machine can increase

  a. distance by decreasing force.

  b. force by decreasing distance.

  c. neither distance nor force.

  d. Either (a) or (b)

8 What is power?

  a. the strength of someone or something

  b. the force that is used

  c. the work that is done

  d. the rate at which work is done

9 What is the unit for power?

  a. newton

  b. kilogram

  c. watt

  d. joule

Short Answer

10 Identify the two simple machines that make up a pair of scissors.

11 Explain why you do work on a bag of groceries when you pick it up but not when you carry it.

12 Why is the work output of a machine always less than the work input?

13 What does the mechanical advantage of a first-class lever depend upon? Describe how it can be changed.

Math Skills

14 You and a friend together apply a force of 1,000 N to a car, which makes the car roll 10 m in 1 min and 40 s.

  a. How much work did you and your friend do together?

  b. What was the power output?

15 A lever allows a 35 N load to be lifted with a force of 7 N. What is the mechanical advantage of the lever?

CRITICAL THINKING

16 Concept Mapping Use the following terms to create a concept map: *work, force, distance, machine,* and *mechanical advantage.*

17 Analyzing Ideas Explain why levers usually have a greater mechanical efficiency than other simple machines do.

18 Making Inferences The amount of work done on a machine is 300 J, and the machine does 50 J of work. What can you say about the amount of friction that the machine has while operating?

19 Applying Concepts The winding road shown below is a series of inclined planes. Describe how a winding road makes it easier for vehicles to travel up a hill.

20 Predicting Consequences Why wouldn't you want to reduce the friction involved in using a winding road?

21 Making Comparisons How does the way that a wedge's mechanical advantage is determined differ from the way that a screw's mechanical advantage is determined?

22 Identifying Relationships If the mechanical advantage of a certain machine is greater than 1, what does that tell you about the relationship between the input force and distance and output force and distance?

INTERPRETING GRAPHICS

For each of the images below, identify the class of lever used and calculate the mechanical advantage of the lever.

23

Output force 120 N

Input force 40 N

Fulcrum

24

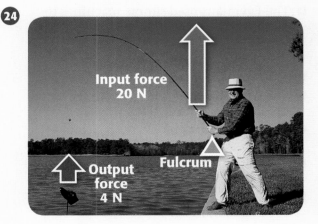

Input force 20 N

Output force 4 N

Fulcrum

Standardized Test Preparation

Read each of the passages below. Then, answer the questions that follow each passage.

Passage 1 The Great Pyramid, located in Giza, Egypt, covers an area the size of 7 city blocks and rises about 40 stories high. The Great Pyramid was built around 2600 BCE and took less than 30 years to complete. During this time, the Egyptians cut and moved more than 2 million stone blocks, most of which average 2,000 kg. The workers did not have cranes, bulldozers, or any other heavy-duty machines. What they did have were two simple machines—the inclined plane and the lever. Archeologists have found the remains of inclined planes, or ramps, made from mud, stone, and wood. The Egyptians pushed or pulled the blocks along ramps to raise the blocks to the proper height. Notches in many blocks indicate that huge levers were used as giant crowbars to lift and move the heavy blocks.

1. What is the main idea of the passage?

A Archeologists have found the remains of inclined planes near the pyramids.

B The Great Pyramid at Giza was built in less than 30 years.

C The Egyptians cut and moved more than 2 million stone blocks.

D The Egyptians used simple machines to build the Great Pyramid at Giza.

2. Which of the following is a fact stated in the passage?

F The Great Pyramid was made using more than 2 million stone blocks.

G Each of the stone blocks used to build the Great Pyramid was exactly 2,000 kg.

H Ancient Egyptians used cranes to build the Great Pyramid.

I The Great Pyramid at Giza has a mass of about 2 million kg.

Passage 2 While riding a bicycle, you have probably experienced vibrations when the wheels of the bicycle hit bumps in the road. The force of the vibrations travels up through the frame to the rider. Slight vibrations can cause discomfort. Large ones can cause you to lose control of the bike and crash. Early bicycle designs made no attempt to dampen the <u>shock</u> of vibrations. Later designs used air-filled rubber tires and softer seats with springs to absorb some of the vibrations. Today's bike designs provide a safer, more comfortable ride. Various new materials—titanium, for example—absorb shock better than traditional steel and aluminum do. More important, designers are putting a variety of shock absorbers—devices that absorb energy—into bike designs.

1. In the passage, what does the term *shock* mean?

A a medical emergency that can be caused by blood loss

B a dry material used in early bicycles

C a feeling of being stunned and surprised

D a jolt or impact

2. Which of the following is a fact stated in the passage?

F You have experienced vibrations while bicycle riding.

G Slight vibrations can cause severe discomfort.

H Titanium absorbs shock better than aluminum does.

I Today's bike designs provide a more fashionable ride.

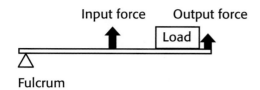

Input force   Output force

Load

Fulcrum

1. How does this lever make work easier?
   A by changing the direction of the force
   B by increasing both force and distance
   C by increasing force and decreasing distance
   D by decreasing force and increasing distance

2. What would the mechanical advantage of this lever be?
   F less than 1
   G 1
   H greater than 1
   I There is not enough information to determine the answer.

3. What type of lever is the lever in the diagram?
   A a first-class lever
   B a second-class lever
   C a third-class lever
   D There is not enough information to determine the answer.

4. Which of the following items is the same type of lever as the lever in the diagram?
   F a seesaw
   G a wheelbarrow
   H a bottle opener
   I an arm lifting a barbell

1. For a special musical number during a school choir concert, 6 students stood in the first row, 10 students stood in the second row, and 14 students stood in the third row. If the pattern continued, how many students stood in the fifth row?
   A 18
   B 22
   C 26
   D 30

2. Michael baked some bread for his friends. He put 2½ cups of flour in each loaf. Altogether, he used 12½ cups of flour. How many loaves did he make?
   F 2 loaves
   G 4 loaves
   H 5 loaves
   I 15 loaves

3. A force of 15 N is exerted over a distance of 6 m. How much work was done? (Use the equation $W = F \times d$.)
   A 21 J
   B 21 N
   C 90 J
   D 90 N

4. If 350 J of work was done in 50 s, what was the power output? (Use the equation $P = W/t$.)
   F 7 W
   G 70 W
   H 1,750 W
   I 17,500 W

Standardized Test Preparation

Science in Action

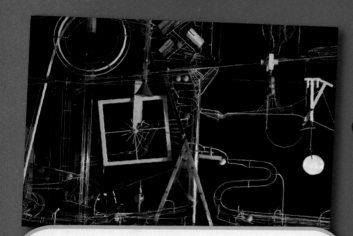

Science, Technology, and Society

Kinetic Sculpture

The collection of tubes, tracks, balls, and blocks of wood shown in the photo is an audio-kinetic sculpture. A conveyor belt lifts the balls to a point high on the track, and the balls wind their way down as they are pulled by the force of gravity and pushed by various other forces. They twist through spirals, drop straight down tubes, and sometimes go up and around loops as if on a roller coaster. All this is made possible by the artist's applications of principles of kinetic energy, the energy of motion.

Math ACTIVITY

A conveyor belt on a kinetic sculpture lifts a ball to a point 0.8 m high. It exerts 0.05 N of force as it does so. How much work does the conveyor belt do on the ball?

Weird Science

Nanomachines

The technology of making things smaller and smaller keeps growing and growing. Powerful computers can now be held in the palm of your hand. But what can motors that are smaller than grains of pepper do? How can gnat-sized robots that can swim through the bloodstream be used? One possible field in which very small machines, *nanomachines,* can be used is in medicine.

Some scientists are looking into the possibility of creating cell-sized machines called *nanobots.* These tiny robots may have many uses in medicine if they can be injected into a person's bloodstream.

Language Arts ACTIVITY

WRITING SKILL Write a short story in which nanobots are used to save someone's life. Describe the machines the nanobots use in destroying deadly bacteria, clearing blood clots, or delivering medicine.

Mike Hensler

The Surf Chair Mike Hensler was a lifeguard at Daytona Beach, Florida, when he realized that it was next to impossible for someone in a wheelchair to come onto the beach. Although he had never invented a machine before, Hensler decided to build a wheelchair that could be driven across sand without getting stuck. He began spending many evenings in his driveway with a pile of lawn-chair parts, designing the chair by trial and error.

The result of Hensler's efforts looks very different from a conventional wheelchair. With huge rubber wheels and a thick frame of white PVC pipe, the Surf Chair not only moves easily over sandy terrain but also is weather resistant and easy to clean. The newest models of the Surf Chair come with optional attachments, such as a variety of umbrellas, detachable armrests and footrests, and even places to attach fishing rods.

Social Studies ACTIVITY

List some simple and compound machines that are used as access devices for people who are disabled. Research how these machines came to be in common use.

go.hrw.com

To learn more about these Science in Action topics, visit **go.hrw.com** and type in the keyword **HP5WRKF.**

Current Science

Check out Current Science® articles related to this chapter by visiting **go.hrw.com**. Just type in the keyword **HP5CS08.**

Energy and Energy Resources

SECTION **1** What Is Energy? 240

SECTION **2** Energy Conversions . . . 248

SECTION **3** Conservation of Energy 254

SECTION **4** Energy Resources. 258

Chapter Lab 264
Chapter Review 266
Standardized Test Preparation 268
Science in Action. 270

About the

Imagine that you're a driver in this race. Your car needs a lot of energy to finish. So, it probably needs a lot of gasoline, right? No, it just needs a lot of sunshine! This car runs on solar energy. Solar energy is one of the many forms of energy. Energy is needed to drive a car, turn on a light bulb, play sports, and walk to school. Energy is always being changed into different forms for different uses.

FOLDNOTES **Layered Book** Before you read the chapter, create the FoldNote entitled "Layered Book" described in the **Study Skills** section of the Appendix. Label the tabs of the layered book with "Types of energy," "Energy conversions," "Conservation of energy," and "Energy resources." As you read the chapter, write information you learn about each category under the appropriate tab.

Energy Swings!

In this activity, you'll observe a moving pendulum to learn about energy.

Procedure

1. Make a pendulum by tying a **50 cm long string** around the hook of a **100 g hooked mass.**

2. Hold the string with one hand. Pull the mass slightly to the side, and let go of the mass without pushing it. Watch it swing at least 10 times.

3. Record your observations. Note how fast and how high the pendulum swings.

4. Repeat step 2, but pull the mass farther to the side.

5. Record your observations. Note how fast and how high the pendulum swings.

Analysis

1. Does the pendulum have energy? Explain your answer.

2. What causes the pendulum to move?

3. Do you think the pendulum had energy before you let go of the mass? Explain your answer.

What Is Energy?

It's match point. The crowd is silent. The tennis player tosses the ball into the air and then slams it with her racket. The ball flies toward her opponent, who swings her racket at the ball. THWOOSH!! The ball goes into the net, causing it to shake. Game, set, and match!!

The tennis player needs energy to slam the ball with her racket. The ball also must have energy in order to cause the net to shake. Energy is around you all of the time. But what, exactly, is energy?

Energy and Work: Working Together

In science, **energy** is the ability to do work. Work is done when a force causes an object to move in the direction of the force. How do energy and work help you play tennis? The tennis player in **Figure 1** does work on her racket by exerting a force on it. The racket does work on the ball, and the ball does work on the net. When one object does work on another, energy is transferred from the first object to the second object. This energy allows the second object to do work. So, work is a transfer of energy. Like work, energy is expressed in units of joules (J).

✓ **Reading Check** What is energy? (*See the Appendix for answers to Reading Checks.*)

energy the capacity to do work

Figure 1 *The tennis player does work and transfers energy to the racket. With this energy, the racket can then do work on the ball.*

Kinetic Energy

In tennis, energy is transferred from the racket to the ball. As it flies over the net, the ball has kinetic (ki NET ik) energy. **Kinetic energy** is the energy of motion. All moving objects have kinetic energy. Like all forms of energy, kinetic energy can be used to do work. For example, kinetic energy allows a hammer to do work on a nail, as shown in **Figure 2.**

kinetic energy the energy of an object that is due to the object's motion

Kinetic Energy Depends on Mass and Speed

An object's kinetic energy can be found by the following equation:

$$kinetic\ energy = \frac{mv^2}{2}$$

The *m* stands for the object's mass in kilograms. The *v* stands for the object's speed. The faster something is moving, the more kinetic energy it has. Also, the greater the mass of a moving object, the greater its kinetic energy is.

A large car has more kinetic energy than a car that has less mass and that is moving at the same speed does. But as you can see from the equation, speed is squared. So speed has a greater effect on kinetic energy than mass does. For this reason, car crashes are much more dangerous at higher speeds than at lower speeds. A moving car has *4 times* the kinetic energy of the same car going half the speed! This is because it's going twice the speed of the slower car, and 2 squared is 4.

Figure 2 *When you swing a hammer, you give it kinetic energy, which does work on the nail.*

MATH FOCUS

Kinetic Energy What is the kinetic energy of a car that has a mass of 1,200 kg and is moving at a speed of 20 m/s?

Step 1: Write the equation for kinetic energy.
$$KE = \frac{mv^2}{2}$$

Step 2: Replace *m* and *v* with the measurements given, and solve.

$$KE = \frac{1,200\ kg \times (20\ m/s)^2}{2}$$

$$KE = \frac{1,200\ kg \times 400\ m^2/s^2}{2}$$

$$KE = \frac{480,000\ kg{\bullet}m^2/s^2}{2}$$

$$KE = 240,000\ kg{\bullet}m^2/s^2 = 240,000\ J$$

Now It's Your Turn

1. What is the kinetic energy of a car that has a mass of 2,400 kg and is moving at 20 m/s? How does this kinetic energy compare to the kinetic energy of the car in the example given at left?

2. What is the kinetic energy of a 4,000 kg elephant that is running at 2 m/s? at 4 m/s? How do the two kinetic energies compare with one another?

3. What is the kinetic energy of a 2,000 kg bus that is moving at 30 m/s?

4. What is the kinetic energy of a 3,000 kg bus that is moving at 20 m/s?

Potential Energy

Not all energy has to do with motion. **Potential energy** is the energy an object has because of its position. For example, the stretched bow shown in **Figure 3** has potential energy. The bow has energy because work has been done to change its shape. The energy of that work is turned into potential energy.

Gravitational Potential Energy

When you lift an object, you do work on it. You use a force that is against the force of gravity. When you do this, you transfer energy to the object and give the object *gravitational potential energy*. Books on a shelf have gravitational potential energy. So does your backpack after you lift it on to your back. The amount of gravitational potential energy that an object has depends on its weight and its height.

Calculating Gravitational Potential Energy

You can find gravitational potential energy by using the following equation:

gravitational potential energy = weight × height

Because weight is expressed in newtons and height in meters, gravitational potential energy is expressed in newton-meters (N•m), or joules (J).

Recall that *work = force × distance*. Weight is the amount of force that you must use on an object to lift it, and height is a distance. So, gravitational potential energy is equal to the amount of work done on the object to lift it to a certain height. Or, you can think of gravitational potential energy as equal to the work that would be done by the object if it were dropped from its height.

Figure 3 *The stored potential energy of the bow and string allows them to do work on the arrow when the string is released.*

Gravitational Potential Energy What is the gravitational potential energy of a book with a weight of 13 N at a height of 1.5 m off the ground?

Step 1: Write the equation for gravitational potential energy (*GPE*).

GPE = weight × height

Step 2: Replace the weight and height with the measurements given in the problem, and solve.

GPE = 13 N × 1.5 m
GPE = 19.5 N•m = 19.5 J

Now It's Your Turn

1. What is the gravitational potential energy of a cat that weighs 40 N standing on a table that is 0.8 m above the ground?
2. What is the gravitational potential energy of a diver who weighs 500 N standing on a platform that is 10 m off the ground?
3. What is the gravitational potential energy of a diver who weighs 600 N standing on a platform that is 8 m off the ground?

Height Above What?

When you want to find out an object's gravitational potential energy, the "ground" that you measure the object's height from depends on where it is. For example, what if you want to measure the gravitational potential energy of an egg sitting on the kitchen counter? In this case, you would measure the egg's height from the floor. But if you were holding the egg over a balcony several stories from the ground, you would measure the egg's height from the ground! You can see that gravitational potential energy depends on your point of view. So, the height you use in calculating gravitational potential energy is a measure of how far an object has to fall.

Mechanical Energy

How would you describe the energy of the juggler's pins in **Figure 4**? To describe their total energy, you would state their mechanical energy. **Mechanical energy** is the total energy of motion and position of an object. Both potential energy and kinetic energy are kinds of mechanical energy. Mechanical energy can be all potential energy, all kinetic energy, or some of each. You can use the following equation to find mechanical energy:

mechanical energy = potential energy + kinetic energy

✓ **Reading Check** What two kinds of energy can make up the mechanical energy of an object?

Mechanical Energy in a Juggler's Pin

The mechanical energy of an object remains the same unless it transfers some of its energy to another object. But even if the mechanical energy of an object stays the same, the potential energy or kinetic energy it has can increase or decrease.

Look at **Figure 4.** While the juggler is moving the pin with his hand, he is doing work on the pin to give it kinetic energy. But as soon as the pin leaves his hand, the pin's kinetic energy starts changing into potential energy. How can you tell that the kinetic energy is decreasing? The pin slows down as it moves upwards. Eventually, all of the pin's kinetic energy turns into potential energy, and it stops moving upward.

As the pin starts to fall back down again, its potential energy starts changing back into kinetic energy. More and more of its potential energy turns into kinetic energy. You can tell because the pin speeds up as it falls towards the ground.

potential energy the energy that an object has because of the position, shape, or condition of the object

mechanical energy the amount of work an object can do because of the object's kinetic and potential energies

Figure 4 *As a pin is juggled, its mechanical energy is the sum of its potential energy and its kinetic energy at any point.*

Figure 5   Thermal Energy in Water

The particles in an ice cube vibrate in fixed positions and do not have a lot of kinetic energy.

The particles of water in a lake can move more freely and have more kinetic energy than water particles in ice do.

The particles of water in steam move rapidly, so they have more energy than the particles in liquid water do.

Other Forms of Energy

Energy can come in a number of forms besides mechanical energy. These forms of energy include thermal, chemical, electrical, sound, light, and nuclear energy. As you read the next few pages, you will learn what these different forms of energy have to do with kinetic and potential energy.

Thermal Energy

All matter is made of particles that are always in random motion. Because the particles are in motion, they have kinetic energy. *Thermal energy* is all of the kinetic energy due to random motion of the particles that make up an object.

As you can see in **Figure 5,** particles move faster at higher temperatures than at lower temperatures. The faster the particles move, the greater their kinetic energy and the greater the object's thermal energy. Thermal energy also depends on the number of particles. Water in the form of steam has a higher temperature than water in a lake does. But the lake has more thermal energy because the lake has more water particles.

Chemical Energy

Where does the energy in food come from? Food is made of chemical compounds. When compounds such as sugar form, work is done to join the different atoms together. *Chemical energy* is the energy of a compound that changes as its atoms are rearranged. Chemical energy is a form of potential energy because it depends on the position and arrangement of the atoms in a compound.

For another activity related to this chapter, go to **go.hrw.com** and type in the keyword **HP5ENGW.**

Quick Lab

Hear That Energy!

1. Make a simple drum by covering the open end of an **empty coffee can** with **wax paper.** Secure the wax paper with a **rubber band.**

2. Using the eraser end of a **pencil,** tap lightly on the wax paper. Describe how the paper responds. What do you hear?

3. Repeat step 2, but tap the paper a bit harder. Compare your results with those of step 2.

4. Cover half of the wax paper with one hand. Now, tap the paper. What happened? How can you describe sound energy as a form of mechanical energy?

Electrical Energy

The electrical outlets in your home allow you to use electrical energy. *Electrical energy* is the energy of moving electrons. Electrons are the negatively charged particles of atoms.

Suppose you plug an electrical device, such as the amplifier shown in **Figure 6,** into an outlet and turn it on. The electrons in the wires will transfer energy to different parts inside the amplifier. The electrical energy of moving electrons is used to do work that makes the sound that you hear from the amplifier.

The electrical energy used in your home comes from power plants. Huge generators turn magnets inside loops of wire. The changing position of a magnet makes electrical energy run through the wire. This electrical energy can be thought of as potential energy that is used when you plug in an electrical appliance and use it.

Figure 6 *The movement of electrons produces the electrical energy that an amplifier and a microphone use to produce sound.*

Sound Energy

Figure 7 shows how a vibrating object transmits energy through the air around it. Sound energy is caused by an object's vibrations. When you stretch a guitar string, the string stores potential energy. When you let the string go, this potential energy is turned into kinetic energy, which makes the string vibrate. The string also transmits some of this kinetic energy to the air around it. The air particles also vibrate, and transmit this energy to your ear. When the sound energy reaches your ear, you hear the sound of the guitar.

✓ Reading Check What does sound energy consist of?

Figure 7 *As the guitar strings vibrate, they cause particles in the air to vibrate. These vibrations transmit sound energy.*

Figure 8 *The energy used to cook food in a microwave is a form of light energy.*

Light Energy

Light allows you to see, but did you know that not all light can be seen? **Figure 8** shows a type of light that we use but can't see. *Light energy* is produced by the vibrations of electrically charged particles. Like sound vibrations, light vibrations cause energy to be transmitted. But the vibrations that transmit light energy don't need to be carried through matter. In fact, light energy can move through a vacuum (an area where there is no matter).

Nuclear Energy

There is a form of energy that comes from a tiny amount of matter. It is used to generate electrical energy, and it gives the sun its energy. It is *nuclear* (NOO klee uhr) *energy*, the energy that comes from changes in the nucleus (NOO klee uhs) of an atom.

Atoms store a lot of potential energy because of the positions of the particles in the nucleus of the atoms. When two or more small nuclei (NOO klee ie) join together, or when the nucleus of a large atom splits apart, energy is given off.

The energy given off by the sun comes from nuclear energy. In the sun, shown in **Figure 9,** hydrogen nuclei join together to make a larger helium nucleus. This reaction, known as *fusion,* gives off a huge amount of energy. The sun's light and heat come from these reactions.

When a nucleus of a heavy element such as uranium is split apart, the potential energy in the nucleus is given off. This kind of nuclear energy is called *fission*. Fission is used to generate electrical energy at nuclear power plants.

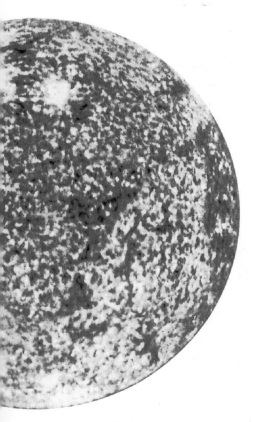

Figure 9 *Without the nuclear energy from the sun, life on Earth would not be possible.*

✔ Reading Check Where does nuclear energy come from?

Summary

- Energy is the ability to do work, and work equals the transfer of energy. Energy and work are expressed in units of joules (J).
- Kinetic energy is energy of motion and depends on speed and mass.
- Potential energy is energy of position. Gravitational potential energy depends on weight and height.

- Mechanical energy is the sum of kinetic energy and potential energy.
- Thermal energy and sound energy can be considered forms of kinetic energy.
- Chemical energy, electrical energy, and nuclear energy can be considered forms of potential energy.

Using Key Terms

1. In your own words, write a definition for the term *energy*.

2. Use the following terms in the same sentence: *kinetic energy*, *potential energy*, and *mechanical energy*.

Understanding Key Ideas

3. What determines an object's thermal energy?
   a. the motion of its particles
   b. its size
   c. its potential energy
   d. its mechanical energy

4. How are energy and work related?

5. What two factors determine gravitational potential energy?

6. Describe why chemical energy is a form of potential energy.

Critical Thinking

7. **Identifying Relationships** When you hit a nail into a board by using a hammer, the head of the nail gets warm. In terms of kinetic and thermal energy, describe why you think the nail head gets warm.

8. **Applying Concepts** Explain why a high-speed collision may cause more damage to vehicles than a low-speed collision does.

Interpreting Graphics

9. Which part of mechanical energy does the girl in the picture below have the most of?

For a variety of links related to this chapter, go to www.scilinks.org

Topic: What Is Energy? ; Forms of Energy
SciLinks code: HSM1660; HSM0612

Energy Conversions

Imagine you're finishing a clay mug in art class. You turn around, and your elbow knocks the mug off the table. Luckily, you catch the mug before it hits the ground.

The mug has gravitational potential energy while it is on the table. As the mug falls, its potential energy changes into kinetic energy. This change is an example of an energy conversion. An **energy conversion** is a change from one form of energy to another. Any form of energy can change into any other form of energy. Often, one form of energy changes into more than one other form.

energy conversion a change from one form of energy to another

Kinetic Energy and Potential Energy

Look at **Figure 1.** At the instant this picture was taken, the skateboarder on the left side of the picture was hardly moving. How did he get up so high in the air? As you might guess, he was moving at a high speed on his way up the half-pipe. So, he had a lot of kinetic energy. What happened to that energy? His kinetic energy changed into potential energy. Imagine that the picture below is a freeze-frame of a video. What happens once the video starts running again? The skateboarder's potential energy will become kinetic energy once again as he speeds down the side of the half-pipe.

Figure 1 **Potential Energy and Kinetic Energy**

When the skateboarder reaches the top of the half-pipe, his potential energy is at a maximum.

As he speeds down through the bottom of the half-pipe, the skateboarder's kinetic energy is at a maximum.

Elastic Potential Energy

A rubber band can be used to show another example of an energy conversion. Did you know that energy can be stored in a rubber band? Look at **Figure 2.** The wound-up rubber band in the toy airplane has a kind of potential energy called *elastic potential energy.* When the rubber band is let go, the stored energy becomes kinetic energy, spins the propeller, and makes the airplane fly.

You can change the shape of a rubber band by stretching it. Stretching the rubber band takes a little effort. The energy you put into stretching it becomes elastic potential energy. Like the skateboarder at the top of the half-pipe, the stretched rubber band stores potential energy. When you let the rubber band go, it goes back to its original shape. It releases its stored-up potential energy as it does so, as you know if you have ever snapped a rubber band against your skin!

Reading Check How is elastic potential energy stored and released? (*See the Appendix for answers to Reading Checks.*)

Figure 2 *The wound-up rubber band in this model airplane has potential energy because its shape has been changed.*

Conversions Involving Chemical Energy

You may have heard someone say, "Breakfast is the most important meal of the day." Why is eating breakfast so important? As shown in **Figure 3,** chemical energy comes from the food you eat. Your body uses chemical energy to function. Eating breakfast gives your body the energy needed to help you start the day.

Figure 3 Chemical energy of food is converted into kinetic energy when you are active. It is converted into thermal energy to maintain body temperature.

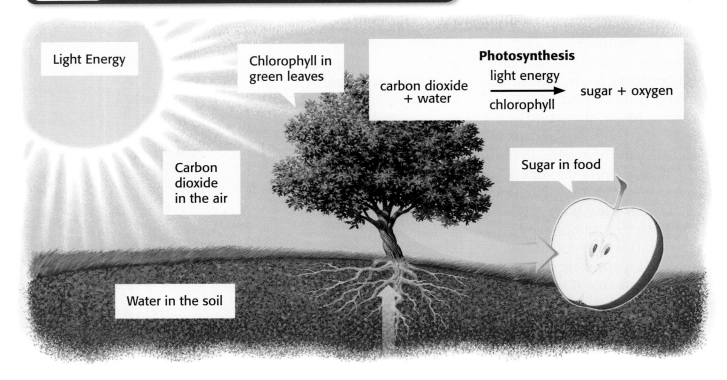

Figure 4 From Light Energy to Chemical Energy

Light Energy

Chlorophyll in green leaves

Photosynthesis

carbon dioxide + water $\xrightarrow[\text{chlorophyll}]{\text{light energy}}$ sugar + oxygen

Carbon dioxide in the air

Sugar in food

Water in the soil

CONNECTION TO Biology

WRITING SKILL **Energy from Plants** All living things need energy. Plants play a major role in providing sources of energy that our bodies use, from the oxygen we breathe to the food we eat. Research the different ways that plants help provide the energy requirements of all living things, and write a one-page report in your **science journal** describing what you learn.

Energy Conversions in Plants

Did you know that the chemical energy in the food you eat comes from the sun's energy? When you eat fruits, vegetables, or grains, you are taking in chemical energy. This energy comes from a chemical change that was made possible by the sun's energy. When you eat meat from animals that ate plants, you are also taking in energy that first came from the sun.

As shown in **Figure 4,** photosynthesis (FOHT oh SIN thuh sis) uses light energy to make new substances that have chemical energy. In this way, light energy is changed into chemical energy. The chemical energy from a tree can be changed into thermal energy when you burn the tree's wood. So, if you follow the conversion of energy back far enough, the energy from a wood fire actually comes from the sun!

Reading Check Where does the energy that plants use to grow come from?

The Process Continues

Let's trace where the energy goes. Plants change light energy into chemical energy. The chemical energy in the food you eat is changed into another kind of chemical energy that your body can use. Your body then uses that energy to give you the kinetic energy that you use in everything you do. It's an endless process—energy is always going somewhere!

Figure 5 Energy Conversions in a Hair Dryer

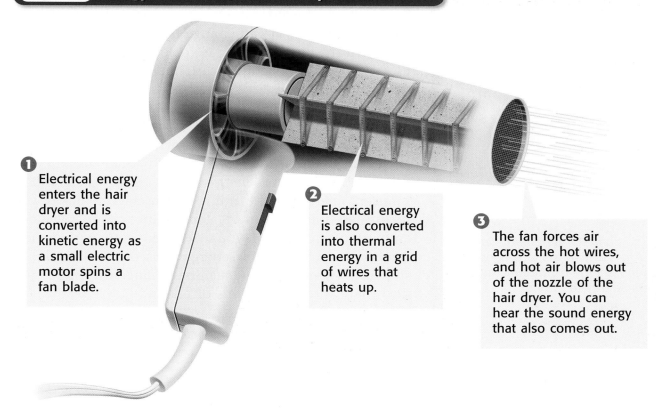

1 Electrical energy enters the hair dryer and is converted into kinetic energy as a small electric motor spins a fan blade.

2 Electrical energy is also converted into thermal energy in a grid of wires that heats up.

3 The fan forces air across the hot wires, and hot air blows out of the nozzle of the hair dryer. You can hear the sound energy that also comes out.

Why Energy Conversions Are Important

Energy conversions are needed for everything we do. Heating our homes, getting energy from a meal, and many other things use energy conversions. Machines, such as the hair dryer shown in **Figure 5,** help harness energy and make that energy work for you. Electrical energy by itself won't dry your hair. But you can use a hair dryer to change electrical energy into the thermal energy that will help you dry your hair.

Conversions Involving Electrical Energy

You use electrical energy all of the time. When you listen to the radio, when you make toast, and when you take a picture with a camera, you use electrical energy. Electrical energy can easily be changed into other forms of energy. **Table 1** lists some common energy conversions that involve electrical energy.

Table 1 Some Conversions of Electrical Energy	
Alarm clock	electrical energy ⟶ light energy and sound energy
Battery	chemical energy ⟶ electrical energy
Light bulb	electrical energy ⟶ light energy and thermal energy
Blender	electrical energy ⟶ kinetic energy and sound energy

Figure 6 *Some of the energy you transfer to a nutcracker is converted into sound energy as the nutcracker transfers energy to the nut.*

Energy and Machines

You've been learning about energy, its different forms, and the ways that it can change between forms. Another way to learn about energy is to look at how machines use energy. A machine can make work easier by changing the size or direction (or both) of the force needed to do the work.

Suppose you want to crack open a walnut. Using a nutcracker, such as the one shown in **Figure 6,** would be much easier (and less painful) than using your fingers. You transfer energy to the nutcracker, and it transfers energy to the nut. The nutcracker allows you to use less force over a greater distance to do the same amount of work as if you had used your bare hands. Another example of how energy is used by a machine is shown in **Figure 7.** Some machines change the energy put into them into other forms of energy.

✓ *Reading Check* **What are two things that machines can do to force that is put into them?**

Figure 7 **Energy Conversions in a Bicycle**

For your bike to start and keep moving, energy must be transferred and converted.

❶ Chemical energy in your body is converted into kinetic energy when your muscle fibers contract and relax.

❷ Your legs transfer this kinetic energy to the pedals by pushing them around in a circle.

❹ The chain moves and transfers energy to the back wheel, which gets you moving!

❸ The pedals transfer this kinetic energy to the gear wheel, which transfers kinetic energy to the chain.

Machines as Energy Converters

Machines help you use energy by converting it into the form that you need. **Figure 8** shows a device called a *radiometer*. It was invented to measure energy from the sun. Inside the glass bulb are four small vanes that absorb light energy. The vanes are dark on one side and light on the other. The dark sides absorb light energy better than the light sides do. As gases next to the dark sides of the vanes heat up, the gas molecules move faster, which causes the vanes to turn. The radiometer shows how a machine can convert energy from one form into another. It changes light energy into heat energy into kinetic energy.

Figure 8 *Machines can change energy into different forms. This radiometer converts light energy into kinetic energy.*

SECTION Review

Summary

- An energy conversion is a change from one form of energy to another. Any form of energy can be converted into any other form of energy.

- Kinetic energy is converted to potential energy when an object is moved against gravity.

- Elastic potential energy is another example of potential energy.

- Your body uses the food you eat to convert chemical energy into kinetic energy.

- Plants convert light energy into chemical energy.

- Machines can transfer energy and can convert energy into a more useful form.

Using Key Terms

1. In your own words, write a definition for the term *energy conversion*.

Understanding Key Ideas

2. In plants, energy is transformed from
   a. kinetic to potential.
   b. light to chemical.
   c. chemical to electrical.
   d. chemical to light.

3. Describe a case in which electrical energy is converted into thermal energy.

4. How does your body get the energy that it needs?

5. What is the role of machines in energy conversions?

Critical Thinking

6. **Applying Concepts** Describe the kinetic-potential energy conversions that occur when a basketball bounces.

7. **Applying Concepts** A car that brakes suddenly comes to a screeching halt. Is the sound energy produced in this conversion a useful form of energy? Explain your answer.

Interpreting Graphics

Look at the diagram below, and answer the following questions.

8. What kind of energy does the skier have at the top of the slope?

9. What happens to that energy after the skier races down the slope of the mountain?

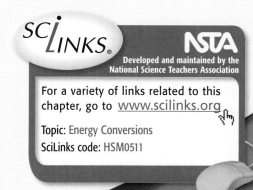

Conservation of Energy

Many roller coasters have a mechanism that pulls the cars up to the top of the first hill. But the cars are on their own for the rest of the ride.

As the cars go up and down the hills on the track, their potential energy is converted into kinetic energy and back again. But the cars never return to the same height at which they started. Does energy get lost somewhere along the way? No, it is just converted into other forms of energy.

Where Does the Energy Go?

To find out where a roller coaster's original potential energy goes, you have to think about more than just the hills of the roller coaster. Friction plays a part too. **Friction** is a force that opposes motion between two surfaces that are touching. For the roller coaster to move, energy must be used to overcome friction. There is friction between the cars' wheels and the track and between the cars and the air around them. As a result, not all of the potential energy of the cars changes into kinetic energy as the cars go down the first hill. Likewise, as you can see in **Figure 1,** not all of the kinetic energy of the cars changes back into potential energy.

READING WARM-UP

Objectives

- Explain how energy is conserved within a closed system.
- Explain the law of conservation of energy.
- Give examples of how thermal energy is always a result of energy conversion.
- Explain why perpetual motion is impossible.

Terms to Learn

friction
law of conservation of energy

READING STRATEGY

Paired Summarizing Read this section silently. In pairs, take turns summarizing the material. Stop to discuss ideas that seem confusing.

Figure 1 **Energy Conversions in a Roller Coaster**

Not all of the cars' potential energy (*PE*) is converted into kinetic energy (*KE*) as the cars go down the first hill. In addition, not all of the cars' kinetic energy is converted into potential energy as the cars go up the second hill. Some of it is changed into thermal energy because of friction.

ⓐ *PE* is greatest at the top of the first hill.

ⓑ *KE* at the bottom of the first hill is less than the *PE* at the top was.

ⓒ *PE* at the top of the second hill is less than *KE* and *PE* from the first hill.

Energy Is Conserved Within a Closed System

A *closed system* is a group of objects that transfer energy only to each other. For example, a closed system that involves a roller coaster consists of the track, the cars, and the air around them. On a roller coaster, some mechanical energy (the sum of kinetic and potential energy) is always converted into thermal energy because of friction. Sound energy also comes from the energy conversions in a roller coaster. If you add together the cars' kinetic energy at the bottom of the first hill, the thermal energy due to overcoming friction, and the sound energy made, you end up with the same total amount of energy as the original amount of potential energy. In other words, energy is conserved and not lost.

friction a force that opposes motion between two surfaces that are in contact

law of conservation of energy the law that states that energy cannot be created or destroyed but can be changed from one form to another

Law of Conservation of Energy

Energy is conserved in all cases. Because no exception to this rule has been found, this rule is described as a law. According to the **law of conservation of energy,** energy cannot be created or destroyed. The total amount of energy in a closed system is always the same. As **Figure 2** shows, energy can change from one form to another. But all of the different forms of energy in a system always add up to the same total amount of energy. It does not matter how many energy conversions take place.

Reading Check Why is the conservation of energy considered a scientific law? (*See the Appendix for answers to Reading Checks.*)

Figure 2 Energy Conservation in a Light Bulb

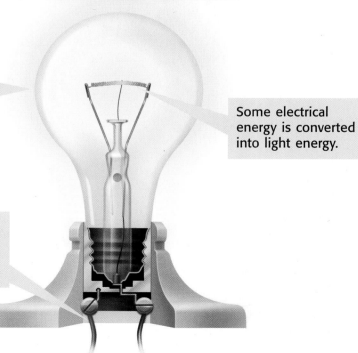

Some energy is converted into thermal energy, which makes the bulb feel warm.

Some electrical energy is converted into light energy.

As electrical energy is carried through the wire, some of it is converted into thermal energy.

No Conversion Without Thermal Energy

Any time one form of energy is converted into another form, some of the original energy always gets converted into thermal energy. The thermal energy due to friction that results from energy conversions is not useful energy. That is, this thermal energy is not used to do work. Think about a car. You put gas into a car. But not all of the gasoline's chemical energy makes the car move. Some wasted thermal energy will always result from the energy conversions. Much of this energy leaves through the radiator and the exhaust pipe.

Perpetual Motion? No Way!

People have sometimes tried to make a machine that would run forever without any additional energy. This perpetual (puhr PECH oo uhl) motion machine would put out exactly as much energy as it takes in. But that's impossible, because some waste thermal energy always results from energy conversions. The only way a machine can keep moving is to have a constant supply of energy. For example, the "drinking bird" shown in **Figure 3** uses thermal energy from the air to evaporate the water from its head. So, it is not a perpetual motion machine.

Reading Check Why is "perpetual motion" impossible?

Figure 3 The "Drinking Bird"

❶ When the bird "drinks," the felt covering its head gets wet.

❷ When the bird is upright, water evaporates from the felt, which decreases the temperature and pressure in the head. Fluid is drawn up from the tail, where pressure is higher, and the bird tips downward.

❸ After the bird "drinks," fluid returns to the tail, the bird flips upright, and the cycle repeats.

Making Conversions Efficient

You may have heard that a car is energy efficient if it gets good gas mileage, and that your home may be energy efficient if it is well insulated. In terms of energy conversions, *energy efficiency* (e FISH uhn see) is a comparison of the amount of energy before a conversion with the amount of useful energy after a conversion. A car with high energy efficiency can go farther than other cars with the same amount of gas.

Energy conversions that are more efficient end up wasting less energy. Look at **Figure 4.** Newer cars tend to be more energy efficient than older cars. One reason is the smooth, aerodynamic (ER oh die NAM ik) shape of newer cars. The smooth shape reduces friction between the car and the surrounding air. Because these cars move through air more easily, they use less energy to overcome friction. So, they are more efficient. Improving the efficiency of machines, such as cars, is important because greater efficiency results in less waste. If less energy is wasted, less energy is needed to operate a machine.

Figure 4 *The shape of newer cars reduces friction between the body of the car and the air.*

More aerodynamic car

Less aerodynamic car

SECTION Review

Summary

- Because of friction, some energy is always converted into thermal energy during an energy conversion.

- Energy is conserved within a closed system. According to the law of conservation of energy, energy cannot be created or destroyed.

- Perpetual motion is impossible because some of the energy put into a machine is converted into thermal energy because of friction.

Using Key Terms

1. Use the following terms in the same sentence: *friction* and *the law of conservation of energy.*

Understanding Key Ideas

2. Perpetual motion is impossible because

   a. things tend to slow down.

   b. energy is lost.

   c. machines are very inefficient.

   d. machines have friction.

3. Describe the energy conversions that take place on a roller coaster, and explain how energy is conserved.

Math Skills

4. A bike is pedaled with 80 J of energy and then coasts. It does 60 J of work in moving forward until it stops. How much of the energy that was put into the bike became thermal energy?

Critical Thinking

5. **Evaluating Conclusions** Imagine that you drop a ball. It bounces a few times and then it stops. Your friend says that the energy that the ball had is gone. Where did the energy go? Evaluate your friend's statement based on energy conservation.

6. **Evaluating Assumptions** If someone says that a car has high energy output, can you conclude that the car is efficient? Explain.

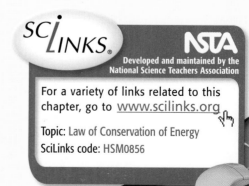

SCI**LINKS**

NSTA
Developed and maintained by the National Science Teachers Association

For a variety of links related to this chapter, go to www.scilinks.org

Topic: Law of Conservation of Energy
SciLinks code: HSM0856

Energy Resources

Energy is used to light and warm our homes. It is used to make food, clothing, and other things. It is also used to transport people and products from place to place. Where does all of this energy come from?

An *energy resource* is a natural resource that can be converted into other forms of energy in order to do useful work. In this section, you will learn about several energy resources, including the one that most other energy resources come from—the sun.

Nonrenewable Resources

Some energy resources, called **nonrenewable resources,** cannot be replaced or are replaced much more slowly than they are used. Fossil fuels are the most important nonrenewable resources.

Oil and natural gas, shown in **Figure 1,** as well as coal, are the most common fossil fuels. **Fossil fuels** are energy resources that formed from the buried remains of plants and animals that lived millions of years ago. These plants stored energy from the sun by photosynthesis. Animals used and stored this energy by eating the plants. So, fossil fuels are concentrated forms of the sun's energy. Now, millions of years later, energy from the sun is released when these fossil fuels are burned.

✓ **Reading Check** Why are fossil fuels considered nonrenewable resources? *(See the Appendix for answers to Reading Checks.)*

nonrenewable resource a resource that forms at a rate that is much slower than the rate at which it is consumed

fossil fuel a nonrenewable energy resource formed from the remains of organisms that lived long ago

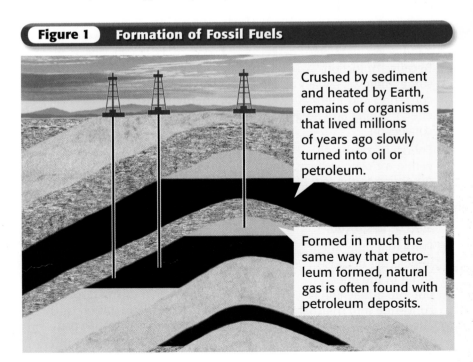

Figure 1   Formation of Fossil Fuels

Crushed by sediment and heated by Earth, remains of organisms that lived millions of years ago slowly turned into oil or petroleum.

Formed in much the same way that petroleum formed, natural gas is often found with petroleum deposits.

Uses of Fossil Fuels

All fossil fuels contain stored energy from the sun, which can be converted into other kinds of energy. **Figure 2** shows some different ways that fossil fuels are used in our society.

People have been getting energy from the burning of coal, a fossil fuel, for hundreds of years. Today, burning coal is still a very common way to generate electrical energy. Many products, such as gasoline, wax, and plastics, are made from petroleum, another fossil fuel. A third kind of fossil fuel, natural gas, is often used in home heating.

Figure 2 **Everyday Uses of Some Fossil Fuels**

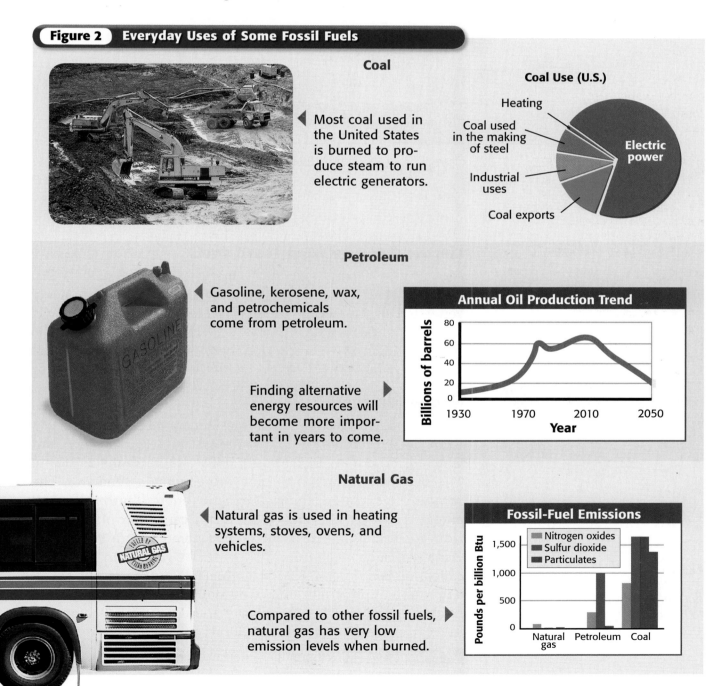

Coal

Most coal used in the United States is burned to produce steam to run electric generators.

Coal Use (U.S.)

Heating
Coal used in the making of steel
Industrial uses
Coal exports
Electric power

Petroleum

Gasoline, kerosene, wax, and petrochemicals come from petroleum.

Finding alternative energy resources will become more important in years to come.

Annual Oil Production Trend

Billions of barrels

Natural Gas

Natural gas is used in heating systems, stoves, ovens, and vehicles.

Compared to other fossil fuels, natural gas has very low emission levels when burned.

Fossil-Fuel Emissions

Pounds per billion Btu

- Nitrogen oxides
- Sulfur dioxide
- Particulates

Natural gas   Petroleum   Coal

Figure 3 Converting Fossil Fuels into Electrical Energy

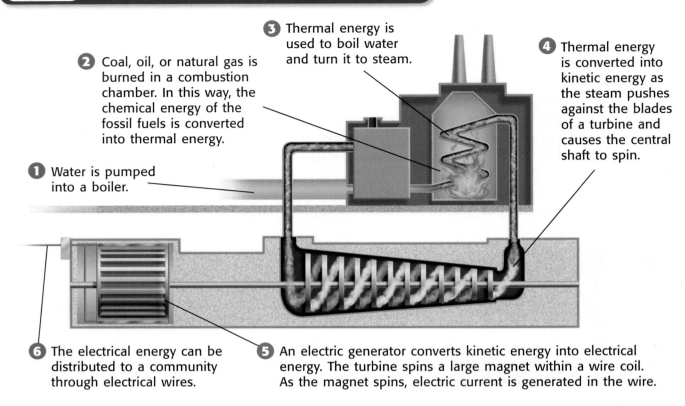

3 Thermal energy is used to boil water and turn it to steam.

2 Coal, oil, or natural gas is burned in a combustion chamber. In this way, the chemical energy of the fossil fuels is converted into thermal energy.

4 Thermal energy is converted into kinetic energy as the steam pushes against the blades of a turbine and causes the central shaft to spin.

1 Water is pumped into a boiler.

6 The electrical energy can be distributed to a community through electrical wires.

5 An electric generator converts kinetic energy into electrical energy. The turbine spins a large magnet within a wire coil. As the magnet spins, electric current is generated in the wire.

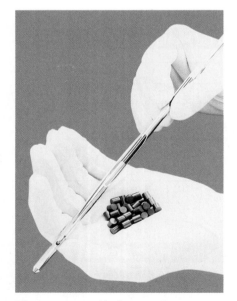

Figure 4 *A single uranium fuel pellet contains the energy equivalent of about 1 metric ton of coal.*

Electrical Energy from Fossil Fuels

One way to generate electrical energy is to burn fossil fuels. In fact, fossil fuels are the main source of electrical energy generated in the United States. *Electric generators* convert the chemical energy in fossil fuels into electrical energy by the process shown in **Figure 3.** The chemical energy in fossil fuels is changed into the electrical energy that you use every day.

Nuclear Energy

Another way to generate electrical energy is to use nuclear energy. Like fossil-fuel power plants, a nuclear power plant generates thermal energy that boils water to make steam. The steam then turns a turbine, which runs a generator. The spinning generator changes kinetic energy into electrical energy. However, the fuels used in nuclear power plants differ from fossil fuels. Nuclear energy is generated from radioactive elements, such as uranium, shown in **Figure 4.** In a process called *nuclear fission* (NOO klee uhr FISH uhn), the nucleus of a uranium atom is split into two smaller nuclei, which releases nuclear energy. Because the supply of these elements is limited, nuclear energy is a nonrenewable resource.

✓ Reading Check Where does nuclear energy come from?

Renewable Resources

Some energy resources, called **renewable resources,** are naturally replaced more quickly than they are used. Some renewable resources, such as solar energy and wind energy, are considered practically limitless.

Solar Energy

Sunlight can be changed into electrical energy through solar cells. These cells can be used in devices such as calculators. Solar cells can also be placed on the roof of a house to provide electrical energy. Some houses can use solar energy by allowing sunlight into the house through large windows. The sun's energy can then be used to heat the house.

Energy from Water

The sun causes water to evaporate and fall again as rain that flows through rivers. The potential energy of water in a reservoir can be changed into kinetic energy as the water flows through a dam. **Figure 5** shows a hydroelectric dam. Falling water turns turbines in a dam. The turbines are connected to a generator that changes kinetic energy into electrical energy.

Wind Energy

Wind is caused by the sun's heating of Earth's surface. Because Earth's surface is not heated evenly, wind is created. The kinetic energy of wind can turn the blades of a windmill. Wind turbines are shown in **Figure 6.** A wind turbine changes the kinetic energy of the air into electrical energy by turning a generator.

renewable resource a natural resource that can be replaced at the same rate at which the resource is consumed

Figure 5 *This dam converts the energy from water going downstream into electrical energy.*

Figure 6 *These wind turbines are converting wind energy into electrical energy.*

Geothermal Energy

Thermal energy caused by the heating of Earth's crust is called *geothermal energy.* Some geothermal power plants pump water underground next to hot rock. The water returns to the surface as steam, which can then turn the turbine of a generator.

✓ Reading Check Where does geothermal energy come from?

Biomass

Plants use and store energy from the sun. Organic matter, such as plants, wood, and waste, that can be burned to release energy is called *biomass.* **Figure 7** shows an example. Some countries depend on biomass for energy.

The Two Sides to Energy Resources

All energy resources have advantages and disadvantages. How can you decide which energy resource to use? **Table 1** compares several energy resources. Depending on where you live, what you need energy for, and how much energy you need, one energy resource may be a better choice than another.

Figure 7 *Plants capture the sun's energy. When wood is burned, it releases the energy it got from the sun, which can be used to generate electrical energy.*

Table 1 Advantages and Disadvantages of Energy Resources		
Energy Resource	**Advantages**	**Disadvantages**
Fossil fuels	• provide a large amount of thermal energy per unit of mass • are easy to get and transport • can be used to generate electricity and to make products such as plastic	• is nonrenewable • produces smog • releases substances that can cause acid precipitation • creates a risk of oil spills
Nuclear	• is a very concentrated form of energy • does not produce air pollution	• produces radioactive waste • is nonrenewable
Solar	• is an almost limitless source of energy • does not produce pollution	• is expensive to use for large-scale energy production • is practical only in sunny areas
Water	• is renewable • does not produce air pollution	• requires dams, which disrupt a river's ecosystem • is available only where there are rivers
Wind	• is renewable • is relatively inexpensive to generate • does not produce air pollution	• is practical only in windy areas
Geothermal	• is an almost limitless source of energy • power plants require little land	• is practical only in areas near hot spots • produces wastewater, which can damage soil
Biomass	• is renewable • is inexpensive	• requires large areas of farmland • produces smoke

Choosing the Right Energy Resource

As **Table 1** shows, each source of energy that we know about on Earth has advantages and disadvantages. For example, you have probably heard that fossil fuels pollute the air. They will also run out after they are used up. Even renewable resources have their drawbacks. Generating lots of energy from solar energy is difficult. So it cannot be used to meet the energy needs of large cities. Geothermal energy is limited to the "hot spots" in the world where it is available. Hydroelectric energy requires large dams, which can affect the ecology of river life. Energy planning in all parts of the world requires careful consideration of energy needs and the availability and responsible use of resources.

CONNECTION TO Social Studies

WRITING SKILL **Earth's Energy Resources** Find examples of places in the world where the various energy resources mentioned in this chapter are used. List them in your **science journal**. Discuss any patterns that you notice, such as which regions of the world use certain energy resources.

SECTION Review

Summary

- An energy resource is a natural resource that can be converted into other forms of energy in order to do useful work.

- Nonrenewable resources cannot be replaced after they are used or can be replaced only after long periods of time. They include fossil fuels and nuclear energy.

- Renewable resources can be replaced in nature over a relatively short period of time. They include energy from the sun, wind, and water; geothermal energy; and biomass.

- The sun is the source of most energy on Earth.

- Choices about energy resources depend on where you live and what you need energy for.

Using Key Terms

1. In your own words, write a definition for the term *fossil fuel*.

Complete each of the following sentences by choosing the correct term from the word bank.

nonrenewable resources
renewable resources

2. There is a practically limitless supply of ___.

3. ___ are used up more quickly than they are being replaced.

Understanding Key Ideas

4. Which of the following is a renewable resource?
   a. wind
   b. coal
   c. nuclear energy
   d. petroleum

5. Compare fossil fuels and biomass as energy resources.

6. Trace electrical energy back to the sun.

Critical Thinking

7. **Making Comparisons** Describe the similarities and differences between transforming energy in a hydroelectric dam and a wind turbine.

8. **Analyzing Ideas** Name an energy resource that does NOT depend on the sun.

Interpreting Graphics

9. Use the pie chart below to explain why renewable resources are becoming more important to the United States.

U.S. Energy Sources

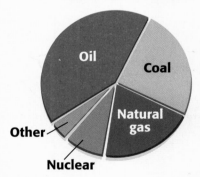

SciLINKS.

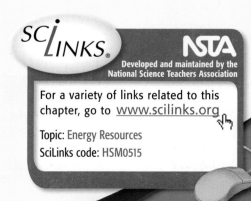

NSTA
Developed and maintained by the National Science Teachers Association

For a variety of links related to this chapter, go to www.scilinks.org

Topic: Energy Resources
SciLinks code: HSM0515

Finding Energy

When you coast down a hill on a bike or skateboard, you may notice that you pick up speed, or go faster and faster. Because you are moving, you have kinetic energy—the energy of motion. Where does that energy come from? When you pedal the bike or push the skateboard, you are the source of the kinetic energy. But where does the kinetic energy come from when you roll down a hill without making any effort? In this lab, you will find out where such kinetic energy comes from.

OBJECTIVES

Form a hypothesis about where kinetic energy comes from.

Test your hypothesis by collecting and analyzing data.

MATERIALS

- books (2 or 3)
- masking tape
- meterstick
- metric balance
- rolling cart
- stopwatch
- wooden board

Ask a Question

1 Where does the kinetic energy come from when you roll down a hill?

Form a Hypothesis

2 Write a hypothesis that is a possible answer to the question above. Explain your reasoning.

Test the Hypothesis

3 Copy the Data Collection Table below.

Data Collection Table							
Height of ramp (m)	Length of ramp (m)	Mass of cart (kg)	Weight of cart (N)	Time of trial (s)			Average time (s)
				1	2	3	

DO NOT WRITE IN BOOK

4 Use your books and board to make a ramp.

5 Use masking tape to mark a starting line at the top of the ramp. Be sure the starting line is far enough down from the top of the ramp to allow the cart to be placed behind the line.

6 Use masking tape to mark a finish line at the bottom of the ramp.

7 Find the height of the ramp by measuring the height of the starting line and subtracting the height of the finish line. Record the height of the ramp in your Data Collection Table.

8 Measure the distance in meters between the starting line and the finish line. In the Data Collection Table, record this distance as the length of the ramp.

9 Use the balance to find the mass of the cart in grams. Convert this measurement to kilograms by dividing it by 1,000. In your Data Collection Table, record the mass in kilograms.

10 Multiply the mass by 10 to get the weight of the cart in newtons. Record this weight in your Data Collection Table.

11 Set the cart behind the starting line, and release it. Use a stopwatch to time how long the cart takes to reach the finish line. Record the time in your Data Collection Table.

12 Repeat step 11 twice more, and average the results. Record the average time in your Data Collection Table.

Analyze the Results

1 **Organizing Data** Copy the Calculations Table shown at right onto a separate sheet of paper.

2 **Analyzing Data** Calculate and record the quantities for the cart in the Calculations Table by using your data and the four equations that follow.

Calculations Table			
Average speed (m/s)	Final speed (m/s)	Kinetic energy at bottom (J)	Gravitational potential energy at top (J)
DO NOT WRITE IN BOOK			

$$average\ speed = \frac{length\ of\ ramp}{average\ time}$$

Final speed = 2 × *average speed*
(This equation works because the cart accelerates smoothly from 0 m/s.)

$$kinetic\ energy = \frac{mass \times (final\ speed)^2}{2}$$

(Remember that 1 kg • m²/s² = 1 J, the unit used to express energy.)

Gravitational potential energy =
weight × height
(Remember that 1 N = 1 kg • m/s²,
so 1 N × 1 m = 1 kg • m²/s² = 1 J)

Draw Conclusions

3 **Drawing Conclusions** How does the cart's gravitational potential energy at the top of the ramp compare with its kinetic energy at the bottom? Does this support your hypothesis? Explain your answer.

4 **Evaluating Data** You probably found that the gravitational potential energy of the cart at the top of the ramp was almost, but not exactly, equal to the kinetic energy of the cart at the bottom of the ramp. Explain this finding.

5 **Applying Conclusions** Suppose that while riding your bike, you coast down both a small hill and a large hill. Compare your final speed at the bottom of the small hill with your final speed at the bottom of the large hill. Explain your answer.

Chapter Review

USING KEY TERMS

For each pair of terms, explain how the meanings of the terms differ.

1 *potential energy* and *kinetic energy*

2 *mechanical energy* and *energy conversion*

3 *friction* and *the law of conservation of energy*

4 *renewable resources* and *nonrenewable resources*

5 *energy resources* and *fossil fuels*

UNDERSTANDING KEY IDEAS

Multiple Choice

6 Kinetic energy depends on
a. mass and volume.
b. velocity and weight.
c. weight and height.
d. velocity and mass.

7 Gravitational potential energy depends on
a. mass and velocity.
b. weight and height.
c. mass and weight.
d. height and distance.

8 Which of the following types of energy is not a renewable resource?
a. wind energy
b. nuclear energy
c. solar energy
d. geothermal energy

9 Which of the following sentences describes a conversion from chemical energy to thermal energy?
a. Food is digested and used to regulate body temperature.
b. Charcoal is burned in a barbecue pit.
c. Coal is burned to produce steam.
d. All of the above

10 When energy changes from one form to another, some of the energy always changes into
a. kinetic energy.
b. potential energy.
c. thermal energy.
d. mechanical energy.

Short Answer

11 Name two forms of energy, and relate them to kinetic or potential energy.

12 Give three examples of one form of energy being converted into another form.

13 Explain what a closed system is, and how energy is conserved within it.

14 How are fossil fuels formed?

Math Skills

15 A box has 400 J of gravitational potential energy.
a. How much work had to be done to give the box that energy?
b. If the box weighs 100 N, how far above the ground is it?

16 Concept Mapping Use the following terms to create a concept map: *energy, machines, sound energy, hair dryer, electrical energy, energy conversions, thermal energy,* and *kinetic energy*.

17 Applying Concepts Describe what happens in terms of energy when you blow up a balloon and release it.

18 Identifying Relationships After you coast down a hill on your bike, you will eventually come to a complete stop. Use this fact to explain why perpetual motion is impossible.

19 Predicting Consequences Imagine that the sun ran out of energy. What would happen to our energy resources on Earth?

20 Analyzing Processes Look at the photo below. Beginning with the pole vaulter's breakfast, trace the energy conversions necessary for the event shown to take place.

21 Forming Hypotheses Imagine two cars, one of which is more efficient than the other. Suggest two possible reasons one car is more efficient.

22 Evaluating Hypotheses Describe how you would test the two hypotheses you proposed in item 21. How would you determine whether one, both, or neither hypothesis is a factor in the car's efficiency?

Use the graphic below to answer the questions that follow.

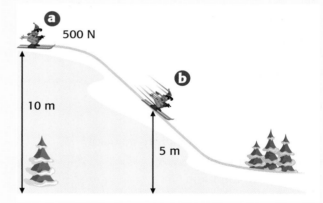

23 What is the skier's gravitational potential energy at point *A*?

24 What is the skier's gravitational potential energy at point *B*?

25 What is the skier's kinetic energy at point *B*? (Hint: mechanical energy = potential energy + kinetic energy)

Standardized Test Preparation

Read each of the passages below. Then, answer the questions that follow each passage.

Passage 1 Gas hydrates are icy formations of water and methane. Methane is the main component of natural gas. The methane in gas hydrates is made by bacteria in the ocean. Large areas of hydrates have been found off the coasts of North Carolina and South Carolina in marine sediments. In just two areas that are each about the size of Rhode Island, scientists think there may be 70 times the amount of natural gas used by the United States in 1 year. The energy from gas hydrates could be used to drive machinery or generate electrical energy.

1. How large are each of the two gas hydrate deposits mentioned in this article?
   A about the size of the United States
   B about the size of South Carolina
   C about the size of North Carolina
   D about the size of Rhode Island

2. What are gas hydrates mainly made of?
   F bacteria and sediments
   G water and methane
   H natural gas and water
   I ice and sediments

3. How long could U.S. natural gas needs be met by all the gas in both deposits mentioned?
   A 1 year
   B 2 years
   C 70 years
   D 140 years

4. Where do methane gas hydrates come from?
   F ocean water
   G bacteria
   H sediments
   I ice

Passage 2 Two new technologies may reduce the price of electric cars. One is called a *hybrid electric vehicle*. This vehicle has a small gasoline engine that provides extra power and recharges the batteries. The other technology uses hydrogen fuel cells instead of batteries. These cells use the hydrogen present in more-conventional fuels, such as gasoline or ethanol, to produce an electric current that powers the car.

1. In this passage, what does *vehicle* mean?
   A electric
   B hybrid
   C car
   D current

2. Which of the following are conventional fuels?
   F gasoline and ethanol
   G hydrogen and ethanol
   H gasoline and hydrogen
   I only hydrogen

3. Which of the following is a fact in this passage?
   A A hybrid electric vehicle runs partly on gasoline.
   B All electric cars are hybrid.
   C All electric cars use hydrogen fuel cells.
   D Hydrogen fuel cells use conventional fuel.

4. What do the two new technologies described in the passage have in common?
   F They do not use conventional fuels.
   G They may reduce the price of electric cars.
   H They use hybrid engines.
   I They use hydrogen to produce an electric current.

The pie chart below shows U.S. energy use by source of energy. Use the chart below to answer the questions that follow.

U.S. Energy Sources

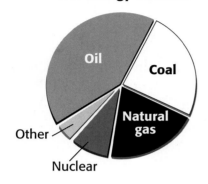

1. According to the graph, the United States relies on fossil fuels for about what percentage of its energy?

  A 30%

  B 45%

  C 60%

  D 80%

2. Nuclear energy represents about what percentage of U.S. energy sources?

  F 15%

  G 30%

  H 50%

  I 70%

3. Which energy source accounts for about 25% of U.S. energy?

  A oil

  B coal

  C natural gas

  D nuclear energy

Read each question below, and choose the best answer.

1. Gerald bought 2.5 kg of apples. How many grams of apples did he buy?

  A 0.0025 g

  B 0.25 g

  C 25 g

  D 2,500 g

2. Which group contains ratios that are equivalent to 3/8?

  F 6/16, 9/24, 12/32

  G 6/16, 12/24, 12/32

  H 6/24, 12/32, 15/40

  I 6/9, 9/24, 15/40

3. Carmen went to a bookstore. She bought three books for $7.99 each and four books for $3.35 each. Which number sentence can be used to find c, the total cost of the books?

  A $c = 3 + (7.99 \times 1) + (4 \times 3.35)$

  B $c = (1 \times 7.99) + (3 \times 3.35)$

  C $c = (3 \times 7.99) + (4 \times 3.35)$

  D $c = (3 \times 7.99) \times (4 \times 3.35)$

4. Rhonda's Mobile Car Washing charges $15 to wash a customer's car. Vacuuming the car costs an extra $10. Rhonda wants to know how much money she earned last week. When she looks at her appointment book, Rhonda finds that she washed a total of 50 cars. Only 20 of these cars were vacuumed after being washed. How much money did Rhonda earn last week?

  F $500

  G $750

  H $950

  I $1050

Standardized Test Preparation

Science in Action

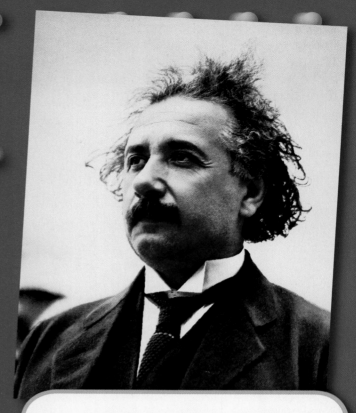

Science, Technology, and Society

Underwater Jet Engines
Almost all boats that have engines use propellers. But in 2002, a British company announced that it had developed an underwater jet engine.

The underwater jet engine works by producing steam in a gasoline-powered boiler. When the steam hits the water, it condenses to a very small volume, which creates a vacuum. This vacuum causes thrust by sucking in water from the front of the tube. The underwater jet engine is extremely energy-efficient, produces a great amount of thrust, and creates very little pollution.

Social Studies ACTIVITY

Research the kinds of water propulsion people have used throughout history. Note which kinds were improvements on previous technology and which were completely new.

Scientific Discoveries

$E = mc^2$
The famous 20th-century scientist Albert Einstein discovered an equation that is almost as famous as he is. That equation is $E = mc^2$. You may have heard of it before. But what does it mean?

The equation represents a relationship between mass and energy. E represents energy, m represents mass, and c represents the speed of light. So, $E = mc^2$ means that a small amount of mass has a very large amount of energy! Nuclear reactors harness this energy, which is given off when radioactive atoms split.

Math ACTIVITY

The speed of light is approximately 300,000,000 m/s. How much energy is equivalent to the mass of 0.00000002 g of hydrogen?

Cheryl Mele

Power-Plant Manager Cheryl Mele is the manager of the Decker Power Plant in Austin, Texas, where she is in charge of almost 1 billion watts of electric power generation. Most of the electric power is generated by a steam-driven turbine system that uses natural gas fuel. Gas turbines are also used. Together, the systems make enough electrical energy for many homes and businesses.

Cheryl Mele says her job as plant manager is to do "anything that needs doing." Her training as a mechanical engineer allows her to run tests and to find problems in the plant. Previously, Mele had a job helping to design more-efficient gas turbines. That job helped prepare her for the job of plant manager.

Mele believes that engineering and power-plant management are interesting jobs because they allow you to work with many new technologies. Mele thinks young people should pursue what interests them. "Be sure to connect the math you learn to the science you are doing," she says. "This will help you to understand both."

Language Arts ACTIVITY

Look up the word *energy* in a dictionary. Compare the different definitions you find to the definition given in this chapter.

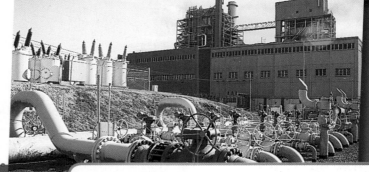

To learn more about these Science in Action topics, visit go.hrw.com and type in the keyword **HP5ENGF.**

Current Science

Check out Current Science® articles related to this chapter by visiting go.hrw.com. Just type in the keyword **HP5CS09.**

Heat and Heat Technology

SECTION **1** Temperature 274

SECTION **2** What Is Heat? 280

SECTION **3** Matter and Heat 288

SECTION **4** Heat Technology 292

Chapter Lab 300
Chapter Review 302
Standardized Test Preparation 304
Science in Action 306

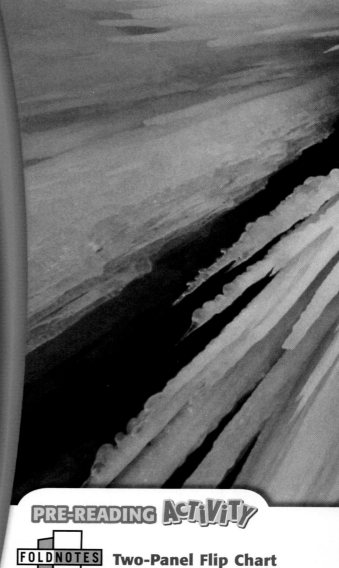

About the PHOTO

This ice climber is using a lot of special equipment. This equipment includes a rope, a safety helmet, an ice pick, and warm clothing. The climber's clothing, which includes insulating layers inside a protective outer layer, keeps his body heat from escaping into the cold air. If he weren't wearing enough protective clothing, he would be feeling very cold, because thermal energy always moves into areas of lower temperature.

PRE-READING ACTIVITY

FOLDNOTES **Two-Panel Flip Chart**
Before you read the chapter, create the FoldNote entitled "Two-Panel Flip Chart" described in the **Study Skills** section of the Appendix. Label the flaps of the two-panel flip chart with "Heat" and "Temperature." As you read the chapter, write information you learn about each category under the appropriate flap.

START-UP ACTIVITY

Some Like It Hot

Sometimes, you can estimate an object's temperature by touching the object. In this activity, you will find out how well your hand works as a thermometer!

Procedure

1. Gather small pieces of the following materials: **metal, wood, plastic foam, rock, plastic,** and **cardboard.** Allow the materials to sit untouched on a table for a few minutes.

2. Put the palms of your hands on each of the materials. List the materials in order from coolest to warmest.

3. Place a **thermometer strip** on the surface of each material. Record the temperature of each material.

Analysis

1. Which material felt the warmest to your hands?

2. Which material had the highest temperature? Was it the same material that felt the warmest?

3. Why do you think some materials felt warmer than others?

4. Was your hand a good thermometer? Explain why or why not.

Temperature

You probably put on a sweater or a jacket when it's cold. Likewise, you probably wear shorts in the summer when it gets hot. But how hot is hot, and how cold is cold?

Think about the knobs on a water faucet: they are labeled "H" for hot and "C" for cold. But does only hot water come out when the hot-water knob is on? You may have noticed that when you first turn on the hot water, the water is warm or even cool. Is the label on the knob wrong? The terms *hot* and *cold* are not scientific terms. If you really want to specify how hot or cold something is, you must use temperature.

What Is Temperature?

You probably think of temperature as a measure of how hot or cold something is. But using the terms *hot* and *cold* can be confusing. Imagine that you are outside on a hot day. You step onto a shady porch where a fan is blowing. You think it feels cool there. Then, your friend comes out onto the porch from an air-conditioned house. She thinks it feels warm! Using the word *temperature* instead of words such as *cool* or *warm* avoids confusion. Scientifically, **temperature** is a measure of the average kinetic energy of the particles in an object.

Temperature and Kinetic Energy

All matter is made of atoms or molecules that are always moving, even if it doesn't look like they are. Because the particles are in motion, they have kinetic energy. The faster the particles are moving, the more kinetic energy they have. Look at **Figure 1.** The more kinetic energy the particles of an object have, the higher the temperature of the object is.

temperature a measure of how hot (or cold) something is; specifically, a measure of the average kinetic energy of the particles in an object

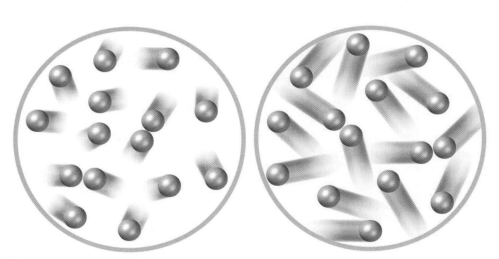

Figure 1 *The gas particles on the right have a higher average kinetic energy than those on the left. So, the gas on the right is at a higher temperature.*

Quick Lab

Hot or Cold?

1. Put both your hands into a **bucket of warm water,** and note how the water feels.
2. Now, put one hand into a **bucket of cold water** and the other into a **bucket of hot water.**
3. After a minute, take your hands out of the hot and cold water and put them back in the warm water. Note how the water feels to each hand.
4. Can you rely on your hands to determine temperature? Explain your observations.

Average Kinetic Energy of Particles

Particles of matter are always moving. But they move in different directions and at different speeds. The motion of particles is random. Because particles are moving at different speeds, individual particles have different amounts of kinetic energy. But the *average* kinetic energy of all the particles in an object can be measured. When you measure an object's temperature, you measure the average kinetic energy of all the particles in the object.

The temperature of a substance depends on the average kinetic energy of all its particles. Its temperature does not depend on how much of it you have. Look at **Figure 2.** A pot of tea and a cup of tea each have a different amount of tea. But their atoms have the same average kinetic energy. So, the pot of tea and the cup of tea are at the same temperature.

Reading Check How is temperature related to kinetic energy? *(See the Appendix for answers to Reading Checks.)*

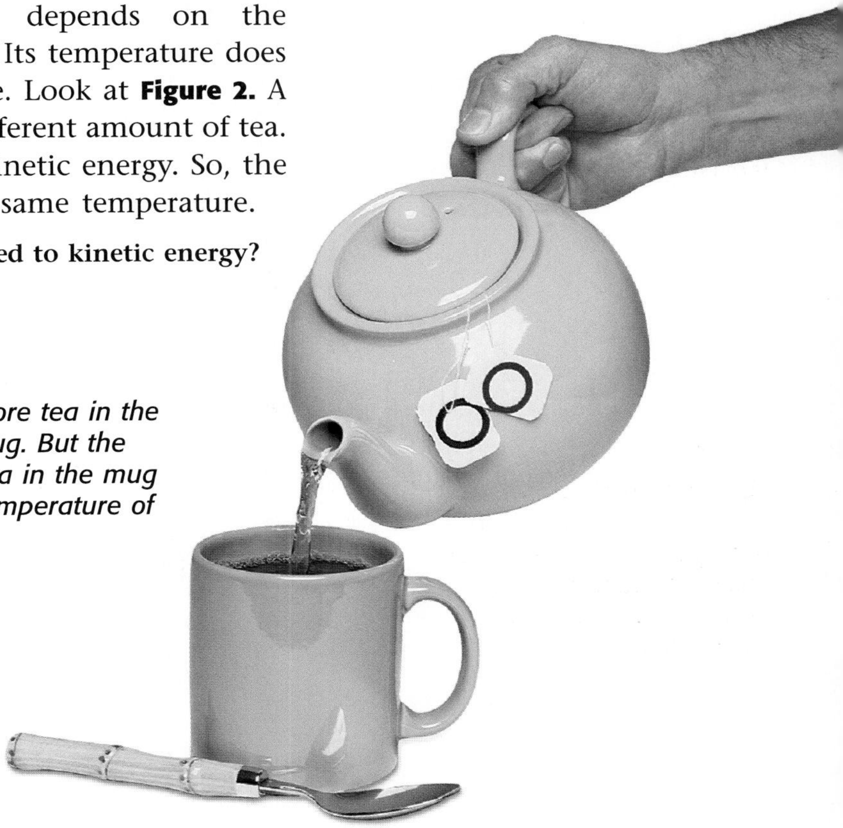

Internet Activity

For another activity related to this chapter, go to **go.hrw.com** and type in the keyword **HP5HOTW.**

Figure 2 *There is more tea in the teapot than in the mug. But the temperature of the tea in the mug is the same as the temperature of the tea in the teapot.*

Measuring Temperature

How would you measure the temperature of a steaming cup of hot chocolate? Would you take a sip of it or stick your finger in it? You probably would not. You would use a thermometer.

Using a Thermometer

Many thermometers are thin glass tubes filled with a liquid. Mercury and alcohol are often used in thermometers because they remain in liquid form over a large temperature range.

Thermometers can measure temperature because of a property called thermal expansion. **Thermal expansion** is the increase in volume of a substance because of an increase in temperature. As a substance's temperature increases, its particles move faster and spread out. So, there is more space between them, and the substance expands. Mercury and alcohol expand by constant amounts for a given change in temperature.

Look at the thermometers in **Figure 3.** They are all at the same temperature. So, the alcohol in each thermometer has expanded the same amount. But the number for each thermometer is different because a different temperature scale is marked on each one.

✓ **Reading Check** What property makes thermometers work?

thermal expansion an increase in the size of a substance in response to an increase in the temperature of the substance

absolute zero the temperature at which molecular energy is at a minimum (0 K on the Kelvin scale or −273.16°C on the Celsius scale)

Figure 3 Three Temperature Scales

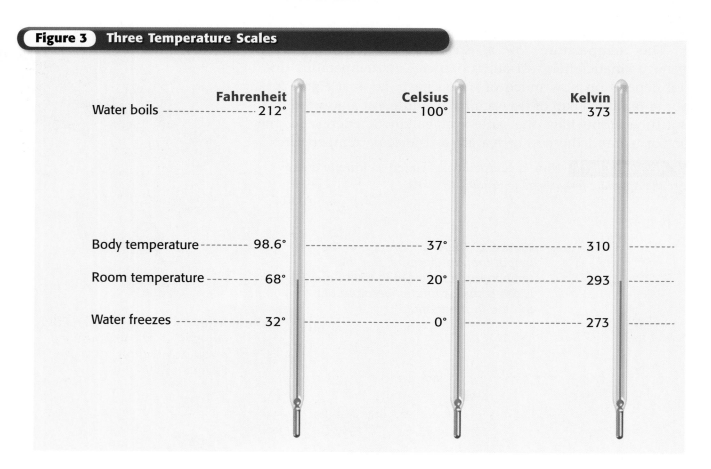

	Fahrenheit	Celsius	Kelvin
Water boils	212°	100°	373
Body temperature	98.6°	37°	310
Room temperature	68°	20°	293
Water freezes	32°	0°	273

Temperature Scales

Look at **Figure 4.** When a weather report is given, you will probably hear the temperature given in degrees Fahrenheit (°F). Scientists, however, often use the Celsius scale. In the Celsius scale, the temperature range between the freezing point and boiling point of water is divided into 100 equal parts, called degrees Celsius (°C). A third scale, the Kelvin (or absolute) scale, is the official SI temperature scale. The Kelvin scale is divided into units called kelvins (K)—not degrees kelvin.

The lowest temperature on the Kelvin scale is 0 K, which is called **absolute zero.** Absolute zero (about −459°F) is the temperature at which all molecular motion stops. It is not possible to actually reach absolute zero, although temperatures very close to 0 K have been reached in laboratories.

Temperature Conversion

As shown by the thermometers on the previous page, a given temperature is represented by different numbers on the three temperature scales. For example, the freezing point of water is 32°F, 0°C, or 273 K.

The temperature 0°C is actually much higher than 0 K. But a *change* of one kelvin is equal to a change of one Celsius degree. The temperature 0°C is higher than 0°F, but a change of one Fahrenheit degree is *not* equal to a change of one Celsius degree. You can convert from one scale to another using the equations shown in **Table 1** below.

MATH PRACTICE

Converting Temperatures

Use the equations in **Table 1** to answer the following questions:

1. What temperature on the Celsius scale is equivalent to 373 K?

2. Absolute zero is 0 K. What is the equivalent temperature on the Celsius scale? on the Fahrenheit scale?

3. Which temperature is colder, 0°F or 200 K?

Table 1 Converting Between Temperature Units		
To convert	**Use the equation**	**Example**
Celsius to Fahrenheit °C ⟶ °F	$°F = \left(\frac{9}{5} \times °C\right) + 32$	Convert 45°C to degrees Fahrenheit. $°F = \left(\frac{9}{5} \times 45°C\right) + 32 = 113°F$
Fahrenheit to Celsius °F ⟶ °C	$°C = \frac{5}{9} \times (°F - 32)$	Convert 68°F to degrees Celsius. $°C = \frac{5}{9} \times (68°F - 32) = 20°C$
Celsius to Kelvin °C ⟶ K	$K = °C + 273$	Convert 45°C to Kelvins. $K = 45°C + 273 = 318 K$
Kelvin to Celsius K ⟶ °C	$°C = K - 273$	Convert 32 K to degrees Celsius. $°C = 32 K - 273 = -241°C$

Figure 4 *Weather reports that you see on the news usually give temperatures in degrees Fahrenheit (°F).*

More About Thermal Expansion

You have learned about how thermal expansion works in the liquids that fill thermometers. Thermal expansion has many other applications. Below, you will read about a case in which thermal expansion can be dangerous, one in which it can be useful, and one in which it can carry you into the air!

Expansion Joints on Highways

Have you ever gone across a highway bridge in a car? You probably heard and felt a "thuh-thunk" every couple of seconds as you went over the bridge. That sound is made when the car goes over small gaps called *expansion joints,* shown in **Figure 5.**

If the weather is very hot, the bridge can heat up enough to expand. As it expands, there is a danger of the bridge breaking. Expansion joints keep segments of the bridge apart so that they have room to expand without the bridge breaking.

✔ Reading Check What is the purpose of expansion joints in a bridge?

Bimetallic Strips in Thermostats

Thermal expansion also occurs in a thermostat, the device that controls the heater in your home. Some thermostats have a bimetallic strip inside. A *bimetallic strip* is made of two different metals stacked in a thin strip. Because different materials expand at different rates, one of the metals expands more than the other when the strip gets hot. This makes the strip coil and uncoil in response to changes in temperature. This coiling and uncoiling closes and opens an electric circuit that turns the heater on and off in your home, as shown in **Figure 6.**

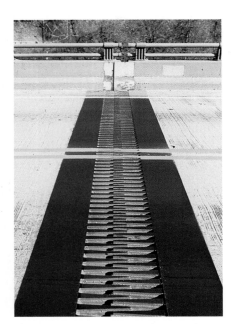

Figure 5 *This gap in the bridge allows the concrete to expand and contract without breaking.*

Figure 6 **How a Thermostat Works**

Electrical contacts   **Bimetallic strip**

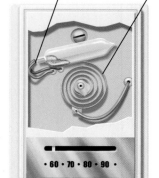

a As the room temperature drops below the desired level, the bimetallic strip coils more tightly, and the glass tube tilts. A drop of mercury closes an electric circuit that turns the heater on.

b As the room temperature rises above the desired level, the bimetallic strip uncoils slightly, becoming larger. The drop of mercury rolls back in the tube, opening the electric circuit, and the heater turns off.

Thermal Expansion in Hot-Air Balloons

You may have heard the expression "Hot air rises." If you have ever seen hot-air balloons peacefully gliding through the sky, you have seen this principle at work. But why does hot air rise?

When a gas is heated, as shown in **Figure 7,** its particles have more kinetic energy. They move around more quickly, so there is more space between them. The gas is then able to expand if it is not kept at the same volume by its container. When air (which is a mixture of gases) inside a hot-air balloon is heated, the air expands. As it expands, it becomes less dense than the air outside the balloon. So, the balloon goes up, up, and away!

Figure 7 *Thermal expansion helps get these hot-air balloons off the ground.*

SECTION Review

Summary

- Temperature is a measure of the average kinetic energy of the particles of a substance.
- Fahrenheit, Celsius, and Kelvin are three temperature scales.
- Thermal expansion is the increase in volume of a substance due to an increase in temperature.
- Absolute zero (0 K, or −273°C) is the lowest possible temperature.
- A thermostat works because of the thermal expansion of a bimetallic strip.

Using Key Terms

1. In your own words, write a definition for the term *temperature.*

2. Use each of the following terms in a separate sentence: *thermal expansion* and *absolute zero.*

Understanding Key Ideas

3. Which of the following is the coldest temperature possible?
   a. 0 K
   b. 0°C
   c. 0°F
   d. −273°F

4. Does temperature depend on the amount of the substance? Explain.

5. Describe the process of thermal expansion.

Math Skills

6. Convert 35°C to degrees Fahrenheit.

7. Convert 34°F to degrees Celsius.

8. Convert 0°C to kelvins.

9. Convert 100 K to degrees Celsius.

Critical Thinking

10. **Predicting Consequences** Why do you think heating a full pot of soup on the stove could cause the soup to overflow?

11. **Analyzing Processes** During thermal expansion, what happens to the density of a substance?

12. **Forming Hypotheses** A glass of cold water whose particles had a low average kinetic energy was placed on a table. The average kinetic energy in the cold water increased, while the average kinetic energy of the part of the table under the glass decreased. What do you think happened?

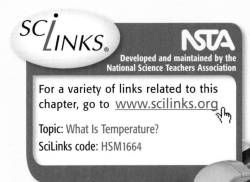

SCI LINKS.

NSTA

Developed and maintained by the
National Science Teachers Association

For a variety of links related to this chapter, go to www.scilinks.org

Topic: What Is Temperature?
SciLinks code: HSM1664

What Is Heat?

It's time for your annual physical. The doctor comes in and begins her exam by placing a metal stethoscope on your back. You jump a little and say, "Whoa! That's cold!"

What is it about the stethoscope that made it feel cold? The answer has to do with how energy moves between the metal and your skin. In this section, you'll learn about this kind of energy transfer.

Transferred Thermal Energy

You might think of the word *heat* as having to do with things that feel hot. But heat also has to do with things that feel cold—such as the stethoscope. In fact, heat is what causes objects to feel hot or cold or to get hot or cold under the right conditions. You probably use the word *heat* every day to mean different things. However, in this chapter, you will use only one specific meaning for *heat*. **Heat** is the energy transferred between objects that are at different temperatures.

Why do some things feel hot, while others feel cold? When two objects at different temperatures come into contact, energy is always transferred from the object that has the higher temperature to the object that has the lower temperature. Look at **Figure 1.** The doctor's stethoscope touches your back. Energy is transferred from your back to the stethoscope because your back has a higher temperature (about 37°C) than the stethoscope (probably room temperature, about 20°C) has. This energy is transferred quickly, so the stethoscope feels cold to you.

heat the energy transferred between objects that are at different temperatures

Figure 1 *The metal stethoscope feels cold because of heat!*

Heat and Thermal Energy

If heat is transferred energy, what form of energy is being transferred? The answer is thermal energy. **Thermal energy** is the total kinetic energy of the particles that make up a substance. Thermal energy, which is measured in joules (J), depends partly on temperature. Something at a high temperature has more thermal energy than it would have at a lower temperature. Thermal energy also depends on how much of a substance there is. Look at **Figure 2.** The more particles there are in a substance at a given temperature, the greater the thermal energy of the substance is.

Figure 2 *Although both soups are at the same temperature, there is more soup in the pan. So, the soup in the pan has more thermal energy than the soup in the bowl.*

Reaching the Same Temperature

Look at **Figure 3.** When objects that have different temperatures come into contact, energy will always be transferred. Energy will pass from the warmer object to the cooler object until both have the same temperature. When objects that are touching each other have the same temperature, there is no net change in the thermal energy of either one. Although one object may have more thermal energy than the other object, both objects will be at the same temperature.

thermal energy the kinetic energy of a substance's atoms

✔ **Reading Check** What will happen if two objects at different temperatures come into contact? (*See the Appendix for answers to Reading Checks.*)

Figure 3 **Transfer of Thermal Energy**

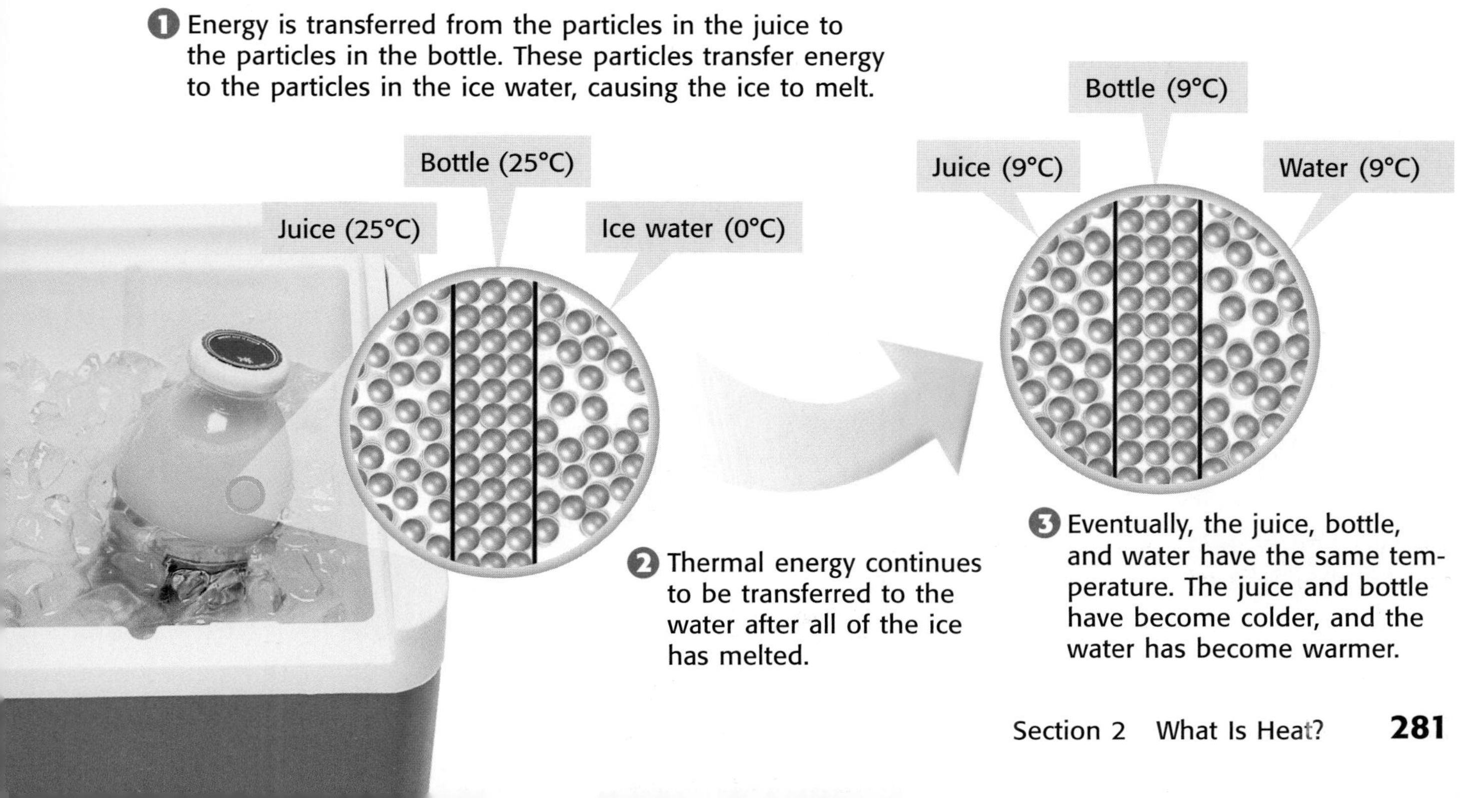

❶ Energy is transferred from the particles in the juice to the particles in the bottle. These particles transfer energy to the particles in the ice water, causing the ice to melt.

Bottle (25°C)

Juice (25°C)

Ice water (0°C)

Bottle (9°C)

Juice (9°C)

Water (9°C)

❷ Thermal energy continues to be transferred to the water after all of the ice has melted.

❸ Eventually, the juice, bottle, and water have the same temperature. The juice and bottle have become colder, and the water has become warmer.

Conduction, Convection, and Radiation

You already know several examples of energy transfer. You know that stoves transfer energy to soup in a pot. You adjust the temperature of your bath water by adding cold or hot water to the tub. And the sun warms your skin. In the next few pages, you'll learn about three ways to transfer thermal energy: *conduction, convection,* and *radiation.*

Conduction

Imagine that you have put a cold metal spoon in a bowl of hot soup, as shown in **Figure 4.** Soon, the handle of the spoon warms up—even though it is not in the soup! The entire spoon gets warm because of conduction. **Thermal conduction** is the transfer of thermal energy from one substance to another through direct contact. Conduction can also occur within a substance, such as the spoon in **Figure 4.**

How does conduction work? When objects touch each other, their particles collide. Thermal energy is transferred from the higher-temperature substance to the lower-temperature substance. Remember that particles of substances at different temperatures have different average kinetic energies. So, when particles collide, particles with higher kinetic energy transfer energy to those with lower kinetic energy. This transfer makes some particles slow down and other particles speed up until all particles have the same average kinetic energy. As a result, the substances have the same temperature.

thermal conduction the transfer of energy as heat through a material

Figure 4 The end of this spoon will warm up because conduction, the transfer of energy through direct contact, occurs all the way up the handle.

Conductors and Insulators

Substances that conduct thermal energy very well are called **thermal conductors.** For example, the metal in a doctor's stethoscope is a conductor. Energy is transferred rapidly from your warm skin to the cool stethoscope. That's why the stethoscope feels cold. Substances that do not conduct thermal energy very well are called **thermal insulators.** For example, a doctor's wooden tongue depressor is an insulator. It is at the same temperature as the stethoscope. But the tongue depressor doesn't feel cold. The reason is that thermal energy is transferred very slowly from your tongue to the wood. Some typical conductors and insulators are shown in **Table 1** at right.

✓ **Reading Check** How can two objects that are the same temperature feel as if they are at different temperatures?

Table 1 Conductors and Insulators	
Conductors	**Insulators**
Curling iron	Flannel shirt
Cookie sheet	Oven mitt
Iron skillet	Plastic spatula
Copper pipe	Fiberglass insulation
Stove coil	Ceramic bowl

Convection

A second way thermal energy is transferred is **convection,** the transfer of thermal energy by the movement of a liquid or a gas. Look at **Figure 5.** When you boil water in a pot, the water moves in roughly circular patterns because of convection. The water at the bottom of a pot on a stove burner gets hot because it is touching the pot (conduction). As it heats, the water becomes less dense because its higher-energy particles spread apart. The warmer water rises through the denser, cooler water above it. At the surface, the warm water begins to cool. The particles move closer together, making the water denser. The cooler water then sinks back to the bottom. It is heated again, and the cycle begins again. This circular motion of liquids or gases due to density differences that result from temperature differences is called a *convection current.*

thermal conductor a material through which energy can be transferred as heat

thermal insulator a material that reduces or prevents the transfer of heat

convection the transfer of thermal energy by the circulation or movement of a liquid or gas

Figure 5 *The repeated rising and sinking of water during boiling are due to convection.*

Radiation

radiation the transfer of energy as electromagnetic waves

A third way thermal energy is transferred is **radiation,** the transfer of energy by electromagnetic waves, such as visible light and infrared waves. Unlike conduction and convection, radiation can involve either an energy transfer between particles of matter or an energy transfer across empty space.

All objects, including the heater in **Figure 6,** radiate electromagnetic waves. The sun emits visible light, which you can see, and waves of other frequencies, such as infrared and ultraviolet waves, which you cannot see. When your body absorbs infrared waves, you feel warmer.

Radiation and the Greenhouse Effect

Earth's atmosphere acts like the windows of a greenhouse. It allows the sun's visible light to pass through it. A greenhouse also traps heat energy, keeping the inside warm. The atmosphere traps some energy, too. This process, called the *greenhouse effect,* is illustrated in **Figure 7.** If our atmosphere did not trap the sun's energy in this way, most of the sun's energy that reached Earth would be radiated immediately back into space. Earth would be a cold, lifeless planet.

The atmosphere traps the sun's energy because of *greenhouse gases,* such as water vapor, carbon dioxide, and methane, which trap energy especially well. Some scientists are concerned that high levels of greenhouse gases in the atmosphere may trap too much energy and make Earth too warm.

✓ Reading Check What is the greenhouse effect?

Figure 6 *The coils of this portable heater warm a room partly by radiating visible light and infrared waves.*

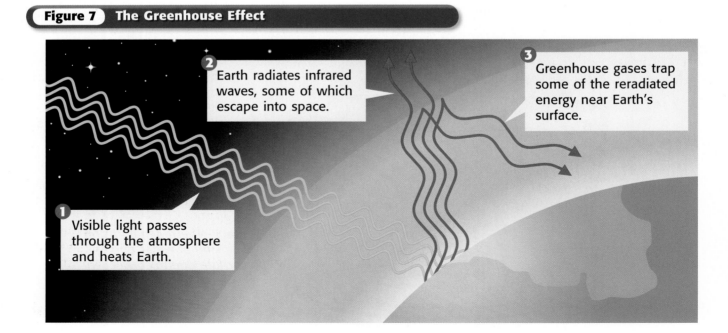

Figure 7 **The Greenhouse Effect**

1 Visible light passes through the atmosphere and heats Earth.

2 Earth radiates infrared waves, some of which escape into space.

3 Greenhouse gases trap some of the reradiated energy near Earth's surface.

Heat and Temperature Change

On a hot summer day, have you ever fastened your seat belt in a car? If so, you may have noticed that the metal buckle felt hotter than the cloth belt. Why?

Thermal Conductivity

Different substances have different thermal conductivities. *Thermal conductivity* is the rate at which a substance conducts thermal energy. The metal buckle of a seat belt, such as the one shown in **Figure 8,** has a higher thermal conductivity than the cloth belt has. Because of its higher thermal conductivity, the metal transfers energy more rapidly to your hand when you touch it than the cloth does. So, even if the cloth and metal are at the same temperature, the metal feels hotter.

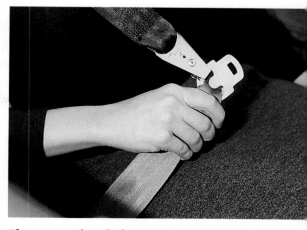

Figure 8 *The cloth part of a seat belt does not feel as hot as the metal part.*

Specific Heat

Another difference between the metal and the cloth is how easily each changes temperature when it absorbs or loses energy. When equal amounts of energy are transferred to or from equal masses of different substances, the change in temperature for each substance will differ. **Specific heat** is the amount of energy needed to change the temperature of 1 kg of a substance by 1°C.

Look at **Table 2.** The specific heat of the cloth of a seat belt is more than twice that of the metal buckle. So, for equal masses of metal and cloth, the same thermal energy will increase the temperature of the metal twice as much as the cloth. The higher the specific heat of something is, the more energy it takes to increase its temperature. **Table 2** shows that most metals have very low specific heats. On the other hand, the specific heat of water is very high. This is why swimming-pool water usually feels cool, even on a hot day. The same energy heats up the air more than it heats up the water.

specific heat the quantity of heat required to raise a unit mass of homogeneous material 1 K or 1°C in a specified way given constant pressure and volume

CONNECTION TO Social Studies

WRITING SKILL **Living near Coastlines** Water has a higher specific heat than land does. Because of water's high specific heat, the ocean has a moderating effect on the weather of coastal areas. The mild weather of coastal areas is one reason they tend to be heavily populated. Find out what the weather is like in various coastal areas in the world. Research the various reasons why coastal areas tend to be heavily populated, and write a brief report in your **science journal.**

Table 2 Specific Heat of Some Common Substances

Substance	Specific heat (J/kg•°C)	Substance	Specific heat (J/kg•°C)
Lead	128	Glass	837
Gold	129	Aluminum	899
Copper	387	Cloth of seat belt	1,340
Iron	448	Ice	2,090
Metal of seat belt	500	Water	4,184

Mass of water = 0.2 kg
Temperature (before) = 25°C
Temperature (after) = 80°C
Specific heat of
    water = 4,184 J/kg•°C

Figure 9 *Information used to calculate heat, the amount of energy transferred to the water, is shown above.*

Heat, Temperature, and Amount

Unlike temperature, energy transferred between objects can not be measured directly. Instead, it must be calculated. When calculating energy transferred between objects, you can use the definition of *heat* as the amount of energy that is transferred between two objects that are at different temperatures. Heat can then be expressed in joules (J).

How much energy is needed to heat a cup of water to make tea? To answer this question, you have to consider the water's mass, its change in temperature, and its specific heat. These are all listed in **Figure 9.** In general, if you know an object's mass, its change in temperature, and its specific heat, you can use the equation below to calculate heat.

$$heat \text{ (J)} = specific\ heat \text{ (J/kg•°C)} \times mass \text{ (kg)}$$
$$\times\ change\ in\ temperature \text{ (°C)}$$

Calculating Heat

Using the equation above, you can calculate the heat transferred to the water. Because the water's temperature increases, the value of heat is positive. You can also use this equation to calculate the heat transferred from an object when it cools down. The value for heat would then be negative because the temperature decreases.

✓ Reading Check What are the three pieces of information needed to calculate heat?

Calculating Heat Calculate the heat transferred to a mass of 0.2 kg of water to change the temperature of the water from 25°C to 80°C. (The specific heat of water is 4,184 J/kg•°C.)

Step 1: Write the equation for calculating heat.

heat = specific heat × mass × change in temperature

Step 2: Replace the specific heat, mass, and temperature change with the values given in the problem, and solve.

heat = 4,184 J/kg•°C × 0.2 kg × (80°C − 25°C)

heat = 46,024 J

Now It's Your Turn

1. Imagine that you heat 2.0 kg of water to make pasta. The temperature of the water before you heat it is 40°C, and the temperature after is 100°C. How much heat was transferred to the water?

Summary

- Heat is energy transferred between objects that are at different temperatures.

- Thermal energy is the total kinetic energy of the particles that make up a substance.

- Thermal energy will always be transferred from higher to lower temperature.

- Transfer of thermal energy ends when two objects that are in contact are at the same temperature.

- Conduction, convection, and radiation are three ways thermal energy is transferred.

- Specific heat is the amount of energy needed to change the temperature of 1 kg of a substance by 1°C.

- Energy transferred by heat cannot be measured directly. It must be calculated using specific heat, mass, and change in temperature.

- Energy transferred by heat is expressed in joules (J) and is calculated as follows:
  heat (J) = *specific heat* (J/kg•°C) × *mass* (kg) × *change in temperature* (°C).

Using Key Terms

For each pair of terms, explain how the meanings of the terms differ.

1. *thermal conductor* and *thermal insulator*

2. *convection* and *radiation*

Understanding Key Ideas

3. Two objects at different temperatures are in contact. Which of the following happens to their thermal energy?

   a. Their thermal energies remain the same.

   b. Thermal energy passes from the cooler object to the warmer object.

   c. Thermal energy passes from the warmer object to the cooler object.

   d. Thermal energy passes back and forth equally between the two objects.

4. What is heat?

Math Skills

5. The specific heat of lead is 128 J/kg•°C. How much heat is needed to raise the temperature of a 0.015 kg sample of lead by 10°C?

Critical Thinking

6. **Making Inferences** Two objects have the same total thermal energy. They are different sizes. Are they at the same temperature? Explain.

7. **Applying Concepts** Why do many metal cooking utensils have wooden handles?

Interpreting Graphics

8. Look at the photo below. It shows examples of heat transfer by conduction, convection, and radiation. Indicate which type of heat transfer is happening next to each letter.

SciLINKS.

NSTA
Developed and maintained by the
National Science Teachers Association

For a variety of links related to this chapter, go to www.scilinks.org

Topic: What Is Heat?
SciLinks code: HSM1661

Matter and Heat

Have you ever eaten a frozen juice bar outside on a hot summer day? It's pretty hard to finish the entire thing before it starts to drip and make a big mess!

The juice bar melts because the sun radiates energy to the frozen juice bar. The energy absorbed by the juice bar increases the kinetic energy of the molecules in the juice bar, which starts to change to a liquid.

States of Matter

The matter that makes up a frozen juice bar has the same identity whether the juice bar is frozen or has melted. The matter is just in a different form, or state. The **states of matter** are the physical forms in which a substance can exist. Matter consists of particles that can move around at different speeds. The state a substance is in depends on the speed of its particles, the attraction between them, and the pressure around them. Three familiar states of matter are solid, liquid, and gas, shown in **Figure 1.**

Thermal energy is the total energy of all the particles that make up a substance. Suppose that you have equal masses of a substance in its three states, each at a different temperature. The substance will have the most thermal energy as a gas and the least thermal energy as a solid. The reason is that the particles of a gas move around fastest.

READING WARM-UP

Objectives
- Identify three states of matter.
- Explain how heat affects matter during a change of state.
- Describe how heat affects matter during a chemical change.
- Explain what a *calorimeter* is used for.

Terms to Learn

states of matter
change of state

READING STRATEGY

Brainstorming The key idea of this section is the relationship between matter and heat. Brainstorm words and phrases related to matter and heat.

Figure 1 Particles of a Solid, a Liquid, and a Gas

Particles of a gas, such as carbon dioxide, move fast enough to overcome nearly all of the attraction between them. The particles move independently of one another.

Particles of a liquid move fast enough to overcome some of the attraction between them. The particles are able to slide past one another.

Particles of a solid, such as ice, do not move fast enough to overcome the strong attraction between them, so they are held tightly together. The particles vibrate in place.

Changes of State

When you melt cheese to make a cheese dip, such as that shown in **Figure 2,** the cheese changes from a solid to a thick, gooey liquid. A **change of state** is a change of a substance from one state of matter to another. A change of state is a *physical change* that affects one or more physical properties of a substance without changing the identity of the substance. Changes of state include *freezing* (liquid to solid), *melting* (solid to liquid), *boiling* (liquid to gas), and *condensing* (gas to liquid).

Energy and Changes of State

Suppose that you put an ice cube in a pan and set the pan on a stove burner. Soon, the ice will turn to water and then to steam. If you made a graph of the temperature of the ice versus the energy involved during this process, it would look something like the graph in **Figure 3.**

As the ice is heated, its temperature increases from –25°C to 0°C. As the ice melts, its temperature remains at 0°C even as more energy is added. This added energy changes the arrangement of the molecules in the ice. The temperature of the ice remains the same until all of the ice has become liquid water. At that point, the water's temperature starts to increase from 0°C to 100°C. At 100°C, the water begins to change to steam. Even as more energy is added, the water's temperature stays at 100°C as long as there is liquid water present. When all of the water has become steam, the temperature again increases.

Reading Check What happens to the temperature of a substance while it is undergoing a change of state? (*See the Appendix for answers to Reading Checks.*)

Figure 2 *When you melt cheese, you change the state of the cheese but not its identity.*

states of matter the physical forms of matter, which include solid, liquid, and gas

change of state the change of a substance from one physical state to another

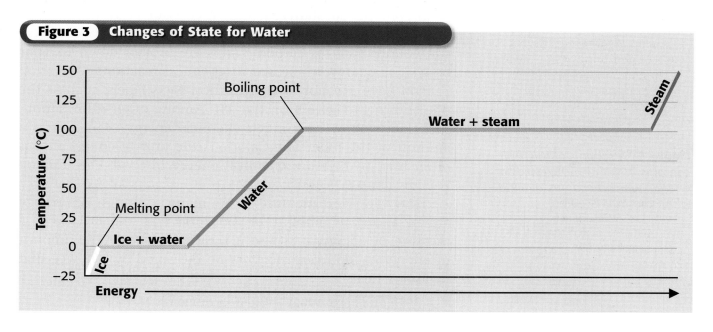

Figure 3 Changes of State for Water

Graph: Temperature (°C) versus Energy. Ice warms to Melting point; Ice + water; Water; Boiling point; Water + steam; Steam. Temperature axis marked –25, 0, 25, 50, 75, 100, 125, 150.

Figure 4 *In a natural-gas fireplace, the methane in natural gas and the oxygen in air change into carbon dioxide and water. As a result of the change, energy is given off, making a room feel warmer.*

Heat and Chemical Changes

Heat is involved not only in changes of state, which are physical changes, but also in *chemical changes*—changes that occur when one or more substances are changed into entirely new substances that have different properties. During a chemical change, new substances are formed.

For a new substance to form, old bonds between particles must be broken, and new bonds must be formed. The breaking and creating of bonds between particles involves energy. Sometimes, a chemical change requires that thermal energy be put into substances for a reaction to occur. Other times, a chemical change, such as the one shown in **Figure 4,** will result in a release of energy.

Food and Chemical Energy

Food contains substances from which your body gets energy. Energy that your body can use is released when chemical compounds such as carbohydrates are broken down in your body. The energy is released in chemical reactions.

You have probably seen Nutrition Facts labels, such as the one shown in **Figure 5** on the left. Among other information, such labels show how much chemical energy is in a certain amount of the food. The Calorie is the unit of energy that is often used to measure chemical energy in food. One Calorie is equivalent to 4,184 J.

How do you measure how many Calories of energy are in a certain amount of food? Because the Calorie is a measure of energy, it is also a measure of heat. The amount of energy in food can therefore be measured by a device that measures heat.

Figure 5 *A serving of this fruit contains 120 Cal (502,080 J) of energy, which becomes available when the fruit is eaten.*

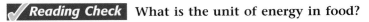 **Reading Check** What is the unit of energy in food?

Calorimeters

A *calorimeter* (KAL uh RIM uht uhr) is a device that measures heat. When one object transfers thermal energy to another object, the energy lost by one object is gained by the other object. This is the key to how a calorimeter works. Inside a calorimeter, shown in **Figure 6,** thermal energy is transferred from a known mass of a test substance to a known mass of another substance, usually water.

The energy of food, in Calories, is found in this way. In a special kind of calorimeter called a *bomb calorimeter,* a food sample is burned. The energy that is released is transferred to the water. By measuring the temperature change of the water and using water's specific heat, you can determine the exact amount of energy transferred by the food sample to the water. This amount of energy (heat) equals the energy content of the food.

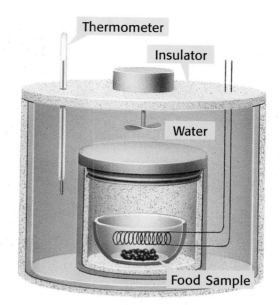

Figure 6 *A bomb calorimeter can measure energy content in food by measuring how much heat is given off by a food sample when it is burned.*

SECTION Review

Summary

- States of matter include solid, liquid, and gas.
- Thermal energy transferred during a change of state does not change a substance's temperature. Rather, it causes a substance's particles to be rearranged.
- Chemical changes can cause thermal energy to be released or absorbed.
- A calorimeter can measure energy changes by measuring heat.

Using Key Terms

1. Use each of the following terms in a separate sentence: *states of matter* and *change of state.*

Understanding Key Ideas

2. What determines a substance's state?
   a. the size of its particles
   b. the amount of the substance
   c. the speed of its particles and the attraction between them
   d. the chemical energy that the substance has

3. During a change of state, why doesn't the temperature of the substance change?

Math Skills

4. When burned in a calorimeter, a sample of popcorn released 627,600 J. How much energy, in Calories, did the popcorn have?

Critical Thinking

5. **Applying Concepts** Many cold packs used for sports injuries are activated by bending the package, causing the substances inside to chemically react. How is heat involved in this process?

6. **Analyzing Processes** When water evaporates (changes from a liquid to a gas), the air near the water's surface becomes cooler. Explain why.

SCiLINKS®

NSTA
Developed and maintained by the National Science Teachers Association

For a variety of links related to this chapter, go to www.scilinks.org

Topic: Heat Energy
SciLinks code: HSM0727

Heat Technology

You probably wouldn't be surprised to learn that the heater in your home is an example of heat technology. But did you know that automobiles, refrigerators, and air conditioners are also examples of heat technology?

It's true! You can travel long distances, you can keep your food cold, and you can feel comfortable indoors during the summer—all because of heat technology.

Heating Systems

Many homes and buildings have a central heating system that controls the temperature in every room. On the next few pages, you will see some different central heating systems.

Hot-Water Heating

The high specific heat of water makes it useful for heating systems. A hot-water heating system is shown in **Figure 1.** A hot-water heater raises the temperature of water, which is pumped through pipes that lead to radiators in each room. The radiators then heat the colder air surrounding them. The water returns to the hot-water heater to be heated again.

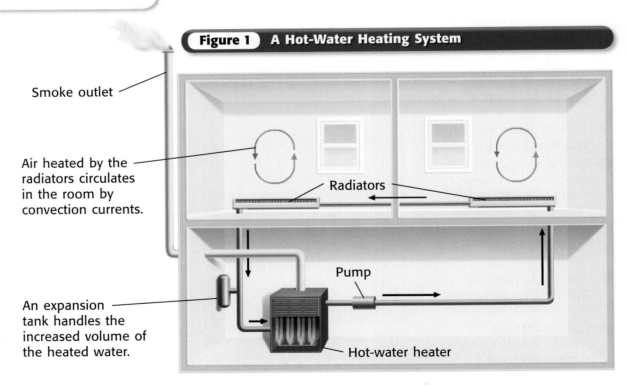

Figure 1 A Hot-Water Heating System

Smoke outlet

Air heated by the radiators circulates in the room by convection currents.

Radiators

Pump

An expansion tank handles the increased volume of the heated water.

Hot-water heater

Figure 2 A Warm-Air Heating System

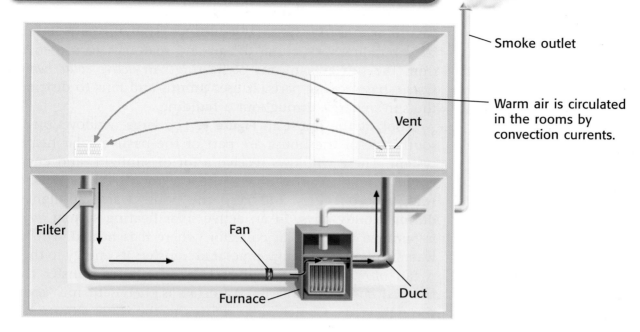

Smoke outlet

Warm air is circulated in the rooms by convection currents.

Vent

Filter

Fan

Furnace

Duct

Warm-Air Heating

Air cannot hold as much thermal energy as water can. But warm-air heating systems are used in many homes and offices in the United States. In a warm-air heating system, shown in **Figure 2,** air is heated by burning fuel (usually natural gas) in a furnace. The warm air travels through ducts to different rooms. The warm air heats air in the rooms. Cooler air sinks below the warm air and enters a vent near the floor. Then, a fan forces the cooler air into the furnace. The air is heated and returned to the ducts. An air filter cleans the air as it moves through the system.

Heating and Insulation

Heat may quickly escape out of a house during cold weather, and during hot weather a house may heat up. To keep the house comfortable, a heating system must run much of the time during the winter. Air conditioners often must run most of the time in the summer to keep a house cool. This can be wasteful. Insulation can help reduce the energy needed to heat and cool buildings. Fiberglass insulation is shown in **Figure 3. Insulation** is a material that reduces the transfer of thermal energy. When insulation is used in walls, ceilings, and floors, less heat passes into or out of the building. Insulation helps a house stay warm in the winter and cool in the summer.

insulation a substance that reduces the transfer of electricity, heat, or sound

Figure 3 *Millions of tiny air pockets in this insulation help prevent thermal energy from flowing into or out of a building.*

✓ **Reading Check** How does insulation help reduce energy costs? (*See the Appendix for answers to Reading Checks.*)

Figure 4 *Passive and active solar heating systems work together to use the sun's energy to heat an entire house.*

Solar Heating

The sun gives off a huge amount of energy. Solar heating systems use this energy to heat houses and buildings. A *passive solar heating system* does not have moving parts. It relies on a building's structural design and materials to use energy from the sun as a means of heating. An *active solar heating system* has moving parts. It uses pumps and fans to distribute the sun's energy throughout a building.

Look at the house in **Figure 4.** The large windows on the south side of the house are part of the passive solar heating system. These windows receive a lot of sunlight, and energy enters through the windows into the rooms. Thick concrete walls absorb energy and keep the house warm at night or during cloudy days. In an active solar heating system, water is pumped to the solar collector, where it is heated. The hot water is pumped through pipes and transfers its energy to them. A fan blowing over the pipes helps the pipes transfer their thermal energy to the air. Warm air is then sent into rooms through vents. Cooler water returns to the water storage tank to be pumped back through the solar collector.

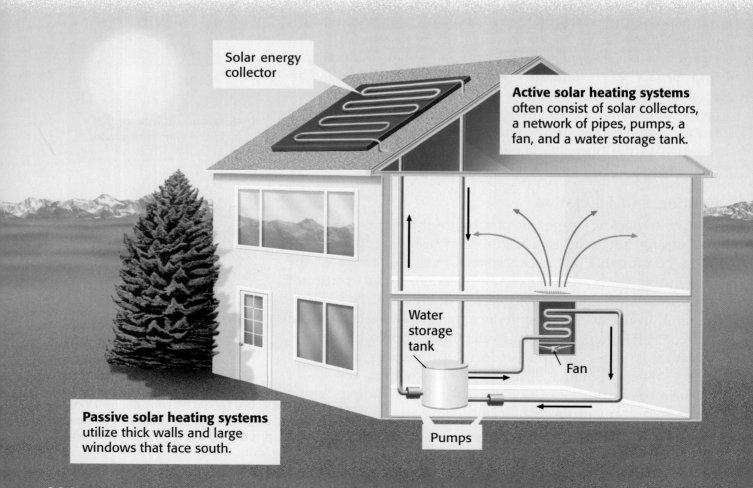

Solar energy collector

Active solar heating systems often consist of solar collectors, a network of pipes, pumps, a fan, and a water storage tank.

Water storage tank

Fan

Pumps

Passive solar heating systems utilize thick walls and large windows that face south.

Heat Engines

Did you know that automobiles work because of heat? A car has a **heat engine,** a machine that uses heat to do work. In a heat engine, fuel combines with oxygen in a chemical change that releases thermal energy. Heat engines burn fuel through this process, called *combustion*. Heat engines that burn fuel outside the engine are called *external combustion engines*. Heat engines that burn fuel inside the engine are called *internal combustion engines*. In both types of engines, fuel is burned to release thermal energy that can be used to do work.

Reading Check What kind of energy do combustion engines use?

External Combustion Engines

A simple steam engine, shown in **Figure 5,** is an example of an external combustion engine. Coal is burned to heat water in a boiler and change the water to steam. The steam expands, which pushes a piston. The piston can be attached to other parts of the machine that do work.

Modern steam engines, such as those used to generate electrical energy at a power plant, drive turbines instead of pistons. In the case of generators that use steam to do work, thermal energy is converted into electrical energy.

heat engine a machine that transforms heat into mechanical energy, or work

CONNECTION TO Oceanography

Energy from the Ocean
Ocean engineers are developing a new technology called *Ocean Thermal Energy Conversion*, or OTEC. OTEC uses temperature differences between surface water and deep water in the ocean to generate electrical energy. Research more information about OTEC, and make a model or a poster demonstrating how it works.

ACTIVITY

Figure 5 An External Combustion Engine

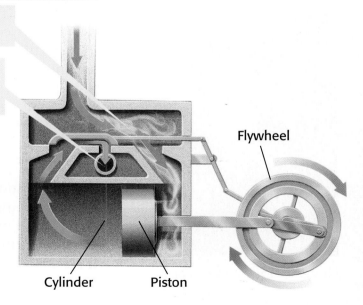

Steam enters through the open valve.

Steam exits the cylinder through an exhaust outlet.

Flywheel

Cylinder   Piston   Flywheel

Cylinder   Piston

① The expanding steam enters the cylinder from one side. The steam does work on the piston, forcing the piston to move.

② As the piston moves to the other side, a second valve opens, and steam enters. The steam does work on the piston and moves it back. The motion of the piston turns a flywheel.

Section 4   Heat Technology   **295**

Wire to spark plug

Cylinder

Piston

Crankshaft

Figure 6 *The continuous cycling of the four strokes in the cylinders converts thermal energy into the kinetic energy needed to make a car move.*

Figure 7 *This air-conditioning unit keeps a building cool by moving thermal energy from inside the building to the outside.*

Internal Combustion Engines

The six-cylinder car engine shown in **Figure 6** is an internal combustion engine. Fuel is burned inside the engine. The fuel used is gasoline, which is burned inside the cylinders. The cylinders go through a series of steps in burning the fuel.

First, a mixture of gasoline and air enters each cylinder as the piston moves down. This step is called the *intake stroke.* Next, the crankshaft turns and pushes the piston up, compressing the fuel mixture. This step is called the *compression stroke.* Next comes the *power stroke,* in which the spark plug uses electrical energy to ignite the compressed fuel mixture. As the mixture of fuel and air burns, it expands and forces the piston down. Finally, during the *exhaust stroke,* the crankshaft turns, and the piston is forced back up, pushing exhaust gases out of the cylinder.

Cooling Systems

When the summer gets hot, an air-conditioned room can feel very refreshing. Cooling systems are used to transfer thermal energy out of a particular area so that it feels cooler. An air conditioner, shown in **Figure 7,** is a cooling system that transfers thermal energy from a warm area inside a building or car to an area outside. Thermal energy naturally tends to go from areas of higher temperature to areas of lower temperature. So, to transfer thermal energy outside where it is warmer, the air-conditioning system must do work. It's like walking uphill: if you are going against gravity, you must do work.

Figure 8 How a Refrigerator Works

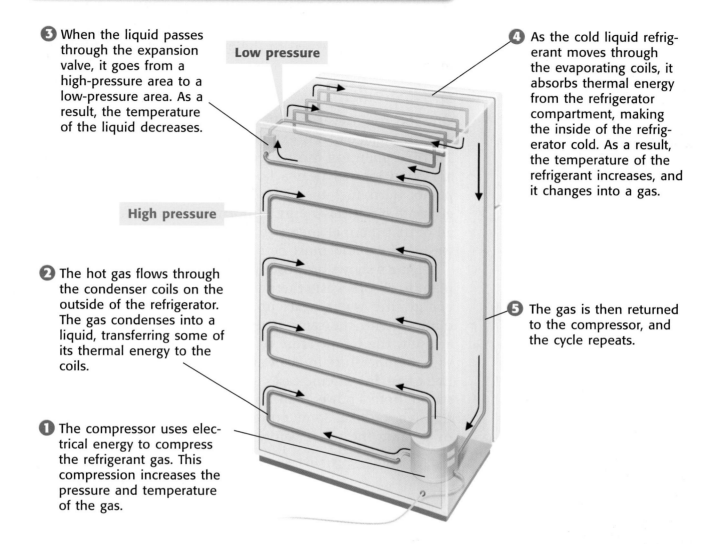

❸ When the liquid passes through the expansion valve, it goes from a high-pressure area to a low-pressure area. As a result, the temperature of the liquid decreases.

Low pressure

High pressure

❹ As the cold liquid refrigerant moves through the evaporating coils, it absorbs thermal energy from the refrigerator compartment, making the inside of the refrigerator cold. As a result, the temperature of the refrigerant increases, and it changes into a gas.

❷ The hot gas flows through the condenser coils on the outside of the refrigerator. The gas condenses into a liquid, transferring some of its thermal energy to the coils.

❺ The gas is then returned to the compressor, and the cycle repeats.

❶ The compressor uses electrical energy to compress the refrigerant gas. This compression increases the pressure and temperature of the gas.

Cooling and Energy

Most cooling systems require electrical energy to do the work of cooling. The electrical energy is used by a device called a compressor. The *compressor* does the work of compressing the refrigerant. The *refrigerant* is a gas that has a boiling point below room temperature, which allows it to condense easily.

To keep many foods fresh, you store them in a refrigerator. A refrigerator is another example of a cooling system. **Figure 8** shows how a refrigerator continuously transfers thermal energy from inside the refrigerator to the condenser coils on the outside of the refrigerator. That's why the area near the back of a refrigerator feels warm.

✔**Reading Check** How does the inside of a refrigerator stay at a temperature that is cooler than the temperature outside the refrigerator?

Heat Technology and Thermal Pollution

Heating systems, car engines, and cooling systems all transfer thermal energy to the environment. Unfortunately, too much thermal energy released to the environment can have a negative effect.

Thermal Pollution

thermal pollution a temperature increase in a body of water that is caused by human activity and that has a harmful effect on water quality and on the ability of that body of water to support life

One of the negative effects of excess thermal energy is **thermal pollution,** the excessive heating of a body of water. Thermal pollution can happen near large power plants, which are often located near a body of water. Many electric-power plants burn fuel to release thermal energy that is used to generate electrical energy. Unfortunately, it is not possible for all of that thermal energy to do work. So, some thermal energy waste results and must be released to the environment.

Figure 9 shows how cool water is circulated through a power plant to absorb waste thermal energy. As the cool water absorbs energy, the water heats up. Sometimes the heated water is dumped into the same body of water that it came from. As a result, the temperature of the water can increase. Increased water temperature in lakes and streams can harm animals that live there. In extreme cases, the increase in temperature downstream from a power plant can adversely affect the ecosystem of the river or lake. Some power plants reduce thermal pollution by cooling the water before it is returned to the river.

Reading Check Give an example of thermal pollution.

Figure 9 *Thermal pollution from power plants can result if the plant raises the water temperature of lakes and streams.*

Cool water

Warm water

Summary

- Central heating systems include hot-water heating systems and warm-air heating systems.

- Solar heating systems can be passive or active. In passive solar heating, a building takes advantage of the sun's energy without the use of moving parts. Active solar heating uses moving parts to aid the flow of solar energy throughout a building.

- Heat engines use heat to do work.

- The two kinds of heat engines are external combustion engines, which burn fuel outside the engine, and internal combustion engines, which burn fuel inside the engine.

- A cooling system transfers thermal energy from cooler temperatures to warmer temperatures by doing work.

- Transferring excess thermal energy to lakes and rivers can result in thermal pollution.

Using Key Terms

1. Use each of the following terms in a separate sentence: *insulation, heat engine,* and *thermal pollution.*

Understanding Key Ideas

2. Which of the following describes how cooling systems transfer thermal energy?

   a. Thermal energy naturally flows from cooler areas to warmer areas.

   b. Thermal energy naturally flows from warmer areas to cooler areas.

   c. Work is done to transfer thermal energy from warmer areas to cooler areas.

   d. Work is done to transfer thermal energy from cooler areas to warmer areas.

3. Compare a hot-water heating system with a warm-air heating system.

4. What is the difference between an external combustion engine and an internal combustion engine?

Critical Thinking

5. **Identifying Relationships** How are changes of state important in how a refrigerator works?

6. **Expressing Opinions** Compare the advantages and disadvantages of solar heating systems. What do you think their overall benefits are, compared with those of other heating systems?

Interpreting Graphics

7. Look at the graph below. It shows the cost of heating a certain house month by month over the course of a year. During which times of the year is the most energy used for heating? Explain your answer.

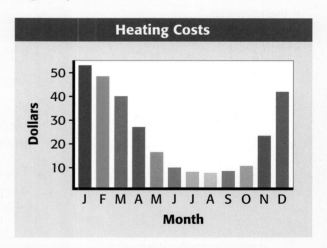

Heating Costs

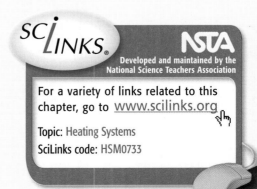

For a variety of links related to this chapter, go to www.scilinks.org

Topic: Heating Systems
SciLinks code: HSM0733

Using Scientific Methods

Skills Practice Lab

Feel the Heat

Heat is the energy transferred between objects at different temperatures. Energy moves from objects at higher temperatures to objects at lower temperatures. If two objects are left in contact for a while, the warmer object will cool down and the cooler object will warm up until they eventually reach the same temperature. In this activity, you will combine equal masses of water and nails at different temperatures to determine which has a greater effect on the final temperature.

OBJECTIVES

Measure the temperature change when hot and cold objects come into contact.

Compare materials for their ability to hold thermal energy.

MATERIALS

- balance, metric
- cups, plastic-foam, 9 oz (2)
- cylinder, graduated, 100 mL
- nails (10 to 12)
- string, 30 cm length
- paper towels
- rubber band
- thermometer
- water, cold
- water, hot

SAFETY

Ask a Question

1 When you combine substances at two different temperatures, will the final temperature be closer to the initial temperature of the warmer substance or of the colder substance, or halfway in between?

Form a Hypothesis

2 Write a prediction that answers the question in item 1.

Test the Hypothesis

3 Copy the table below onto a separate sheet of paper.

4 Use the rubber band to bundle the nails together. Find and record the mass of the bundle. Tie a length of string around the bundle, leaving one end of the string 15 cm long.

5 Put the bundle of nails into one of the cups, letting the string dangle outside the cup. Fill the cup with enough hot water to cover the nails, and set it aside for at least 5 min.

		Data Collection Table			
Trial	**Mass of nails (g)**	**Volume of water that equals mass of nails (mL)**	**Initial temp. of water and nails (°C)**	**Initial temp. of water to which nails will be transferred (°C)**	**Final temp. of water and nails combined (°C)**
1					
2					

DO NOT WRITE IN BOOK

6. Use the graduated cylinder to measure enough cold water to exactly equal the mass of the nails (1 mL of water = 1 g). Record this volume in the table.

7. Measure and record the temperature of the hot water with the nails and the temperature of the cold water.

8. Use the string to transfer the bundle of nails to the cup of cold water. Use the thermometer to monitor the temperature of the water-nail mixture. When the temperature stops changing, record this final temperature in the table.

9. Empty the cups, and dry the nails.

10. For Trial 2, repeat steps 4 through 9, but switch the hot and cold water. Record all of your measurements.

Analyze the Results

1. **Analyzing Results** In Trial 1, you used equal masses of cold water and nails. Did the final temperature support your initial prediction? Explain.

2. **Analyzing Results** In Trial 2, you used equal masses of hot water and nails. Did the final temperature support your initial prediction? Explain.

3. **Explaining Events** In Trial 1, which material—the water or the nails—changed temperature the most after you transferred the nails? What about in Trial 2? Explain your answers.

Draw Conclusions

4. **Drawing Conclusions** The cold water in Trial 1 gained energy. Where did the energy come from?

5. **Evaluating Results** How does the energy gained by the nails in Trial 2 compare with the energy lost by the hot water in Trial 2? Explain.

6. **Applying Conclusions** Which material seems to be able to hold energy better? Explain your answer.

7. **Interpreting Information** Specific heat is a property of matter that indicates how much energy is required to change the temperature of 1 kg of a material by 1°C. Which material in this activity has a higher specific heat (changes temperature less for the same amount of energy)?

8. **Making Predictions** Would it be better to have pots and pans made from a material with a high specific heat or a low specific heat? Explain your answer.

Communicating Your Data

Share your results with your classmates. Discuss how you would change your prediction to include your knowledge of specific heat.

Chapter Review

USING KEY TERMS

For each pair of terms, explain how the meanings of the terms differ.

1 *temperature* and *thermal energy*

2 *conduction* and *heat*

3 *conductor* and *insulator*

4 *states of matter* and *change of state*

5 *heat engine* and *thermal pollution*

UNDERSTANDING KEY IDEAS

Multiple Choice

6 Which of the following temperatures is the lowest?

a. 100°C

b. 100°F

c. 100 K

d. They are all the same.

7 Which of the following materials would NOT be a good insulator?

a. wood

b. cloth

c. metal

d. rubber

8 In an air conditioner, thermal energy is

a. transferred from areas of higher temperatures to areas of lower temperatures.

b. transferred from areas of lower temperatures to areas of higher temperatures.

c. used to do work.

d. transferred into the building.

9 The units of energy that you read on a food label are

a. Newtons.

b. Calories.

c. Joules.

d. Both (b) and (c)

10 Compared wih the Pacific Ocean, a cup of hot chocolate has

a. more thermal energy and a higher temperature.

b. less thermal energy and a higher temperature.

c. more thermal energy and a lower temperature.

d. less thermal energy and a lower temperature.

Short Answer

11 How does temperature relate to kinetic energy?

12 What are the differences between conduction, convection, and radiation?

13 Explain how heat affects matter during a change of state.

Math Skills

14 The weather forecast calls for a temperature of 84°F. What is the corresponding temperature in degrees Celsius? in kelvins?

15 Suppose 1.3 kg of water is heated from 20°C to 100°C. How much energy was transferred to the water? (Water's specific heat is 4,184 J/kg•°C.)

CRITICAL THINKING

16 Concept Mapping Create a concept map using the following terms: *thermal energy, temperature, radiation, heat, conduction,* and *convection.*

17 Applying Concepts The metal lid is stuck on a glass jar of jelly. Explain why running hot water over the lid will help you get the lid off.

18 Applying Concepts How does a down jacket keep you warm? (Hint: Think about what insulation does.)

19 Predicting Consequences Would opening the refrigerator cool a room in a house? Explain your answer.

20 Evaluating Assumptions Someone claims that a large bowl of soup has more thermal energy than a small bowl of soup. Is this always true? Explain.

21 Analyzing Processes In a hot-air balloon, air is heated by a flame. Explain how this enables the balloon to float in the air.

22 Analyzing Processes What is different about the two kinds of metal on the bimetallic strip of a thermostat coil?

23 Making Comparisons How is radiation different from both conduction and convection?

INTERPRETING GRAPHICS

Examine the graph below, and then answer the questions that follow.

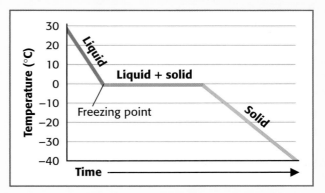

24 What physical change does this graph illustrate?

25 What is the freezing point of this liquid?

26 What is happening at the point where the line is horizontal?

Standardized Test Preparation

Read each of the passages below. Then, answer the questions that follow each passage.

Passage 1 All matter is made up of particles. Temperature is a measure of the average kinetic energy of these particles. The colder a substance gets, the less kinetic energy its particles have, and the slower the particles move. In theory, at absolute zero (–273°C), all movement of particles should stop. Scientists are working in laboratories to cool matter so much that the temperature approaches absolute zero.

1. What is the purpose of this text?
   A to entertain
   B to influence
   C to express
   D to inform

2. What does information in the passage suggest?
   F Matter at absolute zero no longer exists.
   G No one knows what would happen to matter at absolute zero.
   H It is currently not possible to cool matter to absolute zero.
   I Scientists have cooled matter to absolute zero.

3. What information does the passage give about the relationship between kinetic energy and temperature?
   A The higher the temperature, the more kinetic energy a substance has.
   B There is no relationship between temperature and kinetic energy.
   C The higher the temperature, the less kinetic energy a substance has.
   D No one knows what the relationship between kinetic energy and temperature is.

Passage 2 Birds and mammals burn fuel to maintain body temperatures that are usually greater than the air temperature of their surroundings. A lot of energy is necessary to maintain a high body temperature. Tiny animals such as shrews and hummingbirds maintain high body temperatures only during the day. At night or when the air temperature falls significantly, these tiny creatures go into a state called torpor. When an animal is in torpor, its respiration and heart rate are slow. Circulation continues primarily to major organs. Body temperature drops. Because their body processes are slowed, animals in torpor use much less energy than they usually need.

1. Which of the following would be the **best** summary of this passage?
   A Some animals use less energy than other animals.
   B Some animals use more energy than other animals.
   C Some animals maintain high body temperatures only during the day, going into torpor at night.
   D Going into torpor at night is necessary for some animals to maintain high body temperatures.

2. What happens when an animal goes into torpor?
   F Respiration and heart rate slow, and body temperature drops.
   G Normal respiration and heart rate are maintained, and body temperature drops.
   H Respiration and heart rate increase, and body temperature drops.
   I Respiration and heart rate increase, and body temperature rises.

The figure below shows a thermometer in each of two graduated cylinders holding water. Use the figure below to answer the questions that follow.

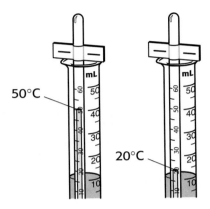

50°C

20°C

1. Which graduated cylinder contains more water?

A The cylinder on the left contains more.

B The cylinder on the right contains more.

C The cylinders contain equal amounts.

D There is not enough information to determine the answer.

2. If the two cylinders are touching each other, what will happen to the thermal energy in the cylinders?

F It will pass from the left cylinder to the right cylinder.

G It will pass from the right cylinder to the left cylinder.

H It will pass equally between the two cylinders.

I Nothing will happen.

3. If the water in the graduated cylinders is mixed together, which of the following will most likely be the temperature of the mixture?

A 25°C

B 35°C

C 50°C

D 70°C

Read each question below, and choose the best answer.

1. Elena has a bag containing 4 blue marbles, 6 red marbles, and 3 green marbles. She picks 1 marble at random. What is the probability of her picking a blue marble?

A 1 in 13

B 1 in 4

C 4 in 13

D 9 in 13

2. If $8 - 2n = -30$, what is the value of n?

F 7

G 19

H 68

I 120

3. A rectangle has sides of 4 cm and 10 cm. If the lengths of each of its sides are reduced by half, what will the change in the area of the rectangle be?

A 1/4 as much area

B 1/2 as much area

C 2 times as much area

D 4 times as much area

4. The specific heat of copper is 387 J/kg•°C. If the temperature of 0.05 kg of copper is raised from 25°C to 30°C, how much heat was put into the copper?

F 96.8 J

G 484 J

H 581 J

I 96,800 J

5. A change in temperature of 1°C is equal to a change in temperature of 1 K. The temperature 0°C is equal to the temperature 273 K. If the temperature is 300 K, what is the temperature in degrees Celsius?

A −27°C

B 27°C

C 54°C

D 73°C

Standardized Test Preparation

Science in Action

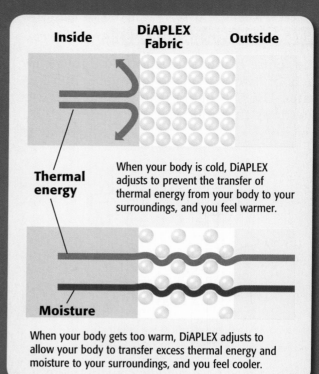

Inside | DiAPLEX Fabric | Outside

Thermal energy

When your body is cold, DiAPLEX adjusts to prevent the transfer of thermal energy from your body to your surroundings, and you feel warmer.

Moisture

When your body gets too warm, DiAPLEX adjusts to allow your body to transfer excess thermal energy and moisture to your surroundings, and you feel cooler.

Scientific Discoveries

The Deep Freeze

All matter is made up of tiny, constantly vibrating particles. Temperature is a measure of the average kinetic energy of particles. The colder a substance gets, the slower its particles move. Scientists are interested in how matter behaves when it is cooled to almost absolute zero, the absence of all thermal energy, which is about –273°C. In one method, scientists aim lasers at gas particles, holding them so still that their temperature is less than one-millionth of a degree from absolute zero. It's like turning on several garden hoses and pointing each from a different angle at a soccer ball so that the ball won't move in any direction.

Math ACTIVITY

Think of the coldest weather you have ever been in. What was the temperature? Convert this temperature to kelvins. Compare this temperature with absolute zero.

Science, Technology, and Society

DiAPLEX®: The Intelligent Fabric

Wouldn't it be great if you had a winter coat that could automatically adjust to keep you cozy regardless of the outside temperature? Well, scientists have developed a new fabric called DiAPLEX that can be used to make such a coat!

Like most winter coats, DiAPLEX is made from nylon. But whereas most nylon fabrics have thousands of tiny pores, or openings, DiAPLEX doesn't have pores. It is a solid film. This film makes DiAPLEX even more waterproof than other nylon fabrics.

Language Arts ACTIVITY

WRITING SKILL Think of two different items of clothing that you wear when the weather is cool or cold. Write a paragraph explaining how you think each of them works in keeping you warm when it is cold outside. Does one keep you warmer than the other? How does it do so?

Michael Reynolds

Earthship Architect Would you want to live in a house without a heating system? You could if you lived in an Earthship! Earthships are the brainchild of Michael Reynolds, an architect in Taos, New Mexico. These houses are designed to make the most of our planet's most abundant source of energy, the sun.

Each Earthship takes full advantage of passive solar heating. For example, large windows face south in order to maximize the amount of energy the house receives from the sun. Each home is partially buried in the ground. The soil helps keep the energy that comes in through the windows inside the house.

To absorb the sun's energy, the outer walls of Earthships are massive and thick. The walls may be made with crushed aluminum cans or stacks of old automobile tires filled with dirt. These materials absorb the sun's energy and naturally heat the house. Because an Earthship maintains a temperature around 15°C (about 60°F), it can keep its occupants comfortable through all but the coldest winter nights.

Social Studies ACTIVITY

Find out more about Michael Reynolds and other architects who have invented unique ways of building houses that are energy-efficient. Present your findings.

go.hrw.com

To learn more about these Science in Action topics, visit go.hrw.com and type in the keyword **HP5HOTF.**

Current Science

Check out Current Science® articles related to this chapter by visiting go.hrw.com. Just type in the keyword **HP5CS10.**

TIMELINE

The Atom

Thousands of years ago, people began asking the question, "What is matter made of?" This unit follows the discoveries and ideas that have led to our current theories about what makes up matter. You will learn about the atom—the building block of all matter—and its structure. You will also learn how the periodic table is used to classify and organize elements according to patterns in atomic structure and other properties. This timeline illustrates some of the events that have brought us to our current understanding of atoms and of the periodic table in which they are organized.

Around 400 BCE
The Greek philosopher Democritus proposes that small particles called *atoms* make up all matter.

1897
British scientist J.J. Thomson identifies electrons as particles that are present in every atom.

1911
Ernest Rutherford, a physicist from New Zealand, discovers the positively charged nucleus of the atom.

1981
Scientists in Switzerland develop a scanning tunneling microscope, which is used to see atoms for the first time.

1803

British scientist and school teacher John Dalton reintroduces the concept of atoms with evidence to support his ideas.

1848

James Marshall finds gold while building Sutter's Mill, starting the California gold rush.

1869

Russian chemist Dmitri Mendeleev develops a periodic table that organizes the elements known at the time.

1932

The neutron, one of the particles in the nucleus of an atom, is discovered by British physicist James Chadwick.

1945

The United Nations is formed. Its purpose is to maintain world peace and develop friendly relations between countries.

1989

Germans celebrate when the Berlin Wall ceases to function as a barrier between East and West Germany.

1996

Another element is added to the periodic table after a team of German scientists synthesize an atom containing 112 protons in its nucleus.

2001

Researchers use electron beam technology to create a tiny silicon transistor that is only 80 atoms wide and that can run at speeds of almost 20 gigahertz.

11

Introduction to Atoms

SECTION 1 Development of the Atomic Theory 312

SECTION 2 The Atom 318

Chapter Lab 326
Chapter Review 328
Standardized Test Preparation 330
Science in Action 332

About the PHOTO

You have probably made bubbles with a plastic wand and a soapy liquid. Some scientists make bubbles by using a bubble chamber. A bubble chamber is filled with a pressurized liquid that forms bubbles when a charged particle moves through it. This photo shows the tracks made by charged particles moving through a bubble chamber. Bubble chambers help scientists learn about particles called *atoms,* which make up all objects.

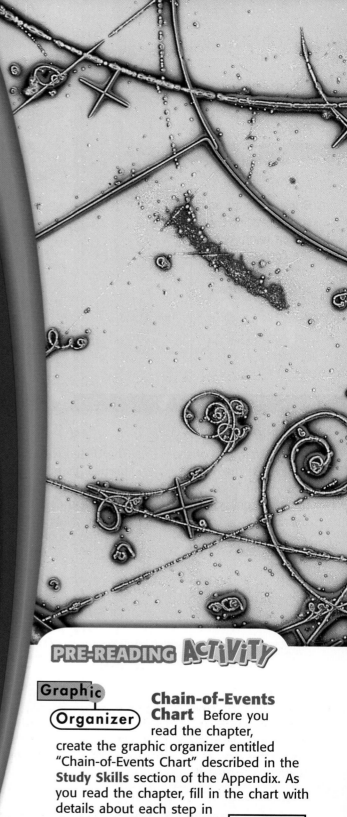

PRE-READING ACTIVITY

Graphic Organizer

Chain-of-Events Chart Before you read the chapter, create the graphic organizer entitled "Chain-of-Events Chart" described in the **Study Skills** section of the Appendix. As you read the chapter, fill in the chart with details about each step in the historical development of ideas about atoms.

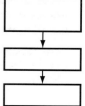

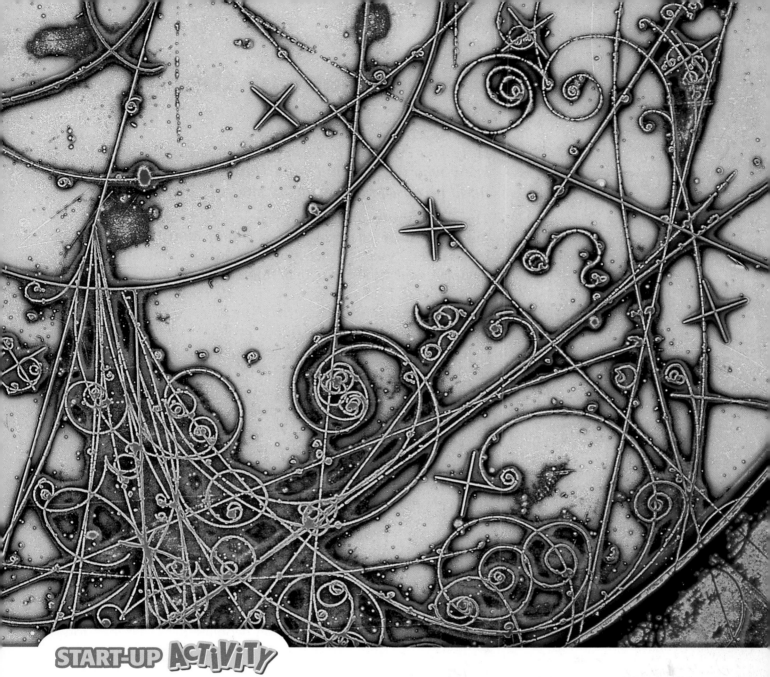

START-UP ACTIVITY

Where Is It?

Scientists have been able to gather information about atoms without actually seeing them. In this activity, you will do something similar: you will form an idea about the location and size of a hidden object by rolling marbles at it.

Procedure

1. Place a **rectangular piece of cardboard** on **four books or blocks** so that each corner of the cardboard rests on a book or block.

2. Your teacher will place an **unknown object** under the cardboard. Be sure that you cannot see the object.

3. Place a **large piece of paper** on top of the cardboard.

4. Carefully roll a **marble** under the cardboard. Record on the paper the position where the marble enters and exits. Also, record the direction it travels.

5. Keep rolling the marble from different directions to collect data about the shape and location of the object. Write down all of your observations.

Analysis

1. Form a conclusion about the object's shape, size, and location. Record your conclusion.

2. Lift the cardboard, and look at the object. Compare your conclusions with the object's actual size, shape, and location.

Development of the Atomic Theory

Have you ever watched a mystery movie and thought you knew who the criminal was? Have you ever changed your mind because of a new fact or clue?

The same thing happens in science! Sometimes an idea or model must be changed as new information is gathered. In this section, you will see how our ideas about atoms have changed over time. Your first stop is ancient Greece.

The Beginning of Atomic Theory

Imagine that you cut something in half. Then, you cut each half in half again, and so on. Could you keep cutting the pieces in half forever? Around 440 BCE, a Greek philosopher named Democritus (di MAHK ruh tuhs) thought that you would eventually end up with a particle that could not be cut. He called this particle an atom. The word *atom* is from the Greek word *atomos*, meaning "not able to be divided." Democritus said that all atoms are small, hard particles. He thought that atoms were made of a single material formed into different shapes and sizes.

From Aristotle to Modern Science

Aristotle (AR is TAHT'l), another Greek philosopher, disagreed with Democritus's ideas. He believed that you would never end up with a particle that could not be cut. He had such a strong influence on people's ideas that for a long time, most people thought he was right.

Democritus was right, though: Matter is made of particles, which we call atoms. An **atom** is the smallest particle into which an element can be divided and still be the same substance. **Figure 1** shows a picture of aluminum atoms taken with an electron microscope. Long before actually being able to see atoms, scientists had ideas about them.

READING WARM-UP

Objectives

● Describe some of the experiments that led to the current atomic theory.

● Compare the different models of the atom.

● Explain how the atomic theory has changed as scientists have discovered new information about the atom.

Terms to Learn

atom   nucleus
electron   electron cloud

READING STRATEGY

Reading Organizer As you read this section, create an outline of the section. Use the headings from the section in your outline.

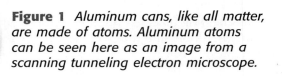

Figure 1 *Aluminum cans, like all matter, are made of atoms. Aluminum atoms can be seen here as an image from a scanning tunneling electron microscope.*

Dalton's Atomic Theory Based on Experiments

By the late 1700s, scientists had learned that elements combine in certain proportions based on mass to form compounds. For example, hydrogen and oxygen always combine in the same proportion to form water. John Dalton, a British chemist and schoolteacher, wanted to know why. He experimented with different substances. His results suggested that elements combine in certain proportions because they are made of single atoms. Dalton, shown in **Figure 2,** published his atomic theory in 1803. His theory stated the following ideas:

- All substances are made of atoms. Atoms are small particles that cannot be created, divided, or destroyed.
- Atoms of the same element are exactly alike, and atoms of different elements are different.
- Atoms join with other atoms to make new substances.

✓ Reading Check Why did Dalton think that elements are made of single atoms? (*See the Appendix for answers to Reading Checks.*)

Not Quite Correct

Toward the end of the 1800s, scientists agreed that Dalton's theory explained much of what they saw. However, new information was found that did not fit some of Dalton's ideas. The atomic theory was then changed to describe the atom more correctly. As you read on, you will learn how Dalton's theory has changed, step by step, into the modern atomic theory.

atom the smallest unit of an element that maintains the properties of that element

Figure 2 *John Dalton developed his atomic theory from observations gathered from many experiments.*

Figure 3 Thomson's Cathode-Ray Tube Experiment

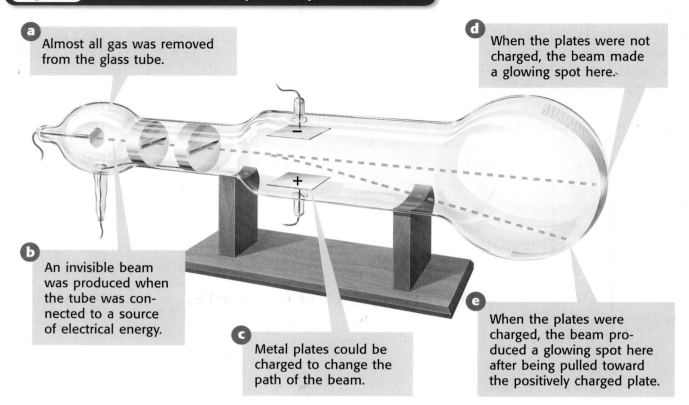

a Almost all gas was removed from the glass tube.

d When the plates were not charged, the beam made a glowing spot here.

b An invisible beam was produced when the tube was connected to a source of electrical energy.

c Metal plates could be charged to change the path of the beam.

e When the plates were charged, the beam produced a glowing spot here after being pulled toward the positively charged plate.

Thomson's Discovery of Electrons

electron a subatomic particle that has a negative charge

In 1897, a British scientist named J. J. Thomson showed that there was a mistake in Dalton's theory. Thomson discovered that there are small particles *inside* the atom. This means that atoms can be divided into even smaller parts.

Thomson experimented with a cathode-ray tube like the one shown in **Figure 3.** He discovered that a positively charged plate (marked with a plus sign in the drawing) attracted the beam. Thomson concluded that the beam was made of particles that have negative electric charges. He also concluded that these negatively charged particles are present in every kind of atom. The negatively charged particles that Thomson discovered are now called **electrons.**

Like Plums in a Pudding

Figure 4 *Thomson proposed that electrons were located throughout an atom like plums in a pudding, as shown in this model.*

After learning that atoms contain electrons, Thomson proposed a new model of the atom. This model is shown in **Figure 4.** It is sometimes called the *plum-pudding model,* after a dessert that was popular in Thomson's day. Thomson thought that electrons were mixed throughout an atom, like plums in a pudding. Today, you might call Thomson's model the *chocolate chip ice-cream model.*

Rutherford's Atomic "Shooting Gallery"

In 1909, a former student of Thomson's named Ernest Rutherford decided to test Thomson's theory. He designed an experiment to study the parts of the atom. He aimed a beam of small, positively charged particles at a thin sheet of gold foil. **Figure 5** shows Rutherford's experiment. Rutherford put a special coating behind the foil. The coating glowed when hit by the positively charged particles. Rutherford could then see where the particles went after hitting the gold.

✓ Reading Check How could Rutherford tell where the positively charged particles went after hitting the gold foil?

Surprising Results

Rutherford started with Thomson's idea that atoms are soft "blobs" of matter. He expected the particles to pass right through the gold in a straight line. Most of the particles did just that. But to Rutherford's great surprise, some of the particles were deflected (turned to one side). Some even bounced straight back. Rutherford reportedly said,

"It was quite the most incredible event that has ever happened to me in my life. It was almost as if you fired a fifteen-inch shell into a piece of tissue paper and it came back and hit you."

CONNECTION TO Language Arts

WRITING SKILL **Solving Mysteries** Scientists who made discoveries about the atom had to do so by gathering clues and drawing conclusions from experiments. Read a short mystery story, and write a one-page paper in which you discuss the methods that were used to solve the mystery in the story. Compare these methods with those used by scientists finding out about what atoms are like.

Figure 5 Rutherford's Gold-Foil Experiment

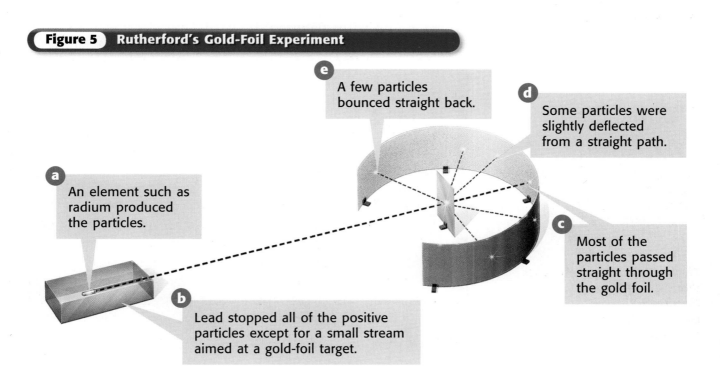

e A few particles bounced straight back.

d Some particles were slightly deflected from a straight path.

a An element such as radium produced the particles.

c Most of the particles passed straight through the gold foil.

b Lead stopped all of the positive particles except for a small stream aimed at a gold-foil target.

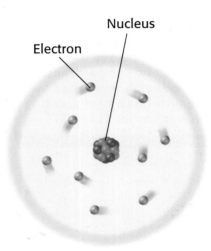

Figure 6 *Rutherford's model of the atom had electrons surrounding the nucleus at a distance. (This model does not show the true scale of sizes and distances.)*

Where Are the Electrons?

The plum-pudding model of the atom did not explain what Rutherford saw. Most of the tiny particles went straight through the gold foil, with a small number being deflected. He realized that in order to explain this, atoms must be considered mostly empty space, with a tiny part made of highly dense matter.

Far from the Nucleus

In 1911, Rutherford revised the atomic theory. He made a new model of the atom, as shown in **Figure 6.** Rutherford proposed that in the center of the atom is a tiny, extremely dense, positively charged part called the **nucleus** (NOO klee uhs). Because like charges repel, Rutherford reasoned that positively charged particles that passed close by the nucleus were pushed away by the positive charges in the nucleus. A particle that headed straight for a nucleus would be pushed almost straight back in the direction from which it came. From his results, Rutherford calculated that the diameter of the nucleus was 100,000 times smaller than the diameter of the gold atom. To get an idea of this kind of difference in size, look at **Figure 7.**

Reading Check How did Rutherford change Thomson's model of the atom?

Bohr's Electron Levels

In 1913, Niels Bohr, a Danish scientist who worked with Rutherford, studied the way that atoms react to light. Bohr's results led him to propose that electrons move around the nucleus in certain paths, or energy levels. In Bohr's model, there are no paths between the levels. But electrons can jump from a path in one level to a path in another level. Think of the levels as rungs on a ladder. You can stand on the rungs of a ladder but not *between* the rungs. Bohr's model was a valuable tool in predicting some atomic behavior, but the atomic theory still had room for improvement.

Figure 7 *The diameter of this pinhead is 100,000 times smaller than the diameter of the stadium. The pinhead represents the size of a nucleus, and the stadium represents the size of an atom.*

The Modern Atomic Theory

Many 20th-century scientists added to our current understanding of the atom. An Austrian physicist named Erwin Schrödinger (SHROH ding uhr) and a German physicist named Werner Heisenberg (HIE zuhn berkh) did especially important work. They further explained the nature of electrons in the atom. For example, electrons do not travel in definite paths as Bohr suggested. In fact, the exact path of an electron cannot be predicted. According to the current theory, there are regions inside the atom where electrons are *likely* to be found. These regions are called **electron clouds.** The electron-cloud model of the atom is shown in **Figure 8.**

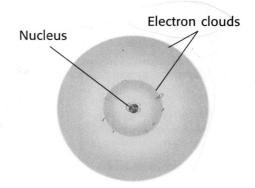

Figure 8 *In the current model of the atom, electrons surround the nucleus in electron clouds.*

SECTION Review

Summary

- Democritus thought that matter is composed of atoms.
- Dalton based his theory on observations of how elements combine.
- Thomson discovered electrons in atoms.
- Rutherford discovered that atoms are mostly empty space with a dense, positive nucleus.
- Bohr proposed that electrons are located in levels at certain distances from the nucleus.
- The electron-cloud model represents the current atomic theory.

Using Key Terms

1. In your own words, write a definition for the term *atom*.

The statements below are false. For each statement, replace the underlined term to make a true statement.

2. A <u>nucleus</u> is a particle with a negative electric charge.

3. The <u>electron</u> is where most of an atom's mass is located.

Understanding Key Ideas

4. Which of the following scientists discovered that atoms contain electrons?
   a. Dalton
   b. Thomson
   c. Rutherford
   d. Bohr

5. What did Dalton do in developing his theory that Democritus did not do?

6. What discovery demonstrated that atoms are mostly empty space?

7. What refinements did Bohr make to Rutherford's proposed atomic theory?

Critical Thinking

8. **Making Comparisons** Compare the location of electrons in Bohr's theory with the location of electrons in the current atomic theory.

9. **Analyzing Methods** How does the design of Rutherford's experiment show what he was trying to find out?

Interpreting Graphics

10. What about the atomic model shown below was shown to be incorrect?

SciLINKS.

NSTA
Developed and maintained by the
National Science Teachers Association

For a variety of links related to this chapter, go to www.scilinks.org
Topic: Development of the Atomic Theory;
Current Atomic Theory
SciLinks code: HSM0399; HSM0371

The Atom

SECTION

2

Atoms are very small, and atoms are made up of even smaller things. But you can still learn a lot about the parts that make up an atom and what holds an atom together.

In this section, you'll learn about how atoms are alike and how they are different. But first you'll find out just how small an atom really is.

How Small Is an Atom?

Think about a penny. A penny contains about 2×10^{22} atoms (which can be written as 20,000,000,000,000,000,000,000 atoms) of copper and zinc. That's 20 thousand billion billion atoms—over 3,000,000,000,000 times more atoms than there are people on Earth! If there are that many atoms in a penny, each atom must be very small.

Scientists know that aluminum is made of average-sized atoms. An aluminum atom has a diameter of about 0.00000003 cm. That's three one-hundred-millionths of a centimeter. Take a look at **Figure 1.** Even things that are very thin, such as aluminum foil, are made up of very large numbers of atoms.

Figure 1 *This aluminum foil might seem thin to you. But it is about 50,000 atoms thick!*

Figure 2 Parts of an Atom

Electrons are negatively charged particles found in electron clouds outside the nucleus. The size of the electron clouds determines the size of the atom.

Protons are positively charged particles in the nucleus of an atom.

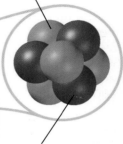

The **nucleus** is the small, dense, positively charged center of the atom. It contains most of the atom's mass.

Neutrons are particles in the nucleus of an atom that have no charge.

The diameter of the nucleus is 1/100,000 the diameter of the atom.

What Is an Atom Made Of?

As tiny as an atom is, it is made up of even smaller particles. These particles are protons, neutrons, and electrons, shown in the model in **Figure 2.** (The particles in the pictures are not shown in their correct proportions. If they were, the electrons would be too small to see.)

The Nucleus

Protons are positively charged particles in the nucleus. The mass of a proton is about 1.7×10^{-24} g. This number can also be written as 0.0000000000000000000000017 g. Because the masses of particles in atoms are so small, scientists made a new unit for them. The SI unit used to express the masses of particles in atoms is the **atomic mass unit** (amu). Each proton has a mass of about 1 amu.

Neutrons are the particles of the nucleus that have no electrical charge. Neutrons are a little more massive than protons are. But the difference in mass is so small that the mass of a neutron can be thought of as 1 amu.

Protons and neutrons are the most massive particles in an atom. But the volume of the nucleus is very small. So, the nucleus is very dense. If it were possible to have a nucleus the volume of a grape, that nucleus would have a mass greater than 9 million metric tons!

✓ Reading Check Name the two kinds of particles that can be found in the nucleus. (*See the Appendix for answers to Reading Checks.*)

proton a subatomic particle that has a positive charge and that is found in the nucleus of an atom

atomic mass unit a unit of mass that describes the mass of an atom or molecule

neutron a subatomic particle that has no charge and that is found in the nucleus of an atom

Outside the Nucleus

Electrons are the negatively charged particles in atoms. Electrons are found around the nucleus within electron clouds. Compared with protons and neutrons, electrons are very small in mass. It takes more than 1,800 electrons to equal the mass of 1 proton. The mass of an electron is so small that it is usually thought of as almost zero.

The charges of protons and electrons are opposite but equal, so their charges cancel out. Because an atom has no overall charge, it is neutral. What happens if the numbers of electrons and protons are not equal? The atom becomes a charged particle called an *ion* (IE ahn). An atom that loses one or more electrons becomes a positively-charged ion. An atom that gains one or more electrons becomes a negatively-charged ion.

Reading Check **How does an atom become a positively-charged ion?**

CONNECTION TO Astronomy

Hydrogen Hydrogen is the most abundant element in the universe. It is the fuel for the sun and other stars. It is currently believed that there are roughly 2,000 times more hydrogen atoms than oxygen atoms and 10,000 times more hydrogen atoms than carbon atoms.

Make a model of a hydrogen atom using materials of your choice to represent a hydrogen atom's proton and electron. Present the model to the class, and explain in what ways your model resembles a hydrogen atom.

ACTIVITY

How Do Atoms of Different Elements Differ?

There are more than 110 different elements. The atoms of each of these elements are different from the atoms of all other elements. What makes atoms different from each other? To find out, imagine that you could build an atom by putting together protons, neutrons, and electrons.

Starting Simply

It's easiest to start with the simplest atom. Protons and electrons are found in all atoms. The simplest atom is made of just one of each. It's so simple it doesn't even have a neutron. To "build" this atom, put just one proton in the center of the atom for the nucleus. Then, put one electron in the electron cloud. Congratulations! You have just made a hydrogen atom.

Now for Some Neutrons

Now, build an atom that has two protons. Both of the protons are positively charged, so they repel one another. You cannot form a nucleus with them unless you add some neutrons. For this atom, two neutrons will do. To have a neutral charge, your new atom will also need two electrons outside the nucleus. What you have is an atom of the element helium. A model of this atom is shown in **Figure 3.**

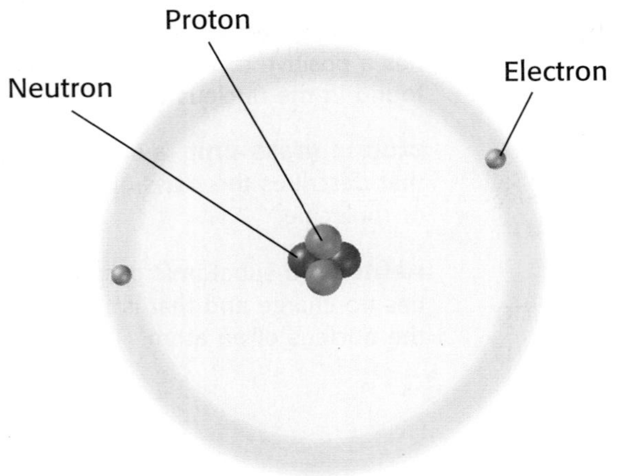

Figure 3 *A helium nucleus must have neutrons in it to keep the protons from moving apart.*

Building Bigger Atoms

You could build a carbon atom using 6 protons, 6 neutrons, and 6 electrons. You could build an oxygen atom using 8 protons, 9 neutrons, and 8 electrons. You could even build a gold atom with 79 protons, 118 neutrons, and 79 electrons! As you can see, an atom does not have to have equal numbers of protons and neutrons.

Protons and Atomic Number

How can you tell which elements these atoms represent? The key is the number of protons. The number of protons in the nucleus of an atom is the **atomic number** of that atom. All atoms of an element have the same atomic number. Every hydrogen atom has only one proton in its nucleus, so hydrogen has an atomic number of 1. Every carbon atom has six protons in its nucleus. So, carbon has an atomic number of 6.

Isotopes

An atom that has one proton, one electron, and one neutron is shown in **Figure 4.** The atomic number of this new atom is 1, so the atom is hydrogen. However, this hydrogen atom's nucleus has two particles. Therefore, this atom has a greater mass than the hydrogen atom you made.

The new atom is another isotope (IE suh TOHP) of hydrogen. **Isotopes** are atoms that have the same number of protons but have different numbers of neutrons. Atoms that are isotopes of each other are always the same element, because isotopes always have the same number of protons. They have different numbers of neutrons, however, which gives them different masses.

INTERNET ACTIVITY

For another activity related to this chapter, go to **go.hrw.com** and type in the keyword **HP5ATSW.**

atomic number the number of protons in the nucleus of an atom; the atomic number is the same for all atoms of an element

isotope an atom that has the same number of protons (or the same atomic number) as other atoms of the same element do but that has a different number of neutrons (and thus a different atomic mass)

Figure 4   Isotopes of Hydrogen

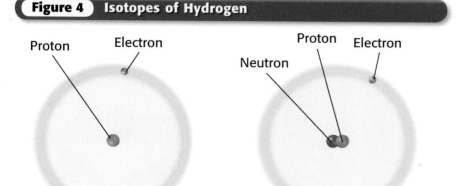

Proton   Electron   Proton   Electron

Neutron

This isotope is a hydrogen atom that has one proton in its nucleus.

This isotope is a hydrogen atom that has one proton and one neutron in its nucleus.

mass number the sum of the numbers of protons and neutrons in the nucleus of an atom

Properties of Isotopes

Each element has a limited number of isotopes that are found in nature. Some isotopes of an element have special properties because they are unstable. An unstable atom is an atom with a nucleus that will change over time. This type of isotope is *radioactive*. Radioactive atoms spontaneously fall apart after a certain amount of time. As they do, they give off smaller particles, as well as energy.

However, isotopes of an element share most of the same chemical and physical properties. For example, the most common oxygen isotope has 8 neutrons in the nucleus. Other isotopes of oxygen have 9 or 10 neutrons. All three isotopes are colorless, odorless gases at room temperature. Each isotope has the chemical property of combining with a substance as it burns. Different isotopes of an element even behave the same in chemical changes in your body.

✓ **Reading Check** In what cases are differences between isotopes important?

Telling Isotopes Apart

You can identify each isotope of an element by its mass number. The **mass number** is the sum of the protons and neutrons in an atom. Electrons are not included in an atom's mass number because their mass is so small that they have very little effect on the atom's total mass. Look at the boron isotope models shown in **Figure 5** to see how to calculate an atom's mass number.

Figure 5 | **Isotopes of Boron**

Each of these boron isotopes has five protons. But because each has a different number of neutrons, each has a different mass number.

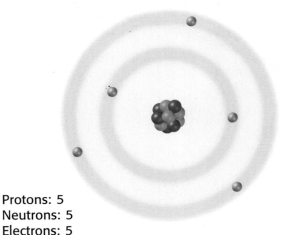

Protons: 5
Neutrons: 5
Electrons: 5
Mass number = protons + neutrons = 10

Protons: 5
Neutrons: 6
Electrons: 5
Mass number = protons + neutrons = 11

Naming Isotopes

To identify a specific isotope of an element, write the name of the element followed by a hyphen and the mass number of the isotope. A hydrogen atom with one proton and no neutrons has a mass number of 1. Its name is hydrogen-1. Hydrogen-2 has one proton and one neutron. The carbon isotope with a mass number of 12 is called carbon-12. If you know that the atomic number for carbon is 6, you can calculate the number of neutrons in carbon-12 by subtracting the atomic number from the mass number. For carbon-12, the number of neutrons is 12 − 6, or 6.

$$\begin{array}{rl} 12 & \text{Mass number} \\ -\ 6 & \text{Number of protons (atomic number)} \\ \hline 6 & \text{Number of neutrons} \end{array}$$

Calculating the Mass of an Element

Most elements contain a mixture of two or more isotopes. For example, all copper is composed of copper-63 atoms and copper-65 atoms. The **atomic mass** of an element is the weighted average of the masses of all the naturally occurring isotopes of that element. A weighted average accounts for the percentages of each isotope that are present. Copper, including the copper in the Statue of Liberty, shown in **Figure 6,** is 69% copper-63 and 31% copper-65. The atomic mass of copper is 63.6 amu.

Figure 6 *The copper used to make the Statue of Liberty includes both copper-63 and copper-65. Copper's atomic mass is 63.6 amu.*

atomic mass the mass of an atom expressed in atomic mass units

MATH FOCUS

Atomic Mass Chlorine-35 makes up 76% of all the chlorine in nature, and chlorine-37 makes up the other 24%. What is the atomic mass of chlorine?

Step 1: Multiply the mass number of each isotope by its percentage abundance in decimal form.

$$(35 \times 0.76) = 26.60$$
$$(37 \times 0.24) = 8.88$$

Step 2: Add these amounts together to find the atomic mass.

$$\begin{array}{rl} (35 \times 0.76) = & 26.60 \\ (37 \times 0.24) = & +\ 8.88 \\ \hline & 35.48 \text{ amu} \end{array}$$

Now It's Your Turn

1. Calculate the atomic mass of boron, which occurs naturally as 20% boron-10 and 80% boron-11.
2. Calculate the atomic mass of rubidium, which occurs naturally as 72% rubidium-85 and 28% rubidium-87.
3. Calculate the atomic mass of gallium, which occurs naturally as 60% gallium-69 and 40% gallium-71.
4. Calculate the atomic mass of silver, which occurs naturally as 52% silver-107 and 48% silver-109.
5. Calculate the atomic mass of silicon, which occurs naturally as 92% silicon-28, 5% silicon-29, and 3% silicon-30.

Forces in Atoms

You have seen that atoms are made of smaller particles. But what are the *forces* (the pushes or pulls between objects) acting between these particles? Four basic forces are at work everywhere, even within the atom. These forces are gravitational force, electromagnetic force, strong force, and weak force. These forces work together to give an atom its structure and properties. Look at **Figure 7** to learn about each one.

✓ **Reading Check** What are the four basic forces at work everywhere in nature?

Figure 7 | **Forces in the Atom**

Gravitational Force Probably the most familiar of the four forces is *gravitational force*. Gravitational force acts between all objects all the time. The amount of gravitational force between objects depends on their masses and the distance between them. Gravitational force pulls objects, such as the sun, Earth, cars, and books, toward one another. However, because the masses of particles in atoms are so small, the gravitational force within atoms is very small.

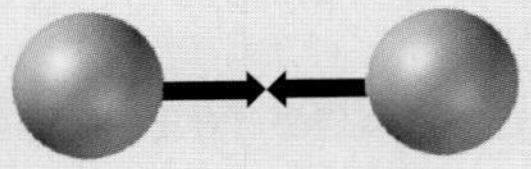

Electromagnetic Force As mentioned earlier, objects that have the same charge repel each other, while objects with opposite charge attract each other. This is due to the *electromagnetic force*. Protons and electrons are attracted to each other because they have opposite charges. The electromagnetic force holds the electrons around the nucleus.

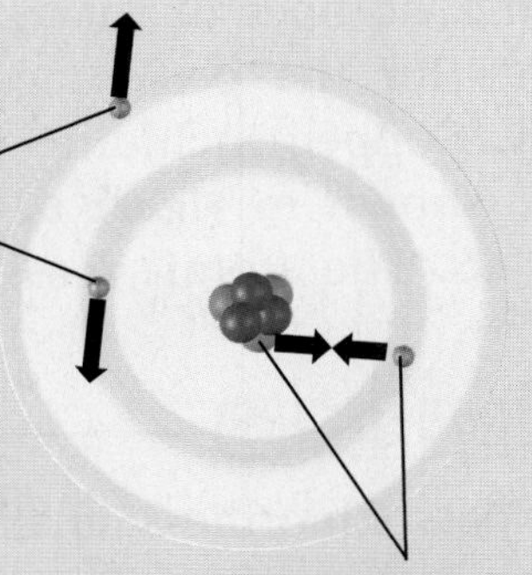

Particles with the same charges repel each other.

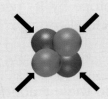

Particles with opposite charges attract each other.

Strong Force Protons push away from one another because of the electromagnetic force. A nucleus containing two or more protons would fly apart if it were not for the *strong force*. At the close distances between protons and neutrons in the nucleus, the strong force is greater than the electromagnetic force, so the nucleus stays together.

Weak Force The *weak force* is an important force in radioactive atoms. In certain unstable atoms, a neutron can change into a proton and an electron. The weak force plays a key role in this change.

SECTION Review

Summary

- Atoms are extremely small. Ordinary-sized objects are made up of very large numbers of atoms.

- Atoms consist of a nucleus, which has protons and usually neutrons, and electrons, located in electron clouds around the nucleus.

- The number of protons in the nucleus of an atom is that atom's atomic number. All atoms of an element have the same atomic number.

- Different isotopes of an element have different numbers of neutrons in their nuclei. Isotopes of an element share most chemical and physical properties.

- The mass number of an atom is the sum of the atom's neutrons and protons.

- Atomic mass is a weighted average of the masses of natural isotopes of an element.

- The forces at work in an atom are gravitational force, electromagnetic force, strong force, and weak force.

Using Key Terms

1. Use the following terms in the same sentence: *proton, neutron,* and *isotope.*

Complete each of the following sentences by choosing the correct term from the word bank.

| atomic mass unit | atomic number |
| mass number | atomic mass |

2. An atom's ___ is equal to the number of protons in its nucleus.

3. An atom's ___ is equal to the weighted average of the masses of all the naturally occurring isotopes of that element.

Understanding Key Ideas

4. Which of the following particles has no electric charge?
   - **a.** proton
   - **b.** neutron
   - **c.** electron
   - **d.** ion

5. Name and describe the four forces that are at work within the nucleus of an atom.

Math Skills

6. The metal thallium occurs naturally as 30% thallium-203 and 70% thallium-205. Calculate the atomic mass of thallium.

Critical Thinking

7. **Analyzing Ideas** Why is gravitational force in the nucleus so small?

8. **Predicting Consequences** Could a nucleus of more than one proton but no neutrons exist? Explain.

Interpreting Graphics

9. Look at the two atomic models below. Do the two atoms represent different elements or different isotopes? Explain.

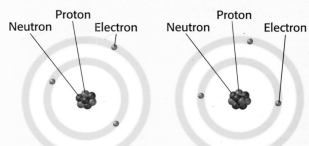

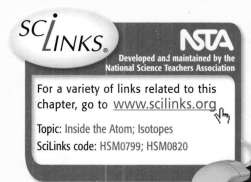

For a variety of links related to this chapter, go to www.scilinks.org

Topic: Inside the Atom; Isotopes
SciLinks code: HSM0799; HSM0820

Model-Making Lab

Made to Order

Imagine that you are an employee at the Elements-4-U Company, which custom builds elements. Your job is to construct the atomic nucleus for each element ordered by your clients. You were hired for the position because of your knowledge about what a nucleus is made of and your understanding of how isotopes of an element differ from each other. Now, it's time to put that knowledge to work!

Procedure

1 Copy the table below onto another sheet of paper. Be sure to leave room to expand the table to include more elements.

2 Your first assignment is the nucleus of hydrogen-1. Pick up one proton (a white plastic-foam ball). Congratulations! You have built a hydrogen-1 nucleus, the simplest nucleus possible.

3 Count the number of protons and neutrons in the nucleus, and fill in rows 1 and 2 for this element in the table.

4 Use the information in rows 1 and 2 to determine the atomic number and mass number of the element. Record this information in the table.

Data Collection Table						
	Hydrogen-1	**Hydrogen-2**	**Helium-3**	**Helium-4**	**Beryllium-9**	**Beryllium-10**
Number of protons						
Number of neutrons						
Atomic number						
Mass number						

DO NOT WRITE IN BOOK

⑤ Draw a picture of your model.

⑥ Hydrogen-2 is an isotope of hydrogen that has one proton and one neutron. Using a strong-force connector, add a neutron to your hydrogen-1 nucleus. (Remember that in a nucleus, the protons and neutrons are held together by the strong force, which is represented in this activity by the toothpicks.) Repeat steps 3–5.

⑦ Helium-3 is an isotope of helium that has two protons and one neutron. Add one proton to your hydrogen-2 nucleus to create a helium-3 nucleus. Each particle should be connected to the other two particles so that they make a triangle, not a line. Protons and neutrons always form the smallest arrangement possible because the strong force pulls them together. Then, repeat steps 3–5.

⑧ For the next part of the lab, you will need to use information from the periodic table of the elements. Look at the illustration below. It shows the periodic table entry for carbon. You can find the atomic number of any element at the top of its entry on the periodic table. For example, the atomic number of carbon is 6.

Atomic number —— 6
C
Carbon

⑨ Use the information in the periodic table to build models of the following isotopes of elements: helium-4, lithium-7, beryllium-9, and beryllium-10. Remember to put the protons and neutrons as close together as possible—each particle should attach to at least two others. Repeat steps 3–5 for each isotope.

Analyze the Results

❶ **Examining Data** What is the relationship between the number of protons and the atomic number?

❷ **Analyzing Data** If you know the atomic number and the mass number of an isotope, how could you figure out the number of neutrons in its nucleus?

Draw Conclusions

❸ **Applying Conclusions** Look up uranium on the periodic table. What is the atomic number of uranium? How many neutrons does the isotope uranium-235 have?

❹ **Evaluating Models** Compare your model with the models of your classmates. How are the models similar? How are they different?

Applying Your Data

Combine your model with one that another student has made to create a single nucleus. Identify the element (and isotope) you have created.

Chapter Review

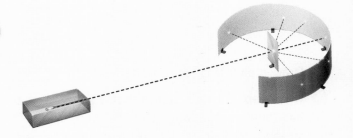

USING KEY TERMS

The statements below are false. For each statement, replace the underlined term to make a true statement.

1 <u>Electrons</u> have a positive charge.

2 All atoms of the same element contain the same number of <u>neutrons</u>.

3 <u>Protons</u> have no electrical charge.

4 The <u>atomic number</u> of an element is the number of protons and neutrons in the nucleus.

5 The <u>mass number</u> is an average of the masses of all naturally occurring isotopes of an element.

UNDERSTANDING KEY IDEAS

Multiple Choice

6 The discovery of which particle proved that the atom is not indivisible?

a. proton

b. neutron

c. electron

d. nucleus

7 How many protons does an atom with an atomic number of 23 and a mass number of 51 have?

a. 23

b. 28

c. 51

d. 74

8 In Rutherford's gold-foil experiment, Rutherford concluded that the atom is mostly empty space with a small, massive, positively charged center because

a. most of the particles passed straight through the foil.

b. some particles were slightly deflected.

c. a few particles bounced straight back.

d. All of the above

9 Which of the following determines the identity of an element?

a. atomic number

b. mass number

c. atomic mass

d. overall charge

10 Isotopes exist because atoms of the same element can have different numbers of

a. protons.

b. neutrons.

c. electrons.

d. None of the above

Short Answer

11 What force holds electrons in atoms?

12 In two or three sentences, describe Thomson's plum-pudding model of the atom.

Math Skills

13 Calculate the atomic mass of gallium, which consists of 60% gallium-69 and 40% gallium-71.

14 Calculate the number of protons, neutrons, and electrons in an atom of zirconium-90 that has no overall charge and an atomic number of 40.

CRITICAL THINKING

15 Concept Mapping Use the following terms to create a concept map: *atom, nucleus, protons, neutrons, electrons, isotopes, atomic number,* and *mass number.*

16 Analyzing Processes Particle accelerators, such as the one below, are devices that speed up charged particles in order to smash them together. Scientists use these devices to make atoms. How can scientists determine whether the atoms formed are a new element or a new isotope of a known element?

17 Analyzing Ideas John Dalton made a number of statements about atoms that are now known to be incorrect. Why do you think his atomic theory is still found in science textbooks?

18 Analyzing Methods If scientists had tried to repeat Thomson's experiment and found that they could not, would Thomson's conclusion still have been valid? Explain your answer.

INTERPRETING GRAPHICS

Use the diagrams below to answer the questions that follow.

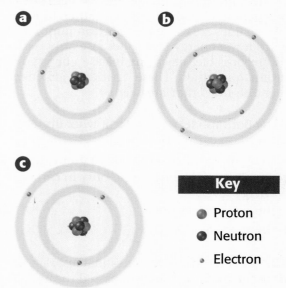

19 Which diagrams represent isotopes of the same element?

20 What is the atomic number for A?

21 What is the mass number for B?

Standardized Test Preparation

Read each of the passages below. Then, answer the questions that follow each passage.

Passage 1 In the Bohr model of the atom, electrons can be found only in certain energy levels. Electrons "jump" from one level to the next level without passing through any of the regions in between. When an electron moves from one level to another, it gains or loses energy, depending on the direction of its jump. Bohr's model explained an unusual event. When electric charges pass through atoms of a gaseous element, the gas produces a glowing light, like in a neon sign. If this light is passed through a prism, a pattern of lines appears, each line having a different color. The pattern depends on the element—neon has one pattern, and helium has another. In Bohr's model, the lines are caused by electron jumps from higher to lower energy levels. Because only certain jumps are possible, electrons release energy only in certain quantities. These "packets" of energy produce the lines that are seen.

1. In the Bohr model of the atom, what limitation is placed on electrons?

  A the number of electrons in an atom

  B the electrons' being found only in certain energy levels

  C the size of electrons

  D the speed of electrons

2. What causes the colored lines that appear when the light from a gas is passed through a prism?

  F packets of energy released by electron jumps

  G electrons changing color

  H atoms of the gas exchanging electrons

  I There is not enough information to determine the answer.

Passage 2 No one has ever seen a living dinosaur, but scientists have determined the appearance of *Tyrannosaurus rex* by studying fossilized skeletons. Scientists theorize that these extinct creatures had big hind legs, small front legs, a long, whip-like tail, and a mouth full of dagger-shaped teeth. However, theories of how *T. rex* walked have been harder to develop. For many years, most scientists thought that *T. rex* plodded slowly like a big, lazy lizard. However, after studying well-preserved dinosaur tracks and noticing skeletal similarities between certain dinosaur fossils and living creatures like the ostrich, many scientists now theorize that *T. rex* could turn on the speed. Some scientists estimate that *T. rex* had bursts of speed of 32 km/h (20 mi/h)!

1. According to this passage, where does most of what we know about the appearance of *Tyrannosaurus rex* come from?

  A fossilized skeletons

  B dinosaur tracks

  C living organisms such as the ostrich

  D living specimens of *T. rex*

2. How did scientists conclude that *T. rex* could probably move very quickly?

  F They measured the speed at which it could run.

  G They compared fossilized *T. rex* tracks with *T. rex* skeletons.

  H They studied dinosaur tracks and noted similarities between ostrich skeletons and *T. rex* skeletons.

  I They measured the speed at which ostriches could run.

Use the diagram of an atom below to answer the questions that follow.

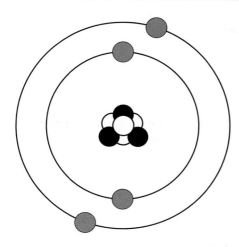

Read each question below, and choose the best answer.

1. The black circles in the center of the model represent neutrons. What do the white circles in the center represent?
   A electrons
   B protons
   C nuclei
   D atoms

2. What is the mass number of the atom shown in the model?
   F 3
   G 7
   H 9
   I 11

3. What is the overall charge of the atom shown in the model?
   A +2
   B +1
   C 0
   D −1

1. Aimee, Mari, and Brooke are 163 cm, 171 cm, and 175 cm tall. Which of the following measurements is a reasonable average height of these three friends?
   A 170 cm
   B 175 cm
   C 255 cm
   D 509 cm

2. A certain school has 40 classrooms. Most of the classrooms have 25 to 30 students. Which of the following is a reasonable estimate of the number of students that go to this school?
   F 40 students
   G 100 students
   H 1,100 students
   I 2,000 students

3. Jenna is setting up a fish tank in her room. The tank is the shape of a rectangular prism. The height of the tank is 38 cm, the width is 23 cm, and the length is 62 cm. The tank is filled with water to a point that is 7 cm from the top. How much water is in the tank?
   A 44,206 cm^3
   B 48,070 cm^3
   C 54,188 cm^3
   D 64,170 cm^3

4. Which of the following is equal to 8^5?
   F $8 + 8 + 8 + 8 + 8$
   G $5 \times 5 \times 5 \times 5 \times 5 \times 5 \times 5 \times 5$
   H 5×8
   I $8 \times 8 \times 8 \times 8 \times 8$

Standardized Test Preparation

Science in Action

Scientific Discoveries

Modern Alchemy

Hundreds of years ago, many people thought that if you treated lead with certain chemicals, it would turn into gold. People called *alchemists* often spent their whole lives trying to find a way to make gold from other metals, such as lead. We now know that the methods alchemists tried to change one element to another did not work. But in the 20th century, scientists learned that you really could change one element to another! In a nuclear reaction, small particles can be collided with atomic nuclei. This process makes the nuclei split apart to form two nuclei of different elements.

Math ACTIVITY

If you split apart an atom of lead (atomic number = 82) and one of the atoms left was gold (atomic number = 79), what would be the atomic number of the other atom that resulted from this change?

Weird Science

Mining on the Moon?

Since the end of the Apollo moon missions in 1972, no one has set foot on the surface of the moon. But today, an isotope of helium known as *helium-3* is fueling new interest in returning to the moon. Some scientists speculate that helium-3 can be used as a safe and nonpolluting fuel for a new kind of power plant. Helium-3 is very rare on Earth, but a huge amount of the isotope exists on the surface of the moon. But how can helium-3 be brought to Earth? Some researchers imagine a robotic lunar mining operation that will harvest the helium-3 and transport it to Earth.

Language Arts ACTIVITY

WRITING SKILL Write a paragraph in which you rephrase the information above in your own words. Be sure to include what helium-3 is, where it can be found, and how it could be used.

Melissa Franklin

Experimental Physicist In the course of a single day, you could find experimental physicist Melissa Franklin running a huge drill or showing her lab to a 10-year-old child. You could see her putting together a huge piece of electronic equipment or even telling a joke. Then you'd see her really get down to business—studying the smallest particles of matter in the universe.

"I am trying to understand the forces that describe how everything in the world moves—especially the smallest things," Franklin explains. Franklin and her team helped discover a particle called the top quark. (Quarks are the tiny particles that make up protons and neutrons.) "You can understand the ideas without having to be a math genius," Franklin says. "Anyone can have ideas," she says, "absolutely anyone." Franklin also has some advice for young people interested in physics. "Go and bug people at the local university. Just call up a physics person and say, 'Can I come visit you for a couple of hours?' Kids do that with me, and it's really fun."

Social Studies ACTiViTY

WRITING SKILL Find out about an experimental physicist who made an important discovery. Write a one-page report about how that discovery affected the ideas of other scientists.

To learn more about these Science in Action topics, visit **go.hrw.com** and type in the keyword **HP5ATSF.**

Current Science

Check out Current Science® articles related to this chapter by visiting go.hrw.com. Just type in the keyword **HP5CS11.**

12

The Periodic Table

SECTION ① Arranging the Elements 336

SECTION ② Grouping the Elements 344

Chapter Lab 352
Chapter Review 354
Standardized Test Preparation 356
Science in Action. 358

About the PHOTO

You already know or have heard about elements on the periodic table, such as oxygen, carbon, and neon. Neon gas was discovered in 1898. In 1902, a French engineer, chemist, and inventor named Georges Claude made the first neon lamp. In 1910, Claude made the first neon sign, and in 1923, he introduced neon signs to the United States. Now, artists such as Eric Ehlenberger use glass and neon to create interesting works of art, such as these neon jellyfish.

PRE-READING ACTIVITY

FOLDNOTES **Three-Panel Flip Chart**
Before you read the chapter, create the FoldNote entitled "Three-Panel Flip Chart" described in the **Study Skills** section of the Appendix. Label the flaps of the three-panel flip chart with "Metal," "Nonmetal," and "Metalloid." As you read the chapter, write information you learn about each category under the appropriate flap.

START-UP ACTIVITY

Placement Pattern

In this activity, you will identify the pattern your teacher used to create a new classroom seating arrangement.

Procedure

1. Draw a seating chart for the new classroom arrangement that your teacher gave to you. Write the name of each of your classmates in the place on the chart that corresponds to his or her seat.

2. Write information about yourself, such as your name, date of birth, hair color, and height, in the space that represents you on the chart.

3. Gather the same information about the people near you, and write it in the spaces on the chart.

Analysis

1. From the information you gathered, identify a pattern that might explain the order of people in the chart. Collect more information if needed.

2. Test your pattern by gathering information from a person you did not talk to before.

3. If the new information does not support your pattern, reanalyze your data and collect more information to determine another pattern.

Arranging the Elements

Suppose you went to the video store and all the videos were mixed together. How could you tell the comedies from the action movies? If the videos were not arranged in a pattern, you wouldn't know what kind of movie you had chosen!

Scientists in the early 1860s had a similar problem. At that time, scientists knew some of the properties of more than 60 elements. However, no one had organized the elements according to these properties. Organizing the elements according to their properties would help scientists understand how elements interact with each other.

Discovering a Pattern

Dmitri Mendeleev (duh MEE tree MEN duh LAY uhf), a Russian chemist, discovered a pattern to the elements in 1869. First, he wrote the names and properties of the elements on cards. Then, he arranged his cards, as shown in **Figure 1,** by different properties, such as density, appearance, and melting point. After much thought, he arranged the elements in order of increasing atomic mass. When he did so, a pattern appeared.

✓ **Reading Check** How had Mendeleev arranged elements when he noticed a pattern? (*See the Appendix for answers to Reading Checks.*)

Figure 1 *By playing "chemical solitaire" on long train rides, Mendeleev organized the elements according to their properties.*

Table 1 Properties of Germanium

	Mendeleev's predictions (1869)	Actual properties
Atomic mass	70	72.6
Density*	5.5 g/cm³	5.3 g/cm³
Appearance	dark gray metal	gray metal
Melting point*	high melting point	937°C

* at room temperature and pressure

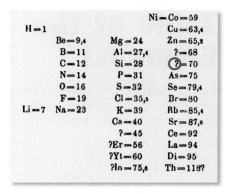

Figure 2 *Mendeleev used question marks to mark some elements that he thought would be found later.*

Periodic Properties of the Elements

Mendeleev saw that when the elements were arranged in order of increasing atomic mass, those that had similar properties occurred in a repeating pattern. That is, the pattern was periodic. **Periodic** means "happening at regular intervals." The days of the week are periodic. They repeat in the same order every 7 days. Similarly, Mendeleev found that the elements' properties followed a pattern that repeated every seven elements. His table became known as the *periodic table of the elements*.

Predicting Properties of Missing Elements

Figure 2 shows part of Mendeleev's first try at arranging the elements. The question marks show gaps in the pattern. Mendeleev predicted that elements yet to be found would fill these gaps. He used the pattern he found to predict their properties. **Table 1** compares his predictions for one missing element—germanium—with its actual properties. By 1886, all of the gaps had been filled. His predictions were right.

periodic describes something that occurs or repeats at regular intervals

periodic law the law that states that the repeating chemical and physical properties of elements change periodically with the atomic numbers of the elements

Changing the Arrangement

A few elements' properties did not fit the pattern in Mendeleev's table. Mendeleev thought that more-accurate atomic masses would fix these flaws in his table. But new atomic mass measurements showed that the masses he had used were correct. In 1914, Henry Moseley (MOHZ lee), a British scientist, determined the number of protons—the atomic number—in an atom. All elements fit the pattern in Mendeleev's periodic table when they were arranged by atomic number.

Look at the periodic table on the next two pages. All of the more than 30 elements discovered since 1914 follow the periodic law. The **periodic law** states that the repeating chemical and physical properties of elements change periodically with the elements' atomic numbers.

CONNECTION TO Language Arts

WRITING SKILL **Hidden Help** You may be asked to memorize some of the chemical symbols. A story or poem that uses the symbols might be helpful. In your **science journal,** write a short story, poem, or just a few sentences in which the words correspond to and bring to mind the chemical symbols of the first 20 elements.

✓ **Reading Check** What property is used to arrange elements in the periodic table?

Periodic Table of the Elements

Each square on the table includes an element's name, chemical symbol, atomic number, and atomic mass.

The color of the chemical symbol indicates the physical state at room temperature. Carbon is a solid.

6	Atomic number
C	Chemical symbol
Carbon	Element name
12.0	Atomic mass

The background color indicates the type of element. Carbon is a nonmetal.

Background

Metals	
Metalloids	
Nonmetals	

Chemical symbol

Solid	
Liquid	
Gas	

Period 1

1
H
Hydrogen
1.0

Group 1	Group 2										

Period 2

3	4
Li	**Be**
Lithium	Beryllium
6.9	9.0

Period 3

11	12
Na	**Mg**
Sodium	Magnesium
23.0	24.3

		Group 3	Group 4	Group 5	Group 6	Group 7	Group 8	Group 9

Period 4

19	20	21	22	23	24	25	26	27
K	**Ca**	**Sc**	**Ti**	**V**	**Cr**	**Mn**	**Fe**	**Co**
Potassium	Calcium	Scandium	Titanium	Vanadium	Chromium	Manganese	Iron	Cobalt
39.1	40.1	45.0	47.9	50.9	52.0	54.9	55.8	58.9

Period 5

37	38	39	40	41	42	43	44	45
Rb	**Sr**	**Y**	**Zr**	**Nb**	**Mo**	**Tc**	**Ru**	**Rh**
Rubidium	Strontium	Yttrium	Zirconium	Niobium	Molybdenum	Technetium	Ruthenium	Rhodium
85.5	87.6	88.9	91.2	92.9	95.9	(98)	101.1	102.9

Period 6

55	56	57	72	73	74	75	76	77
Cs	**Ba**	**La**	**Hf**	**Ta**	**W**	**Re**	**Os**	**Ir**
Cesium	Barium	Lanthanum	Hafnium	Tantalum	Tungsten	Rhenium	Osmium	Iridium
132.9	137.3	138.9	178.5	180.9	183.8	186.2	190.2	192.2

Period 7

87	88	89	104	105	106	107	108	109
Fr	**Ra**	**Ac**	**Rf**	**Db**	**Sg**	**Bh**	**Hs**	**Mt**
Francium	Radium	Actinium	Rutherfordium	Dubnium	Seaborgium	Bohrium	Hassium	Meitnerium
(223)	(226)	(227)	(261)	(262)	(263)	(264)	(265)†	(268)†

† Estimated from currently available IUPAC data.

A row of elements is called a *period*.

A column of elements is called a *group* or *family*.

Values in parentheses are of the most stable isotope of the element.

These elements are placed below the table to allow the table to be narrower.

Lanthanides

58	59	60	61	62
Ce	**Pr**	**Nd**	**Pm**	**Sm**
Cerium	Praseodymium	Neodymium	Promethium	Samarium
140.1	140.9	144.2	(145)	150.4

Actinides

90	91	92	93	94
Th	**Pa**	**U**	**Np**	**Pu**
Thorium	Protactinium	Uranium	Neptunium	Plutonium
232.0	231.0	238.0	(237)	(244)

Topic: **Periodic Table**
Go To: **go.hrw.com**
Keyword: **HN0 PERIODIC**
Visit the HRW Web site for
updates on the periodic table.

This zigzag line reminds you where the metals, nonmetals, and metalloids are.

			Group 13	Group 14	Group 15	Group 16	Group 17	Group 18
								2 **He** Helium 4.0
			5 **B** Boron 10.8	6 **C** Carbon 12.0	7 **N** Nitrogen 14.0	8 **O** Oxygen 16.0	9 **F** Fluorine 19.0	10 **Ne** Neon 20.2
Group 10	Group 11	Group 12	13 **Al** Aluminum 27.0	14 **Si** Silicon 28.1	15 **P** Phosphorus 31.0	16 **S** Sulfur 32.1	17 **Cl** Chlorine 35.5	18 **Ar** Argon 39.9
28 **Ni** Nickel 58.7	29 **Cu** Copper 63.5	30 **Zn** Zinc 65.4	31 **Ga** Gallium 69.7	32 **Ge** Germanium 72.6	33 **As** Arsenic 74.9	34 **Se** Selenium 79.0	35 **Br** Bromine 79.9	36 **Kr** Krypton 83.8
46 **Pd** Palladium 106.4	47 **Ag** Silver 107.9	48 **Cd** Cadmium 112.4	49 **In** Indium 114.8	50 **Sn** Tin 118.7	51 **Sb** Antimony 121.8	52 **Te** Tellurium 127.6	53 **I** Iodine 126.9	54 **Xe** Xenon 131.3
78 **Pt** Platinum 195.1	79 **Au** Gold 197.0	80 **Hg** Mercury 200.6	81 **Tl** Thallium 204.4	82 **Pb** Lead 207.2	83 **Bi** Bismuth 209.0	84 **Po** Polonium (209)	85 **At** Astatine (210)	86 **Rn** Radon (222)
110 **Ds** Darmstadtium (269)†	111 **Uuu** Unununium (272)†	112 **Uub** Ununbium (277)†		114 **Uuq** Ununquadium (285)†				

The names and three-letter symbols of elements are temporary. They are based on the atomic numbers of the elements. Official names and symbols will be approved by an international committee of scientists.

63 **Eu** Europium 152.0	64 **Gd** Gadolinium 157.2	65 **Tb** Terbium 158.9	66 **Dy** Dysprosium 162.5	67 **Ho** Holmium 164.9	68 **Er** Erbium 167.3	69 **Tm** Thulium 168.9	70 **Yb** Ytterbium 173.0	71 **Lu** Lutetium 175.0
95 **Am** Americium (243)	96 **Cm** Curium (247)	97 **Bk** Berkelium (247)	98 **Cf** Californium (251)	99 **Es** Einsteinium (252)	100 **Fm** Fermium (257)	101 **Md** Mendelevium (258)	102 **No** Nobelium (259)	103 **Lr** Lawrencium (262)

The Periodic Table and Classes of Elements

At first glance, you might think studying the periodic table is like trying to explore a thick jungle without a guide—you can easily get lost! However, the table itself contains a lot of information that will help you along the way.

Elements are classified as metals, nonmetals, and metalloids, according to their properties. The number of electrons in the outer energy level of an atom is one characteristic that helps determine which category an element belongs in. The zigzag line on the periodic table can help you recognize which elements are metals, which are nonmetals, and which are metalloids.

Metals

Most elements are metals. Metals are found to the left of the zigzag line on the periodic table. Atoms of most metals have few electrons in their outer energy level. Most metals are solid at room temperature. Mercury, however, is a liquid at room temperature. Some additional information on properties shared by most metals is shown in **Figure 3.**

✓ **Reading Check** What are four properties shared by most metals?

Quick Lab

Conduction Connection

1. Fill a **plastic-foam cup** with **hot water.**

2. Stand a **piece of copper wire** and a **graphite lead** from a mechanical pencil in the water.

3. After 1 min, touch the top of each object. Record your observations.

4. Which material conducted thermal energy the best? Why?

Figure 3   Properties of Metals

Metals tend to be **shiny.** You can see a reflection in a mirror because light reflects off the shiny surface of a thin layer of silver behind the glass.

Most metals are **ductile,** which means that they can be drawn into thin wires. All metals are **good conductors of electric current.** The wires in the electrical devices in your home are made of copper.

Most metals are **malleable,** which means that they can be flattened with a hammer and will not shatter. Aluminum is flattened into sheets to make cans and foil.

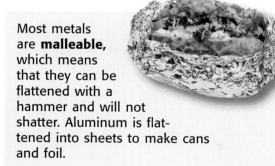

Most metals are **good conductors of thermal energy.** This iron griddle conducts thermal energy from a stove top to cook your favorite foods.

Figure 4 — Properties of Nonmetals

Nonmetals are **not malleable or ductile.** In fact, solid nonmetals, such as carbon in the graphite of the pencil lead, are brittle and will break or shatter when hit with a hammer.

Sulfur, like most nonmetals, is **not shiny.**

Nonmetals are **poor conductors of thermal energy and electric current.** If the gap in a spark plug is too wide, the nonmetals nitrogen and oxygen in the air will stop the spark and a car's engine will not run.

Nonmetals

Nonmetals are found to the right of the zigzag line on the periodic table. Atoms of most nonmetals have an almost complete set of electrons in their outer level. Atoms of the elements in Group 18, the noble gases, have a complete set of electrons. More than half of the nonmetals are gases at room temperature. Many properties of nonmetals are the opposite of the properties of metals, as shown in **Figure 4.**

Metalloids

Metalloids, also called *semiconductors,* are the elements that border the zigzag line on the periodic table. Atoms of metalloids have about half of a complete set of electrons in their outer energy level. Metalloids have some properties of metals and some properties of nonmetals, as shown in **Figure 5.**

Percentages

Elements are classified as metals, nonmetals, and metalloids. Use the periodic table to determine the percentage of elements in each of the three categories.

Figure 5 — Properties of Metalloids

Tellurium is **shiny,** but it is **brittle** and can easily be smashed into a powder.

Boron is almost as **hard** as diamond, but it is also **very brittle.** At high temperatures, it is a **good conductor of electric current.**

period in chemistry, a horizontal row of elements in the periodic table

group a vertical column of elements in the periodic table; elements in a group share chemical properties

Decoding the Periodic Table

The periodic table may seem to be in code. In a way, it is. But the colors and symbols will help you decode the table.

Each Element Is Identified by a Chemical Symbol

Each square on the periodic table includes an element's name, chemical symbol, atomic number, and atomic mass. The names of the elements come from many sources. Some elements, such as mendelevium, are named after scientists. Others, such as californium, are named after places. Some element names vary by country. But the chemical symbols are the same worldwide. For most elements, the chemical symbol has one or two letters. The first letter is always capitalized. Any other letter is always lowercase. The newest elements have temporary three-letter symbols.

Rows Are Called *Periods*

Each horizontal row of elements (from left to right) on the periodic table is called a **period.** Look at Period 4 in **Figure 6.** The physical and chemical properties of elements in a row follow a repeating, or periodic, pattern as you move across the period. Properties such as conductivity and reactivity change gradually from left to right in each period.

Columns Are Called *Groups*

Each vertical column of elements (from top to bottom) on the periodic table is called a **group.** Elements in the same group often have similar chemical and physical properties. For this reason, a group is also called a *family*.

Reading Check Why is a group sometimes called a family?

Figure 6 *As you move from left to right across a row, the elements become less metallic.*

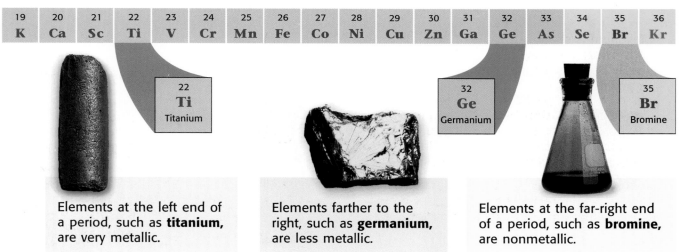

Elements at the left end of a period, such as **titanium,** are very metallic.

Elements farther to the right, such as **germanium,** are less metallic.

Elements at the far-right end of a period, such as **bromine,** are nonmetallic.

Summary

- Mendeleev developed the first periodic table by listing the elements in order of increasing atomic mass. He used his table to predict that elements with certain properties would be discovered later.

- Properties of elements repeat in a regular, or periodic, pattern.

- Moseley rearranged the elements in order of increasing atomic number.

- The periodic law states that the repeating chemical and physical properties of elements relate to and depend on elements' atomic numbers.

- Elements in the periodic table are classified as metals, nonmetals, and metalloids.

- Each element has a chemical symbol.

- A horizontal row of elements is called a *period*.

- Physical and chemical properties of elements change across each period.

- A vertical column of elements is called a *group* or *family*.

- Elements in a group usually have similar properties.

Using Key Terms

1. In your own words, write a definition for the term *periodic*.

Understanding Key Ideas

2. Which of the following elements should be the best conductor of electric current?
   a. germanium
   b. sulfur
   c. aluminum
   d. helium

3. Compare a period and a group on the periodic table.

4. What property did Mendeleev use to position the elements on the periodic table?

5. State the periodic law.

Critical Thinking

6. **Identifying Relationships** An atom that has 117 protons in its nucleus has not yet been made. Once this atom is made, to which group will element 117 belong? Explain your answer.

7. **Applying Concepts** Are the properties of sodium, Na, more like the properties of lithium, Li, or magnesium, Mg? Explain your answer.

Interpreting Graphics

8. The image below shows part of a periodic table. Compare the image below with the similar part of the periodic table in your book.

1	1 H 1.0079 水素			
2	3 Li 6.941 リチウム	4 Be 9.01218 ベリリウム		
3	11 Na 22.98977 ナトリウム	12 Mg 24.305 マグネシウム		
4	19 K	20 Ca	21 Sc	22 Ti

SCiLINKS®

NSTA
Developed and maintained by the
National Science Teachers Association

For a variety of links related to this chapter, go to www.scilinks.org

Topic: Periodic Table; Metals
SciLinks code: HSM1125; HSM0947

Grouping the Elements

You probably know a family with several members who look a lot alike. The elements in a family or group in the periodic table often—but not always—have similar properties.

The properties of the elements in a group are similar because the atoms of the elements have the same number of electrons in their outer energy level. Atoms will often take, give, or share electrons with other atoms in order to have a complete set of electrons in their outer energy level. Elements whose atoms undergo such processes are called *reactive* and can combine to form compounds.

Group 1: Alkali Metals

	Group contains: metals
3 **Li** Lithium	**Electrons in the outer level:** 1
11 **Na** Sodium	**Reactivity:** very reactive **Other shared properties:** softness; color of silver; shininess; low density

| **19** **K** Potassium |
| **37** **Rb** Rubidium |
| **55** **Cs** Cesium |
| **87** **Fr** Francium |

Alkali metals (AL kuh LIE MET uhlz) are elements in Group 1 of the periodic table. They share physical and chemical properties, as shown in **Figure 1.** Alkali metals are the most reactive metals because their atoms can easily give away the one outer-level electron. Pure alkali metals are often stored in oil. The oil keeps them from reacting with water and oxygen in the air. Alkali metals are so reactive that in nature they are found only combined with other elements. Compounds formed from alkali metals have many uses. For example, sodium chloride (table salt) is used to flavor your food. Potassium bromide is used in photography.

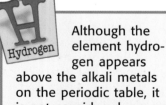

Although the element hydrogen appears above the alkali metals on the periodic table, it is not considered a member of Group 1. It will be described separately at the end of this section.

Figure 1 **Properties of Alkali Metals**

 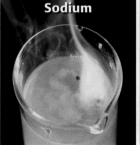 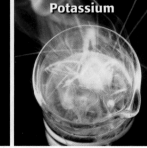

▲ Alkali metals are soft enough to be cut with a knife.

▲ Alkali metals react with water to form hydrogen gas.

Group 2: Alkaline-Earth Metals

4 **Be** Beryllium	**Group contains:** metals **Electrons in the outer level:** 2 **Reactivity:** very reactive but less reactive than alkali metals **Other shared properties:** color of silver; higher densities than alkali metals

4 **Be** Beryllium
12 **Mg** Magnesium
20 **Ca** Calcium
38 **Sr** Strontium
56 **Ba** Barium
88 **Ra** Radium

Alkaline-earth metals (AL kuh LIEN UHRTH MET uhlz) are less reactive than alkali metals are. Atoms of alkaline-earth metals have two outer-level electrons. It is more difficult for atoms to give two electrons than to give one when joining with other atoms. Group 2 elements and their compounds have many uses. For example, magnesium can be mixed with other metals to make low-density materials used in airplanes. And compounds of calcium are found in cement, chalk, and even you, as shown in **Figure 2.**

Figure 2 *Calcium, an alkaline-earth metal, is an important part of a compound that keeps your bones and teeth healthy.*

Groups 3–12: Transition Metals

21 **Sc**	22 **Ti**	23 **V**	24 **Cr**	25 **Mn**	26 **Fe**	27 **Co**	28 **Ni**	29 **Cu**	30 **Zn**
39 **Y**	40 **Zr**	41 **Nb**	42 **Mo**	43 **Tc**	44 **Ru**	45 **Rh**	46 **Pd**	47 **Ag**	48 **Cd**
57 **La**	72 **Hf**	73 **Ta**	74 **W**	75 **Re**	76 **Os**	77 **Ir**	78 **Pt**	79 **Au**	80 **Hg**
89 **Ac**	104 **Rf**	105 **Db**	106 **Sg**	107 **Bh**	108 **Hs**	109 **Mt**	110 **Ds**	111 **Uuu**	112 **Uub**

Group contains: metals
Electrons in the outer level: 1 or 2
Reactivity: less reactive than alkaline-earth metals
Other shared properties: shininess; good conductors of thermal energy and electric current; higher densities and melting points than elements in Groups 1 and 2 (except for mercury)

alkali metal one of the elements of Group 1 of the periodic table (lithium, sodium, potassium, rubidium, cesium, and francium)

alkaline-earth metal one of the elements of Group 2 of the periodic table (beryllium, magnesium, calcium, strontium, barium, and radium)

Groups 3–12 do not have individual names. Instead, all of these groups are called *transition metals*. The atoms of transition metals do not give away their electrons as easily as atoms of the Group 1 and Group 2 metals do. So, transition metals are less reactive than alkali metals and alkaline-earth metals are.

✓ Reading Check **Why are alkali metals more reactive than transition metals are?** (*See the Appendix for answers to Reading Checks.*)

Figure 3 Properties of Transition Metals

Mercury is used in thermometers. Unlike the other transition metals, mercury is liquid at room temperature.

Many transition metals—but not all—are silver colored! This **gold** ring proves it!

Some transition metals, such as **titanium** in the artificial hip at right, are not very reactive. But others, such as **iron**, are reactive. The iron in the steel trowel on the left has reacted to form rust.

Properties of Transition Metals

The properties of the transition metals vary widely, as shown in **Figure 3.** But, because these elements are metals, they share the properties of metals. Transition metals tend to be shiny and to conduct thermal energy and electric current well.

Lanthanides and Actinides

Some transition metals from Periods 6 and 7 appear in two rows at the bottom of the periodic table to keep the table from being too wide. The elements in each row tend to have similar properties. Elements in the first row follow lanthanum and are called *lanthanides*. The lanthanides are shiny, reactive metals. Some of these elements are used to make steel. An important use of a compound of one lanthanide element is shown in **Figure 4.**

Elements in the second row follow actinium and are called *actinides*. All atoms of actinides are radioactive, or unstable. The atoms of a radioactive element can change into atoms of another element. Elements listed after plutonium, element 94, do not occur in nature. They are made in laboratories. Very small amounts of americium (AM uhr ISH ee uhm), element 95, are used in some smoke detectors.

Reading Check Are lanthanides and actinides transition metals?

Figure 4 *Do you see red? The color red appears on a computer monitor because of a compound formed from europium that coats the back of the screen.*

57
La
Lanthanum

89
Ac
Actinium

	58	59	60	61	62	63	64	65	66	67	68	69	70	71
Lanthanides	**Ce**	**Pr**	**Nd**	**Pm**	**Sm**	**Eu**	**Gd**	**Tb**	**Dy**	**Ho**	**Er**	**Tm**	**Yb**	**Lu**
	90	91	92	93	94	95	96	97	98	99	100	101	102	103
Actinides	**Th**	**Pa**	**U**	**Np**	**Pu**	**Am**	**Cm**	**Bk**	**Cf**	**Es**	**Fm**	**Md**	**No**	**Lr**

Group 13: Boron Group

5 **B** Boron
13 **Al** Aluminum
31 **Ga** Gallium
49 **In** Indium
81 **Tl** Thallium

Group contains: one metalloid and four metals
Electrons in the outer level: 3
Reactivity: reactive
Other shared properties: solids at room temperature

The most common element from Group 13 is aluminum. In fact, aluminum is the most abundant metal in Earth's crust. Until the 1880s, however, aluminum was considered a precious metal because the process used to make pure aluminum was very expensive. During the 1850s and 1860s, Emperor Napoleon III of France used aluminum dinnerware because aluminum was more valuable than gold.

Today, the process of making pure aluminum is easier and less expensive than it was in the 1800s. Aluminum is now an important metal used in making aircraft parts. Aluminum is also used to make lightweight automobile parts, foil, cans, and siding.

Like the other elements in the boron group, aluminum is reactive. Why can it be used in so many things? A thin layer of aluminum oxide quickly forms on aluminum's surface when aluminum reacts with oxygen in the air. This layer prevents further reaction of the aluminum.

CONNECTION TO Environmental Science

WRITING SKILL **Recycling Aluminum**

Aluminum recycling is a very successful program. In your **science journal**, write a one-page report that describes how aluminum is processed from its ore. In your report, identify the ore and compare the energy needed to extract aluminum from the ore with the energy needed to process recycled aluminum.

Group 14: Carbon Group

6 **C** Carbon
14 **Si** Silicon
32 **Ge** Germanium
50 **Sn** Tin
82 **Pb** Lead
114 **Uuq** Ununquadium

Group contains: one nonmetal, two metalloids, and two metals
Electrons in the outer level: 4
Reactivity: varies among the elements
Other shared properties: solids at room temperature

The nonmetal carbon can be found uncombined in nature, as shown in **Figure 5.** Carbon also forms a wide variety of compounds. Some of these compounds, such as proteins, fats, and carbohydrates, are necessary for living things on Earth.

The metalloids silicon and germanium, also in Group 14, are used to make computer chips. The metal tin is useful because it is not very reactive. For example, a tin can is really made of steel coated with tin. Because the tin is less reactive than the steel is, the tin keeps the iron in the steel from rusting.

✔ **Reading Check** What metalloids from Group 14 are used to make computer chips?

Figure 5 *Diamond and soot have very different properties, yet both are natural forms of carbon.*

Diamond is the hardest material known. It is used as a jewel and on cutting tools, such as saws, drills, and files.

Soot is formed from burning oil, coal, and wood and is used as a pigment in paints and crayons.

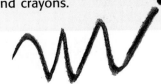

Group 15: Nitrogen Group

Figure 6 *Simply striking a match on the side of this box causes chemicals on the match to react with phosphorus on the box and begin to burn.*

| 7
 N
 Nitrogen |
| 15
 P
 Phosphorus |
| 33
 As
 Arsenic |
| 51
 Sb
 Antimony |
| 83
 Bi
 Bismuth |

Group contains: two nonmetals, two metalloids, and one metal
Electrons in the outer level: 5
Reactivity: varies among the elements
Other shared properties: solids at room temperature (except for nitrogen)

Nitrogen, which is a gas at room temperature, makes up about 80% of the air you breathe. Nitrogen removed from air can be reacted with hydrogen to make ammonia for fertilizers.

Although nitrogen is not very reactive, phosphorus is extremely reactive, as shown in **Figure 6.** In fact, in nature phosphorus is only found combined with other elements.

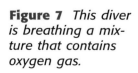

INTERNET ACTIVITY

For another activity related to this chapter, go to **go.hrw.com** and type in the keyword **HP5PRTW.**

Group 16: Oxygen Group

| 8
 O
 Oxygen |
| 16
 S
 Sulfur |
| 34
 Se
 Selenium |
| 52
 Te
 Tellurium |
| 84
 Po
 Polonium |

Group contains: three nonmetals, one metalloid, and one metal
Electrons in the outer level: 6
Reactivity: Reactive
Other shared properties: All but oxygen are solid at room temperature.

Oxygen makes up about 20% of air. Oxygen is necessary for substances to burn. Oxygen is also important to most living things, such as the diver in **Figure 7.** Sulfur is another commonly found member of Group 16. Sulfur can be found as a yellow solid in nature. It is used to make sulfuric acid, the most widely used compound in the chemical industry.

✓ **Reading Check** Which gases from Groups 15 and 16 make up most of the air you breathe?

Figure 7 *This diver is breathing a mixture that contains oxygen gas.*

Figure 8 Physical Properties of Some Halogens

Chlorine is a yellowish green gas.

Bromine is a dark red liquid.

Iodine is a dark gray solid.

Group 17: Halogens

9	F	Fluorine
17	Cl	Chlorine
35	Br	Bromine
53	I	Iodine
85	At	Astatine

Group contains: nonmetals
Electrons in the outer level: 7
Reactivity: very reactive
Other shared properties: poor conductors of electric current; violent reactions with alkali metals to form salts; never in uncombined form in nature

Halogens (HAL oh juhnz) are very reactive nonmetals because their atoms need to gain only one electron to have a complete outer level. The atoms of halogens combine readily with other atoms, especially metals, to gain that missing electron. The reaction of a halogen with a metal makes a salt, such as sodium chloride. Both chlorine and iodine are used as disinfectants. Chlorine is used to treat water. Iodine mixed with alcohol is used in hospitals.

Although the chemical properties of the halogens are similar, the physical properties are quite different, as shown in **Figure 8.**

halogen one of the elements of Group 17 of the periodic table (fluorine, chlorine, bromine, iodine, and astatine); halogens combine with most metals to form salts

CONNECTION TO Biology

Water Treatment Chlorine has been used to treat drinking water since the early 20th century. Chlorinating water helps protect people from many diseases by killing the organisms in water that cause the diseases. But there is much more to water treatment than just adding chlorine. Research how a water treatment plant purifies water for your use. Construct a model of a treatment plant. Use labels to describe the role of each part of the plant in treating the water you use each day.

ACTiViTY

Group 18: Noble Gases

2 **He** Helium	**Group contains:** nonmetals
10 **Ne** Neon	**Electrons in the outer level:** 8 (except helium, which has 2)
18 **Ar** Argon	**Reactivity:** unreactive
36 **Kr** Krypton	**Other shared properties:** colorless, odorless gases at room temperature
54 **Xe** Xenon	
86 **Rn** Radon	

Figure 9 *In addition to neon, other noble gases can be used to make "neon" lights.*

noble gas one of the elements of Group 18 of the periodic table (helium, neon, argon, krypton, xenon, and radon); noble gases are unreactive

Noble gases are unreactive nonmetals and are in Group 18 of the periodic table. The atoms of these elements have a full set of electrons in their outer level. So, they do not need to lose or gain any electrons. Under normal conditions, they do not react with other elements. Earth's atmosphere is almost 1% argon. But all the noble gases are found in small amounts.

The unreactivity of the noble gases makes them useful. For example, ordinary light bulbs last longer when they are filled with argon. Because argon is unreactive, it does not react with the metal filament in the light bulb even when the filament gets hot. A more reactive gas might react with the filament, causing the light to burn out. The low density of helium makes blimps and weather balloons float. Another popular use of noble gases is shown in **Figure 9.**

✓ **Reading Check** Why are noble gases unreactive?

Hydrogen

1 **H** Hydrogen	**Electrons in the outer level:** 1
	Reactivity: reactive
	Other properties: colorless, odorless gas at room temperature; low density; explosive reactions with oxygen

Figure 10 *Hydrogen reacts violently with oxygen. The hot water vapor that forms as a result of this reaction helps guide the space shuttle into orbit.*

The properties of hydrogen do not match the properties of any single group, so hydrogen is set apart from the other elements in the table. Hydrogen is above Group 1 because atoms of the alkali metals also have only one electron in their outer level. Atoms of hydrogen can give away one electron when they join with other atoms. However, the physical properties of hydrogen are more like those of nonmetals than those of metals. So, hydrogen really is in a group of its own. Hydrogen is found in stars. In fact, it is the most abundant element in the universe. Its reactive nature makes it useful as a fuel in rockets, as shown in **Figure 10.**

Summary

- Alkali metals (Group 1) are the most reactive metals. Atoms of the alkali metals have one electron in their outer level.

- Alkaline-earth metals (Group 2) are less reactive than the alkali metals are. Atoms of the alkaline-earth metals have two electrons in their outer level.

- Transition metals (Groups 3–12) include most of the well-known metals and the lanthanides and actinides.

- Groups 13–16 contain the metalloids and some metals and nonmetals.

- Halogens (Group 17) are very reactive non-metals. Atoms of the halogens have seven electrons in their outer level.

- Noble gases (Group 18) are unreactive nonmetals. Atoms of the noble gases have a full set of electrons in their outer level.

- Hydrogen is set off by itself in the periodic table. Its properties do not match the properties of any one group.

Using Key Terms

Complete each of the following sentences by choosing the correct term from the word bank.

noble gas   alkaline-earth metal

halogen   alkali metal

1. An atom of a(n) ___ has a full set of electrons in its outermost energy level.

2. An atom of a(n) ___ has one electron in its outermost energy level.

3. An atom of a(n) ___ tends to gain one electron when it combines with another atom.

4. An atom of a(n) ___ tends to lose two electrons when it combines with another atom.

Understanding Key Ideas

5. Which group contains elements whose atoms have six electrons in their outer level?
   a. Group 2   c. Group 16
   b. Group 6   d. Group 18

6. What are two properties of the alkali metals?

7. What causes the properties of elements in a group to be similar?

8. What are two properties of the halogens?

9. Why is hydrogen set apart from the other elements in the periodic table?

10. Which group contains elements whose atoms have three electrons in their outer level?

Interpreting Graphics

11. Look at the model of an atom below. Does the model represent a metal atom or a nonmetal atom? Explain your answer.

Critical Thinking

12. **Making Inferences** Why are neither the alkali metals nor the alkaline-earth metals found uncombined in nature?

13. **Making Comparisons** Compare the element hydrogen with the alkali metal sodium.

SCLINKS.

NSTA

Developed and maintained by the National Science Teachers Association

For a variety of links related to this chapter, go to www.scilinks.org

Topic: Alkali Metals; Halogens and Noble Gases

SciLinks code: HSM0043; HSM0711

Model-Making Lab

Create a Periodic Table

You probably have classification systems for many things in your life, such as your clothes, your books, and your CDs. One of the most important classification systems in science is the periodic table of the elements. In this lab, you will develop your own classification system for a collection of ordinary objects. You will analyze trends in your system and compare your system with the periodic table of the elements.

Procedure

1 Your teacher will give you a bag of objects. Your bag is missing one item. Examine the items carefully. Describe the missing object in as many ways as you can. Be sure to include the reasons why you think the missing object has the characteristics you describe.

2 Lay the paper squares out on your desk or table so that you have a grid of five rows of four squares each.

3 Arrange your objects on the grid in a logical order. (You must decide what order is logical!) You should end up with one blank square for the missing object.

4 Record a description of the basis for your arrangement.

5 Measure the mass (g) and diameter (mm) of each object, and record your results in the appropriate square. Each square (except the empty one) should have one object and two written measurements on it.

6 Examine your pattern again. Does the order in which your objects are arranged still make sense? Explain.

7 Rearrange the squares and their objects if necessary to improve your arrangement. Record a description of the basis for the new arrangement.

8 Working across the rows, number the squares 1 to 20. When you get to the end of a row, continue numbering in the first square of the next row.

9 Copy your grid. In each square, be sure to list the type of object and label all measurements with appropriate units.

Analyze the Results

1 **Constructing Graphs** Make a graph of mass (*y*-axis) versus object number (*x*-axis). Label each axis, and title the graph.

2 **Constructing Graphs** Now make a graph of diameter (*y*-axis) versus object number (*x*-axis).

Draw Conclusions

3 **Analyzing Graphs** Discuss each graph with your classmates. Try to identify any important features of the graph. For example, does the graph form a line or a curve? Is there anything unusual about the graph? What do these features tell you? Record your answers.

4 **Evaluating Models** How is your arrangement of objects similar to the periodic table of the elements found in this textbook? How is your arrangement different from that periodic table?

5 **Making Predictions** Look again at your prediction about the missing object. Do you think your prediction is still accurate? Try to improve your description by estimating the mass and diameter of the missing object. Record your estimates.

6 **Evaluating Methods** Mendeleev created a periodic table of elements and predicted characteristics of missing elements. How is your experiment similar to Mendeleev's work?

Chapter Review

USING KEY TERMS

Complete each of the following sentences by choosing the correct term from the word bank.

group   period
alkali metals   halogens
alkaline-earth metals   noble gases

1 Elements in the same vertical column on the periodic table belong to the same ___.

2 Elements in the same horizontal row on the periodic table belong to the same ___.

3 The most reactive metals are ___.

4 Elements that are unreactive are called ___.

UNDERSTANDING KEY IDEAS

Multiple Choice

5 Mendeleev's periodic table was useful because it

  a. showed the elements arranged by atomic number.

  b. had no empty spaces.

  c. showed the atomic number of the elements.

  d. allowed for the prediction of the properties of missing elements.

6 Most nonmetals are

  a. shiny.

  b. poor conductors of electric current.

  c. flattened when hit with a hammer.

  d. solids at room temperature.

7 Which of the following items is NOT found on the periodic table?

  a. the atomic number of each element

  b. the name of each element

  c. the date that each element was discovered

  d. the atomic mass of each element

8 Which of the following statements about the periodic table is false?

  a. There are more metals than non-metals on the periodic table.

  b. Atoms of elements in the same group have the same number of electrons in their outer level.

  c. The elements at the far left of the periodic table are nonmetals.

  d. Elements are arranged by increasing atomic number.

9 Which of the following statements about alkali metals is true?

  a. Alkali metals are generally found in their uncombined form.

  b. Alkali metals are Group 1 elements.

  c. Alkali metals should be stored underwater.

  d. Alkali metals are unreactive.

10 Which of the following statements about elements is true?

  a. Every element occurs naturally.

  b. All elements are found in their uncombined form in nature.

  c. Each element has a unique atomic number.

  d. All of the elements exist in approximately equal quantities.

Short Answer

11 How is Moseley's basis for arranging the elements different from Mendeleev's?

12 How is the periodic table like a calendar?

Math Skills

Examine the chart of the percentages of elements in the Earth's crust below. Then, answer the questions that follow.

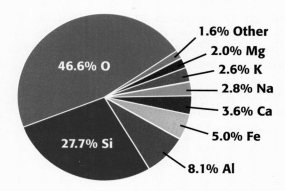

13 Excluding the "Other" category, what percentage of the Earth's crust are alkali metals?

14 Excluding the "Other" category, what percentage of the Earth's crust are alkaline-earth metals?

CRITICAL THINKING

15 Concept Mapping Use the following terms to create a concept map: *periodic table, elements, groups, periods, metals, nonmetals,* and *metalloids.*

16 Forming Hypotheses Why was Mendeleev unable to make any predictions about the noble gas elements?

17 Identifying Relationships When an element that has 115 protons in its nucleus is synthesized, will it be a metal, a nonmetal, or a metalloid? Explain your answer.

18 Applying Concepts Your classmate offers to give you a piece of sodium that he found on a hiking trip. What is your response? Explain.

19 Applying Concepts Identify each element described below.

a. This metal is very reactive, has properties similar to those of magnesium, and is in the same period as bromine.

b. This nonmetal is in the same group as lead.

INTERPRETING GRAPHICS

20 Study the diagram below to determine the pattern of the images. Predict the missing image, and draw it. Identify which properties are periodic and which properties are shared within a group.

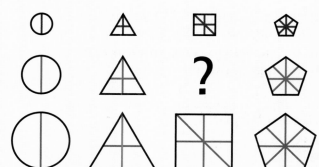

Standardized Test Preparation

Read each of the passages below. Then, answer the questions that follow each passage.

Passage 1 Napoleon III (1808–1873) ruled as emperor of France from 1852 to 1870. Napoleon III was the nephew of the famous French military leader and emperor Napoleon I. Early in his reign, Napoleon III was an <u>authoritarian</u> ruler. France's economy did well under his dictatorial rule, so the French rebuilt cities and built railways. During the 1850s and 1860s, Napoleon III used aluminum dinnerware because aluminum was more valuable than gold. Despite his wealth and French economic prosperity, Napoleon III lost public support and popularity. So, in 1860, he began a series of reforms that allowed more individual freedoms in France.

1. What is the meaning of the word *authoritarian* in the passage?
  A controlling people's thoughts and actions
  B writing books and stories
  C being an expert on a subject
  D being very wealthy

2. Which of the following statements best describes why Napoleon III probably changed the way he ruled France?
  F He was getting old.
  G He was unpopular and had lost public support.
  H He had built as many railroads as he could.
  I He used aluminum dinnerware.

3. According to the passage, in what year did Napoleon III die?
  A 1808
  B 1873
  C 1860
  D 1852

Passage 2 Named after architect Buckminster Fuller, buckyballs resemble the geodesic domes that are characteristic of the architect's work. Excitement over buckyballs began in 1985, when scientists projected light from a laser onto a piece of graphite. In the soot that remained, researchers found a completely new kind of molecule! Buckyballs are also found in the soot from a candle flame. Some scientists claim to have detected buckyballs in space. In fact, one suggestion is that buckyballs are at the center of the condensing clouds of gas, dust, and debris that form galaxies.

1. Which of the following statements correctly describes buckyballs?
  A They are a kind of dome-shaped building.
  B They are shot from lasers.
  C They were unknown before 1985.
  D They are named for the scientist who discovered them.

2. Based on the passage, which of the following statements is an opinion?
  F Buckyballs might be in the clouds that form galaxies.
  G Buckyballs are named after an architect.
  H Scientists found buckyballs in soot.
  I Buckyballs are a kind of molecule.

3. According to the passage, why were scientists excited?
  A Buckyballs were found in space.
  B An architect created a building that resembled a molecule.
  C Buckyballs were found to be in condensing clouds of gas that form galaxies.
  D A new kind of molecule was found.

INTERPRETING GRAPHICS

Use the image of the periodic table below to answer the questions that follow.

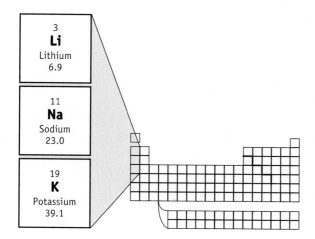

1. Which of the following statements is correct for the elements shown?

   A Lithium has the greatest atomic number.

   B Sodium has the least atomic mass.

   C Atomic number decreases as you move down the column.

   D Atomic mass increases as you move down the column.

2. Which of the following statements best describes the outer electrons in atoms of the elements shown?

   F The atoms of each element have 1 outer-level electron.

   G Lithium atoms have 3 outer-level electrons, sodium atoms have 11, and potassium atoms have 19.

   H Lithium atoms have 7 outer-level electrons, sodium atoms have 23, and potassium atoms have 39.

   I The atoms of each element have 11 outer-level electrons.

3. The elements featured in the image belong to which of the following groups?

   A noble gases

   B alkaline-earth metals

   C halogens

   D alkali metals

1. Elvira's house is 7.3 km from her school. What is this distance expressed in meters?

   A 0.73 m

   B 73 m

   C 730 m

   D 7,300 m

2. A chemical company is preparing a shipment of 10 g each of four elements. Each element must be shipped in its own container that is completely filled with the element. Which container will be the largest?

Element	Density (g/cm³)	Mass (g)
Aluminum	2.702	10
Arsenic	5.727	10
Germanium	5.350	10
Silicon	2.420	10

   F the container of aluminum

   G the container of arsenic

   H the container of germanium

   I the container of silicon

3. Arjay has samples of several common elements. Each element has a unique atomic mass (expressed in amu). Which of the following lists shows the atomic masses in order from least to greatest?

   A 63.55, 58.69, 55.85, 58.93

   B 63.55, 58.93, 58.69, 55.85

   C 55.85, 58.69, 58.93, 63.55

   D 55.85, 63.55, 58.69, 58.93

Standardized Test Preparation

Science in Action

Weird Science

Buckyballs

In 1985, scientists found a completely new kind of molecule! This carbon molecule has 60 carbon atoms linked together in a shape similar to that of a soccer ball. This molecule is called a buckyball. Buckyballs have also been found in the soot from candle flames. And some scientists claim to have detected buckyballs in space. Chemists have been trying to identify the molecules' properties. One property is that a buckyball can act like a cage and hold smaller substances, such as individual atoms. Buckyballs are both slippery and strong. Scientists are exploring their use in tough plastics and cutting tools.

Language Arts ACTIVITY

WRITING SKILL Imagine that you are trapped within a buckyball. Write a one-page short story describing your experience. Describe the windows in your molecular prison.

Science, Technology, and Society

The Science of Fireworks

Explosive and dazzling, a fireworks display is both a science and an art. More than 1,000 years ago, the Chinese made black powder, or gunpowder. The powder was used to set off firecrackers and primitive missiles. The shells of fireworks contain several different chemicals. Black powder at the bottom of the shell launches the shell into the sky. A second layer of black powder ignites the rest of the chemicals and causes an explosion that lights up the sky! Colors can be created by mixing chemicals such as strontium (for red), magnesium (for white), or copper (for blue) with the gunpowder.

Math ACTIVITY

Fireworks can cost between $200 and $2,000 each. If a show uses 20 fireworks that cost $200 each, 12 fireworks that cost $500 each, and 10 fireworks that cost $1,200 each, what is the total cost for the fireworks?

Glenn T. Seaborg

Making Elements When you look at the periodic table, you can thank Dr. Glenn Theodore Seaborg and his colleagues for many of the actinide elements. While working at the University of California at Berkeley, Seaborg and his team added a number of elements to the periodic table. His work in identifying properties of plutonium led to his working on the top-secret Manhattan Project at the University of Chicago. He was outspoken about the beneficial uses of atomic energy and, at the same time, opposed the production and use of nuclear weapons.

Seaborg's revision of the layout of the periodic table—the actinide concept—is the most significant since Mendeleev's original design. For his scientific achievements, Dr. Seaborg was awarded the 1951 Nobel Prize in Chemistry jointly with his colleague, Dr. Edwin M. McMillan. Element 106, which Seaborg neither discovered nor created, was named seaborgium in his honor. This was the first time an element had been named after a living person.

Social Studies ACTIVITY

WRITING SKILL Write a newspaper editorial to express an opinion for or against the Manhattan Project. Be sure to include information to support your view.

To learn more about these Science in Action topics, visit **go.hrw.com** and type in the keyword **HP5PRTF.**

Current Science

Check out Current Science® articles related to this chapter by visiting go.hrw.com. Just type in the keyword HP5CS12.

UNIT 5

TIMELINE

Interactions of Matter

In this unit you will study the interactions through which matter can change its identity. You will learn how atoms bond with one another to form compounds and how atoms join in different combinations to form new substances through chemical reactions. You will also learn about the properties of several categories of compounds. Finally, you will learn how nuclear interactions can actually change the identity of an atom. This timeline includes some of the events leading to the current understanding of these interactions of matter.

1828

Urea, a compound found in urine, is produced in a laboratory. Until this time, chemists had believed that compounds created by living organisms could not be produced in the laboratory.

1858

German chemist Friedrich August Kekulé suggests that carbon forms four chemical bonds and can form long chains.

1942

The first nuclear chain reaction is carried out in a squash court under the football stadium at the University of Chicago.

1979

Public fear about nuclear power grows after an accident occurs at the Three Mile Island nuclear power station located in Pennsylvania.

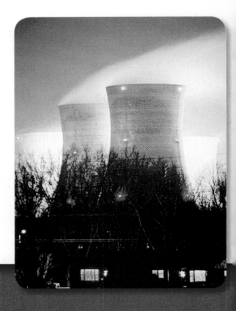

1867

Swedish chemist Alfred Nobel develops dynamite. Dynamite's explosive power is a result of the decomposition reaction of nitroglycerin.

1898

The United States defeats Spain in the Spanish-American War.

1903

Marie Curie, Pierre Curie, and Henri Becquerel are awarded the Nobel Prize in physics for the discovery of radioactivity.

1964

Dr. Martin Luther King, Jr., American civil rights leader, is awarded the Nobel Peace Prize.

1969

The *Nimbus III* weather satellite is launched by the United States, representing the first civilian use of nuclear batteries.

1996

Evidence of organic compounds in a meteorite leads scientists to speculate that life may have existed on Mars more than 3.6 billion years ago.

2001

The first total solar eclipse of the millenium occurs on June 21.

2002

Hy-wire, the world's first drivable vehicle to combine a hydrogen fuel cell with by-wire technology, is introduced.

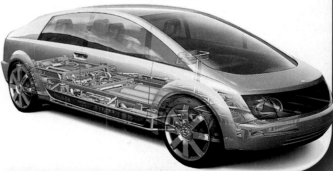

13

Chemical Bonding

SECTION **1** **Electrons and Chemical Bonding** 364

SECTION **2** **Ionic Bonds** 368

SECTION **3** **Covalent and Metallic Bonds** 372

Chapter Lab 378
Chapter Review 380
Standardized Test Preparation 382
Science in Action 384

About the PHOTO

What looks like a fantastic "sculpture" is really a model of deoxyribonucleic acid (DNA). DNA is one of the most complex molecules in living things. In DNA, atoms are bonded together in two very long spiral strands. These strands join to form a double spiral. The DNA in living cells has all the coding for passing on the traits of that cell and that organism.

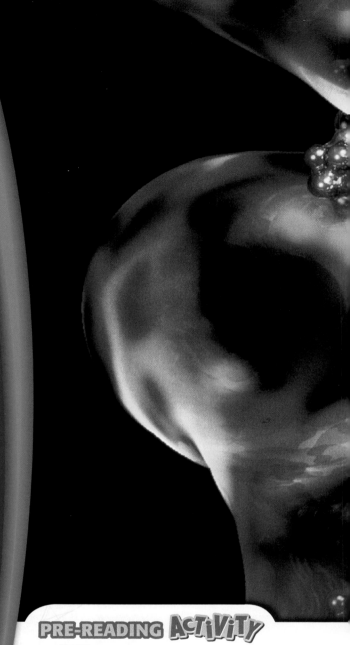

PRE-READING ACTIVITY

Three-Panel Flip Chart
Before you read the chapter, create the FoldNote entitled "Three-Panel Flip Chart" described in the **Study Skills** section of the Appendix. Label the flaps of the three-panel flip chart with "Ionic bond," "Covalent bond," and "Metallic bond." As you read the chapter, write information you learn about each category under the appropriate flap.

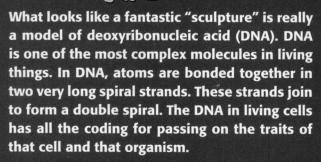

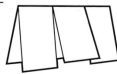

From Glue to Goop

Particles of glue can bond to other particles and hold objects together. Different types of bonds create differences in the properties of substances. In this activity, you will see how the formation of bonds causes a change in the properties of white glue.

Procedure

1. Fill a **small paper cup** 1/4 full of **white glue.** Record the properties of the glue.

2. Fill a **second small paper cup** 1/4 full of **borax solution.**

3. Pour the borax solution into the cup of white glue, and stir well using a **plastic spoon** or a **wooden craft stick.**

4. When the material becomes too thick to stir, remove it from the cup and knead it with your fingers. Record the properties of the material.

Analysis

1. Compare the properties of the glue with those of the new material.

2. The properties of the material resulted from bonds between the borax and the glue. Predict the properties of the material if less borax is used.

Electrons and Chemical Bonding

Have you ever stopped to consider that by using only the 26 letters of the alphabet, you make all of the words you use every day?

Although the number of letters is limited, combining the letters in different ways allows you to make a huge number of words. In the same way that words can be formed by combining letters, substances can be formed by combining atoms.

Combining Atoms Through Chemical Bonding

Look at **Figure 1.** Now, look around the room. Everything you see—desks, pencils, paper, and even your friends—is made of atoms of elements. All substances are made of atoms of one or more of the approximately 100 elements. For example, the atoms of carbon, hydrogen, and oxygen combine in different patterns to form sugar, alcohol, and citric acid. **Chemical bonding** is the joining of atoms to form new substances. The properties of these new substances are different from the properties of the original elements. An interaction that holds two atoms together is called a **chemical bond.** When chemical bonds form, electrons are shared, gained, or lost.

READING WARM-UP

Objectives

● Describe chemical bonding.
● Identify the number of valence electrons in an atom.
● Predict whether an atom is likely to form bonds.

Terms to Learn

chemical bonding
chemical bond
valence electron

READING STRATEGY

Discussion Read this section silently. Write down questions that you have about this section. Discuss your questions in a small group.

Discussing Bonding Using Theories and Models

We cannot see atoms and chemical bonds with the unaided eye. For more than 150 years, scientists have done many experiments that have led to a theory of chemical bonding. Remember that a theory is an explanation for some phenomenon that is based on observation, experimentation, and reasoning. The use of models helps people discuss the theory of how and why atoms form bonds.

Figure 1 *Everything you see in this photo is formed by combining atoms.*

Figure 2 Electron Arrangement in an Atom

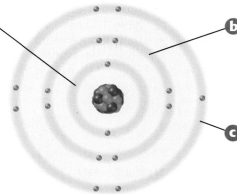

a The **first energy level** is closest to the nucleus and can hold up to 2 electrons.

b Electrons will begin filling the **second energy level** only after the first level is full. The second energy level can hold up to 8 electrons.

c The **third energy level** in this model of a chlorine atom has only 7 electrons, so the atom has a total of 17 electrons. This outer level of the atom is not full.

Electron Number and Organization

To understand how atoms form chemical bonds, you need to know about the electrons in an atom. The number of electrons in an atom can be determined from the atomic number of the element. The *atomic number* is the number of protons in an atom. But atoms have no charge. So, the atomic number also represents the number of electrons in the atom.

Electrons in an atom are organized in energy levels. **Figure 2** shows a model of the arrangement of electrons in a chlorine atom. This model and models like it are useful for counting electrons in energy levels of atoms. But, these models do not show the true structure of atoms.

chemical bonding the combining of atoms to form molecules or ionic compounds

chemical bond an interaction that holds atoms or ions together

valence electron an electron that is found in the outermost shell of an atom and that determines the atom's chemical properties

Outer-Level Electrons and Bonding

Not all of the electrons in an atom make chemical bonds. Most atoms form bonds using only the electrons in the outermost energy level. An electron in the outermost energy level of an atom is a **valence electron** (VAY luhns ee LEK TRAHN). The models in **Figure 3** show the valence electrons for two atoms.

Reading Check Which electrons are used to form bonds? *(See the Appendix for answers to Reading Checks.)*

Figure 3 Counting Valence Electrons

Oxygen
Electron total: 8
First level: 2 electrons
Second level: 6 electrons

An oxygen atom has 6 valence electrons.

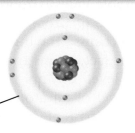

Sodium
Electron total: 11
First level: 2 electrons
Second level: 8 electrons
Third level: 1 electron

A sodium atom has 1 valence electron.

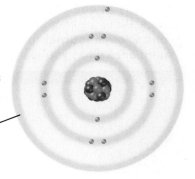

Figure 4 Determining the Number of Valence Electrons

Atoms of elements in **Groups 1 and 2** have the same number of valence electrons as their group number.

Atoms of elements in **Groups 13–18** have 10 fewer valence electrons than their group number. However, helium atoms have only 2 valence electrons.

Atoms of elements in **Groups 3–12** do not have a rule relating their valence electrons to their group number.

H																	18
1	2											13	14	15	16	17	He
Li	Be											B	C	N	O	F	Ne
Na	Mg	3	4	5	6	7	8	9	10	11	12	Al	Si	P	S	Cl	Ar
K	Ca	Sc	Ti	V	Cr	Mn	Fe	Co	Ni	Cu	Zn	Ga	Ge	As	Se	Br	Kr
Rb	Sr	Y	Zr	Nb	Mo	Tc	Ru	Rh	Pd	Ag	Cd	In	Sn	Sb	Te	I	Xe
Cs	Ba	La	Hf	Ta	W	Re	Os	Ir	Pt	Au	Hg	Tl	Pb	Bi	Po	At	Rn
Fr	Ra	Ac	Rf	Db	Sg	Bh	Hs	Mt	Ds	Uuu	Uub		Uuq				

CONNECTION TO Social Studies

WRITING SKILL **History of a Noble Gas** When Dmitri Mendeleev organized the first periodic table, he did not include the noble gases. The noble gases had not been discovered at that time. Research the history of the discovery of one of the noble gases. Write a paragraph in your **science journal** to summarize what you learned.

Valence Electrons and the Periodic Table

You can use a model to determine the number of valence electrons of an atom. But what would you do if you didn't have a model? You can use the periodic table to determine the number of valence electrons for atoms of some elements.

Elements are grouped based on similar properties. Within a group, or family, the atoms of each element have the same number of valence electrons. So, the group numbers can help you determine the number of valence electrons for some atoms, as shown in **Figure 4.**

To Bond or Not to Bond

Not all atoms bond in the same manner. In fact, some atoms rarely bond at all! The number of electrons in the outermost energy level of an atom determines whether an atom will form bonds.

Atoms of the noble gases (Group 18) do not usually form chemical bonds. Atoms of Group 18 elements (except helium) have 8 valence electrons. Having 8 valence electrons is a special condition. In fact, atoms that have 8 electrons in their outermost energy level do not usually form bonds. The outermost energy level of an atom is considered to be full if the energy level contains 8 electrons.

✓ Reading Check The atoms of which group in the periodic table rarely form chemical bonds?

Filling The Outermost Level

An atom that has fewer than 8 valence electrons is much more likely to form bonds than an atom that has 8 valence electrons is. Atoms bond by gaining, losing, or sharing electrons to have a filled outermost energy level. A filled outermost level contains 8 valence electrons. **Figure 5** describes how atoms can achieve a filled outermost energy level.

Is Two Electrons a Full Set?

Not all atoms need 8 valence electrons to have a filled outermost energy level. Helium atoms need only 2 valence electrons. The outermost energy level in a helium atom is the first energy level. The first energy level of any atom can hold only 2 electrons. So, the outermost energy level of a helium atom is full if the energy level has only 2 electrons. Atoms of hydrogen and lithium also form bonds by gaining, losing, or sharing electrons to achieve 2 electrons in the first energy level.

Figure 5 **Filling Outermost Energy Levels**

Sulfur
An atom of sulfur has 6 valence electrons. It can have 8 valence electrons by sharing 2 electrons with or gaining 2 electrons from other atoms.

Magnesium
An atom of magnesium has 2 valence electrons. It can have a full outer level by losing 2 electrons. The second energy level becomes the outermost energy level and contains 8 electrons.

SECTION Review

Summary

- Chemical bonding is the joining of atoms to form new substances. A chemical bond is an interaction that holds two atoms together.

- A valence electron is an electron in the outermost energy level of an atom.

- Most atoms form bonds by gaining, losing, or sharing electrons until they have 8 valence electrons. Atoms of some elements need only 2 electrons to fill their outermost level.

Using Key Terms

1. Use the following terms in the same sentence: *chemical bond* and *valence electron*.

Understanding Key Ideas

2. Which of the following atoms do not usually form bonds?
   a. calcium   **c.** hydrogen
   b. neon   **d.** oxygen

3. Describe chemical bonding.

4. Explain how to use the valence electrons in an atom to predict if the atom will form bonds.

Critical Thinking

5. **Making Inferences** How can an atom that has 5 valence electrons achieve a full set of valence electrons?

6. **Applying Concepts** Identify the number of valence electrons in a barium atom.

Interpreting Graphics

7. Look at the model below. How many valence electrons are in a fluorine atom? Will fluorine atoms form bonds? Explain.

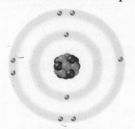

Fluorine

ionic bond a bond that forms when electrons are transferred from one atom to another, which results in a positive ion and a negative ion

ion a charged particle that forms when an atom or group of atoms gains or loses one or more electrons

Ionic Bonds

Have you ever accidentally tasted sea water? If so, you probably didn't enjoy it. What makes sea water taste different from the water in your home?

Sea water tastes different because salt is dissolved in it. One of the salts in sea water is the same as the salt that you eat. The chemical bonds in salt are ionic (ie AHN ik) bonds.

Forming Ionic Bonds

An **ionic bond** is a bond that forms when electrons are transferred from one atom to another atom. During ionic bonding, one or more valence electrons are transferred from one atom to another. Like all chemical bonds, ionic bonds form so that the outermost energy levels of the atoms in the bonds are filled. **Figure 1** shows another substance that contains ionic bonds.

Charged Particles

An atom is neutral because the number of electrons in an atom equals the number of protons. So, the charges of the electrons and protons cancel each other. A transfer of electrons between atoms changes the number of electrons in each atom. But the number of protons stays the same in each atom. The negative charges and positive charges no longer cancel out, and the atoms become ions. **Ions** are charged particles that form when atoms gain or lose electrons. An atom normally cannot gain electrons without another atom nearby to lose electrons (or cannot lose electrons without a nearby atom to gain them). But it is easier to study the formation of ions one at a time.

✓ Reading Check Why are atoms neutral? (*See the Appendix for answers to Reading Checks.*)

Figure 1 *Calcium carbonate in this snail's shell contains ionic bonds.*

Figure 2 Forming Positive Ions

Here's How It Works: During chemical changes, a sodium atom can lose its 1 electron in the third energy level to another atom. The filled second level becomes the outermost level, so the resulting sodium ion has 8 valence electrons.

Here's How It Works: During chemical changes, an aluminum atom can lose its 3 electrons in the third energy level to another atom. The filled second level becomes the outermost level, so the resulting aluminum ion has 8 valence electrons.

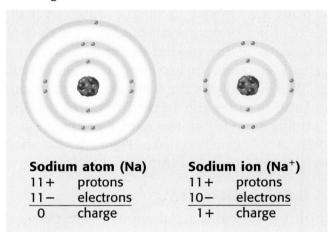

Sodium atom (Na)
11+ protons
11− electrons
0 charge

Sodium ion (Na$^+$)
11+ protons
10− electrons
1+ charge

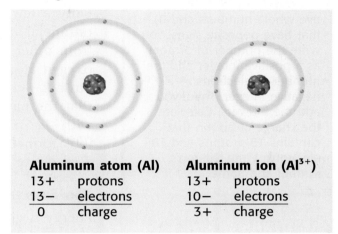

Aluminum atom (Al)
13+ protons
13− electrons
0 charge

Aluminum ion (Al^{3+})
13+ protons
10− electrons
3+ charge

Forming Positive Ions

Ionic bonds form during chemical changes when atoms pull electrons away from other atoms. The atoms that lose electrons form ions that have fewer electrons than protons. Because the positive charges outnumber the negative charges, these ions have a positive charge.

Metal Atoms and the Loss of Electrons

Atoms of most metals have few valence electrons. Metal atoms tend to lose these valence electrons and form positive ions. Look at the models in **Figure 2.** When a sodium atom loses its only valence electron to another atom, the sodium atom becomes a sodium ion. A sodium ion has 1 more proton than it has electrons. So, the sodium ion has a 1+ charge. The chemical symbol for this ion is written as Na$^+$. Notice that the charge is written to the upper right of the chemical symbol. **Figure 2** also shows a model for the formation of an aluminum ion.

The Energy Needed to Lose Electrons

Energy is needed to pull electrons away from atoms. Only a small amount of energy is needed to take electrons from metal atoms. In fact, the energy needed to remove electrons from atoms of elements in Groups 1 and 2 is so small that these elements react very easily. The energy needed to take electrons from metals comes from the formation of negative ions.

Studying Salt

Spread several grains of salt on a dark sheet of construction paper. Use a magnifying lens to examine the salt. Ask an adult at home to examine the salt. Discuss what you saw. Then, gently tap the salt with a small hammer. Examine the salt again. Describe your observations in your **science journal.**

Forming Negative Ions

Some atoms gain electrons from other atoms during chemical changes. The ions that form have more electrons than protons. So, these ions have a negative charge.

Nonmetal Atoms Gain Electrons

The outermost energy level of nonmetal atoms is almost full. Only a few electrons are needed to fill the outer level of a nonmetal atom. So, atoms of nonmetals tend to gain electrons from other atoms. Look at the models in **Figure 3.** When an oxygen atom gains 2 electrons, it becomes an oxide ion that has a 2− charge. The symbol for the oxide ion is O^{2-}. Notice that the name of the negative ion formed from oxygen ends with -*ide*. This ending is used for the names of the negative ions formed when atoms gain electrons. **Figure 3** also shows a model of how a chloride ion is formed.

The Energy of Gaining Electrons

Energy is given off by most nonmetal atoms when they gain electrons. The more easily an atom gains an electron, the more energy the atom releases. Atoms of Group 17 elements give off the most energy when they gain an electron. These elements are very reactive. An ionic bond will form between a metal and a nonmetal if the nonmetal releases more energy than is needed to take electrons from the metal.

✓ Reading Check Atoms of which group on the periodic table give off the most energy when forming negative ions?

Figure 3 **Forming Negative Ions**

Here's How It Works: During chemical changes, an oxygen atom gains 2 electrons in the second energy level from another atom. An oxide ion that has 8 valence electrons is formed. Thus, its outermost energy level is filled.

Here's How It Works: During chemical changes, a chlorine atom gains 1 electron in the third energy level from another atom. A chloride ion that has 8 valence electrons is formed. Thus, its outermost energy level is filled.

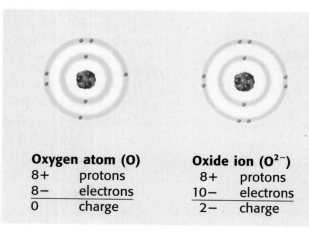

Oxygen atom (O)		**Oxide ion (O^{2-})**	
8+	protons	8+	protons
8−	electrons	10−	electrons
0	charge	2−	charge

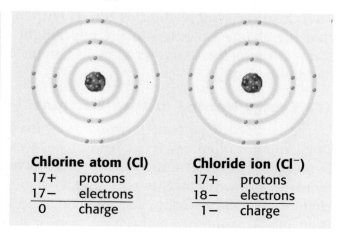

Chlorine atom (Cl)		**Chloride ion (Cl^-)**	
17+	protons	17+	protons
17−	electrons	18−	electrons
0	charge	1−	charge

Ionic Compounds

When ionic bonds form, the number of electrons lost by the metal atoms equals the number gained by the nonmetal atoms. The ions that bond are charged, but the compound formed is neutral because the charges of the ions cancel each other. When ions bond, they form a repeating three-dimensional pattern called a **crystal lattice** (KRIS tuhl LAT is), like the one shown in **Figure 4.** The strong attraction between ions in a crystal lattice gives ionic compounds certain properties, which include brittleness, high melting points, and high boiling points.

crystal lattice the regular pattern in which a crystal is arranged

Figure 4 *This model of the crystal lattice of sodium chloride, or table salt, shows a three-dimensional view of the bonded ions. In the model, the sodium ions are pink and the chloride ions are green.*

SECTION Review

Summary

- An ionic bond is a bond that forms when electrons are transferred from one atom to another. During ionic bonding, the atoms become oppositely charged ions.

- Ionic bonding usually occurs between atoms of metals and atoms of nonmetals.

- Energy is needed to remove electrons from metal atoms. Energy is released when most nonmetal atoms gain electrons.

Using Key Terms

1. Use the following terms in the same sentence: *ion* and *ionic bond*.

2. In your own words, write a definition for the term *crystal lattice*.

Understanding Key Ideas

3. Which types of atoms usually become negative ions?

   a. metals

   b. nonmetals

   c. noble gases

   d. All of the above

4. How does an atom become a positive ion? a negative ion?

5. What are two properties of ionic compounds?

Math Skills

6. What is the charge of an ion that has 12 protons and 10 electrons? Write the ion's symbol.

Critical Thinking

7. **Applying Concepts** Which group of elements gains two valence electrons when the atoms form ionic bonds?

8. **Identifying Relationships** Explain why ionic compounds are neutral even though they are made up of charged particles.

9. **Making Comparisons** Compare the formation of positive ions with the formation of negative ions in terms of energy changes.

SCiLINKS®

Developed and maintained by the National Science Teachers Association

For a variety of links related to this chapter, go to www.scilinks.org

Topic: Types of Chemical Bonds
SciLinks code: HSM1565

SECTION 3

Covalent and Metallic Bonds

Imagine bending a wooden coat hanger and a wire coat hanger. The wire one would bend easily, but the wooden one would break. Why do these things behave differently?

One reason is that the bonds between the atoms of each object are different. The atoms of the wooden hanger are held together by covalent bonds (KOH VAY luhnt BAHNDZ). But the atoms of the wire hanger are held together by metallic bonds. Read on to learn about the difference between these kinds of chemical bonds.

Covalent Bonds

Most things around you, such as water, sugar, oxygen, and wood, are held together by covalent bonds. Substances that have covalent bonds tend to have low melting and boiling points and are brittle in the solid state. For example, oxygen has a low boiling point, which is why it is a gas at room temperature. And wood is brittle, so it breaks when bent.

A **covalent bond** forms when atoms share one or more pairs of electrons. When two atoms of nonmetals bond, a large amount of energy is needed for either atom to lose an electron. So, two nonmetals don't transfer electrons to fill the outermost energy levels of their atoms. Instead, two nonmetal atoms bond by sharing electrons with each another, as shown in the model in **Figure 1**.

✓ **Reading Check** What is a covalent bond? (*See the Appendix for answers to Reading Checks.*)

READING WARM-UP

Objectives
● Explain how covalent bonds form.
● Describe molecules.
● Explain how metallic bonds form.
● Describe the properties of metals.

Terms to Learn
covalent bond
molecule
metallic bond

READING STRATEGY

Reading Organizer As you read this section, create an outline of the section. Use the headings from the section in your outline.

covalent bond a bond formed when atoms share one or more pairs of electrons

Figure 1 *By sharing electrons in a covalent bond, each hydrogen atom (the smallest atom) has a full outermost energy level containing two electrons.*

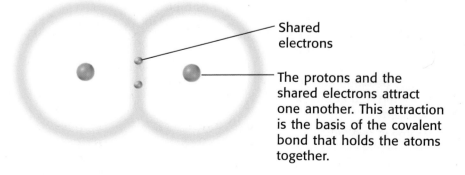

Shared electrons

The protons and the shared electrons attract one another. This attraction is the basis of the covalent bond that holds the atoms together.

Figure 2 **Covalent Bonds in a Water Molecule**

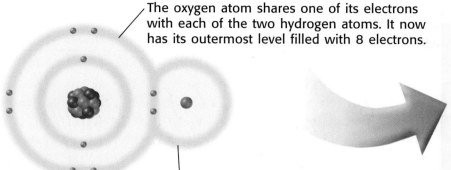

The oxygen atom shares one of its electrons with each of the two hydrogen atoms. It now has its outermost level filled with 8 electrons.

Each hydrogen atom shares its 1 electron with the oxygen atom. Each hydrogen atom now has an outer level filled with 2 electrons.

This electron-dot diagram for water shows only the outermost level of electrons for each atom. But you still see how the atoms share electrons.

Covalent Bonds and Molecules

Substances containing covalent bonds consist of individual particles called molecules (MAHL i KYOOLZ). A **molecule** usually consists of two or more atoms joined in a definite ratio. A hydrogen molecule is composed of two covalently bonded hydrogen atoms. However, most molecules are composed of atoms of two or more elements. The models in **Figure 2** show two ways to represent the covalent bonds in a water molecule.

One way to represent atoms and molecules is to use electron-dot diagrams. An electron-dot diagram is a model that shows only the valence electrons in an atom. Electron-dot diagrams can help you predict how atoms might bond. To draw an electron-dot diagram, write the symbol of the element and place one dot around the symbol for every valence electron in the atom, as shown in **Figure 3.** Place the first 4 dots alone on each side, and then pair up any remaining dots.

molecule the smallest unit of a substance that keeps all of the physical and chemical properties of that substance

Figure 3 **Using Electron–Dot Diagrams**

Carbon atoms have 4 valence electrons. A carbon atom needs 4 more electrons to have a filled outermost energy level.

Oxygen atoms have 6 valence electrons. An oxygen atom needs only 2 more electrons to have a filled outermost energy level.

Krypton atoms have 8 valence electrons. Krypton is nonreactive. Krypton atoms do not need any more electrons.

This diagram represents a hydrogen molecule. The dots between the letters represent a pair of shared electrons.

Figure 4 *The water in this fishbowl is made up of many tiny water molecules. Each molecule is the smallest particle that has the chemical properties of water.*

INTERNET ACTIVITY

For another activity related to this chapter, go to **go.hrw.com** and type in the keyword **HP5BNDW**.

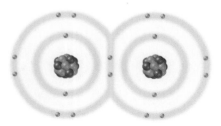

Figure 5 *Two covalently bonded fluorine atoms have filled outermost energy levels. The two electrons shared by the atoms are counted as valence electrons for each atom.*

Covalent Compounds and Molecules

An atom is the smallest particle into which an element can be divided and still be the same element. Likewise, a molecule is the smallest particle into which a covalently bonded compound can be divided and still be the same compound. Look at the three-dimensional models in **Figure 4.** They show how a sample of water is made up of many individual molecules of water. Imagine dividing water over and over. You would eventually end up with a single molecule of water. What would happen if you separated the hydrogen and oxygen atoms that make up a water molecule? Then, you would no longer have water.

The Simplest Molecules

Molecules are composed of at least two covalently bonded atoms. The simplest molecules are made up of two bonded atoms. Molecules made up of two atoms of the same element are called *diatomic molecules.* Elements that are found in nature as diatomic molecules are called *diatomic elements.* Hydrogen is a diatomic element. Oxygen, nitrogen, and the halogens fluorine, chlorine, bromine, and iodine are also diatomic elements. Look at **Figure 5.** The shared electrons are counted as valence electrons for each atom. So, both atoms of the molecule have filled outermost energy levels.

✓ Reading Check How many atoms are in a diatomic molecule?

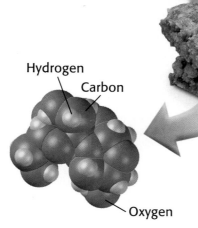

Hydrogen

Carbon

Oxygen

Figure 6 *A granola bar contains sucrose, or table sugar. A molecule of sucrose is composed of carbon atoms, hydrogen atoms, and oxygen atoms joined by covalent bonds.*

More-Complex Molecules

Diatomic molecules are the simplest molecules. They are also some of the most important molecules. You could not live without diatomic oxygen molecules. But other important molecules are much more complex. Soap, plastic bottles, and even proteins in your body are examples of complex molecules. Carbon atoms are the basis of many of these complex molecules. Each carbon atom needs to make four covalent bonds to have 8 valence electrons. These bonds can be with atoms of other elements or with other carbon atoms, as shown in the model in **Figure 6.**

Metallic Bonds

Look at the unusual metal sculptures shown in **Figure 7.** Some metal pieces have been flattened, while other metal pieces have been shaped into wires. How could the artist change the shape of the metal into all of these different forms without breaking the metal into pieces? Metal can be shaped because of the presence of a metallic bond, a special kind of chemical bond. A **metallic bond** is a bond formed by the attraction between positively charged metal ions and the electrons in the metal. Positively charged metal ions form when metal atoms lose electrons.

CONNECTION TO Biology

Proteins Proteins perform many functions throughout your body. A single protein can have thousands of covalently bonded atoms. Proteins are built from smaller molecules called *amino acids.* Make a poster showing how amino acids are joined to make proteins.

ACTIVITY

metallic bond a bond formed by the attraction between positively charged metal ions and the electrons around them

Figure 7 *The different shapes of metal in these sculptures are possible because of the bonds that hold the metal together.*

375

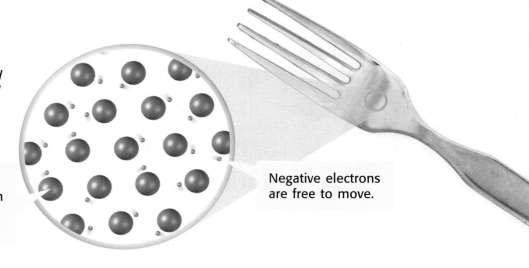

Figure 8 *Moving electrons are attracted to the metal ions, and the attraction forms metallic bonds.*

The positive metal ions are in fixed positions in the metal.

Negative electrons are free to move.

Movement of Electrons Throughout a Metal

Bonding in metals is a result of the metal atoms being so close to one another that their outermost energy levels overlap. This overlapping allows valence electrons to move throughout the metal, as shown in **Figure 8.** You can think of a metal as being made up of positive metal ions that have enough valence electrons "swimming" around to keep the ions together. The electrons also cancel the positive charge of the ions. Metallic bonds extend throughout the metal in all directions.

Properties of Metals

Metallic bonding is what gives metals their particular properties. These properties include electrical conductivity, malleability, and ductility.

Conducting Electric Current

Metallic bonding allows metals to conduct electric current. For example, when you turn on a lamp, electrons move within the copper wire that connects the lamp to the outlet. The electrons that move are the valence electrons in the copper atoms. These electrons are free to move because the electrons are not connected to any one atom.

Reshaping Metals

Because the electrons swim freely around the metal ions, the atoms in metals can be rearranged. As a result, metals can be reshaped. The properties of *ductility* (the ability to be drawn into wires) and *malleability* (the ability to be hammered into sheets) describe a metal's ability to be reshaped. For example, copper is made into wires for use in electrical cords. Aluminum can be pounded into thin sheets and made into aluminum foil.

Reading Check What is ductility?

Bending Without Breaking

When a piece of metal is bent, some of the metal ions are forced closer together. You might expect the metal to break because all of the metal ions are positively charged. Positively charged ions repel one another. However, positive ions in a metal are always surrounded by and attracted to the electrons in the metal—even if the metal ions move. The electrons constantly move around and between the metal ions. The moving electrons maintain the metallic bonds no matter how the shape of the metal changes. So, metal objects can be bent without being broken, as shown in **Figure 9.**

Figure 9 *Metal can be reshaped without breaking because metallic bonds occur in many directions.*

SECTION Review

Summary

- In covalent bonding, two atoms share electrons. A covalent bond forms when atoms share one or more pairs of electrons.

- Covalently bonded atoms form a particle called a *molecule*. A molecule is the smallest particle of a compound that has the chemical properties of the compound.

- In metallic bonding, the valence electrons move throughout the metal. A bond formed by the attraction between positive metal ions and the electrons in the metal is a metallic bond.

- Properties of metals include conductivity, ductility, and malleability.

Using Key Terms

1. Use each of the following terms in a separate sentence: *covalent bond* and *metallic bond*.

2. In your own words, write a definition for the term *molecule*.

Understanding Key Ideas

3. Between which of the following atoms is a covalent bond most likely to occur?
   a. calcium and lithium
   b. sodium and fluorine
   c. nitrogen and oxygen
   d. helium and argon

4. What happens to the electrons in covalent bonding?

5. How many dots does an electron-dot diagram of a sulfur atom have?

6. List three properties of metals that are a result of metallic bonds.

7. Describe how the valence electrons in a metal move.

8. Explain the difference between ductility and malleability. Give an example of when each property is useful.

Critical Thinking

9. **Identifying Relationships** How do the metallic bonds in a staple allow it to function properly?

10. **Applying Concepts** Draw an electron-dot diagram for ammonia (a nitrogen atom covalently bonded to three hydrogen atoms).

Interpreting Graphics

11. This electron-dot diagram is not complete. Which atom needs to form another bond? Explain.

$$H$$
$$H : \ddot{C} : H$$

Model-Making Lab

Covalent Marshmallows

A hydrogen atom has 1 electron in its outermost energy level, but 2 electrons are required to fill its outermost level. An oxygen atom has 6 electrons in its outermost level, but 8 electrons are required to fill its outermost level. To fill their outermost energy levels, two atoms of hydrogen and one atom of oxygen can share electrons, as shown below. Such a sharing of electrons to fill the outermost level of atoms is called *covalent bonding*. When hydrogen and oxygen bond in this manner, a molecule of water is formed. In this lab, you will build a three-dimensional model of water to better understand the covalent bonds formed in a water molecule.

OBJECTIVES

Build a three-dimensional model of a water molecule.

Draw an electron-dot diagram of a water molecule.

MATERIALS

- marshmallows (two of one color, one of another color)
- toothpicks

SAFETY

A Model of a Water Molecule

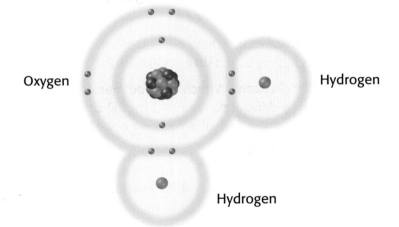

Oxygen   Hydrogen

Hydrogen

Procedure

1 Using the marshmallows and toothpicks, create a model of a water molecule. Use the diagram above for guidance in building your model.

2 Draw a sketch of your model. Be sure to label the hydrogen and oxygen atoms on your sketch.

3 Draw an electron-dot diagram of the water molecule.

Analyze the Results

1 **Classifying** What do the marshmallows represent? What do the toothpicks represent?

2 **Evaluating Models** Why are the marshmallows different colors?

3 **Analyzing Results** Compare your model with the diagram on the previous page. How might your model be improved to more accurately represent a water molecule?

Draw Conclusions

4 **Making Predictions** Hydrogen in nature can covalently bond to form hydrogen molecules, H$_2$. How could you use the marshmallows and toothpicks to model this bond?

5 **Applying Conclusions** Draw an electron-dot diagram of a hydrogen molecule.

6 **Drawing Conclusions** Which do you think would be more difficult to create—a model of an ionic bond or a model of a covalent bond? Explain your answer.

Applying Your Data

Create a model of a carbon dioxide molecule, which consists of two oxygen atoms and one carbon atom. The structure is similar to the structure of water, although the three atoms bond in a straight line instead of at angles. The bond between each oxygen atom and the carbon atom in a carbon dioxide molecule is a *double bond,* so use two connections. Do the double bonds in carbon dioxide appear stronger or weaker than the single bonds in water? Explain your answer.

Chapter Review

USING KEY TERMS

Complete each of the following sentences by choosing the correct term from the word bank.

crystal lattice
molecule
chemical bonding
valence electron
covalent bond

ionic bond
chemical bond
metallic bond
ion

1 An interaction that holds two atoms together is a(n) ___.

2 A charged particle that forms when an atom transfers electrons is a(n) ___.

3 A bond formed when atoms share electrons is a(n) ___.

4 Electrons free to move throughout a material are associated with a(n) ___.

5 An electron in the outermost energy level of an atom is a(n) ___.

6 Ionic compounds are bonded in a three-dimensional pattern called a(n) ___.

UNDERSTANDING KEY IDEAS

Multiple Choice

7 Which element has a full outermost energy level containing only two electrons?

a. fluorine, F
b. helium, He
c. hydrogen, H
d. oxygen, O

8 Which of the following describes what happens when an atom becomes an ion with a 2– charge?

a. The atom gains 2 protons.
b. The atom loses 2 protons.
c. The atom gains 2 electrons.
d. The atom loses 2 electrons.

9 The properties of ductility and malleability are associated with which type of bonds?

a. ionic
b. covalent
c. metallic
d. All of the above

10 What type of element tends to lose electrons when it forms bonds?

a. metal
b. metalloid
c. nonmetal
d. noble gas

11 Which pair of atoms can form an ionic bond?

a. sodium, Na, and potassium, K
b. potassium, K, and fluorine, F
c. fluorine, F, and chlorine, Cl
d. sodium, Na, and neon, Ne

Short Answer

12 List two properties of covalent compounds.

13 Explain why an iron ion is attracted to a sulfide ion but not to a zinc ion.

14 Compare the three types of bonds based on what happens to the valence electrons of the atoms.

Math Skills

15 For each atom below, write the number of electrons it must gain or lose to have 8 valence electrons. Then, calculate the charge of the ion that would form.

a. calcium, Ca

b. phosphorus, P

c. bromine, Br

d. sulfur, S

CRITICAL THINKING

16 Concept Mapping Use the following terms to create a concept map: *chemical bonds, ionic bonds, covalent bonds, metallic bonds, molecule,* and *ions.*

17 Identifying Relationships Predict the type of bond each of the following pairs of atoms would form:

a. zinc, Zn, and zinc, Zn

b. oxygen, O, and nitrogen, N

c. phosphorus, P, and oxygen, O

d. magnesium, Mg, and chlorine, Cl

18 Applying Concepts Draw electron-dot diagrams for each of the following atoms, and state how many bonds it will have to make to fill its outer energy level.

a. sulfur, S

b. nitrogen, N

c. neon, Ne

d. iodine, I

e. silicon, Si

19 Predicting Consequences Using your knowledge of valence electrons, explain the main reason so many different molecules are made from carbon atoms.

20 Making Inferences Does the substance being hit in the photo below contain ionic or metallic bonds? Explain your answer.

INTERPRETING GRAPHICS

Use the picture of a wooden pencil below to answer the questions that follow.

21 In which part of the pencil are metallic bonds found?

22 List three materials in the pencil that are composed of molecules that have covalent bonds.

23 Identify two differences between the properties of the material that has metallic bonds and the materials that have covalent bonds.

Standardized Test Preparation

Read each of the passages below. Then, answer the questions that follow each passage.

Passage 1 In 1987, pilots Richard Rutan and Jeana Yeager flew the *Voyager* aircraft around the world without refueling. The record-breaking trip lasted a little more than nine days. To carry enough fuel for the trip, the plane had to be as lightweight as possible. Using fewer bolts than the number of bolts usually used to attach parts would make the airplane lighter. But without bolts, what would hold the parts together? The designers decided to use glue!

They could not use regular glue. They used superglue. When superglue is applied, it combines with water from the air to form chemical bonds. So, the materials stick together as if they were one material. Superglue is so strong that the weight of a two-ton elephant cannot separate two metal plates glued together with just a few drops!

1. Who are Richard Rutan and Jeana Yeager?
   A the designers of the *Voyager* aircraft
   B the pilots of the *Voyager* aircraft
   C the inventors of superglue
   D chemists that study superglue

2. In the passage, what does *aircraft* mean?
   F an airplane
   G a helicopter
   H a hot-air balloon
   I an airplane that doesn't need fuel

3. The author probably wrote this passage to
   A encourage people to fly airplanes.
   B tell airplane designers how to make airplanes that need less fuel.
   C explain why superglue was a good substitute for bolts in the *Voyager* aircraft.
   D explain why people should buy superglue instead of regular glue.

Passage 2 One of the first contact lenses was developed by a Hungarian physician named Joseph Dallos in 1929. He came up with a way to make a mold of the human eye. He used these molds to make a glass lens that followed the shape of the eye. Unfortunately, the glass lenses he made were not very comfortable.

Many years later, in an effort to solve the comfort problem of contact lenses, Czechoslovakian chemists Otto Wichterle and Drahoslav Lim invented a water-absorbing plastic gel. The lenses made from this gel were soft and <u>pliable</u>, and they allowed air to pass through the lens to the eye. These characteristics made the lenses more comfortable to wear than glass lenses.

1. In the passage, what does *pliable* mean?
   A able to be bent
   B very stiff
   C spongelike
   D similar to glass

2. Which of the following statements is a fact from the passage?
   F The first contact lenses were plastic.
   G Two Hungarian physicians developed a way of making molds of human eyes.
   H Glass contact lenses were not comfortable.
   I Joseph Dallos was a chemist.

3. What is a possible reason that glass contact lenses were not comfortable?
   A Glass contact lenses allow air to pass through the lens to the eye.
   B Glass contact lenses did not follow the shape of the human eye.
   C Glass contact lenses absorb water.
   D Glass contact lenses are very hard.

The graph below shows chemicals used by the science department at Harding Middle School. Use the graph below to answer the questions that follow.

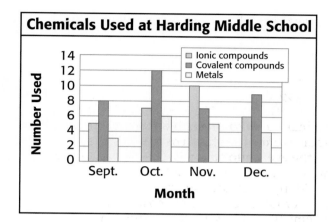

Chemicals Used at Harding Middle School

1. In which month were the most ionic compounds used?

    A September

    B October

    C November

    D December

2. Which type of chemical was used the least number of times?

    F ionic compounds

    G covalent compounds

    H metals

    I both ionic compounds and metals

3. How many covalent compounds were used during all four months?

    A 16

    B 25

    C 28

    D 36

4. In which month were the most compounds used?

    F September

    G October

    H November

    I December

Read each question below, and choose the best answer.

1. Protons have a charge of 1+ and electrons have a charge of 1−. A magnesium ion has 12 protons and 10 electrons. What is the charge of the ion?

    A 2+

    B 2−

    C 10−

    D 12+

2. Fructose is the chemical name for a sugar found in some fruits. The chemical formula for fructose is $C_6H_{12}O_6$. The C is the symbol for carbon, the O is the symbol for oxygen, and the H is the symbol for hydrogen. The numbers after each letter tell you how many atoms of each element are in one molecule of fructose. What percentage of the atoms in fructose are carbon atoms?

    F 0.25%

    G 6%

    H 25%

    I 33%

3. The density of an object is found by dividing its mass by its volume. Katie has a piece of silver metal that has a mass of 5.4 g and a volume of 2.0 cm³. What is the density of Katie's metal?

    A 0.37 cm³/g

    B 2.7 g/cm³

    C 7.4 g/cm³

    D 10.8 g•cm³

4. Ms. Mazza is a chemistry teacher. During class, her students ask her four to six questions every 10 min. What is a reasonable estimate of the number of questions asked during a 45 min class period?

    F 12 questions

    G 15 questions

    H 23 questions

    I 40 questions

Standardized Test Preparation

Science in Action

Science, Technology, and Society

Superglue Bandages and Stitches

If you aren't careful when using superglue, you may accidentally learn that superglue quickly bonds skin together! This property of superglue led to the development of new kinds of superglue that can be used as alternatives for bandages and stitches. Using superglue to close wounds has several advantages over using bandages and stitches. For example, superglue bandages can cover cuts on parts of the body that are difficult to cover with regular bandages. And superglue stitches are less painful than regular stitches. Finally, wounds closed with superglue are easier to care for than wounds covered by bandages or closed with stitches.

Math ACTIVITY

A wound can be closed 3 times faster with glue than it can be with stitches. If it takes a doctor 27 min to close a wound by using stitches, how long would it take to close the same wound by using glue?

Weird Science

How Geckos Stick to Walls

Geckos are known for their ability to climb up smooth surfaces. Recently, scientists found the secret to the gecko's sticky talent. Geckos have millions of microscopic hairs on the bottom of their feet. Each hair splits into as many as 1,000 tinier hairs called *hairlets*. At the end of each hairlet is a small pad. As the gecko walks, each pad forms a van der Waals force with the surface on which the gecko is walking. A van der Waals force is an attraction similar to an ionic bond, but the van der Waals force is much weaker than an ionic bond and lasts for only an instant. But because there are so many pads on a gecko's foot, the van der Waals forces are strong enough to keep the gecko from falling.

Language Arts ACTIVITY

WRITING SKILL Imagine that you could stick to walls as well as a gecko can. Write a five-paragraph short story describing what you would do with your wall-climbing ability.

Roberta Jordan

Analytical Chemist Have you ever looked at something and wondered what chemicals it contained? That's what analytical chemists do for a living. They use tests to find the chemical makeup of a sample. Roberta Jordan is an analytical chemist at the Idaho National Engineering and Environmental Laboratory in Idaho Falls, Idaho.

Jordan's work focuses on the study of radioactive waste generated by nuclear power plants and nuclear-powered submarines. Jordan works with engineers to develop safe ways to store the radioactive waste. She tells the engineers which chemicals need to be studied and which techniques to use to study those chemicals.

Jordan enjoys her job because she is always learning new techniques. "One of the things necessary to be a good chemist is you have to be creative. You have to be able to think above and beyond the normal ways of doing things to come up with new ideas, new experiments," she explains. Jordan believes that a person interested in a career in chemistry has many opportunities. "There are a lot of things out there that need to be discovered," says Jordan.

Social Studies ACTIVITY

Many elements in the periodic table were discovered by analytical chemists. Pick an element from the periodic table, and research its history. Make a poster about the discovery of that element.

go.hrw.com

To learn more about these Science in Action topics, visit go.hrw.com and type in the keyword **HP5BNDF.**

Current Science

Check out Current Science® articles related to this chapter by visiting go.hrw.com. Just type in the keyword HP5CS13.

14

Chemical Reactions

SECTION ① Forming New
Substances 388

SECTION ② Chemical Formulas
and Equations 392

SECTION ③ Types of Chemical
Reactions 398

SECTION ④ Energy and Rates of
Chemical Reactions . . . 402

Chapter Lab 408
Chapter Review 410
Standardized Test Preparation 412
Science in Action 414

About the PHOTO

Dazzling fireworks and the Statue of Liberty are great examples of chemical reactions. Chemical reactions cause fireworks to soar, explode, and light up the sky. And the Statue of Liberty has its distinctive green color because of the reaction between the statue's copper and chemicals in the air.

PRE-READING ACTIVITY

FOLDNOTES **Four-Corner Fold**
Before you read the chapter, create the FoldNote entitled "Four-Corner Fold" described in the **Study Skills** section of the Appendix. Label the flaps of the four-corner fold with "Chemical formulas," "Chemical equations," "Types of chemical reactions," and "Rates of chemical reactions." Write what you know about each topic under the appropriate flap. As you read the chapter, add other information that you learn.

START-UP ACTIVITY

A Model Formula

Chemicals react in very precise ways. In this activity, you will model a chemical reaction and will predict how chemicals react.

Procedure

1. You will receive **several marshmallow models.** The models are marshmallows attached by **toothpicks.** Each of these models is a Model A.

2. Your teacher will show you an example of Model B and Model C. Take apart one or more Model As to make copies of Model B and Model C.

3. If you have marshmallows left over, use them to make more Model Bs and Model Cs. If you need more parts to complete a Model B or Model C, take apart another Model A.

4. Repeat step 3 until you have no parts left over.

Analysis

1. How many Model As did you use to make copies of Model B and Model C?

2. How many Model Bs did you make? How many Model Cs did you make?

3. Suppose you needed to make six Model Bs. How many Model As would you need? How many Model Cs could you make with the leftover marshmallows?

Forming New Substances

Each fall, a beautiful change takes place when leaves turn colors. You see bright oranges and yellows that had been hidden by green all summer. What causes this change?

To answer this question, you need to know what causes leaves to be green. Leaves are green because they contain a green substance, or *pigment*. This pigment is called *chlorophyll* (KLAWR uh FIL). During the spring and summer, the leaves have a large amount of chlorophyll in them. But in the fall, when temperatures drop and there are fewer hours of sunlight, chlorophyll breaks down to form new substances that have no color. The green chlorophyll is no longer present to hide the other pigments. You can now see the orange and yellow colors that were present all along.

Chemical Reactions

A chemical change takes place when chlorophyll breaks down into new substances. This change is an example of a chemical reaction. A **chemical reaction** is a process in which one or more substances change to make one or more new substances. The chemical and physical properties of the new substances differ from those of the original substances. Some results of chemical reactions are shown in **Figure 1.**

READING WARM-UP

Objectives

● Describe how chemical reactions produce new substances that have different chemical and physical properties.

● Identify four signs that indicate that a chemical reaction might be taking place.

● Explain what happens to chemical bonds during a chemical reaction.

Terms to Learn

chemical reaction
precipitate

READING STRATEGY

Reading Organizer As you read this section, create an outline of the section. Use the headings from the section in your outline.

chemical reaction the process by which one or more substances change to produce one or more different substances

Figure 1 Results of Chemical Reactions

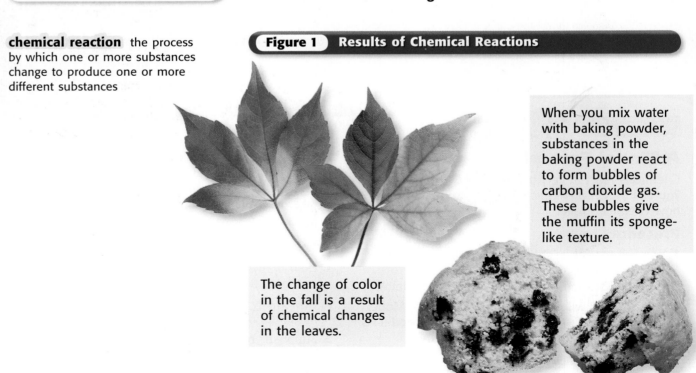

The change of color in the fall is a result of chemical changes in the leaves.

When you mix water with baking powder, substances in the baking powder react to form bubbles of carbon dioxide gas. These bubbles give the muffin its sponge-like texture.

Signs of Chemical Reactions

How can you tell when a chemical reaction is taking place? **Figure 2** shows some signs that tell you that a reaction may be taking place. In some chemical reactions, gas bubbles form. Other reactions form solid precipitates (pree SIP uh TAYTS). A **precipitate** is a solid substance that is formed in a solution. During other chemical reactions, energy is given off. This energy may be in the form of light, thermal energy, or electricity. Reactions often have more than one of these signs. And the more of these signs that you see, the more likely that a chemical reaction is taking place.

precipitate a solid that is produced as a result of a chemical reaction in solution

✓ Reading Check What is a precipitate? (*See the Appendix for answers to Reading Checks.*)

Figure 2 Some Signs of Chemical Reactions

Gas Formation
The chemical reaction in the beaker has formed a brown gas, nitrogen dioxide. This gas is formed when a strip of copper is placed into nitric acid.

Solid Formation
Here you see potassium chromate solution being added to a silver nitrate solution. The dark red solid is a precipitate of silver chromate.

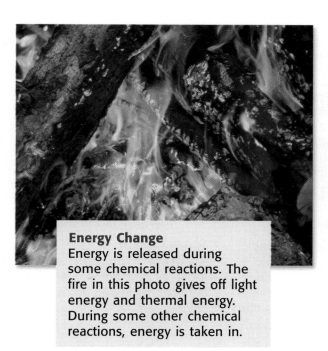

Energy Change
Energy is released during some chemical reactions. The fire in this photo gives off light energy and thermal energy. During some other chemical reactions, energy is taken in.

Color Change
Don't spill chlorine bleach on your jeans! The bleach reacts with the blue dye on the fabric and causes the color of the material to change.

A Change of Properties

Even though the signs we look for to see if a reaction is taking place are good signals of chemical reactions, they do not guarantee that a reaction is happening. For example, gas can be given off when a liquid boils. But this example is a physical change, not a chemical reaction.

So, how can you be sure that a chemical reaction is occurring? The most important sign is the formation of new substances that have different properties. Look at **Figure 3.** The starting materials in this reaction are sugar and sulfuric acid. Several things tell you that a chemical reaction is taking place. Bubbles form, a gas is given off, and the beaker becomes very hot. But most important, new substances form. And the properties of these substances are very different from those of the starting substances.

Figure 3 *The top photo shows the starting substances: table sugar and sulfuric acid, a clear liquid. The substances formed in this chemical reaction are very different from the starting substances.*

Bonds: Holding Molecules Together

A *chemical bond* is a force that holds two atoms together in a molecule. For a chemical reaction to take place, the original bonds must break and new bonds must form.

Breaking and Making Bonds

How do new substances form in a chemical reaction? First, chemical bonds in the starting substances must break. Molecules are always moving. If the molecules bump into each other with enough energy, the chemical bonds in the molecules break. The atoms then rearrange, and new bonds form to make the new substances. **Figure 4** shows how bonds break and form in the reaction between hydrogen and chlorine.

✓ **Reading Check** What happens to the bonds of substances during a chemical reaction?

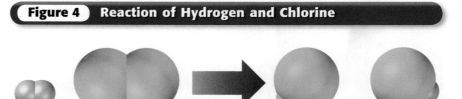

Figure 4   Reaction of Hydrogen and Chlorine

hydrogen   +   chlorine   hydrogen chloride

Breaking Bonds Hydrogen and chlorine are diatomic. Diatomic molecules are two atoms bonded together. The bonds joining these atoms must first break before the atoms can react with each other.

Making Bonds A new substance, hydrogen chloride, forms as new bonds are made between hydrogen atoms and chlorine atoms.

New Bonds, New Substances

What happens when hydrogen and chlorine are combined? A chlorine gas molecule is a diatomic (DIE uh TAHM ik) molecule. That is, a chlorine molecule is made of two atoms of chlorine. Chlorine gas has a greenish yellow color. Hydrogen gas is also a diatomic molecule. Hydrogen gas is a flammable, colorless gas. When chlorine gas and hydrogen gas react, the bond between the hydrogen atoms breaks. And the bond between the chlorine atoms also breaks. A new bond forms between each hydrogen and chlorine atom. A new substance, hydrogen chloride, is formed. Hydrogen chloride is a nonflammable, colorless gas. Its properties differ from the properties of both of the starting substances.

Let's look at another example. Sodium is a metal that reacts violently in water. Chlorine gas is poisonous. When chlorine gas and sodium react, the result is a familiar compound—table salt. Sodium chloride, or table salt, is a harmless substance that almost everyone uses. The salt's properties are very different from sodium's or chlorine's. Salt is a new substance.

Quick Lab

Reaction Ready

1. Place a **piece of chalk** in a **plastic cup.**
2. Add **5 mL of vinegar** to the cup. Record your observations.
3. What evidence of a chemical reaction do you see?
4. What type of new substance was formed?

SECTION Review

Summary

- A chemical reaction is a process by which substances change to produce new substances with new chemical and physical properties.

- Signs that indicate a chemical reaction has taken place are a color change, formation of a gas or a solid, and release of energy.

- During a reaction, bonds are broken, atoms are rearranged, and new bonds are formed.

Using Key Terms

1. Use the following terms in the same sentence: *chemical reaction* and *precipitate*.

Understanding Key Ideas

2. Most chemical reactions
   a. have starting substances that collide with each other.
   b. do not break bonds.
   c. do not rearrange atoms.
   d. cannot be seen.

3. If the chemical properties of a substance have not changed, has a chemical reaction occurred?

Critical Thinking

4. **Analyzing Processes** Steam is escaping from a teapot. Is this a chemical reaction? Explain.

5. **Applying Concepts** Explain why charcoal burning in the grill is a chemical change.

Interpreting Graphics

Use the photo below to answer the questions that follow.

6. What evidence of a chemical reaction is shown in the photo?

7. What is happening to the bonds of the starting substances?

SCiLINKS

NSTA
Developed and maintained by the
National Science Teachers Association

For a variety of links related to this chapter, go to www.scilinks.org

Topic: Chemical Reactions
SciLinks code: HSM0274

Chemical Formulas and Equations

How many words can you make using the 26 letters of the alphabet? Many thousands? Now, think of how many sentences you can make with all of those words.

Letters are used to form words. In the same way, chemical symbols are put together to make chemical formulas that describe substances. Chemical formulas can be placed together to describe a chemical reaction, just like words can be put together to make a sentence.

Chemical Formulas

All substances are formed from about 100 elements. Each element has its own chemical symbol. A **chemical formula** is a shorthand way to use chemical symbols and numbers to represent a substance. A chemical formula shows how many atoms of each kind are present in a molecule.

As shown in **Figure 1,** the chemical formula for water is H_2O. This formula tells you that one water molecule is made of two atoms of hydrogen and one atom of oxygen. The small 2 in the formula is a subscript. A *subscript* is a number written below and to the right of a chemical symbol in a formula. Sometimes, a symbol, such as O for oxygen in water's formula, has no subscript. If there is no subscript, only one atom of that element is present. Look at **Figure 1** for more examples of chemical formulas.

Figure 1 **Chemical Formulas of Different Substances**

Water	**Oxygen**	**Glucose**
H_2O	O_2	$C_6H_{12}O_6$
Water molecules are made up of 3 atoms—2 atoms of hydrogen bonded to 1 atom of oxygen.	**Oxygen** is a diatomic molecule. Each molecule has 2 atoms of oxygen bonded together.	**Glucose** molecules have 6 atoms of carbon, 12 atoms of hydrogen, and 6 atoms of oxygen.

Carbon dioxide

CO_2

The *absence of a prefix* indicates one carbon atom.

The prefix *di-* indicates two oxygen atoms.

Dinitrogen monoxide

N_2O

The prefix *di-* indicates two nitrogen atoms.

The prefix *mono-* indicates one oxygen atom.

Figure 2 *The formulas of these covalent compounds can be written by using the prefixes in the names of the compounds.*

Writing Formulas for Covalent Compounds

If you know the name of the covalent compound, you can often write the chemical formula for that compound. Covalent compounds are usually composed of two nonmetals. The names of many covalent compounds use prefixes. Each prefix represents a number, as shown in **Table 1.** The prefixes tell you how many atoms of each element are in a formula. **Figure 2** shows you how to write a chemical formula from the name of a covalent compound.

Writing Formulas for Ionic Compounds

If the name of a compound contains the name of a metal and the name of a nonmetal, the compound is ionic. To write the formula for an ionic compound, make sure the compound's charge is 0. In other words, the formula must have subscripts that cause the charges of the ions to cancel out. **Figure 3** shows you how to write a chemical formula from the name of an ionic compound.

✓ **Reading Check** What kinds of elements make up an ionic compound? (*See the Appendix for answers to Reading Checks.*)

Table 1 Prefixes Used in Chemical Names			
mono-	1	hexa-	6
di-	2	hepta-	7
tri-	3	octa-	8
tetra-	4	nona-	9
penta-	5	deca-	10

Sodium chloride

NaCl

A sodium ion has a **1+ charge.**

A chloride ion has a **1− charge.**

One sodium ion and one chloride ion have an overall **charge of (1+) + (1−) = 0**

Magnesium chloride

$MgCl_2$

A magnesium ion has a **2+ charge.**

A chloride ion has a **1− charge.**

One magnesium ion and two chloride ions have an overall **charge of (2+) + 2(1−) = 0.**

Figure 3 *The formula of an ionic compound is written by using enough of each ion so that the overall charge is 0.*

Figure 4 *Like chemical symbols, the symbols on this musical score are understood around the world!*

chemical equation a representation of a chemical reaction that uses symbols to show the relationship between the reactants and the products

reactant a substance or molecule that participates in a chemical reaction

product the substance that forms in a chemical reaction

Chemical Equations

Think about a piece of music, such as the one in **Figure 4.** Someone writing music must tell the musician what notes to play, how long to play each note, and how each note should be played. Words aren't used to describe the musical piece. Instead, musical symbols are used. The symbols can be understood by anyone who can read music.

Describing Reactions by Using Equations

In the same way that composers use musical symbols, chemists around the world use chemical symbols and chemical formulas. Instead of changing words and sentences into other languages to describe reactions, chemists use chemical equations. A **chemical equation** uses chemical symbols and formulas as a shortcut to describe a chemical reaction. A chemical equation is short and is understood by anyone who understands chemical formulas.

From Reactants to Products

When carbon burns, it reacts with oxygen to form carbon dioxide. **Figure 5** shows how a chemist would use an equation to describe this reaction. The starting materials in a chemical reaction are **reactants** (ree AK tuhnts). The substances formed from a reaction are **products.** In this example, carbon and oxygen are reactants. Carbon dioxide is the product.

✓ **Reading Check** What is the difference between reactants and products in a chemical reaction?

Figure 5 **The Parts of a Chemical Equation**

Charcoal is used to cook food on a barbecue grill. When carbon in charcoal reacts with oxygen in the air, the primary product is carbon dioxide, as shown by the chemical equation.

The formulas of the **reactants** are written before the arrow.

The formulas of the **products** are written after the arrow.

$$C + O_2 \longrightarrow CO_2$$

A **plus sign** separates the formulas of two or more reactants or products from one another.

The **arrow,** also called the *yields sign,* separates the formulas of the reactants from the formulas of the products.

Figure 6 Examples of Similar Symbols and Formulas

CO_2

The chemical formula for the compound **carbon dioxide** is CO_2. Carbon dioxide is a colorless, odorless gas that you exhale.

CO

The chemical formula for the compound **carbon monoxide** is CO. Carbon monoxide is a colorless, odorless, and poisonous gas.

Co

The chemical symbol for the element **cobalt** is Co. Cobalt is a hard, bluish gray metal.

The Importance of Accuracy

The symbol or formula for each substance in the equation must be written correctly. For a compound, use the correct chemical formula. For an element, use the proper chemical symbol. An equation that has the wrong chemical symbol or formula will not correctly describe the reaction. In fact, even a simple mistake can make a huge difference. **Figure 6** shows how formulas and symbols can be mistaken.

The Reason Equations Must Be Balanced

Atoms are never lost or gained in a chemical reaction. They are just rearranged. Every atom in the reactants becomes part of the products. When writing a chemical equation, make sure the number of atoms of each element in the reactants equals the number of atoms of those elements in the products. This is called balancing the equation.

Balancing equations comes from the work of a French chemist, Antoine Lavoisier (lah vwah ZYAY). In the 1700s, Lavoisier found that the total mass of the reactants was always the same as the total mass of the products. Lavoisier's work led to the **law of conservation of mass.** This law states that mass is neither created nor destroyed in ordinary chemical and physical changes. This law means that a chemical equation must show the same numbers and kinds of atoms on both sides of the arrow.

Counting Atoms

Some chemical formulas contain parentheses. When counting atoms, multiply everything inside the parentheses by the subscript. For example, $Ca(NO_3)_2$ has one calcium atom, two (2 × 1) nitrogen atoms, and six (2 × 3) oxygen atoms. Find the number of atoms of each element in the formulas $Mg(OH)_2$ and $Al_2(SO_4)_3$.

law of conservation of mass
the law that states that mass cannot be created or destroyed in ordinary chemical and physical changes

How to Balance an Equation

To balance an equation, you must use coefficients (KOH uh FISH uhnts). A *coefficient* is a number that is placed in front of a chemical symbol or formula. For example, 2CO represents two carbon monoxide molecules. The number *2* is the coefficient.

For an equation to be balanced, all atoms must be counted. So, you must multiply the subscript of each element in a formula by the formula's coefficient. For example, $2H_2O$ contains a total of four hydrogen atoms and two oxygen atoms. Only coefficients—not subscripts—are changed when balancing equations. Changing the subscripts in the formula of a compound would change the compound. **Figure 7** shows you how to use coefficients to balance an equation.

✓ Reading Check If you see $4O_2$ in an equation, what is the coefficient?

CONNECTION TO Language Arts

WRITING SKILL **Diatomic Molecules** Seven of the chemical elements exist as diatomic molecules. Do research to find out which seven elements these are. Write a short report that describes each diatomic molecule. Be sure to include the formula for each molecule.

Figure 7 Balancing a Chemical Equation

Follow these steps to write a balanced equation for $H_2 + O_2 \longrightarrow H_2O$.

① Count the atoms of each element in the reactants and in the products. You can see that there are fewer oxygen atoms in the product than in the reactants.

Reactants	Products
$H_2 + O_2$	H_2O

H = 2   O = 2   H = 2   O = 1

② To balance the oxygen atoms, place the coefficient 2 in front of H_2O. Doing so gives you two oxygen atoms in both the reactants and the products. But now there are too few hydrogen atoms in the reactants.

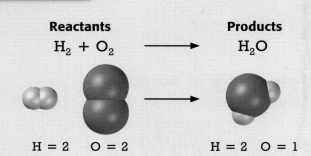

Reactants	Products
$H_2 + O_2$	$2H_2O$

H = 2   O = 2   H = 4   O = 2

③ To balance the hydrogen atoms, place the coefficient 2 in front of H_2. But to be sure that your answer is correct, always double-check your work!

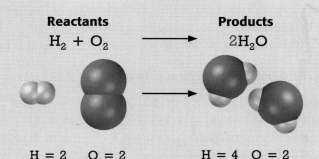

Reactants	Products
$2H_2 + O_2$	$2H_2O$

H = 4   O = 2   H = 4   O = 2

Quick Lab

Conservation of Mass

1. Place **5 g of baking soda** into a **sealable plastic bag.**

2. Place **5 mL of vinegar** into a **plastic film canister.** Put the lid on the canister.

3. Place the canister into the bag. Squeeze the air out of the bag. Seal the bag tightly.

4. Use a **balance** to measure the mass of the bag and its contents. Record the mass.

5. Keeping the bag closed, open the canister in the bag. Mix the vinegar with the baking soda. Record your observations.

6. When the reaction has stopped, measure the mass of the bag and its contents. Record the mass.

7. Compare the mass of the materials before the reaction and the mass of the materials after the reaction. Explain your observations.

SECTION Review

Summary

- A chemical formula uses symbols and subscripts to describe the makeup of a compound.

- Chemical formulas can often be written from the names of covalent and ionic compounds.

- A chemical equation uses chemical formulas, chemical symbols, and coefficients to describe a reaction.

- Balancing an equation requires that the same numbers and kinds of atoms be on each side of the equation.

- A balanced equation illustrates the law of conservation of mass: mass is neither created nor destroyed during ordinary physical and chemical changes.

Using Key Terms

The statements below are false. For each statement, replace the underlined word to make a true statement.

1. A chemical <u>formula</u> describes a chemical reaction.

2. The substances formed from a chemical reaction are <u>reactants</u>.

Understanding Key Ideas

3. The correct chemical formula for carbon tetrachloride is
   a. CCl_3.   c. CCl.
   b. C_3Cl.   d. CCl_4.

4. Calcium oxide is used to make soil less acidic. Its formula is
   a. Ca_2O_2.   c. CaO_2.
   b. CaO.   d. Ca_2O.

5. Balance the following equations by adding the correct coefficients.
   a. $Na + Cl_2 \longrightarrow NaCl$
   b. $Mg + N_2 \longrightarrow Mg_3N_2$

6. How does a balanced chemical equation illustrate that mass is never lost or gained in a chemical reaction?

7. What is the difference between a subscript and a coefficient?

Math Skills

8. Calculate the number of atoms of each element represented in each of the following: $2Na_3PO_4$, $4Al_2(SO_4)_3$, and $6PCl_5$.

Critical Thinking

9. **Analyzing Methods** Describe how to write a formula for a covalent compound. Give an example of a covalent compound.

10. **Applying Concepts** Explain why the subscript in a formula of a chemical compound cannot be changed when balancing an equation.

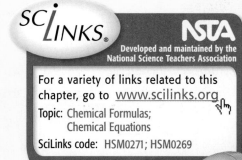

SCILINKS®

NSTA
Developed and maintained by the National Science Teachers Association

For a variety of links related to this chapter, go to www.scilinks.org
Topic: Chemical Formulas; Chemical Equations
SciLinks code: HSM0271; HSM0269

Types of Chemical Reactions

There are thousands of known chemical reactions. Can you imagine having to memorize even 50 of them?

Remembering all of them would be impossible! But fortunately, there is help. In the same way that the elements are divided into groups based on their properties, reactions can be classified based on what occurs during the reaction.

Most reactions can be placed into one of four categories: synthesis (SIN thuh sis), decomposition, single-displacement, and double-displacement. Each type of reaction has a pattern that shows how reactants become products. One way to remember what happens in each type of reaction is to imagine people at a dance. As you learn about each type of reaction, study the models of students at a dance. The models will help you recognize each type of reaction.

Synthesis Reactions

A **synthesis reaction** is a reaction in which two or more substances combine to form one new compound. For example, a synthesis reaction takes place when sodium reacts with chlorine. This synthesis reaction produces sodium chloride, which you know as table salt. A synthesis reaction would be modeled by two people pairing up to form a dancing couple, as shown in **Figure 1.**

✓ **Reading Check** What is a synthesis reaction? (*See the Appendix for answers to Reading Checks.*)

synthesis reaction a reaction in which two or more substances combine to form a new compound

$$2Na + Cl_2 \longrightarrow 2NaCl$$

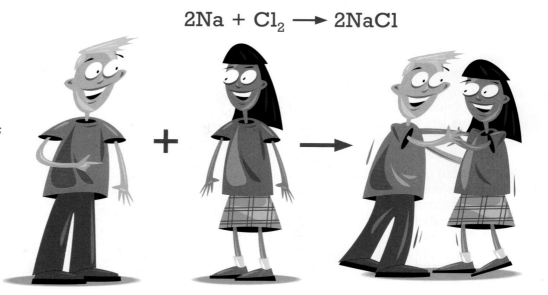

Figure 1 *Sodium reacts with chlorine to form sodium chloride in this synthesis reaction.*

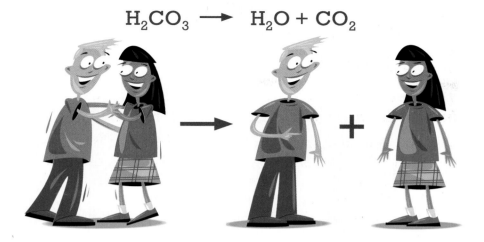

$$H_2CO_3 \longrightarrow H_2O + CO_2$$

Figure 2 *In this decomposition reaction, carbonic acid, H_2CO_3, decomposes to form water and carbon dioxide.*

Decomposition Reactions

A **decomposition reaction** is a reaction in which a single compound breaks down to form two or more simpler substances. Decomposition is the reverse of synthesis. The dance model for a decomposition reaction would be a couple that finishes a dance and separates, as shown in **Figure 2.**

✓ Reading Check How is a decomposition reaction different from a synthesis reaction?

Single-Displacement Reactions

Sometimes, an element replaces another element that is a part of a compound. This type of reaction is called a **single-displacement reaction.** The products of single-displacement reactions are a new compound and a different element. The dance model for a single-displacement reaction would show a person cutting in on a couple who is dancing. A new couple is formed. And a different person is left alone, as shown in **Figure 3.**

decomposition reaction a reaction in which a single compound breaks down to form two or more simpler substances

single-displacement reaction a reaction in which one element or radical takes the place of another element or radical in a compound

Figure 3 *Zinc replaces the hydrogen in hydrochloric acid to form zinc chloride and hydrogen gas in this single-displacement reaction.*

$$Zn + 2HCl \longrightarrow ZnCl_2 + H_2$$

Figure 4 Reactivity of Elements

Cu + 2AgNO₃ → 2Ag + Cu(NO₃)₂
Copper is more reactive than silver.

Ag + Cu(NO₃)₂ → no reaction
Silver is less reactive than copper.

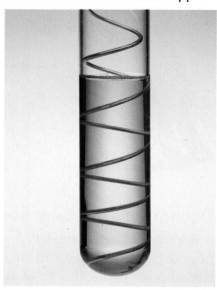

For another activity related to this chapter, go to **go.hrw.com** and type in the keyword **HP5REAW.**

Reactivity of Elements

In a single-displacement reaction, a more reactive element can displace a less reactive element in a compound. For example, **Figure 4** shows that copper is more reactive than silver. Copper (Cu) can replace the silver (Ag) ion in the compound silver nitrate. But the opposite reaction does not occur, because silver is less reactive than copper.

The elements in Group 1 of the periodic table are the most reactive metals. Very few nonmetals are involved in single-displacement reactions. In fact, only Group 17 nonmetals participate in single-displacement reactions.

✓ Reading Check Why can one element sometimes replace another element in a single-displacement reaction?

Identifying Reactions

1. Study each of the following equations:

$4Na + O_2 \rightarrow 2Na_2O$

$2Ag_3N \rightarrow 6Ag + N_2$

$P_4 + 5O_2 \rightarrow 2P_2O_5$

$Zn + 2HCl \rightarrow ZnCl_2 + H_2$

2. Build models of each of these reactions using **colored clay.** Choose a different color of clay to represent each kind of atom.

3. Identify each type of reaction as a synthesis, decomposition, or single-displacement reaction.

Double-Displacement Reactions

A **double-displacement reaction** is a reaction in which ions from two compounds exchange places. One of the products of this type of reaction is often a gas or a precipitate. A dance model of a double-displacement reaction would be two couples dancing and then trading partners, as shown in **Figure 5**.

double-displacement reaction
a reaction in which a gas, a solid precipitate, or a molecular compound forms from the exchange of ions between two compounds

$$NaCl + AgF \longrightarrow NaF + AgCl$$

Figure 5 *A double-displacement reaction occurs when sodium chloride reacts with silver fluoride to form sodium fluoride and silver chloride (a precipitate).*

SECTION Review

Summary

- A synthesis reaction is a reaction in which two or more substances combine to form a compound.

- A decomposition reaction is a reaction in which a compound breaks down to form two or more simpler substances.

- A single-displacement reaction is a reaction in which an element takes the place of another element that is part of a compound.

- A double-displacement reaction is a reaction in which ions in two compounds exchange places.

Using Key Terms

1. In your own words, write a definition for each of the following terms: *synthesis reaction* and *decomposition reaction*.

Understanding Key Ideas

2. What type of reaction does the following equation represent?

$$FeS + 2HCl \longrightarrow FeCl_2 + H_2S$$

   a. synthesis reaction
   b. double-displacement reaction
   c. single-displacement reaction
   d. decomposition reaction

3. Describe the difference between single- and double-displacement reactions.

Math Skills

4. Write the balanced equation in which potassium iodide, KI, reacts with chlorine to form potassium chloride, KCl, and iodine.

Critical Thinking

5. **Analyzing Processes** The first reaction below is a single-displacement reaction that could occur in a laboratory. Explain why the second single-displacement reaction could not occur.

$$CuCl_2 + Fe \longrightarrow FeCl_2 + Cu$$
$$CaS + Al \longrightarrow \text{no reaction}$$

6. **Making Inferences** When two white compounds are mixed in a solution, a yellow solid forms. What kind of reaction has taken place? Explain your answer.

SCiLINKS®

NSTA
Developed and maintained by the National Science Teachers Association

For a variety of links related to this chapter, go to www.scilinks.org

Topic: Reaction Types
SciLinks code: HSM1272

Energy and Rates of Chemical Reactions

What is the difference between eating a meal and running a mile? You could say that a meal gives you energy, while running "uses up" energy.

Chemical reactions can be described in the same way. Some reactions release energy, and other reactions absorb energy.

Reactions and Energy

Chemical energy is part of all chemical reactions. Energy is needed to break chemical bonds in the reactants. As new bonds form in the products, energy is released. By comparing the chemical energy of the reactants with the chemical energy of the products, you can decide if energy is released or absorbed in the overall reaction.

Exothermic Reactions

A chemical reaction in which energy is released is called an **exothermic reaction.** *Exo* means "go out" or "exit." *Thermic* means "heat" or "energy." Exothermic reactions can give off energy in several forms, as shown in **Figure 1.** The energy released in an exothermic reaction is often written as a product in a chemical equation, as in this equation:

$$2Na + Cl_2 \longrightarrow 2NaCl + energy$$

Figure 1 **Types of Energy Released in Exothermic Reactions**

Light energy is released in the exothermic reaction that is taking place in these light sticks.

Electrical energy is released in the exothermic reaction that will take place in this battery.

Light and thermal energy are released in the exothermic reaction taking place in this campfire.

Endothermic Reactions

A chemical reaction in which energy is taken in is called an **endothermic reaction.** *Endo* means "go in." The energy that is taken in during an endothermic reaction is often written as a reactant in a chemical equation. Energy as a reactant is shown in the following equation:

$$2H_2O + energy \longrightarrow 2H_2 + O_2$$

An example of an endothermic process is photosynthesis. In photosynthesis, plants use light energy from the sun to produce glucose. Glucose is a simple sugar that is used for nutrition. The equation that describes photosynthesis is the following:

$$6CO_2 + 6H_2O + energy \longrightarrow C_6H_{12}O_6 + 6O_2$$

Reading Check What is an endothermic reaction? (*See the Appendix for answers to Reading Checks.*)

exothermic reaction a chemical reaction in which heat is released to the surroundings

endothermic reaction a chemical reaction that requires heat

law of conservation of energy the law that states that energy cannot be created or destroyed but can be changed from one form to another

The Law of Conservation of Energy

Neither mass nor energy can be created or destroyed in chemical reactions. The **law of conservation of energy** states that energy cannot be created or destroyed. However, energy can change forms. And energy can be transferred from one object to another in the same way that a baton is transferred from one runner to another runner, as shown in **Figure 2.**

The energy released in exothermic reactions was first stored in the chemical bonds in the reactants. And the energy taken in during endothermic reactions is stored in the products. If you could measure all the energy in a reaction, you would find that the total amount of energy (of all types) is the same before and after the reaction.

Figure 2 *Energy can be transferred from one object to another object in the same way that a baton is transferred from one runner to another runner in a relay race.*

Endo Alert

1. Fill a **plastic cup** half full with **calcium chloride solution.**
2. Measure the temperature of the solution by using a **thermometer.**
3. Carefully add **1 tsp of baking soda.**
4. Record your observations.
5. When the reaction has stopped, record the temperature of the solution.
6. What evidence that an endothermic reaction took place did you observe?

Figure 3 *Chemical reactions need energy to get started in the same way that a bowling ball needs a push to get rolling.*

Rates of Reactions

A reaction takes place only if the particles of reactants collide. But there must be enough energy to break the bonds that hold particles together in a molecule. The speed at which new particles form is called the *rate of a reaction*.

Activation Energy

activation energy the minimum amount of energy required to start a chemical reaction

Before the bowling ball in **Figure 3** can roll down the alley, the bowler must first put in some energy to start the ball rolling. A chemical reaction must also get a boost of energy before the reaction can start. This boost of energy is called activation energy. **Activation energy** is the smallest amount of energy that molecules need to react.

Another example of activation energy is striking a match. Before a match can be used to light a campfire, the match has to be lit! A strike-anywhere match has all the reactants it needs to burn. The chemicals on a match react and burn. But, the chemicals will not light by themselves. You must strike the match against a surface. The heat produced by this friction provides the activation energy needed to start the reaction.

✓ **Reading Check** What is activation energy?

Sources of Activation Energy

Friction is one source of activation energy. In the match example, friction provides the energy needed to break the bonds in the reactants and allow new bonds to form. An electric spark in a car's engine is another source of activation energy. This spark begins the burning of gasoline. Light can also be a source of activation energy for a reaction. **Figure 4** shows how activation energy relates to exothermic reactions and endothermic reactions.

CONNECTION TO Social Studies

WRITING SKILL **The Strike-Anywhere Match**
Research the invention of the strike-anywhere match. Find out who invented it, who patented it, and when the match was introduced to the public. In your **science journal,** write a short report about what you learn from your research.

Figure 4 Energy Diagrams

Exothermic Reaction Once an exothermic reaction starts, it can continue. The energy given off as the product forms continues to supply the activation energy needed for the substances to react.

Endothermic Reaction An endothermic reaction continues to absorb energy. Energy must be used to provide the activation energy needed for the substances to react.

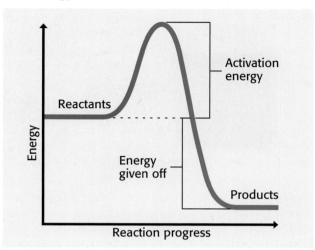

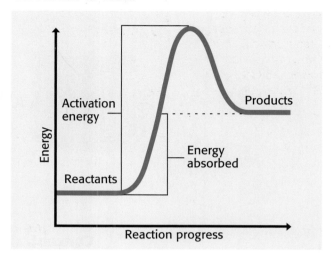

Factors Affecting Rates of Reactions

The rate of a reaction is a measure of how fast the reaction takes place. Recall that the rate of a reaction depends on how fast new particles form. There are four factors that affect the rate of a reaction. These factors are: temperature, concentration, surface area, and the presence of an inhibitor or catalyst.

Temperature

A higher temperature causes a faster rate of reaction, as shown in **Figure 5.** At high temperatures, particles of reactants move quickly. The rapid movement causes the particles to collide often and with a lot of energy. So, many particles have the activation energy to react. And many reactants can change into products in a short time.

Figure 5 *The light stick on the right glows brighter than the one on the left because the one on the right is warmer. The higher temperature causes the rate of the reaction to increase.*

Which Is Quicker?

1. Fill a **clear plastic cup** with **250 mL of warm water.** Fill a **second clear plastic cup** with **250 mL of cold water.**
2. Place **one-quarter of an effervescent tablet** in each of the two cups of water at the same time. Using a **stopwatch,** time each reaction.
3. Observe each reaction, and record your observations.
4. In which cup did the reaction occur at a faster rate?

Figure 6 **Concentration of Solutions**

▼ When the amount of copper sulfate crystals dissolved in water is **small,** the concentration of the copper sulfate solution is **low.**

▼ When the amount of copper sulfate crystals dissolved in water is **large,** the concentration of the copper sulfate solution is **high.**

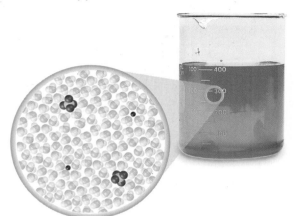 

CONNECTION TO Biology

Enzymes and Inhibitors
Enzymes are proteins that speed up reactions in your body. Sometimes, chemicals called *inhibitors* stop the action of enzymes. Research how inhibitors are beneficial in reactions in the human body. Make a poster or a model that explains what you have learned, and present it to your class.

ACTiViTY

inhibitor a substance that slows down or stops a chemical reaction

catalyst a substance that changes the rate of a chemical reaction without being used up or changed very much

Concentration

In general, a high concentration of reactants causes a fast rate of a reaction. *Concentration* is a measure of the amount of one substance dissolved in another substance, as shown in **Figure 6.** When the concentration is high, there are many reactant particles in a given volume. So, there is a small distance between particles. The particles run into each other often. Thus, the particles react faster.

✓ **Reading Check** How does a high concentration of reactants increase the rate of a reaction?

Surface Area

Surface area is the amount of exposed surface of a substance. Increasing the surface area of solid reactants increases the rate of a reaction. Grinding a solid into a powder makes a larger surface area. Greater surface area exposes more particles of the reactant to other reactant particles. This exposure to other particles causes the particles of the reactants to collide with each other more often. So, the rate of the reaction is increased.

Inhibitors

An **inhibitor** is a substance that slows down or stops a chemical reaction. Slowing down or stopping a reaction may sometimes be useful. For example, preservatives are added to foods to slow down the growth of bacteria and fungi. The preservatives prevent bacteria and fungi from producing substances that can spoil food. Some antibiotics are examples of inhibitors. For example, penicillin prevents certain kinds of bacteria from making a cell wall. So, the bacteria die.

Catalysts

Some chemical reactions would be too slow to be useful without a catalyst (KAT uh LIST). A **catalyst** is a substance that speeds up a reaction without being permanently changed. Because it is not changed, a catalyst is not a reactant. A catalyst lowers the activation energy of a reaction, which allows the reaction to happen more quickly. Catalysts called *enzymes* speed up most reactions in your body. Catalysts are even found in cars, as seen in **Figure 7.** The catalytic converter decreases air pollution. It does this by increasing the rate of reactions that involve the harmful products given off by cars.

Figure 7 *This catalytic converter contains platinum and palladium. These two catalysts increase the rate of reactions that make the car's exhaust less harmful.*

SECTION Review

Summary

- Energy is given off in exothermic reactions.
- Energy is absorbed in an endothermic reaction.
- The law of conservation of energy states that energy is neither created nor destroyed.
- Activation energy is the energy needed for a reaction to occur.
- The rate of a chemical reaction is affected by temperature, concentration, surface area, and the presence of an inhibitor or catalyst.

Using Key Terms

The statements below are false. For each statement, replace the underlined term to make a true statement.

1. An <u>exothermic</u> reaction absorbs energy.

2. The rate of a reaction can be <u>increased</u> by adding an inhibitor.

Understanding Key Ideas

3. Which of the following will not increase the rate of a reaction?
   a. adding a catalyst
   b. increasing the temperature of the reaction
   c. decreasing the concentration of reactants
   d. grinding a solid into powder

4. How does the concentration of a solution affect the rate of reaction?

Critical Thinking

5. **Making Comparisons** Compare exothermic and endothermic reactions.

6. **Applying Concepts** Explain how chewing your food thoroughly can help your body digest food.

Interpreting Graphics

Use the diagram below to answer the questions that follow.

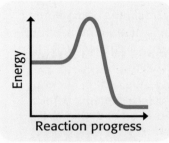

7. Does this energy diagram show an exothermic or an endothermic reaction? How can you tell?

8. A catalyst lowers the amount of activation energy needed to get a reaction started. What do you think the diagram would look like if a catalyst were added?

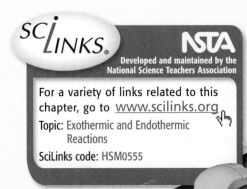

SCILINKS®

NSTA
Developed and maintained by the
National Science Teachers Association

For a variety of links related to this chapter, go to www.scilinks.org
Topic: Exothermic and Endothermic Reactions
SciLinks code: HSM0555

Skills Practice Lab

OBJECTIVES

Describe how the surface area of a solid affects the rate of a reaction.

Explain how concentration of reactants will speed up or slow down a reaction.

MATERIALS

- funnels (2)
- graduated cylinders, 10 mL (2)
- hydrochloric acid, concentrated
- hydrochloric acid, dilute
- strips of aluminum, about 5 cm x 1 cm each (6)
- scissors
- test-tube rack
- test tubes, 30 mL (6)

SAFETY

Speed Control

The reaction rate (how fast a chemical reaction happens) is an important factor to control. Sometimes, you want a reaction to take place rapidly, such as when you are removing tarnish from a metal surface. Other times, you want a reaction to happen very slowly, such as when you are depending on a battery as a source of electrical energy.

In this lab, you will discover how changing the surface area and concentration of the reactants affects reaction rate. In this lab, you can estimate the rate of reaction by observing how fast bubbles form.

Part A: Surface Area

Ask a Question

1 How does changing the surface area of a metal affect reaction rate?

Form a Hypothesis

2 Write a statement that answers the question above. Explain your reasoning.

Test the Hypothesis

3 Use three identical strips of aluminum. Put one strip into a test tube. Place the test tube in the test-tube rack. **Caution:** The strips of metal may have sharp edges.

4 Carefully fold a second strip in half and then in half again. Use a textbook or other large object to flatten the folded strip as much as possible. Place the strip in a second test tube in the test-tube rack.

5 Use scissors to cut a third strip of aluminum into the smallest possible pieces. Place all of the pieces into a third test tube, and place the test tube in the test-tube rack.

6 Use a funnel and a graduated cylinder to pour 10 mL of concentrated hydrochloric acid into each of the three test tubes. **Caution:** Hydrochloric acid is corrosive. If any acid should spill on you, immediately flush the area with water and notify your teacher.

7 Observe the rate of bubble formation in each test tube. Record your observations.

Analyze the Results

1 **Organizing Data** Which form of aluminum had the greatest surface area? the smallest surface area?

2 **Analyzing Data** The amount of aluminum and the amount of acid were the same in all three test tubes. Which form of the aluminum seemed to react the fastest? Which form reacted the slowest? Explain your answers.

3 **Analyzing Results** Do your results support the hypothesis you made? Explain.

Draw Conclusions

4 **Making Predictions** Would powdered aluminum react faster or slower than the forms of aluminum you used? Explain your answer.

Part B: Concentration

Ask a Question

1 How does changing the concentration of acid affect the reaction rate?

Form a Hypothesis

2 Write a statement that answers the question above. Explain your reasoning.

Test the Hypothesis

3 Place one of the three remaining aluminum strips in each of the three clean test tubes. (Note: Do not alter the strips.) Place the test tubes in the test-tube rack.

4 Using the second funnel and graduated cylinder, pour 10 mL of water into one of the test tubes. Pour 10 mL of dilute acid into the second test tube. Pour 10 mL of concentrated acid into the third test tube.

5 Observe the rate of bubble formation in the three test tubes. Record your observations.

Analyze the Results

1 **Explaining Events** In this set of test tubes, the strips of aluminum were the same, but the concentration of the acid was different. Was there a difference between the test tube that contained water and the test tubes that contained acid? Which test tube formed bubbles the fastest? Explain.

2 **Analyzing Results** Do your results support the hypothesis you made? Explain.

Draw Conclusions

3 **Applying Conclusions** Why should spilled hydrochloric acid be diluted with water before it is wiped up?

Chapter Review

USING KEY TERMS

Complete each of the following sentences by choosing the correct term from the word bank.

subscript	exothermic reaction
inhibitor	synthesis reaction
coefficient	reactant

1 Adding a(n) ___ will slow down a chemical reaction.

2 A chemical reaction that gives off heat is called a(n) ___.

3 A chemical reaction that forms one compound from two or more substances is called a(n) ___.

4 The 2 in the formula Ag_2S is a (an) ___.

UNDERSTANDING KEY IDEAS

Multiple Choice

5 Balancing a chemical equation so that the same number of atoms of each element is found in both the reactants and the products is an example of

a. activation energy.

b. the law of conservation of energy.

c. the law of conservation of mass.

d. a double-displacement reaction.

6 Which of the following is the correct chemical formula for dinitrogen tetroxide?

a. N_4O_2

b. NO_2

c. N_2O_5

d. N_2O_4

7 In which type of reaction do ions in two compounds switch places?

a. a synthesis reaction

b. a decomposition reaction

c. a single-displacement reaction

d. a double-displacement reaction

8 Which of the following actions is an example of the use of activation energy?

a. plugging in an iron

b. playing basketball

c. holding a lit match to paper

d. eating

9 Enzymes in your body act as catalysts. Thus, the role of enzymes is

a. to increase the rate of chemical reactions.

b. to decrease the rate of chemical reactions.

c. to help you breathe.

d. to inhibit chemical reactions.

Short Answer

10 Name the type of reaction that each of the following equations represents.

a. $2Cu + O_2 \rightarrow 2CuO$

b. $2Na + MgSO_4 \rightarrow Na_2SO_4 + Mg$

c. $Ba(CN)_2 + H_2SO_4 \rightarrow BaSO_4 + 2HCN$

11 Describe what happens to chemical bonds during a chemical reaction.

12 Name four ways that you can change the rate of a chemical reaction.

13 Describe four clues that signal that a chemical reaction is taking place.

1. inhibitor
2.
3.
4. Subscript
5. C
6. D
7. D
8. A
9. A

exo

23. exo   exo   endo

Yulisy

1. endothermic
2. decreased
3. D

4

5

6

7

8. It wouldn't go up as high.

Math Skills

14 Write balanced equations for the following:

a. $Fe + O_2 \rightarrow Fe_2O_3$

b. $Al + CuSO_4 \rightarrow Al_2(SO_4)_3 + Cu$

c. $Mg(OH)_2 + HCl \rightarrow MgCl_2 + H_2O$

15 Calculate the number of atoms of each element shown in the formulas below:

a. $CaSO_4$

b. $4NaOCl$

c. $Fe(NO_3)_2$

d. $2Al_2(CO_3)_3$

CRITICAL THINKING

16 Concept Mapping Use the following terms to create a concept map: *products, chemical reaction, chemical equation, chemical formulas, reactants, coefficients,* and *subscripts.*

17 Evaluating Assumptions Your friend is very worried by rumors that he has heard about a substance called *dihydrogen monoxide* in the city's water system. What could you say to your friend to calm his fears? (Hint: Write the formula of the substance.)

18 Analyzing Ideas As long as proper safety precautions have been taken, why can explosives be transported long distances without exploding?

19 Applying Concepts You measured the mass of a steel pipe before leaving it outdoors. One month later, the pipe had rusted, and its mass had increased. Does this change violate the law of conservation of mass? Explain your answer.

20 Applying Concepts Acetic acid, a compound found in vinegar, reacts with baking soda to produce carbon dioxide, water, and sodium acetate. Without writing an equation, identify the reactants and the products of this reaction.

INTERPRETING GRAPHICS

Use the photo below to answer the questions that follow.

21 What evidence in the photo supports the claim that a chemical reaction is taking place?

22 Is this reaction an exothermic or endothermic reaction? Explain your answer.

23 Draw and label an energy diagram of both an exothermic and endothermic reaction. Identify the diagram that describes the reaction shown in the photo above.

Standardized Test Preparation

Read each of the passages below. Then, answer the questions that follow each passage.

Passage 1 The key to an air bag's success during a crash is the speed at which it inflates. Inside the bag is a gas generator that contains the compounds sodium azide, potassium nitrate, and silicon dioxide. At the moment of a crash, an electronic sensor in the car detects the sudden change in speed. The sensor sends a small electric current to the gas generator. This electric current provides the activation energy for the chemicals in the gas generator. The rate at which the reaction happens is very fast. In 1/25 of a second, the gas formed in the reaction inflates the bag. The air bag fills upward and outward. By filling the space between a person and the car's dashboard, the air bag protects him or her from getting hurt.

1. Which of the following events happens first?
   A The sensor sends an electric current to the gas generator.
   B The air bag inflates.
   C The air bag fills the space between the person and the dashboard.
   D The sensor detects a change in speed.

2. What provides the activation energy for the reaction to occur?
   F the speed of the car
   G the inflation of the air bag
   H the hot engine
   I the electric current from the sensor

3. What is the purpose of this passage?
   A to convince the reader to wear a seat belt
   B to describe the series of events that inflate an air bag
   C to explain why air bags are an important safety feature in cars
   D to show how chemical reactions protect pedestrians

Passage 2 An important tool in fighting forest fires is a slimy, red goop. This mixture of powder and water is a very powerful fire retardant. The burning of trees, grass, and brush is an exothermic reaction. The fire retardant slows or stops this self-feeding reaction by increasing the activation energy for the materials to which it sticks. A plane can carry between 4,500 and 11,000 L of the goop. The plane then drops it all in front of the raging flames of a forest fire when the pilot presses the button. Firefighters on the ground can gain valuable time when a fire is slowed with a fire retardant. This extra time allows the ground team to create a fire line that will finally stop the fire.

1. Which of the following sentences best summarizes the passage?
   A The burning of forests and other brush is an exothermic reaction.
   B Dropping fire retardants ahead of a flame can help firefighters on the ground stop a fire.
   C Firefighters on the ground create a fire line that will help stop the fire from spreading.
   D The slimy, red goop used as a fire retardant is made of a mixture of powder and water.

2. Based on the passage, which of the following statements is a fact?
   F Fire retardants are always successful in putting out fires.
   G No more than 4,500 L of red goop are loaded onto a plane.
   H A fire retardant works by increasing the activation energy for the materials that it sticks on.
   I The burning of trees is an endothermic reaction.

Use the energy diagram below to answer the questions that follow.

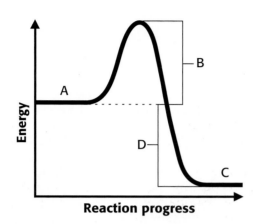

Reaction progress

1. Which letter represents the energy of the products?
   A A
   B B
   C C
   D D

2. Which letter represents the activation energy of the reaction?
   F A
   G B
   H C
   I D

3. Which of the following statements best describes the reaction represented by the graph?
   A The reaction is endothermic because the energy of the products is greater than the energy of the reactants.
   B The reaction is endothermic because the energy of the reactants is greater than the energy of the products.
   C The reaction is exothermic because the energy of the products is greater than the energy of the reactants.
   D The reaction is exothermic because the energy of the reactants is greater than the energy of the products.

Read each question below, and choose the best answer.

1. Nina has 15 pens in her backpack. She has 3 red pens, 10 black pens, and 2 blue pens. If Ben selects a pen to borrow at random, what is the probability that the pen selected is red?
   A 2/15
   B 1/5
   C 1/3
   D 2/3

2. How many atoms of nitrogen, N, are in the formula for calcium nitrate, $Ca(NO_3)_2$?
   F 3
   G 2
   H 6
   I 1

3. Which letter best represents the number 2 3/5 on the number line?

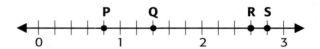

   A P
   B Q
   C R
   D S

4. According to the following chemical equation, how many reactants are needed to form water and carbon dioxide?

$$H_2CO_3 \longrightarrow H_2O + CO_2$$

   F one
   G two
   H three
   I four

Standardized Test Preparation

Science in Action

Science, Technology, and Society

Bringing Down the House!

Have you ever watched a building being demolished? It takes only minutes to demolish it, but a lot of time was spent planning the demolition. And it takes time to remove hazardous chemicals from the building. For example, asbestos, which is found in insulation, can cause lung cancer. Mercury found in thermostats can cause brain damage, birth defects, and death. It is important to remove these substances because most of the rubble is sent to a landfill. If hazardous chemicals are not removed, they could leak into the groundwater and enter the water supply.

Math ACTiViTY

A city produces 4 million tons of waste in 1 year. Of this waste, 82% is solid waste. If 38% of the solid waste comes from the construction and demolition of buildings, how many tons of waste does this represent?

Weird Science

Light Sticks

Have you ever seen light sticks at a concert? Your family may even keep them in the car for emergencies. But how do light sticks work? To activate the light stick, you have to bend it. Most light sticks are made of a plastic tube that contains a mixture of two chemicals. Also inside the tube is a thin glass vial, which contains hydrogen peroxide. As long as the glass vial is unbroken, the two chemicals are kept separate. But bending the ends of the tube breaks the glass vial. This action releases the hydrogen peroxide into the other chemicals and a chemical reaction occurs, which makes the light stick glow.

Social Studies ACTiViTY

Who invented light sticks? What was their original purpose? Research the answers to these questions. Make a poster that shows what you have learned.

Larry McKee

Arson Investigator Once a fire dies down, you might see an arson investigator like Lt. Larry McKee on the scene. "After the fire is out, I can investigate the fire scene to determine where the fire started and how it started," says McKee, who questions witnesses and firefighters about what they have seen. He knows that the color of the smoke can indicate certain chemicals. He also has help detecting chemicals from an accelerant-sniffing dog, Nikki. Nikki has been trained to detect about 11 different chemicals. If Nikki finds one of these chemicals, she begins to dig. McKee takes a sample of the suspicious material to the laboratory. He treats the sample so that any chemicals present will dissolve in a liquid. A sample of this liquid is placed into an instrument called a *gas chromatograph* and tested. The results of this test are printed out in a graph, from which the suspicious chemical is identified. Next, McKee begins to search for suspects. By combining detective work with scientific evidence, fire investigators can help find clues that can lead to the conviction of the arsonist.

Language Arts ACTiViTY

WRITING SKILL Write a one-page story about an arson investigator. Begin the story at the scene of a fire. Take the story through the different steps that you think an investigator would have to go through to solve the crime.

To learn more about these Science in Action topics, visit go.hrw.com and type in the keyword **HP5REAF.**

Current Science

Check out Current Science® articles related to this chapter by visiting go.hrw.com. Just type in the keyword **HP5CS14.**

15

Chemical Compounds

SECTION **1** **Ionic and Covalent Compounds**. **418**

SECTION **2** **Acids and Bases**. **422**

SECTION **3** **Solutions of Acids and Bases**. **428**

SECTION **4** **Organic Compounds** . . **432**

Chapter Lab **438**

Chapter Review **440**

Standardized Test Preparation **442**

Science in Action **444**

About the PHOTO

The bean weevil feeds on bean seeds, which are rich in chemical compounds such as proteins, carbohydrates, and lipids. The bean weevil begins life as a tiny grub that lives in the seed where it eats starch and protein. The adult then cuts holes in the seed coat and crawls out, as you can see in this photo.

PRE-READING ACTIVITY

FOLDNOTES **Layered Book** Before you read the chapter, create the FoldNote entitled "Layered Book" described in the **Study Skills** section of the Appendix. Label the tabs of the layered book with "Ionic and covalent compounds," "Acids and bases," "Solutions of acids and bases," and "Organic compounds." As you read the chapter, write information you learn about each category under the appropriate tab.

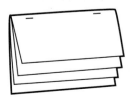

START-UP ACTIVITY

Sticking Together

In this activity, you will demonstrate the force that keeps particles together in some compounds.

Procedure

1. Rub **two balloons** with a **wool cloth.** Move the balloons near each other. Describe what you see.
2. Put one balloon against a wall. Record your observations.

Analysis

1. The balloons are charged by rubbing them with the wool cloth. Like charges repel each other. Opposite charges attract each other. Do the balloons have like or opposite charges? Explain.
2. If the balloon that was placed against the wall has a negative charge, what is the charge on the wall? Explain your answer.
3. The particles that make up compounds are attracted to each other in the same way that the balloon is attracted to the wall. What can you infer about the particles that make up such compounds?

Ionic and Covalent Compounds

When ions or molecules combine, they form compounds. Because there are millions of compounds, it is helpful to organize them into groups. But how can scientists tell the difference between compounds?

One way to group compounds is by the kind of chemical bond they have. A **chemical bond** is the combining of atoms to form molecules or compounds. Bonding can occur between valence electrons of different atoms. *Valence electrons* are electrons in the outermost energy level of an atom. The behavior of valence electrons determines if an ionic compound or a covalent compound is formed.

Ionic Compounds and Their Properties

The properties of ionic compounds are a result of strong attractive forces called ionic bonds. An *ionic bond* is an attraction between oppositely charged ions. Compounds that contain ionic bonds are called **ionic compounds.** Ionic compounds can be formed by the reaction of a metal with a nonmetal. Metal atoms become positively charged ions when electrons are transferred from the metal atoms to the nonmetal atoms. This transfer of electrons also causes the nonmetal atom to become a negatively charged ion. Sodium chloride, commonly known as *table salt,* is an ionic compound.

Brittleness

Ionic compounds tend to be brittle solids at room temperature. So, they usually break apart when hit. This property is due to the arrangement of ions in a repeating three-dimensional pattern called a *crystal lattice,* shown in **Figure 1.** Each ion in a lattice is surrounded by ions of the opposite charge. And each ion is bonded to the ions around it. When an ionic compound is hit, the pattern of ions shifts. Ions that have the same charge line up and repel one another, which causes the crystal to break.

Figure 1 *The sodium ions, shown in purple, and the chloride ions, shown in green, are bonded in the crystal lattice structure of sodium chloride.*

READING WARM-UP

Objectives

● Describe the properties of ionic and covalent compounds.

● Classify compounds as ionic or covalent based on their properties.

Terms to Learn

chemical bond
ionic compound
covalent compound

READING STRATEGY

Reading Organizer As you read this section, create an outline of the section. Use the headings from the section in your outline.

chemical bond the combining of atoms to form molecules or compounds

ionic compound a compound made of oppositely charged ions

Figure 2 **Melting Points of Some Ionic Compounds**

Potassium dichromate
Melting point: 398°C

Magnesium oxide
Melting point: 2,800°C

Nickel(II) oxide
Melting point: 1,984°C

High Melting Points

Because of the strong ionic bonds that hold ions together, ionic compounds have high melting points. These high melting points are the reason that most ionic compounds are solids at room temperature. For example, solid sodium chloride must be heated to 801°C before it will melt. The melting points of three other ionic compounds are given in **Figure 2.**

Solubility and Electrical Conductivity

Many ionic compounds are highly soluble. So, they dissolve easily in water. Water molecules attract each of the ions of an ionic compound and pull the ions away from one another. The solution that forms when an ionic compound dissolves in water can conduct an electric current, as shown in **Figure 3.** The solution can conduct an electric current because the ions are charged and are able to move freely past one another. However, an undissolved crystal of an ionic compound does not conduct an electric current.

Reading Check Why do ionic solutions conduct an electric current? (*See the Appendix for answers to Reading Checks.*)

For another activity related to this chapter, go to **go.hrw.com** and type in the keyword **HP5CMPW.**

Figure 3 *The pure water does not conduct an electric current. However, the solution of salt water conducts an electric current, so the bulb lights up.*

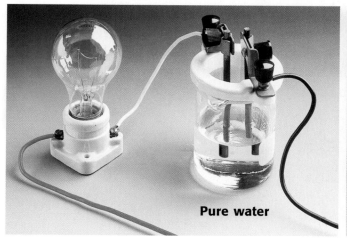

Pure water

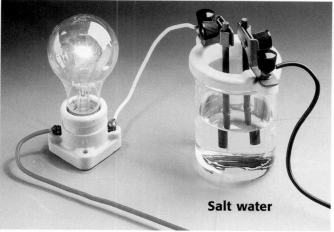

Salt water

Covalent Compounds and Their Properties

Most compounds are covalent compounds. **Covalent compounds** are compounds that form when a group of atoms shares electrons. This sharing of electrons forms a covalent bond. A *covalent bond* is a weaker attractive force than an ionic bond is. The group of atoms that make up a covalent compound is called a molecule. A *molecule* is the smallest particle into which a covalently bonded compound can be divided and still be the same compound. Properties of covalent compounds are very different from the properties of ionic compounds.

covalent compound a chemical compound formed by the sharing of electrons

Low Solubility

Many covalent compounds are not soluble in water, which means that they do not dissolve well in water. You may have noticed this if you have ever left off the top of a soda bottle. The carbon dioxide gas that gives the soda its fizz eventually escapes, and your soda pop goes "flat." The attraction between water molecules is much stronger than their attraction to the molecules of most other covalent compounds. So, water molecules stay together instead of mixing with the covalent compounds. If you have ever made salad dressing, you probably know that oil and water don't mix. Oils, such as the oil in the salad dressing in **Figure 4,** are made of covalent compounds.

✓ **Reading Check** Why won't most covalent compounds dissolve in water?

Figure 4 *Olive oil, which is used in salad dressings, is made of very large covalent molecules that do not mix with water.*

Low Melting Points

The forces of attraction between molecules of covalent compounds are much weaker than the bonds holding ionic solids together. Less heat is needed to separate the molecules of covalent compounds, so these compounds have much lower melting and boiling points than ionic compounds do.

Electrical Conductivity

Although most covalent compounds don't dissolve in water, some do. Most of the covalent compounds that dissolve in water form solutions that have uncharged molecules. Sugar is a covalent compound that dissolves in water and that does not form ions. So, a solution of sugar and water does not conduct an electric current, as shown in **Figure 5.** However, some covalent compounds do form ions when they dissolve in water. Many acids, for example, form ions in water. These solutions, like ionic solutions, conduct an electric current.

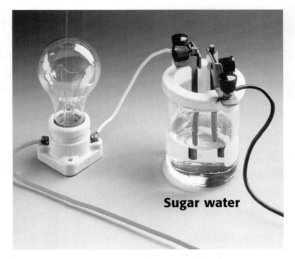

Sugar water

Figure 5 *This solution of sugar, a covalent compound, and water does not conduct an electric current because the molecules of sugar are not charged.*

SECTION
Review

Summary

- Ionic compounds have ionic bonds between ions of opposite charges.
- Ionic compounds are usually brittle, have high melting points, dissolve in water, and often conduct an electric current.
- Covalent compounds have covalent bonds and consist of particles called molecules.
- Covalent compounds have low melting points, don't dissolve easily in water, and do not conduct an electric current.

Using Key Terms

1. Use each of the following terms in a separate sentence: *ionic compound, covalent compound,* and *chemical bond.*

Understanding Key Ideas

2. Which of the following describes an ionic compound?

   a. It has a low melting point.

   b. It consists of shared electrons.

   c. It conducts electric current in water solutions.

   d. It consists of two nonmetals.

3. List two properties of covalent compounds.

Math Skills

4. A compound contains 39.37% chromium, 38.10% oxygen, and potassium. What percentage of the compound is potassium?

Critical Thinking

5. **Making Inferences** Solid crystals of ionic compounds do not conduct an electric current. But when the crystals dissolve in water, the solution conducts an electric current. Explain.

6. **Applying Concepts** Some white solid crystals are dissolved in water. If the solution does not conduct an electric current, is the solid an ionic compound or a covalent compound? Explain.

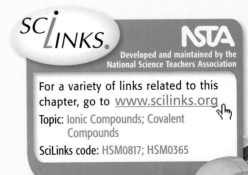

SCiLINKS **NSTA**
Developed and maintained by the
National Science Teachers Association

For a variety of links related to this chapter, go to www.scilinks.org
Topic: Ionic Compounds; Covalent Compounds
SciLinks code: HSM0817; HSM0365

Acids and Bases

Would you like a nice, refreshing glass of acid? This is just what you get when you have a glass of lemonade.

Lemons contain a substance called an *acid*. One property of acids is a sour taste. In this section, you will learn about the properties of acids and bases.

Acids and Their Properties

A sour taste is not the only property of an acid. Have you noticed that when you squeeze lemon juice into tea, the color of the tea becomes lighter? This change happens because acids cause some substances to change color. An **acid** is any compound that increases the number of hydronium ions, H_3O^+, when dissolved in water. Hydronium ions form when a hydrogen ion, H^+, separates from the acid and bonds with a water molecule, H_2O, to form a hydronium ion, H_3O^+.

✓ **Reading Check** How is a hydronium ion formed? (*See the Appendix for answers to Reading Checks.*)

Acids Have a Sour Flavor

Have you ever taken a bite of a lemon or lime? If so, like the boy in **Figure 1,** you know the sour taste of an acid. The taste of lemons, limes, and other citrus fruits is a result of citric acid. However, taste, touch, or smell should NEVER be used to identify an unknown chemical. Many acids are *corrosive,* which means that they destroy body tissue, clothing, and many other things. Most acids are also poisonous.

acid any compound that increases the number of hydronium ions when dissolved in water

NEVER touch or taste a concentrated solution of a strong acid.

Figure 1 *Foods that have a sour taste usually contain acids.*

Figure 2 Detecting Acids with Indicators

The indicator, bromthymol blue, is pale blue in water.

When acid is added, the color changes to yellow because of the presence of the indicator.

indicator a compound that can reversibly change color depending on conditions such as pH

Acids Change Colors in Indicators

A substance that changes color in the presence of an acid or base is an **indicator.** Look at **Figure 2.** The flask on the left contains water and an indicator called *bromthymol blue* (BROHM THIE MAWL BLOO). Acid has been added to the flask on the right. The color changes from pale blue to yellow because the indicator detects the presence of an acid.

Another indicator commonly used in the lab is litmus. Paper strips containing litmus are available in both blue and red. When an acid is added to blue litmus paper, the color of the litmus changes to red.

Acids React with Metals

Acids react with some metals to produce hydrogen gas. For example, hydrochloric acid reacts with zinc metal to produce hydrogen gas, as shown in **Figure 3.** The equation for the reaction is the following:

$$2HCl + Zn \longrightarrow H_2 + ZnCl_2$$

In this reaction, zinc displaces hydrogen in the compound, hydrochloric acid. This displacement happens because zinc is an active metal. But if the element silver were put into hydrochloric acid, nothing would happen. Silver is not an active metal, so no reaction would take place.

Figure 3 *Bubbles of hydrogen gas form when zinc metal reacts with hydrochloric acid.*

Acids Conduct Electric Current

When acids are dissolved in water, they break apart and form ions in the solution. The ions make it possible for the solution to conduct an electric current. A car battery is one example of how an acid can be used to produce an electric current. The sulfuric acid in the battery conducts electricity to help start the car's engine.

Uses of Acids

Acids are used in many areas of industry and in homes. Sulfuric acid is the most widely made industrial chemical in the world. It is used to make many products, including paper, paint, detergents, and fertilizers. Nitric acid is used to make fertilizers, rubber, and plastics. Hydrochloric acid is used to make metals from their ores by separating the metals from the materials with which they are combined. It is also used in swimming pools to help keep them free of algae. Hydrochloric acid is even found in your stomach, where it aids in digestion. Hydrofluoric acid is used to etch glass, as shown in **Figure 4.** Citric acid and ascorbic acid (Vitamin C) are found in orange juice. And carbonic acid and phosphoric acid help give a sharp taste to soft drinks.

Reading Check What are three uses of acids?

Figure 4 *The image of the swan was etched into the glass through the use of hydrofluoric acid.*

Figure 5   Examples of Bases

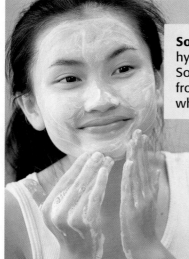

Soaps are made from sodium hydroxide, which is a base. Soaps remove dirt and oils from skin and feel slippery when you touch them.

Baking soda is a very mild base. It is used in toothpastes and mouthwashes to neutralize acids, which can produce unpleasant odors.

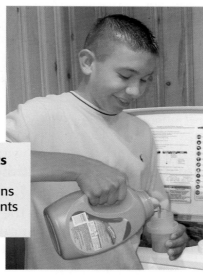

Bleach and detergents contain bases and are used for removing stains from clothing. Detergents feel slippery like soap.

Bases and Their Properties

A **base** is any compound that increases the number of hydroxide ions, OH⁻, when dissolved in water. For example, sodium hydroxide breaks apart to form sodium ions and hydroxide ions as shown below.

$$NaOH \longrightarrow Na^+ + OH^-$$

Hydroxide ions give bases their properties. **Figure 5** shows examples of bases that you are probably familiar with.

base any compound that increases the number of hydroxide ions when dissolved in water

Bases Have a Bitter Flavor and a Slippery Feel

The properties of a base solution include a bitter taste and a slippery feel. If you have ever accidentally tasted soap, you know the bitter taste of a base. Soap will also have the slippery feel of a base. However, taste, touch or smell should NEVER be used to identify an unknown chemical. Like acids, many bases are corrosive. If your fingers feel slippery when you are using a base in an experiment, you may have gotten the base on your hands. You should immediately rinse your hands with large amounts of water and tell your teacher.

NEVER touch or taste a concentrated solution of a strong base.

Figure 6 Detecting Bases with Indicators

The indicator, bromthymol blue, is pale blue in water.

When a base is added to the indicator, the indicator turns dark blue.

Bases Change Color in Indicators

Like acids, bases change the color of an indicator. Most indicators turn a different color in the presence of bases than they do in the presence of acids. For example, bases change the color of red litmus paper to blue. And the indicator, bromthymol blue, turns blue when a base is added to it, as shown in **Figure 6.**

Bases Conduct Electric Current

Solutions of bases conduct an electric current because bases increase the number of hydroxide ions, OH^-, in a solution. A hydroxide ion is actually a hydrogen atom and an oxygen atom bonded together. The extra electron gives the hydroxide ion a negative charge.

Blue to Red—Acid!

1. Pour about 5 mL of **test solution** into a **spot plate.** Test the solution using **red litmus paper** and **blue litmus paper** by dipping a **stirring rod** into it and then touching the rod to a piece of litmus paper.

2. Record any color changes. Clean the stirring rod.

3. Repeat the above steps with each solution. Use new pieces of litmus paper as needed.

4. Identify each solution as acidic or basic.

Uses of Bases

Like acids, bases have many uses. Sodium hydroxide is a base used to make soap and paper. It is also used in oven cleaners and in products that unclog drains. Calcium hydroxide, $Ca(OH)_2$, is used to make cement and plaster. Ammonia is found in many household cleaners and is used to make fertilizers. And magnesium hydroxide and aluminum hydroxide are used in antacids to treat heartburn. **Figure 7** shows some of the many products that contain bases. Carefully follow the safety instructions when using these products. Remember that bases can harm your skin.

Reading Check What three ways can bases be used at home?

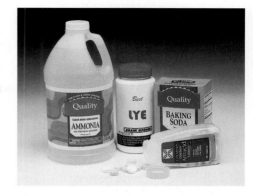

Figure 7 *Bases are common around the house. They are useful as cleaning agents, as cooking aids, and as medicines.*

SECTION Review

Summary

- An acid is a compound that increases the number of hydronium ions in solution.

- Acids taste sour, turn blue litmus paper red, react with metals to produce hydrogen gas, and may conduct an electric current when in solution.

- Acids are used for industrial purposes and in household products.

- A base is a compound that increases the number of hydroxide ions in solution.

- Bases taste bitter, feel slippery, and turn red litmus paper blue. Most solutions of bases conduct an electric current.

- Bases are used in cleaning products and acid neutralizers.

Using Key Terms

1. In your own words, write a definition for each of the following terms: *acid, base,* and *indicator.*

Understanding Key Ideas

2. A base is a substance that
   a. feels slippery.
   b. tastes sour.
   c. reacts with metals to produce hydrogen gas.
   d. turns blue litmus paper red.

3. Acids are important in
   a. making antacids.
   b. preparing detergents.
   c. keeping algae out of swimming pools.
   d. manufacturing cement.

4. What happens to red litmus paper when when it touches a base?

Math Skills

5. A cake recipe calls for 472 mL of milk. You don't have a metric measuring cup at home, so you need to convert milliliters to cups. You know that 1 L equals 1.06 quarts and that there are 4 cups in 1 quart. How many cups of milk will you need to use?

Critical Thinking

6. **Making Comparisons** Compare the properties of acids and bases.

7. **Applying Concepts** Why would it be useful for a gardener or a vegetable farmer to use litmus paper to test soil samples?

8. **Analyzing Processes** Suppose that your teacher gives you a solution of an unknown chemical. The chemical is either an acid or a base. You know that touching or tasting acids and bases is not safe. What two tests could you perform on the chemical to determine whether it is an acid or a base? What results would help you decide if the chemical was an acid or a base?

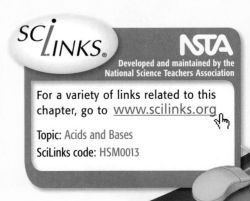

SC/LINKS®

NSTA

Developed and maintained by the National Science Teachers Association

For a variety of links related to this chapter, go to www.scilinks.org

Topic: Acids and Bases
SciLinks code: HSM0013

Solutions of Acids and Bases

Suppose that at your friend's party, you ate several large pieces of pepperoni pizza followed by cake and ice cream. Now, you have a terrible case of indigestion.

If you have ever had an upset stomach, you may have felt very much like the boy in **Figure 1.** And you may have taken an antacid. But do you know how antacids work? An antacid is a weak base that neutralizes a strong acid in your stomach. In this section, you will learn about the strengths of acids and bases. You will also learn about reactions between acids and bases.

Strengths of Acids and Bases

Acids and bases can be strong or weak. The strength of an acid or a base is not the same as the concentration of an acid or a base. The concentration of an acid or a base is the amount of acid or base dissolved in water. But the strength of an acid or a base depends on the number of molecules that break apart when the acid or base is dissolved in water.

Strong Versus Weak Acids

As an acid dissolves in water, the acid's molecules break apart and produce hydrogen ions, H^+. If all of the molecules of an acid break apart, the acid is called a *strong acid*. Strong acids include sulfuric acid, nitric acid, and hydrochloric acid. If only a few molecules of an acid break apart, the acid is a weak acid. Weak acids include acetic (uh SEET ik) acid, citric acid, and carbonic acid.

✓ **Reading Check** What is the difference between a strong acid and a weak acid? (*See the Appendix for answers to Reading Checks.*)

Figure 1 *Antacids may help relieve your stomachache by reacting with the acid in your stomach.*

Strong Versus Weak Bases

When all molecules of a base break apart in water to produce hydroxide ions, OH⁻, the base is a strong base. Strong bases include sodium hydroxide, calcium hydroxide, and potassium hydroxide. When only a few molecules of a base break apart, the base is a weak base, such as ammonium hydroxide and aluminum hydroxide.

Acids, Bases, and Neutralization

When the base in an antacid meets stomach acid, a reaction occurs. The reaction between acids and bases is a **neutralization reaction** (NOO truhl i ZA shuhn ree AK shuhn). Acids and bases neutralize one another because the hydrogen ions (H^+), which are present in an acid, and the hydroxide ions (OH^-), which are present in a base, react to form water, H_2O, which is neutral. Other ions from the acid and base dissolve in the water. If the water evaporates, these ions join to form a compound called a *salt*.

The pH Scale

An *indicator*, such as litmus, can identify whether a solution contains an acid or base. To describe how acidic or basic a solution is, the pH scale is used. The **pH** of a solution is a measure of the hydronium ion concentration in the solution. A solution that has a pH of 7 is neutral, which means that the solution is neither acidic nor basic. Pure water has a pH of 7. Basic solutions have a pH greater than 7. Acidic solutions have a pH less than 7. **Figure 2** shows the pH values for many common materials.

pHast Relief!

1. Pour **vinegar** into a **small plastic cup** until the cup is half full. Test the vinegar with **red and blue litmus paper.** Record your results.

2. Crush one **antacid tablet,** and mix it with the vinegar. Test the mixture with litmus paper. Record your results.

3. Compare the acidity of the solution before the antacid was added with the acidity of the solution after it was added.

neutralization reaction the reaction of an acid and a base to form a neutral solution of water and a salt

pH a value that is used to express the acidity or basicity (alkalinity) of a system

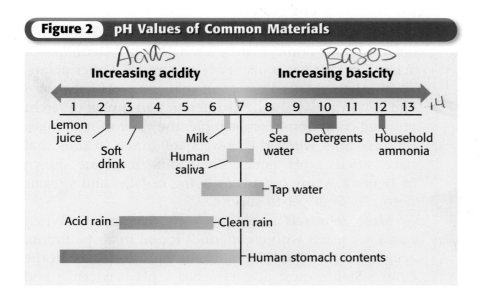

Figure 2 pH Values of Common Materials

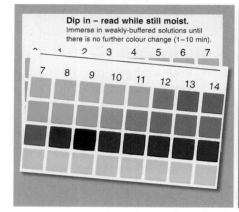

Figure 3 Using Indicators to Find pH

pH Indicator Scale

Dip in – read while still moist.
Immerse in weakly-buffered solutions until
there is no further colour change (1–10 min).

1 2 3 4 5 6 7
7 8 9 10 11 12 13 14

pH 4

pH 10

CONNECTION TO Biology

WRITING SKILL **Blood and pH**
Human blood has a pH between 7.38 and 7.42. If the blood pH is lower or higher, the body cannot function properly. Research what can cause the pH of blood to rise above or fall below normal ranges. Write a one-page paper that details your findings.

Figure 4 *To grow blue flowers, plant hydrangeas in soil that has a low pH. To grow pink flowers, use soil that has a high pH.*

Using Indicators to Determine pH

A combination of indicators can be used to find out how basic or how acidic a solution is. This can be done if the colors of the indicators are known at different pH values. **Figure 3** shows strips of pH paper, which contains several different indicators. These strips were dipped into two different solutions. The pH of each solution is found by comparing the colors on each strip with the colors on the indicator scale provided. This kind of indicator is often used to test the pH of water in pools and aquariums. Another way to find the pH of a solution is to use a pH meter. These meters can detect and measure hydronium ion concentration electronically.

✓ **Reading Check** How can indicators determine pH?

pH and the Environment

Living things depend on having a steady pH in their environment. Some plants, such as pine trees, prefer acidic soil that has a pH between 4 and 6. Other plants, such as lettuce, need basic soil that has a pH between 8 and 9. Plants may also have different traits under different growing conditions. For example, the color of hydrangea flowers varies when the flowers are grown in soils that have different pH values. These differences are shown in **Figure 4.** Many organisms living in lakes and streams need a neutral pH to survive.

Most rain has a pH between 5.5 and 6. When rainwater reacts with compounds found in air pollution, acids are formed and the rainwater's pH decreases. In the United States, most acid rain has a pH between 4 and 4.5, but some precipitation has a pH as low as 3.

Salts

When an acid neutralizes a base, a salt and water are produced. A **salt** is an ionic compound formed from the positive ion of a base and the negative ion of an acid. When you hear the word *salt*, you probably think of the table salt you use to season your food. But the sodium chloride found in your salt shaker is only one example of a large group of compounds called *salts*.

Uses of Salts

Salts have many uses in industry and in homes. You already know that sodium chloride is used to season foods. It is also used to make other compounds, including lye (sodium hydroxide) and baking soda. Sodium nitrate is a salt that is used to preserve food. And calcium sulfate is used to make wallboard, which is used in construction. Another use of salt is shown in **Figure 5.**

Figure 5 *Salts help keep roads free of ice by decreasing the freezing point of water.*

salt an ionic compound that forms when a metal atom replaces the hydrogen of an acid

---

SECTION Review

Summary

- Every molecule of a strong acid or base breaks apart to form ions. Few molecules of weak acids and bases break apart to form ions.
- An acid and a base can neutralize one another to make salt and water.
- pH is a measure of hydronium ion concentration in a solution.
- A salt is an ionic compound formed in a neutralization reaction. Salts have many industrial and household uses.

Using Key Terms

1. Use the following terms in the same sentence: *neutralization reaction* and *salt*.

Understanding Key Ideas

2. A neutralization reaction
   a. includes an acid and a base.
   b. produces a salt.
   c. forms water.
   d. All of the above

3. Explain the difference between a strong acid and a weak acid.

Math Skills

4. For each point lower on the pH scale, the hydrogen ions in solution increase tenfold. For example, a solution of pH 3 is not twice as acidic as a solution of pH 6 but is 1,000 times as acidic. How many times more acidic is a solution of pH 2 than a solution of pH 4?

Critical Thinking

5. **Analyzing Processes** Predict what will happen to the hydrogen ion concentration and the pH of water if hydrochloric acid is added to the water.

6. **Analyzing Relationships** Would fish be healthy in a lake that has a low pH? Explain.

7. **Applying Concepts** Soap is made from a strong base and oil. Would you expect the pH of soap to be 4 or 9? Explain.

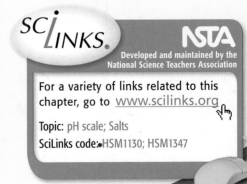

SCiLINKS®

NSTA

Developed and maintained by the National Science Teachers Association

For a variety of links related to this chapter, go to www.scilinks.org

Topic: pH scale; Salts
SciLinks code: HSM1130; HSM1347

Organic Compounds

Can you believe that more than 90% of all compounds are members of a single group of compounds? It's true!

Most compounds are members of a group called organic compounds. **Organic compounds** are covalent compounds composed of carbon-based molecules. Fuel, rubbing alcohol, and sugar are organic compounds. Even cotton, paper, and plastic belong to this group. Why are there so many kinds of organic compounds? Learning about the carbon atom can help you understand why.

The Four Bonds of a Carbon Atom

All organic compounds contain carbon. Each carbon atom has four valence electrons. So, each carbon atom can make four bonds with four other atoms.

Carbon Backbones

The models in **Figure 1** are called *structural formulas*. They are used to show how atoms in a molecule are connected. Each line represents a pair of electrons that form a covalent bond. Many organic compounds are based on the types of carbon backbones shown in **Figure 1.** Some compounds have hundreds or thousands of carbon atoms as part of their backbone! Organic compounds may also contain hydrogen, oxygen, sulfur, nitrogen, and phosphorus.

✓ Reading Check What is the purpose of structural formulas? (*See the Appendix for answers to Reading Checks.*)

Figure 1 **Three Models of Carbon Backbones**

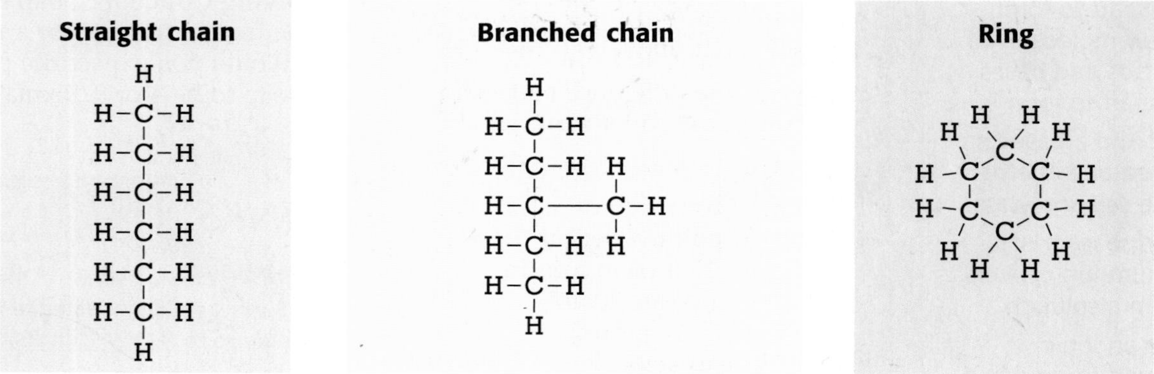

Straight chain

▲ All carbon atoms are connected in a straight line.

Branched chain

▲ The chain of carbon atoms branches into different directions when a carbon atom is bonded to more than one other carbon atom.

Ring

▲ The chain of carbon atoms forms a ring.

Figure 2 Three Types of Hydrocarbons

Alkane

The **propane** in this camping stove is a saturated hydrocarbon.

Alkene

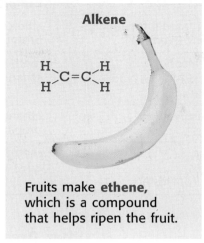

Fruits make **ethene**, which is a compound that helps ripen the fruit.

Alkyne

$$H-C\equiv C-H$$

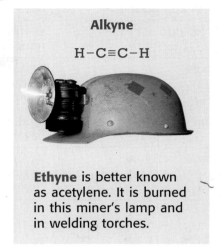

Ethyne is better known as acetylene. It is burned in this miner's lamp and in welding torches.

Hydrocarbons and Other Organic Compounds

Although many organic compounds contain several kinds of atoms, some contain only two. Organic compounds that contain only carbon and hydrogen are called **hydrocarbons.**

Saturated Hydrocarbons

The propane shown in **Figure 2** is a saturated hydrocarbon. A *saturated hydrocarbon,* or *alkane,* is a hydrocarbon in which each carbon atom in the molecule shares a single bond with each of four other atoms. A single bond is a covalent bond made up of one pair of shared electrons.

Unsaturated Hydrocarbons

An *unsaturated hydrocarbon,* such as ethene or ethyne shown in **Figure 2,** is a hydrocarbon in which at least one pair of carbon atoms shares a double bond or a triple bond. A double bond is a covalent bond made up of two pairs of shared electrons. A triple bond is a covalent bond made up of three pairs of shared electrons. Hydrocarbons that contain double or triple bonds are unsaturated because these bonds can be broken and more atoms can be added to the molecules.

Compounds that contain two carbon atoms connected by a double bond are called *alkenes.* Hydrocarbons that contain two carbon atoms connected by a triple bond are called *alkynes.*

Aromatic Hydrocarbons

Most aromatic (AR uh MAT ik) compounds are based on benzene. As shown in **Figure 3,** benzene has a ring of six carbons that have alternating double and single bonds. Aromatic hydrocarbons often have strong odors.

organic compound a covalently bonded compound that contains carbon

hydrocarbon an organic compound composed only of carbon and hydrogen

Figure 3 *Benzene is the starting material for manufacturing many products, including medicines.*

Table 1 Types and Uses of Organic Compounds

Type of compound	Uses	Examples
Alkyl halides	starting material for Teflon™ refrigerant (Freon™)	chloromethane, CH_3Cl bromoethane, C_2H_5Br
Alcohols	rubbing alcohol gasoline additive antifreeze	methanol, CH_3OH ethanol, C_2H_5OH
Organic acids	food preservatives flavorings	ethanoic acid, CH_3COOH propanoic acid, C_2H_5COOH
Esters	flavorings fragrances clothing (polyester)	methyl ethanoate, CH_3COOCH_3 ethyl propanoate, $C_2H_5COOC_2H_5$

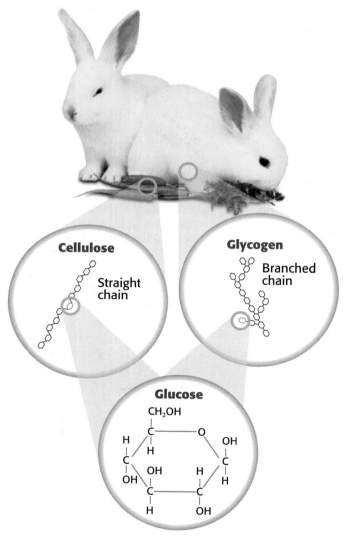

Figure 4 *Glucose molecules, represented by hexagons, can bond to form complex carbohydrates, such as cellulose and glycogen.*

Other Organic Compounds

There are many other kinds of organic compounds. Some have atoms of halogens, oxygen, sulfur, and phosphorus in their molecules. A few of these compounds and their uses are listed in **Table 1.**

Biochemicals: The Compounds of Life

Organic compounds that are made by living things are called *biochemicals*. Biochemicals are divided into four categories: carbohydrates, lipids, proteins, and nucleic acids (noo KLEE ik AS idz).

Carbohydrates

Carbohydrates are biochemicals that are composed of one or more simple sugar molecules bonded together. Carbohydrates are used as a source of energy. There are two kinds of carbohydrates: simple carbohydrates and complex carbohydrates.

Simple carbohydrates include simple sugars, such as glucose. **Figure 4** shows how glucose molecules can bond to form different complex carbohydrates. Complex carbohydrates may be made of hundreds or thousands of sugar molecules bonded together. *Cellulose* gives plant cell walls their rigid structure, and *glycogen* supplies energy to muscle cells.

Lipids

Lipids are biochemicals that do not dissolve in water. Fats, oils, and waxes are kinds of lipids. Lipids have many functions, including storing energy and making up cell membranes. Although too much fat in your diet can be unhealthy, some fat is important to good health. The foods in **Figure 5** are sources of lipids.

Lipids store excess energy in the body. Animals tend to store lipids as fats, while plants store lipids as oils. When an organism has used up most of its carbohydrates, it can obtain energy by breaking down lipids. Lipids are also used to store some vitamins.

Proteins

Most of the biochemicals found in living things are proteins. In fact, after water, proteins are the most common molecules in your cells. **Proteins** are biochemicals that are composed of "building blocks" called *amino acids*.

Amino acids are small molecules made up of carbon, hydrogen, oxygen, and nitrogen atoms. Some amino acids also include sulfur atoms. Amino acids bond to form proteins of many shapes and sizes. The shape of a protein determines the function of the protein. If even a single amino acid is missing or out of place, the protein may not function correctly or at all. Proteins have many functions. They regulate chemical activities, transport and store materials, and provide structural support.

Reading Check What are proteins made of?

carbohydrate a class of energy-giving nutrients that includes sugars, starches, and fiber; composed of one or more simple sugars bonded together

lipid a type of biochemical that does not dissolve in water; fats and steroids are lipids

protein a molecule that is made up of amino acids and that is needed to build and repair body structures and to regulate processes in the body

Food Facts

1. Select **four empty food packages.**

2. Without reading the Nutrition Facts labels, rank the items from most carbohydrate content to least carbohydrate content.

3. Rank the items from most fat content to least fat content.

4. Read the Nutrition Facts labels, and compare your rankings with the real rankings.

5. Why do you think your rankings were right, or why were they wrong? Explain your answers.

Figure 5 *Vegetable oil, meat, cheese, nuts, eggs, and milk are sources of lipids in your diet.*

Figure 6 *Spider webs are made up of proteins that are shaped like long fibers.*

nucleic acid a molecule made up of subunits called *nucleotides*

Examples of Proteins

Proteins have many roles in your body and in living things. Enzymes (EN ZIEMZ) are proteins that are catalysts. *Catalysts* regulate chemical reactions in the body by increasing the rate at which the reactions occur. Some hormones are proteins. For example, insulin is a protein hormone that helps regulate your blood-sugar level. Another kind of protein, called *hemoglobin,* is found in red blood cells and delivers oxygen throughout the body. There are also large proteins that extend through cell membranes. These proteins help control the transport of materials into and out of cells. Some proteins, such as those in your hair, provide structural support. The structural proteins of silk fibers make the spider web shown in **Figure 6** strong and lightweight.

Nucleic Acids

The largest molecules made by living organisms are nucleic acids. **Nucleic acids** are biochemicals made up of *nucleotides* (NOO klee oh TIEDZ). Nucleotides are molecules made of carbon, hydrogen, oxygen, nitrogen, and phosphorus atoms. There are only five kinds of nucleotides. But nucleic acids may have millions of nucleotides bonded together. The only reason living things differ from each other is that each living thing has a different order of nucleotides.

Nucleic acids have several functions. One function of nucleic acids is to store genetic information. They also help build proteins and other nucleic acids. Nucleic acids are sometimes called *the blueprints of life,* because they contain all the information needed for a cell to make all of its proteins.

Reading Check What are two functions of nucleic acids?

CONNECTION TO Social Studies

DNA "Fingerprinting" and Crime-Scene Investigation The chemical structure of all human DNA is the same. The only difference between one person's DNA and another's is the order, or sequence, of the building blocks in the DNA. The number of ways these building blocks can be sequenced are countless.

DNA fingerprinting is new process. However, it has changed the way that criminal investigations are carried out. Research DNA fingerprinting. Find out when DNA fingerprinting was first used, who developed the process, and how DNA fingerprinting is used in crime-scene investigations. Present your findings in an oral presentation to your class. Include a model or a poster to help explain the process to your classmates.

DNA and RNA

There are two kinds of nucleic acids: DNA and RNA. A model of DNA (**d**eoxyribo**n**ucleic **a**cid) is shown in **Figure 7**. DNA is the genetic material of the cell. DNA molecules can store a huge amount of information because of their length. The DNA molecules in a single human cell have a length of about 2 m—which is more than 6 ft long! When a cell needs to make a certain protein, it copies a certain part of the DNA. The information copied from the DNA directs the order in which amino acids are bonded to make that protein. DNA also contains information used to build the second type of nucleic acid, RNA (**r**ibo**n**ucleic **a**cid). RNA is involved in the actual building of proteins.

Figure 7 *Two strands of DNA are twisted in a spiral shape. Four different nucleotides make up the rungs of the DNA ladder.*

SECTION Review

Summary

- Organic compounds contain carbon, which can form four bonds.
- Hydrocarbons are composed of only carbon and hydrogen.
- Hydrocarbons may be saturated, unsaturated, or aromatic hydrocarbons.
- Carbohydrates are made of simple sugars.
- Lipids store energy and make up cell membranes.
- Proteins are composed of amino acids.
- Nucleic acids store genetic information and help cells make proteins.

Using Key Terms

1. Use the following terms in the same sentence: *organic compound, hydrocarbon,* and *biochemical.*

2. In your own words, write a definition for each of the following terms: *carbohydrate, lipid, protein,* and *nucleic acid.*

Understanding Key Ideas

3. A saturated hydrocarbon has
   a. only single bonds.
   b. double bonds.
   c. triple bonds.
   d. double and triple bonds.

4. List two functions of proteins.

5. What is an aromatic hydrocarbon?

Critical Thinking

6. **Identifying Relationships** Hemoglobin is a protein that is in blood and that transports oxygen to the tissues of the body. Information stored in nucleic acids tells a cell how to make proteins. What might happen if there is a mistake in the information needed to make hemoglobin?

7. **Making Comparisons** Compare saturated hydrocarbons with unsaturated hydrocarbons.

Interpreting Graphics

Use the structural formula of this organic compound to answer the questions that follow.

$$H-\underset{\underset{H}{|}}{\overset{\overset{H}{|}}{C}}-\underset{\underset{H}{|}}{\overset{\overset{H}{|}}{C}}-\underset{\underset{H}{|}}{\overset{\overset{H}{|}}{C}}-H$$

8. What type of bonds are present in this molecule?

9. Can you determine the shape of the molecule from this structural formula? Explain your answer.

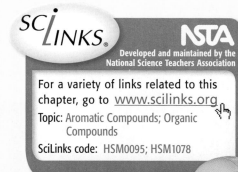

Developed and maintained by the National Science Teachers Association

For a variety of links related to this chapter, go to www.scilinks.org

Topic: Aromatic Compounds; Organic Compounds

SciLinks code: HSM0095; HSM1078

Skills Practice Lab

Cabbage Patch Indicators

OBJECTIVES

Make a natural acid-base indicator solution.

Determine the pH of various common substances.

MATERIALS

- beaker, 250 mL
- beaker tongs
- eyedropper
- hot plate
- litmus paper
- pot holder
- red cabbage leaf
- sample liquids provided by teacher
- tape, masking
- test tubes
- test-tube rack
- water, distilled

SAFETY

Indicators are weak acids or bases that change color due to the pH of the substance to which they are added. Red cabbage contains a natural indicator. It turns specific colors at specific pHs. In this lab you will extract the indicator from red cabbage. Then, you will use it to determine the pH of several liquids.

Procedure

1. Copy the table below. Be sure to include one line for each sample liquid.

Data Collection Table			
Liquid	Color with indicator	pH	Effect on litmus paper
Control			
		DO NOT WRITE IN BOOK	

2 Put on protective gloves. Place 100 mL of distilled water in the beaker. Tear the cabbage leaf into small pieces. Place the pieces in the beaker.

3 Use the hot plate to heat the cabbage and water to boiling. Continue boiling until the water is deep blue. **Caution:** Use extreme care when working near a hot plate.

4 Use tongs to remove the beaker from the hot plate. Turn the hot plate off. Allow the solution to cool on a pot holder for 5 to 10 minutes.

5 While the solution is cooling, use masking tape and a pen to label the test tubes for each sample liquid. Label one test tube as the control. Place the tubes in the rack.

6 Use the eyedropper to place a small amount (about 5 mL) of the indicator (cabbage juice) in the test tube labeled as the control.

7 Pour a small amount (about 5 mL) of each sample liquid into the appropriate test tube.

8 Using the eyedropper, place several drops of the indicator into each test tube. Swirl gently. Record the color of each liquid in the table.

9 Use the chart below to the find the pH of each sample. Record the pH values in the table.

10 Litmus paper has an indicator that turns red in an acid and blue in a base. Test each liquid with a strip of litmus paper. Record the results.

Analyze the Results

1 **Analyzing Data** What purpose does the control serve? What is the pH of the control?

2 **Examining Data** What colors in your samples indicate the presence of an acid? What colors indicate the presence of a base?

3 **Analyzing Results** Why is red cabbage juice considered a good indicator?

Draw Conclusions

4 **Interpreting Information** Which do you think would be more useful to help identify an unknown liquid—litmus paper or red cabbage juice? Why?

Applying Your Data

Unlike distilled water, rainwater has some carbon dioxide dissolved in it. Is rainwater acidic, basic, or neutral? To find out, place a small amount of the cabbage juice indicator (which is water-based) in a clean test tube. Use a straw to gently blow bubbles in the indicator. Continue blowing bubbles until you see a color change. What can you conclude about the pH of your "rainwater?" What is the purpose of blowing bubbles in the cabbage juice?

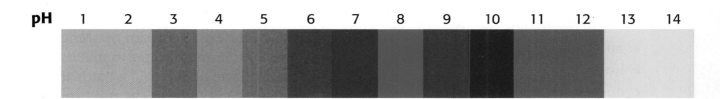

| pH | 1 | 2 | 3 | 4 | 5 | 6 | 7 | 8 | 9 | 10 | 11 | 12 | 13 | 14 |

Chapter Review

USING KEY TERMS

For each pair of terms, explain how the meanings of the terms differ.

1 *ionic compound* and *covalent compound*

2 *acid* and *base*

3 *pH* and *indicator*

4 *hydrocarbon* and *organic compound*

5 *carbohydrate* and *lipid*

6 *protein* and *nucleic acid*

UNDERSTANDING KEY IDEAS

Multiple Choice

7 Which of the following statements describes lipids?

  a. Lipids are used to store energy.

  b. Lipids do not dissolve in water.

  c. Lipids make up part of the cell membrane.

  d. All of the above

8 Ionic compounds

  a. have a low melting point.

  b. are often brittle.

  c. do not conduct electric current in water.

  d. do not dissolve easily in water.

9 An increase in the concentration of hydronium ions in solution

  a. raises the pH.

  b. lowers the pH.

  c. does not affect the pH.

  d. doubles the pH.

10 The compounds that store information for building proteins are

  a. lipids.

  b. hydrocarbons.

  c. nucleic acids.

  d. carbohydrates.

Short Answer

11 What type of compound would you use to neutralize a solution of potassium hydroxide?

12 Explain why the reaction of an acid with a base is called *neutralization*.

13 What characteristic of carbon atoms helps to explain the wide variety of organic compounds?

14 What kind of ions are produced when an acid is dissolved in water and when a base is dissolved in water?

Math Skills

15 Most of the vinegar used to make pickles is 5% acetic acid. So, in 100 mL of vinegar, 5 mL is acid diluted with 95 mL of water. If you bought a 473 mL bottle of 5% vinegar, how many milliliters of acetic acid would be in the bottle? How many milliliters of water were used to dilute the acetic acid?

16 If you dilute a 75 mL can of orange juice with enough water to make a total volume of 300 mL, what is the percentage of juice in the mixture?

17 Concept Mapping Use the following terms to create a concept map: *acid, base, salt, neutral,* and *pH.*

18 Applying Concepts Fish give off the base, ammonia, NH_3, as waste. How does the release of ammonia affect the pH of the water in the aquarium? What can be done to correct the pH of the water?

19 Analyzing Methods Many insects, such as fire ants, inject formic acid, a weak acid, when they bite or sting. Describe the type of compound that should be used to treat the bite.

20 Making Comparisons Organic compounds are also covalent compounds. What properties would you expect organic compounds to have as a result?

21 Applying Concepts Farmers have been known to taste their soil to determine whether the soil has the correct acidity for their plants. How would taste help the farmer determine the acidity of the soil?

22 Analyzing Ideas A diet that includes a high level of lipids is unhealthy. Why is a diet containing no lipids also unhealthy?

Use the structural formulas below to answer the questions that follow.

23 A saturated hydrocarbon is represented by which structural formula(s)?

24 An unsaturated hydrocarbon is represented by which structural formula(s)?

25 An aromatic hydrocarbon is represented by which structural formula(s)?

READING

Read each of the passages below. Then, answer the questions that follow each passage.

Passage 1 Spider webs often resemble a bicycle wheel. The "spokes" of the web are made of a silk thread called *dragline silk*. The sticky, stretchy part of the web is called *capture silk* because the spiders use this silk to <u>capture</u> their prey. Spider silk is made of proteins, and proteins are made of amino acids. There are 20 naturally occurring amino acids, but spider silk has only 7 of them. Scientists used a technique called *nuclear magnetic resonance* (NMR) to see the structure of dragline silk. The silk fiber is made of two tough strands of alanine-rich protein embedded in a glycine-rich substance. This protein resembles tangled spaghetti. Scientists believe that this tangled part makes the silk springy and that a repeating sequence of 5 amino acids makes the protein stretchy.

1. According to the passage, how many types of amino acids does spider silk contain?

A 20 amino acids

B 5 amino acids

C 7 amino acids

D all naturally occurring amino acids

2. Based on the passage, which of the following statements is a fact?

F Capture silk makes up the "spokes" of the web.

G The silk fiber is made of two strands of glycine-rich protein.

H Proteins are made of amino acids.

I Spider webs are strong because of a repeating sequence of 5 amino acids.

3. In this passage, what does *capture* mean?

A to kill

B to eat

C to free

D to trap

Passage 2 The earliest evidence of soapmaking dates back to 2,800 BCE. A soaplike material was found in clay cylinders in ancient Babylon. According to Roman legend, soap was named after Mount Sapo, where animals were sacrificed. A soaplike substance was made when rain washed the melted animal fat and wood ashes into the clay soil along the Tiber River. In 1791, a major step toward large scale <u>commercial</u> soapmaking began when Nicholas Leblanc, a French chemist, patented a process for making soda ash from salt. About 20 years later, the science of modern soapmaking was born. At that time, Michel Chevreul, another French chemist, discovered how fats, glycerin, and fatty acids interact. This interaction is the basis of saponification, or soap chemistry, today.

1. In this passage, what does *commercial* mean?

A for advertising purposes

B for public sale

C from French manufacturers

D for a limited time period

2. Based on the passage, which of the following statements is a fact?

F Saponification is a process used to make soap.

G The word *soap* probably originated from the French.

H Modern soapmaking began around 1791.

I Soapmaking began 2,000 years ago.

3. Which of the following statements is the best summary for the passage?

A The process of soapmaking has a history of at least 4,000 years.

B Most of the scientists responsible for soapmaking were from France.

C Commercial soapmaking began in 1791.

D Soap chemistry is called *saponification*.

The diagram below shows a model of a water molecule (H_2O). Use the diagram to answer the questions that follow.

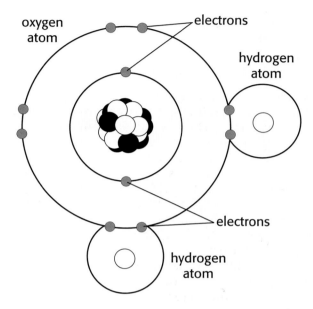

oxygen atom

electrons

hydrogen atom

electrons

hydrogen atom

1. Which statement best describes the oxygen atom?

A The oxygen atom has four valence electrons.

B The oxygen atom is sharing two electrons with two other atoms.

C The oxygen atom lost two electrons.

D The oxygen atom has two valence electrons.

2. Which of the following features cannot be determined by looking at the model?

F the number of atoms in the molecule

G the number of electrons in each atom

H the type of bonds joining the atoms

I the physical state of the substance

3. Which statement best describes each of the smaller atoms in the molecule?

A Each atom has eight total electrons.

B Each atom has two protons.

C Each atom has two valence electrons.

D Each atom has lost two electrons.

Read each question below, and choose the best answer.

1. Marty is making 8 gal of lemonade. How much sugar does he need if 1 1/2 cups of sugar are needed for every 2 gal of lemonade?

A 4 cups

B 6 cups

C 3 cups

D 8 cups

2. The Jimenez family went to the science museum. They bought four tickets at $12.95 each, four snacks at $3 each, and two souvenirs at $7.95 each. What is the best estimate of the total cost of tickets, snacks, and souvenirs?

F $24

G $50

H $63

I $80

3. Each whole number on the pH scale represents a tenfold change in the concentration of hydronium ions. An acid that has a pH of 2 has how many times more hydronium ions than an acid that has a pH of 5?

A 30 times more hydronium ions

B 100 times more hydronium ions

C 1,000 times more hydronium ions

D 10,000 times more hydronium ions

Science in Action

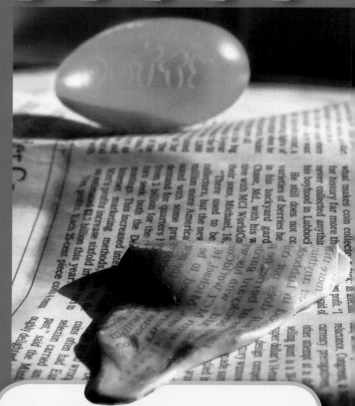

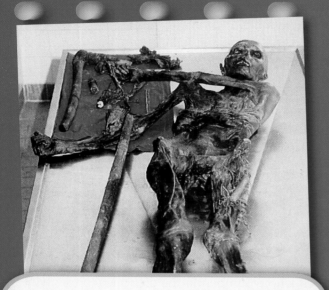

Science, Technology, and Society

Molecular Photocopying

To learn about our human ancestors, scientists can use DNA from mummies. Well-preserved DNA can be copied using a technique called polymerase chain reaction (PCR). PCR uses enzymes called *polymerases,* which make new strands of DNA using old strands as templates. Thus, PCR is called molecular photocopying. However, scientists have to be very careful when using this process. If just one of their own skin cells falls into the PCR mixture, it will contaminate the ancient DNA with their own DNA.

Weird Science

Silly Putty™

During World War II, the supply of natural rubber was very low. So, James Wright, at General Electric, tried to make a synthetic rubber. The putty he made could be molded, stretched, and bounced. But it did not work as a rubber substitute and was ignored. Then, Peter Hodgson, a consultant for a toy company, had a brilliant idea. He marketed the putty as a toy in 1949. It was an immediate success. Hodgson created the name Silly Putty™. Although Silly Putty™ was invented more than 50 years ago, it has not changed much. More than 300 million eggs of Silly Putty have been sold since 1950.

Social Studies ACTiViTY

WRITING SKILL DNA analysis of mummies is helping archeologists study human history. Write a research paper about what scientists have learned about human history through DNA analysis.

Math ACTiViTY

In 1949, Mr. Hodgson bought 9.5 kg of putty for $147. The putty was divided into balls, each having a mass of 14 g. What was his cost for one 14 g ball of putty?

Jeannie Eberhardt

Forensic Scientist Jeannie Eberhardt says that her job as a forensic scientist is not really as glamorous as it may seem on popular TV shows. "If they bring me a garbage bag from the crime scene, then my job is to dig through the trash and look for evidence," she laughs. Jeannie Eberhardt explains that her job is to "search for, collect, and analyze evidence from crime scenes." Eberhardt says that one of the most important qualities a forensic scientist can have is the ability to be unbiased. She says that she focuses on the evidence and not on any information she may have about the alleged crime or the suspect. Eberhardt advises students who think they might be interested in a career as a forensic scientist to talk to someone who works in the field. She also recommends that students develop a broad science background. And she advises students that most of these jobs require extensive background checks. "Your actions now could affect your ability to get a job later on," she points out.

Language Arts ACTiViTY

WRITING SKILL Jeannie Eberhardt says that it is very important to be unbiased when analyzing a crime scene. Write a one-page essay explaining why it is necessary to focus on the evidence in a crime and not on personal feelings or news reports.

go.hrw.com

To learn more about these Science in Action topics, visit go.hrw.com and type in the keyword **HP5CMPF**

Current Science

Check out Current Science® articles related to this chapter by visiting go.hrw.com. Just type in the keyword **HP5CS15**

16

Atomic Energy

SECTION ① Radioactivity......... 448

SECTION ② Energy from
the Nucleus.......... 456

Chapter Lab 462
Chapter Review 464
Standardized Test Preparation 466
Science in Action............... 468

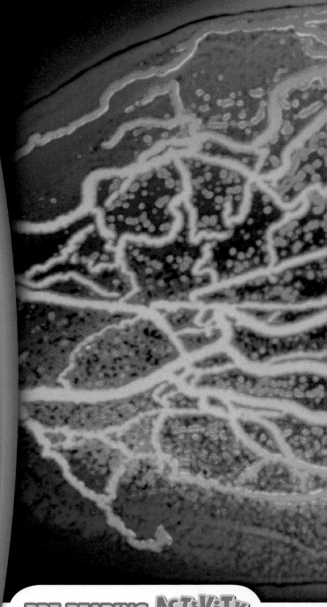

About the PHOTO

Look closely at the blood vessels that show up clearly in this image of a human hand. Doctors sometimes inject radioactive substances into a patient's body to help locate tumors and measure the activity of certain organs. Radioactive emissions from the substances are measured using a scanning device. Then, computers turn the data into an image.

PRE-READING ACTIVITY

Graphic Organizer

Spider Map Before you read the chapter, create the graphic organizer entitled "Spider Map" described in the **Study Skills** section of the Appendix. Label the circle "Radioactive Decay." Create a leg for each type of radioactive decay. As you read the chapter, fill in the map with details about each type of decay.

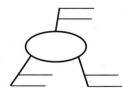

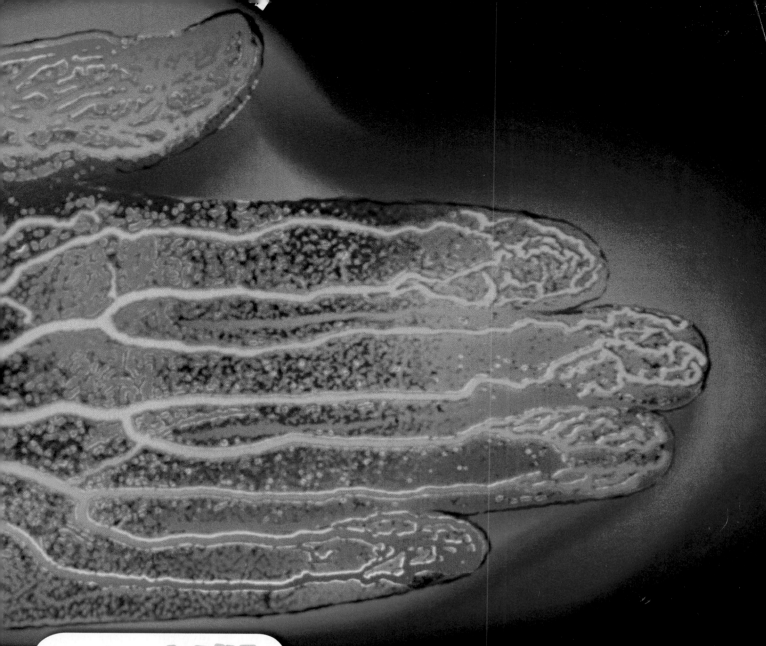

START-UP ACTIVITY

Watch Your Headsium!

In this activity, you will model the decay of unstable nuclei into stable nuclei.

Procedure

1. Place **100 pennies** with the heads' side up in a **box with a lid.** The pennies represent radioactive nuclei. Record 100 "headsium" nuclei as "Trial 0."

2. Close the box. Shake it up and down for 5 s.

3. Open the box. Remove the stable tails-up nuclei, or "tailsium" nuclei. Count the number of headsium nuclei remaining, and record it as "Trial 1."

4. Perform trials until you don't have any more pennies in the box or until you have finished five trials. Record your results.

Analysis

1. On a piece of **graph paper,** graph your data by plotting "Number of headsium nuclei" on the *y*-axis and "Trial number" on the *x*-axis. What trend do you see in the number of headsium nuclei?

2. Compare your graph with the graphs made by the other students in your class.

Radioactivity

When scientists do experiments, they don't always find what they expect to find.

In 1896, a French scientist named Henri Becquerel found much more than he expected. He found a new area of science.

Discovering Radioactivity

Becquerel's hypothesis was that fluorescent minerals give off X rays. (*Fluorescent* materials glow when light shines on them.) To test his idea, he put a fluorescent mineral on top of a photographic plate wrapped in paper. After putting his setup in bright sunlight, he developed the plate and saw the strong image of the mineral he expected, as shown in **Figure 1.**

An Unexpected Result

Becquerel tried to do the experiment again, but the weather was cloudy. So, he put his materials in a drawer. He developed the plate anyway a few days later. He was shocked to see a strong image. Even without light, the mineral gave off energy. The energy passed through the paper and made an image on the plate. After more tests, Becquerel concluded that this energy comes from uranium, an element in the mineral.

Naming the Unexpected

This energy is called *nuclear radiation,* high-energy particles and rays that are emitted by the nuclei of some atoms. Marie Curie, a scientist working with Becquerel, named the process by which some nuclei give off nuclear radiation. She named the process **radioactivity,** which is also called *radioactive decay.*

Figure 1 *Sunlight could not pass through the paper. So, the image on the plate must have been made by energy given off by the mineral.*

Figure 2 Alpha Decay of Radium-226

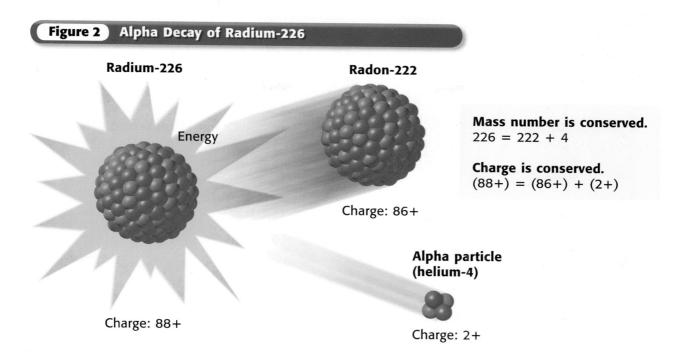

Radium-226

Radon-222

Energy

Mass number is conserved.
226 = 222 + 4

Charge is conserved.
(88+) = (86+) + (2+)

Charge: 86+

Charge: 88+

Alpha particle
(helium-4)

Charge: 2+

Kinds of Radioactive Decay

During *radioactive decay,* an unstable nucleus gives off particles and energy. Three kinds of radioactive decay are alpha decay, beta decay, and gamma decay.

Alpha Decay

The release of an alpha particle from a nucleus is called *alpha decay.* An *alpha particle* is made up of two protons and two neutrons. It has a mass number of 4 and a charge of 2+. The **mass number** is the sum of the numbers of protons and neutrons in the nucleus of an atom. An alpha particle is the same as the nucleus of a helium atom. Many large radioactive nuclei give off alpha particles and become nuclei of atoms of different elements. One example of a nucleus that gives off alpha particles is radium-226. (The number that follows the name of an element is the mass number of the atom.)

Conservation in Decay

Look at the model of alpha decay in **Figure 2.** This model shows two important things about radioactive decay. First, the mass number is conserved. The sum of the mass numbers of the starting materials is always equal to the sum of the mass numbers of the products. Second, charge is conserved. The sum of the charges of the starting materials is always equal to the sum of the charges of the products.

✓ **Reading Check** What two things are conserved in radioactive decay? (*See the Appendix for answers to Reading Checks.*)

radioactivity the process by which an unstable nucleus gives off nuclear radiation

mass number the sum of the numbers of protons and neutrons in the nucleus of an atom

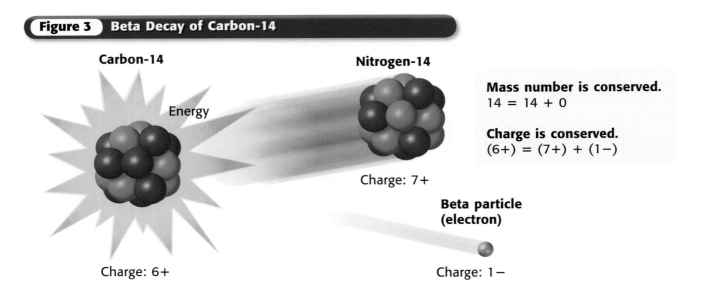

Figure 3 Beta Decay of Carbon-14

Carbon-14

Nitrogen-14

Energy

Charge: 7+

Charge: 6+

Beta particle
(electron)

Charge: 1−

Mass number is conserved.
14 = 14 + 0

Charge is conserved.
(6+) = (7+) + (1−)

Beta Decay

The release of a beta particle from a nucleus is called *beta decay*. A *beta particle* can be an electron or a positron. An electron has a charge of 1−. A positron has a charge of 1+. But electrons and positrons have a mass of almost 0. The mass number of a beta particle is 0 because it has no protons or neutrons.

Two Types of Beta Decay

A carbon-14 nucleus undergoes beta decay, as shown in the model in **Figure 3.** During this kind of decay, a neutron breaks into a proton and an electron. Notice that the nucleus becomes a nucleus of a different element. And both mass number and charge are conserved.

Not all isotopes of an element decay in the same way. **Isotopes** are atoms that have the same number of protons as other atoms of the same element do but that have different numbers of neutrons. A carbon-11 nucleus undergoes beta decay when a proton breaks into a positron and a neutron. But during any beta decay, the nucleus changes into a nucleus of a different element. And both mass number and charge are conserved.

isotope an atom that has the same number of protons (or the same atomic number) as other atoms of the same element do but that has a different number of neutrons (and thus a different atomic mass)

Gamma Decay

Energy is also given off during alpha decay and beta decay. Some of this energy is in the form of light that has very high energy called *gamma rays*. The release of gamma rays from a nucleus is called *gamma decay*. This decay happens as the particles in the nucleus shift places. Gamma rays have no mass or charge. So, gamma decay alone does not cause one element to change into another element.

The Penetrating Power of Radiation

The three forms of nuclear radiation have different abilities to penetrate, or go through, matter. This difference is due to their mass and charge, as you can see in **Figure 4.**

Effects of Radiation on Matter

Atoms that are hit by nuclear radiation can give up electrons. Chemical bonds between atoms can break when hit by nuclear radiation. Both of these things can cause damage to living and nonliving matter.

Damage to Living Matter

When an organism absorbs radiation, its cells can be damaged. Radiation can cause burns like those caused by touching something that is hot. A single large exposure to radiation can lead to *radiation sickness*. Symptoms of this sickness include fatigue, loss of appetite, and hair loss. Destruction of blood cells and even death can result. Exposure to radiation can also increase the risk of cancer because of the damage done to cells. People who work near radioactive materials often wear a film badge. Radiation will make an image on the film to warn the person if the levels of radiation are too high.

✓ Reading Check Name three symptoms of radiation sickness.

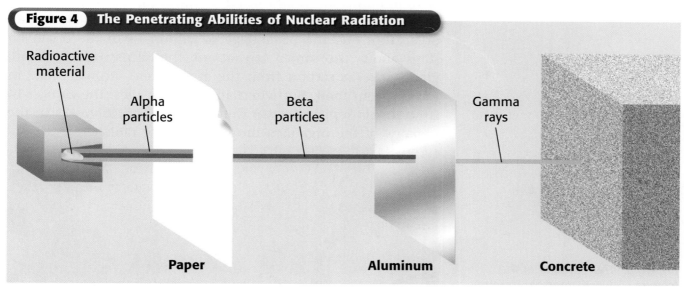

Figure 4 The Penetrating Abilities of Nuclear Radiation

Radioactive material

Alpha particles

Beta particles

Gamma rays

Paper

Aluminum

Concrete

▲ **Alpha particles** have a greater charge and mass than beta particles and gamma rays do. Alpha particles travel about 7 cm through air and are stopped by paper or clothing.

▲ **Beta particles** have a 1– or 1+ charge and almost no mass. They are more penetrating than alpha particles. Beta particles travel about 1 m through air but are stopped by 3 mm of aluminum.

▲ **Gamma rays** have no charge or mass and are the most penetrating. They are blocked by very dense, thick materials, such as a few centimeters of lead or a few meters of concrete.

Damage to Nonliving Matter

Radiation can also damage nonliving matter. When metal atoms lose electrons, the metal is weakened. For example, radiation can cause the metal structures of buildings, such as nuclear power plants, to become unsafe. High levels of radiation from the sun can damage spacecraft.

Damage at Different Depths

Gamma rays go through matter easily. They can cause damage deep within matter. Beta particles cause damage closer to the surface. Alpha particles cause damage very near the surface. But alpha particles are larger and more massive than the particles of other kinds of radiation. So, if a source of alpha particles enters an organism, the particles can cause the most damage.

Finding a Date by Decay

Finding a date for someone can be tough—especially if the person is several thousand years old! Hikers in the Italian Alps found the remains of the Iceman, shown in **Figure 5,** in 1991. Scientists were able to estimate the time of death—about 5,300 years ago! How did the scientists do this? The decay of radioactive carbon was the key.

Carbon-14—It's in You!

Carbon atoms are found in all living things. A small percentage of these atoms is radioactive carbon-14 atoms. During an organism's life, the percentage of carbon-14 in the organism stays about the same. Any atoms that decay are replaced. Plants take in carbon from the atmosphere. Animals take in carbon from food. But when an organism dies, the carbon-14 is no longer replaced. Over time, the level of carbon-14 in the remains of the organism drops because of radioactive decay.

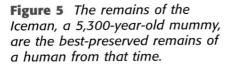

CONNECTION TO Environmental Science

WRITING SKILL **Radon in the Home** Radioactive radon-222 forms from the radioactive decay of uranium found in soil and rocks. Because radon is a gas, it can enter buildings through gaps in the walls and floors. Research the hazards of radon. Identify methods used to detect it and to prevent exposure to it. Present your findings by writing a pamphlet in the form of a public service announcement.

Figure 5 *The remains of the Iceman, a 5,300-year-old mummy, are the best-preserved remains of a human from that time.*

Figure 6 Radioactive Decay and Half-Life

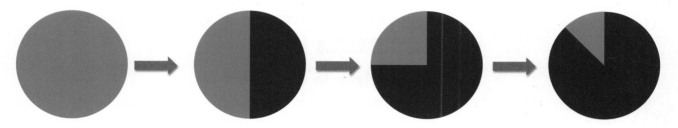

The **original sample** contains a certain amount of radioactive isotope.

After **one half-life,** one-half of the original sample has decayed, and half is unchanged.

After **two half-lives,** one-fourth of the original sample remains unchanged.

After **three half-lives,** only one-eighth of the original sample remains unchanged.

A Steady Rate of Decay

Scientists have found that every 5,730 years, half of the carbon-14 in a sample decays. The rate of decay is constant. The rate is not changed by other conditions, such as temperature or pressure. Each radioactive isotope has its own rate of decay, called half-life. A **half-life** is the amount of time it takes one-half of the nuclei of a radioactive isotope to decay. **Figure 6** is a model of this process. **Table 1** lists some isotopes that have a wide range of half-lives.

half-life the time needed for half of a sample of a radioactive substance to undergo radioactive decay

> ✓ **Reading Check** What is the half-life of carbon-14?

Determining Age

Scientists measured the number of decays in the Iceman's body each minute. They found that a little less than half of the carbon-14 in the body had changed. In other words, not quite one half-life of carbon-14 (5,730 years) had passed since the Iceman died.

Carbon-14 can be used to find the age of objects up to 50,000 years old. To find the age of older things, other elements must be used. For example, potassium-40 has a half-life of 1.3 billion years. It is used to find the age of dinosaur fossils.

How Old Is It?

One-fourth of the original carbon-14 of an antler is unchanged. As shown in **Figure 6,** two half-lives have passed. To determine the age of the antler, multiply the number of half-lives that have passed by the half-life of carbon-14. The antler's age is 2 times the half-life of carbon-14:

age = 2 × 5,730 years
age = 11,460 years

Determine the age of a wooden spear that contains one-eighth of its original amount of carbon-14.

Table 1 Examples of Half-Lives

Isotope	Half-life	Isotope	Half-life
Uranium-238	4.5 billion years	Polonium-210	138 days
Oxygen-21	3.4 s	Nitrogen-13	10 min
Hydrogen-3	12.3 years	Calcium-36	0.1 s

Uses of Radioactivity

You have learned how radioactive isotopes are used to determine the age of objects. But radioactivity is used in many areas for many things. The smoke detectors in your home might even use a small amount of radioactive material! Some isotopes can be used as tracers. *Tracers* are radioactive elements whose paths can be followed through a process or reaction.

> ✓ **Reading Check** What is a tracer?

Radioactivity in Healthcare

Doctors use tracers to help diagnose medical problems. Radioactive tracers that have short half-lives are fed to or injected into a patient. Then, a detector is used to follow the tracer as it moves through the patient's body. The image in **Figure 7** shows an example of the results of a tracer study. Radioactive materials are also used to treat illnesses, including cancer. Radioactive materials can even help prevent illness. For example, many food and healthcare products are sterilized using radiation.

Radioactivity in Industry

Radioactive isotopes can also help detect defects in structures. For example, radiation is used to test the thickness of metal sheets as they are made. Another way radioactive isotopes are used to test structures is shown in **Figure 7.**

Some space probes have been powered by radioactive materials. The energy given off as nuclei decay is converted into electrical energy for the probe.

INTERNET ACTIVITY

For another activity related to this chapter, go to **go.hrw.com** and type in the keyword **HP5RADW.**

Figure 7 Uses of Radioactivity in Healthcare and in Industry

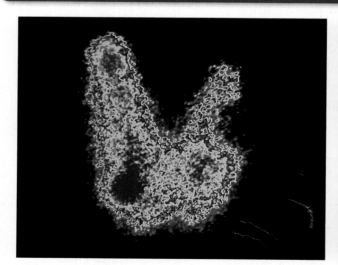

Radioactive iodine-131 was used to make this scan of a thyroid gland. The dark area shows the location of a tumor.

Tracers are used to find weak spots in materials and leaks in pipes. A Geiger counter is often used to detect the tracer.

Summary

- Henri Becquerel discovered radioactivity while trying to study X rays. Radioactivity is the process by which a nucleus gives off nuclear radiation.

- An alpha particle is composed of two protons and two neutrons. A beta particle can be an electron or a positron. Gamma rays are a form of light with very high energy.

- Gamma rays penetrate matter better than alpha or beta particles do. Beta particles penetrate matter better than alpha particles do.

- Nuclear radiation can damage living and nonliving matter.

- Half-life is the amount of time it takes for one-half of the nuclei of a radioactive isotope to decay. The age of some objects can be determined using half-lives.

- Uses of radioactive materials include detecting defects in materials, sterilizing products, diagnosing illness, and generating electrical energy.

Using Key Terms

1. Use the following terms in the same sentence: *mass number* and *isotope*.

Understanding Key Ideas

2. Which of the following statements correctly describes the changes that happen in radioactive decay?

   a. Alpha decay changes the atomic number and the mass number of a nucleus.

   b. Gamma decay changes the atomic number but not the mass number of a nucleus.

   c. Gamma decay changes the mass number but not the atomic number of a nucleus.

   d. Beta decay changes the mass number but not the atomic number of a nucleus.

3. Describe the experiment that led to the discovery of radioactivity.

4. Give two examples of how radioactivity is useful and two examples of how it is harmful.

Math Skills

5. A rock contains one-fourth of its original amount of potassium-40. The half-life of potassium-40 is 1.3 billion years. Calculate the rock's age.

6. How many half-lives have passed if a sample contains one-sixteenth of its original amount of radioactive material?

Critical Thinking

7. **Making Comparisons** Compare the penetrating power of the following nuclear radiation: alpha particles, beta particles, and gamma rays.

8. **Making Inferences** Why would uranium-238 not be useful in determining the age of a spear that is thought to be 5,000 years old? Explain your reasoning.

Interpreting Graphics

9. Look at the figure below. Which nucleus could not undergo alpha decay? Explain your answer.

Beryllium-10   **Hydrogen-3**

6 neutrons   2 neutrons
4 protons   1 proton

Developed and maintained by the
National Science Teachers Association

For a variety of links related to this chapter, go to www.scilinks.org

Topic: Discovering Radioactivity; Radioactive Isotopes

SciLinks code: HSM0412; HSM1256

Energy from the Nucleus

From an early age, you were probably told not to play with fire. But fire itself is neither good nor bad. It simply has benefits and hazards.

Likewise, getting energy from the nucleus of an atom has benefits and hazards. In this section, you will learn about two ways to get energy from the nucleus—fission (FISH uhn) and fusion (FYOO zhuhn). Gaining an understanding of the advantages and disadvantages of fission and fusion is important for people who will make decisions about the use of this energy—people like you!

READING WARM-UP

Objectives
- Describe nuclear fission.
- Identify advantages and disadvantages of fission.
- Describe nuclear fusion.
- Identify advantages and disadvantages of fusion.

Terms to Learn
nuclear fission
nuclear chain reaction
nuclear fusion

READING STRATEGY

Reading Organizer As you read this section, make a table comparing nuclear fission and nuclear fusion.

Nuclear Fission

The nuclei of some atoms decay by breaking into two smaller, more stable nuclei. **Nuclear fission** is the process by which a large nucleus splits into two small nuclei and releases energy.

The nuclei of some uranium atoms, as well as the nuclei of other large atoms, can undergo nuclear fission naturally. Large atoms can also be forced to undergo fission by hitting the atoms with neutrons, as shown by the model in **Figure 1.**

✓ **Reading Check** What happens to a nucleus that undergoes nuclear fission? (*See the Appendix for answers to Reading Checks.*)

Figure 1 Fission of a Uranium-235 Nucleus

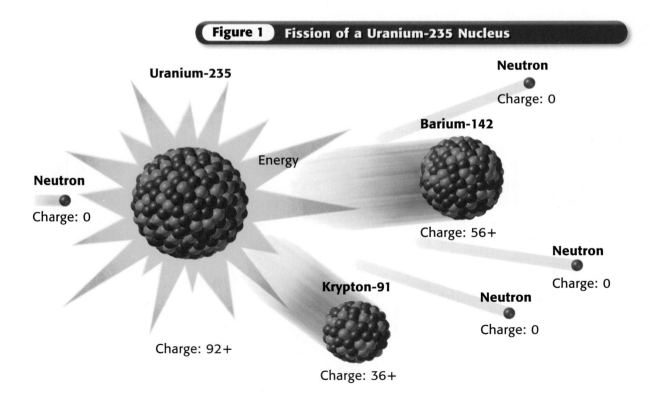

Uranium-235

Neutron
Charge: 0

Neutron
Charge: 0

Energy

Barium-142
Charge: 56+

Neutron
Charge: 0

Krypton-91
Charge: 36+

Neutron
Charge: 0

Charge: 92+

Energy from Matter

Did you know that matter can be changed into energy? It's true! If you could find the total mass of the products in **Figure 1** and compare it with the total mass of the reactants, you would find something strange. The total mass of the products is slightly less than the total mass of the reactants. Why are the masses different? Some of the matter was converted into energy.

The amount of energy given off when a single uranium nucleus splits is very small. But this energy comes from a very small amount of matter. The amount of matter converted into energy is only about one-fifth the mass of a hydrogen atom. And hydrogen is the smallest atom that exists! Look at **Figure 2.** The nuclear fission of the uranium nuclei in one fuel pellet releases as much energy as the chemical change of burning about 1,000 kg of coal.

Figure 2 *Each of these small fuel pellets can generate a large amount of energy through the process of nuclear fission.*

Nuclear Chain Reactions

Look at **Figure 1** again. Suppose that two or three of the neutrons produced split other uranium-235 nuclei. So, energy and more neutrons are given off. And then suppose that two or three of the neutrons that were given off split other nuclei and so on. This example is one type of **nuclear chain reaction,** a continuous series of nuclear fission reactions. A model of an uncontrolled chain reaction is shown in **Figure 3.**

nuclear fission the splitting of the nucleus of a large atom into two or more fragments; releases additional neutrons and energy

nuclear chain reaction a continuous series of nuclear fission reactions

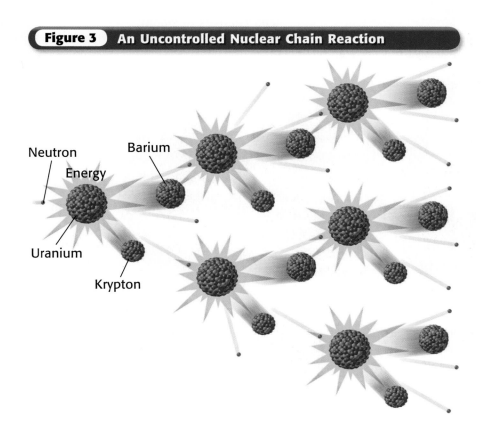

Figure 3 **An Uncontrolled Nuclear Chain Reaction**

Neutron

Barium

Energy

Uranium

Krypton

Energy from a Chain Reaction

In an *uncontrolled chain reaction,* huge amounts of energy are given off very quickly. For example, the tremendous energy of an atomic bomb is the result of an uncontrolled chain reaction. On the other hand, nuclear power plants use *controlled chain reactions.* The energy released from the nuclei in the uranium fuel within the nuclear power plants is used to generate electrical energy. **Figure 4** shows how a nuclear power plant works.

Advantages and Disadvantages of Fission

Every form of energy has advantages and disadvantages. To make informed decisions about energy use, you need to know both sides. For example, burning wood to keep warm on a cold night could save your life. But a spark from the fire could start a forest fire. Nuclear fission has advantages and disadvantages that you should think about.

Figure 4 How a Nuclear Power Plant Works

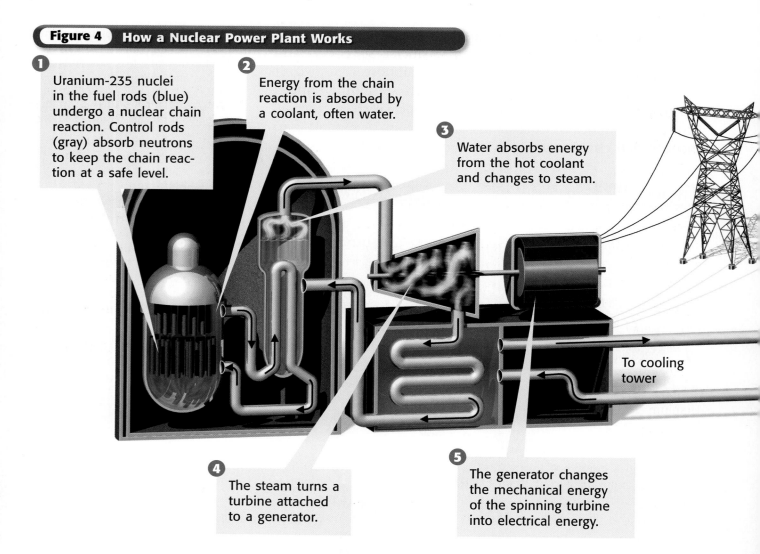

❶ Uranium-235 nuclei in the fuel rods (blue) undergo a nuclear chain reaction. Control rods (gray) absorb neutrons to keep the chain reaction at a safe level.

❷ Energy from the chain reaction is absorbed by a coolant, often water.

❸ Water absorbs energy from the hot coolant and changes to steam.

To cooling tower

❹ The steam turns a turbine attached to a generator.

❺ The generator changes the mechanical energy of the spinning turbine into electrical energy.

Accidents

A concern that many people have about nuclear power is the risk of an accident. In Chernobyl, Ukraine, on April 26, 1986, an accident happened, as shown in **Figure 5.** An explosion put large amounts of radioactive uranium fuel and waste products into the atmosphere. The cloud of radioactive material spread over most of Europe and Asia. It reached as far as North America.

Figure 5 *During a test at the Chernobyl nuclear power plant, the emergency protection system was turned off. The reactor overheated, which resulted in an explosion.*

What Waste!

Another concern about nuclear power is nuclear waste. This waste includes used fuel rods, chemicals used to process uranium, and even shoe covers and overalls worn by workers. Controlled fission has been carried out for only about 50 years. But the waste will give off high levels of radiation for thousands of years. The rate of radioactive decay cannot be changed. So, the nuclear waste must be stored until it becomes less radioactive. Most of the used fuel rods are stored in huge pools of water. Some of the liquid wastes are stored in underground tanks. However, scientists continue to look for better ideas for long-term storage of nuclear waste.

Nuclear Versus Fossil Fuel

Nuclear power plants cost more to build than power plants that use fossil fuels. But nuclear power plants often cost less to run than plants that use fossil fuels because less fuel is needed. Also, nuclear power plants do not release gases, such as carbon dioxide, into the atmosphere. The use of fission allows our supply of fossil fuels to last longer. However, the supply of uranium is limited.

✓ Reading Check What are two advantages of using nuclear fission to generate electrical energy?

CONNECTION TO Language Arts

WRITING SKILL **Storage Site** The government of the United States is required by law to build underground storage for nuclear waste. The waste must be stored for a very long time and cannot escape into the environment. In your **science journal,** write a one-page paper describing the characteristics of a good location for these underground storage sites.

Quick Lab

Gone Fission

1. Make two paper balls from a **sheet of paper.**
2. Stand in a group with your classmates. Make sure you are an arm's length from your other classmates.
3. Your teacher will gently toss a paper ball at the group. If you are touched by a ball, gently toss your paper balls at the group.
4. Explain how this activity is a model of a chain reaction. Be sure to explain what the students and the paper balls represent.

Figure 6 Nuclear Fusion of Hydrogen

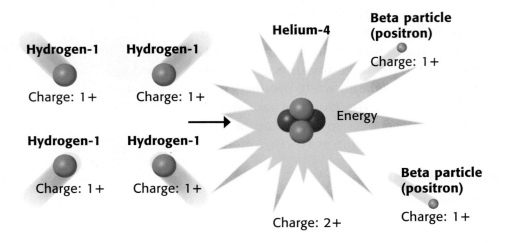

Nuclear Fusion

Fusion is another nuclear reaction in which matter is converted into energy. In **nuclear fusion,** two or more nuclei that have small masses combine, or fuse, to form a larger nucleus.

nuclear fusion the combination of the nuclei of small atoms to form a larger nucleus; releases energy

Plasma Needed

In order for fusion to happen, the repulsion between positively charged nuclei must be overcome. Very high temperatures are needed—more than 100,000,000°C! At these high temperatures, matter is a plasma. *Plasma* is the state of matter in which electrons have been removed from atoms. So, plasma is made up of ions and electrons. One place that has such temperatures is the sun. In the sun's core, hydrogen nuclei fuse to form a helium nucleus, as shown in the model in **Figure 6.**

✓ **Reading Check** Describe the process of nuclear fusion.

Advantages and Disadvantages of Fusion

Energy for your home cannot yet be generated using nuclear fusion. First, very high temperatures are needed. Second, more energy is needed to make and hold the plasma than is generated by fusion. But scientists predict that fusion will provide electrical energy in the future—maybe in your lifetime!

Less Accident Prone

The concern about an accident such as the one at Chernobyl is much lower for fusion reactors. If a fusion reactor exploded, very little radioactive material would be released. Fusion products are not radioactive. And the hydrogen-3 used for fuel in experimental fusion reactors is much less radioactive than the uranium used in fission reactors.

CONNECTION TO Astronomy

Elements of the Stars
Hydrogen is not the only fuel that stars use for fusion. Research other elements that stars can use as fuels and the fusion reactions that make these elements. Make a poster showing what you learn.

ACTiViTY

Oceans of Fuel

Scientists studying fusion use hydrogen-2 and hydrogen-3 in their work. Hydrogen-1 is much more common than these isotopes. But there is enough of them in Earth's waters to provide fuel for millions of years. Also, a fusion reaction releases more energy per gram of fuel than a fission reaction does. So, fusion saves more resources than fission does, as shown in **Figure 7.**

Less Waste

The products of fusion reactions are not radioactive. So, fusion is a "cleaner" source of energy than fission is. There would be much less radioactive waste. But to have the benefits of fusion, scientists need money to pay for research.

Figure 7 *Fusing the hydrogen-2 in 3.8 L of water would release about the same amount of energy as burning 1,140 L of gasoline!*

SECTION Review

Summary

- In nuclear fission, a massive nucleus breaks into two nuclei.

- In nuclear fusion, two or more nuclei combine to form a larger nucleus.

- Nuclear fission is used in power plants to generate electrical energy. A limited fuel supply and radioactive waste products are disadvantages of fission.

- Nuclear fusion cannot yet be used as an energy source, but plentiful fuel and little waste are advantages of fusion.

Using Key Terms

Complete each of the following sentences by choosing the correct term from the word bank.

> nuclear fission
> nuclear fusion
> nuclear chain reaction

1. During ___, small nuclei combine.

2. During ___, nuclei split one after another.

Understanding Key Ideas

3. Which of the following is an advantage nuclear fission has over fossil fuels?

   a. unlimited supply of fuel
   b. less radioactive waste
   c. fewer building expenses
   d. less released carbon dioxide

4. Which kind of nuclear reaction is currently used to generate electrical energy?

5. Which kind of nuclear reaction is the source of the sun's energy?

6. What particle is needed to begin a nuclear chain reaction?

7. In both fission and fusion, what is converted into energy?

Math Skills

8. Imagine that a uranium nucleus splits and releases three neutrons and that each neutron splits another nucleus. If the first split occurs in stage 1, how many nuclei will split during stage 4?

Critical Thinking

9. **Making Comparisons** Compare nuclear fission with nuclear fusion.

10. **Analyzing Processes** The floor of a room is covered in mousetraps that each hold two table-tennis balls. One ball is dropped onto a trap. The trap snaps shut, and the balls on it fly into the air and fall on other traps. What nuclear process is modeled here? Explain your answer.

SCILINKS.

NSTA
Developed and maintained by the
National Science Teachers Association

For a variety of links related to this chapter, go to www.scilinks.org

Topic: Nuclear Fission; Nuclear Fusion
SciLinks code: HSM1048; HSM1050

Model-Making Lab

OBJECTIVES

Build models to represent controlled and uncontrolled nuclear chain reactions.

Compare models of controlled and uncontrolled nuclear chain reactions.

MATERIALS

- dominoes (15)
- stopwatch

Domino Chain Reactions

Fission of uranium-235 is a process that relies on neutrons. When a uranium-235 nucleus splits into two smaller nuclei, it releases two or three neutrons that can cause neighboring nuclei to undergo fission. This fission can result in a nuclear chain reaction. In this lab, you will build two models of nuclear chain reactions, using dominoes.

Procedure

1 For the first model, set up the dominoes as shown below. When pushed over, each domino should hit two dominoes in the next row.

2 Measure the time it takes for all the dominoes to fall. To do this, start the stopwatch as you tip over the front domino. Stop the stopwatch when the last domino falls. Record this time.

3 If some of the dominoes do not fall, repeat steps 1 and 2. You may have to adjust the setup a few times.

4 For the second model, set up the dominoes as shown at left. The domino in the first row should hit both of the dominoes in the second row. Beginning with the second row, only one domino from each row should hit both of the dominoes in the next row.

5 Repeat step 2. Again, you may have to adjust the setup a few times to get all the dominoes to fall.

Analyze the Results

1 **Classifying** Which model represents an uncontrolled chain reaction? Which represents a controlled chain reaction? Explain your answers.

2 **Analyzing Results** Imagine that each domino releases a certain amount of energy as it falls. Compare the total amount of energy released in the two models.

3 **Analyzing Data** Compare the time needed to release the energy in the models. Which model took longer to release its energy?

Draw Conclusions

4 **Evaluating Models** In a nuclear power plant, a chain reaction is controlled by using a material that absorbs neutrons. Only enough neutrons to continue the chain reaction are allowed to continue splitting uranium-235 nuclei. Explain how your model of a controlled nuclear chain reaction modeled this process.

5 **Applying Conclusions** Why must uranium nuclei be close to each other in order for a nuclear chain reaction to happen? (Hint: What would happen in your model if the dominoes were too far apart?)

Chapter Review

USING KEY TERMS

The statements below are false. For each statement, replace the underlined term to make a true statement.

1 <u>Nuclear fusion</u> involves splitting a nucleus.

2 During one <u>beta decay</u>, half of a radioactive sample will decay.

3 <u>Radioactivity</u> involves the joining of nuclei.

4 Isotopes of an element have different <u>atomic numbers</u>.

UNDERSTANDING KEY IDEAS

Multiple Choice

5 Which of the following is a use of radioactive material?

a. detecting smoke

b. locating defects in materials

c. generating electrical energy

d. All of the above

6 Which particle both begins and is produced by a nuclear chain reaction?

a. positron   **c.** alpha particle

b. neutron   **d.** beta particle

7 Which nuclear radiation can be stopped by paper?

a. alpha particles   **c.** gamma rays

b. beta particles   **d.** None of the above

8 The half-life of a radioactive atom is 2 months. If you start with 1 g of the element, how much will remain after 6 months?

a. One-half of a gram will remain.

b. One-fourth of a gram will remain.

c. One-eighth of a gram will remain.

d. None of the sample will remain.

9 The waste products of nuclear fission

a. are harmless.

b. are safe after 20 years.

c. can be destroyed by burning them.

d. remain radioactive for thousands of years.

10 Which statement about nuclear fusion is false?

a. Nuclear fusion happens in the sun.

b. Nuclear fusion is the joining of the nuclei of atoms.

c. Nuclear fusion is currently used to generate electrical energy.

d. Nuclear fusion can use hydrogen as fuel.

Short Answer

11 What are two dangers associated with nuclear fission?

12 What are two of the problems that need to be solved in order to make nuclear fusion a usable energy source?

13 In fission, the products have less mass than the starting materials do. Explain why this happens.

Math Skills

14 A scientist used 10 g of phosphorus-32 in a test on plant growth but forgot to record the date. When measured some time later, only 2.5 g of phosphorus-32 remained. If phosphorus-32 has a half-life of 14 days, how many days ago did the experiment begin?

CRITICAL THINKING

15 **Concept Mapping** Use the following terms to create a concept map: *radioactive decay, alpha particle, beta particle, gamma ray,* and *nuclear radiation*.

16 **Expressing Opinions** Smoke detectors often use americium-243 to detect smoke particles in the air. Americium-243 undergoes alpha decay. Do you think that these smoke detectors are safe to have in your home if used properly? Explain. (Hint: Think about how penetrating alpha particles are.)

17 **Applying Concepts** How can radiation cause cancer?

18 **Analyzing Processes** Explain why nuclei of carbon, oxygen, and iron can be found in stars.

19 **Making Inferences** If you could block all radiation from sources outside your body, explain why you would still be exposed to some radiation.

INTERPRETING GRAPHICS

20 The image below was made in a manner similar to that of Becquerel's original experiment. What conclusions can be drawn from this image about the penetrating power of radiation?

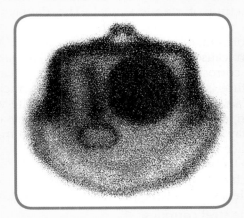

Use the graph below to answer the questions that follow.

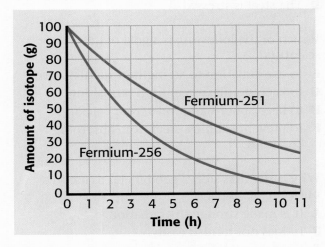

21 What is the half-life of fermium-256?

22 What is the half-life of fermium-251?

READING

Read each of the passages below. Then, answer the questions that follow each passage.

Passage 1 Have you noticed that your forks, knives, and spoons don't tarnish easily? Most metal utensils are made of stainless steel. Because it doesn't tarnish, stainless steel is also used in nuclear reactors. Some scientists study radiation's effects on metals and other substances. An important focus of their studies is radiation's effect on the structure of stainless steel. The damage to stainless steel is caused mainly by neutron and heavy ion radiation inside nuclear reactors. The radiation causes stress in the metal. The stress leads to corrosion and finally to cracking. Clearly, this feature is not desirable in parts of a nuclear reactor! Scientists hope that by studying the way radiation affects the atoms of metals, they can find a way to use the incoming radiation to make the surface stronger instead of weaker.

1. Which of the following happens last as stainless steel is damaged in a nuclear reactor?

 A The steel corrodes.

 B The steel is exposed to radiation.

 C The steel cracks.

 D The steel is stressed.

2. Which of the following is a goal of the scientists?

 F to use radiation to strengthen stainless steel

 G to keep stainless steel from tarnishing

 H to keep spoons and forks from cracking

 I to prevent stainless steel from absorbing radiation

3. Why is stainless steel a good metal to use in a nuclear reactor?

 A It is made stronger by radiation.

 B It does not tarnish easily.

 C It cracks under stress.

 D It is not affected by radiation.

Passage 2 A space probe takes about 7 years to reach Saturn. What could supply energy for the cameras and equipment after that time in space? The answer is the radioactive element plutonium! The nuclei (singular, *nucleus*) of plutonium atoms are <u>radioactive</u>, so the nuclei are unstable. They become stable by giving off radiation in the form of particles and rays. This process heats the materials surrounding the plutonium, and the thermal energy of the materials is converted into electrical energy by a radioisotope thermoelectric generator (RTG). Spacecraft such as *Voyager, Galileo,* and *Ulysses* depended on RTGs for electrical energy. Because an RTG can generate electrical energy for 10 or more years by using one sample of plutonium, an RTG provides energy longer than any battery can. In fact, the RTGs on *Voyager* were still providing energy after 20 years!

1. Plutonium in an RTG can be expected to provide energy for how long?

 A much less than 7 years

 B about 7 years

 C 10 years or more

 D 20 years

2. Which of the following terms has the most similar meaning to the term *radioactive*?

 F thermoelectric

 G plutonium

 H radiation

 I unstable

3. What is the final form of energy provided by RTGs?

 A thermal

 B electrical

 C particles and rays

 D nuclear

The table below shows the half-lives of some radioactive isotopes. Use the table below to answer the questions that follow.

Examples of Half-Lives

Isotope	Half-life
Hydrogen-3	12.3 years
Nitrogen-13	10 min
Oxygen-21	3.4 s
Calcium-36	0.1 s
Polonium-210	138 days
Uranium-238	4.5 billion years

1. Half of a sample of which of the following isotopes would take the longest to decay?

A uranium-238

B hydrogen-3

C polonium-210

D calcium-36

2. How old is an artifact if only one-fourth of the hydrogen-3 in the sample remains?

F 3.075 years

G 6.15 years

H 12.3 years

I 24.6 years

3. How many days will it take for three-fourths of a sample of radioactive polonium-210 to decay?

A 69 days

B 103.5 days

C 138 days

D 276 days

4. How many isotopes have shorter half-lives than polonium-210?

F two

G three

H four

I five

Read each question below, and choose the best answer.

1. The Butterfly Society spent 1.5 h planting a butterfly garden on Saturday and twice as many hours on Sunday. Which equation could be used to find the total number of hours they spent planting on those 2 days?

A $n = 2(1.5)$

B $n = 1.5 + 2(1.5)$

C $n = 1.5 + 1.5 + 2$

D $n = 2 \times 2 \times 1.5$

2. How many half-lives have passed if one-eighth of a sample of radioactive carbon-14 remains?

F two

G three

H four

I eight

3. Which of the following shows the correct fraction of the original sample of radioactive isotope that remains after four half-lives?

A $4(1/2)$

B $(1/2)(1/4)$

C $4\ 1/2$

D $(1/2)(1/2)(1/2)(1/2)$

4. To find the area of a circle, use the equation $area = \pi r^2$. If the radius of circle A is doubled, how will the area of the circle change?

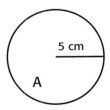

F The area will be 1/4 as large.

G The area will be 1/2 as large.

H The area will be 2 times larger.

I The area will be 4 times larger.

Science in Action

Science, Technology, and Society

Irradiated Food

One way to help keep food fresh for longer periods of time is to irradiate it. Exposing food to radiation can kill organisms such as mold or bacteria that cause food to spoil. In addition, irradiated potatoes and onions can be stored for a longer time without sprouting. Radiation can even be used to control pests such as beetles that could cause a lot of damage to stored grains.

Social Studies ACTIVITY

WRITING SKILL Food preservation is an important development of history. Write a one-page report that compares methods that you use to keep food from spoiling with methods used in the late 1800s.

Weird Science

Nuclear-Powered Bacteria

Deep under Earth's surface, there is no light. Temperatures are high, water is scarce, and oxygen is difficult to find. For many years, scientists thought that nothing could live under these extreme conditions. But in 1989, a team of scientists found bacteria living in rocks that are 500 m below Earth's surface. Since then, bacteria have been found living in rocks that are as deep as 3.5 km below Earth's surface! Scientists wondered what these bacteria use for food. These bacteria seem to get their food from an unusual source—the radioactive decay of uranium. The idea that radioactive decay can be a food source is new to science and is changing the way that scientists think about life.

Math ACTIVITY

How deep is 3.5 km? To help you imagine this depth, calculate how many Statues of Liberty could be stacked in a hole that is 3.5 km deep. The Statue of Liberty in New York is about 46 m tall.

Marie and Pierre Curie

A Great Team You may have heard the saying "Two heads are better than one." For scientific discoveries, this saying is quite true. The husband and wife team Pierre and Marie Curie put their heads together and discovered the elements radium and polonium. Their work also helped them describe radioactivity.

Working side by side for long hours under poor conditions, Marie and Pierre Curie studied the mysterious rays given off by the element uranium. They processed huge amounts of an ore called *pitchblende* to collect the uranium from it. Strangely, the leftover material was more active than uranium. They spent several more months working with the material and discovered an element that was 300 times more active than uranium. Marie called it *polonium* in honor of Poland, which was the country in which she was born. For their research on radiation, the Curies were awarded the Nobel Prize in physics in 1903.

Language Arts ACTiViTY

WRITING SKILL Think of a time that you and a friend solved a problem together that neither of you could solve alone. Write a one-page story about how you each helped solve the problem.

To learn more about these Science in Action topics, visit go.hrw.com and type in the keyword **HP5RADF**.

Current Science

Check out Current Science® articles related to this chapter by visiting go.hrw.com. Just type in the keyword **HP5CS16**.

UNIT 6

TIMELINE

Electricity

Can you imagine a world without computers, motors, or even light bulbs? Your life would be very different indeed without electricity and the devices that depend on it. In this unit, you will learn how electricity results from tiny charged particles, how electricity and magnetism interact, and how electronic technology has revolutionized the world in a relatively short amount of time. This timeline includes some of the events leading to our current understanding of electricity, electromagnetism, and electronic technology.

1751

Benjamin Franklin flies a kite to which a key is attached in a thunderstorm to demonstrate that lightning is a form of electricity.

1903

Dutch physician Willem Einthoven develops the first electrocardiograph machine to record the tiny electric currents that pass through the body's tissues.

1947

The transistor is invented.

1958

The invention of the integrated circuit, which uses millions of transistors, revolutionizes electronic technology.

1773

American colonists hold the "Boston Tea Party" and dump 342 chests of British tea into Boston Harbor.

1831

British scientist Michael Faraday and American physicist Joseph Henry separately demonstrate the principle of electromagnetic induction in which magnetism is used to generate electricity.

1876

The telephone is officially invented by Alexander Graham Bell, who beats Elisha Gray to the patent office by only a few hours.

1911

Superconductivity is discovered. Superconductivity is the ability some metals and alloys have to carry electric current without resistance under certain conditions.

1945

Grace Murray Hopper, a pioneer in computers and computer languages, coins the phrase "debugging the computer" after removing from the wiring of her computer a moth that caused the computer to fail.

1984

The first portable CD player is introduced.

1997

Garry Kasparov, reigning world chess champion, loses a historic match to a computer named Deep Blue.

2003

One of the largest electricity blackouts in North American history started in the afternoon on August 14, 2003. The blackout left several large cities, including New York City; Detroit, Michigan; and Toronto, Canada, in the dark. Several days passed before electrical energy was fully restored to the millions of people affected in eight U.S. states and Canada.

Introduction to Electricity

SECTION **1** Electric Charge
and Static Electricity .. 474

SECTION **2** Electric Current and
Electrical Energy...... 482

SECTION **3** Electrical Calculations 490

SECTION **4** Electric Circuits 494

Chapter Lab 500
Chapter Review 502
Standardized Test Preparation 504
Science in Action................. 506

About the PHOTO

This incredible light display is not an indoor lightning storm, but it's close! When scientists at the Sandia National Laboratory fire this fusion device, a huge number of electrons move across the room and make giant sparks.

PRE-READING ACTIVITY

FOLDNOTES **Layered Book** Before you read the chapter, create the FoldNote entitled "Layered Book" described in the **Study Skills** section of the Appendix. Label the tabs of the layered book with "Charge," "Current," "Voltage," and "Resistance." As you read the chapter, write information you learn about each category under the appropriate tab.

START-UP ACTiViTY

Stick Together

In this activity, you will see how a pair of electrically charged objects interact.

Procedure

1. Take **two strips of cellophane tape.** Each strip should be 20 cm long. Fold over a small part of the end of each strip to form a tab.

2. Hold each piece of tape by its tab. Bring the two pieces of tape close together, but do not let them touch. Record your observations.

3. Tape one of the strips to your lab table. Tape the second strip on top of the first strip.

4. Pull the strips of tape off the table together.

5. Quickly pull the strips apart. Bring the two pieces of tape close together, but do not let them touch. Record your observations.

Analysis

1. Compare how the pieces of tape behaved when you first brought them together with how they behaved after you pulled the pieces apart.

2. As you pulled the pieces of tape apart, electrons from one piece of tape moved onto the other piece of tape. Describe the charge on each piece of tape after you pulled the two pieces apart.

3. From your observations, draw a conclusion about how objects having the charges that you described behave toward one another.

Introduction to Electricity   **473**

Electric Charge and Static Electricity

Have you ever reached out to open a door and received a shock from the doorknob? Why did that happen?

On dry days, you might get a shock when you open a door, put on a sweater, or touch another person. These shocks come from static electricity. To understand static electricity, you need to learn about atoms and charge.

Electric Charge

All matter is made up of very small particles called *atoms*. Atoms are made of even smaller particles called protons, neutrons, and electrons, which are shown in **Figure 1.** How do these particles differ? For one thing, protons and electrons are charged particles, and neutrons are not.

✔ **Reading Check** What are the two types of charged particles in atoms? (*See the Appendix for answers to Reading Checks.*)

Charges Exert Forces

Charge is a physical property. An object can have a positive charge, a negative charge, or no charge. Charge is best understood by learning how charged objects interact. Charged objects exert a force—a push or a pull—on other charged objects. The **law of electric charges** states that like charges repel, or push away, and opposite charges attract. **Figure 2** illustrates this law.

READING WARM-UP

Objectives
- Describe how charged objects interact by using the law of electric charges.
- Describe three ways in which an object can become charged.
- Compare conductors with insulators.
- Give two examples of static electricity and electric discharge.

Terms to Learn
law of electric charges
electric force
electric field
electrical conductor
electrical insulator
static electricity
electric discharge

READING STRATEGY

Reading Organizer As you read this section, create an outline of the section. Use the headings from the section in your outline.

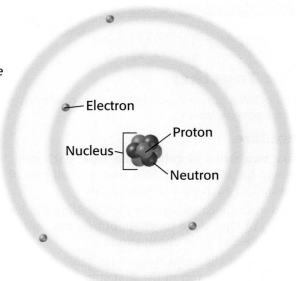

Figure 1 *Protons and neutrons make up the center of the atom, the nucleus. Electrons are found outside the nucleus.*

Electron

Proton

Nucleus

Neutron

Figure 2 The Law of Electric Charges

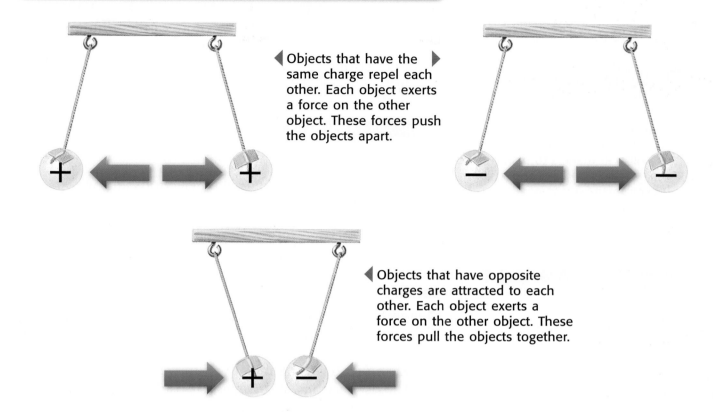

Objects that have the same charge repel each other. Each object exerts a force on the other object. These forces push the objects apart.

Objects that have opposite charges are attracted to each other. Each object exerts a force on the other object. These forces pull the objects together.

The Force Between Protons and Electrons

Protons are positively charged. Electrons are negatively charged. Because protons and electrons have opposite charges, they are attracted to each other. Without this attraction, electrons could not be held in atoms.

The Electric Force and the Electric Field

The force between charged objects is an **electric force.** The size of the electric force depends on two things. The first thing is the amount of charge on each object. The greater the charge is, the greater the electric force is. The other thing that determines the size of the electric force is the distance between the charges. The closer together the charges are, the greater the electric force is.

Charged things are affected by electric force because charged things have an electric field around them. An **electric field** is the region around a charged object in which an electric force is exerted on another charged object. A charged object in the electric field of another charged object is attracted or repelled by the electric force acting on it.

law of electric charges the law that states that like charges repel and opposite charges attract

electric force the force of attraction or repulsion on a charged particle that is due to an electric field

electric field the space around a charged object in which another charged object experiences an electric force

Charge It!

Atoms have equal numbers of protons and electrons. Because an atom's positive and negative charges cancel each other out, atoms do not have a charge. So, how can anything made of atoms be charged? An object becomes positively charged when it loses electrons. An object becomes negatively charged when it gains electrons. Objects can become charged by friction, conduction, and induction, as shown in **Figure 3.**

✓ Reading Check What are three ways of charging an object?

Friction

Charging by *friction* happens when electrons are "wiped" from one object onto another. If you use a cloth to rub a plastic ruler, electrons move from the cloth to the ruler. The ruler gains electrons and becomes negatively charged. At the same time, the cloth loses electrons and becomes positively charged.

Conduction

Charging by *conduction* happens when electrons move from one object to another by direct contact. Suppose you touch an uncharged piece of metal with a positively charged glass rod. Electrons from the metal will move to the glass rod. The metal loses electrons and becomes positively charged.

CONNECTION TO
Environmental Science

WRITING SKILL **Painting Cars**
Research how charge and electric force are used by car makers to paint cars. Then, in your **science journal,** write a one-page report describing the process and explaining how the use of charge to paint cars helps protect the environment.

Figure 3 **Three Ways to Charge an Object**

Friction	Conduction	Induction

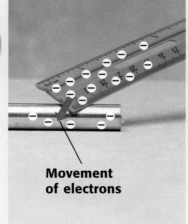

Movement of electrons

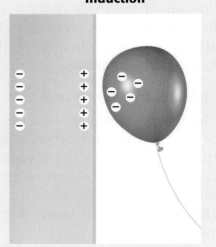

The friction of rubbing a balloon on your hair causes electrons to move from your hair to the balloon. Your hair and the balloon become oppositely charged and attract each other.

When a negatively charged plastic ruler touches an uncharged metal rod, the electrons in the ruler travel to the rod. The rod becomes negatively charged by conduction.

A negatively charged balloon makes a small section of a metal beam have a positive charge through induction. Electrons in the metal are repelled by and move away from the balloon.

Induction

Charging by *induction* happens when charges in an uncharged metal object are rearranged without direct contact with a charged object. Suppose you hold a metal object near a positively charged object. The electrons in the metal are attracted to and move toward the positively charged object. This movement causes (or induces) an area of negative charge on the surface of the metal.

Conservation of Charge

When you charge something by any method, no charges are created or destroyed. The numbers of electrons and protons stay the same. Electrons simply move from one atom to another, which makes areas that have different charges. Because charges are not created or destroyed, charge is said to be conserved.

Detecting Charge

You can use a device called an *electroscope* to see if something is charged. An electroscope is a glass flask that has a metal rod in its rubber stopper. Two metal leaves are attached to the bottom of the rod. When the electroscope is not charged, the leaves hang straight down. When the electroscope is charged, the leaves repel each other, or spread apart.

Figure 4 shows a negatively charged ruler touching the rod of an electroscope. Electrons move from the ruler to the electroscope. The leaves become negatively charged and repel each other. If something that is positively charged touches the neutral rod, electrons move off the electroscope. Then, the leaves become positively charged and repel each other. An electroscope can show that an object is charged. However, it cannot show whether the charge is positive or negative.

Reading Check What can you do with an electroscope?

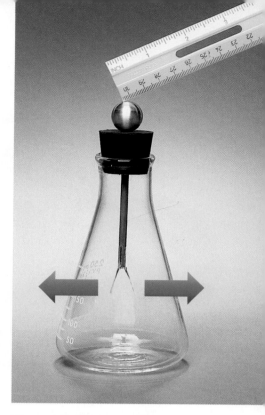

Figure 4 *When an electroscope is charged, the metal leaves have the same charge and repel each other.*

Detecting Charge

1. Use **scissors** to cut **two strips of aluminum foil** that are 1 cm × 4 cm each.
2. Bend a **paper clip** to make a hook. (The clip will look like an upside-down question mark.)
3. Push the end of the hook through the middle of an **index card,** and tape the hook so that it hangs straight down from the card.
4. Lay the two foil strips on top of one another, and hang them on the hook by gently pushing the hook through them.
5. Lay the card over the top of a **glass jar.**
6. Bring **various charged objects** near the top of the paper-clip hook, and observe what happens. Explain your observations.

Moving Charges

Look at **Figure 5.** Have you ever noticed that electrical cords are often made from metal and plastic? Different materials are used because electric charges move through some materials more easily than they move through others. Most materials are either conductors or insulators based on how easily charges move in them.

Conductors

An **electrical conductor** is a material in which charges can move easily. Most metals are good conductors because some of their electrons are free to move. Conductors are used to make wires. For example, a lamp cord has metal wire and metal prongs. Copper, aluminum, and mercury are good conductors.

Insulators

An **electrical insulator** is a material in which charges cannot move easily. Insulators do not conduct charges very well because their electrons cannot flow freely. The electrons are tightly held in the atoms of the insulator. The insulating material in a lamp cord stops charges from leaving the wire and protects you from electric shock. Plastic, rubber, glass, wood, and air are good insulators.

Static Electricity

After you take your clothes out of the dryer, they sometimes are stuck together. They stick together because of static electricity. **Static electricity** is the electric charge at rest on an object.

When something is *static,* it is not moving. The charges of static electricity do not move away from the object that they are in. So, the object keeps its charge. Your clothes are charged by friction as they rub against each other inside a dryer. As the clothes tumble, negative charges are lost by some clothes and build up on other clothes. When the dryer stops, the transfer of charges also stops. And because clothing is an insulator, the built-up electric charges stay on each piece of clothing. The result of this buildup of charges is static cling.

Figure 5 *These jumper cables are made of metal, which carries electric charges, and plastic, which keeps the charges away from your hands.*

electrical conductor a material in which charges can move freely

electrical insulator a material in which charges cannot move freely

static electricity electric charge at rest; generally produced by friction or induction

Electric Discharge

Charges that build up as static electricity on an object eventually leave the object. The loss of static electricity as charges move off an object is called **electric discharge.** Sometimes, electric discharge happens slowly. For example, clothes stuck together by static electricity will eventually separate on their own. Over time, their electric charges move to water molecules in the air.

Sometimes, electric discharge happens quickly. It may happen with a flash of light, a shock, or a crackling noise. For example, when you wear rubber-soled shoes and walk on carpet, negative charges build up on your body. When you reach out for a metal doorknob, the negative charges on your body can jump to the doorknob. The electric discharge happens quickly, and you feel a small shock.

One of the most dramatic examples of electric discharge is lightning. How does lightning form through a buildup of static electricity? **Figure 6** shows the answer.

Reading Check What is electric discharge?

electric discharge the release of electricity stored in a source

Figure 6 How Lightning Forms

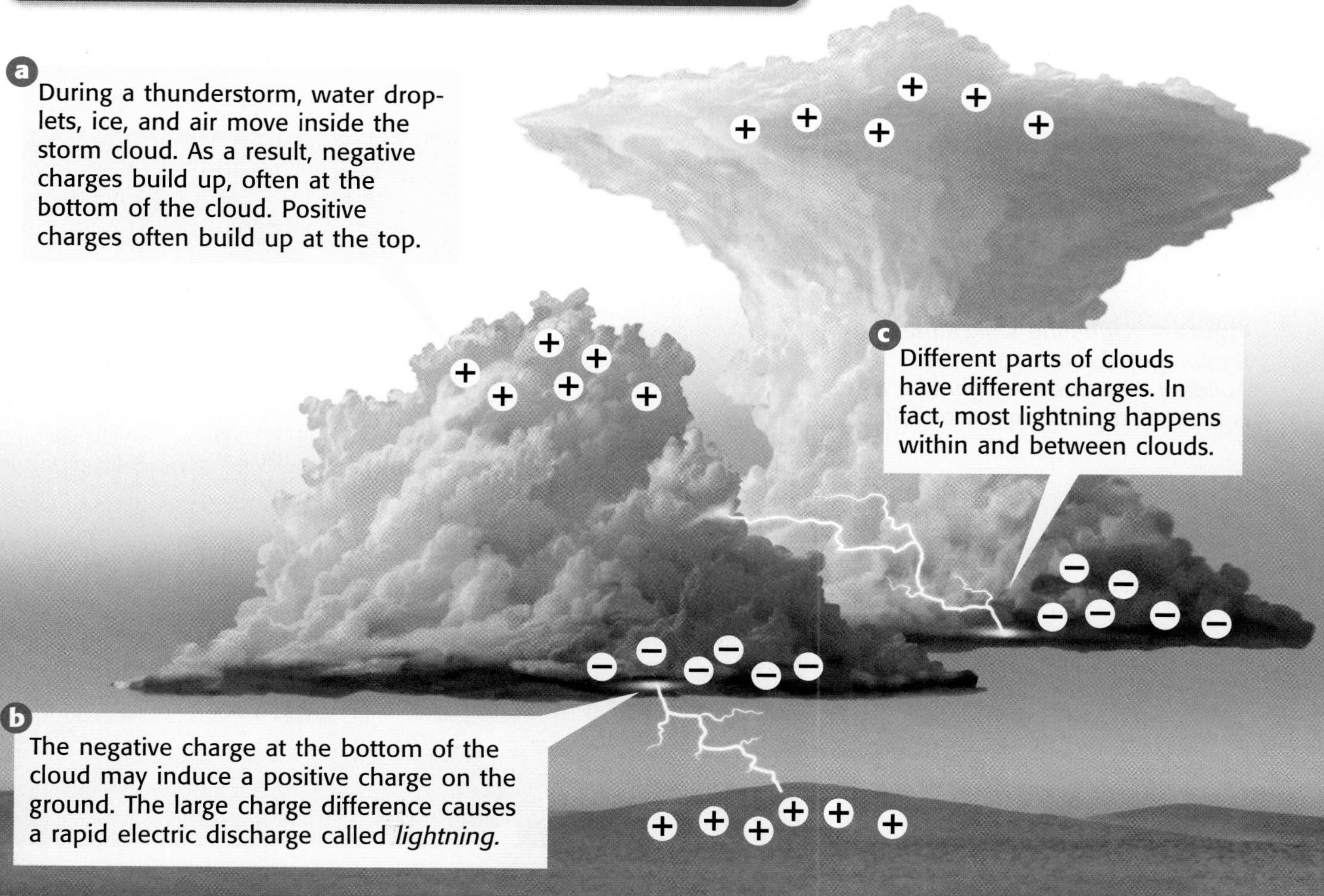

a During a thunderstorm, water droplets, ice, and air move inside the storm cloud. As a result, negative charges build up, often at the bottom of the cloud. Positive charges often build up at the top.

c Different parts of clouds have different charges. In fact, most lightning happens within and between clouds.

b The negative charge at the bottom of the cloud may induce a positive charge on the ground. The large charge difference causes a rapid electric discharge called *lightning.*

Lightning Dangers

Lightning usually strikes the highest point in a charged area because that point provides the shortest path for the charges to reach the ground. Anything that sticks up or out in an area can provide a path for lightning. Trees and people in open areas are at risk of being struck by lightning. For this reason, it is particularly dangerous to be at the beach or on a golf course during a lightning storm. Even standing under a tree during a storm is dangerous. The charges from lightning striking a tree can jump to your body.

Reading Check Why is it dangerous to be outside in an open area during a storm?

Lightning Rods

A lightning rod is a pointed rod connected to the ground by a wire. Lightning rods are often mounted so that they are the tallest point on a building, as shown in **Figure 7.** Objects, such as a lightning rod, that are joined to Earth by a conductor, such as a wire, are *grounded.* Any object that is grounded provides a path for electric charges to move to Earth. Because Earth is so large, it can give up or absorb charges without being damaged. When lightning strikes a lightning rod, the electric charges are carried safely to Earth through the rod's wire. By directing the charge to Earth, the rods prevent lightning from damaging buildings.

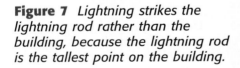

Figure 7 *Lightning strikes the lightning rod rather than the building, because the lightning rod is the tallest point on the building.*

Summary

- The law of electric charges states that like charges repel and opposite charges attract.
- The size of the electric force between two objects depends on the size of the charges exerting the force and the distance between the objects.
- Charged objects exert a force on each other and can cause each other to move.
- Objects become charged when they gain or lose electrons.
- Objects may become charged by friction, conduction, or induction.
- Charges are not created or destroyed and are said to be conserved.
- Charges move easily in conductors but do not move easily in insulators.
- Static electricity is the buildup of electric charges on an object. It is lost through electric discharge.

Using Key Terms

For each pair of terms, explain how the meanings of the terms differ.

1. *static electricity* and *electric discharge*

2. *electric force* and *electric field*

3. *electrical conductor* and *electrical insulator*

Understanding Key Ideas

4. Which of the following is an insulator?
   a. copper
   b. rubber
   c. aluminum
   d. iron

5. Compare the three methods of charging.

6. What does the law of electric charges say about two objects that are positively charged?

7. Give two examples of static electricity.

8. List two examples of electric discharge.

Critical Thinking

9. **Analyzing Processes** Imagine that you touch the top of an electroscope with an object. The metal leaves spread apart. Can you determine whether the charge is positive or negative? Explain your answer.

10. **Applying Concepts** Why is it important to touch a charged object to the metal rod of an electroscope and not to the rubber stopper?

Interpreting Graphics

The photograph below shows two charged balloons. Use the photograph below to answer the questions that follow.

11. Do the balloons have the same charge or opposite charges? Explain your answer.

12. How would the photograph look if each balloon were given the charge opposite to the charge it has now? Explain your answer.

SCILINKS.

NSTA
Developed and maintained by the
National Science Teachers Association

For a variety of links related to this chapter, go to www.scilinks.org

Topic: Static Electricity
SciLinks code: HSM1451

Electric Current and Electrical Energy

You might not realize that when you watch TV, use a computer, or even turn on a light bulb, you depend on moving charges for the electrical energy that you need.

Electrical energy is the energy of electric charges. In most of the things that use electrical energy, the electric charges flow through wires. As you read on, you will learn more about how this flow of charges—called *electric current*—is made and how it is controlled in the things that you use every day.

READING WARM-UP

Objectives

● Describe electric current.

● Describe voltage and its relationship to electric current.

● Describe resistance and its relationship to electric current.

● Explain how a cell generates electrical energy.

● Describe how thermocouples and photocells generate electrical energy.

Terms to Learn

electric current
voltage
resistance
cell
thermocouple
photocell

READING STRATEGY

Reading Organizer As you read this section, make a table comparing electric current, voltage, and resistance.

Electric Current

An **electric current** is the rate at which charges pass a given point. The higher the current is, the greater the number of charges that pass the point each second. Electric current is expressed in units called *amperes* (AM PIRZ), which is often shortened to *amps*. The symbol for *ampere* is A. And in equations, the symbol for current is the letter *I*.

✔ **Reading Check** What is the unit of measurement for electric current? (*See the Appendix for answers to Reading Checks.*)

Making Charges Move

When you flip the switch on a flashlight, the light comes on instantly. But do charges in the battery instantly reach the bulb? No, they don't. When you flip the switch, an electric field is set up in the wire at the speed of light. And the electric field causes the free electrons in the wire to move. The energy of each electron is transferred instantly to the next electron, as shown in **Figure 1.**

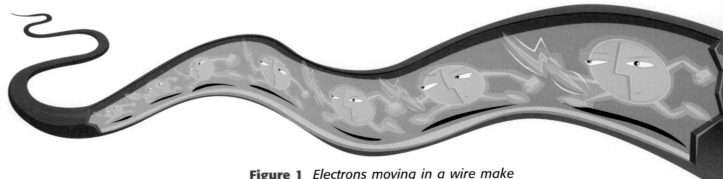

Figure 1 *Electrons moving in a wire make up current and provide energy to the things that you use each day.*

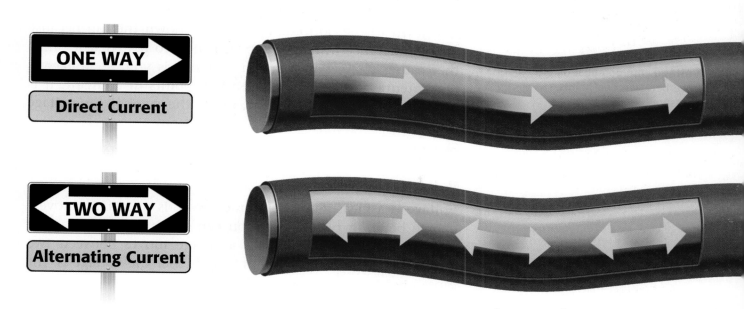

ONE WAY
Direct Current

TWO WAY
Alternating Current

Figure 2 *Charges move in one direction in DC, but charges continually change direction in AC.*

Commanding Electrons to Move

This electric field is created so quickly that all electrons start moving through the wire at the same instant. Think of the electric field as a command to the electrons to charge ahead. The light comes on instantly because all of the electrons obey this command at the same time. So, the current that lights the bulb is established very quickly even though each electron moves quite slowly. In fact, a single electron may take more than an hour to travel 1 m through a wire.

electric current the rate at which charges pass through a given point; measured in amperes

AC and DC

There are two kinds of electric current—direct current (DC) and alternating current (AC). Look at **Figure 2.** In direct current, the charges always flow in the same direction. In alternating current, the charges continually shift from flowing in one direction to flowing in the reverse direction.

The electric current from the batteries used in a camera is DC. The electric current from outlets in your home is AC. In the United States, the alternating current changes directions 120 times each second, or has 60 cycles each second.

Both kinds of current can give you electrical energy. For example, if you connect a flashlight bulb to a battery, the light bulb will light. And you can light a household light bulb by putting it in a lamp and turning the lamp on.

✓ Reading Check What are two kinds of electric current?

Voltage

If you are on a bike at the top of a hill, you know that you can roll down to the bottom. You can roll down the hill because of the difference in height between the two points. The "hill" that causes charges in a circuit to move is voltage. **Voltage** is the potential difference between two points in a circuit. It is expressed in volts (V). In equations, the symbol for voltage is the letter V.

voltage the potential difference between two points; measured in volts

✓ Reading Check What is the unit of measurement for voltage?

Voltage and Energy

Voltage is a measure of how much work is needed to move a charge between two points. You can think of voltage as the amount of energy released as a charge moves between two points in the path of a current. The higher the voltage is, the more energy is released per charge.

Voltage and Electric Current

As long as there is a voltage between two points on a wire, charges will flow in the wire. The size of the current depends on the voltage. The greater the voltage is, the greater the current is. A greater current means that more charges move in the wire each second. A large current is needed to start a car. So, the battery in a car has a fairly high voltage of 12 V. **Figure 3** shows batteries that have a number of different voltages. If you have a device that uses direct current, one of these batteries might help.

Figure 3 *Batteries are made with various voltages for use in many different devices.*

Figure 4 *An electric eel can create a voltage of more than 600 V!*

Varying Nature of Voltage

Things that run on batteries usually need a low voltage. For example, a portable radio might need only 3 V. Compare the voltage of such a radio with the voltage created by the eel in **Figure 4.** Most devices in your home use alternating current from an outlet. In the United States, electrical outlets usually supply AC at 120 V. So, most electrical devices, such as televisions, toasters, and alarm clocks, are made to run on 120 V.

Resistance

Resistance is another factor that determines the amount of current in a wire. **Resistance** is the opposition to the flow of electric charge. Resistance is expressed in ohms (Ω, the Greek letter *omega*). In equations, the symbol for resistance is the letter *R*.

You can think of resistance as "electrical friction." The higher the resistance of a material is, the lower the current in the material is. So, if the voltage doesn't change, as resistance goes up, current goes down. An object's resistance depends on the object's material, thickness, length, and temperature.

Resistance and Material

Good conductors, such as copper, have low resistance. Poor conductors, such as iron, have higher resistance. The resistance of insulators is so high that electric charges cannot flow in them. Materials with low resistance, such as copper, are used to make wires. But materials with high resistance are also helpful. For example, the high resistance of the filament in a light bulb causes the light bulb to heat up and give off light.

resistance in physical science, the opposition presented to the current by a material or device

Figure 5 A Model of Resistance

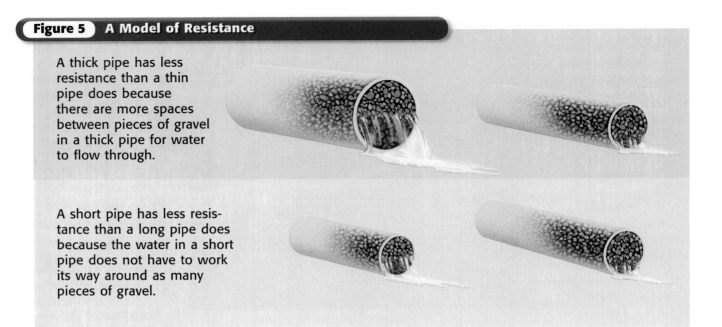

A thick pipe has less resistance than a thin pipe does because there are more spaces between pieces of gravel in a thick pipe for water to flow through.

A short pipe has less resistance than a long pipe does because the water in a short pipe does not have to work its way around as many pieces of gravel.

Resistance, Thickness, and Length

To understand how the thickness and length of a wire affect the wire's resistance, look at the model in **Figure 5.** The pipe filled with gravel represents a wire. The water flowing through the pipe represents electric charges.

Resistance and Temperature

Resistance also depends on temperature. In general, the resistance of metals increases as temperature rises. The atoms vibrate faster at higher temperatures and get in the way of the flowing electric charges. If you cool certain materials to a very low temperature, resistance will drop to 0 Ω. Materials in this state are called *superconductors*. A small superconductor is shown in **Figure 6.** Very little energy is wasted when electric charges move in a superconductor. However, a large amount of energy is needed to cool them. Scientists are studying how superconductors can be used to store and transmit energy.

Figure 6 *One interesting property of superconductors is that they repel magnets. The superconductor in this photo is repelling the magnet so strongly that the magnet is floating.*

Figure 7 How a Cell Works

Flow

a A chemical reaction with the electrolyte leaves extra electrons on one electrode. This electrode is made of zinc.

b A different chemical reaction causes electrons to be pulled off the other electrode. In this cell, this electrode is made of copper.

c If the electrodes are connected by a wire, electrons flow through the wire and ions move in the electrolyte. The moving charges make an electric current.

Generating Electrical Energy

You know that energy cannot be created or destroyed. It can only be changed into other kinds of energy. Many things change different kinds of energy into electrical energy. For example, generators convert mechanical energy into electrical energy. **Cells** change chemical or radiant energy into electrical energy. Batteries are made of one or more cells.

Parts of a Cell

A cell, such as the one in **Figure 7,** contains a mixture of chemicals called an *electrolyte* (ee LEK troh LIET). Electrolytes allow charges to flow. Every cell also has a pair of electrodes made from conducting materials. An *electrode* (ee LEK TROHD) is the part of a cell through which charges enter or exit. Chemical changes between the electrolyte and the electrodes convert chemical energy into electrical energy.

Kinds of Cells

Two kinds of cells are wet cells and dry cells. Wet cells, such as the one in **Figure 7,** have liquid electrolytes. A car battery is made of several wet cells that use sulfuric acid as the electrolyte. You can make your own wet cell by poking strips of zinc and copper into a lemon. When the metal strips are connected, enough electrical energy is generated to run a small clock, as shown in **Figure 8.** Dry cells work in a similar way. But the electrolytes in dry cells are solid or pastelike. The cells used in small radios and flashlights are types of dry cells.

Reading Check What are two kinds of cells?

cell in electricity, a device that produces an electric current by converting chemical or radiant energy into electrical energy

Figure 8 *This cell uses the juice of a lemon as an electrolyte and uses strips of zinc and copper as electrodes.*

Thermocouples

Thermal energy can be converted into electrical energy by a **thermocouple.** A simple thermocouple, shown in **Figure 9,** is made by joining wires of two different metals into a loop. The temperature difference within the loop causes charges to flow through the loop. The greater the temperature difference is, the greater the current is. Thermocouples usually do not generate much energy. But they are useful for monitoring the temperatures of car engines, furnaces, and ovens.

Photocells

If you look at a solar-powered calculator, you will see a dark strip called a *solar panel*. This panel is made of several photocells. A **photocell** converts light energy into electrical energy. How do photocells work? Most photocells contain silicon atoms. As long as light shines on the photocell, electrons gain enough energy to move between atoms. The electrons are then able to move through a wire to provide electrical energy to power a device, such as a calculator.

In larger panels, photocells can provide energy to buildings and cars. Large panels of photocells are even used on satellites. By changing light energy from the sun into electrical energy, the photocells provide energy to the many devices on the satellite to keep the devices working.

☑ Reading Check What device converts light energy into electrical energy?

thermocouple a device that converts thermal energy into electrical energy

photocell a device that converts light energy into electrical energy

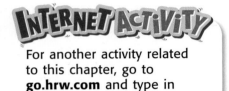

For another activity related to this chapter, go to **go.hrw.com** and type in the keyword **HP5ELEW.**

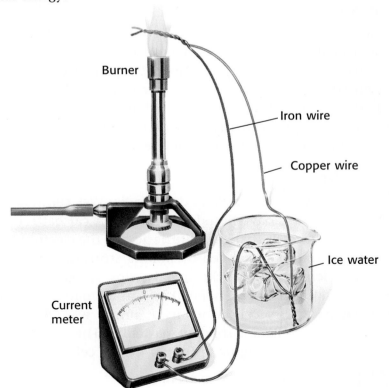

Burner

Iron wire

Copper wire

Ice water

Current meter

Figure 9 *In a simple thermocouple, one section of the loop is heated and one section is cooled.*

Summary

- Electric current is the rate at which charges pass a given point.
- An electric current can be made when there is a potential difference between two points.
- As voltage, or potential difference increases, current increases.
- An object's resistance varies depending on the object's material, thickness, length, and temperature. As resistance increases, current decreases.
- Cells and batteries convert chemical energy or radiant energy into electrical energy.
- Thermocouples and photocells are devices used to generate electrical energy.

Using Key Terms

Complete each of the following sentences by choosing the correct term from the word bank.

voltage	electric current
resistance	cell

1. The rate at which charges pass a point is a(n) ___.

2. The opposition to the flow of charge is ___.

3. Another term for *potential difference* is ___.

4. A device that changes chemical energy into electrical energy is a(n) ___.

Understanding Key Ideas

5. Which of the following factors affects the resistance of an object?
   a. thickness of the object
   b. length of the object
   c. temperature of the object
   d. All of the above

6. Name the parts of a cell, and explain how they work together to produce an electric current.

7. Compare alternating current with direct current.

8. How do the currents produced by a 1.5 V flashlight cell and a 12 V car battery compare if the resistance is the same?

9. How does increasing the resistance affect the current?

Critical Thinking

10. **Making Comparisons** A friend is having trouble studying the types of cells in this section. Explain to your friend how the terms *photocell* and *thermocouple* hold clues that can help him or her remember the type of energy taken in by each device.

11. **Making Inferences** Why do you think some calculators that contain photocells also contain batteries?

12. **Applying Concepts** Which wire would have the lowest resistance: a long, thin iron wire at a high temperature or a short, thick copper wire at a low temperature?

Interpreting Graphics

13. The wires shown below are made of copper and have the same temperature. Which wire should have the lower resistance? Explain your answer.

Ⓐ   Ⓑ

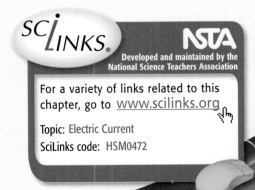

For a variety of links related to this chapter, go to www.scilinks.org

Topic: Electric Current
SciLinks code: HSM0472

Electrical Calculations

A German school teacher named Georg Ohm wondered how electric current, voltage, and resistance are related.

Connecting Current, Voltage, and Resistance

Ohm (1789–1854) studied the resistances of materials. He measured the current that resulted from different voltages applied to a piece of metal wire. The graph on the left in **Figure 1** is similar to the graph of his results.

Ohm's Law

Ohm found that the ratio of voltage (V) to current (I) is a constant for each material. This ratio is the resistance (R) of the material. When the voltage is expressed in volts (V) and the current is in amperes (A), the resistance is in ohms (Ω). The equation below is often called *Ohm's law* because of Ohm's work.

$$R = \frac{V}{I}, \text{ or } V = I \times R$$

As the resistance goes up, the current goes down. And as the resistance decreases, the current increases. The second graph in **Figure 1** shows this relationship. Notice that if you multiply the current and the resistance for any point, you get 16 V.

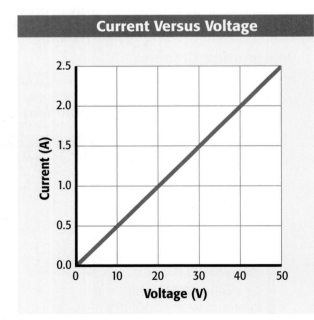

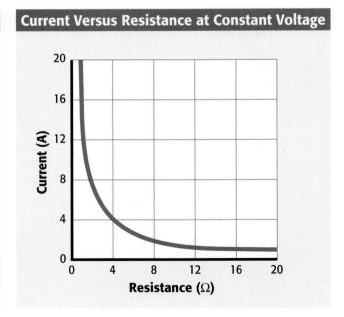

Figure 1 *The relationship between current and voltage is different from the relationship between current and resistance.*

Using Ohm's Law What is the voltage if the current is 2 A and the resistance is 12 Ω?

Step 1: Write the equation for voltage.

$$V = I \times R$$

Step 2: Replace the current and resistance with the measurements given in the problem, and solve.

$$V = 2 \text{ A} \times 12 \text{ Ω}$$
$$V = 24 \text{ V}$$

Now It's Your Turn

1. Find the voltage if the current is 0.2 A and the resistance is 2 Ω.
2. The resistance of an object is 4 Ω. If the current in the object is 9 A, what voltage must be used?
3. An object has a resistance of 20 Ω. Calculate the voltage needed to produce a current of 0.5 A.

Electric Power

The rate at which electrical energy is changed into other forms of energy is **electric power.** The unit for power is the watt (W), and the symbol for power is the letter *P.* Electric power is expressed in watts when the voltage is in volts and the current is in amperes. Electric power is calculated by using the following equation:

power = voltage × current, or P = V × I

electric power the rate at which electrical energy is converted into other forms of energy

Watt: The Unit of Power

If you have ever changed a light bulb, you probably know about watts. Light bulbs, such as the ones in **Figure 2,** have labels such as "60 W," "75 W," or "120 W." As electrical energy is supplied to a light bulb, the light bulb glows. As power increases, the bulb burns brighter because more electrical energy is converted into light energy. The higher power rating of a 120 W bulb tells you that it burns brighter than a 60 W bulb.

Another common unit of power is the kilowatt (kW). One kilowatt is equal to 1,000 W. Kilowatts are used to express high values of power, such as the power needed to heat a house.

✓ Reading Check What are two common units for electric power? (*See the Appendix for answers to Reading Checks.*)

Figure 2 These light bulbs have different wattages, so they use different amounts of electric power.

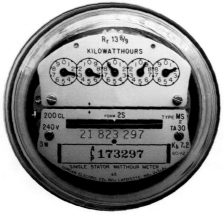

Figure 3 *These photographs were taken 10 days apart. According to the dials on the meter, 101 kWh of energy were used.*

Measuring Electrical Energy

Electric power companies sell electrical energy to homes and businesses. Such companies determine how much a home or business has to pay based on power and time. For example, the amount of electrical energy used in a home depends on the power of the electrical devices in the house and the length of time that those devices are on. The equation for electrical energy is as follows:

$$\textit{electrical energy} = \textit{power} \times \textit{time, or } E = P \times t$$

Measuring Household Energy Use

Different amounts of electrical energy are used each day in a home. Electric companies usually calculate electrical energy by multiplying the power in kilowatts by the time in hours. The unit of electrical energy is usually kilowatt-hours (kWh). If 2,000 W (2 kW) of power are used for 3 h, then 6 kWh of energy were used.

Electric power companies use meters, such as the one in **Figure 3,** to determine how many kilowatt-hours of energy are used by a household. These meters are often outside of buildings so that someone from the power company can read them.

✓ **Reading Check** What unit of measurement is usually used to express electrical energy?

MATH FOCUS

Power and Energy A small television set draws a current of 0.42 A at 120 V. What is the power rating for the television? How much energy is used if the television is on for 3 h?

Step 1: Write the equation for power.

$$P = V \times I$$

Step 2: Replace the voltage and current with the measurements given in the problem, and solve.

$$P = 120 \text{ V} \times 0.42 \text{ A}$$
$$P = 50.4 \text{ W, or } 0.0504 \text{ kW}$$

Step 3: Write the equation for electrical energy.

$$E = P \times t$$

Step 4: Replace the power and time with the measurements given in the problem, and solve.

$$E = 0.0504 \text{ kW} \times 3 \text{ h}$$
$$E = 0.1512 \text{ kWh}$$

Now It's Your Turn
1. A computer monitor draws 1.2 A at a voltage of 120 V. What is the power rating of the monitor?
2. A light bulb draws a 0.5 A current at a voltage of 120 V. What is the power rating of the light bulb?
3. How much electrical energy does a 100 W light bulb use if it is left on for 24 h?

How to Save Energy

Every appliance uses energy. But a fan, such as the one in **Figure 4,** could actually help you save energy. If you use a fan, you can run an air conditioner less. Replacing items that have high power ratings with items that have lower ratings is another way to save energy. Turning off lights when they are not in use will also help.

Figure 4 *Using a fan to stay cool and using a small toaster instead of a larger toaster oven are ways to save energy.*

SECTION Review

Summary

- Ohm's law describes the relationship between current, resistance, and voltage.
- Electric power is the rate at which electrical energy is changed into other forms of energy.
- Electrical energy is electric power multiplied by time. It is usually expressed in kilowatt-hours.

Using Key Terms

1. In your own words, write a definition for the term *electric power*.

Understanding Key Ideas

2. Which of the following is Ohm's law?
   a. $E = P \times t$
   b. $I = V \times R$
   c. $P = V \times I$
   d. $V = I \times R$

3. Circuit A has twice the resistance of circuit B. The voltage is the same in each circuit. Which circuit has the higher current?

Math Skills

4. Use Ohm's law to find the voltage needed to make a current of 3 A in a resistance of 9 Ω.

5. How much electrical energy does a 40 W light bulb use if it is left on for 12 h?

Critical Thinking

6. **Applying Concepts** Explain why increasing the voltage applied to a wire can have the same effect on the current in the wire that decreasing the resistance of the wire does.

7. **Identifying Relationships** Using the equations in this section, develop an equation to find electrical energy from time, current, and resistance.

Electric Circuits

Think about a roller coaster. You start out nice and easy. Then, you roar around the track. A couple of exciting minutes later, you are right back where you started!

A roller-coaster car follows a fixed pathway. The ride's starting point and ending point are the same place. This kind of closed pathway is called a *circuit*.

Parts of an Electric Circuit

Just like a roller coaster, an electric circuit always forms a loop—it begins and ends in the same place. Because a circuit forms a loop, a circuit is a closed path. So, an *electric circuit* is a complete, closed path through which electric charges flow.

All circuits need three basic parts: an energy source, wires, and a load. Loads, such as a light bulb or a radio, are connected to the energy source by wires. Loads change electrical energy into other forms of energy. These other forms might include thermal energy, light energy, or mechanical energy. As loads change electrical energy into other forms, they offer some resistance to electric currents. **Figure 1** shows examples of the parts of a circuit.

✓ **Reading Check** What are the three parts of an electric circuit? (*See the Appendix for answers to Reading Checks.*)

Figure 1   **Necessary Parts of a Circuit**

The **energy source** can be a battery, a photocell, a thermocouple, or an electric generator at a power plant.

Wires connect the other parts of a circuit. Wires are made of conducting materials that have low resistance, such as copper.

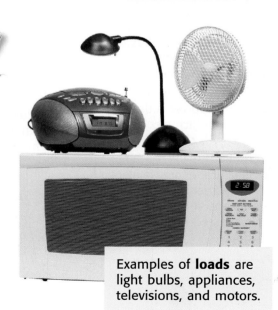

Examples of **loads** are light bulbs, appliances, televisions, and motors.

Figure 2 Using a Switch

When the **switch is closed,** the two pieces of conducting material touch, which allows the electric charges to flow through the circuit.

When the **switch is open,** the gap between the two pieces of conducting material prevents the electric charges from traveling through the circuit.

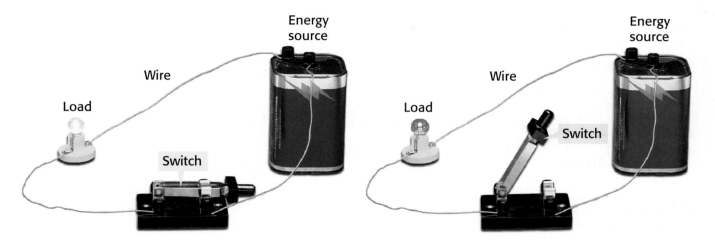

A Switch To Control a Circuit

Sometimes, a circuit also contains a switch, such as the one shown in **Figure 2.** A switch is used to open and close a circuit. Usually, a switch is made of two pieces of conducting material, one of which can be moved. For charges to flow through a circuit, the switch must be closed, or "turned on." If a switch is open, or "off," the loop of the circuit is broken. Charges cannot flow through a broken circuit. Light switches, power buttons on radios, and even the keys on calculators and computers open and close circuits.

Types of Circuits

Look around the room. Count the number of objects that use electrical energy. You might have found things, such as lights, a clock, and maybe a computer. All of the things you counted are loads in a large circuit. The circuit may connect more than one room in the building. In fact, most circuits have more than one load.

The loads in a circuit can be connected in different ways. As a result, circuits are often divided into two types. A circuit can be a series circuit or a parallel circuit. One of the main differences in these circuits is the way in which the loads are connected to one another. As you read about each type of circuit, look closely at how the loads are connected.

✔ **Reading Check** What are two types of electric circuits?

CONNECTION TO Biology

WRITING SKILL **Nervous Impulses** Believe it or not, your body is controlled and monitored by electrical impulses. Research the electrical impulses that travel between your brain and the muscles and organs in your body. Then, in your **science journal,** write a one-page comparison of your nervous system and an electric circuit.

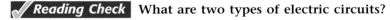

Series Circuits

A **series circuit** is a circuit in which all parts are connected in a single loop. There is only one path for charges to follow, so the charges moving through a series circuit must flow through each part of the circuit.

All of the loads in a series circuit share the same current. The four identical light bulbs in **Figure 3** are joined in series. Because the current in each bulb is the same, the lights glow with the same brightness. But if you add more light bulbs, the resistance of the whole circuit would go up and the current would drop. Therefore, all of the bulbs would be dimmer.

✓ **Reading Check** How are loads connected in a series circuit?

Uses for Series Circuits

A series circuit has only one pathway for moving charges. If there is any break in the circuit, the charges will stop flowing. For example, if one light bulb in a series circuit burns out, there is a break in the circuit. None of the light bulbs in the circuit would light. Using series circuits would not be a very convenient way to wire your home. Imagine if your refrigerator and a lamp were in a series circuit together. Your refrigerator would run only when the lamp was on. And when the bulb burns out, the refrigerator would stop working!

But series circuits are useful in some ways. For example, series circuits are useful in wiring burglar alarms. If any part of the circuit in a burglar alarm fails, there will be no current in the system. The lack of current signals that a problem exists, and the alarm will sound.

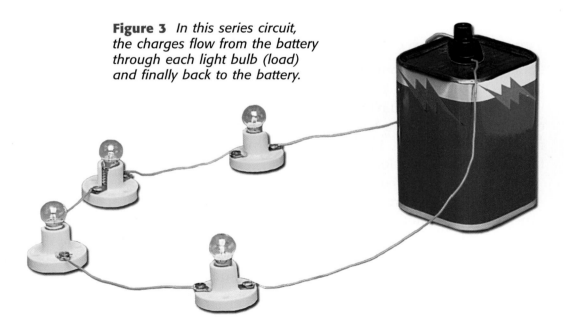

Figure 3 In this series circuit, the charges flow from the battery through each light bulb (load) and finally back to the battery.

Parallel Circuits

Think about what would happen if all of the lights in your home were connected in series. If you needed to turn on a light in your room, all other lights in the house would have to be turned on, too! Instead of being wired in series, circuits in buildings are wired in parallel. A **parallel circuit** is a circuit in which loads are connected side by side. Charges in a parallel circuit have more than one path on which they can travel.

Unlike the loads in a series circuit, the loads in a parallel circuit do not have the same current. Instead, each load in a parallel circuit uses the same voltage. For example, each bulb in **Figure 4** uses the full voltage of the battery. As a result, each light bulb glows at full brightness no matter how many bulbs are connected in parallel. You can connect loads that need different currents to the same parallel circuit. For example, you can connect a hair dryer, which needs a high current to run, to the same circuit as a lamp, which needs less current.

Reading Check How are loads connected in a parallel circuit?

Uses for Parallel Circuits

In a parallel circuit, each branch of the circuit can work by itself. If one load is broken or missing, charges will still run through the other branches. So, the loads on those branches will keep working. In your home, each electrical outlet is usually on its own branch and has its own switch. Imagine if each time a light bulb went out your television or stereo stopped working. With parallel circuits, you can use one light or appliance at a time, even if another load fails.

parallel circuit a circuit in which the parts are joined in branches such that the potential difference across each part is the same

A Parallel Lab

1. Connect a **6 V battery** and **two flashlight bulbs** in a parallel circuit. Draw a picture of your circuit.

2. Add **another flashlight bulb** in parallel with the other two bulbs. How does the brightness of the light bulbs change?

3. Replace one of the light bulbs with a **burned-out light bulb.** What happens to the other lights in the circuit? Why?

Figure 4 *In this parallel circuit, the electric charges flow from the battery and branch off through each bulb. The charges then flow back to the battery.*

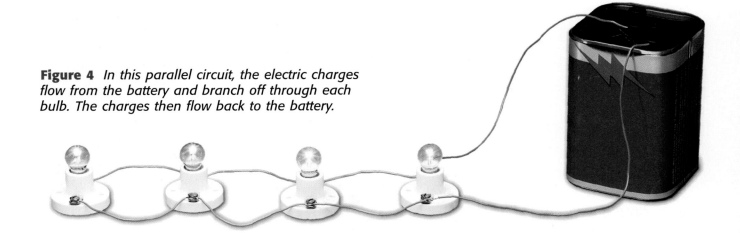

Household Circuit Safety

In every home, several circuits connect all of the lights, appliances, and outlets. The circuits branch out from a breaker box or a fuse box that acts as the "electrical headquarters" for the building. Each branch receives a standard voltage, which is 120 V in the United States.

Circuit Failure

Broken wires or water can cause a short circuit. In a short circuit, charges do not go through one or more loads in the circuit. The resistance decreases, so the current increases. The wires can heat up, and the circuit could fail. The wires might even get hot enough to start a fire. Circuits also may fail if they are overloaded. When too many loads are in a circuit, the current increases, and a fire might start. Safety features, such as fuses and circuit breakers, help prevent electrical fires.

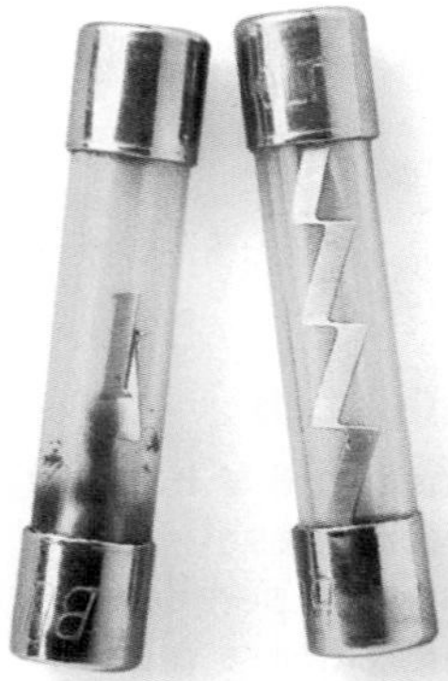

Fuses

A fuse has a thin strip of metal. The charges in the circuit flow through this strip. If the current is too high, the metal strip melts, as shown in **Figure 5.** As a result, the circuit is broken, and charges stop flowing.

Circuit Breakers

A circuit breaker is a switch that automatically opens if the current is too high. A strip of metal in the breaker warms up, bends, and opens the switch, which opens the circuit. Charges stop flowing. Open circuit breakers can be closed by flipping a switch after the problem has been fixed.

A ground fault circuit interrupter (GFCI), shown in **Figure 6,** acts as a small circuit breaker. If the current in one side of an outlet differs even slightly from the current in the other side, the GFCI opens the circuit and the charges stop flowing. To close the circuit, you must push the reset button.

Reading Check What are two safety devices used in circuits?

Figure 5 *The blown fuse on the left must be replaced with a new fuse, such as the one on the right.*

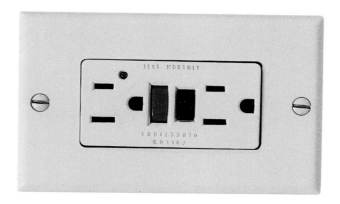

Figure 6 *GFCIs are often found on outlets in bathrooms and kitchens to protect you from electric shock.*

Electrical Safety Tips

You use electrical devices every day. So, remembering that using electrical energy can be hazardous is important. Warning signs, such as the one in **Figure 7,** can help you avoid electrical dangers. To stay safe while you use electrical energy, follow these tips:

- Make sure the insulation on cords is not worn.
- Do not overload circuits by plugging in too many electrical devices.
- Do not use electrical devices while your hands are wet or while you are standing in water.
- Never put objects other than a plug into an electrical outlet.

Figure 7 *Obeying signs that warn of high voltage can keep you safe from electrical dangers.*

SECTION Review

Summary

- Circuits consist of an energy source, a load, wires, and, in some cases, a switch.
- All parts of a series circuit are connected in a single loop. The loads in a parallel circuit are on separate branches.
- Circuits fail through a short circuit or an overload. Fuses or circuit breakers protect against circuit failure.
- It is important to follow safety tips when using electrical energy.

Using Key Terms

1. In your own words, write a definition for each of the following terms: *series circuit* and *parallel circuit.*

Understanding Key Ideas

2. Which part of a circuit changes electrical energy into another form of energy?
   a. energy source
   b. wire
   c. switch
   d. load

3. Name and describe the three essential parts of a circuit.

4. How do fuses and circuit breakers protect your home against electrical fires?

Critical Thinking

5. **Forming Hypotheses** Suppose that you turn on the heater in your room and all of the lights in your room go out. Propose a reason why the lights went out.

6. **Applying Concepts** Will a fuse work successfully if it is connected in parallel with the device it is supposed to protect? Explain your answer.

Interpreting Graphics

7. Look at the circuits below. Identify each circuit as a parallel circuit or a series circuit.

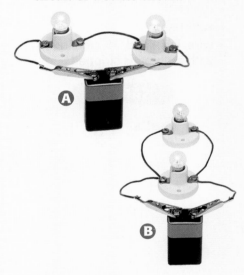

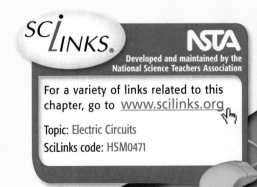

SCLINKS®

NSTA

Developed and maintained by the
National Science Teachers Association

For a variety of links related to this chapter, go to www.scilinks.org

Topic: Electric Circuits
SciLinks code: HSM0471

Skills Practice Lab

Circuitry 101

OBJECTIVES

Build a series circuit and a parallel circuit.

Use Ohm's law to calculate the resistance of a circuit from voltage and current.

MATERIALS

- ammeter
- energy source—dry cell(s)
- light-bulb holders (3)
- light bulbs (3)
- switch
- voltmeter
- wire, insulated, 15 cm lengths with both ends stripped

SAFETY

There are two basic types of electric circuits. A series circuit connects all of the parts in a single loop, and a parallel circuit connects each part on a separate branch. A switch wired in series with the energy source can control the whole circuit. If you want each part of the circuit to work on its own, the loads must be wired in parallel. In this lab, you will use an ammeter to measure current and a voltmeter to measure voltage. For each circuit, you will use Ohm's law (resistance equals voltage divided by current) to determine the overall resistance.

Procedure

1. Build a series circuit with an energy source, a switch, and three light bulbs. Draw a diagram of your circuit. **Caution:** Always leave the switch open when building or changing the circuit. Close the switch only when you are testing or taking a reading.

2. Test your circuit. Do all three bulbs light up? Are all bulbs the same brightness? What happens if you carefully unscrew one light bulb? Does it make any difference which bulb you unscrew? Record your observations.

3. Connect the ammeter between the power source and the switch. Close the switch, and record the current on your diagram. Be sure to show where you measured the current.

4. Reconnect the circuit so that the ammeter is between the first and second bulbs. Record the current, as you did in step 3.

5. Move the ammeter so that it is between the second and third bulbs, and record the current again.

6. Remove the ammeter from the circuit. Connect the voltmeter to the two ends of the power source. Record the voltage on your diagram.

7. Use the voltmeter to measure the voltage across each bulb. Record each reading.

8. Take apart your series circuit. Reassemble the same items so that the bulbs are wired in parallel. (Note: The switch must remain in series with the power source to be able to control the whole circuit.) Draw a diagram of your circuit.

9 Test your circuit, and record your observations, as you did in step 2.

10 Connect the ammeter between the power source and the switch. Record the current.

11 Reconnect the circuit so that the ammeter is right next to one of the three bulbs. Record the current.

12 Repeat step 11 for the two remaining bulbs.

13 Remove the ammeter from your circuit. Connect the voltmeter to the two ends of the power source. Record the voltage.

14 Measure and record the voltage across each light bulb.

Analyze the Results

1 **Recognizing Patterns** Was the current the same at all places in the series circuit? Was it the same everywhere in the parallel circuit?

2 **Analyzing Data** For each circuit, compare the voltage across each light bulb with the voltage at the power source.

3 **Identifying Patterns** What is the relationship between the voltage at the power source and the voltages at the light bulbs in a series circuit?

4 **Analyzing Data** Use Ohm's law and the readings for current (*I*) and voltage (*V*) at the power source for both circuits to calculate the total resistance (*R*) in both the series and parallel circuits.

Draw Conclusions

5 **Drawing Conclusions** Was the total resistance for both circuits the same? Explain your answer.

6 **Interpreting Information** Why did the bulbs differ in brightness?

7 **Making Predictions** Based on your results, what do you think might happen if too many electrical appliances are plugged into the same series circuit? What might happen if too many electrical appliances are plugged into the same parallel circuit?

Chapter Review

USING KEY TERMS

The statements below are false. For each statement, replace the underlined term to make a true statement.

1 Charges flow easily in an <u>electrical insulator</u>.

2 Lightning is a form of <u>static electricity</u>.

3 A <u>thermocouple</u> converts chemical energy into electrical energy.

4 <u>Voltage</u> is the opposition to the current by a material.

5 <u>Electric force</u> is the rate at which electrical energy is converted into other forms of energy.

6 Each load in a <u>parallel circuit</u> has the same current.

UNDERSTANDING KEY IDEAS

Multiple Choice

7 Two objects repel each other. What charges might the objects have?

a. positive and positive

b. positive and negative

c. negative and negative

d. Both (a) and (c)

8 Which device converts chemical energy into electrical energy?

a. lightning rod

b. cell

c. light bulb

d. switch

9 Which of the following wires has the lowest resistance?

a. a short, thick copper wire at 25°C

b. a long, thick copper wire at 35°C

c. a long, thin copper wire at 35°C

d. a short, thick iron wire at 25°C

10 An object becomes charged when the atoms in the object gain or lose

a. protons.

b. neutrons.

c. electrons.

d. All of the above

11 Which of the following devices does NOT protect you from electrical fires?

a. electric meter

b. circuit breaker

c. fuse

d. ground fault circuit interrupter

12 For a cell to produce a current, the electrodes of the cell must

a. have a potential difference.

b. be in a liquid.

c. be exposed to light.

d. be at two different temperatures.

13 The outlets in your home provide

a. direct current.

b. alternating current.

c. electric discharge.

d. static electricity.

Short Answer

14 Describe how a switch controls a circuit.

15 Name the two factors that affect the strength of electric force, and explain how they affect electric force.

16 Describe how direct current differs from alternating current.

Math Skills

17 What voltage is needed to produce a 6 A current in an object that has a resistance of 3 Ω?

18 Find the current produced when a voltage of 60 V is applied to a resistance of 15 Ω.

19 What is the resistance of an object if a voltage of 40 V produces a current of 5 A?

20 A light bulb is rated at 150 W. How much current is in the bulb if 120 V is applied to the bulb?

21 How much electrical energy does a 60 W light bulb use if it is used for 1,000 hours?

CRITICAL THINKING

22 **Concept Mapping** Use the following terms to create a concept map: *electric current, battery, charges, photocell, thermocouple, circuit, parallel circuit,* and *series circuit.*

23 **Making Inferences** Suppose your science classroom was rewired over the weekend. On Monday, you notice that the lights in the room must be on for the fish-tank bubbler to work. And if you want to use the computer, you must turn on the overhead projector. Describe what mistake the electrician made when working on the circuits in your classroom.

24 **Applying Concepts** You can make a cell by using an apple, a strip of copper, and a strip of silver. Explain how you would construct the cell, and identify the parts of the cell. What type of cell did you make? Explain your answer.

25 **Applying Concepts** Your friend shows you a magic trick. First, she rubs a plastic pipe on a piece of wool. Then, she holds the pipe close to an empty soda can that is lying on its side. When the pipe is close to the can, the can rolls toward the pipe. Explain how this trick works.

INTERPRETING GRAPHICS

26 Classify the objects in the photograph below as electrical conductors or electrical insulators.

READING

Read each of the passages below. Then, answer the questions that follow each passage.

Passage 1 In 1888, Frank J. Sprague developed a way to operate trolleys by using electrical energy. These electric trolleys ran on a metal track and were connected by a pole to an overhead power line. Electric charges flowed down the pole to motors in the trolley. A wheel at the top of the pole, called a <u>shoe</u>, rolled along the power line and allowed the trolley to move along its track without losing contact with its source of electrical energy. The charges passed through the motor and then returned to a generator by way of the metal track.

1. In this passage, what does the word *shoe* mean?

  A a type of covering that you wear on your foot

  B a device that allowed a trolley to get electrical energy

  C a flat, U-shaped metal plate nailed to a horse's hoof

  D the metal track on which trolleys ran

2. What is the main purpose of this passage?

  F to inform the reader

  G to influence the reader's opinion

  H to express the author's opinion

  I to make the reader laugh

3. Which of the following statements describes what happens first in the operation of a trolley?

  A Charges flow down the pole.

  B Charges pass through the motor.

  C Charges enter the shoe from the power line.

  D Charges return to the generator through the tracks.

Passage 2 Benjamin Franklin (1706–1790) first suggested the terms *positive* and *negative* for the two types of charge. At the age of 40, Franklin was a successful printer and journalist. He saw some experiments on electricity and was so fascinated by them that he began to devote much of his time to experimenting. Franklin was the first person to realize that lightning is a huge electric discharge, or spark. He invented the first lightning rod, for which he became famous. He also flew a kite into thunderclouds—at great risk to his life—to collect charge from them. During and after the Revolutionary War, Franklin gained fame as a politician and a statesman.

1. Which of the following happened earliest in Franklin's life?

  A He gained fame as a politician.

  B He flew a kite into thunderclouds.

  C He saw experiments on electricity.

  D He was a successful journalist.

2. Which of the following statements is a fact according to the passage?

  F Franklin became interested in electricity in 1706.

  G There is no connection between lightning and an electric discharge.

  H Franklin became a successful journalist after he performed experiments with electricity.

  I Flying a kite into thunderclouds is dangerous.

Use the diagram below to answer the questions that follow.

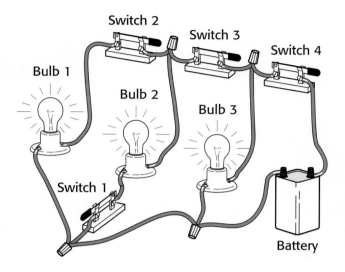

1. Opening which switch will turn off only light bulb 2?

  A switch 1

  B switch 2

  C switch 3

  D switch 4

2. Opening which switch will turn off exactly two light bulbs?

  F switch 1

  G switch 2

  H switch 3

  I switch 4

3. If only switches 2 and 3 are open, which of the following will happen?

  A All three bulbs will remain lit.

  B Only bulb 1 will remain lit.

  C Only bulb 3 will remain lit.

  D All three bulbs will turn off.

4. Which of the following statements is false?

  F Bulb 2 will be off when bulb 1 is off.

  G Bulb 3 will be on if any other bulb is on.

  H Bulbs 1 and 3 can be on when bulb 2 is off.

  I Bulb 3 can be on when bulbs 1 and 2 are off.

Read each question below, and choose the best answer.

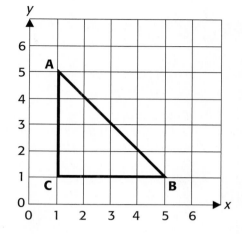

1. Look at triangle *ABC*. If you want to draw square *ADBC*, what would the coordinates of *D* be?

  A (1, 5)

  B (3, 3)

  C (5, 5)

  D (5, 1)

2. The equation *voltage = current × resistance* is often called *Ohm's law*. If the current in an object is 0.5 A and the voltage across the object is 12 V, what is the resistance of the object?

  F 0.042 Ω

  G 6 Ω

  H 12.5 Ω

  I 24 Ω

3. Heather has six large dogs. In one day, each of the dogs eats 2.1 kg of dog food. Which is the best estimate of the total number of kilograms of food all of the dogs eat in 4 weeks?

  A less than 150 kg

  B between 150 and 225 kg

  C between 225 and 300 kg

  D more than 300 kg

Science in Action

Weird Science

Electric Eels

Electric eels are freshwater fish from Central and South America. They can produce powerful jolts of electrical energy. Electric discharges from eels are strong enough to stun or kill smaller fish and frogs in the water. The eels then swallow their motionless prey whole. Early travelers to the Amazon River basin wrote that in shallow pools, the eels' discharges could knock horses and humans over. Within the body of an eel, which is 2.5 m long, are a series of electroplates, or modified muscle tissues that generate low voltages. An eel has 5,000 to 6,000 connected electroplates. In lab experiments, the bursts of voltage from a fully grown eel have been measured to be about 600 V.

Math ACTiViTY

The battery in a car provides 12 V. How many times more voltage can a fully grown eel provide than can a car battery? If the voltage provided by the eel were used in a circuit that had a resistance of 200 Ω, what would the current in the circuit be?

Scientific Discoveries

Sprites and Elves

Imagine that you are in a plane on a moonless night. You notice a thunderstorm 80 km away and see lightning move between the clouds and the Earth. Then, suddenly, a ghostly red glow stretches many kilometers above the clouds! You did not expect that!

In 1989, scientists captured the first image of this strange, red, glowing lightning. Since then, photographs from space shuttles, airplanes, telescopes, and observers on the ground have shown several types of electrical glows. Two were named sprites and elves because, like the mythical creatures, they disappear just as the eye begins to see them. Sprites and elves last only a few thousandths of a second.

Language Arts ACTiViTY

WRITING SKILL Imagine that you are a hunter living in about 5000 BCE. On a hunt, you see a sprite as described above. Write a two-page short story explaining what you saw, what your reaction was, and why you think the sprite happened.

Pete Perez

Electrician Sometimes, you forget just how much of daily life is dependent on electricity—until the electricity goes out! Then, you call an electrician, such as Pete Perez. Perez has been installing electrical systems and solving electricity problems in commercial and residential settings since 1971. "I'm in this work because of the challenge. Everywhere you go it's something new."

An electrician performs a wide variety of jobs that may include repairs, routine maintenance, or disaster prevention. One day, he or she might install wiring in a new house. The next day, he or she might replace wiring in an older house. Jobs can be as simple as replacing a fuse or as complicated as restoring an industrial machine. Also, electricians may work under many different conditions, including in a dark basement or at the top of an electrical tower. Perez's advice to aspiring young electricians is, "Open up your mind." You never know what kind of job is waiting for you around the corner, because every day brings stranger and more interesting challenges.

Social Studies ACTIVITY

Imagine that you are helping run a job fair at your school. Research the requirements for becoming an electrician. Make a brochure that tells what an electrician does and what training is needed. Describe how much the training and basic equipment to get started will cost. Include the starting salary and information about any testing or certification that is needed.

To learn more about these Science in Action topics, visit **go.hrw.com** and type in the keyword **HP5ELEF**.

Current Science

Check out Current Science® articles related to this chapter by visiting go.hrw.com. Just type in the keyword HP5CS17.

18

Electromagnetism

SECTION **1** Magnets and
Magnetism 510

SECTION **2** Magnetism from
Electricity 518

SECTION **3** Electricity from
Magnetism 524

Chapter Lab 530
Chapter Review 532
Standardized Test Preparation 534
Science in Action................ 536

About the PHOTO

Superhot particles at millions of degrees Celsius shoot out of the sun. But they do not escape. They loop back and crash into the sun's surface at more than 100 km/s (223,000 mi/h). The image of Earth has been added to show how large these loops can be. What directs the particles? The particles follow along the path of the magnetic field lines of the sun. You depend on magnetic fields in electric motors and generators. And you can use them to show off a good report card on the refrigerator.

PRE-READING ACTIVITY

Graphic Organizer

Comparison Table Before you read the chapter, create the graphic organizer entitled "Comparison Table" described in the **Study Skills** section of the Appendix. Label the columns with "Motor" and "Generator." Label the rows with "Energy in" and "Energy out." As you read the chapter, fill in the table with details about the energy conversion that happens in each device.

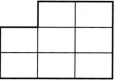

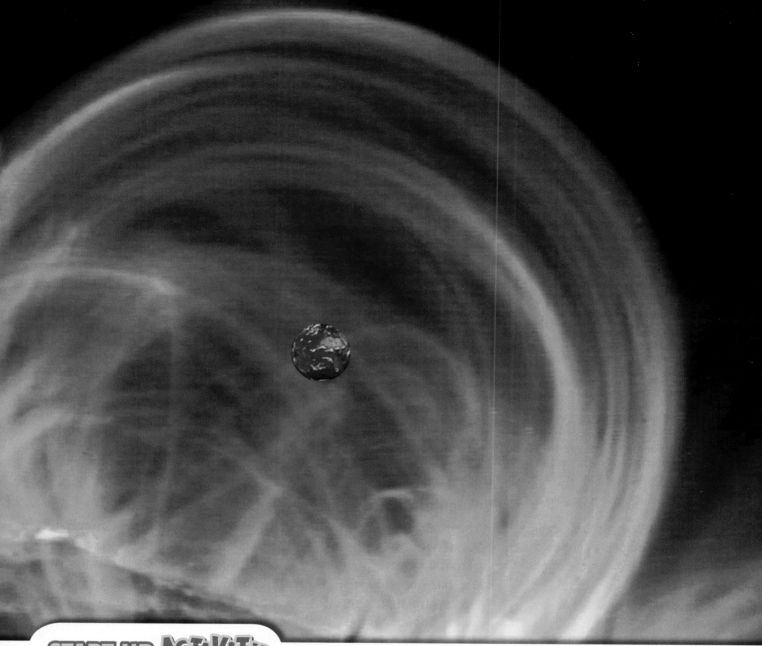

START-UP ACTIVITY

Magnetic Attraction

In this activity, you will investigate ways you can use a magnet to lift steel.

Procedure

1. Put **5 steel paper clips** on your desk. Touch the clips with an **unmagnetized iron nail.** Record the number of clips that stick to it.

2. Touch the clips with the end of a **strong bar magnet.** Record the number of clips that stick to the magnet.

3. While holding the magnet against the head of the nail, touch the tip of the nail to the paper clips. Count the number of paper clips that stick to the nail.

4. Remove the magnet from the end of the nail. Record the number of paper clips you counted in step 3 and your observations when you removed the magnet.

5. Drag one end of the bar magnet 50 times down the nail. Drag the magnet in only one direction.

6. Set the magnet aside. Touch the nail to the clips. Record the number of clips that stick to it.

Analysis

1. What caused the difference between the number of paper clips that you picked up in step 1 and in step 3?

2. What effect did the magnet have on the nail in step 5?

Magnets and Magnetism

You've probably seen magnets stuck to a refrigerator door. These magnets might be holding notes or pictures. Or they might be just for looks.

If you have ever experimented with magnets, you know that they stick to each other and to some kinds of metals. You also know that magnets can stick to things without directly touching them—such as a magnet used to hold a piece of paper to a refrigerator door.

Properties of Magnets

More than 2,000 years ago, the Greeks discovered a mineral that attracted things made of iron. Because this mineral was found in a part of Turkey called Magnesia, the Greeks called it magnetite. Today, any material that attracts iron or things made of iron is called a **magnet.** All magnets have certain properties. For example, all magnets have two poles. Magnets exert forces on each other and are surrounded by a magnetic field.

✓ **Reading Check** What is a magnet? (*See the Appendix for answers to Reading Checks.*)

Magnetic Poles

The magnetic effects are not the same throughout a magnet. What would happen if you dipped a bar magnet into a box of paper clips? Most of the clips would stick to the ends of the bar, as shown in **Figure 1.** This shows that the strongest effects are near the ends of the bar magnet. Each end of the magnet is a magnetic pole. As you will see, **magnetic poles** are points on a magnet that have opposite magnetic qualities.

magnet any material that attracts iron or materials containing iron

magnetic pole one of two points, such as the ends of a magnet, that have opposing magnetic qualities

Figure 1 *More paper clips stick to the ends, or magnetic poles, of a magnet because the magnetic effects are strongest there.*

North and South

Suppose you hang a magnet by a string so that the magnet can spin. You will see that one end of the magnet always ends up pointing to the north, as shown in **Figure 2.** The pole of a magnet that points to the north is called the magnet's *north pole*. The opposite end of the magnet points to the south. It is called the magnet's *south pole*. Magnetic poles are always in pairs. You will never find a magnet that has only a north pole or only a south pole.

Figure 2 *The needle in a compass is a magnet that is free to rotate.*

Magnetic Forces

When you bring two magnets close together, the magnets each exert a **magnetic force** on the other. These magnetic forces result from spinning electric charges in the magnets. The force can either push the magnets apart or pull them together. The magnetic force is a universal force. It is always present when magnetic poles come near one another.

Think of the last time you worked with magnets. If you held two magnets in a certain way, they pulled together. When you turned one of the magnets around, they pushed apart. Why? The magnetic force between magnets depends on how the poles of the magnets line up. Like poles repel, and opposite poles attract, as shown in **Figure 3.**

magnetic force the force of attraction or repulsion generated by moving or spinning electric charges

✓ Reading Check If two magnets push each other away, what can you conclude about their poles?

Figure 3 **Magnetic Force Between Magnets**

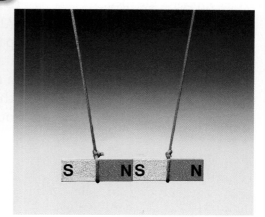

▲ If you hold the north poles of two magnets close together, the magnetic force will push the magnets apart. The same is true if you hold the south poles close together.

▲ If you hold the north pole of one magnet close to the south pole of another magnet, the magnetic force will pull the magnets together.

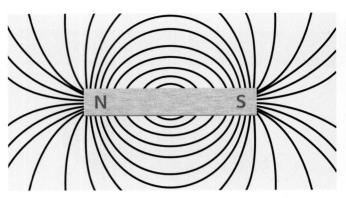
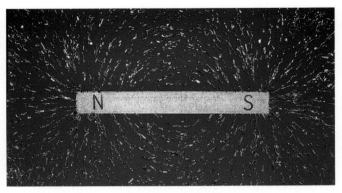

Figure 4 *Magnetic field lines show the shape of a magnetic field around a magnet. You can model magnetic field lines by sprinkling iron filings around a magnet.*

Magnetic Fields

A *magnetic field* exists in the region around a magnet in which magnetic forces can act. The shape of a magnetic field can be shown with lines drawn from the north pole of a magnet to the south pole, as shown in **Figure 4.** These lines map out the magnetic field and are called *magnetic field lines*. The closer together the field lines are, the stronger the magnetic field is. The lines around a magnet are closest together at the poles, where the magnetic force on an object is strongest.

The Cause of Magnetism

Some materials are magnetic. Some are not. For example, a magnet can pick up paper clips and iron nails. But it cannot pick up paper, plastic, pennies, or aluminum foil. What causes the difference? Whether a material is magnetic depends on the material's atoms.

Atoms and Domains

All matter is made of atoms. Electrons are negatively charged particles of atoms. As an electron moves around, it makes, or induces, a magnetic field. The atom will then have a north and a south pole. In most materials, such as copper and aluminum, the magnetic fields of the individual atoms cancel each other out. Therefore, these materials are not magnetic.

But in materials such as iron, nickel, and cobalt, groups of atoms are in tiny areas called *domains*. The north and south poles of the atoms in a domain line up and make a strong magnetic field. Domains are like tiny magnets of different sizes within an object. The arrangement of domains in an object determines whether the object is magnetic. **Figure 5** shows how the arrangement of domains works.

Reading Check Why are copper and aluminum not magnetic?

Figure 5 Arrangement of Domains in an Object

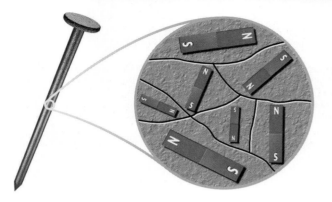

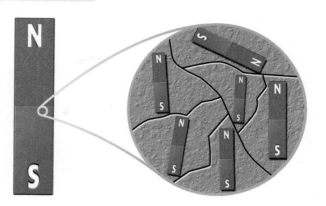

If the domains in an object are randomly arranged, the magnetic fields of the individual domains cancel each other out, and the object has no magnetic properties.

If most of the domains in an object are aligned, the magnetic fields of the individual domains combine to make the whole object magnetic.

Losing Alignment

The domains of a magnet may not always stay lined up. When domains move, the magnet is demagnetized, or loses its magnetic properties. Dropping a magnet or hitting it too hard can move the domains. Putting the magnet in a strong magnetic field that is opposite to its own can also move domains. Increasing the temperature of a magnet can also demagnetize it. At higher temperatures, atoms in the magnet vibrate faster. As a result, the atoms in the domains may no longer line up.

✓ Reading Check Describe two ways a magnet can lose its magnetic properties.

Making Magnets

You can make a magnet from something made of iron, cobalt, or nickel. You just need to line up the domains in it. For example, you can magnetize an iron nail if you rub it in one direction with one pole of a magnet. The domains in the nail line up with the magnetic field of the magnet. So, the domains in the nail become aligned. As more domains line up, the magnetic field of the nail grows stronger. The nail will become a magnet, as shown in **Figure 6.**

The process of making a magnet also explains how a magnet can pick up an unmagnetized object, such as a paper clip. When a magnet is close to a paper clip, some domains in the paper clip line up with the field of the magnet. So, the paper clip becomes a temporary magnet. The north pole of the paper clip points toward the south pole of the magnet. The paper clip is attracted to the magnet. When the magnet is removed, the domains of the paper clip become scrambled again.

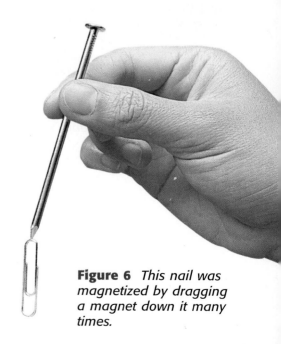

Figure 6 *This nail was magnetized by dragging a magnet down it many times.*

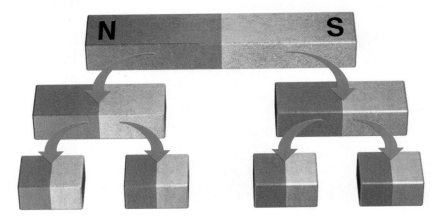

Figure 7 *If you cut a magnet in pieces, each piece will still be a magnet with two poles.*

Cutting a Magnet

What do you think would happen if you cut a magnet in half? You might think that you would end up with one north-pole piece and one south-pole piece. But that's not what happens. When you cut a magnet in half, you end up with two magnets. Each piece has its own north pole and south pole, as shown in **Figure 7.** A magnet has poles because its domains are lined up. Each domain within a magnet is like a tiny magnet with a north pole and a south pole. Even the smallest pieces of a magnet have two poles.

Kinds of Magnets

There are different ways to describe magnets. Some magnets are made of iron, nickel, cobalt, or mixtures of those metals. Magnets made with these metals have strong magnetic properties and are called *ferromagnets*. Look at **Figure 8.** The mineral magnetite is an example of a naturally occurring ferromagnet. Another kind of magnet is the *electromagnet*. This is a magnet made by an electric current. An electromagnet usually has an iron core.

Figure 8 *Magnetite attracts objects containing iron and is a ferromagnet.*

✔ **Reading Check** What are ferromagnets?

Temporary and Permanent Magnets

Magnets can also be described as temporary magnets or permanent magnets. *Temporary magnets* are made from materials that are easy to magnetize. But they tend to lose their magnetization easily. Soft iron is iron that is not mixed with any other materials. It can be made into temporary magnets. *Permanent magnets* are difficult to magnetize. But they tend to keep their magnetic properties longer than temporary magnets do. Some permanent magnets are made with alnico (AL ni KOH)—an alloy of aluminum, nickel, cobalt, and iron.

Earth as a Magnet

One end of every magnet points to the north if the magnet can spin. For more than 2,000 years, travelers have used this property to find their way. In fact, you use this when you use a compass, because a compass has a freely spinning magnet.

One Giant Magnet

In 1600, an English physician named William Gilbert suggested that magnets point to the north because Earth is one giant magnet. In fact, Earth behaves as if it has a bar magnet running through its center. The poles of this imaginary magnet are located near Earth's geographic poles.

Poles of a Compass Needle

If you put a compass on a bar magnet, the marked end of the needle points to the south pole of the magnet. Does that surprise you? Opposite poles of magnets attract each other. A compass needle is a small magnet. And the tip that points to the north is the needle's north pole. Therefore, the point of a compass needle is attracted to the south pole of a magnet.

South Magnetic Pole near North Geographic Pole

Look at **Figure 9.** A compass needle points north because the magnetic pole of Earth that is closest to the geographic North Pole is a magnetic *south* pole. A compass needle points to the north because its north pole is attracted to a very large magnetic south pole.

Model of Earth's Magnetic Field

1. Place a **bar magnet** on a **sheet of butcher paper.** Draw a circle on the paper with a diameter larger than the bar magnet. This represents the surface of the Earth. Label Earth's North Pole and South Pole.

2. Place the bar magnet under the butcher paper, and line up the bar magnet with the poles.

3. Sprinkle some **iron filings** lightly around the perimeter of the circle. Describe and sketch the pattern you see.

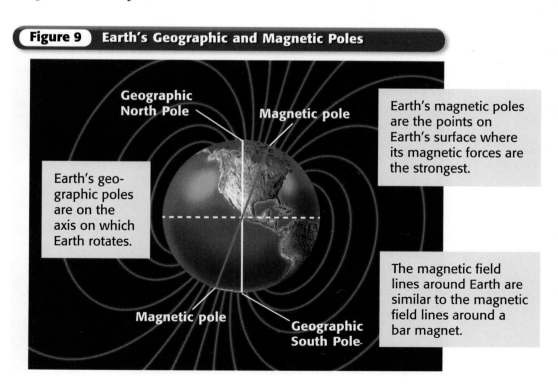

Figure 9 Earth's Geographic and Magnetic Poles

Geographic North Pole

Magnetic pole

Earth's magnetic poles are the points on Earth's surface where its magnetic forces are the strongest.

Earth's geographic poles are on the axis on which Earth rotates.

Magnetic pole

Geographic South Pole

The magnetic field lines around Earth are similar to the magnetic field lines around a bar magnet.

The Core of the Matter

Although you can think of Earth as having a giant bar magnet through its center, there isn't really a magnet there. The temperature of Earth's core (or center) is very high. The atoms in it move too violently to stay lined up in domains.

Scientists think that the Earth's magnetic field is made by the movement of electric charges in the Earth's core. The Earth's core is made mostly of iron and nickel. The inner core is solid because it is under great pressure. The outer core is liquid because the pressure is less. As Earth rotates, the liquid in the core flows. Electric charges move, which makes a magnetic field.

✓ Reading Check What do scientists think causes the Earth's magnetic field?

A Magnetic Light Show

Look at **Figure 10.** The beautiful curtain of light is called an *aurora* (aw RAWR uh). Earth's magnetic field plays a part in making auroras. An aurora is formed when charged particles from the sun hit oxygen and nitrogen atoms in the air. The atoms become excited and then give off light of many colors.

Earth's magnetic field blocks most of the charged particles from the sun. But the field bends inward at the magnetic poles. As a result, the charged particles can crash into the atmosphere at and near the poles. Auroras seen near Earth's North Pole are called the *northern lights,* or aurora borealis (aw RAWR uh BAWR ee AL is). Auroras seen near the South Pole are called the *southern lights,* or aurora australis (aw RAWR uh aw STRAY lis).

Figure 10 *An aurora is an amazing light show in the sky.*

Summary

- All magnets have two poles. The north pole will always point to the north if allowed to rotate freely. The other pole is called the south pole.

- Like magnetic poles repel each other. Opposite magnetic poles attract.

- Every magnet is surrounded by a magnetic field. The shape of the field can be shown with magnetic field lines.

- A material is magnetic if its domains line up.

- Magnets can be classified as ferromagnets, electromagnets, temporary magnets, and permanent magnets.

- Earth acts as if it has a big bar magnet through its core. Compass needles and the north poles of magnets point to Earth's magnetic south pole, which is near Earth's geographic North Pole.

- Auroras are most commonly seen near Earth's magnetic poles because Earth's magnetic field bends inward at the poles.

Using Key Terms

1. Use the following terms in the same sentence: *magnet, magnetic force,* and *magnetic pole.*

Understanding Key Ideas

2. What metal is used to make ferromagnets?
   a. iron
   b. cobalt
   c. nickel
   d. All of the above

3. Name three properties of magnets.

4. Why are some iron objects magnetic and others not magnetic?

5. How are temporary magnets different from permanent magnets?

Critical Thinking

6. **Forming Hypotheses** Why are auroras more commonly seen in places such as Alaska and Australia than in places such as Florida and Mexico?

7. **Applying Concepts** Explain how you could use magnets to make a small object appear to float in air.

8. **Making Inferences** Earth's moon has no atmosphere and has a cool, solid core. Would you expect to see auroras on the moon? Explain your answer.

Interpreting Graphics

The image below shows a model of Earth as a large magnet. Use the image below to answer the questions that follow.

9. Which magnetic pole is closest to the geographic North Pole?

10. Is the magnetic field of Earth stronger near the middle of Earth (in Mexico) or at the bottom of Earth (in Antarctica)? Explain your answer.

SCiLINKS

NSTA
Developed and maintained by the
National Science Teachers Association

For a variety of links related to this chapter, go to www.scilinks.org

Topic: Magnetism; Types of Magnets
SciLinks code: HSM0900; HSM1566

Magnetism from Electricity

Most of the trains you see roll on wheels on top of a track. But engineers have developed trains that have no wheels. The trains actually float above the track.

They float because of magnetic forces between the track and the train cars. Such trains are called maglev trains. The name *maglev* is short for magnetic levitation. To levitate, maglev trains use a kind of magnet called an electromagnet. Electromagnets can make strong magnetic fields. In this section, you will learn how electricity and magnetism are related and how electromagnets are made.

The Discovery of Electromagnetism

Danish physicist Hans Christian Oersted (UHR STED) discovered the relationship between electricity and magnetism in 1820. During a lecture, he held a compass near a wire carrying an electric current. Oersted noticed that when the compass was close to the wire, the compass needle no longer pointed to the north. The result surprised Oersted. A compass needle is a magnet. It moves from its north-south orientation only when it is in a magnetic field different from Earth's. Oersted tried a few experiments with the compass and the wire. His results are shown in **Figure 1.**

Figure 1 Oersted's Experiment

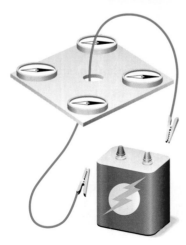

a If no electric current exists in the wire, the compass needles point in the same direction.

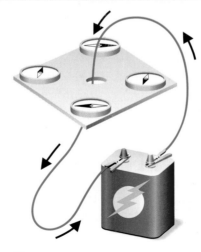

b Electric current in one direction in the wire causes the compass needles to deflect in a clockwise direction.

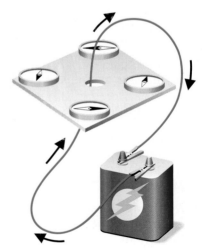

c Electric current in the opposite direction makes the compass needles deflect in a counterclockwise direction.

More Research

From his experiments, Oersted concluded that an electric current produces a magnetic field. He also found that the direction of the field depends on the direction of the current. The French scientist André-Marie Ampère heard about Oersted's findings. Ampère did more research with electricity and magnetism. Their work was the first research of electromagnetism. **Electromagnetism** is the interaction between electricity and magnetism.

> ✓ **Reading Check** What is electromagnetism? (*See the Appendix for answers to Reading Checks.*)

electromagnetism the interaction between electricity and magnetism

solenoid a coil of wire with an electric current in it

Using Electromagnetism

The magnetic field generated by an electric current in a wire can move a compass needle. But the magnetic field is not strong enough to be very useful. However, two devices, the solenoid and the electromagnet, strengthen the magnetic field made by a current-carrying wire. Both devices make electromagnetism more useful.

Solenoids

A single loop of wire carrying a current does not have a very strong magnetic field. But suppose you form many loops into a coil. The magnetic fields of the individual loops will combine to make a much stronger field. A **solenoid** is a coil of wire that produces a magnetic field when carrying an electric current. In fact, the magnetic field around a solenoid is very similar to the magnetic field of a bar magnet, as shown in **Figure 2.** The strength of the magnetic field of a solenoid increases as more loops per meter are used. The magnetic field also becomes stronger as the current in the wire is increased.

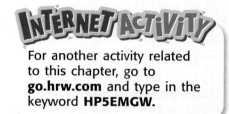

For another activity related to this chapter, go to **go.hrw.com** and type in the keyword **HP5EMGW.**

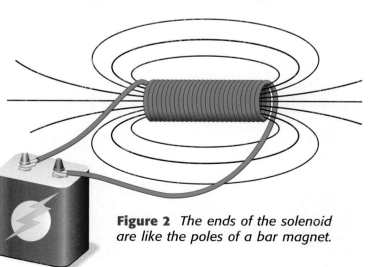

Figure 2 *The ends of the solenoid are like the poles of a bar magnet.*

electromagnet a coil that has a soft iron core and that acts as a magnet when an electric current is in the coil

Figure 3 *Electromagnets used in salvage yards are turned on to pick up metal objects and turned off to put them down again.*

Electromagnets

An **electromagnet** is made up of a solenoid wrapped around an iron core. The magnetic field of the solenoid makes the domains inside the iron core line up. The magnetic field of the electromagnet is the field of the solenoid plus the field of the magnetized core. As a result, the magnetic field of an electromagnet may be hundreds of times stronger than the magnetic field of just the solenoid.

You can make an electromagnet even stronger. You can increase the number of loops per meter in the solenoid. You can also increase the electric current in the wire. Some electromagnets are strong enough to lift a car or levitate a train! Maglev trains levitate because strong magnets on the cars are pushed away by powerful electromagnets in the rails.

✓ Reading Check What happens to the magnetic field of an electromagnet if you increase the current in the wire?

Turning Electromagnets On and Off

Electromagnets are very useful because they can be turned on and off as needed. The solenoid has a field only when there is electric current in it. So, electromagnets attract things only when a current exists in the wire. When there is no current in the wire, the electromagnet is turned off. **Figure 3** shows an example of how this property can be useful.

Applications of Electromagnetism

Electromagnetism is useful in your everyday life. You already know that electromagnets can be used to lift heavy objects containing iron. But did you know that you use a solenoid whenever you ring a doorbell? Or that there are electromagnets in motors? Keep reading to learn how electromagnetism makes these things work.

Doorbells

Look at **Figure 4.** Have you ever noticed a doorbell button that has a light inside? Have you noticed that when you push the button, the light goes out? Two solenoids in the doorbell allow the doorbell to work. Pushing the button opens the circuit of the first solenoid. The current stops, causing the magnetic field to drop and the light to go out. The change in the field causes a current in the second solenoid. This current induces a magnetic field that pushes an iron rod that sounds the bell.

Magnetic Force and Electric Current

An electric current can cause a compass needle to move. The needle is a small magnet. The needle moves because the electric current in a wire creates a magnetic field that exerts a force on the needle. If a current-carrying wire causes a magnet to move, can a magnet cause a current-carrying wire to move? **Figure 5** shows that the answer is yes. This property is useful in electric motors.

> **✓ Reading Check** Why does a current-carrying wire cause a compass needle to move?

Figure 4 *Ringing this doorbell requires two solenoids.*

Figure 5 **Magnetic Force on a Current-Carrying Wire**

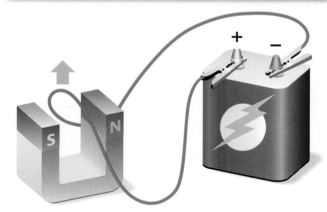

ⓐ When a current-carrying wire is placed between two poles of a magnet, the wire will jump up.

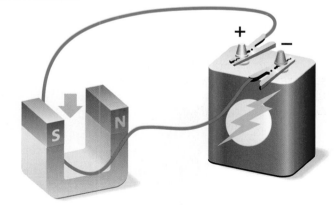

ⓑ Switching the wires at the battery reverses the direction of the current, and the wire is pushed down.

Electric Motors

An **electric motor** is a device that changes electrical energy into mechanical energy. All electric motors have an *armature*—a loop or coil of wire that can rotate. The armature is mounted between the poles of a permanent magnet or electromagnet.

In electric motors that use direct current, a device called a *commutator* is attached to the armature to reverse the direction of the electric current in the wire. A commutator is a ring that is split in half and connected to the ends of the armature. Electric current enters the armature through brushes that touch the commutator. Every time the armature and the commutator make a half turn, the direction of the current in the armature is reversed. **Figure 6** shows how a direct-current motor works.

Figure 6   A Direct-Current Electric Motor

Getting Started An electric current in the armature causes the magnet to exert a force on the armature. Because of the direction of the current on either side of the armature, the magnet pulls up on one side and down on the other side. This pulling makes the armature rotate.

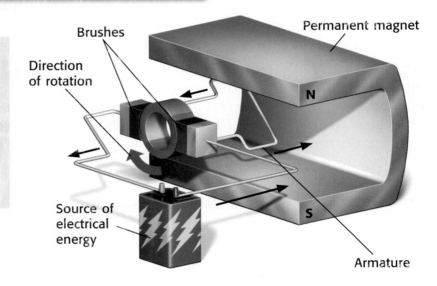

Running the Motor As the armature rotates, the commutator causes the electric current in the coil to change directions. When the electric current is reversed, the side of the coil that was pulled up is pulled down and the side that was pulled down is pulled up. This change of direction keeps the armature rotating.

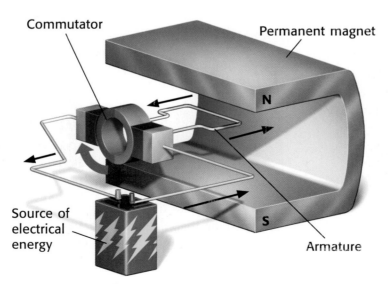

Galvanometers

A galvanometer (GAL vuh NAHM uht uhr) measures current. Galvanometers are sometimes found in equipment used by electricians, such as ammeters and voltmeters, as shown in **Figure 7.** A galvanometer has an electromagnet placed between the poles of a permanent magnet. The poles of the electromagnet are pushed away by the poles of the permanent magnet. The electromagnet is free to rotate and is attached to a pointer. The pointer moves along a scale that shows the size and direction of the current.

✓ **Reading Check** What does a galvanometer measure?

Figure 7 *This ammeter uses a galvanometer to measure electric current.*

SECTION Review

Summary

- Oersted discovered that a wire carrying a current makes a magnetic field.

- Electromagnetism is the interaction between electricity and magnetism.

- An electromagnet is a solenoid that has an iron core.

- A magnet can exert a force on a wire carrying a current.

- A doorbell, an electric motor, and a galvanometer all make use of electromagnetism.

Using Key Terms

For each pair of terms, explain how the meanings of the terms differ.

1. *electromagnet* and *solenoid*

Understanding Key Ideas

2. Which of the following actions will decrease the strength of the magnetic field of an electromagnet?
   a. using fewer loops of wire per meter in the coil
   b. decreasing the current in the wire
   c. removing the iron core
   d. All of the above

3. Describe what happens when you hold a compass close to a wire carrying a current.

4. What is the relationship between an electric current and a magnetic field?

5. What makes the armature in an electric motor rotate?

Critical Thinking

6. **Applying Concepts** What do Hans Christian Oersted's experiments have to do with a galvanometer? Explain your answer.

7. **Making Comparisons** Compare the structures and magnetic fields of solenoids with those of electromagnets.

Interpreting Graphics

8. Look at the image below. Your friend says that the image shows an electromagnet because there are loops with a core in the middle. Is your friend correct? Explain your reasoning.

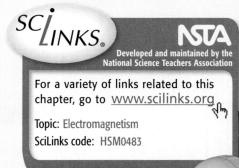

For a variety of links related to this chapter, go to www.scilinks.org

Topic: Electromagnetism
SciLinks code: HSM0483

Electricity from Magnetism

When you use an electrical appliance or turn on a light in your home, you probably don't think about where the electrical energy comes from.

For most people, an electric power company supplies their home with electrical energy. In this section, you'll learn how a magnetic field can induce an electric current and how power companies use this process to supply electrical energy.

Electric Current from a Changing Magnetic Field

Hans Christian Oersted discovered that an electric current could make a magnetic field. Soon after, scientists wondered if a magnetic field could make an electric current. In 1831, two scientists each solved this problem. Joseph Henry, of the United States, made the discovery first. But Michael Faraday, from Great Britain, published his results first. Faraday also reported them in great detail, so his results are better known.

Faraday's Experiment

Faraday used a setup like the one shown in **Figure 1.** Faraday hoped that the magnetic field of the electromagnet would make—or induce—an electric current in the second wire. But no matter how strong the electromagnet was, he could not make an electric current in the second wire.

✓ Reading Check What was Faraday trying to do in his experiment? (*See the Appendix for answers to Reading Checks.*)

Figure 1 Faraday's Experiment with Magnets and Induction

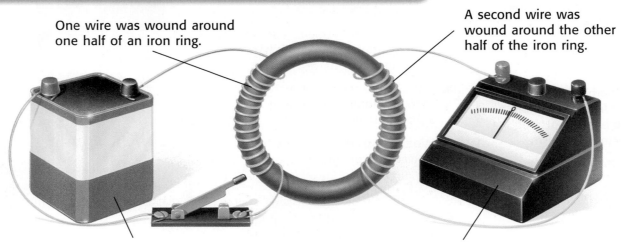

One wire was wound around one half of an iron ring.

A second wire was wound around the other half of the iron ring.

A battery supplied an electric current to the wire, making an electromagnet.

A galvanometer measured any current produced in the second wire by the magnetic field.

Figure 2 **Factors that Affect an Induced Current**

a An electric current is induced when you move a magnet through a coil of wire.

b A greater electric current is induced if you move the magnet faster through the coil because the magnetic field is changing faster.

c A greater electric current is induced if you add more loops of wire. This magnet is moving at the same speed as the magnet in **b.**

d The induced electric current reverses direction if the magnet is pulled out rather than pushed in.

Success for an Instant

As Faraday experimented with the electromagnetic ring, he noticed something interesting. At the instant he connected the wires to the battery, the galvanometer pointer moved. This movement showed that an electric current was present. The pointer moved again at the instant he disconnected the battery. But as long as the battery was fully connected, the galvanometer measured no electric current.

Faraday realized that electric current in the second wire was made only when the magnetic field was changing. The magnetic field changed as the battery was connected and disconnected. The process by which an electric current is made by changing a magnetic field is called **electromagnetic induction.** Faraday did many more experiments in this area. Some of his results are shown in **Figure 2.**

electromagnetic induction the process of creating a current in a circuit by changing a magnetic field

Inducing Electric Current

Faraday's experiments also showed that moving either the magnet or the wire changes the magnetic field around the wire. So, an electric current is made when a magnet moves in a coil of wire or when a wire moves between the poles of a magnet.

Consider the magnetic field lines between the poles of the magnet. An electric current is induced only when a wire crosses the magnetic field lines, as shown in **Figure 3.** An electric current is induced because a magnetic force can cause electric charges to move. But the charges move in a wire only when the wire moves through the magnetic field.

Figure 3 *As the wire moves between the poles of the magnet, it cuts through magnetic field lines, and an electric current is induced.*

electric generator a device that converts mechanical energy into electrical energy

Electric Generators

Electromagnetic induction is very important for the generation of electrical energy. An **electric generator** uses electromagnetic induction to change mechanical energy into electrical energy. **Figure 4** shows the parts of a simple generator. **Figure 5** explains how the generator works.

✓ *Reading Check* What energy change happens in an electric generator?

Figure 4 **Parts of a Simple Generator**

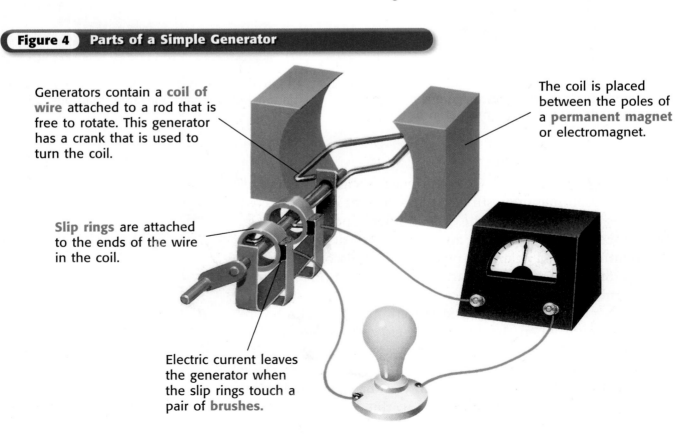

Generators contain a **coil of wire** attached to a rod that is free to rotate. This generator has a crank that is used to turn the coil.

The coil is placed between the poles of a **permanent magnet** or electromagnet.

Slip rings are attached to the ends of the wire in the coil.

Electric current leaves the generator when the slip rings touch a pair of **brushes.**

Figure 5 How a Generator Works

1 As the crank is turned, the rotating coil crosses the magnetic field lines of the magnet, and an electric current is induced in the wire.

2 When the coil is not crossing the magnetic field lines, no electric current is induced.

3 As the coil continues to rotate, the magnetic field lines are crossed in a different direction. An electric current is induced in the opposite direction.

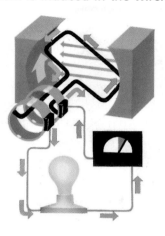  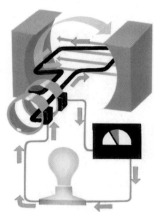

Alternating Current

The electric current produced by the generator shown in **Figure 5** changes direction each time the coil makes a half turn. Because the electric current changes direction, it is an alternating current. Generators in power plants also make alternating current. But generators in power plants are very large. They have many coils of wire instead of just one. In most large generators, the magnet is turned instead of the coils.

Generating Electrical Energy

The energy that generators convert into electrical energy comes from different sources. The source in nuclear power plants is thermal energy from a nuclear reaction. The energy boils water into steam. The steam turns a turbine. The turbine turns the magnet of the generator, which induces an electric current and generates electrical energy. Other kinds of power plants burn fuel such as coal or gas to release thermal energy.

Energy from wind can also be used to turn turbines. **Figure 6** shows how the energy of falling water is converted into electrical energy in a hydroelectric power plant.

Reading Check What are three sources of energy that are used to generate electrical energy?

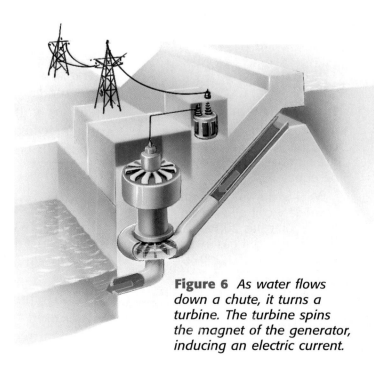

Figure 6 *As water flows down a chute, it turns a turbine. The turbine spins the magnet of the generator, inducing an electric current.*

Section 3 Electricity from Magnetism **527**

Figure 7 How Transformers Change Voltage

The primary coil of a **step-up transformer** has fewer loops than the secondary coil. So, the voltage of the electric current in the secondary coil is higher than the voltage of the electric current in the primary coil. Therefore, voltage is increased.

The primary coil of a **step-down transformer** has more loops than the secondary coil. So, the voltage of the electric current in the secondary coil is lower than the voltage of the electric current in the primary coil. Therefore, voltage is decreased.

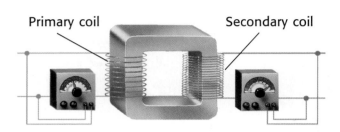

Primary coil   Secondary coil

Primary coil   Secondary coil

transformer a device that increases or decreases the voltage of alternating current

Transformers

Another device that relies on induction is a transformer. A **transformer** increases or decreases the voltage of alternating current. A simple transformer is made up of two coils of wire wrapped around an iron ring. The primary coil gets alternating current from an electrical energy source. The current makes the ring an electromagnet. But the current in the primary coil is alternating. The magnetic field of the electromagnet changes as the direction of the current changes. The changing magnetic field in the iron ring induces a current in the secondary coil.

Reading Check What does a transformer do?

Step-Up, Step-Down

The number of loops in the primary and secondary coils of a transformer determines whether it increases or decreases the voltage, as shown in **Figure 7.** A step-up transformer increases voltage and decreases current. A step-down transformer decreases voltage and increases current. However, the amount of energy going into and out of the transformer does not change.

Electrical Energy for Your Home

The electric current that brings electrical energy to your home is usually transformed three times, as shown in **Figure 8.** At the power plants, the voltage is increased. This decreases power loss that happens as the energy is sent over long distances. Of course, the voltage must be decreased again before the current is used. Two step-down transformers are used before the electric current reaches your house.

Transformers and Voltage

In a transformer, for each coil, the voltage divided by the number of loops must be equal.

What is the voltage in the secondary coil of a transformer that has 20 loops if the primary coil has 10 loops and a voltage of 1,200 V?

Figure 8 **Getting Energy to Your Home**

① The voltage is stepped up thousands of times at the power plant.

② The voltage is stepped down at a local power distribution center.

③ The voltage is stepped down again at a transformer near your house.

SECTION Review

Summary

- Electromagnetic induction is the process of making an electric current by changing a magnetic field.

- An electric generator converts mechanical energy into electrical energy through electromagnetic induction.

- A step-up transformer increases the voltage of an alternating current. A step-down transformer decreases the voltage.

- The side of a transformer that has the greater number of loops has the higher voltage.

Using Key Terms

For each pair of terms, explain how the meanings of the terms differ.

1. *electric generator* and *transformer*

Understanding Key Ideas

2. Which of the following will induce an electric current in a wire?

   a. moving a magnet into a coil of wire

   b. moving a wire between the poles of a magnet

   c. turning a loop of wire between the poles of a magnet

   d. All of the above

3. How does a generator produce an electric current?

4. Compare a step-up transformer with a step-down transformer based on the number of loops in the primary and secondary coils.

Math Skills

5. A transformer has 500 loops in its primary coil and 5,000 loops in its secondary coil. What is the voltage in the primary coil if the voltage in the secondary coil is 20,000 V?

6. A transformer has 3,000 loops in its primary coil and 1,500 loops in its secondary coil. What is the voltage in the secondary coil if the voltage in the primary coil is 120 V?

Critical Thinking

7. **Analyzing Ideas** One reason that electric power plants do not send out electrical energy as direct current is that direct current cannot be transformed. Explain why not.

8. **Analyzing Processes** Explain why rotating either the coil or the magnet in a generator induces an electric current.

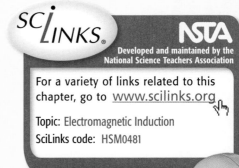

Developed and maintained by the
National Science Teachers Association

For a variety of links related to this chapter, go to www.scilinks.org

Topic: Electromagnetic Induction
SciLinks code: HSM0481

Model-Making Lab

OBJECTIVES

Build a model of an electric motor.

Analyze the workings of the parts of a motor.

MATERIALS

- battery, 4.5 V
- cup, plastic-foam
- magnet, disc (4)
- magnet wire, 100 cm
- marker, permanent
- paper clips, large (2)
- sandpaper
- tape
- tube, cardboard
- wire, insulated, with alligator clips, approximately 30 cm long (2)

SAFETY

Build a DC Motor

Electric motors can be used for many things. Hair dryers, CD players, and even some cars and buses are powered by electric motors. In this lab, you will build a direct current electric motor—the basis for the electric motors you use every day.

Procedure

1 To make the armature for the motor, wind the wire around the cardboard tube to make a coil like the one shown below. Wind the ends of the wire around the loops on each side of the coil. Leave about 5 cm of wire free on each end.

2 Hold the coil on its edge. Sand the enamel from only the top half of each end of the wire. This acts like a commutator, except that it blocks the electric current instead of reversing it during half of each rotation.

3 Partially unfold the two paper clips from the middle. Make a hook in one end of each paper clip to hold the coil, as shown below.

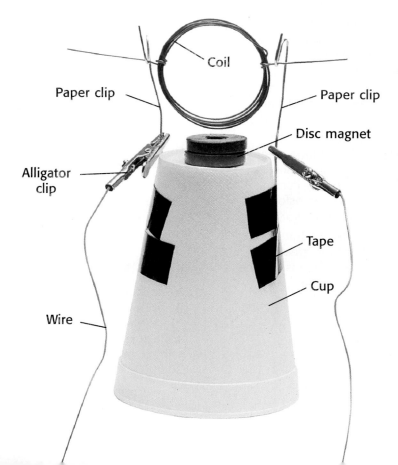

4. Place two disc magnets in the bottom of the cup, and place the other magnets on the outside of the bottom of the cup. The magnets should remain in place when the cup is turned upside down.

5. Tape the paper clips to the sides of the cup. The hooks should be at the same height, and should keep the coil from hitting the magnet.

6. Test your coil. Flick the top of the coil lightly with your finger. The coil should spin freely without wobbling or sliding to one side.

7. Make adjustments to the ends of the wire and the hooks until your coil spins freely.

8. Use the alligator clips to attach one wire to each paper clip.

9. Attach the free end of one wire to one terminal of the battery.

10. Connect the free end of the other wire to the second battery terminal, and give your coil a gentle spin. Record your observations.

11. Stop the coil, and give it a gentle spin in the opposite direction. Record your observations.

12. If the coil does not keep spinning, check the ends of the wire. Bare wire should touch the paper clips during half of the spin, and only enamel should touch the paper clips for the other half of the spin.

13. If you removed too much enamel, color half of the wire with a permanent marker.

14. Switch the connections to the battery, and repeat steps 10 and 11.

Analyze the Results

1. **Describing Events** Did your motor always spin in the direction you started it? Explain.

2. **Explaining Events** Why was the motor affected by switching the battery connections?

3. **Explaining Events** Some electric cars run on solar power. Which part of your model would be replaced by the solar panels?

Draw Conclusions

4. **Drawing Conclusions** Some people claim that electric-powered cars produce less pollution than gasoline-powered cars do. Why might this be true?

5. **Evaluating Models** List some reasons that electric cars are not ideal.

6. **Applying Conclusions** How could your model be used to help design a hair dryer?

7. **Applying Conclusions** Make a list of at least three other items that could be powered by an electric motor like the one you built.

Chapter Lab **531**

Chapter Review

USING KEY TERMS

Complete each of the following sentences by choosing the correct term from the word bank.

electric motor   transformer
magnetic force   electric generator
magnetic pole   electromagnetism
electromagnetic induction

1 Each end of a bar magnet is a(n) ___.

2 A(n) ___ converts mechanical energy into electrical energy.

3 ___ occurs when an electric current is made by a changing magnetic field.

4 The relationship between electricity and magnetism is called ___.

UNDERSTANDING KEY IDEAS

Multiple Choice

5 In the region around a magnet in which magnetic forces act exists the
  a. magnetic field.
  b. domain.
  c. pole.
  d. solenoid.

6 An electric fan has an electric motor inside to change
  a. mechanical energy into electrical energy.
  b. thermal energy into electrical energy.
  c. electrical energy into thermal energy.
  d. electrical energy into mechanical energy.

7 The marked end of a compass needle always points directly to
  a. Earth's geographic South Pole.
  b. Earth's geographic North Pole.
  c. a magnet's south pole.
  d. a magnet's north pole.

8 A device that increases the voltage of an alternating current is called a(n)
  a. electric motor.
  b. galvanometer.
  c. step-up transformer.
  d. step-down transformer.

9 The magnetic field of a solenoid can be increased by
  a. adding more loops per meter.
  b. increasing the current.
  c. putting an iron core inside the coil to make an electromagnet.
  d. All of the above

10 What do you end up with if you cut a magnet in half?
  a. one north-pole piece and one south-pole piece
  b. two unmagnetized pieces
  c. two pieces each with a north pole and a south pole
  d. two north-pole pieces

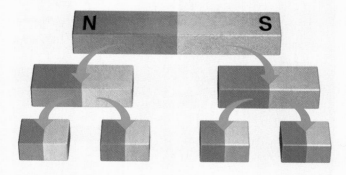

Short Answer

11 Explain why auroras are seen mostly near the North Pole and South Pole.

12 Compare the function of an electric generator with the function of an electric motor.

13 Explain why some pieces of iron are more magnetic than others are.

Math Skills

14 A step-up transformer increases voltage 20 times. If the voltage of the primary coil is 1,200 V, what is the voltage of the secondary coil?

CRITICAL THINKING

15 **Concept Mapping** Use the following terms to create a concept map: *electromagnetism, electricity, magnetism, electromagnetic induction, generators,* and *transformers.*

16 **Applying Concepts** You win a hand-powered flashlight as a prize in your school science fair. The flashlight has a clear plastic case, so you can look inside to see how it works. When you press the handle, a gray ring spins between two coils of wire. The ends of the wire are connected to the light bulb. So, when you press the handle, the light bulb glows. Explain how an electric current is produced to light the bulb. (Hint: Paper clips are attracted to the gray ring.)

17 **Identifying Relationships** Closed fire doors can slow the spread of fire between rooms. In some buildings, electromagnets controlled by the building's fire-alarm system hold the fire doors open. If a fire is detected, the doors automatically shut. Explain why electromagnets are used instead of permanent magnets.

INTERPRETING GRAPHICS

18 Look at the solenoids and electromagnets shown below. Identify which of them has the strongest magnetic field and which has the weakest magnetic field. Explain your reasoning.

a
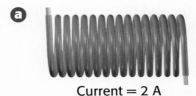
Current = 2 A

b
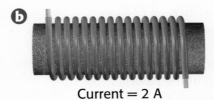
Current = 2 A

c

Current = 4 A

d
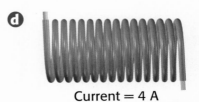
Current = 4 A

Standardized Test Preparation

Read each of the passages below. Then, answer the questions that follow each passage.

Passage 1 Place a small disk of plastic foam in a bowl of water. Hold the eye of a sewing needle in one hand and a bar magnet in the other. Starting near your fingers, drag one end of the magnet down the needle from the eye to the point and off the end of the needle. Drag the magnet down the needle in the same direction about 20 times. Be sure each stroke uses the same end of the magnet and moves in the same direction down the needle. Carefully place the needle on the plastic foam. The needle and foam should float. Bring the south pole of the magnet near the needle. Note which end of the needle points toward the magnet. Remove the magnet, and observe how the needle turns. The end of the needle that pointed toward the south pole of the magnet will point in a northerly direction.

1. What is the purpose of the passage?

   A to express

   B to instruct

   C to convince

   D to direct

2. What can a person build by following the steps described in the passage?

   F a fishing float

   G a bar magnet

   H an electromagnet

   I a compass

Passage 2 Frogs have been seen floating in midair! No, it's not a magic trick. It's part of an experiment on magnetic levitation. Every object, living or nonliving, contains atoms that act like magnets. These atomic magnets are millions of times weaker than ordinary household magnets. But the atomic magnets are still strong enough to be influenced by other magnets. If an object, such as a frog, is exposed to a magnet that is strong enough, the magnetic force between the object and the magnet can lift the object and make it float. A large solenoid is used in these experiments. A solenoid is a coil of wire that acts like a magnet when an electric current is in the wire. The solenoid has a magnetic field with a north pole and a south pole. The interaction of the magnetic field of the solenoid and the magnetic fields of the atoms in the object causes the object to float.

1. Why can objects be made to float in a magnetic field?

   A Every object has a strong magnetic field.

   B Every object has atoms that have magnetic fields.

   C Every object acts like a solenoid.

   D Every object makes a magnetic field when it is exposed to a household magnet.

2. Which of the following can be inferred from information in the passage?

   F Household magnets cannot levitate in the solenoid used in the experiment.

   G Atomic magnets are stronger than the solenoid used in the experiment.

   H Household magnets are strong enough to levitate a frog.

   I Household magnets are stronger than atomic magnets but weaker than the solenoid used in the experiment.

The graph below shows current versus rotation angle for the output of an alternating-current generator. Use the graph below to answer the questions that follow.

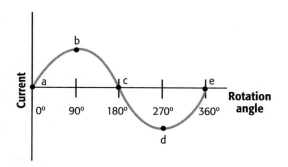

1. Which of the following describes points at which the generator produces no current?

A a and b

B b and d

C c and d

D a and e

2. Between which points is current increasing?

F between a and b

G between b and c

H between c and e

I between b and d

3. At which points is the same amount of current produced but the direction of the current reversed?

A a and b

B b and d

C a and c

D b and e

Read each question below, and choose the best answer.

1. The voltage across the secondary coil of a transformer is found by multiplying the voltage across the primary coil by the number of turns in the secondary coil and then dividing by the number of turns in the primary coil. A certain transformer has a primary coil with 1,000 turns and a voltage of 1,200 V. What is the voltage across the secondary coil if it has 2,000 turns?

A 600 V

B 1,000 V

C 2,400 V

D 2,400,000 V

2. Laura cuts a magnetic strip into thirds. She then cuts each third into halves. How many small magnets does she have?

F 1.5

G 3

H 5

I 6

3. Mrs. Welch is ordering magnets for her science class. She has 24 students in her class, who work in pairs. Each pair of lab partners needs three magnets for the experiment. If Mrs. Welch can order a pack of six magnets for $5.00, what is the cost for her order?

A $2.50

B $30.00

C $60.00

D $120.00

4. A disc magnet is 0.5 cm thick and has a diameter of 2.5 cm. The volume of this magnet in cubic centimeters (cm³) can be calculated using which of the following equations?

F $V = \pi(2.5)^2 \times 0.5$

G $V = \pi(2.5/2)^2 \times 0.5$

H $V = \pi(0.5)^2 \times 2.5$

I $V = \pi(0.5/2)^2 \times 2.5$

Science in Action

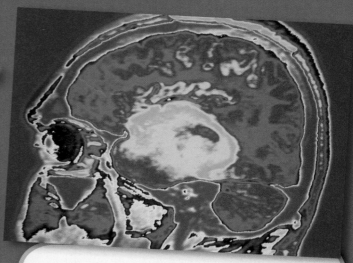

Science, Technology, and Society

Magnets in Medicine

Like X rays, magnetic resonance imaging (MRI) creates pictures of a person's internal organs and skeleton. But MRI produces clearer pictures than X rays do, and MRI does not expose the body to the potentially harmful radiation of X rays. Instead, MRI uses powerful electromagnets and radio waves to create images. MRI allows doctors to find small tumors, see subtle changes in the brain, locate blockages in blood vessels, and observe damage to the spinal cord.

Weird Science

Geomagnetic Storms

On March 13, 1989, a geomagnetic storm hit Montreal, Quebec. It caused an electrical blackout that left about 6 million people without electricity for nine hours.

A geomagnetic storm occurs when gusts of solar wind smash into Earth's magnetic field. Powerful eruptions from the sun, called coronal mass ejections (CME), happen periodically, sending charged particles outward at high speeds. Solar winds usually travel between 300 km/s and 600 km/s. But the gusts of solar wind from a CME can travel as fast as 2,000 km/s.

Language Arts ACTiViTY

WRITING SKILL Write a two-page story about a student who undergoes an MRI scan. In your story, include the reason he or she must have the scan, a description of the procedure, and the information the doctor can determine by looking at the scan.

Math ACTiViTY

Earth is approximately 150,000,000 km from the sun. Calculate how long it takes a solar wind that travels at 500 km/s to reach Earth from the sun.

James Clerk Maxwell

Magnetic Math James Clerk Maxwell was a Scottish mathematician who lived in the 1800s. Maxwell's research led to advances in electromagnetism and in many other areas of science. He proposed that light is an electromagnetic wave—a wave that consists of electric and magnetic fields that vibrate at right angles to each other. His work on electromagnetic fields provided the foundation for Einstein's theory of relativity.

After college, Maxwell decided to study the work of Michael Faraday. Many physicists of the time thought that Faraday's work was not scientific enough. Faraday described his experiments but did not try to apply any scientific or mathematical theory to the results. Maxwell felt that this was a strength. He decided not to read any of the mathematical descriptions of electricity and magnetism until he had read all of Faraday's work. The first paper Maxwell wrote about electricity, called "On Faraday's Lines of Force," brought Faraday's experimental results together with a mathematical analysis of the magnetic field surrounding a current. This paper described a few simple mathematical equations that could be used to describe the interactions between electric and magnetic fields. Maxwell continued to work with Faraday's results and to publish papers that gave scientific explanations of some of Faraday's most exciting observations.

Social Studies ACTIVITY

Study the life of James Clerk Maxwell. Make a timeline that shows major events in his life. Include three or four historic events that happened during his lifetime.

To learn more about these Science in Action topics, visit go.hrw.com and type in the keyword **HP5EMGF.**

Current Science

Check out Current Science® articles related to this chapter by visiting go.hrw.com. Just type in the keyword **HP5CS18.**

19

Electronic Technology

SECTION **1** **Electronic Devices** 540

SECTION **2** **Communication Technology** 546

SECTION **3** **Computers** 554

Chapter Lab 562
Chapter Review 564
Standardized Test Preparation 566
Science in Action 568

About the PHOTO

Can you read the expression on Kismet's face? This robot's expression can be sad, happy, angry, interested, surprised, disgusted, or just plain calm. Kismet was developed by MIT researchers to interact with humans. Electronic devices in cameras, motors, and computers allow Kismet to change its expression as it responds to its surroundings.

PRE-READING ACTIVITY

FOLDNOTES **Booklet** Before you read the chapter, create the FoldNote entitled "Booklet" described in the **Study Skills** section of the Appendix. Label each page of the booklet with a main idea from the chapter. As you read the chapter, write what you learn about each main idea on the appropriate page of the booklet.

START-UP ACTIVITY

Talking Long Distance

In this activity, you'll build a model of a telephone.

Procedure

1. Thread one end of a **piece of string** through the hole in the bottom of one **empty food can.**

2. Tie a knot in the end of the string inside the can. The knot should be large enough to keep the string in place. The rest of the string should come out of the bottom of the can.

3. Repeat steps 1 and 2 with **another can** and the other end of the string.

4. Hold one can, and have a classmate hold the other. Walk away from each other until the string is fairly taut.

5. Speak into your can while your classmate holds the other can at his or her ear. Switch roles.

Analysis

1. Describe what you heard.

2. Compare your model with a real telephone.

3. How are signals sent back and forth along the string?

4. Why do you think it was important to pull the string taut?

Electronic Devices

Electronic devices use electrical energy. But they do not use electrical energy in the same way that machines do.

Some machines can change electrical energy into other forms of energy in order to do work. Electronic devices use it to handle information.

Inside an Electronic Device

For example, a remote control sends information to a television. **Figure 1** shows the inside of a remote control. The large green board is a circuit board. A **circuit board** is a collection of many circuit parts on a sheet of insulating material. A circuit board connects the parts of the circuit to supply electric current and send signals to the parts of an electronic device.

Sending Information to Your Television

To change the channel or volume on the television, you push buttons on the remote control. When you push a button, you send a signal to the circuit board. The components of the circuit board process the signal to send the correct information to the television. The information is sent to the television in the form of infrared light by a tiny bulb called a *light-emitting diode* (DIE OHD), or LED. In this section, you'll learn about diodes and other components and learn about how they work.

READING WARM-UP

Objectives

- Identify the role of a circuit board in an electronic device.
- Describe semiconductors and how their conductivity can be changed.
- Describe diodes and how they are used in circuits.
- Describe transistors and how they are used in circuits.
- Explain how integrated circuits have influenced electronic technology.

Terms to Learn

circuit board   diode
semiconductor   transistor
doping   integrated
                 circuit

READING STRATEGY

Reading Organizer As you read this section, make a concept map by using the terms above.

circuit board a sheet of insulating material that carries circuit elements and that is inserted in an electronic device

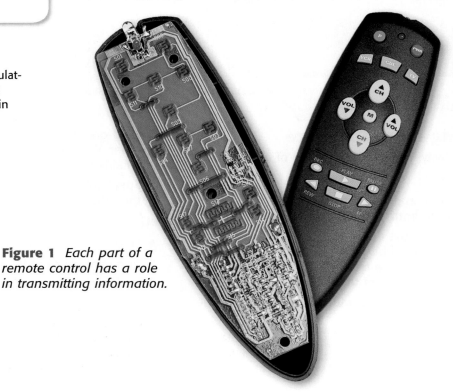

Figure 1 *Each part of a remote control has a role in transmitting information.*

Semiconductors

Semiconductors (SEM i kuhn DUHK tuhrz) are used in many electronic components. A **semiconductor** is a substance that conducts an electric current better than an insulator does but not as well as a conductor does. Semiconductors have allowed people to make incredible advances in electronic technology.

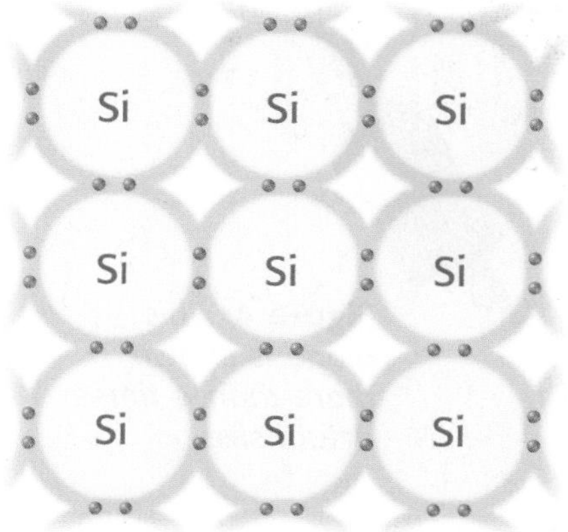

How Do Semiconductors Work?

The way a semiconductor conducts electric current is based on how its electrons are arranged. Silicon, Si, is a widely used semiconductor. As shown in **Figure 2,** when silicon atoms bond, they share all of their valence electrons. There are no electrons free to make much electric current. So, why are semiconductors such as silicon used? They are used because their conductivity can be changed.

Doping

You can change the conductivity of a semiconductor through doping (DOHP eeng). **Doping** is the addition of an impurity to a semiconductor. Adding the impurity changes the arrangement of electrons. A few atoms of the semiconductor are replaced with a few atoms of another element that has a different number of electrons, as shown in **Figure 3.**

✔️ **Reading Check** What is the result of doping a semiconductor? (*See the Appendix for answers to Reading Checks.*)

Figure 2 *Each silicon atom shares its four valence electrons with other silicon atoms.*

semiconductor an element or compound that conducts electric current better than an insulator does but not as well as a conductor does

doping the addition of an impurity element to a semiconductor

Figure 3 Types of Doped Semiconductors

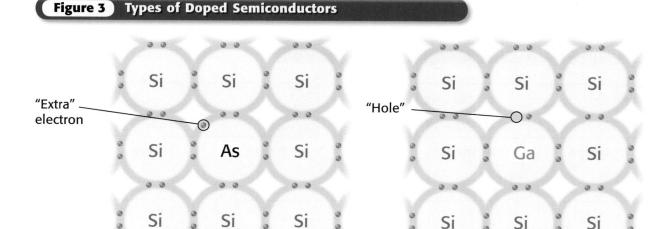

"Extra" electron

"Hole"

N-Type Semiconductor An atom of arsenic, As, has five electrons in its outermost energy level. Replacing a silicon atom with an arsenic atom results in an "extra" electron.

P-Type Semiconductor An atom of gallium, Ga, has three electrons in its outermost energy level. Replacing a silicon atom with a gallium atom results in a "hole" where an electron could be.

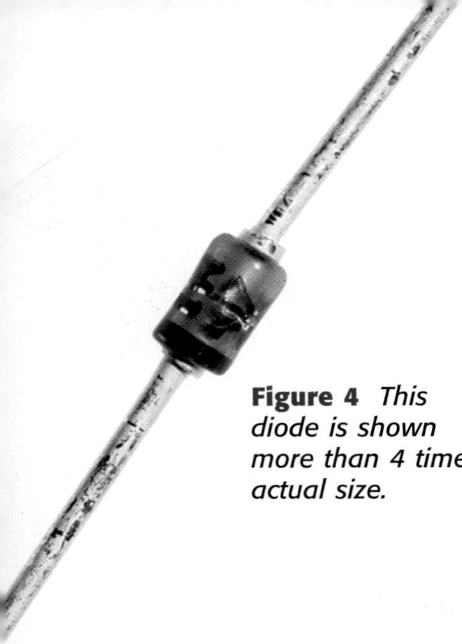

Diodes

Layers of semiconductors can be put together like sandwiches to make electronic components. Joining an n-type semiconductor with a p-type semiconductor forms a diode. A **diode** is an electronic component that allows electric charge to move mainly in one direction. Look at **Figure 4.** Each wire joins to one of the layers in the diode.

Figure 4 *This diode is shown more than 4 times actual size.*

diode an electronic device that allows electric charge to move more easily in one direction than in the other

The Flow of Electrons in Diodes

Where the two layers in a diode meet, some "extra" electrons move from the n-type layer to fill some "holes" in the p-type layer. This change gives the n-type layer a positive charge and the p-type layer a negative charge. If a diode is connected to a source of electrical energy, such as a battery, so that the positive terminal is closer to the p-type layer, a current is made. If the connections are switched so that the negative terminal is closer to the p-type layer, there is no current. **Figure 5** shows how a diode works.

Using Diodes to Change AC to DC

Power plants send electrical energy to homes by means of alternating current (AC). But many things, such as radios, use direct current (DC). Diodes can help change AC to DC. Alternating current switches direction many times each second. The diodes in an AC adapter block the current in one direction. Other components average the current in the direction that remains. As a result, AC is changed to DC.

✓ *Reading Check* Why can a diode change AC to DC?

Figure 5 How a Diode Works

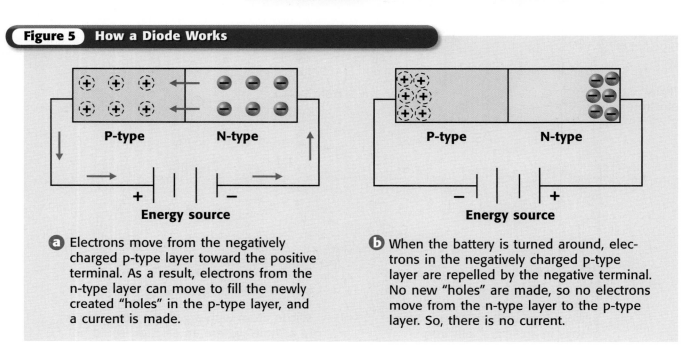

ⓐ Electrons move from the negatively charged p-type layer toward the positive terminal. As a result, electrons from the n-type layer can move to fill the newly created "holes" in the p-type layer, and a current is made.

ⓑ When the battery is turned around, electrons in the negatively charged p-type layer are repelled by the negative terminal. No new "holes" are made, so no electrons move from the n-type layer to the p-type layer. So, there is no current.

Transistors

What do you get when you sandwich three layers of semiconductors together? You get a transistor! A **transistor** is an electronic component that amplifies, or increases, current. It can be used in many circuits, including an amplifier and a switch. Transistors can be NPN or PNP transistors. An NPN transistor has a p-type layer between two n-type layers. A PNP transistor has an n-type layer between two p-type layers. Look at **Figure 6**. Each wire joins to one of the layers in the transistor.

✓ Reading Check Name two kinds of transistors made from semiconductors.

Transistors as Amplifiers

A microphone does not make a current that is large enough to run a loudspeaker. But a transistor can be used in an amplifier to make a larger current. Look at **Figure 7**. In the circuit, there is a small electric current in the microphone. This current triggers the transistor to allow a larger current in the loudspeaker. The electric current can be larger because of a large source of electrical energy in the loudspeaker side of the circuit.

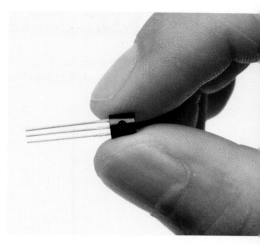

Figure 6 *This transistor is smaller than a pencil eraser!*

transistor a semiconductor device that can amplify current and that is used in amplifiers, oscillators, and switches

Figure 7 **A Transistor as an Amplifier**

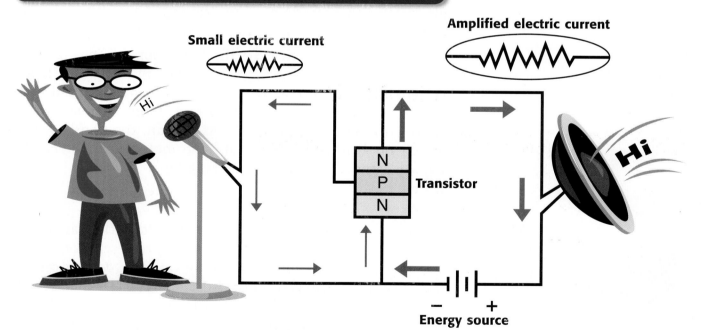

❶ Sound waves from your voice enter the microphone. As a result, a small electric current is made in the microphone side of the circuit.

❷ A transistor allows the small electric current to control a larger electric current that operates the loudspeaker.

❸ The current in the loudspeaker is larger than the current produced by the microphone. Otherwise, the two currents are identical.

Figure 8 A Transistor as a Switch

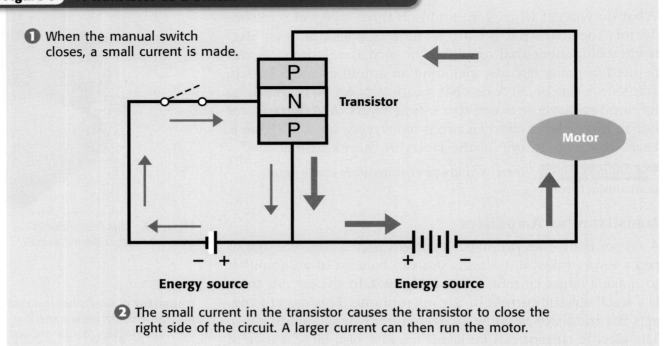

1 When the manual switch closes, a small current is made.

P
N
P

Transistor

Motor

– +
Energy source

+ –
Energy source

2 The small current in the transistor causes the transistor to close the right side of the circuit. A larger current can then run the motor.

Transistors in Switches

Remote-controlled toy cars use transistors in switches. Look at **Figure 8.** When the manual switch in the circuit is closed, a small current is made in the small loop. The small current causes the transistor to close the large loop on the right. As a result, a larger current is made in the large loop. The larger current runs the motor. You switch on a small current. The transistor switches on a larger current. If the manual switch is opened, the circuit is broken. As a result, the transistor will switch off the current that runs the motor. Computers also rely on transistors that work in switches.

integrated circuit a circuit whose components are formed on a single semiconductor

Integrated Circuits

An **integrated circuit** (IN tuh GRAYT id SUHR kit) is an entire circuit that has many components on a single semiconductor. The parts of the circuit are made by carefully doping certain spots. Look at **Figure 9.** Integrated circuits and circuit boards have helped shrink electronic devices. Many complete circuits can fit into one integrated circuit. So, complicated electronic systems can be made very small. Because the circuits are so small, the electric charges moving through them do not have to travel very far. Devices that use integrated circuits can run at very high speeds.

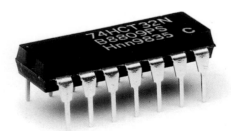

Figure 9 *This integrated circuit contains many electronic components, yet its dimensions are only about 1 cm × 3 cm!*

✓ **Reading Check** Describe two benefits of using integrated circuits in electronic devices.

Smaller and Smarter Devices

Before transistors and semiconductor diodes were made, vacuum tubes, like the one in **Figure 10,** were used. Vacuum tubes can amplify electric current and change AC to DC. But vacuum tubes are much larger than semiconductor components are. They also get hotter and don't last as long. Early radios had to be large. Space was needed to hold the vacuum tubes and to keep them from overheating. Modern radios are very small. They use transistors and integrated circuits. And your radio might have other features, such as a clock or a CD player. But even more importantly than waking you up to your favorite music, integrated circuits have changed the world through their use in computers.

Figure 10 *Vacuum tubes are much larger than the transistors used today. So, radios that used the tubes were very large also.*

SECTION Review

Summary

- Circuit boards contain circuits that supply current to different parts of electronic devices.
- Semiconductors are often used in electronic devices because their conductivity can be changed by doping.
- Diodes allow current in one direction and can change AC to DC.
- Transistors are used in amplifiers and switches.
- Integrated circuits have made smaller, smarter electronic devices possible.

Using Key Terms

For each pair of terms, explain how the meanings of the terms differ.

1. *circuit board* and *integrated circuit*

2. *semiconductor* and *doping*

3. *diode* and *transistor*

Understanding Key Ideas

4. Which element forms the basis for semiconductors?
   a. oxygen
   b. gallium
   c. arsenic
   d. silicon

5. Describe how p-type and n-type semiconductors are made.

6. Explain how a diode changes AC to DC.

7. What are two purposes transistors serve?

Math Skills

8. An integrated circuit that was made in 1974 contained 6,000 transistors. An integrated circuit that was made in 2000 contained 42,000,000 transistors. How many times more transistors did the circuit made in 2000 have?

Critical Thinking

9. **Making Comparisons** How might an electronic system that uses vacuum tubes be different from one that uses integrated circuits?

10. **Applying Concepts** Would modern computers be possible without integrated circuits? Explain.

Interpreting Graphics

11. The graph below represents electric current in a series circuit. Does the circuit contain a diode? Explain your reasoning.

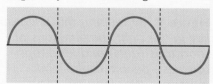

For a variety of links related to this chapter, go to www.scilinks.org

Topic: Transistors
SciLinks code: HSM1550

Communication Technology

What electronic devices do you use to send or receive information? Your answer might include telephones, radios, or televisions.

In this section, you'll study these and other electronic devices that are used for communication. You'll also learn about two kinds of signals used to send and store information.

Communicating with Signals

One of the first electronic communication devices was the telegraph. It was invented in the 1830s. It used an electric current to send messages between places joined by wires. People sent messages in Morse code through the wires. **Table 1** shows the patterns of dots and dashes that stand for each letter and number in Morse code. The message was sent by tapping a telegraph key, like the one in **Figure 1.** This tapping closed a circuit, causing "clicks" at the receiving end of the telegraph.

Signals and Carriers

Electronic communication devices, including the telegraph, send information by using signals. A *signal* is anything, such as a movement, a sound, or a set of numbers and letters, that can be used to send information. Often, one signal is sent using another signal called a *carrier*. Electric current is the carrier of the signals made by tapping a telegraph key. Two kinds of signals are analog signals and digital signals.

READING WARM-UP

Objectives
- Identify how signals transmit information.
- Describe analog signals and their use in telephones and records.
- Describe digital signals and their use in compact discs.
- Describe how information is transmitted and received in radios and televisions.

Terms to Learn
analog signal
digital signal

READING STRATEGY

Discussion Read this section silently. Write down questions that you have about this section. Discuss your questions in a small group.

Figure 1 *By tapping this telegraph key in the right combinations of short taps (dots) and long taps (dashes), people could send messages over long distances.*

Table 1	International Morse Code						
A	·–	G	––·	Q	––·–	1	·––––
B	–···	H	····	R	·–·	2	··–––
C	–·–·	I	··	S	···	3	···––
D	–··	J	·–––	T	–	4	····–
E	·	K	–·–	U	··–	5	·····
F	··–·	L	·–··	V	···–	6	–····
		M	––	W	·––	7	––···
		N	–·	X	–··–	8	–––··
		O	–––	Y	–·––	9	––––·
		P	·––·	Z	––··	0	–––––

Analog Signals

An **analog signal** (AN uh LAWG SIG nuhl) is a signal whose properties change without a break or jump between values. Think of a dimmer switch on a light. You can continuously change the brightness of the light using the dimmer switch.

The changes in an analog signal are based on changes in the original information. For example, when you talk on the phone, the sound of your voice is changed into changing electric current in the form of a wave. This wave is an analog signal that is similar to the original sound wave. But remember that sound waves do not travel down your phone line!

☑ **Reading Check** What is an analog signal? (*See the Appendix for answers to Reading Checks.*)

Talking on the Phone

Look at the telephone in **Figure 2.** You talk into the transmitter. You listen to the receiver. The transmitter changes the sound waves made when you speak into an analog signal. This signal moves through phone wires to the receiver of another phone. The receiver changes the analog signal back into the sound of your voice. Sometimes, the analog signals are changed to digital signals and back again before they reach the other person. You will learn about digital signals later in this section.

analog signal a signal whose properties can change continuously in a given range

CONNECTION TO Geology

Seismograms A *seismograph* is a device used by scientists to record waves made by earthquakes. It makes a *seismogram*—wavy lines on paper that record ground movement. Draw an example of a seismogram that shows changes in the wave, and explain why this is an example of an analog signal.

ACTIVITY

Figure 2 How a Telephone Works

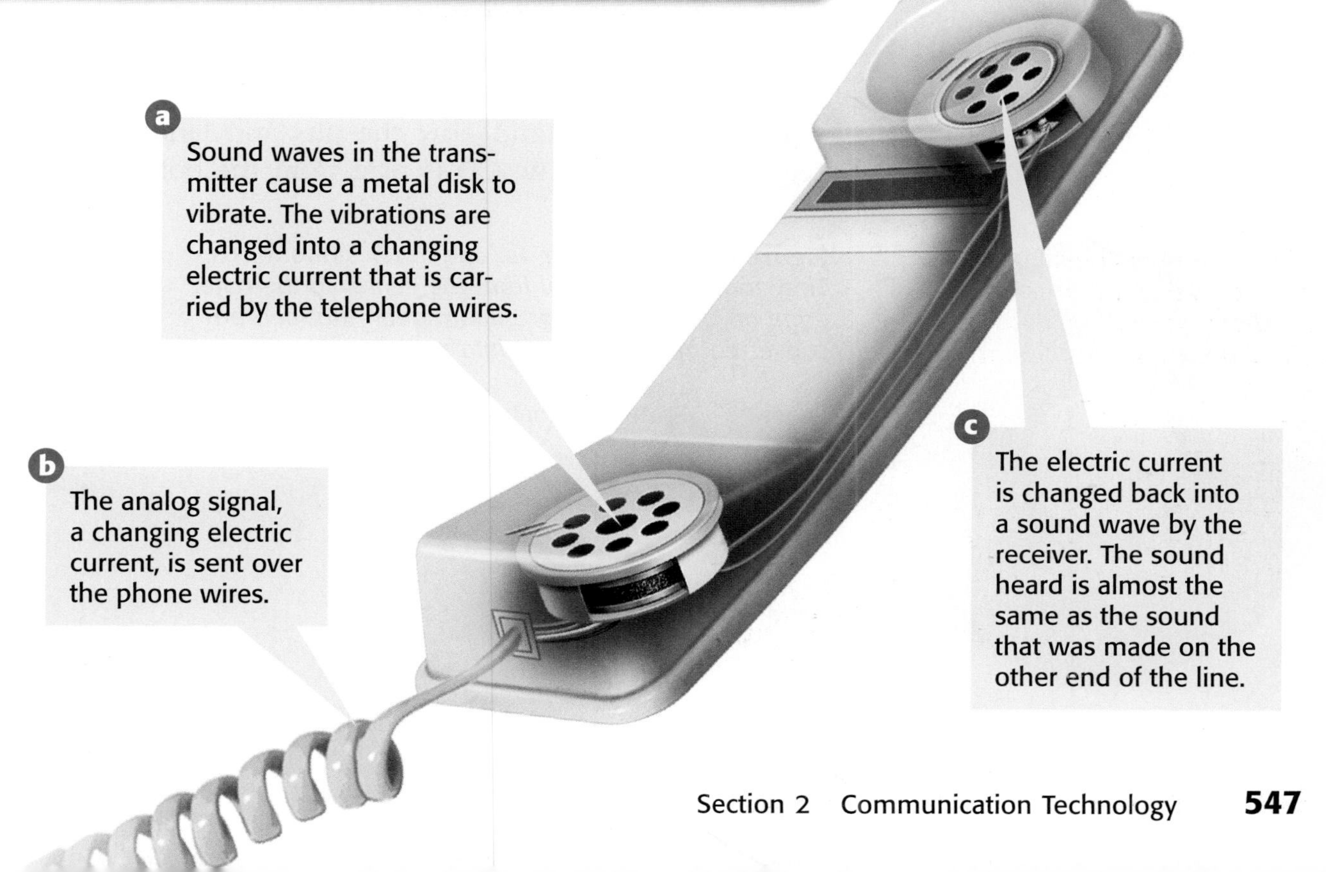

a Sound waves in the transmitter cause a metal disk to vibrate. The vibrations are changed into a changing electric current that is carried by the telephone wires.

b The analog signal, a changing electric current, is sent over the phone wires.

c The electric current is changed back into a sound wave by the receiver. The sound heard is almost the same as the sound that was made on the other end of the line.

Analog Recording

If you want to save a sound, you can store an analog signal of the sound wave. In vinyl records, the signal is made into grooves on a plastic disk. The sound's properties are represented by the number and depth of the contours in the disk.

Playing a Record

Figure 3 shows a record being played. The stylus (STIE luhs), or needle, makes an electromagnet vibrate. The vibrating electromagnet induces an electric current that is used to make sound. Analog recording makes sound that is very close to the original. But unwanted sounds are sometimes recorded and are not easy to remove. Also, the stylus touches the record to play it. So, the record wears out, and the sound changes over time.

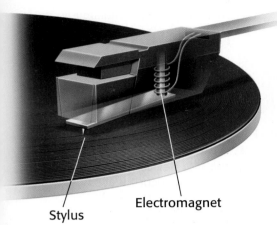

Stylus   Electromagnet

Figure 3 *As the stylus rides in the record's grooves, it causes an electromagnet to vibrate.*

digital signal a signal that can be represented as a sequence of discrete values

Digital Signals

A **digital signal** is a signal that is represented as a sequence of separate values. It does not change continuously. Think of a regular light switch. It can be either on or off. Information in a digital signal is represented as binary (BIE nuh ree) numbers. *Binary* means "two." Numbers in binary are made up of only two digits, 1 and 0. Each digit is a *bit,* which is short for *binary digit.* Computers process digital signals that are in the form of a pattern of electric pulses. Each pulse stands for a 1. Each missing pulse stands for a 0.

Digital Storage on a CD

You've probably heard digital sound from a compact disc, or CD. Sound is recorded to a CD by means of a digital signal. A CD stores the signals in a thin layer of aluminum. Look at **Figure 4.** To understand how the pits and lands are named, keep in mind that the CD is read from the bottom.

Figure 4 *Pits stand for 1s, and lands stand for 0s. They form a tight spiral from the center to the outer edge on a CD. They store information that can be converted by a CD player into sound.*

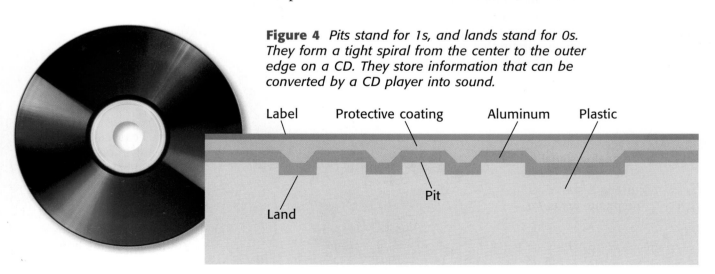

Label   Protective coating   Aluminum   Plastic

Pit

Land

Digital Recording

In a digital recording, the sound wave is measured many times each second. **Figure 5** shows how these sample values represent the original sound. These numbers are then changed into binary values using 1s and 0s. The 1s and 0s are stored as pits and lands on a CD.

In digital recording, the sample values don't exactly match the original sound wave. So, the number of samples taken each second is important to make sure the recording sounds the way it should sound. Taking more sample values each second makes a digital sound that is closer to the original sound.

✓ Reading Check How can a digital recording be made to sound more like the original sound?

Playing a CD

In a CD player, the CD spins around while a laser shines on the CD from below. As shown in **Figure 6,** light reflected from the CD enters a detector. The detector changes the pattern of light and dark into a digital signal. The digital signal is changed into an analog signal, which is used to make a sound wave. Because only light touches the CD, the CD doesn't wear out. But errors can happen from playing a dirty or scratched CD.

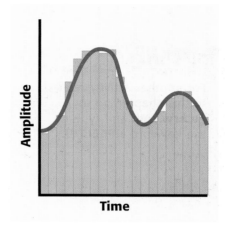

Figure 5 *Each of the bars represent a digital sample of the sound wave.*

Figure 6 **How a CD Player Works**

Different sequences and sizes of pits and lands will register different patterns of numbers that are converted into different sounds.

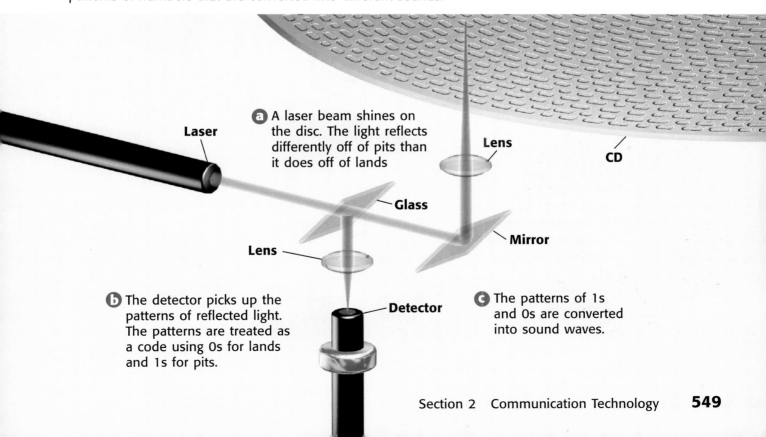

Laser

a A laser beam shines on the disc. The light reflects differently off of pits than it does off of lands

Lens

CD

Glass

Lens

Mirror

b The detector picks up the patterns of reflected light. The patterns are treated as a code using 0s for lands and 1s for pits.

Detector

c The patterns of 1s and 0s are converted into sound waves.

Radio and Television

You hear or see shows on your radio or television that are broadcast from a station that may be many kilometers away. The radio and TV signals can be either analog or digital. An *electromagnetic* (EM) *wave* is a wave that consists of changing electric and magnetic fields. EM waves are used as carriers.

Radio

Radio waves are one kind of EM wave. Radio stations use radio waves to carry signals that represent sound. Look at **Figure 7.** Radio waves are transmitted by a radio tower. They travel through the air and are picked up by a radio antenna.

INTERNET ACTIVITY

For another activity related to this chapter, go to **go.hrw.com** and type in the keyword **HP5ELTW.**

Figure 7 How a Radio Works

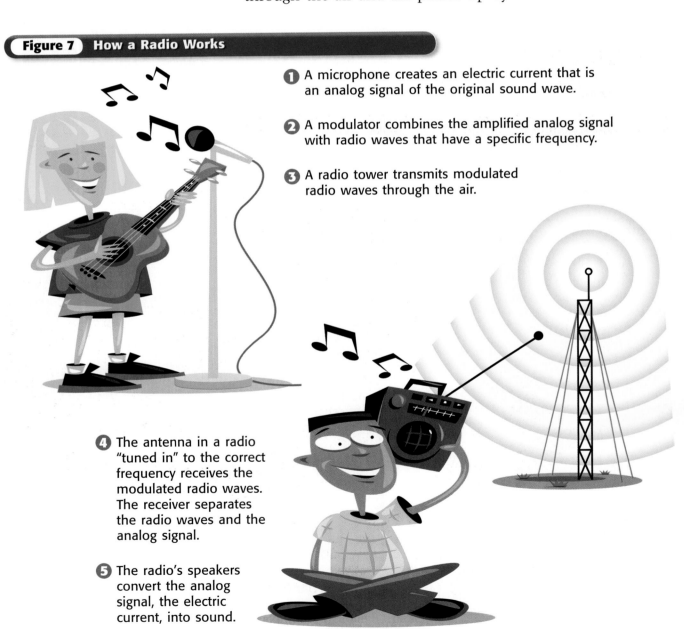

❶ A microphone creates an electric current that is an analog signal of the original sound wave.

❷ A modulator combines the amplified analog signal with radio waves that have a specific frequency.

❸ A radio tower transmits modulated radio waves through the air.

❹ The antenna in a radio "tuned in" to the correct frequency receives the modulated radio waves. The receiver separates the radio waves and the analog signal.

❺ The radio's speakers convert the analog signal, the electric current, into sound.

Television

The pictures you see on your television are made by beams of electrons hitting the screen, as described in **Figure 8.** Video signals hold the information to make a picture. Audio signals hold the information to make the sound. These signals can be sent as analog or digital signals to your television. The signals can be broadcast using EM waves as carriers. The signals can be sent through cables or from satellites or broadcast towers.

More and more, television programs are going digital. This means that they are filmed using digital cameras and transmitted to homes as digital signals. You can watch digital shows on an analog TV. However, on a digital display, the images and sound of these programs are much clearer than on a television made for analog broadcasts.

Reading Check What kinds of signals can be picked up by a color television?

TV Screen

With an adult, use a magnifying lens to look at a television screen. How are the fluorescent materials arranged? Hold the lens at various distances from the screen. What effects do you see? How does the screen's changing picture affect what you see?

ACTIVITY

Figure 8 Images on a Color Television

❶ Video signals transmitted from a TV station are received by the antenna of a TV receiver.

❷ Electronic circuits divide the video signal into separate signals for each of three electron beams. The beams, one for each primary color of light (red, green, and blue), strike the screen in varying strengths determined by the video signal.

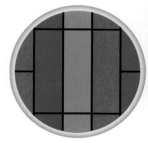

❸ The screen has stripes or dots of three fluorescent (FLOO uh RES uhnt) materials. These materials glow when hit by electrons. The electron beams sweep the screen 30 times every second and activate the fluorescent materials. These materials then emit colored light that is viewed as a picture.

Plasma Display

Standard televisions must be deep enough so that the electron beams can reach all parts of the screen. So, televisions are bulky and heavy. A newer kind of screen, called a *plasma display,* is much thinner. It can be as thin as 15 cm. So, it is not much thicker than a painting on the wall!

Figure 9 shows how a plasma display works. Plasma displays do not use electron tubes. Instead, they have thousands of tiny cells with gases in them. A computer charges the cells, making a current in the gases. The current generates colored lights. Each light can be red, green, blue, or a combination. As in a regular television, these three colors are combined to make every picture on the screen.

✓ **Reading Check** Why is a plasma display thinner than a regular television?

Figure 9 How a Plasma Display Works

❶ Video signals transmitted from a TV station are received by a device, such as a VCR, that has a television tuner in it. The signals are then sent to the plasma display.

❷ The signal includes commands to charge conductors on either side of small wells in the screen. The atoms of gas in the wells become charged and form a plasma.

❸ Each well contains one of three fluorescent materials. The materials give off red, blue, or green light after absorbing energy given off by the plasma.

❹ The colored light from each group of three wells blends together and makes a small dot of light in the picture on the screen.

SECTION Review

Summary

- Signals transmit information in electronic devices. Signals can be transmitted using a carrier. Signals can be analog or digital.

- Analog signals have continuous values. Telephones, record players, radios, and regular TV sets use analog signals.

- In a telephone, a transmitter changes sound waves to electric current. The current is sent across a phone line. The receiving telephone converts the signal back into a sound wave.

- Analog signals of sounds are used to make vinyl records. Changes in the groove reflect changes in the sound.

- Digital signals have discrete values, such as 0 and 1. CD players use digital signals.

- Radios and televisions use electromagnetic waves. These waves travel through the atmosphere. In a radio, the signals are converted to sound waves. In a television, electron beams convert the signals into images on the screen.

Using Key Terms

1. In your own words, write a definition for each of the following terms: *analog signal* and *digital signal*.

Understanding Key Ideas

2. Which of the following objects changes sound waves into an electric current in order to transmit information?
   a. telephone
   b. radio
   c. television
   d. telegraph

3. Why are carriers used to transmit signals?

4. What is an early example of an electrical device used for sending information over long distances? How did this device work?

Critical Thinking

5. **Applying Concepts** Is Morse code an example of an analog signal or a digital signal? Explain your reasoning.

6. **Making Comparisons** Compare how a telephone and a radio tower transmit information.

7. **Making Inferences** Does a mercury thermometer provide information in an analog or digital way? Explain your reasoning.

Interpreting Graphics

8. Look at the graphs below. They represent a sound wave that is being changed into a digital signal. Each bar represents a digital sample of the sound wave. Which graph represents the digital signal that is closer to the original sound wave? Explain your reasoning.

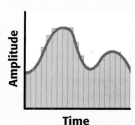

SCiLINKS®

NSTA
Developed and maintained by the
National Science Teachers Association

For a variety of links related to this chapter, go to www.scilinks.org

Topic: Telephone Technology;
Television Technology

SciLinks code: HSM1499; HSM1501

Computers

Did you use a computer to wake up this morning?

You might think of a computer as something you use to send e-mail or to surf the Internet. But computers are around you all the time. Computers are in automobiles, VCRs, and telephones. Even an alarm clock is an example of a simple computer!

What Is a Computer?

A **computer** is an electronic device that performs tasks by following instructions given to it. A computer does a task when it is given a command and has the instructions necessary to carry out that command. Computers can do tasks very quickly.

Basic Functions

The basic functions of a computer are shown in **Figure 1.** The information you give to a computer is called *input*. The computer *processes* the input. Processing could mean adding a list of numbers, making a drawing, or even moving a piece of equipment. Input doesn't have to be processed right away. It can be stored until it is needed. The computer *stores* information in its memory. *Output* is the final result of the job done by the computer.

✓ **Reading Check** What are the basic functions of a computer?
(See the Appendix for answers to Reading Checks.)

READING WARM-UP

Objectives

● List a computer's basic functions, and describe its development.
● Identify the main components of computer hardware.
● Explain how information can be stored on CD-Rs and CD-RWs.
● Describe what computer software allows a computer to do.
● Describe computer networks.

Terms to Learn

computer   software
microprocessor   Internet
hardware

READING STRATEGY

Prediction Guide Before reading this section, write the title of each heading in this section. Next, under each heading, write what you think you will learn.

Figure 1 **Basic Computer Functions**

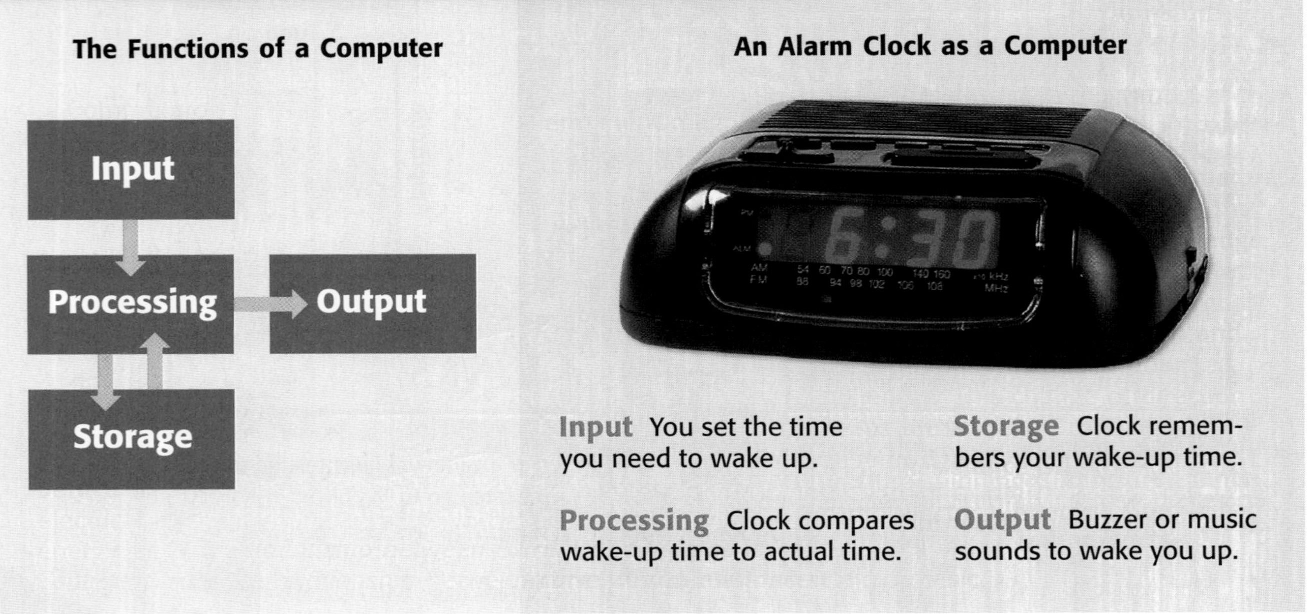

The Functions of a Computer

Input → Processing → Output
Processing ↔ Storage

An Alarm Clock as a Computer

Input You set the time you need to wake up.

Processing Clock compares wake-up time to actual time.

Storage Clock remembers your wake-up time.

Output Buzzer or music sounds to wake you up.

The First Computers

Your pocket calculator is a simple computer. But computers were not always so small and easy to use. The first computers were huge! They were made up of large pieces of equipment that could fill a room. The first general-purpose computer is shown in **Figure 2.** This is the ENIAC. ENIAC stands for Electronic Numerical Integrator and Computer. It was made in 1946 by the U.S. Army. The ENIAC was made up of thousands of vacuum tubes. As a result, it had to be cooled while in use. It also cost a lot to build and to run.

Figure 2 *Fast for its time, the ENIAC could add 5,000 numbers per second.*

Modern Computers

Computers have become much smaller because of integrated circuits. Computers today use microprocessors. A **microprocessor** is a single chip that controls and carries out a computer's instructions. The first widely available microprocessor had only 4,800 transistors. But microprocessors made today may have more than 40 million transistors. Computers are now made so small that we can carry them around like a book!

computer an electronic device that can accept data and instructions, follow the instructions, and output the results

microprocessor a single semiconductor chip that controls and executes a microcomputer's instructions

Reading Check What is a microprocessor?

The Speed of a Simple Computer

1. With a partner, use a **clock** to measure the time it takes each of you to solve the following items by hand.
   a. $(108 \div 9) + 231 - 19$
   b. $1 \times 2 \times 3 \times 4 \times 5$
   c. $(4 \times 6 \times 8) \div 2$
   d. $3 \times (5 + 12) - 2$
2. Repeat step 1 using a **calculator.**
3. Which method was faster?
4. Which method was more accurate?
5. Will the calculator always give you the correct answer? Explain.

Computer Hardware

hardware the parts or pieces of equipment that make up a computer

Different parts of a computer do different jobs. **Hardware** is the parts or pieces of equipment that make up a computer. As you read about each piece of hardware, look at **Figure 3** and **Figure 4** to see what the hardware looks like.

Input Devices

An *input device* gives information, or input, to the computer. You can enter information into a computer using a keyboard, a mouse, a scanner, or a digitizing pad and pen. You can even enter information using a microphone.

Central Processing Unit

A computer does tasks in the *central processing unit,* or CPU. In a personal computer, the CPU is a microprocessor. Input goes through the CPU for processing on the spot or for storage in memory. In the CPU, the computer does calculations, solves problems, and carries out instructions given to it.

Reading Check What does *CPU* stand for?

CONNECTION TO
Social Studies

WRITING SKILL **ENIAC** ENIAC was developed for use by the U.S. Army during World War II. Research what ENIAC was to be used for in the war and what plans were made for ENIAC after the war. Write a one-page report in your **science journal** to report your findings.

Figure 3 Computer Hardware

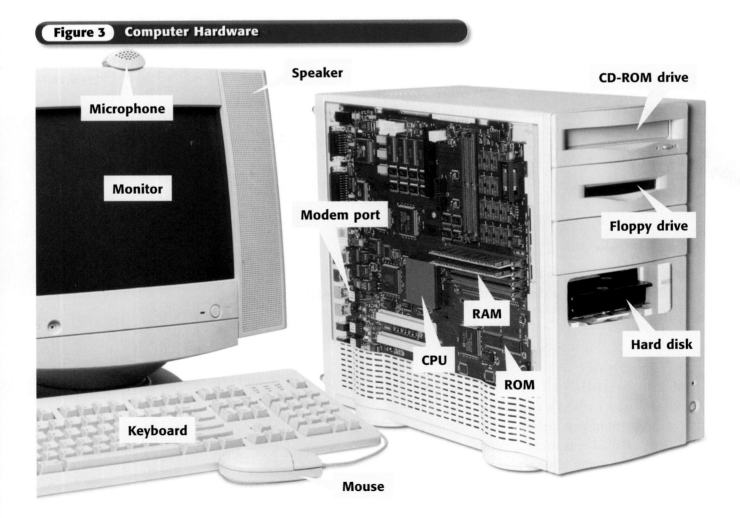

Speaker

CD-ROM drive

Microphone

Monitor

Modem port

Floppy drive

RAM

CPU

ROM

Hard disk

Keyboard

Mouse

Memory

Information can be stored in the computer's memory until it is needed. Hard disks inside a computer and floppy disks or CDs that are put into a computer have memory to store information. Two other types of memory are *ROM* (read-only memory) and *RAM* (random-access memory).

ROM is permanent. It handles jobs such as start-up, maintenance, and hardware management. ROM normally cannot be added to or changed. It also cannot be lost when the computer is turned off. RAM is temporary. RAM stores information only while it is being used. RAM is sometimes called *working memory.* Information in RAM is lost if the power is shut off. So, it is a good habit to save your work to a hard drive or to a disk every few minutes.

Output Devices

Once a computer does a job, it shows the results on an *output device.* Monitors, printers, and speaker systems are all examples of output devices.

Modems and Interface Cards

Computers can exchange information if they are joined by modems or interface cards. Modems send information through telephone lines. Modems convert information from a digital signal to an analog signal and vice versa. Interface cards use cables or wireless connections.

Computer Memory

Suppose you download a document from the Internet that uses 25 kilobytes of memory. How many of those documents could you fit on a disk that has 1 gigabyte of memory? A kilobyte is 1,024 bytes, and a gigabyte is 1,073,741,824 bytes.

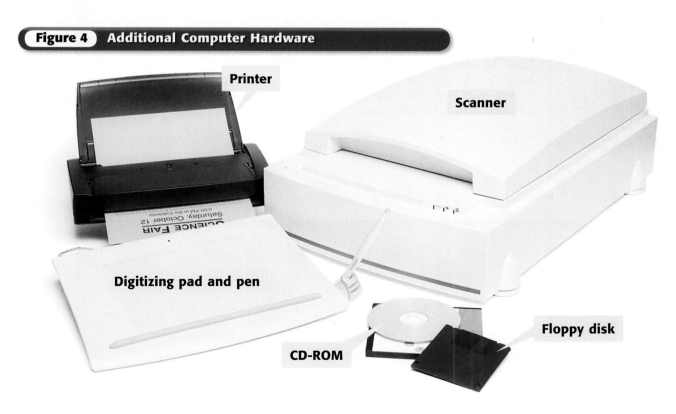

Figure 4 **Additional Computer Hardware**

Printer

Scanner

Digitizing pad and pen

CD-ROM

Floppy disk

Compact Discs

Today, you can use a CD burner to make your own compact discs. A CD can hold about 500 times more information than a floppy disk. It can store digital photos, music files, and any other type of computer file.

Burning and Erasing CDs

The first kind of CD that you could put information onto, or "burn," is a CD-recordable (CD-R) disc. CD-R discs use a dye to block light. When the dye is heated, light cannot pass through to reflect off the aluminum. To burn a CD, a special laser heats some places and not others. This burning creates a pattern of "on" and "off" spots on the CD-R. These spots store information just as the pits and lands do on a regular CD. You can burn a CD-R disc only once.

A CD-rewritable (CD-RW) disc can be used more than once. CD-RW discs use a special compound that can be erased and written over again. CD-RW discs cost more than CD-R discs. But CD-RW discs cannot be read by all CD players. Look at **Figure 5** to see how CD-R and CD-RW discs work.

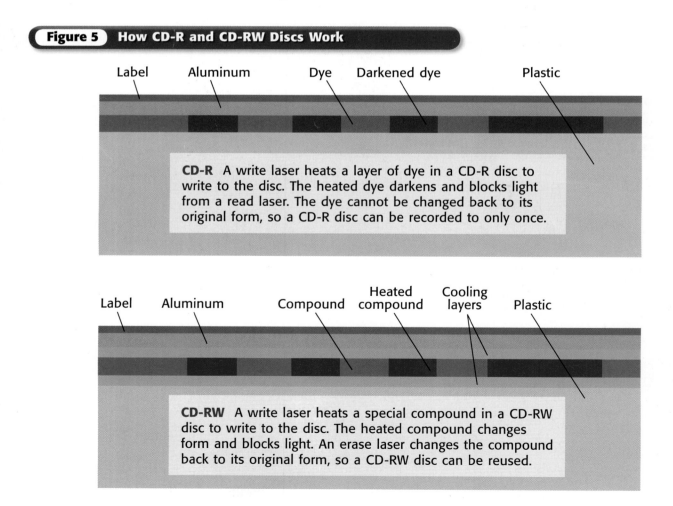

Figure 5 How CD-R and CD-RW Discs Work

Label   Aluminum   Dye   Darkened dye   Plastic

CD-R A write laser heats a layer of dye in a CD-R disc to write to the disc. The heated dye darkens and blocks light from a read laser. The dye cannot be changed back to its original form, so a CD-R disc can be recorded to only once.

Label   Aluminum   Compound   Heated compound   Cooling layers   Plastic

CD-RW A write laser heats a special compound in a CD-RW disc to write to the disc. The heated compound changes form and blocks light. An erase laser changes the compound back to its original form, so a CD-RW disc can be reused.

Computer Software

Computers need instructions before they can do any given task. **Software** is a set of instructions or commands that tells a computer what to do. A computer program is software.

Kinds of Software

Software can be split into two kinds: operating-system software and application software. Operating-system software handles basic operations needed by the computer. It helps the software and hardware communicate. It also handles commands from an input device. It can find programming instructions on a hard disk to be loaded into memory.

Application software tells the computer to run a utility, such as the ones shown in **Figure 6.** The pages in this book were made using many kinds of application software!

software a set of instructions or commands that tells a computer what to do; a computer program

✓**Reading Check** What are the two main kinds of software?

Figure 6 Common Types of Computer Software

Word Processing

Video Games

Interactive Instruction

Graphics

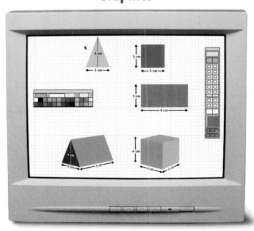

Computer Networks

By using modems and software, many computers can be connected, which allows them to communicate with one another. The **Internet** is a huge computer network made up of millions of computers that can all share information.

Internet a large computer network that connects many local and smaller networks all over the world

The Internet

Figure 7 shows some ways computers can be connected. Computers can connect on the Internet by using modems to dial into an Internet Service Provider, or ISP. A home computer often connects to an ISP over a phone or cable line. Computers in a school or business can be joined in a Local Area Network, or LAN. These computers connect to an ISP through only one line. ISPs around the world are connected by fiber optic cables.

The World Wide Web

The part of the Internet that people know best is called the *World Wide Web*. When you use a Web browser to look at pages on the Internet, you are on the World Wide Web. Web pages share a format that is simple enough that any computer can view them. They are grouped into Web sites. Clicking on a link takes you from one page or site to another. You can use a search engine to find Web pages on a topic for a report or to find out about your favorite movie!

Figure 7 *Internet Service Providers allow computers in your home or school to connect to large routing computers that are linked around the world.*

✓ **Reading Check** Describe the World Wide Web.

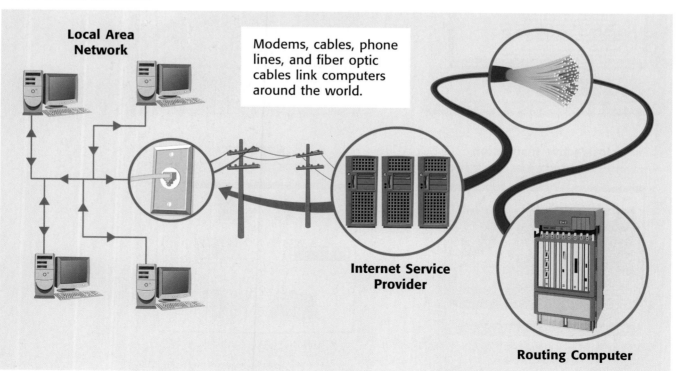

Local Area Network

Modems, cables, phone lines, and fiber optic cables link computers around the world.

Internet Service Provider

Routing Computer

Summary

- All computers have four basic functions: input, processing, storage, and output.

- The first general-purpose computer, ENIAC, was made of thousands of vacuum tubes and filled an entire room. Microprocessors have made it possible to have computers the size of notebooks.

- Computer hardware includes input devices, the CPU, memory, output devices, and modems.

- CD burners can store information on recordable CDs, or CD-Rs. Rewritable CDs, or CD-RWs, can be erased and reused. Both use patterns of light and dark spots.

- Computer software is a set of instructions that tell a computer what to do. The two main types are operating systems and applications. Applications include word processors, spreadsheets, and games.

- The Internet is a huge network that allows millions of computers to share information.

Using Key Terms

The statements below are false. For each statement, replace the underlined term to make a true statement.

1. A word-processing application is an example of <u>hardware</u>.

2. An ISP allows you to connect to the <u>microprocessor</u>.

Understanding Key Ideas

3. Which of the following is an example of hardware used for input?
   - **a.** monitor
   - **b.** keyboard
   - **c.** printer
   - **d.** speaker

4. How are modern computers different from ENIAC? How are they the same?

5. What is the difference between hardware and software?

6. Explain how a CD burner works.

7. What is the Internet?

Critical Thinking

8. **Applying Concepts** Using the terms *input, output, processing,* and *store,* explain how you use a pocket calculator to add numbers.

9. **Predicting Consequences** If no phone lines were working, would there be any communication on the Internet? Explain.

Math Skills

10. How many 800 KB digital photos could you burn onto a CD-R disc that can hold 700 MB of information? (Note: 1,024 KB = 1 MB)

Interpreting Graphics

11. Look at the image of a RAM module below. Each of the black rectangles on the module is 32 MB of RAM. Each side of the module has the same number of rectangles. How much total RAM does the module have?

For a variety of links related to this chapter, go to www.scilinks.org

Topic: Computer Technology; Internet
SciLinks code: HSM0334; HSM0808

Skills Practice Lab

Sending Signals

With a telegraph, you can use electric current to send signals between two telegraph keys connected by wires. In this lab, you will build a model of a telegraph that allows you to use Morse code to transmit messages to a friend.

Procedure

1 Build a switch on the wood block, as shown below. Use a thumbtack to tack down a paper clip so that one end of the paper clip hangs over the edge of the wood block.

2 Unfold a second paper clip so that it looks like an *s*. Use the second thumbtack to tack down one end of the open paper clip on top of the remaining paper clip. The free end of the closed paper clip should hang off of the edge of the wood block opposite the first paper clip. The free end of the open paper clip should touch the thumbtack below it when pushed down.

3 Build the rest of the circuit, as shown below. Use a wire to connect one terminal of the battery to one of the paper clips that hangs over the edge of the wood block.

4 Use a second wire to connect the other paper clip that hangs over the edge of the wood block to the bulb holder.

5 Use a third wire to connect the other side of the bulb holder with the second terminal of the battery.

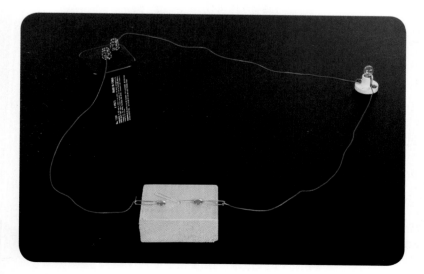

6 Test your circuit by gently pressing down on the open paper clip so that it touches the thumbtack below it. The light bulb should light. This is your model of a telegraph key.

7 Connect your model to another team's model. Use the remaining wire in each team's materials to connect the bulb holders, as shown on the next page. Test your circuit by closing each switch one at a time.

8 Write a short, four- or five-word message in Morse code. Take turns sending messages to the other team using the telegraph. To send a dot, press the paper clip down for two seconds. To send a dash, hold the clip down for four seconds. Decode the message you receive, and check to see if you got the correct message.

9 Remove one of the batteries. Test your circuit again by closing each switch one at a time.

Analyze the Results

1 **Describing Events** When both batteries are attached, what happens to the flashlight bulbs when you close your switch?

2 **Describing Events** When both batteries are attached, what happens to the flashlight bulbs when the other team closes their switch?

3 **Describing Events** How does removing one of the batteries change the way you can send or receive messages on the telegraph?

4 **Analyzing Results** Did you receive the correct message from the other team? If not, what problems did you have?

Draw Conclusions

5 **Drawing Conclusions** When the two models are connected, are the flashlight bulbs part of a series circuit or a parallel circuit?

6 **Making Predictions** How might using a telegraph to transmit messages overseas be difficult?

Table 1 International Morse Code

A ·‑	J ·‑‑‑	S ···	2 ··‑‑‑
B ‑···	K ‑·‑	T ‑	3 ···‑‑
C ‑·‑·	L ·‑··	U ··‑	4 ····‑
D ‑··	M ‑‑	V ···‑	5 ·····
E ·	N ‑·	W ·‑‑	6 ‑····
F ··‑·	O ‑‑‑	X ‑··‑	7 ‑‑···
G ‑‑·	P ·‑‑·	Y ‑·‑‑	8 ‑‑‑··
H ····	Q ‑‑·‑	Z ‑‑··	9 ‑‑‑‑·
I ··	R ·‑·	1 ·‑‑‑‑	0 ‑‑‑‑‑

Chapter Review

USING KEY TERMS

For each pair of terms, explain how the meanings of the terms differ.

1 *semiconductor* and *integrated circuit*

2 *transistor* and *doping*

3 *analog signal* and *digital signal*

4 *computer* and *microprocessor*

5 *hardware* and *software*

UNDERSTANDING KEY IDEAS

Multiple Choice

6 All electronic devices transmit information using
  a. signals.
  b. electromagnetic waves.
  c. radio waves.
  d. modems.

7 Semiconductors are used to make
  a. transistors.
  b. integrated circuits.
  c. diodes.
  d. All of the above

8 Which of the following is an example of a telecommunication device?
  a. vacuum tube
  b. telephone
  c. radio
  d. Both (b) and (c)

9 A monitor, a printer, and a speaker are examples of
  a. input devices.
  b. memory.
  c. computers.
  d. output devices.

10 Record players play sounds that were recorded in the form of
  a. digital signals.
  b. electric currents.
  c. analog signals.
  d. radio waves.

11 Memory in a computer that is permanent and cannot be changed is called
  a. RAM.
  b. ROM.
  c. CPU.
  d. None of the above

12 Beams of electrons that shine on fluorescent materials are used in
  a. telephones.
  b. telegraphs.
  c. televisions.
  d. radios.

Short Answer

13 How is an electronic device different from other machines that use electrical energy?

14 In one or two sentences, describe how a television works.

15 Give three examples of how computers are used in your everyday life.

16 Explain the advantages that transistors have over vacuum tubes.

Math Skills

17 How many bits can be stored on a 20 GB hard disk? (Hint: 1 GB = 1,073,741,824 bytes; 1 byte = 8 bits.)

CRITICAL THINKING

18 **Concept Mapping** Use the following terms to create a concept map: *electronic devices, radio waves, electric current, signals,* and *information.*

19 **Applying Concepts** Your friend is preparing an oral report on the history of radio and finds the photograph shown below. He asks you why the radio is so large. Using what you know about electronic devices, how do you explain the size of this vintage radio?

20 **Making Comparisons** Using what you know about the differences between analog signals and digital signals, compare the sound from a record player to the sound from a CD player.

21 **Making Comparisons** What do Morse code and digital signals have in common?

INTERPRETING GRAPHICS

The diagram below shows a circuit that contains a transistor. Use the diagram below to answer the questions that follow.

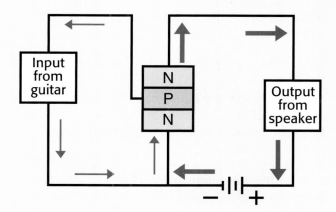

22 What purpose does the transistor serve in this diagram?

23 Compare the current in the left side of the circuit with the current in the right side of the circuit.

24 Compare the sound from the speaker with the sound from the guitar.

Standardized Test Preparation

READING

Read each of the passages below. Then, answer the questions that follow each passage.

Passage 1 The first televisions hit the market in the 1940s. At about $625 each, they were too expensive for most families to afford. Although the sets were large and bulky, the screens were small, and images were fuzzy and in black and white. Today's televisions have bigger screens and sharper pictures—in full color. Modern televisions are also generally less expensive. A typical television today costs less than half what it cost in the 1940s, and that cost is not accounting for inflation. Many modern televisions are cable ready and have remote controls. You can buy televisions with built-in DVD or videotape players. You could even install theater-quality surround sound. But even these improvements may seem out of date in 20 years.

1. Which of the following can be inferred from the passage?

  A Color movies are better than black-and-white movies.

  B In the 1940s, television sets did not have remote controls.

  C Today's televisions are not much better than the TVs made in the 1940s.

  D Televisions are much more expensive today than they were in the past.

2. Which of the following statements is a fact in the passage?

  F The first television sets had small screens with fuzzy, black-and-white images.

  G Televisions with built-in videotape players are very expensive.

  H Television screens are too large.

  I Although televisions are improving, the quality of TV programming is getting worse.

Passage 2 One of the first electronic communication devices was the telegraph, which was invented in the 1830s. The telegraph used an electric current to send messages between two distant places linked by wires. Telegraph operators sent messages in Morse code, which uses combinations of short taps and long taps to represent numbers and letters. When operators tapped the telegraph key, this closed a circuit, causing "clicks" at the receiving end of the telegraph. Although telegraphs are not used much today, they were an important step in the development of electronic <u>telecommunication</u>.

1. What is the meaning of the word *telecommunication* in this passage?

  A using telephones to communicate

  B sending messages to someone within hearing distance

  C trying to decipher codes without a key

  D communicating with someone over a long distance

2. What happens first when an operator sends a telegraph message?

  F A circuit opens and closes with the pattern of short and long taps.

  G There are short and long clicks on the receiving end.

  H The operator taps the telegraph key with a pattern of short and long taps.

  I The message is deciphered and interpreted by the receiver.

The table below gives the cost of parts to build your own personal computer. Use the table below to answer the questions that follow.

Cost of Computer Parts	
Part	**Cost**
Case	$50–$200
Power supply (300–400 W)	$30–$50
CPU (1.7–2.26 GHz)	$80–$250
Cooling equipment (may come with case)	$0–$50
Motherboard	$50–$200
RAM (256–512 MB)	$50–$150
Floppy drive	$20
Hard drive (60–100 GB)	$80–$125
CD-ROM drive or DVD-ROM drive or CD-RW/DVD combo	$35–$120
Video card	$40–$175
Sound card (may be optional)	$0–$200
Speakers	$10–$150
Microphone (optional)	$0–$50
Keyboard and mouse	$50–$80
Monitor	$200–$600

1. Which of the following items is optional when building a computer?

   A a CPU

   B a hard drive

   C RAM

   D a microphone

2. What is the total cost to purchase the most expensive CPU, the most expensive mother-board, and the least expensive monitor?

   F $330

   G $650

   H $730

   I $1,050

Read each question below, and choose the best answer.

1. A plasma television is 15 cm thick. What is this value in inches? (1 in. = 2.5 cm)

   A 6 in.

   B 12 in.

   C 17.5 in.

   D 37.5 in.

2. The radius of a compact disc is about 6 cm. What is the approximate area of a compact disc? (Estimate the value of π to be 3.)

   F 36 cm

   G 36 cm^2

   H 108 cm

   I 108 cm^2

3. When sound is recorded digitally onto a CD, the sound waves are converted to electric current. The current is sampled about 44,000 times per second to make a digital signal. About how many samples would be taken in 1 min?

   A 733

   B 264,000

   C 733,000

   D 2,640,000

4. The first general-purpose computer, ENIAC, was made of 18,000 vacuum tubes. ENIAC used about 180,000 W of power. About how much power was consumed by each vacuum tube?

   F 0.1 W

   G 1.8 W

   H 10 W

   I 18 W

Science in Action

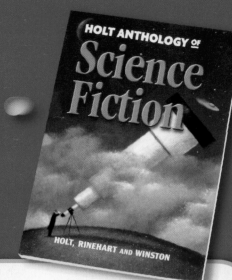

Science, Technology, and Society

Wearable Computers

Today's thin, portable laptop computers are extremely tiny compared to the first general-purpose computer, ENIAC, which filled an entire room. But today's laptops may look bulky next to the computers of tomorrow. In the future, you might wear your computer! A wearable computer is always with you, like clothing or eyeglasses. It is easy to operate. You can even use it while moving around. You might use a wearable computer to take notes in class, look up a phone number, check e-mail, or browse the Internet. These computers are already being used today by a number of companies. As the technology evolves, wearable computers will become even easier to use and more advanced in the types of tasks they perform.

Math ACTIVITY

One wearable computer that is available today can operate from 0°C to 50°C. You can convert temperature measurements from Celsius to Fahrenheit with this equation: Fahrenheit temperature = (9/5 × Celsius temperature) + 32. What is the operating range of this computer in degrees Fahrenheit?

Science Fiction

"There Will Come Soft Rains" by Ray Bradbury

Ticktock, seven o'clock, time to get up, seven o'clock. The voice clock in the living room sent out the wake-up message, gently calling to the family to get up and begin their new day. A few minutes later, the automatic stove in the kitchen began the family breakfast. A soft rain was falling outside, so the weather box by the front door suggested that raincoats were necessary today.

But no family sounds come from the house. The house goes on talking to itself as if it were keeping itself company. Why doesn't anyone answer? Find out when you read Ray Bradbury's "There Will Come Soft Rains" in the *Holt Anthology of Science Fiction*.

Language Arts ACTIVITY

WRITING SKILL The story described above takes place in 2026. The author has imagined how the future world might be. Write a short story about how you think life will be different in the year 2050.

Agnes Riley

Computer Technician Some people take it for granted how smoothly a computer works—until it breaks down. When that happens, you may need to call in an expert, such as Agnes Riley. Agnes is a computer technician from Budapest, Hungary. When a computer isn't working properly, she will take it apart, find the problem, and fix it.

Many people go to school to learn about computer repair, but Agnes taught herself. In Hungary, the company she worked for had a set of old, run-down computers. Agnes started experimenting, trying to repair them. The more she tinkered, the more she learned.

When Agnes moved to New York City in 1999, she wanted to become a computer technician. She started out as a computer salesperson. Eventually, she got the technician training materials. Her earlier experimenting and her studying paid off. She passed the exam to become a licensed technician. Agnes enjoys solving problems and likes helping people. If you are the same type of person, you might want to become a computer technician, too!

Social Studies ACTIVITY

WRITING SKILL Agnes Riley is from Budapest, Hungary. What might you see if you visited Budapest? Do some research to find out, and then design a travel brochure to encourage tourists to visit the city. You might include information about local points of interest or Budapest's history.

go.hrw.com
To learn more about these Science in Action topics, visit **go.hrw.com** and type in the keyword **HP5ELTF.**

Current Science
Check out Current Science® articles related to this chapter by visiting go.hrw.com. Just type in the keyword **HP5CS19.**

UNIT 7

TIMELINE

Waves, Sound, and Light

When you hear the word *waves*, you probably think of waves in the ocean. But waves that you encounter every day have a much bigger effect on your life than do water waves! In this unit, you will learn about different types of waves, how waves behave and interact, and how sound energy and light energy travel in waves. This timeline shows some events and discoveries that have occurred throughout history as scientists have sought to learn more about the energy of waves.

Around 1600

Italian astronomer and physicist Galileo Galilei attempts to calculate the speed of light by using lanterns and shutters. He writes that the speed is "extraordinarily rapid."

1903

The popularity of an early movie called *The Great Train Robbery* leads to the establishment of permanent movie theaters.

1960

The first working laser is demonstrated.

1971

Hungarian physicist Dennis Gabor wins the Nobel Prize in physics for his invention of holography, the method used to make holograms.

1704

Sir Isaac Newton publishes his book *Optiks*, which contains his theories about light and color.

1711

English trumpeter John Shore invents the tuning fork, an instrument that produces a single-frequency note.

1801

British scientist Thomas Young is the first to provide experimental data showing that light behaves as a wave.

1905

Physicist Albert Einstein suggests that light sometimes behaves as a particle.

1929

American astronomer Edwin Hubble uses the Doppler effect of light to determine that the universe is expanding.

1947

Anne Frank's *The Diary of a Young Girl* is published. The book is an edited version of the diary kept by a Jewish teenager while in hiding during World War II.

1983

A "mouse" is first used on personal computers.

1997

British pilot Andy Green drives a jet-powered car at 341 m/s, when he becomes the first person to travel faster than the speed of sound on land.

2002

Scientists develop a thermoacoustic refrigerator. The device is cooled using high amplitude sound instead of chemical refrigerants.

20

The Energy of Waves

SECTION **1** The Nature of Waves . . 574

SECTION **2** Properties of Waves . . 580

SECTION **3** Wave Interactions 584

Chapter Lab 590
Chapter Review 592
Standardized Test Preparation 594
Science in Action 596

About the PHOTO

A surfer takes advantage of a wave's energy to catch an exciting ride. The ocean wave that this surfer is riding is just one type of wave. You are probably familiar with water waves. But did you know that light, sound, and even earthquakes are waves? From music to television, waves play an important role in your life every day.

PRE-READING ACTIVITY

FOLDNOTES **Three-Panel Flip Chart**
Before you read the chapter, create the FoldNote entitled "Three-Panel Flip Chart" described in the **Study Skills** section of the Appendix. Label the flaps of the three-panel flip chart with "The nature of waves," "Properties of waves," and "Wave interactions." As you read the chapter, write information you learn about each category under the appropriate flap.

Energetic Waves

In this activity, you will observe the movement of a wave. Then, you will determine the source of the wave's energy.

Procedure

1. Tie one end of a **piece of rope** to the back of a **chair.**

2. Hold the other end in one hand, and stand away from the chair so that the rope is almost straight but is not pulled tight.

3. Move the rope up and down quickly to create a wave. Repeat this step several times. Record your observations.

Analysis

1. In which direction does the wave move?

2. How does the movement of the rope compare with the movement of the wave?

3. Where does the energy of the wave come from?

The Nature of Waves

Imagine that your family has just returned home from a day at the beach. You had fun playing in the ocean under a hot sun. You put some cold pizza in the microwave for dinner, and you turn on the radio. Just then, the phone rings. It's your friend calling to ask about homework.

In the events described above, how many different waves were present? Believe it or not, there were at least five! Can you name them? Here's a hint: A **wave** is any disturbance that transmits energy through matter or empty space. Okay, here are the answers: water waves in the ocean; light waves from the sun; microwaves inside the microwave oven; radio waves transmitted to the radio; and sound waves from the radio, telephone, and voices. Don't worry if you didn't get very many. You will be able to name them all after you read this section.

✓ **Reading Check** What do all waves have in common? (*See the Appendix for answers to Reading Checks.*)

Wave Energy

Energy can be carried away from its source by a wave. You can observe an example of a wave if you drop a rock in a pond. Waves from the rock's splash carry energy away from the splash. However, the material through which the wave travels does not move with the energy. Look at **Figure 1.** Can you move a leaf on a pond if you are standing on the shore? You can make the leaf bob up and down by making waves that carry enough energy through the water. But you would not make the leaf move in the same direction as the wave.

wave a periodic disturbance in a solid, liquid, or gas as energy is transmitted through a medium

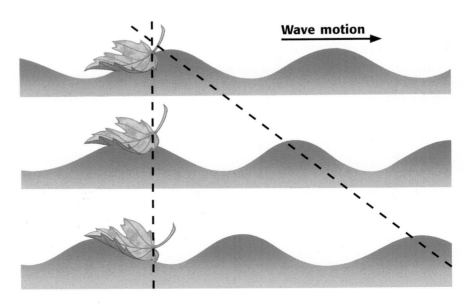

Figure 1 *Waves on a pond move toward the shore, but the water and the leaf floating on the surface only bob up and down.*

Waves and Work

As a wave travels, it does work on everything in its path. The waves in a pond do work on the water to make it move up and down. The waves also do work on anything floating on the water's surface. For example, boats and ducks bob up and down with waves. The fact that these objects move tells you that the waves are transferring energy.

Energy Transfer Through a Medium

Most waves transfer energy by the vibration of particles in a medium. A **medium** is a substance through which a wave can travel. A medium can be a solid, a liquid, or a gas. The plural of *medium* is *media*.

When a particle vibrates (moves back and forth, as in **Figure 2**), it can pass its energy to a particle next to it. The second particle will vibrate like the first particle does. In this way, energy is transmitted through a medium.

Sound waves need a medium. Sound energy travels by the vibration of particles in liquids, solids, and gases. If there are no particles to vibrate, no sound is possible. If you put an alarm clock inside a jar and remove all the air from the jar to create a vacuum, you will not be able to hear the alarm.

Other waves that need a medium include ocean waves, which move through water, and waves that are carried on guitar and cello strings when they vibrate. Waves that need a medium are called *mechanical waves*. **Figure 3** shows the effect of a mechanical wave in Earth's crust: an earthquake.

Figure 2 *A vibration is one complete back-and-forth motion of an object.*

medium a physical environment in which phenomena occur

Figure 3 *Earthquakes cause seismic waves to travel through Earth's crust. The energy they carry can be very destructive to anything on the ground.*

Figure 4 *Light waves are electromagnetic waves, which do not need a medium. Light waves from the Crab nebula, shown here, travel through the vacuum of space billions of miles to Earth, where they can be detected with a telescope.*

Energy Transfer Without a Medium

Some waves can transfer energy without going through a medium. Visible light is one example. Other examples include microwaves made by microwave ovens, TV and radio signals, and X rays used by dentists and doctors. These waves are *electromagnetic waves*.

Although electromagnetic waves do not need a medium, they can go through matter, such as air, water, and glass. The energy that reaches Earth from the sun comes through electromagnetic waves, which go through space. As shown in **Figure 4,** you can see light from stars because electromagnetic waves travel through space to Earth. Light is an electromagnetic wave that your eyes can see.

Reading Check How do electromagnetic waves differ from mechanical waves?

CONNECTION TO Astronomy

Light Speed Light waves from stars and galaxies travel great distances that are best expressed in light-years. A light-year is the distance a ray of light can travel in one year. Some of the light waves from these stars have traveled billions of light-years before reaching Earth. Do the following calculation in your **science journal:** If light travels at a speed of 300,000,000 m/s, what distance is a light-minute? (Hint: There are 60 s in a minute.)

ACTIVITY

Types of Waves

All waves transfer energy by repeated vibrations. However, waves can differ in many ways. Waves can be classified based on the direction in which the particles of the medium vibrate compared with the direction in which the waves move. The two main types of waves are *transverse waves* and *longitudinal* (LAHN juh TOOD'n uhl) *waves.* Sometimes, a transverse wave and a longitudinal wave can combine to form another kind of wave called a *surface wave.*

Transverse Waves

Waves in which the particles vibrate in an up-and-down motion are called **transverse waves.** *Transverse* means "moving across." The particles in this kind of wave move across, or perpendicularly to, the direction that the wave is going. To be *perpendicular* means to be "at right angles."

A wave moving on a rope is an example of a transverse wave. In **Figure 5,** you can see that the points along the rope vibrate perpendicularly to the direction the wave is going. The highest point of a transverse wave is called a *crest,* and the lowest point between each crest is called a *trough* (TRAWF). Although electromagnetic waves do not travel by vibrating particles in a medium, all electromagnetic waves are considered transverse waves. The reason is that the waves are made of vibrations that are perpendicular to the direction of motion.

INTERNET ACTIVITY

For another activity related to this chapter, go to **go.hrw.com** and type in the keyword **HP5WAVW.**

transverse wave a wave in which the particles of the medium move perpendicularly to the direction the wave is traveling

---

Figure 5 Motion of a Transverse Wave

A wave on a rope is a transverse wave because the particles of the medium vibrate perpendicularly to the direction the wave moves.

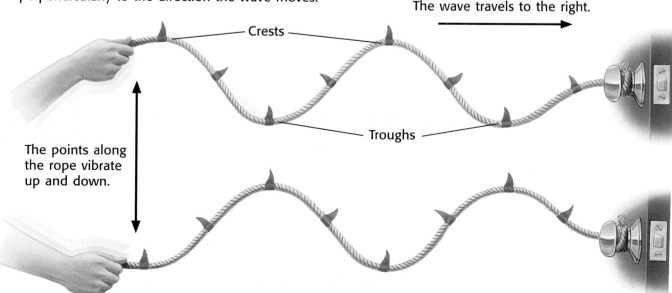

The wave travels to the right.

Crests

Troughs

The points along the rope vibrate up and down.

Figure 6 **Comparing Longitudinal and Transverse Waves**

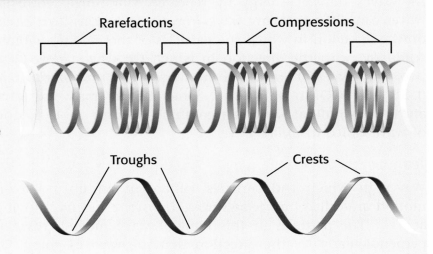

Pushing a spring back and forth creates a longitudinal wave, much the same way that shaking a rope up and down creates a transverse wave.

Rarefactions   Compressions

Longitudinal wave

Troughs   Crests

Tranverse wave

Longitudinal Waves

longitudinal wave a wave in which the particles of the medium vibrate parallel to the direction of wave motion

In a **longitudinal wave,** the particles of the medium vibrate back and forth along the path that the wave moves. You can make a longitudinal wave on a spring. When you push on the end of the spring, the coils of the spring crowd together. A part of a longitudinal wave where the particles are crowded together is called a *compression*. When you pull back on the end of the spring, the coils are pulled apart. A part where the particles are spread apart is a *rarefaction* (RER uh FAK shuhn). Compressions and rarefactions are like the crests and troughs of a transverse wave, as shown in **Figure 6.**

Sound Waves

A sound wave is an example of a longitudinal wave. Sound waves travel by compressions and rarefactions of air particles. **Figure 7** shows how a vibrating drum forms compressions and rarefactions in the air around it.

✓ Reading Check What kind of wave is a sound wave?

Figure 7 *Sound energy is carried away from a drum by a longitudinal wave through the air.*

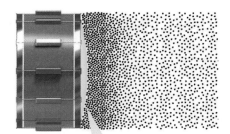

When the drumhead moves out after being hit, a compression is created in the air particles.

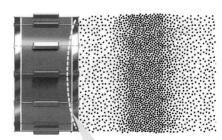

When the drumhead moves back in, a rarefaction is created.

Combinations of Waves

When waves form at or near the boundary between two media, a transverse wave and a longitudinal wave can combine to form a *surface wave*. An example is shown in **Figure 8.** Surface waves look like transverse waves, but the particles of the medium in a surface wave move in circles rather than up and down. The particles move forward at the crest of each wave and move backward at the trough.

Figure 8 *Ocean waves are surface waves. A floating bottle shows the circular motion of particles in a surface wave.*

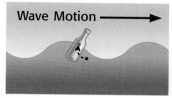
Wave Motion →

SECTION Review

Summary

- A wave is a disturbance that transmits energy.
- The particles of a medium do not travel with the wave.
- Mechanical waves require a medium, but electromagnetic waves do not.
- Particles in a transverse wave vibrate perpendicularly to the direction the wave travels.
- Particles in a longitudinal wave vibrate parallel to the direction that the wave travels.

Using Key Terms

Complete each of the following sentences by choosing the correct term from the word bank.

transverse wave	wave
longitudinal wave	medium

1. In a ___, the particles vibrate parallel to the direction that the wave travels.

2. Mechanical waves require a ___ through which to travel.

3. Any ___ transmits energy through vibrations.

4. In a ___, the particles vibrate perpendicularly to the direction that the wave travels.

Understanding Key Ideas

5. Waves transfer
   a. matter.
   b. energy.
   c. particles.
   d. water.

6. Name a kind of wave that does not require a medium.

Critical Thinking

7. **Applying Concepts** Sometimes, people at a sports event do "the wave." Is this a real example of a wave? Why or why not?

8. **Making Inferences** Why can supernova explosions in space be seen but not heard on Earth?

Interpreting Graphics

9. Look at the figure below. Which part of the wave is the crest? Which part of the wave is the trough?

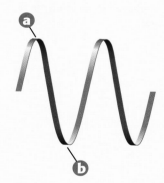

For a variety of links related to this chapter, go to www.scilinks.org
Topic: The Nature of Waves; Types of Waves
SciLinks code: HSM1017; HSM1574

Developed and maintained by the National Science Teachers Association

Properties of Waves

You are in a swimming pool, floating on your air mattress, enjoying a gentle breeze. Your friend does a "cannonball" from the high dive nearby. Suddenly, your mattress is rocking wildly on the waves generated by the huge splash.

The breeze generates waves in the water as well, but they are very different from the waves created by your diving friend. The waves made by the breeze are shallow and close together, while the waves from your friend's splash are tall and widely spaced. Properties of waves, such as the height of the waves and the distance between crests, are useful for comparing and describing waves.

Amplitude

If you tie one end of a rope to the back of a chair, you can create waves by moving the free end up and down. If you shake the rope a little, you will make a shallow wave. If you shake the rope hard, you will make a tall wave.

The **amplitude** of a wave is related to its height. A wave's amplitude is the maximum distance that the particles of a medium vibrate from their rest position. The rest position is the point where the particles of a medium stay when there are no disturbances. The larger the amplitude is, the taller the wave is. **Figure 1** shows how the amplitude of a transverse wave may be measured.

Larger Amplitude—More Energy

When using a rope to make waves, you have to work harder to create a wave with a large amplitude than to create one with a small amplitude. The reason is that it takes more energy to move the rope farther from its rest position. Therefore, a wave with a large amplitude carries more energy than a wave with a small amplitude does.

amplitude the maximum distance that the particles of a wave's medium vibrate from their rest position

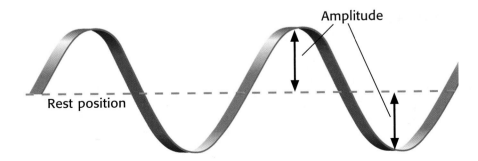

Figure 1 *The amplitude of a transverse wave is measured from the rest position to the crest or to the trough of the wave.*

Amplitude

Rest position

Wavelength

Another property of waves is wavelength. A **wavelength** is the distance between any two crests or compressions next to each other in a wave. The distance between two troughs or rarefactions next to each other is also a wavelength. In fact, the wavelength can be measured from any point on a wave to the next corresponding point on the wave. Wavelength is measured the same way in both a longitudinal wave and a transverse wave, as shown in **Figure 2.**

Shorter Wavelength—More Energy

If you are making waves on either a spring or a rope, the rate at which you shake it will determine whether the wavelength is short or long. If you shake it rapidly back and forth, the wavelength will be shorter. If you are shaking it rapidly, you are putting more energy into it than if you were shaking it more slowly. So, a wave with a shorter wavelength carries more energy than a wave with a longer wavelength does.

> **✓ Reading Check** How does shaking a rope at different rates affect the wavelength of the wave that moves through the rope? (*See the Appendix for answers to Reading Checks.*)

wavelength the distance from any point on a wave to an identical point on the next wave

Springy Waves

1. Hold a coiled **spring toy** on the floor between you and a classmate so that the spring is straight. This is the rest position.

2. Move one end of the spring back and forth at a constant rate. Note the wavelength of the wave you create.

3. Increase the amplitude of the waves. What did you have to do? How did the change in amplitude affect the wavelength?

4. Now, shake the spring back and forth about twice as fast as you did before. What happens to the wavelength? Record your observations.

Figure 2 Measuring Wavelengths

Wavelength can be measured from any two corresponding points that are adjacent on a wave.

Longitudinal wave

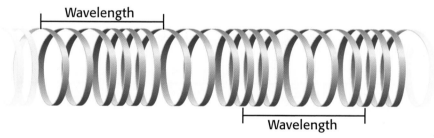

Transverse wave

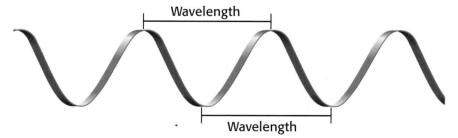

Frequency

Think about making rope waves again. The number of waves that you can make in 1 s depends on how quickly you move the rope. If you move the rope slowly, you make only a small number of waves each second. If you move it quickly, you make a large number of waves. The number of waves produced in a given amount of time is the **frequency** of the wave. Frequency is usually expressed in *hertz* (Hz). For waves, one hertz equals one wave per second (1 Hz = 1/s). **Figure 3** shows a wave with a frequency of 0.2 Hz.

✓ **Reading Check** If you make three rope waves per second, what is the frequency of the wave?

Higher Frequency—More Energy

To make high-frequency waves in a rope, you must shake the rope quickly back and forth. To shake a rope quickly takes more energy than to shake it slowly. Therefore, if the amplitudes are equal, high-frequency waves carry more energy than low-frequency waves.

Wave Speed

Wave speed is the speed at which a wave travels. Wave speed (v) can be calculated using wavelength (λ, the Greek letter *lambda*) and frequency (f), by using the *wave equation*, which is shown below:

$$v = \lambda \times f$$

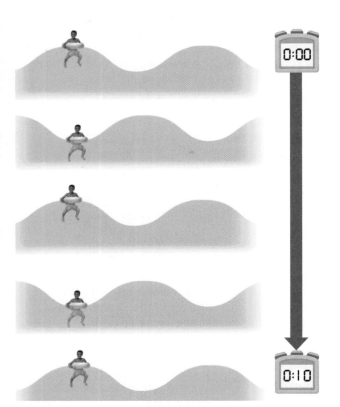

Figure 3 *Frequency can be measured by counting how many waves pass by in a certain amount of time. Here, two waves went by in 10 s, so the frequency is 2/10 s = 0.2 Hz.*

Wave Calculations   Determine the wave speed of a wave that has a wavelength of 5 m and a frequency of 4 Hz.

Step 1: Write the equation for wave speed.

$$v = \lambda \times f$$

Step 2: Replace the λ and f with the values given in the problem, and solve.

$$v = 5 \text{ m} \times 4 \text{ Hz} = 20 \text{ m/s}$$

The equation for wave speed can also be rearranged to determine wavelength or frequency, as shown at top right.

$\lambda = \dfrac{v}{f}$ (Rearranged by dividing by f.)

$f = \dfrac{v}{\lambda}$ (Rearranged by dividing by λ.)

Now It's Your Turn

1. What is the frequency of a wave if the wave has a speed of 12 cm/s and a wavelength of 3 cm?

2. A wave has a frequency of 5 Hz and a wave speed of 18 m/s. What is its wavelength?

Frequency and Wavelength Relationship

Three of the basic properties of a wave are related to one another in the wave equation—wave speed, frequency, and wavelength. If you know any two of these properties of a wave, you can use the wave equation to find the third.

One of the things the wave equation tells you is the relationship between frequency and wavelength. If a wave is traveling a certain speed and you double its frequency, its wavelength will be cut in half. Or if you were to cut its frequency in half, the wavelength would be double what it was before. So, you can say that frequency and wavelength are *inversely* related. Think of a sound wave, traveling underwater at 1,440 m/s, given off by the sonar of a submarine like the one shown in **Figure 4.** If the sound wave has a frequency of 360 Hz, it will have a wavelength of 4.0 m. If the sound wave has twice that frequency, the wavelength will be 2.0 m, half as big.

The wave speed of a wave in a certain medium is the same no matter what the wavelength is. So, the wavelength and frequency of a wave depend on the wave speed, not the other way around.

Figure 4 *Submarines use sonar, sound waves in water, to locate underwater objects.*

frequency the number of waves produced in a given amount of time

wave speed the speed at which a wave travels through a medium

SECTION
Review

Summary

- Amplitude is the maximum distance the particles of a medium vibrate from their rest position.
- Wavelength is the distance between two adjacent corresponding parts of a wave.
- Frequency is the number of waves that pass a given point in a given amount of time.
- Wave speed can be calculated by multiplying the wave's wavelength by the frequency.

Using Key Terms

1. In your own words, write a definition for each of the following terms: *amplitude, frequency,* and *wavelength.*

Understanding Key Ideas

2. Which of the following results in more energy in a wave?
   a. a smaller wavelength
   b. a lower frequency
   c. a shallower amplitude
   d. a lower speed

3. Draw a transverse wave, and label how the amplitude and wavelength are measured.

Math Skills

4. What is the speed (*v*) of a wave that has a wavelength (*λ*) of 2 m and a frequency (*f*) of 6 Hz?

Critical Thinking

5. **Making Inferences** A wave has a low speed but a high frequency. What can you infer about its wavelength?

6. **Analyzing Processes** Two friends blow two whistles at the same time. The first whistle makes a sound whose frequency is twice that of the sound made by the other whistle. Which sound will reach you first?

SCiLINKS.

NSTA

Developed and maintained by the
National Science Teachers Association

For a variety of links related to this chapter, go to www.scilinks.org

Topic: Properties of Waves
SciLinks code: HSM1236

Wave Interactions

If you've ever seen a planet in the night sky, you may have had a hard time telling it apart from a star. Both planets and stars shine brightly, but the light waves that you see are from very different sources.

All stars, including the sun, produce light. But planets do not produce light. So, why do planets shine so brightly? The planets and the moon shine because light from the sun *reflects* off them. Without reflection, you would not be able to see the planets. Reflection is one of the wave interactions that you will learn about in this section.

Reflection

Reflection happens when a wave bounces back after hitting a barrier. All waves—including water, sound, and light waves—can be reflected. The reflection of water waves is shown in **Figure 1.** Light waves reflecting off an object allow you to see that object. For example, light waves from the sun are reflected when they strike the surface of the moon. These reflected waves allow us to enjoy moonlit nights. A reflected sound wave is called an *echo*.

Waves are not always reflected when they hit a barrier. If all light waves were reflected when they hit your eyeglasses, you would not be able to see anything! A wave is *transmitted* through a substance when it passes through the substance.

reflection the bouncing back of a ray of light, sound, or heat when the ray hits a surface that it does not go through

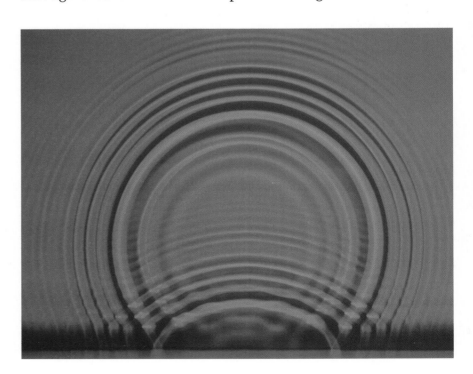

Figure 1 *These water waves are reflecting off the side of the container.*

Figure 2 *A light wave passing at an angle into a new medium—such as water—is refracted because the speed of the wave changes.*

Refraction

Try this simple activity: Place a pencil in a half-filled glass of water. Now, look at the pencil from the side. The pencil appears to be broken into two pieces! But as you can see when you take the pencil out of the water, it is still in one piece.

What you saw in this experiment was the result of the *refraction* of light waves. **Refraction** is the bending of a wave as the wave passes from one medium to another at an angle. Refraction of a flashlight beam as the beam passes from air to water is shown in **Figure 2.**

When a wave moves from one medium to another, the wave's speed changes. When a wave enters a new medium, the wave changes wavelength as well as speed. As a result, the wave bends and travels in a new direction.

refraction the bending of a wave as the wave passes between two substances in which the speed of the wave differs

✓ **Reading Check** What happens to a wave when it moves from one medium to another at an angle? (*See the Appendix for answers to Reading Checks.*)

Refraction of Different Colors

When light waves from the sun pass through a droplet of water in a cloud or through a prism, the light is refracted. But the different colors in sunlight are refracted by different amounts, so the light is *dispersed,* or spread out, into its separate colors. When sunlight is refracted this way through water droplets, you can see a rainbow. Why does that happen?

Although all light waves travel at the same speed through empty space, when light passes through a medium such as water or glass, the speed of the light wave depends on the wavelength of the light wave. Because the different colors of light have different wavelengths, their speeds are different, and they are refracted by different amounts. As a result, the colors are spread out, so you can see them individually.

CONNECTION TO Language Arts

WRITING SKILL **The Colors of the Rainbow** People have always been fascinated by the beautiful array of colors that results when sunlight strikes water droplets in the air to form a rainbow. The knowledge science gives us about how they form makes them no less breathtaking.

In the library, find a poem that you like about rainbows. In your **science journal,** copy the poem, and write a paragraph in which you discuss how your knowledge of refraction affects your opinion about the poem.

Figure 3 Diffraction Through an Opening

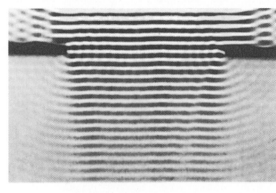

If the barrier or opening is larger than the wavelength of the wave, there is only a small amount of diffraction.

If the barrier or opening is the same size or smaller than the wavelength of an approaching wave, the amount of diffraction is large.

diffraction a change in the direction of a wave when the wave finds an obstacle or an edge, such as an opening

Diffraction

Suppose you are walking down a city street and you hear music. The sound seems to be coming from around the corner, but you cannot see where the music is coming from because a building on the corner blocks your view. Why do sound waves travel around a corner better than light waves do?

Most of the time, waves travel in straight lines. For example, a beam of light from a flashlight is fairly straight. But in some circumstances, waves curve or bend when they reach the edge of an object. The bending of waves around a barrier or through an opening is known as **diffraction.**

If You Can Hear It, Why Can't You See It?

The amount of diffraction of a wave depends on its wavelength and the size of the barrier or opening the wave encounters, as shown in **Figure 3.** You can hear music around the corner of a building because sound waves have long wavelengths and are able to diffract around corners. However, you cannot see who is playing the music because the wavelengths of light waves are much shorter than sound waves, so light is not diffracted very much.

Interference

You know that all matter has volume. Therefore, objects cannot be in the same space at the same time. But waves are energy, not matter. So, more than one wave can be in the same place at the same time. In fact, two waves can meet, share the same space, and pass through each other! When two or more waves share the same space, they overlap. The result of two or more waves overlapping is called **interference**. **Figure 4** shows what happens when waves occupy the same space and interfere with each other.

interference the combination of two or more waves that results in a single wave

Constructive Interference

Constructive interference happens when the crests of one wave overlap the crests of another wave or waves. The troughs of the waves also overlap. When waves combine in this way, the energy carried by the waves is also able to combine. The result is a new wave that has higher crests and deeper troughs than the original waves had. In other words, the resulting wave has a larger amplitude than the original waves had.

✓ Reading Check How does constructive interference happen?

Figure 4 Constructive and Destructive Interference

Constructive Interference When waves combine by constructive interference, the combined wave has a larger amplitude.

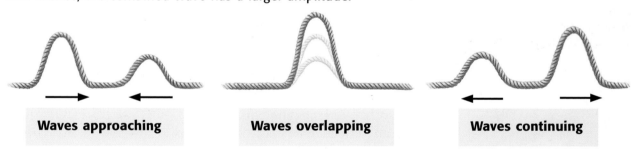

| Waves approaching | Waves overlapping | Waves continuing |

Destructive Interference When two waves with the same amplitude combine by destructive interference, they cancel each other out.

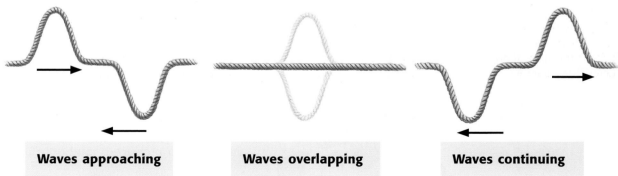

| Waves approaching | Waves overlapping | Waves continuing |

Destructive Interference

Destructive interference happens when the crests of one wave and the troughs of another wave overlap. The new wave has a smaller amplitude than the original waves had. When the waves involved in destructive interference have the same amplitude and meet each other at just the right time, the result is no wave at all.

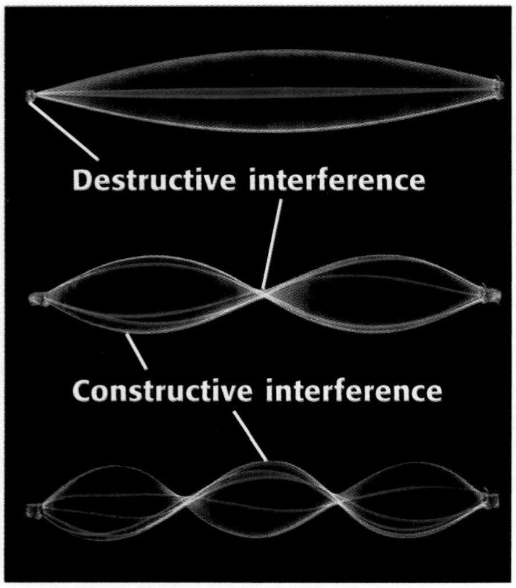

Standing Waves

If you tie one end of a rope to the back of a chair and move the other end up and down, the waves you make go down the rope and are reflected back. If you move the rope at certain frequencies, the rope appears to vibrate in loops, as shown in **Figure 5.** The loops come from the interference between the wave you made and the reflected wave. The resulting wave is called a **standing wave.** In a standing wave, certain parts of the wave are always at the rest position because of total destructive interference between all the waves. Other parts have a large amplitude because of constructive interference.

A standing wave only *looks* as if it is standing still. Waves are actually going in both directions. Standing waves can be formed with transverse waves, such as when a musician plucks a guitar string, as well as with longitudinal waves.

✓ **Reading Check** How can interference and reflection cause standing waves?

Figure 5 *When you move a rope at certain frequencies, you can create different standing waves.*

Figure 6 *A marimba produces notes through the resonance of air columns.*

a The marimba bars are struck with a mallet, causing the bars to vibrate.

b The vibrating bars cause the air in the columns to vibrate.

c The lengths of the columns have been adjusted so that the resonant frequency of the air column matches the frequency of the bar.

d The air column resonates with the bar, increasing the amplitude of the vibrations to produce a loud note.

Resonance

The frequencies at which standing waves are made are called *resonant frequencies*. When an object vibrating at or near the resonant frequency of a second object causes the second object to vibrate, **resonance** occurs. A resonating object absorbs energy from the vibrating object and vibrates, too. An example of resonance is shown in **Figure 6** on the previous page.

You may be familiar with another example of resonance at home—in your shower. When you sing in the shower, certain frequencies create standing waves in the air that fills the shower stall. The air resonates in much the same way that the air column in a marimba does. The amplitude of the sound waves becomes greater. So your voice sounds much louder.

standing wave a pattern of vibration that simulates a wave that is standing still

resonance a phenomenon that occurs when two objects naturally vibrate at the same frequency; the sound produced by one object causes the other object to vibrate

SECTION Review

Summary

- Waves reflect after hitting a barrier.
- Refraction is the bending of a wave when it passes through different media.
- Waves bend around barriers or through openings during diffraction.
- The result of two or more waves overlapping is called interference.
- Amplitude increases during constructive interference and decreases during destructive interference.
- Resonance occurs when a vibrating object causes another object to vibrate at one of its resonant frequencies.

Using Key Terms

Complete each of the following sentences by choosing the correct term from the word bank.

refraction   reflection
diffraction   interference

1. ___ happens when a wave passes from one medium to another at an angle.

2. The bending of a wave around a barrier is called ___.

3. We can see the moon because of the ___ of sunlight off it.

Understanding Key Ideas

4. The combining of waves as they overlap is known as
   a. interference.
   b. diffraction.
   c. refraction.
   d. resonance.

5. Name two wave interactions that can occur when a wave encounters a barrier.

6. Explain why you can hear two people talking even after they walk around a corner.

7. Explain what happens when two waves encounter one another in destructive interference.

Critical Thinking

8. **Making Inferences** Sometimes, when music is played loudly, you can feel your body shake. Explain what is happening in terms of resonance.

9. **Applying Concepts** How could two waves on a rope interfere so that the rope did not move at all?

Interpreting Graphics

10. In the image below, what sort of wave interaction is happening?

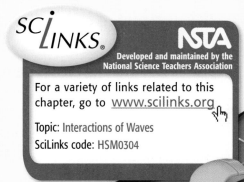

Developed and maintained by the National Science Teachers Association

For a variety of links related to this chapter, go to www.scilinks.org

Topic: Interactions of Waves
SciLinks code: HSM0304

Skills Practice Lab

OBJECTIVES

Form hypotheses about the energy and speed of waves.

Test your hypotheses by performing an experiment.

MATERIALS

- beaker, small
- newspaper
- pan, shallow, approximately 20 cm × 30 cm
- pencils (2)
- stopwatch
- water

SAFETY

Wave Energy and Speed

If you threw a rock into a pond, waves would carry energy away from the point of origin. But if you threw a large rock into a pond, would the waves carry more energy away from the point of origin than waves caused by a small rock? And would a large rock make waves that move faster than waves made by a small rock? In this lab, you'll answer these questions.

Ask a Question

1 In this lab, you will answer the following questions: Do waves made by a large disturbance carry more energy than waves made by a small disturbance? Do waves created by a large disturbance travel faster than waves created by a small disturbance?

Form a Hypothesis

2 Write a few sentences that answer the questions above.

Test the Hypothesis

3 Place the pan on a few sheets of newspaper. Using the small beaker, fill the pan with water.

4 Make sure that the water is still. Tap the surface of the water with the eraser end of one pencil. This tap represents the small disturbance. Record your observations about the size of the waves that are made and the path they take.

5 Repeat step 4. This time, use the stopwatch to record the amount of time it takes for one of the waves to reach the side of the pan. Record your data.

6 Using two pencils at once, repeat steps 4 and 5. These taps represent the large disturbance. (Try to use the same amount of force to tap the water that you used with just one pencil.) Observe and record your results.

Analyze the Results

1 **Describing Events** Compare the appearance of the waves created by one pencil with that of the waves created by two pencils. Were there any differences in amplitude (wave height)?

2 **Describing Events** Compare the amount of time required for the waves to reach the side of the pan. Did the waves travel faster when two pencils were used?

Draw Conclusions

3 **Drawing Conclusions** Do waves made by a large disturbance carry more energy than waves made by a small one? Explain your answer, using your results to support your answer. (Hint: Remember the relationship between amplitude and energy.)

4 **Drawing Conclusions** Do waves made by a large disturbance travel faster than waves made by a small one? Explain your answer.

Applying Your Data

A tsunami is a giant ocean wave that can reach a height of 30 m. Tsunamis that reach land can cause injury and enormous property damage. Using what you learned in this lab about wave energy and speed, explain why tsunamis are so dangerous. How do you think scientists can predict when tsunamis will reach land?

Chapter Review

USING KEY TERMS

For each pair of terms, explain how the meanings of the terms differ.

1 *longitudinal wave* and *transverse wave*

2 *wavelength* and *amplitude*

3 *reflection* and *refraction*

UNDERSTANDING KEY IDEAS

Multiple Choice

4 As the wavelength increases, the frequency

a. decreases.

b. increases.

c. remains the same.

d. increases and then decreases.

5 Waves transfer

a. matter.   c. particles.

b. energy.   d. water.

6 Refraction occurs when a wave enters a new medium at an angle because

a. the frequency changes.

b. the amplitude changes.

c. the wave speed changes.

d. None of the above

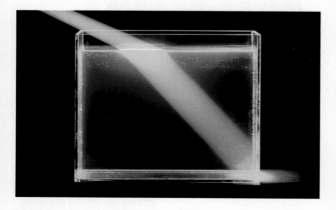

7 The wave property that is related to the height of a wave is the

a. wavelength.

b. amplitude.

c. frequency.

d. wave speed.

8 During constructive interference,

a. the amplitude increases.

b. the frequency decreases.

c. the wave speed increases.

d. All of the above

9 Waves that don't require a medium are

a. longitudinal waves.

b. electromagnetic waves.

c. surface waves.

d. mechanical waves.

Short Answer

10 Draw a transverse wave and a longitudinal wave. Label a crest, a trough, a compression, a rarefaction, and wavelengths. Also, label the amplitude on the transverse wave.

11 What is the relationship between frequency, wave speed, and wavelength?

Math Skills

12 A fisherman in a row boat notices that one wave crest passes his fishing line every 5 s. He estimates the distance between the crests to be 1.5 m and estimates that the crests of the waves are 0.5 m above the troughs. Using this data, determine the amplitude and speed of the waves.

13 Concept Mapping Use the following terms to create a concept map: *wave, refraction, transverse wave, longitudinal wave, wavelength, wave speed,* and *diffraction.*

14 Analyzing Ideas You have lost the paddles for the canoe you rented, and the canoe has drifted to the center of a pond. You need to get it back to the shore, but you do not want to get wet by swimming in the pond. Your friend suggests that you drop rocks behind the canoe to create waves that will push the canoe toward the shore. Will this solution work? Why or why not?

15 Applying Concepts Some opera singers can use their powerful voices to break crystal glasses. To do this, they sing one note very loudly and hold it for a long time. While the opera singer holds the note, the walls of the glass move back and forth until the glass shatters. Explain in terms of resonance how the glass shatters.

16 Analyzing Processes After setting up stereo speakers in your school's music room, you notice that in certain areas of the room, the sound from the speakers is very loud. In other areas, the sound is very soft. Using the concept of interference, explain why the sound levels in the music room vary.

17 Predicting Consequences A certain sound wave travels through water with a certain wavelength, frequency, and wave speed. A second sound wave with twice the frequency of the first wave then travels through the same water. What is the second wave's wavelength and wave speed compared to those of the first wave?

18 Look at the waves below. Rank the waves from highest energy to lowest energy, and explain your reasoning.

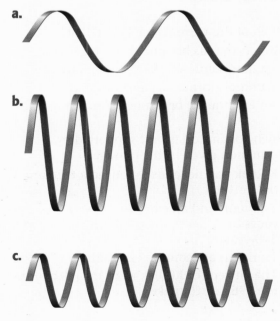

a.

b.

c.

Standardized Test Preparation

Read each of the passages below. Then, answer the questions that follow each passage.

Passage 1 On March 27, 1964, a powerful earthquake rocked Alaska. The earthquake started on land near Anchorage, and the seismic waves spread quickly in all directions. The earthquake created a series of ocean waves called <u>tsunamis</u> in the Gulf of Alaska. In the deep water of the gulf, the tsunamis were short and far apart. But as these waves entered the shallow water surrounding Kodiak Island, off the coast of Alaska, they became taller and closer together. Some reached heights of nearly 30 m! The destructive forces of the earthquake and tsunamis killed 21 people and caused $10 million in damage to Kodiak, which made this marine disaster the worst in the town's 200-year history.

1. In the passage, what does *tsunami* mean?
A a seismic wave
B an earthquake
C an ocean wave
D a body of water

2. Which of these events happened first?
F The tsunamis became closer together.
G Tsunamis entered the shallow water.
H Tsunamis formed in the Gulf of Alaska.
I An earthquake began near Anchorage.

3. Which conclusion is **best** supported by information given in the passage?
A Kodiak had never experienced a tsunami before 1964.
B Tsunamis and an earthquake were the cause of Kodiak's worst marine disaster in 200 years.
C Tsunamis are common in Kodiak.
D The citizens of Kodiak went into debt after the 1964 earthquake.

Passage 2 Resonance was partially responsible for the destruction of the Tacoma Narrows Bridge, in Washington. The bridge opened in July 1940 and soon earned the nickname Galloping Gertie because of its wavelike motions. These motions were created by wind that blew across the bridge. The wind caused vibrations that were close to a resonant frequency of the bridge. Because the bridge was in resonance, it absorbed a large amount of energy from the wind, which caused it to vibrate with a large amplitude. On November 7, 1940, a supporting cable slipped, and the bridge began to twist. The twisting of the bridge, combined with high winds, further increased the amplitude of the bridge's motion. Within hours, the amplitude became so great that the bridge collapsed. Luckily, all of the people on the bridge that day were able to escape before it crashed into the river below.

1. What caused wavelike motions in the Tacoma Narrows Bridge?
A wind that caused vibrations that were close to the resonant frequency of the bridge
B vibrations from cars going over the bridge
C twisting of a broken support cable
D an earthquake

2. Why did the bridge collapse?
F A supporting cable slipped.
G It absorbed a great amount of energy from the wind.
H The amplitude of the bridge's vibrations became great enough.
I Wind blew across it.

Use the figure below to answer the questions that follow.

Read each question below, and choose the best answer.

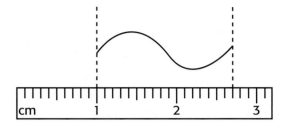

1. This wave was generated in a laboratory investigation. What is the wavelength of the wave?

A 1.5 cm

B 1.7 cm

C 2.0 cm

D 2.7 cm

2. If the frequency of the wave shown were doubled, what would the wavelength of the wave be?

F 0.85 cm

G 1.35 cm

H 3.4 cm

I 5.4 cm

3. What is the amplitude of the wave shown?

A 0.85 cm

B 1.7 cm

C 2.7 cm

D There is not enough information to determine the answer.

1. How is the product of $5 \times 5 \times 5 \times 2 \times 2 \times 2 \times 2$ expressed in exponential notation?

A $3^5 \times 4^2$

B $5^3 \times 2^4$

C $5^7 \times 2^7$

D 10^7

2. Mannie purchased 8.9 kg of dog food from the veterinarian. How many grams of dog food did he purchase?

F 8,900 g

G 890 g

H 89 g

I 0.89 g

3. What is the area of a rectangle whose sides are 3 cm long and 7.5 cm long?

A 10.5 cm^2

B 12 cm^2

C 21 cm^2

D 22.5 cm^2

4. An underwater sound wave traveled 1.5 km in 1 s. How far would it travel in 4 s?

F 5.0 km

G 5.5 km

H 6.0 km

I 6.5 km

5. During a tennis game, the person serving the ball is allowed only 2 serves to start a point. Hannah plays a tennis match and is able to use 50 of her 63 first serves to start a point. What is the **best** estimate of Hannah's first-service percentage?

A 126%

B 88%

C 81.5%

D 79%

Science in Action

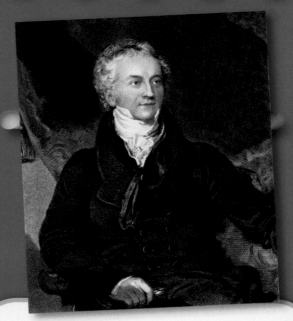

Science, Technology, and Society

The Ultimate Telescope

The largest telescopes in the world don't depend on visible light, lenses, or mirrors. Instead, they collect radio waves from the far reaches of outer space. One radio telescope, called the Very Large Array (VLA), is located in a remote desert in New Mexico.

Just as you can detect light waves from stars with your eyes, radio waves emitted from objects in space can be detected with radio telescopes. The Very Large Array consists of 27 radio telescopes like the ones in the photo above.

Math ACTiViTY

Radio waves travel about 300,000,000 m/s. The M100 galaxy is about 5.68×10^{23} m away from Earth. How long, in years, does it take radio waves from M100 to be detected by the VLA?

Scientific Discoveries

The Wave Nature of Light

Have you ever wondered what light really is? Many early scientists did. One of them, the great 17th-century scientist Isaac Newton, did some experiments and decided that light consisted of particles. But when experimenting with lenses, Newton observed some things that he could not explain.

Around 1800, the scientist Thomas Young did more experiments on light and found that it diffracted when it passed through slits. Young concluded that light could be thought of as waves. Although scientists were slow to accept this idea, they now know that light is both particle-like and wavelike.

Language Arts ACTiViTY

WRITING SKILL Thomas Young said, "The nature of light is a subject of no material importance to the concerns of life or to the practice of the arts, but it is in many other respects extremely interesting." Write a brief essay in which you answer the following questions: What do you think Young meant? Do you agree with him? How would you respond to his statement?

Estela Zavala

Ultrasonographer Estela Zavala is a registered diagnostic medical ultrasonographer who works at Austin Radiological Association in Austin, Texas. Most people have seen a picture of a sonogram showing an unborn baby inside its mother's womb. Ultrasound technologists make these images with an ultrasound machine, which sends harmless, high-frequency sound waves into the body. Zavala uses ultrasound to form images of organs in the body. Zavala says about her education, "After graduating from high school, I went to an X-ray school to be licensed as an X-ray technologist. First, I went to an intensive one-month training program. After that, I worked for a licensed radiologist for about a year. Finally, I attended a year-long ultrasound program at a local community college before becoming fully licensed." What Zavala likes best about her job is being able to help people by finding out what is wrong with them without surgery. Before ultrasound, surgery was the only way to find out about the health of someone's organs.

Social Studies ACTiViTY

WRITING SKILL Research the different ways in which ultrasound technology is used in medical practice today. Write a few paragraphs about what you learn.

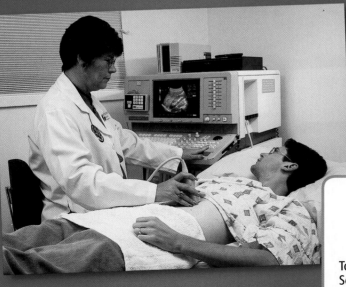

To learn more about these Science in Action topics, visit **go.hrw.com** and type in the keyword **HP5WAVF.**

Current Science

Check out Current Science® articles related to this chapter by visiting **go.hrw.com. Just type in the keyword HP5CS20.**

21

The Nature of Sound

SECTION **1** What Is Sound? 600

SECTION **2** Properties of Sound. . . 606

SECTION **3** Interactions of
Sound Waves 612

SECTION **4** Sound Quality. 618

Chapter Lab 622
Chapter Review 624
Standardized Test Preparation 626
Science in Action. 628

About the PHOTO

Look at these dolphins swimming swiftly and silently through their watery world. Wait a minute—swiftly? Yes. Silently? No way! Dolphins use sound—clicks, squeaks, and other noises—to communicate. Dolphins also use sound to locate their food by echolocation and to find their way through murky water.

PRE-READING ACTIVITY

Graphic Organizer

Concept Map Before you read the chapter, create the graphic organizer entitled "Concept Map" described in the **Study Skills** section of the Appendix. As you read the chapter, fill in the concept map with details about each type of sound interaction.

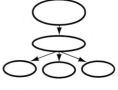

START-UP ACTIVITY

A Homemade Guitar

In this chapter, you will learn about sound. You can start by making your own guitar. It won't sound as good as a real guitar, but it will help you explore the nature of sound.

Procedure

1. Stretch a **rubber band** lengthwise around an empty **shoe box.** Place the box hollow side up. Pluck the rubber band gently. Describe what you hear.

2. Stretch **another rubber band of a different thickness** around the box. Pluck both rubber bands. Describe the differences in the sounds.

3. Put a **pencil** across the center of the box and under the rubber bands, and pluck again. Compare this sound with the sound you heard before the pencil was used.

4. Move the pencil closer to one end of the shoe box. Pluck on both sides of the pencil. Describe the differences in the sounds you hear.

Analysis

1. How did the thicknesses of the rubber bands affect the sound?

2. In steps 3 and 4, you changed the length of the vibrating part of the rubber bands. What is the relationship between the vibrating length of the rubber band and the sound that you hear?

The Nature of Sound   **599**

SECTION 1

What Is Sound?

You are in a restaurant, and without warning, you hear a loud crash. A waiter dropped a tray of dishes. What a mess! But why did dropping the dishes make such a loud sound?

READING WARM-UP

Objectives

- Describe how vibrations cause sound.
- Explain how sound is transmitted through a medium.
- Explain how the human ear works, and identify its parts.
- Identify ways to protect your hearing.

Terms to Learn

sound wave
medium

READING STRATEGY

Prediction Guide Before reading this section, predict whether each of the following statements is true or false:

- Sound waves are made by vibrations.
- Sound waves push air particles along until they reach your ear.

In this section, you'll find out what causes sound and what characteristics all sounds have in common. You'll also learn how your ears detect sound and how you can protect your hearing.

Sound and Vibrations

As different as they are, all sounds have some things in common. One characteristic of sound is that it is created by vibrations. A *vibration* is the complete back-and-forth motion of an object. **Figure 1** shows one way sound is made by vibrations.

Figure 1 Sounds from a Stereo Speaker

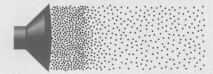

a Electrical signals make the speaker vibrate. As the speaker cone moves forward, it pushes the air particles in front of it closer together, creating a region of higher density and pressure called a *compression.*

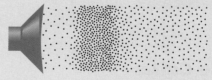

b As the speaker cone moves backward, air particles close to the cone become less crowded, creating a region of lower density and pressure called a *rarefaction.*

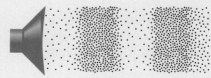

c For each vibration, a compression and a rarefaction are formed. As the compressions and rarefactions travel away from the speaker, sound is transmitted through the air.

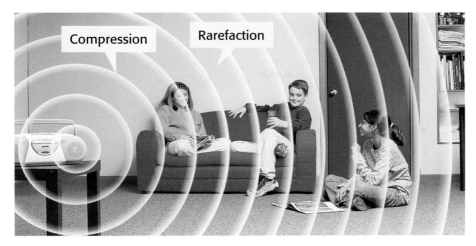

Figure 2 *You can't actually see sound waves, but they can be represented by spheres that spread out in all directions.*

Sound Waves

Longitudinal (LAHN juh TOOD'n uhl) waves are made of compressions and rarefactions. A **sound wave** is a longitudinal wave caused by vibrations and carried through a substance. The particles of the substance, such as air particles, vibrate back and forth along the path that the sound wave travels. Sound is transmitted through the vibrations and collisions of the particles. Because the particles vibrate back and forth along the paths that sound travels, sound travels as longitudinal waves.

Sound waves travel in all directions away from their source, as shown in **Figure 2.** However, air or other matter does not travel with the sound waves. The particles of air only vibrate back and forth. If air did travel with sound, wind gusts from music speakers would blow you over at a school dance!

✓ Reading Check What do sound waves consist of? (*See the Appendix for answers to Reading Checks.*)

sound wave a longitudinal wave that is caused by vibrations and that travels through a material medium

Good Vibrations

1. Gently strike a **tuning fork** on a **rubber eraser.** Watch the prongs, and listen for a sound. Describe what you see and what you hear.

2. Lightly touch the fork with your fingers. What do you feel?

3. Grasp the prongs of the fork firmly with your hand. What happens to the sound?

4. Strike the tuning fork on the eraser again, and dip the prongs in a **cup of water.** Describe what happens to the water.

5. Record your observations.

Figure 3 Tubing is connected to a pump that is removing air from the jar. As the air is removed, the ringing alarm clock sounds quieter and quieter.

medium a physical environment in which phenomena occur

Sound and Media

Another characteristic of sound is that all sound waves require a medium (plural, *media*). A **medium** is a substance through which a wave can travel. Most of the sounds that you hear travel through air at least part of the time. But sound waves can also travel through other materials, such as water, glass, and metal.

In a vacuum, however, there are no particles to vibrate. So, no sound can be made in a vacuum. This fact helps to explain the effect described in **Figure 3.** Sound must travel through air or some other medium to reach your ears and be detected.

✓ *Reading Check* What does sound need in order to travel?

How You Detect Sound

Imagine that you are watching a suspenseful movie. Just before a door is opened, the background music becomes louder. You know that there is something scary behind that door! Now, imagine watching the same scene without the sound. You would have more difficulty figuring out what's going on if there were no sound.

Figure 4 shows how your ears change sound waves into electrical signals that allow you to hear. First, the outer ear collects sound waves. The vibrations then go to your middle ear. Very small organs increase the size of the vibrations here. These vibrations are then picked up by organs in your inner ear. Your inner ear changes vibrations into electrical signals that your brain interprets as sound.

Figure 4 How the Human Ear Works

ⓐ The **outer ear** acts as a funnel for sound waves. The *pinna* collects sound waves and directs them into the *ear canal.*

ⓑ In the **middle ear,** three bones—the *hammer, anvil,* and *stirrup*—act as levers to increase the size of the vibrations.

ⓒ In the **inner ear,** vibrations created by sound are changed into electrical signals for the brain to interpret.

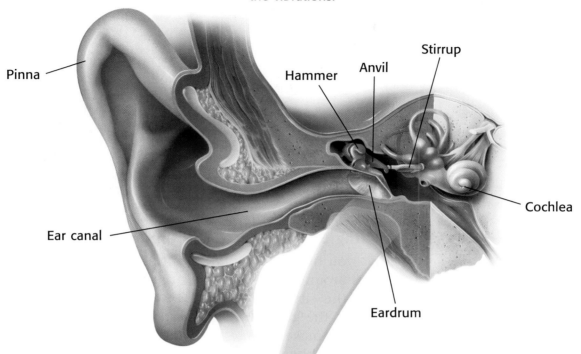

Pinna

Ear canal

Hammer Anvil Stirrup

Cochlea

Eardrum

❶ Sound waves vibrate the *eardrum*—a lightly stretched membrane that is the entrance to the middle ear.

❷ The vibration of the eardrum makes the hammer vibrate, which, in turn, makes the anvil and stirrup vibrate.

❸ The stirrup vibrates the *oval window*—the entrance to the inner ear.

❹ The vibrations of the oval window create waves in the liquid inside the *cochlea.*

❺ Movement of the liquid causes tiny hair cells inside the cochlea to bend.

❻ The bending of the hair cells stimulates nerves, which send electrical signals to the brain.

Figure 5 *Sound is made whether or not anyone is around to hear it.*

INTERNET ACTIVITY

For another activity related to this chapter, go to **go.hrw.com** and type in the keyword **HP5SNDW.**

Making Sound Versus Hearing Sound

Have you heard this riddle? If a tree falls in the forest and no one is around to hear it, does the tree make a sound? Think about the situation pictured in **Figure 5.** When a tree falls and hits the ground, the tree and the ground vibrate. These vibrations make compressions and rarefactions in the surrounding air. So, there would be a sound!

Making sound is separate from detecting sound. The fact that no one heard the tree fall doesn't mean that there wasn't a sound. A sound was made—it just wasn't heard.

Hearing Loss and Deafness

The many parts of the ear must work together for you to hear sounds. If any part of the ear is damaged or does not work properly, hearing loss or deafness may result.

One of the most common types of hearing loss is called *tinnitus* (ti NIET us), which results from long-term exposure to loud sounds. Loud sounds can cause damage to the hair cells and nerve endings in the cochlea. Once these hairs are damaged, they do not grow back. Damage to the cochlea or any other part of the inner ear usually results in permanent hearing loss.

People who have tinnitus often say they have a ringing in their ears. They also have trouble understanding other people and hearing the difference between words that sound alike. Tinnitus can affect people of any age. Fortunately, tinnitus can be prevented.

✓ Reading Check What causes tinnitus?

Protecting Your Hearing

Short exposures to sounds that are loud enough to be painful can cause hearing loss. Your hearing can also be damaged by loud sounds that are not quite painful, if you are exposed to them for long periods of time. There are some simple things you can do to protect your hearing. Loud sounds can be blocked out by earplugs. You can listen at a lower volume when you are using headphones, as in **Figure 6.** You can also move away from loud sounds. If you are near a speaker playing loud music, just move away from it. When you double the distance between yourself and a loud sound, the sound's intensity to your ears will be one-fourth of what it was before.

Figure 6 *Turning your radio down can help prevent hearing loss, especially when you use headphones.*

SECTION Review

Summary

- All sounds are generated by vibrations.
- Sounds travel as longitudinal waves consisting of compressions and rarefactions.
- Sound waves travel in all directions away from their source.
- Sound waves require a medium through which to travel. Sound cannot travel in a vacuum.
- Your ears convert sound into electrical impulses that are sent to your brain.
- Exposure to loud sounds can cause hearing damage.
- Using earplugs and lowering the volume of sounds can prevent hearing damage.

Using Key Terms

1. Use the following terms in the same sentence: *sound wave* and *medium.*

Understanding Key Ideas

2. Sound travels as
   a. transverse waves.
   b. longitudinal waves.
   c. shock waves.
   d. airwaves.

3. Which part of the ear increases the size of the vibrations of sound waves entering the ear?
   a. outer ear
   b. ear canal
   c. middle ear
   d. inner ear

4. Name two ways of protecting your hearing.

Critical Thinking

5. **Analyzing Processes** Explain why a person at a rock concert will not feel gusts of wind coming out of the speakers.

6. **Analyzing Ideas** If a meteorite crashed on the moon, would you be able to hear it on Earth? Why, or why not?

7. **Identifying Relationships** Recall the breaking dishes mentioned at the beginning of this section. Why was the sound that they made so loud?

Interpreting Graphics

Use the diagram of a wave below to answer the questions that follow.

8. What kind of wave is this?

9. Draw a sketch of the diagram on a separate sheet of paper, and label the compressions and rarefactions.

10. How do vibrations make these kinds of waves?

For a variety of links related to this chapter, go to www.scilinks.org

Topic: The Ear; What Is Sound?
SciLinks code: HSM0440; HSM1663

Properties of Sound

Imagine that you are swimming in a neighborhood pool. You can hear the high, loud laughter of small children and the soft splashing of the waves at the edge of the pool.

Why are some sounds loud, soft, high, or low? The differences between sounds depend on the properties of the sound waves. In this section, you will learn about properties of sound.

The Speed of Sound

Suppose you are standing at one end of a pool and two people from the opposite end of the pool yell at the same time. You would hear their voices at the same time. The reason is that the speed of sound depends only on the medium in which the sound is traveling. So, you would hear them at the same time—even if one person yelled louder!

How the Speed of Sound Can Change

Table 1 shows how the speed of sound varies in different media. Sound travels quickly through air, but it travels even faster in liquids and even faster in solids.

Temperature also affects the speed of sound. In general, the cooler the medium is, the slower the speed of sound. Particles of cool materials move more slowly and transmit energy more slowly than particles do in warmer materials. In 1947, pilot Chuck Yeager became the first person to travel faster than the speed of sound. Yeager flew the airplane shown in **Figure 1** at 293 m/s (about 480 mi/h) at 12,000 m above sea level. At that altitude, the temperature of the air is so low that the speed of sound is only 290 m/s.

READING WARM-UP

Objectives

● Compare the speed of sound in different media.

● Explain how frequency and pitch are related.

● Describe the Doppler effect, and give examples of it.

● Explain how amplitude and loudness are related.

● Describe how amplitude and frequency can be "seen" on an oscilloscope.

Terms to Learn

pitch   loudness
Doppler effect   decibel

READING STRATEGY

Reading Organizer As you read this section, create an outline of the section. Use the headings from the section in your outline.

Table 1 **Speed of Sound in Different Media**

Medium	Speed (m/s)
Air (0°C)	331
Air (20°C)	343
Air (100°C)	366
Water (20°C)	1,482
Steel (20°C)	5,200

Figure 1 *The X-1 airplane was the first vehicle to move faster than the speed of sound.*

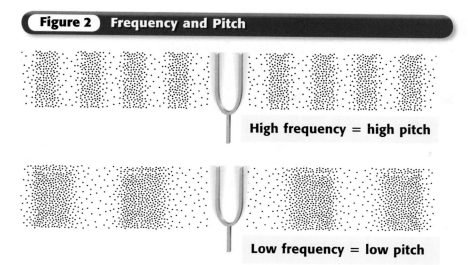

Figure 2 Frequency and Pitch

High frequency = high pitch

Low frequency = low pitch

Pitch and Frequency

How low or high a sound seems to be is the **pitch** of that sound. The *frequency* of a wave is the number of crests or troughs that are made in a given time. The pitch of a sound is related to the frequency of the sound wave, as shown in **Figure 2.** Frequency is expressed in hertz (Hz), where 1 Hz = 1 wave per second. For example, the lowest note on a piano is about 40 Hz. The screech of a bat is 10,000 Hz or higher.

✓ Reading Check What is frequency? (*See the Appendix for answers to Reading Checks.*)

Frequency and Hearing

If you see someone blow a dog whistle, the whistle seems silent to you. The reason is that the frequency of the sound wave is out of the range of human hearing. But the dog hears the whistle and comes running! **Table 2** compares the range of frequencies that humans and animals can hear. Sounds that have a frequency too high for people to hear are called *ultrasonic.*

pitch a measure of how high or low a sound is perceived to be, depending on the frequency of the sound wave

The Speed of Sound
The speed of sound depends on the medium through which sound is traveling and the medium's temperature. Sound travels at 343 m/s through air at a temperature of 20°C. How far will sound travel in 20°C air in 5 s?
  The speed of sound in steel at 20°C is 5,200 m/s. How far can sound travel in 5 s through steel at 20°C?

Table 2 Frequencies Heard by Different Animals	
Animal	**Frequency range (Hz)**
Bat	2,000 to 110,000
Porpoise	75 to 150,000
Cat	45 to 64,000
Beluga whale	1,000 to 123,000
Elephant	16 to 12,000
Human	20 to 20,000
Dog	67 to 45,000

Figure 3 The Doppler Effect

a A car with its horn honking moves toward the sound waves going in the same direction. A person in front of the car hears sound waves that are closer together.

b The car moves away from the sound waves going in the opposite direction. A person behind the car hears sound waves that are farther apart and have a lower frequency.

The Doppler Effect

Have you ever been passed by a car with its horn honking? If so, you probably noticed the sudden change in pitch—sort of an *EEEEEOOoooowwn* sound—as the car went past you. The pitch you heard was higher as the car moved toward you than it was after the car passed. This higher pitch was a result of the Doppler effect. For sound waves, the **Doppler effect** is the apparent change in the frequency of a sound caused by the motion of either the listener or the source of the sound. **Figure 3** shows how the Doppler effect works.

In a moving sound source, such as a car with its horn honking, sound waves that are moving forward are going the same direction the car is moving. As a result, the compressions and rarefactions of the sound wave will be closer together than they would be if the sound source was not moving. To a person in front of the car, the frequency and pitch of the sound seem high. After the car passes, it is moving in the opposite direction that the sound waves are moving. To a person behind the car, the frequency and pitch of the sound seem low. The driver always hears the same pitch because the driver is moving with the car.

Doppler effect an observed change in the frequency of a wave when the source or observer is moving

Loudness and Amplitude

If you gently tap a drum, you will hear a soft rumbling. But if you strike the drum with a large force, you will hear a much louder sound! By changing the force you use to strike the drum, you change the loudness of the sound that is created. **Loudness** is a measure of how well a sound can be heard.

Energy and Vibration

Look at **Figure 4.** The harder you strike a drum, the louder the boom. As you strike the drum harder, you transfer more energy to the drum. The drum moves with a larger vibration and transfers more energy to the air around it. This increase in energy causes air particles to vibrate farther from their rest positions.

Increasing Amplitude

When you strike a drum harder, you are increasing the amplitude of the sound waves being made. The *amplitude* of a wave is the largest distance the particles in a wave vibrate from their rest positions. The larger the amplitude, the louder the sound. And the smaller the amplitude, the softer the sound. One way to increase the loudness of a sound is to use an amplifier, shown in **Figure 5.** An amplifier receives sound signals in the form of electric current. The amplifier then increases the energy and makes the sound louder.

✓ Reading Check What is the relationship between the amplitude of a sound and its energy of vibration?

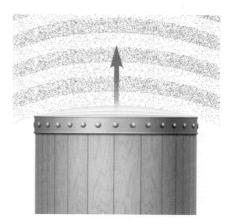

Figure 4 *When a drum is struck hard, it vibrates with a lot of energy, making a loud sound.*

loudness the extent to which a sound can be heard

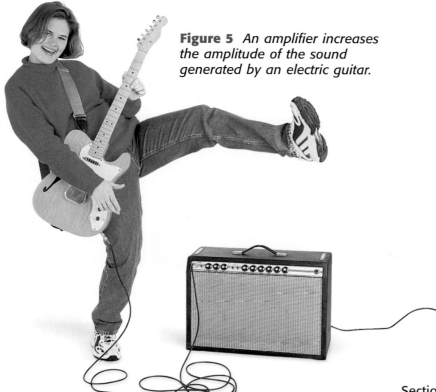

Figure 5 *An amplifier increases the amplitude of the sound generated by an electric guitar.*

Quick Lab

Sounding Board

1. With one hand, hold a **ruler** on your **desk** so that one end of it hangs over the edge.

2. With your other hand, pull the free end of the ruler up a few centimeters, and let go.

3. Try pulling the ruler up different distances. How does the distance affect the sounds you hear? What property of the sound wave are you changing?

4. Change the length of the part that hangs over the edge. What property of the sound wave is affected? Record your answers and observations.

Table 3 Decibel Levels of Common Sounds

Decibel level	Sound
0	the softest sounds you can hear
20	whisper
25	purring cat
60	normal conversation
80	lawn mower, vacuum cleaner, truck traffic
100	chain saw, snowmobile
115	sandblaster, loud rock concert, automobile horn
120	threshold of pain
140	jet engine 30 m away
200	rocket engine 50 m away

decibel the most common unit used to measure loudness (symbol, dB)

Measuring Loudness

The most common unit used to express loudness is the **decibel** (dB). The softest sounds an average human can hear are at a level of 0 dB. Sounds that are at 120 dB or higher can be painful. **Table 3** shows some common sounds and their decibel levels.

"Seeing" Amplitude and Frequency

Sound waves are invisible. However, technology can provide a way to "see" sound waves. A device called an *oscilloscope* (uh SIL uh SKOHP) can graph representations of sound waves, as shown in **Figure 6.** Notice that the graphs look like transverse waves instead of longitudinal waves.

 **Reading Check** What does an oscilloscope do?

Figure 6 "Seeing" Sounds

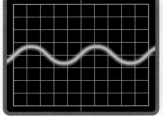 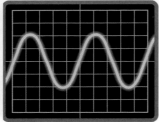 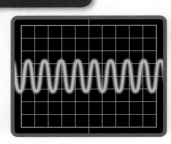 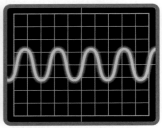

The graph on the right has a **larger amplitude** than the graph on the left. So, the sound represented on the right is **louder** than the one represented on the left.

The graph on the right has a **lower frequency** than the one on the left. So, the sound represented on the right has a **lower pitch** than the one represented on the left.

From Sound to Electrical Signal

An oscilloscope is shown in **Figure 7**. A microphone is attached to the oscilloscope and changes a sound wave into an electrical signal. The electrical signal is graphed on the screen in the form of a wave. The graph shows the sound as if it were a transverse wave. So, the sound's amplitude and frequency are easier to see. The highest points (crests) of these waves represent compressions, and the lowest points (troughs) represent rarefactions. By looking at the displays on the oscilloscope, you can quickly see the differences in amplitude and frequency of different sound waves.

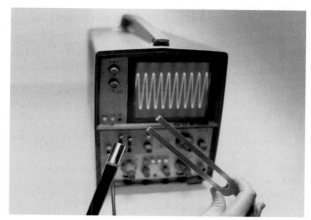

Figure 7 *An oscilloscope can be used to represent sounds.*

SECTION Review

Summary

- The speed of sound depends on the medium and the temperature.
- The pitch of a sound becomes higher as the frequency of the sound wave becomes higher. Frequency is expressed in units of Hertz (Hz), which is equivalent to waves per second.
- The Doppler effect is the apparent change in frequency of a sound caused by the motion of either the listener or the source of the sound.
- Loudness increases with the amplitude of the sound. Loudness is expressed in decibels.
- The amplitude and frequency of a sound can be measured electronically by an oscilloscope.

Using Key Terms

1. In your own words, write a definition for the term *pitch*.

2. Use the following terms in the same sentence: *loudness* and *decibel*.

Understanding Key Ideas

3. At the same temperature, in which medium does sound travel fastest?
   a. air
   b. liquid
   c. solid
   d. It travels at the same speed through all media.

4. In general, how does the temperature of a medium affect the speed of sound through that medium?

5. What property of waves affects the pitch of a sound?

6. How does an oscilloscope allow sound waves to be "seen"?

Math Skills

7. You see a distant flash of lightning, and then you hear a thunderclap 2 s later. The sound of the thunder moves at 343 m/s. How far away was the lightning?

8. In water that is near 0°C, a submarine sends out a sonar signal (a sound wave). The signal travels 1500 m/s and reaches an underwater mountain in 4 s. How far away is the mountain?

Critical Thinking

9. **Analyzing Processes** Will a listener notice the Doppler effect if both the listener and the source of the sound are traveling toward each other? Explain your answer.

10. **Predicting Consequences** A drum is struck gently, then is struck harder. What will be the difference in the amplitude of the sounds made? What will be the difference in the frequency of the sounds made?

Interactions of Sound Waves

Have you ever heard of a sea canary? It's not a bird! It's a whale! Beluga whales are sometimes called sea canaries because of the many different sounds they make.

Dolphins, beluga whales, and many other animals that live in the sea use sound to communicate. Beluga whales also rely on reflected sound waves to find fish, crabs, and shrimp to eat. In this section, you will learn about reflection and other interactions of sound waves. You will also learn how bats, dolphins, and whales use sound to find food.

Reflection of Sound Waves

Reflection is the bouncing back of a wave after it strikes a barrier. You're probably already familiar with a reflected sound wave, otherwise known as an **echo.** The strength of a reflected sound wave depends on the reflecting surface. Sound waves reflect best off smooth, hard surfaces. Look at **Figure 1.** A shout in an empty gymnasium can produce an echo, but a shout in an auditorium usually does not.

The difference is that the walls of an auditorium are usually designed so that they absorb sound. If sound waves hit a flat, hard surface, they will reflect back. Reflection of sound waves doesn't matter much in a gymnasium. But you don't want to hear echoes while listening to a musical performance!

echo a reflected sound wave

Figure 1   **Sound Reflection and Absorption**

Sound waves easily reflect off the smooth, hard walls of a gymnasium. For this reason, you hear an echo.

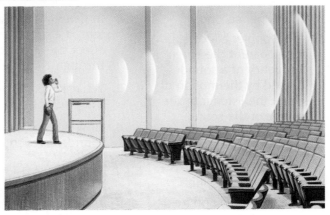

In well-designed auditoriums, echoes are reduced by soft materials that absorb sound waves and by irregular shapes that scatter sound waves.

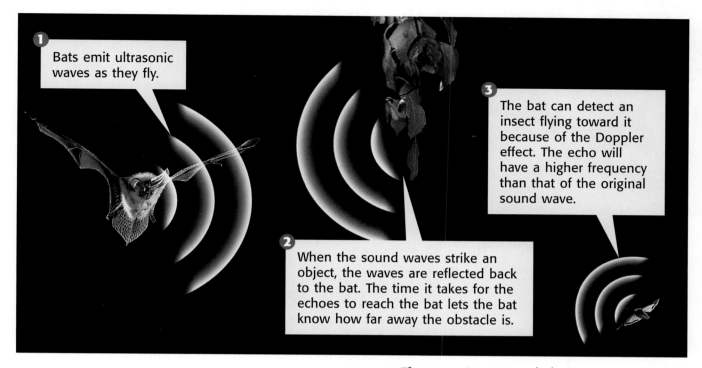

1 Bats emit ultrasonic waves as they fly.

2 When the sound waves strike an object, the waves are reflected back to the bat. The time it takes for the echoes to reach the bat lets the bat know how far away the obstacle is.

3 The bat can detect an insect flying toward it because of the Doppler effect. The echo will have a higher frequency than that of the original sound wave.

Figure 2 *Bats use echolocation to navigate around barriers and to find insects to eat.*

Echolocation

Beluga whales use echoes to find food. The use of reflected sound waves to find objects is called **echolocation.** Other animals—such as dolphins, bats, and some kinds of birds—also use echolocation to hunt food and to find objects in their paths. **Figure 2** shows how echolocation works. Animals that use echolocation can tell how far away something is based on how long it takes sound waves to echo back to their ears. Some animals, such as bats, also make use of the Doppler effect to tell if another moving object, such as an insect, is moving toward it or away from it.

echolocation the process of using reflected sound waves to find objects; used by animals such as bats

✓ *Reading Check* **How is echolocation useful to some animals?** (*See the Appendix for answers to Reading Checks.*)

Echolocation Technology

People use echoes to locate objects underwater by using sonar (which stands for **s**ound **n**avigation **a**nd **r**anging). *Sonar* is a type of electronic echolocation. **Figure 3** shows how sonar works. Ultrasonic waves are used because their short wavelengths give more details about the objects they reflect off. Sonar can also help navigators on ships avoid icebergs and can help oceanographers map the ocean floor.

Figure 3 *A fish finder sends ultrasonic waves down into the water. The time it takes for the echo to return helps determine the location of the fish.*

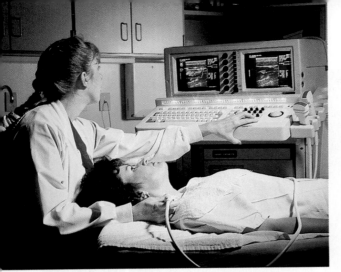

Figure 4 *Images created by ultrasonography are fuzzy, but they are a safe way to see inside a patient's body.*

Ultrasonography

Ultrasonography (UHL truh soh NAHG ruh fee) is a medical procedure that uses echoes to "see" inside a patient's body without doing surgery. A special device makes ultrasonic waves with a frequency that can be from 1 million to 10 million hertz, which reflect off the patient's internal organs. These echoes are then changed into images that can be seen on a television screen, as shown in **Figure 4.** Ultrasonography is used to examine kidneys, gallbladders, and other organs. It is also used to check the development of an unborn baby in a mother's body. Ultrasonic waves are less harmful to human tissue than X rays are.

Interference of Sound Waves

Sound waves also interact through interference. **Interference** happens when two or more waves overlap. **Figure 5** shows how two sound waves can combine by both constructive and destructive interference.

Orchestras and bands make use of constructive interference when several instruments of the same kind play the same notes. Interference of the sound waves causes the combined amplitude to increase, resulting in a louder sound. But destructive interference may keep some members of the audience from hearing the concert well. In certain places in an auditorium, sound waves reflecting off the walls interfere destructively with the sound waves from the stage.

interference the combination of two or more waves that results in a single wave

sonic boom the explosive sound heard when a shock wave from an object traveling faster than the speed of sound reaches a person's ears

✓ **Reading Check** What are the two kinds of sound wave interference?

Figure 5 **Constructive and Destructive Interference**

Sound waves from two speakers producing sound of the same frequency combine by both constructive and destructive interference.

Constructive Interference
As the compressions of one wave overlap the compressions of another wave, the sound will be louder because the amplitude is increased.

Destructive Interference
As the compressions of one wave overlap the rarefactions of another wave, the sound will be softer because the amplitude is decreased.

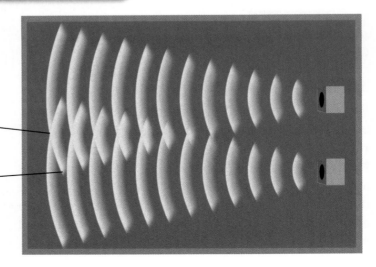

Interference and the Sound Barrier

As the source of a sound—such as a jet plane—gets close to the speed of sound, the sound waves in front of the jet plane get closer and closer together. The result is constructive interference. **Figure 6** shows what happens as a jet plane reaches the speed of sound.

For the jet in **Figure 6** to go faster than the speed of sound, the jet must overcome the pressure of the compressed sound waves. **Figure 7** shows what happens as soon as the jet reaches supersonic speeds—speeds faster than the speed of sound. At these speeds, the sound waves trail off behind the jet. At their outer edges, the sound waves combine by constructive interference to form a *shock wave*.

A **sonic boom** is the explosive sound heard when a shock wave reaches your ears. Sonic booms can be so loud that they can hurt your ears and break windows. They can even make the ground shake as it does during an earthquake.

Figure 6 *When a jet plane reaches the speed of sound, the sound waves in front of the jet combine by constructive interference. The result is a high-density compression that is called the sound barrier.*

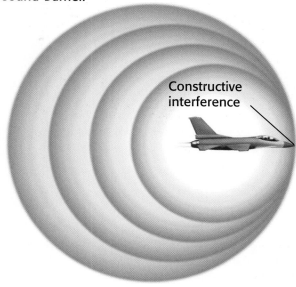

Constructive interference

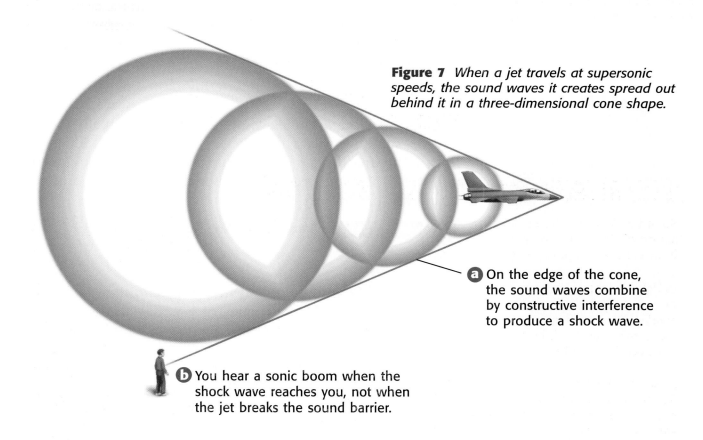

Figure 7 *When a jet travels at supersonic speeds, the sound waves it creates spread out behind it in a three-dimensional cone shape.*

ⓐ On the edge of the cone, the sound waves combine by constructive interference to produce a shock wave.

ⓑ You hear a sonic boom when the shock wave reaches you, not when the jet breaks the sound barrier.

Figure 8 Resonant Frequencies of a Plucked String

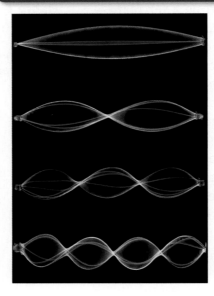

The lowest resonant frequency is called the *fundamental*.

Higher resonant frequencies are called *overtones*. The first overtone is twice the frequency of the fundamental.

The second overtone is 3 times the fundamental.

The third overtone is 4 times the fundamental.

standing wave a pattern of vibration that simulates a wave that is standing still

resonance a phenomenon that occurs when two objects naturally vibrate at the same frequency; the sound produced by one object causes the other object to vibrate

Interference and Standing Waves

When you play a guitar, you can make some pleasing sounds, and you might even play a tune. But have you ever watched a guitar string after you've plucked it? You may have noticed that the string vibrates as a standing wave. A **standing wave** is a pattern of vibration that looks like a wave that is standing still. Waves and reflected waves of the same frequency are going through the string. Where you see maximum amplitude, waves are interfering constructively. Where the string seems to be standing still, waves are interfering destructively.

Although you can see only one standing wave, which is at the *fundamental* frequency, the guitar string actually creates several standing waves of different frequencies at the same time. The frequencies at which standing waves are made are called *resonant frequencies*. Resonant frequencies and the relationships between them are shown in **Figure 8.**

✓ Reading Check What is a standing wave?

Resonance

If you have a tuning fork, shown in **Figure 9,** that vibrates at one of the resonant frequencies of a guitar string, you can make the string make a sound without touching it. Strike the tuning fork, and hold it close to the string. The string will start to vibrate and produce a sound.

Using the vibrations of the tuning fork to make the string vibrate is an example of resonance. **Resonance** happens when an object vibrating at or near a resonant frequency of a second object causes the second object to vibrate.

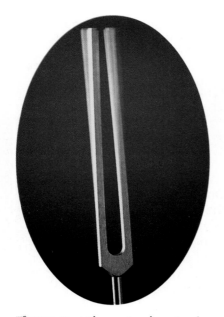

Figure 9 *When struck, a tuning fork can make another object vibrate if they both have the same resonant frequency.*

Resonance in Musical Instruments

Musical instruments use resonance to make sound. In wind instruments, vibrations are caused by blowing air into the mouthpiece. The vibrations make a sound, which is amplified when it forms a standing wave inside the instrument.

String instruments also resonate when they are played. An acoustic guitar, such as the one shown in **Figure 10,** has a hollow body. When the strings vibrate, sound waves enter the body of the guitar. Standing waves form inside the body of the guitar, and the sound is amplified.

Figure 10 *The body of a guitar resonates when the guitar is strummed.*

SECTION Review

Summary

- Echoes are reflected sound waves.
- Some animals can use echolocation to find food or to navigate around objects.
- People use echolocation technology in many underwater applications.
- Ultrasonography uses sound reflection for medical applications.
- Sound barriers and shock waves are created by interference.
- Standing waves form at an object's resonant frequencies.
- Resonance happens when a vibrating object causes a second object to vibrate at one of its resonant frequencies.

Using Key Terms

1. Use the following terms in the same sentence: *echo* and *echolocation*.

Complete each of the following sentences by choosing the correct term from the word bank.

interference	standing wave
sonic boom	resonance

2. When you pluck a string on a musical instrument, a(n) _____ forms.

3. When a vibrating object causes a nearby object to vibrate, _____ results.

Understanding Key Ideas

4. What causes an echo?
   a. reflection
   b. resonance
   c. constructive interference
   d. destructive interference

5. Describe a place in which you would expect to hear echoes.

6. How do bats use echoes to find insects to eat?

7. Give one example each of constructive and destructive interference of sound waves.

Math Skills

8. Sound travels through air at 343 m/s at 20°C. A bat emits an ultrasonic squeak and hears the echo 0.05 s later. How far away was the object that reflected it? (Hint: Remember that the sound must travel *to* the object and *back to* the bat.)

Critical Thinking

9. **Applying Concepts** Your friend is playing a song on a piano. Whenever your friend hits a certain key, the lamp on top of the piano rattles. Explain why the lamp rattles.

10. **Making Comparisons** Compare sonar and ultrasonography in locating objects.

SCI**LINKS**®

NSTA
Developed and maintained by the National Science Teachers Association

For a variety of links related to this chapter, go to www.scilinks.org

Topic: Interactions of Sound Waves
SciLinks code: HSM0804

READING WARM-UP

Objectives

● Explain why different instruments have different sound qualities.

● Describe how each family of musical instruments produces sound.

● Explain how noise is different from music.

Terms to Learn

sound quality
noise

READING STRATEGY

Reading Organizer As you read this section, make a table comparing the way different instruments produce sound.

Sound Quality

Have you ever been told that the music you really like is just a lot of noise? If you have, you know that people can disagree about the difference between noise and music.

You might think of noise as sounds you don't like and music as sounds that are pleasant to hear. But the difference between music and noise does not depend on whether you like the sound. The difference has to do with sound quality.

What Is Sound Quality?

Imagine that the same note is played on a piano and on a violin. Could you tell the instruments apart without looking? The notes played have the same frequency. But you could probably tell them apart because the instruments make different sounds. The notes sound different because a single note on an instrument actually comes from several different pitches: the fundamental and several overtones. The result of the combination of these pitches is shown in **Figure 1.** The result of several pitches mixing together through interference is **sound quality.** Each instrument has a unique sound quality. **Figure 1** also shows how the sound quality differs when two instruments play the same note.

Figure 1 *Each instrument has a unique sound quality that results from the particular blend of overtones that it has.*

Fundamental

First overtone

Second overtone

Resulting sound

Piano

Violin

Sound Quality of Instruments

The difference in sound quality among different instruments comes from their structural differences. All instruments produce sound by vibrating. But instruments vary in the part that vibrates and in the way that the vibrations are made. There are three main families of instruments: string instruments, wind instruments, and percussion instruments.

sound quality the result of the blending of several pitches through interference

✔ **Reading Check** How do musical instruments differ in how they produce sound? (*See the Appendix for answers to Reading Checks.*)

String Instruments

Violins, guitars, and banjos are examples of string instruments. They make sound when their strings vibrate after being plucked or bowed. **Figure 2** shows how two different string instruments produce sounds.

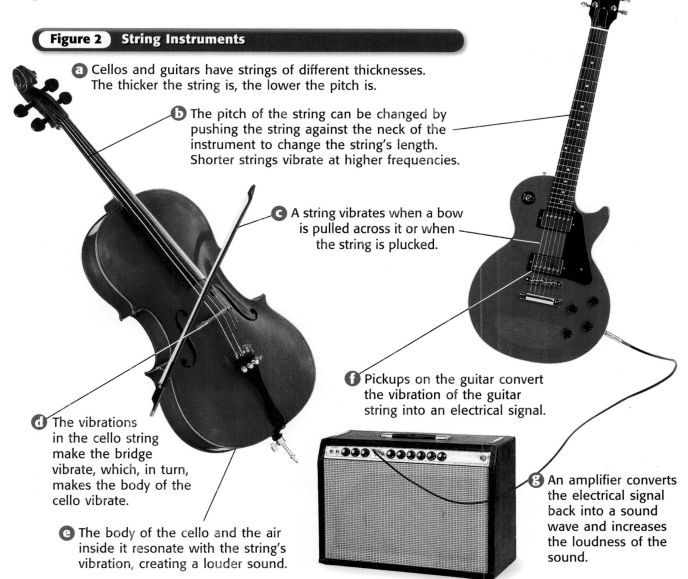

Figure 2 **String Instruments**

a Cellos and guitars have strings of different thicknesses. The thicker the string is, the lower the pitch is.

b The pitch of the string can be changed by pushing the string against the neck of the instrument to change the string's length. Shorter strings vibrate at higher frequencies.

c A string vibrates when a bow is pulled across it or when the string is plucked.

d The vibrations in the cello string make the bridge vibrate, which, in turn, makes the body of the cello vibrate.

e The body of the cello and the air inside it resonate with the string's vibration, creating a louder sound.

f Pickups on the guitar convert the vibration of the guitar string into an electrical signal.

g An amplifier converts the electrical signal back into a sound wave and increases the loudness of the sound.

Figure 3 Wind Instruments

a A trumpet player's lips vibrate when the player blows into a trumpet.

b The reed vibrates back and forth when a musician blows into a clarinet.

c Standing waves are formed in the air columns of the instruments. The pitch of the instrument depends in part on the length of the air column. The longer the column is, the lower the pitch is.

d The length of the air column in a trumpet is changed by pushing the valves.

e The length of the air column in a clarinet is changed by closing or opening the finger holes.

Wind Instruments

A wind instrument produces sound when a vibration is created at one end of its air column. The vibration causes standing waves inside the air column. Pitch is changed by changing the length of the air column. Wind instruments are sometimes divided into two groups—woodwinds and brass. Examples of woodwinds are saxophones, oboes, and recorders. French horns, trombones, and tubas are brass instruments. A brass instrument and a woodwind instrument are shown in **Figure 3.**

Percussion Instruments

Drums, bells, and cymbals are percussion instruments. They make sound when struck. Instruments of different sizes are used to get different pitches. Usually, the larger the instrument is, the lower the pitch is. The drums and cymbals in a trap set, shown in **Figure 4,** are percussion instruments.

Figure 4 Percussion Instruments

The skins of the drums vibrate when struck with drumsticks.

Cymbals vibrate when struck together or when struck with drumsticks.

Each drum in the set is a different size. The larger the drum is, the lower the pitch is.

Music or Noise?

Most of the sounds we hear are noises. The sound of a truck roaring down the highway, the slam of a door, and the jingle of keys falling to the floor are all noises. **Noise** can be described as any sound, especially a nonmusical sound, that is a random mix of frequencies (or pitches). **Figure 5** shows on an oscilloscope the difference between a musical sound and noise.

noise a sound that consists of a random mix of frequencies

✓ **Reading Check** What is the difference between music and noise?

French horn

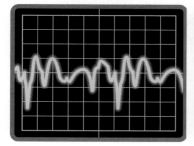

A sharp clap

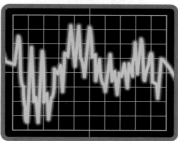

Figure 5 *A note from a French horn produces a sound wave with a repeating pattern, but noise from a clap produces complex sound waves with no regular pattern.*

SECTION Review

Summary

● Different instruments have different sound qualities.

● Sound quality results from the blending through interference of the fundamental and several overtones.

● The three families of instruments are string, wind, and percussion instruments.

● Noise is a sound consisting of a random mix of frequencies.

Using Key Terms

1. Use each of the following terms in a separate sentence: *sound quality* and *noise*.

Understanding Key Ideas

2. What interaction of sound waves determines sound quality?
   a. reflection   c. pitch
   b. diffraction   d. interference

3. Why do different instruments have different sound qualities?

Critical Thinking

4. **Making Comparisons** What do string instruments and wind instruments have in common in how they produce sound?

5. **Identifying Bias** Someone says that the music you are listening to is "just noise." Does the person mean that the music is a random mix of frequencies? Explain your answer.

Interpreting Graphics

6. Look at the oscilloscope screen below. Do you think the sound represented by the wave on the screen is noise or music? Explain your answer.

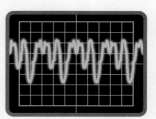

SCI**LINKS**®

NSTA
Developed and maintained by the
National Science Teachers Association

For a variety of links related to this chapter, go to www.scilinks.org

Topic: Sound Quality
SciLinks code: HSM1427

Skills Practice Lab

Easy Listening

Pitch describes how low or high a sound is. A sound's pitch is related to its frequency—the number of waves per second. Frequency is measured in hertz (Hz), where 1 Hz equals 1 wave per second. Most humans can hear frequencies in the range from 20 Hz to 20,000 Hz. But not everyone detects all pitches equally well at all distances. In this activity, you will collect data to see how well you and your classmates hear different frequencies at different distances.

OBJECTIVES

Measure your classmates' ability to detect different pitches at different distances.

Graph the average class data.

Form a conclusion about how easily pitches of different frequencies are heard at different distances.

MATERIALS

- eraser, hard rubber
- meterstick
- paper, graph
- tuning forks, different frequencies (4)

Ask a Question

1 Do most of the students in your classroom hear low-, mid-, or high-frequency sounds best?

Form a Hypothesis

2 Write a hypothesis that answers the question above. Explain your reasoning.

Test the Hypothesis

3 Choose one member of your group to be the sound maker. The others will be the listeners.

4 Copy the data table below onto another sheet of paper. Be sure to include a column for every listener in your group.

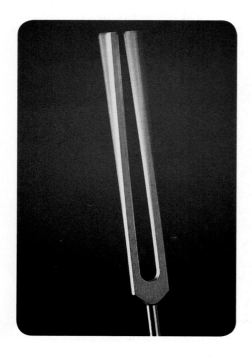

Data Collection Table				
	Distance (m)			
Frequency	Listener 1	Listener 2	Listener 3	Average
1 (_____Hz)				
2 (_____Hz)		DO NOT WRITE IN BOOK		
3 (_____Hz)				
4 (_____Hz)				

5 The sound maker will choose one of the tuning forks, and record the frequency of the tuning fork in the data table.

6 The listeners should stand 1 m from the sound maker with their backs turned.

7 The sound maker will create a sound by striking the tip of the tuning fork gently with the eraser.

8 Listeners who hear the sound should take one step away from the sound maker. The listeners who do not hear the sound should stay where they are.

9 Repeat steps 7 and 8 until none of the listeners can hear the sound or the listeners reach the edge of the room.

10 Using the meterstick, the sound maker should measure the distance from his or her position to each of the listeners. All group members should record this data.

11 Repeat steps 5 through 10 with a tuning fork of a different frequency.

12 Continue until all four tuning forks have been tested.

Analyze the Results

1 **Organizing Data** Calculate the average distance for each frequency. Share your group's data with the rest of the class to make a data table for the whole class.

2 **Analyzing Data** Calculate the average distance for each frequency for the class.

3 **Constructing Graphs** Make a graph of the class results, plotting average distance (*y*-axis) versus frequency (*x*-axis).

Draw Conclusions

4 **Drawing Conclusions** Was everyone in the class able to hear all of frequencies equally? (Hint: Was the average distance for each frequency the same?)

5 **Evaluating Data** If the answer to question 4 is no, which frequency had the longest average distance? Which frequency had the shortest final distance?

6 **Analyzing Graphs** Based on your graph, do your results support your hypothesis? Explain your answer.

7 **Evaluating Methods** Do you think your class sample is large enough to confirm your hypothesis for all people of all ages? Explain your answer.

Chapter Review

Complete each of the following sentences by choosing the correct term from the word bank.

loudness   echoes
pitch   noise
sound quality

1 The _____ of a sound wave depends on its amplitude.

2 Reflected sound waves are called _____.

3 Two different instruments playing the same note sound different because of _____.

UNDERSTANDING KEY IDEAS

Multiple Choice

4 If a fire engine is traveling toward you, the Doppler effect will cause the siren to sound

   a. higher.   **c.** louder.
   b. lower.   **d.** softer.

5 Sound travels fastest through

   a. a vacuum.   **c.** air.
   b. sea water.   **d.** glass.

6 If two sound waves interfere constructively, you will hear

   a. a high-pitched sound.
   b. a softer sound.
   c. a louder sound.
   d. no change in sound.

7 You will hear a sonic boom when

   a. an object breaks the sound barrier.
   b. an object travels at supersonic speeds.
   c. a shock wave reaches your ears.
   d. the speed of sound is 290 m/s.

8 Resonance can happen when an object vibrates at another object's

   a. resonant frequency.
   b. fundamental frequency.
   c. second overtone frequency.
   d. All of the above

9 A technological device that can be used to see sound waves is a(n)

   a. sonar.   **c.** ultrasound.
   b. oscilloscope.   **d.** amplifier.

Short Answer

10 Describe how the Doppler effect helps a beluga whale determine whether a fish is moving away from it or toward it.

11 How do vibrations cause sound waves?

12 Briefly describe what happens in the different parts of the ear.

Math Skills

13 A submarine that is not moving sends out a sonar sound wave traveling 1,500 m/s, which reflects off a boat back to the submarine. The sonar crew detects the reflected wave 6 s after it was sent out. How far away is the boat from the submarine?

624   Chapter 21

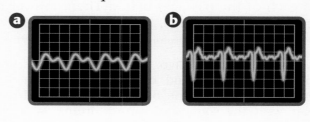

CRITICAL THINKING

14 Concept Mapping Use the following terms to create a concept map: *sound waves, pitch, loudness, decibels, frequency, amplitude, oscilloscope, hertz,* and *interference.*

15 Analyzing Processes An *anechoic chamber* is a room where there is almost no reflection of sound waves. Anechoic chambers are often used to test sound equipment, such as stereos. The walls of such chambers are usually covered with foam triangles. Explain why this design eliminates echoes in the room.

16 Applying Concepts Would the pilot of an airplane breaking the sound barrier hear a sonic boom? Explain why or why not.

17 Forming Hypotheses After working in a factory for a month, a man you know complains about a ringing in his ears. What might be wrong with him? What do you think may have caused his problem? What can you suggest to him to prevent further hearing loss?

INTERPRETING GRAPHICS

Use the oscilloscope screens below to answer the questions that follow:

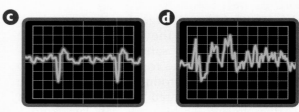

18 Which sound is noise?

19 Which represents the softest sound?

20 Which represents the sound with the lowest pitch?

21 Which two sounds were produced by the same instrument?

Standardized Test Preparation

Read each of the passages below. Then, answer the questions that follow each passage.

Passage 1 Centuries ago, Marco Polo wrote about the booming sand dunes of the Asian desert. He wrote that the booming sands filled the air with the sounds of music, drums, and weapons of war. Booming sands are most often found in the middle of large deserts. They have been discovered all over the world, including the United States. Booming sands make loud, low-pitched sounds when the top layers of sand slip over the layers below, producing vibrations. The sounds have been compared to foghorns, cannon fire, and moaning. The sounds can last from a few seconds to 15 min and can be heard more than 10 km away!

1. Which is a fact in this passage?
 A Marco Polo loved traveling.
 B Booming sands always sound like moaning people.
 C Booming sands are the most interesting thing in Asia.
 D Some booming sands are found in the United States.

2. Which of the following phrases **best** describes booming sands?
 F found in Asia
 G noisy
 H slippery
 I discovered by Marco Polo

3. What causes booming sands?
 A vibrations caused by top layers of sand slipping over layers below
 B battles in the desert
 C animals that live beneath sand dunes
 D There is not enough information to determine the answer.

Passage 2 People who work in the field of architectural acoustics are concerned with controlling sound that travels in a closed space. Their goal is to make rooms and buildings quiet yet suitable for people to enjoy talking and listening to music. One major factor that affects the acoustical quality of a room is the way the room reflects sound waves. Sound waves bounce off surfaces such as doors, ceilings, and walls. Using materials that absorb sound reduces the reflection of sound waves. Materials that have small pockets of air that can trap the sound vibrations and keep them from reflecting are the most sound absorbent. Sound-absorbing floor and ceiling tiles, curtains, and upholstered furniture all help to control the reflection of sound waves.

1. The field of architectural acoustics is concerned with which of the following?
 A making buildings earthquake safe
 B controlling sound in closed spaces
 C designing sound-absorbing materials
 D making buildings as quiet as possible

2. Which of the following is a major factor in the acoustical quality of a room?
 F the size of the room
 G the furnishings in the room
 H the walls of the room
 I the noise level in the room

3. Which of the following materials is **most** likely to absorb sounds the best?
 A materials that have small pockets of air
 B surfaces such as doors, ceilings, and walls
 C materials that keep the room as quiet as possible
 D furniture that is made of wood

Use the pictures of standing waves below to answer the questions that follow.

(a)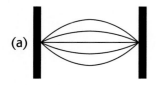

(c)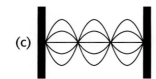

(b)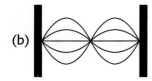

(d)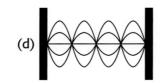

1. Which of the standing waves has the lowest frequency?

A a

B b

C c

D d

2. Which of the standing waves has the highest frequency?

F a

G b

H c

I d

3. Which of the standing waves represents the first overtone?

A a

B b

C c

D d

4. In which of the following pairs of standing waves is the frequency of the second wave twice the frequency of the first?

F a, b

G a, c

H b, c

I c, d

Read each question below, and choose the best answer.

1. The speed of sound in copper is 3,560 m/s. Which is another way to express this measure?

A 356×10^2 m/s

B 0.356×10^3 m/s

C 3.56×10^3 m/s

D 3.56×10^4 m/s

2. The speed of sound in sea water is 1,522 m/s. How far can a sound wave travel underwater in 10 s?

F 152.2 m

G 1,522 m

H 15,220 m

I 152,220 m

3. Claire likes to go swimming after work. She warms up for 120 s before she begins swimming, and it takes her an average of 55 s to swim one lap. Which equation could be used to find w, the number of seconds it takes for Claire to warm up and swim 15 laps?

A $w = (15 \times 120) + 55$

B $w = (15 \times 55) + 120$

C $w = 120 + 55 + 15$

D $w = (15 \times 55) \times 120$

4. The Vasquez family went bowling. They rented 6 pairs of shoes for $3 a pair and bowled for 2 h at a rate of $8.80/h. Which is the best estimate of the total cost of the shoes and bowling?

F $24

G $30

H $36

I $45

Science in Action

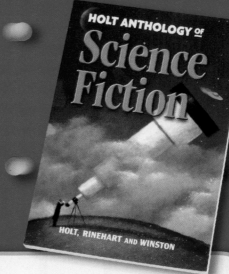

Scientific Discoveries

Jurassic Bark

Imagine you suddenly hear a loud honking sound, such as a trombone or a tuba. "Must be band tryouts," you think. You turn to find the noise and find yourself face to face with a 10 m long, 2,800 kg dinosaur with a huge tubular crest on its snout. Do you run? No—your musical friend, *Parasaurolophus,* is a vegetarian. In 1995, an almost-complete fossil skull of an adult *Parasaurolophus* was found in New Mexico. Scientists studied the noise-making qualities of *Parasaurolophus*'s crest and found that it contained many internal tubes and chambers.

Math ACTiViTY

Imagine that a standing wave with a frequency of 80 Hz is made inside the crest of a *Parasaurolophus*. What would be the frequency of the first overtone of this standing wave? the second? the third?

Science Fiction

"Ear" by Jane Yolen

Jily and her friends, Sanya and Feeny, live in a time not too far in the future. It is a time when everyone's hearing is damaged. People communicate using sign language—unless they put on their Ear. Then, the whole world is filled with sounds.

Jily and her friends visit a club called The Low Down. It is too quiet for Jily's tastes, and she wants to leave. But Sanya is dancing by herself, even though there is no music. When Jily finds Feeny, they notice some Earless kids their own age. Earless people never go to clubs, and Jily finds their presence offensive. But Feeny is intrigued.

Everyone is given an Ear at the age of 12 but has to give it up at the age of 30. Why would these kids want to go out without their Ears before the age of 30? Jily thinks the idea is ridiculous and doesn't stick around to find out the answer to such a question. But it is an answer that will change her life by the end of the next day.

Language Arts ACTiViTY

WRITING SKILL Read "Ear," by Jane Yolen, in the *Holt Anthology of Science Fiction.* Write a one-page report that discusses how the story made you think about the importance of hearing in your everyday life.

Adam Dudley

Sound Engineer Adam Dudley uses the science of sound waves every day at his job. He is the audio supervisor for the Performing Arts Center of the University of Texas at Austin. Dudley oversees sound design and technical support for campus performance spaces, including an auditorium that seats over 3,000 people.

To stage a successful concert, Dudley takes many factors into account. The size and shape of the room help determine how many speakers to use and where to place them. It is a challenge to make sure people seated in the back row can hear well enough and also to make sure that the people up front aren't going deaf from the high volume.

Adam Dudley loves his job—he enjoys working with people and technology and prefers not to wear a coat and tie. Although he is invisible to the audience, his work backstage is as crucial as the musicians and actors on stage to the success of the events.

Social Studies ACTIVITY

Research the ways in which concert halls were designed before the use of electricity for amplification. Make a model or diorama, and present it to the class, explaining the acoustical factors involved in the design.

To learn more about these Science in Action topics, visit go.hrw.com and type in the keyword **HP5SNDF.**

Current Science

Check out Current Science® articles related to this chapter by visiting go.hrw.com. Just type in the keyword **HP5CS21.**

22

The Nature of Light

SECTION 1 What Is Light? 632

SECTION 2 The Electromagnetic Spectrum 636

SECTION 3 Interactions of Light Waves 644

SECTION 4 Light and Color 652

Chapter Lab 658

Chapter Review 660

Standardized Test Preparation 662

Science in Action 664

About the PHOTO

What kind of alien life lives on this planet? Actually, this isn't a planet at all. It's an ordinary soap bubble! The brightly colored swirls on this bubble are reflections of light. Light waves combine through interference so that you see different colors on this soap bubble.

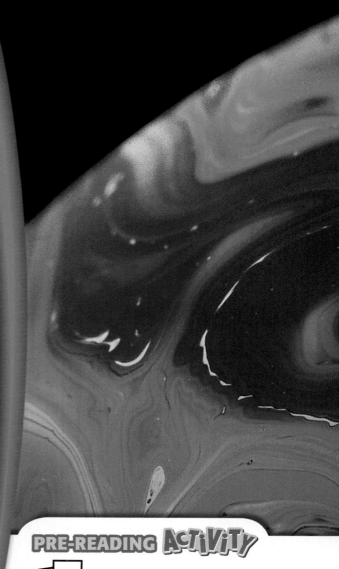

PRE-READING ACTIVITY

FOLDNOTES **Booklet** Before you read the chapter, create the FoldNote entitled "Booklet" described in the **Study Skills** section of the Appendix. Label each page of the booklet with a main idea from the chapter. As you read the chapter, write what you learn about each main idea on the appropriate page of the booklet.

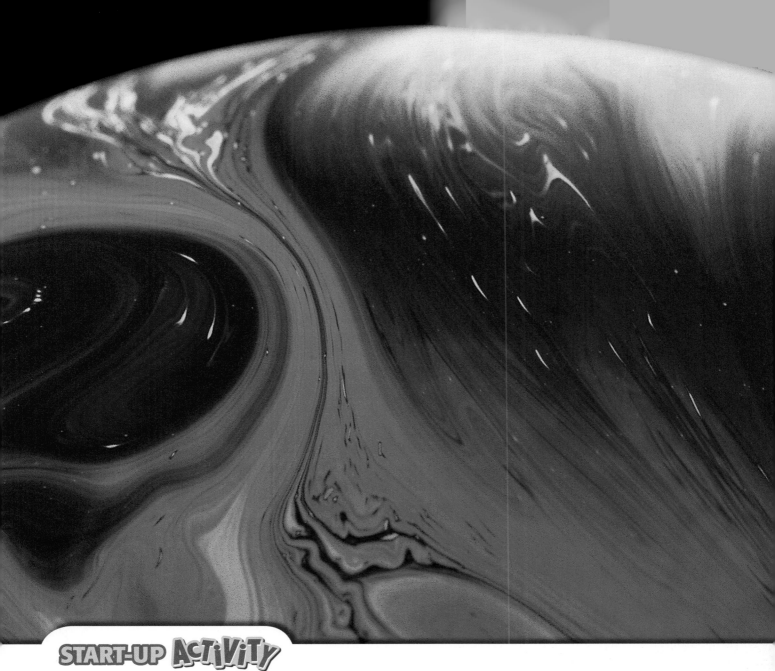

START-UP ACTIVITY

Colors of Light

Is white light really white? In this activity, you will use a spectroscope to answer that question.

Procedure

1. Your teacher will give you a **spectroscope** or instructions for making one.

2. Turn on an **incandescent light bulb.** Look at the light bulb through your spectroscope. Write a description of what you see.

3. Repeat step 2, looking at a **fluorescent light.** Again, describe what you see.

Analysis

1. Compare what you saw with the incandescent light bulb with what you saw with the fluorescent light bulb.

2. Both kinds of bulbs produce white light. What did you learn about white light by using the spectroscope?

3. Light from a flame is yellowish but is similar to white light. What do you think you would see if you used a spectroscope to look at light from a flame?

What Is Light?

You can see light. It's everywhere! Light comes from the sun and from other sources, such as light bulbs. But what exactly is light?

Scientists are still studying light to learn more about it. A lot has already been discovered about light, as you will soon find out. Read on, and be enlightened!

READING WARM-UP

Objectives

● Describe light as an electromagnetic wave.

● Calculate distances traveled by light by using the speed of light.

● Explain why light from the sun is important.

Terms to Learn

electromagnetic wave
radiation

READING STRATEGY

Brainstorming The key idea of this section is light. Brainstorm words and phrases related to light.

Light: An Electromagnetic Wave

Light is a type of energy that travels as a wave. But light is different from other kinds of waves. Other kinds of waves, like sound waves and water waves, must travel through matter. Light does not require matter through which to travel. Light is an electromagnetic wave (EM wave). An **electromagnetic wave** is a wave that can travel through empty space or matter and consists of changing electric and magnetic fields.

Fields exist around certain objects and can exert a force on another object without touching that object. For example, Earth is a source of a gravitational field. This field pulls you and all things toward Earth. But keep in mind that this field, like all fields, is not made of matter.

Figure 1 shows a diagram of an electromagnetic wave. Notice that the electric and magnetic fields are at right angles—or are *perpendicular*—to each other. These fields are also perpendicular to the direction of the wave motion.

electromagnetic wave a wave that consists of electric and magnetic fields that vibrate at right angles to each other

Figure 1 *Electromagnetic waves are made of vibrating electric and magnetic fields.*

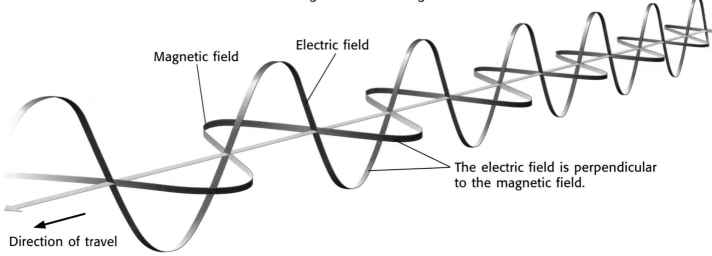

Magnetic field

Electric field

The electric field is perpendicular to the magnetic field.

Direction of travel

Figure 2 *The hair on the girl's head stands up because of an electric field and the iron filings form arcs around the magnet because of a magnetic field.*

Electric and Magnetic Fields

Electromagnetic waves are changing electric and magnetic fields. But what are electric and magnetic fields? An *electric field* surrounds every charged object. The electric field around a charged object pulls oppositely charged objects toward it and repels like-charged objects. You can see the effect of electric fields whenever you see objects stuck together by static electricity. **Figure 2** shows another effect of an electric field.

A *magnetic field* surrounds every magnet. Because of magnetic fields, paper clips and iron filings are pulled toward magnets. You can feel the effect of magnetic fields when you hold two magnets close together. The iron filings around the magnet in **Figure 2** form arcs in the presence of the magnet's magnetic field.

✓ Reading Check Where can electric fields be found? (*See the Appendix for answers to Reading Checks.*)

How EM Waves Are Produced

An EM wave can be produced by the vibration of an electrically charged particle. When the particle vibrates, or moves back and forth, the electric field around it also vibrates. When the electric field starts vibrating, a vibrating magnetic field is created. The vibration of an electric field and a magnetic field together produces an EM wave that carries energy released by the original vibration of the particle. The transfer of energy as electromagnetic waves is called **radiation.**

CONNECTION TO Social Studies

WRITING SKILL **The Particle Model of Light**
Thinking of light as being an electromagnetic wave can explain many properties of light. But some properties of light can be explained only by using a particle model of light. In the particle model of light, light is thought of as a stream of particles called *photons*. Research the history of the particle model of light. Write a one-page paper on what you learn.

radiation transfer of energy as electromagnetic waves

Figure 3 *Thunder and lightning are produced at the same time. But you usually see lightning before you hear thunder, because light travels much faster than sound.*

The Speed of Light

Scientists have yet to discover anything that travels faster than light. In the near vacuum of space, the speed of light is about 300,000,000 m/s, or 300,000 km/s. Light travels slightly slower in air, glass, and other types of matter. (Keep in mind that even though electromagnetic waves do not need to travel through matter, they can travel through many substances.)

Believe it or not, light can travel about 880,000 times faster than sound! This fact explains the phenomenon described in **Figure 3.** If you could run at the speed of light, you could travel around Earth 7.5 times in 1 s.

✓ **Reading Check** How does the speed of light compare with the speed of sound?

MATH FOCUS

How Fast Is Light? The distance from Earth to the moon is 384,000 km. Calculate the time it takes for light to travel that distance.

Step 1: Write the equation for speed.

$$speed = \frac{distance}{time}$$

Step 2: Rearrange the equation by multiplying by time and dividing by speed.

$$time = \frac{distance}{speed}$$

Step 3: Replace *distance* and *speed* with the values given in the problem, and solve.

$$time = \frac{384,000 \text{ km}}{300,000 \text{ km/s}}$$

$$time = 1.28 \text{ s}$$

Now It's Your Turn

1. The distance from the sun to Venus is 108,000,000 km. Calculate the time it takes for light to travel that distance.

Light from the Sun

Even though light travels quickly, it takes about 8.3 min for light to travel from the sun to Earth. It takes this much time because Earth is 150,000,000 km away from the sun.

The EM waves from the sun are the major source of energy on Earth. For example, plants use photosynthesis to store energy from the sun. And animals use and store energy by eating plants or by eating other animals that eat plants. Even fossil fuels, such as coal and oil, store energy from the sun. Fossil fuels are formed from the remains of plants and animals that lived millions of years ago.

Although Earth receives a large amount of energy from the sun, only a very small part of the total energy given off by the sun reaches Earth. Look at **Figure 4.** The sun gives off energy as EM waves in all directions. Most of this energy travels away in space.

Figure 4 *Only a small amount of the sun's energy reaches the planets in the solar system.*

SECTION Review

Summary

● Light is an electromagnetic (EM) wave. An EM wave is a wave that consists of changing electric and magnetic fields. EM waves require no matter through which to travel.

● EM waves can be produced by the vibration of charged particles.

● The speed of light in a vacuum is about 300,000,000 m/s.

● EM waves from the sun are the major source of energy for Earth.

Using Key Terms

1. Use the following terms in the same sentence: *electromagnetic wave* and *radiation*.

Understanding Key Ideas

2. Electromagnetic waves are different from other types of waves because they can travel through
   a. air.
   b. glass.
   c. space.
   d. steel.

3. Describe light in terms of electromagnetic waves.

4. Why is light from the sun important?

5. How can electromagnetic waves be produced?

Math Skills

6. The distance from the sun to Jupiter is 778,000,000 km. How long does it take for light from the sun to reach Jupiter?

Critical Thinking

7. **Making Inferences** Why is it important that EM waves can travel through empty space?

8. **Making Comparisons** How does the amount of energy produced by the sun compare with the amount of energy that reaches Earth from the sun?

9. **Applying Concepts** Explain why the energy produced by burning wood in a campfire is energy from the sun.

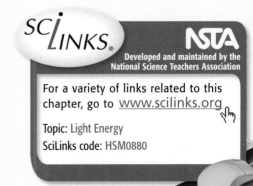

For a variety of links related to this chapter, go to www.scilinks.org

Topic: Light Energy
SciLinks code: HSM0880

The Electromagnetic Spectrum

When you look around, you can see things that reflect light to your eyes. But a bee might see the same things differently. Bees can see a kind of light—called ultraviolet light—*that you can't see!*

It might seem odd to call something you can't see *light*. The light you are most familiar with is called *visible light*. Ultraviolet light is similar to visible light. Both are kinds of electromagnetic (EM) waves. In this section, you will learn about many kinds of EM waves, including X rays, radio waves, and microwaves.

Characteristics of EM Waves

All EM waves travel at the same speed in a vacuum—300,000 km/s. How is this possible? The speed of a wave is found by multiplying its wavelength by its frequency. So, EM waves having different wavelengths can travel at the same speed as long as their frequencies are also different. The entire range of EM waves is called the **electromagnetic spectrum.** The electromagnetic spectrum is shown in **Figure 1.** The electromagnetic spectrum is divided into regions according to the length of the waves. There is no sharp division between one kind of wave and the next. Some kinds even have overlapping ranges.

✓ **Reading Check** How is the speed of a wave determined? (*See the Appendix for answers to Reading Checks.*)

READING WARM-UP

Objectives

● Identify how electromagnetic waves differ from each other.

● Describe some uses for radio waves and microwaves.

● List examples of how infrared waves and visible light are important in your life.

● Explain how ultraviolet light, X rays, and gamma rays can be both helpful and harmful.

Terms to Learn

electromagnetic spectrum

READING STRATEGY

Mnemonics As you read this section, create a mnemonic device to help you remember the kinds of EM waves.

Figure 1 **The Electromagnetic Spectrum**

The electromagnetic spectrum is arranged from long to short wavelength or from low to high frequency.

Radio waves
All radio and television stations broadcast radio waves.

Microwaves
Despite their name, microwaves are not the shortest EM waves.

Infrared
Infrared means "below red."

Radio Waves

Radio waves cover a wide range of waves in the EM spectrum. Radio waves have some of the longest wavelengths and the lowest frequencies of all EM waves. In fact, radio waves are any EM waves that have wavelengths longer than 30 cm. Radio waves are used for broadcasting radio signals.

Broadcasting Radio Signals

Figure 2 shows how radio signals are broadcast. Radio stations encode sound information into radio waves by varying either the waves' amplitude or their frequency. Changing amplitude or frequency is called *modulation* (MAHJ uh LAY shuhn). You probably know that there are AM radio stations and FM radio stations. The abbreviation *AM* stands for "amplitude modulation," and the abbreviation *FM* stands for "frequency modulation."

Comparing AM and FM Radio Waves

AM radio waves are different from FM radio waves. For example, AM radio waves have longer wavelengths than FM radio waves do. And AM radio waves can bounce off the atmosphere and thus can travel farther than FM radio waves. But FM radio waves are less affected by electrical noise than AM radio waves are. So, music broadcast from FM stations sounds better than music broadcast from AM stations.

❶ A radio station converts sound into an electric current. The current produces radio waves that are sent out in all directions by the antenna.

❷ A radio receives radio waves and then converts them into an electric current, which is then converted to sound.

Figure 2 *Radio waves cannot be heard, but they can carry energy that can be converted into sound.*

electromagnetic spectrum all of the frequencies or wavelengths of electromagnetic radiation

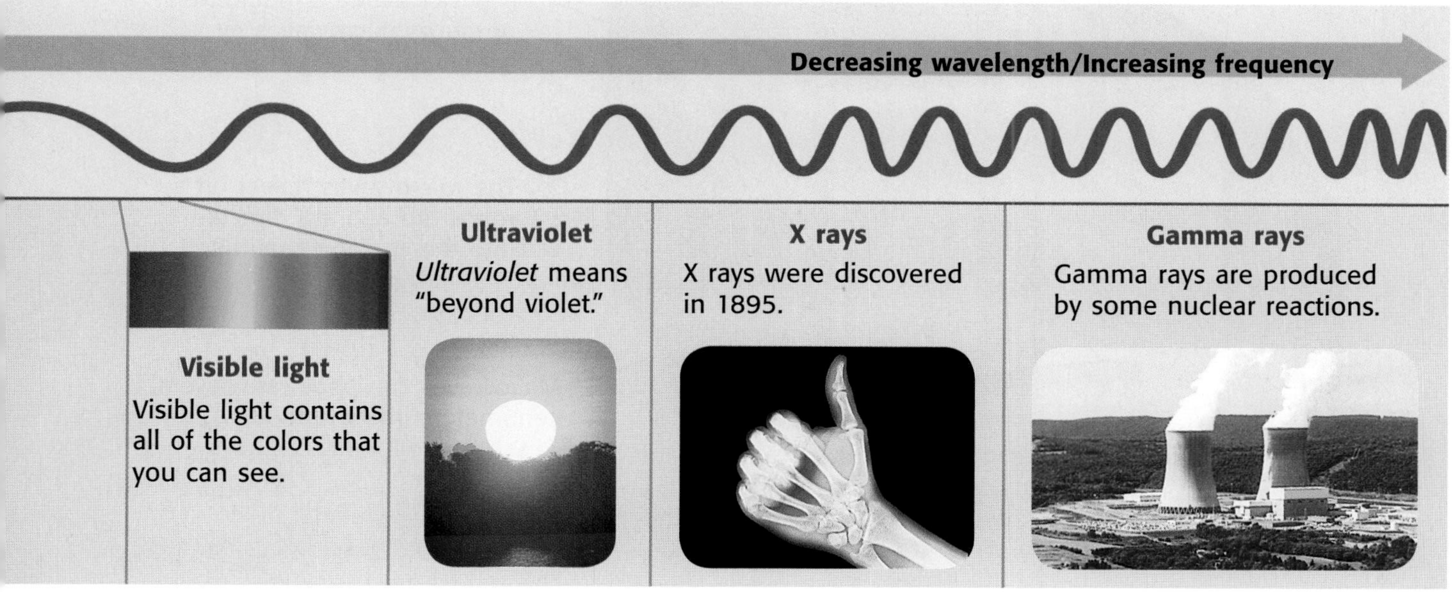

Decreasing wavelength/Increasing frequency

Visible light
Visible light contains all of the colors that you can see.

Ultraviolet
Ultraviolet means "beyond violet."

X rays
X rays were discovered in 1895.

Gamma rays
Gamma rays are produced by some nuclear reactions.

Radio Waves and Television

Television signals are also carried by radio waves. Most television stations broadcast radio waves that have shorter wavelengths and higher frequencies than those broadcast by radio stations. Like radio signals, television signals are broadcast using amplitude modulation and frequency modulation. Television stations use frequency-modulated waves to carry sound and amplitude-modulated waves to carry pictures.

Some waves carrying television signals are transmitted to artificial satellites orbiting Earth. The waves are amplified and sent to ground antennas. They then travel through cables to televisions in homes. Cable television works by this process.

Reading Check Which EM waves can carry television signals?

Microwaves

Microwaves have shorter wavelengths and higher frequencies than radio waves do. Microwaves have wavelengths between 1 mm and 30 cm. You are probably familiar with microwaves—they are created in a microwave oven, such as the one shown in **Figure 3.**

Microwaves and Communication

Like radio waves, microwaves are used to send information over long distances. For example, cellular phones send and receive signals using microwaves. And signals sent between Earth and artificial satellites in space are also carried by microwaves.

Figure 3 How a Microwave Oven Works

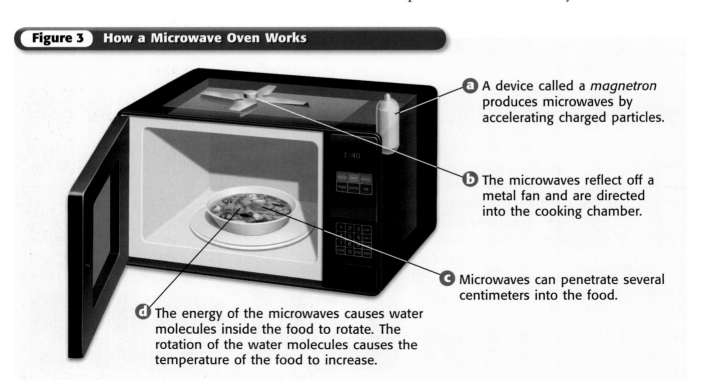

a A device called a *magnetron* produces microwaves by accelerating charged particles.

b The microwaves reflect off a metal fan and are directed into the cooking chamber.

c Microwaves can penetrate several centimeters into the food.

d The energy of the microwaves causes water molecules inside the food to rotate. The rotation of the water molecules causes the temperature of the food to increase.

Figure 4 *Police officers use radar to detect cars going faster than the speed limit.*

Radar

Microwaves are also used in radar. *Radar* (**ra**dio **d**etection **a**nd **r**anging) is used to detect the speed and location of objects. The police officer in **Figure 4** is using radar to check the speed of a car. The radar gun sends out microwaves that reflect off the car and return to the gun. The reflected waves are used to calculate the speed of the car. Radar is also used to watch the movement of airplanes and to help ships navigate at night.

Infrared Waves

Infrared waves have shorter wavelengths and higher frequencies than microwaves do. The wavelengths of infrared waves vary between 700 nanometers and 1 mm. A nanometer (nm) is equal to 0.000000001 m.

On a sunny day, you may be warmed by infrared waves from the sun. Your skin absorbs infrared waves striking your body. The energy of the waves causes the particles in your skin to vibrate more, and you feel an increase in temperature. The sun is not the only source of infrared waves. Almost all things give off infrared waves, including buildings, trees, and you! The amount of infrared waves an object gives off depends on the object's temperature. Warmer objects give off more infrared waves than cooler objects do.

You can't see infrared waves, but some devices can detect infrared waves. For example, infrared binoculars change infrared waves into light you can see. Such binoculars can be used to watch animals at night. **Figure 5** shows a photo taken with film that is sensitive to infrared waves.

Figure 5 *In this photograph, brighter colors indicate higher temperatures.*

Figure 6 *Water droplets can separate white light into visible light of different wavelengths. As a result, you see all the colors of visible light in a rainbow.*

Visible Light

Visible light is the very narrow range of wavelengths and frequencies in the electromagnetic spectrum that humans can see. Visible light waves have shorter wavelengths and higher frequencies than infrared waves do. Visible light waves have wavelengths between 400 nm and 700 nm.

Visible Light from the Sun

Some of the energy that reaches Earth from the sun is visible light. The visible light from the sun is white light. *White light* is visible light of all wavelengths combined. Light from lamps in your home as well as from the fluorescent bulbs in your school is also white light.

✓ Reading Check What is white light?

Colors of Light

Humans see the different wavelengths of visible light as different colors, as shown in **Figure 6.** The longest wavelengths are seen as red light. The shortest wavelengths are seen as violet light.

The range of colors is called the *visible spectrum.* You can see the visible spectrum in **Figure 7.** When you list the colors, you might use the imaginary name *ROY G. BiV* to help you remember their order. The capital letters in Roy's name represent the first letter of each color of visible light: **r**ed, **o**range, **y**ellow, **g**reen, **b**lue, and **v**iolet. What about the *i* in Roy's last name? You can think of *i* as standing for the color indigo. Indigo is a dark blue color.

SCHOOL to HOME

Making a Rainbow

On a sunny day, ask a parent to use a hose or a spray bottle to make a mist of water outside. Move around until you see a rainbow in the water mist. Draw a diagram showing the positions of the water mist, the sun, the rainbow, and yourself.

ACTIVITY

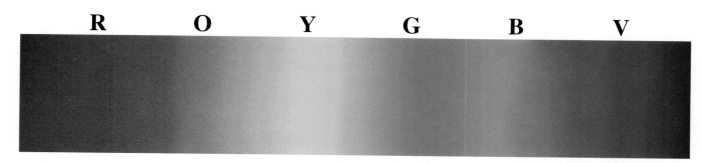

R   O   Y   G   B   V

Figure 7 *The visible spectrum contains all colors of light.*

Ultraviolet Light

Ultraviolet light (UV light) is another type of electromagnetic wave produced by the sun. Ultraviolet waves have shorter wavelengths and higher frequencies than visible light does. The wavelengths of ultraviolet light waves vary between 60 nm and 400 nm. Ultraviolet light affects your body in both bad and good ways.

✓ Reading Check How do ultraviolet light waves compare with visible light waves?

Bad Effects

On the bad side, too much ultraviolet light can cause sunburn, as you can see in **Figure 8.** Too much ultraviolet light can also cause skin cancer, wrinkles, and damage to the eyes. Luckily, much of the ultraviolet light from the sun does not reach Earth's surface. But you should still protect yourself against the ultraviolet light that does reach you. To do so, you should use sunscreen with a high SPF (**s**un **p**rotection **f**actor). You should also wear sunglasses that block out UV light to protect your eyes. Hats, long-sleeved shirts, and long pants can protect you, too. You need this protection even on overcast days because UV light can travel through clouds.

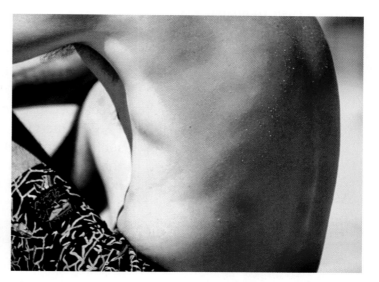

Figure 8 *Too much exposure to ultraviolet light can lead to a painful sunburn. Using sunscreen will help protect your skin.*

Good Effects

On the good side, ultraviolet waves produced by ultraviolet lamps are used to kill bacteria on food and surgical tools. In addition, small amounts of ultraviolet light are beneficial to your body. When exposed to ultraviolet light, skin cells produce vitamin D. This vitamin allows the intestines to absorb calcium. Without calcium, your teeth and bones would be very weak.

X Rays and Gamma Rays

X rays and gamma rays have some of the shortest wavelengths and highest frequencies of all EM waves.

X Rays

X rays have wavelengths between 0.001 nm and 60 nm. They can pass through many materials. This characteristic makes X rays useful in the medical field, as shown in **Figure 9.** But too much exposure to X rays can also damage or kill living cells. A patient getting an X ray may wear special aprons to protect parts of the body that do not need X-ray exposure. These aprons are lined with lead because X rays cannot pass through lead.

X-ray machines are also used as security devices in airports and other public buildings. The machines allow security officers to see inside bags and other containers without opening the containers.

Reading Check How are patients protected from X rays?

Gamma Rays

Gamma rays are EM waves that have wavelengths shorter than 0.1 nm. They can penetrate most materials very easily. Gamma rays are used to treat some forms of cancer. Doctors focus the rays on tumors inside the body to kill the cancer cells. This treatment often has good effects, but it can have bad side effects because some healthy cells may also be killed.

Gamma rays are also used to kill harmful bacteria in foods, such as meat and fresh fruits. The gamma rays do not harm the treated food and do not stay in the food. So, food that has been treated with gamma rays is safe for you to eat.

Figure 9 How a Bone Is X Rayed

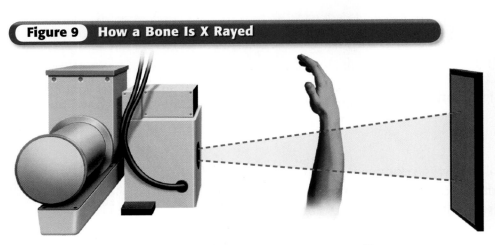 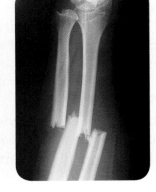

❶ X rays travel easily through skin and muscle but are absorbed by bones.

❷ The X rays that are not absorbed strike the film.

❸ Bright areas appear on the film where X rays are absorbed by the bones.

Summary

- All electromagnetic (EM) waves travel at the speed of light. EM waves differ only by wavelength and frequency.
- The entire range of EM waves is called the *electromagnetic spectrum*.
- Radio waves are used for communication.
- Microwaves are used in cooking and in radar.
- The absorption of infrared waves is felt as an increase in temperature.

- Visible light is the narrow range of wavelengths that humans can see. Different wavelengths are seen as different colors.
- Ultraviolet light is useful for killing bacteria and for producing vitamin D in the body. Overexposure to ultraviolet light can cause health problems.
- X rays and gamma rays are EM waves that are often used in medicine. Overexposure to these kinds of rays can damage or kill living cells.

Using Key Terms

1. In your own words, write a definition for the term *electromagnetic spectrum*.

Understanding Key Ideas

2. Which of the following electromagnetic waves are produced by the sun?
   - **a.** infrared waves
   - **b.** visible light
   - **c.** ultraviolet light
   - **d.** All of the above

3. How do the different kinds of EM waves differ from each other?

4. Describe two ways of transmitting information using radio waves.

5. Explain why ultraviolet light, X rays, and gamma rays can be both helpful and harmful.

6. What are two common uses for microwaves?

7. What is white light? What are two sources of white light?

8. What is the visible spectrum?

Critical Thinking

9. **Applying Concepts** Describe how three different kinds of electromagnetic waves have been useful to you today.

10. **Making Comparisons** Compare the wavelengths of infrared waves, ultraviolet light, and visible light.

Interpreting Graphics

The waves in the diagram below represent two different kinds of EM waves. Use the diagram below to answer the questions that follow.

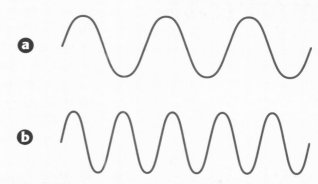

11. Which wave has the longest wavelength?

12. Suppose that one of the waves represents a microwave and one of the waves represents a radio wave. Which wave represents the microwave?

Developed and maintained by the National Science Teachers Association

For a variety of links related to this chapter, go to www.scilinks.org

Topic: Electromagnetic Spectrum
SciLinks code: HSM0482

Interactions of Light Waves

Have you ever seen a cat's eyes glow in the dark when light shines on them? Cats have a special layer of cells in the back of their eyes that reflects light.

This layer helps the cat see better by giving the eyes another chance to detect the light. Reflection is one interaction of electromagnetic waves. Because we can see visible light, it is easier to explain all wave interactions by using visible light.

Reflection

Reflection happens when light waves bounce off an object. Light reflects off objects all around you. When you look in a mirror, you are seeing light that has been reflected twice—first from you and then from the mirror. If light is reflecting off everything around you, why can't you see your image on a wall? To answer this question, you must learn the law of reflection.

The Law of Reflection

Light reflects off surfaces the same way that a ball bounces off the ground. If you throw the ball straight down against a smooth surface, it will bounce straight up. If you bounce it at an angle, it will bounce away at an angle. The *law of reflection* states that the angle of incidence is equal to the angle of reflection. *Incidence* is the arrival of a beam of light at a surface. **Figure 1** shows this law.

✓ **Reading Check** What is the law of reflection? (*See the Appendix for answers to Reading Checks.*)

READING WARM-UP

Objectives

● Describe how reflection allows you to see things.
● Describe absorption and scattering.
● Explain how refraction can create optical illusions and separate white light into colors.
● Explain the relationship between diffraction and wavelength.
● Compare constructive and destructive interference of light.

Terms to Learn

reflection   refraction
absorption   diffraction
scattering   interference

READING STRATEGY

Reading Organizer As you read this section, make a concept map by using the terms above.

Figure 1 **The Law of Reflection**

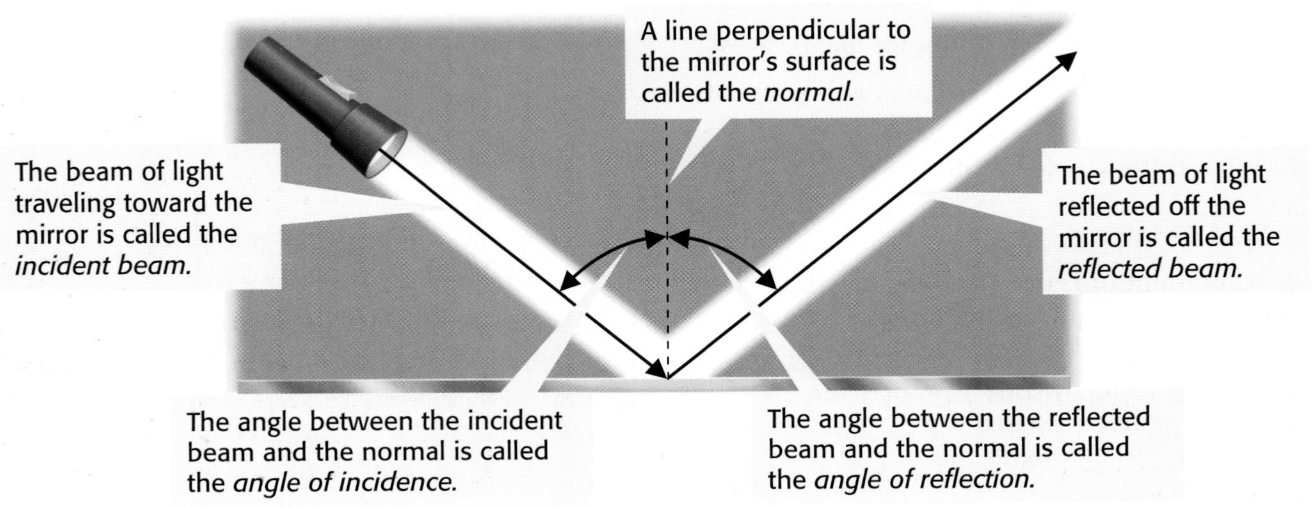

A line perpendicular to the mirror's surface is called the *normal*.

The beam of light traveling toward the mirror is called the *incident beam*.

The beam of light reflected off the mirror is called the *reflected beam*.

The angle between the incident beam and the normal is called the *angle of incidence*.

The angle between the reflected beam and the normal is called the *angle of reflection*.

Figure 2 Regular Reflection Vs. Diffuse Reflection

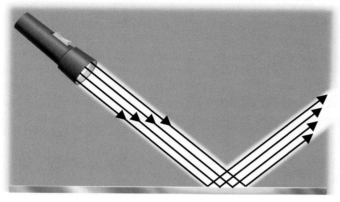

Regular reflection occurs when light beams are reflected at the same angle. When your eye detects the reflected beams, you can see a reflection on the surface.

Diffuse reflection occurs when light beams reflect at many different angles. You can't see a reflection because not all of the reflected light is directed toward your eyes.

Types of Reflection

So, why can you see your image in a mirror but not in a wall? The answer has to do with the differences between the two surfaces. A mirror's surface is very smooth. Thus, light beams reflect off all points of the mirror at the same angle. This kind of reflection is called *regular reflection*. A wall's surface is slightly rough. Light beams will hit the wall's surface and reflect at many different angles. This kind of reflection is called *diffuse reflection*. **Figure 2** shows the difference between the two kinds of reflection.

reflection the bouncing back of a ray of light, sound, or heat when the ray hits a surface that it does not go through

Light Source or Reflection?

If you look at a TV set in a bright room, you see the cabinet around the TV and the image on the screen. But if you look at the same TV in the dark, you see only the image on the screen. The difference is that the screen is a light source, but the cabinet around the TV is not.

You can see a light source even in the dark because its light passes directly into your eyes. The tail of the firefly in **Figure 3** is a light source. Flames, light bulbs, and the sun are also light sources. Objects that produce visible light are called *luminous* (LOO muh nuhs).

Most things around you are not light sources. But you can still see them because light from light sources reflects off the objects and then travels to your eyes. A visible object that is not a light source is *illuminated*.

Figure 3 You can see the tail of this firefly because it is luminous. But you see its body because it is illuminated.

✔ **Reading Check** List four different light sources.

Absorption and Scattering

absorption in optics, the transfer of light energy to particles of matter

scattering an interaction of light with matter that causes light to change its energy, direction of motion, or both

Have you noticed that when you use a flashlight, the light shining on things closer to you appears brighter than the light shining on things farther away? The light is less bright the farther it travels from the flashlight. The light is weaker partly because the beam spreads out and partly because of absorption and scattering.

Absorption of Light

The transfer of energy carried by light waves to particles of matter is called **absorption.** When a beam of light shines through the air, particles in the air absorb some of the energy from the light. As a result, the beam of light becomes dim. The farther the light travels from its source, the more it is absorbed by particles, and the dimmer it becomes.

Scattering of Light

Scattering is an interaction of light with matter that causes light to change direction. Light scatters in all directions after colliding with particles of matter. Light from the ship shown in **Figure 4** is scattered out of the beam by air particles. This scattered light allows you to see things that are outside the beam. But, because light is scattered out of the beam, the beam becomes dimmer.

Scattering makes the sky blue. Light with shorter wavelengths is scattered more than light with longer wavelengths. Sunlight is made up of many different colors of light, but blue light (which has a very short wavelength) is scattered more than any other color. So, when you look at the sky, you see a background of blue light.

Figure 4 *A beam of light becomes dimmer partly because of scattering.*

✓ **Reading Check** Why can you see things outside a beam of light?

Quick Lab

Scattering Milk

1. Fill a **2 L clear plastic bottle** with **water**.
2. Turn the lights off, and shine a **flashlight** through the water. Look at the water from all sides of the bottle. Write a description of what you see.
3. Add **3 drops of milk** to the water, and shake the bottle to mix it up.
4. Repeat step 2. Describe any color changes. If you don't see any, add more milk until you do.
5. How is the water-and-milk mixture like air particles in the atmosphere? Explain your answer.

Refraction

Imagine that you and a friend are at a lake. Your friend wades into the water. You look at her, and her feet appear to have separated from her legs! What has happened? You know her feet did not fall off, so how can you explain what you see? The answer has to do with refraction.

Refraction and Material

Refraction is the bending of a wave as it passes at an angle from one substance, or material, to another. **Figure 5** shows a beam of light refracting twice. Refraction of light waves occurs because the speed of light varies depending on the material through which the waves are traveling. In a vacuum, light travels at 300,000 km/s, but it travels more slowly through matter. When a wave enters a new material at an angle, the part of the wave that enters first begins traveling at a different speed from that of the rest of the wave.

refraction the bending of a wave as the wave passes between two substances in which the speed of the wave differs

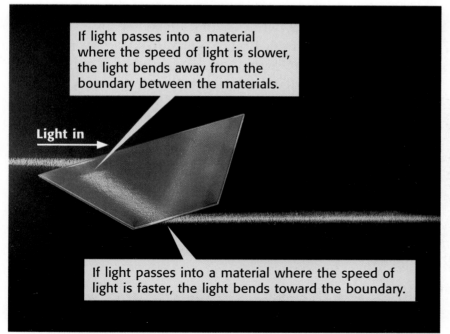

If light passes into a material where the speed of light is slower, the light bends away from the boundary between the materials.

Light in

If light passes into a material where the speed of light is faster, the light bends toward the boundary.

Figure 5 *Light travels more slowly through glass than it does through air. So, light refracts as it passes at an angle from air to glass or from glass to air. Notice that the light is also reflected inside the prism.*

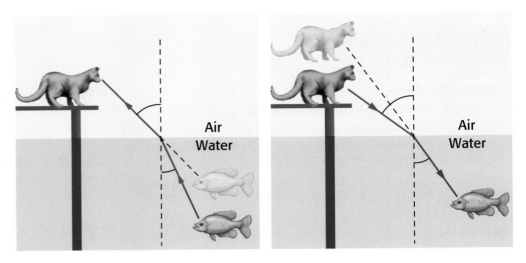

Figure 6 *Because of refraction, the cat and the fish see optical illusions. To the cat, the fish appears closer than it really is. To the fish, the cat appears farther away than it actually is.*

Air
Water

Air
Water

Refraction and Optical Illusions

Usually, when you look at an object, the light reflecting off the object travels in a straight line from the object to your eye. Your brain always interprets light as traveling in straight lines. But when you look at an object that is underwater, the light reflecting off the object does not travel in a straight line. Instead, it refracts. **Figure 6** shows how refraction creates an optical illusion. This kind of illusion causes a person's feet to appear separated from the legs when the person is wading.

Refraction and Color Separation

White light is composed of all the wavelengths of visible light. The different wavelengths of visible light are seen by humans as different colors. When white light is refracted, the amount that the light bends depends on its wavelength. Waves with short wavelengths bend more than waves with long wavelengths. As shown in **Figure 7,** white light can be separated into different colors during refraction. Color separation by refraction is responsible for the formation of rainbows. Rainbows are created when sunlight is refracted by water droplets.

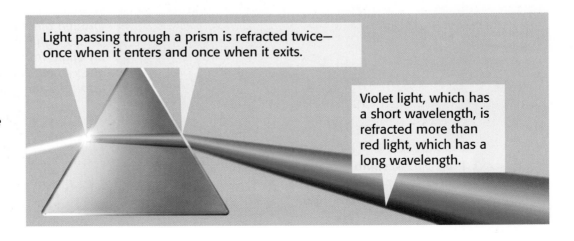

Light passing through a prism is refracted twice—once when it enters and once when it exits.

Violet light, which has a short wavelength, is refracted more than red light, which has a long wavelength.

Figure 7 *A prism is a piece of glass that separates white light into the colors of visible light by refraction.*

Quick Lab

Refraction Rainbow

1. **Tape** a **piece of construction paper** over the end of a **flashlight.** Use **scissors** to cut a slit in the paper.

2. Turn on the flashlight, and lay it on a table. Place a **prism** on end in the beam of light.

3. Slowly rotate the prism until you can see a rainbow on the surface of the table. Draw a diagram of the light beam, the prism, and the rainbow.

Diffraction

Refraction isn't the only way light waves are bent. **Diffraction** is the bending of waves around barriers or through openings. The amount a wave diffracts depends on its wavelength and the size of the barrier or the opening. The greatest amount of diffraction occurs when the barrier or opening is the same size or smaller than the wavelength.

diffraction a change in the direction of a wave when the wave finds an obstacle or an edge, such as an opening

✓ Reading Check The amount a wave diffracts depends on what two things?

Diffraction and Wavelength

The wavelength of visible light is very small—about 100 times thinner than a human hair! So, a light wave cannot bend very much by diffraction unless it passes through a narrow opening, around sharp edges, or around a small barrier, as shown in **Figure 8.**

Light waves cannot diffract very much around large obstacles, such as buildings. Thus, you can't see around corners. But light waves always diffract a small amount. You can observe light waves diffracting if you examine the edges of a shadow. Diffraction causes the edges of shadows to be blurry.

Figure 8 *This diffraction pattern is made by light of a single wavelength shining around the edges of a very tiny disk.*

Interference

Interference is a wave interaction that happens when two or more waves overlap. Overlapping waves can combine by constructive or destructive interference.

Constructive Interference

When waves combine by *constructive interference,* the resulting wave has a greater amplitude, or height, than the individual waves had. Constructive interference of light waves can be seen when light of one wavelength shines through two small slits onto a screen. The light on the screen will appear as a series of alternating bright and dark bands, as shown in **Figure 9.** The bright bands result from light waves combining through constructive interference.

Reading Check What is constructive interference?

Destructive Interference

When waves combine by *destructive interference,* the resulting wave has a smaller amplitude than the individual waves had. So, when light waves interfere destructively, the result will be dimmer light. Destructive interference forms the dark bands seen in **Figure 9.**

You do not see constructive or destructive interference of white light. To understand why, remember that white light is composed of waves with many different wavelengths. The waves rarely line up to combine in total destructive interference.

Figure 9 Constructive and Destructive Interference

① Red light of one wavelength passes between two tiny slits.

② The light waves diffract as they pass through the tiny slits.

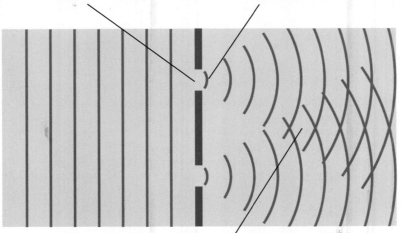

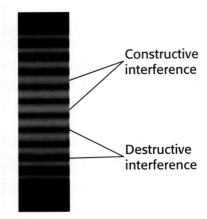

Constructive interference

Destructive interference

③ The diffracted light waves interfere both constructively and destructively.

④ The interference shows up on a screen as bright and dark bands.

SECTION Review

Summary

- The law of reflection states that the angle of incidence is equal to the angle of reflection.

- Things that are luminous can be seen because they produce their own light. Things that are illuminated can be seen because light reflects off them.

- Absorption is the transfer of light energy to particles of matter. Scattering is an interaction of light with matter that causes light to change direction.

- Refraction of light waves can create optical illusions and can separate white light into separate colors.

- How much light waves diffract depends on the light's wavelength. Light waves diffract more when traveling through a narrow opening.

- Interference can be constructive or destructive. Interference of light waves can cause bright and dark bands.

Using Key Terms

For each pair of terms, explain how the meanings of the terms differ.

1. *refraction* and *diffraction*

2. *absorption* and *scattering*

Understanding Key Ideas

3. Which light interaction explains why you can see things that do not produce their own light?

   a. absorption
   b. reflection
   c. refraction
   d. scattering

4. Describe how absorption and scattering can affect a beam of light.

5. Why do objects that are underwater look closer than they actually are?

6. How does a prism separate white light into different colors?

7. What is the relationship between diffraction and the wavelength of light?

Critical Thinking

8. **Applying Concepts** Explain why you can see your reflection on a spoon but not on a piece of cloth.

9. **Making Inferences** The planet Mars does not produce light. Explain why you can see Mars shining like a star at night.

10. **Making Comparisons** Compare constructive interference and destructive interference.

Interpreting Graphics

Use the image below to answer the questions that follow.

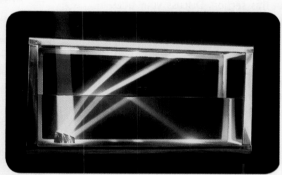

11. Why doesn't the large beam of light bend like the two beams in the middle of the tank?

12. Which light interaction explains what is happening to the bottom light beam?

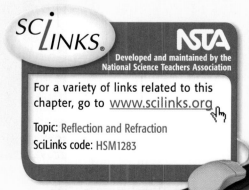

SCI LINKS.

NSTA
Developed and maintained by the
National Science Teachers Association

For a variety of links related to this chapter, go to www.scilinks.org

Topic: Reflection and Refraction
SciLinks code: HSM1283

Light and Color

Why are strawberries red and bananas yellow? How can a soda bottle be green, yet you can still see through it?

If white light is made of all the colors of light, how do things get their color from white light? Why aren't all things white in white light? Good questions! To answer these questions, you need to know how light interacts with matter.

Light and Matter

When light strikes any form of matter, it can interact with the matter in three different ways—the light can be reflected, absorbed, or transmitted.

Reflection happens when light bounces off an object. Reflected light allows you to see things. Absorption is the transfer of light energy to matter. Absorbed light can make things feel warmer. **Transmission** is the passing of light through matter. You see the transmission of light all the time. All of the light that reaches your eyes is transmitted through air. Light can interact with matter in several ways at the same time. Look at **Figure 1.** Light is transmitted, reflected, and absorbed when it strikes the glass in a window.

transmission the passing of light or other form of energy through matter

Figure 1 **Transmission, Reflection, and Absorption**

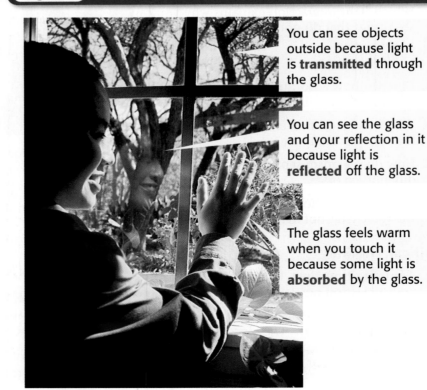

You can see objects outside because light is **transmitted** through the glass.

You can see the glass and your reflection in it because light is **reflected** off the glass.

The glass feels warm when you touch it because some light is **absorbed** by the glass.

Figure 2 Transparent, Translucent, and Opaque

Transparent plastic makes it easy to see what you are having for lunch.

Translucent wax paper makes it a little harder to see exactly what's for lunch.

Opaque aluminum foil makes it impossible to see your lunch without unwrapping it.

Types of Matter

Matter through which visible light is easily transmitted is said to be **transparent.** Air, glass, and water are examples of transparent matter. You can see objects clearly when you view them through transparent matter.

Sometimes, windows in bathrooms are made of frosted glass. If you look through one of these windows, you will see only blurry shapes. You can't see clearly through a frosted window because it is translucent (trans LOO suhnt). **Translucent** matter transmits light but also scatters the light as it passes through the matter. Wax paper is an example of translucent matter.

Matter that does not transmit any light is said to be **opaque** (oh PAYK). You cannot see through opaque objects. Metal, wood, and this book are examples of opaque objects. You can compare transparent, translucent, and opaque matter in **Figure 2.**

Reading Check List two examples of translucent objects. (*See the Appendix for answers to Reading Checks.*)

transparent describes matter that allows light to pass through with little interference

translucent describes matter that transmits light but that does not transmit an image

opaque describes an object that is not transparent or translucent

Colors of Objects

How is an object's color determined? Humans see different wavelengths of light as different colors. For example, humans see long wavelengths as red and short wavelengths as violet. And, some colors, like pink and brown, are seen when certain combinations of wavelengths are present.

The color that an object appears to be is determined by the wavelengths of light that reach your eyes. Light reaches your eyes after being reflected off an object or after being transmitted through an object. When your eyes receive the light, they send signals to your brain. Your brain interprets the signals as colors.

Figure 3 Opaque Objects and Color

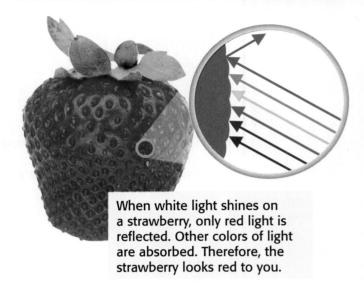

When white light shines on a strawberry, only red light is reflected. Other colors of light are absorbed. Therefore, the strawberry looks red to you.

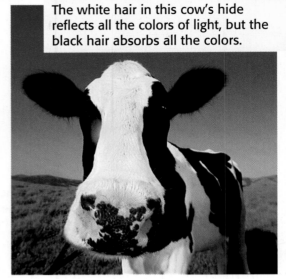

The white hair in this cow's hide reflects all the colors of light, but the black hair absorbs all the colors.

Colors of Opaque Objects

When white light strikes a colored opaque object, some colors of light are absorbed, and some are reflected. Only the light that is reflected reaches your eyes and is detected. So, the colors of light that are reflected by an opaque object determine the color you see. For example, if a sweater reflects blue light and absorbs all other colors, you will see that the sweater is blue. Another example is shown on the left in **Figure 3.**

What colors of light are reflected by the cow shown on the right in **Figure 3**? Remember that white light includes all colors of light. So, white objects—such as the white hair in the cow's hide—appear white because all the colors of light are reflected. On the other hand, black is the absence of color. When light strikes a black object, all the colors are absorbed.

✔ **Reading Check** What happens when white light strikes a colored opaque object?

Colors of Transparent and Translucent Objects

The color of transparent and translucent objects is determined differently than the color of opaque objects. Ordinary window glass is colorless in white light because it transmits all the colors that strike it. But some transparent objects are colored. When you look through colored transparent or translucent objects, you see the color of light that was transmitted through the material. The other colors were absorbed, as shown in **Figure 4.**

Figure 4 *This bottle is green because the plastic transmits green light.*

654

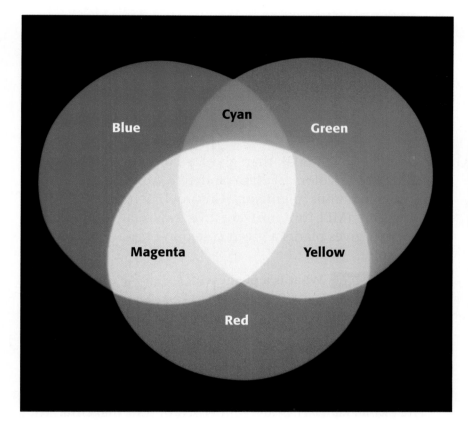

Figure 5 *Primary colors of light—written in white—combine to produce white light. Secondary colors of light—written in black—are the result of two primary colors added together.*

Mixing Colors of Light

In order to get white light, you must combine all colors of light, right? This method is one way of doing it. But you can also get light that appears white by adding just three colors of light together—red, blue, and green. The combination of these three colors is shown in **Figure 5.** In fact, these three colors can be combined in different ratios to produce many colors. Red, blue, and green are called the *primary colors of light.*

Color Addition

When colors of light combine, you see different colors. Combining colors of light is called *color addition.* When two primary colors of light are added together, you see a *secondary color of light.* The secondary colors of light are cyan (blue plus green), magenta (blue plus red), and yellow (red plus green). **Figure 5** shows how secondary colors of light are formed.

Light and Color Television

The colors on a color television are produced by color addition of the primary colors of light. A television screen is made up of groups of tiny red, green, and blue dots. Each dot will glow when the dot is hit by an electron beam. The colors given off by the glowing dots add together to produce all the different colors you see on the screen.

Television Colors

Turn on a color television. Ask an adult to carefully sprinkle a few tiny drops of water onto the television screen. Look closely at the drops of water, and discuss what you see. In your **science journal**, write a description of what you saw.

Mixing Colors of Pigment

If you have ever tried mixing paints in art class, you know that you can't make white paint by mixing red, blue, and green paint. The difference between mixing paint and mixing light is due to the fact that paint contains pigments.

Pigments and Color

A **pigment** is a material that gives a substance its color by absorbing some colors of light and reflecting others. Almost everything contains pigments. Chlorophyll (KLAWR uh FIL) and melanin (MEL uh nin) are two examples of pigments. Chlorophyll gives plants a green color, and melanin gives your skin its color.

 **Reading Check** What is a pigment?

Color Subtraction

Each pigment absorbs at least one color of light. Look at **Figure 6.** When you mix pigments together, more colors of light are absorbed or taken away. So, mixing pigments is called *color subtraction.*

The *primary pigments* are yellow, cyan, and magenta. They can be combined to produce any other color. In fact, every color in this book was produced by using just the primary pigments and black ink. The black ink was used to provide contrast to the images. **Figure 7** shows how the four pigments combine to produce many different colors.

Figure 6 *Primary pigments—written in black—combine to produce black. Secondary pigments—written in white—are the result of the subtraction of two primary pigments.*

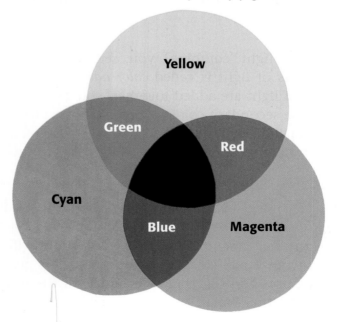

pigment a substance that gives another substance or a mixture its color

Quick Lab

Rose-Colored Glasses?

1. Obtain **four plastic filters**—red, blue, yellow, and green.
2. Look through one filter at an object across the room. Describe the object's color.
3. Repeat step 2 with each of the filters.
4. Repeat step 2 with two or three filters together.
5. Why do you think the colors change when you use more than one filter?
6. Write your observations and answers.

Figure 7 Color Subtraction and Color Printing

The picture of the balloon on the left was made by overlapping yellow ink, cyan ink, magenta ink, and black ink.

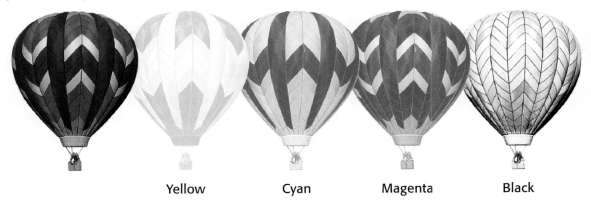

Yellow   Cyan   Magenta   Black

SECTION Review

Summary

- Objects are transparent, translucent, or opaque, depending on their ability to transmit light.

- Colors of opaque objects are determined by the color of light that they reflect.

- Colors of translucent and transparent objects are determined by the color of light they transmit.

- White light is a mixture of all colors of light.

- Light combines by color addition. The primary colors of light are red, blue, and green.

- Pigments give objects color. Pigments combine by color subtraction. The primary pigments are magenta, cyan, and yellow.

Using Key Terms

1. Use the following terms in the same sentence: *transmission* and *transparent*.

2. In your own words, write a definition for each of the following terms: *translucent* and *opaque*.

Understanding Key Ideas

3. You can see through a car window because the window is
   a. opaque.   c. transparent.
   b. translucent. d. transmitted.

4. Name and describe three different ways light interacts with matter.

5. How is the color of an opaque object determined?

6. Describe how the color of a transparent object is determined.

7. What are the primary colors of light, and why are they called *primary colors*?

8. What four colors of ink were used to print this book?

Critical Thinking

9. **Applying Concepts** What happens to the different colors of light when white light shines on an opaque violet object?

10. **Analyzing Ideas** Explain why mixing colors of light is called *color addition* but mixing pigments is called *color subtraction*.

Interpreting Graphics

11. Look at the image below. The red rose was photographed in red light. Explain why the leaves appear black and the petals appear red.

For a variety of links related to this chapter, go to www.scilinks.org

Topic: Colors
SciLinks code: HSM0314

Developed and maintained by the National Science Teachers Association

Use flashlights to mix colors of light by color addition.

Use paints to mix colors of pigments by color subtraction.

MATERIALS

Part A
- colored filters, red, green, and blue (1 of each)
- flashlights (3)
- paper, white
- tape, masking

Part B
- cups, small plastic or paper (2)
- paintbrush
- paper, white
- ruler, metric
- tape, masking
- water
- watercolor paints

SAFETY

Mixing Colors

Mix two colors, such as red and green, and you create a new color. Is the new color brighter or darker? Color and brightness depend on the light that reaches your eye. And what reaches your eye depends on whether you are adding colors (mixing colors of light) or subtracting colors (mixing colors of pigments). In this activity, you will do both types of color formation and see the results firsthand!

Part A: Color Addition

Procedure

1. Tape a colored filter over each flashlight lens.

2. In a darkened room, shine the red light on a sheet of white paper. Then, shine the green light next to the red light. You should have two circles of light, one red and one green, next to each other.

3. Move the flashlights so that the circles overlap by half their diameter. What color is formed where the circles overlap? Is the mixed area brighter or darker than the single-color areas? Record your observations.

Red ? Green

4. Repeat steps 2 and 3 with the red and blue lights.

5. Now, shine all three lights at the same point on the paper. Record your observations.

Analyze the Results

1 Describing Events In general, when you mixed two colors, was the result brighter or darker than the original colors?

2 Explaining Events In step 5, you mixed all three colors. Was the resulting color brighter or darker than when you mixed two colors? Explain your observations in terms of color addition.

Draw Conclusions

3 Making Predictions What do you think would happen if you mixed together all the colors of light? Explain your answer.

Part B: Color Subtraction

Procedure

1 Place a piece of masking tape on each cup. Label one cup "Clean" and the other cup "Dirty." Fill each cup about half full with water.

2 Wet the paintbrush thoroughly in the "Clean" cup. Using the watercolor paints, paint a red circle on the white paper. The circle should be approximately 4 cm in diameter.

3 Clean the brush by rinsing it first in the "Dirty" cup and then in the "Clean" cup.

4 Paint a blue circle next to the red circle. Then, paint half the red circle with the blue paint.

5 Examine the three areas: red, blue, and mixed. What color is the mixed area? Does it appear brighter or darker than the red and blue areas? Record your observations.

6 Clean the brush by repeating Step 3. Paint a green circle 4 cm in diameter, and then paint half the blue circle with green paint.

7 Examine the green, blue, and mixed areas. Record your observations.

8 Now add green paint to the mixed red-blue area so that you have an area that is a mixture of red, green, and blue paint. Clean the brush again.

9 Finally, record your observations of this new mixed area.

Analyze the Results

1 Identifying Patterns In general, when you mixed two colors, was the result brighter or darker than the original colors?

2 Analyzing Results In step 8, you mixed all three colors. Was the result brighter or darker than the result from mixing two colors? Explain what you saw in terms of color subtraction.

Draw Conclusions

3 Drawing Conclusions Based on your results, what do you think would happen if you mixed all the colors of paint? Explain your answer.

Chapter Review

USING KEY TERMS

Complete each of the following sentences by choosing the correct term from the word bank.

interference	radiation
scattering	opaque
translucent	transmission
electromagnetic wave	electromagnetic spectrum

1. _____ is the transfer of energy by electromagnetic waves.

2. This book is a(n) _____ object.

3. _____ is a wave interaction that occurs when two or more waves overlap and combine.

4. Light is a kind of _____ and can therefore travel through matter and space.

5. During _____, light travels through an object.

UNDERSTANDING KEY IDEAS

Multiple Choice

6. Electromagnetic waves transmit
   a. charges.
   b. fields.
   c. matter.
   d. energy.

7. Objects that transmit light easily are
   a. opaque.
   b. translucent.
   c. transparent.
   d. colored.

8. You can see yourself in a mirror because of
   a. absorption.
   b. scattering.
   c. regular reflection.
   d. diffuse reflection.

9. Shadows have blurry edges because of
   a. diffraction.
   b. scattering.
   c. diffuse reflection.
   d. refraction.

10. What color of light is produced when red light is added to green light?
   a. cyan   c. yellow
   b. blue   d. white

11. Prisms produce the colors of the rainbow through
   a. reflection.   c. diffraction.
   b. refraction.   d. interference.

12. Which kind of electromagnetic wave travels fastest in a vacuum?
   a. radio wave
   b. visible light
   c. gamma ray
   d. They all travel at the same speed.

13. Electromagnetic waves are made of
   a. vibrating particles.
   b. vibrating charged particles.
   c. vibrating electric and magnetic fields.
   d. All of the above

Short Answer

14 How are gamma rays used?

15 What are two uses for radio waves?

16 Why is it difficult to see through glass that has frost on it?

Math Skills

17 Calculate the time it takes for light from the sun to reach Mercury. Mercury is 54,900,000 km away from the sun.

CRITICAL THINKING

18 **Concept Mapping** Use the following terms to create a concept map: *light, matter, reflection, absorption,* and *transmission.*

19 **Applying Concepts** A tern is a type of bird that dives underwater to catch fish. When a young tern begins learning to catch fish, the bird is rarely successful. The tern has to learn that when a fish appears to be in a certain place underwater, the fish is actually in a slightly different place. Why does the tern see the fish in the wrong place?

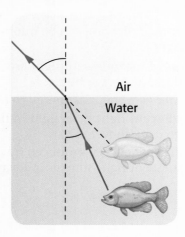

Air
Water

20 **Evaluating Conclusions** Imagine that you are teaching your younger brother about light. You tell him that white light is light of all the colors of the rainbow combined. But your brother says that you are wrong because mixing different colors of paint produces black and not white. Explain why your brother's conclusion is wrong.

21 **Making Inferences** If you look around a parking lot during the summer, you might see sunshades set up in the windshields of cars. How do sunshades help keep the insides of cars cool?

INTERPRETING GRAPHICS

22 Each of the pictures below shows the effects of a wave interaction of light. Identify the interaction involved.

a.

b.

c.

READING

Read each of the passages below. Then, answer the questions that follow each passage.

Passage 1 Jaundice occurs in some infants when bilirubin—a pigment in healthy red blood cells—builds up in the bloodstream as blood cells break down. This excess bilirubin is deposited in the skin, giving the skin a yellowish hue. Jaundice is not dangerous if treated quickly. If left untreated, it can lead to brain damage.

The excess bilirubin in the skin is best broken down by bright blue light. For this reason, hospitals hang special blue fluorescent lights above the cribs of newborns needing treatment. The blue light is sometimes balanced with light of other colors so that doctors and nurses can be sure the baby is not blue from a lack of oxygen.

1. Which of the following is a fact in the passage?
   A Jaundice is always very dangerous.
   B Bilirubin in the skin of infants can be broken down with bright blue light.
   C Excess bilirubin in the skin gives the skin a bright blue hue.
   D Blue lights can make a baby blue from a lack of oxygen.

2. What is the purpose of this passage?
   F to explain what jaundice is and how it is treated
   G to warn parents about shining blue light on their babies
   H to persuade light bulb manufacturers to make blue light bulbs
   I to explain the purpose of bilirubin in red blood cells

Passage 2 If you have ever looked inside a toaster while toasting a piece of bread, you may have seen thin wires or bars glowing red. The wires give off energy as light when heated to a high temperature. Light produced by hot objects is called *incandescent light*. Most of the lamps in your home probably use incandescent light bulbs.

Sources of incandescent light also release a large amount of <u>thermal</u> energy. Thermal energy is sometimes called *heat energy*. Sometimes, thermal energy from incandescent light is used to cook food or to warm a room. But often this thermal energy is not used for anything. For example, the thermal energy given off by light bulbs is not very useful.

1. What does the word *thermal* mean, based on its use in the passage?
   A light
   B energy
   C heat
   D food

2. What is incandescent light?
   F light used for cooking food
   G light that is red in color
   H light that is not very useful
   I light produced by hot objects

3. Which of the following can be inferred from the passage?
   A Sources of incandescent light are rarely found in an average home.
   B A toaster uses thermal energy to toast bread.
   C Incandescent light from light bulbs is often used to cook food.
   D The thermal energy produced by incandescent light sources is always useful.

The angles of refraction in the table were measured when a beam of light entered the material from air at a 45° angle. Use the table below to answer the questions that follow.

Material and Refraction		
Material	Index of refraction	Angle of refraction
Diamond	2.42	17°
Glass	1.52	28°
Quartz	1.46	29°
Water	1.33	32°

1. Which material has the highest index of refraction?
   A diamond
   B glass
   C quartz
   D water

2. Which material has the greatest angle of refraction?
   F diamond
   G glass
   H quartz
   I water

3. Which of the following statements **best** describes the data in the table?
   A The higher the index of refraction, the greater the angle of refraction.
   B The higher the index of refraction, the smaller the angle of refraction.
   C The greater the angle of refraction, the higher the index of refraction.
   D There is no relationship between the index of refraction and the angle of refraction.

4. Which two materials would be the most difficult to separate by observing only their angles of refraction?
   F diamond and glass
   G glass and quartz
   H quartz and water
   I water and diamond

Read each question below, and choose the best answer.

1. A square metal plate has an area of 46.3 cm². The length of one side of the plate is between which two values?
   A 4 cm and 5 cm
   B 5 cm and 6 cm
   C 6 cm and 7 cm
   D 7 cm and 8 cm

2. A jet was flying over the Gulf of Mexico at an altitude of 2,150 m. Directly below the jet, a submarine was at a depth of −383 m. What was the distance between the jet and the submarine?
   F −2,533 m
   G −1,767 m
   H 1,767 m
   I 2,533 m

3. The speed of light in a vacuum is exactly 299,792,458 m/s. Which of the following is a good estimate of the speed of light?
   A 3.0×10^{-8} m/s
   B 2.0×10^{8} m/s
   C 3.0×10^{8} m/s
   D 3.0×10^{9} m/s

4. The wavelength of the yellow light produced by a sodium vapor lamp is 0.000000589 m. Which of the following is equal to the wavelength of the sodium lamp's yellow light?
   F -5.89×10^{7} m
   G 5.89×10^{-9} m
   H 5.89×10^{-7} m
   I 5.89×10^{7} m

5. Amira purchased a box of light bulbs for $3.81. There are three light bulbs in the box. What is the cost per light bulb?
   A $0.79
   B $1.06
   C $1.27
   D $11.43

Science in Action

Weird Science

Fireflies Light the Way

Just as beams of light from lighthouses warn boats of approaching danger, the light of an unlikely source—fireflies—is being used by scientists to warn food inspectors of bacterial contamination.

Fireflies use an enzyme called *luciferase* to make light. Scientists have taken the gene from fireflies that tells cells how to make luciferase. They put this gene into a virus that preys on bacteria. The virus is not harmful to humans and can be mixed into meat. When the virus infects bacteria in the meat, the virus transfers the gene into the genes of the bacteria. The bacteria then produce luciferase and glow! So, if a food inspector sees glowing meat, the inspector knows that the meat is contaminated with bacteria.

Science, Technology, and Society

It's a Heat Wave

In 1946, Percy Spencer visited a laboratory belonging to Raytheon—the company he worked for. When he stood near a device called a *magnetron,* he noticed that a candy bar in his pocket melted. Spencer hypothesized that the microwaves produced by the magnetron caused the candy bar to warm up and melt. To test his hypothesis, Spencer put a bag of popcorn kernels next to the magnetron. The microwaves heated the kernels, causing them to pop! Spencer's simple experiment showed that microwaves could heat foods quickly. Spencer's discovery eventually led to the development of the microwave oven—an appliance found in many kitchens today.

Social Studies ACTiViTY

WRITING SKILL Many cultures have myths to explain certain natural phenomena. Read some of these myths. Then, write your own myth titled "How Fireflies Got Their Fire."

Math ACTiViTY

Popcorn pops when the inside of the kernel reaches a temperature of about 175°C. Convert this temperature to degrees Fahrenheit.

Albert Einstein

A Light Pioneer When Albert Einstein was 15 years old, he asked himself, "What would the world look like if I were speeding along on a motorcycle at the speed of light?" For many years afterward, he would think about this question and about the very nature of light, time, space, and matter. He even questioned the ideas of Isaac Newton, which had been widely accepted for 200 years. Einstein was bold. And he was able to see the universe in a totally new way.

In 1905, Einstein published a paper on the nature of light. He knew from the earlier experiments of others that light was a wavelike phenomenon. But he theorized that light could also travel as particles. Scientists did not readily accept Einstein's particle theory of light. Even 10 years later, the American physicist Robert Millikan, who proved that the particle theory of light was true, was reluctant to believe his own experimental results. Einstein's theory helped pave the way for television, computers, and other important technologies. The theory also earned Einstein a Nobel Prize in physics in 1921.

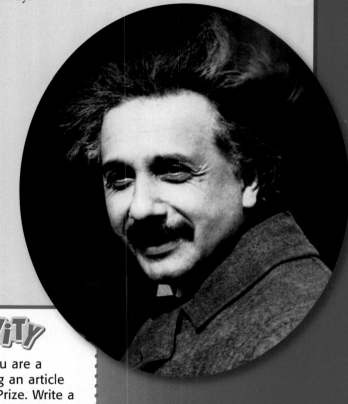

Language Arts ACTiViTY

WRITING SKILL Imagine that it is 1921. You are a newspaper reporter writing an article about Albert Einstein and his Nobel Prize. Write a one-page article about Albert Einstein, his theory, and the award he won.

To learn more about these Science in Action topics, visit go.hrw.com and type in the keyword **HP5LGTF.**

Current Science

Check out Current Science® articles related to this chapter by visiting go.hrw.com. Just type in the keyword **HP5CS22.**

23

Light and Our World

SECTION **1** **Mirrors and Lenses** . . . 668

SECTION **2** **Light and Sight** 674

SECTION **3** **Light and Technology** . . 678

Chapter Lab 686
Chapter Review 688
Standardized Test Preparation 690
Science in Action 692

About the PHOTO

This photo of Earth was taken by a satellite in space. All of the dots of light in this photo are lights in cities around the world. In areas with many dots, people live in cities that are close together. Light is very important in your every-day life. Not only does light help you see at night but light waves can also be used to send information over long distances. In fact, the satellite that took this picture sent the picture to Earth by using light waves!

PRE-READING ACTIVITY

FOLDNOTES **Tri-Fold** Before you read the chapter, create the FoldNote entitled "Tri-Fold" described in the **Study Skills** section of the Appendix. Write what you know about light in the column labeled "Know." Then, write what you want to know in the column labeled "Want." As you read the chapter, write what you learn about light in the column labeled "Learn."

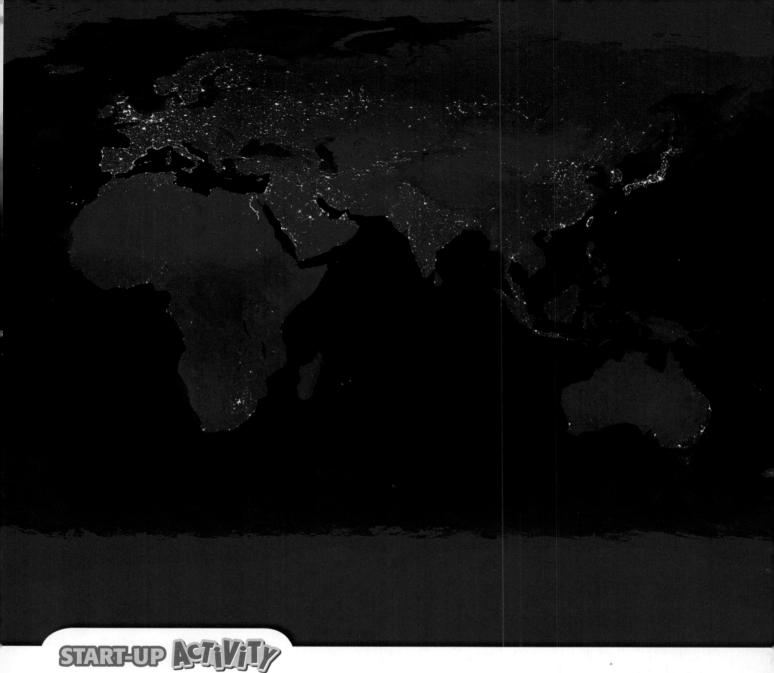

START-UP ACTIVITY

Mirror, Mirror

In this activity, you will study images formed by flat, or plane, mirrors.

Procedure

1. Tape a sheet of **graph paper** on your desk. Stand a **flat mirror** in the middle of the paper. Hold the mirror in place with pieces of **modeling clay.**

2. Place a **pen** four squares in front of the mirror. How many squares behind the mirror is the image of the pen? Move the pen farther away from the mirror. How did the image change?

3. Replace the mirror with **colored glass.** Look at the image of the pen in the glass. Compare the image in the glass with the one in the mirror.

4. Draw a square on the graph paper in front of the glass. Then, look through the glass, and trace the image of the square on the paper behind the glass. Using a **metric ruler,** measure and compare the two squares.

Analysis

1. How does the distance from an object to a plane mirror compare with the apparent distance from the mirror to the object's image behind the mirror?

2. Images formed in the colored glass are similar to images formed in a plane mirror. In general, how does the size of an object compare with that of its image in a plane mirror?

Mirrors and Lenses

When walking by an ambulance, you notice that the letters on the front of the ambulance look strange. Some letters are backward, and they don't seem to spell a word!

Look at **Figure 1.** The letters spell the word *ambulance* when viewed in a mirror. Images in mirrors are reversed left to right. The word *ambulance* is spelled backward so that people driving cars can read it when they see an ambulance in their rearview mirrors. To understand how images are formed in mirrors, you must first learn how to use rays to trace the path of light waves.

Rays and the Path of Light Waves

Light waves are electromagnetic waves. Light waves travel from their source in all directions. If you could trace the path of one light wave as it travels away from a light source, you would find that the path is a straight line. Because light waves travel in straight lines, you can use an arrow called a *ray* to show the path and the direction of a light wave.

Rays and Reflected and Refracted Light

Rays help to show the path of a light wave after it bounces or bends. Light waves that bounce off an object are reflected. Light waves that bend when passing from one medium to another are refracted. So, rays in ray diagrams show changes in the direction light travels after being reflected by mirrors or refracted by lenses.

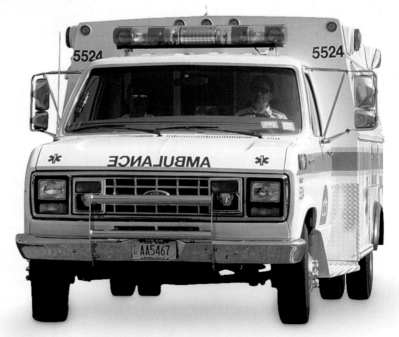

Figure 1 *If you hold this photo up to the mirror in your bathroom, you will see the word* AMBULANCE.

Mirrors and Reflection of Light

Have you ever looked at your reflection in a metal spoon? The spoon is like a mirror but not like a bathroom mirror! If you look on one side of the spoon, your face is upside down. But on the other side, your face is right side up. Why? Read on to find out!

The shape of a mirror affects the way light reflects from it. So, the image you see in your bathroom mirror differs from the image you see in a spoon. Mirrors are classified by their shape. Three shapes of mirrors are plane, concave, and convex.

Plane Mirrors

Most mirrors, such as the one in your bathroom, are plane mirrors. A **plane mirror** is a mirror that has a flat surface. When you look in a plane mirror, your reflection is right side up. The image is also the same size as you are. Images in plane mirrors are reversed left to right, as shown in **Figure 2.**

In a plane mirror, your image appears to be the same distance behind the mirror as you are in front of it. Why does your image seem to be behind the mirror? When light reflects off the mirror, your brain thinks the reflected light travels in a straight line from behind the mirror. The ray diagram in **Figure 3** explains how light travels when you look into a mirror. The image formed by a plane mirror is a virtual image. A *virtual image* is an image through which light does not travel.

Reading Check What is a virtual image? (*See the Appendix for answers to Reading Checks.*)

Figure 2 *Rearview mirrors in cars are plane mirrors. This mirror shows the reflection of the front of the ambulance shown in Figure 1.*

plane mirror a mirror that has a flat surface

Figure 3 **How Images Are Formed in Plane Mirrors**

The rays show how light reaches your eyes. The dotted lines show where the light appears to come from.

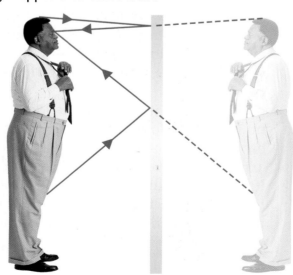

Light reflects off you and strikes the mirror. The light then reflects off the mirror at an angle equal to the angle at which the light hit the mirror. Some of the reflected light enters your eyes.

Your image appears to be behind the mirror because your brain assumes that the light rays that enter your eyes travel in a straight line from an object to your eyes.

Figure 4 *Concave mirrors are curved like the inside of a spoon. The image formed by a concave mirror depends on the optical axis, focal point, and focal length of the mirror.*

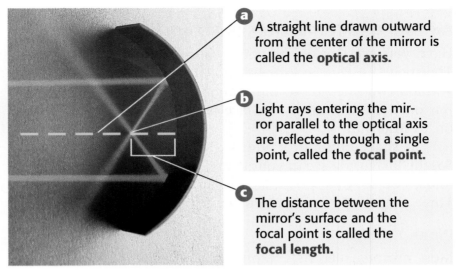

ⓐ A straight line drawn outward from the center of the mirror is called the **optical axis.**

ⓑ Light rays entering the mirror parallel to the optical axis are reflected through a single point, called the **focal point.**

ⓒ The distance between the mirror's surface and the focal point is called the **focal length.**

concave mirror a mirror that is curved inward like the inside of a spoon

convex mirror a mirror that is curved outward like the back of a spoon

For another activity related to this chapter, go to **go.hrw.com** and type in the keyword **HP5LOWW.**

Concave Mirrors

A mirror that is curved inward is called a **concave mirror.** The images formed by concave mirrors differ from the images formed by plane mirrors. The image formed by a concave mirror depends on three things: the optical axis, focal point, and focal length of the mirror. **Figure 4** explains these terms.

You have already learned that plane mirrors can form only virtual images. Concave mirrors also form virtual images. But they can form real images, too. A *real image* is an image through which light passes. A real image can be projected onto a screen, but a virtual image cannot.

Concave Mirrors and Ray Diagrams

To find out what kind of image a concave mirror forms, you can make a ray diagram. Draw two rays from the top of the object to the mirror. Then, draw rays reflecting from the surface of the mirror. If the reflected rays cross in front of the mirror, a real image is formed. If the reflected rays do not cross in front of the mirror, extend the reflected rays in straight lines behind the mirror. Those lines will cross to show where a virtual image is formed. Study **Figure 5** to better understand ray diagrams.

If an object is placed at the focal point of a concave mirror, no image will form. All rays that pass through the focal point on their way to the mirror will reflect parallel to the optical axis. The rays will never cross in front of or behind the mirror. If you put a light source at the focal point of a concave mirror, light will reflect outward in a powerful beam. So, concave mirrors are used in car headlights and flashlights.

✓ Reading Check How can a concave mirror be used to make a powerful beam of light?

Figure 5 *The type of image formed by a concave mirror depends on the distance between the object and the mirror.*

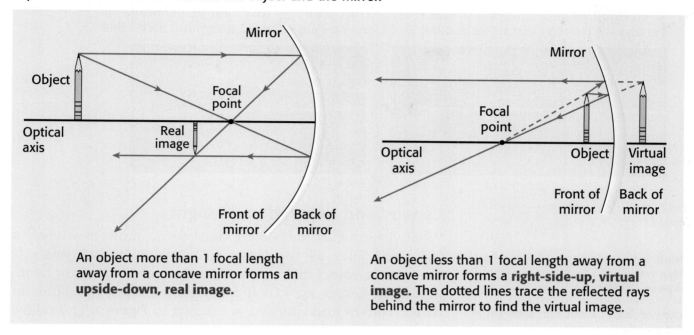

An object more than 1 focal length away from a concave mirror forms an **upside-down, real image.**

An object less than 1 focal length away from a concave mirror forms a **right-side-up, virtual image.** The dotted lines trace the reflected rays behind the mirror to find the virtual image.

Convex Mirrors

If you look at your reflection in the back of a spoon, you will notice that your image is right side up and small. The back of a spoon is a convex mirror. A **convex mirror** is a mirror that curves outward. **Figure 6** shows how an image is formed by a convex mirror. The reflected rays do not cross in front of a convex mirror. So, the reflected rays are extended behind the mirror to find the virtual image. All images formed by convex mirrors are virtual, right side up, and smaller than the original object. Convex mirrors are useful because they make images of large areas. So, convex mirrors are often used for security in stores and factories. Convex mirrors are also used as side mirrors on cars and trucks.

School to Home

Car Mirrors

Sit in the passenger side of a car. Ask an adult at home to stand one car-length behind the car. Look at the adult's reflection in the passenger side mirror. Then, look at the adult's reflection in the rearview mirror. Make a table comparing the two mirrors and the images you saw in each mirror.

ACTIVITY

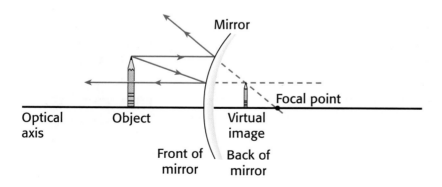

Figure 6 *All images formed by convex mirrors are formed behind the mirror. Therefore, all images formed by convex mirrors are virtual.*

Figure 7 **How Light Passes Through Lenses**

When light rays pass through a **convex lens,** the rays are refracted toward each other.

When light rays pass through a **concave lens,** the rays are refracted away from each other.

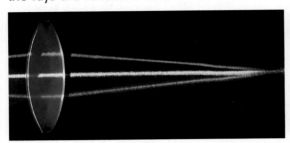 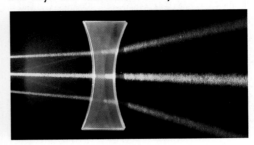

Lenses and Refraction of Light

What do cameras, telescopes, and movie projectors have in common? They all use lenses to create images. A **lens** is a transparent object that forms an image by refracting, or bending, light. Lenses are classified by their shape. Two kinds of lenses, convex and concave, are shown in **Figure 7.** The yellow beams in **Figure 7** show that light rays that pass through the center of any lens are not refracted. Like mirrors, lenses have a focal point and an optical axis.

lens a transparent object that refracts light waves such that they converge or diverge to create an image

convex lens a lens that is thicker in the middle than at the edges

concave lens a lens that is thinner in the middle than at the edges

Convex Lenses

A **convex lens** is a lens that is thicker in the middle than at the edges. Convex lenses form different kinds of images. The ways in which two of these kinds of images are formed are shown in **Figure 8.** In addition, a convex lens can form a real image that is larger than the object if the object is between 1 and 2 focal lengths away from the lens. Convex lenses have many uses. For example, magnifying lenses and camera lenses are convex lenses. And convex lenses are sometimes used in eyeglasses.

Reading Check What is a convex lens?

Figure 8 *The distance between an object and a convex lens determines the size and the kind of image formed.*

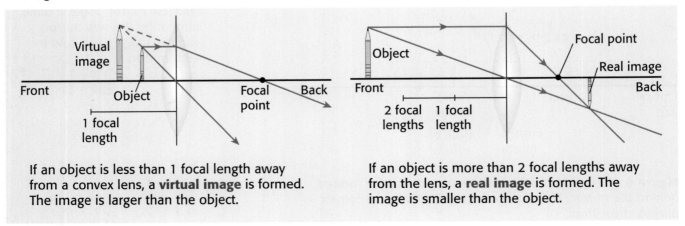

If an object is less than 1 focal length away from a convex lens, a **virtual image** is formed. The image is larger than the object.

If an object is more than 2 focal lengths away from the lens, a **real image** is formed. The image is smaller than the object.

Concave Lenses

A **concave lens** is a lens that is thinner in the middle than at the edges. Light rays entering a concave lens parallel to the optical axis always bend away from each other and appear to come from a focal point in front of the lens. The rays never meet. So, concave lenses never form a real image. Instead, they form virtual images, as shown in **Figure 9.** Concave lenses are sometimes combined with other lenses in telescopes. The combination of lenses produces clearer images of distant objects. Concave lenses are also used in microscopes and eyeglasses.

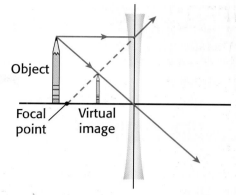

Figure 9 *Concave lenses form virtual images. The image is smaller than the object.*

SECTION Review

Summary

● Rays are arrows that show the path of a single light wave.

● Ray diagrams can be used to find where images are formed by mirrors and lenses.

● Plane mirrors and convex mirrors produce virtual images. Concave mirrors produce both real images and virtual images.

● Convex lenses produce both real images and virtual images. Concave lenses produce only virtual images.

Using Key Terms

For each pair of terms, explain how the meanings of the terms differ.

1. *convex mirror* and *concave mirror*

2. *convex lens* and *concave lens*

Understanding Key Ideas

3. Which of the following can form real images?
   a. a plane mirror
   b. a convex mirror
   c. a convex lens
   d. a concave lens

4. Explain how you can use a ray diagram to determine if a real image or a virtual image is formed by a mirror.

5. Compare the images formed by plane mirrors, concave mirrors, and convex mirrors.

6. Describe the images that can be formed by convex lenses.

7. Explain why a concave lens cannot form a real image.

Critical Thinking

8. **Applying Concepts** Why is an image right side up on the back of a spoon but upside down on the inside of a spoon?

9. **Making Inferences** Teachers sometimes use overhead projectors to show transparencies on a screen. What type of lens does an overhead projector use?

Interpreting Graphics

10. Look at the ray diagram below. Identify the type of lens and the kind of image that is formed.

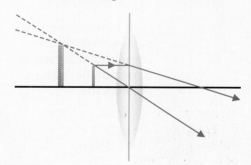

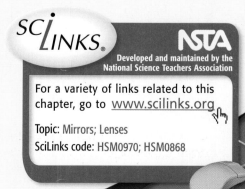

SECTION 2

Light and Sight

When you look around, you can see objects both near and far. You can also see the different colors of the objects.

You see objects that produce their own light because the light is detected by your eyes. You see all other objects because light reflected from the objects enters your eyes. But how do your eyes work, and what causes people to have vision problems?

READING WARM-UP

Objectives

- Identify the parts of the human eye, and describe their functions.
- Describe three common vision problems.
- Describe surgical eye correction.

Terms to Learn

nearsightedness
farsightedness

READING STRATEGY

Reading Organizer As you read this section, make a flowchart of how the eye works.

How You Detect Light

Visible light is the part of the electromagnetic spectrum that can be detected by your eyes. Your eye gathers light to form the images that you see. The steps of this process are shown in **Figure 1.** Muscles around the lens change the thickness of the lens so that objects at different distances can be seen in focus. The light that forms the real image is detected by receptors in the retina called *rods* and *cones*. Rods can detect very dim light. Cones detect colors in bright light.

Figure 1 **How Your Eyes Work**

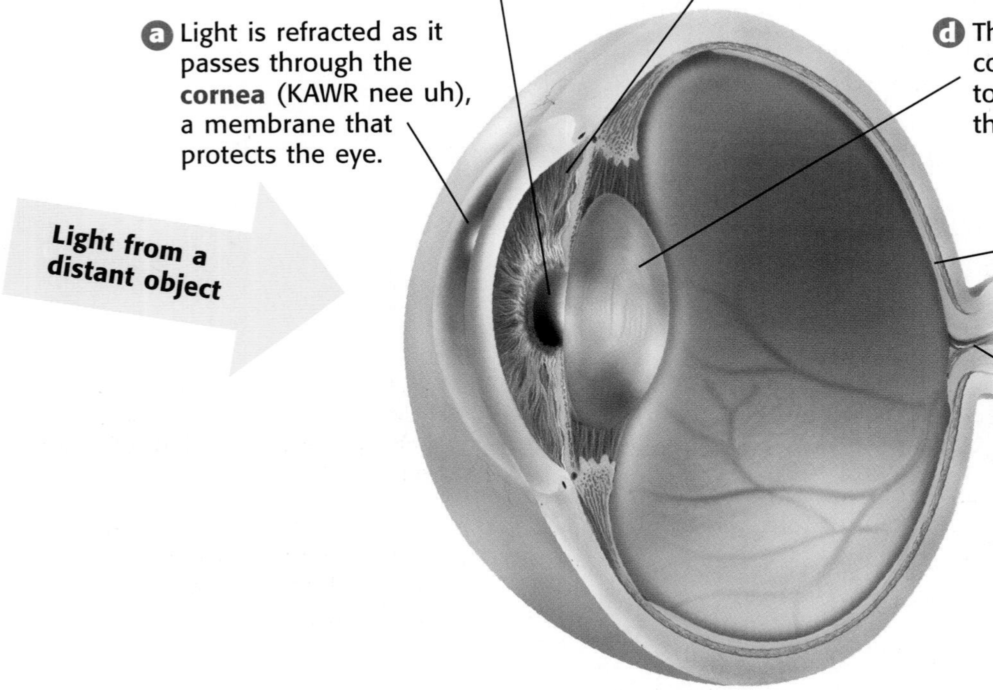

Light from a distant object
a Light is refracted as it passes through the **cornea** (KAWR nee uh), a membrane that protects the eye.
b Light passes through the **pupil,** the opening in the eye.
c The size of the pupil is controlled by the **iris,** which is the colored part of the eye.
d The **lens** of the eye is convex and refracts light to focus a real image on the back of the eye.
e The back surface of the eye is called the **retina** (RET 'n uh). Light is detected by receptors in the retina called *rods* and *cones*.
f Nerves attached to the rods and cones carry information to the brain about the light that strikes the retina.

Figure 2 Correcting Nearsightedness and Farsightedness

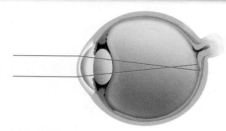

Nearsightedness happens when the eye is too long, which causes the lens to focus light in front of the retina.

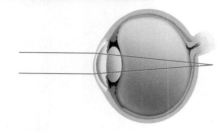

Farsightedness happens when the eye is too short, which causes the lens to focus light behind the retina.

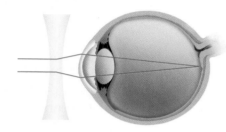

A **concave lens** placed in front of a nearsighted eye refracts the light outward. The lens in the eye can then focus the light on the retina.

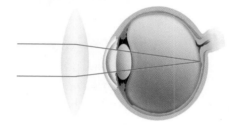

A **convex lens** placed in front of a farsighted eye focuses the light. The lens in the eye can then focus the light on the retina.

Common Vision Problems

People who have normal vision can clearly see objects that are close and objects that are far away. They can also tell the difference between all colors of visible light. But because the eye is complex, it's no surprise that many people have defects in their eyes that affect their vision.

Nearsightedness and Farsightedness

The lens of a properly working eye focuses light on the retina. So, the images formed are always clear. Two common vision problems happen when light is not focused on the retina, as shown in **Figure 2. Nearsightedness** happens when a person's eye is too long. A nearsighted person can see something clearly only if it is nearby. Objects that are far away look blurry. **Farsightedness** happens when a person's eye is too short. A farsighted person can see faraway objects clearly. But things that are nearby look blurry. **Figure 2** also shows how these vision problems can be corrected with glasses.

✔ Reading Check What causes nearsightedness and farsightedness? (*See the Appendix for answers to Reading Checks.*)

nearsightedness a condition in which the lens of the eye focuses distant objects in front of rather than on the retina

farsightedness a condition in which the lens of the eye focuses distant objects behind rather than on the retina

Figure 3 *The photo on the left is what a person who has normal vision sees. The photo on the right is a simulation of what a person who has red-green color deficiency might see.*

Color Deficiency

About 5% to 8% of men and 0.5% of women in the world have *color deficiency,* or colorblindness. The majority of people who have color deficiency can't tell the difference between shades of red and green or can't tell red from green. **Figure 3** compares what a person with normal vision sees with what a person who has red-green color deficiency sees. Color deficiency cannot be corrected.

Color deficiency happens when the cones in the retina do not work properly. The three kinds of cones are named for the colors they detect most—red, green, or blue. But each kind can detect many colors of light. A person who has normal vision can see all colors of visible light. But in some people, the cones respond to the wrong colors. Those people see certain colors, such as red and green, as a different color, such as yellow.

✓ **Reading Check** What are the three kinds of cones?

CONNECTION TO
Biology

Color Deficiency and Genes The ability to see color is a sex-linked genetic trait. Certain genes control which colors of light the cones detect. If these genes are defective in a person, that person will have color deficiency. A person needs one set of normal genes to have normal color vision. Genes that control the red cones and the green cones are on the X chromosome. Women have two X chromosomes, but men have only one. So, men are more likely than women to lack a set of these genes and to have red-green color deficiency. Research two other sex-linked traits, and make a graph comparing the percentage of men and women who have the traits.

ACTiViTY

Surgical Eye Correction

Using surgery to correct nearsightedness or farsight-edness is possible. Surgical eye correction works by reshaping the patient's cornea. Remember that the cornea refracts light. So, reshaping the cornea changes how light is focused on the retina.

To prepare for eye surgery, an eye doctor uses a machine to measure the patient's corneas. A laser is then used to reshape each cornea so that the patient gains perfect or nearly perfect vision. **Figure 4** shows a patient undergoing eye surgery.

Risks of Surgical Eye Correction

Although vision-correction surgery can be helpful, it has some risks. Some patients report glares or double vision. Others have trouble seeing at night. Other patients lose vision permanently. People under 20 years old shouldn't have vision-correction surgery because their vision is still changing.

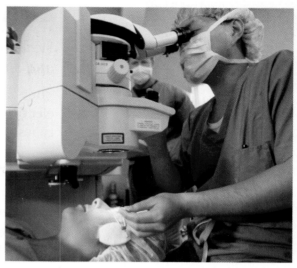

Figure 4 *An eye surgeon uses a very precise laser to reshape this patient's cornea.*

SECTION Review

Summary

- The human eye has several parts, including the cornea, the pupil, the iris, the lens, and the retina.

- Nearsightedness and farsightedness happen when light is not focused on the retina. Both problems can be corrected with glasses or eye surgery.

- Color deficiency is a condition in which cones in the retina respond to the wrong colors.

- Eye surgery can correct some vision problems.

Using Key Terms

1. Use each of the following terms in a separate sentence: *nearsightedness* and *farsightedness*.

Understanding Key Ideas

2. A person who is nearsighted will have the most trouble reading
   a. a computer screen in front of him or her.
   b. a book in his or her hands.
   c. a street sign across the street.
   d. the title of a pamphlet on a nearby table.

3. List the parts of the eye, and describe what each part does.

4. What are three common vision problems?

5. How are nearsightedness and farsightedness corrected?

6. Describe surgical eye correction.

7. What do the rods and cones in the eye do?

Math Skills

8. About 0.5% of women have a color deficiency. How many women out of 200 have a color deficiency?

Critical Thinking

9. **Forming Hypotheses** Why do you think color deficiency cannot be corrected?

10. **Expressing Opinions** Would you have surgical eye correction? Explain your reasons.

Light and Technology

What do cameras, telescopes, lasers, cellular telephones, and satellite televisions have in common?

They are all types of technology that use light or other electromagnetic waves. Read on to learn how these and other types of light technology are useful in your everyday life.

Optical Instruments

Optical instruments are devices that use mirrors and lenses to help people make observations. Some optical instruments help you see things that are very far away. Others help you see things that are very small. Some optical instruments record images. The optical instrument that you are probably most familiar with is the camera.

Cameras

Cameras are used to record images. **Figure 1** shows the parts of a 35 mm camera. A digital camera has a lens, a shutter, and an aperture (AP uhr chuhr) like a 35 mm camera has. But instead of using film, a digital camera uses light sensors to record images. The sensors send an electrical signal to a computer in the camera. This signal contains data about the image that is stored in the computer, on a memory stick, card, or disk.

Figure 1 How a Camera Works

The **shutter** opens and closes behind the lens to control how much light enters the camera. The longer the shutter is open, the more light enters the camera.

The **lens** of a camera is a convex lens that focuses light on the film. Moving the lens focuses light from objects at different distances.

The **film** is coated with chemicals that react when they are exposed to light. The result is an image stored on the film.

The **aperture** is an opening that lets light into the camera. The larger the aperture is, the more light enters the camera.

Figure 2 | How Refracting and Reflecting Telescopes Work

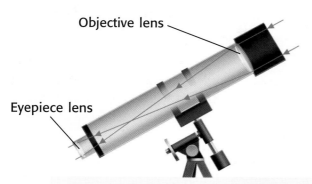

Objective lens

Eyepiece lens

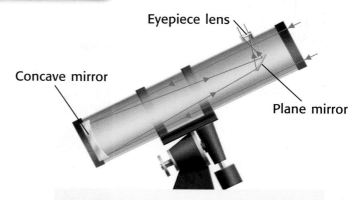

Eyepiece lens

Concave mirror

Plane mirror

A **refracting telescope** has two convex lenses. Light enters through the objective lens and forms a real image. This real image is then magnified by the eyepiece lens. You see this magnified image when you look through the eyepiece lens.

A **reflecting telescope** has a concave mirror that collects and focuses light to form a real image. The light strikes a plane mirror that directs the light to the convex eyepiece lens, which magnifies the real image.

Telescopes

Telescopes are used to see detailed images of large, distant objects. Astronomers use telescopes to study things in space, such as the moon, planets, and stars. Telescopes are classified as either refracting or reflecting. *Refracting telescopes* use lenses to collect light. *Reflecting telescopes* use mirrors to collect light. **Figure 2** shows how these two kinds of telescopes work.

Light Microscopes

Simple light microscopes are similar to refracting telescopes. These microscopes have two convex lenses. An objective lens is close to the object being studied. An eyepiece lens is the lens you look through. Microscopes are used to see magnified images of tiny, nearby objects.

Lasers and Laser Light

A **laser** is a device that produces intense light of only one color and wavelength. Laser light is different from nonlaser light in many ways. One important difference is that laser light is *coherent*. When light is coherent, light waves move together as they travel away from their source. The crests and troughs of coherent light waves are aligned. So, the individual waves behave as one wave.

✓ **Reading Check** What does it mean for light to be coherent? (*See the Appendix for answers to Reading Checks.*)

Microscope Magnification
Some microscopes use more than one lens to magnify objects. The power of each lens indicates the amount of magnification the lens gives. For example, a 10× lens magnifies objects 10 times. To find the amount of magnification given by two or more lenses used together, multiply the powers of the lenses. What is the magnification given by a 5× lens used with a 20× lens?

laser a device that produces intense light of only one wavelength and color

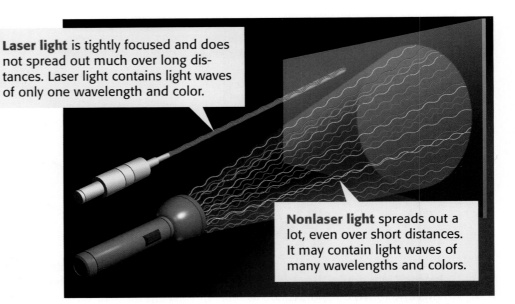

Laser light is tightly focused and does not spread out much over long distances. Laser light contains light waves of only one wavelength and color.

Figure 3 *Laser light is very different from nonlaser light.*

Nonlaser light spreads out a lot, even over short distances. It may contain light waves of many wavelengths and colors.

How Lasers Produce Light

Figure 3 compares laser and nonlaser light. The word *laser* stands for **l**ight **a**mplification by **s**timulated **e**mission of **r**adiation. *Amplification* is the increase in the brightness of the light. *Radiation* is energy transferred as electromagnetic waves.

What is stimulated emission? In an atom, an electron can move from one energy level to another. A photon (a particle of light) is released when an electron moves from a higher energy level to a lower energy level. The release of photons is called *emission*. *Stimulated emission* occurs when a photon strikes an atom that is in an excited state and makes the atom emit another photon. The newly emitted photon is identical to the first photon. The two photons travel away from the atom together. **Figure 4** shows how laser light is produced.

Figure 4 How a Helium-Neon Laser Works

ⓐ The inside of the laser is filled with helium and neon gases. An electric current in the laser excites the atoms of the gases.

ⓑ Excited neon atoms release photons of red light. When these photons strike other excited neon atoms, stimulated emission occurs.

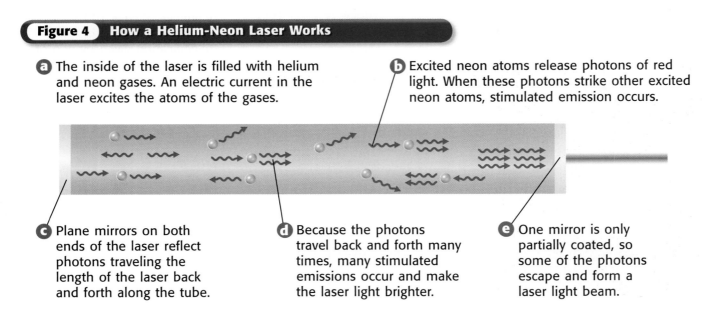

ⓒ Plane mirrors on both ends of the laser reflect photons traveling the length of the laser back and forth along the tube.

ⓓ Because the photons travel back and forth many times, many stimulated emissions occur and make the laser light brighter.

ⓔ One mirror is only partially coated, so some of the photons escape and form a laser light beam.

Uses for Lasers

Lasers are used to make holograms, such as the one shown in **Figure 5.** A **hologram** is a piece of film that produces a three-dimensional image of an object. Holograms are similar to photographs because both are images recorded on film. However, unlike photographs, the images you see in holograms are not on the surface of the film. The images appear in front of or behind the film. If you move the hologram, you will see the image from different angles.

Lasers are also used for other tasks. For example, lasers are used to cut materials such as metal and cloth. Doctors sometimes use lasers for surgery. And CD players have lasers. Light from the laser in a CD player reflects off patterns on a CD's surface. The reflected light is converted to a sound wave.

Reading Check How are holograms like photographs?

Optical Fibers

Imagine a glass thread that transmits more than 1,000 telephone conversations at the same time with flashes of light. This thread, called an *optical fiber,* is a thin, glass wire that transmits light over long distances. Some optical fibers are shown in **Figure 6.** Transmitting information through telephone cables is the most common use of optical fibers. Optical fibers are also used to network computers. And they allow doctors to see inside patients' bodies without performing major surgery.

Light in a Pipe

Optical fibers are like pipes that carry light. Light stays inside an optical fiber because of total internal reflection. *Total internal reflection* is the complete reflection of light along the inside surface of the material through which it travels. **Figure 6** shows total internal reflection in an optical fiber.

hologram a piece of film that produces a three-dimensional image of an object; made by using laser light

Figure 5 *Some holograms make three-dimensional images that look so real that you might want to reach out and touch them!*

Figure 6 **How Optical Fibers Work**

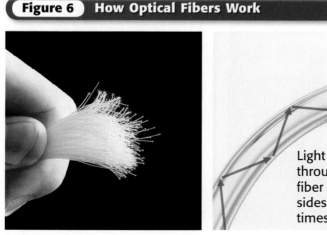

Light traveling through an optical fiber reflects off the sides thousands of times each meter.

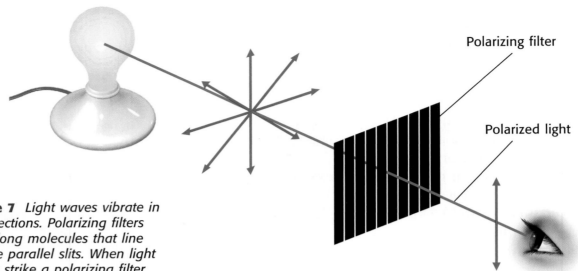

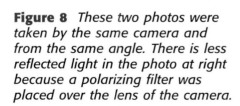

Figure 7 *Light waves vibrate in all directions. Polarizing filters have long molecules that line up like parallel slits. When light waves strike a polarizing filter, only the light waves vibrating in the same direction as the slits pass through.*

Polarized Light

The next time you shop for sunglasses, look for some that have lenses that polarize light. Such sunglasses are good for reducing glare. *Polarized light* consists of light waves that vibrate in only one plane. **Figure 7** illustrates how light is polarized.

When light reflects off a horizontal surface, such as a car hood or a body of water, the light is polarized horizontally. You see this polarized light as glare. Polarizing sunglasses reduce glare from horizontal surfaces because the lenses have vertically polarized filters. These filters allow only vertically vibrating light waves to pass through them. Polarizing filters are also used by photographers to reduce glare in their photographs, as shown in **Figure 8.**

Figure 8 *These two photos were taken by the same camera and from the same angle. There is less reflected light in the photo at right because a polarizing filter was placed over the lens of the camera.*

Quick Lab

Blackout!

1. Hold a **lens from a pair of polarizing sunglasses** up to your eye, and look through the lens. Record your observations.

2. Put a **second polarizing lens** over the first lens. Make sure both lenses are right side up. Look through both lenses, and describe your observations.

3. Rotate one lens slowly as you look through both lenses, and describe what happens.

4. Why can't you see through the lenses when they are aligned a certain way?

Communication Technology

You may think that talking on the telephone has nothing to do with light. But if you are talking on a cordless telephone or a cellular telephone, you are using a form of light technology! Light is an electromagnetic wave. There are many different kinds of electromagnetic waves. Radio waves and microwaves are kinds of electromagnetic waves. And cordless telephones and cellular telephones use radio waves and microwaves to send signals.

Cordless Telephones

Cordless telephones are a combination of a regular telephone and a radio. There are two parts to a cordless telephone—the base and the handset. The base is connected to a telephone jack in the wall of a building. The base receives calls through the phone line. The base then changes the signal to a radio wave and sends the signal to the handset. The handset changes the radio signal to sound for you to hear. The handset also changes your voice to a radio wave that is sent back to the base.

Figure 9 *You can make and receive calls with a cellular telephone almost everywhere you go.*

✔ **Reading Check** What kind of electromagnetic wave does a cordless telephone use?

Cellular Telephones

The telephone in **Figure 9** is a cellular telephone. Cellular telephones are similar to the handset part of a cordless telephone because they send and receive signals. But a cellular telephone receives signals from tower antennas located across the country instead of from a base. And instead of using radio waves, cellular telephones use microwaves to send information.

Satellite Television

Another technology that uses electromagnetic waves to transmit data is satellite television. Satellite television companies broadcast microwave signals from human-made satellites in space. Broadcasting from space allows more people to receive the signals than broadcasting from an antenna on Earth. Small satellite dishes on the roofs of houses or outside apartments collect the signals. The signals are then sent to the customer's television set. People who have satellite television usually have better TV reception than people who receive broadcasts from antennas on Earth.

The Global Positioning System

The Global Positioning System (GPS) is a network of 27 satellites that orbit Earth. These satellites continuously send microwave signals. The signals can be picked up by a GPS receiver on Earth and used to measure positions on the Earth's surface. **Figure 10** explains how GPS works. GPS was originally used by the United States military. But now, anyone in the world who has a GPS receiver can use the system. People use GPS to avoid getting lost and to have fun. Some cars have GPS road maps that can tell the car's driver how to get to a certain place. Hikers and campers use GPS receivers to find their way in the wilderness. And some people use GPS receivers for treasure-hunt games.

Reading Check What are two uses for GPS?

CONNECTION TO
Social Studies

Navigation GPS is a complex navigation system. Before GPS was developed, travelers and explorers used other techniques, such as compasses and stars, to find their way. Research an older form of navigation, and make a poster that summarizes what you learn.

ACTIVITY

Figure 10 The Global Positioning System

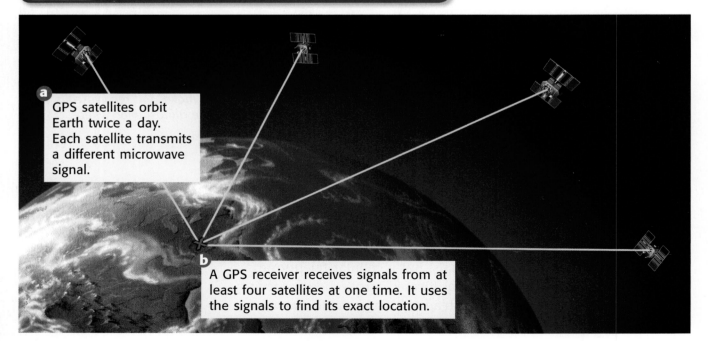

a GPS satellites orbit Earth twice a day. Each satellite transmits a different microwave signal.

b A GPS receiver receives signals from at least four satellites at one time. It uses the signals to find its exact location.

Summary

- Optical instruments, such as cameras, telescopes, and microscopes, are devices that help people make observations.

- Lasers are devices that produce intense, coherent light of only one wavelength and color. Lasers produce light by a process called *stimulated emission*.

- Optical fibers transmit light over long distances.

- Polarized light contains light waves that vibrate in only one direction.

- Cordless telephones are a combination of a telephone and a radio. Information is transmitted in the form of radio waves between the handset and the base.

- Cellular phones transmit information in the form of microwaves to and from antennas.

- Satellite television is broadcast by microwaves from satellites in space.

- GPS is a navigation system that uses microwave signals sent by a network of satellites in space.

Using Key Terms

1. Use each of the following terms in a separate sentence: *laser* and *hologram*.

Understanding Key Ideas

2. Which of the following statements about laser light is NOT true?
   a. Laser light is coherent.
   b. Laser light contains light of only one wavelength.
   c. Laser light is produced by stimulated emission.
   d. Laser light spreads out over short distances.

3. List three optical instruments, and describe what they do.

4. What are four uses for lasers?

5. Describe how optical fibers work.

6. What is polarized light?

7. Describe two ways that satellites in space are useful in everyday life.

Critical Thinking

8. **Making Comparisons** Compare how a cordless telephone works with how a cellular telephone works.

9. **Making Inferences** Why do you think optical fibers can transmit information over long distances without losing much of the signal?

Interpreting Graphics

Use the graph below to answer the questions that follow.

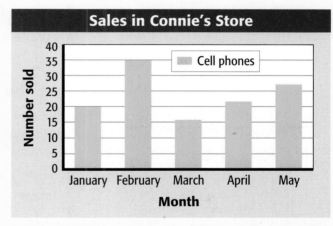

Sales in Connie's Store

10. In which two months did Connie's store sell the most cellular telephones?

11. How many cellular telephones were sold in January?

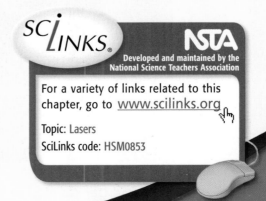

Developed and maintained by the National Science Teachers Association

For a variety of links related to this chapter, go to www.scilinks.org

Topic: Lasers
SciLinks code: HSM0853

Skills Practice Lab

OBJECTIVES

Use a convex lens to form images.

Determine the characteristics of real images formed by convex lenses.

MATERIALS

- candle
- card, index, 4 × 6 in. or larger
- clay, modeling
- convex lens
- jar lid
- matches
- meterstick

SAFETY

Images from Convex Lenses

A convex lens is thicker in the center than at the edges. Light rays passing through a convex lens come together at a focal point. Under certain conditions, a convex lens will create a real image of an object. This image will have certain characteristics, depending on the distance between the object and the lens. In this experiment, you will determine the characteristics of real images created by a convex lens—the kind of lens used as a magnifying lens.

Ask a Question

① What are the characteristics of real images created by a convex lens? For example, are the images upright or inverted (upside down)? Are the images larger or smaller than the object?

Form a Hypothesis

② Write a hypothesis that is a possible answer to the questions above. Explain your reasoning.

Test the Hypothesis

③ Copy the table below.

Data Collection				
Image	Orientation (upright/ inverted)	Size (larger/ smaller)	Image distance (cm)	Object distance (cm)
1				
2	DO NOT WRITE IN BOOK			
3				

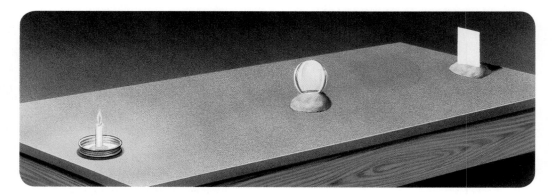

4 Use modeling clay to make a base for the lens. Place the lens and base in the middle of the table.

5 Stand the index card upright in some modeling clay on one side of the lens.

6 Place the candle in the jar lid, and anchor it with some modeling clay. Place the candle on the table so that the lens is halfway between the candle and the card. Light the candle.
Caution: Use extreme care around an open flame.

7 In a darkened room, slowly move the card and the candle away from the lens while keeping the lens exactly halfway between the card and the candle. Continue until you see a clear image of the candle flame on the card. This is image 1.

8 Measure and record the distance between the lens and the card (image distance) and between the lens and the candle (object distance).

9 Is the image upright or inverted? Is it larger or smaller than the candle? Record this information in the table.

10 Move the lens toward the candle. The new object distance should be less than half the object distance measured in step 8. Move the card back and forth until you find a sharp image (image 2) of the candle on the card.

11 Repeat steps 8 and 9 for image 2.

12 Leave the card and candle in place and move the lens toward the card to get the third image (image 3).

13 Repeat steps 8 and 9 for image 3.

Analyze the Results

1 **Recognizing Patterns** Describe the trend between image distance and image size.

2 **Examining Data** What are the similarities between the real images that are formed by a convex lens?

Draw Conclusions

3 **Making Predictions** The lens of your eye is a convex lens. Use the information you collected to describe the image projected on the back of your eye when you look at an object.

Applying Your Data

Convex lenses are used in film projectors. Explain why your favorite movie stars are truly "larger than life" on the screen in terms of image distance and object distance.

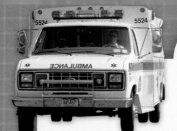

Chapter Review

USING KEY TERMS

In each of the following sentences, replace the incorrect term with the correct term from the word bank.

nearsightedness   hologram
concave mirror   laser
plane mirror   convex lens
convex mirror   farsightedness

1 A convex mirror is a mirror shaped like the inside of a spoon.

2 Eye surgeons use a hologram to reshape the cornea of an eye.

3 A person who has nearsightedness has trouble reading a book.

4 A concave lens refracts light and focuses it inward to a focal point.

5 If you move a lens around, you can see its three-dimensional image from different angles.

UNDERSTANDING KEY IDEAS

Multiple Choice

6 Which of the following parts of the eye refracts light?

a. pupil   **c.** lens
b. iris   **d.** retina

7 A vision problem that happens when light is focused in front of the retina is

a. farsightedness.
b. nearsightedness.
c. color deficiency.
d. None of the above

8 What kind of mirror provides images of large areas and is used for security?

a. a plane mirror
b. a concave mirror
c. a convex mirror
d. All of the above

9 A simple refracting telescope has

a. a convex lens and a concave lens.
b. a concave mirror and a convex lens.
c. two convex lenses.
d. two concave lenses.

10 Light waves in a laser beam interact and act as one wave. This light is called

a. coherent light.   **c.** polarized light.
b. emitted light.   **d.** reflected light.

11 When you look at yourself in a plane mirror, you see a

a. real image behind the mirror.
b. real image on the surface of the mirror.
c. virtual image that appears to be behind the mirror.
d. virtual image that appears to be in front of the mirror.

Short Answer

12 What kind of eyeglass lens should be prescribed for a person who cannot focus on nearby objects? Explain.

13 How is a hologram different from a photograph?

14 Why might a scientist who is working at the North Pole need polarizing sunglasses?

Math Skills

15 Ms. Welch's class conducted a poll about vision problems. Of the 150 students asked, 21 reported that they are nearsighted. Six of the nearsighted students wear contact lenses to correct their vision, and the rest wear glasses.

a. What percentage of the students asked is nearsighted?

b. What percentage of the students asked wears glasses?

CRITICAL THINKING

16 **Concept Mapping** Use the following terms to create a concept map: *lens, telescope, camera, real image, virtual image,* and *optical instrument.*

17 **Analyzing Ideas** Stoplights are usually mounted so that the red light is on the top and the green light is on the bottom. Why is it important for a person who has red-green color deficiency to know this arrangement?

18 **Applying Concepts** How could you find out if a device that produces red light is a laser or if it is just a red flashlight?

19 **Making Inferences** Imagine that you have a GPS receiver. When you use your receiver in the park and are surrounded by tall trees, the receiver easily finds your location. But when you use your receiver downtown and are surrounded by tall buildings, the receiver cannot determine your location. Why do you think there is a difference in reception? Describe a situation in which poor GPS reception around tall buildings could cause problems.

INTERPRETING GRAPHICS

20 Look at the ray diagrams below. For each diagram, identify the type of mirror that is being used and the kind of image that is being formed.

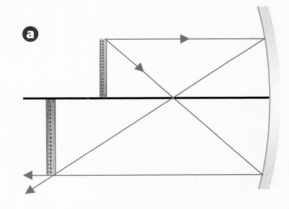

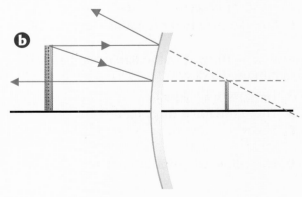

Standardized Test Preparation

Read each of the passages below. Then, answer the questions that follow each passage.

Passage 1 One day in the 1920s, an automobile collided with a horse and carriage. Garrett Morgan witnessed this, and the accident gave him an idea. Morgan designed a signal that included signs to direct traffic at busy intersections. The signal could be seen from a distance and could be clearly understood. Morgan patented the first traffic signal in 1923. Unlike the small, three-bulb signal boxes used today, the early <u>versions</u> were T shaped and had the words *stop* and *go* printed on them.

Morgan's invention was an immediate success. Morgan sold the patent to General Electric Corporation for $40,000—a large sum in those days. Since then, later versions of Morgan's traffic signal have been a mainstay of traffic control.

1. In the passage, what does the word *versions* refer to?
  A automobiles
  B accidents
  C light bulbs
  D traffic signals

2. Which of the following statements is a fact?
  F Morgan still makes money selling traffic signals today.
  G Traffic signals were confusing and caused a lot of accidents.
  H Morgan came up with the idea of a traffic signal after seeing a traffic accident.
  I Morgan patented the traffic signal in 1920.

3. How were the first traffic signals similar to the signals used today?
  A They were T shaped.
  B They contained three light bulbs.
  C The words *stop* and *go* were printed on them.
  D They directed traffic at busy intersections.

Passage 2 Twenty years ago, stars were very visible, even above large cities. Now, the stars above large cities are <u>obscured</u> by the glow from city lights. This glow, called sky glow, is created when light reflects off dust and particles in the atmosphere. Sky glow is also called light pollution.

The majority of light pollution comes from outdoor lights, such as headlights, street lights, porch lights, and parking-lot lights. Unlike other kinds of pollution, light pollution can easily be reduced. For example, using covered outdoor lights keeps the light angled downward, which prevents most of the light from reaching particles in the sky. Also, using motion-sensitive lights and timed lights helps eliminate unnecessary light.

1. Which of the following **best** describes the reason the author wrote the passage?
  A to explain light pollution and to explain how to reduce it
  B to convince people to look at stars
  C to explain why people should not live in cities
  D to describe the beauty of sky glow

2. Which of the following contributes the least amount to light pollution?
  F headlights on cars
  G lights inside homes
  H lights used in outdoor stadiums
  I lights in large parking lots

3. In the passage, what does the word *obscured* mean?
  A made brighter
  B reflected
  C polluted
  D made difficult to see

The table below shows details about four lasers sold by a laser company. Use the table below to answer the questions that follow.

Laser Specifications			
Color	Power (mW)	Wavelength (nm)	Mass (kg)
Blue	15	488	2.8
Yellow	5	568	5.8
Red	18	633	0.9
Red	10	633	0.6

1. What is the mass of the laser that has the most power?

A 0.6 kg

B 0.9 kg

C 2.8 kg

D 5.8 kg

2. The company also sells a laser that has a wavelength of 633 nm and a power of 5 mW. Which of the following statements **best** predicts the mass of this laser?

F The laser has a mass of less than 0.6 kg.

G The laser has a mass between 0.6 kg and 0.9 kg.

H The laser has a mass greater than 0.9 kg.

I The laser has a mass of 5.8 kg.

3. Based on the information in the table, which statement is most likely true?

A The power of the laser determines the color of light.

B The wavelength of the laser determines the color of light.

C The mass of the laser determines the color of light.

D There is not enough information to determine the answer.

Read each question below, and choose the best answer.

1. Micah has a box that has a length of 16 cm, a width of 10 cm, and a height of 5 cm. What is the volume of the box?

A 1,600 cm³

B 800 cm³

C 700 cm³

D 500 cm³

2. The table below shows the low temperature in Minneapolis, Minnesota, for five days in December.

Day	Temperature (°C)
Monday	−12
Tuesday	−8
Wednesday	7
Thursday	−3
Friday	11

Which list shows the temperatures from lowest to highest?

F −3°C, −8°C, −12°C, 7°C, 11°C

G −3°C, 7°C, −8°C, 11°C, −12°C

H −12°C, 11°C, 7°C, −8°C, −3°C

I −12°C, −8°C, −3°C, 7°C, 11°C

3. The power of a microscope lens is the amount of magnification the lens gives. For example, a 10× lens magnifies objects 10 times. How many times is an object magnified if it is viewed with both a 5× lens and a 30× lens?

A 35 times

B 60 times

C 150 times

D 350 times

Science in Action

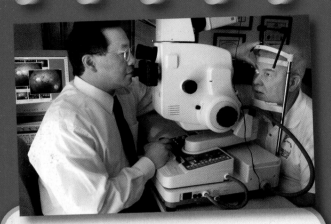

Science, Technology, and Society

Bionic Eyes

Imagine bionic eyes that allow a person who is blind to see. Researchers working on artificial vision think that the technology will be available soon. Many companies are working on different ways to restore sight to people who are blind. Some companies are developing artificial corneas, while other companies are building artificial retinas. One item that has already been tested on people is a pair of glasses that provides limited vision. The glasses have a camera that sends a signal to an electrode implanted in the person's brain. The images are black and white and are not detailed, but the person who is wearing the glasses can see obstacles in his or her path.

Language Arts ACTiViTY

WRITING SKILL Write a one-page story about a teen who has his or her eyesight restored by a bionic eye. What would the teen want to see first? What would the teen do that he or she couldn't do before?

Scientific Debate

Do Cellular Telephones Cause Cancer?

As cellular telephones became popular, people began to wonder if the phones were dangerous. Some cell-phone users claimed that the microwave energy from their cell phones caused them to develop brain cancer. So far, most research shows that the microwave energy emitted by cell phones is too low and too weak to damage human tissue. However, some studies have shown negative effects. There is some evidence that the low-power microwave energy used by cell phones may damage DNA and may cause cells to shrink. Because so many people use cellular phones, research continues around the world.

Math ACTiViTY

The American Cancer Society estimates that 0.006% of people in the United States will be diagnosed with brain cancer each year. If a city has a population of 50,000 people, how many people in that city will be diagnosed with brain cancer in one year?

Sandra Faber

Astronomer What do you do when you send a telescope into space and then find out that it is broken? You call Dr. Sandra Faber, a professor of astronomy at the University of California, Santa Cruz (UCSC). In April 1990, after the *Hubble Space Telescope* went into orbit, scientists found that the images the telescope collected were not turning out as expected. Dr. Faber's team at UCSC was in charge of a device on *Hubble* called the *Wide Field Planetary Camera*. Dr. Faber and her team decided to test the telescope to determine what was wrong.

To perform the test, they centered *Hubble* onto a bright star and took several photos. From those photos, Dr. Faber's team created a model of what was wrong. After reporting the error to NASA and presenting the model they had developed, Dr. Faber and a group of experts began to correct the problem. The group's efforts were a success and put *Hubble* back into operation so that astronomers could continue researching stars and other objects in space.

Social Studies ACTIVITY

Research the history of the telescope. Make a timeline with the dates of major events in telescope history. For example, you could include the first use of a telescope to see the rings of Saturn in your timeline.

go.hrw.com

To learn more about these Science in Action topics, visit go.hrw.com and type in the keyword **HP5LOWF.**

Current Science

Check out Current Science® articles related to this chapter by visiting go.hrw.com. Just type in the keyword **HP5CS23.**

Contents

CHAPTER **1** **The World of Physical Science**

Skills Practice Exploring the Unseen 696
Model Making Off to the Races 697
Skills Practice Coin Operated 698

CHAPTER **2** **The Properties of Matter**

Skills Practice Volumania! 700
Skills Practice Determining Density 702
Skills Practice Layering Liquids 703

CHAPTER **3** **States of Matter**

Skills Practice Full of Hot Air! 704
Skills Practice Can Crusher 705

CHAPTER **4** **Elements, Compounds, and Mixtures**

Skills Practice A Sugar Cube Race! 706
Skills Practice Making Butter 707
Model Making Unpolluting Water 708

CHAPTER **5** **Matter in Motion**

Skills Practice Built for Speed 710
Skills Practice Relating Mass
    and Weight 711
Skills Practice Science Friction 712

CHAPTER **6** **Forces and Motion**

Skills Practice A Marshmallow
    Catapult 714
Model Making Blast Off! 715
Skills Practice Quite a Reaction 716

CHAPTER **7** **Forces in Fluids**

Skills Practice Density Diver 718

CHAPTER **8** **Work and Machines**

Skills Practice Inclined to Move 719
Skills Practice Wheeling and Dealing 720
Inquiry Building Machines 722

CHAPTER **9** **Energy and Energy Resources**

Skills Practice Energy of a Pendulum..... 723

CHAPTER **10** **Heat and Heat Technology**

Inquiry Save the Cube! 724
Model Making Counting Calories 725

CHAPTER **14** **Chemical Reactions**

Model Making Finding a Balance 726
Skills Practice Cata-what? Catalyst! 727
Skills Practice Putting Elements
    Together 728

CHAPTER **15** **Chemical Compounds**

Skills Practice Making Salt 730

CHAPTER **17** **Introduction to Electricity**

Skills Practice Stop the
    Static Electricity! 732
Model Making Potato Power 733

CHAPTER **18** **Electromagnetism**

Skills Practice Magnetic Mystery 734
Skills Practice Electricity from
    Magnetism 735

CHAPTER **19** **Electronic Technology**

Model Making Tune In! 736

CHAPTER **20** **The Energy of Waves**

Skills Practice Wave Speed, Frequency,
    and Wavelength 740

CHAPTER **21** **The Nature of Sound**

Inquiry The Speed of Sound 742
Skills Practice Tuneful Tube 743
Skills Practice The Energy of Sound 744

CHAPTER **22** **The Nature of Light**

Skills Practice What Color of Light Is
    Best for Green Plants? 746
Skills Practice Which Color Is
    Hottest? 747

CHAPTER **23** **Light and Our World**

Skills Practice Mirror Images 748

Skills Practice Lab

Exploring the Unseen

Your teacher will give you a box in which a special divider has been created. Your task is to describe this divider as precisely as possible—without opening the box! Your only aid is a marble that is also inside the box. This task will allow you to demonstrate your understanding of the scientific method. Good luck!

MATERIALS

• mystery box, sealed

Ask a Question

1 Record the question that you are trying to answer by doing this experiment. (Hint: Read the introductory paragraph again if you are not sure what your task is.)

Form a Hypothesis

2 Before you begin the experiment, think about what's required. Do you think you will be able to easily determine the shape of the divider? Can you determine its texture or color? Write a hypothesis that states how much you think you will be able to determine about the divider during the experiment. (Remember that you can't open the box!)

Test the Hypothesis

3 Using all the methods you can think of (except opening the box), test your hypothesis. Make careful notes about your testing and observations.

Analyze the Results

1 What characteristics of the divider were you able to identify? Draw or write your best description of the interior of the box.

2 Do your observations support your hypothesis? Explain. If your results do not support your hypothesis, write a new hypothesis, and test it.

3 With your teacher's permission, open the box, and look inside. Record your observations.

Draw Conclusions

4 Write a paragraph summarizing your experiment. Be sure to include what methods you used, whether your results supported your hypothesis, and how you could improve your methods.

Model-Making Lab

Off to the Races!

Scientists often use models—representations of objects or systems. Physical models, such as a model airplane, are generally a different size than the objects they represent. In this lab, you will build a model car, test its design, and then try to improve the design.

MATERIALS

- board
- clothes-hanger wire, 16 cm
- eraser, pink rubber, or small wood block
- glue
- paper, typing (2 sheets)
- pliers (or wire cutters)
- ruler, metric
- stopwatch
- textbooks

SAFETY

Procedure

1 Using the materials listed, design and build a car that will carry the load (the eraser or block of wood) down the ramp as quickly as possible. Your car must be no wider than 8 cm, it must have room to carry the load, and it must roll.

2 As you test your design, do not be afraid to rebuild or re-design your car. Improving your methods is an important part of scientific progress.

3 When you have a design that works well, measure the time required for your car to roll down the ramp. Record this time. Test your car with this design several times for accuracy.

4 Try to improve your model. Find one thing that you can change to make your model car roll faster down the ramp. Write a description of the change.

5 Test your model again as you did in step 3 and make additional improvements if needed.

Analyze the Results

1 Why is it important to have room in the model car for the eraser or wood block? (Hint: Think about the function of a real car.)

2 Before you built the model car, you created a design for it. Do you think this design is also a model? Explain.

3 Based on your observations in this lab, list three reasons why it is helpful for automobile designers to build and test small model cars rather than immediately build a full-size car.

Draw Conclusions

4 In this lab, you built a model that was smaller than the object it represented. Some models are larger than the objects they represent. List three examples of larger models that are used to represent objects. Why is it helpful to use a larger model in these cases?

Skills Practice Lab

Coin Operated

All pennies are exactly the same, right? Probably not! After all, each penny was made in a certain year at a specific mint, and each has traveled a unique path to reach your classroom. But all pennies are similar. In this lab, you will investigate differences and similarities among a group of pennies.

Procedure

1. Write the numbers 1 through 10 on a page, and place a penny next to each number.

2. Use the metric balance to find the mass of each penny to the nearest 0.1 g. Record each measurement next to the number of that penny.

3. On a table that your teacher will provide, make a mark in the correct column of the table for each penny you measured.

4. Separate your pennies into piles, based on the class data. Place each pile on its own sheet of paper.

5. Measure and record the mass of each pile. Write the mass on the paper you are using to identify the pile.

6. Fill a graduated cylinder halfway with water. Carefully measure the volume in the cylinder, and record it.

MATERIALS

- balance, metric
- graduated cylinder, 100 mL
- paper, notebook (10 sheets)
- paper towels
- pennies (10)
- water

SAFETY

7 Carefully place the pennies from one pile into the graduated cylinder. Measure and record the new volume.

8 Carefully pour out the water into the sink, and remove the pennies from the graduated cylinder. With a paper towel, dry off the pile of pennies.

9 Repeat steps 6 through 8 for each pile of pennies.

Analyze the Results

1 Determine the volume of the displaced water by subtracting the initial volume from the final volume. This amount is equal to the volume of the pennies. Record the volume of each pile of pennies.

2 Calculate the density of each pile. To make this calculation, divide the total mass of the pennies by the volume of the pennies. Record the density.

3 What differences, if any, did you note in the mass, volume, and density of the pennies?

Draw Conclusions

4 If you noted differences, what do you think might be the cause of these differences?

5 How is it possible for the pennies to have different densities?

6 What clues might allow you to separate the pennies into the same groups without experimentation? Explain.

Skills Practice Lab

Volumania!

You have learned how to measure the volume of a solid object that has square or rectangular sides. But there are lots of objects in the world that have irregular shapes. In this lab activity, you'll learn some ways to find the volume of objects that have irregular shapes.

MATERIALS

Part A
- graduated cylinder
- water
- various small objects supplied by your teacher

Part B
- bottle, plastic (or similar container), 2L, bottom half
- funnel
- graduated cylinder
- pan, aluminum pie
- paper towels
- water

SAFETY

Part A: Finding the Volume of Small Objects

Procedure

1 Fill a graduated cylinder half full with water. Read and record the volume of the water. Be sure to look at the surface of the water at eye level and to read the volume at the bottom of the meniscus, as shown below.

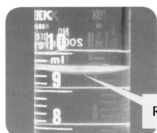

Read volume here

2 Carefully slide one of the objects into the tilted graduated cylinder, as shown below.

3 Read the new volume, and record it.

4 Subtract the old volume from the new volume. The resulting amount is equal to the volume of the solid object.

5 Use the same method to find the volume of the other objects. Record your results.

Analyze the Results

1 What changes do you have to make to the volumes you determine in order to express them correctly?

2 Do the heaviest objects always have the largest volumes? Why or why not?

Part B: Finding the Volume of Your Hand

Procedure

1. Completely fill the container with water. Put the container in the center of the pie pan. Be sure not to spill any of the water into the pie pan.

2. Make a fist, and put your hand into the container up to your wrist.

3. Remove your hand, and let the excess water drip into the container, not the pie pan. Dry your hand with a paper towel.

4. Use the funnel to pour the overflow water into the graduated cylinder. Measure the volume. This measurement is the volume of your hand. Record the volume. (Remember to use the correct unit of volume for a solid object.)

5. Repeat this procedure with your other hand.

Analyze the Results

1. Was the volume the same for both of your hands? If not, were you surprised? What might account for a person's hands having different volumes?

2. Would it have made a difference if you had placed your open hand into the container instead of your fist? Explain your reasoning.

3. Compare the volume of your right hand with the volume of your classmates' right hands. Create a class graph of right-hand volumes. What is the average right-hand volume for your class?

Applying Your Data

Design an experiment to determine the volume of a person's body. In your plans, be sure to include the materials needed for the experiment and the procedures that must be followed. Include a sketch that shows how your materials and methods would be used in this experiment.

Using an encyclopedia, the Internet, or other reference materials, find out how the volumes of very large samples of matter—such as an entire planet—are determined.

Skills Practice Lab

Determining Density

The density of an object is its mass divided by its volume. But how does the density of a small amount of a substance relate to the density of a larger amount of the same substance? In this lab, you will calculate the density of one marble and of a group of marbles. Then, you will confirm the relationship between the mass and volume of a substance.

Procedure

1 Copy the table below. Include one row for each marble.

Mass of marble (g)	Total mass of marbles (g)	Total volume (mL)	Volume of marbles (mL) (total volume minus 50.0 mL)	Density of marbles (g/mL) (total mass divided by volume)
		DO NOT WRITE IN BOOK		

2 Fill the graduated cylinder with 50 mL of water. If you put in too much water, twist one of the paper towels, and use it to absorb excess water.

3 Measure the mass of a marble as accurately as you can (to at least .01 g). Record the mass in the table.

4 Carefully drop the marble in the tilted cylinder, and measure the total volume. Record the volume in the third column.

5 Measure and record the mass of another marble. Add the masses of the marbles together, and record this value in the second column of the table.

6 Carefully drop the second marble in the graduated cylinder. Complete the row of information in the table.

7 Repeat steps 5 and 6. Add one marble at a time. Stop when you run out of marbles, the water no longer completely covers the marbles, or the graduated cylinder is full.

Analyze the Results

1 Examine the data in your table. As the number of marbles increases, what happens to the total mass of the marbles? What happens to the volume of the marbles? What happens to the density of the marbles?

2 Graph the total mass of the marbles (*y*-axis) versus the volume of the marbles (*x*-axis). Is the graph a straight line?

Draw Conclusions

3 Does the density of a substance depend on the amount of substance present? Explain how your results support your answer.

Applying Your Data

Calculate the slope of the graph. How does the slope compare with the values in the column entitled "Density of marbles"? Explain.

Skills Practice Lab

Layering Liquids

You have learned that liquids form layers according to the densities of the liquids. In this lab, you'll discover whether it matters in which order you add the liquids.

Ask a Question

1 Does the order in which you add liquids of different densities to a container affect the order of the layers formed by those liquids?

Form a Hypothesis

2 Write a possible answer to the question above.

Test the Hypothesis

3 Using the graduated cylinders, add 10 mL of each liquid to the clear container. Remember to read the volume at the bottom of the meniscus, as shown below. Record the order in which you added the liquids.

4 Observe the liquids in the container. Sketch what you see. Be sure to label the layers and the colors.

5 Add 10 mL more of liquid C. Observe what happens, and record your observations.

6 Add 20 mL more of liquid A. Observe what happens, and record your observations.

Analyze the Results

1 Which of the liquids has the greatest density? Which has the least density? How can you tell?

2 Did the layers change position when you added more of liquid C? Explain your answer.

3 Did the layers change position when you added more of liquid A? Explain your answer.

MATERIALS

- beaker (or other small, clear container)
- funnel (3)
- graduated cylinder, 10 mL (3)
- liquid A
- liquid B
- liquid C

SAFETY

4 Find out in what order your classmates added the liquids to the container. Compare your results with those of a classmate who added the liquids in a different order. Were your results different? Explain why or why not.

Draw Conclusions

5 Based on your results, evaluate your hypothesis from step 2.

Skills Practice Lab

Full of Hot Air!

Why do hot-air balloons float gracefully above Earth, but balloons you blow up fall to the ground? The answer has to do with the density of the air inside the balloon. *Density* is mass per unit volume, and volume is affected by changes in temperature. In this experiment, you will investigate the relationship between the temperature of a gas and its volume. Then, you will be able to determine how the temperature of a gas affects its density.

MATERIALS

- balloon
- beaker, 250 mL
- gloves, heat-resistant
- hot plate
- ice water
- pan, aluminum (2)
- ruler, metric
- water

SAFETY

Ask a Question

1 How does an increase or decrease in temperature affect the volume of a balloon?

Form a Hypothesis

2 Write a hypothesis that answers the question above.

Test the Hypothesis

3 Fill an aluminum pan with water about 4 cm to 5 cm deep. Put the pan on the hot plate, and turn the hot plate on.

4 Fill the other pan 4 cm to 5 cm deep with ice water.

5 Blow up a balloon inside the 500 mL beaker, as shown. The balloon should fill the beaker but should not extend outside the beaker. Tie the balloon at its opening.

6 Place the beaker and balloon in the ice water. Observe what happens. Record your observations.

7 Remove the balloon and beaker from the ice water. Observe the balloon for several minutes. Record any changes.

8 Put on heat-resistant gloves. When the hot water begins to boil, put the beaker and balloon in the hot water. Observe the balloon for several minutes, and record your observations.

9 Turn off the hot plate. When the water has cooled, carefully pour it into a sink.

Analyze the Results

1 Summarize your observations of the balloon. Relate your observations to Charles's law.

2 Was your hypothesis from step 2 supported? If not, revise your hypothesis.

Draw Conclusions

3 Based on your observations, how is the density of a gas affected by an increase or decrease in temperature?

Skills Practice Lab

Can Crusher

Condensation can occur when gas particles come near the surface of a liquid. The gas particles slow down because they are attracted to the liquid. This reduction in speed causes the gas particles to condense into a liquid. In this lab, you'll see that particles that have condensed into a liquid don't take up as much space and therefore don't exert as much pressure as they did in the gaseous state.

MATERIALS

- beaker, 1 L
- can, aluminum (2)
- gloves, heat-resistant
- hot plate
- tongs
- water

SAFETY

Procedure

1. Fill the beaker with room-temperature water.

2. Place just enough water in an aluminum can to slightly cover the bottom.

3. Put on heat-resistant gloves. Place the aluminum can on a hot plate turned to the highest temperature setting.

4. Heat the can until the water is boiling. Steam should be rising vigorously from the top of the can.

5. Using tongs, quickly pick up the can, and place the top 2 cm of the can upside down in the 1 L beaker filled with water.

6. Describe your observations.

Analyze the Results

1. The can was crushed because the atmospheric pressure outside the can became greater than the pressure inside the can. Explain what happened inside the can to cause the difference in pressure.

Draw Conclusions

2. Inside every popcorn kernel is a small amount of water. When you make popcorn, the water inside the kernels is heated until it becomes steam. Explain how the popping of the kernels is the opposite of what you saw in this lab. Be sure to address the effects of pressure in your explanation.

Applying Your Data

Try the experiment again, but use ice water instead of room-temperature water. Explain your results in terms of the effects of temperature.

Skills Practice Lab

A Sugar Cube Race!

If you drop a sugar cube into a glass of water, how long will it take to dissolve? What can you do to speed up the rate at which it dissolves? Should you change something about the water, the sugar cube, or the process? In other words, what variable should you change? Before reading further, make a list of variables that could be changed in this situation. Record your list.

MATERIALS

- beakers or other clear containers (2)
- clock or stopwatch
- graduated cylinder
- sugar cubes (2)
- water
- other materials approved by your teacher

SAFETY

Ask a Question

1. Write a question you can test about factors that affect the rate sugar dissolves.

Form a Hypothesis

2. Choose one variable to test. Record your choice, and predict how changing your variable will affect the rate of dissolving.

Test the Hypothesis

3. Pour 150 mL of water into one of the beakers. Add one sugar cube, and use the stopwatch to measure how long it takes for the sugar cube to dissolve. You must not disturb the sugar cube in any way! Record this time.

4. Be sure to get your teacher's approval before you begin. You may need additional equipment.

5. Prepare your materials to test the variable you have picked. When you are ready, start your procedure for speeding up the rate at which the sugar cube dissolves. Use the stopwatch to measure the time. Record this time.

Analyze the Results

1. Compare your results with the prediction you made in step 2. Was your prediction correct? Why or why not?

Draw Conclusions

2. Why was it necessary to observe the sugar cube dissolving on its own before you tested the variable?

3. Do you think changing more than one variable would speed up the rate of dissolving even more? Explain your reasoning.

4. Discuss your results with a group that tested a different variable. Which variable had a greater effect on the rate of dissolving?

Skills Practice Lab

Making Butter

A colloid is an interesting substance. It has properties of both solutions and suspensions. Colloidal particles are not heavy enough to settle out, so they remain evenly dispersed throughout the mixture. In this activity, you will make butter—a very familiar colloid—and observe the characteristics that classify butter as a colloid.

MATERIALS

- clock or stopwatch
- container with lid, small, clear
- heavy cream
- marble

SAFETY

Procedure

1. Place a marble inside the container, and fill the container with heavy cream. Put the lid tightly on the container.

2. Take turns shaking the container vigorously and constantly for 10 min. Record the time when you begin shaking. Every minute, stop shaking the container, and hold it up to the light. Record your observations.

3. Continue shaking the container, taking turns if necessary. When you see, hear, or feel any changes inside the container, note the time and change.

4. After 10 min of shaking, you should have a lump of "butter" surrounded by liquid inside the container. Describe both the butter and the liquid in detail.

5. Let the container sit for about 10 min. Observe the butter and liquid again, and record your observations.

Analyze the Results

1. When you noticed the change inside the container, what did you think was happening at that point?

2. Based on your observations, explain why butter is classified as a colloid.

3. What kind of mixture is the liquid that is left behind? Explain.

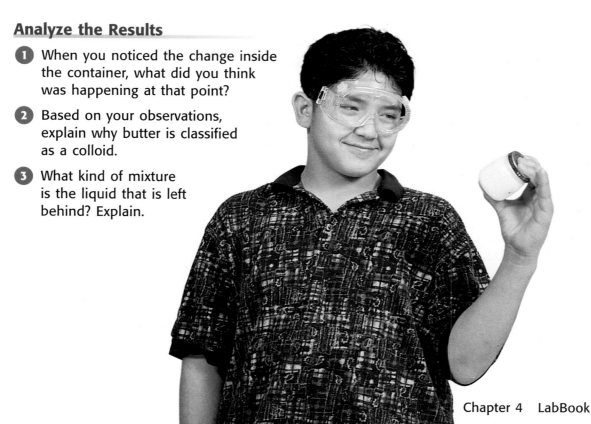

Model-Making Lab

Unpolluting Water

In many cities, the water supply comes from a river, lake, or reservoir. This water may include several mixtures, including suspensions (with suspended dirt, oil, or living organisms) and solutions (with dissolved chemicals). To make the water safe to drink, your city's water supplier must remove impurities. In this lab, you will model the procedures used in real water treatment plants.

MATERIALS

- beaker, 250 mL (4)
- charcoal, activated, washed
- cup, plastic-foam, 8 oz (2)
- graduated cylinder
- nail, small
- paper, filter (2 pieces)
- rubber band
- ruler, metric
- sand, fine, washed
- scissors
- spoon, plastic (2)
- water, "polluted"

SAFETY

Part A: Untreated Water

Procedure

1. Measure 100 mL of "polluted" water into a graduated cylinder. Be sure to shake the bottle of water before you pour so your sample will include all the impurities.

2. Pour the contents of the graduated cylinder into one of the beakers.

3. Copy the table below, and record your observations of the water in the "Before treatment" row.

Observations						
	Color	Clearness	Odor	Any layers?	Any solids?	Water volume
Before treatment						
After oil separation						
After sand filtration						
After charcoal						

DO NOT WRITE IN BOOK

Part B: Settling In

If a suspension is left standing, the suspended particles will settle to the top or bottom. You should see a layer of oil at the top.

Procedure

1. Separate the oil by carefully pouring the oil into another beaker. You can use a plastic spoon to get the last bit of oil from the water. Record your observations.

Part C: Filtration

Cloudy water can be a sign of small particles still in suspension. These particles can usually be removed by filtering. Water treatment plants use sand and gravel as filters.

Procedure

1 Make a filter as follows:

   a. Use the nail to poke 5 to 10 small holes in the bottom of one of the cups.

   b. Cut a circle of filter paper to fit inside the bottom of the cup. (This filter will keep the sand in the cup.)

   c. Fill the cup to 2 cm below the rim with wet sand. Pack the sand tightly.

   d. Set the cup inside an empty beaker.

2 Pour the polluted water on top of the sand, and let the water filter through. Do not pour any of the settled mud onto the sand. (Dispose of the mud as instructed by your teacher.) In your table, record your observations of the water collected in the beaker.

Part D: Separating Solutions

Something that has been dissolved in a solvent cannot be separated using filters. Water treatment plants use activated charcoal to absorb many dissolved chemicals.

Procedure

1 Place activated charcoal about 3 cm deep in the unused cup. Pour the water collected from the sand filtration into the cup, and stir with a spoon for 1 min.

2 Place a piece of filter paper over the top of the cup, and fasten it in place with a rubber band. With the paper securely in place, pour the water through the filter paper and back into a clean beaker. Record your observations in your table.

Analyze the Results

1 Is your unpolluted water safe to drink? Why or why not?

2 When you treat a sample of water, do you get out exactly the same amount of water that you put in? Explain your answer.

3 Some groups may still have cloudy water when they finish. Explain a possible cause for this.

Skills Practice Lab

Built for Speed

Imagine that you are an engineer at GoCarCo, a toy-vehicle company. GoCarCo is trying to beat the competition by building a new toy vehicle. Several new designs are being tested. Your boss has given you one of the new toy vehicles and instructed you to measure its speed as accurately as possible with the tools you have. Other engineers (your classmates) are testing the other designs. Your results could decide the fate of the company!

Procedure

1. How will you accomplish your goal? Write a paragraph to describe your goal and your procedure for this experiment. Be sure that your procedure includes several trials.

2. Show your plan to your boss (teacher). Get his or her approval to carry out your procedure.

3. Perform your stated procedure. Record all data. Be sure to express all data in the correct units.

Analyze the Results

1. What was the average speed of your vehicle? How does your result compare with the results of the other engineers?

2. Compare your technique for determining the speed of your vehicle with the techniques of the other engineers. Which technique do you think is the most effective?

3. Was your toy vehicle the fastest? Explain why or why not.

Applying Your Data

Think of several conditions that could affect your vehicle's speed. Design an experiment to test your vehicle under one of those conditions. Write a paragraph to explain your procedure. Be sure to include an explanation of how that condition changes your vehicle's speed.

Skills Practice Lab

Relating Mass and Weight

Why do objects with more mass weigh more than objects with less mass? All objects have weight on Earth because their mass is affected by Earth's gravitational force. Because the mass of an object on Earth is constant, the relationship between the mass of an object and its weight is also constant. You will measure the mass and weight of several objects to verify the relationship between mass and weight on the surface of Earth.

MATERIALS

- balance, metric
- classroom objects, small
- paper, graph
- scissors
- spring scale (force meter)
- string

SAFETY

Procedure

1 Copy the table below.

Mass and Weight Measurements		
Object	Mass (g)	Weight (N)

DO NOT WRITE IN BOOK

2 Using the metric balance, find the mass of five or six small classroom objects designated by your teacher. Record the masses.

3 Using the spring scale, find the weight of each object. Record the weights. (You may need to use the string to create a hook with which to hang some objects from the spring scale, as shown at right.)

Analyze the Results

1 Using your data, construct a graph of weight (y-axis) versus mass (x-axis). Draw a line that best fits all your data points.

2 Does the graph confirm the relationship between mass and weight on Earth? Explain your answer.

Skills Practice Lab

Science Friction

In this experiment, you will investigate three types of friction—static, sliding, and rolling—to determine which is the largest force and which is the smallest force.

MATERIALS

- rods, wood or metal (3–4)
- scissors
- spring scale (force meter)
- string
- textbook (covered)

SAFETY

Ask a Question

1 Which type of friction is the largest force—static, sliding, or rolling? Which is the smallest?

Form a Hypothesis

2 Write a statement or statements that answer the questions above. Explain your reasoning.

Test the Hypothesis

3 Cut a piece of string, and tie it in a loop that fits in the textbook, as shown on the next page. Hook the string to the spring scale.

4 Practice the next three steps several times before you collect data.

5 To measure the static friction between the book and the table, pull the spring scale very slowly. Record the largest force on the scale before the book starts to move.

6 After the book begins to move, you can determine the sliding friction. Record the force required to keep the book sliding at a slow, constant speed.

7 Place two or three rods under the book to act as rollers. Make sure the rollers are evenly spaced. Place another roller in front of the book so that the book will roll onto it. Pull the force meter slowly. Measure the force needed to keep the book rolling at a constant speed.

Analyze the Results

1 Which type of friction was the largest? Which was the smallest?

2 Do the results support your hypothesis? If not, how would you revise or retest your hypothesis?

Draw Conclusions

3 Compare your results with those of another group. Are there any differences? Working together, design a way to improve the experiment and resolve possible differences.

Skills Practice Lab

A Marshmallow Catapult

Catapults use projectile motion to launch objects. In this lab, you will build a simple catapult and determine the angle at which the catapult will launch an object the farthest.

Ask a Question

1 At what angle, from 10° to 90°, will a catapult launch a marshmallow the farthest?

Form a Hypothesis

2 Write a hypothesis that is a possible answer to your question.

Angle	Distance 1 (cm)	Distance 2 (cm)	Average distance	Data Collection
10°	DO NOT WRITE IN BOOK			

MATERIALS

- marshmallows, miniature (2)
- meterstick
- protractor
- spoon, plastic
- tape, duct
- wood block, 3.5 cm × 3.5 cm × 1 cm

SAFETY

Test the Hypothesis

3 Copy the table above. In your table, add one row each for 20°, 30°, 40°, 50°, 60°, 70°, 80°, and 90° angles.

4 Using duct tape, attach the plastic spoon to the 1 cm side of the block. Use enough tape to attach the spoon securely.

5 Place one marshmallow in the center of the spoon, and tape it to the spoon. This marshmallow serves as a ledge to hold the marshmallow that will be launched.

6 Line up the bottom corner of the block with the bottom center of the protractor, as shown in the photograph. Start with the block at 10°.

7 Place a marshmallow in the spoon, on top of the taped marshmallow. Pull the spoon back lightly, and let go. Measure and record the distance from the catapult that the marshmallow lands. Repeat the measurement, and calculate an average.

8 Repeat step 7 for each angle up to 90°.

Analyze the Results

1 At what angle did the catapult launch the marshmallow the farthest? Explain any differences from your hypothesis.

Draw Conclusions

2 At what angle should you throw a ball or shoot an arrow so that it will fly the farthest? Why? Support your answer with your data.

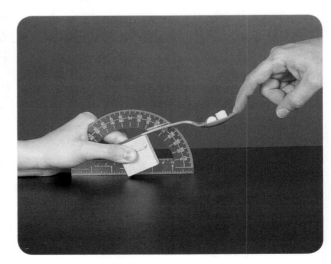

Model-Making Lab

Blast Off!

You have been hired as a rocket scientist for NASA. Your job is to design a rocket that will have a controlled flight while carrying a payload. Keep in mind that Newton's laws will have a powerful influence on your rocket.

Procedure

1. When you begin your experiment, your teacher will tape one end of the fishing line to the ceiling.

2. Use a pencil to poke a small hole in each side of the cup near the top. Place a 15 cm piece of string through each hole, and tape down the ends inside.

3. Inflate the balloon, and use the twist tie to hold it closed.

4. Tape the free ends of the strings to the sides of the balloon near the bottom. The cup should hang below the balloon. Your model rocket should look like a hot-air balloon.

5. Thread the fishing line that is hanging from the ceiling through the straw. Tape the balloon securely to the straw. Tape the loose end of the fishing line to the floor.

6. Untie the twist tie while holding the end of the balloon closed. When you are ready, release the end of the balloon. Mark and record the maximum height of the rocket.

7. Repeat the procedure, adding a penny to the cup each time until your rocket cannot lift any more pennies.

Analyze the Results

1. In a paragraph, describe how all three of Newton's laws influenced the flight of your rocket.

Draw Conclusions

2. Draw a diagram of your rocket. Label the action and reaction forces.

Applying Your Data

Brainstorm ways to modify your rocket so that it will carry the most pennies to the maximum height. Select the best design. When your teacher has approved all the designs, build and launch your rocket. Which variable did you modify? How did this variable affect your rocket's flight?

MATERIALS

- balloon, long, thin
- cup, paper, small
- fishing line, 3 m
- meterstick
- pencil
- pennies
- straw, straight plastic
- string, 15 cm (2)
- tape, masking
- twist tie

SAFETY

Skills Practice Lab

Quite a Reaction

Catapults have been used for centuries to throw objects great distances. According to Newton's third law of motion (whenever one object exerts a force on a second object, the second object exerts an equal and opposite force on the first), when an object is launched, something must also happen to the catapult. In this activity, you will build a kind of catapult that will allow you to observe the effects of Newton's third law of motion and the law of conservation of momentum.

MATERIALS

- cardboard rectangles, 10 cm × 15 cm (3)
- glue
- marble
- meterstick
- pushpins (3)
- rubber band
- scissors
- straws, plastic (6)
- string

SAFETY

Procedure

1. Glue the cardboard rectangles together to make a stack of three.

2. Push two of the pushpins into the cardboard stack near the corners at one end, as shown below. These pushpins will be the anchors for the rubber band.

3. Make a small loop of string.

4. Put the rubber band through the loop of string, and then place the rubber band over the two pushpin anchors. The rubber band should be stretched between the two anchors with the string loop in the middle.

5. Pull the string loop toward the end of the cardboard stack opposite the end with the anchors, and fasten the loop in place with the third pushpin.

6. Place the six straws about 1 cm apart on a tabletop or on the floor. Then, carefully center the catapult on top of the straws.

7. Put the marble in the closed end of the V formed by the rubber band.

8. Use scissors to cut the string holding the rubber band, and observe what happens. (Be careful not to let the scissors touch the cardboard catapult when you cut the string.)

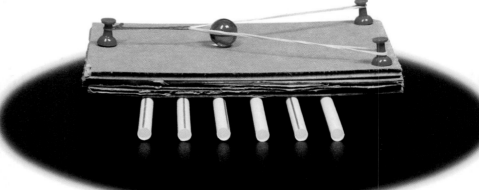

9 Reset the catapult with a new piece of string. Try launching the marble several times to be sure that you have observed everything that happens during a launch. Record all your observations.

Analyze the Results

1 Which has more mass, the marble or the catapult?

2 What happened to the catapult when the marble was launched?

3 How far did the marble fly before it landed?

4 Did the catapult move as far as the marble did?

Draw Conclusions

5 Explain why the catapult moved backward.

6 If the forces that made the marble and the catapult move apart are equal, why didn't the marble and the catapult move apart the same distance? (Hint: The fact that the marble can roll after it lands is not the answer.)

7 The momentum of an object depends on the mass and velocity of the object. What is the momentum of the marble before it is launched? What is the momentum of the catapult? Explain your answers.

8 Using the law of conservation of momentum, explain why the marble and the catapult move in opposite directions after the launch.

Applying Your Data

How would you modify the catapult if you wanted to keep it from moving backward as far as it did? (It still has to rest on the straws.) Using items that you can find in the classroom, design a catapult that will move backward less than the one originally designed.

Skills Practice Lab

Density Diver

Crew members of a submarine can control the submarine's density underwater by allowing water to flow into and out of special tanks. These changes in density affect the submarine's position in the water. In this lab, you'll control a "density diver" to learn for yourself how the density of an object affects its position in a fluid.

MATERIALS

- bottle, plastic, with screw-on cap, 2 L
- dropper, medicine
- water

SAFETY

Ask a Question

1 How does the density of an object determine whether the object floats, sinks, or maintains its position in a fluid?

Form a Hypothesis

2 Write a possible answer to the question above.

Test the Hypothesis

3 Completely fill the 2 L plastic bottle with water.

4 Fill the diver (medicine dropper) approximately halfway with water, and place it in the bottle. The diver should float with only part of the rubber bulb above the surface of the water. If the diver floats too high, carefully remove it from the bottle, and add a small amount of water to the diver. Place the diver back in the bottle. If you add too much water and the diver sinks, empty out the bottle and diver, and go back to step 3.

5 Put the cap on the bottle tightly so that no water leaks out.

6 Apply various pressures to the bottle. Carefully watch the water level inside the diver as you squeeze and release the bottle. Record what happens.

7 Try to make the diver rise, sink, or stop at any level. Record your technique and your results.

Analyze the Results

1 How do the changes inside the diver affect its position in the surrounding fluid?

2 What relationship did you observe between the diver's density and the diver's position in the fluid?

Draw Conclusions

3 Explain how your density diver is like a submarine.

4 Explain how pressure on the bottle is related to the diver's density. Be sure to include Pascal's principle in your explanation.

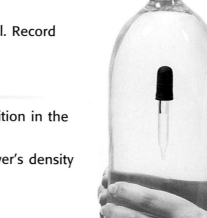

Skills Practice Lab

Inclined to Move

In this lab, you will examine a simple machine—an inclined plane. Your task is to compare the work done with and without the inclined plane and to analyze the effects of friction.

MATERIALS

- board, wooden
- blocks
- book, small
- meterstick
- paper, graph
- spring scale
- string

SAFETY

Ask a Question

1 Write a question that you can test regarding inclined planes.

Form a Hypothesis

2 Write a possible answer to the question you wrote.

Test the Hypothesis

3 Copy the table at right.

4 Tie a piece of string around a book. Attach the spring scale to the string. Use the spring scale to slowly lift the book to a height of 50 cm. Record the output force (the force needed to lift the book). The output force is constant throughout the lab.

5 Use the board and blocks to make a ramp 10 cm high at the highest point. Measure and record the ramp length.

6 Keeping the spring scale parallel to the ramp, as shown, slowly raise the book. Record the input force (the force needed to pull the book up the ramp).

7 Increase the height of the ramp by 10 cm. Repeat step 6. Repeat this step for each ramp height up to 50 cm.

Analyze the Results

1 The real work done includes the work done to overcome friction. Calculate the real work at each height by multiplying the ramp length (converted to meters) by the input force. Graph your results, plotting work (*y*-axis) versus height (*x*-axis).

Force Versus Height			
Ramp height (cm)	Output force (N)	Ramp length (cm)	Input force (N)
10			
20			
30		*DO NOT WRITE IN BOOK*	
40			
50			

2 The ideal work is the work you would do if there were no friction. Calculate the ideal work at each height by multiplying the ramp height (cm) by the output force. Plot the data on your graph.

Draw Conclusions

3 Does it require more or less force and work to raise the book by using the ramp? Explain, using your calculations.

4 What is the relationship between the height of the inclined plane and the input force?

Skills Practice Lab

Wheeling and Dealing

A crank handle, such as that used in pencil sharpeners, ice-cream makers, and water wells, is one kind of wheel and axle. In this lab, you will use a crank handle to find out how a wheel and axle helps you do work. You will also determine what effect the length of the handle has on the operation of the machine.

Ask a Question

1 What effect does the length of a handle have on the operation of a crank?

Form a Hypothesis

2 Write a possible answer to the question above.

Test the Hypothesis

3 Copy Table 1.

4 Measure the radius (in meters) of the large dowel in the wheel-and-axle assembly. Record this in Table 1 as the axle radius, which remains constant throughout the lab. (Hint: Measure the diameter, and divide by 2.)

5 Using the spring scale, measure the weight of the large mass. Record this in Table 1 as the output force, which remains constant throughout the lab.

6 Use two C-clamps to secure the wheel-and-axle assembly to the table, as shown.

7 Measure the length (in meters) of handle 1. Record this length as a wheel radius in Table 1.

8 Insert the handle into the hole in the axle. Attach one end of the string to the large mass and the other end to the screw in the axle. The mass should hang down, and the handle should turn freely.

9 Turn the handle to lift the mass off the floor. Hold the spring scale upside down, and attach it to the end of the handle. Measure the force (in newtons) as the handle pulls up on the spring scale. Record this as the input force.

MATERIALS

- C-clamps (2)
- handles (4)
- mass, large
- meterstick
- spring scale
- string, 0.5 m
- wheel-and-axle assembly

SAFETY

Table 1 Data Collection

Handle	Axle radius (m)	Output force (N)	Wheel radius (m)	Input force (N)
1				
2				
3		*DO NOT WRITE IN BOOK*		
4				

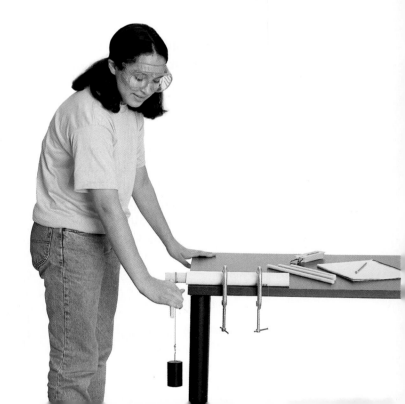

10 Remove the spring scale, and lower the mass to the floor. Remove the handle.

11 Repeat steps 7 through 10 with the other three handles. Record all data in Table 1.

Analyze the Results

1 Copy Table 2.

Table 2 Calculations						
Handle	Axle distance (m)	Wheel distance (m)	Work input (J)	Work output (J)	Mechanical efficiency (%)	Mechanical advantage
1						
2						
3						
4						

DO NOT WRITE IN BOOK

2 Calculate the following for each handle, using the equations given. Record your answers in Table 2.

a. *Distance axle rotates = 2 × π × axle radius*

Distance wheel rotates = 2 × π × wheel radius

(Use 3.14 for the value of π.)

b. *Work input = input force × wheel distance*

Work output = output force × axle distance

c. *Mechanical efficiency =* $\frac{work\ output}{work\ input} × 100$

d. *Mechanical advantage =* $\frac{wheel\ radius}{axle\ radius}$

Draw Conclusions

3 What happens to work output and work input as the handle length increases? Why?

4 What happens to mechanical efficiency as the handle length increases? Why?

5 What happens to mechanical advantage as the handle length increases? Why?

6 What will happen to mechanical advantage if the handle length is kept constant and the axle radius gets larger?

7 What factors were controlled in this experiment? What was the variable?

Inquiry Lab

Building Machines

You are surrounded by machines. Some are simple machines, such as ramps for wheelchair access to a building. Others are compound machines, such as elevators and escalators, that are made of two or more simple machines. In this lab, you will design and build several simple machines and a compound machine.

Ask a Question

1 How can simple machines be combined to make compound machines?

Form a Hypothesis

2 Write a possible answer to the question above.

Test the Hypothesis

3 Use the listed materials to build a model of each simple machine: inclined plane, lever, wheel and axle, pulley, screw, and wedge. Describe and draw each model.

4 Design a compound machine by using the materials listed. You may design a machine that already exists, or you may invent your own machine. Be creative!

5 After your teacher approves your design, build your compound machine.

Analyze the Results

1 List a possible use for each of your simple machines.

2 How many simple machines are in your compound machine? List them.

3 Compare your compound machine with those created by your classmates.

4 What is a possible use for your compound machine? Why did you design it as you did?

5 A compound machine is listed in the materials list. What is it?

Applying Your Data

Design a compound machine that has all the simple machines in it. Explain what the machine will do and how it will make work easier. With your teacher's approval, build your machine.

MATERIALS

- bottle caps
- cardboard
- clay, modeling
- craft sticks
- glue
- paper
- pencils
- rubber bands
- scissors
- shoe boxes
- stones
- straws
- string
- tape
- thread spools, empty
- other materials available in your classroom that are approved by your teacher

SAFETY

Skills Practice Lab

Energy of a Pendulum

A pendulum clock is a compound machine that uses stored energy to do work. A spring stores energy, and with each swing of the pendulum, some of that stored energy is used to move the hands of the clock. In this lab, you will take a close look at the energy conversions that occur as a pendulum swings.

MATERIALS

- marker
- mass, hooked, 100 g
- meterstick
- string, 1 m

SAFETY

Procedure

1. Make a pendulum by tying the string around the hook of the mass. Use the marker and the meterstick to mark points on the string that are 50 cm, 70 cm, and 90 cm away from the mass.

2. Hold the string at the 50 cm mark. Gently pull the mass to the side, and release it without pushing it. Observe at least 10 swings of the pendulum.

3. Record your observations. Be sure to note how fast and how high the pendulum swings.

4. Repeat steps 2 and 3 while holding the string at the 70 cm mark and again while holding the string at the 90 cm mark.

Analyze the Results

1. List similarities and differences in the motion of the pendulum during all three trials.

2. At which point (or points) of the swing was the pendulum moving the slowest? the fastest?

Draw Conclusions

3. In each trial, at which point (or points) of the swing did the pendulum have the greatest potential energy? the least potential energy? (Hint: Think about your answers to question 2.)

4. At which point (or points) of the swing did the pendulum have the greatest kinetic energy? the least kinetic energy? Explain your answers.

5. Describe the relationship between the pendulum's potential energy and its kinetic energy on its way down. Explain.

6. What improvements might reduce the amount of energy used to overcome friction so that the pendulum would swing for a longer period of time?

Inquiry Lab

Save the Cube!

The biggest enemy of an ice cube is the transfer of thermal energy—heat. Energy can be transferred to an ice cube in three ways: conduction (the transfer of energy through direct contact), convection (the transfer of energy by the movement of a liquid or gas), and radiation (the transfer of energy through matter or space). Your challenge in this activity is to design a way to protect an ice cube as much as possible from all three types of energy transfer.

MATERIALS

- bag, plastic, small
- balance, metric
- cup, plastic or paper, small
- ice cube
- milk carton, empty, half-pint
- assorted materials provided by your teacher

Ask a Question

1 What materials prevent energy transfer most efficiently?

Form a Hypothesis

2 Design a system that protects an ice cube against each type of energy transfer. Describe your proposed design.

Test the Hypothesis

3 Use a plastic bag to hold the ice cube and any water if the ice cube melts. You may use any of the materials to protect the ice cube. The whole system must fit inside a milk carton.

4 Find the mass of the empty cup, and record it. Then, find and record the mass of an empty plastic bag.

5 Find and record the mass of the ice cube and cup together.

6 Quickly wrap the bag (and the ice cube inside) in its protection. Remember that the package must fit in the milk carton.

7 Place your ice cube in the "thermal zone" set up by your teacher. After 10 min, remove the ice cube from the zone.

8 Open the bag. Pour any water into the cup. Find and record the mass of the cup and water together.

9 Find and record the mass of the water by subtracting the mass of the empty cup from the mass of the cup and water.

10 Use the same method to determine the mass of the ice cube.

11 Using the following equation, find and record the percentage of the ice cube that melted:

$$\% \; melted = \frac{mass \; of \; water}{mass \; of \; ice \; cube} \times 100$$

Analyze the Results

1 Compared with other designs in your class, how well did your design protect against each type of energy transfer? How could you improve your design?

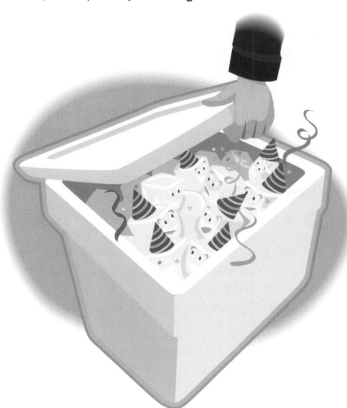

Model-Making Lab

Counting Calories

Energy transferred by heat is often expressed in units called *calories.* In this lab, you will build a model of a device called a *calorimeter.* Scientists often use calorimeters to measure the amount of energy that can be transferred by a substance. In this experiment, you will construct your own calorimeter and test it by measuring the energy released by a hot penny.

Procedure

1 Copy the table below.

Data Collection Table									
Seconds	0	15	30	45	60	75	90	105	120
Water temperature (°C)									

DO NOT WRITE IN BOOK

2 Place the lid on the small plastic-foam cup, and insert a thermometer through the hole in the top of the lid. (The thermometer should not touch the bottom of the cup.) Place the small cup inside the large cup to complete the calorimeter.

3 Remove the lid from the small cup, and add 50 mL of room-temperature water to the cup. Measure the water's temperature, and record the value in the first column (0 s) of the table.

4 Using tongs, heat the penny carefully. Add the penny to the water in the small cup, and replace the lid. Start your stopwatch.

5 Every 15 s, measure and record the temperature. Gently swirl the large cup to stir the water, and continue recording temperatures for 2 min (120 s).

Analyze the Results

1 What was the total temperature change of the water after 2 min?

2 The number of calories absorbed by the water is the mass of the water (in grams) multiplied by the temperature change (in °C) of the water. How many calories were absorbed by the water? (Hint: 1 mL water = 1 g water)

3 In terms of heat, explain where the calories to change the water temperature came from.

Model-Making Lab

Finding a Balance

Usually, balancing a chemical equation involves just writing. But in this activity, you will use models to practice balancing chemical equations, as shown below. By following the rules, you will soon become an expert equation balancer!

MATERIALS

• envelopes, each labeled with an unbalanced equation

Example

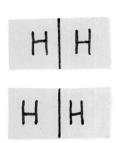

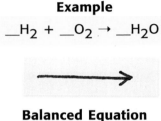

$$\_H_2 + \_O_2 \rightarrow \_H_2O$$

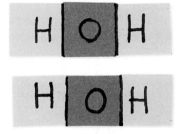

Balanced Equation

$$2H_2 + O_2 \rightarrow 2H_2O$$

Procedure

1. The rules are as follows:
   a. Reactant-molecule models may be placed only to the left of the arrow.
   b. Product-molecule models may be placed only to the right of the arrow.
   c. You may use only complete molecule models.
   d. At least one of each of the reactant and product molecules shown in the equation must be included in the model when you are finished.

2. Select one of the labeled envelopes. Copy the unbalanced equation written on the envelope.

3. Open the envelope, and pull out the molecule models and the arrow. Place the arrow in the center of your work area.

4. Put one model of each molecule that is a reactant on the left side of the arrow and one model of each product on the right side.

5. Add one reactant-molecule or product-molecule model at a time until the number of each of the different-colored squares on each side of the arrow is the same. Remember to follow the rules.

6. When the equation is balanced, count the number of each of the molecule models you used. Write these numbers as coefficients, as shown in the balanced equation above.

7. Select another envelope, and repeat the steps until you have balanced all of the equations.

Analyze the Results

1. The rules specify that you are allowed to use only complete molecule models. How are these rules similar to what occurs in a real chemical reaction?

2. In chemical reactions, energy is either released or absorbed. Devise a way to improve the model to show energy being released or absorbed.

Skills Practice Lab

Cata-what? Catalyst!

Catalysts increase the rate of a chemical reaction without being changed during the reaction. In this experiment, hydrogen peroxide, H_2O_2, decomposes into oxygen, O_2, and water, H_2O. An enzyme present in liver cells acts as a catalyst for this reaction. You will investigate the relationship between the amount of the catalyst and the rate of the decomposition reaction.

Ask a Question

1. How does the amount of a catalyst affect reaction rate?

Form a Hypothesis

2. Write a statement that answers the question above. Explain your reasoning.

Test the Hypothesis

3. Put a small piece of masking tape near the top of each test tube, and label the tubes "1," "2," and "3."

4. Create a hot-water bath by filling the beaker half full with hot water.

5. Using the funnel and graduated cylinder, measure 5 mL of the hydrogen peroxide solution into each test tube. Place the test tubes in the hot-water bath for 5 min.

6. While the test tubes warm up, grind one liver cube with the mortar and pestle.

7. After 5 min, use the tweezers to place the cube of liver in test tube 1. Place the ground liver in test tube 2. Leave test tube 3 alone.

8. Observe the reaction rate (the amount of bubbling) in all three test tubes, and record your observations.

Analyze the Results

1. Does liver appear to be a catalyst? Explain your answer.

2. Which type of liver (whole or ground) produced a faster reaction? Why?

3. What is the purpose of test tube 3?

MATERIALS

- beaker, 600 mL
- funnel
- graduated cylinder, 10 mL
- hydrogen peroxide, 3% solution
- liver cubes, small (2)
- mortar and pestle
- tape, masking
- test tubes, 10 mL (3)
- tweezers
- water, hot

SAFETY

Draw Conclusions

4. How do your results support or disprove your hypothesis?

5. Why was a hot-water bath used? (Hint: Look in your book for a definition of *activation energy*.)

Skills Practice Lab

Putting Elements Together

A synthesis reaction is a reaction in which two or more substances combine to form a single compound. The resulting compound has different chemical and physical properties than the substances from which it is composed. In this activity, you will synthesize, or create, copper(II) oxide from the elements copper and oxygen.

MATERIALS

- balance, metric
- Bunsen burner (or portable burner)
- copper powder
- evaporating dish
- gauze, wire
- gloves, protective
- igniter
- paper, weighing
- ring stand and ring
- tongs

SAFETY

Procedure

1 Copy the table below.

Data Collection Table	
Object	**Mass (g)**
Evaporating dish	
Copper powder	
Copper + evaporating dish after heating	*DO NOT WRITE IN BOOK*
Copper(II) oxide	

2 Use the metric balance to measure the mass (to the nearest 0.1 g) of the empty evaporating dish. Record this mass in the table.

3 Place a piece of weighing paper on the metric balance, and measure approximately 10 g of copper powder. Record the mass (to the nearest 0.1 g) in the table. **Caution:** Wear protective gloves when working with copper powder.

4 Use the weighing paper to place the copper powder in the evaporating dish. Spread the powder over the bottom and up the sides as much as possible. Discard the weighing paper.

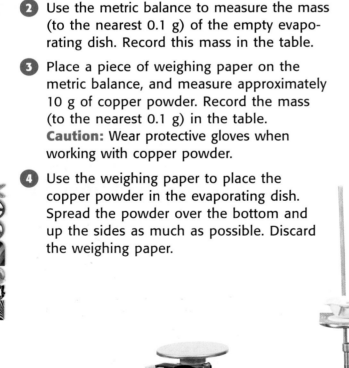

5 Set up the ring stand and ring. Place the wire gauze on top of the ring. Carefully place the evaporating dish on the wire gauze.

6 Place the Bunsen burner under the ring and wire gauze. Use the igniter to light the Bunsen burner. **Caution:** Use extreme care when working near an open flame.

7 Heat the evaporating dish for 10 min.

8 Turn off the burner, and allow the evaporating dish to cool for 10 min. Use tongs to remove the evaporating dish and to place it on the balance to determine the mass. Record the mass in the table.

9 Determine the mass of the reaction product—copper(II) oxide—by subtracting the mass of the evaporating dish from the mass of the evaporating dish and copper powder after heating. Record this mass in the table.

Analyze the Results

1 What evidence of a chemical reaction did you observe after the copper was heated?

2 Explain why there was a change in mass.

3 How does the change in mass support the idea that this reaction is a synthesis reaction?

Draw Conclusions

4 Why was powdered copper used rather than a small piece of copper? (Hint: How does surface area affect the rate of the reaction?)

5 Why was the copper heated? (Hint: Look in your book for the discussion of activation energy.)

6 The copper bottoms of cooking pots can turn black when used. How is that similar to the results you obtained in this lab?

Applying Your Data

Rust, shown below, is iron(III) oxide—the product of a synthesis reaction between iron and oxygen. How does painting a car help prevent this type of reaction?

Skills Practice Lab

Making Salt

A neutralization reaction between an acid and a base produces water and a salt. In this lab, you will react an acid with a base and then let the water evaporate. You will then examine what is left for properties that tell you that it is indeed a salt.

Ask a Question

1 Write a question about reactions between acids and bases.

Form a Hypothesis

2 Write a hypothesis that may answer the question you asked in the step above.

Test the Hypothesis

3 Put on protective gloves. Carefully measure 25 mL of hydrochloric acid in a graduated cylinder, and then pour it into the beaker. Carefully rinse the graduated cylinder with distilled water to clean out any leftover acid. **Caution:** Hydrochloric acid is corrosive. If any should spill on you, immediately flush the area with water, and notify your teacher.

4 Add 3 drops of phenolphthalein indicator to the acid in the beaker. You will not see anything happen yet because this indicator won't show its color unless too much base is present.

5 Measure 20 mL of sodium hydroxide (base) in the graduated cylinder, and add it slowly to the beaker with the acid. Use the stirring rod to mix the substances completely. **Caution:** Sodium hydroxide is also corrosive. If any should spill on you, immediately flush the area with water, and notify your teacher.

6 Use an eyedropper to add more base, a few drops at a time, to the acid-base mixture in the beaker. Be sure to stir the mixture after each few drops. Continue adding drops of base until the mixture remains colored after stirring.

MATERIALS

- beaker, 100 mL
- eyedroppers (2)
- evaporating dish
- gloves, protective
- graduated cylinder, 100 mL
- hydrochloric acid
- magnifying lens
- phenolphthalein solution in a dropper bottle
- stirring rod, glass
- sodium hydroxide
- water, distilled

SAFETY

7. Use another eyedropper to add acid to the beaker, 1 drop at a time, until the color just disappears after stirring.

8. Pour the mixture carefully into an evaporating dish, and place the dish where your teacher tells you to allow the water to evaporate overnight.

9. The next day, examine your evaporating dish, and with a magnifying lens, study the crystals that were left. Identify the color, shape, and other properties of the crystals.

Analyze the Results

1. The following equation is for the reaction that occurred in this experiment:

$$HCl + NaOH \longrightarrow H_2O + NaCl$$

NaCl is ordinary table salt and forms very regular cubic crystals that are white. Did you find white cubic crystals?

2. The phenolphthalein indicator changes color in the presence of a base. Why did you add more acid in step 7 until the color disappeared?

Applying Your Data

Another neutralization reaction occurs between hydrochloric acid and potassium hydroxide, KOH. The equation for this reaction is as follows:

$$HCl + KOH \longrightarrow H_2O + KCl$$

What are the products of this neutralization reaction? How do they compare with those you discovered in this experiment?

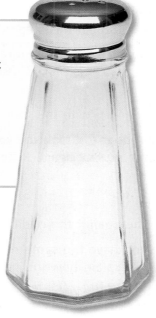

Skills Practice Lab

Stop the Static Electricity!

Imagine this scenario: Some of your clothes cling together when they come out of the dryer. This annoying problem is caused by static electricity—the buildup of electric charges on an object. In this lab, you'll discover how this buildup occurs.

Ask a Question

1 How do electric charges build up on clothes in a dryer?

Form a Hypothesis

2 Write a statement that answers the question above. Explain your reasoning.

Test the Hypothesis

3 Tie a piece of thread approximately 30 cm in length to a packing peanut. Hang the peanut by the thread from the edge of a table. Tape the thread to the table.

4 Rub the rubber rod with the wool cloth for 10 to 15 s. Bring the rod near, but do not touch, the peanut. Observe the peanut, and record your observations. If nothing happens, repeat this step.

5 Touch the peanut with the rubber rod. Pull the rod away from the peanut, and then bring it near again. Record your observations.

6 Repeat steps 4 and 5 with the glass rod and silk cloth.

7 Now, rub the rubber rod with the wool cloth, and bring the rod near the peanut again. Record your observations.

Analyze the Results

1 What caused the peanut to act differently in steps 4 and 5?

2 Did the glass rod have the same effect on the peanut as the rubber rod did? Explain how the peanut reacted in each case.

3 Was the reaction of the peanut the same in steps 5 and 7? Explain.

Draw Conclusions

4 Based on your results, was your hypothesis correct? Explain your answer, and write a new statement if necessary.

MATERIALS

- cloth, silk
- cloth, woolen
- packing peanut, plastic-foam
- rod, glass
- rod, rubber
- tape
- thread, 30 cm

SAFETY

Applying Your Data

Do some research to find out how a dryer sheet helps stop the buildup of electric charges in the dryer.

Model-Making Lab

Potato Power

Have you ever wanted to look inside a D cell from a flashlight or an AA cell from a portable radio? All cells include the same basic components, as shown below. There is a metal "bucket," some electrolyte (a paste), and a rod of some other metal (or solid) in the middle. Even though cell construction is simple, companies that manufacture cells are always trying to make a product with the highest voltage possible from the least expensive materials. Sometimes, companies try different pastes, and sometimes they try different combinations of metals. In this lab, you will make your own cell. Using inexpensive materials, you will try to produce the highest voltage you can.

MATERIALS

- metal strips, labeled
- potato
- ruler, metric
- voltmeter

SAFETY

Procedure

1. Choose two metal strips. Carefully push one of the strips into the potato at least 2 cm deep. Insert the second strip the same way, and measure how far apart the two strips are. (If one of your metal strips is too soft to push into the potato, push a harder strip in first, remove it, and then push the soft strip into the slit.) Record the two metals you have used and the distance between the strips. **Caution:** The strips of metal may have sharp edges.

2. Connect the voltmeter to the two strips, and record the voltage.

3. Move one of the strips closer to or farther from the other. Measure the new distance and voltage. Record your results.

4. Repeat steps 1 through 3, using different combinations of metal strips and distances until you find the combination that produces the highest voltage.

Metal "bucket"

Electrolyte

Metal or carbon rod

D cell

Analyze the Results

1. What combination of metals and distance produced the highest voltage?

2. If you change only the distance but use the same metal strips, what is the effect on the voltage?

3. One of the metal strips tends to lose electrons, and the other tends to gain electrons. What do you think would happen if you used two strips of the same metal?

Skills Practice Lab

Magnetic Mystery

Every magnet is surrounded by a magnetic field. Magnetic field lines show the shape of the magnetic field. These lines can be modeled by using iron filings. The iron filings are affected by the magnetic field, and they fall into lines showing the field. In this lab, you will first learn about magnetic fields, and then you will use this knowledge to identify a mystery magnet's shape and orientation based on observations of the field lines.

MATERIALS

- acetate, clear (1 sheet)
- iron filings
- magnets, different shapes (2)
- shoe box
- tape, masking

SAFETY

Ask a Question

1 Can a magnet's shape and orientation be determined without seeing the magnet?

Form a Hypothesis

2 Write a possible answer to the question above. Explain your reasoning.

Test the Hypothesis

3 Lay one of the magnets flat on a table.

4 Place a sheet of clear acetate over the magnet. Sprinkle some iron filings on the acetate to see the magnetic field lines.

5 Draw the magnet and the magnetic field lines.

6 Remove the acetate, and return the filings to the container.

7 Place your magnet so that one end is pointing up. Repeat steps 4 through 6.

8 Place your magnet on its side. Repeat steps 4 through 6.

9 Repeat steps 3 through 8 with the other magnet.

10 Remove the lid from a shoe box, and tape a magnet underneath the lid. Once the magnet is secure, place the lid on the box.

11 Exchange boxes with another team.

12 Without opening the box, use the sheet of acetate and the iron filings to determine the shape of the magnetic field.

13 Draw the magnetic field lines.

Analyze the Results

1 Use your drawings from steps 3 through 9 to find the shape and orientation of the magnet in your box. Draw a picture of your conclusion.

Applying Your Data

Examine your drawings. Can you identify the north and south poles of a magnet from the shape of the magnetic field lines? Design a procedure that would allow you to determine the poles of a magnet.

Skills Practice Lab

Electricity from Magnetism

You use electricity every day. But did you ever wonder where it comes from? Some of the electrical energy you use is converted from chemical energy in cells or batteries. But where does the electrical energy come from when you plug a lamp into a wall outlet? In this lab, you will see how electricity can be generated from magnetism.

Ask a Question

1 How can electricity be generated from magnetism?

Form a Hypothesis

2 Write a statement to answer question 1.

Test the Hypothesis

3 Sand the enamel off the last 2 cm or 3 cm of each end of the magnet wire. Wrap the magnet wire around the tube to make a coil, as illustrated below. Using the insulated wires, attach the bare ends of the wire to the galvanometer.

4 While watching the galvanometer, move a bar magnet into the coil, hold it there for a moment, and then remove it. Record your observations.

5 Repeat step 4 several times, moving the magnet at different speeds. Observe the galvanometer carefully.

6 Hold the magnet still, and pass the coil over the magnet. Record your observations.

Analyze the Results

1 How does the speed of the magnet affect the size of the electric current?

MATERIALS

- alligator clip (2)
- cardboard tube
- galvanometer, commercial
- magnet, bar, strong
- magnet wire, 150 cm
- sandpaper
- wires, insulated, 30 cm long (2)

SAFETY

2 How is the direction of the electric current affected by the motion of the magnet?

3 Examine your hypothesis. Is your hypothesis accurate? Explain. If necessary, write a new hypothesis to answer question 1.

Draw Conclusions

4 Would an electric current still be generated if the wire were broken? Why or why not?

5 Could a stationary magnet be used to generate an electric current? Explain.

6 What energy conversions occur in this investigation?

7 Write a short paragraph that explains the requirements for generating electricity from magnetism.

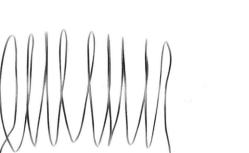

Model-Making Lab

Tune In!

You probably have listened to radios many times in your life. Modern radios are complicated electronic devices. However, radios do not have to be so complicated. The basic parts of all radios include a diode, an inductor, a capacitor, an antenna, a ground wire, and an earphone (or a speaker and amplifier on a large radio). In this activity, you will examine each of these components one at a time as you build a working model of a radio-wave receiver.

Ask a Question

❶ Write a question you can test using the procedure in this lab.

Form a Hypothesis

❷ Write a possible answer to the question you wrote in the step above. Explain your reasoning.

Test the Hypothesis

❸ Examine the diode. Describe it on another sheet of paper.

❹ A diode carries current in only one direction. Draw the inside of a diode, and illustrate how the diode might allow current in only one direction.

❺ An inductor controls the amount of electric current because of the resistance of the wire. Make an inductor by winding the insulated wire around a cardboard tube approximately 100 times. Wind the wire so that all the turns of the coil are neat and in an orderly row, as shown below. Leave about 25 cm of wire on each end of the coil. The coil of wire may be held on the tube using tape.

MATERIALS

- aluminum foil
- antenna
- cardboard, 20 cm × 30 cm
- cardboard tubes (2)
- connecting wires, 30 cm each (7)
- diode
- earphone
- ground wire
- paper (1 sheet)
- paper clips (3)
- scissors
- tape
- wire, insulated, 2 m

SAFETY

6 Now, you will construct the variable capacitor. A capacitor stores electrical energy when an electric current is applied. A variable capacitor is a capacitor in which the amount of energy stored can be changed. Cut a piece of aluminum foil to go around the tube but only half the length of the tube, as shown at right. Keep the foil as wrinkle-free as possible as you wrap it around the tube, and tape the foil to itself. Now, tape the foil to the tube.

7 Use the sheet of paper and tape to make a sliding cover on the tube. The paper should completely cover the foil on the tube with about 1 cm extra.

8 Cut another sheet of aluminum foil to wrap completely around the paper. Leave approximately 1 cm of paper showing at each end of the foil. Tape this foil sheet to the paper sleeve. If you have done this correctly, you have a paper/foil sheet that will slide up and down the tube over the stationary foil. The two pieces of foil should not touch.

9 Stand your variable capacitor on its end so that the stationary foil is at the bottom. The amount of stored energy is greater when the sleeve is down than when the sleeve is up.

10 Use tape to attach one connecting wire to the stationary foil at the end of the tube. Use tape to attach another connecting wire to the sliding foil sleeve. Be sure that the metal part of the wire touches the foil.

Capacitor

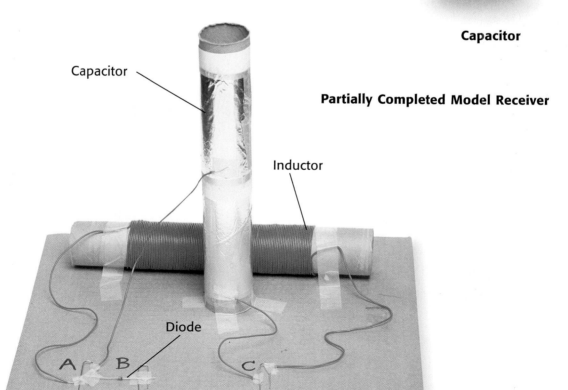

Partially Completed Model Receiver

11. Hook three paper clips on one edge of the cardboard, as shown below. Label one paper clip "A," the second one "B," and the third one "C."

12. Lay the inductor on the piece of cardboard, and tape it to the cardboard.

13. Stand the capacitor next to the inductor, and tape the tube to the cardboard. Be sure not to tape the sleeve—it must be free to slide.

14. Use tape to connect the diode to paper clips A and B. The cathode should be closest to paper clip B. (The cathode end of the diode is the one with the dark band.) Make sure that all connections have good metal-to-metal contact.

15. Connect one end of the inductor to paper clip A and the other end to paper clip C. Use tape to hold the wires in place.

16. Connect the wire from the sliding part of the capacitor to paper clip A. Connect the other wire (from the stationary foil) to paper clip C.

17. The antenna receives radio waves transmitted by a radio station. Tape a connecting wire to your antenna. Then, connect this wire to paper clip A.

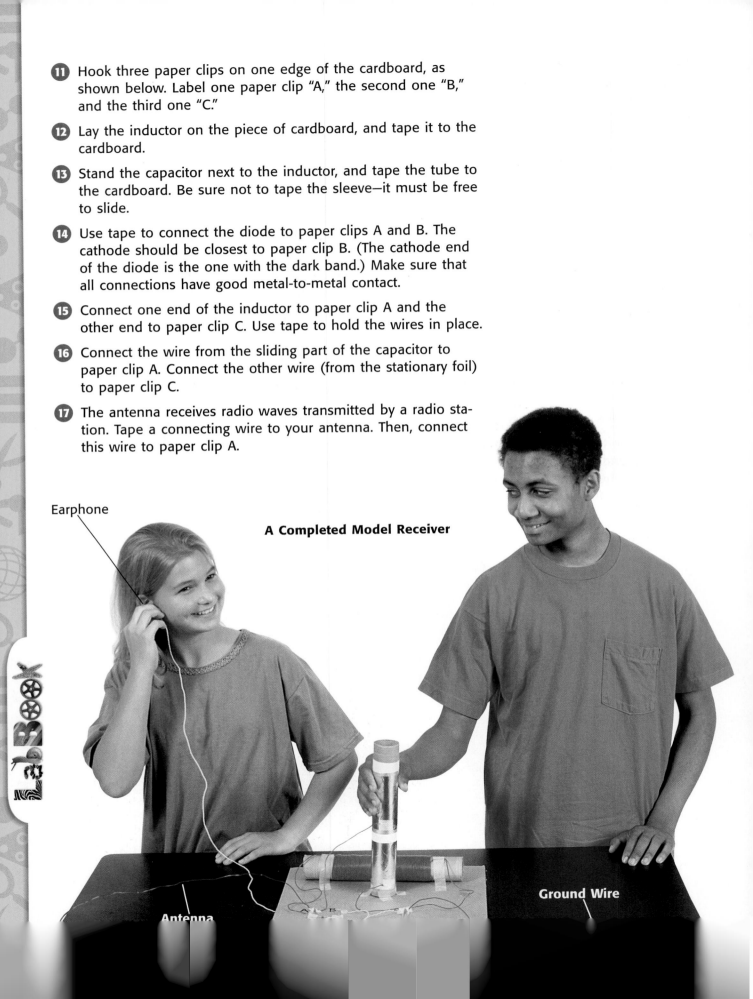

Earphone

A Completed Model Receiver

Ground Wire

Antenna

18 Use tape to connect one end of the ground wire to paper clip C. The other end of the ground wire should be connected to an object specified by your teacher.

19 The earphone will allow you to detect the radio waves you receive. Connect one wire from the earphone to paper clip B and the other wire to paper clip C.

20 You are now ready to begin listening. With everything connected and the earphone in your ear, slowly slide the paper/foil sheet of the capacitor up and down. Listen for a very faint sound. You may have to troubleshoot many of the parts to get your receiver to work. As you troubleshoot, check to be sure there is good contact between all the connections.

Analyze the Results

1 Describe the process of operating your receiver.

2 Considering what you have learned about a diode, why is it important to have the diode connected the correct way?

3 A function of the inductor on a radio is to "slow the current down." Why does the inductor you made slow the current down more than does a straight wire the length of your coil?

4 A capacitor consists of any two conductors separated by an insulator. For your capacitor, list the two conductors and the insulator.

Draw Conclusions

5 Explain why the amount of stored energy is increased down when you slide the foil sleeve and decreased when you slide the foil sleeve up.

6 Make a list of ways that your receiver is similar to a modern radio. Make a second list of ways that your receiver is different from a modern radio.

Skills Practice Lab

Wave Speed, Frequency, and Wavelength

Wave speed, frequency, and wavelength are three related properties of waves. In this lab, you will make observations and collect data to determine the relationship among these properties.

Part A: Wave Speed

Procedure

1 Copy Table 1.

Table 1	Wave Speed Data		
Trial	Length of spring (m)	Time for wave (s)	Speed of wave (m/s)
1			
2			
3		DO NOT WRITE IN BOOK	
Average			

2 Two students should stretch the spring to a length of 2 m to 4 m on the floor or on a table. A third student should measure the length of the spring. Record the length in Table 1.

3 One student should pull part of the spring sideways with one hand, as shown at right, and release the pulled-back portion. This action will cause a wave to travel down the spring.

4 Using a stopwatch, the third student should measure how long it takes for the wave to travel down the length of the spring and back. Record this time in Table 1.

5 Repeat steps 3 and 4 two more times.

Part B: Wavelength and Frequency

Procedure

1 Keep the spring the same length that you used in Part A.

2 Copy Table 2.

Table 2 Wavelength and Frequency Data				
Trial	Length of spring (m)	Time for 10 cycles (s)	Wave frequency (Hz)	Wavelength (m)
1				
2		*DO NOT WRITE IN BOOK*		
3				
Average				

3 One of the two students holding the spring should start shaking the spring from side to side until a wave pattern appears that resembles one of those shown.

4 Using the stopwatch, the third student should measure and record how long it takes for 10 cycles of the wave pattern to occur. (One back-and-forth shake is 1 cycle.) Keep the pattern going so that measurements for three trials can be made.

Analyze the Results

Part A

1 Calculate and record the wave speed for each trial. (Speed equals distance divided by time; distance is twice the spring length.)

2 Calculate and record the average time and the average wave speed.

Part B

3 Calculate the frequency for each trial by dividing the number of cycles (10) by the time. Record the answers in Table 2.

4 Determine the wavelength using the equation at right that matches your wave pattern. Record your answer in Table 2.

5 Calculate and record the average time and frequency.

Draw Conclusions: Parts A and B

6 Analyze the relationship among speed, wavelength, and frequency. Multiply or divide any two of them to see if the result equals the third. (Use the averages from your data tables.) Write the equation that shows the relationship.

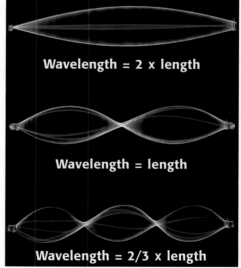

Wave Patterns

Wavelength = 2 x length

Wavelength = length

Wavelength = 2/3 x length

Inquiry Lab

The Speed of Sound

In the chapter entitled "The Nature of Sound," you learned that the speed of sound in air is 343 m/s at 20°C (approximately room temperature). In this lab, you'll design an experiment to measure the speed of sound yourself—and you'll determine if you're "up to speed"!

MATERIALS

- items to be determined by the students and approved by the teacher

Procedure

1. Brainstorm with your teammates to come up with a way to measure the speed of sound. Consider the following as you design your experiment:

   a. You must have a method of making a sound. Some simple examples include speaking, clapping your hands, and hitting two boards together.

   b. Remember that speed is equal to distance divided by time. You must devise methods to measure the distance that a sound travels and to measure the amount of time it takes for that sound to travel that distance.

   c. Sound travels very rapidly. A sound from across the room will reach your ears almost before you can start recording the time! You may wish to have the sound travel a long distance.

   d. Remember that sound travels in waves. Think about the interactions of sound waves. You might be able to include these interactions in your design.

2. Discuss your experimental design with your teacher, including any equipment you need. Your teacher may have questions that will help you improve your design.

3. Once your design is approved, carry out your experiment. Be sure to perform several trials. Record your results.

Analyze the Results

1. Was your result close to the value given in the introduction to this lab? If not, what factors may have caused you to get such a different value?

2. Why was it important for you to perform several trials in your experiment?

Draw Conclusions

3. Compare your results with those of your classmates. Determine which experimental design provided the best results. Explain why you think this design was so successful.

Skills Practice Lab

Tuneful Tube

If you have seen a singer shatter a crystal glass simply by singing a note, you have seen an example of resonance. For the glass to shatter, the note has to match the resonant frequency of the glass. A column of air within a cylinder can also resonate if the air column is the proper length for the frequency of the note. In this lab, you will investigate the relationship between the length of an air column, the frequency, and the wavelength during resonance.

MATERIALS

- eraser, pink, rubber
- graduated cylinder, 100 mL
- paper, graph
- plastic tube, supplied by your teacher
- ruler, metric
- tuning forks, different frequencies (4)
- water

SAFETY

Procedure

1. Copy the data table below.

Data Collection Table			
Frequency (Hz)			
Length (cm)	DO NOT WRITE IN BOOK		

2. Fill the graduated cylinder with water.

3. Hold a plastic tube in the water so that about 3 cm is above the water.

4. Record the frequency of the first tuning fork. Gently strike the tuning fork with the eraser, and hold the tuning fork so that the prongs are just above the tube, as shown at right. Slowly move the tube
and fork up and down until you hear the loudest sound.

5. Measure the distance from the top of the tube to the water. Record this length in your data table.

6. Repeat steps 3–5 using the other three tuning forks.

Analyze the Results

1. Calculate the wavelength (in centimeters) of each sound wave by dividing the speed of sound in air (343 m/s at 20°C) by the frequency and multiplying by 100.

2. Make the following graphs: air column length versus frequency and wavelength versus frequency. On both graphs, plot the frequency on the x-axis.

3. Describe the trend between the length of the air column and the frequency of the tuning fork.

4. How are the pitches you heard related to the wavelengths of the sounds?

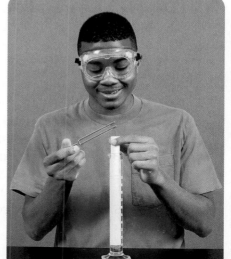

Skills Practice Lab

The Energy of Sound

In the chapter entitled "The Nature of Sound," you learned about various properties and interactions of sound. In this lab, you will perform several activities that will demonstrate that the properties and interactions of sound all depend on one thing—the energy carried by sound waves.

MATERIALS

- cup, plastic, small, filled with water
- eraser, pink, rubber
- rubber band
- string, 50 cm
- tuning forks, same frequency (2), different frequency (1)

SAFETY

Part A: Sound Vibrations

Procedure

1. Lightly strike a tuning fork with the eraser. Slowly place the prongs of the tuning fork in the plastic cup of water. Record your observations.

Part B: Resonance

Procedure

1. Strike a tuning fork with the eraser. Quickly pick up a second tuning fork in your other hand, and hold it about 30 cm from the first tuning fork.

2. Place the first tuning fork against your leg to stop the tuning fork's vibration. Listen closely to the second tuning fork. Record your observations, including the frequencies of the two tuning forks.

3. Repeat steps 1 and 2, using the remaining tuning fork as the second tuning fork.

Part C: Interference

Procedure

1. Use the two tuning forks that have the same frequency, and place a rubber band tightly over the prongs near the base of one tuning fork, as shown at right. Strike both tuning forks against the eraser. Hold the stems of the tuning forks against a table, 3 cm to 5 cm apart. If you cannot hear any differences, move the rubber band up or down the prongs. Strike again. Record your observations.

Part D: The Doppler Effect

Procedure

1 Your teacher will tie the piece of string securely to the base of one tuning fork. Your teacher will then strike the tuning fork and carefully swing the tuning fork in a circle overhead. Record your observations.

Analyze the Results

1 How do your observations demonstrate that sound waves are carried through vibrations?

2 Explain why you can hear a sound from the second tuning fork when the frequencies of the tuning forks used are the same.

3 When using tuning forks of different frequencies, would you expect to hear a sound from the second tuning fork if you strike the first tuning fork harder? Explain your reasoning.

4 Did you notice the sound changing back and forth between loud and soft? A steady pattern like this one is called a *beat frequency.* Explain this changing pattern of loudness and softness in terms of interference (both constructive and destructive).

5 Did the tuning fork make a different sound when your teacher was swinging it than when he or she was holding it? If yes, explain why.

6 Is the actual pitch of the tuning fork changing when it is swinging? Explain.

Draw Conclusions

7 Explain how your observations from each part of this lab verify that sound waves carry energy from one point to another through a vibrating medium.

8 Particularly loud thunder can cause the windows of your room to rattle. How is this evidence that sound waves carry energy?

Skills Practice Lab

What Color of Light Is Best for Green Plants?

Plants grow well outdoors under natural sunlight. However, some plants are grown indoors under artificial light. A variety of colored lights are available for helping plants grow indoors. In this experiment, you'll test several colors of light to discover which color best meets the energy needs of green plants.

Ask a Question

1 Which color of light is best for growing green plants?

Form a Hypothesis

2 Write a hypothesis that answers the question above. Explain your reasoning.

Test the Hypothesis

3 Use the masking tape and marker to label the side of each Petri dish with your name and the type of light under which you will place the dish.

4 Place a moist paper towel in each Petri dish. Place 5 seedlings on top of the paper towel. Cover each dish.

5 Record your observations of the seedlings, such as length, color, and number of leaves.

6 Place each dish under the appropriate light.

7 Observe the Petri dishes every day for at least 5 days. Record your observations.

Analyze the Results

1 Based on your results, which color of light is best for growing green plants? Which color of light is worst?

Draw Conclusions

2 Remember that the color of an opaque object (such as a plant) is determined by the colors the object reflects. Use this information to explain your answer to question 1 above.

3 Would a purple light be good for growing purple plants? Explain.

MATERIALS

- bean seedlings
- colored lights, supplied by your teacher
- marker, felt-tip
- paper towels
- Petri dishes with covers
- tape, masking
- water

SAFETY

Skills Practice Lab

Which Color Is Hottest?

Will a navy blue hat or a white hat keep your head warmer in cool weather? Colored objects absorb energy, which can make the objects warmer. How much energy is absorbed depends on the object's color. In this experiment, you will test several colors under a bright light to determine which colors absorb the most energy.

MATERIALS

- light source
- paper, colored, squares
- paper, graph
- paper towels
- pencils or pens, colored
- tape, transparent
- thermometer
- water, room-temperature

SAFETY

Procedure

1 Copy the table below. Be sure to have one column for each color of paper you use and enough rows to end at 3 min.

Data Collection Table				
Time (s)	White	Red	Blue	Black
0				
15				
30		DO NOT WRITE IN BOOK		
45				
etc.				

2 Tape a piece of colored paper around the bottom of a thermometer, and hold it under the light source. Record the temperature every 15 s for 3 min.

3 Cool the thermometer by removing the piece of paper and placing the thermometer in the cup of room-temperature water. After 1 min, remove the thermometer, and dry it with a paper towel.

4 Repeat steps 2 and 3 with each color, making sure to hold the thermometer at the same distance from the light source.

Analyze the Results

1 Prepare a graph of temperature (y-axis) versus time (x-axis). Using a different colored pencil or pen for each set of data, plot all data on one graph.

2 Rank the colors you used in order from hottest to coolest.

Draw Conclusions

3 Compare the colors, based on the amount of energy each absorbs.

4 In this experiment, a white light was used. How would your results be different if you used a red light? Explain.

5 Use the relationship between color and energy absorbed to explain why different colors of clothing are used for different seasons.

Skills Practice Lab

Mirror Images

When light actually passes through an image, the image is a real image. When light does not pass through the image, the image is a virtual image. Recall that plane mirrors produce only virtual images because the image appears to be behind the mirror where no light can pass through it.

In fact, all mirrors can form virtual images, but only some mirrors can form real images. In this experiment, you will explore the virtual images formed by concave and convex mirrors, and you will try to find a real image using both types of mirrors.

MATERIALS

- candle
- card, index
- clay, modeling
- jar lid
- matches
- mirror, concave
- mirror, convex

SAFETY

Part A: Finding Virtual Images

Procedure

1. Hold the convex mirror at arm's length away from your face. Observe the image of your face in the mirror.

2. Slowly move the mirror toward your face, and observe what happens to the image. Record your observations.

3. Move the mirror very close to your face. Record your observations.

4. Slowly move the mirror away from your face, and observe what happens to the image. Record your observations.

5. Repeat steps 1 through 4 with the concave mirror.

Analyze the Results

1. For each mirror, did you find a virtual image? How can you tell?

2. Describe the images you found. Were they smaller than, larger than, or the same size as your face? Were they right side up or upside down?

Draw Conclusions

3. Describe at least one use for each type of mirror. Be creative, and try to think of inventions that might use the properties of the two types of mirrors.

Part B: Finding a Real Image

Procedure

1. In a darkened room, place a candle in a jar lid near one end of a table. Use modeling clay to hold the candle in place. Light the candle. **Caution:** Use extreme care around an open flame.

2. Use more modeling clay to make a base to hold the convex mirror upright. Place the mirror at the other end of the table, facing the candle.

3. Hold the index card between the candle and the mirror but slightly to one side so that you do not block the candlelight, as shown below.

4. Move the card slowly from side to side and back and forth to see whether you can focus an image of the candle on it. Record your results.

5. Repeat steps 2–4 with the concave mirror.

Analyze the Results

1. For each mirror, did you find a real image? How can you tell?

2. Describe the real image you found. Was it smaller than, larger than, or the same size as the object? Was it right side up or upside down?

Draw Conclusions

3. Astronomical telescopes use large mirrors to reflect light to form a real image. Based on your results, do you think a concave or a convex mirror would be better for this instrument? Explain your answer.

Contents

Reading Check Answers 751
Study Skills 757
SI Measurement 763
Temperature Scales 764
Measuring Skills 765
Scientific Methods 766
Periodic Table of the Elements 768
Making Charts and Graphs 770
Math Refresher 773
Physical Science Laws and Principles 777

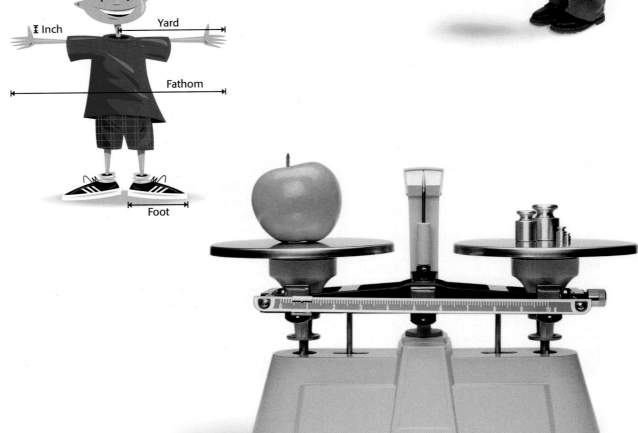

✓ *Reading Check* Answers

Chapter 1   The World of Physical Science

Section 1

Page 6: The first step in gathering knowledge is asking a question.

Page 8: how matter interacts with other matter, what the structure and properties of matter are, and how substances change

Page 10: A geochemist studies the chemistry of rocks, minerals, and soil.

Section 2

Page 13: Asking questions helps focus the purpose of the investigation.

Page 14: Boat efficiency is important because it saves resources, such as fuel.

Page 17: Information is easier to see and understand when it is organized into charts and graphs.

Page 18: The results of an investigation can be communicated by writing a scientific paper, making a presentation, or creating a Web site.

Section 3

Page 21: One possible limitation of a mathematical model is that complex models may have unknown variables. If the unknown variables change, a mathematical model could fail.

Page 22: A theory can explain a hypothesis or an observation.

Section 4

Page 24: Scientists use tools to make measurements and analyze data.

Page 26: The SI unit for temperature is the kelvin (K).

Chapter 2   The Properties of Matter

Section 1

Page 39: liters (L) and milliliters (mL)

Page 40: You could measure the volume of an apple by submerging the apple in a container of water and measuring the volume of the water that the apple displaces.

Page 42: kilograms (kg), grams (g), and milligrams (mg)

Section 2

Page 44: Some physical properties are color, shape, odor, weight, volume, texture, state, and density.

Page 46: If the object's density is less than the water's density, the object will float.

Page 49: A physical change is a change that occurs to a substance or object that does not change the identity of the substance.

Section 3

Page 50: Reactivity describes the ability of two or more substances to combine and form one or more new substances.

Page 52: Chemical changes occur when one or more substances are changed into entirely new substances that have different properties. A chemical property of a substance determines whether a chemical change will occur.

Chapter 3   States of Matter

Section 1

Page 67:
The particles in a crystalline solid are arranged in a repeating pattern of rows that forms an orderly, three-dimensional arrangement.

Page 68:
Viscosity is a liquid's resistance to flow.

Section 2

Page 71:
There are more particles of gas in the basketball than there are in the beach ball. More particles hit the inside surface of the basketball, which causes increased force.

Page 72:
Charles's law states that the volume of a gas in a closed container changes as the temperature of the gas changes. If the temperature increases, the volume increases. If the temperature decreases, the volume decreases.

Section 3

Page 74: A change of state is the change of a substance from one physical form to another.

Page 76: Evaporation is the change of a substance from a liquid to a gas.

Page 78: As a substance changes state, its temperature remains constant until the change of state is complete.

Chapter 4   Elements, Compounds, and Mixtures

Section 1

Page 90: An element is a pure substance because it contains only one type of particle.

Page 92: Metals are shiny, conduct heat energy, and conduct electric current.

Section 2

Page 95: Three physical properties used to identify compounds are melting point, density, and color.

Page 96: Compounds can be broken down into elements or simpler compounds.

Section 3

Page 98: Substances in a mixture keep their identities because no chemical change takes place when a mixture is made.

Page 101: An alloy is a solid solution of metal or nonmetal dissolved in another metal.

Page 103: As temperature increases, the solubility of a gas decreases.

Page 104: The particles of a suspension can be separated by passing the suspension through a filter.

Chapter 5 Matter in Motion

Section 1
Page 118: A reference point is an object that appears to stay in place.

Page 120: Velocity can change by changing speed or changing direction.

Page 122: The unit for acceleration is meters per second per second (m/s^2).

Section 2
Page 125: If all of the forces act in the same direction, you must add the forces to determine the net force.

Page 126: 2 N north

Section 3
Page 129: Friction is greater between rough surfaces because rough surfaces have more microscopic hills and valleys.

Page 131: *Static* means "not moving."

Page 132: Three common lubricants are oil, grease, and wax.

Section 4
Page 135: You must exert a force to overcome the gravitational force between the object and Earth.

Page 136: Gravitational force increases as mass increases.

Page 138: The weight of an object is a measure of the gravitational force on the object.

Chapter 6 Forces and Motion

Section 1
Page 151: The acceleration due to gravity is 9.8 m/s^2.

Page 152: Air resistance will have more of an effect on the acceleration of a falling leaf.

Page 154: The word *centripetal* means "toward the center."

Page 156: Gravity gives vertical motion to an object in projectile motion.

Section 2
Page 159: When the bus is moving, both you and the bus are in motion. When the bus stops moving, no unbalanced force acts on your body, so your body continues to move forward.

Page 161: The acceleration of an object increases as the force exerted on the object increases.

Page 163: The forces in a force pair are equal in size and opposite in direction.

Page 164: Objects accelerate toward Earth because the force of gravity pulls them toward Earth.

Section 3
Page 167: When two objects collide, some or all of the momentum of each object can be transferred to the other object.

Page 168: After a collision, objects can stick together or can bounce off each other.

Chapter 7 Forces in Fluids

Section 1
Page 181: Two gases in the atmosphere are nitrogen and oxygen.

Page 182: Pressure increases as depth increases.

Page 184: You decrease pressure inside a straw by removing some of the air inside the straw.

Section 2
Page 187: An object is buoyed up if the buoyant force on the object is greater than the object's weight.

Page 188: Helium is less dense than air.

Page 190: Crew members control the density of a submarine by controlling the amount of water in the ballast tanks.

Section 3
Page 193: Lift is an upward force on an object that is moving in a fluid.

Page 195: An irregular or unpredictable flow of fluids is known as *turbulence.*

Page 196: Airplanes can reduce turbulence by changing the shape or area of the wings.

Chapter 8 Work and Machines

Section 1
Page 210: No, work is done on an object only if force causes the object to move in a direction that is parallel to the force.

Page 213: Work is calculated as force times distance.

Page 214: Power is calculated as work done (in joules) divided by the time (in seconds) in which the work was done.

Section 2
Page 217: Machines make work easier by allowing a decreased force to be applied over a greater distance.

Page 218: Machines can change the force or the distance through which force is applied.

Page 220: mechanical efficiency = (work output ÷ work input) × 100

Section 3
Page 223: Each class of lever has a different set of mechanical advantage possibilities.

Page 225: the radius of the wheel divided by the radius of the axle

Page 226: a slanted surface that makes the raising of loads easier, such as a ramp

Page 228: They have more moving parts than simple machines do, so they tend to be less efficient than simple machines are.

Chapter 9 Energy and Energy Resources

Section 1
Page 240: Energy is the ability to do work.

Page 243: kinetic energy and potential energy

Page 245: Sound energy consists of vibrations carried through the air.

Page 246: Nuclear energy comes from changes in the nucleus of an atom.

Section 2

Page 249: Elastic potential energy can be stored by stretching a rubber band. Elastic potential energy is released when the rubber band goes back to its original shape.

Page 250: Plants get their energy from the sun.

Page 252: Machines can change the size or direction of the input force.

Section 3

Page 255: Conservation of energy is considered a scientific law because no exception to it has ever been observed.

Page 256: Perpetual motion is impossible because energy conversions always result in the production of waste thermal energy.

Section 4

Page 258: Fossil fuels are nonrenewable resources because they are used up more quickly than they are replaced.

Page 260: Nuclear energy comes from radioactive elements that give off energy during nuclear fission.

Page 262: Geothermal energy comes from the thermal energy given off by underground areas of hot rock.

Chapter 10   Heat and Heat Technology

Section 1

Page 275: Temperature is a measure of the average kinetic energy of the particles of a substance.

Page 276: Thermal expansion makes thermometers work.

Page 279: Expansion joints on a bridge allow the bridge to undergo thermal expansion without breaking.

Section 2

Page 281: If two objects at different temperatures come into contact, thermal energy will be transferred from the higher-temperature object to the lower-temperature object until both objects are at the same temperature.

Page 283: Two objects that are at the same temperature can feel as though they are at different temperatures if one object is a better thermal conductor than the other is. The better conductor will feel colder because it will draw thermal energy away from your hand faster.

Page 284: The greenhouse effect is the trapping of thermal energy from the sun in Earth's atmosphere.

Page 286: Specific heat, mass, and the change in temperature are needed to calculate heat.

Section 3

Page 289: While a substance is undergoing a change of state, the temperature of the substance remains the same.

Page 291: The Calorie is the unit of food energy.

Section 4

Page 293: Insulation helps save energy costs by keeping thermal energy from passing into or escaping from a building.

Page 295: Combustion engines use thermal energy.

Page 297: The inside of a refrigerator is able to stay cooler than the outside because thermal energy inside the refrigerator is continuously being transferred outside of the refrigerator.

Page 298: Sample answer: Thermal pollution can take place when heated water from an electrical generating plant is returned to the river from which the water came. The heated water that is returned to the river raises the temperature of the river water.

Chapter 11   Introduction to Atoms

Section 1

Page 313: Dalton thought that elements are made of single atoms because elements always combine in specific proportions to form compounds.

Page 315: Rutherford could tell where the positively charged particles went because they hit a special coating that glowed where it was hit.

Page 316: Rutherford changed Thomson's model of the atom by proposing that the nucleus is a tiny, dense, positively charged area surrounded by electrons.

Section 2

Page 319: Protons and neutrons can be found in the nucleus.

Page 320: An atom becomes a positively charged ion when it loses an electron.

Page 322: Differences between isotopes are important when a certain isotope is radioactive.

Page 324: The four basic forces are the gravitational force, electromagnetic force, strong force, and weak force.

Chapter 12   The Periodic Table

Section 1

Page 336: Mendeleev had arranged elements based on increasing atomic mass.

Page 337: atomic number

Page 340: Most metals are solid at room temperature, ductile, malleable, and shiny. In addition, they are good conductors of electric current and thermal energy.

Page 342: Elements in a group often have similar chemical and physical properties.

Section 2

Page 345: It is easier for atoms of alkali metals to lose their outer electron than for atoms of transition metals to lose their outer electrons. Therefore, alkali metals are more reactive than transition metals.

Page 346: Yes, lanthanides and actinides are transition metals.

Page 347: silicon and germanium

Page 348: nitrogen and oxygen

Page 350: Atoms of noble gases have a full set of electrons in their outer level.

Chapter 13   Chemical Bonding

Section 1

Page 365: Most atoms form bonds only with their valence electrons.

Page 366: Atoms in Group 18 (the noble gases) rarely form chemical bonds.

Section 2

Page 367: Atoms are neutral because the number of protons in an atom always equals the number of electrons in the atom.

Page 369: Atoms in Group 17 give off the most energy when forming negative ions.

Section 3

Page 372: A covalent bond is a bond that forms when atoms share one or more pairs of electrons.

Page 374: There are two atoms in a diatomic molecule.

Page 376: Ductility is the ability to be drawn into wires.

Chapter 14   Chemical Reactions

Section 1

Page 389: A precipitate is a solid substance that is formed in a solution.

Page 390: In a chemical reaction, the chemical bonds in the starting substances break, and then new bonds form to make new substances.

Section 2

Page 393: Ionic compounds are made up of a metal and a nonmetal.

Page 394: Reactants are the starting substances in a chemical reaction, and products are the substances that are formed.

Page 396: 4

Section 3

Page 398: A synthesis reaction is a reaction in which two or more substances combine to form one new compound.

Page 399: In a decomposition reaction, a substance breaks down into simpler substances. In a synthesis reaction, two or more substances combine to form one new compound.

Page 400: In a single-displacement reaction, an element may replace another element if the replacing element is more reactive than the original element.

Section 4

Page 403: An endothermic reaction is a chemical reaction in which energy is taken in.

Page 404: Activation energy is the energy that is needed to start a chemical reaction.

Page 406: A high concentration of reactants allows the particles of the reactants to run into each other more often, so the reaction proceeds at a faster rate.

Chapter 15   Chemical Compounds

Section 1

Page 419: Ionic solutions conduct an electric current because the ions in the solution are charged and are able to move past each other easily.

Page 420: Most covalent compounds will not dissolve in water because the attraction of the water molecules to each other is much stronger than their attraction to the compound.

Section 2

Page 422: A hydronium ion forms when a hydrogen ion bonds to a water molecule in a water solution.

Page 424: Sulfuric acid is used in car batteries to conduct electric current. Hydrochloric acid is used as an algaecide in swimming pools. Nitric acid is used to make fertilizers.

Page 427: Bases can be used at home in the form of soap, oven cleaner, or antacid.

Section 3

Page 428: In a strong acid, all of the molecules of the acid break apart when the acid is dissolved in water. In a weak acid, only a few of the acid molecules break apart when the acid is dissolved in water.

Page 430: Indicators turn different colors at different pH levels. The color on the pH strip can be compared with the colors on the indicator scale to determine the pH of the solution being tested.

Section 4

Page 432: Structural formulas show how atoms in a molecule are connected.

Page 435: Proteins are made of building blocks called *amino acids.*

Page 436: Nucleic acids store genetic information and build proteins.

Chapter 16   Atomic Energy

Section 1

Page 449: mass number and charge

Page 451: fatigue, loss of appetite, and hair loss

Page 453: 5,730 years

Page 454: A tracer is a radioactive element whose path can be followed through a process or reaction.

Section 2

Page 456: A nucleus that undergoes nuclear fission splits into two smaller, more stable nuclei.

Page 459: Sample answer: Using nuclear fission to generate electrical energy can help our supply of fossil fuels last longer, can help protect the environment because gases such as carbon dioxide are not released during fission, and can save money because nuclear power plants often cost less to run than power plants that use fossil fuels.

Page 460: In nuclear fusion, two or more nuclei that have small masses combine to form a larger nucleus. During fusion, energy is released.

Chapter 17 Introduction to Electricity
Section 1
Page 474: protons and electrons

Page 476: friction, conduction, and induction

Page 477: You can use an electroscope to detect whether an object is charged.

Page 479: Electric discharge is the release of electricity stored in a source.

Page 480: Sample answer: A person in an open area might be the tallest object and might provide a path for lightning.

Section 2
Page 482: amperes (A)

Page 483: alternating current (AC) and direct current (DC)

Page 484: volts (V)

Page 487: wet cells and dry cells

Page 488: a photocell

Section 3
Page 491: watt (W) and kilowatt (kW)

Page 492: kilowatt-hour (kWh)

Section 4
Page 494: an energy source, wires, and a load

Page 495: series circuits and parallel circuits

Page 496: Loads are connected in a single loop in a series circuit.

Page 497: Loads are connected side by side in branches in a parallel circuit.

Page 498: fuses and circuit breakers

Chapter 18 Electromagnetism
Section 1
Page 510: A magnet is any material that attracts iron or things made of iron.

Page 511: The poles of the magnets are identical.

Page 512: The magnetic fields of the individual atoms cancel each other out.

Page 513: A magnet can lose its magnetic properties if it is dropped, hit, placed in a strong magnetic field that is opposite to its own, or heated.

Page 514: Ferromagnets are magnets made of iron, nickel, cobalt, or mixtures of these metals.

Page 516: Scientists think that the Earth's magnetic field is caused by the movement of electric charges in the Earth's liquid outer core.

Section 2
Page 519: the interaction between electricity and magnetism

Page 520: The magnetic field gets stronger.

Page 521: The electric current creates a magnetic field that exerts a force on the compass needle and causes the compass needle to move.

Page 523: electric current

Section 3
Page 524: Faraday was trying to induce a current in a wire by using the magnetic field of an electromagnet.

Page 526: Mechanical energy is converted into electrical energy in an electric generator.

Page 527: A nuclear reaction, fossil fuels, and wind are sources of energy that are used to generate electrical energy.

Page 528: A transformer increases or decreases the voltage of alternating current.

Chapter 19 Electronic Technology
Section 1
Page 541: The conductivity of the semiconductor is changed by doping.

Page 542: A diode allows current in only one direction, so it blocks current that is in the other direction.

Page 543: NPN and PNP

Page 544: Devices can be made smaller and can run faster by using integrated circuits.

Section 2
Page 547: An analog signal is a signal whose properties can change continuously in a given range.

Page 549: A digital recording can be made to sound more like the original sound by taking more samples each second.

Page 551: analog signals and digital signals

Page 552: A plasma display does not use electron beams to activate the fluorescent materials. Instead, each tiny cell is activated individually.

Section 3
Page 554: input, processing, storage, and output

Page 555: A microprocessor is a single semiconductor chip that controls and executes a microcomputer's instructions.

Page 556: central processing unit

Page 559: operating-system software and application software

Page 560: Sample answer: The World Wide Web is a collection of pages that share a format that can be viewed on any computer.

Chapter 20 The Energy of Waves
Section 1
Page 574: All waves are disturbances that transmit energy.

Page 576: Electromagnetic waves do not require a medium.

Page 578: A sound wave is a longitudinal wave.

Section 2
Page 581: Shaking the rope faster makes the wavelength shorter; shaking the rope more slowly makes the wavelength longer.

Page 582: 3 Hz

Section 3

Page 585: It refracts.

Page 587: Constructive interference occurs when the crests of one wave overlap the crests of another wave.

Page 588: A standing wave results from a wave that is reflected between two fixed points. Interference from the wave and reflected waves cause certain points to remain at rest and certain points to remain at a large amplitude.

Chapter 21   The Nature of Sound

Section 1

Page 601: Sound waves consist of longitudinal waves carried through a medium.

Page 602: Sound needs a medium in order to travel.

Page 604: Tinnitus is caused by long-term exposure to loud sounds.

Section 2

Page 607: Frequency is the number of crests or troughs made in a given time.

Page 609: The amplitude of a sound increases as the energy of the vibrations that caused the sound increases.

Page 610: An oscilloscope turns sounds into electrical signals and graphs the signals.

Section 3

Page 613: Echolocation helps some animals find food.

Page 614: Sound wave interference can be either constructive or destructive.

Page 616: A standing wave is a pattern of vibration that looks like a wave that is standing still.

Section 4

Page 619: Musical instruments differ in the part of the instrument that vibrates and in the way that the vibrations are made.

Page 621: Music consists of sound waves that have regular patterns, and noise consists of a random mix of frequencies.

Chapter 22   The Nature of Light

Section 1

Page 633: Electric fields can be found around every charged object.

Page 634: The speed of light is about 880,000 times faster than the speed of sound.

Section 2

Page 636: The speed of a wave is determined by multiplying the wavelength and frequency of the wave.

Page 638: Radio waves carry TV signals.

Page 640: White light is the combination of visible light of all wavelengths.

Page 641: Ultraviolet light waves have shorter wavelengths and higher frequencies than visible light waves do.

Page 642: Patients are protected from X rays by special lead-lined aprons.

Section 3

Page 644: The law of reflection states that the angle of incidence equals the angle of reflection.

Page 645: Sample answer: Four light sources are a television screen, a fluorescent light in the classroom, a light bulb, and the tail of a firefly.

Page 646: You can see things outside of a beam of light because light is scattered outside of the beam.

Page 649: The amount that a wave diffracts depends on the wavelength of the wave and the size of the barrier or opening.

Page 650: Constructive interference is interference in which the resulting wave has a greater amplitude than the original waves had.

Section 4

Page 653: Sample answer: Two translucent objects are a frosted window and wax paper.

Page 654: When white light shines on a colored opaque object, some of the colors of light are absorbed and some are reflected.

Page 656: A pigment is a material that gives color to a substance by absorbing some colors of light and reflecting others.

Chapter 23   Light and Our World

Section 1

Page 669: A virtual image is an image through which light does not travel.

Page 670: A concave mirror can be used to make a powerful beam of light by putting a light source at the focal point of the mirror.

Page 672: A convex lens in thicker in the middle than it is at the edges.

Section 2

Page 675: Nearsightedness happens when a person's eye is too long. Farsightedness happens when a person's eye is too short.

Page 676: The three kinds of cones are red, blue, and green.

Section 3

Page 679: When light is coherent, light waves move together as they travel away from their source. Individual waves behave as one wave.

Page 681: Holograms are like photographs because both are images recorded on film.

Page 683: A cordless telephone sends signals by using radio waves.

Page 684: Sample answer: GPS can be used by hikers and campers to find their way in the wilderness. GPS can also be used for treasure hunt games.

Study Skills

FoldNote Instructions

Have you ever tried to study for a test or quiz but didn't know where to start? Or have you read a chapter and found that you can remember only a few ideas? Well, FoldNotes are a fun and exciting way to help you learn and remember the ideas you encounter as you learn science!

FoldNotes are tools that you can use to organize concepts. By focusing on a few main concepts, FoldNotes help you learn and remember how the concepts fit together. They can help you see the "big picture." Below you will find instructions for building 10 different FoldNotes.

Pyramid

1. Place a sheet of paper in front of you. Fold the lower left-hand corner of the paper diagonally to the opposite edge of the paper.

2. Cut off the tab of paper created by the fold (at the top).

3. Open the paper so that it is a square. Fold the lower right-hand corner of the paper diagonally to the opposite corner to form a triangle.

4. Open the paper. The creases of the two folds will have created an X.

5. Using scissors, cut along one of the creases. Start from any corner, and stop at the center point to create two flaps. Use tape or glue to attach one of the flaps on top of the other flap.

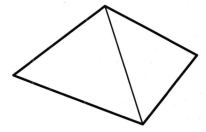

Double Door

1. Fold a sheet of paper in half from the top to the bottom. Then, unfold the paper.

2. Fold the top and bottom edges of the paper to the crease.

Booklet

1. Fold a sheet of paper in half from left to right. Then, unfold the paper.

2. Fold the sheet of paper in half again from the top to the bottom. Then, unfold the paper.

3. Refold the sheet of paper in half from left to right.

4. Fold the top and bottom edges to the center crease.

5. Completely unfold the paper.

6. Refold the paper from top to bottom.

7. Using scissors, cut a slit along the center crease of the sheet from the folded edge to the creases made in step 4. Do not cut the entire sheet in half.

8. Fold the sheet of paper in half from left to right. While holding the bottom and top edges of the paper, push the bottom and top edges together so that the center collapses at the center slit. Fold the four flaps to form a four-page book.

Layered Book

1. Lay one sheet of paper on top of another sheet. Slide the top sheet up so that 2 cm of the bottom sheet is showing.

2. Hold the two sheets together, fold down the top of the two sheets so that you see four 2 cm tabs along the bottom.

3. Using a stapler, staple the top of the FoldNote.

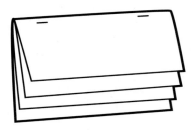

Key-Term Fold

1. Fold a sheet of lined notebook paper in half from left to right.

2. Using scissors, cut along every third line from the right edge of the paper to the center fold to make tabs.

Four-Corner Fold

1. Fold a sheet of paper in half from left to right. Then, unfold the paper.

2. Fold each side of the paper to the crease in the center of the paper.

3. Fold the paper in half from the top to the bottom. Then, unfold the paper.

4. Using scissors, cut the top flap creases made in step 3 to form four flaps.

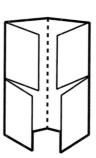

Three-Panel Flip Chart

1. Fold a piece of paper in half from the top to the bottom.

2. Fold the paper in thirds from side to side. Then, unfold the paper so that you can see the three sections.

3. From the top of the paper, cut along each of the vertical fold lines to the fold in the middle of the paper. You will now have three flaps.

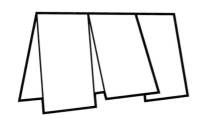

Table Fold

1. Fold a piece of paper in half from the top to the bottom. Then, fold the paper in half again.

2. Fold the paper in thirds from side to side.

3. Unfold the paper completely. Carefully trace the fold lines by using a pen or pencil.

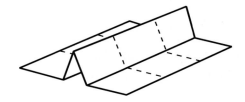

Two-Panel Flip Chart

1. Fold a piece of paper in half from the top to the bottom.

2. Fold the paper in half from side to side. Then, unfold the paper so that you can see the two sections.

3. From the top of the paper, cut along the vertical fold line to the fold in the middle of the paper. You will now have two flaps.

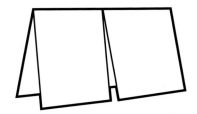

Tri-Fold

1. Fold a piece a paper in thirds from the top to the bottom.

2. Unfold the paper so that you can see the three sections. Then, turn the paper sideways so that the three sections form vertical columns.

3. Trace the fold lines by using a pen or pencil. Label the columns "Know," "Want," and "Learn."

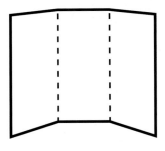

Appendix

Graphic Organizer Instructions

Have you ever wished that you could "draw out" the many concepts you learn in your science class? Sometimes, being able to *see* how concepts are related really helps you remember what you've learned. Graphic Organizers do just that! They give you a way to draw or map out concepts.

All you need to make a Graphic Organizer is a piece of paper and a pencil. Below you will find instructions for four different Graphic Organizers designed to help you organize the concepts you'll learn in this book.

Spider Map

1. Draw a diagram like the one shown. In the circle, write the main topic.

2. From the circle, draw legs to represent different categories of the main topic. You can have as many categories as you want.

3. From the category legs, draw horizontal lines. As you read the chapter, write details about each category on the horizontal lines.

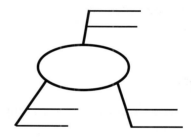

Comparison Table

1. Draw a chart like the one shown. Your chart can have as many columns and rows as you want.

2. In the top row, write the topics that you want to compare.

3. In the left column, write characteristics of the topics that you want to compare. As you read the chapter, fill in the characteristics for each topic in the appropriate boxes.

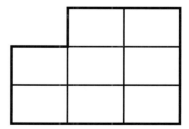

Chain-of-Events-Chart

1. Draw a box. In the box, write the first step of a process or the first event of a timeline.

2. Under the box, draw another box, and use an arrow to connect the two boxes. In the second box, write the next step of the process or the next event in the timeline.

3. Continue adding boxes until the process or timeline is finished.

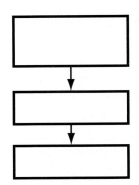

Concept Map

1. Draw a circle in the center of a piece of paper. Write the main idea of the chapter in the center of the circle.

2. From the circle, draw other circles. In those circles, write characteristics of the main idea. Draw arrows from the center circle to the circles that contain the characteristics.

3. From each circle that contains a characteristic, draw other circles. In those circles, write specific details about the characteristic. Draw arrows from each circle that contains a characteristic to the circles that contain specific details. You may draw as many circles as you want.

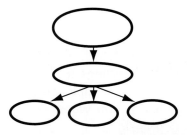

Appendix

SI Measurement

The International System of Units, or SI, is the standard system of measurement used by many scientists. Using the same standards of measurement makes it easier for scientists to communicate with one another.

SI works by combining prefixes and base units. Each base unit can be used with different prefixes to define smaller and larger quantities. The table below lists common SI prefixes.

SI Prefixes

Prefix	Symbol	Factor	Example
kilo-	k	1,000	kilogram, 1 kg = 1,000 g
hecto-	h	100	hectoliter, 1 hL = 100 L
deka-	da	10	dekameter, 1 dam = 10 m
		1	meter, liter, gram
deci-	d	0.1	decigram, 1 dg = 0.1 g
centi-	c	0.01	centimeter, 1 cm = 0.01 m
milli-	m	0.001	milliliter, 1 mL = 0.001 L
micro-	μ	0.000 001	micrometer, 1 μm = 0.000 001 m

SI Conversion Table

SI units	From SI to English	From English to SI
Length		
kilometer (km) = 1,000 m	1 km = 0.621 mi	1 mi = 1.609 km
meter (m) = 100 cm	1 m = 3.281 ft	1 ft = 0.305 m
centimeter (cm) = 0.01 m	1 cm = 0.394 in.	1 in. = 2.540 cm
millimeter (mm) = 0.001 m	1 mm = 0.039 in.	
micrometer (μm) = 0.000 001 m		
nanometer (nm) = 0.000 000 001 m		
Area		
square kilometer (km^2) = 100 hectares	1 km^2 = 0.386 mi^2	1 mi^2 = 2.590 km^2
hectare (ha) = 10,000 m^2	1 ha = 2.471 acres	1 acre = 0.405 ha
square meter (m^2) = 10,000 cm^2	1 m^2 = 10.764 ft^2	1 ft^2 = 0.093 m^2
square centimeter (cm^2) = 100 mm^2	1 cm^2 = 0.155 in.^{2}	1 in.^{2} = 6.452 cm^2
Volume		
liter (L) = 1,000 mL = 1 dm^3	1 L = 1.057 fl qt	1 fl qt = 0.946 L
milliliter (mL) = 0.001 L = 1 cm^3	1 mL = 0.034 fl oz	1 fl oz = 29.574 mL
microliter (μL) = 0.000 001 L		
Mass		
kilogram (kg) = 1,000 g	1 kg = 2.205 lb	1 lb = 0.454 kg
gram (g) = 1,000 mg	1 g = 0.035 oz	1 oz = 28.350 g
milligram (mg) = 0.001 g		
microgram (μg) = 0.000 001 g		

Temperature Scales

Temperature can be expressed by using three different scales: Fahrenheit, Celsius, and Kelvin. The SI unit for temperature is the kelvin (K).

Although 0 K is much colder than 0°C, a change of 1 K is equal to a change of 1°C.

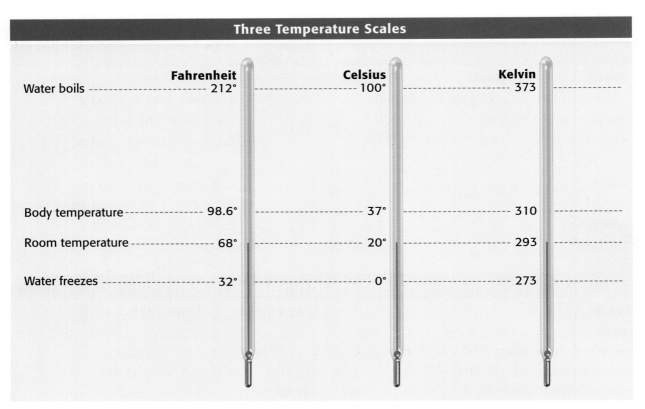

Three Temperature Scales

	Fahrenheit	Celsius	Kelvin
Water boils	212°	100°	373
Body temperature	98.6°	37°	310
Room temperature	68°	20°	293
Water freezes	32°	0°	273

Temperature Conversions Table		
To convert	**Use this equation:**	**Example**
Celsius to Fahrenheit °C → °F	$°F = \left(\dfrac{9}{5} \times °C\right) + 32$	Convert 45°C to °F. $°F = \left(\dfrac{9}{5} \times 45°C\right) + 32 = 113°F$
Fahrenheit to Celsius °F → °C	$°C = \dfrac{5}{9} \times (°F - 32)$	Convert 68°F to °C. $°C = \dfrac{5}{9} \times (68°F - 32) = 20°C$
Celsius to Kelvin °C → K	$K = °C + 273$	Convert 45°C to K. $K = 45°C + 273 = 318\ K$
Kelvin to Celsius K → °C	$°C = K - 273$	Convert 32 K to °C. $°C = 32K - 273 = -241°C$

Measuring Skills

Using a Graduated Cylinder

When using a graduated cylinder to measure volume, keep the following procedures in mind:

1 Place the cylinder on a flat, level surface before measuring liquid.

2 Move your head so that your eye is level with the surface of the liquid.

3 Read the mark closest to the liquid level. On glass graduated cylinders, read the mark closest to the center of the curve in the liquid's surface.

Using a Meterstick or Metric Ruler

When using a meterstick or metric ruler to measure length, keep the following procedures in mind:

1 Place the ruler firmly against the object that you are measuring.

2 Align one edge of the object exactly with the 0 end of the ruler.

3 Look at the other edge of the object to see which of the marks on the ruler is closest to that edge. (Note: Each small slash between the centimeters represents a millimeter, which is one-tenth of a centimeter.)

Using a Triple-Beam Balance

When using a triple-beam balance to measure mass, keep the following procedures in mind:

1 Make sure the balance is on a level surface.

2 Place all of the countermasses at 0. Adjust the balancing knob until the pointer rests at 0.

3 Place the object you wish to measure on the pan. **Caution:** Do not place hot objects or chemicals directly on the balance pan.

4 Move the largest countermass along the beam to the right until it is at the last notch that does not tip the balance. Follow the same procedure with the next-largest countermass. Then, move the smallest countermass until the pointer rests at 0.

5 Add the readings from the three beams together to determine the mass of the object.

6 When determining the mass of crystals or powders, first find the mass of a piece of filter paper. Then, add the crystals or powder to the paper, and remeasure. The actual mass of the crystals or powder is the total mass minus the mass of the paper. When finding the mass of liquids, first find the mass of the empty container. Then, find the combined mass of the liquid and container. The mass of the liquid is the total mass minus the mass of the container.

Scientific Methods

The ways in which scientists answer questions and solve problems are called **scientific methods.** The same steps are often used by scientists as they look for answers. However, there is more than one way to use these steps. Scientists may use all of the steps or just some of the steps during an investigation. They may even repeat some of the steps. The goal of using scientific methods is to come up with reliable answers and solutions.

Six Steps of Scientific Methods

1 Ask a Question

Good questions come from careful **observations.** You make observations by using your senses to gather information. Sometimes, you may use instruments, such as microscopes and telescopes, to extend the range of your senses. As you observe the natural world, you will discover that you have many more questions than answers. These questions drive investigations.

Questions beginning with *what, why, how,* and *when* are important in focusing an investigation. Here is an example of a question that could lead to an investigation.

Question: How does acid rain affect plant growth?

2 Form a Hypothesis

After you ask a question, you need to form a **hypothesis.** A hypothesis is a clear statement of what you expect the answer to your question to be. Your hypothesis will represent your best "educated guess" based on what you have observed and what you already know. A good hypothesis is testable. Otherwise, the investigation can go no further. Here is a hypothesis based on the question, "How does acid rain affect plant growth?"

Hypothesis: Acid rain slows plant growth.

The hypothesis can lead to predictions. A prediction is what you think the outcome of your experiment or data collection will be. Predictions are usually stated in an if-then format. Here is a sample prediction for the hypothesis that acid rain slows plant growth.

Prediction: If a plant is watered with only acid rain (which has a pH of 4), then the plant will grow at half its normal rate.

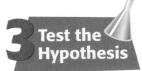

3 Test the Hypothesis

After you have formed a hypothesis and made a prediction, your hypothesis should be tested. One way to test a hypothesis is with a controlled experiment. A **controlled experiment** tests only one factor at a time. In an experiment to test the effect of acid rain on plant growth, the **control group** would be watered with normal rain water. The **experimental group** would be watered with acid rain. All of the plants should receive the same amount of sunlight and water each day. The air temperature should be the same for all groups. However, the acidity of the water will be a variable. In fact, any factor that is different from one group to another is a **variable.** If your hypothesis is correct, then the acidity of the water and plant growth are *dependant variables.* The amount a plant grows is dependent on the acidity of the water. However, the amount of water each plant receives and the amount of sunlight each plant receives are *independent variables.* Either of these factors could change without affecting the other factor.

Sometimes, the nature of an investigation makes a controlled experiment impossible. For example, the Earth's core is surrounded by thousands of meters of rock. Under such circumstances, a hypothesis may be tested by making detailed observations.

4 Analyze the Results

After you have completed your experiments, made your observations, and collected your data, you must analyze all the information you have gathered. Tables and graphs are often used in this step to organize the data.

5 Draw Conclusions

After analyzing your data, you can determine if your results support your hypothesis. If your hypothesis is supported, you (or others) might want to repeat the observations or experiments to verify your results. If your hypothesis is not supported by the data, you may have to check your procedure for errors. You may even have to reject your hypothesis and make a new one. If you cannot draw a conclusion from your results, you may have to try the investigation again or carry out further observations or experiments.

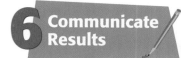

6 Communicate Results

After any scientific investigation, you should report your results. By preparing a written or oral report, you let others know what you have learned. They may repeat your investigation to see if they get the same results. Your report may even lead to another question and then to another investigation.

Scientific Methods in Action

Scientific methods contain loops in which several steps may be repeated over and over again. In some cases, certain steps are unnecessary. Thus, there is not a "straight line" of steps. For example, sometimes scientists find that testing one hypothesis raises new questions and new hypotheses to be tested. And sometimes, testing the hypothesis leads directly to a conclusion. Furthermore, the steps in scientific methods are not always used in the same order. Follow the steps in the diagram, and see how many different directions scientific methods can take you.

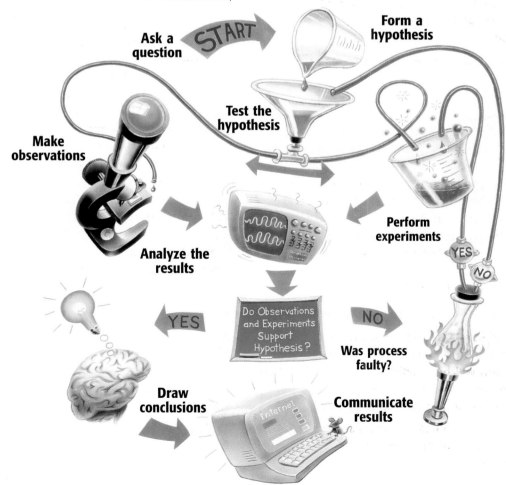

Appendix

Periodic Table of the Elements

Each square on the table includes an element's name, chemical symbol, atomic number, and atomic mass.

The color of the chemical symbol indicates the physical state at room temperature. Carbon is a solid.

6	Atomic number
C	Chemical symbol
Carbon	Element name
12.0	Atomic mass

The background color indicates the type of element. Carbon is a nonmetal.

Background
Metals
Metalloids
Nonmetals

Chemical symbol
Solid
Liquid
Gas

Period 1

1
H
Hydrogen
1.0

Group 1   Group 2

Period 2

3	4
Li	**Be**
Lithium	Beryllium
6.9	9.0

Period 3

11	12
Na	**Mg**
Sodium	Magnesium
23.0	24.3

Group 3   Group 4   Group 5   Group 6   Group 7   Group 8   Group 9

Period 4

19	20	21	22	23	24	25	26	27
K	**Ca**	**Sc**	**Ti**	**V**	**Cr**	**Mn**	**Fe**	**Co**
Potassium	Calcium	Scandium	Titanium	Vanadium	Chromium	Manganese	Iron	Cobalt
39.1	40.1	45.0	47.9	50.9	52.0	54.9	55.8	58.9

Period 5

37	38	39	40	41	42	43	44	45
Rb	**Sr**	**Y**	**Zr**	**Nb**	**Mo**	**Tc**	**Ru**	**Rh**
Rubidium	Strontium	Yttrium	Zirconium	Niobium	Molybdenum	Technetium	Ruthenium	Rhodium
85.5	87.6	88.9	91.2	92.9	95.9	(98)	101.1	102.9

Period 6

55	56	57	72	73	74	75	76	77
Cs	**Ba**	**La**	**Hf**	**Ta**	**W**	**Re**	**Os**	**Ir**
Cesium	Barium	Lanthanum	Hafnium	Tantalum	Tungsten	Rhenium	Osmium	Iridium
132.9	137.3	138.9	178.5	180.9	183.8	186.2	190.2	192.2

Period 7

87	88	89	104	105	106	107	108	109
Fr	**Ra**	**Ac**	**Rf**	**Db**	**Sg**	**Bh**	**Hs**	**Mt**
Francium	Radium	Actinium	Rutherfordium	Dubnium	Seaborgium	Bohrium	Hassium	Meitnerium
(223)	(226)	(227)	(261)	(262)	(263)	(264)	(265)†	(268)†

† Estimated from currently available IUPAC data.

A row of elements is called a *period*.

A column of elements is called a *group* or *family*.

Values in parentheses are of the most stable isotope of the element.

These elements are placed below the table to allow the table to be narrower.

Lanthanides

58	59	60	61	62
Ce	**Pr**	**Nd**	**Pm**	**Sm**
Cerium	Praseodymium	Neodymium	Promethium	Samarium
140.1	140.9	144.2	(145)	150.4

Actinides

90	91	92	93	94
Th	**Pa**	**U**	**Np**	**Pu**
Thorium	Protactinium	Uranium	Neptunium	Plutonium
232.0	231.0	238.0	(237)	(244)

Topic: **Periodic Table**
Go To: **go.hrw.com**
Keyword: **HN0 PERIODIC**
Visit the HRW Web site for
updates on the periodic table.

Group 18

						2 **He** Helium 4.0

+3   −3   −2   −1

| Group 13 | Group 14 | Group 15 | Group 16 | Group 17 | |

This zigzag line
reminds you where
the metals, nonmetals,
and metalloids are.

Group 13	Group 14	Group 15	Group 16	Group 17	
5 **B** Boron 10.8	6 **C** Carbon 12.0	7 **N** Nitrogen 14.0	8 **O** Oxygen 16.0	9 **F** Fluorine 19.0	10 **Ne** Neon 20.2
13 **Al** Aluminum 27.0	14 **Si** Silicon 28.1	15 **P** Phosphorus 31.0	16 **S** Sulfur 32.1	17 **Cl** Chlorine 35.5	18 **Ar** Argon 39.9

Group 10	Group 11	Group 12					
28 **Ni** Nickel 58.7	29 **Cu** Copper 63.5	30 **Zn** Zinc 65.4	31 **Ga** Gallium 69.7	32 **Ge** Germanium 72.6	33 **As** Arsenic 74.9	34 **Se** Selenium 79.0	35 **Br** Bromine 79.9	36 **Kr** Krypton 83.8
46 **Pd** Palladium 106.4	47 **Ag** Silver 107.9	48 **Cd** Cadmium 112.4	49 **In** Indium 114.8	50 **Sn** Tin 118.7	51 **Sb** Antimony 121.8	52 **Te** Tellurium 127.6	53 **I** Iodine 126.9	54 **Xe** Xenon 131.3
78 **Pt** Platinum 195.1	79 **Au** Gold 197.0	80 **Hg** Mercury 200.6	81 **Tl** Thallium 204.4	82 **Pb** Lead 207.2	83 **Bi** Bismuth 209.0	84 **Po** Polonium (209)	85 **At** Astatine (210)	86 **Rn** Radon (222)
110 **Ds** Darmstadtium (269)†	111 **Uuu** Unununium (272)†	112 **Uub** Ununbium (277)†		114 **Uuq** Ununquadium (285)†				

The names and three-letter symbols of elements are temporary. They
are based on the atomic numbers of the elements. Official names and
symbols will be approved by an international committee of scientists.

63 **Eu** Europium 152.0	64 **Gd** Gadolinium 157.2	65 **Tb** Terbium 158.9	66 **Dy** Dysprosium 162.5	67 **Ho** Holmium 164.9	68 **Er** Erbium 167.3	69 **Tm** Thulium 168.9	70 **Yb** Ytterbium 173.0	71 **Lu** Lutetium 175.0
95 **Am** Americium (243)	96 **Cm** Curium (247)	97 **Bk** Berkelium (247)	98 **Cf** Californium (251)	99 **Es** Einsteinium (252)	100 **Fm** Fermium (257)	101 **Md** Mendelevium (258)	102 **No** Nobelium (259)	103 **Lr** Lawrencium (262)

Appendix

Making Charts and Graphs

Pie Charts

A pie chart shows how each group of data relates to all of the data. Each part of the circle forming the chart represents a category of the data. The entire circle represents all of the data. For example, a biologist studying a hardwood forest in Wisconsin found that there were five different types of trees. The data table at right summarizes the biologist's findings.

Wisconsin Hardwood Trees	
Type of tree	Number found
Oak	600
Maple	750
Beech	300
Birch	1,200
Hickory	150
Total	3,000

How to Make a Pie Chart

1 To make a pie chart of these data, first find the percentage of each type of tree. Divide the number of trees of each type by the total number of trees, and multiply by 100.

$$\frac{600 \text{ oak}}{3,000 \text{ trees}} \times 100 = 20\%$$

$$\frac{750 \text{ maple}}{3,000 \text{ trees}} \times 100 = 25\%$$

$$\frac{300 \text{ beech}}{3,000 \text{ trees}} \times 100 = 10\%$$

$$\frac{1,200 \text{ birch}}{3,000 \text{ trees}} \times 100 = 40\%$$

$$\frac{150 \text{ hickory}}{3,000 \text{ trees}} \times 100 = 5\%$$

2 Now, determine the size of the wedges that make up the pie chart. Multiply each percentage by 360°. Remember that a circle contains 360°.

$20\% \times 360° = 72°$ $25\% \times 360° = 90°$

$10\% \times 360° = 36°$ $40\% \times 360° = 144°$

$5\% \times 360° = 18°$

3 Check that the sum of the percentages is 100 and the sum of the degrees is 360.

$20\% + 25\% + 10\% + 40\% + 5\% = 100\%$

$72° + 90° + 36° + 144° + 18° = 360°$

4 Use a compass to draw a circle and mark the center of the circle.

5 Then, use a protractor to draw angles of 72°, 90°, 36°, 144°, and 18° in the circle.

6 Finally, label each part of the chart, and choose an appropriate title.

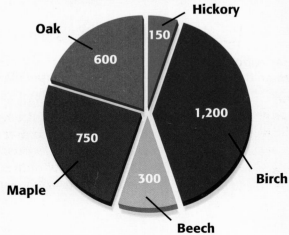

A Community of Wisconsin Hardwood Trees

Line Graphs

Line graphs are most often used to demonstrate continuous change. For example, Mr. Smith's students analyzed the population records for their hometown, Appleton, between 1900 and 2000. Examine the data at right.

Because the year and the population change, they are the *variables*. The population is determined by, or dependent on, the year. Therefore, the population is called the **dependent variable,** and the year is called the **independent variable.** Each set of data is called a **data pair.** To prepare a line graph, you must first organize data pairs into a table like the one at right.

Population of Appleton, 1900–2000	
Year	Population
1900	1,800
1920	2,500
1940	3,200
1960	3,900
1980	4,600
2000	5,300

How to Make a Line Graph

1. Place the independent variable along the horizontal (*x*) axis. Place the dependent variable along the vertical (*y*) axis.

2. Label the *x*-axis "Year" and the *y*-axis "Population." Look at your largest and smallest values for the population. For the *y*-axis, determine a scale that will provide enough space to show these values. You must use the same scale for the entire length of the axis. Next, find an appropriate scale for the *x*-axis.

3. Choose reasonable starting points for each axis.

4. Plot the data pairs as accurately as possible.

5. Choose a title that accurately represents the data.

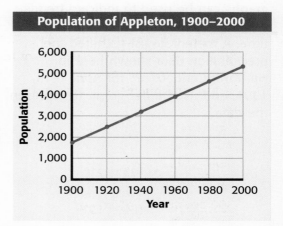

How to Determine Slope

Slope is the ratio of the change in the *y*-value to the change in the *x*-value, or "rise over run."

1. Choose two points on the line graph. For example, the population of Appleton in 2000 was 5,300 people. Therefore, you can define point *a* as (2000, 5,300). In 1900, the population was 1,800 people. You can define point *b* as (1900, 1,800).

2. Find the change in the *y*-value. (*y* at point *a*) − (*y* at point *b*) = 5,300 people − 1,800 people = 3,500 people

3. Find the change in the *x*-value. (*x* at point *a*) − (*x* at point *b*) = 2000 − 1900 = 100 years

4. Calculate the slope of the graph by dividing the change in *y* by the change in *x*.

$$slope = \frac{change\ in\ y}{change\ in\ x}$$

$$slope = \frac{3,500\ people}{100\ years}$$

$$slope = 35\ people\ per\ year$$

In this example, the population in Appleton increased by a fixed amount each year. The graph of these data is a straight line. Therefore, the relationship is **linear.** When the graph of a set of data is not a straight line, the relationship is **nonlinear.**

Using Algebra to Determine Slope

The equation in step 4 may also be arranged to be

$$y = kx$$

where y represents the change in the y-value, k represents the slope, and x represents the change in the x-value.

$$slope = \frac{change\ in\ y}{change\ in\ x}$$

$$k = \frac{y}{x}$$

$$k \times x = \frac{y \times x}{x}$$

$$kx = y$$

Bar Graphs

Bar graphs are used to demonstrate change that is not continuous. These graphs can be used to indicate trends when the data cover a long period of time. A meteorologist gathered the precipitation data shown here for Hartford, Connecticut, for April 1–15, 1996, and used a bar graph to represent the data.

Precipitation in Hartford, Connecticut April 1–15, 1996			
Date	Precipitation (cm)	Date	Precipitation (cm)
April 1	0.5	April 9	0.25
April 2	1.25	April 10	0.0
April 3	0.0	April 11	1.0
April 4	0.0	April 12	0.0
April 5	0.0	April 13	0.25
April 6	0.0	April 14	0.0
April 7	0.0	April 15	6.50
April 8	1.75		

How to Make a Bar Graph

1. Use an appropriate scale and a reasonable starting point for each axis.

2. Label the axes, and plot the data.

3. Choose a title that accurately represents the data.

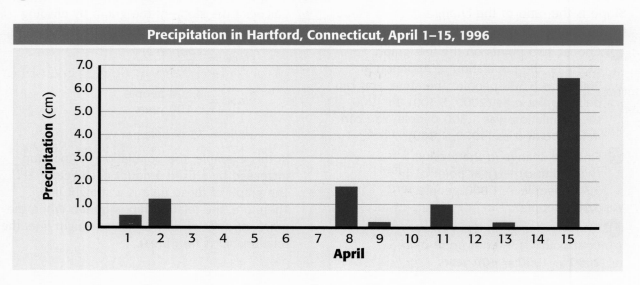

Math Refresher

Science requires an understanding of many math concepts. The following pages will help you review some important math skills.

Averages

An **average,** or **mean,** simplifies a set of numbers into a single number that *approximates* the value of the set.

Example: Find the average of the following set of numbers: 5, 4, 7, and 8.

Step 1: Find the sum.
$$5 + 4 + 7 + 8 = 24$$

Step 2: Divide the sum by the number of numbers in your set. Because there are four numbers in this example, divide the sum by 4.
$$\frac{24}{4} = 6$$

The average, or mean, is **6.**

Ratios

A **ratio** is a comparison between numbers, and it is usually written as a fraction.

Example: Find the ratio of thermometers to students if you have 36 thermometers and 48 students in your class.

Step 1: Make the ratio.
$$\frac{36 \text{ thermometers}}{48 \text{ students}}$$

Step 2: Reduce the fraction to its simplest form.
$$\frac{36}{48} = \frac{36 \div 12}{48 \div 12} = \frac{3}{4}$$

The ratio of thermometers to students is **3 to 4,** or $\frac{3}{4}$. The ratio may also be written in the form 3:4.

Proportions

A **proportion** is an equation that states that two ratios are equal.
$$\frac{3}{1} = \frac{12}{4}$$

To solve a proportion, first multiply across the equal sign. This is called *cross-multiplication.* If you know three of the quantities in a proportion, you can use cross-multiplication to find the fourth.

Example: Imagine that you are making a scale model of the solar system for your science project. The diameter of Jupiter is 11.2 times the diameter of the Earth. If you are using a plastic-foam ball that has a diameter of 2 cm to represent the Earth, what must the diameter of the ball representing Jupiter be?
$$\frac{11.2}{1} = \frac{x}{2 \text{ cm}}$$

Step 1: Cross-multiply.
$$\frac{11.2}{1} \diagdown\!\!\!\!\!\diagup \frac{x}{2}$$
$$11.2 \times 2 = x \times 1$$

Step 2: Multiply.
$$22.4 = x \times 1$$

Step 3: Isolate the variable by dividing both sides by 1.
$$x = \frac{22.4}{1}$$
$$x = 22.4 \text{ cm}$$

You will need to use a ball that has a diameter of **22.4** cm to represent Jupiter.

Percentages

A **percentage** is a ratio of a given number to 100.

> **Example:** What is 85% of 40?

Step 1: Rewrite the percentage by moving the decimal point two places to the left.

$$0.85$$

Step 2: Multiply the decimal by the number that you are calculating the percentage of.

$$0.85 \times 40 = 34$$

85% of 40 is **34.**

Decimals

To **add** or **subtract decimals,** line up the digits vertically so that the decimal points line up. Then, add or subtract the columns from right to left. Carry or borrow numbers as necessary.

> **Example:** Add the following numbers: 3.1415 and 2.96.

Step 1: Line up the digits vertically so that the decimal points line up.

$$\begin{array}{r} 3.1415 \\ + 2.96 \\ \hline \end{array}$$

Step 2: Add the columns from right to left, and carry when necessary.

$$\begin{array}{r} {}^{1\ 1} \\ 3.1415 \\ + 2.96 \\ \hline 6.1015 \end{array}$$

The sum is **6.1015.**

Fractions

Numbers tell you how many; **fractions** tell you *how much of a whole.*

> **Example:** Your class has 24 plants. Your teacher instructs you to put 5 plants in a shady spot. What fraction of the plants in your class will you put in a shady spot?

Step 1: In the denominator, write the total number of parts in the whole.

$$\frac{?}{24}$$

Step 2: In the numerator, write the number of parts of the whole that are being considered.

$$\frac{5}{24}$$

So, $\frac{5}{24}$ of the plants will be in the shade.

Reducing Fractions

It is usually best to express a fraction in its simplest form. Expressing a fraction in its simplest form is called *reducing* a fraction.

> **Example:** Reduce the fraction $\frac{30}{45}$ to its simplest form.

Step 1: Find the largest whole number that will divide evenly into both the numerator and denominator. This number is called the *greatest common factor* (GCF).

Factors of the numerator 30:
    1, 2, 3, 5, 6, 10, **15,** 30

Factors of the denominator 45:
    1, 3, 5, 9, **15,** 45

Step 2: Divide both the numerator and the denominator by the GCF, which in this case is 15.

$$\frac{30}{45} = \frac{30 \div 15}{45 \div 15} = \frac{2}{3}$$

Thus, $\frac{30}{45}$ reduced to its simplest form is $\frac{2}{3}$.

Appendix

Adding and Subtracting Fractions

To **add** or **subtract fractions** that have the **same denominator,** simply add or subtract the numerators.

Examples:

$$\frac{3}{5} + \frac{1}{5} = ? \quad \text{and} \quad \frac{3}{4} - \frac{1}{4} = ?$$

Step 1: Add or subtract the numerators.

$$\frac{3}{5} + \frac{1}{5} = \frac{4}{\quad} \quad \text{and} \quad \frac{3}{4} - \frac{1}{4} = \frac{2}{\quad}$$

Step 2: Write the sum or difference over the denominator.

$$\frac{3}{5} + \frac{1}{5} = \frac{4}{5} \quad \text{and} \quad \frac{3}{4} - \frac{1}{4} = \frac{2}{4}$$

Step 3: If necessary, reduce the fraction to its simplest form.

$\frac{4}{5}$ cannot be reduced, and $\frac{2}{4} = \frac{1}{2}$.

To **add** or **subtract fractions** that have **different denominators,** first find the least common denominator (LCD).

Examples:

$$\frac{1}{2} + \frac{1}{6} = ? \quad \text{and} \quad \frac{3}{4} - \frac{2}{3} = ?$$

Step 1: Write the equivalent fractions that have a common denominator.

$$\frac{3}{6} + \frac{1}{6} = ? \quad \text{and} \quad \frac{9}{12} - \frac{8}{12} = ?$$

Step 2: Add or subtract the fractions.

$$\frac{3}{6} + \frac{1}{6} = \frac{4}{6} \quad \text{and} \quad \frac{9}{12} - \frac{8}{12} = \frac{1}{12}$$

Step 3: If necessary, reduce the fraction to its simplest form.

The fraction $\frac{4}{6} = \frac{2}{3}$, and $\frac{1}{12}$ cannot be reduced.

Multiplying Fractions

To **multiply fractions,** multiply the numerators and the denominators together, and then reduce the fraction to its simplest form.

Example:

$$\frac{5}{9} \times \frac{7}{10} = ?$$

Step 1: Multiply the numerators and denominators.

$$\frac{5}{9} \times \frac{7}{10} = \frac{5 \times 7}{9 \times 10} = \frac{35}{90}$$

Step 2: Reduce the fraction.

$$\frac{35}{90} = \frac{35 \div 5}{90 \div 5} = \frac{7}{18}$$

Dividing Fractions

To **divide fractions,** first rewrite the divisor (the number you divide by) upside down. This number is called the *reciprocal* of the divisor. Then multiply and reduce if necessary.

Example:

$$\frac{5}{8} \div \frac{3}{2} = ?$$

Step 1: Rewrite the divisor as its reciprocal.

$$\frac{3}{2} \rightarrow \frac{2}{3}$$

Step 2: Multiply the fractions.

$$\frac{5}{8} \times \frac{2}{3} = \frac{5 \times 2}{8 \times 3} = \frac{10}{24}$$

Step 3: Reduce the fraction.

$$\frac{10}{24} = \frac{10 \div 2}{24 \div 2} = \frac{5}{12}$$

Appendix

Scientific Notation

Scientific notation is a short way of representing very large and very small numbers without writing all of the place-holding zeros.

> **Example:** Write 653,000,000 in scientific notation.

Step 1: Write the number without the place-holding zeros.

653

Step 2: Place the decimal point after the first digit.

6.53

Step 3: Find the exponent by counting the number of places that you moved the decimal point.

6.53000000

The decimal point was moved eight places to the left. Therefore, the exponent of 10 is positive 8. If you had moved the decimal point to the right, the exponent would be negative.

Step 4: Write the number in scientific notation.

6.53×10^8

Area

Area is the number of square units needed to cover the surface of an object.

> **Formulas:**
>
> *area of a square = side × side*
> *area of a rectangle = length × width*
> *area of a triangle = $\frac{1}{2}$ × base × height*
>
> **Examples:** Find the areas.

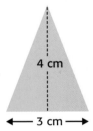

Triangle

area = $\frac{1}{2}$ × base × height
area = $\frac{1}{2}$ × 3 cm × 4 cm
*area = **6 cm²***

4 cm

← 3 cm →

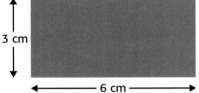

3 cm

6 cm

Rectangle
area = length × width
area = 6 cm × 3 cm
*area = **18 cm²***

3 cm

← 3 cm →

Square
area = side × side
area = 3 cm × 3 cm
*area = **9 cm²***

Volume

Volume is the amount of space that something occupies.

> **Formulas:**
>
> *volume of a cube = side × side × side*
>
> *volume of a prism = area of base × height*
>
> **Examples:**
>
> Find the volume of the solids.

Cube
volume = side × side × side
volume = 4 cm × 4 cm × 4 cm
*volume = **64 cm³***

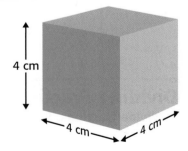

4 cm

4 cm

4 cm

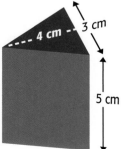

4 cm

3 cm

5 cm

Prism
volume = area of base × height
volume = (area of triangle) × height
volume = ($\frac{1}{2}$ × 3 cm × 4 cm) × 5 cm
volume = 6 cm² × 5 cm
*volume = **30 cm³***

Appendix

776   Appendix

Physical Science Laws and Principles

Law of Conservation of Energy

The law of conservation of energy states that energy can be neither created nor destroyed.

The total amount of energy in a closed system is always the same. Energy can be changed from one form to another, but all of the different forms of energy in a system always add up to the same total amount of energy no matter how many energy conversions occur.

Law of Universal Gravitation

The law of universal gravitation states that all objects in the universe attract each other by a force called *gravity*. The size of the force depends on the masses of the objects and the distance between objects.

The first part of the law explains why a bowling ball is much harder to lift than a table-tennis ball. Because the bowling ball has a much larger mass than the table-tennis ball does, the amount of gravity between the Earth and the bowling ball is greater than the amount of gravity between the Earth and the table-tennis ball.

The second part of the law explains why a satellite can remain in orbit around the Earth. The satellite is carefully placed at a distance great enough to prevent the Earth's gravity from immediately pulling the satellite down but small enough to prevent the satellite from completely escaping the Earth's gravity and wandering off into space.

Newton's Laws of Motion

Newton's first law of motion states that an object at rest remains at rest and an object in motion remains in motion at constant speed and in a straight line unless acted on by an unbalanced force.

The first part of the law explains why a football will remain on a tee until it is kicked off or until a gust of wind blows it off.

The second part of the law explains why a bike rider will continue moving forward after the bike comes to an abrupt stop. Gravity and the friction of the sidewalk will eventually stop the rider.

Newton's second law of motion states that the acceleration of an object depends on the mass of the object and the amount of force applied.

The first part of the law explains why the acceleration of a 4 kg bowling ball will be greater than the acceleration of a 6 kg bowling ball if the same force is applied to both.

The second part of the law explains why the acceleration of a bowling ball will be larger if a larger force is applied to the bowling ball.

The relationship of acceleration (*a*) to mass (*m*) and force (*F*) can be expressed mathematically by the following equation:

$$acceleration = \frac{force}{mass}, \text{ or } a = \frac{F}{m}$$

This equation is often rearranged to the form

$$force = mass \times acceleration$$
$$\text{or}$$
$$F = m \times a$$

Newton's third law of motion states that whenever one object exerts a force on a second object, the second object exerts an equal and opposite force on the first.

This law explains that a runner is able to move forward because of the equal and opposite force that the ground exerts on the runner's foot after each step.

Law of Reflection

The law of reflection states that the angle of incidence is equal to the angle of reflection. This law explains why light reflects off a surface at the same angle that the light strikes the surface.

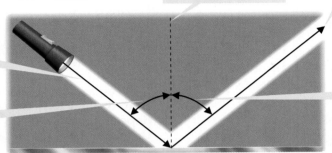

A line perpendicular to the mirror's surface is called the *normal.*

The beam of light reflected off the mirror is called the *reflected beam.*

The beam of light traveling toward the mirror is called the *incident beam.*

The angle between the incident beam and the normal is called the *angle of incidence.*

The angle between the reflected beam and the normal is called the *angle of reflection.*

Charles's Law

Charles's law states that for a fixed amount of gas at a constant pressure, the volume of the gas increases as the temperature of the gas increases. Likewise, the volume of the gas decreases as the temperature of the gas decreases.

If a basketball that was inflated indoors is left outside on a cold winter day, the air particles inside the ball will move more slowly. They will hit the sides of the basketball less often and with less force. The ball will get smaller as the volume of the air decreases.

Boyle's Law

Boyle's law states that for a fixed amount of gas at a constant temperature, the volume of a gas increases as the pressure of the gas decreases. Likewise, the volume of a gas decreases as its pressure increases.

If an inflated balloon is pulled down to the bottom of a swimming pool, the pressure of the water on the balloon increases. The pressure of the air particles inside the balloon must increase to match that of the water outside, so the volume of the air inside the balloon decreases.

Pascal's Principle

Pascal's principle states that a change in pressure at any point in an enclosed fluid will be transmitted equally to all parts of that fluid.

When a mechanic uses a hydraulic jack to raise an automobile off the ground, he or she increases the pressure on the fluid in the jack by pushing on the jack handle. The pressure is transmitted equally to all parts of the fluid-filled jacking system. As fluid presses the jack plate against the frame of the car, the car is lifed off the ground.

Archimedes' Principle

Archimedes' principle states that the buoyant force on an object in a fluid is equal to the weight of the volume of fluid that the object displaces.

A person floating in a swimming pool displaces 20 L of water. The weight of that volume of water is about 200 N. Therefore, the buoyant force on the person is 200 N.

Bernoulli's Principle

Bernoulli's principle states that as the speed of a moving fluid increases, the fluid's pressure decreases.

The lift on an airplane wing or on a Frisbee® can be explained in part by using Bernoulli's principle. Because of the shape of the Frisbee, the air moving over the top of the Frisbee must travel farther than the air below the Frisbee in the same amount of time. In other words, the air above the Frisbee is moving faster than the air below it. This faster-moving air above the Frisbee exerts less pressure than the slower-moving air below it does. The resulting increased pressure below exerts an upward force and pushes the Frisbee up.

Useful Equations

Average speed

$$\text{average speed} = \frac{\text{total distance}}{\text{total time}}$$

Example: A bicycle messenger traveled a distance of 136 km in 8 h. What was the messenger's average speed?

$$\frac{136 \text{ km}}{8 \text{ h}} = 17 \text{ km/h}$$

The messenger's average speed was **17 km/h.**

Average acceleration

$$\frac{\text{average}}{\text{acceleration}} = \frac{\text{final velocity} - \text{starting velocity}}{\text{time it takes to change velocity}}$$

Example: Calculate the average acceleration of an Olympic 100 m dash sprinter who reaches a velocity of 20 m/s south at the finish line. The race was in a straight line and lasted 10 s.

$$\frac{20 \text{ m/s} - 0 \text{ m/s}}{10\text{s}} = 2 \text{ m/s/s}$$

The sprinter's average acceleration is **2 m/s/s south.**

Net force

Forces in the Same Direction

When forces are in the same direction, add the forces together to determine the net force.

Example: Calculate the net force on a stalled car that is being pushed by two people. One person is pushing with a force of 13 N northwest, and the other person is pushing with a force of 8 N in the same direction.

$$13 \text{ N} + 8 \text{ N} = 21 \text{ N}$$

The net force is **21 N northwest.**

Forces in Opposite Directions

When forces are in opposite directions, subtract the smaller force from the larger force to determine the net force. The net force will be in the direction of the larger force.

Example: Calculate the net force on a rope that is being pulled on each end. One person is pulling on one end of the rope with a force of 12 N south. Another person is pulling on the opposite end of the rope with a force of 7 N north.

$$12 \text{ N} - 7 \text{ N} = 5 \text{ N}$$

The net force is **5 N south.**

Work

Work is done by exerting a force through a distance. Work has units of joules (J), which are equivalent to Newton-meters.

$$Work = F \times d$$

Example: Calculate the amount of work done by a man who lifts a 100 N toddler 1.5 m off the floor.

$Work = 100 \text{ N} \times 1.5 \text{ m} = 150 \text{ N} \bullet \text{m} = 150 \text{ J}$

The man did **150 J** of work.

Power

Power is the rate at which work is done. Power is measured in watts (W), which are equivalent to joules per second.

$$P = \frac{Work}{t}$$

Example: Calculate the power of a weightlifter who raises a 300 N barbell 2.1 m off the floor in 1.25 s.

$Work = 300 \text{ N} \times 2.1 \text{ m} = 630 \text{ N} \bullet \text{m} = 630 \text{ J}$

$P = \dfrac{630 \text{ J}}{1.25 \text{ s}} = \dfrac{504 \text{ J}}{\text{s}} = 504 \text{ W}$

The weightlifter has **504 W** of power.

Pressure

Pressure is the force exerted over a given area. The SI unit for pressure is the pascal (Pa).

$$pressure = \frac{force}{area}$$

Example: Calculate the pressure of the air in a soccer ball if the air exerts a force of 25,000 N over an area of 0.15 m².

$pressure = \dfrac{25{,}000 \text{ N}}{0.15 \text{ m}^2} = \dfrac{167{,}000 \text{ N}}{\text{m}^2} = 167{,}000 \text{ Pa}$

The pressure of the air inside the soccer ball is **167,000 Pa.**

Density

$$density = \frac{mass}{volume}$$

Example: Calculate the density of a sponge that has a mass of 10 g and a volume of 40 cm³.

$\dfrac{10 \text{ g}}{40 \text{ cm}^3} = \dfrac{0.25 \text{ g}}{\text{cm}^3}$

The density of the sponge is $\dfrac{0.25 \text{ g}}{\text{cm}^3}$.

Concentration

$$concentration = \frac{mass \ of \ solute}{volume \ of \ solvent}$$

Example: Calculate the concentration of a solution in which 10 g of sugar is dissolved in 125 mL of water.

$\dfrac{10 \text{ g of sugar}}{125 \text{ mL of water}} = \dfrac{0.08 \text{ g}}{\text{mL}}$

The concentration of this solution is $\dfrac{0.08 \text{ g}}{\text{mL}}$.

Glossary

A

absolute zero the temperature at which molecular energy is at a minimum (0 K on the Kelvin scale or -273.16°C on the Celsius scale) (277)

absorption in optics, the transfer of light energy to particles of matter (646)

acceleration (ak SEL uhr AY shuhn) the rate at which velocity changes over time; an object accelerates if its speed, direction, or both change (121)

acid any compound that increases the number of hydronium ions when dissolved in water (422)

activation energy the minimum amount of energy required to start a chemical reaction (404)

alkali metal (AL kuh LIE MET uhl) one of the elements of Group 1 of the periodic table (lithium, sodium, potassium, rubidium, cesium, and francium) (344)

alkaline-earth metal (AL kuh LIEN UHRTH MET uhl) one of the elements of Group 2 of the periodic table (beryllium, magnesium, calcium, strontium, barium, and radium) (345)

amplitude the maximum distance that the particles of a wave's medium vibrate from their rest position (580)

analog signal (AN uh LAWG SIG nuhl) a signal whose properties can change continuously in a given range (547)

Archimedes' principle (AHR kuh MEE DEEZ PRIN suh puhl) the principle that states that the buoyant force on an object in a fluid is an upward force equal to the weight of the volume of fluid that the object displaces (186)

atmospheric pressure the pressure caused by the weight of the atmosphere (181)

atom the smallest unit of an element that maintains the properties of that element (312)

atomic mass the mass of an atom expressed in atomic mass units (323)

atomic mass unit a unit of mass that describes the mass of an atom or molecule (319)

atomic number the number of protons in the nucleus of an atom; the atomic number is the same for all atoms of an element (321)

B

base any compound that increases the number of hydroxide ions when dissolved in water (425)

Bernoulli's principle (ber NOO leez PRIN suh puhl) the principle that states that the pressure in a fluid decreases as the fluid's velocity increases (192)

boiling the conversion of a liquid to a vapor when the vapor pressure of the liquid equals the atmospheric pressure (76)

Boyle's law the law that states that the volume of a gas is inversely proportional to the pressure of a gas when temperature is constant (72)

buoyant force (BOY uhnt FAWRS) the upward force that keeps an object immersed in or floating on a liquid (186)

C

carbohydrate a class of energy-giving nutrients that includes sugars, starches, and fiber; contains carbon, hydrogen, and oxygen (434)

catalyst (KAT uh LIST) a substance that changes the rate of a chemical reaction without being used up or changed very much (407)

cell in electricity, a device that produces an electric current by converting chemical or radiant energy into electrical energy (487)

change of state the change of a substance from one physical state to another (74, 289)

Charles's law the law that states that the volume of a gas is directly proportional to the temperature of a gas when pressure is constant (72)

chemical bond an interaction that holds atoms or ions together (364, 418)

chemical bonding the combining of atoms to form molecules or ionic compounds (364)

chemical change a change that occurs when one or more substances change into entirely new substances with different properties (52)

chemical equation a representation of a chemical reaction that uses symbols to show the relationship between the reactants and the products (394)

chemical formula a combination of chemical symbols and numbers to represent a substance (392)

chemical property a property of matter that describes a substance's ability to participate in chemical reactions (50)

chemical reaction the process by which one or more substances change to produce one or more different substances (388)

circuit board a sheet of insulating material that carries circuit elements and that is inserted in an electronic device (540)

colloid (KAHL OYD) a mixture consisting of tiny particles that are intermediate in size between those in solutions and those in suspensions and that are suspended in a liquid, solid, or gas (104)

compound a substance made up of atoms of two or more different elements joined by chemical bonds (94)

compound machine a machine made of more than one simple machine (228)

computer an electronic device that can accept data and instructions, follow the instructions, and output the results (554)

concave lens a lens that is thinner in the middle than at the edges (673)

concave mirror a mirror that is curved inward like the inside of a spoon (670)

concentration the amount of a particular substance in a given quantity of a mixture, solution, or ore (102)

condensation the change of state from a gas to a liquid (77)

convection the transfer of thermal energy by the circulation or movement of a liquid or gas (283)

convex lens a lens that is thicker in the middle than at the edges (672)

convex mirror a mirror that is curved outward like the back of a spoon (671)

covalent bond (koh VAY luhnt BAHND) a bond formed when atoms share one or more pairs of electrons (372)

covalent compound a chemical compound that is formed by the sharing of electrons (420)

crystal lattice (KRIS tuhl LAT is) the regular pattern in which a crystal is arranged (371)

D

data any pieces of information acquired through observation or experimentation (17)

decibel the most common unit used to measure loudness (symbol, dB) (610)

decomposition reaction a reaction in which a single compound breaks down to form two or more simpler substances (399)

density the ratio of the mass of a substance to the volume of the substance (26, 45)

diffraction a change in the direction of a wave when the wave finds an obstacle or an edge, such as an opening (586, 649)

digital signal a signal that can be represented as a sequence of discrete values (548)

diode an electronic device that allows electric charge to move more easily in one direction than in the other (542)

doping (DOHP eeng) the addition of an impurity element to a semiconductor (541)

Doppler effect an observed change in the frequency of a wave when the source or observer is moving (608)

double-displacement reaction a reaction in which a gas, a solid precipitate, or a molecular compound forms from the exchange of ions between two compounds (401)

drag a force parallel to the velocity of the flow; it opposes the direction of an aircraft and, in combination with thrust, determines the speed of the aircraft (195)

E

echo a reflected sound wave (612)

echolocation the process of using reflected sound waves to find objects; used by animals such as bats (613)

electrical conductor a material in which charges can move freely (478)

electrical insulator a material in which charges cannot move freely (478)

electric current the rate at which charges pass through a given point; measured in amperes (482)

electric discharge the release of electricity stored in a source (479)

electric field the space around a charged object in which another charged object experiences an electric force (475)

electric force the force of attraction or repulsion on a charged particle that is due to an electric field (475)

electric generator a device that converts mechanical energy into electrical energy (526)

electric motor a device that converts electrical energy into mechanical energy (522)

electric power the rate at which electrical energy is converted into other forms of energy (491)

electromagnet a coil that has a soft iron core and that acts as a magnet when an electric current is in the coil (520)

electromagnetic induction the process of creating a current in a circuit by changing a magnetic field (525)

electromagnetic spectrum all of the frequencies or wavelengths of electromagnetic radiation (636)

electromagnetic wave a wave that consists of electric and magnetic fields that vibrate at right angles to each other (632)

electromagnetism the interaction between electricity and magnetism (519)

electron a subatomic particle that has a negative charge (314)

electron cloud a region around the nucleus of an atom where electrons are likely to be found (317)

element a substance that cannot be separated or broken down into simpler substances by chemical means (90)

endothermic reaction a chemical reaction that requires heat (403)

energy the capacity to do work (240)

energy conversion a change from one form of energy to another (248)

evaporation (ee vap uh RAY shuhn) the change of a substance from a liquid to a gas (76)

exothermic reaction a chemical reaction in which heat is released to the surroundings (402)

F

farsightedness a condition in which the lens of the eye focuses distant objects behind rather than on the retina (675)

fluid a nonsolid state of matter in which the atoms or molecules are free to move past each other, as in a gas or liquid (180)

force a push or a pull exerted on an object in order to change the motion of the object; force has size and direction (124)

fossil fuel a nonrenewable energy resource formed from the remains of organisms that lived long ago (258)

free fall the motion of a body when only the force of gravity is acting on the body (153)

frequency the number of waves produced in a given amount of time (582)

friction a force that opposes motion between two surfaces that are in contact (128, 254)

G

gas a form of matter that does not have a definite volume or shape (69)

gravity a force of attraction between objects that is due to their masses (134)

group a vertical column of elements in the periodic table; elements in a group share chemical properties (342)

H

half-life the time needed for half of a sample of a radioactive substance to undergo radioactive decay (453)

halogen (HAL oh juhn) one of the elements of Group 17 of the periodic table (fluorine, chlorine, bromine, iodine, and astatine); halogens combine with most metals to form salts (349)

hardware the parts or pieces of equipment that make up a computer (556)

heat the energy transferred between objects that are at different temperatures (280)

heat engine a machine that transforms heat into mechanical energy, or work (295)

hologram a piece of film that produces a three-dimensional image of an object; made by using laser light (681)

hydrocarbon an organic compound composed only of carbon and hydrogen (433)

hypothesis (hie PAHTH uh sis) an explanation that is based on prior scientific research or observations and that can be tested (15)

I

inclined plane a simple machine that is a straight, slanted surface, which facilitates the raising of loads; a ramp (226)

indicator a compound that can reversibly change color depending on conditions such as pH (423)

inertia (in UHR shuh) the tendency of an object to resist being moved or, if the object is moving, to resist a change in speed or direction until an outside force acts on the object (42, 160)

inhibitor a substance that slows down or stops a chemical reaction (406)

insulation a substance that reduces the transfer of electricity, heat, or sound (293)

integrated circuit (IN tuh GRAYT id SUHR kit) a circuit whose components are formed on a single semiconductor (544)

interference the combination of two or more waves that results in a single wave (587, 614, 650)

Internet a large computer network that connects many local and smaller networks all over the world (560)

ion a charged particle that forms when an atom or group of atoms gains or loses one or more electrons (368)

ionic bond (ie AHN ik BAHND) a bond that forms when electrons are transferred from one atom to another, which results in a positive ion and a negative ion (368)

ionic compound a compound made of oppositely charged ions (418)

isotope (IE suh TOHP) an atom that has the same number of protons (or the same atomic number) as other atoms of the same element do but that has a different number of neutrons (and thus a different atomic mass) (321, 450)

J

joule the unit used to express energy; equivalent to the amount of work done by a force of 1 N acting through a distance of 1 m in the direction of the force (symbol, J) (213)

K

kinetic energy (ki NET ik EN uhr jee) the energy of an object that is due to the object's motion (241)

L

laser a device that produces intense light of only one wavelength and color (679)

law a summary of many experimental results and observations; a law tells how things work (23)

law of conservation of energy the law that states that energy cannot be created or destroyed but can be changed from one form to another (255, 403)

law of conservation of mass the law that states that mass cannot be created or destroyed in ordinary chemical and physical changes (395)

law of electric charges the law that states that like charges repel and opposite charges attract (474)

lens a transparent object that refracts light waves such that they converge or diverge to create an image (672)

lever a simple machine that consists of a bar that pivots at a fixed point called a *fulcrum* (222)

lift an upward force on an object that moves in a fluid (193)

lipid a type of biochemical that does not dissolve in water; fats and steroids are lipids (435)

liquid the state of matter that has a definite volume but not a definite shape (68)

longitudinal wave a wave in which the particles of the medium vibrate parallel to the direction of wave motion (578)

loudness the extent to which a sound can be heard (609)

M

machine a device that helps do work by either overcoming a force or changing the direction of the applied force (216)

magnet any material that attracts iron or materials containing iron (510)

magnetic force the force of attraction or repulsion generated by moving or spinning electric charges (511)

magnetic pole one of two points, such as the ends of a magnet, that have opposing magnetic qualities (510)

mass a measure of the amount of matter in an object (25, 41, 138)

mass number the sum of the numbers of protons and neutrons in the nucleus of an atom (322, 449)

matter anything that has mass and takes up space (38)

mechanical advantage a number that tells how many times a machine multiplies force (219)

mechanical efficiency (muh KAN i kuhl e FISH uhn see) the ratio of output to input of energy or of power; it can be calculated by dividing work output by work input (220)

mechanical energy the amount of work an object can do because of the object's kinetic and potential energies (243)

medium a physical environment in which phenomena occur (575, 602)

melting the change of state in which a solid becomes a liquid by adding heat (75)

meniscus (muh NIS kuhs) the curve at a liquid's surface by which one measures the volume of the liquid (39)

metal an element that is shiny and that conducts heat and electricity well (92)

metallic bond a bond formed by the attraction between positively charged metal ions and the electrons around them (375)

metalloid elements that have properties of both metals and nonmetals (92)

meter the basic unit of length in the SI (symbol, m) (25)

microprocessor a single semiconductor chip that controls and executes a microcomputer's instructions (555)

mixture a combination of two or more substances that are not chemically combined (98)

model a pattern, plan, representation, or description designed to show the structure or workings of an object, system, or concept (20)

molecule (MAHL i KYOOL) the smallest unit of a substance that keeps all of the physical and chemical properties of that substance (373)

momentum (moh MEN tuhm) a quantity defined as the product of the mass and velocity of an object (166)

motion an object's change in position relative to a reference point (118)

N

nearsightedness a condition in which the lens of the eye focuses distant objects in front of rather than on the retina (675)

net force the combination of all of the forces acting on an object (125)

neutralization reaction (NOO truhl i ZA shuhn ree AK shuhn) the reaction of an acid and a base to form a neutral solution of water and a salt (429)

neutron a subatomic particle that has no charge and that is found in the nucleus of an atom (319)

newton the SI unit for force (symbol, N) (124)

noble gas one of the elements of Group 18 of the periodic table (helium, neon, argon, krypton, xenon, and radon); noble gases are unreactive (350)

noise a sound that consists of a random mix of frequencies (621)

nonmetal an element that conducts heat and electricity poorly (92)

nonrenewable resource a resource that forms at a rate that is much slower than the rate at which it is consumed (258)

nuclear chain reaction a continuous series of nuclear fission reactions (457)

nuclear fission (NOO klee uhr FISH uhn) the splitting of the nucleus of a large atom into two or more fragments; releases additional neutrons and energy (456)

nuclear fusion (NOO klee uhr FYOO zhuhn) the combination of the nuclei of small atoms to form a larger nucleus; releases energy (460)

nucleic acid (noo KLEE ik AS id) a molecule made up of subunits called *nucleotides* (436)

nucleus (NOO klee uhs) in physical science, an atom's central region, which is made up of protons and neutrons (316)

O

observation the process of obtaining information by using the senses (13)

opaque (oh PAYK) describes an object that is not transparent or translucent (653)

organic compound a covalently bonded compound that contains carbon (432)

P

parallel circuit a circuit in which the parts are joined in branches such that the potential difference across each part is the same (497)

pascal the SI unit of pressure (symbol, Pa) (180)

Pascal's principle the principle that states that a fluid in equilibrium contained in a vessel exerts a pressure of equal intensity in all directions (196)

period in chemistry, a horizontal row of elements in the periodic table (342)

periodic describes something that occurs or repeats at regular intervals (337)

periodic law the law that states that the repeating chemical and physical properties of elements change periodically with the atomic numbers of the elements (337)

pH a value that is used to express the acidity or basicity (alkalinity) of a system (429)

photocell a device that converts light energy into electrical energy (488)

physical change a change of matter from one form to another without a change in chemical properties (48)

physical property a characteristic of a substance that does not involve a chemical change, such as density, color, or hardness (44)

physical science the scientific study of nonliving matter (7)

pigment a substance that gives another substance or a mixture its color (656)

pitch a measure of how high or low a sound is perceived to be, depending on the frequency of the sound wave (607)

plane mirror a mirror that has a flat surface (669)

potential energy the energy that an object has because of the position, shape, or condition of the object (242)

power the rate at which work is done or energy is transformed (214)

precipitate (pree SIP uh TAYT) a solid that is produced as a result of a chemical reaction in solution (389)

pressure the amount of force exerted per unit area of a surface (71, 180)

product a substance that forms in a chemical reaction (394)

projectile motion (proh JEK tuhl MOH shuhn) the curved path that an object follows when thrown, launched, or otherwise projected near the surface of Earth (155)

protein a molecule that is made up of amino acids and that is needed to build and repair body structures and to regulate processes in the body (435)

proton a subatomic particle that has a positive charge and that is found in the nucleus of an atom (319)

pulley a simple machine that consists of a wheel over which a rope, chain, or wire passes (224)

pure substance a sample of matter, either a single element or a single compound, that has definite chemical and physical properties (90)

R

radiation the transfer of energy as electromagnetic waves (284, 633)

radioactivity the process by which an unstable nucleus gives off nuclear radiation (448)

reactant (ree AK tuhnt) a substance or molecule that participates in a chemical reaction (394)

reflection the bouncing back of a ray of light, sound, or heat when the ray hits a surface that it does not go through (584, 644)

refraction the bending of a wave as the wave passes between two substances in which the speed of the wave differs (585, 647)

renewable resource a natural resource that can be replaced at the same rate at which the resource is consumed (261)

resistance in physical science, the opposition presented to the current by a material or device (485)

resonance a phenomenon that occurs when two objects naturally vibrate at the same frequency; the sound produced by one object causes the other object to vibrate (589, 616)

S

salt an ionic compound that forms when a metal atom replaces the hydrogen of an acid (431)

scattering an interaction of light with matter that causes light to change its energy, direction of motion, or both (646)

science the knowledge obtained by observing natural events and conditions in order to discover facts and formulate laws or principles that can be verified or tested (6)

scientific methods a series of steps followed to solve problems (12)

screw a simple machine that consists of an inclined plane wrapped around a cylinder (227)

semiconductor (SEM i kuhn DUHK tuhr) an element or compound that conducts electric current better than an insulator does but not as well as a conductor does (541)

series circuit a circuit in which the parts are joined one after another such that the current in each part is the same (496)

single-displacement reaction a reaction in which one element takes the place of another element in a compound (399)

software a set of instructions or commands that tells a computer what to do; a computer program (559)

solenoid a coil of wire with an electric current in it (519)

solid the state of matter in which the volume and shape of a substance are fixed (67)

solubility the ability of one substance to dissolve in another at a given temperature and pressure (102)

solute in a solution, the substance that dissolves in the solvent (100)

solution a homogeneous mixture of two or more substances uniformly dispersed throughout a single phase (100)

solvent in a solution, the substance in which the solute dissolves (100)

sonic boom the explosive sound heard when a shock wave from an object traveling faster than the speed of sound reaches a person's ears (615)

sound quality the result of the blending of several pitches through interference (618)

sound wave a longitudinal wave that is caused by vibrations and that travels through a material medium (601)

specific heat the quantity of heat required to raise a unit mass of homogeneous material 1 K or 1°C in a specified way given constant pressure and volume (285)

speed the distance traveled divided by the time interval during which the motion occurred (119)

standing wave a pattern of vibration that simulates a wave that is standing still (588, 616)

states of matter the physical forms of matter, which include solid, liquid, and gas (66, 288)

static electricity electric charge at rest; generally produced by friction or induction (478)

sublimation (SUHB luh MAY shuhn) the process in which a solid changes directly into a gas (78)

surface tension the force that acts on the surface of a liquid and that tends to minimize the area of the surface (68)

suspension a mixture in which particles of a material are more or less evenly dispersed throughout a liquid or gas (104)

synthesis reaction (SIN thuh sis ree AK shuhn) a reaction in which two or more substances combine to form a new compound (398)

T

temperature a measure of how hot (or cold) something is; specifically, a measure of the average kinetic energy of the particles in an object (26, 70, 274)

terminal velocity the constant velocity of a falling object when the force of air resistance is equal in magnitude and opposite in direction to the force of gravity (152)

theory an explanation that ties together many hypotheses and observations (22)

thermal conduction the transfer of energy as heat through a material (282)

thermal conductor a material through which energy can be transferred as heat (283)

thermal energy the kinetic energy of a substance's atoms (281)

thermal expansion an increase in the size of a substance in response to an increase in the temperature of the substance (276)

thermal insulator a material that reduces or prevents the transfer of heat (283)

thermal pollution a temperature increase in a body of water that is caused by human activity and that has a harmful effect on water quality and on the ability of that body of water to support life (298)

thermocouple a device that converts thermal energy into electrical energy (488)

thrust the pushing or pulling force exerted by the engine of an aircraft or rocket (194)

transformer a device that increases or decreases the voltage of alternating current (528)

transistor a semiconductor device that can amplify current and that is used in amplifiers, oscillators, and switches (543)

translucent (trans LOO suhnt) describes matter that transmits light but that does not transmit an image (653)

transmission the passing of light or other form of energy through matter (652)

transparent describes matter that allows light to pass through with little interference (653)

transverse wave a wave in which the particles of the medium move perpendicularly to the direction the wave is traveling (577)

V

valence electron (VAY luhns ee LEK TRAHN) an electron that is found in the outermost shell of an atom and that determines the atom's chemical properties (365)

velocity (vuh LAHS uh tee) the speed of an object in a particular direction (120)

viscosity the resistance of a gas or liquid to flow (68)

voltage the potential difference between two points; measured in volts (484)

volume a measure of the size of a body or region in three-dimensional space (26, 38, 71)

W

watt the unit used to express power; equivalent to joules per second (symbol, W) (214)

wave a periodic disturbance in a solid, liquid, or gas as energy is transmitted through a medium (574)

wavelength the distance from any point on a wave to an identical point on the next wave (581)

wave speed the speed at which a wave travels through a medium (582)

wedge a simple machine that is made up of two inclined planes and that moves; often used for cutting (227)

Glossary

weight a measure of the gravitational force exerted on an object; its value can change with the location of the object in the universe (41, 138)

wheel and axle a simple machine consisting of two circular objects of different sizes; the wheel is the larger of the two circular objects (225)

work the transfer of energy to an object by using a force that causes the object to move in the direction of the force (210)

work input the work done on a machine; the product of the input force and the distance through which the force is exerted (217)

work output the work done by a machine; the product of the output force and the distance through which the force is exerted (217)

Glossary

Spanish Glossary

A

absolute zero/cero absoluto la temperatura a la que la energía molecular es mínima (0 K en la escala de Kelvin ó −273.16°C en la escala de Celsius) (277)

absorption/absorción en la óptica, la transferencia de energía luminosa a las partículas de materia (646)

acceleration/aceleración la tasa a la que la velocidad cambia con el tiempo; un objeto acelera si su rapidez cambia, si su dirección cambia, o si tanto su rapidez como su dirección cambian (121)

acid/ácido cualquier compuesto que aumenta el número de iones de hidrógeno cuando se disuelve en agua (422)

activation energy/energía de activación la cantidad mínima de energía que se requiere para iniciar una reacción química (404)

alkali metal/metal alcalino uno de los elementos del Grupo 1 de la tabla periódica (litio, sodio, potasio, rubidio, cesio y francio) (344)

alkaline-earth metal/metal alcalinotérreo uno de los elementos del Grupo 2 de la tabla periódica (berilio, magnesio, calcio, estroncio, bario y radio) (345)

amplitude/amplitud la distancia máxima a la que vibran las partículas del medio de una onda a partir de su posición de reposo (580)

analog signal/señal análoga una señal cuyas propiedades cambian continuamente en un rango determinado (547)

Archimedes' principle/principio de Arquímedes el principio que establece que la fuerza flotante de un objeto que está en un fluido es una fuerza ascendente cuya magnitud es igual al peso del volumen del fluido que el objeto desplaza (186)

atmospheric pressure/presión atmosférica la presión producida por el peso de la atmósfera (181)

atom/átomo la unidad más pequeña de un elemento que conserva las propiedades de ese elemento (312)

atomic mass/masa atómica la masa de un átomo, expresada en unidades de masa atómica (323)

atomic mass unit/unidad de masa atómica una unidad de masa que describe la masa de un átomo o una molécula (319)

atomic number/número atómico el número de protones en el núcleo de un átomo; el número atómico es el mismo para todos los átomos de un elemento (321)

B

base/base cualquier compuesto que aumenta el número de iones de hidróxido cuando se disuelve en agua (425)

Bernoulli's principle/principio de Bernoulli el principio que establece que la presión de un fluido disminuye a medida que la velocidad del fluido aumenta (192)

boiling/ebullición la conversión de un líquido en vapor cuando la presión de vapor del líquido es igual a la presión atmosférica (76)

Boyle's law/ley de Boyle la ley que establece que el volumen de un gas es inversamente proporcional a su presión cuando la temperatura es constante (72)

buoyant force/fuerza boyante la fuerza ascendente que hace que un objeto se mantenga sumergido en un líquido o flotando en él (186)

C

carbohydrate/carbohidrato una clase de nutrientes que proporcionan energía; incluye los azúcares, los almidones y las fibras; contiene carbono, hidrógeno y oxígeno (434)

catalyst/catalizador una substancia que cambia la tasa de una reacción química sin consumirse ni cambiar demasiado (407)

cell/celda en electricidad, un aparato que produce una corriente eléctrica transformando la energía química o radiante en energía eléctrica (487)

change of state/cambio de estado el cambio de una substancia de un estado físico a otro (74, 289)

Charles's law/ley de Charles la ley que establece que el volumen de un gas es directamente proporcional a su temperatura cuando la presión es constante (72)

chemical bond/enlace químico una interacción que mantiene unidos los átomos o los iones (364, 418)

chemical bonding/formación de un enlace químico la combinación de átomos para formar moléculas o compuestos iónicos (364)

chemical change/cambio químico un cambio que ocurre cuando una o más substancias se transforman en substancias totalmente nuevas con propiedades diferentes (52)

chemical equation/ecuación química una representación de una reacción química que usa símbolos para mostrar la relación entre los reactivos y los productos (394)

chemical formula/fórmula química una combinación de símbolos químicos y números que se usan para representar una substancia (392)

chemical property/propiedad química una propiedad de la materia que describe la capacidad de una substancia de participar en reacciones químicas (50)

chemical reaction/reacción química el proceso por medio del cual una o más substancia cambian para producir una o más substancias distintas (388)

circuit board/cuadro del circuito una lámina de material aislante que lleva elementos del circuito y que es insertado en un aparato electrónico (540)

colloid/coloide una mezcla formada por partículas diminutas que son de tamaño intermedio entre las partículas de las soluciones y las de las suspensiones y que se encuentran suspendidas en un líquido, sólido o gas (104)

compound/compuesto una substancia formada por átomos de dos o más elementos diferentes unidos por enlaces químicos (94)

compound machine/máquina compuesta una máquina hecha de más de una máquina simple (228)

computer/computadora un aparato electrónico que acepta información e instrucciones, sigue instrucciones y produce una salida para los resultados (554)

concave lens/lente cóncava una lente que es más delgada en la parte media que en los bordes (673)

concave mirror/espejo cóncavo un espejo que está curvado hacia adentro como la parte interior de una cuchara (670)

concentration/concentración la cantidad de una cierta substancia en una cantidad determinada de mezcla, solución o mena (102)

condensation/condensación el cambio de estado de gas a líquido (77)

convection/convección la transferencia de energía térmica mediante la circulación o el movimiento de un líquido o gas (283)

convex lens/lente convexa una lente que es más gruesa en la parte media que en los bordes (672)

convex mirror/espejo convexo un espejo que está curvado hacia fuera como la parte de atrás de una cuchara (671)

covalent bond/enlace covalente un enlace formado cuando los átomos comparten uno más pares de electrones (372)

covalent compound/compuesto covalente un compuesto químico que se forma al compartir electrones (420)

crystal lattice/red cristalina el patrón regular en el que un cristal está ordenado (371)

D

data/datos cualquier parte de la información que se adquiere por medio de la observación o experimentación (17)

decibel/decibel la unidad más común que se usa para medir el volumen del sonido (símbolo: dB) (610)

decomposition reaction/reacción de descomposición una reacción en la que un solo compuesto se descompone para formar dos o más substancias más simples (399)

density/densidad la relación entre la masa de una substancia y su volumen (26, 45)

diffraction/difracción un cambio en la dirección de una onda cuando ésta se encuentra con un obstáculo o un borde, tal como una abertura (586, 649)

digital signal/señal digital una señal que se puede representar como una secuencia de valores discretos (548)

diode/diodo un aparato electrónico que permite que la corriente eléctrica pase más fácilmente en una dirección que en otra (542)

doping/adulteración la adición de un elemento impuro a un semiconductor (541)

Doppler effect/efecto Doppler un cambio que se observa en la frecuencia de una onda cuando la fuente o el observador está en movimiento (608)

double-displacement reaction/reacción de doble desplazamiento una reacción en la que se forma un gas, un precipitado sólido o un compuesto molecular a partir del intercambio de iones entre dos compuestos (401)

drag/resistencia aerodinámica una fuerza paralela a la velocidad del flujo; se opone a la dirección de un avión y, en combinación con el empuje, determina la velocidad del avión (195)

E

echo/eco una onda de sonido reflejada (612)

echolocation/ecolocación el proceso de usar ondas de sonido reflejadas para buscar objetos; utilizado por animales tales como los murciélagos (613)

electrical conductor/conductor eléctrico un material en el que las cargas se mueven libremente (478)

electrical insulator/aislante eléctrico un material en el que las cargas no pueden moverse libremente (478)

electric current/corriente eléctrica la tasa a la que las cargas pasan por un punto determinado; se mide en amperes (482)

electric discharge/descarga eléctrica la liberación de electricidad almacenada en una fuente (479)

electric field/campo eléctrico el espacio que se encuentra alrededor de un objeto con carga y en el que otro objeto con carga experimenta una fuerza eléctrica (475)

electric force/fuerza eléctrica la fuerza de atracción o repulsión en una partícula con carga debido a un campo eléctrico (475)

electric generator/generador eléctrico un aparato que transforma la energía mecánica en energía eléctrica (526)

electric motor/motor eléctrico un aparato que transforma la energía eléctrica en energía mecánica (522)

electric power/potencia eléctrica la tasa a la que la energía eléctrica se transforma en otras formas de energía (491)

electromagnet/electroimán una bobina que tiene un centro de hierro suave y que funciona como un imán cuando hay una corriente eléctrica en la bobina (520)

electromagnetic induction/inducción electromagnética el proceso de crear una corriente en un circuito por medio de un cambio en el campo magnético (525)

electromagnetic spectrum/espectro electromagnético todas las frecuencias o longitudes de onda de la radiación electromagnética (636)

electromagnetic wave/onda electromagnética una onda que está formada por campos eléctricos y magnéticos que vibran formando un ángulo recto unos con otros (632)

electromagnetism/electromagnetismo la interacción entre la electricidad y el magnetismo (519)

electron/electrón una partícula subatómica que tiene carga negativa (314)

electron cloud/nube de electrones una región que rodea al núcleo de un átomo en la cual es probable encontrar a los electrones (317)

element/elemento una substancia que no se puede separar o descomponer en substancias más simples por medio de métodos químicos (90)

endothermic reaction/reacción endotérmica una reacción química que necesita calor (403)

energy/energía la capacidad de realizar un trabajo (240)

energy conversion/transformación de energía un cambio de un tipo de energía a otro (248)

evaporation/evaporación el cambio de una substancia de líquido a gas (76)

exothermic reaction/reacción exotérmica una reacción química en la que se libera calor a los alrededores (402)

F

farsightedness/hipermetropía condición en la que el cristalino del ojo enfoca los objetos lejanos detrás de la retina en lugar de en ella (675)

fluid/fluido un estado no sólido de la materia en el que los átomos o moléculas tienen libertad de movimiento, como en el caso de un gas o un líquido (180)

force/fuerza una acción de empuje o atracción que se ejerce sobre un objeto con el fin de cambiar su movimiento; la fuerza tiene magnitud y dirección (124)

fossil fuel/combustible fósil un recurso energético no renovable formado a partir de los restos de organismos que vivieron hace mucho tiempo (258)

free fall/caída libre el movimiento de un cuerpo cuando la única fuerza que actúa sobre él es la fuerza de gravedad (153)

frequency/frecuencia el número de ondas producidas en una cantidad de tiempo determinada (582)

friction/fricción una fuerza que se opone al movimiento entre dos superficies que están en contacto (128, 254)

G

gas/gas un estado de la materia que no tiene volumen ni forma definidos (69)

gravity/gravedad una fuerza de atracción entre dos objetos debido a sus masas (134)

group/grupo una columna vertical de elementos de la tabla periódica; los elementos de un grupo comparten propiedades químicas (342)

H

half-life/vida media el tiempo que tarda la mitad de la muestra de una substancia radiactiva en desintegrarse por desintegración radiactiva (453)

halogen/halógeno uno de los elementos del Grupo 17 de la tabla periódica (flúor, cloro, bromo, yodo y ástato); los halógenos se combinan con la mayoría de los metales para formar sales (349)

hardware/hardware las partes o piezas de equipo que forman una computadora (556)

heat/calor la transferencia de energía entre objetos que están a temperaturas diferentes (280)

heat engine/motor térmico una máquina que transforma el calor en energía mecánica, o trabajo (295)

hologram/holograma una porción de película que produce una imagen tridimensional de un objeto mediante luz láser (681)

hydrocarbon/hidrocarburo un compuesto orgánico compuesto únicamente por carbono e hidrogeno (433)

hypothesis/hipótesis una explicación que se basa en observaciones o investigaciones científicas previas y que se puede probar (15)

I

inclined plane/plano inclinado una máquina simple que es una superficie recta e inclinada, que facilita el levantamiento de cargas; una rampa (226)

indicator/indicador un compuesto que puede cambiar de color de forma reversible dependiendo de condiciones tales como el pH (423)

inertia/inercia la tendencia de un objeto a no moverse o, si el objeto se está moviendo, la tendencia a resistir un cambio en su rapidez o dirección hasta que una fuerza externa actúe en el objeto (42, 160)

inhibitor/inhibidor una substancia que desacelera o detiene una reacción química (406)

insulation/aislante una substancia que reduce la transferencia de electricidad, calor o sonido (293)

integrated circuit/circuito integrado un circuito cuyos componentes están formados en un solo semiconductor (544)

interference/interferencia la combinación de dos o más ondas que resulta en una sola onda (587, 614, 650)

Internet/Internet una amplia red de computadoras que conecta muchas redes locales y redes más pequeñas por todo el mundo (560)

ion/ion una partícula cargada que se forma cuando un átomo o grupo de átomos gana o pierde uno o más electrones (368)

ionic bond/enlace iónico un enlace que se forma cuando los electrones se transfieren de un átomo a otro, y que produce un ion positivo y uno negativo (368)

ionic compound/compuesto iónico un compuesto formado por iones con cargas opuestas (418)

isotope/isótopo un átomo que tiene el mismo número de protones (o el mismo número atómico) que otros átomos del mismo elemento, pero que tiene un número diferente de neutrones (y, por lo tanto, otra masa atómica) (321, 450)

J

joule/joule la unidad que se usa para expresar energía; equivale a la cantidad de trabajo realizada por una fuerza de 1 N que actúa a través de una distancia de 1 m en la dirección de la fuerza (símbolo: J) (213)

K

kinetic energy/energía cinética la energía de un objeto debido al movimiento del objeto (241)

L

laser/láser un aparato que produce una luz intensa de únicamente una longitud de onda y color (679)

law/ley un resumen de muchos resultados y observaciones experimentales; una ley dice cómo funcionan las cosas (23)

law of conservation of energy/ley de la conservación de la energía la ley que establece que la energía ni se crea ni se destruye, sólo se transforma de una forma a otra (255, 403)

law of conservation of mass/ley de la conservación de la masa la ley que establece que la masa no se crea ni se destruye por cambios químicos o físicos comunes (395)

law of electric charges/ley de las cargas eléctricas la ley que establece que las cargas iguales se repelen y las cargas opuestas se atraen (474)

lens/lente un objeto transparente que refracta las ondas de luz de modo que converjan o diverjan para crear una imagen (672)

lever/palanca una máquina simple formada por una barra que gira en un punto fijo llamado *fulcro* (222)

lift/propulsión una fuerza hacia arriba en un objeto que se mueve en un fluido (193)

lipid/lípido un tipo de substancia bioquímica que no se disuelve en agua; las grasas y los esteroides son lípidos (435)

liquid/líquido el estado de la materia que tiene un volumen definido, pero no una forma definida (68)

longitudinal wave/onda longitudinal una onda en la que las partículas del medio vibran paralelamente a la dirección del movimiento de la onda (578)

loudness/volumen el grado al que se escucha un sonido (609)

M

machine/máquina un aparato que ayuda a realizar un trabajo, ya sea venciendo una fuerza o cambiando la dirección de la fuerza aplicada (216)

magnet/imán cualquier material que atrae hierro o materiales que contienen hierro (510)

magnetic force/fuerza magnética la fuerza de atracción o repulsión generadas por cargas eléctricas en movimiento o que giran (511)

magnetic pole/polo magnético uno de dos puntos, tales como los extremos de un imán, que tienen cualidades magnéticas opuestas (510)

mass/masa una medida de la cantidad de materia que tiene un objeto (25, 41, 138)

mass number/número de masa la suma de los números de protones y neutrones que hay en el núcleo de un átomo (322, 449)

matter/materia cualquier cosa que tiene masa y ocupa un lugar en el espacio (38)

mechanical advantage/ventaja mecánica un número que dice cuántas veces una máquina multiplica una fuerza (219)

mechanical efficiency/eficiencia mecánica la relación entre la entrada y la salida de energía o potencia; se calcula dividiendo la salida de trabajo por la entrada de trabajo (220)

mechanical energy/energía mecánica la cantidad de trabajo que un objeto realiza debido a las energías cinética y potencial del objeto (243)

medium/medio un ambiente físico en el que ocurren fenómenos (575, 602)

melting/fusión el cambio de estado en el que un sólido se convierte en líquido al añadirse calor (75)

meniscus/menisco la curva que se forma en la superficie de un líquido, la cual sirve para medir el volumen de un líquido (39)

metal/metal un elemento que es brillante y conduce bien el calor y la electricidad (92)

metallic bond/enlace metálico un enlace formado por la atracción entre iones metálicos cargados positivamente y los electrones que los rodean (375)

metalloid/metaloides elementos que tienen propiedades tanto de metales como de no metales (92)

meter/metro la unidad fundamental de longitud en el sistema internacional de unidades (símbolo: m) (25)

microprocessor/microprocesador un chip único de un semiconductor, el cual controla y ejecuta las instrucciones de una microcomputadora (555)

mixture/mezcla una combinación de dos o más substancias que no están combinadas químicamente (298)

model/modelo un diseño, plan, representación o descripción cuyo objetivo es mostrar la estructura o funcionamiento de un objeto, sistema o concepto (20)

molecule/molécula la unidad más pequeña de una substancia que conserva todas las propiedades físicas y químicas de esa substancia (373)

momentum/momento una cantidad que se define como el producto de la masa de un objeto por su velocidad (166)

motion/movimiento el cambio en la posición de un objeto respecto a un punto de referencia (118)

N

nearsightedness/miopía condición en la que el cristalino del ojo enfoca los objetos lejanos delante de la retina en lugar de en ella (675)

net force/fuerza neta la combinación de todas las fuerzas que actúan sobre un objeto (125)

neutralization reaction/reacción de neutralización la reacción de un ácido y una base que forma una solución neutra de agua y una sal (429)

neutron/neutrón una partícula subatómica que no tiene carga y que se encuentra en el núcleo de un átomo (319)

newton/newton la unidad de fuerza del sistema internacional de unidades (símbolo: N) (124)

noble gas/gas noble uno de los elementos del Grupo 18 de la tabla periódica (helio, neón, argón, criptón, xenón y radón); los gases nobles son no reactivos (350)

noise/ruido un sonido que está constituido por una mezcla aleatoria de frecuencias (621)

nonmetal/no metal un elemento que es mal conductor del calor y la electricidad (92)

nonrenewable resource/recurso no renovable un recurso que se forma a una tasa que es mucho más lenta que la tasa a la que se consume (258)

nuclear chain reaction/reacción nuclear en cadena una serie continua de reacciones nucleares de fisión (457)

nuclear fission/fisión nuclear la partición del núcleo de un átomo grande en dos o más fragmentos; libera neutrones y energía adicionales (456)

nuclear fusion/fusión nuclear combinación de los núcleos de átomos pequeños para formar un núcleo más grande; libera energía (460)

nucleic acid/ácido nucleico una molécula formada por subunidades llamadas *nucleótidos* (436)

nucleus/núcleo en ciencias físicas, la región central de un átomo, la cual está constituida por protones y neutrones (316)

O

observation/observación el proceso de obtener información por medio de los sentidos (13)

opaque/opaco término que describe un objeto que no es transparente ni translúcido (653)

organic compound/compuesto orgánico un compuesto enlazado de manera covalente que contiene carbono (432)

P

parallel circuit/circuito paralelo un circuito en el que las partes están unidas en ramas de manera tal que la diferencia de potencial entre cada parte es la misma (497)

pascal/pascal la unidad de presión del sistema internacional de unidades (símbolo: Pa) (180)

Pascal's principle/principio de Pascal el principio que establece que un fluido en equilibro que esté contenido en un recipiente ejerce una presión de igual intensidad en todas las direcciones (196)

period/período en química, una hilera horizontal de elementos en la tabla periódica (342)

periodic/periódico término que describe algo que ocurre o que se repite a intervalos regulares (337)

periodic law/ley periódica la ley que establece que las propiedades químicas y físicas repetitivas de un elemento cambian periódicamente en función del número atómico de los elementos (337)

pH/pH un valor que expresa la acidez o la basicidad (alcalinidad) de un sistema (429)

photocell/fotocelda un aparato que transforma la energía luminosa en energía eléctrica (488)

physical change/cambio físico un cambio de materia de una forma a otra sin que ocurra un cambio en sus propiedades químicas (48)

physical property/propiedad física una característica de una substancia que no implica un cambio químico, tal como la densidad, el color o la dureza (44)

physical science/ciencias físicas el estudio científico de la materia sin vida (7)

pigment/pigmento una substancia que le da color a otra substancia o mezcla (656)

pitch/altura tonal una medida de qué tan agudo o grave se percibe un sonido, dependiendo de la frecuencia de la onda sonora (607)

plane mirror/espejo plano un espejo que tiene una superficie plana (669)

potential energy/energía potencial la energía que tiene un objeto debido a su posición, forma o condición (242)

power/potencia la tasa a la que se realiza un trabajo o a la que se transforma la energía (214)

precipitate/precipitado un sólido que se produce como resultado de una reacción química en una solución (389)

pressure/presión la cantidad de fuerza ejercida en una superficie por unidad de área (71, 180)

product/producto una substancia que se forma en una reacción química (394)

projectile motion/movimiento proyectil la trayectoria curva que sigue un objeto cuando es aventado, lanzado o proyectado de cualquier otra manera cerca de la superficie de la Tierra (155)

protein/proteína una molécula formada por aminoácidos que es necesaria para construir y reparar estructuras corporales y para regular procesos del cuerpo (435)

proton/protón una partícula subatómica que tiene una carga positiva y que se encuentra en el núcleo de un átomo (319)

pulley/polea una máquina simple formada por una rueda sobre la cual pasa una cuerda, cadena o cable (224)

pure substance/substancia pura una muestra de materia, ya sea un solo elemento o un solo compuesto, que tiene propiedades químicas y físicas definidas (90)

R

radiation/radiación la transferencia de energía en forma de ondas electromagnéticas (284, 633)

radioactivity/radiactividad el proceso por medio del cual un núcleo inestable emite radiación nuclear (448)

reactant/reactivo una substancia o molécula que participa en una reacción química (394)

reflection/reflexión el rebote de un rayo de luz, sonido o calor cuando el rayo golpea una superficie pero no la atraviesa (584, 644)

refraction/refracción el curvamiento de una onda cuando ésta pasa entre dos substancias en las que su velocidad difiere (585, 647)

renewable resource/recurso renovable un recurso natural que puede reemplazarse a la misma tasa a la que se consume (261)

resistance/resistencia en ciencias físicas, la oposición que un material o aparato presenta a la corriente (485)

resonance/resonancia un fenómeno que ocurre cuando dos objetos vibran naturalmente a la misma frecuencia; el sonido producido por un objeto hace que el otro objeto vibre (589, 616)

S

salt/sal un compuesto iónico que se forma cuando un átomo de un metal reemplaza el hidrógeno de un ácido (431)

scattering/dispersión una interacción de la luz con la materia que hace que la luz cambie su energía, la dirección del movimiento o ambas (646)

science/ciencia el conocimiento que se obtiene por medio de la observación natural de acontecimientos y condiciones con el fin de descubrir hechos y formular leyes o principios que puedan ser verificados o probados (6)

scientific methods/métodos científicos una serie de pasos que se siguen para solucionar problemas (12)

screw/tornillo una máquina simple formada por un plano inclinado enrollado a un cilindro (227)

semiconductor/semiconductor un elemento o compuesto que conduce la corriente eléctrica mejor que un aislante, pero no tan bien como un conductor (541)

series circuit/circuito en serie un circuito en el que las partes están unidas una después de la otra de manera tal que la corriente en cada parte es la misma (496)

single-displacement reaction/reacción de sustitución simple una reacción en la que un elemento toma el lugar de otro elemento en un compuesto (399)

software/software un conjunto de instrucciones o comandos que le dicen qué hacer a una computadora; un programa de computadora (559)

solenoid/solenoide una bobina de alambre que tiene una corriente eléctrica (519)

solid/sólido el estado de la materia en el cual el volumen y la forma de una sustancia están fijos (67)

solubility/solubilidad la capacidad de una substancia de disolverse en otra a una temperatura y una presión dadas (102)

solute/soluto en una solución, la sustancia que se disuelve en el solvente (100)

solution/solución una mezcla homogénea de dos o más sustancias dispersas de manera uniforme en una sola fase (100)

solvent/solvente en una solución, la sustancia en la que se disuelve el soluto (100)

sonic boom/estampido sónico el sonido explosivo que se escucha cuando la onda de choque de un objeto que se desplaza a una velocidad superior a la de la luz llega a los oídos de una persona (615)

sound quality/calidad del sonido el resultado de la combinación de varios tonos por medio de la interferencia (618)

sound wave/onda de sonido una onda longitudinal que se origina debido a vibraciones y que se desplaza a través de un medio material (601)

specific heat/calor específico la cantidad de calor que se requiere para aumentar una unidad de masa de un material homogéneo 1 K ó 1°C de una manera especificada, dados un volumen y una presión constantes (285)

speed/rapidez la distancia que un objeto se desplaza dividida entre el intervalo de tiempo durante el cual ocurrió el movimiento (119)

standing wave/onda estacionaria un patrón de vibración que simula una onda que está parada (588, 616)

states of matter/estados de la material las formas físicas de la materia, que son sólida, líquida y gaseosa (66, 288)

static electricity/electricidad estática carga eléctrica en reposo; por lo general se produce por fricción o inducción (478)

sublimation/sublimación el proceso por medio del cual un sólido se transforma directamente en un gas (78)

surface tension/tensión superficial la fuerza que actúa en la superficie de un líquido y que tiende a minimizar el área de la superficie (68)

suspension/suspensión una mezcla en la que las partículas de un material se encuentran dispersas de manera más o menos uniforme a través de un líquido o de un gas (104)

synthesis reaction/reacción de síntesis una reacción en la que dos o más sustancias se combinan para formar un compuesto nuevo (398)

T

temperature/temperatura una medida de qué tan caliente (o frío) está algo; específicamente, una medida de la energía cinética promedio de las partículas de un objeto (26, 70, 274)

terminal velocity/velocidad terminal la velocidad constante de un objeto en caída cuando la fuerza de resistencia del aire es igual en magnitud y opuesta en dirección a la fuerza de gravedad (152)

theory/teoría una explicación que relaciona muchas hipótesis y observaciones (22)

thermal conduction/conducción térmica la transferencia de energía en forma de calor a través de un material (282)

thermal conductor/conductor térmico un material a través del cual es posible transferir energía en forma de calor (283)

thermal energy/energía térmica la energía cinética de los átomos de una sustancia (281)

thermal expansion/expansión térmica un aumento en el tamaño de una sustancia en respuesta a un aumento en la temperatura de la sustancia (276)

thermal insulator/aislante térmico un material que reduce o evita la transferencia de calor (283)

thermal pollution/contaminación térmica un aumento en la temperatura de una masa de agua, producido por las actividades humanas y que tieneun efecto dañino en la calidad del agua y en la capacidad de esa masa de agua para permitir que se desarrolle la vida (298)

thermocouple/termopar un aparato que transforma la energía térmica en energía eléctrica (488)

thrust/empuje la fuerza de empuje o arrastre ejercida por el motor de un avión o cohete (194)

transformer/transformador un aparato que aumenta o disminuye el voltaje de la corriente alterna (528)

transistor/transistor un aparato semiconductor que puede amplificar la corriente y se usa en los amplificadores, osciladores e interruptores (543)

translucent/traslúcido término que describe la materia que transmite luz, pero que no transmite una imagen (653)

transmission/transmisión el paso de la luz u otra forma de energía a través de la materia (652)

transparent/transparente término que describe materia que permite el paso de la luz con poca interferencia (653)

transverse wave/onda transversal una onda en la que las partículas del medio se mueven perpendicularmente respecto a la dirección en la que se desplaza la onda (577)

V

valence electron/electrón de valencia un electrón que se encuentra en el orbital más externo de un átomo y que determina las propiedades químicas del átomo (365)

velocity/velocidad la rapidez de un objeto en una dirección dada (120)

viscosity/viscosidad la resistencia de un gas o un líquido a fluir (68)

voltage/voltaje la diferencia de potencial entre dos puntos, medida en voltios (484)

volume/volumen una medida del tamaño de un cuerpo o región en un espacio de tres dimensiones (26, 38, 71)

W

watt/watt (o vatio) la unidad que se usa para expresar potencia; es equivalente a un joule por segundo (símbolo: W) (214)

wave/onda una perturbación periódica en un sólido, líquido o gas que se transmite a través de un medio en forma de energía (574)

wavelength/longitud de onda la distancia entre cualquier punto de una onda y un punto idéntico en la onda siguiente (581)

wave speed/rapidez de onda la rapidez a la cual viaja una onda a través de un medio (582)

wedge/cuña una máquina simple que está formada por dos planos inclinados y que se mueve; normalmente se usa para cortar (227)

weight/peso una medida de la fuerza gravitacional ejercida sobre un objeto; su valor puede cambiar en función de la ubicación del objeto en el universo (41, 138)

wheel and axle/eje y rueda una máquina simple que está formada por dos objetos circulares de diferente tamaño; la rueda es el mayor de los dos objetos circulares (225)

work/trabajo la transferencia de energía a un objeto mediante una fuerza que hace que el objeto se mueva en la dirección de la fuerza (210)

work input/trabajo de entrada el trabajo realizado en una máquina; el producto de la fuerza de entrada por la distancia a través de la que se ejerce la fuerza (217)

work output/trabajo producido el trabajo realizado por una máquina; el producto de la fuerza de salida por la distancia a través de la que se ejerce la fuerza (217)

Index

Boldface page numbers refer to illustrative material, such as figures, tables, margin elements, photographs, and illustrations.

A

absolute zero, **276,** 277, 306
absorption of light, 646, **646, 647, 652**
absorption of sound waves, 612, **612**
AC (alternating current), 483, **483**
   diodes and, 542
   generators of, 527, **527**
   voltage of, 485
acceleration, 121, **121**
   air pollution and, 161
   average, 122, 779
   calculating, 122, **122, 151,** 162
   circular motion, 123, **123**
   detecting, 140–141
   graphs of, 122, **122**
   gravity and, 150–151, **150, 151, 162,** 164
   in Newton's second law, 161–162, **161, 162, 777**
accelerometers, 140–141
acetylene, **433**
acid rain, **54,** 430
acids, 422–424, **422,** 428–431
   labs on, 429, 438–439
   pH scale, 429, **429**
   properties of, 422–423, **422, 423**
   strong vs. weak, 428
   uses of, 424, **424**
actinides, 346, **346,** 359
activation energy, 404, **404, 405,** 407
active solar heating systems, 294, **294**
adaptations, **15**
aerodynamic shapes, 257, **257**
age dating, 452–453, **452**
air. *See also* air pressure
   as mixture, **101**
   pollution, **161,** 430
   resistance, 152–153, **152, 153**
   speed of sound in, 606, **606, 607**
air conditioning, 296, **296**
airplane flight, 193–194, **193, 194,** 606
air pollution, **161,** 430
air pressure
   air flow and, 184–185, **184, 185**

airplane flight and, 193, **193**
   floating and sinking and, 188, **188**
   in tires, 180, **180**
   tornadoes and, 185, **185**
air resistance, 152–153, **152, 153**
alarm clocks, **554**
alchemy, 332
alkali metals, 344, **344**
alkaline-earth metals, 345, **345**
alkanes, 433, **433**
alkenes, 433, **433**
alkynes, 433, **433**
alloys, 101, **101**
alnico, 514
alpha decay, 449, **449**
alpha particles, 449, **449, 451,** 452
alternating current (AC), 483, **483**
   diodes and, 542
   generators of, 527, **527**
   voltage of, 485
aluminum
   foil, 318, **318**
   ions, **369**
   malleability of, **45, 340,** 376
   properties of, **347**
   recycling of, **347**
   uses of, 96
aluminum hydroxide, 426
americium, 346
amino acids, **375,** 435
ammeters, 500–501
ammonia, 96–97, 426
amorphous solids, 67, **67**
Ampère, André-Marie, 519
amperes (A), 482
amplification, from lasers, 680
amplifiers
   electrical energy in, 245, **245, 609, 609**
   for string instruments, **619**
   transistors as, 543, **543**
amplitude, 580, **580**
   interference and, **587**
   loudness and, 609, **609**
   on oscilloscopes, 610–611, **610, 611**
amplitude modulation, 637–638
AM radio waves, 637–638
analog recording, 548, **548**
analog signals, 547–548, **547, 550**
analytical chemists, 385
angle of incidence, 644, **644**
angle of reflection, 644, **644**
animal compasses, **512**
antacids, 426, 428, **428, 429**
antennas, **550**
antibiotics, 406

antifreeze, **101**
antimony, **93**
anvils, in ears, **603**
apertures, **678**
Apollo astronauts, **134**
Archimedes' principle, 186–187, **186, 187,** 778
area, **763,** 776
argon, 350
Aristotle, 150, 312
armatures, 522, **522,** 530
aromatic hydrocarbons, 433, **433**
arrows, in equations, **394**
arsenic, 541
arson investigators, 415
artificial bones, 62
asbestos, 414
ascorbic acid, 424
astronomers, 693
atmospheric pressure, **180,** 181
   balloons and, 181, **181**
   boiling point and, 77
   variations in, 182, **182**
atomic diagrams, **322**
atomic energy, 448–461
   advantages and disadvantages of, **262,** 458–461
   age-dating by decay, **452, 453**
   chain reactions and, 457–458, **457,** 462–463
   Einstein's equation on, 270
   from matter, 457
   nuclear fission, 456–459, **456, 457, 458, 459**
   nuclear fusion, 246, **246,** 460–461, **460, 461**
   nuclear power plants, **458**
   radioactivity and, 448–454
   in the sun, 246, **246**
atomic mass, 323, **323,** 337
atomic mass unit (amu), 319, **319**
atomic number, 321, **321,** 365
atomic theory, 312–317
   beginnings of, 312
   Bohr's, 316
   Dalton's, 313, **313**
   modern, 317, **317**
   Rutherford's, 315–316, **315**
   Thomson's, 314, **314**
atoms, 312, **313,** 318–325
   chemical bonding of, 364
   differences between elements, 320–321, **320**
   in domains, 512, **513**
   in early atomic theory, 312
   electric force and electric fields in, 475

electron clouds in, **316, 317, 317, 319,** 320

electron-dot diagrams of, 373, **373**

electron number and organization in, 365, **365**

four basic forces in, 324, **324**

ions and, 368–370 **369, 370**

isotopes, 321–323, **321, 322, 323, 450** (see also isotopes)

law of electric charges in, 474, **474, 475**

magnetism and, 512

mass number of, 449, **449**

in molecules, 373, **373**

neutrons in, 319, **319**

nuclear fusion of, 246, **246,** 460–461, **460, 461**

nucleus of, 316, **316,** 319, **319**

protons in, 319, **319**

size of, 318, **318**

states of matter and, 66, **66**

auroras, 516, **516**

average acceleration, 122, 779

averages, 773

average speed, 119, **120,** 265, 779

B

bacteria, **97,** 468, 664

baking soda, **425**

balanced forces, 126, **126**

balances, triple-beam, **41,** 765

ballast tanks, 190, **190**

balloons, 181, **181,** 188, **188**

bar graphs, 772, **772**

baseball, 195, **195**

bases, 425–427, **425,** 429–431

labs on, **429,** 438–439

pH scale, 429, **429**

properties of, **247,** 425–426, **425, 426**

strong vs. weak, 429

uses of, 426, **427**

bats, echolocation by, 613, **613**

batteries, **251,** 484, **484**

Becquerel, Henri, 448

beluga whales, 612

benzene, 433, **433**

Bernoulli, Daniel, 192

Bernoulli's principle, 192, **193**

curveballs and, 195, **195**

flight and, 193–194, **193, 194**

Frisbees® and, 204

statement of, 779

water streams and, 192, **192**

beta decay, 450, **450**

beta particles, 450, **450, 451,** 452

bicycles, energy conversions in, **252**

big bang theory, 21, **21**

bimetallic strips, 278, **278**

binary numbers, 548

biochemicals, 434–435, **434, 435**

biology, 11, **11**

biomass, energy from, 262, **262**

bionic eyes, 692

birds, flight in, 194, 196

bitterness, 425

black holes, **136**

black powder, 358

bleach, **425**

block and tackle, 224, **224**

blood, **99, 430,** 436

blue sky, 646

boat propulsion, 13–14, **13, 14, 16, 17**

body temperature, **764**

Boeing 737 jets, 193, **193**

Bohr, Niels, 316

boiling, 76, **76, 78**

boiling points, 76–77, **76, 79**

bomb calorimeters, 291, **291**

bonding, chemical, 364–377. See also chemical bonds

bonds. See chemical bonds; covalent bonds; ionic bonds; metallic bonds

bones, 62, **642**

boron, **93, 322, 341**

boron group elements, 347, **347**

Bova, Ben, 34

bowling, 168, **168,** 210

Boyle, Robert, 72

Boyle's law, 72, **72,** 778

Bracken, Alisha, 205

Bradbury, Ray, 568

brain cancer, 692

brakes, hydraulic, 196, **197**

braking systems on snowboards and skis, 147

brass, **101**

breathing, **184**

brittleness, 418

bromine, **342, 349**

bromthymol blue, 423, **423,** 426, **426**

brushes, **526**

buckyballs, 358

building demolition, 414

bumper cars, 159, **159**

buoyancy. See also buoyant force

in diving, 183, **183,** 205

in flight, 193–194, **193, 194**

buoyant force, 186–191, **186**

Archimedes' principle, 186–187, **186, 187,** 778

density and, 188, **188**

determining, 186, **186**

labs on, **190,** 198–199

mass and, 190, **190**

shape and, 189, **189**

volume and, 191, **191**

weight and, 187, **187**

burglar alarms, 496

C

cabbage, pH and color of, 438–439

cake, baking a, 53, **53**

calcium, 345, **345, 453**

calcium carbonate, **368**

calcium hydroxide, 426

Calories, 290–291, **291**

calorimeters, 291, **291**

cameras, 678, **678**

cancer, cell phones and, 692

can openers, 228, **228**

carbohydrates, 434, **434**

carbon

in backbones of organic compounds, 432, **432**

beta decay of, 450, **450**

in buckyballs, 348

covalent bonding of, 375

as graphite, **341**

isotopes, 452–453, **452**

properties of, 91, 347, **347**

carbon-14 dating, 452–453, **452**

carbon dioxide

from carbonated beverages, 96

chemical formula of, **393**

as dry ice, 78, **78**

in photosynthesis, 97

properties of, **395**

carbon group elements, 347, **347**

carbonic acid, 96, 424

carbon monoxide, **395**

carriers, 546

cars

acceleration in, **161**

catalytic converters in, 407, **407**

as compound machines, 228

Doppler effect in, 608, **608**

energy conversions in, 256

energy efficiency of, 257, **257**

friction and, 131

high-speed crashes of, 241

horsepower in, 215, **215**

hydraulic brakes in, 196, **197**

jumper cables for, 478, **478**

mirrors in, 669, **669,** 671, **671**

momentum of, 166

pollution and size of, **161**

remote-controlled toy, 544, **544**

sparks as activation energy in, 404

voltages in, 484, **484**

catalysts, **406,** 407, **407,** 436

catalytic converters, 407, **407**

cathode-ray tube experiment, 314, **314**

Index

CD-R (CD-recordable), 558, **558**
CD-RW (CD-rewritable), 558, **558**
CDs (compact discs), 548–549, **548, 549,** 558, **558**
cellos, 616–617, **616, 617,** 619, **619**
cells, electrical, 487–488, **487, 488**
cellular phones, 638, 683, **683,** 692
cellulose, 434
Celsius scale, **25, 26, 276,** 277, **764**
   conversion equation, **277**
central processing units (CPUs), 556, **556**
centrifuges, **99**
centripetal acceleration, 123, **123**
centripetal force, 154, **154**
cerium sulfate, **103**
chain reactions, 457–458, **457,** 462–463
changes of state, 74, **74,** 289, **289**
   condensation, 77, **77**
   energy and, 74–78, **79,** 289, **289**
   evaporation, 48, 76, **76**
   freezing, 75, **75**
   melting, 75
   sublimation, 78, **78**
   temperature and, 78, **79**
   of water, **74, 289**
characteristic properties, 51, 76, 91, **91**
charge, electric
   calculation of, **370**
   charging objects, 476–477, **476, 477**
   conservation of, 449, **449,** 477
   detection of, 477, **477**
   lab on, **477**
   law of electric charges, 474, **475**
   moving charges, 478, **478**
   static electricity, 478–480
charged particles, 368
Charles's law, 72, **72, 73,** 778
charts, 770–772, **770, 771, 772**
cheetahs, **7**
chemical bonds, 364–377, **365,** 418, **418**
   in chemical reactions, 390–391, **390**
   covalent, 372–373, **372, 373**
   double and triple, 433, **433**
   electron number and organization, 365–367, **365, 366, 367**
   energy in, 402–403
   ionic, 368–371, **369, 370, 371**
   labs on, **376,** 378–379
   marshmallow models of, 378–379
   metallic, 375–377, **376**
   noble gases and, 366
   van der Waals force in, 384

chemical changes, 52, **52**
   to break down compounds, 96, **96**
   clues to, 53
   in composition, 54, **54**
   heat and, 290–291, **290**
   new substances from, 52, **52**
   in photosynthesis, 250, **250**
   reversing, 55, **55**
chemical compounds, 418–437. *See also* compounds
chemical energy
   in chemical reactions, 389, **389**
   conversions involving, 249–250, **249**
   in food, 244, **244,** 290–291, **290, 291**
   from fossil fuels, 260, **260**
   in plants, 250, **250**
chemical equations, 392–397, **394**
   balancing, 395–396, **396**
   importance of accuracy in, **395**
   reactants and products in, 394, **394**
chemical formulas, 392–397, **392, 393, 395**
chemical properties, 50, **50**
   characteristic properties, 51, 76, 91, **91**
   chemical change and, 52–55, **52, 54, 55**
   during chemical reactions, 388–390, **388, 389, 390**
   composition and, 54
   lab on, 56–57
   physical properties compared with, 51, **51**
   reactivity, 50, **50,** 91, 400, **400**
chemical reactions, 388–407, **389**
   activation energy in, 404, **405**
   chemical and physical properties during, 388
   chemical bonds during, 390–391, **390**
   decomposition, 399, **399**
   double-displacement, 401, **401**
   endothermic, 403, **403, 405**
   equations of, 394–396, **394, 396**
   exothermic, 402, **402, 403, 405**
   labs on, **391, 403, 405,** 408–409
   neutralization, 429, **429**
   rates of, 405–407, **405, 406, 407**
   reactants and products in, 394, **394**
   reactivity of elements, 400, **400**
   signs of, 389–390, **389, 390**
   single-displacement, 399, **399**
   synthesis, 398, **398**

chemical symbols, **338–339,** 342, 392, **395**
chemistry, 8, **8,** 385
Chernobyl nuclear accident, 459, **459**
chloride ions, **370**
chlorine
   atomic mass of, 323
   negative ions of, **370**
   properties of, **95,** 349, **349**
   reaction with hydrogen, **390,** 391
   water treatment by, **349**
chlorophyll, 388, 656
circle graphs, 770, **770**
circuit boards, 540, **540**
circuit breakers, 498, **498**
circuits, electric, 494–499
   integrated, 544, **544**
   labs on, **496–497,** 500–501
   parts of, 494–495, **494, 495**
   safety tips and, 498–499, **498, 499**
   switches in, 495, **495**
   types of, 495–497, **496, 497,** 500–501
circular motion, 123, **123**
citric acid, 424
clapping, **621**
clarinets, 620, **620**
classes, of elements, 340–341, **340, 341**
CMEs (coronal mass ejections), 536
coal, 258–260, **258, 259, 260**
cobalt, **91, 395**
cochlea, **603**
coefficients, in equations, 396
coils, wire, **526, 527**
collisions, 167–168, **167, 168**
colloids, 104, **104**
color addition, 655, **655,** 658–659
color deficiency, 676, **676**
colors
   in acid-base indicators, 423, **423,** 426, **426**
   colorblindness, 676, **676**
   mixing light, 655, **655,** 658–659
   mixing pigments, 656–657, **656, 657,** 658–659
   of objects, 653–654, **654**
   in rainbows, 585, **585**
   separation by refraction, 585, 648, **648**
   in televisions, **655**
   visible light and, 640, **640, 641**
color subtraction, 656–657, **657,** 658–659
color television, 551–552, **551, 552**

communication, 18, **18**
communication technology, 546–553, 683, **683**
   analog signals, 547–548, **547, 548**
   digital signals, 548–549, **548, 549**
   labs on, **555,** 562–563
   microwaves and, 638, 683, 692
   Morse code, 546, **546,** 562–563
   plasma displays, 552, **552**
   radios, 545, **545,** 550, **550,** 605
   television, 540, 551–552, **551, 552, 655**
commutators, 522, **522,** 530
compact discs (CDs), 548–549, **548, 549,** 558, **558**
compasses
   animals and, **512**
   Earth and, 515–516, **515**
   electric currents and, 518, **518**
   north and south poles of, 511, **511**
compound machines, 228, **228**
compounds, 94–97, **95,** 418–437
   breaking down, 96, **96**
   covalent, 374–375, **374,** 420–421, **420, 421** (*see also* covalent compounds)
   flame tests of, 106–107
   in industry, 96
   ionic, 317, **317,** 418–419, **418, 419** (*see also* ionic compounds)
   labs on, **95,** 106–107
   in nature, 97, **97**
   ratio of elements in, 94, **94**
compression, in longitudinal waves, 578, **578, 600, 601**
compressors, 297, **297**
computers, 554–561, **555**
   basic functions of, 554, **554**
   binary digits in, 548
   burning and erasing CDs using, 558, **558**
   hardware, 556–557, **556, 557**
   history of, 555, **555, 556**
   lab on, **555**
   networks, 560, **560**
   software, 559, **559**
   technicians, 569
   wearable, 568
computer technicians, 569
concave lenses, **672,** 673, **673, 675**
concave mirrors, 670, **670, 671**
concentration, 102, **102**
   calculating, **102,** 780
   reaction rates and, 406, **406,** 409
   in solutions, 102–103, **102, 103**

conceptual models, 21, **21**
conclusions, 767
condensation, 77, **77**
condensation points, 77
conduction, thermal, 282, **282.** *See also* conductivity, thermal
conductivity, electrical. *See also* conductors, electrical
   charging by conduction, 476, **476**
   of elements, 91, **91**
   of metalloids, **93**
   of metals, **93**
   of semiconductors, 541, **541**
conductivity, thermal, **45**
   of metalloids, **93**
   of metals, **93, 340**
   of nonmetals, **341**
   as physical property, **45**
   temperature and, 285, **285**
   thermal conduction, 282, **282**
   thermal conductors, 283, **283, 340, 341**
conductors, electrical, 478, **478.** *See also* conductivity, electrical
   acids, 424
   bases, 426
   covalent compounds, 421, **421**
   ionic compounds, 419, **419**
   metals, 340, **340,** 376
   resistance and, **485**
   semiconductors, 341, **341,** 541, **541**
   temperature and, 486
conductors, thermal, 283, **283, 340, 341**
cones, 674, 676
conservation, in decay, 449
conservation of energy, 254–257
   in chemical reactions, 403
   conversions and, 254, **254**
   efficiency and, 257, **257**
   law of, 255, **255,** 403, **403,** 777
   roller-coaster example, 254, **254**
   thermal energy in, 256, **256**
conservation of mass, 23, 395, **395, 397**
conservation of momentum, law of, 167–168, **167, 168**
constructive interference, 587, **587**
   in light waves, 650, **650**
   in sound waves, 614–615, **614, 615**
   in standing waves, **588**
control groups, 767
controlled experiments, 16, 767
convection, thermal, 283, **283**
convection currents, 283, **283,** 293, **293**

conversions, unit, **277, 763, 764**
convex lenses, 672, **672, 675,** 686–687
convex mirrors, **670,** 671, **671**
cooking at high altitudes, **77**
cooling systems, 296, **296**
copper
   atomic mass of, 323, **323**
   chemical changes in, **52**
   electrical conductivity of, 485
   in fireworks, 358
   mining of, 113
   properties of, **45, 93, 340,** 376
copper mining, 113
cordless telephones, 683
coronal mass ejections (CMEs), 536
corrosive, 422
covalent bonds, 372–373, **372, 373,** 378–379, 420
covalent compounds, 420–421, **420**
   covalent bonds in, 372–373, **372, 373,** 378–379, 420
   formulas for, 393, **393**
   molecules of, 374–375, **374, 375, 420**
   properties of, 420–421, **420, 421**
CPUs (central processing units), 556, **556**
Crab nebula, **576**
crests, 577, **577, 578**
crime-scene investigations, **436**
cross-multiplication, 773
crushing, rate of dissolution and, **103**
crystal lattices, 371, **371**
crystalline solids, 67, **67**
cube volume, 776
cubic centimeters, 40, **40, 763**
cubic meters, 25, **25,** 40, **40, 763**
cubic units, 40, **40, 70**
Curie, Marie, 448, 469
Curie, Pierre, 469
current, electric, 482, **482**
   alternating current, 483, **483,** 485, 527, 542
   in breaking down compounds, 96, **96**
   diodes and, 542, **542**
   direct current, 483, **483,** 542
   discovery of electromagnetism, 518–519, **518**
   electrical cells, 487–488, **487, 488**
   induction by magnetism, 524–526, **524, 525, 526**
   magnetic force and, 521, **521**
   measurement by galvanometers, 523
   Ohm's law, 490, **490**
   resistance and, 485–486, **486**

Index

current, electric (*continued*)
 in series and parallel circuits, 495–497, **496, 497,** 500–501
 solenoids and, 519, **519**
 voltage and, 484–485, **484**
curveballs, 195, **195**
Czarnowski, James, 12–18, **13**

D

Dalton's atomic theory, 313, **313**
data, 17, **17,** 771, **771**
dating, age, 452–453, **452**
DC (direct current), 483, **483,** 542
DC electric motors, 522, **522,** 530–531
deafness, 604
deceleration, 121
decibels, 610, **610**
decimals, 774
decomposition reactions, 399, **399**
deep-sea diving, 86
Democritus, 312
demolition, 414
density, 26, **26,** 45, **45**
 calculation of, 47, **47, 188,** 780
 of elements, 91, **91**
 examples of, **47**
 floating and sinking and, 188, **188**
 of gases, **47**
 identifying substances through, 47, **47**
 liquid layers and, 46, **46**
 overall, 189–190, **189, 190**
 of rocks, **189**
 of solids, 46
 water pressure and, 183
deoxyribonucleic acid (DNA), **436,** 437, **437,** 444
dependent variables, 771, **771**
destructive interference, **587,** 588
 in light waves, 650, **650**
 in sound waves, 614, **614**
detergents, **425**
diamonds, 347, **347**
DiAPLEX®, 306
diatomic elements, 374, **374, 396**
diatomic molecules, 374, **374, 390**
diffraction, 586, **586,** 649, **649**
diffuse reflection, 645, **645**
digital cameras, 678
digital recording, 549, **549**
digital signals, 548–549, **548, 549,** 551
dilute solutions, 102, **102**
dinitrogen monoxide, **393**
dinosaurs, sound from, 628
diodes, 542, **542**

direct current (DC), 483, **483,** 542
direct current electric motors, 522, **522,** 530–531
displacement, 40, **40**
dissolving, 48, 103, **103.** *See also* solutions
distance
 determined with GPS watch system, 146
 gravitational force and, 137, **137**
 in light-years, **576**
distillation, **99**
diving, 183, **183,** 205
DNA (deoxyribonucleic acid), **436,** 437, **437,** 444
DNA fingerprinting, **436**
dog whistles, 607
domains, 512, **513**
doorbells, 521, **521**
doping, 541, **541**
Doppler effect, 608, **608,** 613, **613**
double-displacement reactions, 401, **401**
drag, 195–196, **195, 196**
drinking bird, 256, **256**
drums, **245,** 609, **609**
dry cells, 487
dry cleaning, 112
dry ice, 78, **78**
ductility, **45, 93, 340,** 376
Dudley, Adam, 629

E

"Ear," 628
ears, 182, **603**
Earth, 135, 137, 515–516, **515, 516**
earthquakes, **547,** 575, **575**
Earthship architects, 307
Eberhardt, Jeannie, 445
echoes, 584, 612, **612**
echolocation, 613, **613**
effervescent tablets, **52**
efficiency
 energy, 13–14, **14, 17,** 257, **257**
 mechanical, 220–221, **220**
Einstein, Albert, 34, 270, 665
Einstein's equation, 270
elastic potential energy, 249, **249**
electrical calculations, 490–493
electrical cells, 487–488, **487, 488**
electrical conductivity
 charging by conduction, 476, **476**
 of elements, 91, **91**
 of metalloids, **93**
 of metals, **93**
 of semiconductors, 541, **541**
electrical conductors, 478, **478**
 acids, 424

bases, 426
 covalent compounds, 421, **421**
 ionic compounds, 419, **419**
 metals, 340, **340,** 376
 resistance and, **485**
 semiconductors, 341, **341,** 541, **541**
 temperature and, 486
electrical current, 482–489
electrical energy, 482–489
 conversions involving, 251, **251**
 from exothermic reactions, **402**
 from fossil fuels, 260, **260**
 generating, 487–488, **487, 488,** 527, **527**
 household, 245, **245**
 measuring, 492, **492,** 500–501
 from nuclear energy, 260, **260,** 458–459, **458, 459**
electrical insulators, 478, **478**
electrical outlets, 485
electric charge, 474–481
 calculation of, **370**
 charging objects, 476–477, **476, 477**
 conservation of, 449, **449,** 477
 detection of, 477, **477**
 lab on, **477**
 law of electric charges, 474
 moving charges, 478, **478**
 in static electricity, 478–480
electric circuits, 494–499
 integrated, 544, **544**
 labs on, **497,** 500–501
 parts of, 494–495, **494, 495**
 safety tips, 498–499, **498, 499**
 switches in, 495, **495**
 types of, 495–497, **496, 497,** 500–501
electric current, 482, **482**
 alternating current, 483, **483,** 485, 527, 542
 in breaking down compounds, 96, **96**
 diodes and, 542, **542**
 direct current, 483, **483,** 542
 discovery of electromagnetism, 518–519, **518**
 electrical cells, 487–488, **487, 488**
 induction by magnetism, 524–526, **524, 525, 526**
 magnetic force and, 521, **521**
 measurement by galvanometers, 523
 Ohm's law, 490, **490**
 resistance and, 485–486, **486**
 in series and parallel circuits, 495–497, **496, 497,** 500–501
 solenoids and, 519, **519**
 voltage and, 484–485, **484**

electric discharges, 479–480, **479, 480,** 506
electric eels, **485,** 506
electric fields, 475, **475,** 632–633, **632, 633**
electric force, 475, **475**
electric generators, 260, **260,** 526–527, **526, 527**
electricians, 507
electricity, 474–499. *See also* electric current; electromagnetism
  electrical cells, 487–488, **487, 488**
  electric charge, 449, 474–478, **476, 477**
  electric circuits, 494–499, **494, 495, 496, 497**
  electric power, 491–492
  generators, 260, **260,** 526–527, **526, 527**
  magnetism and, 518–529
  measuring, 492–493, **492,** 500–501
  nervous impulses, **495**
  Ohm's law, 490, **491,** 500–501
  resistance, 485–486, **485, 486,** 490, **490**
  safety tips, 498–499, **498, 499**
  static, 478–480, **479, 480**
  switches, 495, **495**
  transformers, 528, **528, 529**
  voltage, 484–485
  ways to save, 493, **493**
electric meters, 492, **492**
electric motors, 522, **522,** 530–531
electric power, 214–215, **214, 215,** 491, **491**
electrodes, 487, **487**
electrolysis, 54, **96**
electrolytes, 487
electromagnetic force, **324,** 511, **511**
electromagnetic induction, 524–526, **524, 525, 526**
electromagnetic spectrum, **636–637,** 636–642
electromagnetic waves (EM waves), 632, **632.** *See also* light; sound waves; waves
  energy transfer by, 576, **576**
  light as, 632, **632**
  longitudinal, 578, **578, 581, 600,** 601
  producing, 633
  in radios, 550, **550**
  sound waves as, 578, **578**
  transverse, 577, **577, 578, 581**
electromagnetism, 508–529, **519**
  applications of, 521–523, **521, 522,** 536
  auroras and, 516, **516**

discovery of, 518, **518**
  Earth as a magnet, 515–516, **515**
  electric generators, 260, **260,** 526–527, **526, 527**
  electric motors, 522, **522,** 530–531
  electromagnets, 514, 520, **520**
  induction of electric current, 524–526, **524, 525, 526**
  labs on, **520,** 530–531
  losing alignment, 513
  maglev trains, 221, **221,** 518, 520
  magnet cutting, 514, **514**
  magnetic fields, 512, **512, 513,** 515, **515**
  magnetic force, 511, **511,** 521, **521**
  magnet making, 513, **513**
  magnet properties, 510–511, **510, 511**
  in record players, 548, **548**
  solenoids, 519, **519**
  transformers, 528, **528, 529**
electromagnets, 514, 520, **520**
electron clouds, **316,** 317, **317, 319,** 320
electron-dot diagrams, 373, **373**
electronic devices, 540–545
electronics engineers, 35
electronic technology, 540–561
  analog signals, 547–548, **547, 548**
  circuit boards, 540, **540**
  computers, 554–560, **554, 556, 558, 560**
  digital signals, 548–549, **548, 549**
  diodes, 542, **542**
  integrated circuits, 544, **544**
  labs on, **555,** 562–563
  plasma displays, 552, **552**
  semiconductors, 541, **541**
  transistors, 543–544, **543, 544,** 555
  vacuum tubes and, 545, **545**
electrons, 314, **314,** 364–367
  chemical bonding and, 366–367, **367**
  in covalent bonds, 372, **372**
  in diodes, 542, **542**
  discovery of, 314, **314**
  in electric current, 482–483, **483**
  electron clouds, **316,** 317, **317, 319,** 320
  energy levels, 365, **365**
  magnetic fields, 512
  movement within metals, 376–377, **376**
  positrons and, 450

properties of, 320
  in semiconductors, 541, **541**
  in televisions, 551, **551**
  valence, 365–367, **365, 366**
electroscopes, 477, **477**
elements, 90–93, **91**
  atom differences, 320–321, **320**
  characteristic properties of, 91, **91**
  classes of, 340–341, **340, 341**
  classification by properties, 92–93, **92, 93**
  diatomic, 374, **374**
  identification of, 91, **91**
  isotopes of, 321, **321,** 450, **450** (*see also* isotopes)
  labs on, **91,** 326–327
  mass calculations, 323, **323**
  periodic properties of, 337
  periodic table of, 336–351, **338–339, 768–769**
  predicting properties of missing, 337, **337**
  as pure substances, 90
  ratios in compounds, 94, **94**
  reactivity of, 400, **400**
elves, 506
EM waves (electromagnetic waves), 632, **632.** *See also* light; sound waves; waves
  energy transfer by, 576, **576**
  light as, 632, **632**
  longitudinal, 578, **578, 581, 600,** 601
  producing, 633
  in radios, 550, **550**
  sound waves as, 578, **578**
  transverse, 577, **577, 578, 581**
endothermic changes, 75, 78, **79**
endothermic reactions, 403, **403, 405**
energy, 240–263, **240.** *See also* conservation of energy; energy conversions
  activation, 404, **404, 405,** 407
  atomic, 457–458, **457,** 462–463 (*see also* atomic energy)
  from chain reactions, 457–458, **457**
  changes of state and, 74, **76,** 77–78, 80–81, 289 (*see also* changes of state)
  chemical, 244, **244,** 249–250, **249, 250** (*see also* chemical energy)
  cooling and, 297, **297**
  efficiency, 13–14, **14, 17,** 257, **257**
  elastic potential, 249, **249**

energy (*continued*)
electrical, 487–488, **487, 488,** 527, **527** (*see also* electrical energy)
in endothermic reactions, 75, 78, **79,** 403, **405**
in exothermic reactions, 75, **79,** 402, **402, 405**
to gain electrons, 370
heat and, 280, **280**
kinetic, 210, 241, **241,** 264–265
labs on, **245,** 264–265
light, 246, **246,** 250, **250, 402**
mechanical, 243, **243**
from nonrenewable resources, 258–260, **258, 259, 260**
nuclear, 246, **246, 262,** 270 (*see also* nuclear energy)
from ocean temperature differences, **295**
potential, 242–243, **242,** 261, **261,** 265
power and, 214
to remove electrons, 369
from renewable resources, 261–262, **261, 262**
sound, 245, **245**
from•the sun, 635, **635**
thermal, 244, **244, 249,** 280–281, **281**
wave, 574–576, **574, 575, 576,** 580–582
work and, 240, **240**
energy conversions, 248–253, **248**
of chemical energy, 249–250, **249, 250**
efficiency of, 257, **257**
of elastic potential energy, 249, **249**
of electrical energy, 251, **251**
in food, 290–291, **290, 291**
of fossil fuels, 260, **260**
of kinetic and potential energy, 248–249, **248, 249, 254**
law of conservation of energy and, 255, **255,** 403
in a light bulb, **255**
machines and, 252–253, **252, 253**
in plants, 250, **250**
radiometers, 253, **253**
in roller coasters, 254, **254**
thermal energy from all, 256, **256**
energy diagrams, **405**
energy levels, electron, 365, **365**
engines
external combustion, 295, **295**
heat, 295–296, **295, 296**
internal combustion, 296, **296**
steam, 295, **295**

underwater jet, 270
English units, **763**
ENIAC computer, 555, **555, 556**
enzymes, **406,** 436, 444, 664
equations, chemical, 392–397, **394**
ethene, **433**
ethyne, **433**
evaporation, 48, 76, **76, 99**
Everest, Mount, 182, **182**
exothermic changes, 75
exothermic reactions, 402, **402, 403, 405**
expansion joints, 278, **278**
experimental groups, 767
experimental physicists, 333
experiments, controlled, 16, 767
external combustion engines, 295, **295**
eyes, 674, **674**
bionic, 692
color deficiency, 676, **676**
surgical correction, 676, **676**
vision problems, 675, **675**

F

Faber, Sandra, 693
Fahrenheit scale, **26, 276,** 277, **277, 764**
falling objects, 150–153, **150, 151, 152, 153**
families (groups), **338,** 342, **768–769**
Faraday, Michael, 524–525, **524,** 537
fats, 435, **435**
ferromagnets, 514, **514**
fertilizers, 96–97
fields, electric, 475, **475,** 632–633, **632, 633.** *See also* magnetic fields
film, 678, **678**
filtration, **99**
fingerprinting, DNA, **436**
fireflies, 664
fireworks, 106–107, 358
first-class levers, 222, **222**
first law of motion, Newton's, 158–160, **158, 159**
fish, buoyancy of, 191, **191**
fish finders, **613**
fission, 456, **457**
advantages and disadvantages of, 458–459, **458, 459**
chain reactions, 457–458, **457,** 462–463
electricity from, 246, 260, **260**
lab on, 459
of uranium-235, **456**
fixed pulleys, 224, **224**

flame tests, 106–107
flammability, 50, **50**
flashlights, 670
flight, 193–194, **193, 194,** 196, **196**
floating, 187–188, **187,** 198–199
fluids, 180–185, **180.** *See also* liquids
atmospheric pressure on, **180,** 181–182, **181, 182**
in ballast tanks, 190, **190**
Bernoulli's principle, 192–195, **192, 193, 194, 195**
buoyant force, 186–191, **186, 187, 189, 190**
flight and, 193–194, **193, 194**
flow of, 184–185, **184, 185**
labs on, **184, 190**
Pascal's principle, 196, **197,** 778
pressure from, 180–181, **180, 181**
water pressure, 183, **183**
fluorescent materials, 448, **551, 552**
fluorine, **374**
FM radio waves, 637
focal length, **670**
focal point, 670, **670, 671**
foils, **16**
FoldNotes instuctions, 757–760, **757, 758, 759, 760**
food
chemical energy in, 7, 11, 290–291, **290, 291**
inspection of, 664
preservation of, 468
forces, 124–127, **124.** *See also* gravitational force; gravity
acceleration, 161–162, **161, 162**
action and reaction pairs of, 163–164, **163, 164,** 169
air resistance, 152–153, **152, 153**
balanced and unbalanced, 126–127, **126, 127,** 135
buoyant, 186–191, **186, 187, 189, 190**
calculating, 181
centripetal, 154, **154**
electric, 475, **475**
electromagnetic, **324,** 511, **511**
in fluids, 180–197
force-distance trade-off in machines, 218, **218**
friction and, 128–129, **128, 129**
on gases, 71, **71**
input and output, 217–218, **218, 219**
labs on, 140–141, **156, 159, 160,** 198–199
magnetic, 511, **511**
net, 125–126, **125, 126,** 779
strong, **324**
thrust, 194, **194**
units of, **41,** 42, 124

weak, **324**
work compared with, 210–211, **211**
forensic scientists, 445
formulas, chemical, 392–397, **392, 393, 395**
fossil fuels, 258, **258**
advantages and disadvantages of, **262**
electricity from, 260, **260**
formation of, 258, **258**
nuclear power compared with, 459
uses of, 259, **259**
fractions, 774–775
Franklin, Benjamin, **480**
Franklin, Melissa, 333
free fall, 153–154, **153, 154**
freezing, 75, **75**
freezing points, 75, **764**
frequencies, 582, **582**
electromagnetic spectrum, 636, **636–637**
energy and, 582, **582**
hearing and, 607, **607,** 622–623
on oscilloscopes, 610–611, **610, 611**
resonant, 589, 616, **616**
of sound, 607, **607, 610**
wavelength and, 583
frequency modulation, 637–638
friction, 128–133, **128,** 254, **255**
activation energy from, 404
charging objects by, 476, **476**
energy conversions through, 254, **254**
forces and, 128–129, **129, 130**
harmful and helpful, 131, **220**
increasing, 133
kinetic, 130, **130**
labs on, **129, 132**
Newton's first law and, 159
reducing, 132, **132**
in ski and snowboard braking systems, 147
static, 131, **131**
surface roughness and, 129
Frisbees®, 204
fulcrum, 222, **222, 223**
fundamental frequencies, **616,** 618
fuses, 498, **498**
fusion, 246, **246,** 460–461, **460, 461**

G

Galileo, 150
gallium, 75, **75, 541**
galvanometers, 523
gamma decay, 450

gamma rays, 450, **451,** 452, **637,** 642
gamma ray spectrometers, **642**
gas chromatographs, 415
gases, **68,** 69
Boyle's law, 72, **72**
changes in shape and volume of, 69, **69**
Charles's law, 72, **72, 73**
from chemical reactions, 389, **389**
condensation of, 77
density of, **47**
dissolution in water, 103
greenhouse, 284
as lubricants, 132
noble, 341, 350, **350, 366**
plasma from, 86
pressure and force on, 71–72, **71, 72**
refrigerant, 297
as state of matter, 288, **288**
temperature and, 70, **70**
volume of, **71**
GCF (greatest common factor), 774
geckos, 384
Geiger counters, **454**
gelatin, 104, **104**
gemologists, 63
generators, electric, 260, 260, 526–527, **526, 527**
genetics, 437, **437, 676**
geochemists, 10, **10**
geology, 10, **10**
geomagnetic storms, 536
geothermal energy, 262–263, **262**
germanium, **337, 342,** 347
GFCIs (ground fault circuit interrupters), 498, **498**
gigabytes, **557**
Gilbert, William, 515
glass, 67, **67,** 652–654, **652**
gliders, 194, **194**
global positioning system (GPS), 146, 684, **684**
glucose, **392,** 434, **434**
gold, 63, 332, **346**
gold-foil experiment, 315, **315**
Goldsworthy, Andy, 87
GPS (global positioning system), 146, 684, **684**
GPS watch system, 146
graduated cylinders, 26, 28–29, 39, **39,** 765
grams, **763**
granite, 100, **100**
Graphic Organizers instructions, 761–762, **761, 762**
graphite, **341**
graphs
of acceleration, 122, **122**

bar, 772, **772**
circle, 770, **770**
line, 771–772, **771**
in scientific methods, 17, **17**
slopes of, 119, **119,** 771–772
of speed, 119, **119**
gravitational force. *See also* gravity
atmospheric pressure and, 182, **182**
within atoms, **324**
distance and, 137, **137**
on the Earth, 135
falling objects and, 150, **150**
mass and, 136, **136**
of the sun, 137, **137**
weight as measure of, 41, **41,** 138–139, **138, 139**
gravitational potential energy, 242–243, **242,** 265
gravity, 134–139, **134,** 150–157. *See also* gravitational force
acceleration due to, 150–151, **150, 151, 162,** 164
effects on matter, 134–135, **134**
effects on seeds, **135**
as force, **125**
law of universal gravitation, 135, 136–137, **136, 137,** 777
Newton's second law and, **162**
Newton's third law and, 164, **164**
projectile motion and, 155–156, **155, 156**
weight and, 42, **42**
greatest common factor (GCF), 774
greenhouse effect, 284, **284**
ground fault circuit interrupters (GFCIs), 498, **498**
grounding, 480, **480**
groups, **338,** 342, **342,** 768–769
guitars
pickups on, **619**
resonance of, 616–617, **616, 617**
sound energy from, 245, **245**
sound quality of, 619, **619**
gunpowder, 358

H

hailstones, 152
hair dryers, 251, **251**
Halderman, Jack C., II, 204
half-lives, 453, **453**
halogens, 349, **349**
hammers (part of ear), **603**
hammers (tool), **219**
hardware, computer, 556–557, **556, 557**
hawks, 194
hazardous chemicals, 414

headlights, car, 670
hearing
    deafness and loss of, 604
    detecting sounds, 602
    ears, 182, **603**
    frequency and, 607, **607,** 622–
        623
    protecting, 605, **605**
heat, 96, **96,** 280–299, **280**
    calculating, 286, **286**
    calorimeters, 291, **291**
    changes of state and, 289, **289**
    chemical changes and, 290–291,
        290
    conduction, 282, **282**
    conductors and insulators, 283,
        283
    convection, 283, **283**
    greenhouse effect, 284, **284**
    heat engines, 295–296, **295,**
        296
    infrared radiation, 284, **284,** 636,
        636, 639
    labs on, **282,** 300–301
    refrigerators, 297, **297**
    solubility and, **103**
    specific, 285–286, **285, 286,**
        300–301
    thermal conductivity, **45, 93,**
        285, 340, 341
    thermal energy and, 281, **281**
    thermal pollution, 298, **298**
heat engines, 295–296, **295, 296**
heating systems
    cooling systems and, 296, **296**
    hot-water, 292, **292**
    insulation and, 293, **293**
    solar, 294, **294,** 307
    thermal pollution from, 298, **298**
    warm-air, 293, **293**
heat technology, 292–299
hectares, **763**
Heisenberg, Werner, 317
heliox, 86
helium, 86, 320, **320,** 332
    balloons, **188**
    in deep-sea diving, 86
    density of, **47**
    lasers, **680**
    valence electrons in, 367
helium-neon lasers, **680**
hemoglobin, 436
Henry, Joseph, 524
Hensler, Mike, 237
hertz (Hz), 582, 607
Hodgson, Peter, 444
holograms, 681, **681**
horizontal motion, gravity and, 155,
    155
hormones, 436
horsepower, **215**

hot-air balloons, 279, **279**
hot-water heating systems, 292,
    292
Hubble Space Telescope, 693
hydrangeas, **430**
hydraulic devices, 196, **197**
hydrocarbons, 433–434, **433**
hydrochloric acid, 424
hydroelectric energy, 261, **261,** 263
hydroelectric power plants, 527,
    527
hydrofluoric acid, 424, **424**
hydrogen, 91, **320, 344,** 350, **350**
    hydronium ions, 422
    isotopes of, **321, 453**
    nuclear fusion of, 246, **246,**
        460–461, **460, 461**
    reaction with chlorine, **390,** 391
    valence electrons in, 367
hydrogen peroxide, 414
hydronium ions, 422
hydroxide ion, 425
hypotheses, 15–17, **15, 17,** 766–767

I

Iceman remains, **452**
ice palaces, 34, **34**
ideal machines, 221, **221**
illuminated objects, 645, **645**
images
    real, 670, **671,** 672, **672, 674**
    three-dimensional, 681, **681**
    virtual, 669–673, **671, 672, 673**
incidence, 644, **644**
incident beams, **644**
inclined planes, **218,** 226, **226**
independent variables, 771, **771**
indicators, acid and base, **422,** 423
    examples of, 423, **423,** 426, **426**
    lab on, 438–439
    in neutralization reactions, 429,
        429
    use of, 430, **430**
induction
    by changing magnetic fields,
        524–526, **524, 525, 526**
    charging objects by, **476,** 477
inertia, 42, **42,** 160, **160**
    lab on, 170–171
    mass as measure of, 43, **43,**
        160, **160**
    Newton's first law and, 160,
        160, 777
infrared binoculars, 639
infrared radiation, 284, **284, 636,**
    639, **639**
inhibitors, 405–406, **406**
inner ears, **603**

input, computer, 554, **554,** 556,
    556
input devices, 556, **556**
"Inspiration" (Bova), 34
insulation, thermal, 293, **293**
insulators, electrical, 478, **478**
insulators, thermal, 283, **283**
insulin, 436
integrated circuits, 544, **544**
interface cards, 557
interference, 587, **587,** 614, **614**
    constructive, 587, **587, 614,** 650,
        650
    destructive, 588, **588, 614**
    in light waves, 650, **650**
    resonance and, 589, 616–617,
        616, 617
    sound barrier and, 615, **615**
    in sound waves, 614–616, **614,**
        615
    in standing waves, 588–589,
        588, 589, 616, **616**
internal combustion engines, 296,
    296
International System of Units (SI),
    25–26, **25,** 277, **763**
Internet, 560, **560**
Internet Service Providers (ISPs),
    560, **560**
iodine, **93,** 349, **349, 454**
ionic bonds, 368–371, **368**
    in double-displacement
        reactions, 401, **401**
    formation of, 368
    in ionic compounds, 418–419
    metallic bonds, 375–377, **376**
    negative ions and, 370, **370**
    positive ions and, 369, **369**
ionic compounds, 418–419, **418**
    crystals of, 418, **418**
    formulas for, 393, **393**
    properties of, 418–419, **419**
    salts as, 431, **431**
ions, 320, 368–370, **368,** 401
iron
    magnetic separation of, **99**
    in magnets, 514, **514**
    properties of, **91, 340, 346**
iron oxide, 51
iron pyrite, 47
irradiated food, 468
isotopes, 321–323, **321,** 450, **450**
    age dating by, 452–453, **452**
    beta decay from, 450, **450**
    of boron, **322**
    of carbon, 452–453, **452**
    half-lives of, **453**
    of hydrogen, **321, 453**
    lab on, 326–327
    medical uses of, 454, **454**

Index

radioactive, 322
uses of, 454, **454**
ISPs (Internet Service Providers),
560, **560**

J

jet engines, underwater, 270
jets, 193–194, **193, 194,** 615, **615**
jewelry designers, 63
Jordan, Roberta, 385, **385**
joules (J), 213, 218, 286
juggling, mechanical energy in, 243,
243
jumper cables, 478, **478**

K

kelvins, **25,** 26, **26,** 277, 764
Kelvin scale, **26, 276,** 277, **764**
conversion equations, **277**
kilobytes, 557
kilograms (kg), 25, **25,** 139, **763**
kilowatt-hours (kWh), 492, **492**
kilowatts (kW), 491
kinetic energy, 210, 241, **241,**
264–265
kinetic friction, 130, **130**
kinetic sculpture, 236
Kitty Hawk, first flight at, **194**
knives, as wedges, 227, **227**

L

LANs (Local Area Networks), 560,
560
lanthanides, 346, **346**
lasers, 679, **679**
in CD players, 549, **549**
light from, 680, **680**
transmitters, 35
uses of, 681, **681**
Lavoisier, Antoine, 395
law of conservation of energy, 255,
255, 403, **403,** 777
law of conservation of mass, 23,
395, **395, 397**
law of conservation of momentum,
167–168, **167, 168**
law of electric charges, 474, **475**
law of reflection, 644, **644,** 778
law of universal gravitation, 135,
136–137, **136, 137,** 777
laws, scientific, **22,** 23, 777–779
laws of motion, Newton's, 158–
164, **158, 161, 163,** 777
lead, **47, 93,** 332

least common denominator (LCD),
775
LED (light-emitting diodes), 540
length, 25, **25, 763,** 765, **765**
lenses, 668–673, **672**
in cameras, **678**
concave, **672,** 673, **673, 675**
convex, 672, **672, 675,** 686–687
in the eye, 674, **674**
in microscopes, 679, **679**
in telescopes, **679**
levers, 217, **219,** 222–223, **222, 223**
Lidar, 35
lift, 193–194, **193, 194,** 196, **196**
lifting, power suits for, 176
light, 632–657, 668–685
absorption and scattering, 101,
646, **646, 647, 652**
color addition, 655, **655,** 658–
659
colors of objects, 653–654, **654**
color subtraction, 656–657, **656,
657,** 658–659
color television, 655
communication technology, 683,
683
diffraction, 586, **586,** 649, **649**
Einstein on, 665
electromagnetic spectrum, 636,
636–637
as electromagnetic wave, 576,
576, 632–633, **632, 633**
energy, 246, **246,** 250, **250, 402**
gamma rays, **637,** 642
greenhouse effect and, 284, **284**
infrared radiation, 284, **284, 636,**
639, **639**
interaction with matter, 652–
654, **652, 653, 654**
interference, 587–589, **587, 588,**
650, **650**
labs on, **649, 656,** 658–659,
686–687
from lasers, 679–681, **679, 680,
681**
lenses, 672–673, **672, 673**
luminous vs. illuminated objects,
645, **645**
microwaves, **636,** 638–639, **638,
639,** 664
mirrors, 668–671, **669, 670, 671**
mixing colors, 655–657, **655,
656, 657**
moonlight, **646**
optical fibers, 681, **681**
optical instruments, 678–679,
678, 679
particle and wave characteristics,
596, **633,** 665
polarized, 682, **682**

rays, 668
reflection of, 584, 644–645, **644,
645, 652** (*see also* reflection)
refraction of, 585, **585,** 647–648,
647, 648
sight, 674–677, **674, 675, 676,
677**
speed of, 270, 634, **634**
from the sun, 635, **635**
telescopes, 596, 679, **679**
transmission of, 652, **652, 653**
ultraviolet, **637,** 641, **641**
visible, 636, **637,** 640, **640, 641**
white, 640, 654, **654**
X rays, **637,** 642, **642**
light bulbs
argon gas in, 350
energy conversions in, **251, 255**
in series circuits, 496, **496**
wattage of, 491, **491**
work in, 231
light-emitting diodes (LED), 540
light energy
from exothermic reactions, **402**
in photosynthesis, 250, **250**
production of, 246, **246**
light microscopes, 679, **679**
lightning, 479–480, **479, 480,** 506,
634
lightning rods, 480, **480**
lightsticks, 414
light-years, **576**
linear relationships, 771
line graphs, 771, **771**
lipids, 435, **435**
liquids, 68, **68.** *See also* fluids
density layering in, 46, **46**
as state of matter, 288, **288**
unique characteristics of, 68, **68**
volume measurements of, 28–
29, 39, **39,** 765
liters, **25,** 26, 39, **763**
lithium, 367
litmus paper, 423, 426, 439
loads, electrical, 494–495, **494**
Local Area Networks (LANs), 560,
560
lodestone (magnetite), 510, 514,
514, 516
longitudinal waves, 578, **578, 581,
600,** 601. *See also* sound
waves
loudness, 609–610, **609**
lubricants, 132, **132**
luciferase, 664
luminous objects, 645, **645**
lungs, 184, **184**

M

machines, 216–229, **217**
  compound, 228, **228**
  energy and, 252–253, **252, 253**
  examples of, **216**
  friction in, **220**
  ideal, 221, **221**
  inclined planes, 226, **226, 228**
  levers, 217, **219,** 222–223, **222, 223**
  mechanical advantage in, 219, **219**
  mechanical efficiency in, 220–221, **220**
  perpetual motion in, 256
  pulleys, **219,** 224, **224**
  screws, 227, **227**
  wedges, 227, **227**
  wheel and axle, 225, **225**
  work and, 216–217, **217**
maglev trains, 221, **221,** 518, 520
magnesium, 345, 358, **367**
magnesium chloride, **393**
magnesium hydroxide, 426
magnesium oxide, **94, 419**
magnetic field lines, **512**
magnetic fields
  around the Earth, 515–516, **515**
  around electromagnetic waves, 632–633, **632, 633**
  changing domains with, **513**
  field lines, 512, **512**
  induction of current from, 524–526, **524, 525, 526**
  from solenoids, 519–520, **519**
magnetic force, 511, **511**
magnetic levitation trains, 221, **221,** 518, 520
magnetic poles, 510, **510**
  on Earth, 515, **515**
  north and south, 511, **511**
magnetic resonance imaging (MRI), 536
magnetism, 510–517
  cause of, 512–514
  of Earth, 515–516, **515**
  electric current and, 521, **521,** 524, **524**
  labs on, **515,** 530–531
  loss of alignment, 513
  magnetic forces, 511, **511**
  making magnets, 513, **513**
  medical uses, 536
  as physical property, 44
  superconductors and, **486**
magnetite, 510, 514, **514, 516**
magnetrons, **638,** 664
magnets, 510–517, **510**
  cutting, 514, **514**

Earth as, 515–516, **515**
electromagnets, 514, 520, **520**
  in galvanometers, 523
  kinds of, 514
  losing magnetism, 513
  magnetic fields, 512, **512, 513,** 515–516, **515**
  making, 513, **513,** 530–531
  north and south poles, 510–511, **511,** 514–515, **514, 515**
  properties of, 510–511, **510, 511**
  to separate mixtures, **99**
  solenoids as, 519, **519**
malleability, **45, 93, 340,** 376–377
marimbas, **588**
Mars Odyssey, **642**
mass, 25, **25,** 41, **41,** 138, **138**
  acceleration of, 161–162, **161, 162**
  atomic mass unit, 319
  buoyant force and, 190, **190**
  conservation of, 23, 395, **395, 397**
  effect of gravity on, 134, 136, **136**
  inertia and, 43, **43,** 160, **160**
  kinetic energy and, 241
  measurement of, 765
  of subatomic particles, 319
  units of, 25, **25,** 42, 139, **763**
  weight and, 41–42, **41, 42,** 138, **138**
mass numbers, 322, **322,** 449, **449, 768–769**
materials science, 8, **8**
mathematical models, 21
math refresher, 773–776
matter, 6–27, 38–55, **38,** 66–79
  at absolute zero, 306
  characteristic properties of, 51, 76
  chemical change, 52–53, **52**
  chemical properties of, 50–55, **50, 51**
  density of, 45–47, **46, 47**
  effects of gravity on, 134–135, **134**
  effects of radiation on, 451–452, **451**
  energy from, 457 (*see also* atomic energy)
  heat and, 288–291
  inertia, 42–43
  lab on, 56–57
  light interactions with, 652–654, **652, 653, 654**
  mass and, 41–42, **41, 42**
  in motion, 118–139
  particles of, 66, **66**
  physical changes in, 48–49, **48, 49**

physical properties of, 44–45, **45**
states of, 66–69, **66, 67,** 288, **288**
volume and, 38–40, **39, 40**
Maxwell, James Clerk, 537
McKee, Larry, 415
McMillan, Edwin M., 359
means, 773
measurements
  of current, 523
  of electrical energy, 492, **492,** 500–501
  of heat, 291, **291**
  of length, 765, **765**
  of liquid volume, 28–29, 39, **39,** 765
  of mass and weight, 42, **42,** 138, **138,** 765
  of solid volumes, 40, **40**
  tools of, 24, **24**
mechanical advantage, 219, **219**
  in compound machines, 228, **228**
  in inclined planes, 226, **226**
  in levers, **222, 223**
  in pulleys, **224**
  in screws, 227, **227**
  in wedges, 227, **227**
  in wheel and axle, 225, **225**
mechanical efficiency, 220–221, **220**
mechanical energy, 243, **243**
mechanical waves, 575
medium (plural, *media*), 575, **575,** 602, **602**
melanin, 656
Mele, Cheryl, 271
melting, 75, **75**
melting points, 75
  of covalent compounds, 421
  of elements, 91, **91**
  of ionic compounds, 419, **419**
  state changes and, **79**
memory, computer, 557, **557**
Mendeleev, Dmitri, 336, **336, 337, 366**
meniscus, 39, **39**
mercury
  boiling point of, 76
  density of, **47**
  health hazards of, 414
  as liquid at room temperature, 340
  uses of, **346**
mercury(II) oxide, 96, **96**
metallic bonds, 372–377, **375, 376**
metalloids, 92, **92**
  in the periodic table, **768–769**
  properties of, 92, **93,** 341, **341**
metallurgists, 113

Index

metals, 92, **92**
    active, 423
    alkali, 344, **344**
    alkaline-earth, 345, **345**
    alloys, 101, **101**
    bending without breaking, 377,
        377
    as conductors of electric current,
        340, **340**, 376
    effect of radiation on, 452
    electron movement throughout,
        376–377, **376**
    lanthanides and actinides, 346,
        346
    metallic bonds in, 375–377, **376**
    in the periodic table, **339, 342,
        768–769**
    positive ions of, 369, **369**
    properties of, 92, **93**, 340, **340**,
        376–377
    reactivity of, 400, **400**, 423, **423**
    transition, 345–346, **345, 346**
meteorologists, 10, **10**
meteorology, 10, **10**
meters, 25, **25, 763**
metersticks, 765, **765**
metric rulers, 765, **765**
metric system, 763, **763**
microphones, 543, **543, 550**
microprocessors, 555, **555**
microscopes, 679, **679**
microwave ovens, 246, **246**, 638,
    638, 664
microwaves
    in cellular phones, 683, 692
    in the electromagnetic spectrum,
        636, **636**, 638
    microwave ovens, 246, **246**, 638,
        638, 664
    uses of, 638–639, **638, 639**, 683
Millennium Bridge, 176, **176**
Millikan, Robert, 665
milliliters, 39, **763**
mirrors, 668–673
    car, 671, **671**
    concave, 670, **670, 671**
    convex, **670**, 671, **671**
    image formation, 669, **669**
    plane, 669, **669**
    ray diagrams, 668, **669**, 670,
        670, 671
    regular reflection off, 645, **645**
    reversed images in, 668, **668**
mixing, **103**
mixtures, 98–105, **98**
    colloids in, 104, **104**
    compounds compared with, 100,
        100
    properties of, 98–100, **98, 99**
    separating, 98, **99**

solutions as, 100–103, **101, 102,
    103**
suspensions as, 104, **104**
models, scientific, 20, **21**
    conceptual, 21, **21**
    to illustrate theories, 22, **22**
    mathematical, 21
    physical, 20, **20**
    of scientific laws, 23, **23**
    size of, 22
modems, 557
modulation, 637–638
modulators, **550**
molecular photocopying, 444
molecules, 373, **373**
    in covalent compounds, 420,
        420
    diatomic, 374, **374, 390**
    states of matter and, 66, **66**
momentum, 166–169, **166, 167,
    168, 169**
moon
    mining on, 332
    moonlight, **646**
    orbit of, 154, **154**
    weight on the, 41, **134**, 138, **138**
Morse code, 546, **546**, 562–563
Moseley, Henry, 337
motion, 118, **118**, 150–169
    acceleration, 121–123, **122, 123,
        150–151, 151**
    air resistance, 152–153, **152, 153**
    balanced and unbalanced forces,
        126–127, **126, 127**
    circular, 123, **123**, 154
    falling objects, 150–153, **150,
        151**
    fluids and, 192–197
    friction and, 128–133, **128, 129,
        130, 131**
    momentum, 166–169, **166, 167,
        168, 169**
    net force and, 125–126, **125,
        126**
    Newton's first law of, 158–160,
        158, 159
    Newton's second law of, 161–
        162, **161, 162**
    Newton's third law of, 163–164,
        163, 164, 169
    orbiting objects, 153–154, **153,
        154**
    projectile, 155–156, **155, 156**
    reference points in, 118, **118**
    speed of, 119, **119, 120**
    velocity of, 120–121, **121**
    work and, 211, **211**
motors, electric, 522, **522**, 530–531
movable pulleys, 224, **224**

MRI (magnetic resonance imaging),
    536
mummies, DNA analysis of, 444
musical instruments
    brass, 620, **620, 621**
    guitars, 245, 616–617, **616, 617**,
        619
    noise vs. music, 621, **621**
    overtones in, **616**, 618, **618**
    percussion, 620, **620**
    pianos, **618**
    resonance, 616–617, **616, 617**
    sound quality, 618, **618**
    string, 616–617, **616, 617**, 619,
        619
    wind, 620, **620**

N

names
    of covalent compounds, 393,
        393
    of ionic compounds, 393, **393**
    of isotopes, 323
    of negative ions, 370
    prefixes in, 393, **393**
nanobots, 236
nanomachines, 236
natural gas, 258–260, **258, 259,
    260**
navigation, 684, **684**
negative acceleration, 121
negative ions, 370, **370**
neon, **93, 350, 680**
nervous impulses, **495**
net force, 125–126, **125, 126**, 779
networks, computer, 560, **560**
neutralization reactions, 429, **429**
neutrons, 319, **319**
    in beta decay, 450
    in different isotopes, 321, **321**
    in nuclear chain reactions, 457,
        457
Newton, Sir Isaac, 135, **135**, 158
Newton ball, **163**
newtons (N), 124, **124**
    as unit of force, 124, **124**
    as unit of weight, **41**, 42, 139,
        139
Newton's laws of motion, 158–165
    first law, 158–160, **158, 159,
        160**, 777
    labs on, **159, 160**
    second law, 161–162, **161, 162**,
        777
    summary of, 777
    third law, 163–164, **163, 164,
        169, 777**

nickel, **91**
nickel(II) oxide, **419**
nitric acid, 424
nitrogen, 86, 97, **450, 453**
nitrogen group elements, 348, **348**
nitrogen narcosis, 86
Nix, Aundra, 113
noble gases, 341, 350, **350, 366**
noise, 621, **621**
nonlinear relationships, 771
nonmetals, 92, **92**
    negative ions of, 370, **370**
    on the periodic table, **339, 342,**
        768–769
    properties of, 92, **93,** 341, **341**
nonrenewable resources, 258–260,
    258, 259, 260
normal lines, **644**
northern lights, 516, **516**
north pole, in magnets, 511, **511,**
    515, **515**
n-type semiconductors, **541,** 542–
    543, **542, 543**
nuclear chain reactions, 457–458,
    457, 462–463
nuclear energy
    advantages and disadvantages
        of, **262,** 458–459
    chain reactions, 457–458, **457,**
        462–463
    discovery of radioactivity, 448,
        448
    Einstein's equation on, 270
    kinds of radioactive decay, 449–
        450, **449, 450**
    from matter, 457
    nuclear fission, 456–459, **456,**
        457, 458, 459
    nuclear fusion, 246, **246,** 460–
        461, **460, 461**
    nuclear power plants, **458**
    penetrating power of radiation,
        451–452, **451**
    in the sun, 246, **246**
    uses of radioactivity, 454, **454**
nuclear fission, 456, **457**
    advantages and disadvantages
        of, 458–459, **458, 459**
    chain reactions, 457–458, **457,**
        462–463
    electricity from, 246, 260, **260**
    lab on, 459
    of uranium-235, **456**
nuclear fusion, 246, **246,** 460–461,
    460, 461
nuclear power plants, 246, 458–
    459, **458,** 527
nuclear radiation, discovery of, 448
nuclear wastes, 385, 459, **459**
nucleic acids, 436–437, **436, 437**
nucleotides, 436

nucleus
    atomic, 316, **316,** 319, **319**
    energy from, 456–461
nutcrackers, **219,** 252, **252**
Nutrition Facts labels, 290, **290**

O

observation, 13, **13**
oceans, water pressure in, 183, **183**
Ocean Thermal Energy Conversion
    (OTEC), **295**
ocean waves, 575, 579, **579,** 591
Oersted, Hans Christian, 518–519,
    518, 524
Ohm, Georg, **491**
Ohm's law, 490, **491,** 500–501
oil, **99,** 258–260, **258, 259, 260**
Okamoto, Steve, 177, **177**
opaque materials, 653–654, **653,**
    654
optical axis, 670, **670, 671**
optical fibers, 681, **681**
optical illusions, 648, **648**
optical instruments, 678–679, **678,**
    679
orbiting, 153–154, **153, 154**
organic compounds, 432–437, **432,**
    433, 434, 435
oscilloscopes, 610–611, **610, 611,**
    621
OTEC (Ocean Thermal Energy
    Conversion), **295**
outlets, electrical, 485
output, computer, 554, **554**
output devices, 557
overall density, 189, **189**
overtones, **616,** 618, **618**
oxide ions, **370**
oxygen
    density of, **47**
    isotopes, **453**
    negative ions of, 370, **370**
    properties of, 348, **348**
oxygen group elements, 348, **348**

P

paint colors, 545–547, **656, 657**
paper bags vs. plastic bags, 62
parallel circuits, 497, **497,** 500–501
Parasaurolophus, 628
parentheses, in chemical names,
    393
particles
    alpha, 449, **449, 451,** 452
    beta, 450, **450, 451,** 452
    charged, 368

kinetic energy of, 274–275, **274,**
    275
    light as, 596, **663,** 665
    reaction rates and sizes of, 406
    in solution, 101, **101**
    states of matter and, 288, **288**
    in waves, 575, 577, **577**
Pascal, Blaise, 196
pascals, 180, **180**
Pascal's principle, 196, **197,** 778
passive solar heating systems, 294,
    294, 307
PCR (polymerase chain reaction),
    444
penguins, 15, **15**
penicillin, 406
percentages, 774
percussion instruments, 620, **620**
Perez, Pete, 507
periodic, definition of, 337, **337**
periodic law, 337, **337**
periodic table, 336–351, **338–339,**
    768–769
    alkali metals, 344, **344**
    alkaline-earth metals, 345, **345**
    arrangement by Mendeleev,
        336–337, **336, 366**
    boron group elements, 347, **347**
    carbon group elements, 347, **347**
    decoding, 342, **342**
    halogens, 349, **349**
    hydrogen, 350, **350**
    lab on, 352–353
    lanthanides and actinides, 346,
        346, 359
    nitrogen group elements, 348,
        348
    noble gases, 341, 350, **350**
    number of valence electrons
        and, 366, **366**
    oxygen group elements, 348,
        348
    periodic law, 337
    transition metals, 345–346, **345,**
        346
periods, **338,** 342, **342, 768–769**
permanent magnets, 514, **526**
permanent waves, **424**
perpendicular, 577
perpetual motion machines, 256
Petrenko, Victor, 147, **147**
petroleum, 258–260, **258, 259, 260**
pH, 429, **429**
    of blood, **430**
    in the environment, 430, **430**
    indicators, **422,** 423, **423,** 426,
        426
    labs on, **429,** 438–439
pH meters, 430
phonograph records, 548, **548**

Index

phosphoric acid, 424
phosphorus, 348, **348**
photocells, 488, **488**
photographs, 678, **678,** 682, **682**
photons, **633,** 680, **680**
photosynthesis, 97, 250, **250,** 403
pH scale, 429, **429.** *See also* pH
physical changes, 48–49, **48, 49,**
    74, 289. *See also* changes of
    state
physical models, 20, **20**
physical properties, 44, **44**
    during chemical reactions, 388–
        390, **388, 389, 390**
    density as, 45–47, **46, 47**
    examples of, 45, **45**
    lab on, 56–57
    physical changes, 48–49, **48, 49,**
        54, **54**
    shape as, **51**
    texture as, **54**
physical science, 7, **7**
    biology and, 11, **11**
    chemistry, 8, **8**
    geology, 10, **10**
    meteorology, 10, **10**
    physics, 9, **9**
physics, 9, **9**
pianos, **618**
pigments, 388, 656–657, **656, 657**
pitch, of sound, 607, **607**
    lab on, 622–623
    on oscilloscopes, **610**
    overtones and, 619, **619**
    in percussion instruments, **620**
    in string instruments, **619**
    in wind instruments, 620, **620**
pitchblende, 469
plane mirrors, 669, **669**
plants, energy conversions in, 250,
    250. *See also* photosynthesis
plasma (state of matter), 86, 460
plasma display, 552, **552**
plastic bags, 62
plus signs, in equations, **394**
plutonium, 359
polarized light, 682, **682**
pollution, thermal, **9,** 298, **298**
polonium, **453,** 469
polymerase chain reaction (PCR),
    444
polymerases, 444
positive acceleration, 121
positive ions, 369, **369,** 376–377,
    376
positrons, 450
potassium, **344,** 453
potassium bromide, **103**
potassium dichromate, **419**

potential energy, 242, **242**
    elastic, 249, **249**
    gravitational, 242–243, **242,** 265
    of water, 261, **261**
power, 210–215, **214**
    calculating, 214, **214,** 230–231,
        780
    electric, 491, **491**
    increasing, 215
    lab on, 230–231
    units of, 214, **215,** 491
power plants
    electrical, 260, **260,** 527
    hydroelectric, 527, **527**
    managers of, 271
    nuclear, 458–459, **458**
    thermal pollution, 298, **298**
power suits, 176
precipitates, 389, **389**
prefixes
    in chemical names, 393, **393**
    in SI units, 25, **25, 763**
preservatives, 406
pressure, 71, **71,** 180–185, **180,**
    780
    air, 180, **180,** 184–185, **184, 185**
    atmospheric, 77, **180,** 181, **181**
    body responses to, 182
    boiling point and, 77
    breathing and, 184, **184**
    bubbles and, 181, **181**
    buoyant force and, 186, **186**
    calculating, 180, **181,** 780
    fluid flow and, 184–185, **184,**
        185
    fluid speed and, 192, **192**
    gas, 71–72, **71, 72**
    lab on, **184**
    Pascal's principle, 778
    tornadoes and, 185, **185**
    water, 183, **183,** 196
primary colors, 655, **655**
primary pigments, 656, **656, 657**
prisms, 648, **648,** 776
processing, computer, 554, **554**
products, of chemical reactions,
    394, **394**
projectile motion, 155–156, **155,**
    156
propane, **433**
propellers, boat, 13–14, **14, 17**
proportions, 773
proteins, **375,** 435–437, **435, 436**
Proteus, **13, 16,** 17–18, **17**
protons, 319, **319,** 321
p-type semiconductors, **541,** 542–
    543, **542, 543**
pulleys, **219,** 224, **224**
pure substances, 90, **91**

Q

quarks, 333

R

radar, 639, **639**
radiation, 284, **284,** 633, **633.** *See*
    also radioactivity
    Curie's research on, 469
    effects of, 451–452, **451**
    as electromagnetic waves, 633
    greenhouse effect and, 284, **284**
    infrared, 284, **284, 636,** 639,
        639
    irradiated food, 468
    from lasers, 680, **680**
    microwaves, **636,** 638–639, **638,**
        639, 664
    radio waves, **636,** 637–638, **637,**
        638
    thermal, 284, **284**
    ultraviolet light, **637,** 641, **641**
    X rays, **637,** 642, **642**
radiation sickness, 451
radioactive wastes, 385, 459, **459**
radioactivity, 448–455, **449**
    age dating by, 452–453, **452,**
        453
    as alchemy, 322
    alpha particles, 449, **449, 451,**
        452
    bacteria getting energy from,
        468
    beta particles, 450, **450, 451,**
        452
    carbon-14 dating, 452–453, **452**
    conservation in decay, 449
    discovery of, 448, **448**
    gamma decay, 450
    half-lives, 453, **453**
    lab on, **459**
    uses of, 454, **454**
radiometers, 253, **253**
radios
    hearing loss and, 605, **605**
    mechanics of, 550, **550**
    radio stations, 637, **637**
    vacuum tubes in, 545, **545**
radio stations, 637, **637**
radio telescopes, 596
radio waves
    AM and FM, 637
    in cordless telephones, 683, **683**
    in the electromagnetic spectrum,
        636, 637, **637**
    in GPSs, 684, **684**

Index

radium, 449, **449,** 469
radius, 225
radon, **449, 452**
rainbows, **585,** 640, **640,** 648
RAM (random-access memory), 557
ramps, **218,** 226, **226**
rarefaction, 578, **578, 600, 601**
rates of reactions
    catalysts and, 407, **407**
    concentration and, 406, **406,**
      409
    inhibitors and, 406
    labs on, **405,** 408–409
    surface area and, 406, 408–409
    temperature and, 405, **405**
ratios, 773
ray diagrams
    for lenses, 668, **672, 673**
    for mirrors, 668, **669,** 670, **671,**
      672
reactants, 394, **394**
reactivity
    with acids, 423, **423**
    of elements, 400, **400**
    with oxygen, 50, **50, 51,** 91, **91**
    with vinegar, **54**
read-only memory (ROM), 557
real images
    in the eye, **674**
    in lenses, 672, **672,** 686–687
    in mirrors, 670, **671**
records, phonograph, 548, **548**
rectangle, area of a, 776
rectangular solids, **40**
recycling, **347**
red-green color deficiency, 676, **676**
reference points, 118, **118**
reflected beam, **644**
reflecting telescopes, 679, **679**
reflection, 584, **585,** 644, **645**
    law of, 644, **644,** 778
    light sources and, 645, **645**
    in mirrors, 669, **669**
    in optical fibers, 681, **681**
    regular vs. diffuse, 645, **645**
    of sound waves, 612–614, **612,**
      613, 614
    transmission and, 652, **652**
    of water waves, **584**
refracting telescopes, 679, **679**
refraction, 585, **585,** 647–648, **647,**
    648
refrigerators, 297, **297**
remote controls, 540, **540**
renewable resources, 261–262,
    261, 262
resistance, 485–486, **485, 486,**
    490, **490**
resonance, 589, **589,** 616–617, **616,**
    617
resonant frequencies, 589, 616, **616**

resources, energy, 258–263
resultant velocity, 121, **121**
Reynolds, Michael, 307
Riley, Agnes, 569
RNA (ribonucleic acid), 437, **437**
roller coasters, 177, 254, **254**
rolling kinetic friction, 130, **130,** 132
ROM (read-only memory), 557
rust, **51**
Rutherford, Ernest, 315–316, **315,**
    316

S

safety symbols, 27, **27**
safety tips on electric circuits, 498–
    499, **498, 499**
salt (sodium chloride), **369, 371,**
    391
salts, 429, 431, **431**
salt water, as mixture, 100, **101**
satellite navigation, 684, **684**
satellite television, 684
saturated hydrocarbons, 433, **433**
scattering of light, 101, **101,** 646,
    646, 647
Schrödinger, Erwin, 317
science, 6, **7.** See also physical
    science
scientific laws, **22,** 23, 777–779
scientific methods, 12, **12**
    analyzing the results, 17, **17**
    communicating results, 18
    drawing conclusions, 18
    forming hypotheses, 15, **15**
    lab on, **16**
    making predictions, 15
    observation, 13–14, **13, 14**
    summary of steps in, **12,** 766–
      767
    testing hypotheses, 16–17, **16**
scientific notation, 776
screws, 227, **227**
scuba instructors, 205
Seaborg, Glenn T., 359
seaborgium, 359
sea level, atmospheric pressure at,
    182, **182**
secondary colors, 655, **655**
second-class levers, 223, **223**
second law of motion, Newton's,
    161–162, **161, 162**
seeds, effect of gravity on, **135**
Segway™ Human Transporter, 146,
    146
seismic waves, 575, **575**
seismograms, **547**
seismographs, **547**
semiconductors, 541, **541**
    doping, 541, **541**

metalloids as, **93**
n-type, **541,** 542–543, **542, 543**
properties of, 341, **341**
p-type, **541,** 542–543, **542, 543**
series circuits, 496, **496,** 500–501
shadows, 649
shape, as physical property, **51**
shiny, metals as, 92, **93,** 340
ships, buoyancy of, 189–190, **189,**
    190
shocks, electric, 479, 498, **498**
shock waves, 615, **615**
shutters, 678, **678**
sight, 674, **674**
    bionic eyes, 692
    color deficiency, 676, **676**
    how eyes work, 674, **674**
    problems in, 675, **675**
    surgical eye correction, 676, **676**
signals, 546, 547, **547,** 562–563
silicon, 93, 347, 541, **541**
Silly Putty®, 444
silver, **47, 340**
single-displacement reactions, 399,
    399
SI units, 25–26, **25,** 277, **763**
skateboards, **159,** 248, **248**
skis, brakes on, 147
sliding kinetic friction, 130, **130,**
    132
slopes, of graphs, 119, **119,** 771–
    772
snowboard brakes, 147
snow globes, 104, **104**
So, Mimi, 63
soaps, **425**
sodium, 91, **95, 344,** 369, **369**
sodium chlorate, **103**
sodium chloride
    crystal lattice of, **371,** 418
    formation of, 391
    properties of, 95, **95**
    solubility of, **103**
sodium hydroxide, 425–426
sodium nitrate, **103**
soft drinks, **101**
software, computer, 559, **559**
soil erosion, **48,** 131
solar energy, 261, **262,** 263
solar heating systems, 294, **294,**
    307
solar panels, 488
solar winds, 536
solenoids, 519–521, **519, 520, 521**
solids, 67, **67**
    from chemical reactions, 389,
      389
    crystalline and amorphous, 67,
      67
    density of, 46
    as state of matter, 67, 288, **288**

Index

solubility, 102, **102**
   of covalent compounds, 420,
     420
   examples of, 103
   of gases in water, 103
   of ionic compounds, 419
   as physical property, **45**
solutes, 100, **100,** 102, **102**
solutions, 100, **100**
   concentration of, 102–103, **102,**
     103
   examples of, 101, **101**
   particles in, 101, **101**
   rate of dissolution in, 103, **103**
solvents, 100, **100,** 102, **102,** 112
sonar, 583, **583,** 613, **613**
sonic booms, 615, **615**
soot, 347, **347**
sound, 600–621. *See also* sound
    waves
   detecting, 602
   from dinosaurs, 628
   Doppler effect, 608, **608**
   human ears and, **603,** 604
   labs on, **601, 609,** 622–623
   loudness and amplitude, 609–
     610, **609, 610**
   making vs. hearing, 604
   musical instruments, 616–621,
     616, 617, 618, 619, 620
   noise compared with, 621, **621**
   on oscilloscopes, 610–611, **610,**
     611, 621
   overtones, **616,** 618, **618**
   pitch and frequency, 607, **607**
   quality of, 618–621, **618, 619,**
     620, 621
   resonance, 589, **589,** 616–617,
     616, 617
   sonic booms, 615, **615**
   speed of, 606, **606, 607,** 615,
     615
   units of, 610, **610**
   in a vacuum, 602, **602**
   vocal, **602**
sound barrier, 615, **615**
sound energy, 245, **245**
sound engineers, 629
sound quality, 618–621, **618, 619,**
   620, 621
sound waves, 601, **601.** *See also*
    sound
   amplifiers and, 543, **543**
   in CDs, 549, **549**
   compression and rarefaction in,
     600, 601
   Doppler effect, 608, **608**
   echolocation, 613, **613**
   frequency, 607, **607, 610**
   frequency and wavelength rela-
     tionship, 583, **583**

   interference of, 614–616, **614,**
     615
   labs on, **601, 609**
   as longitudinal waves, 578, **578**
   medium for, 575, **575,** 602, **602**
   on oscilloscopes, 610–611, **610,**
     611, 621
   in radios, **550**
   reflection of, 612–614, **612, 613,**
     614
   standing waves, 616, **616**
   telephones and, 547, **547**
   vibrations, 600
southern lights, 516, **516**
south pole, in magnets, 511, **511,**
   515, **515**
space shuttle, 20, **20**
speakers, stereo, **600,** 605
specific heat, **284,** 285–286, **285,**
   286, 300–301
speed, 119, **119**
   average, 119, **120,** 265, 779
   flight and, 194, **194**
   from GPS watch system, 146
   on graphs, 119, **119**
   kinetic energy and, 241
   of light, 270, 634, **634**
   of simple computers, **555**
   of sound, 606, **606, 607**
   supersonic, 615, **615**
   velocity and, 120, **120**
   of a wave, 582–583
Spencer, Percy, 664
SPF (sun protection factor), 641,
   641
spider webs, **436**
springs, longitudinal waves in, 578,
   578
spring scales, **41**
sprites, 506
square, area of a, 776
standing waves, 588, **588, 589,**
   616–617, **616**
stars, nuclear fusion in, **460**
states of matter, 66, **67,** 288, **289.**
   See also changes of state
   changes of state, 74–79, **75, 76,**
     78, 79
   gases, 69, **69**
   of glass, **67**
   liquids, 68, **68**
   models of, **66**
   particle movement in, 66, **66,**
     69, 70
   physical changes, 48–49, **48, 49**
   as physical property, **45**
   plasma, 86
   solids, 67, **67**
static electricity, 474–481, **478**
   electric discharge and, 479–480,
     479, 480

   from electric fields, 633, **633**
static friction, 131, **131**
Statue of Liberty, **52,** 323, **323**
steam engines, 295, **295**
steel, speed of sound in, **606**
step-up/step-down transformers,
   528, **528, 529**
Stevenson, Robert Louis, 112
stimulated emission, 680, **680**
stirrups, in ears, **603**
storage, computer, 554, **554**
"The Strange Case of Dr. Jekyll and
   Mr. Hyde," 112
strike-anywhere matches, **404**
string instruments, 616–617, **616,**
   617, 619, **619**
strong force, **324**
strontium, 358
stylus, 548, **548**
sublimation, 78, **78**
submarines, buoyancy of, 190, **190**
subscripts, 392, 396
sugars, **375,** 434, **434**
sulfur, **54, 93, 341,** 348, **367**
sulfur dioxide, **54**
sulfuric acid, 424
sun
   geomagnetic storms and, 536
   gravitational force of, 137, **137**
   light from, 635, **635**
   nuclear energy in, 246, **246**
   solar heating from, 294, **294,**
     307
sunglasses, polarized, 682
sun protection factor (SPF), 641,
   641
sunscreen, 641, **641**
superconductors, 486, **486**
superglue, 384
surface area, reaction rates and,
   406, 408–409
surface tension, 68, **68**
surface waves, 577, 579, **579**
Surf Chair, 237
suspensions, 104, **104**
swimming, forces in, 15, **15,** 163,
   163
switches, 495, **495,** 544, **544**
synthesis reactions, 398, **398**

T

telegraphs, 546, **546,** 562–563
telephones
   analog signals in, 547, **547**
   cellular, 638, 683, **683,** 692
telescopes, 596, 679, **679,** 693
television
   colors on, **655**
   images on, 551, **551**

television (continued)
  plasma displays, 552, **552**
  radio waves and, 638
  remote controls, 540, **540**
  satellite, 684
tellurium, 341
temperature, 70, **71**, 274–279, **274**
  absolute zero, **276**, 277, 306
  calculating heat, 286, **286**
  changes of state and, 78, **79,**
    80–81, 289
  electrical resistance and, 486,
    486
  gas behavior and, 70, **70**, 72, **73**
  infrared waves and, 639, **639**
  kinetic energy and, 274–275,
    274, 275
  lab on, **275**
  magnetism and, 513
  plasma and, 86
  reaction rates and, 405, **405**
  solubility and, 103
  specific heat and, 285–286, **285,**
    286
  speed of sound and, 606, **606,**
    607
  temperature scales, **26**, 276–277,
    276, 277, 764
  thermal expansion, 276, **276,**
    278–279, **278**
  unit conversions, 277, **764**
temperature scales, **26**, 276–277,
  276, 277, 764
temporary magnets, 514
terminal velocity, 152
theories, scientific, 22, **22**, 364
"There Will Come Soft Rains," 568
thermal conduction, 282, **282**
thermal conductivity
  in metalloids, **93**
  in metals, **93, 340**
  in nonmetals, **341**
  as physical property, **45**
  temperature and, 285, **285**
thermal conductors, **45**, 283, **283**
thermal convection, 283, **283**
thermal energy, 281, **281**
  from all energy conversions,
    249, 256, **256**
  conductors of, **340, 341**
  in electrical energy conversion,
    260, **260**
  from exothermic reactions, **402**
  in food, 249, **249**
  heat as transfer of, 281, **281**
  in water, 244, **244**
thermal expansion, 276, **276**, 278–
  279, **278**
thermal insulators, 283, **283**
thermal pollution, **9**, 298, **298**

thermocouples, 488, **488**
thermometers, 276
thermostats, 278, **278**
third-class levers, 223, **223**
third law of motion, Newton's,
  163–164, **163, 164,** 169
Thomson, J. J., 314, **314**
thrust, 194, **194**, 204
thunderstorms, 479–480, **479, 480,**
  506, **634**
"The Time Machine," 34
time travel, 34
tin, **93**, 347
tinnitus, 604
tires, air pressure in, 180, **180**
Titanic, **183**
titanium, 62, **342, 346**
tons, metric, 25
top quarks, 333
tornadoes, 10, **10**, 185, **185**
total internal reflection, 681
transformers, 528, **528, 529**
transistors, 543–544, **543, 544,** 555
transition metals, 345–346, **345,**
  346
translucent materials, 653–654,
  653, 654
transmission of light, 652, **652, 653**
transmitted waves, 584
transparent materials, 653–654,
  653, 654
transverse waves, 577, **577, 578,**
  581
triangle, area of a, 776
Triantafyllou, Michael, 12–18, **13**
Trieste, **183**
triple-beam balances, **41**, 765
troughs, 577, **577, 578**
trumpets, 620, **620**
tsunamis, 591
tuning forks, **601**, 616, **616**
turbines, 527, **527**
turbulence, 195–196, **196**

U

ultrasonographers, 597
ultrasonography, 597, 614, **614**
ultraviolet light, **637**, 641, **641**
unbalanced forces, 127, **127**, 135
underwater jet engines, 270
units
  cubic, 40, **40**
  of density, 47
  of electric current, 482
  of energy, 240
  of force, **41**, 42, 124
  of frequency, 582, 607

  of household energy use, 492,
    492
  of length, 25, **25**
  of liquid volume, **25**, 39
  of mass, 25, **25**, 42, 139, 319
  of power, 214, **215**, 491
  prefixes, **763**
  of pressure, 180, **180**
  SI conversion table, **763**
  of sound, 610, **610**
  of speed, 119
  of temperature, **25, 26, 276**, 277,
    277
  of volume, **25**, 26, 39, **763**
  of weight, **41**, 42, 139
  of work, 213, 780
universal gravitation, law of, 135,
  136–137, **136, 137,** 777
unsaturated hydrocarbons, 433, **433**
uranium, 260, **260, 453, 458**

V

vacuum, free fall in a, 153, **153**
vacuum tubes, 545, **545**, 555
valence electrons, 365, **365**
  bonding and, 365, 366–367, **367**
  determining number of, **365,**
    366, **366**
  in electron-dot diagrams, 373,
    373
  in metals, 376–377, **376**
van der Waals force, 384
variables, 16, 767, 771
velocity, 120, **120**
  combining velocities, 121, **121**
  of falling objects, 151–152, **151**
  horizontal, 155, **155**
  speed and, 120
  terminal, 152
  vertical, 156, **156**
vertical motion, 156, **156**
Very Large Array (VLA), 596
vibrations, 600, 609, 616
vinyl records, 548, **548**
violins, 616–617, **616, 617,** 619, **619**
viper fish, **183**
virtual images
  in lenses, 672–673, **672, 673**
  in mirrors, 669–671, **671**
viscosity, 68, **68**
visible light, 636, **637**, 640, **640,**
  641
vision
  bionic eyes, 692
  color deficiency, 676, **676**
  how eyes work, 674, **674**
  problems in, 675, **675**

surgical eye correction, 676, **676**
vitamin D, 641
VLA (Very Large Array), 596
vocal sounds, **602**
voltage, 484, **484**
  from electric eels, **485,** 506
  energy and, 484
  measuring, 500–501
  Ohm's law, 490, **490**
  in parallel circuits, 497
  transformers and, 528, **528, 529**
  varying, **484,** 485
voltmeters, 500–501
volume, 26, **26,** 38, **38**
  buoyant force and, 191, **191**
  of cubes, 776
  formulas for, 776
  of a gas, 71–72, **72, 73,** 778
  lab on, 28–29
  of liquids, **25,** 28–29, 39, **39,** 765
  of solids, 40, **40**
  units of, **25,** 26, 39, **763**

W

warm-air heating systems, 293, **293**
water
  boiling point of, 76–77, **78, 79**
  changes of state of, 74, **74, 75, 79**
  covalent bonds in, 373, **373,** 378–379
  density of, **47**
  electrolysis of, **96**
  electron-dot diagram for, **373**
  energy from, 261, **261, 262**
  freezing point of, **764**
  hot-water heating systems, 292, **292**
  light refraction in, 647
  pressure, 183, **183,** 196
  refraction of light in, 647–648, **648**
  specific heat of, **285**
  speed of sound in, **606**
  thermal energy in, 244, **244**
water pressure, 183, **183,** 196
water treatment, **349**
watts (W), 214, **214,** 491
wave equation, 582–583
wavelength, 581, **581**
  diffraction and, 586, **586**
  electromagnetic spectrum, 636, **636–637**
  energy and, 581

frequency and, 583
measuring, 581, **581**
waves, 574–589, **574.** *See also* wavelength
  absorption and scattering, 612, 646, **646, 647, 652**
  amplitude of, 580, **580,** 609, **609**
  diffraction of, 586, **586,** 649, **649**
  electromagnetic, 576, **576**
  frequency of, 582–583, **582** (*see also* frequencies)
  infrared, 284, **284, 636,** 639, **639**
  interference, 587–589, **587, 588,** 650, **650**
  labs on, **581,** 590–591
  longitudinal, 578, **578, 581, 600,** 601
  mechanical, 575, **575**
  microwaves, **636,** 638–639, **638, 639,** 664
  radio, **636,** 637–638, **683**
  reflection of, 584, **585,** 644–645, **644, 645**
  refraction of, 585, **585,** 647–648, **647, 648**
  resonance, 589
  sound, 575, 578, **578,** 601, **601** (*see also* sound waves)
  standing, 588, **588, 589,** 616–617, **616**
  surface, 577, 579, **579**
  transverse, 577, **577, 578, 581**
  ultraviolet, **637,** 641, **641**
  visible light, 636, **637,** 640, **640, 641**
  wave energy, 574–576, **574, 575, 576,** 580–582
  wave speed, 582–583
  work and, 575
  X rays, **637,** 642, **642**
wave speed, 582–583, **582**
weak force, **324**
wearable computers, 568
weather forecasting, 10, 21, **21**
wedges, 227, **227**
weight, 41, **41,** 138, **138**
  from atmospheric pressure, 181
  buoyant force and, 187, **187**
  calculating, **181**
  gravitational potential energy and, 242
  mass and, 41–42, **41, 42,** 138, **138**
  as measure of gravitational force, 138–139, **138, 139,** 153
  on the moon, 41, **134,** 138, **138**

units of, **41,** 42, 139
weighted averages, 323
weightlessness, **153**
Wells, H. G., 34
"Wet Behind the Ears," 204
wet cells, 487, **487**
wheel and axle, 225, **225**
wheelchairs, for beaches, 237
wheels, invention of, **131**
white light, 640, 654, **654**
Williams-Byrd, Julie, 35
wind energy, 261, **261**
wind instruments, 620, **620, 621**
wing shape, 193–194, **193, 194**
wires, **494**
work, 210–228, **210**
  amount of, 212–213, **212, 213**
  calculating, 213, **213,** 780
  energy and, 240, **240**
  examples of, 210, **211,** 231
  force compared with, 210–211, **211**
  force-distance trade-off, 218, **218**
  in the human body, **211**
  by machines, 216–217, **217**
  power and, 214–215, 230–231
  units of, 213, 780
  waves and, 575
  work input/work output, 217–218, **217, 218, 219**
working memory, 557
work input, 217–218, **217, 218, 219**
work output, 217, **217**
World Wide Web, 560
Wright, James, 444
Wright, Orville, **194**

X

X chromosomes, **676**
X rays, **637,** 642, **642**
X-ray technologists, 597

Y

Yeager, Chuck, 606
Yolen, Jane, 628
Young, Thomas, 596

Z

Zavala, Estela, 597
zero, absolute, **276,** 277, 306
zinc, **47,** 91, 423, **423**

Index

Acknowledgments
continued from page ii

Lab Testing

Barry L. Bishop
Science Teacher and Dept. Chair
San Rafael Junior High School
Ferron, Utah

Paul Boyle
Science Teacher
Perry Heights Middle School
Evansville, Indiana

Vicky Farland
Science Teacher and Dept. Chair
Centennial Middle School
Yuma, Arizona

Rebecca Ferguson
Science Teacher
North Ridge Middle School
North Richland Hills, Texas

Laura Fleet
Science Teacher
Alice B. Landrum Middle School
Ponte Verde Beach, Florida

Jennifer Ford
Science Teacher and Dept. Chair
North Ridge Middle School
North Richland Hills, Texas

Susan Gorman
Science Teacher
North Ridge Middle School
North Richland Hills, Texas

C. John Graves
Science Teacher
Monforton Middle School
Bozeman, Montana

Dennis Hanson
Science Teacher and Dept. Chair
Big Bear Middle School
Big Bear Lake, California

Norman E. Holcomb
Science Teacher
Marion Local Schools
Maria Stein, Ohio

Kenneth J. Horn
Science Teacher and Dept. Chair
Fallston Middle School
Fallston, Maryland

Tracy Jahn
Science Teacher
Berkshire Junior-Senior High School
Canaan, New York

Edith C. McAlanis
Science Teacher and Dept. Chair
Socorro Middle School
El Paso, Texas

Kevin McCurdy, Ph.D.
Science Teacher
Elmwood Junior High School
Rogers, Arkansas

Alyson Mike
Science Teacher
East Valley Middle School
East Helena, Montana

Joseph W. Price
Science Teacher and Dept. Chair
H.M. Browne Junior High School
Washington, D.C.

Terry J. Rakes
Science Teacher
Elmwood Junior High School
Rogers, Arkansas

Rodney A. Sandefur
Science Teacher
Naturita Middle School
Naturita, Colorado

Bert J. Sherwood
Science Teacher
Socorro Middle School
El Paso, Texas

Patricia McFarlane Soto
Science Teacher and Dept. Chair
G. W. Carver Middle School
Miami, Florida

David M. Sparks
Science Teacher
Redwater Junior High School
Redwater, Texas

Larry Tackett
Science Teacher and Dept. Chair
R. H. Terrell Junior High School
Washington, D.C.

Elsie N. Waynes
Science Teacher and Dept. Chair
R. H. Terrell Junior High School
Washington, D.C.

Sharon L. Woolf
Science Teacher
Langston Hughes Middle School
Reston, Virginia

Lee Yassinski
Science Teacher
Sun Valley Middle School
Sun Valley, California

John Zambo
Science Teacher
Elizabeth Ustach Middle School
Modesto, California

Teacher Reviewers

Diedre S. Adams
Physical Science Instructor
Science Department
West Vigo Middle School
West Terre Haute, Indiana

Trisha Elliott
Science and Mathematics Teacher
Chain of Lakes Middle School
Orlando, Florida

Liza M. Guasp
Science Teacher
Celebration K–8 School
Celebration, Florida

Ronald W. Hudson
Science Teacher
Batchelor Middle School
Bloomington, Indiana

Denise Hulette
Teacher
Conway Middle School
Orlando, Florida

Tiffany Kracht
Science Teacher
Chain of Lakes Middle School
Orlando, Florida

Stacy Loeak
Science Teacher and Department Chair
Baker Middle School
Columbus, Georgia

Bill Martin
Science Teacher
Southeast Middle School
Kernersville, North Carolina

Maureen Martin
Science Teacher
Jackson Creek Middle School
Bloomington, Indiana

Thomas Lee Reed
Science Teacher
Rising Starr Middle School
Fayetteville, Georgia

Shannon Ripple
Science Teacher
Science Department
Canyon Vista Middle School
Round Rock, Texas

Mark Schnably
Science Instructor
Jefferson Middle School
Winston-Salem, North Carolina

Martha Tedrow
Science Teacher
Thomas Jefferson Middle School
Winston-Salem, North Carolina

Martha B. Trisler
Science Teacher
Rising Starr Middle School
Fayetteville, Georgia

Sherrye Valenti
Curriculum Leader
Science Department
Wildwood Middle School, Rockwood School District
Wildwood, Missouri

Louise Whealton
Science Teacher
Wiley Middle School
Winston-Salem, North Carolina

Roberta Young
Science Teacher
Gunn Junior High School
Arlington, Texas

Lab Development

Phillip G. Bunce
Former Physics Teacher
Austin, Texas

Kenneth E. Creese
Science Teacher
White Mountain Junior High School
Rock Springs, Wyoming

William G. Lamb, Ph.D.
Winningstad Chair in the Physical Sciences
Oregon Episcopal School
Portland, Oregon

Alyson Mike
Science Teacher
East Valley Middle School
East Helena, Montana

Joseph W. Price
Science Teacher and
Department Chair
Science and Math Instructor
for Pre-College Program
H. M. Browne Junior High
School
Howard University
Washington, D.C.

Denice Lee Sandefur
Science Chairperson
Nucla High School
Nucla, Colorado

John Spadafino
Mathematics and Physics
Teacher
Hackensack High School
Hackensack, New Jersey

Walter Woolbaugh
Science Teacher
Manhattan Junior
High School
Manhattan, Montana

Feature Development
Katy Z. Allen
Hatim Belyamani
John A. Benner
David Bradford
Jennifer Childers
Mickey Coakley
Susan Feldkamp
Jane Gardner
Erik Hahn
Christopher Hess
Deena Kalai

Charlotte W. Luongo, MSc
Michael May
Persis Mehta, Ph.D.
Eileen Nehme, MPH
Catherine Podeszwa
Dennis Rathnaw
Daniel B. Sharp
John M. Stokes
April Smith West
Molly F. Wetterschneider

Answer Checking
John A. Benner
Austin, Texas

Staff Credits

Editorial
Robert Todd, *Vice President,*
Editorial Science
Debbie Starr,
Managing Editor
Laura Zapanta,
Senior Editor

Editorial Development Team
Amy Fry
Michael Mazza
Micah Newman
Laura Prescott
Dyanne Semerjibashian
Ann Welch

Copyeditors
Dawn Marie Spinozza,
Copyediting Manager
Anne-Marie De Witt
Jane A. Kirschman
Kira J. Watkins

Editorial Support Staff
Mary Anderson
Suzanne Krejci
Shannon Oehler

Online Products
Bob Tucek,
Executive Editor
Wesley M. Bain

Design
Book Design
Kay Selke,
Director of Book Design
Sonya Mendeke, *Designer*
Lisa Woods, *Designer*
Holly Whittaker, *Project*
Administrator

Media Design
Richard Metzger,
Design Director
Chris Smith,
Senior Designer

Image Acquisitions
Curtis Riker, *Director*
Jeannie Taylor,
Photo Research Manager
Diana Goetting,
Senior Photo Researcher
Elaine Tate,
Art Buyer Supervisor
Angela Boehm,
Senior Art Buyer

Design New Media
Ed Blake, *Director*
Kimberly Cammerata, *Design*
Manager
Michael Rinella,
Senior Designer

Cover Design
Bill Smith Studio

Publishing Services
Carol Martin, *Director*

Graphic Services
Bruce Bond, *Director*
Jeff Bowers, *Graphic Services*
Manager
Cathy Murphy, *Senior*
Graphics Specialist
JoAnn Stringer, *Senior*
Graphics Specialist II
Nanda Patel,
Graphics Specialist
Katrina Gnader,
Graphics Specialist

Technology Services
Laura Likon, *Director*
Juan Baquera, *Technology*
Services Manager
Lana Kaupp,
Senior Technology Services
Analyst
Margaret Sanchez, *Senior*
Technology Services Analyst
Sarah Buller, *Technology*
Services Analyst
Patty Zepeda, *Technology*
Services Analyst
Jeff Robinson, *Ancillary*
Design Manager

New Media
Armin Gutzmer, *Director*
Melanie Baccus,
New Media Coordinator

Lydia Doty,
Senior Project Manager
Cathy Kuhles, *Technical*
Assistant
Marsh Flournoy, *Quality*
Assurance Analyst
Tara F. Ross, *Senior Project*
Manager

Production
Eddie Dawson,
Production Manager
Sherry Sprague, *Senior*
Production Coordinator
Suzanne Brooks, *Production*
Coordinator

Teacher Edition
Alicia Sullivan
David Hernandez
April Litz

Manufacturing and Inventory
Ivania Quant Lee
Wilonda Ieans

Ancillary Development and Production
General Learning
Communications,
Northbrook, Illinois

Credits

PHOTOGRAPHY

Front Cover (tl), Corbis; (tr), Creatas/PictureQuest; (br), Douglas E. Walker/Masterfile; (bl), Leroy Grannis/Getty Images; (owl), Kim Taylor/Bruce Coleman

Skills Practice Lab Teens Sam Dudgeon/HRW

Connection to Astrology Corbis Images; **Connection to Biology** David M. Phillips/Visuals Unlimited; **Connection to Chemistry** Digital Image copyright © 2005 PhotoDisc; **Connection to Environment** Digital Image copyright © 2005 PhotoDisc; **Connection to Geology** Letraset Phototone; **Connection to Language Arts** Digital Image copyright © 2005 PhotoDisc; **Connection to Meteorology** Digital Image copyright © 2005 PhotoDisc; **Connection to Oceanography** © ICONOTEC; **Connection to Physics** Digital Image copyright © 2005 PhotoDisc

Table of Contents iii (tr), Sam Dudgeon/HRW; iii (br), © Lawrence Livermore National Laboratory/Photo Researchers, Inc.; iv (cl), Peter Van Steen/HRW; iv (bl), Richard Megna/Fundamental Photographs; v (bl), Victoria Smith/HRW; v (tl), © Royalty-free/CORBIS; vi (tl), age fotostock/Fabio Cardoso; vi (bl), NASA; vii (tl), Larry L. Miller/Photo Researchers, Inc.; vii (cl), Sam Dudgeon/HRW; vii (bl), © Galen Rowell/CORBIS; viii (tl), CORBIS Images/HRW; viii (bl), John Langford/HRW; ix (bl), Victoria Smith/HRW; ix (tl), Corbis Images; x (bl), Victoria Smith/HRW; x (tl), © Konrad Wothe/Minden Pictures; xi (tl), ©Bob Thomason/Getty Images; xii (tl), John Langford/HRW; xii (bl), Gamma Photo/Central Scientific Company; xiii (tl), © Reuters NewMedia Inc./CORBIS; xiii (b), Pete Saloutos/The Stock Market; xiv (cl), Sam Dudgeon/HRW; xiv (b), ©Cameron Davidson/Getty Images; xv (tl), ©Digital Vision Ltd.; xvi (bl), Peter Van Steen/HRW ; xvi (tr), Richard Megna/Fundamental Photographs; xvi-xvii (b), Peter Van Steen/HRW ; xvii (br), Sam Dudgeon/HRW; xviii-xxii (all), Sam Dudgeon/HRW; xxvi (bl), Sam Dudgeon/HRW; xxvii (tl), John Langford/HRW; xxvii (b), Sam Dudgeon/HRW; xxviii (tl), Victoria Smith/HRW; xxviii (bl), Stephanie Morris/HRW; xxviii (br), Sam Dudgeon/HRW; xxix (tl), Patti Murray/Animals, Animals; xxix (tr), Jana Birchum/HRW; xxix (b), Peter Van Steen/HRW

Unit One 2 (t), Corbis-Bettmann; 2 (bl), Enrico Tedeschi; 2 (c), UPI/CORBIS/Bettman; 3 (cr), Getty Images; 3 (cl), Sam Dudgeon/HRW; 3 (tr), Brown Brothers/HRW Photo Library; 3 (bl), ©Natalie Fobes/Getty Images; 3 (br), REUTERS/Charles W. Luzier/NewsCom

Chapter One 4-5 (all), © Kevin Schafer/Getty Images; 6 (bl), Peter Van Steen/HRW; 7 (tl), © Jeff Hunter/Getty Images; 7 (br), Roy Ooms/Masterfile; 8 (bl), © Lawrence Livermore National Laboratory/Photo Researchers, Inc.; 9 (tl), © Gunnar Kullenberg/Stock Connection/PNI; 10 (tl), Howard B. Bluestein; 10 (bc, br), Andy Christiansen/HRW; 11 (tr), John Langford/HRW; 13 (br), Stephen Maclone/HRW; 13 (bl), Barry Chin/Boston Globe; 16 (b), Donna Coveney/MIT News; 20 (cl), Digital Image copyright © 2005 PhotoDisc; 20 (bl), Peter Van Steen/HRW; 21 (bl), © JULIAN BAUM/Photo Researchers, Inc.; 22 (tl), Victoria Smith/HRW; 23 (all), Victoria Smith/HRW; 24 (all), Victoria Smith/HRW; 28 (bc), Sam Dudgeon/HRW; 29 (bl), Digital Image copyright © 2005 PhotoDisc; 30 (bl), Sam Dudgeon/HRW; 30 (tl), Victoria Smith/HRW; 31 (c), John Langford/HRW; 31 (cr), Victoria Smith/HRW; 34 (tr), © Layne Kennedy/CORBIS; 35 (all), Louis Fronkier/Art Louis Photographics/HRW

Chapter Two 36-37 (all), Mark Renders/Getty Images; 38 (b), Sam Dudgeon/HRW; 38 (bc), Digital Image copyright © 2005 PhotoDisc; 39 (cr), Sam Dudgeon/HRW; 40 (cl), Sam Dudgeon/HRW; 40 (cl), Victoria Smith/HRW; 41 (all), Sam Dudgeon/HRW; 42 (tl), John Langford/HRW; 42 (br), Corbis Images; 44 (b), Sam Dudgeon/HRW; 45 (tl), Victoria Smith/HRW; 45 (tr, tc, c), Sam Dudgeon/HRW; 45 (cr, bl), John Morrison/Morrison Photography; 46 (tl), Richard Megna/Fundamental Photographs; 46 (bl), Victoria Smith/HRW; 48 (tr), Lance Schriner/HRW; 48 (tl), John Langford/HRW; 49 (tl), Victoria Smith/HRW; 49 (inset), Sam Dudgeon/HRW; 50 (br), Rob Boudreau/Getty Images; 51 (cl, cr), Charlie Winters/HRW; 51 (tl, tr), Sam Dudgeon/HRW; 52 (c, cr), Morrison Photography; 52 (bl), Joseph Drivas/Getty Images; 52 (br), © SuperStock; 53 (all), Sam Dudgeon/HRW; 54 (all), Charlie Winters/HRW; 55 (tr), CORBIS Images/HRW; 56 (b), Sam Dudgeon/HRW; 58 (bc), Richard Megna/Fundamental Photographs; 59 (cr), Lance Schriner/HRW; 62 (tl), © David Young-Wolff/PhotoEdit; 63 (cr), Courtesy Mimi So; 63 (b), Steve Cole/PhotoDisc/PictureQuest

Chapter Three 64-65 (all), Teresa Nouri Rishel/Dale Chihuly Studio; 67 (bl), Digital Image copyright © 2005 PhotoDisc; 67 (br), Susumu Nishinaga/Science Photo Library/Photo Researchers, Inc.; 68 (tr), Victoria Smith/HRW; 68 (bl), © Dr Jeremy Burgess/Photo Researchers, Inc.; 69 (tr), Scott Van Osdol/HRW; 70 (br), AP Photo/Beth Keiser; 71 (bl), Corbis Images; 71 (br), Victoria Smith/HRW; 75 (bc), Scott Van Osdol/HRW; 75 (tr), Richard Megna/Fundamental Photographs, 77 (bl), Ed Reschke/Peter Arnold, Inc.; 78 (tl), Omni Photo Communications, Inc./Index Stock Imagery, 80 (br), Victoria Smith/HRW; 81 (br), Sam Dudgeon/HRW; 82 (bc), Sam Dudgeon/HRW; 83 (bl), Charles D. Winters/Photo Researchers, Inc.; 86 (tr), CORBIS Images/HRW; 86 (tl), Scoones/SIPA Press; 87 (cr), Susanna Frohman/San Jose Mercury News/NewsCom; 87 (bl), Andrew Goldsworthy

Chapter Four 88-89 (all), Scott Van Osdol/HRW; 90 (br), Jonathan Blair/Woodfin Camp & Associates, Inc.; 90 (bl), Victoria Smith/HRW; 91 (br), Russ Lappa/Photo Researchers, Inc.; 91 (bl, bc), Charles D. Winters/Photo Researchers, Inc.; 92 (tl), © Zack Burris/Zack Burris, Inc.; 92 (tcl), Yann Arthus-Bertrand/CORBIS; 92 (tcr, tr), Walter Chandoha; 93 (lead), Victoria Smith/HRW; 93 (copper, tin, sulfur), Sam Dudgeon/HRW; 93 (neon), Runk/Shoenberger/Grant Heilman Photography Inc.; 93 (silicon), Joyce Photographics/Photo Researchers, Inc.; 93 (boron), Russ Lappa/Photo Researchers, Inc.; 93 (antimony), Charles D. Winters/Photo Researchers, Inc.; 93 (iodine), Larry Stepanowicz; 94 (bl), Runk/Schoenberger/Grant Heilman Photography Inc.; 95 (bl), Runk/Shoenberger/Grant Heilman Photography; 95 (br), Sam Dudgeon/HRW; 96 (tl), Richard Megna/Fundamental Photographs; 97 (tr), John Kaprielian/Photo Researchers, Inc.; 98 (tr), Sam Dudgeon/HRW; 99 (tl), Charles D. Winters; 99 (cl), Sam Dudgeon/HRW; 99 (bc), Charles D. Winters/Photo Researchers, Inc.; 99 (bl), Klaus Guldbrandsen/Science Photo Library/Photo Researchers, Inc.; 99 (tr, cr, br), John Langford/HRW; 100 (tl), Sam Dudgeon/HRW; 101 (bl), Richard Haynes/HRW; 102 (tr), Sam Dudgeon/HRW; 103 (all), John Langford/HRW; 104 (bl), HRW; 104 (br), Lance Schriner/HRW; 105 (tr), Sam Dudgeon/HRW; 106 (bl), © Stuart Westmoreland/Getty Images; 107 (bl), Sam Dudgeon/HRW; 108 (tr), Sam Dudgeon/HRW; 108 (tl), Walter Chandoha; 109 (tr), Sam Dudgeon/HRW; 112 (tl), Peter Van Steen/HRW; 113 (tr), Courtesy of Aundra Nix; 113 (cr), Astrid & Hans-Frieder Michler/SPL/Photo Researchers, Inc.

Unit Two 114 (c), W.A. Mozart at the age of 7: oil on canvas, 1763, by P.A. Lorenzoni/The Granger Collection; 114 (bl), Photo Researchers, Inc.; 114 (t), © SPL/Photo Researchers, Inc.; 115 (tc), The Vittoria, colored line engraving, 16th century/The Granger Collection; 115 (tr), Stock Montage, Inc.; 115 (cl), Getty Images; 115 (cr), Underwood & Underwood/Corbis-Bettmann; 115 (br), © AFP/CORBIS

Chapter Five 116-117 (all), © AFP/CORBIS; 118 (all), © SuperStock; 120 (bl), Robert Ginn/PhotoEdit; 122 (t), Sergio Purtell/Foca; 123 (tr), Digital Image copyright © 2005 PhotoDisc; 124 (b), Michelle Bridwell/HRW; 125 (b), Michelle Bridwell/HRW; 125 (tr), © Roger Ressmeyer/CORBIS; 126 (r), Daniel Schaefer/HRW; 126 (bl), Sam Dudgeon/HRW; 127 (tr), age fotostock/Fabio Cardoso; 130 (bl, br), Michelle Bridwell/HRW; 130 (inset), Stephanie Morris/HRW; 132 (br), © Annie Griffiths Belt/CORBIS; 133 (tr), Sam Dudgeon/HRW; 133 (cr), Victoria Smith/HRW; 134 (br), NASA; 139 (tr), Digital Image copyright © 2005 PhotoDisc; 140 (bl), Sam Dudgeon/HRW; 141 (br), Sam Dudgeon/HRW; 142 (br), © Roger Ressmeyer/CORBIS; 142 (tl), Digital Image copyright © 2005 PhotoDisc 143 (br), Sam Dudgeon/HRW; 146 (tl, c), Sam Dudgeon/HRW; 146 (tr), Justin Sullivan/Getty Images; 147 (bl), Allsport Concepts/Getty Images; 147 (cr), Courtesy Dartmouth University

Chapter Six 148-149 (all), NASA; 149 (br), NASA; 150 (bl), Richard Megna/Fundamental Photographs; 152 (cl), Toby Rankin/Masterfile; 153 (tr), James Sugar/Black Star; 153 (bl), NASA; 155 (bl), Michelle Bridwell/Frontera Fotos; 155 (br), Image copyright © 2005 PhotoDisc, Inc.; 156 (tc), Richard Megna/Fundamental Photographs; 157 (tr), Toby Rankin/Masterfile; 158 (b), John Langford/HRW; 160 (br), Mavournea Hay/HRW; 160 (bc), Michelle Bridwell/Frontera Fotos; 161 (bl), Victoria Smith/HRW; 162 (all), Image copyright © 2005 PhotoDisc, Inc.; 163 (b), David Madison; 164 (tc), Gerard Lacz/Animals Animals/Earth Scenes; 164 (tr), Sam Dudgeon/HRW; 164 (tr), Image copyright © 2005 PhotoDisc, Inc.; 164 (tr), NASA; 165 (br), Lance Schriner/HRW; 165 (tr), Victoria Smith/HRW; 167 (all), Michelle Bridwell/HRW; 168 (br), Zigy Kaluzny/Getty Images; 168 (bl), © SuperStock; 169 (cl), Michelle Bridwell/HRW; 170 (bl), Image ©2001 PhotoDisc, Inc.; 171 (all), Sam Dudgeon/HRW; 172 (tc), Gerard Lacz/Animals Animals/Earth Scenes; 173 (all), Sam Dudgeon/HRW; 176 (tl), AP Photo/Martyn Hayhow; 176 (tr), Junko Kimura/Getty Images/NewsCom; 177 (tr), Steve Okamoto; 177 (br), Lee Schwabe

Chapter Seven 178-179 (all), © Nicholas Pinturas/Getty Images; 182 (tl), © I.M. House/Getty Images; 182 (tcl), David R. Frazier Photolibrary; 182 (cl), Dieter and Mary Plage/Bruce Coleman, Inc.; 182 (bcl), Wolfgang Kaehler/CORBIS; 182 (bl), © Martin Barraud/Getty Images; 183 (tr), © SuperStock; 183 (tcr), Daniel A. Nord; 183 (cr), © Ken Marschall/Madison Press Books; 183 (bcr), Dr. Paul A. Zahl/Photo Researchers, Inc.; 183 (br), CORBIS/Bettman; 185 (tr), © Charles Doswell III/Getty Images; 188 (tl), Bruno P. Zehnder/Peter Arnold, Inc.; 192 (br), Richard Megna/Fundamental Photographs/HRW Photo; 194 (tl), Larry L. Miller/Photo Researchers, Inc.; 194 (tr), Richard Neville/Check Six; 196 (tr), John Neubauer/PhotoEdit; 197 (br), Check Six; 199 (b), Sam Dudgeon/HRW; 200 (tr), © SuperStock; 204 (tc), © Victor Malafronte; 204 (tl), Sam Dudgeon/HRW; 205 (bl), Corbis Images; 205 (tr), Courtesy of Alisha Bracken

Unit Three 206 (t), The Granger Collection, New York; 206 (c), Corbis-Bettmann; 206 (br), Conley Photography, Inc./American Solar Energy Society; 207 (tr), Phil Degginger/Color-Pic, Inc.; 207 (cl), Robert Wolf/HRW; 207 (c), The Granger Collection, New York; 207 (c), David Madison; 207 (br), Courtesy of DEKA Research and Development/PRNewsFoto/NewsCom

Chapter Eight 208-209 (all), age fotostock/Photographer, Year; 210 (bl), John Langford/HRW; 211 (all), John Langford/HRW; 212 (all), © Galen Rowell/CORBIS; 213 (all), Sam Dudgeon/HRW; 214 (all), John Langford/HRW; 216 (cr), Scott Van Osdol/HRW; 216 (br), Robert Wolf/HRW; 216 (bc), Digital Image copyright © 2005 Artville; 217 (br), Sam Dudgeon/HRW; 218 (all), Scott Van Osdol/HRW; 219 (tr, cr), Sam Dudgeon/HRW; 219 (tl), John Langford/HRW; 220 (br), CC Studio/Science Photo Library/Photo Researchers, Inc.; 221 (tr), © Reuters NewMedia Inc./CORBIS; 222 (all), Robert Wolf/HRW; 223 (tr), Robert Wolf/HRW; 223 (br), Scott Van Osdol/HRW; 223 (bc), Sam Dudgeon/HRW; 223 (tc), Robert Wolf/HRW; 225 (tr), Robert Wolf/HRW; 226 (tr), Lisa Davis/HRW; 227 (tl, cr), Sam Dudgeon/HRW; 227 (br), Peter Van Steen/HRW ; 228 (b), Robert Wolf/HRW; 229 (tr), Robert Wolf/HRW; 229 (br), John Langford/HRW; 230 (bl), Stephanie Morris/HRW; 230 (br), Paul Dance/Getty Images; 232 (tl), John Langford/HRW; 233 (cl), Helmut Gritscher/Peter Arnold, Inc.; 233 (tr), Robert Wolf/HRW; 233 (cr), John Langford/HRW; 233 (br), Stephanie Morris/HRW; 236 (tr), © Visuals Unlimited; 236 (tl), Wayne Sorce; 237 (cr), A.W. Stegmeyer/Upstream; 237 (bl), Digital Image copyright © 2005 PhotoDisc

Chapter Nine 238-239 (all), © AFP/CORBIS; 240 (br), Tim Kiusalaas/Masterfile; 241 (cr), Sam Dudgeon/HRW; 242 (tl), Earl Kowall/CORBIS; 243 (br), Sam Dudgeon/HRW; 244 (tl), John Langford/HRW; 244 (tc), Corbis Images; 244 (tr), David Phillips/HRW; 245 (br), Sam Dudgeon/HRW; 245 (cr), Peter Van Steen/HRW; 246 (tr), John Langford/HRW; 246 (bl), NASA; 247 (cr), Peter Van Steen/HRW; 248 (br), © Duomo/CORBIS; 249 (bl, br), John Langford/HRW; 249 (tr), Peter Van Steen/HRW; 252 (all), John Langford/HRW; 253 (tr), © Martin Bond/Photo Researchers, Inc.; 256 (bl), Sam Dudgeon/HRW; 257 (all), Courtesy of Honda; 259 (tl), Robert Brook/Photo Researchers, Inc.; 259 (cl), Sam Dudgeon/HRW; 259 (bl), John Langford/HRW; 260 (bl), D.O.E./Science Source/Photo Researchers, Inc.; 261 (tr), © John D. Cunningham/Visuals Unlimited; 261 (b), CORBIS Images/HRW; 262 (tl), Digital Image copyright © 2005 PhotoDisc; 266 (tl), Courtesy of Honda; 266 (bc), Digital Image copyright © 2005 PhotoDisc; 267 (bl), Mike Powell/Allsport/Getty Images; 270 (bl), Courtesy Pursuit Dynamics; 270 (tr), © Bettman/CORBIS; 271 (all), Robert Wolf/HRW

Chapter Ten 272-273 (all), © Vandystadt/Allsport/Getty Images; 275 (br), John Langford/HRW; 277 (tr), Michelle Bridwell/HRW; 278 (tl), Mark Burnett/Photo Researchers, Inc.; 279 (tr), AP Photo/Joe Giblin; 280 (tl), Sam Dudgeon/HRW; 281 (all), John Langford/HRW; 282 (b), John Langford/HRW; 284 (cl), John Langford/HRW; 285 (tr), Sam Dudgeon/HRW; 286 (tl), John Langford/HRW; 287 (cr), © Simon Watson/FoodPix/Getty Images; 288 (bc), Sam Dudgeon/HRW; 289 (all), John Langford/HRW; 290 (cl), John Langford/HRW; 290 (tr), Peter Van Steen/HRW; 293 (br), John Langford/HRW; 296 (tl), Dorling Kindersley Ltd.; 296 (bl), © COMSTOCK; 299 (tr), John Langford/HRW; 301 (br), Victoria Smith/HRW; 302 (tl), John Langford/HRW; 303 (bl), AP Photo/Joe Giblin; 306 (tl), Dan Winters/Discover Magazine; 307 (b), Solar Survival Architecture; 307 (tr), Singeli Agnew/Taos News

Unit Four 308 (t), The Granger Collection, New York; 308 (bl), Science VU/© IBM/Visuals Unlimited; 308 (cr), © SCIENCE PHOTO LIBRARY/Photo Researchers, Inc.; 309 (tl), SuperStock; 309 (cr), REUTERS/Mark Cardwell/Hulton Archive/Getty Images; 309 (bl), B. Bisson/Sygma; 309 (br), AP Photo/ The Albuquerque Tribune, KayLynn Deveney

Chapter Eleven 310-311 (all), P. Loiez Cern/Science Photo Library/Photo Researchers, Inc.; 312 (bl), Victoria Smith/HRW; 313 (b), Corbis-Bettmann; 316 (br), John Zoiner; 316 (bl), Mavournea Hay/HRW; 318 (b), Sam Dudgeon/HRW; 323 (tr), Corbis Images; 325 (b), Sam Dudgeon/HRW; 326 (br), Victoria Smith/HRW; 327 (br), Sam Dudgeon/HRW; 328 (bl), Corbis-Bettmann; 329 (bl), Fermilab; 332 (tr), NASA; 332 (tl), Giraudon/Art Resource, NY; 333 (br), Fermi National Accelerator Laboratory/CORBIS; 333 (tr), Stephen Maclone

Chapter Twelve 334-335 (all), Gerard Perrone/Courtesy of Eric Ehlenberger; 337 (tr), Sam Dudgeon/HRW; 340 (all), Sam Dudgeon/HRW; 341 (tr), Sam Dudgeon/HRW; 341 (tc), Richard Megna/Fundamental Photographs; 341 (bl), Russ Lappa/Photo Researchers, Inc.; 341 (bc), Lester V. Bergman/Corbis-Bettmann; 341 (tl), Sally Anderson-Bruce/HRW; 342 (bc, br), Richard Megna/Fundamental Photographs; 342 (bl), Tom Pantages Photography; 343 (br), HRW; 343 (tr), Sam Dudgeon/HRW; 344 (bl), Charles D. Winters/Photo Researchers, Inc.; 344 (bc, br), Richard Megna/Fundamental Photographs; 345 (tr), Sam Dudgeon/HRW; 346 (tl, cl), Sam Dudgeon/HRW; 346 (tr), ©1990 P. Petersen/Custom Medical Stock Photo; 346 (tc, bl), Victoria Smith/HRW; 347 (tr), Phillip Hayson/Photo Researchers, Inc.; 347 (br), Sam Dudgeon/HRW; 348 (tl), Sam Dudgeon/HRW; 348 (b), CORBIS Images/HRW; 349 (tl, tc), Richard Megna/Fundamental Photographs; 349 (tr), Charlie Winters/HRW; 350 (bl), NASA; 350 (tl), © Jeff Greenberg/Visuals Unlimited ; 351 (tr), Sam Dudgeon/HRW; 352 (b), Sam Dudgeon/HRW; 353 (br), John Langford/HRW; 354 (tl), Sam Dudgeon/HRW; 358 (tr), CORBIS Images/HRW; 359 (cr), © Lawrence Berkeley National Laboratory/Photo Researchers, Inc.; 359 (cl), © Bettmann/CORBIS

Unit Five 360 (c), Argonne National Laboratory/Corbis-Bettmann; 360 (b), Wally McNamee/Corbis; 361 (tr), Sygma; 361 (bl), Reuters/Nasa/Hulton Archive/Getty Images; 361 (c), Archive France/Hulton Archive/Getty Images; 361 (br), General Motors Corporation. Used with permission, GM Media Archives.

Chapter Thirteen 362-363 (all), © Doug Struthers/Getty Images; 364 (bl), © Charles Gupton/CORBIS; 368 (br), © Konrad Wothe/Minden Pictures; 371 (cl), Paul Silverman/Fundamental Photographs; 374 (tr), Sam Dudgeon/HRW; 375 (tc), Sam Dudgeon/HRW; 375 (bl), © Jonathan Blair/CORBIS; 376 (tr), Victoria Smith/HRW; 377 (tr), John Langford/HRW; 379 (b), Sam Dudgeon/HRW; 380 (br), Victoria Smith/HRW; 381 (cr, br), Sam Dudgeon/HRW; 381 (tc), © Konrad Wothe/Minden Pictures; 384 (tr), Peter Oxford/Nature Picture Library; 384 (tl), Diaphor Agency/Index Stock Imagery, Inc.; 385 (cr), Steve Fischbach/HRW; 385 (bl), W. & D. McIntyre/Photo Researchers, Inc.

Chapter Fourteen 386-387 (all), Corbis Images; 388 (bl), Rob Matheson/The Stock Market; 388 (br), Sam Dudgeon/HRW; 389 (cl, cr), Richard Megna/Fundamental Photographs, New York; 389 (br), Scott Van Osdol/HRW; 389 (bl), J.T. Wright/Bruce Coleman Inc./Picture Quest; 390 (all), Charlie Winters; 391 (br), Charlie Winters/HRW; 394 (tl), John Langford/HRW; 394 (bl), Richard Haynes/HRW; 395 (tr), Charles D. Winters/Photo Researchers, Inc.; 395 (tc), John Langford/HRW; 395 (tl), © Ingram Publishing; 400 (tl), Peticolas/Megna/Fundamental Photographs; 400 (tr), Richard Megna/Fundamental Photographs; 402 (tl), Victoria Smith/HRW; 402 (bc), Peter Van Steen/HRW; 402 (br), © Tom Stewart/The Stock Market; 403 (br), © David Stoecklein/CORBIS; 404 (t), Michael Newman/PhotoEdit; 405 (cr), Richard Megna/Fundamental Photographs; 406 (t), Sam Dudgeon/HRW; 407 (tr), Dorling Kindersley Limited courtesy of the Science Museum, London/CORBIS; 407 (bl), Victoria Smith/HRW; 408 (b), Victoria Smith/HRW; 410 (tr), Richard Megna/Fundamental Photographs; 411 (cr), Richard Megna/Fundamental Photographs; 411 (br), Rob Matheson/The Stock Market; 414 (tr), Tony Freeman/PhotoEdit; 414 (tl), Henry Bargas/Amarillo Globe-News/AP/Wide World Photos; 415 (all), Bob Parker/Austin Fire Investigation

Chapter Fifteen 416-417 (all), © Dr. Dennis Kunkel/Visuals Unlimited; 418 (bl), © Andrew Syred/Getty Images; 419 (all), Richard Megna/Fundamental Photographs; 420 (b), Victoria Smith/HRW; 421 (tr), Richard Megna/Fundamental Photographs; 422 (br), Jack Newkirk/HRW; 423 (br), Charles D. Winters/Timeframe Photography, Inc.; 423 (tl, tr), Peter Van Steen/HRW ; 424 (br), Tom Tracy/The Stock Shop/Medichrome ; 425 (tc), Victoria Smith/HRW; 425 (tr), © Peter Cade/Getty Images; 425 (tl), © Bob Thomason/Getty Images; 426 (all), Peter Van Steen/HRW ; 427 (tr), Peter Van Steen/HRW ; 430 (bl), Digital Image copyright © 2005 PhotoDisc; 430 (tl), Victoria Smith/HRW; 430 (tc, tr), Scott Van Osdol/HRW 431 (tr), Miro Vinton/Stock Boston/PictureQuest; 433 (tl), Sam Dudgeon/HRW; 433 (tc), John Langford/HRW; 433 (tr), Charles D. Winters/Timeframe Photography, Inc.; 434 (tc), Digital Image copyright © 2005 PhotoDisc; 435 (bl), Sam Dudgeon/HRW; 436 (tl), Hans Reinhard/Bruce Coleman, Inc. ; 437 (tr), CORBIS Images/HRW; 438 (b), Sam Dudgeon/HRW; 440 (tr), Peter Van Steen/HRW ; 441 (all), Digital Image copyright © 2005 PhotoDisc; 444 (tr), Dan Loh/AP/Wide World Photos; 444 (tl), Sygma; 445 (tr), Nicole Guglielmo; 445 (bl), Corbis Images

Chapter Sixteen 446-447 (all), GJLP/CNRI/PhotoTake; 448 (br), Henri Becquerel/ The Granger Collection; 448 (bl), Roberto De Gugliemo/Science Photo Library/Photo Researchers, Inc.; 449 (tr), Digital Image copyright © 2005 PhotoDisc; 452 (br), Sygma; 454 (br), Tim Wright/CORBIS; 454 (bl), Custom Medical Stock Photo; 455 (tr), Roberto De Gugliemo/Science Photo Library/Photo Researchers, Inc.; 457 (tr), Emory Kristof/National Geographic Society Image Collection; 459 (tr), © Shone/ Gamma; 461 (tc), Sam Dudgeon/HRW; 461 (tr), John Langford/HRW; 462 (all), Sam Dudgeon/HRW; 463 (b), Sam Dudgeon/HRW; 464 (tl), Tim Wright/CORBIS; 465 (bl), John Langford/HRW; 465 (cr), Science Photo Library/Photo Researchers, Inc.; 468 (tl), Courtesy USDA; 468 (tr), SABA Press Photos, Inc.; 469 (cr), © Underwood & Underwood/CORBIS; 469 (bl), © The Nobel Foundation

Unit Six 470 (t), AKG Photo, London; 470 (c), Getty Images; 470 (bl), Enrico Tedeschi; 471 (t), Property of AT&T Archives. Printed with permission of AT&T.; 471 (c), Peter Southwick/AP/Wide World Photos; 471 (bl), Enrico Tedeschi; 471 (bc), Ilkka Uimonen/Sygma

Chapter Seventeen 472-473 (all), Courtesy Sandia National Laboratories; 476 (bc), John Langford/HRW; 476 (bl), Sam Dudgeon/HRW; 477 (tr), John Langford/HRW; 478 (tl), © COMSTOCK, Inc.; 480 (br), Paul Katz/Index Stock Imagery/PictureQuest; 481 (cr), Michelle Bridwell/HRW; 481 (tr), Sam Dudgeon/HRW; 484 (br), Sam Dudgeon/HRW; 485 (tl), © National Geographic Image Collection/Richard T. Nowitz; 486 (br), Takeshi Takahara/Photo Researchers, Inc.; 487 (br), John Langford/HRW; 489 (tr), John Langford/HRW; 491 (br), Sam Dudgeon/HRW; 492 (tl, tc), Sam Dudgeon/HRW; 493 (cl), Digital Image copyright © 2005 PhotoDisc; 493 (c), © Brand X Pictures; 494 (bl), Richard T. Nowitz/Photo Researchers, Inc.; 494 (bc, br, inset), Sam Dudgeon/HRW; 495 (all), John Langford/HRW; 496 (b), John Langford/ HRW; 497 (b), Sam Dudgeon/HRW; 498 (tl), Paul Silverman/Fundamental Photographs; 498 (bc), Sam Dudgeon/HRW; 499 (all), Sam Dudgeon/HRW; 500 (bl), John Langford/HRW; 501 (b), Victoria Smith/HRW; 502 (br), Sam Dudgeon/HRW; 503 (br), John Langford/HRW; 503 (tl), © COMSTOCK, Inc.; 506 (tr), Daniel L. Osborne, University of Alaska/Detlev Ban Ravenswaay/Science Photo Library/Photo Researchers, Inc.; 506 (tl), Sonia S. Wasco/Grant Heilman Photography, Inc.; 506 (cr), STARLab, Stanford University; 507 (cr), Sam Dudgeon/HRW

Chapter Eighteen 508-509 (all), © NASA/Photo Researchers, Inc.; 510 (bc), Sam Dudgeon/HRW; 511 (tr, bc, br), Richard Megna/Fundamental Photographs; 511 (cr), Sam Dudgeon/HRW; 512 (tr), Richard Megna/Fundamental Photographs; 513 (br), Sam Dudgeon/HRW; 514 (cl), Sam Dudgeon/HRW; 516 (br), Pekka Parviainen/ Science Photo Library/Photo Researchers, Inc.; 517 (tr), Sam Dudgeon/HRW; 520 (br), © Tom Tracy/The Stock Shop; 521 (tr), Victoria Smith/HRW; 523 (cr), Gamma Photo/Central Scientific Company; 523 (tr), Sam Dudgeon/HRW; 530 (cr), Sam Dudgeon/HRW; 531 (bl), David Young Wolf/PhotoEdit; 532 (tl), Sam Dudgeon/HRW; 536 (cl), © Getty Images; 536 (tr), Howard Sochurek; 537 (tr), © Baldwin Ward/ CORBIS

Chapter Nineteen 538-539 (all), © Peter Menzel Photography; 540 (all), Sam Dudgeon/HRW; 542 (tl), Sam Dudgeon/HRW; 543 (tr), Sam Dudgeon/HRW; 544 (bl), Sam Dudgeon/HRW; 545 (all), Sam Dudgeon/HRW; 546 (bl), Digital Image copyright © 2005 PhotoDisc; 548 (tl), Digital Image copyright © 2005 PhotoDisc; 551 (inset), Corbis Images; 552 (inset), Corbis Images; 554 (br), Sam Dudgeon/HRW; 555 (tr), Corbis-Bettmann; 556 (b), Sam Dudgeon/HRW; 557 (b), Sam Dudgeon/ HRW; 561 (all), Sam Dudgeon/HRW; 562 (bl), Sam Dudgeon/HRW; 563 (b), Sam Dudgeon/HRW; 564 (br), Sam Dudgeon/HRW; 565 (bl), Sam Dudgeon/HRW; 568 (tl), © Reuters NewMedia Inc./CORBIS; 569 (cr), Courtesy Agnes Riley; 569 (bl), Digital Image copyright © 2005 PhotoDisc

Unit Seven 570 (c), Photofest; 570 (bl), Hughes Research Laboratories; 570 (br), Sam Dudgeon/HRW; 570 (tr), Archivo Iconografico, S.A./CORBIS; 571 (tl), David Parker/Science Photo Library/Photo Researchers, Inc.; 571 (tr), Dr. E.R. Degginger; 571 (cr), Fotos International/Hulton Archive/Getty Images; 571 (bl), Victoria Smith/ HRW; 571 (br), Kieran Doherty/REUTERS /NewsCom

Chapter Twenty 572-573 (all), © Jason Childs/Getty Images; 575 (tr), Robert Mathena/Fundamental Photographs, New York; 575 (bl), © Albert Copley/Visuals Unlimited; 576 (t), NASA; 583 (tr), © Steve Kaufman/CORBIS; 584 (br), Erich Schrempp/Photo Researchers, Inc.; 585 (tl), Richard Megna/Fundamental Photographs; 586 (tc), Educational Development Center; 588 (tl), Richard Megna/ Fundamental Photographs; 588 (bl), John Langford/HRW; 590 (br), James H. Karales/ Peter Arnold, Inc.; 591 (b), Sam Dudgeon/HRW; 592 (bl), Richard Megna/ Fundamental Photographs; 593 (bl), Martin Bough/Fundamental Photographs; 596 (tl), Pete Saloutos/The Stock Market; 596 (tr), The Granger Collection, New York; 597 (all), Peter Van Steen/HRW

Chapter Twenty One 598-599 (all), © Flip Nicklin/Minden Pictures; 601 (tl), John Langford/HRW; 602 (tr), Sam Dudgeon/HRW; 604 (tr), Sam Dudgeon/HRW; 605 (tr), Mary Kate Denny/PhotoEdit; 606 (tl), Archive Photos; 608 (t), John Langford/HRW; 609 (bl), John Langford/HRW; 611 (tr), Charles D. Winters; 613 (t), © Stephen Dalton/Photo Researchers, Inc.; 614 (tl), Matt Meadows/Photo Researchers, Inc.; 616 (all), Richard Megna/Fundamental Photographs; 617 (tr), Sam Dudgeon/HRW; 618 (bc), Sam Dudgeon/HRW; 619 (bl), Digital Image copyright © 2005 EyeWire ; 619 (br), John Langford/HRW; 620 (tr, tl), Digital Image copyright © 2005 EyeWire ; 620 (bc), Bob Daemmrich/HRW; 622 (bl), Richard Megna/Fundamental Photographs; 623 (br), Sam Dudgeon/HRW; 624 (tl), © Flip Nicklin/Minden Pictures; 624 (bc), Sam Dudgeon/HRW; 625 (tc), © Ross Harrison Koty/Getty Images; 625 (cl), Dick Luria/ Photo Researchers, Inc.; 625 (br), John Langford/HRW; 629 (all), Victoria Smith/HRW

Chapter Twenty Two 630-631 (all), Matt Meadows/Peter Arnold, Inc.; 633 (tl), Charlie Winters/Photo Researchers, Inc.; 633 (tr), Richard Megna/Fundamental Photographs; 634 (t), © A.T. Willett/Getty Images; 635 (tr), © Detlev Van Ravenswaay/Photo Researchers, Inc.; 636 (bc), Sam Dudgeon/HRW; 636 (br, bl), John Langford/HRW; 637 (bcr), Hugh Turvey/Science Photo Library/Photo Researchers, Inc.; 637 (br), Blair Seitz/Photo Researchers, Inc.; 637 (bcl), Leonide Principe/Photo Researchers, Inc.; 637 (tc, tr), Sam Dudgeon/HRW; 639 (br), © Tony Mcconnell/Photo Researchers, Inc.; 639 (tl), © Najlah Feanny/CORBIS SABA; 640 (t), © Cameron Davidson/Getty Images; 641 (cr), © Sinclair Stammers/SPL/Photo Researchers, Inc.; 642 (br), © Michael English/Custom Medical Stock Photo; 643 (tr), Hugh Turvey/Science Photo Library/Photo Researchers, Inc.; 645 (br), © Darwin Dale/ Photo Researchers, Inc.; 646 (bl), Sovfoto/Eastfoto; 647 (bl), Richard Megna/ Fundamental Photographs; 649 (br), Ken Kay/Fundamental Photographs; 651 (cr), Ken Kay/Fundamental Photographs; 652 (br), Stephanie Morris/HRW; 653 (all), John Langford/HRW; 654 (tl), Image copyright ©1998 PhotoDisc; 654 (tr), Renee Lynn/Davis/Lynn Images; 654 (bl), Robert Wolf/HRW; 655 (tl), Leonard Lessin/Peter Arnold, Inc.; 656 (br), Sam Dudgeon/HRW; 657 (t), Index Stock Photography, Inc.; 657 (cr), Peter Van Steen/HRW; 659 (tr), Sam Dudgeon/HRW; 660 (br), Matt Meadows/Peter Arnold, Inc.; 660 (tl), Image copyright © 2005 PhotoDisc, Inc.; 661 (cr), Charles D. Winters/Photo Researchers, Inc.; 661 (bcr), © Mark E. Gibson; 661 (br), Richard Megna/Fundamental Photographs; 664 (tl), Dr. E. R. Degginger; 664 (tr), courtesy of the Raytheon Company; 665 (cr), © Underwood & Underwood/CORBIS

Chapter Twenty Three 666-667 (all), Data courtesy Marc Imhoff of NASA GSFC and Christopher Elvidge of NOAA NGDC. Image by Craig Mayhew and Robert Simmon, NASA GSFC.; 668 (b), Yoav Levy/Phototake; 669 (tr), Stephanie Morris/HRW; 669 (bl, br), John Langford/HRW; 670 (tl), John Langford/HRW; 670 (tr), Richard Megna/ Fundamental Photographs, New York; 676 (tl), © Digital Vision Ltd.; 676 (tr), Courtesy www.vischeck.com (program)/©Digital Vision Ltd. (frogs); 677 (tr), Yoav Levy/Phototake; 681 (tr), Sam Dudgeon/HRW; 681 (bl), Don Mason/The Stock Market; 682 (all), Victoria Smith/HRW; 683 (cr), © Steve Dunwell/Getty Images; 687 (br), Sam Dudgeon/HRW; 688 (tl), Yoav Levy/Phototake; 688 (br), © Digital Vision Ltd.; 692 (tr), Digital Image copyright © 2005; 692 (tl), M. Spencer Green/AP/Wide World Photos; 693 (bc), Photo courtesy R.R. Jones, Hubble Deep field team, NASA; 693 (cr), NASA

Lab Book/Appendix "LabBook Header", "L", Corbis Images; "a", Letraset Phototone; "b", and "B", HRW; "o", and "k", images ©2006 PhotoDisc/HRW; 694 (l, tr, br), Sam Dudgeon/HRW; 694 (c), Scott Van Osdol/HRW; 696 (br), Victoria Smith/HRW; 697 (br), Scott Van Osdol/HRW; 700 (all), Sam Dudgeon/HRW; 701 (tr), John Langford/ HRW; 701 (cr), NASA; 702 (all), Sam Dudgeon/HRW; 703 (br), Sam Dudgeon/HRW; 704 (bl), Sam Dudgeon/HRW; 705 (br), Sam Dudgeon/HRW; 707 (bc), Sam Dudgeon/HRW; 708 (br), Gareth Trevor/Getty Images; 709 (tr), Sam Dudgeon/HRW; 710 (all), Sam Dudgeon/HRW; 711 (br), Sam Dudgeon/HRW; 713 (c), Sam Dudgeon/HRW; 718 (br), Sam Dudgeon/HRW; 719 (b), Sam Dudgeon/HRW; 720 (br), John Langford/HRW; 722 (tr, cr), Robert Wolf; 722 (br), John Langford/HRW; 723 (br), Victoria Smith/HRW; 725 (br), Sam Dudgeon/HRW; 726 (all), Sam Dudgeon/HRW; 727 (br), Sam Dudgeon/HRW; 728 (b), Sam Dudgeon/HRW; 729 (br), Rob Boudreau/Getty Images; 730 (br), Victoria Smith/HRW; 731 (cr), John Langford/HRW; 732 (cr), Sam Dudgeon/HRW; 734 (br), Sam Dudgeon/HRW; 735 (b), Sam Dudgeon/HRW; 736 (b), Sam Dudgeon/HRW; 737 (all), Sam Dudgeon/HRW; 738 (b), Sam Dudgeon/HRW; 739 (b), Sam Dudgeon/HRW; 740 (br), Sam Dudgeon/ HRW; 741 (all), Richard Megna/Fundamental Photographs; 743 (br), Sam Dudgeon/ HRW; 744 (br), HRW Photo; 745 (r), Sam Dudgeon/HRW; 747 (br), Sam Dudgeon/ HRW; 748 (br), Sam Dudgeon/HRW; 750 (all), Sam Dudgeon; 758 (br), Victoria Smith; 759 (br), Victoria Smith; 765 (tr), Peter Van Steen/HRW; 765 (br), Sam Dudgeon/HRW; 779 (tr), Sam Dudgeon/HRW